ENFORCEMENT OF INTELLECTUAL PROPERTY RIGHTS THROUGH BORDER MEASURES

ENFORCEMENT OF INTELLECTUAL PROPERTY RIGHTS THROUGH BORDER MEASURES

FIRST EDITION

Olivier Vrins and Marius Schneider

OXFORD
UNIVERSITY PRESS

OXFORD
UNIVERSITY PRESS

Great Clarendon Street, Oxford OX2 6DP

Oxford University Press is a department of the University of Oxford.
It furthers the University's objective of excellence in research, scholarship,
and education by publishing worldwide in

Oxford New York

Auckland Cape Town Dar es Salaam Hong Kong Karachi
Kuala Lumpur Madrid Melbourne Mexico City Nairobi
New Delhi Shanghai Taipei Toronto

With offices in

Argentina Austria Brazil Chile Czech Republic France Greece
Guatemala Hungary Italy Japan Poland Portugal Singapore
South Korea Switzerland Thailand Turkey Ukraine Vietnam

Oxford is a registered trade mark of Oxford University Press
in the UK and in certain other countries

Published in the United States
by Oxford University Press Inc., New York

First published 2006

British Library Cataloguing in Publication Data

Data available

Library of Congress Cataloging in Publication Data

Data available

Typeset by Newgen Imaging Systems (P) Ltd., Chennai, India
Printed in Great Britain
on acid-free paper by
Hanway Press Limited

ISBN 0–19–928879–8   978–0–19–928879–3

3 5 7 9 10 8 6 4 2

To Annabelle & Sigrid
Camille, Jean-Didier & Maximilian

CONTENTS

DETAILED CONTENTS

PART IV BORDER MEASURES AT THE
NATIONAL LEVEL

4. Austria

PART V CONCLUSION

29. Intellectual property: borders and crossroads

APPENDICES

FOREWORD[1]

> Counterfeiting and piracy cannot be fought with words but with concrete actions because in this context, only the invisible part of the iceberg can be seen.
>
> Mr László Kovács, EC Commissioner in charge of
> Taxation and Customs Union.

The fight against counterfeiting and piracy is now a top priority for the EU customs administrations seeking to avert the potentially dangerous effects of counterfeit goods.

Anything that can be bought and sold can now be counterfeited: apples, waffles, mineral water, sphygmomanometers, medicines, car spare parts, sweets, ink cartridges, and so on. Counterfeiters have turned their attention from high value products to mass-market consumer goods.

This insidious fraud is not easy to quantify and describe. The European Commission, in collaboration with the Member States, therefore publishes annual reports of the customs administrations on the fight against counterfeiting and piracy. These statistics can be used to analyse the development of counterfeiting. Thus, in 1998, when the first report was published, about 10 million objects were seized, but in 2004 the number of items reached over 106 million, an increase of nearly 1000 per cent. The Commission reacted firmly to this alarming increase by launching various legislative initiatives. Nevertheless, the fight against fake goods cannot be won solely through legislation. Risk analysis techniques must also be improved and lessons must be drawn from experience.

Counterfeiting is best understood and analysed as part of an evolving problem related to the nature of the goods. In the past, most pirated products were luxury goods, but today nothing escapes counterfeiting. This creates ever greater risks to consumers' health and safety. In 2004, nearly 4.5 million counterfeit food products including tea, jam, instant soup, and alcohol were seized by customs administrations at the EU external border, an increase of nearly 200 per cent compared to 2003.

The evolving problem of counterfeiting embraces both copying techniques and organizations: internationalization and globalization of trade leads to

---

[1] The views expressed by the authors in this book are purely personal and do not purport to be necessarily shared by the European Commission.

internationalization and globalization of fraud. Criminal organizations gain control of the trade and improve their counterfeiting techniques as customs control techniques change.

The new strategy employed by such organizations is characterized by several striking facts. First, these organizations now often use the same tactic as that used in drug trafficking, that is, the use of an indirect route (*ruptures de charges*). In other words, counterfeit goods are no longer transported directly from the point of production to the point of consumption but pass in transit through neutral territories, sometimes using more than one means of transport, in order to conceal their place of origin and/or their true destination. Thus, one product may pass through several countries, even several continents, before reaching its destination.

Second, various techniques are used to conceal the counterfeit goods. For instance, it is not uncommon for cardboard boxes full of counterfeit cigarettes to be discovered under several tons of potatoes or for false labels to be sewn into clothes in order to hide a counterfeit famous trade mark.

Last but not least, counterfeiters have changed their tactics following the sad events of 11 September 2001. Since then, the relevant authorities have tightened their controls, notably on payments of large amounts into bank accounts. As it has become more and more difficult for counterfeiters to invest large sums of money, they have been forced to resort to money-laundering. This has given rise to a worldwide trade in counterfeit goods.

Such developments have necessitated an improvement in customs control. Two new anti-counterfeiting strategies, drawing from customs techniques used in the fight against drug trafficking, have been developed: zoning and selection.

The work of a customs officer may be satisfying, but it can also be very complicated. Nowadays, the main role of customs administrations is to facilitate external trade. Trade must liberalize but customs administrations must still control illegal cross-border trade. Today, customs administrations are expected to exert less, but better, control. They have had to adapt control techniques to the new requirements, using zoning, a technique which consists of analysing transportation documents by looking for inconsistencies or errors aimed at concealing the true facts.

The second technique used today by customs administrations is selection, a visual analysis of the packaging. The country of origin can be recognized from, for example, wrapping paper, the colour of cellulose tape, or the shape of the packages. Thus, the true origin of a package can be detected by a simple analysis of the cardboard container, even if the transportation documents have been falsified.

Within this context, the regulatory framework needed to be modified to build on the results of the fight against counterfeiting and piracy and to enable right-holders, notably SMIs and SMEs, to have a free and more flexible access to that framework.

The European Commission, in collaboration with the Member States, therefore proposed the new EC Regulation No 1383/2003 which was adopted on 22 July 2003 and came into force on 1 July 2004, and its implementing Regulation No 1891/2004 of 21 October 2004. These new Regulations differ considerably from their predecessors.

The new regulatory framework, referred to above, is intended to tackle the evolving problem of counterfeiting by enabling customs officers and right-holders to work together within a wider legal system.

Collaboration between rights holders and customs administrations should be enhanced by the following significant improvements: widening of the scope of EC Regulation No 1383/2003 to cover new intellectual property rights such as plant variety rights, geographical indications, or designations of origin; harmonization of the form of the new applications for action and the data required; widening of the scope of the *ex officio* procedure; an option for the right-holder to obtain more information and samples for analysis; the power, if implemented in national law, to destroy counterfeit goods without the need to obtain approval from the relevant authority; and abolition of guarantees and fees. This should all render use of the new framework easier for SMIs/SMEs.

Only one year after the new regulatory framework came into force is too soon for a realistic assessment of its true impact. Nevertheless, it is generally acknowledged that the new legislation has led to the seizure of several hundreds of thousands of products which would not have been seized under the previous EC Regulation No 3295/94. The powers of intervention under the new legislation should lead to significant improvements. For instance, over 60,000 counterfeit roses and hundreds of bottles of alcohol which were in breach of the law relating to geographical indications have recently been seized.

Looking beyond the statistics, right-holders' confidence in the new legislation is also proof of its success. The first figures for 2004 show a great rise in the number of applications for action, from 981 in 2000 to about 2,888 in 2004. This indicates the awareness of the problem by economic groups.

The fight against counterfeiting and piracy will only succeed if there is closer collaboration between the relevant supervisory authority and the right-holders. Over 1,000 regular airline flights land every week at EU airports from areas where counterfeit goods are produced and several thousand containers arrive every day in the Community ports, so the 150,000 customs officers of the 25 Member States need the support of economic operators.

Counterfeiting and piracy deprive companies of the fruits of their creativity and their investments. They also undermine the free-market economy and healthy competition, resulting in a loss of income for the Member States. Moreover, they increasingly endanger consumers' health and safety. Indeed, although some consumers knowingly buy counterfeit products, others increasingly are the innocent victims of counterfeiting, which can put fake goods on their plates or in their first aid kit. Counterfeiting kills!

Dear Reader, you must give customs administrations the power, by filing applications for action, to intervene to defend and protect your rights.

It is to be hoped that this book will contribute to spreading this message and the word about the EC and national approaches to the combating of counterfeiting and piracy.

Brussels,   *Christophe Zimmermann*
8 July 2005   *DG Taxation and Customs Union (TAXUD)*
                                          Unity C1—Customs Policy and Customs Controls
                              Head of Sector: 'Fight against counterfeiting and piracy'

PREFACE

Why this book?

This publication contains an in-depth examination of the European system of border measures that has been put in place to protect against goods that infringe certain intellectual property rights, as laid down in Regulation (EC) 1383/2003.

Border measures allow the customs authorities to retain goods suspected of infringing certain intellectual property rights—either on their own initiative, or at the request of right-holders—in order to allow the latter to take action against such products and the persons involved in such traffic, the final aim being to obtain the destruction of all the infringing items.

This European system of border measures has proved to be very efficient, and many right-holders and practitioners make abundant use of it.

We therefore thought that it would be useful to publish a thorough commentary on this new Regulation 1383/2003.

This would not be possible without examining the international legal framework on border measures and, more generally, the economic and social consequences of the phenomenon of counterfeiting and piracy. Two introductory chapters have thus been dedicated to these subjects.

Although the Regulation on border measures has direct effect, it can be seen that a certain amount of discretion is left to the Member States. Consequently, diverse national laws and practices have developed in each European country. It was thus in our view important to set out for our readers an overview of the border measures as they have been applied nationally. These sections have been written by experienced practitioners from all 25 Member States. In order to ensure that the national experts did not merely parrot the rules of the Regulation, we asked our authors to answer a series of questions. The result of this extensive effort can be seen in the 'national' chapters of this book.

A final chapter has been included which examines the roles of the different players in this cat and mouse game. This chapter had to be witty to incentivize readers to continue reading until the very last page . . . We hope that we have succeeded in this worthy aim.

We have tried to include for our readers a cocktail of authors both practising lawyers and from the world of academia, so as to render this publication attractive to both scholars and practitioners. For practical reasons, we have also endeavoured to include reflections from the point of view of both trade mark and patent attorneys and litigators. This is why certain national chapters have been co-signed by several authors.

How to use this book?

Obviously, readers may decide to study this book from the first to the last page.

Right-holders and practitioners can also use this book as a guide to find out how Regulation 1383/2003 has been applied in a particular Member State. For these purposes, it will be sufficient just to read the corresponding national chapter.

Thanks to the uniform structure of both the chapter dedicated to the border measure Regulation and the different national chapters, it is even possible to find out how a particular issue has been resolved in various Member States. The index will enable readers to carry out this form of research. The reader will simply have to look up the topic of interest in the index which indicates the paragraph in which the subject is discussed.

Acknowledgements

We express our sincere gratitude to the authors who have agreed to participate in this project. Without their contribution this book could not have come into existence. Everybody knows that academics and practitioners have numerous commitments and obligations, and precious little time left for writing. All of them have spent many hours of this valuable time drafting and reshaping their chapters. Their efforts have been hugely appreciated! We sincerely hope that the relationships and friendships that we have built up with these co-authors—and of course those that have been formed between the contributors themselves—will further grow and develop.

In both our respective offices we would like to thank Gaëlle Gevers, Paul Maeyaert and Christophe Ronse, for their support for this project; David Tatham, Jeremy Philips, Christophe Zimmermann and numerous officials from the national customs administrations for the time they have devoted to discussing many issues of interest to this book; and, in particular, Christophe Ronse, Florent Gevers, and Bruno Verdonck, who contributed to awaking our curiosity in this field of law, which has now turned into a passion, a fervour, a rage, and, occasionally, a fever.

We have also very much appreciated our collaboration with Louise Kavanagh and Chris Rycroft from Oxford University Press, who have placed their faith in two young lawyers who were relatively inexperienced in the editing world! We strongly hope that the trust they have placed in us will be repaid.

Our special thanks go to our families and friends for their ongoing encouragement in our work on this book. In particular our spouses and children who have agreed to make many concessions, including spending plentiful weekends and evenings, in the company of this and other books. Now that this publication has gone to press, we are elated to have more time again to enjoy life with them, for whom our love—as, hopefully, the readers' interest in this book—will never fade.

Brussels,   *Olivier VRINS & Marius SCHNEIDER*
Summer 2005

LIST OF CONTRIBUTORS

The Phenomenon of Counterfeiting and Piracy in the European Union: Factual Overview and Legal and Institutional Framework

Michael Blakeney Director, Queen Mary Intellectual Property Research Institute, Queen Mary University of London, John Vane Science Building, Charterhouse Square, London EC1M 6BQ, United Kingdom, Tel: +44 (0)20 7882 5718, Fax: +44 (0)20 7882 3446, e-mail: m.blakeney@qmul.ac.uk

The International Legal Framework of Border Measures in the Fight Against Counterfeiting and Piracy

Daniel J Gervais University of Ottawa, 57 Louis Pasteur St. Ottawa, Ontario, Canada K1n 6N5, Tel: +1 (613) 562-5800 # 3381, Fax: +1 (613) 562-5124, e-mail: daniel.gervais@uottawa.ca

Regulation (EC) 1383/2003

Marius Schneider Gevers & Partners, Holidaystraat 5, B-1831 Diegem, Tel: +32 2 715 37 11, Fax: +32 2 715 37 00, e-mail: marius.schneider@gevers.com and marius.schneider@bordermeasures.com

Olivier Vrins Altius, Avenue du Port 86C B.414, B-1000 Brussels, Tel: +32 2 426 14 14, Fax: +32 2 426 20 30, e-mail: olivier.vrins@altius.com and olivier.vrins@bordermeasures.com

Border Measures at the National Level

Austria

Helmut Sonn Sonn & Partner Patentanwälte, European and Austrian Patent, Trade Mark and Design Attorneys, Riemergasse 14, A-1010 Wien, Austria, Tel: +43 1 512 84 05, Fax: +43 1 512 98 05, e-mail: office@sonn.at

Belgium

Olivier Vrins Altius, Avenue du Port 86C B.414, B-1000 Brussels, Tel: +32 2 426 14 14, Fax: +32 2 426 20 30, e-mail: olivier.vrins@altius.com

Marius Schneider Gevers & Partners, Holidaystraat 5, B-1831 Diegem, Tel: +32 2 715 37 11, Fax: +32 2 715 37 00, e-mail: marius.schneider@gevers.com

Cyprus

Alecos Markides Markides, Markides & Co., Markides House, 1 Heroes Street, PO Box 24325, CY-1703 Nicosia, Cyprus, Tel: +357-22-779900, Fax: +357-22-778787, e-mail: info@markides.com.cy

Hermione A Markides Markides, Markides & Co., Markides House, 1 Heroes Street, PO Box 24325, CY-1703 Nicosia, Cyprus, Tel: +357-22-779900, Fax: +357-22-778787, e-mail: info@markides.com.cy

Czech Republic

Petra Korejzova Korejzova & Co., Spálená 29, 110 00 Prague 1, Czech Republic, Tel: +420–224 996 285, Fax: +420–224 933 850, e-mail: petra.korejzova@ korejzova.cz

Denmark

Mads Marstrand-Jorgensen Landenmärket 10, 1119, Copenhagen K, Tel: +45 33 43 31 00, Fax: +45 33 13 38 38, e-mail: mmj@norskerco.dk

Bernhard Posner Zacco A/S, Hans Bekkevolds Allé 7, DK-2900 Hellerup, Tel: +45 39 48 80 00, Fax: +45 39 48 80 80, e-mail: bpo@zacco.dk

Estonia

Raivo Koitel Koitel Patent & Trade Mark Agency, Tartu mnt. 65, 10115 Tallinn, Estonia, PO Box 1759, 10902 Tallinn, Estonia, Tel: +372 6 033260, Fax: +372 6 033261, e-mail: koitel@koitel.ee

Finland

Bernt Juthström Attorney-at-law, Roschier Holmberg, Attorneys Ltd., Keskuskatu 7 A, FIN-00100 Helsinki, Tel: +358 20 506 6000, Fax: +358 20 506 6100, e-mail: bernt.juthstrom@roschier.com

Johanna Harsu Associate Lawyer, LL.M., Roschier Holmberg, Attorneys Ltd., Keskuskatu 7 A, FIN-00100 Helsinki, Tel: +358 20 506 6000, Fax: +358 20 506 6100, e-mail: johanna.harsu@roschier.com

France

Juliette Biardeaud Gilbey de Haas, 90 rue d'Amsterdam, F–75009 Paris, Mob: +33 6 61 96 87 85, Tel: +33 1 56 02 62 00, Fax: +33 1 56 02 62 10, e-mail: juliette_biardeaud@yahoo.com, mail@gilbeydehaas.com

Germany

Stefanie Körber   Weber & Sauberschwarz, Königsallee 1, 40212 Düsseldorf, Tel: +49 211 44 03 93 0, Fax: +49 211 44 03 93 99, e-mail: koerber@weber-sauberschwarz.de

Greece

Dimitra Georganda   G S Kostakopoulos & Associates, Law firm, Akadimias 18, GR-10671 Athens, Tel: +30 210 36 11 846, Fax: +30 210 36 39 180, e-mail: assistant@kostakopoulosg-law.gr

Ekaterini Mouzaki   G S Kostakopoulos & Associates, Law firm, Place Jean Jacobs 7, B-1000 Brussels, Tel: +32 2 502 71 88, Fax: +32 2 502 07 54, e-mail: gskb@tiscali.be

Hungary

László Bérczes   S B G. & K Patent and Law Offices, PO Box 360, H-1369 Budapest, Tel: +36 1 354 34 90, Fax: +36 1 301 09 59, e-mail: berczes_l@sbgk.hu

Ireland

Patricia McGovern and Áine Matthews   LK Shields Solicitors, 39/40 Upper Mount Street, Dublin 2, Republic of Ireland, Tel: +353 1 661 0866, Fax: +353 1 661 0883, e-mail: pmcgovern@lkshields.ie, e-mail: amatthews@lkshields.ie

Italy

Raffaella Barbuto   Studio Torta, Via Viotti 9, 10121 Torino, Tel: +39 011 5611320, Fax: +39 011 5622102, e-mail: barbuto@studiotorta.it

Raffaella Arista   Studio Improda, Via Due Macelli 47 00187 Roma, Tel: +39 06 6780312, Fax: +39 06 69941899, e-mail: studio_improda@edl.it

Latvia

Mara Uzulena   Petersona Patents, 2, Ausekla Street, Suite 2, LV-1010 Riga, Latvia, Tel: +371 7324695, Fax: +371 7830030, e-mail: mara@petpat.lv

Gatis Merzvinskis   Petersona Patents, 2, Ausekla Street, Suite 2, LV-1010 Riga, Latvia, Tel: +371 7324695, Fax: +371 7830030, e-mail: gatis@petpat.lv

Lithuania

Asta Lukošiūtė   Metida, Gedimino ave 45–6, LT-01109 Vilnius, Lithuania, Tel: +370 5 24 90 830/ 831/ 832, Fax: +370 5 24 90 833, e-mail: patent@metida.lt

Luxembourg

Gary Cywie   Noble and Scheidecker 398, route d'Esch. L-1471 Luxembourg, Tel: +352 2648 42–1, Fax: +352 2648 42 35 00, e-mail: cywie@mnks.com

Malta

David Tonna Mamo TCV Advocates, Palazzo Pietro Stiges, 90, Strait Street, Valletta VLT 05, Malta, Tel: +356 21 232271, Fax: +356 21 244291, e-mail: david.tonna@mamotcv.com

Antoine Camilleri Mamo TCV Advocates, Palazzo Pietro Stiges, 90, Strait Street, Valletta VLT 05, Malta, Tel: +356 21 232271, Fax: +356 21 244291, e-mail: antoine.camilleri@mamotcv.com

The Netherlands

Christine Noordzij and Marchien Maks Elzas Noordzij Trade Mark Attorneys, De Lairessestraat 159, 1075 HK Amsterdam, Tel: +31 20 305 02 20, Fax: +31 20 305 02 29, e-mail: office@elzasnoordzij.nl.

Frits Mutsaerts and Maaike Grondman BANNING Advocaten, Statenlaan 55, 5223 LA 's-Hertogenbosch, Tel: +31 73 69 27 757, Fax: +31 73 69 27 787, e-mail: f.mutsaerts@banning.nl, m.grondman@banning.nl.

Poland

Dorota Rzążewska Kulikowska & Kulikowski, ul. Żurawia 47/49, 00-680 Warsaw, Tel: +48 22 621 52 02, Fax: +48 22 621 61 50, e-mail: drzazewska@kulikowski.pl

Zofia Senda Kulikowska & Kulikowski, ul. Żurawia 47/49, 00-680 Warsaw, Tel: +48 22 621 52 02, Fax: +48 22 621 61 50, e-mail: kulikowska@ kulikowski.pl

Portugal

Gonçalo Moreira Rato Lawyer & Intellectual Property Consultant, Rua Rodrigo da Fonseca, 72–3º E, 1250-193 Lisbon, Tel: +351 213875201, Fax: +351 213875200, e-mail: gmrato@mail.telepac.pt

Nuno Cruz J. Pereira da Cruz, S.A., Rua Vítor Cordon, 14—3º, 1249-103 Lisbon, Tel: +351 213475020, Fax: +351 213421885, e-mail: jpcruz@mail.telepac.pt

Slovak Republic

Jan Hák Patentservis Bratislava a.s., Hybešova 40, SK–831 06 Bratislava, Tel + 421 2 49 20 17 11, Fax: + 421 2 44 87 20 75, e-mail: patmag@ patentservis.com

Slovenia

Andrej Bukovnik ITEM d.o.o., Patent & Trade Mark Agency, Resljeva 16, 1000 Ljubljana, Slovenia, Tel: + 386 1 432 01 67, Fax: + 386 1 431 53 31, e-mail: andrej.bukovnik@item.si, Website: www.item.si

Gregor Maček   ITEM d.o.o., Patent & Trade Mark Agency, Resljeva 16, 1000 Ljubljana, Slovenia, Tel: + 386 1 432 01 67, Fax: + 386 1 431 53 31, e-mail: gregor.macek@item.si

Spain

Luis H Larramendi   Elzaburu Miguel Angel 21, 28010 Madrid, Tel: +34 91 700 94 00, Fax: +34 91 319 38 10, e-mail: lhl@elzaburu.es

Ignacio Diez de Rivera Elzaburu   Elzaburu, Miguel Angel 21, 28010 Madrid, Tel: 34 91 700 94 00, Fax: 34 91 319 38 10, e-mail: ide@elzaburu.es

Sweden

Bengt Eliasson   Zacco Sweden AB, PO Box 23101, SE-104 35 Stockholm, Tel: +46 8 729 95 00, Fax: +46 8 31 83 15, e-mail: bel@zacco.se

Helena Wassén Öström   Zacco Sweden AB, PO Box 23101, SE-104 35 Stockholm, Tel: +46 8 729 95 00, Fax: +46 8 31 83 15, e-mail: hew@zacco.se

United Kingdom

Alison Firth   Newcastle Law School, University of Newcastle upon Tyne, 21-24 Windsor Terrace, Newscastle upon Tyne, UK-NE1 7RU, Tel: +44 (0) 191 222 7568, Fax: +44 (0) 191 212 0064, e-mail: alison.firth@ncl.ac.uk

Jeremy Phillips   Queen Mary Intellectual Property Research Institute, University of London, John Vane Science Building, Charterhouse Square, UK-London EC 1M 6BQ, Tel: +44(0)7802 701059, Fax: +44 (0)20 8458 0534, e-mail: jjip@btinternet.com

Intellectual Property: Borders and Crossroads

Jeremy Phillips   Queen Mary Intellectual Property Research Institute, University of London, John Vane Science Building, Charterhouse Square UK-London EC1M 6BQ, Tel: +44 (0)7802 701059, Fax: +44 (0)20 8458 0534, e-mail: jjip@btinternet.com

CONTRIBUTOR BIOGRAPHIES

THE EDITORS

Marius Schneider works with Gevers & Partners as an Intellectual Property lawyer. Before joining Gevers he qualified as an attorney at the Brussels bar. He is a graduate of the University of Louvain-la-Neuve (Lic. Jur., 1996), University College London (LL.M. in European Law, 1997) and the Katholieke Universiteit Brussel (Masters in Intellectual Property, 2003). Marius is the director of the Anti-Counterfeiting Department of Gevers & Partners and also handles trade mark and design matters. He lectures on intellectual property at the Ichec and Vlekho colleges and was invited to give seminars on the implementation of EC Intellectual Property law in east and central European countries as part of the EC Commission's PHARE programme. He has served as a consultant on WIPO missions and as an expert on a WCO Commitee. Marius is a member of the ECTA and APRAH Anti-Counterfeiting committee.

Olivier Vrins works at the Altius law firm. He has practised at the Brussels Bar since 2000 and is a graduate of the University of Louvain-la-Neuve (Lic. Jur., 1998), University of Paris II, France (Erasmus Exchange Program, 1998), University of Ghent (Special Degree in European Law, 1999) and the Queen Mary & Westfield College, London (LL.M. in Intellectual Property and Unfair Competition, 2000). Olivier handles intellectual property matters, focusing mainly on anti-counterfeiting and patent litigation. He has published numerous articles on intellectual property related issues and was invited as an external advisor in a WCO IPR Working Group and to give seminars on the implementation of EC Intellectual Property law in east and central European countries as part of the EC Commission's PHARE programme. He is a member of AIPPI, ECTA, and INTA, and has contributed to the INTA Guide on the Madrid Agreement and Protocol.

THE AUTHORS

Raffaella Arista is a *summa cum laude* law graduate of the University of Rome (LUISS). She trained in intellectual property and commercial law, first in a Roman law firm and later in the Rome and London offices of a large international law firm. She is currently a specialist in intellectual property law, commercial law and international law. She lectures at numerous conferences on trade mark, franchising, merchandising, legal protection of software, and semiconductors under Italian and EC law, technology transfer under EC law, and the discipline of consortium agreements. She is the author of several articles in the field of intellectual property law. She is a member of the Lawyers' Bar Association of Rome, and of several intellectual property associations, including LES-Italy, AIPPI, the Italian Association of European Lawyers (AIGE), and Association Internationale des Jeunes Avocats (AIJA).

Raffaella Barbuto graduated from the School of Law of Turin University, where she completed a thesis on Criminal Commercial Law. She started her career in a civil and commercial law firm. In 1996, she moved to a larger Italian law firm, where she specialized in trade mark matters. She joined Studio Torta in 2001 and became a partner in January 2003. She is a registered Italian trade mark attorney, a Community trade mark and design attorney, and a member of LES-Italy. In addition, she is Studio Torta's designate member of MARQUES, ECTA, and INDICAM, and the author of numerous articles in the field of industrial property. She regularly lectures on trade mark protection issues at conferences, seminars, and round tables. She currently works in Studio Torta's Milan office, where she handles the search, filing, and prosecution of Italian, Community, and foreign trade marks, as well as proceedings and contracts concerning industrial property matters on behalf of Italian and foreign clients.

László Bérczes has been working with S B G & K Patent and Law Offices as a lawyer since 1994, the year he graduated from Eötvös Lóránd University of Budapest. Before that, he studied at the Faculty of Law of the Rijksuniversiteit Limburg, Maastricht (the Netherlands) in 1991 and worked in barristers' chambers and a solicitors' firm in London on the Blanche Lucas Placement Scheme organized by the British Hungarian Law Association. He is currently head of the anti-counterfeiting department of S B G & K; in addition he handles mostly parallel import and copyright infringement matters. He is a member of the Anti-Counterfeiting Committee and the Council of the European Communities Trade Mark Association (ECTA). He is the author of several articles on intellectual property related issues. He gives seminars on intellectual property law for customs and police officers on a regular basis. In June 2004, he was an adviser in the drafting procedure of the new Government Decree laying down the provisions for the implementation of EC Regulation 1383/2003 in Hungary.

Juliette Biardeaud worked as a trade mark attorney before joining the law firm Gilbey de Haas following qualification as a barrister at the Paris Bar in 2001. She graduated from Limoges University in 1997, after successful completion of an Erasmus Exchange at Birmingham University, and subsequently obtained an intellectual property postgraduate degree at Strasbourg in 1998. Juliette specializes in intellectual property infringement matters, and is a member of the APRAM (Association des Praticiens du Droit des Marques et des Modèles), and ECTA (European Community Trademark Association) Anti-Counterfeiting Commissions.

Michael Blakeney is Herchel Smith Professor of Intellectual Property Law at Queen Mary, University of London and Director of the Queen Mary Intellectual Property Research Institute. He has held academic positions at a number of universities in Australia and the UK and formerly worked in the Asia Pacific Bureau of the World Intellectual Property Organization. His consultancy work has been in the fields of access to genetic resources and biotechnological patenting. He has advised the FAO, and the international agricultural research centres of the Consulting Group for International Agricultural Research, including the International Rice Research Institute, International Centre for Living Resource Management, the Centre for International Forestry Research, the International Livestock Research Institute and the International Service for National Agricultural Research on intellectual property management. Michael is General Editor of Perspectives on Intellectual Property and a member of the Editorial Boards of International Trade Law and Regulation and Digital Technology Law Journal, and *Cyberspazio e Diritto*—Cyberspace and Law. He is also the editor of *Border Control of Intellectual Property Rights* (2001), as well as the *Guidebook on Enforcement of Intellectual Property Rights* commissioned by the European Commission (Directorate-General Trade) to assist developing countries (2003).

Andrej Bukovnik graduated in Law from the University of Ljubljana. He received a United Nations Association of Slovenia award for his outstanding graduation work. His practice covers all areas of intellectual property but specializes in trade mark matters and border measures. He is the author of a contribution dealing with the border measure issue in the local law journal.

Antoine Camilleri is an Associate in the firm Mamo TCV Advocates. He obtained a Bachelor of Arts Degree in Legal & Humanistic Studies (1998), a Diploma of Notary Public (1999), a Doctor of Laws Degree (LL.D.) (2001) and a Master of Law Degree—*Magister Juris* in European & Comparative Law (2002) from the University of Malta. He is a Member of the Malta Chamber of Advocates and is responsible for the intellectual property and the anti-counterfeiting department in the firm. His areas of practice include all aspects of intellectual property law. He is presently a part-time lecturer at the University of Malta in the Master of Law Degree—*Magister Juris* in European & Comparative Law, and an examiner in the Faculty of Laws of the same University.

Nuno Cruz is a partner of J Pereira da Cruz, S.A., where he has been practising since 1979. He graduated at the Livre University of Lisbon, Portugal (Lic. Jur., 1983). He has been a member of the Portuguese Bar Association since 1986, and a Portuguese Official Industrial Property Agent since 1995. He is also a professional representative before the European Patent Office and the OHIM. He handles intellectual property matters, mainly consultancy and litigation, including anti-counterfeiting. He has been invited to lecture at various conferences, especially in the field of intellectual property infringements.

Gary Cywie is a member of the Brussels Bar, and works for Noble & Scheidecker Luxembourg law firm, mainly in the new information and communication technologies sector, which includes digital signature, data protection, electronic commerce, domain names, privacy, computer security, and corporate law. In addition, he handles matters relating to industrial and intellectual property law as well as contract, media, and telecommunications. He obtained his law degree *cum laude* from the University of Liege and attended a training course on Internet Strategic Management at the Laboratory for New Information and Communication Technologies Studies. He is the author or co-author of several publications on new information and communication technologies subjects, and regularly speaks at conferences and seminars about matters related to legal aspects of e-business. He actively participated in the drafting and editing of 'the l.i.n.k.' (the Legal Info-soc News Kiosk), a bi-monthly electronic newsletter on Information Society related legal issues and is a member of the ISOC (Internet Society, Luxembourg).

Ignacio Diez de Rivera Elzaburu was born in Madrid, Spain, in December 1969. He graduated in Law from Madrid University and in Economics from Navarre University. He obtained a Masters in Intellectual Property at Alicante University. He has worked at the Elzaburu firm since 1993. Ignacio was admitted as an industrial property attorney and as a European trade mark attorney in 1999. He is also a European design attorney. He is the former manager of Elzaburu's Alicante office which specialized in the Community trade mark system. He has been involved in intellectual property litigation as a lawyer since 1999 and works in this capacity within the Elzaburu's Litigation Group. He is the Chairman of the Anti-Counterfeiting Committee of ECTA, and a Member of AIPPI, ECTA, and the Anti-Counterfeiting and Enforcement Committee of INTA.

Bengt Eliasson is Master of Law from the University of Uppsala. From 1977 to 1986, he was employed as a lawyer at the Swedish Patent Office where he worked in the department for company registrations as well as trade marks. In 1986, he joined AB Stockholms Patentbyrå Zacco & Bruhn (now Zacco Sweden AB), where he has been the manager of the trade mark & legal division for 10 years. Bengt has more than 25 years' experience within intellectual property. Today he specializes in counselling, litigation, and agreements within the entire intellectual property area. Bengt is an adjudicator for domain name conflicts in Sweden, a member of the Law Committee and Internet Committee of ECTA (European Community Trade Mark Association) and has been an active member of the Community Trade Mark Committee of INTA (International Trademark Association).

Alison Firth read Physics at Oxford and has an MSc in polymer physics. She later qualified as a barrister, practising in intellectual property chambers from 1983. Alison is a European Advisory Board member for the European Intellectual Property Review, and has contributed a number of articles to that and other journals. She was a founding editor of the monograph series 'Perspectives on Intellectual Property' and has edited books on intellectual property and media law. She is co-author (with Jeremy Phillips) of *Introduction to Intellectual Property Law* (Butterworths, 4th edn 2002) and author of *Trade marks—the new law* (2nd edn 2005). Since 1994 she has been Hon Legal adviser to the British Copyright Council. She is Intellectual Property Section Convenor for the Society of Legal Scholars, and enjoys associate membership of the Chartered Institute of Patent Agents and the Institute of Trade Mark Attorneys. In 2000–1 Alison was a Steering Group member for the dTi's Quinquennial review of the UK Patent Office. Her research interests centre on the law of intellectual property in its widest sense and the relationship of intellectual property with other areas of the law, such as competition law and civil procedure. Alison is Professor of Commercial Law at the University of Newcastle upon Tyne.

Dimitra Georganda practises law at the Athens branch of G S Kostakopoulos & Associates. She is a graduate of the University of Athens, Greece (LL.B.) and University of Bristol, England (LL.M. in Commercial Law) and qualified for the Athens bar in 2000. She handles intellectual property matters, specializing in trade mark and design litigation.

Daniel J Gervais is Vice-Dean (Research) and Professor of Intellectual Property and Technology Law at the Faculty of Law (Common Law Section) of the University of Ottawa. He was also visiting scholar at Stanford Law School (spring 2004). He is a former Head of Section of the World Intellectual Property Organization (WIPO) and Legal Officer at GATT/WTO. Professor Gervais is the author of *The TRIPs Agreement: Drafting History and Analysis* (2nd edn) published by Sweet & Maxwell, London, 2003.

Maaike Grondman graduated from Utrecht University (Lic. Jur, 1999), specializing in intellectual property law (on an exchange programme with Geneva University, Switzerland). Since then, she has worked as legal counsel and attorney-at-law, joining Banning Advocaten in 2003. She advises clients and conducts legal proceedings for them primarily in the following areas: trade mark and trade name law (including domain names), anti-counterfeiting, copyright law, designs & models law, and entertainment and advertising law. Maaike is a member of several specialist associations, including the Benelux Association for Trademarks, Designs and Models (BMM).

Jan Hák is a registered patent and trade mark attorney, a European patent attorney, and patent lawyer. He is managing director and senior partner of Patentservis Praha. He graduated from Charles University in Prague, Law Faculty, in 1980. From that year till 1990 he worked at the Patent Office, mainly in the legal department, where he participated in the preparation of the 1990 Patent Act. He also actively worked on the present wording of the Czech Trade Mark Act. Jan Hák joined Patentservis in 1990. Since 1996 he has been included on the list of WIPO mediators and arbitrators. He is a member of the Czech Chamber of Patent Attorneys, AIPPI, LES and also of the editorial board of

European Trade Mark Reports, London. Among his main specializations are trade mark legislation and licensing.

Johanna Harsu is an associate lawyer with Roschier Holmberg, Attorneys Ltd and works in the technology, media and communications practice group. She received her LL.M. in 2004 from the University of Helsinki, after which she joined the Helsinki office of Roschier Holmberg. She is an expert in intellectual property, including intellectual property litigation, anti-counterfeit enforcement, trade marks, and designs. She also specializes in domain names, and marketing and consumer law matters and advises on pharmaceuticals and biosciences. Ms Harsu deals with Finnish Customs in Helsinki and Finnish-Russian border issues on a regular basis. She is also a member of the Finnish Anti-Counterfeiting Group.

Bernt Juthström is a partner at Roschier Holmberg, Attorneys Ltd and works in the technology, media, and communications practice group. He received his LL.M from the University of Helsinki in 1991 and trained at the Bench the following year. Before this he acted as public prosecutor in Helsinki. Mr Juthström joined the firm in 1992 and became a partner in 2001. He specializes in intellectual property, including anti-counterfeit enforcement, trade mark infringement matters, and litigation. He also has a wide range of experience in other fields of intellectual property law such as parallel imports, trade secrets, and domain names. Mr Juthström is a member of the Finnish Bar Association, the Finnish Association for Industrial Property, AIPPI, INTA, ECTA, MARQUES and the Finnish Franchising Association. He is active in the Finnish Anti-Counterfeiting Group and was one of the forces who founded the Association. He has lectured and written on various intellectual property topics in Finland.

Raivo Koitel has a Masters degree in Economics (MAE 2001) from Tallinn Technical University, and is presently completing his legal studies at Tartu University. He works for Koitel Patent and Trade Mark Agency as an Estonian and European patent and trade mark attorney. He has attended several international training sessions, seminars and conferences in the field of industrial property, and has published several articles in the area of intellectual property law.

Stefanie Körber is a partner with Weber & Sauberschwarz and has worked with the firm as a lawyer since 2000. She graduated from the University of Osnabrück in 1997 and passed her bar exam in Düsseldorf in 2000. She handles intellectual property matters, mainly trade mark, design, and copyright litigation, and is a member of AIPPI. She is also experienced in the field of unfair competition law.

Petra Korejzova has been working at the law and patent offices Korejzova & Co since it was established in 1992. After graduating from the Charles University in Prague (MA, 1995), she became a trade mark attorney registered in the Patent Chamber. She has been practising at the Czech Bar since 2003 and in 2004, she became a managing partner of the firm. She handles intellectual property matters, mainly unfair competition, anti-counterfeiting, and trade mark litigation.

Luis H Larramendi was born in Madrid in July 1952. He graduated in Law from Madrid University. He has worked with the Elzaburu firm since 1983, was admitted as an industrial property attorney and European patent attorney in 1986, and as a European trade mark attorney in 1995. He is also a European design attorney. Luis is the President of the Spanish AIPPI Working Group on 'Internet Domain Names, Trade Marks and Trade Names'. He is a Council Member and member of the Anti-Counterfeiting Committee of ECTA, a member of AIPPI, FICPI, ECTA, EPI, AIPLA, IPBA, LES E, AGESORPI, ASIPI, APRAM, AEDC, the Meetings Committee of INTA, and an

International Panellist for Spain, WIPO Arbitration and Mediation Centre. In addition, he is an official sworn translator in English and French.

Asta Lukošiūtė is a lawyer at the Metida patent and trade mark agency. In 2002/2003 she trained in the Office for Harmonization in the Internal Market (OHIM). She graduated from the Vilnius University, Faculty of Law (2000), and Riga Graduate School of Law (LL.M. in European and International Law, 2001). She handles a broad range of intellectual property matters, mainly trade marks, designs, and anti-counterfeiting. She has published several articles on intellectual property issues and lectures on Intellectual Property and Competition Law at the Riga Graduate School of Law.

Gregor Maček is a graduate engineer in electronics and a law graduate, both of the University of Ljubljana. He has a wide range of experience in both contentious and non-contentious matters, especially in the fields of trade marks, patents, and industrial designs. Gregor has been actively involved in border measure procedures as from November 2001, when border measures relating to intellectual property infringements were introduced in Slovenia. Gregor has published several articles and lectured on many occasions on new Slovenian legislation, case law, and expected changes following Slovenia's accession to the European Union. He is also a member of the examination board for new patent attorneys with the Slovenian Intellectual Property Office.

Marchien Maks is a graduate of the University of Amsterdam and Leiden University (Lic. Jur., 2001), and specializes in intellectual property. She joined Elzas Noordzij in 2002, where she advises clients in the field of trade mark law, trade name law, domain names, anti-counterfeiting, copyright law, designs and models law, and advertising law. Marchien is a member of the Benelux Association for Trademarks, Designs and Models.

Alecos Markides is a graduate of the Law School of Athens University. In 1970 he was called to the bar (Middle Temple). From 1971 to 1995, he practised law in Cyprus. From 1985 to 1995, he was a Member of the Cyprus House of Representatives (Parliament) and from 1995 to 2003, Attorney General of Cyprus. In this capacity, he headed the Law Office of Cyprus, which had the task of ensuring harmonization of the legal system of Cyprus with the *acquis communautaire*.

Hermione A Markides is a graduate of the Law School of Athens University. She has been the Secretary General of the Cyprus Bar Council for six years, President of the Society for Scientific and Cultural Studies, and President of the Council of Legal Education, preparing the Pupil Advocates for the Cyprus Bar, in association with Leicester University, for 15 years. She was a lecturer on Cyprus Law and has published articles on intellectual property law and company law. She specializes in litigation in intellectual property law and commercial law, and is a member of the Internet and Anti-Counterfeiting Committee of ECTA. She currently practises as a lawyer and is a Senior Partner at Markides, Markides & Co.

Mads Marstrand-Jorgensen is a partner in Norsker & Co. Law Offices and has practised at the Danish Bar since 1975. He graduated from the University of Copenhagen in 1972. He is the head of the intellectual property department of Norsker & Co. and handles all intellectual property matters including a substantial amount of litigation. He is a member of ECTA's Anti-Counterfeiting Committee.

Áine Matthews has worked with LK Shields Solicitors since 2000. Áine graduated in 1999 with a law degree from University College Galway and with a Master of Laws (Intellectual Property, Commercial and European Law) degree from the University of Edinburgh, Scotland, the following year. Áine was admitted as a solicitor in Ireland in early 2004. Her experience is in the area of intellectual property particularly in the law relating to trade marks, copyright, and industrial designs. She is regularly involved in the protection and enforcement of intellectual property and has written many articles on the areas of intellectual property and e-commerce law. Áine is also a registered Irish trade mark agent and Community trade mark attorney.

Patricia McGovern is one of the founding partners of LK Shields Solicitors. Patricia was admitted as a solicitor in 1987 after graduating with a law degree from Trinity College, Dublin. She is also an Irish trade mark agent and Community trade mark attorney. Patricia is the Head of the Intellectual Property Unit in LK Shields Solicitors and has extensive experience of all aspects of intellectual property and also of general commercial matters. She is a contributor to several publications in the area of intellectual property and is a regular speaker at seminars on these and related subjects. She is a member and former Chairman of the Business Law Committee of the Law Society of Ireland and is a member of numerous intellectual property law associations including INTA (Member of the Publications Board), MARQUES, ECTA, The American Intellectual Property Law Association, the Anti-Counterfeiting Group, The Intellectual Property Institute of Canada, and ITMA. She is a former Law Society of Ireland representative on the Company Law Committee of the CCBE (The Council of the Bars and Law Societies of the European Union).

Gatis Merzvinskis graduated from the Institute of Practical Psychology (Lic. translator and interpreter, 1999) and the University of Latvia, Faculty of Law (2000). He is the head of the legal and licensing departments at Petersona Patents where he handles intellectual property matters, mainly licensing, trade mark oppositions, and litigation. He has published numerous articles on intellectual property related issues. Gatis is a member of the Licensing Executive Society and the Association of Science and Technology Transfer Professionals.

Gonçalo Moreira Rato has his own law firm and has been practising at the Portuguese Bar since 1987. He graduated from the University of Lisbon, Portugal (Lic. Jur., 1985) and the Robert Schuman University—Strasbourg III, France (Master in Intellectual Property and International Contracts, 1988). He is a Portuguese official industrial property agent (1995), European patent attorney (1992), and European trade mark attorney (1996). He handles intellectual property matters, mainly the filing of rights and litigation. He is the author of various works in the field of intellectual and industrial property, and has published several articles on intellectual property matters. He has lectured at various Portuguese and international conferences.

Ekaterini Mouzaki practises law at the Brussels branch of G S Kostakopoulos & Associates. She is a graduate of the University of Lille II, France (LL.B., LL.M. in Political Science, LL.M. in European Defence and Security) and qualified for the Athens Bar in 2000. She handles intellectual property matters, specializing in anti-counterfeiting and patent and trade mark litigation.

Frits Mutsaerts is a partner with the law firm BANNING Advocaten. He graduated from Utrecht University (Lic. Jur., 1977), and has since acquired 25 years' experience as an attorney specializing in intellectual property and information technology. As he represents many national and international well-known trade mark owners, he has been the Netherlands delegate in the Anti-counterfeiting Committee of the European Communities Trademark Association (ECTA) since 2002. He is a preferred supplier to the Dutch IT Federation, co-founder of the Association of IT Lawyers, co-founder and joint editor of the Kluwer publication 'Model ICT Contracts', and Arbiter to the Foundation for the Resolution of IT Disputes.

Christine Noordzij is a partner with the trade mark firm, Elzas Noordzij. She graduated from the University of Amsterdam (Lic. Jur., 1993) and has specialized in the field of intellectual property law since 1993. She is the director of the anti-counterfeiting department of Elzas Noordzij and a member of several specialists' associations. Christine has been the Benelux delegate and the secretary on the Anti-Counterfeiting Committee of the European Communities Trademark Association since 1998.

Jeremy Phillips joined the Queen Mary Intellectual Property Research Institute in 2003 as Visiting Professorial Fellow. He has been Intellectual Property Consultant to London-based solicitors, Slaughter and May since 1994 and is the Founder-Editor of Sweet & Maxwell's *European Trade Mark Reports* and *European Copyright and Design Reports*. Jeremy has been Visiting Professor of Intellectual Property Law at UCL, the University of Alicante, and Bournemouth University, and previously held posts at Trinity College, Dublin and the University of Durham. The author of numerous books and articles on intellectual property, he is Consultant Editor of the *Butterworths Intellectual Property Law Handbook* and the *Butterworths E-commerce and Information Technology Law Handbook* as well as Editor of the *Journal of Intellectual Property Law and Practice* (Oxford University Press). He is also co-author (with Alison Firth) of *Introduction to Intellectual Property Law* (Butterworths, 4th edn 2002). His most recent publications are *Trade Mark Law: a Practical Anatomy* (Oxford University Press, 2003) and *Trade Mark Use* (with Ilanah Simon, Oxford University Press, 2005). He is co-founder of the IPKat weblog (www.ipkat.com), the first European intellectual property law weblog.

Bernhard Posner works with Zacco as European Union and public affairs consultant. Prior to advising the Zacco Group, comprising Zacco Denmark, Zacco Norway, and Zacco Sweden, he worked for approximately 25 years with the European Commission as advisor to the Directorate General in charge of intellectual property. He is a Master of Law of the University of Copenhagen, and a former associate professor at the Copenhagen Business School as well as an attorney-at-law in private practice. He has recently carried out an extensive teaching programme in EU candidate countries prior to the enlargement of the Union in 2004 for the European Commission.

Dorota Rzążewska works at Kulikowska & Kulikowski. She has been an attorney-at-law since 1994 and qualified trade mark and patent attorney since 2002. She graduated from the Faculty of Law and Administration at Warsaw University (Uniwersytet Warszawski) and in 1993 she completed her judge's legal training. She completed a postgraduate course in Copyright and Competition Law Studies at Jagiellonian University in 1998 and 1999 (Competition Law). She is a member of the International League of Competition Law (LIDC). She specializes in litigation with respect to intellectual property and unfair competition, appearing before the Patent Office, courts, public prosecutor, and customs authorities and advises in the area of industrial property protection, competition law, copyright, advertisement law, and domain names.

Zofia Senda has been working with Kulikowska & Kulikowski since 1998 and has been an attorney-at-law since 2003. She graduated from the Faculty of Law and Administration at the Catholic University of Lublin (Katolicki Uniwersytet Lubelski). She handles copyright law and litigation proceedings with respect to intellectual property and unfair competition which are conducted before the courts, public prosecutor and customs authorities and provides legal assistance to clients in these fields. She has published several articles on issues related to copyright law.

Helmut Sonn is an Austrian patent attorney and European patent, trade mark, and design attorney. In 1966 he graduated from the University of Technology in Vienna, and has practised as an Austrian patent attorney since 1971. Since 1975 he has been a judge at the International Arbitration Court of the Austrian Federal Economic Chamber, in

1982 he was nominated Expert Lay Judge at the Vienna Commercial Court, and since 2000 he has acted as a Sworn Certified Court Expert. His activities include trade marks and designs, litigation proceedings, as well as problems arising from the Internet (domain names, etc) and arbitration. He has extensive experience in the field of border measures. He is a member of numerous organizations including the Austrian Chamber of Patent Attorneys, Austrian Intellectual Property Law Association (president since 1995), International Federation of Intellectual Property Attorneys (president of honour as well as councillor since 1994), International Association for the Protection of Intellectual Property (president of honour since 1997; president of AIPPI Austria since 1995), Institute of Professional Representatives before the European Patent Office, and the European Communities Trade Mark Association (Austrian Council member since 1994).

David Tonna is Managing Partner in the firm Mamo TCV Advocates. He graduated (Doctor of Laws—LL.D.) from the University of Malta in 1981. He was admitted to the Bar in March 1982 and is a Member of the Malta Chamber of Advocates, the International Bar Association, the International Maritime Committee (CMI) of Belgium (Antwerp), Founder Member of the Malta Maritime Law Association, Member of the European Communities Trademark Association, AIPPI and the Association of European Trade Mark Proprietors (MARQUES). He is also the Honorary Consul of Luxembourg in Malta. He specializes in shipping and ship finance, intellectual property law, company law, company incorporation for local and overseas clients, tax, banking, and investment services, and co-ordinates work for the EU Law department in the firm. He has advised various local and foreign groups, government, and public corporations.

Mara Uzulena graduated from the Riga Technical University, Faculty of Economics and Engineering (1980) and the Turiba Business School, Faculty of Law (2003). She handles trade mark matters, mainly oppositions, litigation, and customs matters. She is a European Trade Mark and Design Attorney, as well as a member of INTA and the Latvian National Group of AIPPI.

Helena Wassén Öström is Master of Law from the University of Uppsala. From 1998 to 2001, she worked as a trade mark consultant and lawyer at Hynell Patenttjänst AB. Helena joined Zacco Sweden AB in 2001. Helena has experience in advising on legal matters relating to intellectual property law as well as marketing law and competition law. She works both with trade mark prosecution and legal work relating to intellectual property, such as oppositions, litigation, and licensing. She has particular experience in handling counterfeit issues in connection with the Swedish customs authorities.

TABLES OF CASES

CANADA

DENMARK

EUROPEAN COURT OF JUSTICE

FINLAND

FRANCE

GERMANY

GREECE

IRELAND

ITALY

PORTUGAL

SPAIN

SWEDEN

UNITED KINGDOM

TABLE OF LEGISLATION, TREATIES, AND CONVENTIONS

EUROPEAN UNION REGULATIONS

CONVENTIONS AND TREATIES

Part I

INTRODUCTION

1

THE PHENOMENON OF COUNTERFEITING AND PIRACY IN THE EUROPEAN UNION: FACTUAL OVERVIEW AND LEGAL AND INSTITUTIONAL FRAMEWORK

Michael Blakeney

Introduction

In developed countries, there is good evidence that intellectual property is, and **1.01** has been, important for the promotion of invention in some industrial sectors, particularly the pharmaceutical, chemical, and petroleum industries as well as biotechnology and some components of information technology.[1] Copyright has also proven essential for the music, film, and publishing industries. For developing countries, the nurturing of indigenous technological capacity through the intellectual property system has also proved to be a key determinant of economic growth and poverty reduction. The enforcement of intellectual property rights thus protects local commercial and industrial innovation, as well as encouraging technology transfer and foreign investment. The enforcement of IP rights is therefore part of a developing country's economic development strategy. A recent survey conducted by the World Intellectual Property Organization's (WIPO) Advisory Committee on Enforcement indicated an under-estimation of the value of intellectual property rights has contributed to ineffective enforcement.[2] It was suggested that it would be useful for governments to assess the value of the industries based primarily on intellectual property rights in terms of a percentage of the Gross Domestic Product (GDP). This could lead to an appreciation of the value

---

[1] See UNCTAD/ICTSD, *Intellectual Property and Development*, Geneva, 2003.
[2] WIPO Doc, WIPO/EIM/3 para 9.

of intellectual property rights in terms of a country's economic environment, as well as in respect to economic, social, and cultural growth and development.

1.02 Low risk of prosecution and enormous profit potential have made criminal counterfeiting an attractive enterprise for organized crime groups. Highly sophisticated and organized criminal syndicates exert significant influence and control over the manufacturing, distribution and sale of counterfeit and pirate goods. Recently, there have also been reported links between counterfeiting and piracy and terrorist organizations which use the sale of fake and unauthorized goods to raise funds and launder money.[3]

I. THE SOCIAL AND ECONOMIC CONSEQUENCES OF COUNTERFEITING AND PIRACY[4]

A. Definitions

1.03 The terms 'counterfeiting' and 'piracy' in relation to goods refer to the manufacture, distribution, and sale of copies of goods which have been made without the authority of the owner of the intellectual property. These goods are intended to appear to be so similar to the original as to be passed off as genuine items. This includes use of famous brands on pharmaceutical products, clothing, perfumes, and household products, not manufactured by or on behalf of the owner of the trade mark, as well as exact copies of CDs containing music or software, which are traded in a form intended to be indistinguishable to ordinary consumers from the genuine product.

1.04 In a criminal law context, intellectual property counterfeiting and piracy are defined as contraband activities which centre on the illegal production and sale of goods which are intended to pass for the real product. In this context 'contraband' refers to goods whose importation, exportation, or possession is forbidden. Dealings in contraband invariably involve smuggling, where the manufacturers and distributors of these products also seek to evade taxes on the production and wholesaling of these products.

---

[3] International Anticounterfeiting Coalition, *International/Global Intellectual Property Theft: Links to Terrorism and Terrorist Organizations*, Washington, 2003.

[4] An extensive study has been devoted to that issue by the Centre d'études internationales de la propriété industrielle (CEIPI), *Impacts de la contrefaçon et de la piraterie en Europe*, 2004. See also Christophe Zimmermann, *La problématique évolutive de la contrefaçon*, Actes du Colloque 'Les rencontres européennes de la propriété industrielle', April 2004.

B. Causes of piracy and counterfeiting

The principal cause of piracy and counterfeiting is the incentive to unscrupulous **1.05** traders of the considerable business profits which may be made from free-riding on the creative efforts and investment of others, by passing off imitations of desired products at a lower cost than those which are incurred by the producer of genuine products. Obviously, this trade would not exist without consumer demand and the public perception that piracy and counterfeiting are innocuous infractions. The theft of intellectual property is not yet equated in the public mind with other offences against property—crimes such as fraud, theft, or trespass. This is exacerbated by (i) a failure of the public authorities and commercial organizations to communicate to the consuming public the dangers arising from the use of unauthorized products and of the harmful social welfare effects of this trade; and (ii) the imposition of penalties which do not adequately deter offenders.

As the EC 1998 Green Paper, *Combating Counterfeiting and Piracy in the Single* **1.06** *Market* observed, '[s]ince the early 1980s counterfeiting and piracy have grown considerably to a point where they have now become a widespread phenomenon with a global impact'.[5] The reasons for this phenomenon are various. They include developments in reprographic technologies, where digitization has facilitated the rapid and extensive production of copies at a minimal cost; the growth in world demand for branded items; as well as economic and political developments, such as the growth of international trade, the internationalization of the economy, the expansion of means of communication and the opportunism of organized crime following the collapse of the political systems in central and eastern Europe and in the former Soviet Union.

The World Customs Organization[6] observes that the evolution of many contra- **1.07** band markets is typically a progression through one or more of the following stages:

- grey market, or parallel, trading;
- smuggling;
- counterfeiting and piracy.

Thus, some markets, like those for contraband cigarettes, alcohol, and pharmaceuticals, evolve through all three stages. Others—like the contraband markets for branded apparel and software—may move directly from grey market trading to counterfeiting.

In Western Europe and North America, the easiest way to meet consumer **1.08** demand for a cheaper product is through so-called grey market, or parallel,

---

[5] COM (98) 569, October 1998.
[6] See eg World Customs Organization, *Smuggling, Counterfeiting and Piracy: The Rising Tide of Contraband and Organised Crime in Europe*, 2001.

trading. Grey market goods are sold outside established distribution agreements, and their purveyors take advantage of the fact that companies charge different prices for their products in different markets.

1.09 In a number of jurisdictions, strong links have been noted between the grey market and smuggling, and in a number of sectors grey market channels have been used to camouflage counterfeit products. In the fashion sportswear and software sectors, it is not uncommon in the grey market for traders to send genuine samples to the importer and mix the consignment with counterfeits.

1.10 In markets for high tax products, such as tobacco and alcohol, where grey market products may not be available, smuggling becomes the primary means of meeting the demand for those products. In smuggling, organized crime groups establish elaborate means of concealing their diversion of products from the legal to the illegal market. This is to avoid law enforcement initiatives and those by private industries seeking to maintain the integrity of their supply chains. The smuggling techniques are complex and transnational in scope and may involve complex transactions with the involvement of legitimate as well as illicit enterprises. The objective is to make smuggling routes and the structure of transactions as complicated as possible, with the largest possible range of owners in a very short space of time, in order to make police and customs investigations as difficult as possible. The primary objective is to make the final owner untraceable and to make the links between the successive owners extremely ambiguous.

1.11 In some cases, grey market goods may not be available, in which case organized crime groups may decide to ensure a steady source of supply by becoming vertically integrated for the purposes of producing and distributing counterfeit and pirate products. This involves developing a supply chain that is wholly in the hands of organized crime groups from rogue manufacturing, through to smuggling the contraband across international borders, to illegal distribution and retailing to consumers.

1.12 The development of digitization and the availability of used manufacturing equipment has facilitated the counterfeiting and piracy of a variety of products—from traditional industries like cigarettes and apparel to high-tech sectors like computer software and music CDs.

1.13 Rogue manufacturing sectors, which produce counterfeit and pirated products, have much, much lower production costs.

- They are usually located in developing nations with extremely low labour and material costs.
- The quality of material inputs is extremely low.
- Quality control is virtually non-existent and the production facilities are often dirty, squalid workshops.

- They are virtually a cash business. Payment is received either in cash, within 8 to 10 days of a shipment being delivered. There is little need to finance receivables on a long-term basis.
- There is little, if any, inventory. Production is closely tied to orders which reduces the need to finance inventories and makes detection very difficult.
- There are no costs associated with overseeing and accountability such as those under which lawful businesses operate.

C. Economic impacts of counterfeiting and piracy

The costs to those businesses whose products are pirated and counterfeited **1.14** include: (i) loss of sales; (ii) competitive disadvantage to those enterprises which free-ride on the research and development and marketing expenses of legitimate enterprises; (iii) the possibility of product liability from defective imitation products; (iv) loss of goodwill and prestige by a brand, where counterfeits are freely available; and (v) the expense of monitoring the market and instituting legal proceedings against infringers. These costs will be incurred in both developed and developing countries.

The losses sustained by industry will be reflected in losses to the public revenue, as **1.15** well as in unemployment in the affected industries.

The prevalence of infringing activities in a country will also discourage invest- **1.16** ment from those industries in which proprietary rights are important. Thus for example, the pirating of music CDs and computer software will discourage investment in the music and information technology sectors.

As counterfeiting and piracy are illicit activities, they will be engaged in by **1.17** criminals, who will use their gains from these activities to subsidize further criminal activities. As these activities are not engaged in by ethical businesses, they will not observe basic employment standards, they will avoid contributing to public revenues through the payment of taxes and excise and they will have no concern that the products which they produce are of an acceptable consumer standard.

(1) Trade diversion

The 1998 EC Green Paper on counterfeiting and piracy[7] refers to the report of the **1.18** Counterfeiting Intelligence Bureau set up by the International Chamber of Commerce (ICC) that counterfeiting accounts for between 5and 7 per cent of

---

[7] See n 4 above.

world trade in value terms.[8] The immediate impact of this global trade is the loss of sales and the consequent impact upon employment. The US copyright industry puts its losses due to piracy at between USD 12 billion and USD 15 billion a year. According to the International Federation of the Phonographic Industry (IFPI),[9] sales of illegal CDs account for 14 per cent of the relevant market at world level. In May 2003, the UK music industry reported that sales of pirate CDs had outstripped the sales of genuine products. In the light of the responses which the Commission received to its Green Paper on the fight against counterfeiting and piracy in the Internal Market, it transpires that, within the European Union, counterfeit and pirated goods account for 5 to 10 per cent of vehicle spare parts sales, 10 per cent of sales of CDs and MCs, 16 per cent of film (video and DVD) sales, and 22 per cent of those of shoes and clothing.[10] The Commission in the final version of its proposal which became the 'Enforcement Directive'[11] refers to a survey carried out in France in 1998 by KPMG, Sofres, and the Union des Fabricants which reported that the average loss to the businesses which replied to the survey, was put at 6.4 per cent of turnover. It also refers to a 2000 study by the Centre for Economics and Business Research (CEBR) on behalf of the Global Anti-Counterfeiting Group (GACG), which quantified the average annual reduction in profits was: EUR 1,266 million in the clothing and footwear sector; EUR 555 million in the perfumes and cosmetics sector; EUR 627 million in the toys[12] and sports articles sector; and EUR 292 million in the pharmaceuticals sector.[13] Finally it reported a study carried out by the International Planning and Research Corporation (IPR), on behalf of the Business Software Alliance (BSA), which quantified the losses in Western Europe (EU plus Norway plus Switzerland) from software piracy in 2000 to be more than USD 3 billion.[14]

1.19 All countries, whether developed, developing or least developed, are vulnerable to trade diversion from piracy and counterfeiting. For example, the development of extensive computer software and movie industries in India, has spawned equally extensive developments in copyright piracy, affecting those industries. The global market for folkloric works, whether music, art, sculptures, textile products, and

---

[8] Counterfeiting Intelligence Bureau, International Chamber of Commerce, *Countering Counterfeiting. A guide to protecting and enforcing intellectual property rights*, 1997. See also Centre for Economics and Business Research, *Counting Counterfeits: Defining a Method to Collect, Analyse and Compare Data on Counterfeiting and Piracy in the Single Market*, 2002.

[9] Recent publications of IFPI include: *Commercial Piracy Report*, 2003; *Enforcement Bulletin*, 2003; *Music Piracy, Organised Crime and Terrorism*; *Online Music Report*, 2004.

[10] http://europa.eu.int/comm/internal_market/en/indprop/piracy/piracyen.pdf, 14–15.

[11] COM (2003) 46 Final.

[12] In relation to counterfeited toys, see Toy Industries of Europe, *The Importance of IPR Protection in the Fight against Counterfeiting of Toys*, 2000.

[13] Global Anti-Counterfeiting Group, *Economic Impact of Counterfeiting in Europe*, June 2000.

[14] Sixth Annual BSA Global Software. Other recent publications of the BSA include: *Expanding Global Economies: The Benefits of Reducing Software Piracy*, 2003; *Eighth Annual BSA Global Software Piracy Study: Trends in Software Piracy (1994–2002)*, 2003.

other artefacts, has spawned a global industry for the counterfeiting of these products. Likewise, with the development of niche markets for agricultural products, an illicit market has developed in which geographical indications are counterfeited.

(2) Revenue effects of counterfeiting and piracy

It is estimated that the tax and excise losses caused by counterfeiting and piracy are considerable. The paper accompanying the Commission proposal for a Directive on the enforcement of intellectual property rights, estimated that in the phonographic sector VAT losses incurred by EU governments as a result of counterfeiting and piracy amount to EUR 100 million.[15] It refers to the study conducted in June 2000 by the CEBR on behalf of the GACG which estimated the average loss of tax revenue in the EU to be: EUR 7,581 million in the clothing and footwear sector; EUR 3.017 million in the perfumes and cosmetics sector; EUR 3,731 million in the toys and sports articles sector; and EUR 1,554 million in the pharmaceuticals sector. The survey carried out in the United Kingdom in 1999 by the CEBR on behalf of the ACG estimated that counterfeiting led to a reduction in Gross National Product (GNP) of GBP 143 million per year and to a GBP 77 million increase in government borrowing. **1.20**

Revenue losses are also incurred in those countries in which counterfeit and pirated products are produced. As this trade tends to be clandestine, the producers of infringing products will hide the size of their production output from the tax authorities too. False documentation will accompany the false products, understating their sale price, for the purpose of reducing tax imposts in both the producing and importing countries. **1.21**

(3) Investment effects

The major cost to those developing countries in which piracy and counterfeiting occur is the loss of access to foreign investment, because of concerns by investors that intellectual property which is produced as the result of the relevant investment, will be stolen by others. This discouraging of investment has the obvious short-term effect of reducing taxes and revenues and the longer-term effect of stifling economic development. More specifically, the establishment of key industries in developing countries, such as those in the IT, biotechnology, and pharmaceutical areas, where intellectual property rights play a key role, will be difficult to establish in the absence of effective intellectual property laws or enforcement. **1.22**

---

[15] http://europa.eu.int/comm/internal_market/en/indprop/piracy/piracyen.pdf, 16, para 7.2.1.

1.23 Similarly, technology transfer arrangements will be difficult to secure, where the basis of those arrangements is the bundling of proprietary technologies as part of the technology package. If there is an ineffective legal regime for the protection of those technologies, their transfer will be discouraged.

(4) Employment effects

1.24 In social terms, the damage suffered by businesses because of counterfeiting and piracy is reflected ultimately in their impact upon employment. Initially, employment may improve in those countries where pirate and counterfeit goods are produced. However, where local industries are developed which are dependent upon intellectual property rights, the local capacity to produce infringing products may have an ultimately harmful effect upon employment. For example, the development of computer, electronics, and film industries in India are vulnerable to the piratical activities of local imitators, which then have an adverse impact upon investment in those industries. Similarly, local music and art industries are vulnerable to the pirating and counterfeiting activities of copyists.

1.25 To some extent, the production of counterfeited goods in developing countries arises from the fact that the production of legitimate branded products in those countries makes available to the authorized factory outlets the brands and the tools of the trade mark proprietor. Sometimes unauthorized use is made of this equipment in the production of counterfeit products. To recover control over the integrity of their products, the brand proprietors will relocate that production in countries where control over the intellectual property rights can be assured.

1.26 In addition to loss of revenue to the State (customs duties, VAT), there may also be infringements of labour legislation where the counterfeit or pirated goods are made in sweatshops by undeclared workers. The phenomenon is a serious threat to economies in general as it may destabilize the markets, including such fragile markets as those in textiles and clothing.

D. Copyright and piracy and the criminal economy[16]

1.27 Counterfeiting and piracy have an adverse effect upon public security, where profits from this trade are appropriated by organized crime, which uses them as a means of recycling and laundering the proceeds of other unlawful activities (arms, drugs, etc).

---

[16] Several reports are available on this topic, such as, eg: Union des Fabricants, *Contrefaçon et criminalité organisée*, 2nd edn, 2004; International AntiCounterfeiting Coalition (IACC), *White Paper: International/Global Intellectual Property Theft: Links to Terrorism and Terrorist Organizations*, 2003; IACC, *Submission of the International AntiCounterfeiting Coalition Inc. to the United States Trade Representative Special 301 Recommendations*, 2003; Alliance against Counterfeiting and

Counterfeiting and piracy, which were once craft activities, have become almost industrial-scale activities offering criminals the prospect of large economic profit without excessive risk. With the advent of e-commerce the rapidity of illegal operations and the difficulty of tracking the operations further reduce the risks for the criminal. Counterfeiting and piracy carried out on a commercial scale are even said to have become more attractive nowadays than drug trafficking, since high potential profits can be obtained without the risk of major legal penalties. Counterfeiting and piracy thus appear to be factors in promoting crime, including terrorism.

Organized criminals often combine counterfeiting and piracy with smuggling. **1.28**
The trade routes which were developed for the smuggling of drugs and arms have provided an existing infrastructure for the trade in counterfeit and pirate products. Indeed, the profitability of infringing products is now beginning to exceed that of drugs and arms, on a profit/weight basis.

The structure and commercial strategies of these organized crime groups is similar **1.29**
to those of lawful enterprises. In response to market forces, participants in each are equally intent on being profitable. But the key difference between legitimate commercial enterprises and criminal ones involves the manner in which commercial disputes are settled, how contracts are enforced, and the way in which dealings with the authorities are regulated. As those of criminal enterprises have to occur outside the court system, violence, coercion, and corruption are a pronounced feature of this trade. Because manufacture is illegal, labour standards are not observed, reducing labour costs, and taxes are not paid on the illicit manufacture, minimizing revenue expenses, thus those involved in illicit trading in infringing products have a number of economic advantages over legitimate manufacturers, wholesalers, and retailers.

The most serious consequences of the trade in counterfeit and pirate products is **1.30**
the stimulation of organized criminal activity and the consequential effects upon public and private corruption. This penetration of organized crime into otherwise lawful economic sectors also has a pernicious impact on public morality. As a contraband market develops, it puts significant pressure on retailers either to participate or go out of business. If they decide to join in, they may be forced to do other kinds of business with organized crime. Legitimate businesses see their prices undercut by cheaper contraband products and feel obliged to enter the black market to protect their businesses and their livelihoods. Once they have entered this trade it becomes difficult to withdraw.

The World Economic Forum in Davos in January 2003 was informed by the **1.31**
World Customs Organization (WCO) that the trade in counterfeit and pirate

Piracy, *Providing the Connexion: Links between Intellectual Property Theft and Organised Crime,* 2003; Interpol, *The Links between Intellectual Property Crime and Terrorist Financing,* 2003; IFPI, *Music Piracy, Organised Crime and Terrorism,* n 9 above.

products was as high as USD 450 billion per annum, was controlled by organized crime, and was being used to fund terrorist activity.

1.32 To the extent that consumers participate in a contraband market, this undermines respect among ordinary citizens for the law. Studies have shown that the initial act of law breaking can influence subsequent behaviour. Once people develop a taste for cheating, they keep on cheating. Thus, a key societal consequence of participating in a contraband market is that it serves to sanction tax evasion and other forms of law breaking.

1.33 A European survey by the Alliance Against Contraband (AAC) on the significance and influence of organized crime in counterfeiting and piracy identified the penetration of organized crime in the following industries:[17]

- branded goods, including clothing, footwear, perfume, and household consumer products;
- cigarettes;
- alcoholic beverages;
- pharmaceuticals;
- software; and
- recorded music.

1.34 The findings of this survey are outlined below. It should be noted that counterfeiting and piracy will often involve more than one category of product and illicit activity. For example, the survey reported that in Britain, police arrested members of a Russian crime group involved in the smuggling of counterfeit CDs and credit card fraud. In Italy, law enforcement officials believe that 100 Camorra organized crime groups in Naples are now heavily involved in CD piracy, as well as drugs, firearms and extortion, and in the Netherlands, police raids against a multi-million-Euro crime group with a major counterfeit CD operation also yielded firearms.

Branded goods

1.35 A difficulty in detecting this illicit trade is the use of subcontractors or outworkers who produce more goods than those ordered by the trade mark proprietor and for which the subcontractor is licensed. The outworking system is not uncommon in many developing countries, where a consolidator will accept a contract to deliver a quantity of branded products to a right-holder and will then subcontract the production of that quantity to smaller production units. This provides an opportunity for outworkers, who may be provided with moulds and dyes for the

---

[17] Alliance against Contraband, *Providing the Connexion: Links between Intellectual Property Theft and Organised Crime*, 2003. The results of the survey can be found on the website of the World Customs Organization, www.wco.org.

authorized production of protected brands, to produce additional unauthorized quantities, which are counterfeit.

In Europe, clothing and footwear companies are estimated to lose EUR 7.5 billion a year to counterfeiting. Across Europe, it is estimated that about 20 per cent of sales of clothing are counterfeit. In France and Sweden, counterfeit sales of clothing and shoes are estimated to comprise about 25 per cent of the total market, while, in Italy, they are believed to account for as much as 12 per cent of sales. The counterfeit leather goods sector in Italy alone is said to be worth EUR 1.6 billion a year. One-half of the counterfeit clothes sold in the European Union are estimated by the survey to be manufactured in member countries. Italy and Britain have been identified as major producers of counterfeit clothing. Again, a difficulty in detecting this illicit trade is the use of subcontractor or outworkers who produce more goods than those ordered by the trade mark proprietor and for which the subcontractor is licensed. **1.36**

Cigarettes

The trade in contraband cigarettes is identified in the AAC survey as one of the most lucrative organized crime sectors in Europe. Annual losses in tax revenues from cigarette smuggling are estimated at EUR 4.0 billion in Italy, EUR 3.9 billion in the UK, EUR 230 million in Germany, and EUR 208 million in Spain. High taxes in those countries are the root cause of cigarette smuggling. They create a sufficient demand among consumers for a cheaper, untaxed product, and the economic incentive for organized crime groups to supply that demand. The AAC survey identified China as a major source of contraband cigarettes. The major smuggling channels into Europe are: across the Balkans from Asia, from Eastern Europe—either to Germany, or from Baltic ports to Britain and through North Africa into Spain. **1.37**

Alcoholic beverages

The European Commission estimates that European Union members lost EUR 500 million per year from the smuggling of alcoholic beverages. In Britain, Denmark and Sweden the Commission estimates that 50 per cent of all spirits consumed are contraband. As with cigarettes, the smuggling of alcoholic beverages is tax driven. In all countries in which counterfeit alcohol is sold, there are health concerns about noxious additives. **1.38**

Contraband pharmaceuticals

The World Customs Organization estimates that around 5 per cent of the world trade in pharmaceuticals involves counterfeit products. In the EU, counterfeiting and associated activities are estimated to cost the pharmaceutical industry EUR 12.6 billion a year in worldwide losses. The AAC survey reported that within the EU, manufacturers of counterfeit pharmaceuticals have been identified in Italy, **1.39**

Germany, Greece, Spain, and the Netherlands. Outside the EU, China is a major source of counterfeit medicines. Contraband activities in the pharmaceutical sector are an especially grave concern to law enforcement because of the public safety dangers involved.

Contraband software

1.40   The AAC report estimated the annual losses from pirated software at EUR 3.8 billion per year in Western Europe. Software counterfeiters operate on a commercial scale in most parts of the world. There is a major problem, particularly in developing countries, involving small scale manufacturers using relatively low-cost technology that allows duplication of software using recordable CD burners. Pirated software is often sold at flea markets, through mail order and newspaper advertisements, and through the Internet. It has been estimated that as much as 90 per cent of Belgian and Dutch counterfeit software is sold on-line.

Contraband recorded music

1.41   The AAC report estimates that, worldwide, one in three recordings is pirated. The Ukraine and Russia are major suppliers of counterfeit CDs to Europe. Their estimated manufacturing capacity vastly outstrips local market needs. Thus, Ukraine's estimated manufacturing capacity is 70 million units a year, while its total legitimate market is about 5 million units a year, and Russia's estimated capacity is 90 million units a year, while its total legitimate market is about 30 million units per year. The AAC noted the involvement of organized crime in a range of piracy and counterfeiting.

Globalization of the trade in counterfeit and pirate products

1.42   The survey by the AAC on the significance and influence of organized crime in counterfeiting and piracy identifies the established trend of global trading in infringing products. Improvements in transportation, particularly with the development of containerization, has made it far cheaper and easier to ship goods around the world. At the same time, crime groups are able to shift production facilities to take advantage of market opportunities. It reports, by way of example, that a Chinese crime group dismantled a factory in Hong Kong which was producing pirate CDs, rebuilt it in Paraguay and staffed it with Hong Kong engineers. In January 2000, police in Germany seized 500,000 counterfeit CDs manufactured in the Ukraine and destined for Uruguay. In China, 190 billion counterfeit cigarettes are produced each year, making it a major source country for European-destined fakes. Malaysia, Singapore, and Taiwan are major locations for counterfeiters of audio and software products. Major counterfeiters of Western designer apparel goods are located in China and Hong Kong.

E. Consumer Protection

Counterfeiting and piracy likewise have damaging consequences for consumers. **1.43**
They generally involve: (i) extorting a higher price from consumers for the
infringing product than they would be prepared to pay for copies; (ii) consumer
deception about the quality of the counterfeit product, with the consequent risk
to health and safety; and (iii) the absence of after-sales service or any effective
recourse in the event of damage or injury.

Counterfeiting and piracy are generally accompanied by deliberate cheating of **1.44**
the consumer as to the quality the consumer is entitled to expect from branded
products. This is because counterfeit or pirated products are produced without
the quality checks imposed by public standards authorities and by the brand
proprietor, who will inevitably be concerned to protect the quality standards
associated with registered brands.

In addition to their economic impact, counterfeiting and piracy have been **1.45**
identified as having a damaging effect upon public health in both developing and
developed countries.[18] The ICC[19] has reported that:

- Dozens of people died in Cambodia through taking ineffective, counterfeit
  malaria medicines.
- Law enforcement authorities in Zambia seized counterfeit shampoo containing
  acid.
- Body-builders and others buying steroids on the black market in Australia were
  sold repackaged livestock steroids as human steroids.
- Diseased pig meat was used in counterfeit cans of pork luncheon meat in China.
- In India, counterfeit drugs were used to fight antibodies in Rh-D negative
  mothers.

The EC 1998 Green Paper, *Combating Counterfeiting and Piracy in the Single* **1.46**
Market identified the following examples of counterfeiting of medicines.

- In 1998 at least 60 counterfeit drugs, including several popular painkillers and
  antibiotics, were reported by the Brazilian Health Ministry as being distributed
  by Brazil's pharmacies and hospitals.
- In Uganda the National Drug Authority discovered expired anti-bacterial
  drugs labelled as a quinine mixture.
- Asian Pacific markets suffer from trade in vials of injectable antibiotic, retrieved
  from hospital waste and refilled—with low-cost streptomycin, non-sterile

---

[18] See also: International Intellectual Property Institute, *Counterfeit Goods and the Public's Health
and Safety*, 2003.
[19] Counterfeiting Intelligence Bureau, International Chamber of Commerce, *Countering
counterfeiting. a guide to protecting and enforcing intellectual property rights*, 1997.

starch powder, talc, or other ingredients which can have serious, even fatal, consequences when injected.

- Deaths in India, Pakistan, Bangladesh and Philippines have been directly linked to talc-filled vials with clear signs of illicit recycling, plugs, plastic and aluminium blisters re-assembled, and labels replaced to provide new, later expiry dates.

1.47   The World Health Organization (WHO) reported that the use of ethylene glycol instead of glycerine, led to the deaths of more than 500 patients in Argentina, Bangladesh, India, Nigeria, and Haiti. The lack of active ingredients in anti-malarials and the general danger that counterfeit and substandard medicines contribute to global antibiotic resistance have been pointed to in the study.[20] In a report on counterfeit drugs in Brazil, the WHO reported that between 10 per cent and 30 per cent of drugs are counterfeit. It appears that non-generics are counterfeited more than generics.[21] Specifically, the report referred to: birth control pills made with wheat; prostate cancer drug without the active ingredient and diet pills comprising dangerous concoctions of thyroid hormones, tranquilizers, diuretics and laxatives to ensure rapid weight loss, leaving users suffering from anxiety and other side effects like hepatotoxicity.[22]

1.48   A similar WHO report on counterfeit drugs in Nigeria[23] estimated counterfeits to number 40 to 60 per cent of all the drugs in the country. Counterfeit drugs include products with little or no active ingredients, or products for which active ingredients have been replaced by less expensive alternatives, giving as examples: children's deaths at Jos University Teaching Hospital, from ingestion of paracetamol syrup adulterated with diethylene glycol; the seizure of blood pressure medication containing chalk and insulin vials filled with sugar water; analgesics passed off as anti-malarials; and medicines that have long expired put back in the market, relabelled with new dates. Almost 2,500 people were killed in Nigeria in 1995 through injecting a supposed anti-meningitis drug during an international vaccination campaign. A batch of this vaccine was counterfeit. The Anti-Counterfeiting Group (ACG) UK also reported finds in Nigeria of brake shoes

---

[20] WHO, *Counterfeit Drugs in Brazil: The Public Health Dangers and Potential Solutions*, 2001, citing M Reidenberg and B Conner, 'Counterfeit and substandard drugs', [2001] Clinical Pharmacology & Therapeutics, vol 69, no 4, 189–193; R Williams and D Heymann, 'Containment of Antibiotic Resistance', [1998] Science, vol 279, no 5354, 1153–1154. Other WHO studies include: *Counterfeit and Substandard Drugs in Myanmar and Vietnam*, 1999; *Médicaments contrefaits—Guide pour l'élaboration de mesures visant à éliminer les medicaments contrefaits*, 2000.

[21] Citing C Csillag, 'Sao Paulo: Epidemic of counterfeit drugs causes concern in Brazil', [1998] The Lancet (Online), vol 352, no 28, 553, available: Northeastern University (accessed 10 March 2002); D Taylor, 'Counterfeiting drugs can kill', [1992] British Medical Journal (Online), vol 304 no 6823, 334, available: Northeastern University (accessed 10 March 2002).

[22] Citing B Pecoul, P Chirac, P Trouiller, and J Pinel, 'Access to Essential Drugs in Poor Countries: A Lost Battle', 1999; *Wall Street Journal*, 24 August 2001, B1.

[23] Ekinadese E Aburime, *Counterfeit Drugs in Nigeria and Current Interventions*, WHO, 2003.

and linings made from compressed grass rather than friction material and which burst into flames on testing, as well as eye drops which contained no active ingredient and were made from contaminated water, which could cause blindness if put into an infected eye.

The World Customs Organization reported that 89 people were killed in Haiti in 1995, having taken a paracetamol-based syrup contaminated with glycol diethylene (a toxic chemical used in antifreeze).   **1.49**

The International Anticounterfeiting Coalition reported the following instances.[24]   **1.50**

- In 2002, a New York County district attorney charged seven people and five companies in the US, China, and India with selling counterfeit Viagra over the Internet. Undercover officers purchased over 25,000 pills. Some pills were smuggled into the US in stereo speakers and stuffed toys. One supplier told the agents that he could supply 2.5 million tablets a month.[25]

- On 7 June 2001, the chief of security for a major drug company (Novartis International AG) testified before a House Subcommittee that one counterfeit ring they uncovered produced 'millions of yellow tablets that were virtually indistinguishable from the genuine product'. The fake tablets were 'made of boric acid, floor wax and lead-based yellow paint used for road markings'.[26]

- In February 2001, authorities in Los Angeles arrested three people for taking part in an extremely sophisticated counterfeit Viagra ring. A Pfizer analysis of the product ranked counterfeit versions of the drug a nine on a scale of 10. According to a pharmacist from the Los Angeles County Department of Health Services, the counterfeiters copied everything from the packaging, the package inserts, and the lot numbers.[27]

- According to the *Shenzhen Evening News* (a Chinese government owned newspaper), approximately 192,000 people died in China in 2001 because of fake drugs. Since 2001, Johnson & Johnson has established 38 criminal cases against factories that copied its products in China. China is widely regarded as the world leader in terms of the manufacture and export of counterfeit products.[28]

---

[24] *White Paper on International/Global Intellectual Property Theft: Links to Terrorism and Terrorist Organizations*, Washington, 2004.

[25] See US Officials Arrest Viagra Counterfeiters, Scrip, 22 May 2002; Ridgely Ochs, Sounding Alarm on Counterfeit Drugs; FDA Investigating Recent of Fake Drug Cases, New York Newsday, at 6 (12 June 2002).

[26] See Wisconsin State Journal, 'Thompson Should Block Surge in Knockoff Drugs' (22 June 2001).

[27] See Douglas Pasternak, 'Knockoffs on the Pharmacy Shelf, Counterfeit Drugs are Coming to America', US News & World Report at 26 (11 June 2001).

[28] See 'China's Killer Headache: Fake Pharmaceuticals', *Washington Post* (30 August 2002). According to US Customs intellectual property seizure statistics, China has topped the list of source countries for infringing goods for six of the past seven years. From 1996–2002, China accounted for

- The Federal Aviation Authority (FAA) estimates that 2 per cent of the 26 million airline parts installed each year are counterfeit (that equals 520,000 parts).[29]

- The operational life of counterfeit bearing seal spacers removed from a United Airlines plane was found to be 600 hours—the genuine parts had an operational life of 20,000 hours—the fake parts came complete with fake boxes, labels, and paperwork and were discovered only because of a vigilant airline mechanic. In another case, Delta Airlines discovered that an engine mount cone-bolt, (a device which actually fastens the engine to the plane) on one of its planes was counterfeit.[30]

- In 1995, counterfeit versions of infant formula were found on the shelves of grocery stores in 16 different states.[31] More recently, in 1999, the Food and Drug Administration (FDA) issued a warning regarding counterfeit cans of infant formula for infants allergic to milk protein. The warning came after some of the illicit product had already been purchased. The FDA warning stated that infants who ingested the counterfeit formula could experience fevers, skin rashes, or severe allergic reactions.[32]

- In the 1980s, one million counterfeit birth control pills caused internal bleeding in women.[33]

F. Cultural effects

1.51 Intellectual property rights hold particular relevance for the cultural sector, especially in the audiovisual sphere. The audiovisual medium is a particularly potent means for the preservation of records of music, dance, performance, ritual and other non-written folkloric forms. The lack of adequate protection of these cultural forms would not only severely undermine the development of a major economic sector but would, above all, pose a threat to our heritage and cultural

---

approximately 32.5 per cent of the total value of shipments seized based on intellectual property violations. See 2003 Submission of the International AntiCounterfeiting Coalition, Inc to the United States Trade Representative, Special 301 Recommendations (February 13, 2003) at 8, available at http://www.iacc.org/teampublish/109_467_4106.cfm.

[29] See Billy Stern, 'Warning! Bogus Parts Have Turned Up in Commercial Jets. Where's the FAA?' *Business Week*, 10 June 1996 at 90.   [30] See id.

[31] See Marian Burros, 'F.D.A. Target: Baby Formula', *New York Times*, 6 September 1995; 142 Cong Rec 5776 (House).

[32] See 'FDA Warns About Infant Formula Fraudulently Labeled as Nutramigen in Southern California', HHS NEWS (US Department of Health and Human Services), P99-23, 8 October 1999.

[33] See S Rep No 98-526 at 4 (1984), reprinted in 1984 USCCAN 3627. See also Naomi Aoki, 'Biotechnology Counterfeiters Hit Serono', Boston Globe at C4 (31 January 2001) (discussing a case from the late 1980s where the ringleaders were sentenced to 24-year prison terms); Peter Lowe, 'The Scope of the Counterfeiting Problem', International Criminal Police Review No 476–477 (1999) at 94–95, available at http://www.interpol.int/Public/FinancialCrime/IntellectualProperty/Publications/Default.asp.

diversity. This is particularly the case where unauthorized audiovisual works ignore the cultural sensitivity which may be required in the revelation and depiction of these subjects.

This sector is particularly under threat from piracy, particularly in smaller states **1.52** where there are no economies of scale. The replacement of analogue by digital media has considerably exacerbated the problem in that it has rendered copying both cheap and easy.

G. Impacts upon competition[34]

Innovation has become one of the most important factors of sustainable growth **1.53** for businesses, and of economic prosperity for society as a whole. Businesses must constantly improve or renew their products if they wish to keep or capture market shares. Sustained inventive and innovatory activity, leading to the development of new products or services, puts businesses at an advantage in technological terms and is a major factor in their competitiveness. Businesses often invest large amounts of money in research and development and in the advertising and marketing of their products. This investment will not be undertaken unless they are in a position to recoup their expenditure. Appropriate and effective protection of intellectual property helps to establish the confidence of businesses, inventors and creators and is a powerful incentive for investment, and hence for economic progress.

Counterfeiting and piracy are detrimental to the proper functioning of competi- **1.54** tion. Since counterfeit and pirated goods are, by definition, substitutes in the economic sense for the lawfully marketed goods which they imitate, the divergences in the cost base for illegal operators will also give rise to differences in the conditions of competition for the lawful operators. Counterfeiters and the producers of pirate goods save on the research and development costs and the marketing costs of legitimate traders. Their free-riding enables them to capture an increasing share of the market, thereby producing distortions in the conditions of competition and diversions of the natural trade flows of legal goods. The phenomena of counterfeiting and piracy thus lead to the loss of turnover and market shares by legitimate businesses. Additionally, they suffer the loss of future sales from the loss of brand image with their customers. The spread of counterfeit and pirated products leads to a prejudicial downgrading of the reputation and originality of the genuine products particularly when businesses gear their publicity to the quality and rarity of their products. This phenomenon also involves additional transaction costs for businesses (costs of protection, investigations,

---

[34] See also ORGALIME, *Counterfeiting. The Threat to the European Engineering Industry.*

expert opinions and disputes) and in certain cases may even lead to tort actions against the *de facto* right-holder of the products marketed by the counterfeiter or pirate where the proof of good faith is in doubt.

II. LEGISLATION ON THE ENFORCEMENT OF INTELLECTUAL PROPERTY RIGHTS IN THE EUROPEAN UNION

1.55 The European Community legislator has sought to harmonize the substantive intellectual property laws of the Member States through the enactment of a series of Directives and Regulations concerned with intellectual property rights. These include:

- Commission Regulation No 418/85 on the Application of Article 85(3) of the Treaty to categories of research and development agreements (19 December 1984)
- Council Directive No 87/54/EEC on the legal protection of topographies of semiconductor products (16 December 1986)
- Commission Regulation No 4087/88 on the Application of Article 85(3) of the Treaty to categories of franchise agreements (30 November 1988)
- First Council Directive No 89/104 to approximate the laws of the Member States relating to trade marks (21 December 1988)
- Council Directive No 91/250 on the legal protection of computer programs (14 May 1991)
- Council Directive No 92/100 on the rental right and lending right and on certain rights related to copyright (19 November 1992)
- Council Directive No 93/83 on the coordination of certain rules concerning copyright and rights related to copyright applicable to satellite broadcasting and cable retransmission (27 September 1993)
- Council Directive No 93/98 harmonizing the term of protection of copyright and certain related rights (29 October 1993)
- Council Regulation No 40/94 on the Community trade mark (20 December 1993)[35]
- Council Regulation No 2100/94 on Community plant variety rights (27 July 1994)[36]
- Directive No 96/9/EC of the European Parliament and of the Council of 11 March 1996 on the legal protection of databases
- Directive No 98/44/EC on the legal protection of biotechnological inventions (19 December 2002)

---

[35] OJ [1994] L 11/1.   [36] OJ [1994] L 227/1.

- Directive No 2001/84/EC of the European Parliament and of the Council on the resale right for the benefit of an author of an original work of art (27 September 2001)
- Directive No 2001/29/EC of the European Parliament and of the Council on the harmonization of certain aspects of copyright and related rights in the information society (22 May 2001)
- Commission Regulation No 2245/2002 implementing Council Regulation (EC) No 6/2002 on Community designs (21 October 2002)[37]
- Council Regulation (EEC) No 1576/89 of 29 May 1989 laying down general rules on the definition, description and presentation of spirit drinks (29 May 1989)[38]
- Council Regulation (EEC) No 1014/90 laying down general rules on the definition, description and presentation of spirit drinks (24 April 1990)
- Directive 98/71/EC of the European Parliament and of the Council on the legal protection of designs (13 October 1998)
- Council Regulation (EC) No 1493/99 on the common organisation of the market in wine (17 May 1999)[39]
- Council Regulation (EC) No 2081/92 on the protection of geographical indications and designations of origin for agricultural products and foodstuffs (14 July 1992)
- Council Regulation (EC) No 1768/92
- Council Regulation (EC) No 1610/96 concerning the creation of a supplementary protection certificate for plant protection products (23 July 1996)

Of these EC Regulations and Directives, two (or three) are specifically targeted at the enforcement of intellectual property rights. These are: **1.56**

- the Directive of the European Parliament and of the Council on measures and procedures to ensure the enforcement of intellectual property rights (16 February 2004) ('the Enforcement Directive');
- the Council Regulation concerning customs action against goods suspected of infringing certain intellectual property rights and the measures to be taken against goods found to have infringed such rights.[40]

A. Enforcement Directive

(1) Genesis of the Directive

On 15 October 1998, the European Commission presented a Green Paper on *Combating Counterfeiting and Piracy in the Single Market*[41] in order to launch a   **1.57**

---

[37] OJ [2002] L 3/1.   [38] OJ [1989] L 160/1.   [39] OJ [1999] L 179/1.
[40] OJ [2003] L196/7.   [41] COM (98) 569 Final.

debate on this subject with all interested parties. The areas of intervention suggested in the Green Paper related in particular to action by the private sector, the effectiveness of technical security provisions, penalties and other means of ensuring compliance with intellectual property rights, as well as administrative cooperation between the national authorities. On 30 November 2000, the Commission presented a follow-up Communication to the Green Paper in which it indicated, among other things, that it would be presenting a proposal for a Directive aimed at harmonizing the legislative, regulatory, and administrative provisions of the Member States on the means of enforcing intellectual property rights, and at ensuring that the rights available enjoy an equivalent level of protection in the Internal Market.[42] This proposal was submitted on 20 March 2003.[43] Subsequently the Economic and Social Committee gave its Opinion on 29 October 2003.[44] The Committee on Legal Affairs and the Internal Market of the European Parliament voted a number of amendments to the Commission proposal on 27 November 2003. It also informed the Council of Ministers of its hope that the European Parliament and the Council could adopt the Directive at first reading. The Council's Working Party on Intellectual Property met a number of times under the Italian Presidency to consider the proposal. On 9 March 2004 the European Parliament voted to adopt the Directive on Intellectual Property Enforcement. It was endorsed in April 2004 by the Council of Ministers.[45] Member States have two years to implement the new enforcement provisions in their national law.

(2) Scope

1.58 The Enforcement Directive aims at the harmonization of national laws as a means to enforce intellectual property rights. The idea is to create a level playing field for intellectual property right-holders based on the best practices already found in the legislations of the different Member States.

1.59 Article 1 of the Directive provides that it is concerned with 'measures and procedures necessary to ensure the enforcement of intellectual property rights'. For the purposes of the Directive, the term 'intellectual property rights' is defined in Article 2 to include industrial property rights.

1.60 Article 2(3) provides that the Directive shall not affect Community Directives governing the substantive law on intellectual property and Member States' international obligations, particularly those under the TRIPs Agreement.[46]

---

[42] COM (2000) 789 Final.   [43] (6777/03).   [44] (OJ C32 of 5.2.2004, 15).
[45] OJ [2004] L195.
[46] World Trade Organization Agreement on Trade Related Aspects of Intellectual Property Rights, 1994.

(3) General obligation

Article 3 of the Enforcement Directive provides that: **1.61**

> Member States shall provide for the measures, procedures and remedies needed to ensure the enforcement of the intellectual property rights covered by this Directive. These measures, procedures and remedies shall be fair and equitable, and shall not be unnecessarily complicated or costly, nor entail unreasonable time-limits or unwarranted delays.

(4) Persons entitled to apply for the application of the measures and procedures

Article 4 of the Directive requires Member States to recognize as persons entitled **1.62**
to seek application of the measures and procedures provided for by the Directive:

- the holders of intellectual property rights in accordance with the provisions of the applicable law;
- all other persons authorized to use those rights, in particular licensees, in so far as permitted by and in accordance with the provisions of the applicable law;
- intellectual property collective rights management bodies which are regularly recognized as having a right to represent holders of intellectual property rights, in so far as permitted by and in accordance with the applicable law;
- professional defence bodies which are regularly recognized as having a right to represent holders of intellectual property rights, in so far as permitted by and in accordance with the applicable law.

(5) Presumption of authorship or ownership in copyright actions

Article 5 provides, in relation to copyright litigation, the author of a literary or **1.63**
artistic work, in the absence of proof to the contrary, shall be regarded as such and consequently be entitled to institute infringement proceedings. It shall be sufficient for his name to appear on the work in the usual manner.

(6) Preservation of evidence

Article 6(1) of the Enforcement Directive provides that Member States shall **1.64**
ensure that, on application by a party who has presented reasonably available evidence sufficient to support his claims, and has, in substantiating those claims, specified evidence which lies in the control of the opposing party, the competent judicial authorities may order that such evidence be produced by the opposing party, subject to the protection of confidential information.

In the case of an infringement carried out on a commercial scale, Member States are **1.65**
required by Article 6(2) to 'take such measures as are necessary to enable the

competent judicial authorities to order, where appropriate, on application by a party, the communication of banking, financial or commercial documents under the control of the opposing party, subject to the protection of confidential information'.

1.66 In relation to the protection of evidence, Article 7(1) provides that:

> Member States shall ensure that even before the commencement of proceedings on the merits of the case the competent judicial authorities may, on application by a party who has presented reasonably available evidence to support his claims that his intellectual property right has been infringed or is about to be infringed, order prompt and effective provisional measures to preserve relevant evidence in regard to the alleged infringement, subject to the protection of confidential information. Such measures may include the detailed description, with or without the taking of samples, or the physical seizure of the infringing goods, and, in appropriate cases, the materials and implements used in the production and/or distribution of these goods and the documents relating thereto. These measures shall be taken, if necessary without the other party having been heard, in particular where any delay is likely to cause irreparable harm to the right-holder, or where there is a demonstrable risk of evidence being destroyed.

(7) *Security for claims*

1.67 Article 7(2) of the Enforcement Directive provides that 'Member States shall ensure that the evidence-protection measures may be subject to the applicant's lodging of an adequate security or equivalent assurance intended to ensure compensation for any prejudice suffered by the defendant'.

(8) *Indemnification of defendant*

1.68 Article 7(4) of the Enforcement Directive provides that:

> Where the evidence-protection measures have been revoked, or where they lapse due to any act or omission by the applicant, or where it is subsequently found that there has been no infringement or threat of infringement of any intellectual property right, the judicial authorities shall have the authority to order the applicant, upon request of the defendant, to provide the defendant with appropriate compensation for any injury caused by these measures.

(9) *Right of information*

1.69 Article 8(1) of the Enforcement Directive provides that:

Member States shall ensure that, in the context of proceedings concerning an infringement of an intellectual property right and in response to a justified and proportionate request of the claimant, the competent judicial authorities may order that information on the origin and distribution networks of the goods or services which infringe an intellectual property right be provided by the infringer and/or any other person who:

    (a) was found in possession of the infringing goods on a commercial scale;
    (b) was found to be using the infringing services on a commercial scale;
    (c) was found to be providing on a commercial scale services used in infringing activities; or
    (d) was indicated by the person referred to in point (a), (b) or (ba) as being involved in the production, manufacture or distribution of the goods or the provision of the services.

Article 9(2) outlines the sorts of information which may be ordered to be disclosed, as follows: **1.70**

(a) the names and addresses of the producers, manufacturers, distributors, suppliers and other previous holders of the goods or services, as well as the intended wholesalers and retailers;

(b) information on the quantities produced, manufactured, delivered, received or ordered, as well as the price obtained for the goods or services in question.

(10) *Provisional measures*

Article 9(1) of the Enforcement Directive provides that Member States shall ensure that the judicial authorities may, at the request of the applicant: **1.71**

(a) issue against the alleged infringer an interlocutory injunction intended to prevent any impending infringement of an intellectual property right, or to forbid, on a provisional basis and subject, where appropriate, to a recurring penalty payment where provided for by national law, the continuation of the alleged infringements of that right, or to make such continuation subject to the lodging of guarantees intended to ensure the compensation of the right-holder; an interlocutory injunction may also be issued, under the same conditions, against an intermediary whose services are being used by a third party to infringe an intellectual property right; injunctions against intermediaries whose services are used by a third party to infringe a copyright or a related right are covered by Directive 2001/29/EC;

(b) order the seizure or delivery up of the goods suspected of infringing an intellectual property right so as to prevent their entry into or movement within the channels of commerce.

Article 9(2) provides that, in cases of infringement committed on a commercial scale, the Member States shall ensure that, if the injured party demonstrates circumstances likely to endanger the recovery of damages, the judicial authorities may order the precautionary seizure of the movable and immovable property of the alleged infringer, including the blocking of his bank accounts and other assets. To this end, the competent authorities may order the communication of bank, financial, or commercial documents, or appropriate access to the relevant information.   **1.72**

1.73   Under Article 9(3), the judicial authorities shall, in respect of the measures referred to in paragraphs 1 and 1a, have the authority to require the applicant to provide any reasonably available evidence in order to satisfy themselves with a sufficient degree of certainty that the applicant is the right-holder and that the applicant's right is being infringed, or that such infringement is imminent.

1.74   According to Article 9(4):

> Member States shall ensure that the provisional measures referred to in paragraphs 1 and 1a may, in appropriate cases, be taken without the defendant having been heard, in particular when any delay would cause irreparable prejudice to the right-holder. In the event of this happening, the parties shall be so informed without delay after the execution of the measures at the latest.

1.75   A review, including the right to be heard, shall take place upon request of the defendant with a view to deciding, within a reasonable time after notification of the measures, whether these measures shall be modified, revoked or confirmed.

1.76   Article 9 (5) of the Enforcement Directive, which clearly mirrors Article 50(6) of the TRIPs Agreement, further imposes on the Member States to ensure that the provisional measures referred to in paragraphs 1 and 2 shall be revoked, or otherwise cease to have effect, upon request by the defendant, if the applicant does not institute proceedings leading to a decision on the merits of the case before the competent judicial authority within a reasonable period. This reasonable period is to be determined by the judicial authority ordering the measures where the Member State's law so permits or, in the absence of such determination, within a period not to exceed 20 working days or 31 calendar days, whichever is the longer.

1.77   Pursuant to Article 9(6), the competent judicial authorities may make the provisional measures referred to in paragraphs 1 and 1a subject to the lodging by the applicant of adequate security or equivalent assurance intended to ensure any compensation of the prejudice suffered by the defendant as provided for in paragraph 5.

1.78   Finally, Article 9(6) provides that:

> [w]here the provisional measures are revoked or where they lapse due to any act or omission by the applicant, or where it is subsequently found that there has been no infringement or threat of infringement of an intellectual property right, the judicial authorities shall have the authority to order the applicant, upon request of the defendant, to provide the defendant with appropriate compensation for any injury caused by these measures.

(11) Injunctions

1.79   Article 11 of the Enforcement Directive provides for the granting of injunctions to restrain infringers and against 'intermediaries whose services are used by a third party to infringe an intellectual property right.'

(12) Damages

Article 13 of the Enforcement Directive provides that compensatory damages **1.80** shall be paid to right-holders, taking into account all appropriate aspects. These include the negative economic consequences, including lost profits, which the injured party has suffered, any unfair profits made by the infringer and, in appropriate cases, elements other than economic factors, such as the moral prejudice caused to the right-holder by the infringement or as an alternative to setting the damages as a lump sum on the basis of elements such as at least the amount of royalties or fees which would have been due if the infringer had requested authorization to use the intellectual property right in question.

B. Border enforcement of intellectual property rights

The issue of enforcement of intellectual property rights at the borders of the **1.81** European Union constitutes the core of this book and will be addressed extensively in the following chapters. Until 1 July 2004, intellectual property rights were protected at the borders of the European Union by Council Regulation 3295/94 laying down measures to prohibit the release for free circulation, export, re-export, or entry for a suspensive procedure of counterfeit and pirated goods. This Regulation already allowed the holder of certain intellectual property rights to lodge an application with the competent customs authorities to prohibit the entry into the Community and the export or re-export from the Community of counterfeit, pirated, and patent infringing goods. On 20 January 2003, the Commission adopted a proposal to amend Council Regulation 3295/94. This resulted in the adoption by the Council on 22 July 2003 of Regulation (EC) No 1383/2003 concerning customs action against goods suspected of infringing certain intellectual property rights and the measures to be taken against goods found to have infringed such rights (hereafter 'the 2003 Regulation').[47] This Regulation applies with effect from 1 July 2004. The 2003 Regulation is directly applicable in the Member States. It has been accompanied by specific implementing measures.[48]

The 2003 Regulation is also integrated with the Community Customs Code (here- **1.82** after CCC).[49] In particular, the customs operations covered by the 2003 Regulation are defined directly by reference to the CCC.[50] Moreover, the Customs

---

[47] OJ [2003] L196/7.

[48] Commission Reg (EC) No 1891/2004 of 21 October 2004, OJ [2004] L 328/16.

[49] Council Reg (EEC) No 2913/92 of 12 October 1992 establishing the Community Customs Code, OJ [1992] L 302/1, as last amended by Reg (EC) No 2700/2000 of the European Parliament and the European Council, OJ [2000] L 311/17. See also Commission Reg (EEC) No 2454/93 of 2 July 1993 laying down provisions for the implementation of Council Reg (EEC) No 2913/92 establishing the Community Customs Code, OJ [1993] L 253/1.

[50] 2003 Reg, Art 1(1)(a).

Code Committee established by Article 247 of the CCC has an advisory role in relation to the implementation of the 2003 Regulation.[51] Within the Commission, responsibility for the 2003 Regulation rests with the Customs Policy Division of the Directorate-General for Taxation and the Customs Union (TAXUD).[52]

1.83   As will be further explained below by other authors, the 2003 Regulation aims to establish barriers at the external frontiers of the Community to trade in goods that infringe certain intellectual property rights, particularly counterfeit and pirated goods.[53] It does not apply to goods that are already in free circulation (that is, goods that have originated, or have already been entered for free circulation, in the single market). As such, it has no application to trade between Member States, unless goods arriving from another Member State have yet to be entered for free circulation.[54]

1.84   On 12 July 2005 the European Commission published a proposal for a Directive on criminal measures aimed at ensuring the enforcement of intellectual property rights and a proposal for a Council Framework Decision to strengthen the criminal law framework to combat intellectual property offences (COM(2005)276 final). This was intended to supplement the civil and administrative measures, procedures and remedies provided for in Directive 2004/48/EC and is expressed in Article 1 to be without prejudice to any more stringent measures which a country might introduce. Article 3 obliges Member States to consider all intentional infringements of an intellectual property right on a commercial scale as a criminal offence and requires the criminalization of attempting, aiding or abetting, and inciting such offences. The 'commercial scale' criterion is borrowed from Article 61 of the TRIPs Agreement. Article 4 of the draft Directive lays down a range of penalties to be imposed on both natural and legal persons, such as fines and the seizure of goods belonging to the offender, including the infringing goods and the materials, implements or media used predominantly for the manufacture or distribution of the goods in question. Other penalties are provided for specific cases: destruction of infringing goods and goods principally used in the manufacture of the goods in question, total or partial closure, on either a permanent or a temporary basis, of the establishment or shop primarily used to commit the infringement. Provision is also made for a permanent or temporary ban on engaging in commercial activities, placement under judicial supervision or judicial winding-up, and a ban on access to public assistance or subsidies. Finally, the publication of judicial decisions is provided for as a means of dissuasion and as a channel of information both for right-holders and for the public at large. As with

---

[51] 2003 Reg, Art 21.   [52] See under para 1.94.   [53] 2003 Reg, 2nd Recital.
[54] European Court of Justice, *Commission* v *France*, Case C-23/99 [2000] ECR I-7653. See also *Administration des Douanes et Droits Indirects* v *Rioglass SA and Transremar SL*, Case C-115/02, 23 October 2003 (not yet reported).

other Directives, Article 5 provides for an 18-month period within which the measures have to be enacted by Member States.

III. THE EUROPEAN COMMISSION AND ITS INITIATIVE AGAINST PIRACY AND COUNTERFEITING

The European Commission is the politically independent institution that **1.85**
represents and upholds the interests of the European Union (EU). It is the driving
force within the EU's institutional system. It has four main roles:

1. to propose legislation to the European Parliament and Council;
2. to manage and implement EU policies and the budget;
3. to enforce European law (jointly with the Court of Justice);
4. to represent the European Union on the international stage, for example by
   negotiating agreements between the EU and other countries.

In the area of intellectual property, the Commission has promulgated an action **1.86**
plan comprising the following elements:

- harmonization among all EU members of legislation to protect intellectual
  property rights;
- improved law enforcement training programmes;
- education programmes to raise awareness among consumers of the negative
  consequences of purchasing counterfeit and pirated products;
- the launching of a study for defining a methodology for collecting, analysing
  and comparing data on counterfeiting and piracy.

In the long-term, the action plan suggests undertaking studies to determine the **1.87**
advisability and/or need for:

- establishing mechanisms for administrative and operational cooperation;
- harmonizing minimum thresholds for sanctions and criminal proceedings;
- extending the powers of Europol, the European equivalent of Interpol, for
  combating counterfeiting and piracy.

The European Community and its Member States devote substantial resources to **1.88**
technical cooperation with States which wish to accede to membership of the
European Union and with countries of other continents. These include either
specific bilateral cooperation or actions fitting into a more general framework,
such as preparation programmes for WTO accession, general programmes for
developing business skills, PHARE (Poland and Hungary, Assistance for the

Reconstruction of the Economy), and TACIS (Technical Assistance for the Commonwealth of Independent States) programmes.

1.89 The European Commission is organized into 36 departments, known as 'Directorates-General' (DGs) and 'services' (such as the Legal Service). Each DG is responsible for a particular policy area and is headed by a Director-General who is answerable to one of the commissioners. It is the DGs that actually devise and draft the Commission's legislative proposals and technical cooperation activities. A number of the Directorates General of the European Commission are concerned with the enforcement of intellectual property rights; foremost among these are: DG Trade, DG Taxation and Customs Union, DG Internal Market, and DG Enterprise. The technical cooperation undertaken by the DGs of the European Commission include: legislative advice, exchanges on how to organize the administrative infrastructure, awareness promotion in the private sector and civil society, and human resources training and capacity building.

A. Directorate General, Trade

1.90 DG Trade has responsibility, among other things, for devising and monitoring internal or external intellectual property policies in accordance with the trade policies of the European Union. A key policy of the Union is to secure the better recognition and enforcement of intellectual property rights. DG Trade's policy in the field of intellectual property consists of: promoting the implementation of effective standards for intellectual property protection worldwide; promoting an adequate enforcement of intellectual property rights worldwide, and participating in the fight against violations; ensuring that such rights are supportive of public health objectives, innovation and technology transfer; and co-operating with developing and least developed countries, for which the introduction and enforcement of intellectual property laws is quite a challenge. The European Union is currently providing technical cooperation to a significant number of countries in this field.

1.91 DG Trade has recently formulated a *Strategy for the Enforcement of Intellectual Property Rights in Third Countries*. The purposes of the Strategy are to:

- provide a long-term line of action for the Commission services with the goal of achieving a significant reduction of the level of intellectual property rights violations in third countries;
- describe, prioritize and coordinate the mechanisms available to the Commission services for achieving their goal;
- inform right-holders and other entities concerned of the means and actions already available, and raise awareness of the importance of their participation.

The proposed activities under the Strategy include: **1.92**

- identifying the priority countries, that is, creating a mechanism based on a questionnaire that will periodically assess the situation and allow the identification of countries where the efforts of the Commission should be concentrated;

- intellectual property rights mechanisms in multilateral (including TRIPs), bi-regional and bilateral agreements. These would include: (i) raising enforcement concerns at Summit meetings with third countries concerned and in the Councils/ Committees created in the framework of these agreements more systematically; (ii) consulting trading partners with the aim of launching an initiative in the TRIPs Council, sounding the alert on the growing dimension of the problem, identifying the causes and proposing solutions; and (iii) revisiting the European Union approach to the intellectual property rights chapter of bilateral agreements with a view to, inter alia, the strengthening of the enforcement clauses;

- political dialogue: (i) making clear to trading partners that an effective protection of intellectual property, at least at the level set in TRIPs, is essential; (ii) launching joint initiatives focusing on intellectual property rights enforcement with countries sharing/ affected by similar concerns; and (iii) providing training and implementing networking mechanisms for officials in European Community Delegations facing enforcement problems;

- incentives/ technical cooperation: (i) ensuring the inclusion in the relevant programmes of technical assistance initiatives in the field of intellectual property rights enforcement; and (ii) exchanging ideas and information with other key providers of technical cooperation, like the World Intellectual Property Organization, the United States, Japan and certain EU Member States, with the aim of avoiding duplication of efforts and sharing of best-practices;

- dispute settlement/ sanctions: (i) recalling the possibility that right-holders have of making use of the Disputes Resolution mechanism in cases of evidence of violations of TRIPs or of bilateral agreements; and (ii) making *ex officio* use of the dispute settlement mechanisms included in multilateral and/ or bilateral agreements in case of non-compliance with the required standards of intellectual property protection;

- creation of public-private partnerships: (i) supporting/ participating in local intellectual property networks established in relevant third countries; (ii) using mechanisms already put in place by Commission services (IPR Helpdesk and Innovation Relay Centres) to exchange information with right-holders and associations; and (iii) building on the cooperation with companies and associations that are very active in the fight against piracy and counterfeiting, inter alia by ensuring the cross-participation of experts from the Commission and from private entities in events organized by the other party;

- awareness raising/drawing on our own experience, that is, promoting the inclusion in technical cooperation programmes and in public-private partnership initiatives of information destined to: (i) raise public awareness about the impact of counterfeiting (loss of foreign investment and technology transfer, risks to health, link with organized crime, etc), (ii) raise the awareness of Community right-holders doing business in 'problematic' countries about the risks incurred; and (iii) make available to the public and to the authorities of concerned third countries a 'Guidebook on Enforcement of Intellectual Property Rights';

- institutional cooperation: (i) improving the exchange of information and the coordination between the services in charge of the different aspects of intellectual property rights enforcement; and (ii) simplifying the identification and the access of external entities (right-holders, third country authorities, etc) to the service responsible for the specific issue concerning them.

1.93 The *Strategy for the Enforcement of Intellectual Property Rights in Third Countries* was presented to the public in the framework of the Conference celebrating 'The 10th Anniversary of the TRIPs Agreement' organized by DG Trade in Brussels on 23 and 24 June 2004.

B. Directorate General, Taxation and Customs Union

1.94 The Customs Union is an essential element in the creation of an integrated single European market and of a common commercial policy. The role of DG Taxation and Customs Union is to maintain and defend the Customs Union and to ensure the uniform application of the nomenclature and origin rules. The Directorate General takes full part in international commercial negotiations which have an effect on the common customs policy and surveys in particular the application of the rules of origin and the preferential trading systems.

1.95 In addition to their traditional activity of collecting duties, customs administrations are entrusted with new tasks involving the protection of both the consumer and the legitimate trader. The development of electronic and world trade, the current EU enlargement process and the development of fraud and organized crime are many factors forcing the customs administrations to adopt new strategies to deal with counterfeiting and piracy. The 2003 Regulation, drafted (as all previous Regulations on 'border measures') by DG Taxation and Customs Union, is part of the Commission's Action Plan against piracy and counterfeiting of 30 November 2000 under which the Directive on the enforcement of intellectual property rights was framed. This Directorate General is also responsible for keeping up to date the statistics on the number and kinds of goods detained at the borders of the Community by the customs authorities of the Member States.[55]

---

[55] These statistics can be found on the DG's website at http://europa.eu.int/comm/taxation_customs/customs/customs_controls/counterfeit_piracy/statistics/index_en.htm.

C. Directorate General, Internal Market

The internal market is one of the essential cornerstones of the European Union. It **1.96** is the culmination of the Treaty of Rome which provided for the creation of a 'common market' based on the free movement of goods, persons, services and capital. The idea of unifying the markets of Member States ties in with the objective of economic and political integration. The Treaty establishing the European Community[56] provides for the activities of the Community to include 'a system ensuring that competition in the internal market is not distorted' and 'the approximation of the laws of the Member States to the extent required for the functioning of the common market'.

The Internal Market DG focuses in particular on the 'knowledge-based' aspects **1.97** of the Single Market. Its work is partly concerned with traditional instruments regulating the market, such as harmonizing the laws of the Member States relating to industrial property rights to avoid barriers to trade. The aim is also to create unitary systems for the protection of such rights with Community-wide effect through the filing of one single application for protection (Community trade marks, designs and patents). The Internal Market DG is also increasingly concerned with ensuring that the Single Market functions properly in the Information Society and the fight against counterfeiting. A fundamental discussion on the principle of Community exhaustion of trade mark rights and its economic effects on innovation, employment and prices is also controlled by the Internal Market DG, as well as the discussions on enlargement. There has been significant intellectual property harmonization in the European Union to do away with barriers to trade and to adjust the framework to new forms of exploitation. The Internal Market DG's task is to enforce this '*acquis*' and to modernize and adapt it to new developments in technology or the markets concerned (see, for example, the Directive on copyright and related rights in the Information Society). It is also involved in international negotiations to improve intellectual property rights protection internationally.

D. IPR Helpdesk Project (Directorate General, Enterprise)

DG Enterprise has established the IPR Helpdesk (www.IPR-Helpdesk.org). **1.98** Its main objective is to assist potential and current contractors taking part in European Community funded research and technological development projects on intellectual property rights (IPR) issues. The IPR Helpdesk also advises on Community diffusion and protection rules, and other issues relating to intellectual property rights (IPR) in international research projects. Another more global

---

[56] EC Treaty (Treaty of Rome), as amended.

objective of the action is to raise awareness of the European research community on IPR issues, emphasizing their European dimension. Additionally, the IPR Helpdesk runs a number of training courses and information seminars on intellectual property matters.

Conclusion

1.99 As can be seen above there are now a number of different agencies involved in intellectual property enforcement. As a result coordination of action is jeopardized and there is also a danger of duplication of effort and waste of resources. This suggests that stronger partnerships between enforcers and business is the way of the future. For example, the UK has announced a strategy around an annual 'National Enforcement Report' which is designed to draw together the enforcement work carried out by major stakeholders 'to establish the state of play and a better strategic picture'. This Report will then feed into discussion of a high level Strategic Tasking and Coordinating Group which will set priorities and coordinate activities for the following year.[57] Similar initiatives are under discussion in other countries.

1.100 Given current concerns about the linkage between counterfeiting and piracy and organized crime, the economic harm caused by those activities, and the danger to consumer health and safety, it is imperative that national cooperation and coordination is replicated by regional and international cooperation.

---

[57] UK Patent Office, *Counter Offensive: An IP Crime Strategy* London, 2004.

Part II

INTERNATIONAL BACKGROUND AND LEGAL FRAMEWORK

2

THE INTERNATIONAL LEGAL FRAMEWORK OF BORDER MEASURES IN THE FIGHT AGAINST COUNTERFEITING AND PIRACY

Daniel J Gervais[1]

Introduction

As is evident from the first part of this book, sales of counterfeit and pirated **2.01** goods cause a significant amount of economic harm. While manufacturers, importers and retailers of illegal goods may profit from this trade, the fact that no intellectual property payments are included in the purchase price means that no funds will be made available for future innovation and creation. Furthermore, by undercutting prices for legitimate goods, sales of such goods are hampered, again reducing incentives to create and innovate. Use of counterfeit products, whether spare parts for automobiles or drugs, can result in injury and death. Finally, profits from sales of counterfeit and pirated goods often end up in the pockets of organized crime, thus indirectly fuelling drug and human trafficking. It should thus be obvious that debates about enforcement of intellectual property rights, when it is applied to counterfeit or pirate goods, are quite different from legitimate debates about the optimal scope of intellectual property protection, and necessary exceptions to allow true creators and innovators to continue to create new works and invent new products and processes. Those debates should continue, but trade in counterfeit and pirated goods must be stopped.

This chapter will outline the international legal framework on border measures **2.02** in the fight against counterfeiting and piracy. Part I describes the origins of

---

[1] The author is indebted to Ms Marina Pavlovic, LL.D. candidate at the University of Ottawa, for her diligent assistance in the research necessary to prepare this text.

the international framework, namely the Berne and Paris Conventions. This chapter will also discuss the genesis of the Agreement on Trade-Related Aspects of Intellectual Property Rights (TRIPs Agreement) and, in particular, the genesis of the provisions on border measures. Part II will analyse in detail the relevant provisions of the TRIPs Agreement. Part III will outline post-TRIPs developments, including developments in other international fora.

I. THE ORIGINS OF THE INTERNATIONAL FRAMEWORK ON BORDER MEASURES

2.03 The *Paris Convention for the Protection of Industrial Property*[2] and the *Berne Convention for the Protection of Literary and Artistic Works*[3] establish minimum standards for the protection of most intellectual property rights.[4] However, these Conventions had two major flaws, namely a lack of detailed provisions on enforcement of rights and the absence of a binding and effective dispute resolution mechanism.[5] Because of such flaws, the provisions they contain dealing with seizure did not significantly decrease the level of trade in counterfeit and pirated goods.[6]

---

[2] Paris Convention for the Protection of Industrial Property of 20 March 1883, as revised at Brussels on 14 December 1900, at Washington on 2 June 1911, at The Hague on 6 November 1925, at London on 2 June 1934, at Lisbon on 31 October 1958, and at Stockholm on 14 July 1967, and as amended on 28 September 1979.

[3] Berne Convention for the Protection of Literary and Artistic Works of 9 September 1886, completed at Paris on 4 May 1896, revised at Berlin on 13 November 1908, completed at Berne on 20 March 1914, revised at Rome on 2 June 1928, at Brussels on 26 June 1948, at Stockholm on 14 July 1967, and at Paris on 24 July 1971, and amended on 28 September 1979.

[4] One could add to this list the International Convention for the Protection of New Varieties of Plants (UPOV Convention) of 2 December 1961 (as revised at Geneva on 10 November 1972, on 23 October 1978, and on 19 March 1991) and the Washington Treaty on Intellectual Property in Respect of Integrated Circuits of 26 May 1989, which never entered into force as examples of pre-TRIPs instruments protecting other forms of intellectual property. Since TRIPs, a number of treaties were adopted under the aegis of WIPO, including the WIPO Copyright Treaty of 20 December 1996 and the WIPO Performances and Phonograms Treaty (WPPT) of the same day, the Trademark Law Treaty (adopted at Geneva on 27 October 1994), which is of a somewhat more administrative nature, and the Patent Law Treaty (adopted at Geneva on 1 June 2000).

[5] Daniel J Gervais, *The TRIPs Agreement: Drafting History and Analysis* (2nd edn, Sweet & Maxwell, London, 2003) at 1.10.

[6] Rohazar Wati Zuallcobley, Ida Palombella and Riccardo Cecchi, 'Border Measures under TRIPs, EU and Italian Law' (November 2000) on-line http://www.wipo.int/academy/en/research_pub/papers/Turin2000/pdf/Cecchietal.pdf.

Articles 9[7] and 10[8] of the Paris Convention deal with the seizure of 'goods unlawfully   **2.04**
bearing a trade mark or trade name' and goods bearing 'false indications'. The main
provision, namely Article 9, is very weak, normatively speaking. Indeed, while in
principle counterfeit goods are subject to seizure on importation[9] in the country of
origin (production) or in the importation country[10] (though the authorities of
countries of the Paris Union are not bound to effect seizure of goods in transit),[11]
national law does not have to provide for such a seizure. In such cases, seizure may
still occur in the country once the goods have been imported.[12] But countries can
adopt even weaker protection. If none of the specified measures (seizure on importation, seizure in the country, prohibition of importation) are available under national
legislation, which the Convention allows, then they need only be replaced with
actions and remedies that are available under national legislation.[13]

The measures specified in Article 9 are also applicable to goods bearing a false   **2.05**
indication of source or origin of the producer, manufacturer, or merchant.[14]

Article 16[15] of the Berne Convention provides that infringing copies of copyright   **2.06**
works are subject to seizure in any country.[16] Berne defines the proper forum as

---

[7] Art 9 reads as follows:

(1) All goods unlawfully bearing a trade mark or trade name shall be seized on importation into
those countries of the Union where such mark or trade name is entitled to legal protection.
(2) Seizure shall likewise be effected in the country where the unlawful affixation occurred or
in the country into which the goods were imported.
(3) Seizure shall take place at the request of the public prosecutor, or any other competent authority, or any interested party, whether a natural person or a legal entity, in conformity with the
domestic legislation of each country.
(4) The authorities shall not be bound to effect seizure of goods in transit.
(5) If the legislation of a country does not permit seizure on importation, seizure shall be
replaced by prohibition of importation or by seizure inside the country.
(6) If the legislation of a country permits neither seizure on importation nor prohibition of
importation nor seizure inside the country, then, until such time as the legislation is modified accordingly, these measures shall be replaced by the actions and remedies available in
such cases to nationals under the law of such country.

[8] Art 10 reads as follows:

(1) The provisions of the preceding Article shall apply in cases of direct or indirect use of a false -
indication of the source of the goods or the identity of the producer, manufacturer, or merchant.
(2) Any producer, manufacturer, or merchant, whether a natural person or a legal entity,
engaged in the production or manufacture of or trade in such goods and established either
in the locality falsely indicated as the source, or in the region where such locality is situated,
or in the country falsely indicated, or in the country where the false indication of source is
used, shall in any case be deemed an interested party.

[9] Art 9(1).   [10] Art 9(2).   [11] Art 9(4).   [12] Art 9(5).
[13] Art 9(6).   [14] Art 10.
[15] Art 16 reads as follows:

(1) Infringing copies of a work shall be liable to seizure in any country of the Union where the
work enjoys legal protection.
(2) The provisions of the preceding paragraph shall also apply to reproductions coming from a
country where the work is not protected, or has ceased to be protected.
(3) The seizure shall take place in accordance with the legislation of each country.

[16] Art 16(1).

the country *for which* protection is claimed—applying in that case not the *lex fori* but the *lex loci delicti*, which are often one and the same. As such, copies originating from countries in which the work is not protected may also be seized in a country where the work is protected.[17] The seizure takes place in accordance with the provisions of national legislation,[18] subject to the principle of national treatment (non-discrimination). Article 13(3)[19] of the Berne Convention provides that the infringing sound recordings may also be subject to seizure.

2.07 Against this backdrop, it is quite obvious that the TRIPs Agreement was a major departure from the previous set of norms. TRIPs was the first multilateral treaty whose provisions on substantive intellectual property, such as copyrights, trade marks, and patents, were mostly drawn from existing treaties (often as a full incorporation of another treaty's provisions).[20] There were no agreed models on enforcement to use as a common normative basis to draft TRIPs. TRIPs negotiators drew instead on their national legislation and their perception of what were the most striking problems with the enforcement of intellectual property rights. In the end, three sets of measures were agreed upon, as well as general principles applicable to all forms of enforcement. Those three sets of measures cover general civil remedies, provisional civil remedies, and border measures. A provision concerning minimal criminal remedies was also incorporated into the Agreement.

2.08 The evolution of the TRIPs section on border measures, a subset of the enforcement Part, was influenced by two important developments, both of which emphasized the connection between intellectual property rights and trade. Prior to TRIPs, the United States, one of the countries with the largest importation of counterfeit and pirated goods, had enacted s 301 of the Trade Act 1974, which authorized the United States Trade Representative (USTR) to 'impose trade sanctions against foreign countries that maintain acts, policies and practices that violate, or deny U.S. rights or benefits under, trade agreements, or are unjustifiable, unreasonable or discriminatory and burden or restrict U.S. commerce'.[21] Trade sanctions under s 301 played an important role in forcing countries where counterfeit and pirated goods were mass-produced to strengthen the level of intellectual property protection.[22] Consonant with this 'bilateral' approach, the United States

---

[17] Art 16(2). See also WIPO, *Guide to the Berne Convention for the Protection of Literary and Artistic Works* (Paris Act, 1971) (WIPO, Geneva, 1978) at 97–98.   [18] Art 16(3).

[19] Art 13(3) reads as follows:
'Recordings made in accordance with paragraphs (1) and (2) of this Article and imported without permission from the parties concerned into a country where they are treated as infringing recordings shall be liable to seizure.'

[20] Art 2(1) of TRIPs requires compliance with Arts 1 to 12 and 19 of the Paris Convention. Art 9(1) requires compliance with Arts 1 to 21 of and the Appendix to the Berne Convention.

[21] See Trade Act of 1974, s 301, part I.

[22] John Sweeney, Scott D Greenberg and Margaret H Bitler, 'Heading them Off at the Pass—Can Counterfeit Goods of Foreign Origin be Stopped at the Counterfeiter's Border?' [1994] 84 Trademark Reporter 477 at 482–483.

took the lead in multilateral negotiations at the GATT/WTO with a view to establishing a uniform set of rules on the enforcement of intellectual property rights. During the Tokyo round of GATT negotiations, the United States and European Community had put forward a text on *Draft Measures to Discourage the Importation of Counterfeit Goods*, which would have strengthened the enforcement of intellectual property rights.[23] This was followed by a *Draft Agreement to Discourage the Importation of Counterfeit Goods*, which was put forward by the United States, the European Community, Japan, and Canada.[24] This Draft Agreement arguably constituted the basis for what is today the TRIPs Agreement.[25]

II. THE TRIPs AGREEMENT

A. An overview of the TRIPs Agreement

The TRIPs Agreement was adopted at Marrakech on 15 April 1994, as Annex 1C **2.09** of the *Final Act Embodying the Results of the Uruguay Round of Multilateral Trade Negotiations*.[26] It is undoubtedly the most significant milestone in the development of intellectual property in the 20th century. Its scope is much broader than that of any previous international agreement—it not only covers all areas already protected under pre-existing agreements, it also gives new life to treaties that have failed in the past and protects, for the first time, rights that did not benefit from any multilateral protection. In addition, as already mentioned, the TRIPs Agreement enshrines detailed rules on one of the most difficult and, for right-holders, painful aspects of intellectual property rights: enforcement.

Part III of TRIPs provides for detailed enforcement mechanisms and principles **2.10** covering civil (including provisional) measures,[27] criminal,[28] and administrative

---

[23] Draft Agreement on Measures to Discourage the Importation of Counterfeit Goods, 31 July 1979, GATT Doc No L/4817. For details of this Draft Agreement as relating to border measures, see Rohazar Wati Zuallcobley, Ida Palombella, Riccardo Cecchi, 'Border Measures under TRIPs, EU and Italian Law' (2000), on-line http://www.wipo.int/academy/en/research_pub/papers/Turin2000/pdf/Cecchietal.pdf, para 4.

[24] Draft Agreement to Discourage the Importation of Counterfeit Goods, 18 October 1982, GATT Doc No L/5382. The Draft Agreement was redistributed as document MTN.GNG/NG11/W/9 of 25 June 1987. See also Paul Goldstein, *International Copyright: Principles, Law, and Practice* (Oxford University Press, Oxford, 2001) at 53.

[25] For detailed negotiation history of the TRIPs Agreement See Gervais, n 5 above, Part I.

[26] Agreement on Trade-Related Aspects of Intellectual Property Rights, 15 April 1994, Marrakech Agreement Establishing the World Trade Organization (hereinafter 'WTO Agreement'), Annex 1C, Legal Instruments Results of the Uruguay Round vol 31, 33 ILM 81 (1994) (hereinafter 'TRIPs Agreement'), on-line at http://www.wto.org/english/docs_e/legal_e/final_e.htm.

[27] TRIPs Agreement, Art 50.   [28] Ibid, Art 61.

procedures[29] (including border measures).[30] To complete the picture, the TRIPs Agreement was brought under the WTO dispute-settlement umbrella,[31] thus correcting a major shortcoming of both the Paris and Berne Conventions. As a result, disputes as to whether a country correctly implemented the Agreement can now be submitted to a WTO panel of experts, whose decision, once adopted by the WTO Dispute Settlement Body,[32] is binding.

2.11 The TRIPs Agreement entered into force on 1 January 1995. With respect to developed (industrialized) countries, the substantive provisions of TRIPs entered into force on 1 January 1996. Developing countries and those in the transition from centrally planned economies had until 1 January 2000 to implement TRIPs.[33]

2.12 TRIPs is a 'minimum standard' agreement, and WTO Members may thus enact provisions that go beyond TRIPs.[34]

B. The application of TRIPs in domestic law

(1) General provisions

2.13 As stated above, Article 1(1) of TRIPs makes it clear that WTO members may go beyond the TRIPs minimum standards in their national laws. Article 1.1 has been referred to, despite some criticism,[35] as a 'pedestal' on which the Dispute Settlement Body's jurisprudence rests, allowing countries to develop their own law and policies within the framework established by the Agreement.[36]

---

[29] TRIPs Agreement, Art 42–49.   [30] Ibid, Art 52–60.   [31] Ibid, Art 64.

[32] Panel and Appellate Body decisions are adopted unless there is a consensus not to adopt it.

[33] See Art 65 of TRIPs.

[34] Art 1(1) of TRIPs: Members shall give effect to the provisions of this Agreement. Members may, but shall not be obliged to, implement in their law more extensive protection than is required by this Agreement, provided that such protection does not contravene the provisions of this Agreement. Members shall be free to determine the appropriate method of implementing the provisions of this Agreement within their own legal system and practice.

To assist countries unfamiliar with the area, a number of model laws exist, some prepared by trade associations others by organizations such as the World Customs Organization (formerly the Customs Cooperation Council), which represents 159 customs administrations covering approximately 95% of world trade in goods (September 2004).

[35] Criticism stems from the fact that the minimum standard framework leaves TRIPs open to the possibility of divergent interpretations by Members, see Laurence R Helfer, 'Adjudicating Copyright Claims under the TRIPs Agreement: A Case for a European Human Right Analogy' [1998] 39 Harvard International Law Journal 357, 358–363.

[36] Jerome H Reichman, 'Securing compliance with the TRIPs Agreement after US v India', [1998] 1 Journal of International Economic Law 585, 596; JH Reichman, 'The TRIPs Agreement Comes of Age: Conflicts or Cooperation With the Developing Countries?' [2000] 32 Case Western Reserve Journal of International Law 441, 446–447.

Whilst Member States must 'give effect' to the provisions of the Agreement,[37] **2.14** the Agreement does not specify how this should be accomplished,[38] which allows the countries the flexibility to implement TRIPs in accordance with their legal systems and practices. Because of this, TRIPs is generally viewed as a *non* self-executing treaty.[39] It is submitted that TRIPs should instead be viewed as a minimum standard agreement, requiring member countries to take necessary actions to implement it in their national legislation.[40] The expression 'give effect' is also used in Article 25(2) of the Paris Convention, where it has been so interpreted.[41] The implementation measures must be in place at the time of entry into force of the Agreement for a Member, which generally coincides with its becoming a member of the WTO.

The meaning and the scope of TRIPs, Article 1(1) were discussed by the Appellate **2.15** Body in *India—Patent Protection for Pharmaceutical and Agricultural Chemical Products*[42] and by the Panel in *India—Patent Protection for Pharmaceutical and Agricultural Products*.[43] Both decisions established that WTO Members States 'are free to determine how best to meet their obligations under the TRIPs Agreement within the context of their own legal system'.[44]

(2) *The TRIPs Agreement and the European Union*

The European Union's legal regime against piracy and counterfeiting has been in **2.16** existence for almost 20 years.[45] The latest changes to the regime were effected by Council Regulation 1383/2003 of 22 July 2003.[46] Detailed analysis of the EU

---

[37] Art 1(1) of TRIPs: Members shall give effect to the provisions of this Agreement. Members may, but shall not be obliged to, implement in their law more extensive protection than is required by this Agreement, provided that such protection does not contravene the provisions of this Agreement. Members shall be free to determine the appropriate method of implementing the provisions of this Agreement within their own legal system and practice.

[38] J H Reichman, 'Enforcing the Enforcement Procedures of the TRIPs Agreement' [1997] 37 Virginia Journal of International Law 335, at 344.

[39] However, see Robert J Gutowski, 'The Marriage of Intellectual Property and International Trade in the TRIPs Agreement: Strange Bedfellows or a Match Made in Heaven' [1999] 47 Buffalo Law Review 713, 738.

[40] Christine Haight Farely, 'Conflicts Between U.S. Law and International Treaties Concerning Geographical Indications', 22 Whittier Law Review 73, 86, n 86.

[41] G H C Bodenhausen, *Guide to the Application of the Paris Convention for the Protection of Industrial Property* (WIPO, Geneva, 1969). TRIPs is not dependent on national law as much as Paris Convention was, however. See Ruth L Gana, 'Prospects for Developing Countries under the TRIPs Agreement' [1996] 29 Vanderbilt Journal of Transnational Law 735, 737.

[42] WTO document WT/DS50/AB/R.   [43] WTO document WT/DS79/R.

[44] Document WT/DS50/AB/R, para 59; see also document WT/DS79/R, para 7.41.

[45] See Council Reg 3842/86 of 1 December 1986; Council Reg 3295/94 of 22 December 1994; Council Reg 241/1999 of 25 January 1999.

[46] Council Reg (EC) No 1383/2003 of 22 July 2003 concerning customs action against goods suspected of infringing certain intellectual property rights and the measures to be taken against goods found to have infringed such rights, OJ L 196, 02/08/2003, 7. See also implementing Reg 1891/2004. The Regulation entered into force on 1 July 2004.

regime is described in Chapter 3 of this book. However, the following section briefly analyses the Regulation in light of the requirements posed by the TRIPs Agreement.

2.17 The first issue to consider is the extent to which the Union is competent to legislate in this area. A second step is to consider whether it has in fact exercised its competence. Given the adoption of the trade mark and designs regulations,[47] various directives and regulations on geographical indications and copyright, as well as biotechnology and the recent enforcement directive,[48] it seems fair to conclude that this jurisdiction has been exercised in almost all intellectual property areas.

2.18 The competence of the European Community and its Member States with respect to GATT/WTO, and consequently the TRIPs Agreement, was first addressed by the European Court of Justice in 1994.[49] In that Opinion, the ECJ wrote that 'the Community and its member states are jointly competent to conclude the Agreement on the Trade-Related Aspects of Intellectual Property'.[50]

2.19 The issue of the direct applicability of the TRIPs Agreement in EU law and the laws of the Member States was addressed by the Court in three cases—*Hermès*,[51] *Parfums Dior*[52] and *Schieving-Nijstad*.[53] TRIPs, Article 50 (6) was at issue in all three cases examined below.

The *Hermès* decision

2.20 The issue in *Hermès* was whether the preliminary relief available under Dutch procedural law should be considered to be a 'provisional measure' under TRIPs, Article 50 (6). The purpose of TRIPs, Article 50(6) is to provide safeguards against the abuse of provisional measures. Hence, provisional measures should be revoked when a procedure on the merits is not initiated within a reasonable period of time. The 'reasonable period' is defined either by the judicial authority who ordered the

---

[47] Including, on trade marks: Council Reg (EC) No 40/94 of 20 December 1993 as amended; Commission Reg (EC) No 2868/95 of 13 December 1995; and on designs: Council Reg (EC) No 6/2002 of 12 December 2001, as amended; Commission Reg (EC) No 2245/2002 of 21 October 2002; Commission Reg No 2246/2002 of 16 December 2002 and the Directive 98/71/EC of the European Parliament and of the Council of 13 October 1998 on the legal protection of designs.

[48] Directive 98/44/EC of the European Parliament and of the Council on the legal protection of biotechnological inventions; Directive 2004/48/EC of the European Parliament and of the Council of 29 April 2004 on the enforcement of intellectual property rights.

[49] Opinion 1/94 on Community Competence to Conclude Certain International Agreements, 1994 ECR I-5276, [1995].   [50] Ibid.

[51] *Hermès International v FHT Marketing Choice BV*, (case C-53/96), decision of 16 June 1998, available at http://oami.eu.int/en/mark/aspects/pdf/JJ960053.pdf.

[52] *Parfums Christian Dior SA v Tuk Consultancy BV, Assco Gerüste GmbH et al.* (C-300/98 and C-392/98), decision of 14 December 2000, available at http://oami.eu.int/en/mark/aspects/pdf/JJ980300.pdf.

[53] *Schieving-Nijstad vof and Others v Robert Groeneveld* (C-89/99), decision of 13 September 2001, available at http://oami.eu.int/en/mark/aspects/pdf/JJ990089.pdf.

provisional measure or, in the absence of such determination, is a period not exceeding 20 working days, or 31 calendar days, whichever is the longer.[54] The provisional measures do not cease to exist automatically after the prescribed time period elapses; rather the defendant should request that the provisional measure be revoked.[55] In *Hermès*, the ECJ found that the preliminary relief under Dutch law did constitute a provisional measure as contemplated under Article 50(6).[56] 'Thus, proceedings on the merits had to be initiated if the plaintiff wished to prevent the defendant from requesting the revocation of the provisional measures granted by the court.'[57] In interpreting the compliance of Dutch law, the Court did not address the question as to whether TRIPs, Article 50(6) had direct effect in national legislation.[58]

The *Parfums Dior* decision

In *Parfums Dior / Assco*, the ECJ found that 'the provisions of TRIPs, an annex to   **2.21** the WTO Agreement, are not such as to create rights upon which individuals may rely directly before the courts by virtue of Community law'.[59] With respect to the shared authority between the European Community and its Member States, the Court concluded that:

> in a field to which TRIPs applies and in respect of which the Community has already legislated, the judicial authorities of the Member States are required by virtue of Community law, when called upon to apply national rules with a view to ordering provisional measures for the protection of rights falling within such a field, to do so as far as possible in the light of the wording and purpose of Article 50 of TRIPs, but in a field in respect of which the Community has not yet legislated and which consequently falls within the competence of the Member States, the protection of intellectual property rights, and measures adopted for that purpose by the judicial authorities, do not fall within the scope of Community law. Accordingly, Community law neither requires nor forbids that the legal order of a Member State should accord to individuals the right to rely directly on the rule laid down by Article 50(6) of TRIPs or that it should oblige the courts to apply that rule of their own motion.[60]

---

[54] Gervais, n 5 above at 2.425.

[55] Gervais, n 5 above at 2.425. See also *Schieving-Nijstad*, above at para 2.19, 'a request by the defendant is necessary in order for the provisional measures ordered by way of interim relief to lapse on the ground that no substantive action has been brought either within the period prescribed in the provisional measures or, where no period is prescribed, within 20 working days or 31 calendar days, whichever is the longer period.'   [56] *Hermès*, n 51 above at para 45.

[57] Charles Gielen, 'Netherlands: Procedure' EIPR 1999, 21(1), N9-10.

[58] 'It should be stressed at the outset that, although the issue of the direct effect of Article 50 of the TRIPs Agreement has been argued, the Court is not required to give a ruling on that question, but only to answer the question of interpretation submitted to it by the national court so as to enable that court to interpret Netherlands procedural rules in the light of that article.' *Hermès*, above, at para 35.   [59] *Dior* at paras 43–44.

[60] *Dior* at para 49.

The *Schieving-Nijstad* ('Route 66') decision

2.22 In *Schieving-Nijstad*, the ECJ further reaffirmed the main conclusion of its *Parfums Dior* opinion.[61] The Court found that '[i]t follows that, in the absence of any Community rules in the matter, it is for the domestic legal system of each Member State to lay down the detailed procedural rules relating to actions for the enforcement of intellectual property rights'.[62] 'Nevertheless, it is apparent from the Court's jurisprudence that, in a field to which TRIPs applies and in respect of which the Community has already legislated, the judicial authorities of the Member States are required by virtue of Community law, when called upon to apply national rules with a view to ordering provisional measures for the protection of rights falling within such a field, to do so as far as possible in the light of the wording and purpose of Article 50 of TRIPs.'[63]

2.23 In summary then, the ECJ has jurisdiction in most, if not all, intellectual property matters due to existing regulation in this field. The EC has exercised its jurisdiction through various directives and regulations on copyright, trade mark, geographical indications, biotechnology and designs as well as enforcement. As to the direct application of TRIPs provisions, they should serve as a guide to interpret EC and Member States' legislation (especially when they are of such a nature as to be easily applicable, such as national treatment), unless they are in direct conflict with TRIPs. This was confirmed in the above cases (most directly perhaps in *Schieving-Nijstad*)[64] and, indirectly at least, in the more recent *Budweiser* case.[65]

2.24 But the provisions are generally not directly applicable. To quote the Court again:

> The answer . . . must therefore be that the procedural requirements of Article 50 of TRIPs, and in particular Article 50(6), are not such as to create rights upon which individuals may rely directly before the Community courts and the courts of the Member States.[66]

2.25 There are two principal issues that emerge from the Court's jurisprudence, namely the relationship between international agreements and EU law, and the ECJ's ability to interpret international norms such as those contained in TRIPs, or its ability to apply them by interpretation of EU or national laws. The latter is of lesser concern here. As far as the former issue is concerned, the ECJ traditionally interpreted GATT rules (pre-WTO) as not having direct effect within the Community. A number of commentators took the view that this interpretation should change now that GATT rules form part of the WTO because of the negotiation and accession process by the European Communities as an entity

---

[61] *Schieving-Nijstad*, above at para 53.   [62] *Schieving-Nijstad*, above at para 34.
[63] *Schieving-Nijstad*, above at para 35.   [64] N 53 above.
[65] *Anheuser-Busch Inc v Budejovický Budvar, národni podnik* (case C-245/02), decision of 16 November 2004. oami.eu.int/en/marks/aspects/pdf/JJ020245.pdf.
[66] *Schieving-Nijstad*, above at para 56.

separate from the Member States. Those commentators argue that the (partial) recognition of the direct effect of TRIPs in EU law (see the *Schieving-Nijstad* case above) is a welcome development. To quote Gaëlle Bontinck:

> The recognition of direct effect for certain TRIPs provisions referring to rights of individuals should be a welcomed development and could be a useful tool to develop the acceptance of the world trading system by individuals, as well as to reinforce the protection of intellectual property rights' holders within the Community. The Court's recognition of the justiciability (sic) of TRIPs provisions is a promising movement in this direction. However, it has not gone so far as to give Community direct effect to the TRIPs provisions. The ECJ seems to be satisfied by the indirect effect of TRIPs for the time being. In the longer term, much will depend on the manner in which we address the relationship between the individual and the international legal system. From *Parfums Dior*, it appears that the ECJ has already made its choice: the individual is sufficiently protected under Community law by the existing case-law, but dissatisfied Member States remain free to grant a higher level of protection. Whether the national courts will perceive the exercise of this freedom to be necessary remains to be seen.[67]

2.26 Naturally, the issue of direct effect in EU law of WTO and other multilateral rules is much larger than TRIPs.

(3) *TRIPs application in the United States*

2.27 Border enforcement is essentially under federal jurisdiction in the United States. Under US law, border measures are part of a larger strategy of the enforcement of the intellectual property rights. Individual intellectual property statutes contain provisions on the enforcement of the relevant rights by the US Customs and Border Protection service.[68]

2.28 Each of these sections gives Customs officials the authority to enforce the provision of the Act concerned. The customs service also adopted a set of very detailed Directives, which explain the procedures required for the enforcement of each of the statutes.[69]

---

[67] Gaëlle Bontinck, 'The TRIPs Agreement and the ECJ: A New Dawn?@ Some Comments about Joined Cases C-300/98 and C-392/98 *Parfums Dior* and *Assco Gerüste*' Jean Monnet Working Paper 16/01, available at http://www.jeanmonnetprogram.org/papers/01/013901.rtf. See also Jacqueline Nanci Land, 'Global Intellectual Property Protection AS Viewed through the European Community's Treatment of Geographical Indications: What Lessons Can Trips Learn?' 11 Cardozo J Int'l & Comp L 1007 at 1027: 'In a field over which the EC has already legislated, such as the trade marks in both *the Parfums Christian Dior* and *Assco* cases, and to which TRIPs applies, each national authority is required to consider TRIPs when applying its own laws.'

[68] This now forms part of the Department of Homeland Security. Particularly relevant sections of the US Code include: 17 USC §§ 101–120 (Copyright Act), Customs officials enforce the following provisions 37 CFR §§ 201.8 (1995); 19 CFR §§ 133.31–133.53 (1995) [provisions which prohibit or restrict the importation of certain copyrighted works]. 17 USC §§ 901–914 (Semiconductor Chip Production Act of 1984). Customs Officials enforce this Act which excludes articles that infringe the rights of mask work owners. 17 USC §§ 1001–1010 (Audio Home Recording Act of 1992)—prohibits the importation of certain digital audio recording devices or digital audio interface devices. 35 USC §§ 154, 271 (Process Patent Amendments Act of 1988).

[69] The various directives are available at http://www.customs.gov/xp/cgov/toolbox/legal/directives/.

C. The TRIPs provisions relating to border measures

2.29 Part III of the TRIPs Agreement regulates the enforcement of intellectual property rights and section 4 of that Part (namely Articles 51 to 60) deals with 'Special Requirements Related to Border Measures'.

2.30 Before looking at each provision in greater detail, it is worth noting how detailed these provisions are, especially in light of the fact that no international treaty applied to such measures prior to TRIPs. While TRIPs is neither perfect nor complete (see the section B of this chapter), it was a huge normative step up for intellectual property enforcement. TRIPs provisions on border measures could, as some commentators argue, become 'the most promising feature of the TRIPs enforcement exercise'.[70]

(1) Article 51—Suspension of release by customs authorities[71]

2.31 Article 51 requires that WTO Members make available a procedure before a 'competent' authority (judicial or administrative) to a right-holder to lodge an application[72] for suspension of the release of goods. The right-holder must be able to demonstrate, at least prima facie, that it has valid grounds for suspecting the importation of infringing goods. The procedure must be available at a minimum for pirated copyright and counterfeit trade mark goods—which are defined in TRIPs in footnote 14 to Article 51. Counterfeit trade mark goods are:

> any goods, including packaging, bearing without authorization a trade mark which is identical to the trade mark validly registered in respect of such goods, or

---

[70] J H Reichman, 'Enforcing the Enforcement Procedures of the TRIPs Agreement' [1997] 37 Virginia Journal of International Law 335, at 343.

[71] Members shall, in conformity with the provisions set out below, adopt procedures (n 13) to enable a right-holder, who has valid grounds for suspecting that the importation of counterfeit trade mark or pirated copyright goods (n 14) may take place, to lodge an application in writing with competent authorities, administrative or judicial, for the suspension by the customs authorities of the release into free circulation of such goods. Members may enable such an application to be made in respect of goods which involve other infringements of intellectual property rights, provided that the requirements of this Section are met. Members may also provide for corresponding procedures concerning the suspension by the customs authorities of the release of infringing goods destined for exportation from their territories.

(foot note 13) It is understood that there shall be no obligation to apply such procedures to imports of goods put on the market in another country by or with the consent of the right-holder, or to goods in transit.

(footnote 14) For the purposes of this Agreement: (a) 'counterfeit trade mark goods' shall mean any goods, including packaging, bearing without authorization a trade mark which is identical to the trade mark validly registered in respect of such goods, or which cannot be distinguished in its essential aspects from such a trade mark, and which thereby infringes the rights of the owner of the trade mark in question under the law of the country of importation; (b) 'pirated copyright goods' shall mean any goods which are copies made without the consent of the right-holder or person duly authorized by the right-holder in the country of production and which are made directly or indirectly from an article where the making of that copy would have constituted an infringement of a copyright or a related right under the law of the country of importation.   [72] See also Art 52.

which cannot be distinguished in its essential aspects from such a trade mark, and which thereby infringes the rights of the owner of the trade mark in question under the law of the country of importation.

2.32 The definition refers only to *registered* marks and would thus not extend to common law marks in terms of a country's minimal obligations. Pirated copyright goods are defined as:

any goods which are copies made without the consent of the right-holder or person duly authorized by the right-holder in the country of production and which are made directly or indirectly from an article where the making of that copy would have constituted an infringement of a copyright or a related right under the law of the country of importation.

2.33 The application mechanism may also be available for infringements of other intellectual property rights. Measures are normally limited to 'visibly infringing' goods, because customs authorities may not be equipped to identify properly goods which may infringe, for example, a patent claim or layout-design of an integrated circuit. An exception is also provided for goods put on the market by or with the consent of the right-holder in a third country and goods in transit.[73] The provision also makes clear that, in the light of existing obligations under GATT and other WTO Agreements, WTO Members may apply border measures to any intellectual property right and also to goods destined for exportation.

2.34 Practical questions may arise, particularly in large countries, where measures may be required at all customs entry points. This was noted by the World Customs Organisation (WCO), whose Model Legislation provides that:

Customs shall establish a centralised system for managing applications for the suspension of the customs clearance referred to paragraphs 1 and 2 above. The details of centralised system shall be prescribed in regulations issued by [the competent authority].[74]

2.35 In such cases, the competent authority should have the authority to order 'national' measures, but through a single contact point, since multiple applications in a single country may be considered as unnecessarily complicated or costly[75] (though not necessarily in all cases). In addition, it should be noted that Article 41(5) provides that WTO members are not required to divert *law enforcement resources* to intellectual property enforcement—which does not, however, mean they should not devote adequate resources (within reasonably available means) to intellectual property enforcement.

---

[73] Some commentators consider the lack of direct reference to 'grey market goods' as one of the flaws of the TRIPs Agreement. See Paul J Heald, 'Trademarks and Geographical Indications: Exploring the Contours of the TRIPs Agreement' [1996] 29 Vanderbilt Journal of Transnational Law 635 at 656. See also Art 6 of TRIPs.   [74] Art 1(3).

[75] Timothy P Trainer, 'TRIPs Border Measures Implementation: Details to Consider' [1995] 74 Trademark World 24 at 25 et seq.

2.36 Article 2 of EC Regulation 1383/2003[76] extends the protection not only to pirated and counterfeit goods,[77] but also to goods that infringe (in the country where the application is sought) a patent, a national plant variety right, designations of origin or geographical indications and geographical designations.[78] This extension of the protection is consistent with the trend in the Community over the last few years,[79] as well as with the 'minimum standard' rules contained in TRIPs, Article 1(1). Like the Agreement, the EC Regulation exempts goods that have been manufactured with the right-holder's consent[80] and goods contained in a traveller's private luggage.[81]

2.37 The EC Regulation applies to both *ex officio* action by the customs authorities[82] and actions based on a right-holder's application.

(2) Article 52—Application[83]

2.38 Article 52 contains additional details about the right-holder's application referred to in Article 51. Article 51 mentions 'valid grounds for suspecting an importation of pirated or counterfeit goods'. The competent authorities (administrative or judicial) must be satisfied that:

 (i) there is a prima facie infringement of an intellectual property right 'under the laws of the country of importation'. 'Prima facie' means that the evidence reasonably justifies the conclusion the applicant is seeking;[84]

 (ii) the right-holder must supply a sufficiently detailed description of the goods to enable customs authorities to identify the goods in question. 'Sufficiently detailed information' should be determined on a case-by-case basis. Clearly, more information may lead to a speedier and more efficient process. However, the competent authorities should be careful not to require excessive or difficult to obtain information or they may find that those requirements represent the 'creation of barriers to legitimate trade'.[85]

---

[76] N 46 above.   [77] Art 1(a) and (b) of EC Reg 1383/2003.

[78] Art 2(1)(c) of EC Reg 1383/2003.

[79] Karel Daele, 'Regulation 1383/2003: A New Step in the Fight Against Counterfeit and Pirated Goods at the Borders of the European Union' [2004] 26 EIPR 214 at 215.

[80] Art 3.1 of EC Reg 1383/2003.   [81] TRIPs, Art 60; Art 3.2 of EC Reg 1383/2003.

[82] TRIPs, Art 58; Art 4 of EC Reg 1383/2003.

[83] Any right-holder initiating the procedures under Art 51 shall be required to provide adequate evidence to satisfy the competent authorities that, under the laws of the country of importation, there is prima facie an infringement of the right-holder's intellectual property right and to supply a sufficiently detailed description of the goods to make them readily recognizable by the customs authorities. The competent authorities shall inform the applicant within a reasonable period whether they have accepted the application and, where determined by the competent authorities, the period for which the customs authorities will take action.

[84] *Black's Law Dictionary* at 579. 'Prima facie', literally 'at first sight', means that upon provisional examination the evidence submitted by or on behalf of the applicant would, in the absence of evidence to the contrary, be sufficient for the applicant to prevail.

[85] TRIPs, Art 41(1) and (2). See also Timothy P Trainer, *Border Enforcement of Intellectual Property* (Oceana Publications, Inc, Dobbs Ferry, 2000) at 266–267; 'Synthesis of Issues Concerning

The decision of the competent authorities should be communicated 'within a **2.39**
reasonable period'—normally a matter of a few days.[86] The decision should also
indicate a period for which the suspension is ordered, provided that there is one.
The wording of Article 52, unchanged since the early drafts of 1990,[87] provides that
the notice to the applicant should contain 'where determined by the competent
authorities, the period for which the customs authorities will take action'. This
implies that there is no obligation to make such a determination on the part of
the authorities but that any determination concerning the period during which
the matter will be considered 'active' by those authorities, if determined, should
be part of the notice. 'Take action' in this context refers to action pursuant to the
right-holder's application. The action in question should comply with TRIPs'
minimum obligations. If the action taken is broader than the simple suspension
of a single shipment and includes further monitoring of incoming shipments or
similar action for a period of time, then the notice should so specify. Conversely,
if the action is specific (such as the suspension of a single shipment), there may be
no need to specify duration.

The previously mentioned WCO Model Legislation provides as follows in that **2.40**
respect:

> Customs shall specify how long it will provide assistance regarding applications
> made under Article 1. The minimum duration for such assistance shall be no less
> than one year, unless the applicant requests a shorter period for assistance or applies
> for action in cases of specific shipments.[88]

Taken together, Articles 53 and 55 provide that release of the goods, subject to the **2.41**
posting of a security, is possible if no judicial provisional measure is issued confirming
the suspension. If proceedings leading to a decision on the merits have been initiated,
the review of the suspension by the competent authority must take place, at the
defendant's (normally the importer's) request 'within a reasonable period'.[89]

Any communication should preferably be communicated in writing, though that **2.42**
is not a formal requirement in TRIPs.[90]

EC Regulation 1383/2003 goes beyond the minimum requirement of the TRIPs **2.43**
Agreement and provides detailed rules about the form, substance, and respective
timelines for the right-holder's application.[91] It provides that the application

---

Difficulties and Practices in the Field of Enforcement', WIPO document WIPO/CME/3 of 26 July
2002 at 10.
  [86] See also TRIPs, Art 50(4) and (6).   [87] See Gervais, n 5, at 2.432.   [88] Art 2.
  [89] See also Art 8 of Council Reg (EC) No 1383/2003 (n 46 above) which uses the same language,
namely 'take action', but specifies a 12-month maximum.
  [90] TRIPs, Art 41(3) lays out a general principle for communication with the parties. It provides
that the decisions on the merits 'shall preferably be in writing', and that it should be available to
parties 'without undue delay'. Given that the decision on application for suspension is not the
decision on merits, it may be argued that a decision need not be in writing.
  [91] TRIPs, Art 52; Art 5 of EC Reg 1383/2003.

should be in writing or submitted electronically.[92] The decision of the customs authorities is communicated to the applicant within 30 days of the receipt of the application.[93] The EC Regulation also provides a list of the minimum information that a right-holder should provide, as well as additional information that may be helpful to the customs authorities to identify the goods.[94]

2.44 The TRIPs Agreement does not set the period for which the customs authorities should 'take action'. It only requires that the period, if any, be communicated to the applicant. The EC Regulation requires that the period be communicated to the applicant and sets the maximum duration to one year,[95] though it can be subsequently extended on the right-holder's request.

(3) Article 53—Security or equivalent assurance[96]

2.45 Article 53(1) entitles the competent authority to require the provision of a security or equivalent assurance to protect both the defendant and the competent authority.[97] This provision means that the competent authority has the right to require that a security or equivalent assurance be posted, but it has discretion as to whether or not such a security will be required. Article 5 of the WCO Model Legislation uses the word 'may' to make this clear.

2.46 The court (or other competent authority) *may* order the applicant to provide security or other equivalent assurance to protect the defendant and to prevent abuse. The security or equivalent assurance will be required where the court is labouring under some degree of uncertainty. However, even in cases involving large scale infringers the provision of a security may not be necessary where the court is quite certain that an infringement has taken place.

---

[92] Arts 5.1 and 5.3 of EC Reg 1383/2003.
[93] Art 5.7 of EC Reg 1383/2003. TRIPs, Art 52 requires notification 'within reasonable time'.
[94] Art 5.5 of EC Reg 1383/2003.   [95] Art 8 of EC Reg 1383/2003.
[96] Which reads as follows: '(1) The competent authorities shall have the authority to require an applicant to provide a security or equivalent assurance sufficient to protect the defendant and the competent authorities and to prevent abuse. Such security or equivalent assurance shall not unreasonably deter recourse to these procedures.

(2) Where pursuant to an application under this Section the release of goods involving industrial designs, patents, layout-designs or undisclosed information into free circulation has been suspended by customs authorities on the basis of a decision other than by a judicial or other independent authority, and the period provided for in Art 55 has expired without the granting of provisional relief by the duly empowered authority, and provided that all other conditions for importation have been complied with, the owner, importer, or consignee of such goods shall be entitled to their release on the posting of a security in an amount sufficient to protect the right-holder for any infringement. Payment of such security shall not prejudice any other remedy available to the right-holder, it being understood that the security shall be released if the right-holder fails to pursue the right of action within a reasonable period of time'.
[97] Eg, where the owner or importer of the goods has suffered a prejudice due to a suspension that is later found to have been unjustified. See Art 50(3) *in fine*.

Article 6 of the EC Regulation[98] provides for an 'acceptance of liability'. The **2.47** pre-2003 EC regime did require a security, but the rule was changed to benefit small and medium size enterprises.[99] The question as to whether that constitutes an assurance equivalent to a security as provided for in Article 50(3) is unclear. But on the principle of providing protection for the defendant, Article 6 seems to be in line with TRIPs.

In cases where there is no defendant, that is, where customs authorities are **2.48** simply looking for infringing material, but none has been found, a security is not usually essential.[100] Nevertheless, the competent authorities may obtain security 'in advance', in order to protect themselves, as the Article authorizes them so to do.

Article 53(2) provides an additional safeguard expressed as a number of conjunct- **2.49** ive conditions.

(i) A suspension must have been ordered in respect of goods allegedly infringing one of the intellectual property rights mentioned (industrial designs, patents, layout-designs, or undisclosed information), that is, what may be a less than 'visible' infringement.

(ii) The suspension must have been ordered on the basis of a decision by the customs authorities or an authority not independent of customs; it does not apply where the suspension is ordered by a judicial or administrative authority independent of customs.

(iii) Ten working days (as defined by the national law of the WTO Member concerned) must have passed (with the possible extension by another 10 working days) without the granting of provisional relief by the authority empowered in respect of Part III, s 3.

(iv) All the other conditions for importation must have been complied with.

(v) A security ('equivalent assurance' is not mentioned) is posted in an amount to protect the right-holder for any infringement (the one that justified the suspension or any other that may exist in respect of the goods), as determined by the competent authority.

When these conditions are met, the owner, importer, or consignee is entitled to **2.50** the release of the goods, without prejudice to the rights of the right-holder. If the right-holder fails to pursue the matter[101] within a reasonable period, the security is released.

---

[98] See n 89 above.

[99] Karel Daele, 'Regulation 1383/2003: A New Step in the Fight Against Counterfeit and Pirated Goods at the Borders of the European Union' n 79 above at 219.

[100] T Trainer, n 75 above at 27.

[101] In this context, it means to bring the matter before the authorities that can order a provisional measure to continue the suspension.

(4) Article 54—Notice of suspension[102]

2.51 The importer and applicant must be notified 'promptly' (normally within a few days) of the suspension. As regards the importer, notification should preferably, but not necessarily, be in writing.[103] As regards the applicant, notice must be served.[104] The meaning of 'promptly' in this context is similar to 'without undue delay'.[105]

(5) Article 55—Duration of suspension[106]

2.52 Article 55 provides detailed rules concerning the duration of the suspension. It should not exceed 10 working days[107] after the notice of the suspension is served on the applicant. Goods should be released, provided other conditions for importation or exportation, as the case may be, have been complied with, unless:

(i) the customs authorities have been informed that judicial or equivalent proceedings leading to a decision on the merits have been initiated by the applicant or any other party to the proceedings other than a defendant; or

(ii) the suspension has been prolonged by the authority empowered in respect of the provisional measures.[108]

2.53 The authority that first ordered the suspension may prolong the delay by 10 working days 'in appropriate cases', that is, where justified in the circumstances of the particular case.

2.54 Article 55 provides for a review under Article 50(4).[109] This review introduces the necessary balance and fairness concerning measures taken in the absence of, or

---

[102] The importer and the applicant shall be promptly notified of the suspension of the release of goods according to Art 51.   [103] See Art 41(3) for the general principle. Also, see n 90 above.
[104] See TRIPs, Art 55.   [105] This should be interpreted in the light of Art 41(1), (2), and (5).
[106] Which reads as follows; 'If, within a period not exceeding 10 working days after the applicant has been served notice of the suspension, the customs authorities have not been informed that proceedings leading to a decision on the merits of the case have been initiated by a party other than the defendant, or that the duly empowered authority has taken provisional measures prolonging the suspension of the release of the goods, the goods shall be released, provided that all other conditions for importation or exportation have been complied with; in appropriate cases, this time-limit may be extended by another 10 working days. If proceedings leading to a decision on the merits of the case have been initiated, a review, including a right to be heard, shall take place upon request of the defendant with a view to deciding, within a reasonable period, whether these measures shall be modified, revoked or confirmed. Notwithstanding the above, where the suspension of the release of goods is carried out or continued in accordance with a provisional judicial measure, the provisions of paragraph 6 of Article 50 shall apply.'
[107] This is defined according to the national law of the WTO Member concerned.
[108] See TRIPs, Part III, s 3.
[109] (4). Where provisional measures have been adopted *inaudita altera parte*, the parties affected shall be given notice, without delay after the execution of the measures at the latest. A review, including a right to be heard, shall take place upon request of the defendant with a view to deciding, within a reasonable period after the notification of the measures, whether these measures shall be modified, revoked or confirmed.

ordered without the knowledge of, the defendant. Notice of the review should be given immediately—either before the measures are executed or immediately after.[110]

Where suspension results from, or is prolonged by, a provisional judicial measure, **2.55** proceedings leading to the next stage and eventually to a decision on the merits of the case must be initiated within the time period indicated by the judicial or administrative authority that ordered the provisional judicial measure, not to exceed 20 working days or 31 calendar days.[111]

The EC Regulation follows Article 55 and related TRIPs provisions quite closely. **2.56** Goods may be suspended by the customs authorities for a period of 10 days,[112] which may be extended for an additional 10 days in appropriate circumstances. The right-holder should inform the authorities within this timeframe that procedures leading to a decision on the merits have been initiated.[113] Both the applicant (the right-holder) and the importer are informed of the suspension.[114] The right-holder and other persons involved (importer, consignee, etc) may inspect the goods.[115]

If the goods are found to be infringing, the customs authorities may destroy them **2.57** or take any other measure that will deprive the 'persons concerned of any economic gains'.[116] Removal of the infringing mark, except in exceptional circumstances, is not deemed to be a sufficient measure.[117] In addition, the Regulation introduces a simplified procedure by which the goods may be destroyed without a final decision on the merits of the case.[118] The holder and/or the owner of the goods must agree to this procedure, and the expenses are borne by the right-holder. This simplified procedure is a new feature of the EU regime.[119]

(6) Article 56—Indemnification of the importer and the owner of the goods[120]

'Relevant authorities'—customs, administrative or judicial—may order the **2.58** applicant (under Article 51) to pay (a) the importer, (b) the consignee, and (c) the

---

[110] See Analysis of Art 50 in Gervais, n 5 above.   [111] See TRIPs, Art 50(6).

[112] TRIPs, Art 55, Art 13 of EC Reg 1383/2003.

[113] TRIPs, Art 55 sets the maximum duration of this period to 10 days (using the wording 'period not exceeding 10 days'), which means that the Member States may adopt shorter periods. With respect to perishable goods a shorter time period is justified.

[114] TRIPs, Art 54; Art 9.3 of EC Reg 1383/2003.

[115] TRIPs, Art 57; Art 9.3. of EC Reg 1383/2003.

[116] Art 17 of EC Reg 1383/2003. See also TRIPs, Art 59.

[117] Art 17(1)(b) of EC Reg 1383/2003.   [118] Art 11 of EC Reg 1383/2003.

[119] Karel Daele, 'Reg 1383/2003: A New Step in the Fight Against Counterfeit and Pirated Goods at the Borders of the European Union' [2004] 26 EIPR 214 at 221.

[120] Relevant authorities shall have the authority to order the applicant to pay the importer, the consignee, and the owner of the goods appropriate compensation for any injury caused to them through the wrongful detention of goods or through the detention of goods released pursuant to Art 55.

owner of the goods, 'appropriate' compensation[121] for any injury caused by wrongful detention or detention followed by a release due to inaction within the time period laid out in Article 55. Article 56 of the TRIPs Agreement uses 'appropriate compensation', while Article 44 uses the term 'adequate compensation'. 'Appropriate compensation' seems to require a case-by-case analysis.[122] The Article does not refer to expenses or attorneys' fees, but they are not excluded. Within the parameters of Article 41, the matter thus depends on national law.[123]

2.59 According to the EC Regulation, the liability of the right-holder towards the customs authorities and the owner/importer is governed by the national law of the Member State concerned.[124]

(7) Article 57—Right of inspection and information[125]

2.60 WTO Members must provide competent authorities with the power to give the right-holder sufficient opportunity to have the goods inspected in order to substantiate his claims. The same authority applies to the importer, but not the owner or consignee. The inspection need not be carried out by the right-holder or importer themselves. There are cases where using an expert (chosen or accepted by the party concerned) is often more appropriate.

2.61 The last sentence of Article 57 provides for another right, namely, the 'right of information'. It applies after a decision on the merits has been made and is a 'may' provision.[126] This provision allows the competent authorities to order the infringer to give the names of his accomplices, upstream or downstream in the channels of production and distribution, whether in the same country or not. The provision reflects a clear reality: piracy and counterfeiting are well-organized, often multinational industries and combating trade in pirated and counterfeit goods requires effective tools. Whilst counterfeiting always implies a serious financial loss for the legitimate industries whose intellectual property rights are

---

[121] See also analysis of Art 44 in Gervais, n 5 above.

[122] For example, Art XII(c)(ii) of GATT uses the term, 'appropriate in circumstances'.

[123] See also analysis of Arts 48 and 50(7) in Gervais, n 5 above.

[124] Art 19 of EC Reg 1383/2003.

[125] Without prejudice to the protection of confidential information, Members shall provide the competent authorities the authority to give the right-holder sufficient opportunity to have any goods detained by the customs authorities inspected in order to substantiate the right-holder's claims. The competent authorities shall also have authority to give the importer an equivalent opportunity to have any such goods inspected. Where a positive determination has been made on the merits of a case, Members may provide the competent authorities the authority to inform the right-holder of the names and addresses of the consignor, the importer and the consignee and of the quantity of the goods in question.

[126] A 'may' provision often determines how something may be done, if a WTO Member chooses to do it. See also analysis of Art 43(2) in Gervais, n 5 above.

abused, it may also have potentially lethal consequences for the public, for example, in the case of counterfeit pharmaceuticals.

(8) *Article 58*—Ex officio *action*[127]

Article 58 is also, albeit indirectly, a 'may' provision.[128] Its purpose is not to impose **2.62** *ex officio* measures (that is, measures taken upon the initiative of the competent authorities without a request by the right-holder or other interested party) but to provide a framework for such measures where they exist. Where such measures exist in the national law of a WTO Member:

(i) the competent authorities (usually customs) should be entitled to seek relevant information from the right-holder;
(ii) the importer and right-holder must be promptly notified;[129]
(iii) the right-holder or other party other than the defendant must proceed to the next stage within 10 working days[130] if the importer has appealed the suspension; and
(iv) 'remedial measures' may be taken against public authorities and officials who did not act in good faith.

(9) *Article 59*—*Remedies*[131]

Article 59 extends the provisions of Article 46[132] concerning destruction or **2.63** disposal outside the channels of commerce of infringing goods. The restrictions contained in that Article also apply (including the 'existing constitutional

---

[127] Where Members require competent authorities to act upon their own initiative and to suspend the release of goods in respect of which they have acquired prima facie evidence that an intellectual property right is being infringed: (a) the competent authorities may at any time seek from the right-holder any information that may assist them to exercise these powers; (b) the importer and the right-holder shall be promptly notified of the suspension. Where the importer has lodged an appeal against the suspension with the competent authorities, the suspension shall be subject to the conditions, *mutatis mutandis*, set out at Art 55; (c) Members shall only exempt both public authorities and officials from liability to appropriate remedial measures where actions are taken or intended in good faith. [128] See n 126 above.

[129] See under Art 54.
[130] See under Art 55—with the possible extension by another 10 working days.
[131] Without prejudice to other rights of action open to the right-holder and subject to the right of the defendant to seek review by a judicial authority, competent authorities shall have the authority to order the destruction or disposal of infringing goods in accordance with the principles set out in Art 46. In regard to counterfeit trade mark goods, the authorities shall not allow the re-exportation of the infringing goods in an unaltered state or subject them to a different customs procedure, other than in exceptional circumstances.

[132] In order to create an effective deterrent to infringement, the judicial authorities shall have the authority to order that goods that they have found to be infringing be, without compensation of any sort, disposed of outside the channels of commerce in such a manner as to avoid any harm caused to the right-holder, or, unless this would be contrary to existing constitutional requirements, destroyed. The judicial authorities shall also have the authority to order that materials and implements the

requirements'). Any order to destroy or dispose of the goods is subject to a right of review by the defendant (presumably the importer) and without prejudice to the right-holder's rights of action (notably regarding damages).

2.64 As regards specifically counterfeit trade mark goods, re-exportation in an unaltered state (with the infringing mark) is not allowed, except in exceptional circumstances[133] and they may not be admitted under a different customs procedure or channel. Right-holders concerned might feel that such re-exportation is unacceptable, however, due to the likelihood of the re-use of the goods in an infringing activity in a third country. Where such evidence is available or such re-use can be shown to be very likely, the principles of Article 41(1)[134] apply.

2.65 There appears to be a potential conflict between the two provisions, namely the forbidding of the release of counterfeit goods into the channel of commerce in Article 46 *in fine*, and Article 59, which contains a limited prohibition on the re-exportation of infringing goods 'in an unaltered state', other than in exceptional circumstances. Would removing an illegal trade mark constitute an alteration sufficient to justify a re-exportation but not entry into the channels of commerce?

2.66 First, it should be noted that both provisions do allow for either entry into the channels of commerce (including in the originally intended country or region of importation) as well as re-exportation in 'exceptional circumstances'. Such circumstances would need to be exceptional indeed to avoid a violation of the obligation to provide an effective deterrent.

2.67 Second, it seems that Article 46 deals mainly with entry into commerce in the country or region of the initial intended importation. Re-exportation may not cause prejudice to the trade mark holder in a different country or territory. TRIPs seems to provide a slightly higher degree of flexibility for re-exportation to a different territory than for the entry into commerce of goods from which an infringing trade mark is 'simply' removed.

2.68 A third difference is in that Article 59 uses the expression 'alteration', rather than 'simple removal' of a mark as in Article 46. Courts have a certain degree of latitude

---

predominant use of which has been in the creation of the infringing goods be, without compensation of any sort, disposed of outside the channels of commerce in such a manner as to minimize the risks of further infringements. In considering such requests, the need for proportionality between the seriousness of the infringement and the remedies ordered as well as the interests of third parties shall be taken into account. In regard to counterfeit trade mark goods, the simple removal of the trade mark unlawfully affixed shall not be sufficient, other than in exceptional cases, to permit release of the goods into the channels of commerce.

[133] See analysis of Art 46 in Gervais, n 5 above.

[134] Members shall ensure that enforcement procedures as specified in this Part are available under their law so as to permit effective action against any act of infringement of intellectual property rights covered by this Agreement, including expeditious remedies to prevent infringements and remedies which constitute a deterrent to further infringements. These procedures shall be applied in such a manner as to avoid the creation of barriers to legitimate trade and to provide for safeguards against their abuse. See also analysis of Art 41 in Gervais, n 5 above.

in determining appropriate alterations other than the removal of the mark. One such example could be to cover part of packaging.[135]

(10) Article 60— De Minimis *Imports*[136]

This Article reflects the practical difficulty of enforcing customs measures with respect to small non-commercial shipments of infringing goods, in particular in travellers' private luggage. However, the potential damage caused by those imports should not be underestimated, particularly where infringing material (videocassettes, music cassettes, etc) may be further reproduced after importation.[137] Policing *de minimis* imports may impose a high administrative burden on customs authorities and Article 41(5) is thus relevant in this context.[138]

2.69

In a number of cases, it may be more fruitful to tackle the source of the pirated or counterfeit goods. In the age of the Internet, where copies of texts, music, and audiovisual productions are sent between individual users apparently causing significant damage to the industries concerned, the meaning of *de minimis* could be re-examined. There can be no doubt that TRIPs was designed with trade in physical goods in mind and whether border measures can be effective (legally or commercially) in this type of environment is another matter.

2.70

D. Other relevant provisions of TRIPs

In addition to the above provisions, several other TRIPs provisions are relevant. Staying with Enforcement, the sections on civil and administrative measures, as well as the section on provisional measures and criminal procedures, further strengthen the framework for fighting trade in counterfeit and pirated goods.[139]

2.71

Article 69 provides for international cooperation to eliminate trade in counterfeit goods, including contact points in each country for this purpose.[140]

2.72

---

[135] In a recent decision, the Federal Court of Canada ordered a company to cover logos that infringed Kraft Canada's copyright rights in the Toblerone bear within a mountain, and the Côte d'Or elephant designs. The court accepted that 'by covering over the copyrighted material with a self-sticking plastic film, which is opaque in way of the artistic works', the chocolate bars could be sold, even though the cover could be removed, but not without visibly damaging the wrapper. The case is *Kraft Canada Inc v Euro Excellence Inc* 2004 FC 1215, 35 CPR (4th) 193 (FCTD).

[136] Members may exclude from the application of the above provisions small quantities of goods of a non-commercial nature contained in travellers' personal luggage or sent in small consignments.

[137] Trainer, n 75 above at 28.

[138] This provision allows WTO Members to implement measures only as far as normally available judicial or administrative resources are available.

[139] See the analysis of respective Articles in Gervais, n 5 above.

[140] The list of contacts is regularly updated and is published by the WTO as document number IP/N/3.

2.73 The TRIPs Agreement is a minimum standard agreement which requires WTO Member States to implement it in their national legislation.[141] Elsewhere in this book, available border measures in all 25 Member Countries of the European Communities are described in detail.

2.74 The following section addresses certain post-TRIPs developments in international fora that clarify the details of the obligations arising from the TRIPs Agreement regarding border measures.

III. POST-TRIPS AND FUTURE DEVELOPMENTS

2.75 TRIPs provisions on border measures are mirrored in major multilateral and bilateral trade agreements concluded after the TRIPs Agreement. The provisions on border measures have thus been imported with few changes into the North American Free Trade Agreement (NAFTA)[142] as well as in bilateral trade agreements between the United States and Australia, Chile, Morocco, Bahrain, and Central American countries.[143] For developments in the EU, see Part III of this book.

2.76 A number of international organizations have also been active in trying to clarify and improve the enforcement of the TRIPs provisions on border measures.

2.77 At the multilateral level, for instance, the World Intellectual Property Organization (WIPO) continues its work on issues relating to TRIPs implementation. WIPO conducted several surveys and gathered information from its members on the enforcement of intellectual property rights.[144] Based on such information, WIPO outlined a number of areas that are contributing to inadequate enforcement of those rights.

2.78 With respect to border measures,[145] the following problems were highlighted:

(i) the lack of cooperation from right-holders following *ex officio* action;

(ii) the lack of human resources, technical equipment, and storing space for confiscated goods;

---

[141] TRIPs, Art 1(1).   [142] Art 1718 of NAFTA. NAFTA entered into force on 1 January 1994.

[143] Bilateral Trade Agreement with Morocco, on-line http://www.ustr.gov/Trade_Agreements/Bilateral/Morocco_FTA/Final_Text/Section_Index.html; Central American Free Trade Agreement, on-line: http://www.ustr.gov/Trade_Agreements/Bilateral/CAFTA-DR/CAFTA-DR_Final_Texts/Section_Index.html; Bilateral Trade Agreement with Chile, on-line http://www.ustr.gov/Trade_Agreements/Bilateral/Chile_FTA/Final_Texts/ Section_Index.html; Bilateral Trade Agreement with Bahrain, on-line http://www.ustr.gov /Trade_Agreements/Bilateral/Bahrain_FTA/Final_texts/Section_Index.html; and the Bilateral Trade Agreement with Australia, http://www.ustr.gov/Trade_Agreements/Bilateral/ Australia_FTA/ Final_Text/Section_Index.html.

[144] See 'Synthesis of Issues Concerning Difficulties and Practices in the Field of Enforcement', WIPO document WIPO/CME/3 of 26 July 2002.

[145] On the basis of TRIPs provisions on border measures, the World Intellectual Property Organization (WIPO) has provided a definition of border measures. WIPO defines border measures

(iii) infringing items placed back in the channels of commerce;

(iv) requirements for excessive security bonds in provisional remedies; and

 (v) the absence of a legal basis for *ex officio* action.

WIPO outlined a number of recommendations and suggestions to improve **2.79** enforcement of intellectual property rights, including better coordination between the countries and international cooperation in these matters. With respect to border measures, the main recommendations were that right-holders be permitted to place a 'single, continuous security bond' to secure all enforcement actions; 'that right-holders [should] not be charged for the detention of infringing goods', and 'that goods found to be infringing [should] not be re-exported, but destroyed in order to prevent the goods from entering other channels of commerce'.[146]

The World Customs Organization (WCO), in collaboration with WIPO, **2.80** adopted a new Model Law on border measures.[147] A predecessor to this Model Law dating back to 1995 was used to assist a number of countries with the implementation of their TRIPs.[148] The Model Law is not directly binding on the Member Countries of the WCO, but rather contains a set of principles and suggestions for the WTO Member States to implement the TRIPs Agreement. The Model Law addresses the following areas: applications for customs assistance; duration of customs surveillance over suspected infringements; the provision of information, including evidence of right ownership and the grounds for suspicion; indemnity and security; suspension of clearance and time period of suspension; notification to the right-holder; examination of the goods by the right-holder; compensation in the case of wrongful detention of goods; *ex officio* action; and powers of suspension of clearance and disposal of counterfeit goods.

The Model Law provides detailed recommendations for individual countries on the **2.81** implementation of the TRIPs provisions. However, it provides for a level of protection higher than the TRIPs minimum. Its purpose is not limited to TRIPs implementation: it also seeks to enshrine 'best practice' of customs authorities in the area of intellectual property enforcement.[149] The Model Law is regularly updated to better meet the needs of customs in the enforcement of the intellectual property rights.

---

as 'legal procedures enabling owners of copyright and related rights—who have valid grounds for suspecting that the importation of pirated copies of their works or objects of related rights, respectively, may take place—to lodge an application for the suspension by the customs authorities of the release into the circulation of such copies.' See 'A Guide to the Copyright and Related Rights Treaties Administered by WIPO and glossary of copyright and related rights terms' (WIPO, 2003) at 270.

[146] Ibid, at 17.

[147] Model Provisions For National Legislation To Implement Fair And Effective Border Measures Consistent With The Agreement On Trade-Related Aspects Of Intellectual Property Rights, adopted on 20 February 2003. The latest version of the Model Law (May 2004) is available on-line at http://www.wcoipr.org/wcoipr/gfx/ModelLawfinal.doc.

[148] See 'Introduction' of the Model Law.

[149] M Lubik, 'The Role of Customs Authorities in the Enforcement of Copyright and Related Rights', 30 June 2003, WIPO document WIPO-CISAC/CR/MSK/03/1 at 6.

2.82 Other TRIPs shortcomings were identified by the European Union in the process leading to the adaption of its Enforcement Directive,[150] which is said to be a possible part of the Doha discussions.[151] It targets in particular financial flows generated by the trade in counterfeit and pirated goods, a matter not included in TRIPs.

Conclusion

2.83 The provisions of the TRIPs Agreement dealing with border measures provide right-holders with a set of mechanisms for the effective enforcement of their intellectual property rights. Counterfeit and pirated goods are often imported from another country and one of the most effective mechanisms for preventing international trade in counterfeit and pirated goods is the seizure of illicit goods at the border. TRIPs allows right-holders to file applications to stop the importation of the goods in all 148 WTO Members.[152] The provisions were implemented in the national legislation of most WTO Members.

2.84 Legal norms are the necessary foundation of effective enforcement, of course. Yet, even where national legislation does provide a TRIPs-compatible legal framework, actual enforcement is ultimately contingent on the effectiveness of the system put in place as well as actions taken (or not) by right-holders. Additionally, if the existence of the necessary administrative and judicial infrastructure is a *sine qua non* of effective enforcement, such enforcement also depends on the successful partnership between business (right-holders), governments and intergovernmental organizations.

---

[150] Directive 2004/48/EC of the European Parliament and of the Council of 29 April 2004 on the Enforcement of Intellectual Property Rights, OJ L 157 (30.04.2004); Corrigendum, OJ L 195/16 (02.06.2004).

[151] Since the inception of the General Agreement on Tariffs and Trade in 1948, a number of 'rounds' were held to negotiate free(r) trade measures. In the last completed round, namely the Uruguay Round, which began in 1986 and ended in 1994, a treaty establishing the World Trade Organization (WTO) was agreed upon, and, as stated above, TRIPs is an Annex to that Agreement. In November 2001, after the dismal failure of the ministerial conference held in Seattle in December 1999, WTO Members agreed on the launch of a round known as the Doha Development Agenda (see the Ministerial Declaration of 20 November 2001, WTO document WT/MIN(01)/DEC/1). It contains only three paragraphs dealing with TRIPs. One deals with access to medicines and public health; another with geographical indications. They are thus not directly relevant here. The third paragraph (number 19) deals mainly with traditional knowledge, folklore and biological diversity, but it allows the TRIPs Council to examine 'other relevant new developments raised by members pursuant to Art 71(1)'. Art 71(1) provides for a general review of TRIPs and the provisions on enforcement including border measures could thus be reopened, possibly on the basis of the EU Enforcement Directive (see n 48 above).   [152] As at 13 October 2004.

Part III

COMMUNITY LEGAL FRAMEWORK

3

REGULATION (EC) 1383/2003

Marius Schneider and Olivier Vrins

Introduction

Before we study in detail the provisions of Council Regulation (EC) 1383/2003 **3.01** of 22 July 2003 concerning customs action against goods suspected of infringing certain intellectual property rights, and the measures to be taken against goods found to have infringed such rights[1] (hereafter referred to as 'the Regulation') in the substantive sections of this book, we will look at the aims and objectives of the Regulation (section A), and the historical background of border measures in the European Community (section B). We will also examine the relation between the Regulation and the national legal systems of the Member States (section C).

A. Aims and objectives of the Regulation

The Regulation is a very powerful tool in the fight against counterfeited and **3.02** pirated goods.

The system of border measures put in place by the Regulation allows customs **3.03** authorities, either on their own initiative (so called *ex officio* interventions) or upon the request of the right-holders, to retain goods suspected of infringing certain intellectual property rights, in order to enable the right-holders to initiate proceedings to determine whether an intellectual property right has been infringed. Goods found to be infringing an intellectual property right will be destroyed or disposed of outside of commercial channels.

A simplified procedure, which allows goods to be abandoned for destruction **3.04** without the need to determine whether an intellectual property right has been infringed, may be foreseen by the Member States.

---

[1] [2003] OJ L196/7 (2.8.2003).

3.05 The Regulation aims to 'guarantee consumers safety and protection, respect for holders' intellectual property rights and the financial interests of the Community in an economic area that is both competitive and open to free competition'. The system of border measures 'should serve to promote business innovation and competitiveness and safeguard jobs while protecting national economies'. However, 'the main objective of this Regulation is to provide the single market and consumers with more effective protection in a bigger Community'.[2]

3.06 In an enlarged Europe with 25 Member States, wide-ranging external borders, continuous trade-flows, and in the absence of border controls at internal boundaries, it is of paramount importance to prevent counterfeited and pirated products from entering the Community. Only a very efficient system of border measures—'not unnecessarily impeding international trade'[3]—will allow this challenge to be met. Adopted on the basis of Article 133 of the Treaty establishing the European Community, which grants the Community competence in relation to the common commercial policy and external trade, the Regulation is undoubtedly a compromise between the imperatives of international trade, free movement of goods, and protection against intellectual property right infringements.

3.07 The Community legislator also aims to protect the general public against goods infringing intellectual property rights. Even though counterfeited and pirated goods may seem attractive to some consumers hard to educate—for example, because they believe that they can afford what they think is a status symbol at a lower price—there is little doubt that these goods are in many instances 'deceiving and in some cases endangering the health and safety of consumers'.[4]

3.08 The Regulation further aims to protect law-abiding manufacturers, traders, and right-holders as 'counterfeiting and pirating are increasingly damaging the economy, financial interests and employment and severely handicap economic operators'.[5] Fair competition, research and innovation, are the economic pillars of the Community, it is therefore only right that the Community legislature protects economic actors against straightforward infringement of intellectual property rights by unfair traders. It has to be remembered that counterfeiting and piracy generate EUR 250 billion of illegal revenue—this corresponds to at least the same

---

[2] Proposal for a Council Regulation concerning customs action against goods suspected of infringing certain intellectual property rights and the measures to be taken against goods found to have infringed such rights COM (2003) 20 final, Explanatory Memorandum (hereafter referred to as the 'Explanatory Memorandum and Proposal'), points 2.1 and 2.2.   [3] Ibid, point 2.3.

[4] Reg 1383/2003, 2nd Recital.

[5] Explanatory Memorandum and Proposal (n 2 above), point 2.3. Cf also Reg 1383/2003, 2nd Recital.

amount of lost profits for industry—and caused the loss of 100,000 jobs a year in Europe over the past 11 years.[6]

Finally, as demonstrated in the section dedicated to the history of border measures in the Community, the draftsmen of Regulation 1383/2003 have taken into account the particular interests of small and medium-sized industries and enterprises[7] and those of the food and drink industry. **3.09**

B. Historical background

Regulation 1383/2003 is already the fourth generation of Community law on border measures against goods infringing intellectual property rights. **3.10**

The first generation Regulation on border measures, Council Regulation (EEC) No 3842/86 laying down measures to prohibit the release for free circulation of counterfeit goods[8] was adopted by the European Council on 1 December 1986 and entered into force on 1 January 1988. This first set of Community rules allowed trade mark owners to lodge an application with the competent authority designated under national law for requesting the suspension by the customs authorities of the release of goods suspected of infringing trade mark rights entered for free circulation in that Member State.[9] The trade mark owner had to refer the matter to the authority competent to take a substantive decision on the case.[10] Goods found to be counterfeit were destroyed or disposed of outside the channels of commerce.[11] Unfortunately this first generation Regulation on border measures did not prove very efficient, and both national authorities and trade mark owners failed to make full use of the possibilities provided by this tool. **3.11**

In 1993, the Commission planned to extend the scope of Regulation 3842/86 to additional intellectual property rights and customs procedures other than the entry for release for free circulation. An initial proposal to stretch the boundaries of the Regulation to pirated goods (that is, goods infringing copyrights, neighbouring rights, or design rights) and to export goods and goods in transit **3.12**

---

[6] ICC Counterfeiting Intelligence Bureau, *Countering Counterfeiting. A Guide to Protecting and Enforcing Intellectual Property Rights*, 1997 and Commission Green Paper on combating counterfeiting and piracy in the single market COM (98) 569, October 1998. Cf K Daele, 'Reg 1383/2003: A New Step in the Fight against Counterfeit and Pirated Goods at the Borders of the European Union', [2004] EIPR 214.

[7] Explanatory Memorandum and Proposal (n 2 above), point 2.5.

[8] [1986] OJ L 357/1 (18.12.1986). The corresponding Implementing Regulation was Commission Reg (EEC) No 3077/87 of 14 October 1987 laying down provisions for the implementation of Council Reg (EEC) No 3842/86 laying down measures to prohibit the release for free circulation of counterfeit goods, [1987] OJ L 291/19 (15.10.1987).

[9] Reg 3842/86 (n 8 above), Art 3(1).   [10] Cf ibid, Art 5.   [11] Cf ibid, Art 7(1).

was prepared by the Commission.[12] Due to a debate on the legal basis for the adoption of the text, the latter remained embryonic.[13] A second, more successful, proposal followed in 1994.[14]

3.13   Council Regulation (EC) No 3295/94 of 22 December 1994 laying down measures to prohibit the release for free circulation, export, re-export, or entry for a suspensive procedure of counterfeit and pirated goods[15] replaced the first generation Regulation as of 1 July 1995. The scope of this second generation Regulation was extended to copyright, neighbouring rights, designs, and additional customs procedures.[16] The *ex officio* procedure was introduced[17] and rapidly proved to be a success, which was reflected in statistical results.[18]

3.14   Following the amendment of Regulation 3295/94 in 1999[19] the latter was renamed Council Regulation (EC) No 3295/94 of 22 December 1994 laying down measures *'concerning the entry into the Community and the export and re-export from the Community of goods infringing certain intellectual property rights'*. It now applied also to goods infringing patents or supplementary protection certificates.[20] Under this new regime, customs were competent to take border measures against goods suspected of infringing intellectual property rights 'whatever their customs status'.[21] Finally, this third generation Regulation provided for a new 'Community-wide' application for action for holders of a Community trade mark registration 'whereby the granting of a single application for action by the competent authority in one Member State can bind one or more other Member States as well'.[22,23] The Community application was a considerable

---

[12] Proposal for a Council Regulation (EEC) laying down measures to prohibit the release for free circulation, export or transit of counterfeit and pirated goods, COM (93) 329 final, [1993] OJ C 238/9 (2.9.1993).

[13] O Vrins, 'Le règlement (CE) n° 1383/2003 du conseil des communautés européennes du 22 juillet 2003: le droit douanier élargit ses frontières', [2004] Intellectuele Rechten Droits Intellectuels 101 (104).

[14] Amended proposal for a Council Regulation (EC) laying down measures to prohibit the release for free circulation, export, re-export or placing under a suspensive procedure of counterfeit and pirated goods (Amendment to the proposal for a Council Regulation (EEC) laying down measures to prohibit the release for free circulation, export or transit of counterfeit and pirated goods), COM (94) 43 final, [1994] OJ C 86/14 (23.3.1994).

[15] [1994] OJ L 341/8 (30.12.1994). This 'second generation' Regulation had been implemented by Commission Reg (EC) No 1367/95 of 16 June 1995 laying down provisions for the implementation of Council Reg (EC) No 3295/94 laying down measures to prohibit the release for free circulation, export, re-export or entry for a suspensive procedure of counterfeit and pirated goods, [1995] OJ L 133/2 (17.6.1995).   [16] Cf Reg 3295/94, Art 1.

[17] Cf ibid, Art 4.   [18] O Vrins (n 13 above), 104–105.

[19] Council Reg (EC) No 241/1999 of 25 January 1999 amending Reg (EC) No 3295/94 laying down measures to prohibit the release for free circulation, export, re-export or entry for a suspensive procedure of counterfeit and pirated goods, [1999] OJ L 27/1 (2.2.1999).

[20] Reg 3295/94 (consolidated text), Art 1.   [21] Reg 241/1999, 3rd Recital.

[22] Reg 3295/94 (consolidated text), Art 3; Reg 241/1999, 7th Recital.

[23] This Regulation has been implemented by Commission Reg 2549/1999 of 2 December 1999, [1999] OJ L 308/16 (3.12.1999), amending Commission Reg (EC) No 1367/95 of 16 June 1995 laying down provisions for the implementation of Council Reg (EC) No 3295/94 laying down

improvement on the former system, and has since been used on a regular basis by right-holders.[24]

In terms of figures, Regulation 3295/94 proved to be very efficient: between 1998 and 2001 the number of articles infringing an intellectual property right discovered by customs officers in the European Community increased by 900 per cent, from 10 million to 100 million articles.[25] **3.15**

Encouraged by these outstanding results, on 20 January 2003 the Commission submitted a proposal[26] to revise once more the system of border measures. The main novelties of the new proposal were its aims to: **3.16**

- extend the scope of the system of border measures to new intellectual property rights, such as plant variety rights, geographical indications, and designations of origin. The purpose of this widening of scope was to allow the food and drink industry to act efficiently against the increasing infringement of their intellectual property rights by counterfeited foodstuff;
- improve the quality of information provided to customs by right-holders in the application for action, and to harmonize the period of validity of the latter;
- prevent abuse of the information provided by customs to the right-holder for purposes other than those laid down in the Regulation;
- abolish fees and securities and to replace them by an undertaking to accept liability. The idea was to allow small and medium sized undertakings to avail themselves of the system of border measures on a more regular basis;
- extend the use of *ex officio* measures;
- allow right-holders to be provided with samples for analysis;
- provide for a simplified procedure allowing a rapid destruction of goods infringing intellectual property rights, thus resolving storage problems.

Regulation 1383/2003 was finally adopted on 22 July 2003, and became applicable on 1 July 2004. The new Regulation was generally welcomed by right-holders and practitioners. That said, the practical working of the system of border measures was severely distorted for a while as the Commission Regulation (EC) 1891/2004[27] implementing Regulation 1383/2003, which **3.17**

---

measures to prohibit the release for free circulation, export, re-export or entry for a suspensive procedure of counterfeit and pirated goods (n 15 above).

[24] I Dies de Rivera Elzaburu, 'An Analysis of the Evolution of the Enforcement of Rights', in European Communities Trade Mark Association, *The Development of Trade Marks, Designs and Related Rights in Europe*, published on the occasion of the ECTA's 25th anniversary, at 157 (159).

[25] Explanatory Memorandum and Proposal (n 2 above), point 1.   [26] Cf n 2 above.

[27] Commission Reg (EC) 1891/2004 laying down provisions for the implementation of Council Reg 1383/2003 concerning customs action against goods suspected of infringing certain intellectual property rights and the measures to be taken against goods found to have infringed such rights, [2004] OJ L 328/16 (30.10.2004).

was supposed to become applicable on 1 July 2004, was only published in the Official Journal of 30 October 2004. The Commission excused the late publication of this implementing regulation by pleading a backlog of important material at the translation services. The delay in publication caused legal uncertainty and reticence to act both on the side of customs and right-holders for a few months.

3.18   The provisions of the fourth generation Regulation will be examined in detail in the rest of this chapter.

C. Regulation 1383/2003—its relation to national law

3.19   The Regulation is secondary Community law, and therefore directly applicable in all Member States of the European Community.[28]

3.20   Given the principle of supremacy of Community law over national law, the Regulation sets aside provisions of national law that are conflicting with the rules laid down by it. This would be the case, for example, for fees or securities that would still be requested by national customs authorities,[29] or in case a Member State appoints several customs authorities competent to process the application for action.[30] The national legislators do however remain free to enact measures where the Regulation invites them to do so, and where the Regulation does not provide for the contrary. A Member State may decide, for example, to introduce into its national law a procedure analogous to the one foreseen in the Regulation allowing border measures to be taken against parallel imports, overruns or goods infringing intellectual property rights not covered by the Regulation (for example, commercial names, topographies of semiconductors, etc).

3.21   The system put in place by the Regulation relies on national law for its effective functioning. National law determines, for example, the procedure and rules to be applied in the proceedings initiated to determine whether an intellectual property right has been infringed. In other words, the Regulation relies on the national provisions of the Member States, on the jurisdiction of the courts or judicial procedures, which are not affected by the measures contained in the Regulation.[31]

---

[28] EC Treaty, Art 110(2), first indent: 'A regulation shall have general application. It shall be binding in its entirety and directly applicable in all Member States.'

[29] As this would be contrary to Reg 1383/2003, Art 5(7), second indent.

[30] This would be in breach of Reg 1383/2003, Art 5(2).

[31] Reg 1383/2003, 8th Recital, *in fine*: '[. . .] This Regulation does not affect the Member States' provisions on the competence of the courts or judicial procedures.' Cf also in this respect, under Reg 3295/94 (n 15 above), the Hague Court of Appeal (*Gerechtshof te 's-Gravenhage*), *Philips v Postech anor*, 25 October 2001, unreported, point 4, upheld by the Dutch Supreme Court (*Hoge Raad*), 19 March 2004, [2004] Intellectuele Eigensdomrechten 233; cf in particular the Opinion of Advocate General Strikwerda in the latter case, ibid, at 237, points 11 ff.

Likewise, the national law of the Member State in which the customs intervention is requested applies when the scope of protection of national intellectual property rights (including national trade marks, designs, copyrights, patents, plant variety rights, designations of origin, and geographical indications) has to be determined.[32] National law also applies to the notification by the relevant customs office to the customs department responsible for the processing of applications for action that legal proceedings have been initiated.[33]

3.22 With regard to some points, the Regulation compels the Member States to adopt certain measures: for example, to designate the customs department competent to receive and process applications for action.[34] Here again, if the competent authority is not designated by the Member States,[35] or if several authorities are appointed to that effect within one Member State, the system put in place by the Regulation cannot work properly. The same applies to the issue of penalties— since Member States are required to introduce effective, proportionate and dissuasive penalties for breaches of the Regulation[36]—and other measures aimed to deprive the persons involved in the traffics of any economic gains from their transactions.[37]

3.23 In relation to other issues Community law encourages the Member States to enact measures, leaving them nonetheless a certain liberty of action. This is the case, for example, for the simplified procedure, which may be provided for by the Member States, in accordance with their national legislation.[38]

3.24 Certain issues are explicitly provided by the Regulation without there being any freedom of action for the Member States. Thus, for example, no fee may be charged for the administrative costs occasioned by the processing of the application for action.[39] Similarly the filing of an application for action is a prerequisite for obtaining the name and address of the consignee, consignor, the declarant, or the holder of the suspect goods.[40]

3.25 Finally, the in-depth analysis in the national chapters contained in this book will show that some of the Member States have adopted an 'atypical' interpretation of the provisions of the Regulation: in several Member States customs authorities

---

[32] Ibid, Art 2(1)(b) and (c). Cf also the 8th Recital: 'Proceedings initiated to determine whether an intellectual property right has been infringed under national law will be conducted with reference to the criteria used to establish whether goods produced in that Member State infringe intellectual property rights [. . .]'; and Art 10, first indent: 'The law in force in the Member State within the territory of which the goods are placed in one of the situations referred to in Art 1(1) shall apply when deciding whether an intellectual property right has been infringed under national law.'

[33] Ibid, Art 10, second indent.   [34] Cf ibid, Art 5(2).

[35] This has for several years been the case in Belgium, where the national legislator omitted to designate an authority competent to process applications for action under the first generation Regulation on border measures (Part IV, Chapter 5, Belgium, at para 5.02).   [36] Ibid, Art 18.

[37] Ibid, Art 17.   [38] Cf ibid, Art 11.   [39] Ibid, Art 5(7), second indent.

[40] Ibid, Art 9(3).

will ask the applicant to provide certified or legalized copies of the documents filed (for example, a power of attorney form, or a registration certificate for an industrial property right, etc). Others consider that handing over infringing goods to charities meets the requirements of Article 17 of the Regulation. One may of course wonder whether these interpretations are in line with the spirit of the Community legislation.

3.26 It will become evident from the national chapters of this book that most of the Member States have adopted national legislation executing the Regulation. Only very few have adopted national law which *supplements* the Regulation by an analogous national system of border measures, whilst even fewer have provided for no national execution at all (besides, as the case may be, an administrative circular).

3.27 We will go on to examine the subject matter and scope of the Regulation (Part I), the conditions governing the filing and processing of an application for action by the customs authorities (Part II), the conditions governing action by the customs authorities and by the authority having jurisdiction to decide on the case (Part III), as well as provisions applicable to goods found to infringe an intellectual property right (Part IV), penalties (Part V), and finally the liability of the customs authorities and the right-holders in the context of the application of the Regulation (Part VI).

I. SUBJECT MATTER AND SCOPE OF REGULATION 1383/2003

3.28 The application of Regulation 1383/2003 is subject to two cumulative positive conditions: first of all the suspect goods have to fall under one of the customs procedures or status defined in Article 1(1) (cf section A), furthermore the goods have to be infringing an intellectual property right in the sense of Article 2(1) (cf section B). Finally, and this is a negative requirement, the goods may not be excluded from the scope of the Regulation (section C).

A. Customs status of the goods

3.29 Regulation 1383/2003 allows customs to take action in virtually every customs situation, provided the goods suspected of infringing an intellectual property right originate in, or are destined for, a non-member country of the European Community.

'Intra-Community' traffic is thus, at present, excluded from the scope of the **3.30**
Regulation, owing to the sacrosanct principle of free movement of goods.[41] The
exclusion of 'intra-Community' traffic from the scope of the Regulation is
definitely regrettable as the amount of infringing goods originating from within
the Community has risen dramatically with the accession of the 10 new Member
States in 2004.

Although we do not want to bore the reader with highly technical considerations **3.31**
on customs procedures, we will have to examine these situations in more detail,
in order to understand the scope of the Regulation and the issues that may still
be open for discussion.

The situations in which customs of the Member States are to take action **3.32**
when coming across goods suspected of infringing any of the intellectual
property rights defined in Article 2(1) of the Regulation are defined in
Article 1(1). Pursuant to this provision, action by the customs authorities is
required:

  (a) when [such goods] are entered for release for free circulation, export or re-export
      in acccrdance with Article 61 of Council Regulation ([E]EC) No 2913/92 of
      12 October 1992 establishing the Community Customs Code;[42]

  (b) when they are found during checks on goods entering or leaving the
      Community customs territory in accordance with Articles 37 and 183 of
      Regulation (EEC) No 2913/92, placed under a suspensive procedure within the
      meaning of Article 84(1)(a) of that Regulation, in the process of being
      re-exported subject to notification under Article 182(2) of that Regulation or
      placed in a free zone or free warehouse within the meaning of Article 166 of that
      Regulation.

The object of Article 1(1) is not to be confused with that of Article 16 of the **3.33**
Regulation; whilst the former 'sets out the conditions for action by the customs
authorities' where goods are *suspected* of infringing an intellectual property right,
the latter provides that, once goods *have been found to infringe* such a right,
subsequent to a customs intervention according to Article 9 and at the end of
the proceedings referred to in Article 13, they may not be cleared by customs, or
placed onto the market or simply into circulation.

The third Recital of the Regulation clarifies the scope of Articles 1(1) and 16, in **3.34**
that it provides that:

  In cases where counterfeit goods, pirated goods and, more generally, goods infringing an intellectual property right originate in or come from third countries, their
  introduction into the Community customs territory, including their transhipment,

---

[41] Cf paras 3.93–3.112 below.
[42] [1992] OJ L 302/1 (19.10.1992) ('the Community Customs Code'). Regulation as last
amended by Reg (EC) No 2700/2000 of the European Parliament and of the Council ([2000] OJ L
311/17 (12.12.2000)).

release for free circulation in the Community, placing in a free zone or warehouse, should be prohibited and a procedure set up to enable the customs authorities to enforce this prohibition as effectively as possible.

3.35 Reference is made on several occasions in Article 1(1) to the so-called 'Community Customs Code' (containing 253 Articles), which, together with its Implementing Regulation[43] (containing no less than 915 Articles and 113 Annexes), sets forth the European Community's basic customs legislation. The European Commission, assisted by a Community Customs Committee, is in charge of implementing this legislation. The Community Customs Code is currently undergoing a comprehensive revision process.[44]

3.36 Regulation 1383/2003 achieves a significant step forward in the definition of the situations in which customs are to take action against goods suspected of infringing intellectual property rights. As has been pointed out by Professor Daniel Gervais in Chapter 2 of this book, Article 9(4) of the Paris Convention is very restrictive on this point, as it only provides for an obligation on its contracting countries to 'seize' suspect goods on importation, whilst Article 9(6) allows the countries concerned to be relieved of this obligation in some circumstances.[45] Similarly, the first EC Regulation on this subject, that is, Regulation 3842/86/EEC, only applied to goods entered for free circulation in the EC Community.

3.37 Regulation 3842/86/EEC rapidly proved unsatisfactory. Indeed, counterfeiters wishing to circumvent the scope of this legislation simply introduced the goods through the borders of a different Member State from the State of destination.[46]

3.38 Therefore, in 1993, the Commission proposed to broaden the scope of this Regulation to cases of exportation and external transit.[47] Regulation 3295/94 did

---

[43] Commission Reg (EEC) No 2454/93 of 2 July 1993 laying down provisions for the implementation of Council Reg (EEC) No 2913/92 establishing the Community Customs Code [1993] OJ L 253/1 (11.10.1993). Regulation as last amended by Commission Reg (EC) No 2286/2003 of 18 December 2003 [2003] OJ L 343/1 (31.12.2003).

[44] For additional information on this point, cf the Communication of the Commission to the Council and the European Parliament on a simple and paperless environment for customs and trade, COM (2003) 452. The latest draft of the Revised Customs Code (11 November 2004, TAXUD/ 458/2004—Rev 4) can be downloaded at http://europa.eu.int/comm/taxation_customs/resources/ documents/458rev_en.pdf. Cf also http://europa.eu.int/comm/taxation_customs/common/ consultations/customs/index_en.htm.

[45] Cf D Gervais (Chapter 2 of this book), para 2.04. The Lithuanian Supreme Court (case 3K-3-1060, *HD Lee Company Inc v UAB Mita*, 17 November 2003. Commented on in World Trademark Law Report of 4 February 2004) recalled, however, that Art 9(4) of the Paris Convention was not to be interpreted as preventing the countries member of the Paris Union from imposing border measures on suspect goods in transit.

[46] S Billings, 'EEC Council Reg 3842/86: an effective piracy weapon?' [1988] EIPR 346 (347).

[47] Cf para 3.12 above, and Proposal for a Council Regulation (EEC) laying down measures to prohibit the release for free circulation, export or transit of counterfeit and pirated goods (n 12 above) and amended proposal for a Council Regulation (EC) laying down measures to prohibit the

even better, since it applied not only to goods entered for free circulation, export or re-export, but also to goods found during checks made on goods placed under a suspensive procedure (thus including goods in external transit), or re-exported subject to notification. In respect of Article 51 of the TRIPs Agreement,[48] which limits itself to obliging the WTO members to adopt procedures to enable a right-holder who has valid grounds for suspecting that the *importation* of counterfeit or pirated goods could take place, to seek the suspension by the customs authorities of the *release into free circulation* of such goods,[49] this Regulation already proved innovative and far-reaching.

Regulation 1383/2003 clarifies the situation existing under Regulation 3295/94 **3.39** and extends the boundaries of the latter even further. In fact, not only does the new Regulation cover 'all customs procedures'; Article 1(1) also encompasses situations where goods are *not* subject to any customs procedure, and thus need not be cleared.[50] Clearance of the goods is only required on 'importation', that is, for goods entered for release for free circulation (to be assigned to a customs-approved treatment or use),[51] for export,[52] or re-export.

Article 1(1) of Regulation 1383/2003 clearly distinguishes between the situations **3.40** where goods are subject to clearance, that is, entry for release for free circulation, export, or re-export (Article 1(1)(a), with reference to Article 61 of the Community Customs Code, concerning the placing of goods under a customs procedure), and all other situations, where the goods are *not* subject to clearance (Article 1(1)(b)). It would therefore be incorrect to argue that smuggled goods cannot be detained by customs under Regulation 1383/2003.[53] It is worth recalling here that the Regulation aims to tackle, amongst other things, the

---

release for free circulation, export, re-export or placing under a suspensive procedure of counterfeit and pirated goods (n 14 above).

[48] Agreement on trade-related aspects of intellectual property rights, set out in Annex 1C to the Agreement establishing the World Trade Organization; approved on behalf of the European Community by Council Decision 94/800/EC of 22 December 1994 concerning the conclusion on behalf of the European Community, as regards matters within its competence, of the agreements reached in the Uruguay Round multilateral negotiations (1986–1994) [1994] OJ L 336/1.

[49] TRIPs Agreement, Art 51, also *allows* WTO Members to provide for corresponding procedures concerning the suspension by the customs authorities of the release of infringing goods destined for *exportation* from their territories.

[50] 'Clearance' of goods refers to the act whereby a person indicates the wish to place goods under a given customs procedure, as provided for by the Community Customs Code (n 42 above), Art 4(17) and Arts 59–78. The declaration is to be lodged with the customs office where the goods were or will shortly be presented (Reg 2454/93, n 43 above, Art 201). In general the clearance of goods is performed by their owner, or one of the latter's representatives. It may also be performed by the person having control over the goods. These persons may be natural or legal persons. As a general rule, the 'declarant' should be established in the Community.

[51] Community Customs Code (n 42 above), Art 48.   [52] Ibid, Art 161(2).

[53] *Contra* C De Meyer and P Van Den Broecke, 'De douane verordening 1383/2003 en het douane beslag', in MC Janssens (ed), *Combattre les atteintes à la propriété intellectuelle*, CIR 2004, 83 (87–88).

transhipment of unauthentic goods[54]—a situation which is very frequently encountered in practice, and in which the goods are not subject to clearance.

3.41 In substance, Regulation 1383/2003 enables the customs authorities of the Member States to take action in all situations where goods suspected of infringing intellectual property rights are likely to be encountered,[55] except in the case of intra-Community traffic. This includes all customs procedures,[56] but also those cases where goods are *not* subject to a customs procedure, such as, for example, transhipment, with the exception of 'internal' (that is, common or Community) transit.

3.42 The Regulation obviously applies irrespective of whether the goods are found on a plane or a lorry, on board a ship, at the quayside, or in a free zone or free warehouse.

3.43 In 2004, the great majority of customs interventions in the EU took place in respect of goods placed under the import procedure (85 per cent, or 18,888 interventions; that is, 96 per cent of the cases in Portugal, 98 per cent in the Czech Republic, 96 per cent in Austria and 89 per cent in Germany, against only 14 per cent in Hungary, 17 per cent in Finland, or 18 per cent in Luxembourg). Only 128 customs actions (0.5 per cent on average, but 10 per cent in Belgium) were carried out under the export procedure, while checks on re-exportation represented 200 cases (1 per cent on average). External transit accounted for 3.5 per cent of the cases (but 82 per cent in Finland, and in Luxembourg). Customs warehousing represented less than 2 per cent of the total figures, or 356 cases (14 per cent in Estonia). Others: 4 per cent.[57]

3.44 Still in 2004, 70 per cent of the *interventions* against counterfeit and pirated goods concerned products originating in Asia (out of which 20 per cent in Thailand, 30 per cent in China, 7 per cent in Turkey, 8 per cent in Hong Kong, 3 per cent in Malaysia, 2 per cent in India). Owing to the recourse to traffic diversion techniques, the United States represented the country of origin (or provenance) in 4 per cent of the cases. China can be considered the biggest exporter of counterfeit products, with 54 per cent of the *articles* seized in 2004, or over 55 million items.[58]

---

[54] Cf Reg 1383/2003, 3rd Recital.

[55] M de Cock Buning, 'De nieuwe Antipiraterij Verordening', [2004] Bijblad bij de Industriële Eigendom 236; K Daele (n 6 above), 215.

[56] The Community Customs Code (n 42 above) provides for eight customs procedures, ie release for free circulation, transit, customs warehousing, inward processing, processing under customs control, temporary importation, outward processing, and exportation (Art 4(16)).

[57] EC Commision, DG TAXUD, breakdown of the number and percentage of customs procedures—EU 2004, http:europe.eu.int/comm/taxation_customs/resources/documents/customs/customs_controls/counterfeit_piracy/statistics/counterf_comm_2004_en.pdf.

[58] Ibid, breakdown of the number of cases by origin of goods—2004, and breakdown of the number of articles seized by origin of goods by origin and by number of articles seized—2004.

As to the means of transport used, rail traffic remains marginal (2 per cent of the **3.45**
case in 2004). Air freight was used in nearly half of the cases (68 per cent in
Belgium, 77 per cent in France, 99.5 per cent in Luxembourg, against 8 per cent
in Ireland), followed by post (32 per cent on average; 90 per cent in Austria, 62 per
cent in Denmark, 91 per cent in Ireland, against only 3 per cent in Cyprus and in
Poland), sea (11 per cent on average, but 70 per cent in Finland, 46 per cent in
Italy, 46 per cent in Greece, and 52 per cent in Spain, 43 per cent in Sweden, and
37 per cent in Portugal), and road (7 per cent on average, against, for example,
over 50 per cent in Estonia, Hungary, Latvia, Lithuania and Slovakia).[59]

(1) Goods entered for release for free circulation

The Regulation applies, in the first place, to goods that are entered for release **3.46**
for free circulation—that means introduced into the Community in order to
circulate freely within its territory.[60]

Article 23 of the EC Treaty stipulates free movement for Community goods **3.47**
throughout the European Community. This principle applies not only to
goods manufactured in the Community but also to imported goods which have
been *released* for free circulation after payment of the import duties[61] to which
they are liable.

The concept of 'release for free circulation' under the Community Customs **3.48**
Code is therefore tantamount to that of 'importation' under national law, with
the difference that goods which are released for free circulation may in principle freely circulate within the whole Community customs territory, whereas
goods subject to importation are cleared in the territory of the relevant Member
State only.

In other words, 'entry for release for free circulation' refers to the introduction **3.49**
into the Community customs territory of goods originating in, or coming from,

---

[59] Ibid, breakdown by means of transport used for the cases examined by the customs administration of the EU—2004.

[60] Cf ECJ, Case 41/76, *Donckerwolcke*, [1976] ECR 1921, para 16: 'Products in free circulation
are to be understood as meaning those products which, coming from third countries, were duly
imported into any one of the Member States in accordance with the requirements laid down by Art
10 [new Art 24 of the EC Treaty].' Cf also Case C-66/99, *D Wandel* [2001] ECR I-873, para 36:
'[N]on-Community goods declared for release for free circulation do not obtain the status of
Community goods until commercial policy measures have been applied and the other formalities
laid down in respect of the importation of goods have been completed and any import duties legally
due have been not only charged but paid or secured.'

[61] Import duties are customs duties payable on importation according to Reg (EEC) 2658/87 on
the tariff and statistical nomenclature and on the Common Customs Tariff ([1987] OJ L 256/1),
autonomous tariff suspensions and tariff quotas, preferential arrangements, anti-dumping,
countervailing, safeguard and retaliatory duties, as well as import charges laid down under the
common agricultural policy and specific arrangements for processed agricultural products.

countries or areas which are not part of that territory.[62] Under Article 24 of the EC Treaty,

> Products coming from a third country shall be considered to be in free circulation in a Member State if the import formalities have been complied with and any customs duties or charges having equivalent effect which are payable have been levied in that Member State, and if they have not benefited from a total or partial drawback of such duties or charges.

3.50 As a consequence, release for free circulation confers on non-Community goods the customs status of Community goods. The purpose of release for free circulation is to fulfil all import formalities so that the goods can be sold on the Community market like any product made in the European Union. It entails application of commercial policy measures[63] (such as, for example, the presentation of an import authorization for goods subject to quotas), completion of the other formalities laid down in respect of the importation of goods (such as, for example, the presentation of a health certificate in certain cases), and the charging of any duties legally due, that is, where goods are liable to them according to the Community Customs Tariff and no duty relief is applicable.[64]

(2) Goods entered for export or re-export, and goods found during checks on goods in the process of being re-exported subject to notification

3.51 As with the concept of 'entry for release for free circulation', the notions of 'export' and 're-export' laid down in Article 1(1) of Regulation 1383/2003 are defined by reference to Article 61 of the Community Customs Code.

3.52 'Export' refers to the opposite situation to 'release for free circulation', referring to the sending of Community goods outside the Community customs territory, subject to completion of the necessary formalities and the charging of any duties legally due. The export procedure is obligatory for Community goods leaving the Community customs territory,[65] with very few exceptions.

3.53 'Re-exportation' contemplates the situation where non-Community goods leave the Community customs territory after being introduced into this territory *without* ever having been conferred the customs status of Community

---

[62] The Community customs territory is defined in Art 3(1) of the Community Customs Code (n 42 above). It includes not only the 25 Member States of the European Union, but also, among others, their territorial waters, inland maritime waters and airspaces, as well as the territory of the Principality of Monaco, and the overseas departments of Guadeloupe, French-Guiana, Martinique, and Réunion. A few islands, overseas, national waters and municipalities are excluded, however. Albeit dependent on a Member State, overseas countries and territories do not belong to the EC customs territory. They are listed in Annex II to the EC Treaty. On this point, cf M Fallon, *Droit matériel général des Communautés européennes*, Brussels, Bruylant; Paris, LGDJ; 1997, 631 ff.
[63] On the notion of 'commercial policy measures', cf Reg 2454/93 (n 43 above), Art 1(7).
[64] Community Customs Code (n 42 above), Art 79.   [65] Ibid, Art 161.

goods, that is, without ever having been released for free circulation within this territory.

The concept of 're-exportation subject to notification' refers to Article 182(2) of the Community Customs Code. Except in those cases specifically set forth otherwise in accordance with the committee procedure, the re-exportation of goods must in principle *always* be notified first to the customs authorities. **3.54**

The notion of 'customs checks' or 'customs controls' refers to acts performed by the customs authorities of the Member States with a view to ensuring that the customs rules and other applicable trade provisions are observed, such as examining goods, documents or accounts, or carrying out inquiries.[66] **3.55**

The carrying out of customs control on exportation (or re-exportation) is considered more and more as a panacea in the fight against counterfeiting and piracy at a worldwide level. In this context, it is very disappointing to note that the EC Member States seldom rely on Regulation 1383/2003 to carry out such checks under the export or re-export procedures. On the international scene, only very few WTO members have implemented the option provided by Article 51 of the TRIPs Agreement, allowing them to entitle the customs authorities to suspend the release of infringing goods destined for exportation from their territories. In this context, it may come as a surprise that China is one of the countries where customs controls on exportation are strong, particularly in the fight against intellectual property right infringements. **3.56**

Conscious of this challenge, the European Commission has recently entered into negotiations with the WTO members to prompt a modification of Article 51 of TRIPs so as to render the carrying out of customs checks on exportation compulsory. **3.57**

(3) *Goods found during checks on merchandise entering or leaving the Community customs territory*

As stipulated in Article 1(1)(b), Regulation 1383/2003 clearly covers situations where suspect goods are found during checks on goods entering or leaving the Community customs territory in accordance with Articles 37 and 183 of the Community Customs Code. **3.58**

Pursuant to Article 37 of the Community Customs Code, goods brought into the Community customs territory are, from the time of entry, subject to customs supervision. They may therefore be subject to control by customs. Article 38(1)(a) provides that the goods are to be conveyed without delay by the person bringing them into the Community to the customs office designated by the customs **3.59**

---

[66] Ibid, Arts 4(14), 13, 68, and 78(2).

authorities. Article 48 requires non-Community goods presented to customs to be assigned a 'customs-approved treatment or use', which includes placing them under a customs procedure.[67] The goods will remain under such supervision for as long as necessary to determine their customs status, if appropriate, and in the case of non-Community goods, in principle until their customs status is changed, they enter a free zone or free warehouse, or they are re-exported or destroyed in accordance with Article 182 of the Community Customs Code. Non-Community goods brought into the Community customs territory cannot be released from the customs office or other approved place at which they are presented until they are assigned a customs-approved treatment or use. In the meantime, the goods must remain under customs supervision, and are held in 'temporary storage',[68] either at the customs office of presentation, or at any other place designated, approved, and controlled by that office.

3.60 Similarly, under Article 183 of the Community Customs Code, goods *leaving* the Community customs territory are also subject to customs supervision. They may therefore be subject to checks by the customs authorities. On leaving the EC customs territory, goods released for free circulation, like goods manufactured in the Community, lose their status as Community goods.[69]

(4) Goods found during checks on merchandise placed under a suspensive procedure

3.61 Non-Community goods intended for a non-EC Member State and which limit themselves to transiting through the Community customs territory are in principle not released for free circulation: they are placed under a suspensive procedure.

3.62 Article 84(1)(a) of the Community Customs Code distinguishes between different types of suspensive procedures, namely external transit, customs warehousing, inward processing in the form of a system of suspension, processing under customs control, and temporary importation.[70]

External transit

3.63 The external transit procedure is defined in Article 91 of the Community Customs Code as allowing the movement from one point to another within the Community customs territory of:

- non-Community goods, without such goods being subject to import duties and other charges or to commercial policy measures;

---

[67] Community Customs Code (n 42 above), Art 4(15).   [68] Cf ibid, Arts 50–53.
[69] Ibid, Art 4(8).
[70] For a more detailed overview of the suspensive procedures, cf F Rutter and A Serneels, *Handbook douane en internationale handel 2000–2001*, Intersentia, Antwerpen, 2000, ch 9 ff, 127 ff.

- Community goods, in cases and on conditions determined in accordance with the committee procedure, in order to prevent products covered by, or benefiting from, export measures from either evading or benefiting unjustifiably from such measures.

The external transit procedure therefore relates to goods moving from one point located within the customs territory of the Community to another point equally located within that territory, to be exported afterwards (in the case of Community goods) or re-exported (in the case of non-Community goods) outside the internal market, in the conditions set forth in Article 91 of the Community Customs Code: **3.64**

> Goods placed under this procedure are subject neither to the corresponding import duties nor to the other measures of commercial policy; it is as if they had not entered the Community territory. In reality, they are imported from a non-member country and pass through one or more Member States before being exported to another non-member country.[71]

The external transit procedure is to end 'when the goods and the corresponding documents are produced at the customs office of destination in accordance with the provisions of the procedure in question.[72] Non-Community goods placed under this procedure are subject to customs supervision from the moment of entry until they leave the Community.[73] **3.65**

By referring in Article 1(1)(b) to the placing of goods under a suspensive procedure, Regulation 1383/2003 clearly applies to goods in external transit. This was already the case under Regulation 3295/94, as the European Court of Justice emphasized on two occasions. **3.66**

In the *Polo/Lauren* case,[74] the American undertaking, The Polo/Lauren Company LP, owner of the RALPH LAUREN trade mark, relied on Regulation 3295/94 to obtain from the Austrian customs authorities the suspension of the release of several consignments of T-shirts which, so it alleged, infringed its trade mark rights. These consignments originated from Indonesia and were destined for Poland (which was at the time not yet a member of the European Union). Polo/Lauren initiated court proceedings in Austria, seeking an injunction whereby the exporter, the Indonesian company, PT Dwidua, would be banned from marketing the goods in question. On 27 September 1998, the Austrian Supreme Court (*Oberster Gerichtshof*) referred the case to the European Court of Justice for a preliminary ruling on the basis of Article 234 of the EC Treaty.[75] The

---

[71] European Court of Justice, Case C-383/98, *The Polo/Lauren v PT Dwidua Langgeng Pratama International Freight Forwarders*, 6 April 2000, [2000] ECR I-2519, point 34.
[72] Community Customs Code (n 42 above), Art 92.
[73] Ibid, Arts 94 and 96; Reg 2454/93 (n 43 above), Arts 345, 349, 356–357, 361, and 365–366.
[74] Cf n 71 above. [75] Formerly Art 177.

national court questioned whether Regulation 3295/94 applied to infringing goods coming from a non-member country of the European Community and destined for another non-member country, but in transit through the Community. The highest Austrian judicial court also wished to know whether the Regulation could be relied upon by a company not established within the EC. The ECJ answered both questions affirmatively. It stressed that goods in external transit are ultimately liable to be fraudulently brought on to the market in the EC. Therefore, the potential impact of this type of movement appeared sufficient to justify the extension of the scope of Regulation 3295/94 to the case of external transit:

> After all, the external transit of non-Community goods is not completely devoid of effect on the internal market. It is, in fact, based on a legal fiction. Goods placed under this procedure are subject neither to the corresponding import duties nor to the other measures of commercial policy; it is as if they had not entered Community territory. In reality, they are imported from a non-member country and pass through one or more Member States before being exported to another non-member country. This operation is all the more liable to have a direct effect on the internal market as there is a risk that counterfeit goods placed under the external transit procedure may be fraudulently brought on to the Community market, as several Governments pointed out in their written observations and at the hearing.[76]

3.67 The Court also concluded that, although Regulation 3295/94 applied to situations which do not appear to have any direct connection with the internal market, the analysis of the issue had revealed no factor of such a kind as to affect its validity.[77]

3.68 The ECJ recalled this point of view in another case concerning the transit through Austria of goods of Chinese origin and destined for the Slovak market (which was then not yet part of the EU), which were suspected of infringing the trade mark rights of the companies La Chemise Lacoste SA and Guccio Gucci SpA.[78] The only difference in the question referred for preliminary ruling to the ECJ in this case, compared to the *Polo/Lauren* case, was that it was referred by an investigating body having jurisdiction under *criminal* law (that is, the *Landesgericht Eisenstadt*). The ECJ pointed out that the interpretation of the scope of Regulation 3295/94 was not conditional upon the type of national proceedings (civil, criminal, or administrative) in which that interpretation was relied on.[79] The Court stressed that that Regulation did apply to the external transit of goods caught by Article 1, regardless of whether or not the external transit of such goods was considered an intellectual property infringement

---

[76] Case C-383/98 (n 71 above), point 34.
[77] Ibid, points 30–35. For a more extensive comment on the *Polo/Lauren* decision, cf eg [2001] Trade Mark Reporter 385.
[78] Case C-60/02, 7 January 2004, *Montres Rolex SA anors*, [2004] ECR I-651. Cf also Opinion of Advocate General Colomer of 5 June 2003, point 36.   [79] Ibid, point 56.

under the national law of the Member State where the customs intervention took place:

> It is not for the Court of Justice to rule on the interpretation of national law, which is a matter for the national court alone. If the national court were to find that the relevant provisions of national law do not prohibit and, thus, do not penalise the mere transit of counterfeit goods through the Member State concerned, contrary none the less to the requirements under Articles 2 and 11 of Regulation No 3295/94, it would be proper to conclude that those articles preclude the national provisions in question.[80]

It follows from the above case law from the ECJ that goods which would have been considered as infringing any of the intellectual property rights listed in Article 2(1) of Regulation 1383/2003, if they had been manufactured in the country of the customs intervention, and which are intercepted whilst in external transit through the Community territory, may be detained by the customs authorities of the Member State of transit, even if those goods would in fact *not* infringe any intellectual property right in the country of destination. **3.69**

The inclusion of external transit in the situations in which customs may take action against goods suspected of infringing intellectual property rights represents a significant step forward from the Paris Convention and the TRIPs Agreement, which do not provide for an obligation on the contracting countries to intervene at the borders in such cases. **3.70**

In this context, attention should also be paid to the opinion of Advocate General Jacobs in *Class International v Unilever*, discussing the trade mark position of grey market goods in external transit. In his view, trade mark owners cannot oppose the entry into the European Union of non-Community goods bearing their trade marks on the ground of Article 5(1)[81] of the Trade Mark Directive,[82] or an equivalent provision,[83] as such entry would not constitute trade mark use. For as long as such goods remain non-Community goods, storing them in a customs warehouse and/or offering them for sale or selling them (without the consent of the trade mark holder) would not constitute 'using [the mark] in the course of trade' within the meaning of Article 5(1) of the Trade Marks Directive. Rightholders would only be entitled to prevent release into free circulation in the European Community of such goods under this provision.[84] Jacobs considered in **3.71**

---

[80] Ibid, point 58.   [81] In conjunction with Art 5(3)(b) and (c).

[82] First Directive 89/104/EEC of the Council of 21 December 1988 to approximate the laws of the Member States relating to trade marks, [1989] OJ EC L 40/1 (11.2.1989).

[83] Cf, eg, Council Reg (EC) No 40/94 of 20 December 1993 on the Community trade mark ([1994] OJ L 11/1 (14.1.1994)), Art 9(1), in conjunction with Art 9(2)(b) and (c).

[84] Opinion of Advocate General Jacobs of 26 May 2005 in Case C-405/03, *Class International BV v Unilever NV anors*, delivered in the context of a reference from the Regional Court of Appeal of The Hague (*Gerechtshof te 's-Gravenhage*), the Netherlands. At the time of writing, the ECJ had not yet rendered its decision. By the date of receipt of the proofs, the Court had rendered its judgement in this case, dated 18 October 2005. The Court follows, in essence, the approach adopted by AG Jacobs on this point. For a detailed overview of this case (including an update on the ECJ's ruling), of

this respect that, in order to be actionable, 'use' of the trade mark within the meaning of Article 5(1) of the Trade Marks Directive must affect, or be liable to affect the function of the trade mark, which is to guarantee to consumers the origin of the goods.[85] He then opined that the essential function of a trade mark cannot be compromised 'solely by the fact that goods genuinely bearing that mark are subject to the external transit procedure and hence by definition are not in free circulation within the Community',[86] nor can it be compromised 'solely by the storage in a Community customs warehouse of trade marked non-Community goods. Such storage cannot in itself affect or be liable to affect the functions of the trade mark'.[87] AG Jacobs relied in this context on the ECJ's *Rioglass* decision.[88]

3.72 Contrary to *Polo/Lauren* and *Rolex, Class International v Unilever* involved *genuine* goods (toothpaste products bearing the trade mark 'AQUAFRESH'), imported (without the trade mark owner's consent) from South Africa, and shipped to Rotterdam from outside the European Economic Area. Regulation 1383/2003 could thus not be applied to the facts of this case.[89] There is therefore, prima facie, no contradiction between the approach taken by Advocate General Jacobs in this case and the principles adopted by the ECJ in its previous decisions in the *Polo Lauren* and *Rolex* cases.

3.73 Nevertheless, there seems to be an intrinsic inconsistency in the philosophy behind the approach followed by the ECJ and Advocate General Jacob in all these transit cases. Indeed, it appears difficult to sustain at the same time, on the ground of the same legislation,[90] on the one hand—in the case of parallel imports of genuine goods—that the external transit and customs warehousing of trade marked goods do *not* constitute trade mark use, and therefore do not result in a trade mark infringement, and on the other hand—in the case of counterfeit goods—that the Member States are to consider the external transit and customs warehousing procedures as an act of infringement.[91] AG Jacobs stated that the origin of the goods did not matter in this context, and pointed out that if the ECJ took the view, in *Rioglass*, that the mere fact that goods in free circulation in the Community pass through a Member State does not involve any marketing and is therefore not liable to infringe the specific subject matter of the trade mark, it

---

O Vrins and M Schneider, 'Trade Mark Use in Transit: EU-Phony or Cacophony?', *Journal of Intellectual Property Law and Practice* (Oxford University Press), Issue 1, November 2005.

  [85] Ibid, referring to Case C-206/01, *Arsenal Football Club* [2002] ECR I-10273, point 40.
  [86] Opinion of AG Jacobs in *Class International v Unilever*, n 84 above, point 29.
  [87] Ibid, point 43.   [88] Case C-115/02, *Rioglass and Transremar* [2003] ECR I-7653.
  [89] Cf Reg 1383/2003, Art 3(1), first indent (compare Regulation 3295/94, Art 1(4)). In *Class International*, the goods were first detained by the Dutch customs authorities on the basis of Reg 3295/94 (as amended) on suspicion of an infringement. However, it subsequently became clear that they were not counterfeit or pirated products within the meaning of that Regulation.
  [90] Ie the statutory national legislation, as interpreted, where appropriate, in compliance with Art 5 of EC Directive 89/104.   [91] Reg 1383/2003, Art 16.

would apply *a fortiori* to non-Community goods in respect of which import formalities have not been completed.

It is at the very least remarkable that AG Jacobs disregarded the risks put forward **3.74** by the Court in its earlier case law that goods in external transit are liable to be fraudulently brought on to the market in the EC.[92] He considered that the Court's statement in *Polo/Lauren* that 'there is a risk that counterfeit goods placed under the external transit procedure may be fraudulently brought on to the Community market' was made in the context of counterfeit, not genuine, goods. Moreover, the Court's interpretation of Article 1 of EC Regulation 3295/94 in *Polo/Lauren* found the source of validity of this Regulation in Article 113 EC, setting out the principles of the Common Commercial Policy of the EU. He concluded that this statement provided, in any event, 'no basis for the exercise of trade mark rights simply because non-Community goods entered the Community under the external transit procedure'.[93]

In *Class International*, AG Jacobs recalled that the trade mark proprietor may **3.75** not prohibit the use of a sign identical to the trade mark for goods identical to

---

[92] And this in spite of the fact that the referring court had found that it had not been shown that there was already a purchaser for the goods in dispute when they entered the Netherlands or when they were detained. Indeed, the Court of Appeal of The Hague had not been satisfied that the goods had been sold to, and were destined for, a customer in the Ukraine, as the defendant alleged. The Dutch judge did not rule out the possibility that the first purchaser of the products could turn out to be established in the EEA (cf Opinion of AG Jacobs in *Class International BV v Unilever*, n 84 above, point 18).

[93] Ibid, point 35. He went on to say that the defendants' concerns that goods such as those at issue in the main proceedings could be released into free circulation in the Community without their consent, thereby infringing their trade mark rights, must be met by reference to the detailed provisions of the Customs Code (ie Reg 2913/92) and its implementing measure (ie Reg 2454/93) which are designed to ensure that non-Community goods placed under the external transit procedure or in customs warehouses are subject to customs supervision from the moment of entry until they leave the Community. If the goods do not in fact leave the Community but are released into free circulation, at that point the trade mark proprietor will be entitled to oppose their 'importing' in accordance with Art 5(3)(c) of the Trade Marks Directive. It may be noted that Art 50(1)(a) of the TRIPs Agreement requires national judicial authorities to have competence 'to order prompt and effective provisional measures [. . .] to prevent an infringement of any intellectual property right from occurring, and in particular to prevent the entry into the channels of commerce in their jurisdiction of goods, including imported goods immediately after customs clearance'. While he appreciated that enforcement of the trade mark proprietor's rights depends on his knowledge of the impending infringement, AG Jacobs did not see any basis for extending those rights in the case of goods subject to the external transit procedure or to the customs warehousing procedure (ibid, points 36 and 44). 'Such enforcement in the case of directly imported goods equally depends on prior knowledge on the part of the trade mark proprietor' (ibid, point 36). Jacobs admitted, however, that where the final destination of the goods is specified and that destination is within the EEA, 'there will be a real risk that the goods would be released into free circulation within the Community' (ibid, point 47); it will then be evident 'that the goods will have to be released into free circulation before delivery and the trade mark proprietor is in my view entitled to assert his rights to prevent that release or delivery' (ibid, point 68). The same applies where the goods are being offered for sale or sold to a trader established outside the EEA, 'who the (parallel) trader knows or has serious reasons to suppose will resell or supply the goods in question to ultimate consumers within the EEA' (ibid, points 69–70).

those for which the mark is registered if that use cannot affect his own interests having regard to the function of the trade mark. He stated that the essential function of a trade mark cannot be compromised solely by the fact that goods *genuinely* bearing that mark are subject to the external transit or the customs warehousing procedure, and hence by definition are not in free circulation within the Community.[94] One may question whether AG Jacobs would have adopted the same reasoning with respect to *counterfeit* goods subject to external transit or customs warehousing. If so, there would appear to be little consistency between the ECJ's case law in *Polo/Lauren* and *Rolex*, in the first place, and the approach followed in *Commission v France* and *Rioglass*, in the second place.

3.76 There is no doubt that, if the ECJ ever were to adopt AG Jacobs' stance in this case as its own this would, at least facilitate, and perhaps even encourage, another phenomenon which is often closely linked to counterfeiting: contraband.

Customs warehousing

3.77 The customs warehousing procedure refers, in substance, to a situation in which non-Community goods which are brought into the customs territory of the Community are being stored in a place approved by, and under the supervision of, the customs authorities,[95] whilst allowing their owner to choose when he pays the import duties or re-exports the goods.[96]

3.78 Customs warehousing is usually opted for in all cases where, and as long as, the country to which the goods will ultimately be delivered has not yet been determined:[97]

> Customs warehousing is a procedure enabling importers to store imported goods where it is not know at the time of importation how the goods will finally be disposed of. The goods may subsequently be re-exported, in which case there will have been no need to pay import duties, or released for free circulation, at which point import duties will be payable.[98]

3.79 The European Court of Justice has stressed that 'the essential purpose of customs warehouses is to provide for the storage of goods', and not to permit the goods to pass from one stage of marketing to another.[99]

---

[94] Opinion of AG Jacobs in *Class International v Unilever*, paras 29 and 43; emphasis added.

[95] Cf in particular Community Customs Code (n 42 above), Arts 85–86, 101, and 105.

[96] Ibid, Arts 98–113. For additional information, cf also the Guidelines concerning Title III 'Customs procedures with economic impact' of Commission Reg (EEC) No 2454/93 of 2 July 1993 laying down provisions for the implementation of Council Reg (EEC) No 2913/92 establishing the Community Customs Code, [2001] OJ C 269/1 (24.9.2001).

[97] M de Cock Buning (n 55 above), 236, n 26.

[98] Opinion of Advocate General Jacobs in *Class International BV v Unilever NV* (n 84 above), point 12.

[99] Case 49/82 *Commission v The Netherlands* [1983] ECR 1195, point 10, cited by Advocate General Jacobs in *Class International*, n 84 above, point 12.

Use of the customs warehousing procedure is conditional upon authorization **3.80** being issued by the customs authorities.[100] Such authorization will be granted only to persons who offer every guarantee necessary for the proper conduct of the operations, and only where customs can supervise and monitor the procedure without having to introduce administrative arrangements disproportionate to the economic needs involved.[101]

Inward processing

Inward processing covers two different situations:[102] **3.81**

- Inward processing in the form of a system of *suspension* allows non-Community goods to be imported into the Community customs territory with a view to being re-exported from that territory in the form of compensating products, that is, after being used in the customs territory of the Community in one or more processing operations, without such goods being subject to import duties or commercial policy measures;

- Inward processing in the form of a system of *drawback* allows goods released for free circulation in the customs territory of the Community to be used in that territory in one or more processing operations, with repayment or remission of the import duties chargeable on such goods if they are exported from the said territory in the form of compensating products.

Thus, inward processing allows imported raw materials or semi-manufactured **3.82** goods to be processed for re-export within the Community customs territory by Community manufacturers without a requirement that the manufacturers have to pay customs duty and VAT on the goods being used. While under the suspension system one allows the duty to be suspended, under the drawback system it is paid and later repaid or remitted.

The processing operations referred to above may consist of the working of the goods **3.83** (including erecting or assembling them, or fitting them to other goods), their processing, or their repair (including restoring them and putting them in order).[103]

Contrary to inward processing in the form of a system of *suspension*, the drawback **3.84** system is not considered a suspensive arrangement within the meaning of Article 84(1)(a) of the Community Customs Code. However, goods which enjoy this status are in principle subject to customs control, and the customs authorities will therefore be in a position to apply the Regulation toward such goods where they are 'found during checks on goods entering or leaving the Community customs territory'.[104]

---

[100] Community Customs Code (n 42 above), Arts 84(1)(b)–85.   [101] Ibid, Art 86.
[102] Ibid, Arts 114–129.   [103] Ibid, Art 114(2)(c).
[104] Cf Reg 1383/2003, Art 1(1)(b).

Processing under customs control

3.85 The procedure for processing under customs control allows non-Community goods to be used in the customs territory of the Community in operations which alter their nature or state, without their being subject to import duties or commercial policy measures. It also allows the products resulting from such operations (called 'processed products') to be released for free circulation at the rate of import duty appropriate to them.[105]

3.86 The purpose of this procedure is in principle to benefit from lower duty rates (the rates applying to the processed products being lower than the rates which would normally be applied to the goods before processing) and thus to contribute to creating or maintaining processing activities in the EC.

3.87 This procedure benefits, for example, goods brought in large quantities into the customs territory of the Community to be repacked in smaller quantities.

Temporary importation

3.88 Temporary importation means that non-Community goods may be used in the Community customs territory, with total or partial relief from import duties or VAT, under certain conditions, and re-exported afterwards in the same state as they were in at import (with the exception of normal depreciation caused by use).

3.89 The situation envisaged is where, for example, an owner of goods who is located outside the Community wishes to enable a potential buyer to examine them, before re-exporting them from the Community customs territory.[106]

Placing in a free zone or free warehouse

3.90 Pursuant to Article 166 of the Community Customs Code, free zones and free warehouses are parts of the customs territory of the Community or premises situated in that territory and separated from the rest of it, in which:

- non-Community goods are considered, for the purpose of import duties and commercial policy import measures, as not being on the Community customs territory (they are therefore free of import duties, VAT, and other import charges), provided they are not released for free circulation, or placed under another customs procedure or used or consumed under conditions other than those provided for in customs regulations;

- Community goods for which such provision is made under Community legislation governing specific fields qualify, by virtue of being placed in a free zone or free warehouse, for measures normally attaching to the export of goods.

---

[105] Community Customs Code (n 42 above), Arts 130–136.
[106] M de Cock Buning (n 55 above) at 236, n 26.

Import and export declarations only have to be lodged when such goods leave the **3.91** free zone.

The Member States have the option of establishing such free zones or free **3.92** warehouses. When doing so, they must notify the European Commission. The list of free zones and free warehouses in existence and in operation in the Member States, together with the address of the relevant customs authorities, is set out in a Communication[107] from the EC Commission, as required under Article 802 of EEC Regulation 2454/93.[108]

Common transit and Community transit?

The European Community is a common market where goods released for free **3.93** circulation and goods made in the Community move freely, without any boundaries or systematic customs controls.

A distinction is traditionally made between 'common' and 'Community transit', **3.94** although the customs rules are effectively identical in both cases. While the 'common' transit procedure is used for the carriage of goods between the 25 Member States of the European Union and the EFTA countries (that is, Liechtenstein, Iceland, Norway, and Switzerland),[109] and for the movement of goods between the EFTA countries themselves, the 'Community' transit procedure is used for customs transit operations between the EU Member States, and is generally applicable, for example, to the movement of Community goods, which, between their point of departure and point of destination in the European Union, have to pass through the territory of a third member country.

The 'Community' transit is therefore a customs procedure which allows goods to **3.95** be moved from one point in the Community to another, whilst 'the 'common' transit concerns the carriage of goods between the EFTA countries, or the EFTA countries and the EC Member States. Those situations are not to be confused with the 'external transit' procedure, which refers to goods moving from one point located within the customs territory of the Community to another point equally located within this territory, to be exported afterwards (in the case of Community goods) or re-exported (in the case of non-Community goods) outside the internal market.[110]

---

[107] Commission communication publishing the list of free zones in existence and in operation in the Community, [2002] OJ C 50/16 (23.2.2002). This list is available on-line at http://europa.eu.int/comm/taxation_customs/resources/documents/customs/procedural_aspects/imports/free_zones/list_freezones.pdf and is regularly updated.　　　　　　[108] N 43 above.

[109] The 'common' transit procedure is based on the Convention of 20 May 1987 between the European Economic Community, the Republic of Austria, the Republic of Finland, the Republic of Iceland, the Kingdom of Norway, the Kingdom of Sweden, and the Swiss Confederation, on a common transit procedure, [1987] OJ L 226/2 (13.8.1987).

[110] Cf paras 3.63–3.71 above.

3.96 The question arises whether Regulation 1383/2003 applies to such cases. Several situations may be distinguished in this context.

Transit through one or several EC Member States of non-Community goods destined for another Member State

3.97 In a decision of 8 September 2000, *In re Nike*, the President of the Haarlem Regional Court[111] considered that Regulation 3295/94 did not apply in such cases, provided the goods in question could not be seen as infringing an intellectual property right in the country of destination, even though they *would* infringe such a right in the country (or countries) of transit. This case was concerned with the validity of an intervention made by the customs authorities of Schiphol airport against goods originating from China and destined for Spain.

3.98 This decision seems contrary to the spirit, if not the letter, of both Regulation 3295/94 and Regulation 1383/2003. It also contrasts with the reasoning adopted by the European Court of Justice in the *Polo/Lauren*[112] and *Rolex*[113] decisions. Indeed, it is obvious that non-Community goods destined for an EC-Member State are all the more liable than in the case of external transit—owing to the principle of free movement of goods—to be ultimately brought on to the market of the Member State of transit where they are likely to infringe an intellectual property right.[114] On the other hand, to allow customs to retain goods in such situations would probably largely undermine the territoriality principle, which is a basic principle of intellectual property rights.

3.99 In any event, it is indisputable that in the situation referred to the Haarlem Regional Court in *Nike*, the Dutch customs authorities were entitled to retain the goods; those goods had indeed been introduced into the Community, an operation which clearly fell under the scope of Regulation 3295/94 (as amended in 1999), and still does under Regulation 1383/2003. Therefore, the only issue which could possibly be at hand was whether the goods infringed Nike's intellectual property rights under Dutch national law whilst in (Community) transit.

3.100 Whatever the case may be, the *Nike* decision has been overruled by a more recent decision of the President of the same Court,[115] where it was held, by reference to Article 6(2)(b) of EC Regulation 3295/94, that this Regulation assimilated goods in transit to goods manufactured in the country of the customs intervention.

---

[111] '*Arrondissementsrechtbank Haarlem*' (the Netherlands). This decision, rendered in summary proceedings, has been reported in [2001] Bijblad bij de Industriële Eigendom 99.

[112] Cf n 71 above.   [113] Cf n 78 above.

[114] M de Cock Buning (n 55 above), at 237.

[115] *Mobile Accessory Club v Nokia*, 28 December 2001, [2002] Bijblad bij de Industriële Eigendom 305. Cf in particular point 7.5.

The *fictio iuris* of Article 6(2)(b) of Regulation 3295/94 has now been transferred **3.101** into the eighth Recital of Regulation 1383/2003, which provides that

> Proceedings initiated to determine whether an intellectual property right has been infringed under national law will be conducted with reference to the criteria used to establish whether goods produced in that Member State infringe intellectual property rights [. . .].

The effect of this 'provision' is not at all clear. It is not obvious whether it adds **3.102** anything to the definition of infringement of intellectual property rights in Article 2(1) of the Regulation. This issue is much more important than it may seem at first sight. Indeed, many countries are still reluctant to consider the *transit* of infringing goods as an act of 'use' of the right in question, and therefore as constituting an infringement. They may find some comfort in this respect since the recent opinion rendered by AG Jacobs in *Class International BV v Unilever*.[116] We will see below[117] that the European Court of Justice also appears to share this reticence when it comes to 'internal' transit, whereas it clearly does not when it comes to external transit.[118] This approach would lose any significance if the eighth Recital of the Regulation were to be interpreted as requiring national courts to disregard the nature of the movement of the goods and to focus exclusively on whether or not the goods would have been considered an infringement had they been manufactured in the State of transit. This interpretation was adopted in several cases in the Netherlands, including those decided by the Supreme Court,[119] under Article 6(2)(b) of Regulation 3295/94. Under Regulation 1383/2003, however, this provision, without having been disavowed, was shifted into a Recital, the ambit and binding character of which towards the Member States is questionable.

Could the Regulation then be applied when non-Community goods destined for **3.103** an EC Member State where they would infringe an intellectual property right are brought into the Community customs territory through another Member State where they do *not* infringe such rights?

The Regulation cannot apply in such circumstances. Indeed, the introduction **3.104** into the customs territory of the Community is not illicit in such a case, that is, the goods do not infringe any third party's rights in the State where they are found in one of the situations referred to in Article 1(1).[120]

Community transit cases

The Regulation clearly does not apply to goods which have been legally manufac- **3.105** tured within the Community territory, or marketed in that territory, with the

---

[116] Cf para 3.71 above.   [117] Cf para 3.105 below.   [118] Cf para 3.63 above.
[119] Dutch '*Hoge Raad*', 19 March 2004, [2004] Intellectuele Eigendomsrechten 233 (cf in particular point 3.5.3.2).   [120] M de Cock Buning (n 55 above), at 237.

right-holder's consent.[121] It is the same for goods which are the subject of a Community transit procedure, owing to the principle of free movement of goods.[122]

3.106 Following this approach, the European Court of Justice held, in *Commission v France*, that, by providing for an option for the customs authorities to retain goods[123] in transit through the French territory which had been legally manufactured in the Member State of origin (Spain) and were destined for another EC Member State where they could equally be legally offered for sale, on the ground that those goods would infringe a right-holder's design rights under French law, the French Republic had violated former Article 30 (now Article 28) of the EC Treaty—which provides that quantitative restrictions on imports and all measures having equivalent effect are to be prohibited between Member States.[124]

3.107 Similarly, in *Rioglass*, the Court held that Article 28 of the EC Treaty was to be interpreted as precluding the implementation, pursuant to a legislative measure of a Member State concerning intellectual property, of procedures for detention by the customs authorities of goods lawfully manufactured in another Member State and intended, following their transit through the territory of the first Member State, to be placed on the market in a non-member country.[125] That case concerned a situation in which trade marked spare car parts, lawfully manufactured in Spain, had been exported from Spain to Poland under cover of a Community transit certificate which allowed movement between two points in the customs territory of the Community and Poland, free of import duty, tax, or commercial policy measures. The goods were detained by customs officers in France on suspicion of trade mark infringement. The manufacturer and the transporter of the goods sought an order that the detention be lifted.

3.108 In the light of the *Polo/Lauren*[126] and *Rolex*[127] cases, the ECJ's approach in *Commission v France*[128] and *Rioglass*[129] is peculiar to say the least. It is true that, unlike the case of external transit, Community transit cases are subject to the

---

[121] ECJ, Case C-23/99, *Commission v France*, 26 September 2000 [2000] ECR I-7653.

[122] Ibid. It is not without interest to recall here that the principle of free movement of goods applies to products coming from non-member countries only where they are in free circulation within the Community (Art 23(2) EC Treaty). Non-Community goods must therefore be duly imported into the Community before they can benefit from freedom of movement.

[123] In that case, spare parts for cars, which are well-known as being the object of fierce debates from the perspective of design rights protection.

[124] The Court dismissed the French Government's arguments based on former Art 36 (now Art 30) of the EC Treaty (safeguard clause).

[125] Case C-115/02, *Rioglass and Transremar* [2003] ECR I-7653. Again, the Court dismissed the French Government's arguments based on former Art 36 (now, Art 30) EC.

[126] N 71 above.   [127] N 78 above.   [128] N 121 above.   [129] N 125 above.

principle of freedom of movement of goods. In paragraph 18 of its *Rioglass* decision, the Court recalled that:

> the Customs Union established by the EC Treaty necessarily implies that the free movement of goods between Member States should be ensured. That freedom could not itself be complete if it were possible for Member States to impede or interfere in any way with the movement of goods in transit. It is therefore necessary, as a consequence of the Customs Union and in the mutual interest of the Member States, to acknowledge the existence of a general principle of freedom of transit of goods within the Community. That principle is, moreover, confirmed by the reference to transit in Article 30 [new Article 28] EC (see, to that effect, Case 266/81 SIOT [1983] ECR 731, para 16, and Case C-367/89 *Richardt and 'Les Accessoires Scientifiques'* [1991] ECR I-4621, para 14).

However, Article 30 EC sets out a few exceptions to the sacrosanct principle of free movement of goods, including the safeguard of intellectual property rights. Nevertheless, in both *Rioglass* and *Commission v France*, the ECJ considered that the protection of design and trade mark rights respectively did not justify the retention of goods at the intra-Community borders. Indeed, the Court opined that in both trade mark[130] and design cases,[131] the mere *transit* of goods coming from a Member State is not liable to infringe these rights. The Court noted that the point of these rights is to guarantee the owner the exclusive right to use the trade mark or design for the purpose of putting a product on the market for the first time. The Court further pointed out that the right to put a product into circulation was not the mere physical transportation of the goods, but consisted in placing them on the market, that is to say the *marketing* of those goods. 'However, in this case, the product is marketed not in French territory, through which it only passes in transit, but in another Member State, where the product is not protected and may therefore be lawfully sold.'[132] 'Intra-Community transit [. . .] consists of the transportation of goods from one Member State to another across the territory of one or more Member States and involves no use of the appearance of the protected design. [. . .] Intra-Community transit does not therefore form part of the specific subject matter of the right of industrial and commercial property in designs.'[133] Similarly, since transit does not involve any marketing of the goods in question, it is not liable to infringe the specific subject matter of a trade mark.[134] **3.109**

One may question to what extent the approach adopted in the *Rioglass* and *Commission v France* decisions can be reconciled with the principles highlighted **3.110**

---

[130] Cf, eg, ECJ, *Winthrop*, Case 16/74, 31 October 1974 [1974] ECR 1183, point 8; *Hoffman-La Roche*, Case 102/77, 23 May 1978 [1978] ECR 1139, point 7; *Loendersloot*, Case C-349/95, 11 November 1997 [1997] ECR I-6227, point 22.

[131] Cf, eg, ECJ, *Volvo*, Case 238/87, 5 October 1988 [1988] ECR 6211, point 8.

[132] Case C-23/99 (n 121 above), at 44.   [133] Ibid, at 43.

[134] Case C-115/02 (n 125 above), at 27.

in *Polo/Lauren* and *Rolex*. In the latter decisions, the Court had justified the application of the Anti-Piracy Regulation to external transit with the risk of the goods being ultimately placed and commercialized within the internal market. It is therefore surprising that the Court approved, on the one hand, the prohibition of external transit through the Community customs territory of goods infringing an intellectual property right in the Member State of the customs intervention, even where such goods would *not* so infringe in the country of origin and in the country of destination, and oppose, on the other hand, intervention by the customs authorities in the case of Community transit of such goods, even where they would possibly infringe an intellectual property right in the country of destination.[135]

Transit through an EC Member State of goods lawfully manufactured in another Member State and intended to be placed on the market in a non-Member country

3.111 On the same ground as in the *Commission v France* case, the ECJ decided, in *Rioglass*, that Article 28 EC was to be interpreted as precluding the implementation, pursuant to a legislative measure of a Member State (France) concerning intellectual property (a trade mark), of procedures for detention by the customs authorities of goods lawfully manufactured in another Member State (Spain) and intended, following their transit through the territory of the first Member State, to be placed on the market in a non-member country (Poland, which had at that time not yet joined the EC).[136] The Court concluded that the principles it had recalled in *Commission v France* held good 'regardless of the final destination of the goods in transit. The fact that the goods are subsequently placed on the market in a non-member country and not in another Member State does not alter the nature of the transit operation which, by definition, does not constitute a placing on the market.'[137]

3.112 The criticism raised above[138] in respect of the *Commission v France* ruling applies *mutatis mutandis* with regard to the *Rioglass* decision.

Transhipment

3.113 As pointed out above,[139] the transhipment of goods suspected of infringing an intellectual property right clearly falls within the scope of Regulation 1383/2003. Suspect goods which reach the Community for the sole purpose of being transhipped from one means of transport to another with a view to subsequently leaving the Community territory may therefore be the subject of border measures.[140]

---

135 It is doubtful whether the decision rendered in Case C-23/99 can be relied on at all in situations where the goods would infringe an intellectual property right in the country of destination: cf the operational part of this decision as well as points 47–48 (*obiter dictum*). However, this issue was apparently considered irrelevant in Case C-115/02.   136 Case C-115/02, n 125 above.
137 Ibid, point 28.   138 Cf para 3.109.   139 Cf paras 3.40–3.41.
140 Cf Reg 1383/2003, 3rd Recital.

As goods in transhipment need not be cleared with customs, transhipment cannot **3.114** be regarded as a customs procedure, and is for that reason not listed in Article 4(16) of the Community Customs Code. In fact, the ECJ ruling in *Polo/Lauren* had not—or at least not unambiguously—decided on whether Regulation 3295/94 applied to transhipment. The factual background to this case clearly related to external transit, not transhipment. In such a context, the concern voiced by the Court that goods in external transit could possibly be brought into, and commercialized within, the Community customs territory was understandable, since external transit presupposes a movement of the goods from one point to another *within that territory*. The risks highlighted by the Court proved real, as the placing of counterfeit goods in external transit—in particular tobacco products and alcoholic beverages—is a typical means to bring them into the Community for them to be ultimately offered for sale there.

However, the risks raised by the ECJ in cases of external transit may appear much **3.115** more limited in the case of transhipment, where the goods are not supposed to travel via or across the Community.

In any event, Article 1(1)(b) of Regulation 1383/2003 allows the customs **3.116** authorities of the Member States to block transhipped goods 'when they are found during checks on goods entering or leaving the Community customs territory in accordance with Articles 37 and 183 of Regulation (EEC) No 2913/92'. Pursuant to Article 37 of the Community Customs Code, goods brought into the Community customs territory are, from the time of their entry, subject to customs supervision. The same applies to goods leaving that territory by virtue of Article 183 of the Community Customs Code.[141] Transhipment is one of those situations where customs exert supervision over the goods.

Common transit cases

Goods circulating between EU Member States and the EFTA countries are clearly **3.117** subject to Regulation 1383/2003. Indeed, Article 1(1) of this Regulation defines the customs status of the goods to which it applies in the light of the Community customs territory,[142] which does *not* include the EFTA countries. The customs administrations of the EU Member States are therefore empowered to retain goods which originate in the EFTA on suspicion of an intellectual property right infringement.

B. Goods infringing an intellectual property right

Regulation 1383/2003 extends the system of border measures to most intellectual **3.118** property rights, but without covering them all. Article 2(1) of the Regulation

---

[141] Cf para 3.58 above.   [142] Cf n 62 above.

defines 'goods infringing an intellectual property right' and distinguishes between (1) 'counterfeit goods'; (2) 'pirated goods'; and (3) goods infringing other industrial property rights. Moulds and matrices may, under conditions defined in Article 2(3), also be treated as infringing goods.

3.119 According to official figures,[143] 74 per cent of the border measures taken by European customs in 2004 related to trade mark infringements (against 85 per cent in 2003). This does not come as a surprise, as these infringements can easily be identified by customs officers. In the same vein, circa 14 per cent of measures related to infringements of copyrights and related rights. Infringements of rather more 'technical' rights, such as patents and design rights accounted for 2 per cent and 5 per cent respectively of measures taken. It remains to be seen how efficient customs interventions will be in relation to plant variety rights and geographical indications, which have been added to customs competence since the entry into force of Regulation 1383/2003, and are not commonly known by customs officers. The owners of these 'technical' rights are probably well advised to file a detailed and well-documented application for action in order to help customs officers identify infringements.

(1) Counterfeit goods

3.120 Article (2)(1)(a)(i) defines 'counterfeit goods' as:

> goods, including packaging, bearing without authorisation a trade mark[144] identical to the trade mark validly registered in respect of the same type of goods, or which cannot be distinguished in its essential aspects from such a trade mark, and which thereby infringes the trade mark-holder's rights under Community law, as provided for by Council Regulation (EC) No 40/94 of 20 December 1993 on the Community trade mark[145] or the law of the Member State in which the application for action by the customs authorities is made.

3.121 The following objects, even if presented separately, are assimilated into counterfeit goods by Article (2)(1)(a), on the same conditions as the goods referred to in point (i):

  (ii) any trade mark symbol (including a logo, label, sticker, brochure, instructions for use or guarantee document bearing such a symbol);
  (iii) packaging materials bearing the trade marks of counterfeit goods.

---

[143] N 57 above.
[144] It is noteworthy that Reg 1383/2003 spells the term 'trade mark' the American way—in one word—whereas most other pieces of Community legislation spell it the English way in two words.
[145] Cf n 83 above.

Definition of counterfeit goods

From the above definition, it is evident that border measures may only be applied **3.122** to signs that are identical to the trade mark, or which cannot be distinguished in their essential aspects from such a mark. Contrary to Regulation 40/94 on the Community trade mark[146] and the First Directive 89/104/EEC of the Council, of 21 December 1988, to approximate the laws of the Member States relating to trade marks,[147] Regulation 1383/2003 does not make use of the Community concept of 'likelihood of confusion on the [relevant part of the] public'[148] to determine the scope of protection of a trade mark, but to the more limited concept of (quasi) identity of the signs.[149] This requirement of (quasi) identity between the sign and the registered trade mark can already be found in the first generation Regulation,[150] and the aim of Article 2(1)(a)(i) of the current Regulation is certainly to preserve customs from the difficult task of determining the scope of protection of a trade mark right.

Surprisingly, the criteria that will have to be applied when determining whether **3.123** the counterfeited goods infringe a trade mark right are those laid down in the Community trade mark Regulation and under national—harmonized[151]—law. At this stage, the criterion of likelihood of confusion will have to be applied, in accordance with both Community and national law.

Furthermore, the Regulation requires that the trade mark is registered for 'the same **3.124** type of goods'. This requirement is presumably narrower than the previous one, since only *identical* goods fall under this definition: in other words, similar goods to those subject to the trade mark registration,which may cause confusion in the consumer's mind, may not normally be subject to border measures. This narrow wording excludes merchandising articles and other derived products, for which the trade mark owner has not obtained registration, from the scope of the Regulation.

The definition of counterfeit goods under the Regulation only refers to 'validly **3.125** registered' trade marks. Trade mark applications, which have not yet matured into registration, may therefore not be the basis for border measures; nor may (unregistered) common law marks.

The registered trade mark may be a national registration or a Community trade **3.126** mark registration. However, the trade mark must enjoy protection within the national territory in which the application for action is made. For a Community trade mark this requirement is normally fulfilled, as the territorial protection

---

[146] Cf n 83 above.   [147] Cf n 82 above.
[148] Arts 5(1)(b) of Directive 89/104/EEC and 9(1)(b) of Reg 40/94.
[149] C De Meyer and P Van den Broecke (n 53 above), 90.   [150] Cf n 8 above.
[151] Cf Directive 89/104/EEC (n 82 above).

extends, in principle, to all 25 Member States. For a national registration, it should be pointed out that an application for action can only be filed in the country where the mark enjoys protection, and obviously not in a Member State in which the mark is not so protected. A clever counterfeiter may exploit the lack of protection of a right-holder in one Member State of the Community by entering infringing goods for free circulation into this particular country. The right-holder will not be able to take border measures in that country, as he does not own a trade mark right, and the counterfeit goods may subsequently freely cross the national borders within the Community.[152]

3.127 Fortunately, the Community legislator assimilates trade mark symbols and packaging materials bearing the trade marks of counterfeit goods into the counterfeit goods themselves, even if they are presented separately at the border. It is in fact not uncommon that traffickers ship trade mark symbols and packaging materials separately from the goods, and that the goods are 'branded' afterwards, once they are within the Community. This tactic allows the infringers to limit their losses when counterfeit materials are intercepted by customs.[153] The Regulation applies to logos (for example, LACOSTE crocodiles), labels, stickers, brochures, instructions for use, and guarantee documents and packaging. There may be some uncertainty as to the interpretation of the requirement that these objects are to be assimilated into counterfeit goods 'on the same conditions as the goods referred to in point (i)'. Some national customs authorities will only allow right-holders to take action against these objects provided they own a trade mark registration for, for example, packaging material and labels.[154] Although this may be consistent with a strict interpretation of Article 2(1)(a), we are of the opinion that such a literal approach was not the intention of the Community legislator, who wanted to allow the right-holder to react against the separate shipment of infringing material. In our opinion, it is right that the likes of logos and labels which can only be sewn onto garments can be apprehended by a trade mark holder who owns a registration for garments.

Scope of protection of a Community trade mark[155]

3.128 A Community trade mark may consist of any signs capable of being represented graphically, particularly words, including personal names, designs, letters,

---

[152] Of course the trade mark owner may take measures under national law, however the system of border measures may not be applied any more.

[153] It will furthermore allow the traffickers to get away in those countries where the trade mark holder can only act against this type of goods provided he has a registration for packaging materials, labels, logos, etc.

[154] Cf on the practice of UK customs: A Clark, 'The Use of Border Measures to Prevent International Trade in Counterfeit and Pirated Goods: Implementation and Proposed Reform of Council Reg 3295/94' [1998] EIPR 414 at 422.

[155] The scope of protection of a national trade mark is examined in the different national chapters of this book.

numerals, the shape of goods or of their packaging, provided that such signs are capable of distinguishing the goods or services of one undertaking from those of other undertakings.[156]

The exclusive rights conferred by a Community trade mark are defined in **3.129** Article 9(1)(a) to (c) of Regulation 40/94 on the Community trade mark. The trade mark holder may prevent all third parties not having his consent from using in the course of trade:

(a) any sign which is identical with the Community trade mark in relation to goods or services which are identical with those for which the Community trade mark is registered;

(b) any sign where, because of its identity with or similarity to the Community trade mark and the identity or similarity of the goods or services covered by the Community trade mark and the sign, there exists a likelihood of confusion on the part of the public;[157]

(c) any sign which is identical with or similar to the Community trade mark in relation to goods or services which are not similar to those for which the Community trade mark is registered, where the latter has a reputation in the Community and where use of that sign without due cause takes unfair advantage of, or is detrimental to, the distinctive character or the repute of the Community trade mark.

Taking into account the restrictive definition of counterfeit goods contained in **3.130** Article 2(1)(a) of Regulation 1383/2003, there is little doubt that right-holders can request border measures in situations referred to in Article 9(1)(a) of Regulation 40/94 and perhaps in most of the cases described in Article 9(1)(b). Contrary to the situation referred to in Article 9(1)(c), no action can however be taken against goods which are different from most of the cases for which a trade mark with a reputation is registered, whatever the circumstances of the matter, since Regulation 1383/2003 only applies to counterfeit goods that are *of the same type* as those subject to the trade mark registration.

Article 9(2) of the Community trade mark Regulation contains the following **3.131** non-exhaustive list of prohibited acts:

(a) affixing the sign to the goods or to the packaging thereof;
(b) offering the goods, putting them on the market or stocking them for these purposes under that sign, or offering or supplying services thereunder;
(c) importing or exporting the goods under that sign;
(d) using the sign on business papers and in advertising.

---

[156] Reg 40/94 (n 83 above), Art 4.
[157] The likelihood of confusion includes the likelihood of association between the sign and the trade mark.

3.132 Article 9(3) of Regulation 40/94 states that the rights conferred by a Community trade mark shall prevail against third parties only as of the date on which the trade mark is published for registration.[158] An application for action may be filed as of this date.

3.133 Proceedings claiming infringement of a Community trade mark must be initiated before a Community trade mark court.[159] The court with jurisdiction has to be determined in accordance with the rules laid down in Article 93(1) to (5) of Regulation 40/94. In most cases a Community trade mark court will have jurisdiction in relation to acts of infringement in all Member States.[160]

Additional considerations

3.134 The different national chapters of this book will illustrate that national customs authorities do not always interpret the Anti-Piracy Regulation literally. It is not unusual for border measures to be taken against signs that are merely similar to a registered trade mark and that are applied to goods not contained in the specific list of goods of the registration. This may be dangerous for the right-holders, as it is conceivable that the authority having jurisdiction under national law to determine whether a trade mark right has been infringed acknowledges that there is a violation of trade mark rights under the wider criteria handled by Community or national law but that the goods should not have been subject to border measures in the first place as they do not fall under the narrow wording of Article 2(1)(a) of Regulation 1383/2003. Fortunately no such decision has been reported to date. In order to prevent this from happening one day, the Community legislature should harmonize the definition of counterfeit goods under the Regulation so that it accords with the scope of protection of a trade mark under Community and national law. It is noteworthy, in this respect, that as far as the intellectual property rights referred to in Article 2(1)(c) of the Regulation are concerned, the scope of protection is defined by analogy with the statutory and regulatory provisions determining such rights.

3.135 We would also applaud the granting of enlarged protection[161] to the owners of a trade mark with a reputation which would profit the applicant for border measures. Since being copied can be the price of success, most of the owners of trade marks with a reputation are victims of large scale counterfeiting. It would be

---

[158] 'Reasonable compensation may, however, be claimed in respect of matters arising after the date of publication of a Community trade mark application, which matters would, after publication of the registration of the trade mark, be prohibited by virtue of that publication. The court seized of the case may not decide upon the merits of the case until the registration has been published' (Reg 40/94, Art 9(3)).   [159] Reg 40/94, Art 92.

[160] Ibid, Art 94.

[161] Art 9(1)(c) of the Community Trade Mark Regulation (n 83 above) and the optional Art 5(2) of the Harmonization Directive (n 82 above). This enlarged protection is a standard in many national trade mark laws of the Member States.

helpful if such right-holders could call upon the enlarged protection provided by law to enforce their intellectual property against free-riders.

(2) *Pirated goods*

Article 2(2) of the Regulation defines 'pirated goods' as: **3.136**

> goods which are or contain copies made without the consent of the holder of a copyright or related right or design right, regardless of whether it is registered in national law, or of a person authorized by the right-holder in the country of production in case where the making of those copies would constitute an infringement of that right under Council Regulation (EC) No 6/2002 of 12 December 2001 on Community designs[162] or the law of the Member State in which the application for customs action is made.

Definition of 'pirated goods'

'Pirated goods' are defined as goods that are, or contain, unlawful copies. It is not **3.137**
entirely clear why the Regulation refers to the term 'copies', instead of making use of the Community law concepts of 'reproduction'[163] and 'communication to the public'[164] for copyright and neighbouring rights and 'design which for the informed user does not produce a different overall impression'[165] for designs. It is conceivable that the draftsmen of the Regulation did not want customs to engage in complex legal consideration of the infringing nature of the goods, and that they therefore preferred to refer to the term 'copies'. From a legal point of view, the difference in terminology cannot be approved, as it may lead to confusion:[166] how wide is the concept of 'copies'?[167] Does it only apply to slavish copies? How must we interpret goods that 'contain copies'? Many of these questions will have to be answered in the light of national practice.

The discrepancy between the term 'copies' used by the Regulation and the scope **3.138**
of protection of copyrights, neighbouring rights and design rights under Community and national law is regrettable. The different terminology may, theoretically, lead the authority competent under national law to determine whether an intellectual property right has been infringed to acknowledge that the right has been violated (for example, by the unauthorized adaptation of a

---

[162] [2002] OJ L 3/1 (5.1.2002).
[163] Directive 2001/29/EC of the European Parliament and of the Council of 22 May 2001 on the harmonization of certain aspects of copyright and related rights in the information society, [2001] OJ L 165/10 (22.6.2001), Art 2.   [164] Ibid, Art 3.
[165] Directive 98/71/EC of the European Parliament and of the Council of 13 October 1998 on the legal protection of designs, [1998] OJ L 289/28 (28.10.1998), Art 9.
[166] There is even a risk of association with Art 19(2) of Reg 6/2002 which limits the rights conferred by an unregistered Community design to acts of copying.
[167] Some scholars consider that the concept of copies would include *all* infringements of copyrights, related rights or design rights: eg C De Meyer and P Van den Broecke (n 53 above), 91.

work protected under copyright) but that this infringement is not necessarily a 'copy' in the sense of the Regulation. In the worst cases this could lead to the release of the goods and the payment of damages. Fortunately, no such case has been reported yet.

3.139 Article 2(1)(b) of the Regulation states that for border measures to be applied the copies have to be made without the consent of the right-holder or of a 'person authorized by the right-holder in the country of production'.[168] This wording excludes from the scope of the Regulation parallel imported goods from outside the Community (made with the consent of the right-holder but imported into the Community without the latter's consent), and goods produced in violation of a contractual agreement (by a licensee of the right-holder). This phraseology is recurrent with Article 3(1) of the Regulation.

3.140 Border measures may be applied regardless of whether the pirated intellectual property right is 'registered in national law'. This only confirms that copyright, neighbouring rights or design rights do not necessarily have to be registered to serve as a basis for an application for action by customs authorities. It would however have been preferable to add also a reference to Community law (and not only to national law), as Regulation 6/2002 provides for the protection of unregistered Community designs.

3.141 As with counterfeited goods, the right-holder has to enjoy protection under Community law (for a Community design) or under the law of the Member State where the application for action is made to be able to rely on Regulation 1383/2003. Here again, traffickers may abuse the lack of protection in one of the Member States to introduce pirated goods into the Community.

3.142 For the scope of protection of copyrights, neighbouring rights, and design rights the Regulation refers to Community or national law. The scope of protection of national law is examined in the different national chapters of this book.

Scope of protection of a Community design

3.143 Council Regulation (EC) No 6/2002 of 12 December 2001 on Community designs[169] introduced the registered and unregistered Community designs, which can be obtained for the appearance of an industrial or handcraft product to the extent that it is new and has an individual character.

3.144 The scope of protection of a Community design is defined by Article 10 of Regulation 6/2002 and extends to any design which does not produce on the informed user a different overall impression. In assessing the scope of protection,

---

[168] This unusual wording can already be found in the initial version of Reg 3295/94 (n 15 above).
[169] Cf n 162 above.

the degree of freedom of the designer in developing his design must be taken into consideration.

Under Article 19(1) of Regulation 6/2002, the owner of a registered Community **3.145** design has the exclusive right to use it and to prevent any third party using it without his consent. The following acts may be prohibited: the making, offering, putting on the market, importing, exporting or using of a product in which the design is incorporated or to which it is applied, or stocking such a product for those purposes.

The rights conferred by an unregistered Community design are more limited **3.146** under Article 19(2), as the right-holder may only prevent the use of the design provided the contested use results from 'copying' the protected design. The owner of an unregistered design cannot act against 'independent creations',[170] which result from an independent work of creation by a designer who may be reasonably thought not to be familiar with the design made available to the public by the holder.

Articles 20 to 23 of Regulation 6/2002 provide for important limitations on the **3.147** rights conferred by a Community design.

(3) Goods infringing other intellectual property rights

Article 2(1)(c) of the Regulation extends the application of border measures to: **3.148**

goods which, in the Member State in which the application for customs action is made, infringe:
  (i) a patent under that Member State's law;
  (ii) a supplementary protection certificate of the kind provided for in Council Regulation (EEC) No 1768/92[171] or Regulation (EC) No 1610/96 of the European Parliament and of the Council;[172]
  (iii) a national plant variety right under the law of that Member State or a Community plant variety right of the kind provided in Council Regulation (EC) No 2100/94;[173]
  (iv) designations of origin or geographical indications under the law of that Member State or Council Regulations (EEC) No 2081/92[174] and (EC) 1493/1999;[175]
  (v) geographical designations of the kind provided for in Council Regulation (EEC) No 1576/89.[176]

---

[170] Likewise the owner of a registered Community design subject to deferment of publication is, under Art 19(3), not protected against independent creations, as long as the relevant entries in the register and the file have not been made available to the public in accordance with Art 50(4).

[171] Council Reg (EEC) No 1768/92 of 18 June 1992 concerning the creation of a supplementary protection certificate for medicinal products, [1992] OJ L 182/1 (2.7.1992).

[172] Reg (EC) No 1610/96 of the European Parliament and of the Council of 23 July 1996 concerning the creation of a supplementary protection certificate for plant protection products, [1996] OJ L 198/30 (8.8.1996).   [173] [1994] OJ L 227/1 (1.9.1994).

[174] [1992] OJ L 208/1 (24.7.1992).   [175] [1999] OJ L 179/1 (14.7.1999).

[176] [1989] OJ L 160/1 (12.6.1989).

General comments

3.149 It is evident from the above definition that the intellectual property right has to enjoy protection in the Member State in which the application for action is filed for such an application to be admirable. This is *a priori* unproblematic for 'Community' rights. For national rights there may be a lack of protection in one of the Member States. As with all other intellectual property rights, traffickers of infringing goods may be tempted to abuse this situation to introduce the infringing goods for free release into this country and 'export' those goods afterwards towards another Member State where the right-holder does enjoy protection.

Goods infringing a patent

3.150 The scope of protection for a patent is governed by the national law of the Member State where the infringement occurs. This is examined in detail in the different national chapters.

3.151 The same principles apply to the so-called European patents, which are, in fact, simply a bundle of national patents. Therefore, European patents have, in each of the Contracting States of the European Patent Convention for which they are granted, the effect of a national patent granted by that State.[177] It is noteworthy that efforts to set up a system of a unitary 'Community patent' have so far failed.

Goods infringing a supplementary protection certificate

3.152 A supplementary protection certificate extends the protection conferred by a patent for a medicinal product for which a marketing authorization exists, in order to compensate the patent owner for the lapse of time between the filing of the patent and the authorization to place the product on the market.

3.153 Article 5 of both Regulations 1768/92 and 1610/96 clarifies that the supplementary protection certificate confers the same rights as the basic patent—within the boundaries of the marketing authorization—and is subject to the same limitations and the same obligations.[178] The infringement will therefore have to be verified under national law in the Member State where the infringing goods are retained by customs.

Goods infringing a Community plant variety right[179]

3.154 Distinct, uniform, stable, and new botanical genera and species may be protected as a Community plant variety right under Council Regulation (EC) No 2100/94.[180]

---

[177] Convention on the grant of European patents, Munich, 5 October 1973, Art 2(2). Cf Art 64 concerning the rights conferred by a European patent.

[178] Cf Reg 1768/92, Art 19(a) for the provisions relating to the new Member States.

[179] The scope of protection of a national plant variety right is examined in the different national chapters of this book. [180] Cf n 173 above.

Article 13(2) of Regulation 2100/94 grants the holder of a Community plant **3.155**
variety right the exclusive right to accomplish the following acts in relation to
variety constituents, or harvested material of the protected variety or to authorize
third parties to accomplish these acts in return for a fee: production or reproduction (multiplication); conditioning for the purpose of propagation; offering for
sale; selling or other marketing; exporting from the Community; importing to the
Community; and stocking for any of the above-mentioned purposes.

The same applies to harvested material, provided it was obtained through the **3.156**
unauthorized use of variety constituents of the protected variety, and unless the
holder has had reasonable opportunity to exercise his right in relation to the said
variety constituents.[181] In specific cases this may even apply to products obtained
directly from material of the protected variety.

Under Articles 17 and 18 of Regulation 2100/94, the use and abuse of a variety **3.157**
denomination may be considered an infringement under certain conditions.

In infringement claims the malicious intention of the infringer will be taken into **3.158**
account.[182]

Goods infringing a designation of origin or a geographical indication

Regulation 2081/92 applies to foodstuffs and agricultural products. Wines and **3.159**
spirits are excluded from the application of this particular Regulation. A distinction is made between:

- protected geographical indication: meaning the name of a region, specific
  place or country describing a product originating in that region, specific place
  or country and possessing a quality or reputation which may be attributed
  to the geographical environment with its inherent natural and/or human components; and

- protected designation of origin: meaning the name of a region, specific place or
  country referring to a product originating in that region, specific place or country and whose quality or other characteristics are essentially or exclusively due
  to a particular geographical environment.[183]

---

[181] Reg 2100/94, Art 13(3).   [182] Ibid, Art 94.
[183] Art 2(2)(a) and (b) Reg 2081/92. As will be observed, three different wordings have been
used in EC Reg 2081/92, 1493/1999, and 1576/89 (that is, 'designations of origin', 'geographical
indications', and 'geographical designations'). These wordings are more or less the same and refer to
the TRIPs Agreement, Arts 22–24 (cf paras 3.162–3.163 below), where only the words 'geographical indications' are used. It is obvious that these three Regulations must abide by the TRIPs
Agreement. It is also interesting to note that the EU has been condemned by a WTO Panel decision
of 21 December 2004 concerning Reg 2081/92 following a complaint from the United States and
Australia. Read more in this respect in G Goebel, 'Geographical Indications', in European
Communities Trade Mark Association, *The Development of Trade Marks, Designs and Related Rights
in Europe* (n 24 above), at 105.

3.160 To qualify for a protected geographical indication or a protected designation of origin, a product must comply with different specifications[184] and be registered.[185]

3.161 Under Article 13 the owners of a geographical indication or a protected designation of origin may oppose:

- any direct or indirect commercial use of a name registered in respect of products not covered by the registration in so far as those products are comparable to the products registered under that name or in so far as using the name exploits the reputation of the protected name;

- any misuse, imitation, or evocation, even if the true origin of the product is indicated or if the protected name is translated or accompanied by an expression such as 'style', 'type', 'method', 'as produced in', 'imitation', or similar;

- any other false or misleading indication as to the provenance, origin, nature, or essential qualities of the product, on the inner or outer packaging, advertising material, or documents relating to the product concerned, and the packing of the product in a container liable to convey a false impression as to its origin;

- any other practice liable to mislead the public as to the true origin of the product.

3.162 Regulation 1493/1999 applies to geographical indications for wines. This extremely convoluted Regulation—replacing no less than 33 prior Regulations—aims at a common organization of the market in wine and lays down rules governing wine-production potential, market mechanisms, producer organizations and sectoral organizations, oenological practices and processes, description, designation, presentation and protection, quality wine produced in specific regions ('quality wine psr'), and trade with third countries. Article 50 of this Regulation provides that Member States shall take all necessary measures to enable interested parties to prevent, on the terms set out in Articles 23 and 24 of the TRIPs Agreement, the use in the Community of a geographical indication for wines for products not originating in the place indicated by the geographical indication in question, even where the true origin of the goods is indicated or the geographical

---

[184] Reg 2081/92, Art 4 provides for the following: the name and description of the product; the definition of the geographical area; the methods of preparation; factors relating to the geographic environment; the inspection bodies; details of labelling and any legislative requirements that must be met.

[185] An application for registration of a protected geographical indication or a protected designation of origin may be made by any group of producers irrespective of its legal form or composition or, in exceptional circumstances, a natural or legal person. The application is sent to the Member State in which the geographical area in which the product originates is located. The Member State checks that it satisfies the requirements and forwards it to the other Member States and the Commission. The latter examines it and publishes it in the Official Journal of the European Communities. If no objections are notified within three months, the protected geographical indication or protected designation of origin is entered in a register kept by the Commission. Where objections are notified the Commission examines the reasons given before taking a decision.

indication is used in translation or accompanied by expressions such as 'kind', 'type', 'style', 'imitation', or the like.[186]

Goods infringing a geographical designation

Geographical designations are governed by Regulation (EEC) No 1576/89, **3.163** which lays down the general rules on the definition, description, and presentation of spirit drinks. Article 1 of the Regulation defines 'spirit drinks' to which it applies and Annexe II lists nearly 200 protected geographical indications. Article 11(a) compels Member States to adopt all measures necessary to permit those concerned to prevent, under the conditions laid down in Articles 23 and 24 of the TRIPs Agreement, the use within the Community of a geographical designation not originating in the place referred to by the geographical designation in question, including in cases where the actual origin of the product is indicated or where the geographical designation is given in translation or accompanied by expressions such as 'like', 'type', 'style', 'imitation', or other.[187]

(4) Moulds and matrices

Any mould or matrix which is specifically designed or adapted for the **3.164** manufacture of goods infringing an intellectual property right shall be treated

---

[186] Reg 1493/1999 (n 175 above), Art 50. Under Art 22 of TRIPs (n 48 above), geographical indications are 'indications which identify a good as originating in the territory of a Member, or a region or locality in that territory, where a given quality, reputation or other characteristic of the goods is essentially attributable to its geographical origin'. As will be observed, in the TRIPs Agreement, geographical indications cover any kind of goods. The three EC Regulations on the other hand cover respectively agricultural products and foodstuffs, wine, and spirits. For the other goods, it is the TRIPs Agreement which applies in the EU. However, peculiarly enough, TRIPs is not cited in Art 2 of Reg 1383/2003. Nevertheless, the reference to the national laws of the Member States should minimize the consequences of this omission.

Under Art 22(2) of TRIPs, 'In respect of geographical indications, Members shall provide the legal means for interested parties to prevent: (a) the use of any means in the designation or presentation of a good that indicates or suggests that the good in question originates in a geographical area other than the true place of origin in a manner which misleads the public as to the geographical origin of the good; (b) any use which constitutes an act of unfair competition within the meaning of Art 10bis of the Paris convention (1967).'

Pursuant to Art 23(1), 'Each Member shall provide the legal means for interested parties to prevent use of a geographical indication identifying wines for wines not originating in the place indicated by the geographical indication in question or identifying spirits for spirits not originating in the place indicated by the geographical indication in question, even where the true origin of the goods is indicated or the geographical indication is used in translation or accompanied by expressions such as "kind", "type", "style", "imitation" or the like.'

Finally, Art 24 sets out, among other things, the exceptions to the protection of geographical indications.

[187] Reg 1576/89 (n 176 above), Art 11(a). According to Art 1(2) of this Regulation, 'spirit drink' means 'an alcoholic liquid: intended for human consumption, having particular organoleptic qualities and [. . .] a minimum alcoholic strength of 15 per cent vol [. . .], and produced either directly by the distillation [. . .] or by the mixture of the spirit drink [. . .]'.

as infringing goods for the purpose of the Regulation, provided the use of such moulds or matrices infringes the right-holder's rights under Community law or the law of the Member State in which an application for action has been filed.[188]

3.165 The application of border measures to moulds and matrices is thus subordinate to substantive provisions of Community or national law allowing the right-holder to oppose the use and commercialization of such devices.

3.166 Regulation 40/94 on the Community trade mark[189] does not provide any means of taking action against moulds and matrices.

3.167 Under Article 89(1)(c) of Regulation 6/2002[190] the Community design court that finds the defendant has infringed a Community design may order the seizure of materials and implements predominantly used to manufacture the infringing goods, if the owner knew the effect for which such use was intended or if such effect would have been obvious in the circumstances. Therefore the customs authorities of the Member States are entitled to take action against moulds and matrices suspected of infringing a Community design right.

3.168 Regulation 2100/94 on Community plant variety rights does not expressly provide for the seizure of material, used for infringing a plant variety right.[191]

3.169 When determining whether moulds and matrices can be apprehended under national law the practitioner should not only verify the different national provisions on intellectual property rights, but also the national criminal law which may provide for the seizure of materials or implements used to commit an offence.

(5) *Intellectual property rights which do not fall under the scope of Regulation 1383/2003*

3.170 Unfortunately not all intellectual property rights are covered by the scope of Regulation 1383/2003.[192] For example, it has been regretted that utility models may not be subject to border measures under this instrument.[193] The same applies

---

[188] Reg 1383/2003, Art 2(3).   [189] Cf n 83 above.   [190] Cf n 162 above.

[191] That said, Art 89 provides that the infringer's gains may, in accordance with national law and private international law, be subject to restitution to the right-holder. It may therefore be worthwhile to examine the national legislation of the Member State in which the infringing goods have been retained on this subject. It is possible that national law provides for the restitution of materials and implements that have served to commit the infringement.

[192] This does not preclude national legislatures to apply a parallel national system of border measures to these intellectual property rights.

[193] International Trademark Association (INTA)'s Position Paper on the proposed amendments to Reg 3295/94 of 8 April 2002, cf http://www.inta.org/downloads/tap_counterfeit2002.pdf, 1–2 which proposed to add utility models to Art 2 of the new Regulation, having regard to Art 1(2) of the Paris Convention and also to Art 2 of the TRIPs Agreement.

to the *sui generis* protection for non original databases,[194] topographies of semi-conductor products,[195] commercial names, etc.

However, the Community legislator expects to use the experience gained under the current Regulation to consider the possibility of increasing the number of intellectual property rights covered by the system of border measures.[196] This can only be welcomed, particularly as many of these intellectual property rights are harmonized or even Community rights. **3.171**

C. Goods excluded from the scope of the Regulation

Article 3 of the Regulation excludes certain goods from the scope of the Regulation: they cannot be subject to border measures, although they may infringe an intellectual property right. **3.172**

The first two categories of excluded goods relate to goods which are placed in one of the customs situations listed in Article 1(1) of the Regulation in breach of a contract, such as (1) parallel imported goods, and (2) goods which have been manufactured under conditions other than those which have been agreed with the right-holder. **3.173**

The third category of excluded goods relates to goods contained in travellers' personal baggage. **3.174**

(1) Parallel imported goods

Article 3(1) excludes the following goods from the system of border measures put in place by the Regulation: **3.175**

> goods bearing a trade mark with the consent of the holder of that trade mark or [. . .] goods bearing a protected designation of origin or a protected geographical indication or which are protected by a patent or a supplementary protection certificate, by a copyright or related right or by a design right or a plant variety and which have been manufactured with the consent of the right-holder but are placed in one of the situations referred to in Article 1(1) without the latter's consent.

---

[194] Directive 96/9/EC of the European Parliament and of the Council of 11 March 1996 on the legal protection of databases, [1996] OJ L 77/20 (27.3.1996). It is noteworthy that under the Czech national legislation *sui generis* rights to databases are currently protected by customs, 'although this is not thought to be a major practical benefit in practice'. Cf J Rutter and M Rosinski, 'Who is the weakest link? Customs search and seizure in the new Europe', Trademark World, June 2004, 26 (27).

[195] Council Directive 87/54/EEC of 16 December 1986 on the legal protection of topographies of semiconductor products, [1987] OJ L 24/36 (27.1.1987).

[196] Reg 1383/2003, 13th Recital.

3.176 These products are referred to as 'parallel imported goods' or 'grey market goods'. They have been produced with the consent of the right-holder but were not intended for the Community internal market.

3.177 It is surprising to note that Article 3(1) of the Regulation does not refer to the territory where the goods have been placed on the market for the first time. However, it would be erroneous to believe that the Regulation enshrines the principle of internationl exhaustion: exhaustion of intellectual property rights is not a consequence of the Regulation. The Regulation is thus not contrary to the settled case law of the ECJ[197] and the different pieces of Community legislation[198] defining the scope of intellectual property rights with reference to 'Community exhaustion'. Nothing therefore prevents right-holders from taking action against such goods under national law. Ideally it would be preferable to extend the Regulation to allow the apprehension of parallel imported goods from outside the Community.[199] Currently, when a right-holder becomes aware through customs actions that parallel importers are dealing in his goods he may not—under a strict interpretation of the Regulation—make any use of the information received from customs under the Regulation,[200] and must notify customs that the goods are not caught by the Regulation and should therefore be released.

3.178 There is little doubt that the exception of parallel imported goods applies to goods manufactured directly by the right-holder and those produced with his consent under a licence.[201]

3.179 Scholars almost unanimously agree that the exception of parallel imports is in line with the TRIPs Agreement, as TRIPs, Article 51, n 13 confirms that the contracting parties agreed that 'there shall be no obligation' to apply border measures

---

[197] ECJ, Case C-355/96, 16 July 1998, *Silhouette International Schmied v Hartlauer Handelsgesellschaft*, [1998] ECR I-4799; Case C-173/98, 1 July 1999, *Sebago and Maison Dubois*, [1999] ECR I-4103.

[198] Directive 89/104/EEC (n 82 above), Art 7; Regulation 40/94 (n 83 above), Art 13; Reg 6/2002 (n 162 above), Art 21; Directive of 14 May 1991 on the legal protection of computer programs ([1991] OJ L 122/42 (17.5.1991)), Art 4(c); Directive of 19 November 1992 on rental, lending rights and certain related rights ([1992] OJ L 346/62 (27.11.1992), Art 9(2); Reg 2100/94 on the Community plant variety right (n 173 above), Art 16.

[199] A Clark, 'Parallel Imports: A New Job for Customs?' [1999] EIPR 1.

[200] Any violation of this rule can, according to Art 12 of the Regulation, be sanctioned by the suspension of the application for action or, in case of repeated breach, to its non-renewal. If national law in the Member State where the situation arises provides therefore, the civil liability of the right-holder may, in addition, be incurred.

[201] R Knaak reports that some scholars argue that the exception does not apply to goods that have been produced by a licensee with the consent of the right-holder, but only to those produced by the right-holder himself. This argument cannot be accepted. As soon as the contractual link can be laid to the right-holder, the goods will have to be considered as falling under the exception. R Knaak in H Harte-Bavendamm, 'Handbuch der Markenpiraterie in Europa', CH Beck'sche Verlagsbuchhandlung, München, 2000, para 22.

to 'goods put on the market in another country by or with the consent of the right-holder'.[202]

The exclusion of grey market goods from border measures dates back to the first **3.180** generation Regulation 3842/86.[203] Most likely, the European legislature considered that it is too burdensome for customs to differentiate between parallel imports (as well as goods, which have been manufactured under conditions other than those which have been agreed with the right-holder) and non-infringing goods. Another underlying reasoning may be that this kind of contractual infringement should be dealt with directly by courts and not by customs who should only take care of the most flagrant infringements.

(2) Goods which have been manufactured under conditions other than those which have been agreed by the right-holder

Similarly, Article 3(1) second indent provides that the Regulation does not apply **3.181** 'to goods referred to in the first subparagraph and which have been manufactured or are protected by another intellectual property right referred to in Article 2(1) under conditions other than those agreed with the right-holder'.

This wording refers to goods manufactured by a licensee in breach of the contrac- **3.182** tual terms of the licence agreement. This exclusion certainly applies to goods which do not fulfil the quality standards agreed upon between the right-holder and the manufacturer, goods which have been manufactured by the licensee in violation of a territorial limitation, and goods which are of a different kind to those covered by the licence agreement.

Some scholars argue that the text of the Regulation does not clearly state that **3.183** goods that have been produced in excess of the number of licensed merchandise agreed between the right-holder and the licensee and without a royalty payment, called 'overruns', fall under the exclusion of Article 3(2).[204] They argue that these 'overruns' have not been 'manufactured with the consent of the right-holder' in the first place. Yet Article 3(2) is generally interpreted as excluding from the system of border measures all goods that have been manufactured in the factory of a licensee. This interpretation is supported by the fact that it is almost impossible for customs to distinguish between authentic goods and those manufactured in violation of any kind of licence agreement.

With regard to the actions that may be taken by the right-holder who becomes **3.184** aware through border measures that a licensee infringes the contractual terms of an agreement, the same reasoning as above (para 3.177 above) applies.

---

[202] In the same sense: Ibid.   [203] Cf n 8 above, Art 1(3).
[204] Cf, eg, R Knaak in H Harte-Bavendamm, n 201 above, para 23.

(3) Goods contained in travellers' personal baggage

3.185 The exclusion of goods contained in travellers' personal baggage is one of the most contested provisions of the Regulation.[205] Article 3(2) provides for the following:

> Where a traveller's personal baggage contains goods of a non-commercial nature within the limits of the duty-free allowance and there are no material indications to suggest the goods are part of commercial traffic, Member States shall consider such goods to be outside the scope of this Regulation.

Scope of the exception

3.186 To fall under the exclusion provided for in Article 3(2), the infringing goods have to be of a 'non-commercial nature', contained in 'traveller's personal baggage', and fall within the limits of the 'duty free allowance'. The Regulation does not clarify these concepts. Yet, they are defined in Council Regulation (EEC) No 918/83,[206] and it would therefore have been sufficient for the European legislature to refer to this piece of Community law.

3.187 The concept of 'personal luggage', as defined in Article 45(2)(a) of Regulation 918/83, includes the 'whole of the luggage which a traveller is in a position to submit to the customs authorities on his arrival in the customs territory of the Community as well as any luggage submitted to this same authority at a later date, provided that evidence can be produced to prove that it was registered, at the time of the traveller's departure, as accompanied luggage with the company which transported it into the customs territory of the Community from the third country of departure'.

3.188 Subparagraph (b) of that same Article defines 'imports of a non-commercial nature' as being 'of an occasional nature, and consist[ing] exclusively of goods for the personal use of the travellers or their families, or of goods intended as presents; the nature and quantity of such goods should not be such as might indicate that they are being imported for commercial reasons'.

3.189 The 'duty free allowance' is, in principle, granted up to a total value of EUR 175 (Article 47 of Regulation 918/83). However, there are several exceptions.[207] It is regrettable that Regulation 1383/2003 does not provide for a method of calculating the value of the duty free allowance. Obviously, the method of calculating the latter is crucial: if the purchase value of the infringing goods is taken into account the threshold for customs interventions will be far lower than if the value of authentic articles is taken as a basis for the calculation. The value of one fashion handbag or one designer shirt will often exceed the limits of the duty

---

[205] O Vrins (n 13 above), at 111–113.
[206] Council Reg (EEC) No 918/83 of 28 March 1983 setting up a Community system of reliefs from customs duty, [1983] OJ L 105/1 (23.4.1983).   [207] Ibid, Arts 46, 47, 47a, 47c, and 49.

free allowance. In Article 13 of a working document of 7 March 2002[208] the Commission proposed calculating the value of the duty free allowance by taking into account the pre-tax value of the original goods in the Member State where the border measures have been taken. In the absence of specific guidelines in the Regulation this important question is left to the discretion of the national customs authorities. The taking of the value of an original article as the basis of their calculations is to be encouraged. Account should be taken of the fact that Article 3(2) of the Regulation is an exception to the general provisions, and as such must be interpreted narrowly. Therefore customs should calculate the limit of the duty free allowance in such a manner as to permit the application of the Regulation wherever possible.

Since the entry into force of Regulation 1383/2003 in 2004, customs are **3.190** competent to take border measures against goods contained in travellers' personal baggage, whenever there are material indications to suggest that the goods are part of a commercial traffic. Again, the Regulation does not define this term, nor does it give guidance as to how this notion is to be interpreted. This is therefore left to the discretion of the national customs authorities who will certainly take into account the nature of the goods, their quantity, the frequency of the importation, and the commercial documents accompanying the goods.

It is noteworthy that 34 per cent of all border measures taken by European **3.191** customs in 2004 were taken against passenger traffic, and this despite the limited powers of customs to intervene against infringing goods in travellers' baggage.[209]

Article 3(2)—and the corresponding provisions of the previous Regulations[210]— **3.192** has always been subject to intensive lobbying by right-holders' associations. The latter have pointed out that the exception of personal baggage cannot be justified by the principle of free circulation—since this principle does not apply at the external borders of the Community—and that it can therefore only be perceived as an unjustified and inadmissible tolerance of tourists trafficking illicit goods. In the absence of greater public regard for intellectual property rights, selective border controls can and should be taken to discourage these activities. It has been stressed that the cumulative effect of millions of people travelling across borders and carrying with them goods infringing intellectual property rights causes enormous commercial harm to right-holders.[211]

---

[208] European Commission, DG TAXUD, Working Document TAXUD/2001/1003 of 28 January 2001, 'Study aiming to improve customs control regarding intellectual property rights and to facilitate access to an effective customs regulation', set up subsequent to the Paris Forum of 20–21 November 2000, http://europa.eu.int/comm/taxation_customs/resources/documents/modernisation_en.pdf, unpublished.

[209] In 2000 this figure reached 49 per cent. For more details cf http://europa.eu.int/comm/taxation_customs/customs/customs_controls/counterfeit_piracy/statistics/index_en.htm.

[210] Cf, eg, Reg 3295/94 (n 15 above), Art 10.

[211] INTA Position Paper of 8 April 2002, n 193 above.

3.193 In its reply to the right-holders the Commission argued that the system of border measures established by the Regulation was in any case an inappropriate weapon in the fight against tourist trafficking of counterfeited products. Abolishing the exception would bring about a massive rise in customs interventions—for only very few infringing goods per intervention—which, in turn, would result in numerous proceedings to determine whether an intellectual property right had been infringed. There can indeed be little doubt that in the absence of a simplified procedure or a prosecution of customs offences by the national authorities, border measures against small quantities of goods are not economically sustainable for the right-holders. An interesting proposal has been made by the textile industry[212] in this respect: the traveller would be offered the option of abandoning suspect goods discovered in his personal baggage for destruction and, in turn, the right-holder would undertake not to pursue the matter any further.

3.194 Despite such criticism, the exception has been kept in Regulation 1383/2003. However, the Commission recognized that the trafficking of small quantities (*trafic fourmis*) of infringing goods may conceal a much larger phenomenon, and therefore the legislature tempered the exception by adding the option for customs to intervene if there is any doubt whether the goods are part of a commercial traffic.

3.195 It is of paramount importance to note that Article 3(2) does not preclude the national legislator from qualifying tourist traffic of counterfeited and pirated goods as an infringing—and even criminal—act under national law.

No general *de minimis* exception

3.196 It is worth mentioning here that the exclusion of limited quantities of infringing goods discovered in personal baggage is the only *de minimis* rule contained in the Regulation. In other words, the duty free allowance—or any other minimum threshold—should play no role in relation to goods shipped by other means of transportation, such as, for example, postal parcels. Customs should apply border measures to these shipments, irrespective of the quantity of infringing goods contained therein. Such small shipments of infringing goods—for example, infringing goods bought by end-consumers on auction or replica websites—pose two problems: first of all, proceeding against the infringers may not always be economically viable. Yet, it should be for the right-holder to decide whether to pursue the matter.[213] A second problem,

---

[212] European Apparel and Textile Organisation (Euratex), Règlement communautaire anti-contrefaçon: proposition d'amélioration formulée par la Commission, 7 February 2003, unpublished.

[213] It has in this context been proposed that the right-holders could be entitled to specify in their applications for action a minimal threshold under which they do not wish to take action.

which cannot be controlled by the right-holder, is that national legislation will not always provide for effective remedies against small shipments without commercial purpose. Importing a minimum quantity of infringing goods for personal use may not qualify as an infringing act under national law. In such circumstances the right-holder may have no way of acting against this behaviour which is nevertheless an infringement of the Regulation. The most appropriate response to the ever increasing phenomenon of mail traffic—at least as long as the simplified procedure of Article 11 has not been implemented by the Member States—would be to treat intellectual property right infringements as customs offences, thus allowing the national customs authorities to prosecute such matters.

II. APPLICATION FOR ACTION BY THE CUSTOMS AUTHORITIES

The filing of an application for action with customs by a right-holder is one of the cornerstones of the border measures system, as it facilitates the recognition and identification of goods suspected of infringing intellectual property rights for the customs authorities. It is therefore essential that right-holders file applications for action, and that the information contained in the application is as complete as possible. The lodging and processing of applications for customs action are examined below (section B). **3.197**

However right-holders are often unaware that their intellectual property rights have been infringed and so have not taken the precaution of filing an application for customs action. In order to enable these right-holders to benefit from this system, the European legislature has provided customs authorities with the authority to intervene on their own initiative—*ex officio*—provided they have sufficient grounds for suspecting that the goods infringe an intellectual property right. In these circumstances, the suspected goods are retained for a short period to enable the right-holder to file an application for action. We will discuss the *ex officio* procedure in section A below. **3.198**

Cf Euratex, n 212 above. We are of the opinion that this proposal could perhaps be considered in certain sectors, such as the textile industry, but would be inappropriate in more sensitive economic areas where consumers' health and safety are at stake. Nevertheless, trade mark owners should be aware of the risks to which such a 'de minimis' strategy would give rise, eg with respect to the dilution of their trade marks (JJ Evrard and I Taymans, 'Défendre la marque avec l'aide des autorités douanières', in F Gotzen (ed), *Marques et concurrence* (Brussels: Bruylant, 1998), 69).

A. Measures prior to an application for action by the customs authorities (*ex officio* measures)

3.199 Article 4 of the Regulation sets out the circumstances in which the customs authorities may detain goods prior to an application for action being filed (the *ex officio* procedure):

> (1) Where the customs authorities, in the course of action in one of the situations referred to in Article 1(1) and before an application has been lodged by a right-holder or granted, have sufficient grounds for suspecting that the goods infringe an intellectual property right, they may suspend the release of the goods or detain them for a period of three working days from the moment of receipt of the notification by the right-holder and by the declarant or holder of the goods, if the latter are known, in order to enable the right-holder to submit an application for action in accordance with Article 5.

> (2) In accordance with the rules in force in the Member State concerned, the customs authorities may, without divulging any information other than the actual or supposed number of items and their nature and before informing the right-holder of the possible infringement, ask the right-holder to provide them with any information they may need to confirm their suspicions.

3.200 Although customs authorities are not compelled to apply the *ex officio* procedure, most of them make use of this option.[214] It is interesting to note that 19 per cent of all customs interventions in the Community during 2004 were made *ex officio* (against 22 per cent in 2003). The statistics also reveal that the customs authorities in some countries are more reticent when it comes to taking *ex officio* measures—for example, the United Kingdom, Ireland, Germany, Spain, and France—whereas others—for example, Hungary, Denmark, Italy, Latvia, Slovenia, the Czech Republic, Slovakia, the Netherlands, Belgium, and Finland—seem glad to act on their own initiative.[215]

3.201 An *ex officio* procedure will typically start with routine checks, during which the customs authorities may apprehend goods they suspect of infringing intellectual property rights under the terms of the Regulation. In the absence of a valid application for action, the officers will endeavour to find out whether the goods are protected by an intellectual property right. This is often done by consulting official databases, or by liaising with the relevant Intellectual Property Offices. If the intellectual property right is registered, the officials can obtain the name of the right-holder and/or his representative. The customs authorities will then contact the right-holder or his representative and the declarant or holder of the goods and inform them of their suspicions. The latter's contact details will normally be included in the transport documents.

---

[214] Art 6 of the Implementing Regulation (n 27 above) provides that in case of perishable goods border measures will primarily be taken in respect of products for which an application for action has already been lodged.

[215] http://europa.eu.int/comm/taxation_customs/customs/customs_controls/counterfeit_piracy/statistics/index_en.htm.

The suspect goods may then be detained or their release suspended for three **3.202** working days in order to allow the right-holder to file an application for action. The moment of receipt of the notification of the interception of the goods by the right-holder[216] is the starting point for the three-day period.[217]

According to the notes on completion of the application for customs action[218] the **3.203** right-holder is obliged to return the proof of receipt of the notification addressed to him by the customs service immediately on receipt.[219]

A 'working day' is defined as every day other than a public holiday, Saturdays and **3.204** Sundays.[220] It goes without saying that bank holidays which are relevant for the calculation of the term are those which apply in the country where the intervention takes place. The three working days period is calculated excluding the day of receipt of the notification. The term is therefore calculated as from the day after the receipt of the notification.

Before informing the right-holder of the possible infringement, customs autho- **3.205** rities can require him to provide them with any information they may need to confirm their suspicions. In accordance with the rules in force in the relevant Member State, the customs authorities may only inform the right-holder of the actual or supposed number of items and their nature.

No other information is normally communicated at this stage. However, it is **3.206** clear from the different national chapters of this book that, in practice, the customs authorities often communicate more information (for example, country of origin and destination, digital pictures) than that which they are entitled to disclose under Article 4 within the framework of an *ex officio* action. Although this practice is appreciated by the right-holders, it is not entirely consistent with the Regulation.

---

[216] It is not entirely clear how the notion of 'the moment of receipt of the notification by the right-holder' is to be interpreted. Is it sufficient that a person in charge of the intellectual property right (eg, a trade mark or patent attorney on the records of the Intellectual Property Office) is notified or does the notification have to reach the right-holder (*stricto sensu*) in person? Art 2(2)(b) specifies that the concept of 'right-holder' includes the right owners representatives for the purposes of the Regulation. One could however envisage situations in which the person mentioned in the register as being in charge of the intellectual property right is no longer in touch with the right-holder. A strict interpretation of the Regulation leads us to the conclusion that in these cases the three working days term would not start to run. Whatever the case may be, right-holders are advised to keep the registers up to date with accurate information on their representatives.

[217] Reg 1891/2004 (n 27 above), Art 5, second indent.   [218] Ibid, Annexes I-A and II-A.

[219] In the case of an *ex officio* action, the customs authorities should inform the right-holder of this obligation to confirm receipt of the notification. A right-holder confronted for the first time by this system of border measures may not necessarily be aware of this obligation, which only figures in the notes on completion of an application for action. Not all national customs authorities insist on this requirement, although they should.

[220] Reg (EEC, Euratom) No 1182/71 of the Council of 3 June 1971 setting out the rules applicable to periods, dates and time limits, [1971] OJ L 124/1 (8.6.1971), Art 2(2), and notes on completion (n 218 above).

3.207 In some cases the initial discussion between the customs authorities and the right-holder for information to confirm any suspicions the customs authorities may have, may lead in practice to a prolongation of the three working days period, as these initial talks can be time-consuming. It should be noted here that the three working days period only starts to run from the moment of receipt by the right-holder and the declarant or holder of the official notification, and not from the start of these informal talks aimed at confirming or allaying any suspicions.

3.208 From a right-holder or representative's point of view the three working days term may seem very short, especially if the chain of instruction between the right-holder and the local representative is long, or if the right-holder resides abroad. However, one has to bear in mind that the detention or suspension of release of suspect goods for three working days on the customs authorities' own initiative and for which they are responsible is a significant delay in today's transportation environment, where goods have to be delivered from one place to another in the shortest possible time without delay. It is therefore only right that the initial term be very short.

3.209 If the customs authorities' suspicions are confirmed by the right-holder, the latter can file an application for action. Provided this application is accepted, the normal procedure described below (Part III) will ensue.

3.210 If an application for action is lodged by the right-holder before the expiry of the three working days period and this application is accepted by the competent customs department, the period for notifying the customs authorities that either proceedings have been initiated to determine whether an intellectual property right has been infringed[221] or that the right-holder has successfully applied the simplified procedure[222] will only start from the day after the application has been received.[223]

3.211 Under Regulation 1383/2003 the circumstances in which *ex officio* actions can be used have been considerably widened: it is no longer a requirement that the infringement of an intellectual property right appears evident[224] to the customs authorities, it is enough that they have sufficient grounds for *suspecting* that an infringement has occurred. According to the Community legislator this widening of the scope of action should give small and medium enterprises the opportunity to access the facility.[225] It is very often the case that right-holders are not aware that their intellectual property rights have been the subject of counterfeiting or piracy. The *ex officio* procedure enables them to recognize this unpleasant reality and to take the necessary steps to file an application for action. This is why the *ex officio* procedure is extremely important.

---

[221] Reg 1383/2003, Art 13.   [222] Ibid, Art 11.
[223] Reg 1891/2004 (n 27 above), Art 5.   [224] Reg 3295/94 (n 15 above), Art 4.
[225] Explanatory Memorandum and Proposal (n 2 above), point 2.5.

B. The lodging and processing of applications for customs action

The filing of a preventive application for action is vital for the good functioning **3.212**
of the European system of border measures, as it allows the right-holder to inform
customs about how to recognize infringing goods.

In 2003 and 2004, the vast majority—nearly 80 per cent—of European customs **3.213**
interventions were taken after an application for action had been filed. In the
same year a total of 1,886 applications for action were filed, an increase of 47 per
cent in only two years. This figure has again risen considerably since the entry
into force of Regulation 1383/2003: in 2004 2,888 applications for action had
been filed.[226]

In the light of the above, it is astonishing that there are still many business people **3.214**
who rely totally on intellectual property rights for their business who have not
filed any application for action.

We will go on to examine first, who is entitled to file an application for action and **3.215**
the documentary evidence that has to be submitted. We will also discuss where the
application has to be filed (the competent customs department), and look at
the formal requirements that have to be fulfilled. Then we will describe in detail
the type of information to be included in the application which should enable
customs authorities to recognize goods that may infringe an intellectual property
right. The rules regarding the processing of an application for action also have to
be scrutinized and finally we will examine the Community application for action,
which is reserved for the owners of 'Community rights'. It should be borne in
mind that the rules discussed apply equally to preventive applications for action
and those lodged following *ex officio* measures.

(1) Persons entitled to file an application for action

It is important to look at the beneficiaries of the Regulation, namely those who **3.216**
may file an application for action, and the documentary evidence these persons
have to submit together with the application for action.

Definition of 'right-holders' under the Regulation

Rather surprisingly, Article 2(2) of the Regulation defines the 'right-holder' in **3.217**
broad terms, as including:

(a) the holder of a trade mark, copyright or related right, design right, patent,
supplementary protection certificate, plant variety right, protected designation of

---

[226] It should be noted that a Community application for action designating 25 countries is
counted as 25 applications. Cf Community statistics, n 215 above.

origin, protected geographical indication and more generally, any right referred to in [Article 2(1)]; or

(b) any other person authorized to use any of the intellectual property rights mentioned in point (a), or a representative of the right-holder or authorized user.

3.218 This wording includes of course the right-holder *strictu senso*, that is to say the owner of the individual or collective[227] intellectual property right, but also any other person authorized to use the intellectual property right, or a representative of the owner or authorized user.

3.219 The term 'authorized user' certainly embraces producers of goods protected by designations of origin and geographical indications. It also comprises licensees, irrespective of whether the licence is contractual or compulsory, exclusive or non-exclusive.[228] Some scholars argue that this definition even includes distributors and agents of the owner of the right.[229] Whatever the case may be, in several cases or countries the authorization to use an industrial property right will have to be registered with the competent Intellectual Property Office in order to be enforceable against third parties, including customs and the traffickers of infringing goods.[230]

3.220 Representatives of the owner of an intellectual property right or the authorized user can be natural or legal persons,[231] and typically include attorneys at law, trade mark, design, or patent attorneys, consultants, collecting societies,[232] right-holders' associations, etc.

3.221 The very wide definition of the 'right-holder' has been included in the European legislation on border measures ever since the first generation Regulation.[233] There can be little doubt that the draftsmen of the successive Regulations intended to make the system available to as many persons as possible, thus ensuring its success.

3.222 It has perhaps been overlooked that some of the authorized users entitled to file an application for action will not be authorized under national law to defend the intellectual property right in question, because it will be considered that they do not have sufficient interest to act. This category includes non-exclusive licensees. Furthermore, not all of those authorized to file an application will necessarily be aware of matters such as the global strategy of the right-holder *stricto sensu*, of the identities of other authorized users, and of the specifics of the intellectual property right (including whether or not a trade mark is used in a given jurisdiction,

---

[227] Eg the owners of collective or certification marks and the group of producers who have obtained a protected geographical indication or a designation of origin.

[228] O Vrins (n 13 above), 114.

[229] C De Meyer and P Van den Broecke (n 53 above), 92–93.

[230] Cf, eg, Reg 40/94, Art 23(1); Reg 6/2002 (n 162 above), Art 33(2).

[231] Reg 1891/2004 (n 27 above), Art 1.

[232] Including those who have as their sole or principal purpose the management or administration of copyright or related rights (cf Ibid, Art 1).   [233] Reg 3842/86 (n 8 above), Art 1(2)(b).

whether a patent is vulnerable to a cancellation action, etc). Several associations of right-holders have voiced their concerns in this respect before the adoption of the Regulation,[234] but the Community legislator has not taken them into account.

Proof of entitlement to file an application for action

For right-holders stricto sensu

According to Article 5(5), second indent, of the Regulation: **3.223**

> The application for action must [. . .] contain the declaration required of the applicant by Article 6 and proof that the applicant holds the right for the goods in question.

According to Article 2(1) of the Implementing Regulation[235] the following is   **3.224**
considered evidence of ownership:

> (a) in the case of a right that is registered or for which an application has been lodged, proof of registration with the relevant office or proof that the application has been lodged;

> (b) in the case of a copyright, related right or design right which is not registered or for which an application has not been lodged, any evidence of authorship or of the applicant's status as original owner.

For a registered industrial property right, proof of registration is required; for a right   **3.225**
for which an application has been lodged, it is sufficient to provide evidence of filing. It is rather surprising that the Implementing Regulation refers to applications, as Regulation 1383/2003 does not seem to provide for the possibility of filing an application for action on the basis of a mere application for an intellectual property right. The reason for this reference might be found under national law.[236]

The Implementing Regulation further specifies that 'a copy of the registration   **3.226**
from the database of a national or international office[237] may be considered proof' of the right.[238] The Community legislature wanted to lighten the burden of proof by allowing the right-holder to submit simple copies of official databases, and *a fortiori* copies of registration certificates. The requirements of certain national customs authorities who request right-holders to submit original certificates, or certified/legalized copies of official databases, are clearly too burdensome and violate the provision of Article 2 of the Implementing Regulation.

For an application for action based on a protected designation of origin or a   **3.227**
geographical indication the applicant is required to submit—in addition to the

---

[234] INTA Position Paper (n 193 above).   [235] Cf n 27 above.

[236] The authors of the national chapters of this book have discussed the possibility of filing an application for action on the basis of a mere application.

[237] Please refer to the following online databases of international offices: Community trade marks and designs: http://oami.eu.int; International trade mark registrations: http://www.wipo.int/ipdl/en/search/madrid/search-struct.jsp; International design registrations: http://www.wipo.int/ipdl/en/search/hague/search-struct.jsp.

[238] Reg 1891/2004 (n 27 above), Art 2(1), second indent.

proof that the designation or indication is registered—evidence that he is the producer or the group of producers.[239]

3.228 For an unregistered intellectual property right, such as a copyright or related rights or an unregistered design right, it is sufficient if the owner submits prima facie evidence that he is the author or original holder. This is in line with Article 5 of the 'Enforcement Directive'[240] which provides a presumption of authorship or ownership.[241]

3.229 The right-holder will have to show the validity of his right, and he has an obligation to notify the competent customs department if this right ceases to be validly registered or expires.[242]

For persons authorized to use the right

3.230 For persons authorized to use the intellectual property right the proof to be submitted will, in addition to evidence of ownership, be a document showing that the person is authorized to use the right in question.[243] This would typically be a licence agreement.

For representatives

3.231 In addition to the above documents, the representative of the right-holder or of any other person authorized to use the intellectual property right will have to prove his authorization to act.[244] This will generally be a power of attorney form reproduced on the letterhead of the person granting the right of representation.

(2) Competent customs department and formal requirements

3.232 In this section, we will see that each Member State has designated one customs department to receive and process applications for action, and we will also examine the formal requirements in relation to the application for action, which are detailed in the Regulation and the Implementing Regulation.

Responsible customs department

3.233 Since the entry into force of Article 5(2) of Regulation 1383/2003, Member States may only designate one customs department to receive and process

---

[239] Reg 1891/2004 (n 27 above), Art 2 *in fine*.

[240] Directive 2004/48/EC of the European Parliament and of the Council of 29 April 2004 on the enforcement of intellectual property rights, [2004] OJ L 157/45 (30.4.2004).

[241] M Blakeney, 'The Phenomenon of Counterfeiting and Piracy in the European Union: Factual Overview and Legal and Institutional Framework', Chapter 1 of this book, para.1.63.

[242] Reg 1383/2003, Art 8(1), second indent.   [243] Ibid, Art 2(2).

[244] Ibid, Art 2(3), first indent.

applications for action. The list of these departments is published as an enclosure of the Implementing Regulation.[245]

Owners of national intellectual property rights will have to file their 'national applications for action' with the competent customs department in the Member State where the suspect goods are found.[246] The formalities will thus have to be undergone country by country, having regard to the specific national rules. In the event that a right-holder files several national applications he will have to take into account that the applications will have different periods of validity. There is however an exception for the owners of Community rights, who may file one single 'Community application for action' designating different countries[247] (cf (5) 'Community' applications for action below). **3.234**

The designation of several customs departments competent on their limited territory within one Member State, as was the case in Greece, for example, is therefore no longer acceptable under Regulation 1383/2003. The current Greek practice of designating one competent department, but of allowing right-holders to also file applications through several other departments should equally be looked at critically. **3.235**

Up to date information,[248] including e-mail and Internet addresses of these departments will be provided in the national chapters of this publication. **3.236**

Form of the application for action

The Regulation only provides that the application for action has to be submitted in writing[249] on a form established by the Commission and the Customs Code Committee.[250] Provided electronic data interchange systems exist, the Member States should encourage right-holders to lodge applications electronically.[251] It will be evident from the national chapters that electronic data interchange systems are still largely absent. **3.237**

The Implementing Regulation aims at harmonizing and standardizing the format of the applications for action—whether they are national or Community applications—by establishing a standardized version of the application form,[252] **3.238**

---

[245] Reg 1891/2004 (n 27 above), Annexes I-C and II-C.   [246] Reg 1383/2003, Art 5(1).
[247] Ibid, Art 5(4).
[248] It is doubtful whether the publication of the up to date list of competent customs departments is best done as an enclosure of the Implementing Regulation or on a website of DG TAXUD.
[249] Reg 1383/2003, Art 5(1).   [250] Ibid, Art 5(4).
[251] Ibid, Art 5(3). A change in terminology has to be pointed out: under the previous Regulation the Member States were allowed to provide for an electronic submission of the application, today they are encouraged to do so.
[252] Reg 1891/2004 (n 27 above), 5th Recital. It is noteworthy that the use of such a form was already mandatory for Community applications for action under Reg 3295/94 (n 15 above). The said form was published together with Reg 2549/1999 (n 23 above).

the use of which is mandatory under Article 3(1). The right-holder has to complete the form—which shall contain no erasures, overwritten words or other alterations—electronically,[253] mechanically or legibly by hand.[254]

3.239 When the right-holder attaches additional sheets they will be deemed to be an integral part of the application.[255]

Language requirements

3.240 As far as national applications for action are concerned, no language requirements are provided for, neither by the Regulation, nor by the Implementing Regulation. For Community applications for action, Article 3(2) of the Implementing Regulation provides that they have to be printed and completed in one of the official languages of the Community designated by the competent authority of the Member States in which the application for action has to be submitted, together with any translation that may be required by the national authorities. In both cases, applicants will therefore have to refer to national law and practice, commented upon in the national chapters of this book.

(3) Requirements regarding the content of the application for action

3.241 'The application for action [. . .] is crucial to optimising customs action in that it provides particulars and a technical description of the potentially pirated or counterfeited products against which customs administrations are being asked to act [. . .].'[256]

3.242 Article 5(5) and (6) of the Regulation distinguishes between mandatory information, optional information and additional information specific to the type of intellectual property right referred to in the application.

Mandatory information

3.243 According to Article 5(5) of the Regulation, the application for action must contain all the information needed to enable the goods in question to be readily recognized by the customs authorities, and in particular:

- An accurate and detailed technical description of the goods. The thoroughness of the description will depend on the type of goods for which the application is filed. Generally speaking, right-holders are well advised to

---

[253] An electronic version which may be reproduced on private printing equipment is available at http://europa.eu.int/comm/taxation_customs/customs/customs_controls/counterfeit_piracy/right_holders/index_en.htm.

[254] Reg 1891/2004, Art 3(1), second indent. Handwritten forms shall be completed in ink and in block capitals.   [255] Ibid, Art 3(1), third indent.

[256] Explanatory Memorandum and Proposal (n 2 above), 4.

give information which will allow customs to distinguish authentic from infringing goods.

- Any specific information the right-holder may have concerning the type or pattern of fraud. The European legislator clearly wants the right-holder who is aware of cases of infringement to share this information with customs. The information available should be constantly updated with data from infringement cases of which the right-holder becomes aware.

In order to be really useful, the above intelligence on trafficking has to be as detailed as possible to allow customs authorities to identify suspect consignments simply and effectively by using the risk analysis principles. The information may be submitted in the form of documents, photos, etc.[257]

- The name and address of an administrative and a technical contact person. As the name suggests, the administrative contact person will have to deal with administrative or legal matters, whereas the technical contact person is responsible for meeting with the customs authorities to discuss technical details of the goods detained. The latter must be easily contactable at short notice. Under Community law, however, it is not mandatory that the contact person has his base or residence in the Member State where the application for action is filed. Obviously the technical and administrative contact person can be the same individual, such as a lawyer, provided he is familiar not only with the procedure, but also with the technical aspects of the product.[258]

Optional information

Article 5(5), fourth indent, encourages right-holders to communicate other available information in their applications for action, 'by way of indication', such as: **3.244**

- The pre-tax value of the original goods on the legitimate market in the country in which the application for action is lodged. It is submitted that this information may be used inter alia to determine the duty free allowance of goods discovered in a traveller's personal baggage.[259]
- The location of the goods or their intended destination.
- Particulars identifying the consignment or packages. It often happens that right-holders exclusively use a particular type of wrapping or labelling for transporting their goods, in which case this information should be shared with customs.
- The scheduled arrival or departure date of the goods.
- The means of transport used.

---

[257] Reg 1891/2004 (n 27 above), Annexes I-A and II-A, notes on completion of the application for action, point IV.

[258] Therefore, right-holders are well advised to hold regular training sessions for their contact persons. [259] Cf Reg 1383/2003, Art 3(2).

- The identity of the importer, exporter, or holder of the goods.
- The country or countries of production, and the routes used by the traffickers.
- The technical differences, if known, between the authentic and suspect goods.

Additional information specific to the type of intellectual property right referred to in the application

3.245 Article 5(6) allows the department responsible for receiving and processing applications for action to request details which are specific to the type of intellectual property right, such as the place of manufacture or production, and the distribution network or names of licensees, in order to facilitate the technical analysis of the products concerned.[260] The Community legislator justifies this option in view of the highly specialized nature of certain intellectual property rights.[261]

3.246 Although right-holders may be reticent to communicate some of the above mentioned information to customs—the latter is, after all, a part of the financial administration—it is strongly recommended that the application for action is as complete as possible in order to allow for the efficient functioning of the system of border measures.

Declaration accepting liability

3.247 According to Article 6(1) of the Regulation:

> Applications for action shall be accompanied by a declaration from the right-holder, which may be submitted either in writing or electronically, in accordance with national legislation, accepting liability towards the persons involved in a situation referred to in Article 1(1) in the event that a procedure initiated pursuant to Article 9(1) is discontinued owing to an act or omission by the right-holder or in the event that the goods in question are subsequently found not to infringe an intellectual property right.
>
> In that declaration the right-holder shall also agree to bear all costs incurred under this Regulation in keeping goods under customs control pursuant to Article 9 and, where applicable, Article 11.

3.248 The undertaking covers the right-holder's liability and guarantees the payment of all costs arising from keeping the goods under customs control. The reference to Articles 9 and 11 of the Regulation indicates that this provision relates to the initial period of detention, lasting a maximum of 20 working days. It will cover among other things, the storage costs and the costs of sorting and counting the goods.

3.249 The undertaking will also cover the right-holder's liability if the goods are finally found to be non-infringing, or if the customs procedure is discontinued due to an act or omission of the right-holder.

---

[260] Reg 1891/2004 (n 27 above), Art 4.
[261] Explanatory Memorandum and Proposal (n 2 above), at 5.

A declaration form is published as Annexes I-B and II-B of the Implementing **3.250**
Regulation.[262] It is noteworthy that this document also contains an undertaking
to pay the costs for the destruction of the infringing goods pursuant to Article 17
of the Regulation. Article 6 of the Regulation does not explicitly specify that the
right-holder has to sign an undertaking to bear the costs for destruction.[263]
However, Article 3(1) of the Implementing Regulation provides that the
declaration has to conform with the form set out in Annexes I-B and II-B of
the Implementing Regulation. In other words the Implementing Regulation
prescribes the use of a declaration which may go beyond Article 6 of the
Regulation.

Whether the declaration may be submitted electronically will depend on the **3.251**
national legislation in the Member State where the application is filed.

The declaration provided for by Article 6 of Regulation 1383/2003 replaces the **3.252**
guarantees which some customs authorities required under Regulation 3295/94.[264]
The Community legislator wanted to allow free access to the system of border
measures to small and medium sized undertakings.[265] Under the new system, the
filing of an Article 6 declaration will release any deposit and fee payable in the
Member State. However, where proceedings brought before the competent
authority on a matter of substance under Regulation 3295/94 are still under way
on the date of filing of the Article 6 declaration, the deposit will not be released
before the close of those proceedings.[266]

When the application for action is lodged by a representative of the owner or **3.253**
authorized user of the intellectual property right concerned, that representative
must produce the declaration accepting liability signed by the right-holder or the
person authorized to use the right, or may sign this declaration himself provided
he also submits a document authorizing him to bear any costs arising from
customs action on their behalf.[267]

---

[262] Reg 1891/2004 (n 27 above).
[263] C De Meyer and P Van den Broecke (n 53 above), 99, n 40, consider, however, that the
destruction costs would implicitly fall under Art 6(1). Moreover, Art 11 of the Regulation stipulates
that under the simplified procedure the destruction occurs 'at the expense and under the responsibility of the right-holder'. [264] N 15 above.
[265] Explanatory Memorandum and Proposal (n 2 above), at 2.
[266] Reg 1891/2004 (n 27 above), Art 9.
[267] Ibid, Art 2(3), second indent. This provision seems to conflict with the notes on
completion (Annexes I-A and II-A of the same Regulation). The latter provide that the natural
or legal person who fills in box 3 of the application (details of applicant—ie right-holder within
the broad meaning of Art 2(2) of the Regulation) must, in all cases, be the one who will provide
the Art 6 declaration. Several national customs departments insist that the application filed by
a representative contains a liability declaration signed by the representative. Our advice in such
a case is to have the declaration signed by the representative *and* the owner of the intellectual
property right.

(4) Processing and acceptance of the application for action

3.254 Upon receipt of an application for action by the competent customs department, the latter shall process that application and notify the applicant in writing of its decision within no more than 30 working days of its receipt.[268]

3.255 Since the entry into force of Regulation 1383/2003 customs authorities may no longer request the payment of a fee for the administrative costs occasioned by the processing of the application.[269]

3.256 In the event that the application does not contain all the mandatory information listed in Article 5(5) of the Regulation, the competent customs department may decide not to process the application for action.[270] In practice, this will rarely happen, as customs will normally request the right-holder to complete the application for action and resubmit it.[271] In the unlikely event of a refusal, customs shall provide reasons for its decision and include information on the appeal procedure. The national remedies against rejection will be discussed in the national chapters.

3.257 To allow customs to communicate easily decisions on acceptance, the application form provides a box which may be filled in by customs.[272]

3.258 The Implementing Regulation[273] requires customs to retain the application for action once accepted for at least one year longer than its legal period of validity.

(5) 'Community' applications for action

3.259 Regulation 241/1999[274] had already introduced the option of designating several Member States in one single application for action for owners of Community trade mark registrations. In practice however, right-holders did not make full use of this possibility.

3.260 This situation has changed significantly: since the entry into force of Regulation 1383/2003 numerous Community applications for action have been filed. Article 5(4) of the Regulation makes possible of filing an application for action with customs of several Member States to all owners of a 'Community right', whether it is a Community trade mark, a Community

---

[268] Reg 1383/2003, Art 5(7), first indent.   [269] Ibid, second indent.
[270] Ibid, Art 5(8).
[271] Such a course of action is explicitly allowed by Reg 1383/2003, Art 5(8), *in fine*.
[272] Reg 1891/2004 (n 27 above), Art 3(1).   [273] Ibid, Art 3(3), second indent.
[274] Cf n 19 above.

design right, a Community plant variety right, a designation of origin, geographical indication, or geographical designation protected by the Community.

In terms of language requirements, it has to be remembered that the Community **3.261** application for action will have to be printed and completed in one of the official languages of the Community designated by the competent authorities of the Member State in which the application for action has to be submitted, together with any translation that may be required.[275] In practice, for the right-holders this involves submitting one file per Member State designated, completed in the official language of the Member State through which the application is lodged. Should further translations be required, the right-holders have to bear the costs, as provided for in the declaration according to Article 6.[276]

In practice, Community applications for action will first be filed with one of **3.262** the competent customs departments in any Member State. Once granted in the first Member State, the decision is addressed to the other Member States designated in the application for action. The latter will have to complete without delay the 'acknowledgement of receipt' section in the form, indicating the date of receipt.[277]

The main advantages of the Community application for action are the uniform **3.263** expiry date and the simplified renewal procedure: right-holders will no longer have to be aware of several different expiry dates of their applications for action, as the period during which the customs authorities are to take action on the basis of a Community application shall be set at one year in all cases,[278] and one single renewal request is sufficient to apply for the renewal in all of the countries designated.

Furthermore, the right-holder may, as long as the application for Community **3.264** action remains valid, in the Member State where the application was originally lodged, enter a request for action to be taken in another Member State not previously mentioned. In such a case, the period of validity of the new application shall be the period remaining under the original application, and it may be renewed in accordance with the conditions applying to the original application.[279]

Two copies of the Community application have to be submitted, one for the **3.265** competent authority of the Member State where the application is lodged, and the other for the right-holder.[280]

---

[275] Reg 1891/2004 (n 27 above), Art 3(2).   [276] Cf also ibid, Annex II-B, second indent.
[277] Ibid, Art 3(3), third indent.   [278] Reg 1383/2003, Art 8(2), second indent.
[279] Reg 1891/2004 (n 27 above), Art 3(3), last indent.   [280] Ibid, first indent.

III. CONDITIONS GOVERNING ACTION BY CUSTOMS AUTHORITIES AND BY THE AUTHORITIES HAVING JURISDICTION TO DETERMINE WHETHER GOODS INFRINGE AN INTELLECTUAL PROPERTY RIGHT

A. Conditions governing action by customs authorities

3.266 This section deals with the notification of customs interventions under Article 9(1) of the Regulation to the right-holder and the declarant or holder of the goods; the information to be provided to right-holders by the customs authorities; and the inspection of the suspected goods and the provision of samples.

(1) Notification of customs intervention

3.267 When coming across goods in one of the situations or under one of the customs procedures referred to in Article 1(1) of the Regulation, and where they are satisfied, after consulting the right-holder where necessary, that the goods are those suspected of infringing an intellectual property right and for which an application for action has been filed and duly accepted, customs shall suspend the release of the goods or detain them.[281]

3.268 We have seen that, where no such application has yet been filed, or the authority responsible for processing it has not yet decided on the relevant application, customs *may* act *ex officio*.[282] The procedure will then consist of two phases: the goods will first be detained, or their release suspended, for a period of time limited to three working days, during which the right-holder is required to lodge an application under Article 5. Once that application has been accepted, the suspension of release or detention of the goods is upheld for a further 3, 10, or 20 working days, to allow the right-holder to initiate proceedings, and/or to operate the simplified procedure, where applicable.[283]

3.269 The customs office that took action must inform the customs department which processed the application immediately.[284]

---

[281] Reg 1383/2003, Art 9(1), first indent. [282] Cf paras 3.199–3.211 above.
[283] Reg 1383/2003, Arts 11 and 13(1). [284] Ibid, Art 9(1), second indent.

The same customs department, or the customs office which took action, must **3.270** inform the right-holder and the declarant or holder[285] of the goods that the intervention has taken place.[286] The notification to the declarant or holder is mainly aimed at allowing them to contact the owner of the goods and, as the case may be, to abandon the goods with a view to their being destroyed in accordance with the simplified procedure set out in Article 11, where applicable.[287]

It is left to the Member States to decide the means by which these notifications **3.271** must be effected.

(2) Information to be provided by customs to the right-holder

Optional information

Once goods suspected of infringing intellectual property rights are detained by **3.272** customs on an *ex officio* basis, we have seen[288] that customs may, in accordance with the rules in force in the Member State concerned, and without divulging any other information, notify the right-holder of the actual or estimated number of items and their nature.[289] However, the *ex officio* procedure is facultative, as is the communication of information in the context of that procedure.

Similarly, where an application for action has been filed by the right-holder under **3.273** Article 5 and has been accepted by the competent customs department, that department, or the customs office which took action, may equally inform the right-holder of the actual or estimated quantity and the actual or supposed nature of the goods, the release of which has been suspended, or which have been detained in accordance with Article 9(1).[290] Under Regulation 3295/94, the communication by customs to the right-holders of information concerning the quantity of suspect goods was compulsory, but only once these goods had been found to infringe an intellectual property right by the national authorities having jurisdiction to decide on this question.[291]

As under Article 4(2), the communication of this information is purely optional. **3.274**

Article 9(2) stipulates that the communication of this information does not oblige **3.275** the right-holder to notify the authority with jurisdiction to take a substantive

---

[285] Within the meaning of Art 38 of the Community Customs Code (n 42 above), ie the person bringing the goods into the Community (Art 38(1)), as well as any person who assumes responsibility for the carriage of the goods after they have been brought into the customs territory of the Community, eg as a result of a transhipment (Art 38(2)).

[286] Reg 1383/2003, Art 9(2), first indent. Unfortunately, under the new Regulation (contrary to the previous regime: cf Reg 3295/94 (n 15 above), as amended in 1999, Art 6(1), second indent), this notification to the right-holder and to the declarant or holder of the goods no longer has to occur 'forthwith' after the goods have been detained, or their release suspended.

[287] K Daele (n 6 above), at 220.   [288] Cf paras 3.205–3.206 above.

[289] Reg 1383/2003, Art 4(2).   [290] Ibid, Art 9(2).

[291] Reg 3295/94 (n 15 above), Art 8(3).

decision.[292] This does not mean that the right-holder is entitled to use the information thus obtained from customs for any purposes—which would be contrary to Article 12 of the Regulation—but only that the information may be utilized to determine whether, in the right-holder's opinion, the goods do indeed infringe an intellectual property right; if so, the right-holder is required to institute proceedings in accordance with Article 13(1), or alternatively, where relevant, to apply the simplified procedure set out in Article 11.

Compulsory information

3.276   Pursuant to Article 9(3), first indent, of the Regulation:

> With a view to establishing whether an intellectual property right has been infringed under national law, and in accordance with national provisions on the protection of personal data, commercial and industrial secrecy and professional and administrative confidentiality, the customs office or department which processed the application shall inform the right-holder, at his request and if known, of the names and addresses of the consignee, the consignor, the declarant or the holder of the goods and the origin and provenance of goods suspected of infringing an intellectual property right.

3.277   Under Regulation 3842/86 as for the quantity of products, notification to the trade mark owners, at their request, of the names and addresses of the consignor, importer, and consignee of the goods was only possible once the goods had already been found to be counterfeit by the national authorities (and unless running counter to provisions of national law).[293] Regulation 3295/94 left this situation unchanged,[294] although it allowed the right-holder to be advised of the name and address of the declarant and, if known, of the consignee of the goods, prior to the commencement of legal proceedings.[295]

3.278   Moreover, information concerning the *holder* of the goods was omitted in the previous Regulations. This had the effect of depriving the right-holder of the opportunity to institute proceedings in the case of transhipments—where there is no declarant—except in the rare situations where the consignee of the goods could be identified.

3.279   The 'origin' of the goods should be distinguished from their 'provenance', in that the former refers to the place of manufacture of the goods, whereas the latter

---

[292]   Reg 1383/2003, Art 9(2), provides that customs may inform the right-holder, *as well as the declarant or the holder of the goods*, of the quantity and nature of these goods, whilst the French text stipulates that such communication does not oblige *'them'* (ie the right-holder, and the declarant or holder of the goods) to institute proceedings.   [293]   Reg 3842/86 (n 8 above), Art 8(3).
[294]   Reg 3295/94 (n 15 above), Art 8(3). K Daele (n 6 above, at 220, n 48) seems to disagree. See, however, the 'Guide to Border Enforcement of IPRs in the EU', http://www.ipr-helpdesk.org/documentos/docsPublicacion/html_xml/8_BorderEnforcement [0000004202_00].html, n 60.
[295]   Reg 3295/94, Art 6(1).

relates to the different countries the goods came through (or, at least, the last country of export of the goods).[296]

Under the new Regulation, the communication by customs to the right-holder of the names and addresses of the consignee, the consignor, the declarant or the holder of the goods, and the origin and provenance of those goods is obligatory provided that: **3.280**

— such information is known by customs
— the communication of this information has been explicitly requested by the right-holder
— it occurs in accordance with national provisions on the protection of personal data, commercial and industrial secrecy, and professional and administrative confidentiality
— it aims at establishing whether an intellectual property right has been infringed under national law.

Whilst the first two provisos do not require any further elaboration, the last two requirements may seem more obscure, and will be explained further.

The relevance of the 'national provisions on the protection of personal data, commercial and industrial secrecy, and professional and administrative confidentiality' in Article 9(3) is not entirely clear, but has to a large extent been clarified by the European Court of Justice. **3.281**

In Case C-223/98,[297] the Court was consulted on a reference for a preliminary ruling from the Stockholm Administrative Court of Appeal (*Kammarrätten i Stockholm*). The Swedish judges asked the European Court to determine whether Article 6(1) of Council Regulation 3295/94[298] (which mirrors in substance Article 9(3) of Regulation 1383/2003) constituted a bar to the application of rules of Swedish national law under which the identity of declarants or consignees of imported goods, which the trade mark owner has found to be counterfeit, may not be disclosed to the trade mark owner. **3.282**

The Court held that, on a proper construction, this provision *did* preclude a rule of national law under which the identity of declarants or consignees of imported goods which the trade mark owner had found to infringe his rights could not be disclosed to him. **3.283**

There is no doubt that the findings of the Court in this ruling apply, *mutatis mutandis*, to Article 9(3) of the new Regulation. Similarly, one may consider that they extend to all intellectual property rights mentioned in Article 2(1), and not **3.284**

---

[296] Ibid, Art 8(3), referred instead to the names and addresses of the 'manufacturer' and 'exporter' of the goods.   [297] *Adidas AG* [1999] ECR I-7081.
[298] Cf n 15 above.

only to trade marks.[299] Some national courts have accepted this jurisprudence, for example, in respect of goods infringing patent rights.[300]

3.285 In so far as the provisions of the Regulation are directly applicable in all Member States and prevail over the provisions of national legislation, Article 9(3) of the Regulation, as interpreted by analogy with Article 6(1) of Regulation 3295/94 in Case C-223/98, supersedes all rules of national law which might prove contrary to it.[301]

3.286 Unfortunately, there has been non-compliance with the ECJ's *Adidas* decision during the last decade in Belgium, and this proved to be a serious obstacle to the efficient application of the system of border measures set out by the Regulation, and consequently, to the effective enforcement of intellectual property rights.

3.287 Unlike Article 9(2), Article 9(3) of the Regulation does not make clear that the communication of the information to which it relates occurs without the right-holder being bound by such communication to notify 'the authority competent to take a substantive decision'.

3.288 Based on this difference in wording, the EC Commission has repeatedly emphasized in its most recent seminars[302] that, in its view, the communication of the names and addresses listed in Article 9(3) compels the right-holder to initiate proceedings aimed at establishing 'whether an intellectual property right has been infringed under national law', or at the very least to employ the simplified procedure of Article 11, where applicable. This stance seems consistent with Article 12, first indent, of the Regulation, which stipulates that that information may be used only 'for the purposes specified in Articles 10, 11 and 13(1)'. Failure to comply with this requirement could result in the right-holder incurring the sanctions set out in Article 12, and/or civil liability, in accordance with national law, towards the persons involved, for discontinuation of the procedure referred to in Article 9(1).[303]

3.289 It is submitted that such an approach is regrettable—assuming that it were ever to be endorsed by the national courts, and ultimately by the European Court of Justice. Indeed, such an interpretation of Article 9(3) suggests that right-holders may not actually avail themselves of the above-mentioned information to

---

[299] F de Visscher and B Michaux, *Précis du droit d'auteur et des droits voisins* (Brussels: Bruylant, 2000), at 543, para 694, n 12.

[300] In Belgium, cf President of the Antwerp Court of First Instance, 15 October 2002, Case No 02/939/C, *Koninklijke Philips Electronics v Belgian State*, unreported.

[301] S Evrard, commenting on the ECJ's *Adidas* ruling, [1999] Ingénieur Conseil 553 (554).

[302] Such as, eg, the operational seminar held on 4–7 April 2005 in Budapest, and the meeting with right-holders which took place on 13 June 2005 in Brussels.

[303] Cf Reg 1383/2003, Art 6(1), first indent.

judge whether the goods do, in their opinion, infringe an intellectual property right, since the simple fact of asking for this information would imply that the right-holder *already* intends to initiate proceedings or contact the persons involved in the traffic for the purpose of the application of the simplified procedure.

Understood in this way, the Regulation would, in fact, force the right-holder **3.290** to adopt a position vis-à-vis customs as to the genuine or non-authentic nature of the goods exclusively on the basis of the limited information referred to in Article 9(2), and possibly also after inspecting the goods and, where customs agree, after being provided with samples.

Experience has shown that it is sometimes difficult for right-holders to decide on **3.291** the genuine or infringing character of the goods on the basis of the information referred to in Article 9(2). In case of doubt, information on the name and address of the consignee, consignor, declarant or holder of the goods (including potential licensees) will often prove conclusive to ascertain whether the goods consist of parallel imports—excluded from the scope of the Regulation pursuant to Article 3(1)—or of counterfeits.

It is therefore no surprise that some authors interpret the phrase 'with a view to **3.292** establishing whether an intellectual property right has been infringed under national law' in Article 9(3) as actually allowing right-holders to assess whether or not the goods infringe any of their rights, and thus whether or not further action is required or appropriate under Articles 11 or 13.[304]

(3) *Inspection of the suspected goods and provision of samples*

Subsequent to notification of a customs action under Article 9(1) of the **3.293** Regulation, the customs office *must* give the right-holder, as well as all persons concerned,[305] the opportunity to inspect the suspected goods.[306]

Moreover, when examining suspect goods, the customs office may take samples. **3.294** Unlike under the previous Regulation,[307] that office may also, according to the rules in force in the Member State in question, hand them over or send them[308] to the right-holder, at his express request. The Explanatory Memorandum to Article 9 provides that such samples must be 'representative' of the suspect

---

[304] M de Cock Buning (n 55 above), at 240.
[305] Ie 'the persons involved in any of the situations referred to in Art 1(1)' of the Regulation.
[306] Reg 1383/2003, Art 9(3), second indent.
[307] Reg 3295/94 (n 15 above), as amended in 1999, Art 6(1)(3), simply provided that the customs office could 'take samples in order to expedite the procedure'.
[308] The customs office may therefore choose, solely at its discretion, either to deliver samples to the right-holders on the customs premises, or to send them for the right-holder's attention.

consignment.[309] In practice, digital photographs of the products are sometimes sent in lieu of samples.

3.295 It is clear from the wording of Article 9(3) that, whilst customs may not refuse to allow the right-holder to inspect the goods, they may respond unfavourably to a request for samples.

3.296 This new provision might, nevertheless, prove of paramount importance in practice, since under the former regime, the customs authorities from several Member States were reticent to hand samples over to right-holders. The new Regulation now provides unambiguously that this is permitted.

3.297 It should be stressed in this context that in some cases, it is impossible for right-holders to carry out forensic research on the goods on the customs' premises.[310] In such cases, the useful effect of the Regulation would actually *require* that the right-holders be in a position to request samples to examine them in their laboratories.

3.298 It should be pointed out, for the sake of clarity, that the inspection of the goods and, *a fortiori*, the provision of samples, is only possible where an application for action has been filed by the right-holder concerned and such application has been duly accepted. No such possibility exists in the context of a simple *ex officio* action (under Article 4) as long as no application has been lodged under Article 5 and accepted by the competent customs department.

3.299 The communication and use of samples is only permitted 'strictly for the purposes of analysis'—which shall be carried out 'under the sole responsibility of the right-holder'—and 'to facilitate the subsequent procedure'.

3.300 Article 9(3), last indent, further states that:

> [. . .] Where circumstances allow, subject to the requirements of Article 11(1) second indent where applicable, samples must be returned on completion of the technical analysis and, where applicable, before goods are released or their detention ended [. . .].

3.301 It will be remembered that, when considering the terms of a reform of the previous Regulation, right-holders lobbied strongly to be entitled, not only to be provided with samples, but also—and this may seem logical—to use such samples in the framework of legal infringement proceedings.[311] Although Article 9(3), last indent, of the new Regulation leaves some doubt in this respect by stating that the use of samples must be limited to technical analysis and such samples must be returned on completion of that analysis, it also provides that use of samples has to

---

[309] Cf n 2 above.
[310] Consider, eg, the case of tobacco products, electrical components and equipments, etc.
[311] Cf INTA Position Paper of 8 April 2002 (n 193 above), at 7.

be allowed 'to facilitate the subsequent procedure', and that the samples must be returned, 'where applicable', before the goods are released, or their detention ended—which suggests that samples may still be used *beyond* the technical analysis. A narrow interpretation of both requirements (that is, 'strictly for the purposes of analysis' *and* 'provided such analysis facilitates the subsequent procedure') would logically exclude the use of samples in the context of court proceedings. Furthermore, it is not entirely clear what is meant by 'subsequent procedure'; does this refer only to the *customs* procedure, as set out in the Regulation, or does it also extend to the proceedings aimed at determining whether an intellectual property right has been infringed under national law referred to in Article 13(1)?

We see no reason why the Community legislature would have wanted to deprive **3.302** right-holders of the chance to use samples received from customs in accordance with Article 9(3) in the course of legal proceedings. Such use is obviously of paramount importance, as it would have a significant influence on the chances of success of the court proceedings, which constitute the outcome, and thus the reason behind the border measure system set out in the Regulation. Clearly, the proviso 'strictly for the purpose of analysis' aims at preventing reckless right-holders from using samples for purposes which are unrelated to an efficient fight against counterfeiting and piracy, for example, in order to make profit out of them. Conversely, it would seem that the use of samples for purposes which are directly related to the fight against intellectual property infringements should not be prohibited—since, in fact, such use may *condition* the success of the whole procedure. It is very unlikely that the Community legislature ever intended to impose such a prohibition on right-holders.

This view seems all the more tenable as Article 11(1) of the Regulation obliges **3.303** the customs authorities, when application is made of the simplified procedure, to systematically take samples prior to the destruction of the goods for keeping 'in such conditions that they constitute evidence admissible in legal proceedings in the Member State in which they might be needed'. It seems obvious that the objective of this provision is to allow the holder of the proprietary interests over goods which have been destroyed in accordance with Article 11 to claim damages if he can establish that the goods were genuine. The well-settled principle of equality of weapons should then clearly entitle right-holders to also use samples received under Article 9(3) as evidence of the infringing character of the goods in court proceedings.

The issue of the costs arising from the handing over or sending of samples is left up **3.304** to the Member States. In practice, samples are in most cases provided free of charge.

The Regulation provides that the sending or handing over of samples must in **3.305** all cases be subject to compliance with 'the rules in force in the Member State concerned', thus implicitly referring to the statutory provisions of national law concerning administrative and professional confidentiality. An analogy in this respect with the interpretation of the same proviso in Article 9(3), first indent, concerning the communication of personal data to the right-holder, is strictly speaking not possible, since Article 9(3) *obliges* the customs officials to communicate such data.[312] However, one may argue that the useful effect of the Regulation may, in some cases,[313] bar the application of provisions of national law precluding the sending or handing over of samples subject to compliance with the (other) requirements set out in Article 9(3), last indent.

3.306 Problems concerning the sending or handing over of samples have recently been reported in several countries, including Spain, France (where the customs authorities seem more inclined to apply their national provisions on border measures—which do not provide for sending samples to right-holders—than the procedure set out by the Regulation), and in certain Italian customs offices.

3.307 Finally, it should be remembered that the determination by the right-holder of the infringing nature of the goods, and therefore the further detention, or suspension of release, of the goods, occur entirely under the latter's responsibility. When filing an application for action, the applicant undertakes to ensure that customs has no liability if a court were ever to disagree with the right-holder's claim in this respect.

3.308 On the other hand, customs should not impose a burden of proof on the right-holder which would be unreasonably stringent at this stage. Neither the rationale for the procedure set out by the new Regulation, nor the general principles governing burden of proof would justify such an approach. Indeed, in most cases, it is only lack of consent from the right-holder which allows a reproduction to be considered an infringement; as it would be excessive to oblige right-holders to establish a negative fact, that is, that they did not agree to such a reproduction, it is in principle up to the alleged infringer to prove the rights owner's consent.[314]

B. Simplified procedure allowing the destruction of the goods without there being any need to determine whether an intellectual property right has been infringed under national law

(1) The procedure under Article 11

3.309 In numerous circumstances, the commencement of court proceedings proves impossible or burdensome in intellectual property infringement matters. This is often the case where unauthentic goods circulate in transit, or are the subject of a

---

[312] Cf paras 3.281ff above. [313] Cf para 3.297 above.

[314] Cf, as concerns trade marks, Th Van Innis, *Les signes distinctifs* (Brussels: Larcier, 1997), para 589.

transhipment—in which case there is no declarant. It appears to be possible in some countries to institute proceedings against the *holder* of the goods—such as their transporter, freight agent, or sea agent;[315] the new Regulation, which allows right-holders to be provided with the contact details of the holder of the goods, seems to support such an approach. However, this may not exist in some countries, at least where the holder's bad faith cannot be established.

Another recurrent problem which right-holders have to cope with in the fight against intellectual property right infringements relates to small consignments. The requirement imposed on right-holders under Article 7(1) of Regulation 3295/94[316] to initiate court proceedings on the merits of the case or to seek interim measures systematically subsequent to each action by the customs authorities proved particularly oppressive for right-holders who have to face numerous interventions in respect of small quantities of infringing goods. This phenomenon is not unusual in the case of postal traffic.[317] **3.310**

It was mainly to address those concerns that the Community legislature laid down a new 'simplified' procedure in Regulation 1383/2003, which unquestionably constitutes one the major and most profitable improvements to the border measure system as it existed under the previous EC Regulations. Another objective of this procedure was to 'resolve the problems of storage and the associated costs'.[318] **3.311**

The simplified procedure is set out in Article 11 of the new Regulation, which stipulates that: **3.312**

> 1. Where customs authorities have detained or suspended the release of goods which are suspected of infringing an intellectual property right in one of the situations covered by Article 1(1), the Member States may provide, in accordance with their national legislation, for a simplified procedure, to be used with the right-holder's agreement, which enables customs authorities to have such goods

---

[315] For an example in which a claim against the transporter was held to be admissable by a court, cf the Finnish Supreme Court, *Adidas Salomon AG v Scanrapid Oy and Raycom Shipping Ab* (Case No KKO:2002:119, 20 December 2003). In this decision, the Court recalled that the consignor of the goods keeps responsibility for the goods as long as they stay on Finnish territory, and held that, given that the infringer could not be identified, it was appropriate to allow the right-holder to initiate proceedings against the holder of the goods, at least so as to enable the Court to order their destruction.
[316] Cf n 15 above.   [317] Cf para 3.196 above.
[318] Cf Explanatory Memorandum and Proposal (n 2 above), under Art 11: 'To facilitate access to customs rules for SMI/SME right holders and to deprive those concerned effectively of the economic gains of trade in counterfeit and pirated goods, a simplified procedure has been introduced whereby goods can be destroyed at the right holder's request and under his responsibility where the customs authorities receive, within ten working days, written permission from the declarant or holder of the goods to destroy the goods [. . .]. Whereas, in the past, legal proceedings to obtain a substantive decision from the competent authorities were all too often abandoned because neither the consignor nor the consignee were on Community territory, it will now be possible to destroy goods infringing certain intellectual property rights in transit or transhipped on the Community customs territory.'

abandoned for destruction under customs control, without there being any need to determine whether an intellectual property right has been infringed under national law. To this end, Member States shall, in accordance with their national legislation, apply the following conditions:

– that the right-holder informs the customs authorities in writing within ten working days, or three working days in the case of perishable goods, of receipt of the notification provided for in Article 9, that the goods concerned by the procedure infringe an intellectual property right referred to in Article 2(1) and provide those authorities with the written agreement of the declarant, the holder or the owner of the goods to abandon the goods for destruction. With the agreement of the customs authorities, this information may be provided directly to customs by the declarant, the holder or the owner of the goods. This agreement shall be presumed to be accepted when the declarant, the holder or the owner of the goods has not specifically opposed destruction within the prescribed period. This period may be extended by a further ten working days where circumstances warrant it;

– that destruction be carried out, unless otherwise specified in national legislation, at the expense and under the responsibility of the right-holder, and be systematically preceded by the taking of samples for keeping by the customs authorities in such conditions that they constitute evidence admissible in legal proceedings in the Member State in which they might be needed.

2. In all other cases, for example where the declarant, holder or owner objects to or contests the destruction of the goods, the procedure laid down in Article 13 shall apply.

3.313 This procedure is inspired to a large extent by the opposition procedure set out under Article 111(a) of the German Copyright Law and by a similar procedure applied in Austria at the time of Regulation 3295/94—which was also followed *de facto* with some variants in other countries.[319] The former Regulation systematically required the commencement of proceedings or the adoption of interim measures.[320]

3.314 The current Regulation thus provides for a *possibility* for the Member States to individually implement a procedure, the principles and boundaries of which must comply with the terms of Article 11.

3.315 Contrary to the *ex officio* procedure, which, although also optional to the customs authorities, need not be implemented to be applied, the simplified procedure set forth in Article 11 of the Regulation does require implementation measures. Although the Regulation is, by its very nature, directly applicable in all Member States, one of its peculiarities is that it mixes provisions having direct effect, with others which clearly do not have direct effect, as is the case with Article 11.[321]

---

[319] Such as, eg, Belgium, at the criminal level, on the initiative of the Public Prosecutors. Outside the European Union—as it stood before 1 May 2004—the Czech Republic had adopted a comparable procedure in 1999. Whilst this procedure was seldom applied to pirated goods, it led to the destruction of counterfeit goods in 50% of cases (cf J Rutter and M Rosinski (n 194 above), at 27).
[320] Reg 3295/94 (n 15 above), Art 7(1).
[321] This is presumably also the case for Art 18 and possibly—although there is more room for dispute here—for Art 17: cf paras 3.19 ff above.

Although the initial working document submitted to right-holders by the **3.316** Commission prior to the adoption of the new Regulation[322] intended to obtain a consensus from the Member States to render the simplified procedure compulsory, this did not appear feasible, as several countries, including France and Italy, maintained that the destruction of the goods upon an *implicit* abandonment would be contrary to their respective Constitutions, if not by the Human Rights Convention, which confer a sacrosanct status on property rights.

Some authors[323] share these concerns, pointing out that the simplified procedure **3.317** is not exclusively applicable to cases of bad-faith infringements. They emphasize, moreover, that the Regulation extends to intellectual property rights which, by reason of their very nature, may—or at least some of them may—give rise to delicate controversies as to their validity, their scope of protection, and therefore the existence of an infringement.[324] Article 14 of the Regulation, which allows the release of goods suspected of infringing certain rights on provision of a security, acknowledges this. Given that it cannot be ruled out that the actual owner of goods detained by customs is not notified of the 'instigation' of a simplified procedure, and therefore is not in a position to object to the destruction of the goods within the period stipulated in Article 11—which is particularly stringent in the case of perishable goods—one may, still according to those authors, expect abuses in the application of the simplified procedure.

It is submitted that this criticism is probably exaggerated. Article 11 provides that **3.318** the destruction of suspect goods under the application of the simplified procedure shall in principle be applied under the right-holder's sole responsibility. Furthermore, the destruction shall be systematically preceded by the taking of samples for keeping by the customs authorities in such conditions that they constitute evidence admissible in legal proceedings in the Member State in which they might be needed. Right-holders are hereby advised not to rely on the simplified procedure recklessly. The owner whose goods would have been destroyed under Article 11 by virtue of an 'implied consent' could indeed file a motion to have a court declare that the goods did *not* infringe any intellectual property right. If his claim ever proved successful, the owner of the goods would be entitled to damages in accordance with the national law of the Member State where the destruction was carried out.

In any event, it seems excessive to state that the implied consent rule laid down in **3.319** Article 11 of the Regulation simply does (or did) not prove useful at all because the practice of entering into settlement agreements leading to the destruction of the goods had already been approved to a large extent in several Member States under

---

[322] N 208 above.   [323] Cf, eg, M de Cock Buning (n 55 above), at 243.
[324] This is, eg, the case as far as patent rights are concerned, where the assessment of an infringement under the doctrine of equivalents may be very awkward.

Regulation 3295/94.[325] It should be recalled in this context that Regulation 3295/94 did *not* allow the conclusion of such agreements, since it did not permit the communication by customs to the right-holders, and use by the latter, of any information relating to the declarant, consignee or consignor of the goods for that purpose. That information had to be used exclusively for the purpose of initiating proceedings in accordance with Article 7(1) of the former Regulation. The implied consent regime appeared all the more necessary as experience has shown that the persons involved in the traffic of suspect goods have in the huge majority of cases remained silent when notified of border measures. This had the unacceptable result of paralysing all 'traditional' procedures susceptible to result in the destruction of the goods.

3.320 The debate over Article 11 will probably never come to an end since, bearing in mind that the procedure it contemplates falls under the so-called 'third pillar' under Community law, the Community legislature will in principle not be in a position to impose it on the Member States unilaterally.

3.321 The first condition set out in Article 11 is that right-holders inform the customs authorities in writing within 10 working days, or 3 working days in the case of perishable goods, of receipt of the notification of the suspension of release or detention provided for in Article 9, that the goods concerned by the procedure infringe an intellectual property right referred to in Article 2(1).

3.322 The period stipulated in Article 11 corresponds to the term imposed on right-holders under Article 13. It may be extended by a further 10 working days where circumstances so warrant. Although Article 11 does not explicitly provide so, it is reasonable to assume, by analogy with Article 13, that no extension would be granted for perishable goods. The Regulation does not clarify in which cases the 10-day period may be extended. Some authors consider that requests for extension should be granted whenever the right-holder has not been able to liaise with the owner, the declarant, or the holder of the goods within the initial 10 working days period to obtain their express consent to the abandonment and destruction of the goods.[326] Nothing in the Regulation suggests such a broad interpretation of Article 11, although it is obvious that customs will enjoy considerable discretionary power in this respect.

3.323 The second condition imposed on the Member States by Article 11 is that the right-holder must provide the customs administrations with the written agreement of the declarant, the holder, or the owner of the goods to abandon the goods for destruction. With the consent of the customs authorities, this information may be provided directly to the customs administration by the declarant, the holder, or the owner of the goods.

---

[325] M de Cock Buning (n 55 above), at 243.   [326] K Daele (n 6 above), at 222.

Agreement will be implied where the declarant, the holder or the owner of the goods has not specifically opposed destruction within the prescribed period.

Although the wording of Article 11 is not crystal-clear on this point, it seems **3.324** logical to interpret this provision as meaning that the communication by the right-holder of the declarant's, holder's, or owner's explicit or implied consent must also occur within the 3, 10 or, as the case may be, 20 working days periods referred to in Article 11(1).

Finally, the goods must be destroyed at the end of the procedure. The destruction **3.325** must be carried out, 'unless otherwise specified in national legislation', at the expense and within the responsibility of the right-holder, and must be systematically preceded by the taking of samples for storage by the customs authorities in such conditions that they may constitute evidence admissible in legal proceedings in the Member State in which they might be needed.

The requirement that the destruction takes place within the right-holder's sole **3.326** responsibility is obviously aimed at exonerating customs from any possible claims in this respect.

As to the issue of liability for the costs of destruction, one may question why the **3.327** Regulation provides that such costs will be borne by the right-holder in all cases, unless provided for otherwise by national law. As it cannot be the objective of the Regulation to impose such a burden on right-holders and to deprive them of the possibility of claiming back such costs from the infringer, one would not anticipate any Community or national authority opposing an agreement between the right-holder, in the first place, and the owner and declarant or holder of the goods, in the second place, for these purposes—on the understanding of course (as this is presumably the actual objective pursued by the Community legislature in Article 11) that only the right-holder will remain liable for such costs as regards the customs authorities notwithstanding any agreement to the contrary.

Needless to say, to be in a position to apply the simplified procedure, the right- **3.328** holder needs to be entitled to require that customs provide him with the contact details of the owner, declarant, or holder of the goods,[327] so that he can get in touch with them to obtain their consent in relation to the abandonment of the goods for the purpose of destroying them. This possibility, which did not exist under Regulation 3295/94,[328] is now explicitly provided for in Article 12, first indent, of the Regulation.

Where the declarant, holder, or owner of the goods objects to, or contests, the **3.329** destruction of the goods, Article 11(2) stipulates that the 'regular' procedure laid down in Article 13 shall apply. The right-holder will thus have to initiate

---

[327] Cf on this point Reg 1383/2003, Art 9(3), paras 3.276–3.287 above.   [328] N15 above.

proceedings so that the courts determine whether the goods do indeed infringe any of his rights.

3.330   The simplified procedure would have been very promising, had the Member States been more enthusiastic in implementing it. It would have allowed a growing number of SMEs to participate more actively in the fight against counterfeiting and piracy—a war which, when it comes to court proceedings, they sometimes cannot afford. Similarly, it would also have encouraged multinationals to get willingly involved in the battle, irrespective of the size of the consignments.

3.331   Unfortunately to date, only two Member States have reported implementing and applying the simplified procedure: the Netherlands and Austria. In the latter country, 70 per cent of all customs actions under the Regulation come to an end as a result of using this procedure.

3.332   It is disappointing that the other 23 Member States have so far failed to implement Article 11. Even though most of them have plans to do so, it remains to be seen whether the simplified procedure will ever fulfil its promise.

(2)   The lot of settlement agreements other than those under Article 11

3.333   Under Article 12 of the Regulation,

> A right-holder receiving the particulars cited in the first subparagraph of Article 9(3) shall use that information only for the purposes specified in Articles 10, 11 and 13(1).
>
> Any other use, not permitted by the national legislation of the Member State where the situation arose, may, on the basis of the law of the Member State in which the goods in question are located, cause the right-holder to incur civil liability and lead to the suspension of the application for action, for the period of validity remaining before renewal, in the Member State in which the events have taken place.
>
> In the event of a further breach of this rule, the competent customs department may refuse to renew the application. In the case of an application of the kind provided for in Article 5(4), it must also notify the other Member States indicated on the form.

3.334   Pursuant to this provision, the right-holder may thus only use the information provided by the customs authorities concerning the names and addresses of the consignee, the consignor, the declarant or the holder, and the origin and provenance, of goods suspected of infringing an intellectual property right for the purpose of applying the simplified procedure of Article 11, or to institute proceedings aimed at determining whether the goods do indeed infringe an intellectual property right, as provided for under Article 13.

3.335   As has been pointed out above,[329] the simplified procedure set out in Article 11 of the Regulation must have been implemented in the national law of the Member

---

[329]   Cf para 3.314 above.

State of the customs intervention to be applicable, and is subject to several strict requirements. One of those requirements is that the goods be ultimately destroyed. 'Unless otherwise specified in national legislation', the destruction has to be carried out at the expense and subject to the responsibility of the right-holder.

We have already advocated above[330] that it would, in our opinion, be unreasonable to interpret Article 11 as prohibiting the conclusion of agreements with the parties involved in the traffic under which the destruction costs would be borne by the owner of the goods. Having regard to Article 11, however, such a clause would not be enforceable in respect of the customs authorities, and could thus not have the effect of exonerating the right-holder of his responsibility and liability for the destruction costs as against customs. Similarly, amicable agreements fulfilling the requirements of Article 11 which would, in addition, provide for the grant of damages by the infringer to the right-holder (including the reimbursement of the storage costs, attorney's costs, punitive damages) and contain, for example, a clause whereby the former covenants to no longer infringe the latter's rights subject to a mutually agreed penalty, ought not to be barred by Articles 11 and 12 of the Regulation. **3.336**

Conversely, amicable arrangements resulting in the granting of a licence retroactively, and thus leading to the *release* of the goods, would clearly be contrary to Article 11 of the Regulation, and therefore also, consequentially, to Article 12.[331] Although some authors[332] have suggested that such deals actually meet the objectives set out in Article 17 of the Regulation, in that they 'deprive the persons concerned of any economic gain from the transaction', we share the Commission's viewpoint that such arrangements undermine the customs' actions in the fight against intellectual property infringements, and would moreover, in some cases, give rise to serious concerns relating to consumer protection or public health, for example. In the context of this debate, one should not lose sight of the fact that the main objective of the Regulation and customs is not only to protect the right-holder's private interests, but to engage in a battle against practices which have, in many respects, been unanimously considered as harming the most fundamental interests of society as a whole.[333] Moreover, customs are not in a position to determine whether the conclusion of licence agreements is, in the circumstances, of such nature as to effectively deprive the persons concerned of any financial advantage. Finally, it should be recalled that intellectual property infringements are in most cases caught under criminal law. In some **3.337**

---

[330] Cf para 3.327 above.

[331] J Drew, 'New EU Regulation to Fight Counterfeiting and Piracy', World Trademark Law, 23 September 2003 (www.trademarklawreport.com).

[332] Cf, eg, C De Meyer and P Van Den Broecke (n 53 above), at 102.

[333] Cf Explanatory Memorandum and Proposal (n 2 above), and K Daele (n 6 above), at 220.

circumstances, the authorities with jurisdiction to deal with such offences may even initiate proceedings on their own initiative. The legitimization of such crimes by the right-holder does not seem to be desirable.

3.338 In any event, it is worth pointing out in this respect that the same authors concede that Articles 11 and 12 of the Regulation do exclude such 'pacts'.[334]

3.339 It is precisely so as to frustrate any attempts by the right-holder to 'misuse' the simplified procedure in this way that some national legislators intend to provide that, if it were to be implemented, the simplified procedure set out in Article 11 should be closely monitored (if not entirely conducted) by the customs authorities, and not by the right-holder. This would preclude the latter from entering into negotiations with the parties involved in the traffic to divert the simplified procedure from its actual objective.

3.340 Non-compliance with the rule that the right-holder may use the information provided by the customs authorities only for the purposes referred to in Articles 11 and 13 of the Regulation may result in very severe sanctions—which are imposed at customs' discretion—consisting in the suspension of the application for action for the period of validity remaining before renewal in the Member State in which the events have taken place. In the event of a further breach of this rule, customs may even refuse to renew the application. In the case of a 'Community' application filed under Article 5(4), the customs authorities must also notify the other Member States indicated on the form. In addition, the right-holder may incur civil liability in accordance with the provisions of national law.

3.341 The fact that right-holders may use the contact details of the parties involved in the traffic of the goods for the purposes of a 'simplified procedure' so that the products can be destroyed without needing to institute court proceedings constitutes a major improvement on the former regime. Indeed, under Regulation 3295/94, the use of such information with a view to concluding an amicable agreement was strictly forbidden, *irrespective of the terms and conditions of such arrangements*. This was, at least, the opinion of the Commission, support for which can be found in the decision of the European Court of Justice in the *Adidas* case C-223/98.[335]

3.342 However, there seems to be an inconsistency between the first and the second indents of Article 12. Indeed, whilst the first indent systematically prohibits *any* use of the information referred to in Article 9(3) for purposes other than the

---

[334] C De Meyer and P Van Den Broecke (n 53 above), at 102.

[335] Cf n 297 above. The Court stated, in para 31, that by virtue of Art 6(1), second indent, of Reg 3295/94 (n 15 above), 'the holder of the right may use the information disclosed by the customs office only with a view to asking the competent national authority to take a substantive decision. If that information is used for other purposes, the holder of the right may incur liability under the civil law of the Member State in which the goods in question are to be found, pursuant to Art 9(3) of the Regulation.'

simplified procedure or the institution of legal proceedings, the second indent suggests that such 'other' uses would in fact be banned only in those cases where they are 'not permitted by the national legislation where the situation arose'.

This discrepancy may give rise to debates on these finer points. To take one example, whereas pursuant to Article 12, first indent, of the Regulation, the use of the contact details of the consignee, consignor, declarant or holder of the goods, once provided by customs to the right-holder under Article 9(3), in order to come to an amicable settlement would appear to be forbidden where such an agreement would extend beyond the terms of Article 11, this would actually only be the case if by virtue of this Article 12, second indent, such use would be in breach of the applicable national law.[336]   **3.343**

(3) Conditions governing action by the authorities having jurisdiction to determine whether the goods infringe an intellectual property right

Pursuant to Article 13 of the Regulation,   **3.344**

1. If, within ten working days of receipt of the notification of suspension of release or of detention, the customs office referred to in Article 9(1) has not been notified that proceedings have been initiated to determine whether an intellectual property right has been infringed under national law in accordance with Article 10 or has not received the right-holder's agreement provided for in Article 11(1) where applicable, release of the goods shall be granted, or their detention shall be ended, as appropriate, subject to completion of all customs formalities.

This period may be extended by a maximum of 10 working days in appropriate cases.

2. In the case of perishable goods suspected of infringing an intellectual property right, the period referred to in paragraph 1 shall be three working days. This period may not be extended.

Before analysing the terms and deadlines imposed on the right-holders under Article 13, the content of the requirement laid down in this provision needs to be examined.   **3.345**

Authorities having jurisdiction to determine whether the goods infringe an intellectual property right

Under Article 13(1) of the Regulation, the right-holder willing to secure the detention or suspension of the release of goods suspected of infringing its rights,   **3.346**

---

[336] The question as to whether right-holders may use the information provided to them by customs pursuant to Art 9(3) of the Regulation to commence infringement proceedings against (genuine) parallel imported goods should in principle lead to the same ambiguity: this appears to be barred by Art 12, first indent (which permits use of the information communicated by customs only in proceedings aimed at determining *whether an intellectual property right has been infringed* in the sense of Art 2(1), bearing in mind that the Regulation does not apply to grey goods), whilst the second indent of the same provision suggests that it could possibly be permitted in some Member States.

is required (i) either, in those cases where the simplified procedure set out in Article 11 has been implemented in the Member State in question, to provide customs with the written agreement of the declarant, the holder or the owner of the goods to abandon them for destruction (which agreement shall be presumed to be accepted when the declarant, holder and owner of the goods have not specifically opposed destruction within the prescribed period); (ii) or, in all other cases, to notify the customs authorities that proceedings have been initiated to determine whether an intellectual property right has indeed been infringed under national law. Article 7(1) of the Implementing Regulation[337] provides in this respect that:

> Where Article 11(2) of the basic Regulation [ie Regulation 1383/2003] applies,[338] the right-holder shall notify the customs authority that proceedings have been initiated to determine whether, under national law, an intellectual property right has been infringed [. . .].

3.347 Failure to do so will cause the goods to be released, or their detention ended, subject to completion of all customs formalities.

3.348 This provision is aimed at preventing abuse of the procedure laid down in the Regulation by intellectual property rights owners, and thus 'to secure and uphold the rights of all parties under the Regulation'.[339]

3.349 Article 13(1) defines the nature of the proceedings which are permitted to secure the detention or suspension of release of the goods by reference to their aim, which is to *determine whether an intellectual property right has been infringed under national law*. The purpose of the proceedings will therefore be for the authorities to decide on whether the goods in question do indeed satisfy any of the definitions laid down in Article 2(1) of the Regulation, having regard to the limits set to the scope of application of the Regulation, laid down in Article 3.

3.350 Although it may be illogical—given the clear intention of the Community legislature to *extend* the ambit of the existing legal framework on this subject—to suggest that the scope of Article 13(1) of the new Regulation is narrower than that of Article 7(1) of EC Regulation 3295/94,[340] one may however question whether this is effectively the case in practice.

3.351 Article 7(1) of Regulation 3295/94 required in this respect that the right-holder notify customs that the matter had been 'referred to the authority competent to take a substantive decision on the case', or that the duly empowered authority had taken 'interim measures'. The conditions set out in this provision were alternative, not cumulative.

---

[337] Cf n 27 above.
[338] Ie in all cases where the simplified procedure cannot be (successfully) applied, 'for example where the declarant, holder or owner objects to or contests the destruction of the goods'.
[339] Cf Explanatory Memorandum and Proposal (n 2 above), under Art 13.
[340] N 15 above.

The commencement of proceedings seeking a 'substantive decision on the case' probably required, at least in most Member States, the serving of a writ of summons on a defendant before the court having jurisdiction to rule *on the merits* of the case.[341] The taking of 'interim measures' alluded most likely to the imposition of a seizure over the goods, either at the civil or at the criminal level— thus at the initiative of the courts or a Public Prosecutor.[342] Others advocated a more liberal approach, considering that the filing of a criminal complaint was deemed sufficient, even where it actually did not result in the effective commencement of court proceedings.[343]

3.352

When interpreted broadly, Article 7(1) of Regulation 3295/94 imposed stringent requirements on the right-holders—that is, the commencement of court proceedings on the merits of the case, which proved often costly, time-consuming, and unachievable where no defendant could be identified (unless it was possible to obtain a seizure on the goods either from the civil courts, which was sometimes problematic given the strict 10 working days term provided for in Article 7(1), or from the Public Prosecutors, in respect of whose action right-holders have in principle no power). Consequently, the requirements provided for in Article 7(1) of Regulation 3295/94 were very onerous in some Member States.

3.353

That the Community legislature, in Article 13(1) of Regulation 1383/2003, has dropped the requirement for the right-holders to initiate proceedings to obtain a 'substantive decision on the case'[344] is to be welcomed. This may suggest that the new criterion, that is, referring to the commencement of 'proceedings to determine whether an intellectual property right has been infringed under national law', has to be considered in a broader sense than the first alternative requirement previously laid down in Article 7(1) of Regulation 3295/94, in so far as it imposed the institution of proceedings seeking to obtain a 'substantive decision' on the case.

3.354

It remains to be seen, however, whether the national courts will accept that simple 'interim decisions' fulfil this requirement. Indeed, it may prove to be unfortunate

3.355

---

[341] Art 7(1) of the French version of Reg 3295/94 used in this respect the wording '*sur le fond*'. In this respect, under Belgian law, cf Th Van Innis (n 314 above), at 474–476, para 590.

[342] Ibid.

[343] L Weynants, 'Toepassing van de Piraterijverordening in België op het vlak van merkenrechten', [2000] BMM Bulletin 9; C De Meyer and P Van Den Broecke (n 53 above), at 108. For an example where the release of goods detained by the Belgian customs authorities was ordered owing to a violation of Reg 3295/94, Art 7(1), cf Antwerp Court of First Instance, *Mega Data anors v Belgium and Philips*, Case 03/1866/A, 9 March 2004, [2004] Intellectuele Rechten Droits Intellectuels 183, commented on in O Vrins, n 13 above, at 125.

[344] That the new Regulation got rid of this requirement is also evident from the wording of the title of Chapter III of the Regulation, which reads 'Conditions governing action by the customs authorities and by the authority *competent to decide on the case*' (emphasis added). On the other hand, strangely enough, the concept of 'authority competent to take a substantive decision reappears in Art 9(2) of the Regulation, which could be taken to refer in this respect to Art 13(1).

that Article 13(1) of Regulation 1383/2003 has omitted the second alternative requirement of Article 7(1) of the previous Regulation, which at least had the advantage of unambiguously admitting interim measures. It is not at all clear whether interim injunctions or seizure orders will be deemed to fulfil the criterion retained under the new Regulation, as they may not qualify as proceedings to 'determine whether an intellectual property right has been infringed', unless of course one advocates a broad reading of Article 13(1), and considers that *every* remedy aimed at assisting the right-holder in establishing an infringement—such as Anton Piller Orders in the UK, *saisie-contrefaçon* proceedings in Belgium or in France, etc—or at having a court decide on the existence of a prima facie infringement in anticipation of proceedings on the merits—for example, to obtain an interim injunction—should be deemed to comply with Article 13(1). This view is not entirely shared by some authors, who think that, whereas proceedings in the context of which a prima facie assessment of the existence of an infringement takes place would fulfil the requirement of Article 13(1), the filing of a simple criminal complaint which would not result in the effective commencement of court proceedings within the period referred to in this provision, or a mere seizure order, would not be sufficient under the new Regulation.[345] However, since Article 13(1) no longer requires that the proceedings be brought before the authority competent to take a *substantive* decision, one may query whether the filing of a criminal complaint, followed by the taking of interim measures by a Public Prosecutor, would not be acceptable—even though Public Prosecutors are without jurisdiction to decide on the merits of the case.

3.356 It is clear that the serving of a writ of summons before the courts will in principle fulfil the requirement laid down in Article 13(1).

3.357 In practice, it appears that the customs authorities from the 25 Member States are proving to be very flexible in their interpretation of Article 13(1); in most countries, interlocutory proceedings, interim measures, and proceedings on the merits will all be considered satisfactory by customs in the framework of this provision.

3.358 In any event, the legality of the interpretation made of Article 13(1) of the Regulation will have to be appraised in the light of Article 55 of the TRIPs Agreement, which echoes in substance the wording of Regulation 3295/94.[346] The TRIPs Agreement sets out minimum standards with which the contracting states (including the European Union) must comply. Therefore, it seems that the interpretation of Article 13(1) of the new Regulation may not be less favourable to the right-holders than that of Article 55 of TRIPs, and thus under the provisions of Article 7(1) of Regulation 3295/94.

---

[345] C De Meyer and P Van Den Broecke (n 53 above), at 107–109.   [346] N 15 above.

It is noteworthy that the proceedings referred to in Article 13(1) of Regulation 1383/2003 do not necessarily have to be instituted *by the right-holder* himself. Article 14(2), third indent, makes it clear that they may be initiated 'other than on the initiative of the right-holder', whereas Article 10, second indent, specifies that they may be commenced by customs, for example. Nothing would prevent such proceedings from being initiated by some other public authority, such as a Public Prosecutor. **3.359**

Article 13 proceedings may be directed against, for example, the consignee, consignor, or holder of the goods. Claims against holders in good faith will in principle, however, be limited to obtaining their cooperation in respect of the surrender and destruction of the goods.[347] It would seem unfair to allow the holder of the goods to exercise any right over the retention of the goods in such a case.[348] **3.360**

In deciding whether or not an intellectual property right has been infringed in the context of the proceedings provided for in Article 13(1), reference must be made to the law in force in the Member State within whose territory the goods have been placed in accordance with one of the situations listed in Article 1(1) (which is basically in the Member State where the goods at issue have been intercepted).[349] **3.361**

Where the authority charged with the matter decides that an infringement exists, it will in principle order the destruction of the goods, or at least that they be placed outside commercial channels.[350] Save in those few countries where counterfeiting constitutes a customs offence (such as, for example, in France or the United Kingdom), the customs authorities will generally have no power to decide on the lot of the goods; nor will they be entitled to impose fines on counterfeiters. **3.362**

Term for notifying customs that proceedings have been started

Save for perishable goods, where the period referred to in Article 13(1) is reduced to three working days and may not be extended,[351] the period provided for in this provision is, as a rule, 10 working days. This period may be extended by another maximum 10 working days in 'appropriate cases'. **3.363**

This period starts running from the date of *receipt* of the notification of suspension of release or detention referred to in Article 9(2) of the Regulation. It is therefore essential that the right-holder returns the proof of receipt of this notification **3.364**

---

[347] Cf, eg, under the Benelux trade mark and design legislation, M de Cock Buning (n 55 above), at 241.
[348] Thus decided, eg, by the President of the Rotterdam Regional Court (the Netherlands) on 7 January 2000, [2000] BMM Bulletin 23.
[349] Reg 1383/2003, Art 10, first indent. Cf para 3.21 above in this respect.
[350] Ibid, Art 17.   [351] Ibid, Art 13(2).

to its author (which will be either the relevant customs office, or the customs authority having jurisdiction to process applications for action under the Regulation)[352] immediately on receipt, as explicitly required by the Notes on Completion of the forms annexed to EC Regulation 1891/2004.[353]

3.365 If an application for action is lodged further to an *ex officio* intervention in accordance with Article 4(1) of the Regulation before expiry of the time limit of three working days provided for in this provision, and this application is accepted by the customs department designated for that purpose as stipulated in Article 5(7), the time limits referred to in Article 13 will only start to run from the day after the application has been accepted.[354]

3.366 The law in force in the Member State within whose territory the goods have been found in one of the situations listed in Article 1(1) (which will basically be the Member State in which the goods at issue were intercepted) will apply to the notification which states that the proceedings provided for in Article 13(1) have been initiated, unless such proceedings have been initiated by the customs authorities.[355]

3.367 It is not entirely clear what is meant by 'appropriate cases' under Article 13(1), second indent. Presumably the Community legislature intended to leave it to the customs authorities of the Member States to determine, on a case-by-case basis, whether an extension of the period provided for in Article 13 is at all justified, taking into account the specific circumstances of their intervention. The customs officials probably enjoy this discretionary power. In this context, it is unlikely— but not impossible—that a national court might order the release of goods, or the termination of their detention, solely on the grounds of an 'inappropriate' extension of the term of 10 working days laid down in Article 13. In any event, some may regret the retention of this vague and abstract criterion which is used to decide on whether requests for extension lodged under this provision are valid or not. The Implementing Regulation has solved this problem to a certain extent by stipulating that, if insufficient time remains to initiate the proceedings referred to in Article 13(1) within the time period laid down in that provision and it appears that attempts to apply the simplified procedure of Article 11 are doomed to failure, the situation 'may be deemed' an appropriate case within the meaning of

---

[352] Reg 1383/2003, Art 9(2).   [353] N 27 above. Cf para 3.203 above in this respect.

[354] Reg 1891/2004, Art 5, first indent. Although the English version of this provision states that the time limits referred to in Reg 1383/2003, Art 13, will be counted only from the day after the application is '*received*', it is logical and obvious from the context (as well as from the other versions of the text, which use eg the words '*acceptée*' in French, '*Annhame*' in German, or '*aanvaard*' in Dutch) that it is the date of *acceptance* of the application, and not the date of its receipt, which will have to be taken into account when calculating the period in question.

[355] Reg 1383/2003, Art 10, second indent.

the second subparagraph of that provision.[356] However, if an extension of 10 working days has already been granted under Article 11, no further extension may be granted under Article 13.[357]

The term of three working days that applies to perishable goods, which had **3.368** not been provided for under Regulation 3295/94, was rendered necessary due to the extension of the scope of application of the new Regulation to goods—in particular foodstuffs—suspected of infringing a plant variety right, a geographical indication, a designation of origin, or a geographical designation. The Community legislature was mostly concerned here with diminishing as far as possible any risks the customs may incur in the case of a deterioration of goods where these ultimately proved to be genuine. Again, the question of the consistency of this term with Article 55 of the TRIPs Agreement may raise doubts.[358] However, Article 13(1) may very well be TRIPs-compliant in this respect, if one bears in mind that border measures under TRIPs do not extend to, for example, plant variety rights, geographical indications, and designations of origin. It could nevertheless be doubtful in respect of counterfeit or pirated goods.

The computation of the time periods provided for in Article 13 follows the same **3.369** rules and principles as those which have been described above concerning, for example, Articles 4(1), 5(7), and 11 of the Regulation.[359]

(4) *Release of goods suspected of infringing certain rights on provision of a security*

Pursuant to Article 14 of the Regulation,

1. In the case of goods suspected of infringing design rights, patents, supple- **3.370** mentary protection certificates or plant variety rights, the declarant, owner, importer, holder or consignee of the goods shall be able to obtain the release of the goods or an end to their detention on provision of a security, provided that:
   (a) the customs office or department referred to in Article 9(1) has been notified, in accordance with Article 13(1), that a procedure has been initiated within the period provided for in Article 13(1) to establish whether an intellectual property right has been infringed under national law;
   (b) the authority empowered for this purpose has not authorised precautionary measures before the expiry of the time limit laid down in Article 13(1);
   (c) all customs formalities have been completed.
2. The security provided for in paragraph 1 must be sufficient to protect the interests of the right-holder.

---

[356] Reg 1891/2004 (n 27 above), Art 7(1).
[357] Ibid, Art 7(2).   [358] Compare para 3.358 above in this respect.
[359] Cf eg para 3.202 above.

Payment of the security shall not affect the other legal remedies available to the right-holder.

Where the procedure to determine whether an intellectual property right has been infringed under national law has been initiated other than on the initiative of the holder of a design right, patent, supplementary protection certificate or plant variety right, the security shall be released if the person initiating the said procedure does not exercise his right to institute legal proceedings within 20 working days of the date on which he receives notification of the suspension of release or detention.

Where the second subparagraph of Article 13(1) applies, this period may be extended to a maximum of 30 working days.

3.371 Article 14 thus provides for an option of requesting the release of goods suspected of infringing any of the specific rights listed in the first paragraph, that is, design rights, patents, supplementary protection certificates, or plant variety rights, on certain conditions. The inclusion of plant variety rights in the list set out in Article 14—which mirrors for the rest the list contained in Article 7(2) of the former Regulation (3295/94)[360]—is a direct consequence of the broadening of the scope of application of Regulation 1383/2003 to this type of intellectual property rights.

3.372 The release of goods under Article 14 of the new Regulation may therefore not be sought in the case of goods suspected of infringing a geographical indication, geographical designation or designation of origin, a trade mark, or a copyright or related right, in accordance with Article 2 of the Regulation.

3.373 The exclusion of geographical indications, geographical designations, and designations of origin from the ambit of Article 14—whilst the initial working document submitted by the Commission to right-holders as an initial draft in view of the new Regulation[361] did intend to include them in this provision—can probably be explained on the basis of considerations relating to consumer protection.

3.374 The exclusion of counterfeit goods and of goods suspected of infringing a copyright probably has its source in Article 61 of the TRIPs Agreement. Under this provision, the contracting states—including the 25 EU Member States—are to consider trade mark and copyright infringements a criminal offence, at least where they are committed in bad faith. The Community legislature would, obviously, have been reluctant to permit the release onto the market of goods recognised by both the World Trade Organization and its contracting parties as damaging the 'ordre public'.

3.375 Having said that, it is noteworthy that Article 61 of TRIPs does also allow the WTO members to make infringements of any of the intellectual property rights

---

[360] N 15 above.   [361] N 208 above.

referred to in Article 14 of the Regulation a criminal offence. In order to take account of this, Article 14 stipulates that the release of the goods on provision of a security will not be possible where the duly empowered authority—which will include, for example, Public Prosecutors—has ordered interim measures over the goods. It will therefore be for the national authorities, if satisfied that goods are likely to harm public order, to take the appropriate steps within the period specified in Article 13 so as to prevent them from flowing on to the market.

Next to the absence of interim measures in respect of goods, Article 14 of the Regulation imposes three additional requirements for the parties involved to be able to rely on this provision, namely (i) that customs have been notified, in accordance with Article 13(1), that proceedings have been initiated in due time to establish whether an intellectual property right has been infringed under national law; (ii) that all customs formalities have been completed; and (iii) that a security sufficient to protect the right-holder's interests has been paid. **3.376**

Although the Regulation does not provide for any guidance in this respect, the amount of the security will usually be calculated on the basis of the value of the suspect goods.[362] **3.377**

As to the procedure aimed at determining whether an intellectual property right has been infringed under national law, the last two indents of Article 14(2) provide that, where it has been instituted other than on the initiative of the right-holder (for example, by a Public Prosecutor or the customs authorities), the security shall be released if the person initiating the said procedure does not exercise his right to institute legal proceedings within 20 working days of the date on which he receives notification of the suspension of release or detention of the goods. Where the second subparagraph of Article 13(1) applies,[363] this period may be extended to a maximum of 30 working days. **3.378**

As was already the case under Article 7(2) of Regulation 3295/94,[364] this option is open to the owner, importer, or consignee of the goods. It is also available—and this is new under Regulation 1383/2003—to the declarant or holder of the goods. **3.379**

The exporter of the goods is therefore deprived of this option where he no longer owns them. **3.380**

---

[362] K Daele (n 6 above), at 221. The criterion to be relied on in this context will probably be the *customs* value of the goods, defined in Art 29 of the Community Customs Code (n 42 above) as 'the transaction value, that is, the price actually paid or payable for the goods when sold for export to the customs territory of the Community [. . .]'. It is determined in accordance with the provisions of Chapter 3 of the same Code as well as Arts 141–181bis of Reg 2454/93 (n 43 above). It should be noted that the customs value of the goods may sometimes, depending on the case, prove very high.

[363] This provision allows the initial 10 working days period to be extended by another 10 working days.   [364] N 15 above.

3.381 The second indent of Article 14(2) of the Regulation makes it clear that payment of the security shall not affect the other legal remedies available to the right-holder. This probably means that the successful application of Article 14 at the request of the owner, importer, consignee, declarant, or holder of suspect goods will therefore not prevent the right-holder from hindering the further movement of the goods or their commercialization by relying on the remedies available under national law. Goods in external transit could thus presumably be subject to border measures upon importation into the country of destination, just like goods in 'Community' transit could be blocked by virtue of a court order or a criminal seizure—provided of course the right-holder does not abuse or 'misuse' his intellectual property rights by acting in that way.

3.382 We are not aware of one single case where the option of obtaining the release of suspect goods on provision of a security would ever have been successfully applied under Regulation 3295/94. This is probably due to the burdensome requirements imposed by the Community legislature to that effect, and to the fact that the intermediaries involved in the transport of the goods are generally unwilling to rely on this option to avoid appearing personally interested in the traffic.

3.383 Having regard to the fact that Article 14 of the new Regulation keeps both the spirit and the letter of Article 7(2) of the former Regulation fundamentally intact, there is no reason to expect an increase in the use of this option.

(5) Storage of the goods

3.384 Under Article 15 of the Regulation,

> The conditions of storage of the goods during the period of suspension of release or detention shall be determined by each Member State but shall not give rise to costs for the customs administration.

3.385 This principle, which had already been provided for to a large extent in Article 7(3) of Regulation 3295/94,[365] is crystal-clear and does not require much explanation.

3.386 The conditions for storage of the goods during the period of detention or suspension of release under Article 9 of the Regulation, and pending the simplified procedure set out in Article 11 and/or the proceedings referred to in Article 13(1), are governed by the national legislation of the Member States.

3.387 One should not lose sight of the fact that Article 6(1), second indent, of the Regulation requires right-holders to enclose with their application for action a

---

[365] N 15 above. Reg 1383/2003, Art 15, now further specifies that storage of the goods in application of the procedures laid down in the Regulation 'shall not give rise to costs for the customs administration'.

declaration whereby they agree to bear all costs incurred under the Regulation in keeping goods under customs control pursuant to Article 9 and, where applicable, pending the simplified procedure under Article 11. Although Article 6(1), second indent, does not explicitly refer to the right-holder's liability for the destruction costs—since it relates to the costs arising out of the keeping of the goods 'under customs control', some consider that it also covers such costs.[366] This viewpoint may find some support in Article 11 of the Regulation, which stipulates that the destruction of the goods under the simplified procedure shall be carried out at the right-holder's expense.[367]

However, for reasons which have been explained above concerning the simplified procedure, it is submitted that the right-holder will nevertheless be entitled to claim such costs back from the counterfeiter, either in the framework of the settlement agreement concluded under Article 11, or in the context of court proceedings. This compromise is commonly agreed upon, and effectively applied, in the vast majority of the Member States. Some others prove even more efficient and pragmatic in the fight against counterfeiting and piracy, in that they impute transport, storage and destruction costs directly to the importer.[368] **3.388**

The issue of storage and destruction costs gives rise to fierce discussions, as they inevitably constitute an obstacle to an efficient and cost-effective war against counterfeiting and piracy. The budget of right-holders in tackling intellectual property theft is not bottomless, and their main concern is not to lose money. In fact, this question implies that many right-holders are still reluctant to file applications for action by the customs authorities under the Regulation. **3.389**

In its initial working document,[369] the Taxation and Customs Union Directorate-General of the European Commission, TAXUD, attempted to resolve the problems arising out of storage and destruction of infringing goods. To that effect, associations of right-holders proposed that the costs resulting from such operations be charged directly by customs to the holder or declarant (usually the transporter) of the goods. This system would presumably have ultimately allowed such costs to be passed through to the actual infringer through the effect of successive counter-claims starting from the transporter and progressing through the counterfeiting network. This would also have urged the 'good faith' defendants to actively take part in the proceedings instituted under Article 13 of the Regulation to establish their alleged innocence. Finally, it would have had the obvious advantage of clearing customs warehouses and criminal courts on a regular basis. **3.390**

Unfortunately, this issue is subject to the subsidiarity principle under Community law, and will therefore probably long continue to be left to the Member States. **3.391**

---

[366] C De Meyer and P Van Den Broecke (n 53 above), at 99, n 40. [367] Cf para 3.250 above.
[368] This appears to be the case, eg, in the Czech Republic: cf J Rutter and M Rosinski (n 194 above), at 27. [369] N 208 above, at 5.

Consequently, right-holders would be well-advised to lobby at this level to have the Exchequer of the Member States take care of such costs in the future, as already happens in a few (rare) countries. Debate on this subject is far from closed, certainly where one notes that some States are even no longer willing to bear the costs arising from the storage of suspect goods pending criminal investigations, as normally should be the case.[370]

3.392 In what can presumably be considered a last attempt to solve this problem, the TAXUD Directorate-General of the EC Commission informally agreed, on the occasion of the latest seminar held in Brussels on 14 June 2005, to examine the possibility of amending Article 15 of the Regulation in the near future to permit that goods suspected of infringing an intellectual property right be stored on the premises of the right-holder in question, under customs supervision, subject to the goods being sealed, where appropriate. Right-holders will undoubtedly follow those deliberations more closely than ever.

IV. PROVISIONS APPLICABLE TO GOODS FOUND TO INFRINGE AN INTELLECTUAL PROPERTY RIGHT

3.393 Pursuant to Article 16 of the Regulation,

> Goods found to infringe an intellectual property right at the end of the procedure provided for in Article 9 shall not be:
>
> — allowed to enter into the Community customs territory,
> — released for free circulation,
> — removed from the Community customs territory,
> — exported or re-exported,
> — placed under a suspensive procedure, or
> — placed in a free zone or free warehouse.

3.394 The reference to Article 9 in this provision is hardly coherent. Indeed, Chapter V of the Regulation, which Article 16 is a part of, encompasses the provisions 'applicable to goods found to infringe an intellectual property right'. This is presumably only the case at the end of the proceedings aimed at determining 'whether an intellectual property right has been infringed' referred to in Article 13 of the Regulation, and certainly not at the end of the procedure set out in Article 9. Goods are normally *not* 'found to infringe an intellectual property right' at the end of the procedure referred to in

---

[370] Eg, where interim measures are adopted toward the goods by a Public Prosecutor.

Article 9—except perhaps on a unilateral basis, by the right-holder, but this is not the situation contemplated by Article 16, which would in this case be redundant along with Article 9(1).

Despite its relative haziness, right-holders will undoubtedly welcome this Article 16, **3.395** which explicitly prohibits, amongst other things, the exportation, re-exportation, and removal of infringing goods from the Community customs territory. Although Article 8(1) of Regulation 3295/94,[371] as amended in 1999, probably already provided for such a prohibition,[372] this is not the case in Article 59 of the TRIPs Agreement, which entitles the contracting countries to allow the re-exportation of the goods in an unaltered state, or to subject them to a different customs procedure—albeit only 'in exceptional circumstances' as far as counterfeit goods are concerned. As with many other provisions, Article 16 of the Regulation can therefore be regarded as a 'TRIPs-plus' provision. The practice of certain Public Prosecutors who used to order the re-exportation of infringing goods to their consignor under customs control is hereby unmistakably not only disapproved, but also proscribed.

Pursuant to Article 17 of the Regulation, which essentially mirrors the provisions **3.396** of Article 8(2) and (3) of Regulation 3295/94,[373]

1. Without prejudice to the other legal remedies open to the right-holder, Member States shall adopt the measures necessary to allow the competent authorities:
   (a) in accordance with the relevant provisions of national law, to destroy goods found to infringe an intellectual property right or dispose of them outside commercial channels in such a way as to preclude injury to the right-holder, without compensation of any sort and, unless otherwise specified in national legislation, at no cost to the exchequer;
   (b) to take, in respect of such goods, any other measures effectively depriving the persons concerned of any economic gains from the transaction.

Save in exceptional cases, simply removing the trade marks which have been affixed to counterfeit goods without authorization shall not be regarded as effectively depriving the persons concerned of any economic gains from the transaction.

2. Goods found to infringe an intellectual property right may be forfeited to the exchequer. In that event, paragraph 1(a) shall apply.

The gist of, and rationale for, this Article 17 do not require lengthy explanation. **3.397** This provision obliges Member States to ensure that goods which have been found by a judicial body to infringe an intellectual property right be irrevocably precluded from flooding onto the market. This is in fact a direct and inevitable consequence of the general prohibition set out in Article 16.

---

[371] N 15 above.
[372] Similarly, Reg 3842/86 (n 8 above), Art 7(1)(b), already prevented the authorities of the Member States from allowing re-exportation in an unaltered state, or their placing under a different customs procedure, of products recognized as counterfeit goods.　　　　[373] N 15 above.

3.398 An in-depth analysis of the manner in which Article 17 has been implemented into the national legislations of the Member States shows, however, that there is no unanimity as to how it ought to be interpreted. A particularly delicate issue in this context relates to the approach—relatively well-established in some Member States—which consists of allowing the delivery (free of charge) of the infringing goods to contributory organizations or other humanitarian legal entities. As can be seen from the national chapters of this book, many national legislatures have passed provisions with the effect of rendering such practices admissible. Although, at first sight, such a regime certainly has to be praised from an ethical viewpoint for its altruistic dimension, it should presumably be considered contrary to Article 17 of the Regulation. Indeed, this option had been explicitly envisaged in the working document drafted by the Taxation and Customs Directorate-General of the EC Commission in 2001–2002—mainly in respect of counterfeit textile goods, the destruction of which is often condemned by public opinion—and was eventually rejected due to the fierce opposition of most right-holders.[374] Inconsistency with various national law provisions, problems related to consumer protection, risk to public health, and similar grounds have been put forward by rights owners in opposition to this proposal. In the case of counterfeit goods, an additional argument against it is the significant risk of diluting the trade mark.

3.399 Having said that, it is submitted that an investigation of whether or not the objectives pursued by Article 17 of the Regulation would be fulfilled if the Member States were to allow the use of infringing goods for humanitarian purposes subject to the following cumulative conditions would be worthwhile.

— Such use would exclusively consist of the abandonment of the goods to charities as referred to in Article 900(2) of Regulation 2454/93[375]—and thus carrying on their activities within the Community—which are recognized in that capacity by the authorities of the relevant Member State and have been providing humanitarian aid for at least two years.

— It would be subject to the removal and destruction of any elements of the goods which infringe intellectual property rights, and permanent marking of goods with the word 'HUMANITA' or a similar label.

— It would always be subject to the right-holder's prior consent.

— It would obviously be precluded wherever it would entail any risk to consumers' protection, public health, or other similar public policy considerations.

3.400 However, such a proposal would still be likely to encounter resistance from the holders of certain categories of intellectual property rights, which might be somewhat reticent to have their brand—in the broadest sense—associated with

---

[374] Cf, eg, the INTA Position Paper of 8 April 2002 (n 193 above), at 8. [375] N 43 above.

humanitarian associations, and therefore allegedly with poor-quality product lines. In any event, this approach does not find any support under Regulation 1383/2003, unless perhaps one considers the above-mentioned circumstances to constitute one of the 'exceptional cases' in which the simple removal of the trade marks which have been affixed to counterfeit goods can be regarded as effectively depriving the persons concerned of any economic gains from the transaction;[376] unfortunately, neither the Regulation nor the TRIPs Agreement[377] clarify what amounts to an 'exceptional case'.

Article 17(2) offers Member States the option of forfeiting the goods to the Exchequer. Even in such a case, the goods would have to be destroyed by the State concerned, or to be disposed of outside commercial channels. With the exception of very few Member States where the exercise of this option may lead to the destruction of the goods at those States' expense, in the vast majority of cases, forfeiture to the Exchequer will not allow right-holders to avoid bearing destruction costs. **3.401**

V. PENALTIES

Pursuant to Article 18 of the Regulation, **3.402**

> Each Member State shall introduce penalties to apply in cases of violation of this Regulation. Such penalties must be effective, proportionate and dissuasive.

Although apparently clear at first sight, this provision is ambiguous in several respects. **3.403**

First of all, Article 18 does not refer to any specific provision the breach of which must be sanctioned. Not *all* provisions of the Regulation can be subject to penalties in the case of a violation. **3.404**

Article 1(1) of the Regulation recalls that the Regulation sets out the conditions for action by the customs authorities when goods are suspected of infringing an intellectual property right. This is the object of Articles 4 to 15 of the Regulation, which are mainly directed towards the customs authorities of the Member States, and also, to a certain extent, to right-holders. It appears difficult to sustain that Article 18 would relate to breaches of all or any of these provisions. **3.405**

---

[376] Cf Reg 1383/2003, Art 17(1), last indent.
[377] Art 17(1), last indent, of the Regulation mirrors the last sentence of Art 46 of the TRIPs Agreement: 'In regard to counterfeit trade mark goods, the simple removal of the trade mark unlawfully affixed shall not be sufficient, other than in exceptional cases, to permit release of the goods into the channels of commerce.'

3.406 Article 1(2) points out that the Regulation also adopts the measures to be taken by customs authorities when suspect goods are ultimately found to infringe intellectual property rights. This is the object of Chapter IV (Articles 16 and 17) of the Regulation.

3.407 In theory, it seems logical that Article 18 actually intends to oblige the Member States to provide for penalties in all cases where goods are found, at the end of the proceedings referred to in Article 13 by the authorities having jurisdiction, to infringe an intellectual property right covered by the Regulation. Strictly speaking, however, this situation does not amount to an infringement of any provision of the Regulation, unless of course one considers Article 18 to be directly related to breaches of Article 16.[378] This makes little sense as, at the end of the procedure set out in Article 9, the goods are in principle detained, or their release suspended, by customs, so that the further circulation of the goods at this stage, and thus a violation of Article 16, is unlikely to happen.

3.408 Secondly, it is interesting to note that, to date—as can be seen from the national chapters of this book—the national legislation of numerous Member States fails to prohibit explicitly the placing of goods found to be infringing in some of the situations listed in Article 16. Some discrepancies between the national laws of the Member States exist in this sector, in particular concerning the 'civil and penal status' of infringing goods placed under the external transit procedure. The question therefore arises whether Article 16 is to be conferred a direct effect, which would have as a consequence the prohibition of such acts regardless of the national statutory provisions of the Member States.

3.409 Although a few isolated decisions from the national courts seem to reject such a stance,[379] the European Court of Justice has recently recalled that, consistent with its earlier decision in the *Polo/Lauren*[380] case, Article 16 must be considered directly applicable.

3.410 In Case C-60/02,[381] a reference had been made to the ECJ by the *Landesgericht* (Regional Court) *Eisenstadt* for a preliminary ruling on the interpretation of Articles 2[382] and 11[383] of Regulation 3295/94.[384] That question was raised in a

---

[378] It is worth mentioning that, under Reg 3295/94, Art 11 (which mirrors Art 18 of Reg 1383/2003) explicitly provided that each Member State had to introduce penalties to apply 'in the event of infringements of Art 2 [. . .]'. Art 2 was essentially similar to Art 16 of the current Regulation.

[379] Cf, eg, Antwerp Seizure Judge (*Beslagrechter*), 4 September 2002, [2003] Intellectuele Rechten Droits Intellectuels 144 (146): despite Reg 3295/94, the Benelux Trade Marks Act does not allow for the prevention of the placing of counterfeit goods in transit through the Benelux territory.

[380] N 71 above.   [381] N 78 above.

[382] 'The entry into the Community, release for free circulation, export, re-export, placing under a suspensive procedure or placing in a free zone or free warehouse of goods found to be [infringing] goods [. . .] on completion of the procedure provided for in Art 6 shall be prohibited.'

[383] 'Moreover, each Member State shall introduce penalties to apply in the event of infringements of Art 2. Such penalties shall be effective and proportionate and constitute an effective deterrent.'   [384] N 15 above.

number of judicial investigations conducted at the request of several trade mark holders, including Montres Rolex, Tommy Hilfiger Licensing, La Chemise Lacoste, Guccio Gucci SpA and The GAP, following the confiscation by the Kittsee customs authorities (Austria) of shipments of goods presumed to be counterfeit copies of those companies' trade marks. Paragraph 1 of the Strafgesetzbuch (Austrian Criminal Code) provided that '[p]unishments or preventive measures may be imposed only for offences which are expressly classified by statute as punishable under criminal law and which were punishable at the time of their commission', whilst Article 7(1) of the European Convention for the Protection of Human Rights and Fundamental Freedoms, which has the status of a constitutional law in the Austrian legal system, prohibits the punishment of acts which, at the time of their commission, were not illegal under national or international law. Under the Austrian Trade Marks Law, only the import and export of counterfeit goods, and not their mere transit across national territory, constitutes illegal use of a trade mark. The Austrian judge asked the ECJ to determine whether a provision of national law, which may be interpreted as meaning that the mere transit of goods manufactured/distributed in contravention of provisions of the law on trade marks is not punishable under criminal law, is contrary to Article 2 of Regulation 3295/94, as amended by Regulation 241/1999.[385]

The Court recalled that Regulation 3295/94 applied to external transit, and **3.411** pointed out that the interpretation of the scope of that Regulation (referring to the *Polo/Lauren* case) was not conditional upon the type of national proceedings (civil, criminal, or administrative) in which that interpretation was relied on.[386] It further recalled that it was not for it, but for the national court alone, to rule on the interpretation of national law. If the national court were to find that the relevant provisions of national law do not prohibit and, thus, do not penalize the mere transit of counterfeit goods through the Member State concerned, contrary to the requirements under Articles 2 and 11 of Regulation 3295/94, it would be proper to conclude that those Articles precluded the national provisions in question.[387] Since, according to settled case law, 'national courts are required to interpret their national law within the limits set by Community law, in order to achieve the result intended by the Community rule in question',[388] if such a compatible interpretation was possible, it was for the national court, in order to secure for holders of intellectual property rights protection of those rights against abuses prohibited by Article 2 of Regulation 3295/94, to apply to the transit of counterfeit goods across the national territory the *civil law* remedies applicable under national law to other conduct prohibited by that provision, provided that they were effective and proportionate and constituted an effective deterrent.[389]

---

[385] N 15 and 19 above.   [386] Case C-60/02 (n 78 above), at point 56.
[387] Ibid, point 58.   [388] Ibid, point 59.   [389] Ibid, point 60.

3.412 However, the ECJ conceded that a particular problem arises where the principle of compatible interpretation is applied to criminal matters. As the Court has also held, that principle finds its limits in the general principles of law which form part of the Community legal system and, in particular, in the principles of legal certainty and non-retroactivity. In that regard, the Court has decided on several occasions that a Directive cannot, of itself and independently of a national law adopted by a Member State for its implementation, have the effect of determining or aggravating the liability in criminal law of persons who act in contravention of the provisions of that Directive.[390] The same principles were held to be applicable to Community Regulations as well, even though such instruments by their very nature do not require any national implementing measures.

3.413 The Court concluded that, although Article 11 of Regulation 3295/94 compelled Member States to adopt penalties for infringements of Article 2 of that Regulation, 'if the national court reaches the conclusion that national law does not prohibit the transit of counterfeit goods across Austrian territory, the principle of non-retroactivity of penalties, as enshrined in Article 7 of the European Convention for the Protection of Human Rights and Fundamental Freedoms, which is a general principle of Community law common to the constitutional traditions of the Member States, would prohibit the imposition of criminal penalties for such conduct, even if the national rule were contrary to Community law'.[391] To put it another way: 'The duty to interpret national law so as to be compatible with Community law, in the light of its wording and purpose, in order to attain the aim pursued by the latter, cannot, of itself and independently of a law adopted by a Member State, have the effect of determining or aggravating the liability in criminal law of an entity which has failed to observe the requirements of Regulation No 3295/94.'[392]

3.414 Finally, the nature of the 'penalties' referred to in Article 18 is not specified in the Regulation. Case C-60/02 suggests that such penalties must be both civil[393] *and* criminal[394] in nature in all cases. Similarly, the wording of, for example, the

---

[390] Case C-60/02 (n 78 above), point 61. [391] Ibid, points 62–63.

[392] Ibid, point 64.

[393] The ECJ pointed out that the duty for the national courts to interpret their national legislation within the limits set out under Community law whenever possible, implied that those courts, 'in order to secure for holders of intellectual property rights protection of those rights against abuses prohibited by Art 2 of Reg 3295/94', were to apply 'civil-law remedies' applicable under national law to the conducts prohibited by that provision, 'provided that they were effective and proportionate and constitute an effective deterrent' (Decision in Case C-60/02 (n 78 above), points 59–60).

[394] The ECJ held that provisions of national law which 'do not prohibit and, thus, do not penalize' the mere transit of counterfeit goods through the Member State concerned, would be 'contrary to the requirements under Arts 2 and 11 of Reg 3295/94' (which mirror Arts 16 and 18 of Reg 1383/2003) (ibid, point 58), and that 'Art 11 of Reg 3295/94 empowered the Member States to adopt penalties for infringements of Art 2 of that Regulation' (ibid, point 62). Then the same must be true for Arts 16 and 18 of Reg 1383/2003.

French version of the Regulation refers to '*sanctions*', thus suggesting that the 'penalties' contemplated in this provision may have a civil and/or penal character.

One may reasonably doubt whether Article 18 does indeed oblige Member States **3.415** to provide for criminal sanctions in all cases where infringing goods are placed in any of the situations listed in Article 16 (or 1(1)) of the Regulation. Such an interpretation of Article 18 would be extremely far-reaching, as it would in fact require from the Member States that they make any infringement of an intellectual property right, as defined in Article 2(1), a criminal offence. First, this would lead to significant disparities amongst the Member States, since Article 2(1) refers to a large extent to their respective national legislations when defining intellectual property right infringements. Secondly, such an interpretation would raise concerns as to compliance of the Regulation with the basic principles of Community law, under which criminal liability issues fall within the 'third pillar', and may therefore not be the harmonized object of a Council Regulation. If the interpretation adopted by the ECJ were correct, one would have to conclude that the failure of the Community legislature to approximate the laws of the Member States as to the enforcement of intellectual property rights under criminal law so far through the Enforcement *Directive*, would actually have been 'remedied' through the adoption of no less than a Regulation! Moreover, the authors of this chapter have been made aware of the fact that a new proposal for a Council Directive is currently being discussed, which precisely intends to harmonize the laws of the Member States by providing for criminal liability in the case of intellectual property right infringements.

In any event, it is clear that it is of paramount importance to try to eradicate the **3.416** disparities which exist between the national legislations of the Member States concerning sanctions applying to intellectual property infringements. As long as this has not happened, counterfeiters will continue to bring infringing goods destined for the internal market through the borders of the Member States which prove to be the less stringent in this respect, or to export such goods destined for outside the Community customs territory from those countries.

VI. LIABILITY OF CUSTOMS AUTHORITIES AND RIGHT-HOLDERS

In this part we will distinguish between the liabilities incurred by right-holders **3.417** (section A) and customs authorities (section B) in the case of non-compliance with the Regulation and the sanctions which apply in this context.

A. Liability of right-holders and sanctions

3.418 The sanctions applicable in the case of non-compliance with the provisions of Article 12 of the Regulation (non-permitted use of the information provided by customs to right-holders under Article 9(3)) have been discussed above.[395]

3.419 The conditions under which a violation of this provision may cause a right-holder to incur civil liability are governed by the national law of the Member States.

3.420 More generally, right-holders may also incur liability for any other breach of the Regulation. In this respect Article 19(3) of the Regulation provides that,

> A right-holder's civil liability shall be governed by the law of the Member State in which the goods in question were placed in one of the situations referred to in Article 1(1).

3.421 Caught by this provision are all situations where any person (such as the owner, importer, exporter, consignee, declarant, or holder of the goods) may have incurred a prejudice owing to a right-holder's illegitimate intervention under the Regulation. Article 56 of the TRIPs Agreement provides in this relation that the relevant authorities shall have the authority to order to pay the importer, the consignee, and the owner of the goods, appropriate compensation for any injury caused to them through the wrongful detention of goods.

3.422 The same principle already applied under Article 9(3) of Regulation 3295/94.[396]

B. Liability of customs authorities and sanctions

3.423 Article 19 distinguishes between two situations in which liability of customs may potentially arise, namely cases where an application for action has been lodged by the right-holder and accepted by the competent customs department under Article 5 of the Regulation (Article 19(1) and (2)), and cases where no such application has yet been filed or accepted (Article 19(2)). Whilst Article 19(1) deals with liability of customs towards right-holders, Article 19(2) addresses the issue of liability of customs and other public authorities towards the owner, consignee, consignor, exporter, importer, declarant, or holder of the goods:

> 1. Save as provided by the law of the Member State in which an application is lodged or, in the case of an application under Article 5(4), by the law of the Member State in which goods infringing an intellectual property right are not detected by a customs office, the acceptance of an application shall not entitle the right-holder to compensation in the event that such goods are not detected by a customs office and are released or no action is taken to detain them in accordance with Article 9(1).

---

[395] Cf paras 3.333–3.340 above.   [396] N 15 above.

2. The exercise by a customs office or by another duly empowered authority of the powers conferred on them in order to fight against goods infringing an intellectual property right shall not render them liable towards the persons involved in the situations referred to in Article 1(1) or the persons affected by the measures provided for in Article 4 for damages suffered by them as a result of the authority's intervention, except where provided for by the law of the Member State in which the application is made or, in the case of an application under Article 5(4), by the law of the Member State in which loss or damage is incurred.

Where an application for action has been filed by the right-holder and accepted by **3.424** customs, the rules governing liability of the customs authorities for failure to detect suspect goods or to take action against such goods once they have been detected are governed by the national law of the Member State in which such application was lodged—or, in the case of a 'Community' application for action, by the law of the Member State where the alleged customs' negligence occurred. In the absence of any provision to that effect in the national legislation of the relevant Member State, Article 19(1) of the Regulation excludes any liability in the above-mentioned circumstances. To put it another way, the Regulation does not, of itself, confer any basis for such liability. The same principle already resulted in effect from Article 9(1) of Regulation 3295/94.[397] Overall, it appears that the national laws of the Member States all, or nearly all, contain general tort law provisions which allow the aforesaid situation to be dealt with, and may cause customs to incur liability whenever they commit a negligent act which would not have been perpetrated by a reasonably careful customs official. Article 56 of the TRIPs Agreement, the scope of which is not limited to right-holders' liability, supports such an approach (of para 3.421 above).

Although this hypothesis is not explicitly caught by Article 19 of the Regulation, **3.425** there is no reason to consider that the same principles would not apply in the event that customs were to violate in any way the provisions of the Regulation, even where an application for action has been filed by the right-holder in question (and accepted by customs).[398] Thus, for instance, one cannot see why Member States would be precluded from adopting provisions holding customs liable for a breach of Article 9(3) of the Regulation (failure to communicate information concerning the persons involved in the network, to the right-holder, or to allow the latter to inspect the suspect goods).

---

[397] N 15 above.

[398] This is what results from the provisions of Art 19(2) of the Regulation, to the extent that it states that '[t]he exercise by a customs office or by another duly empowered authority of the powers conferred on them in order to fight against goods infringing an intellectual property right shall not render them liable towards the persons involved in the situations referred to in Art 1(1) [. . .] for damages suffered by them as a result of the authority's intervention, except where provided for by the law of the Member State in which the application is made or, in the case of an application under Art 5(4), by the law of the Member State in which loss or damage is incurred'.

3.426   As a rule, under the Regulation, the customs authorities of the Member States may not be held liable for a *failure* to act *ex officio*. Indeed, Article 4 of the Regulation makes it clear that the *ex officio* procedure is merely optional.

3.427   However, the opposite situation is not true. Article 19(2) of the Regulation allows the Member States to hold customs, or any other 'duly empowered authority', liable in respect of the persons involved in the traffic of goods (that is, their owner, consignee, consignor, importer, exporter, declarant, or holder) for harm which they may have incurred as a consequence of their intervention—whether on an *ex officio* basis, or based on a duly accepted application for action. This may be the case where customs take action *ex officio* in a reckless manner, for example, against goods which cannot reasonably be considered as constituting an infringement, or detain items which manifestly do not meet the description made of the suspect goods in the application filed by the right-holder. Article 58(c) of the TRIPs Agreement provides in this respect that Members shall only exempt both public authorities and officials from liability to appropriate remedial measures in the context of *ex officio* actions, where such actions are taken or intended in good faith.

3.428   Except in cases of obvious reckless intervention, any customs' liability in the circumstances referred to in Article 19(2) of the Regulation will in principle be ruled out whenever the customs action is subsequent to the filing and acceptance of an application for action, as in such a case the right-holder will have submitted a declaration together with the said application to the effect of indemnifying customs for, and holding them harmless against, any liability claim 'in the event that a procedure initiated pursuant to Article 9(1) is discontinued owing to an act or omission by the right-holder or in the event that the goods in question are subsequently found not to infringe an intellectual property right'.[399] Once an application for action has been filed pursuant to Article 9(1) of the Regulation, the assessment of whether the goods infringe any of the right-holder's intellectual property rights depends on the latter and is carried out under its sole responsibility.

3.429   As to the customs authorities' liability in the context of *ex officio* interventions, it is precisely in order to reduce such risks that the detention or suspension of release of suspect goods under Article 4 has been limited to three working days, after which the goods will either be released or their detention confirmed—but then under the right-holder's entire responsibility.

3.430   Where the national legislators fail to provide for any grounds of liability in the above situations, any liability will be excluded except perhaps if one considered Article 58(c) of the TRIPs Agreement to be directly applicable. Even in such case, however, some may argue that this provision is most relevant to this discussion as it concerns these cases where Members 'require' customs to act *ex officio*. This is not the case under Article 4 of the Regulation.

---

[399]   Reg 1383/2003, Art 6(1), first indent. Cf paras 3.247–3.253 above.

Although the scope of Article 19(2) suggests that it extends to all cases where a **3.431** prejudice is caused in the context of the exercise by a public authority 'of the powers conferred on them in order to fight against goods infringing an intellectual property right', regardless of the legal basis on which such powers rely, it is obvious from the circumstances that the ambit of this provision does not extend beyond actions taken by customs *under the Regulation* against goods suspected of infringing an intellectual property right in the situations referred to in that Regulation, and to the measures adopted by the competent authorities once such goods have been found to infringe intellectual property rights—which constitutes the very object of the Regulation.[400]

VII. FINAL PROVISIONS

We have already pointed out above,[401] that the measures necessary for the **3.432** application of Regulation 1383/2003 are laid down in Regulation 1891/2004.[402] Pursuant to Article 20 of Regulation 1383/2003, this Implementing Regulation was adopted in accordance with the so-called 'management procedure' provided for in Council Decision No 1999/468/EC.[403] The Commission was assisted to that effect by the Customs Code Committee[404] set up by Article 248bis of the Community Customs Code.[405]

Although it may seem trivial at first sight, Article 22 of the Regulation provides for **3.433** a tool which is probably one of the cornerstones of the whole system laid down by the Regulation. Under this provision, the Member States must communicate 'all relevant information' on the application of the Regulation to the Commission, which must, in turn, forward it at the end of every year[406] to the other Member States. To that effect, the provisions of Regulation (EC) 515/97 on mutual assistance between the administrative authorities of the Member States and cooperation between the latter and the Commission to ensure the correct application of the law on customs and agricultural matters[407] apply.

---

[400] Ibid, Art 1(1) and (2).   [401] Cf para 3.17 and n 27 above.   [402] N 27 above.

[403] Council Decision No 1999/468/EC of 28 June 1999 laying down the procedures for the exercise of implementing powers conferred on the Commission, [1999] OJ L 184/23 (17.7.1999). Under this procedure, the Commission had to be assisted by a management committee composed of the representatives of the Member States, and chaired by the representative of the Commission. The latter had to submit to the committee a draft of the measures to be taken. The management committee then had to deliver its opinion on the draft by the majority laid down in Art 205(2) of the EC Treaty, in the case of decisions which the Council is required to adopt on a proposal from the Commission. The Commission ultimately had to adopt the measures, which had to apply immediately.

[404] As required by Reg 1383/2003, Art 21(1).   [405] N 42 above.

[406] Reg 1891/2004 (n 27 above), Art 8(5).

[407] Council Reg (EC) No 515/97 of 13 March 1997, [1997] OJ L 82/1 (22.3.1997). This Regulation replaced the homonymous Council Reg (EEC) No 1468/81 of 19 May 1981, [1981] OJ L 144/1 (2.6.1981), to which Reg 3295/94 (n 15 above), Art 14, referred in the same context.

3.434 The details of this information procedure are laid down in the implementing provisions of Regulation 1891/2004.[408] Pursuant to Article 8 of the latter, each Member State must, at the end of each calendar year, send the Commission a list of all the applications for action filed under Articles 5(1) and 5(4) of Regulation 1383/2003, giving the name and details of each applicant, the type of right for which each application was submitted, and a summary description of each product concerned. The applications which have not been granted do not have to be included in that list. Moreover, in the month following the end of each quarter, the Member States must send the Commission a list, by product type, giving detailed information on the cases in which the release of goods has been suspended or goods have been detained. This description must include the name of the right-holder and a description (including the quantity) of the goods and of the intellectual property right in question, the customs status and means of transport of each consignment, whether commercial or passenger traffic was involved and whether the procedure was initiated *ex officio* or as a result of an application for action, and, if known, the origin, provenance, and destination of the merchandise.

3.435 This information is compiled by the Commission in the form of Community-wide and 'country-by-country' statistics, which are largely made publicly available on the website of the Directorate-General Taxation and Customs Union of the Commission.[409] This is of paramount importance, not only to assess the efficiency and shortcomings of the new Regulations, but also to provide guidance to the customs administrations concerning risk analysis.

3.436 Under Article 23 of Regulation 1383/2003, the Commission must report annually to the Council on the application of the Regulation on the basis of the information provided by the Member States pursuant to Article 22. This report may, where appropriate, be accompanied by a proposal to amend the Regulation.[410]

3.437 At the time of writing, the European Commission has announced that an extensive Communication will be issued in October 2005 on the future customs policy of the Commission in the fight against counterfeiting and piracy. According to the first whispers that have so far been reported, this Communication should conclude that it is too early to judge the merits and defects of the new Regulation, and hence too early to consider a new reform of the Community system of border measures.

3.438 Article 24 repeals Regulation 3295/94[411] with effect from 1 July 2004, that is, the date on which Regulation 1383/2003 became applicable.[412] Article 25, first

---

[408] N 27 above. Cf also in this respect Reg 1383/2003, Art 22, fourth indent.

[409] http://europa.eu.int/comm/taxation_customs/customs/customs_controls/counterfeit_piracy/statistics/index_en.htm.

[410] Reg 3295/94 (n 15 above), Art 2, provided that the Commission had to report to the European Parliament and the Council on the operation of the system, 'particularly with regard to the economic and social consequences of counterfeiting', and to propose any amendments or additions required, within a period of two years from the implementation of that Regulation.   [411] N 15 above.

[412] Reg 1383/2003, Art 24, first indent, and Art 25, second indent. References to Reg 3295/94 must, since then, be construed as references to the new Regulation (Ibid, Art 24, second indent).

indent, of the new Regulation distinguishes, for that purpose, between the date on which the Regulation became *applicable*, and the date on which it *entered into force*, that is, 9 August 2003. This gap left the Commission plenty of time to draw up the implementing provisions laid down in Regulation 1891/2004[413] under Articles 21 and 22 of Regulation 1383/2003.

Conclusion

It is clear that the legal framework and procedures provided for in Regulation 1383/2003 consolidate the legal remedies available to owners of intellectual property rights prior to 1 July 2004. **3.439**

This is certainly the case regarding the broadening of the scope of the system of border measures to plant variety rights, geographical indications, and designations of origin; the abolition of fees and securities for the processing of applications for action; the improvement of the quality of information to be provided to customs by the right-holders in their applications for action; the extension of the scope of the *ex officio* procedure to cases of reasonable suspicions of an infringement; and the possibility for customs to provide samples of suspect goods to the right-holders for technical analysis purposes. **3.440**

In the first year of application of the current Regulation, customs authorities of the Member States have set a new record in the number of infringing articles stopped at the external borders of the European Union.[414] Contrary to expectation, the figures reached by the new 10 Member States have reportedly surpassed to a large extent the results of several 'old' Member States. **3.441**

However, in some respects, the success of the new Regulation appears to be less significant than anticipated. This is the case with for example, the simplified procedure of Article 11, which is aimed at allowing the rapid destruction of suspect goods. The implementation of this procedure in the Member States of the Community has remained marginal and this is regrettable, since practice shows that in those Member States where the procedure *has* been implemented, it has been extremely successful and much used. **3.442**

A few other problems, which are, at least in part, beyond the control of the Commission, seriously undermine the excellent job of the EC Member States' customs administrations. These include the issue of storage of infringing goods, the reluctance of the national authorities to prosecute intellectual property infringements and to apply dissuasive, proportionate, and deterrent penalties in this regard, **3.443**

---

[413] N 27 above.
[414] Nearly 104,000,000 infringing products have been subject to border measures in 2004, which represents an increase of 960 per cent compared to 1998.

and, more generally, failure by the national legislatures to ensure their statutory provisions are consistent with those of the Regulation. In an internal market dominated by the principle of free movement of goods, the Member States should not lose sight of the fact that they cannot afford to be the 'weakest link' through which infringing goods will spread across a Community which embraces no less than 25 countries!

3.444 Right-holders must also accept that their approach has not always been in line with the spirit, as well as the words, of the Regulation. Many of them are reticent to take action against small consignments of infringing goods, whilst others are simply guilty of not filing applications for action in all, or at least many, of the Member States. However, it is, to a certain extent, understandable that the right-holders' policy, in this sector as in all others, is partly guided by economic considerations, which constitute precisely the reason for having their intellectual property rights portfolio in the first place. It is submitted that right-holders should pay more attention to the quality of applications for action and the need to provide comprehensive training sessions for customs officials.

3.445 But the market players who are the most to blame in this field are probably the consumers, whose carelessness may be thought of as nothing short of irresponsible, when one considers the types of organizations that benefit from counterfeiting and piracy.

3.446 Besides the system for border measures, broader actions should be taken to increase public awareness on counterfeiting and piracy, and attention should be drawn to their damaging consequences. There should be increased collaboration between the customs administrations of the various Member States as well as between customs officials and other law enforcement bodies—for example, within the framework of the RALPH project, a cooperation platform set up between the Rotterdam, Antwerp, Le Havre, Felixstowe, and Hamburg port authorities. Further work should be carried out on the statistical network put in place by the Commission and other valuable tools of interest to risk analysis, risk management, and selection techniques, etc. This is especially needed in the ever-evolving sector of counterfeiting and piracy, where the patterns of fraud, such as the means of transport, dissimulation techniques, and the like, indicate the increasing expertise of the traffickers and cross-border criminal associations.

3.447 If such steps forward could be taken, and all players involved in the battle accepted the need 'to secure and uphold the rights of all parties', which is one of the main objectives of the new Regulation[415], then the Community system of border measures would probably become the universal remedy in this field. The excellent job carried out by the European customs authorities gives us every confidence in the future success of the enterprise.

---

[415] Explanatory Memorandum and Proposal (n 2 above), concerning Art 13.

PART IV

BORDER MEASURES AT THE NATIONAL LEVEL

4

AUSTRIA

Helmut Sonn

Introduction

Prior to the entry into force of EC Regulation 1383/2003[1] ('the Regulation'), **4.01** Austria had already adopted a law on counterfeiting.[2] It was based on the second generation Regulation 3295/94,[3] as amended in 1999.[4]

This old law already provided for the possibility of filing applications for action **4.02** with customs. They were filed by a right-holder or his representative, and normally covered the whole trade mark and (if applicable) design portfolio valid in Austria of the respective right-holder. Whenever a shipment whose contents were suspected of infringing the rights of the applicant was temporarily detained, customs notified the right-holder or his representative of the detention of the shipment, indicating the provenance of the goods and the sender, the country of destination and the addressee, as well as the party who declared the shipment before customs, provided that all these pieces of information were known to customs.

On the occasion of such a notification, Austrian customs also invited the right- **4.03** holder or his representative to inspect the goods at the relevant customs office, and normally gave the telephone number of the customs official in charge of the matter.

---

[1] Council Reg (EC) 1383/2003 of 22 July 2003 concerning customs action against goods suspected of infringing certain intellectual property rights and the measures to be taken against goods found to have infringed such rights [2003] OJ L 196/7 (2.8.2003).

[2] *Produktpirateriegesetz 2001—PPG 2001* BGBl I 65/2001 (Law on Counterfeiting 2001).

[3] Council Reg (EC) 3295/94 of 22 December 1994 laying down measures to prohibit the release for free circulation, export, re-export or entry for a suspensive procedure of counterfeit and pirated goods [1994] OJ L 341/8 (22.12.1994).

[4] Council Reg (EC) 241/1999 of 25 January 1999 amending Reg (EC) 3295/94 laying down measures to prohibit the release for free circulation, export, re-export or entry for a suspensive procedure of counterfeit and pirated goods [1999] OJ L 27/1 (2.2.1999).

4.04   At the same time, a deadline of 10 working days was set for the right-holder to take action. The addressee or holder of the goods was informed of the situation and given a deadline of five working days to oppose the border measures. In the absence of any opposition the goods were destroyed.

4.05   Thus, the right-holder was given sufficient time to prepare for taking action against the counterfeiter once opposition was filed within the term of five working days. In addition, the right-holder had the right to request an extension of time for another 10 working days, so that, in practice, the total time for the right-holder to file an action was 15 working days.

4.06   In most cases, no opposition was filed, and the goods were destroyed automatically. Hence, in such cases there was no need for the right-holder to go to court. In some cases, where an opposition had been filed, the representative still had sufficient time to try and persuade the holder of the goods to withdraw his opposition and to agree to destruction of the goods. This procedure was mainly successful in cases where the holder of the goods was an Austrian citizen, and could therefore be reached quite easily.

4.07   All in all, the simplified procedure under the former law was considered a success, as it was clearly much cheaper and more effective than court proceedings.

4.08   A new law on counterfeiting,[5] effective as of 1 July 2004, was promulgated further to the adoption of the new Regulation. It is in line with, and has the same scope of application as the latter. Under the new law, the time for additional negotiations and preparation of action left to the right-holders has been reduced in practical terms to 10 working days.

I. SUBJECT MATTER AND SCOPE OF THE NATIONAL LAW APPLYING THE REGULATION

4.09   This Part of the chapter will deal mainly with the customs procedures under which border measures are to be applied (section A) and the definitions of infringing goods under Austrian law (section B).

A. Customs procedure of the goods

4.10   The customs authorities in Austria apply the Regulation to *all* situations and customs procedures defined in Article 1(1) of the Regulation, including (re-)exportation, external transit, and transhipment.

---

[5]   *Produktpirateriegesetz 2004—PPG 2004* BGBl I 56/2004 (Law on Counterfeiting 2004).

Most of the customs actions, however, take place in procedures with customs **4.11** declarations.[6] Some counterfeit goods are also detected in the course of criminal proceedings (smuggling).

B. Definition of infringing goods

The majority of interventions by Austrian customs in 2004 had to do with clothing, **4.12** whilst watches and jewellery ranked second according to official statistics.[7] From this it can be gathered that a vast majority of customs interventions (in fact about 95 per cent) relate to goods suspected of infringing trade mark rights.

Only a small percentage of interventions in 2004 related to copyright infringe- **4.13** ments. Copyright infringement will normally involve DVDs, CDs, and the like. Official statistics show 54 such cases in Austria in 2004 compared to a total of approximately 2,400 interventions in that year.

While patents do appear in applications with customs, they play no role whatsoever **4.14** in actual cases.

(1) Counterfeit goods

The Austrian Trade Mark Law[8] ('the Trade Mark Law') mirrors the provisions of **4.15** the Harmonization Directive on trade marks.[9]

Under section 10 of the Trade Mark Law, the owner of a trade mark is entitled to **4.16** prevent a third party from using an identical sign in relation to goods or services that are identical to those for which the trade mark is registered. Moreover, a third party may not use an identical or similar sign for identical or similar goods or services, if this could lead to a risk of confusion on the part of the public, including the risk of association between the sign and the trade mark.

Thus, basically, all goods that bear the trade mark of the right-holder, or a sign **4.17** similar thereto, and are of the same or a similar type as the goods listed in the specification of the relevant trade mark registration can be seen as infringing the trade mark-holder's rights under Austrian law.

---

[6] Bundesministerium für Finanzen, 'Produktpiraterie-Aufgriffe der Österreichischen Zollverwaltung 2004', www.bmf.gv.at/zoll/wirtschaft1446/produktpiraterie2871/produktpiraterie-statistik2004.pdf.

[7] Bundesministerium für Finanzen, 'Produktpiraterie-Aufgriffe der Österreichischen Zollverwaltung 2004', www.bmf.gv.at/zoll/wirtschaft1446/produktpiraterie2871/produktpiraterie-statistik2004.pdf.

[8] *Markenschutzgesetz* 1970 *idF der Markenrechtsnov.* 1999 BGBl I 111/1999 (Trade Mark Law) and *Patentrechts- und Gebührennovelle* 2004 BGBl I 149/2004 (Patent and Fee Law Amendment).

[9] First Directive 89/104/EEC of the Council of 21 December 1988 to approximate the laws of the member states relating to trade marks [1989] OJ L 40/1 (11.2.1989).

4.18 Section 10 of the Trade Mark Law also provides that the owner of a registered trade mark may prohibit third parties from using, in the course of trade and without the owner's consent, a sign identical, or similar, to the trade mark in relation to goods and services not similar to those for which the trade mark is registered, provided that the trade mark has a reputation in Austria and that use of the sign takes unfair advantage of, or is detrimental to, the distinctive character or the reputation of the trade mark.

4.19 Section 10a of the Trade Mark Law lists a few examples for what is understood by use of a sign, namely:

- affixing it to goods, or to the packaging thereof;
- offering the goods under that sign, placing them on the market, or holding them for these purposes;
- importing or exporting the goods under that sign;
- using the sign on business papers, in announcements, or in advertising.

4.20 It will be noted from the above that the scope of trade mark protection under Austrian national law is broader than the definition of counterfeit goods under Article 2(1)(a)(i) of the Regulation. Hence, in accordance with the latter provision, Austrian customs normally take action only in those cases where a sign used without the right-holder's authorization is identical to the trade mark of the right-holder, or cannot be distinguished therefrom in its essential aspects. Customs authorities interpret this latter provision rather broadly. So, for example, they may detain a shipment of goods with the inscription 'John Brown' on suspicion of an infringement of the trade mark 'Brown'. Similarly, Adidas will be notified of any shipment containing relevant goods on which any stripe-designs have been affixed, irrespective of the number of the stripes.

4.21 As to the interpretation of the condition in Article 2(1)(a)(i) of the Regulation that the trade mark on the basis of which border measures are taken must be 'validly registered in respect of the same type of goods', there have so far not been any difficulties. Normally, the goods held by customs are encompassed by the specifications of goods of the trade marks of the respective right-holders.

4.22 As pointed out above, a trade mark with a reputation, that is, a trade mark which is well known at least in Austria, enjoys broader protection, as its protection encompasses not only the goods for which the trade mark is registered, but dissimilar goods as well. However, for the purpose of Article 2(1)(a)(i) of the Regulation, dissimilar goods would normally not be considered as being of the 'same type' as those in respect of which the trade mark has been registered.

4.23 Austrian customs will take action in such circumstances only where they are in a position to determine readily whether the trade mark on the basis of which an intervention is envisaged enjoys a reputation. If a trade mark owner wants to make customs aware of the fame of his mark so as to extend the range of goods to be detained, he would not only have to stress in the application, that his trade mark is 'well known', but also to substantiate this fact on the basis of court decisions and other proof to that effect. The application should define which goods the owner still considers to be of 'the same type'.

Apart from those more or less hypothetical possibilities, conversations with   **4.24** Austrian customs officials indicate that they might intervene in cases of well-known marks on a broad interpretation of 'the same type of goods'. However, in a decision of the Austrian Supreme Court[10] regarding an action of Hugo Boss AG on the basis of their famous mark 'BOSS' registered for clothing against Slovenian cigarettes bearing an identical sign which had not been detained by the customs officials, it was held that the former Regulation—Regulation 3295/94, as amended[11]—would not be directly applicable in such circumstances, since the goods could not be considered 'counterfeit' or 'pirated' goods within the meaning of Article 1 of the Regulation. This case would probably not be decided otherwise under the new Regulation, which leaves the definitions of 'counterfeit goods' and 'pirated goods' unchanged. Having said that, if Austrian customs were to detain goods in such situations, the right-holder would readily be granted a rightful title for destruction by the courts under trade mark law (notwithstanding the provisions of the Regulation) as the Dutch court had done in the case underlying ECJ C-405/03.[12]

One of the interesting conclusions of the *BOSS* decision is that the importation of   **4.25** goods infringing trade mark rights from a non-EC Member State into an Austrian free warehouse and the storing of these goods for the purpose of their later export into other non-EC Member States is to be considered an infringement of trade mark rights in this country. However, it remains to be seen whether this is correct under Community Law.[13]

So far, there has never been a case where border measures have been taken in   **4.26** Austria on the basis of mere trade mark *applications*, and it is doubted that this could be the case in the future. There is no legal basis for such a measure. The Regulation speaks of 'validly registered' trade marks. Moreover, the right to an injunction and seizure is conferred by *registered* trade marks only, which likewise holds for national and Community trade marks.[14]

---

[10] Case 4 Ob 54/01x *Oberster Gerichtshof (OGH)* (Supreme Court) of 16 October 2001 ('*Boss-Zigaretten II*'), ÖBl 147/2002.

[11] Council Reg (EC) 3295/94 of 22 December 1994 laying down measures to prohibit the release for free circulation, export, re-export or entry for a suspensive procedure of counterfeit and pirated goods [1994] OJ L 341/8 (22.12.1994), Council Reg (EC) 241/1999 of 25 January 1999 amending Reg (EC) 3295/94 laying down measures to prohibit the release for free circulation, export, re-export or entry for a suspensive procedure of counterfeit and pirated goods [1999] OJ L 27/1 (2.2.1999).

[12] AG Thomas G Jacob's opinion of 26 May 2005 in ECJ C-405/03.   [13] Ibid.

[14] Cf also on this point Council Reg (EC) 40/94 of 20 December 1993 on the Community Trade Mark [1994] OJ L 11/1 (14.1.1994), Art 9(3).

4.27 The Austrian customs authorities also take measures against trade mark symbols and packaging materials bearing the trade mark of counterfeit goods, on the same conditions as for counterfeit goods themselves, even when delivered separately.[15] So, customs actions have been reported in Austria against, for example, cardboards reproducing a counterfeit trade mark, presented separately, which were presumably intended to be put together with the respective goods in a (transparent) package.

(2) Pirated goods

4.28 Both the Austrian Copyright Law[16] and the Austrian Design Law[17] are in line with Community law.

4.29 The owner of a copyright has the exclusive right to utilize his 'work' in the ways reserved to him under the law (that is, to commercially use the 'work'—cf in particular section 14 and the following sections of the Austrian Copyright Law, which include the right of reproduction and the right to make the work available to the public). The subject matter of such rights has to be shown by samples or by any other means, since it is not defined in a register. The existence of a copyright for the work has to be assumed by the customs office upon an allegation of the right-holder. The same holds for 'related rights', which are also named 'neighbouring rights'.

4.30 Section 4 of the Austrian Design Law provides that the owner of a registered design has the exclusive right to use the protected design and to prevent third parties from using it without his consent. 'Use' in this sense includes in particular the production, offering, placing on the market, importing, exporting, or use of a product incorporating the design in an identical or similar way, and the possession of such a product for these purposes.

4.31 Customs officials in Austria are very cooperative. Accordingly, they frequently call the right-holder concerned, or his representative, to find out whether they should suspend release of certain goods or not. They leave it to them to define whether the goods 'are or contain copies' of the work in respect of which they hold the copyright, related rights, or design rights, within the meaning of Article 2(1)(b) of the Regulation.

4.32 As to design rights, a product is clearly seen as infringing such rights if its outer appearance resembles the outer appearance protected by a registered or unregistered

---

[15] Cf Reg 1383/2003, Art 2(1)(a)(ii)–(iii).
[16] *Bundesgesetz über das Urheberrecht an Werken der Literatur und der Kunst und über verwandte Schutzrechte (Urheberrechtsgesetz) idF der Urheberrechtsgesetz-Nov 2003* BGBl 111/1936 idF BGBl I 32/2003 (Copyright Law).
[17] *Bundesgesetz vom 7. Juni 1990 über den Schutz von Mustern (Musterschutzgesetz—MuSchG) idF der Musterschutzgesetz-Nov 2003* BGBl 497/1990 idF BGBl I 81/2003 and BGBl I 149/2004 (Design Law).

design. This is not so easy with copyright cases, especially where the protection relates to invisible contents (music, software, etc). In such cases, the customs officials have to rely on inscriptions on the packaging when making the risk analysis, for example, to identify the nature of the goods.

(3) *Goods infringing other intellectual property rights*

Goods infringing a patent or a supplementary protection certificate

The Austrian Patent Law,[18] in particular sections 22 and 22a, defines the effect of a patent and the scope of its protection,[19] covering both direct and contributory infringements, literal infringements (that is, infringements by literal reproduction of the patent claims) and infringement under the doctrine of equivalents, as is the case in most other European countries. **4.33**

Under the Austrian Patent Law, a patent entitles the patentee to prevent others from producing the subject matter of the invention, placing it on the market, offering it for sale, using it, or importing or holding it for the above-mentioned purposes. In addition, the protection of process patents also covers any products directly obtained by the patented process. **4.34**

The Austrian Law on Supplementary Protection Certificates ('SPCs')[20] merely supplements Community law.[21] Section 1 of this law provides that SPCs (which extend the term of protection of patents valid in Austria in respect of pharmaceuticals or plant protection products already on the market) are granted by the Austrian Patent Office in accordance with the respective Regulations of the European Community. The exclusive rights arising from such certificates are the same as for patents, except that it is no longer the entire scope of the patent claims that is protected, but a specific product on the market falling under it. **4.35**

The Austrian customs authorities will detain, or suspend the release of, goods under the Regulation by reference to Article 2(1)(c)(i) or (ii) if there is at least some suspicion that a patent or an SPC may be infringed under the Austrian or Community law. However, this would only be done on the basis of an existing application with customs containing specific information as to how to detect such infringements. No search will be carried out *ex officio* for patent or SPC infringements. **4.36**

---

[18] *Patentgesetz—PatG 1970* BGBl 259/1970—WV—*Patenrechts-und Gebührennovelle* 2004, BGBl I 149/2004 (Patent Law).

[19] Cf also European Patent Convention, Art 69.

[20] *Bundesgesetz betreffend ergänzende Schutzzertifikate (Schutzzertifikatsgesetz 1996)* BGBl I 11/1997 idF BGBl I 143/2001 and also BGBl I 149/2004 (Law on Supplementary Protection Certificates).

[21] Cf Council Reg (EEC) 1768/92 of 18 June 1992 concerning the creation of a supplementary protection certificate for medicinal products [1992] OJ L 182/1 (2.7.1992), and Reg (EC) 1610/96 of the European Parliament and of the Council of 23 July 1996 concerning the creation of a supplementary protection certificate for plant protection products [1996] OJ L 198/30 (8.8.1996).

4.37 Therefore, an application for action by the Austrian customs authorities based on a patent or an SPC should preferably indicate the source of the genuine product and its price, and in any case all remarkable outer features of the patented product, like colour or inscriptions, or known outside characteristics of the infringing goods, so as to make it easier for customs officials to judge whether or not goods they come across are authentic.

4.38 Moreover, features of a patented product which can be readily examined should be specified in the application. Thus, for example, if a patent claims protection for a mechanical rubber stamp, the printing plate of which can be locked at a certain level to facilitate exchange of the ink pad, this should be specified in the technical analysis of the goods, so that a customs official can try out the stamp he has before him.

4.39 In the case of chemicals, the patented ingredient or combination of ingredients—as evident from the leaflet and/or packaging—should be indicated.

4.40 Also, in the case of SPCs, the description of the protected subject matter should be such that the specific features can be recognized from outside, especially from documentation sent with the pharmaceuticals or the plant protection products.

Goods infringing a national plant variety right

4.41 The Austrian Plant Variety Law[22] has been approximated to the respective Council Regulation (EC) 2100/94,[23] and is equally consistent with the UPOV[24] Convention.[25]

4.42 Under section 4 of the Plant Variety Law the following acts require the consent of the owner of the protected variety with regard to reproduction material: production and reproduction, processing for the purposes of reproduction, offering for sale, sale, or other placing on the market, export, import, and storing for these purposes.

4.43 No case has been reported to date in Austria concerning the taking of border measures under the Regulation against goods suspected of infringing a national or Community plant variety right.

4.44 To be effective, an application based on a plant variety right will have to include a description of the right as registered. Any plant protected by a plant variety right

---

[22] *Bundesgesetz über den Schutz von Pflanzensorten (Sortenschutzgesetz 2001)* BGBl I 109/2001 and 110/2002 (Plant Variety Law).

[23] Council Reg (EC) 2100/94 on Community plant variety rights [1994] OJ L 227/1 (1.9.1994).

[24] Austria is a member of UPOV, the Union for the Protection of New Varieties of Plants.

[25] International Convention for the Protection of New Varieties of Plants (UPOV Convention) of 2 December 1961, as revised at Geneva on 10 November 1972, on 23 October 1978, and on 19 March 1991. This Convention entered into force in Austria on 1 July 2004, BGBl III 133/2004.

is given a (protected) name. A counterfeiter will usually use that name in the documentation, as he would otherwise encounter difficulties in selling the plants.

Goods infringing a national or Community designation of origin or a geographical indication

As to goods infringing a national designation of origin or a geographical indica-tion, the pertinent EC Regulations[26] may be resorted to for further information. In Austria, there is no specific national law on designations of origin, apart from the provisions in the Trade Mark Law[27] regulating the handling of applications and oppositions referred to in the Community Regulations. However, there are some bilateral treaties protecting foreign indications of origin in Austria.[28]   **4.45**

As to Austrian case law, reference should be made to a Supreme Court decision[29] according to which use of (trade mark protected) 'CAMBOZOLA' may be   **4.46**

---

[26] Council Reg (EEC) 2081/92 of 14 July 1992 on the protection of geographical indications and designations of origin for agricultural products and foodstuffs [1992] OJ L 208/1 (24.7.1992), as amended. Cf also Council Reg (EC) 1493/1999 of 17 June 1999 on the common organization of the market in wine [1999] OJ L 179/1 (14.7.1999), as amended.

[27] *Markenschutzgesetz* 1970 *idF der Markenrechtsnov.* 1999 BGBl I 111/1999 (Trade Mark Law).

[28] Treaty with the Czech Republic: *Vertrag zwischen der Republik Österreich und der Tschechoslowakischen Sozialistischen Republik über den Schutz von Herkunftsangaben, Ursprungsbezeichnungen und sonstigen auf die Herkunft hinweisenden Benennungen land-wirtschaftlicher und gewerblicher Erzeugnisse* BGBl. Nr. 1981/75 idF BGBl. III Nr. 1997/123 and *Übereinkommen zur Durchführung des Vertrages zwischen der Republik Österreich und der Tschechischen Sozialistischen Republik über den Schutz von Herkunftsangaben, Ursprungsbezeichnungen und sonstigen auf die Herkunft hinweisenden Bezeichnungen land-wirtschaftlicher und gewerblicher Erzeugnisse,* BGBl. 1981/76; Treaty with Spain: *Abkommen zwischen der Republik Österreich und dem spanischen Staat über den Schutz von Herkunftsangaben, Ursprungsbezeichnungen und Benennungen landwirtschaftlicher und gewerblicher Erzeugnisse,* BGBl. Nr. 1977/593 and *Protokoll zur Durchführung des Abkommens vom 3. Mai 1976 zwischen der Republik Österreich und dem spanischen Staat über den Schutz von Herkunftsangaben und Benennungen landwirtschaftlicher und gewerblicher Erzeugnisse, BGBl. Nr. 1977/594*; Treaty with France: *Abkommen zwischen der Republik Österreich und der Französischen Republik über den Schutz von Herkunftsangaben, Ursprungsbezeichnungen und Benennungen landwirtschaftlicher und gewerblicher Erzeugnisse,* BGBl. Nr. 1976/196 and *Übereinkommen zwischen der österreichischen Bundesregierung und der französischen Republik zur Durchführung des Abkommens vom 10. Mai 1974 zwischen der Republik Österreich und der französischen Republik über den Schutz von Herkunftsangaben, Ursprungsbezeichnungen und Benennungen landwirtschaftlicher und gewerblicher Erzeugnisse,* BGBl. Nr. 1976/240; Treaty with Greece: *Abkommen zwischen der Republik Österreich und dem Königreich Griechenland über den Schutz von Herkunftsangaben, Ursprungsbezeichnungen und Benennungen von Erzeugnissen der Landwirtschaft und der gewerblichen Wirtschaft,* BGBl. Nr. 1972/378 and *Übereinkommen zur Durchführung des Abkommens vom 5. Juni 1970 zwischen der Republik Österreich und dem Königreich Griechenland über den Schutz von Herkunftsangaben, Ursprungsbezeichnungen und Benennungen von Erzeugnissen der Landwirtschaft und der gewerblichen Wirtschaft,* BGBl. 1972/379; Treaty with Italy: *Abkommen zwischen der österreichischen Bundesregierung und der italienischen Regierung über geographische Herkunftsbezeichnungen und Benennungen bestimmter Erzeugnisse,* BGBl. Nr. 1954/235 and *Zusatzprotokoll zum österreichisch-italienischen Abkommen über geographische Herkunftsbezeichnungen und Benennungen bestimmter Erzeugnisse vom 1. Februar 1952,* BGBl. Nr. 1972/348.

[29] Case 4 Ob 25/01g Supreme Court (*OGH*) 10 July 2001, ÖBl 2002/305, following prelim-inary ruling proceedings before the European Court of Justice in Case C-87/97, *Consorzio per la*

continued in spite of the protected designation of origin 'GORGONZOLA', since the trade mark was older than the EU registration of GORGONZOLA and had been registered in good faith.

4.47 Another example is the recent ECJ case C-216/01[30] on the term BUD for beer, based on the bilateral treaty between Austria and the Czech Republic.

4.48 Even if GORGONZOLA had been included in an application for customs action, no such action would have been taken against the importation of CAMBOZOLA, since the two designations can be readily distinguished.

4.49 Contrary to the above, the protected designation BUD and the name of the imported beer 'American Bud' cannot be distinguished 'in their essential aspects' (the word BUD) so that customs would have to detain 'American Bud' if the geographical designation BUD protected by the bilateral treaty were made the basis for an application under Article 2(1)(c)(iv) of the Regulation.

4.50 A designation of origin or geographical indication, such as 'Ungarische Salami' or 'Budweiser Bier', will usually be apparent on the goods, so that the identification by customs of goods infringing such rights should in principle not give rise to any difficulties.

(4) Moulds and matrices

4.51 To date, there have been no customs interventions under the Regulation in relation to moulds or matrices which are specifically designed or adapted for the manufacture of goods infringing an intellectual property right. Austrian national law, however, provides claims for destruction of such moulds and matrices in all intellectual property laws,[31] so that devices of this type should be detained by Austrian customs authorities when they realize the connection with specific intellectual property rights.

C. Goods excluded by the Regulation

(1) Parallel imported goods

4.52 In principle, in accordance with Article 3(1) of the Regulation, border measures are not taken against goods bearing a trade mark with the right-holder's consent,

---

Tutela del Formaggio Gorgonzola v Käserei Champignon Hofmeister GmbH & Co., KG. [1999] ECR I-1301.

[30] ECJ, Case C-216/01, *Budijovicky Budvar v Rudolf Ammersin GmbH*, unreported, available on www.curia.eu.int.

[31] *Patentgesetz* s 148 (Patent Law), *Schutzzertifikatsgesetz* (Law on Supplementary Protection Certificates) with reference to *Patentgesetz* (Patent Law) in s 7, *Markenschutzgesetz* (Trade Mark Law)

nor against goods bearing a protected designation of origin or a protected geographical indication, or which are protected by a patent, an SPC, a copyright or related right, a design right, or a plant variety right, and which have been manufactured with the consent of the right-holder but are placed in one of the situations referred to in Article 1(1) of the Regulation without the latter's consent. Austrian customs will take action only where they cannot be certain as to whether the goods are genuine. In such a case—which is frequent—they will inform the right-holder and request the latter to confirm whether or not the goods are authentic, that is, they have been placed on the market with his consent.

As already explained at the end of paragraph 4.24 above, once customs detain **4.53** goods, rightfully or not, the right-holder can either agree to their release if he does not think that his rights are infringed or get a court order for further detention by the court (and later destruction) if the goods are infringing.[32] Where the Regulation does not apply, customs cannot take any further action according to the Regulation but follow normal routine and have to obey a court order. As long as customs are not aware that the goods are such as fall under Article 3 of the Regulation, the Regulation is applicable (note the wording 'goods are *suspected* of infringing' in Article 1), so that the information of the right-holder or an extension of time for his statement does not contravene any of the normal obligations like confidentiality.

(2) *Goods which have been manufactured under conditions other than those which have been agreed with the right-holder*

Where the Austrian customs authorities are aware that goods they have come **4.54** across do not comply with the terms of an agreement concluded with the right-holder, they cannot inform the latter since the Regulation is not applicable. The authorities could become so aware as the result of a licence agreement on file with customs or entered in the official register of the right.

In the vast majority of cases, customs will not be in a position to determine **4.55** whether goods violate the terms of a licence, as licence agreements are seldom filed with customs. As long as customs authorities suspect the goods to be infringing (cf Article 1 of the Regulation), the Regulation is to be applied. In principle, doubts can only arise where the goods bear the indication 'produced under licence of XX' where XX is the right-holder. Only such a case could lead to the suspicion that the goods are subject to Article 3; then customs must be more careful. However, in order not to allow pirates an easy way of cheating customs by just affixing a licence

---

s 52, *Musterschutzgesetz* (Design Law) with reference to *Patentgesetz* (Patent Law) in s 34, *Urheberrechtsgesetz* (Copyright Law) s 82.

[32] AG Thomas G Jacob's opinion of 26 May 2005 in ECJ C-405/03.

statement to their imitations, customs would eventually, after consultation of the Patent Office Register, still have to apply the Regulation.

(3) Goods contained in travellers' personal baggage

4.56 Travellers' personal baggage is controlled by Austrian customs sporadically. However, customs are not entitled to take action against goods which infringe an intellectual property right contained in travellers' baggage, provided those goods are of a non-commercial nature, within the limits of the duty-free allowance and there are no material indications to suggest they are part of commercial traffic.[33]

4.57 In order to determine whether the goods are within the limits of the duty-free allowance (currently EUR 175), customs will request a copy of the purchase invoices relating to the goods in question. Where such invoices are not available, the value of the goods will have to be estimated 'in equity'.

4.58 The 'non-commercial nature' of the goods is appraised on the basis of factual indications. The assessment will depend on the nature of the goods. If a traveller carries, for example, 10 identical T-shirts, this would be considered a 'material indication of the existence of a commercial traffic'. However, if a traveller holds 10 different T-shirts in his personal baggage, these will be considered his private possessions, and customs will refrain from any action. Note the difference with, for example, watches or sunglasses, as 10 different items of the same kind may also be indicative of a commercial nature. In the case of new complete men's suits, three of these (being similar) have recently been detained presumably as being part of a commercial traffic.

II. APPLICATION FOR ACTION BY THE CUSTOMS AUTHORITIES

4.59 In this Part, the practice of applications for action by the customs authorities under the Regulation and the new Austrian law (*Produktpirateriegesetz* 2004[34]) will be reviewed.

A. Measures prior to an application for action by the customs authorities ('*ex officio* measures')

4.60 Austrian customs do apply *ex officio* measures under Article 4 of the Regulation. At present, approximately 150 applications for action are pending

---

[33] Reg 1383/2003, Art 3(2).   [34] Cf para 4.08 above.

with Austrian customs. Of these, approximately 90 have come about as a consequence of *ex officio* measures.

As to the interpretation of the notion of 'sufficient grounds for suspecting that the goods infringe an intellectual property right' referred to in Article 4 of the Regulation, it will largely depend upon the condition of the goods, the packaging, the documentation, and the trade marks themselves. Sometimes the goods and/or the packaging look extremely cheap and shoddy compared to the genuine goods of the same brand. Moreover, if one shipment contains goods of different brands of the same kind, such goods will be considered suspect as well. Customs are also aware of known importers of infringing products. **4.61**

In the case of *ex officio* customs interventions only minimum information is supplied to the right-holder, that is, the actual or supposed number of items and their nature. Yet once an application has been filed further to an *ex officio* action, the same information can be requested as in the case of an application already on file.[35] Similarly, without a formal application no samples or digital pictures will be sent or handed over to the right-holder, and the right-holder is not allowed to examine the goods. **4.62**

The deadline of three working days provided for in Article 4 of the Regulation for filing an application for action with customs is strictly applied. Nevertheless, Austrian customs have so far accepted minimum requirement applications with late filing of additional details (for example, extension of the application to additional trade marks or designs of the right-holder, and other information according to Articles 5 and 6 of the Regulation). **4.63**

Whenever a shipment of suspected products is detained, or its release suspended *ex officio* by Austrian customs, the officers get in touch with the Austrian Patent Office to identify the holder of the relevant intellectual property right, or the latter's representative. Where this is the case, they liaise with this contact person immediately so as to enable the right-holder—if appropriate—to file an application with customs under Article 5 of the Regulation in due course. **4.64**

B. The lodging and processing of applications for customs action

(1) *Persons entitled to file an application for action*

Definition of 'right-holders' under the Regulation

Austrian customs are quite liberal in the interpretation of the concept of 'right-holder' (as is the Regulation itself) defining who is entitled to file an **4.65**

---

[35] Cf Reg 1383/2003, Art 9(2) and (3), and paras 4.100–4.101 below.

application for action by virtue of the Regulation. Pursuant to Article 2(2) of the Regulation, this notion includes, in the first place, the owners of any of the intellectual property rights referred to in Article 2(1). It also includes 'any other person authorised to use' such rights, and representatives of the right-holders and 'authorised users'.

4.66 In principle, the application for customs action will be lodged by the holder of the right in question. There are also cases where both the right-holder and the latter's exclusive licensee file an application for action. In such a case, a copy of the licence contract is normally enclosed with the application. In theory also non-exclusive licensees, distributors, commercial agents, etc should be authorized to file an application with Austrian customs as 'authorised users', but up to now no such application has become known. The problem with these parties is that they do not normally enjoy a right to sue for infringement, hence they could not take the required action. So, the liberal concept of the Regulation 'any other person authorised to use any of the intellectual property rights mentioned' will not often be used.

4.67 The authorization to use the right on which the application is based need not be registered with the relevant industrial property office, although this may in some cases be a requirement under national or Community law to secure enforceability of, for example, a licence towards third parties. As a practical matter, there are cases where an application for action with customs was filed both in the name of the right-holder and in the name of the licensee. Customs authorities did not object thereto, even though the licence had not been recorded, but only established by way of a simple copy of the licence contract.

4.68 When there has been a change of name on the part of the right-holder or an assignment of the right on which a customs application is based, copies of the documentation ascertaining this change of status are to be filed with customs, particularly in cases where it does not appear from the registers of the relevant industrial property office (for example, the Austrian or European Patent Office, or the Community Trade Mark Register).

4.69 The term 'representative' is also interpreted broadly by the Austrian customs authorities. It includes both natural and legal persons, as set forth in Article 1 of EC Regulation 1891/2004.[36] Whoever has been granted an authorization or a power of attorney may file an application for action in the name of the owner or authorised user of an intellectual property right, even though a power of attorney need not always materially be produced. Thus in the case of legally acknowledged

---

[36] Commission Reg (EC) 1891/2004 of 21 October 2004 laying down provisions for the implementation of Council Reg (EC) 1383/2003 concerning customs action against goods suspected of infringing certain intellectual property rights and the measures to be taken against goods found to have infringed such rights [2004] OJ L 328/16 (30.10.1994).

representatives inscribed in an official list and governed by special laws on these professions, such as lawyers, patent attorneys and notary publics, reference to the fact that a power of attorney is on file with the representative will suffice since this follows from the intellectual property laws themselves. Since these are specialized laws they have not been suspended by the general rule of Article 2(3) of the Implementation Regulation.[37]

Proof of entitlement to file an application for action

For right-holders stricto sensu

The application should list all the rights on which it is based. Normally, copies of **4.70** the relevant registration certificates (reflecting the type of right, registration particulars including pictures, signs, words, and goods), if any, are to be presented. The Austrian customs officials are not particularly strict as to the formal requirements which such copies should fulfil, and in case of doubt, they may have the Patent Office verify the situation. Moreover, as noted above,[38] in a number of cases it is the customs officers themselves who identify the right-holder, what rights he holds, and who the attorney of record is.

In view of the fact that it is mostly trade mark cases that are involved (besides a **4.71** very few copyright and design cases), the various other proofs required under Article 2(1) of EC Regulation 1891/2004 appear of a more theoretical nature, at least at present. In case of copyright on CDs, etc, the copyright-owner is normally indicated on it and samples are filed. In case of unregistered design rights proofs are filed in respect of the firm having displayed the design for the first time at a specified exhibition including a picture of what was exhibited.

In order to evidence that he holds the rights for the goods in question,[39] the right- **4.72** holder may submit printouts from, for example, the official databases of the Austrian Patent Office,[40] European Patent Office, OHIM, or ROMARIN,[41] or from the Plant Variety Offices, or a copy of the Regulation conferring protection on a geographical name.

No case has been reported to date where a mere trade mark, design or patent **4.73** *application* was used as a basis for the filing of an application for action. In any

---

[37] Commission Reg (EC) 1891/2004 of 21 October 2004 laying down provisions for the implementation of Council Reg (EC) 1383/2003 concerning customs action against goods suspected of infringing certain intellectual property rights and the measures to be taken against goods found to have infringed such rights [2004] OJ L 328/16 (30.10.1994).   [38] Cf para 4.64 above.
[39] Cf Reg 1383/2003, Art 5(5), second indent, and Reg 1891/2004, Art 2(1).
[40] www.patentamt.at.
[41] The ROMARIN (Read-Only-Memory of Madrid Active Registry Information) database contains information on all international trade mark registrations made under the Madrid Agreement concerning the International Registration of Marks and the Protocol Relating to that Agreement that have been entered with the International Register kept by the International Bureau of the World Intellectual Property Organization.

case, such applications for action would not be allowable, since mere trade mark, design or patent applications normally do not confer the necessary rights to prevent the sale or use of similar goods before registration. However, unregistered designs (Community) may form the basis of such actions. For unregistered rights, in general, proof by affidavit would suffice for customs; more extensive proof of the subsistence of the right and the owner thereof would have to be presented to the pertinent court should proceedings be instituted at a later date.

For persons authorized to use the right

4.74 Austrian customs have so far taken it for granted that the person in whose name the application is filed is actually authorized to use the right concerned. The applicants file at their own risk. This liberal attitude may change towards demanding separate or additional proof, for example, by way of affidavit, in view of the requirements of Article 2(2) of Regulation 1891/2004. However, such (separate) proof will not be examined by customs as strictly as they would be examined by the courts later on. The risks will always remain with the applicant. As noted above,[42] the authorization to use an industrial property right need not be registered with the relevant office. Nonetheless, the filing of (an excerpt of) the licence agreement is recommended as a precautionary measure.

For representatives

4.75 Recognized professional representatives are not called upon to submit a power of attorney with the application, but reference is normally made to a power on file with the representative in line with the relevant specialized laws. Other representatives have to file their powers.

4.76 A general power for all customs actions of the same right-holder will suffice.

4.77 Foreign representatives without an office or domicile in Austria may also appear before customs as far as covered by EC law on the freedom of services and the respective Austrian laws on these professions implementing it. A word of caution: Austrian customs officials are not, and need not, be multilingual. So, misunderstandings may arise if someone approaches them in a language other than German, even though they have a working knowledge of English. Even Italian cannot be taken for granted, although the location of the Villach customs office is close to the Italian border. In any case, all correspondence exchanged with customs, and certainly *from* customs, will be in German.

4.78 There are no special requirements in Austria concerning the entitlement to sign the declaration referred to in Article 6 of the Regulation. Theoretically, the representatives could sign on the basis of their power.[43] Usually, the liability declaration is signed by the person or persons in whose name(s) the application is filed, who would then be directly responsible for possible later payments.

---

[42] Cf para 4.66 above.   [43] Cf Reg 1891/2004, Art 2(3), second indent.

(2) *Competent customs department and formal requirements*

The customs department competent under Article 5(2) of the Regulation to process applications for customs action in Austria is: **4.79**

Zollamt Villach
Competence Center Gewerblicher Rechtsschutz
Ackerweg 19
A-9500 Villach
Austria
Tel. +43 4242 3028-39, 40, 41, 44, or 52
Fax: +43 4242 3028-71 or 73
e-mail: post.425-pdp.zaktn@bmf.gv.at

At present, the head of the Villach customs department responsible for border measures against goods infringing intellectual property rights is Mr Peter Herold (direct extension -52).

Form of the application for action

In practice, most applications for action by Austrian customs under the Regulation are filed by fax. They can also be filed by e-mail, mail, or courier. It is normally sufficient to file one single copy of the application or a fax plus confirmation copy, depending on the enclosures.   **4.80**

It should become possible in the future to file applications for action in Austria by electronic means, as it is envisaged that an electronic version of the application for action will be made available to the right-holders by Austrian customs (on-line filing). However, forms can already now be obtained on-line.[44]   **4.81**

It is not absolutely necessary that the originally signed declaration under Article 6 of the Regulation be submitted together with the application. It is, however, recommended to file it as soon as possible, in order to avoid later problems. The declaration accompanying the application must, however, show a signature, so when filed by e-mail the original must be scanned, or a facsimile of the signature be applied to the document. A certified electronic signature is not (yet) required.   **4.82**

Language requirements

In Austria an application for action has to be filed in the German language, which is a constitutional requirement for all administrative bodies and the courts.[45] In the case of a 'Community' application under Article 5(4) of the Regulation which designates   **4.83**

---

[44] http://www.bmf.gv.at/service/formulare/zoll/_start.htm and www.bmf.gv.at/service/formulare/zoll/ZA63.pdf. Cf also http://www.bmf.gv.at/service/formulare/zoll/ZA64-1.pdf for the liability declaration referred to in Art 6 of the Regulation.

[45] Federal Constitutional Law, s 8 (*Bundes-Verfassungsgesetz*) BGBl 1/1930 as amended BGBl I Nr. 100/2003.

Austria and has not been filed in the German language, the right-holder must provide the Villach customs office with the necessary translation at his own cost.

4.84 As to the exhibits submitted together with the application, they should also be mainly in the German language. However, no translation will be needed for the likes of a ROMARIN[46] printout. In the case of a technical analysis or a description of the features according to which genuine goods can be differentiated from counterfeits, translations into German should be provided, and will practically always be requested.

4.85 As regards the liability declaration under Article 6 of the Regulation, a trilingual version of it—in German, English, and French—has been made available on the Austrian customs' website.[47] Usually, such declarations are executed by the right-holders either in German, or in German *and* English, or German *and* French. Customs may accept the declaration in the English or French language alone as well, at least when the official text set out in Annex I-B of Regulation 1891/2004 is used, but it may be questioned whether such documents fulfil the aforesaid constitutional requirements.

(3) Requirements regarding the contents of the application for action

Mandatory information

4.86 Article 5(5) of the Regulation imposes on the right-holders the duty to provide customs with all the information necessary to allow them to recognize readily the goods. In practice, however, Austrian customs are not (currently) particularly strict as to the description of the technical features of the goods or the type or pattern of fraud. But if such information is readily available, customs are eager to get it. They may themselves inspect the website of the right-holders.

4.87 Obviously, it is in the right-holder's interest to provide as many details as possible to customs in order to allow them to identify readily infringing goods. The application for action should be particularly well substantiated where the applicant seeks action by the customs authorities against a broader range of goods on the basis of a well known trade mark,[48] or where the application is based on intellectual property rights involving technical aspects, such as, for example, patents or SPCs,[49] and plant variety rights.[50]

4.88 Nor are Austrian customs very strict regarding the appointment of contact persons in the application. When these are not named, the natural or legal person filing the application will be the primary contact, as long as no one else has been nominated in this capacity.

---

[46] Cf n 41 above.
[47] Cf also http://www.bmf.gv.at/service/formulare/zoll/ZA64-1.pdf for the liability declaration referred to in Art 6 of the Regulation.   [48] Cf para 4.22 above.
[49] Cf para 4.35 above.   [50] Cf para 4.43 above.

What is certainly required in all cases are all data concerning the right-holder, **4.89** naming of the applicant, as well as data regarding the rights themselves, including the naming of the goods concerned.

The liberal attitude of Austrian customs means that they do not normally use the **4.90** power given in Article 5(8) of the Regulation to reject the application when these other statements besides the above mentioned are missing. In omitting to do so, they are clearly acknowledging that without a first detention it is often difficult to give this information.

Optional information

Austrian customs would welcome any additional information enabling them to **4.91** distinguish between the genuine and infringing goods, or to determine the routes used for the distribution of authentic goods—as on that basis, customs will be in a position to suspect goods departing from such paths of infringing the right-holder's rights. Again, it is advisable to provide as much information as possible, since this may in some cases prevent the release of genuine goods being suspended, and is likely to facilitate the interception of the infringing goods.

(4) Processing and acceptance of the application for action

On receiving an application for action, the Villach customs department will **4.92** process it and notify the applicant of its decision within 30 working days of its receipt.[51] In practice, where an application is filed outside the framework of an *ex officio* action, customs will usually decide on the application within two weeks.

Although the customs authorities are entitled, pursuant to Article 5(8) of the **4.93** Regulation, not to process an application for action when it does not contain the mandatory information listed in Article 5(5), no case has been reported to date where this power has been exercised by Austrian customs when the minimum information as stated in pararaph 4.86 above has finally been given.

In practice, where the Austrian customs authorities consider that an application **4.94** is not sufficiently detailed, they would simply request that the right-holder or his representative supplement it.

If Austrian customs did decide not to process an application in the future, the **4.95** right-holder concerned would be entitled to lodge an appeal before the Federal Ministry of Finance (*Bundesministerium für Finanzen*)—since customs are within the jurisdiction of that Ministry[52]—in the first place, and finally with the Administrative Court (*Verwaltungsgerichtshof*) in the second place.

The period for which customs take action once an application is granted is in **4.96** principle one year. If the right-holder wishes action to be taken for a shorter period

---

[51] Cf Reg 1383/2003, Art 5(7).   [52] Law on Counterfeiting 2004, s 8.

of time, he may so indicate in the application.[53] There is no reason, however, to make such a request since any (granted) application can be supplemented, for example, by including further rights at any time.

(5) 'Community' applications for action[54]

4.97 Austrian customs take the view that they can deal with only one application per right-holder covering all his possible rights. When confronted with the filing of both a national application in Austria and a 'Community' application in another Member State, the later application will, for practical reasons, be considered as supplementing the earlier one, so that both will be treated as only one, and the contact person will remain the same. The holder of a Community right is allowed to appoint a contact person established in a country other than Austria, but this may—and indeed often will—deprive him of the possibility of seeking an expedited action in Austria (since it will render, for example, inspections, taking of samples, etc, more complicated).

III. CONDITIONS GOVERNING ACTION BY CUSTOMS AUTHORITIES AND BY THE AUTHORITIES HAVING JURISDICTION TO DETERMINE WHETHER GOODS INFRINGE AN INTELLECTUAL PROPERTY RIGHT

A. Conditions governing action by customs authorities

(1) Factual background

4.98 While in 2002,[55] counterfeit and pirated goods reached Austria mainly by truck, statistics show a change in this regard in 2003[56] and 2004.[57] Indeed, over the last

---

[53] Except in the case of 'Community' applications under Art 5(4) of the Regulation, where this period is one year in all cases: cf Reg 1383/2003, Art 8(2), second indent.

[54] Within the meaning of Reg 1383/2003, Art 5(4). As to the language requirements applicable to such applications, cf paras 4.83–4.85 above.

[55] Bundesministerium für Finanzen, Produktpiraterie-Aufgriffe der Österreichischen Zollverwaltung, www.bmf.gv.at/zoll/wirtschaft1446/produktpiraterie2871/produktpiraterie-statistik2002.pdf.

[56] Bundesministerium für Finanzen, Produktpiraterie-Aufgriffe der Österreichischen Zollverwaltung, www.bmf.gv.at/zoll/wirtschaft1446/produktpiraterie2871/produktpiraterie-statistik2003.pdf.

[57] Bundesministerium für Finanzen, Produktpiraterie-Aufgriffe der Österreichischen Zollverwaltung, www.bmf.gv.at/zoll/wirtschaft1446/produktpiraterie2871/produktpiraterie-statistik2004.pdf.

two years, the majority of intercepted consignments have reached the country by mail. The reason for this change may be seen in the fact that all Austrian borders are now with EC countries, with the exception of the short border with Switzerland and Liechtenstein. Customs interventions, of course, also frequently occur at Austrian airports. There are no statistics available as to that, but it can be assumed that the main airports involved in the fight against infringements of intellectual property rights are the Vienna and Linz airports—at least this is what appears from the matters that have been publicly reported to date.

(2) Notification of customs intervention

The right-holder or his representative is notified of an intervention by Austrian customs at once. This notification takes place by post. The date of receipt of the letter will determine the calculation of the deadlines provided for under the Regulation. The declarant or holder of the goods will also be notified of the detention or suspension of release of the goods immediately.[58] In most cases, it is the forwarder of the goods, or the post office, that is notified of the customs action, and those parties pass the information on to the addressee. No 'standard' procedure has been set concerning such notifications. **4.99**

(3) Information to be provided by customs to the right-holder before the right-holder confirms the infringing nature of the goods

Once goods suspected of infringing intellectual property rights are detained by Austrian customs, the right-holder is informed of the actual or estimated quantity and the nature of the goods.[59] **4.100**

Subsequent to the filing—and acceptance—of an application for action under Article 5 of the Regulation, information on the countries of provenance, origin and/or destination of the goods will also be supplied at the right-holder's specific request. Still on demand, in order to establish whether an intellectual property right has been infringed, information will be communicated to the right-holder on the name and address of the consignee, consignor, declarant or holder of the goods, as far as their contact details are known to customs.[60] **4.101**

While under the former Austrian Law on Counterfeiting[61] customs informed the right-holder immediately and systematically of the name and address of the consignee, declarant, and/or exporter of the goods, because of concerns about data protection,[62] this is now only done at the right-holder's explicit request, and **4.102**

---

[58] Cf Reg 1383/2003, Art 9(2).   [59] Cf Reg 1383/2003, Arts 4(2) and 9(2).
[60] Cf Reg 1383/2003, Art 9(3).
[61] *Produktpirateriegesetz 2001—PPG 2001* BGBl I 65/2001 (Law on Counterfeiting 2001).
[62] Personal data are protected in Austria by virtue of the *Bundesgesetz über den Schutz personenbezogener Daten (Datenschutzgesetz 2000—DSG 2000)* BGBl I 165/1999 (Data Protection Law).

for the purpose of establishing whether an intellectual property right has been infringed.[63] Article 9(3) of the Regulation permits the communication of information necessary for detecting and pursuing infringements of intellectual property rights, but this information must not be used for other purposes. Other information is not provided. This approach is in line with the decision of the European Court of Justice of 14 October 1999.[64]

4.103 The protection of these data is general and the restriction of their use is governed by the Data Protection Law.[65] It gives the aggrieved a right for civil action for injunction, removal and damages, also in the form of a quick provisional injunction. It also provides for a right to criminal action with the sanction of one year's imprisonment. If criminal action is not appropriate, the law provides for an administrative penal sanction of a fine of up to EUR 20,000. Even the attempt is punishable.

(4) Inspection of the suspected goods

4.104 Austrian customs allow the right-holder to inspect the goods once he has been informed of their detention, or of the suspension of their release, provided that he has filed an application for action and specifically requests such inspection.[66] The analysis of the goods is essential, as before seeking destruction of the goods, the right-holder should first have satisfied himself that they are indeed counterfeit.

4.105 On being notified of the detention or suspension of the release of suspect goods, the right-holder or his representative may request that customs provide him with samples of those goods. Depending on the location of the customs office where the goods are being detained, the samples will either be handed over or sent by post by the customs officials.

4.106 Alternatively, some customs offices are equipped to take digital photographs of the goods and send them by e-mail to the right-holder.

4.107 Samples or pictures will only be provided at the right-holder's specific request. They may be used as evidence in the context of legal proceedings.

4.108 Section 6 of the Austrian Law on Counterfeiting[67] provides that the destruction of suspect goods must be preceded by the taking of samples by the customs authorities, which must be kept for a duration of six months in case of court proceedings, as prescribed by Article 11(1), second indent, of the Regulation.

---

[63] Art 12 of the Regulation lists the purposes for which use by the right-holders of the particulars referred to in Art 9(3) is allowed.

[64] Cf ECJ, Case C-223/98 *Adidas AG v Kammarrätten i Stockholm* [1999] ECR I-7081.

[65] *Bundesgesetz über den Schutz personenbezogener Daten (Datenschutzgesetz 2000—DSG 2000)* BGBl I 165/1999 (Data Protection Law).   [66] Cf Reg 1383/2003, Art 9(3), second indent.

[67] *Produktpiraterigesetz 2004—PPG 2004* BGBl I 56/2004 (Law on Counterfeiting 2004).

Samples must be returned after examination, particularly in cases where the goods **4.109** have been, or are to be, destroyed or released.

B. Simplified procedure allowing the destruction of the goods without the need to determine whether an intellectual property right has been infringed under national law

Austria has been applying a simplified procedure, resulting in destruction of the **4.110** goods without the need for the right-holders to institute court proceedings, for several years. As has been pointed out above,[68] under the former regime, two different deadlines were imposed on the parties involved. A first deadline allowed the holder or importer of the goods to oppose the detention or suspension of release within five working days, whilst the relevant right-holder could seek confirmation of such measures by commencing legal proceedings within 10 working days. In the majority of cases, the holder of the goods did not oppose the border measures. The goods were thus forfeited automatically.

This simplified procedure has undergone a few (minor) changes since the entry **4.111** into force of the new 2004 Law on Counterfeiting.[69] Section 4 of this Law implements the option provided to the Member States by Article 11 of the Regulation.

The new procedure can be summarized as follows. **4.112**

First, the Villach customs office notifies the right-holder or his representative of **4.113** the temporary detention, or suspension of the release, of a shipment of goods suspected of infringing a specific intellectual property right. If the right-holder is interested in further measures (which will often depend upon the quantity of goods intercepted), he may request information on the consignee, consignor, declarant or holder of the goods from customs, and to be provided with samples or digital pictures of the goods.

In the majority of cases, this is followed by notification from customs informing **4.114** the right-holder or his representative that the declarant, holder, and/or owner of the goods have agreed to, or at least have not opposed,[70] immediate destruction of the products within the term of 10 working days (instead of 5, under the former regime; 3 working days in the case of perishable goods) from receipt of the notification by post. In such circumstances, the right-holder will usually agree to immediate destruction as well (after ascertaining, of course, that the goods do

---

[68] Cf para 4.04 above.
[69] *Produktpiraterigesetz 2004—PPG 2004* BGBl I 56/2004 (Law on Counterfeiting 2004).
[70] In other words, Austrian law applies the presumption provided for in Art 11 of the Regulation that the destruction of the goods is deemed to be accepted when the declarant, holder, or owner of the goods does not oppose the destruction within the term of 10 working days.

indeed infringe one of his rights). Under the new Law on Counterfeiting, agreement of the right-holder to destruction of the goods is mandatory; without such agreement, the goods would be released—unless of course the right-holder has commenced proceedings to determine whether an intellectual property right has been infringed.

4.115 Where the consignee, consignor, declarant, or holder of the goods oppose(s) the destruction within this time period, the right-holder may try to persuade the latter to change his mind. Where the parties eventually consent to the destruction, their agreement on this point is communicated to the Villach customs office.

4.116 As can be seen, the procedure depends upon cooperation between the right-holder, or his representative, and the customs officials.

4.117 Amicable settlements between right-holders and owners of infringing goods are preferred. Customs authorities do not in any way interfere with the various clauses of such agreements, nor do they object to the possible grant of '*a posteriori*' licenses. They wait to be informed by the parties of the outcome of their negotiations to destroy finally the goods, release them, or store them, and then act accordingly.

4.118 Such settlements can take the form of release of some goods for which infringement is more uncertain while others more clearly infringing are to be destroyed.

4.119 The preference for such negotiations and settlements by the Regulation itself and national law is indicated by the following.

4.120 Article 11, first indent, of the Regulation envisages only the right-holder co-operating with customs (contrary to the procedure followed in practice, described in some detail in paras 4.111–4.115). It is the right-holder who must state when the term starts, he has to certify that the detained goods really infringe his rights and he has to file the written agreement of the declarant, the holder or the owner of the goods that the goods are abandoned for destruction.

4.121 In order to be able to file such agreement, the right-holder must communicate and then negotiate with the declarant, the holder or the owner of the goods and finally arrive at a settlement agreement. Nothing in the Regulation states that these negotiations have to be stopped once the declarant, the holder or the owner of the goods has declared his opposition to destruction. If they are continued and all or some goods finally voluntarily abandoned for destruction customs will still act accordingly as long as the procedure is not finalized.

4.122 The Austrian Code of Civil Procedure[71] favours settlement. According to section 204, the parties can always settle their dispute in or out of court. The courts urge

---

[71] *Gesetz vom 1. August 1895, über das gerichtliche Verfahren in bürgerlichen Rechtsstreitigkeiten.* (*Zivilprozessordnung—ZPO*), RGBl. Nr. 113/1895 as amended (Code of Civil Procedure).

settlement at the first oral hearing of a case. The court should (still under s 204) even refer the parties to other bodies likely to achieve a settlement (such as mediators). It is clear that the agreement reached has to be followed; if goods still with customs are abandoned for possibly being infringing they are to be destroyed even if, as a consequence of the settlement, the case is no longer pursued and no decision will ever be issued.

Moreover, section 433 of the Austrian Code of Civil Procedure makes it possible **4.123** to convert a private amicable settlement into a court settlement by having it ratified by a pertinent lower court (*Bezirksgericht*). The wording of section 433 begins with, 'Who intends to sue is entitled before so doing . . .'. This shows that settlement agreements are rightful legal instruments accepted under national law and enforceable even without instituting an infringement action.

C. Conditions governing action by the authorities having jurisdiction to determine whether the goods infringe an intellectual property right

(1) Authorities having jurisdiction to determine whether goods infringe an intellectual property right

Jurisdiction for infringements of intellectual property rights generally lies with **4.124** the civil courts and criminal courts.[72]

This Section considers whether the civil or criminal courts will have jurisdiction **4.125** to decide on a particular matter. The answer to this question differs depending on the various intellectual property rights. The sanctions which may be imposed by the courts in such matters are dealt with in Part V below.

Whether civil or criminal proceedings are preferable for determining whether an **4.126** intellectual property right has been infringed under national law, depends to a large extent upon the intentions of the right-holder and the information available. The procedural differences under both civil and criminal law, as well as their requirements and possible outcome need to be considered.

Civil procedures

Proceedings on the merits of the case

An action before a civil court is commenced with a complaint filed with the civil **4.127** court having jurisdiction to handle the case. The court serves it on the defendant

---

[72] The jurisdiction for declaratory actions of all 'technical' intellectual property rights lies with the Austrian Patent Office. However, such declaratory actions do not lead to an injunction or destruction. They will therefore be disregarded in the present context.

(inside and outside Austria), setting a four-week term for reply. Thus, to be in a position to choose the route of a civil action, the plaintiff has to know the names and addresses of the infringers. Once the defendant's reply is received by the court, a term for a preparatory hearing is set.

4.128 At the first hearing, it is determined how the case should proceed (for example, first of all whether a settlement seems possible in or out of court; if this is not possible, then which proofs are to be produced, especially documents and witnesses, whether and which experts should be nominated, whether and where goods have to be inspected, whether further writs are allowed, whether parallel procedures for cancellation or revocation of the relevant intellectual property rights before the Patent Office are or will be instituted, whether they are precedents over the court action, and whether the proceedings should be stayed or not, or which further requests are brought forward, etc; in short, a 'programme' for the development of the case is established).

4.129 Where all proofs have been presented, and no further questions need be clarified, the court can close the case immediately. If further steps according to the programme are necessary, terms for presenting matters, questioning witnesses, establishing and examining reports by the court-appointed experts, etc are set, as well as a term for a next hearing. Further hearings can be scheduled until the court, having collected or heard all relevant proofs, closes the case. It will then deliver a judgement, usually in writing (seldom orally) at the end of the last hearing.

4.130 It should be pointed out that all proofs have to be presented by the parties. There are (as yet) no discovery or seizure procedures, Anton Piller orders or the like, available under Austrian law to alleviate the general burden of proof. Such remedies could, however, be introduced in the framework of the implementation process relating to the EC Enforcement Directive[73] into Austrian law.

4.131 However, in the case of detention of goods by customs, the right of access to samples of the goods provided for under Article 9(3) of the Regulation usually suffices to establish the infringement, with or without the assistance of a court-appointed expert.

Preliminary injunctions

4.132 Preliminary injunctions can be requested separately before or during the court proceedings on the merits of the case. In intellectual property cases no urgency has to be proven in this context. The request is dealt with in summary proceedings on the basis of the proofs submitted to the judge (documents, samples, written expertises, and affidavits of readily available witnesses), which must be of

---

[73] Directive 2004/48/EC of the European Parliament and of the Council of 29 April 2004 on the enforcement of intellectual property rights [2004] OJ L 157/45.

such a nature as to render the infringement plausible. The proceedings are mainly handled in writing. They will take place *ex parte* when the serving of the summons to a foreign party would be unreasonably time-consuming, or time, or the fact that the defendant is not informed prematurely is of the essence, but such instances are rare. Since the courts enjoy an appreciable discretionary power as to how to deal with preliminary injunctions, they regularly run such proceedings *inter partes*. When granting the request, the court orders the defendant to refrain from all further commercial activities related to the infringing goods. The court may make its order dependent on a security payment when the likelihood of an infringement is not sufficiently high, or the interference with the business of the defendant is severe. The seizure of the goods can normally not be obtained. However, customs will uphold the suspension of free circulation or detention of the goods, and store them when a preliminary injunction has been granted. To be on the safe side, the court may additionally be requested to order the customs to maintain the border measures. There is no reason why such a request should be dismissed, in view of the power of the court to issue orders against third parties with respect to goods in their custody which are the object of the law suit. The preliminary injunction is usually granted for a requested time period. In intellectual property cases, this period usually runs until the decision in the main proceedings has become final.

Decisions of the first instance courts (*Landesgericht*), whether preliminary or final, **4.133** can always be appealed before the courts of second instance (*Oberlandesgericht*). The introduction of new matter (especially new proofs) is excluded on appeal (save in the case of an appeal lodged by the defendant at first instance against an *ex parte* preliminary injunction). The suspensive effect of an appeal can be requested in both preliminary and final proceedings. A further appeal on questions of law is only available, if accepted by the Austrian Supreme Court (*Oberster Gerichtshof*), which is the case when the question of law is of more general importance, and has not yet been clearly decided upon.

The losing party has to pay the costs incurred by the winning party as a result of **4.134** the whole proceedings, including preliminary injunction proceedings. These costs include the costs payable to the court and the court-appointed experts. They also cover the costs of representation, which are calculated on the basis of an official tariff, plus necessary expenses, which may include private expert opinions. All such costs have to be claimed before the end of the procedure in every instance, and will be awarded in the decisions.

Criminal procedures

'Punitive' procedures can be instituted either before administrative bodies, or **4.135** before the criminal courts. In the circumstances relevant here, administrative penal procedures will only take place in cases of smuggling.[74] In practice, counterfeit and pirated goods are also frequently smuggled. In such cases, the penal procedures against smuggling, and those against intellectual property infringements referred to in Article 13 of the Regulation theoretically run in parallel. The right-holder or his representative is informed by customs when there is also a suspicion of smuggling and this specific penal procedure is started. It should be noted that smuggled goods may be declared forfeited.[75] However, this would not apply if the goods are claimed to be owned by an innocent party.

4.136   In any case, forfeiture will mean that the goods come into the ownership of, and can be sold by, the Federal Republic of Austria. Therefore, the absolute claim for destruction provided for by Article 11 of the Regulation if the smuggler consents thereto, which he regularly does to avoid more severe penal sanctions from the courts, is a means which should always be used and is indeed expected by customs. The task of the financial criminal authorities is lightened in such cases, since they need not undertake any further investigations to determine whether they have to pronounce forfeiture (which is then overruled by destruction), but need solely decide on the penalties (fines and/or jail term) for smuggling.

4.137   Criminal offences can be prosecuted by the Public prosecutor either *ex officio*, or upon application by the injured party. In principle, all intellectual property right infringements are the subject of criminal penalties, which are only applied at the plaintiff's request, without the Public prosecutor intervening.

4.138   In the present context, public prosecution has a very limited application. It is only conceivable in the case of fraud or theft. In cases of fraud, deceit is a major element. If the infringing goods are sold as originals at a much higher price than their value, somehow comparable to the price of the original, that is fraud. If the consumer knows that the goods are fake, or if the price is very low, then there is no deceit and, therefore, also no fraud. Cases of fraud do happen, but it is difficult to see how there can be fraud with regard to goods detained by customs where the customer's deceit normally cannot yet be proven. There is only one known case in Austria where the imitations imported were stolen goods and the case was one for the Public prosecutor.

4.139   The general rule is that the right-holder sues (privately, that is, without the Public prosecutor) for infringement of his intellectual property rights.

4.140   The injured party has to request private penal prosecution within six weeks from the day he is informed of the punishable act and of the suspect. This term is no

---

[74] *Bundesgesetz vom 26. Juni 1958, betreffend das Finanzstrafrecht und das Finanzstrafverfahrensrecht (Finanzstrafgesetz—FinStrG.)*, BGBl I 129/1958, last amended BGBl I 57/2004). (Federal Law of 26 June 1958 relating to Financial Criminal Law, and Code of Financial Criminal Procedure).

[75] *Bundesgesetz vom 26. Juni 1958, betreffend das Finanzstrafrecht und das Finanzstrafverfahrensrecht (Finanzstrafgesetz—FinStrG.)*, BGBl I 129/1958, last amended BGBl I 57/2004). (Federal Law of 26 June 1958 relating to Financial Criminal Law, and Code of Financial Criminal Procedure, s 17.)

problem, since Article 13 of the Regulation sets a shorter term of 20 working days maximum from the day the right-holder is informed of the infringement.[76] However, customs often cannot give information about the infringer, since such matters frequently involve forwarding agents and the like, who are not criminally liable for the illicit nature of the transported goods. In such situations, criminal procedure provides the tool to request prosecution against the unknown.

Criminal prosecution usually involves two phases, namely, juridical investigations   **4.141** before trial, and the main proceedings (trial). The investigatory part before trial need not be requested, if all facts are provable. In the case of requested prosecution against the unknown, the investigatory magistrate has the duty to search for the suspect on the basis of the information available, for example, from customs or via Interpol. If all such efforts are in vain and there are no more leads on how to find the suspect, the procedure will be stayed. However, the claim to confiscate the goods is also available, if the suspect is not identified. Therefore, before the procedure is stayed, an order for confiscation and destruction of the goods may be requested. The investigating magistrate can also order search and seizure proceedings with the police on indicated premises, which often lead to seizure of more pirated goods.

Once the investigations before trial have come to an end, and provided the   **4.142** proceedings have not been stayed because a culprit has been found, the injured party has to file his full complaint and detail his claims. The judge can order further investigations, if he thinks that the proofs are not yet sufficient, for example, with regard to the personal liability of the culprit. Then he orders the main trial. Thereafter, the procedure of taking evidence starts. After the final pleadings for the prosecution and then for the defence, the trial is closed, and verdict is given.

Which to choose?

From the above, one can easily infer that civil proceedings are only realistic in case   **4.143** of border measures if the owner of the goods is known and can be reached in order to be served a complaint within a reasonably short term. Otherwise, a criminal action with investigations before trial is preferable. This is especially so where the goal pursued by the right-holder is retention, and ultimately destruction, of the goods. A disadvantage of this path, however, is that if the suspect successfully establishes that he had acted in good faith, the criminal procedure will not achieve the desired result, as it will then be discontinued. In such circumstances, the injured party has to switch to a civil action, in which he can also request destruction of the infringing goods or moulds designed or adapted for producing them. Since the statute of limitation for civil action is three years, this is regularly possible. Nothing in Article 13 of the Regulation hinders customs from continued

---

[76] Save for perishable goods, where the term is three working days; Reg 1383/2003, Art 13(2).

detention of the goods if the initially notified criminal procedure is followed by a notification of a newly initiated civil procedure, at least as long as the two are overlapping at the time of initiating civil procedures.

4.144 Whenever the infringer is an Austrian individual, so that a complaint can be served in time, civil proceedings can be initiated as stated above. In this context, the emphasis is on injunction, publication of the decision, damages, and finally destruction of the goods. One of the very few cases where a decision by the Austrian Supreme Court has been rendered in civil proceedings in the field was against an Austrian businessman who had bought counterfeit goods with the intention of placing them on the market in Austria. The Court held that the latter was to be considered the immediate infringer of the trade mark in question, even though the goods had in fact been imported by a third party and customs had suspended their release at a time when the defendant was not yet in the possession of the goods.[77]

4.145 Regardless of which measures are taken, the costs may be quite high, and it may be difficult to estimate realistically how long the proceedings will take. Reference can be made, for example, to a case where the addressee of counterfeit goods repeatedly did not appear before the criminal court, and eventually simply disappeared, which caused the plaintiff to withdraw from the criminal proceedings for consideration of cost after destruction of the goods.

4.146 Only very rarely can damages actually be obtained, since the persons bringing counterfeit or pirated products into Austria or through Austria will in most cases not be in a position to pay for any costs or damages which the courts may order. Experience shows that in many cases the holder of such goods becomes bankrupt. The defendants may also deny that they have anything at all to do with the shipment, and, where the commercial police conduct a house search, no counterfeit goods can be found. Nonetheless, in these cases, the criminal courts always order destruction at the right-holder's request, which a civil court cannot do.

Determination of the jurisdiction of the courts

Counterfeit goods

4.147 In the case of goods infringing national trade mark rights, the matter will have to be brought before a Criminal Regional Court (*Straflandesgericht*). The location where the goods are being detained by customs will decide which court will rule on the matter. Thus, for example, the Korneuburg Straflandesgericht will have to deal with the matter, if the goods have been detained at Vienna Airport.

4.148 Civil cases will be handled by the Commercial Courts (*Handelsgericht*), whose territorial jurisdiction depends on the residence of the defendant.

---

[77] Case 4 Ob 121/04d *Oberster Gerichtshof (OGH)* (Supreme Court) of 18 August 2004, ecolex 2005/62.

For goods infringing a Community trade mark, the Vienna Criminal Regional **4.149**
Court (*Straflandesgericht Wien*) or the Vienna Commercial Court (*Handelsgericht
Wien*) have exclusive jurisdiction, in criminal and civil cases, respectively.

Pirated goods

Whenever pirated goods infringe a copyright, proceedings will fall within the **4.150**
jurisdiction of the same courts specified above for counterfeit goods infringing
national trade marks.[78]

Design right infringements (regardless of whether or not the design has been **4.151**
registered) fall exclusively within the jurisdiction of the Vienna Criminal Regional
Court (*Straflandesgericht Wien*) for criminal procedures and the Vienna Commercial
Court (*Handelsgericht Wien*) for civil procedures. However, the parties may agree
to transfer a civil action to another (Austrian) commercial court.

Goods infringing a patent or supplementary protection certificate

Here again, the *Straflandesgericht Wien* and the *Handelsgericht Wien*, respectively, **4.152**
have exclusive jurisdiction. As with designs, transfer of a civil case is possible.[79]

Goods infringing a plant variety right

In cases involving goods suspected of infringing plant variety rights, the courts' **4.153**
jurisdiction over criminal cases depends upon the location of the infringement,
while, in civil cases, exclusive jurisdiction lies with the Vienna Commercial Court
(which again can refer the case to another commercial court if both parties
agree).[80]

Goods infringing a designation of origin or a geographical indication

For proceedings involving goods infringing a designation of origin or a geographi- **4.154**
cal indication, criminal proceedings will have to be instituted before the criminal
court established in the district where the infringement has occurred—thus, in the
case of border measures, it will be the court in the district of the customs office where
the goods are being detained—while the residence of the defendant will be decisive
in determining the commercial court having jurisdiction to handle civil actions.

(2) *Term for notifying customs that proceedings have been started*

Where it turns out to be impossible to follow the simplified procedure of Article **4.155**
11, Article 13 of the Regulation sets an initial term of 10 working days (3 for perishable goods) 'of receipt of the notification of suspension of release or detention
of the goods', within which the relevant customs office has to be notified that (civil
or criminal) proceedings have been initiated.

---

[78] Cf para 4.147 above.   [79] Cf para 4.151 above.   [80] Ibid.

4.156   The notification which starts the term is sent by post. Ordinary mail is used for all such notifications throughout the European Union, which means that it can take quite some time in the different countries before such a notification reaches the relevant right-holder. Since there is no requirement to acknowledge service, as is the case in Austria (it is more expensive and takes even more time), even through parallel authorities in other EC Member States (as the courts have to do for deliveries into other Member States), the customs office cannot know when the term has started. Customs are, therefore, dependent on the right-holder to inform them of the date of receipt. Further communication can, however, be made through any available means. Where customs are not informed about a date of receipt within a reasonable period of time, they enquire about it by telephone, fax, or e-mail, if the necessary data are available to them. When they are informed that the letter was not received, they re-send it. Ultimately, they have no option but to post it with acknowledgement of service in order to set a starting date for the term. If the goods are not infringing, and the declarant or holder of the goods needs them urgently, this is a very unfortunate and time-consuming procedure, which should in one way or another be ameliorated without depriving the right-holder of his right for further suspension of release or detention of the goods. However, in practice no such problem has yet been reported.

4.157   The possibility of an extension of the deadline for notifying the customs office that appropriate measures have been taken by the right-holder for another 10 working days 'in appropriate cases', as provided for by Article 13(1), second indent, of the Regulation, is handled quite liberally by Austrian customs. Such requests for extensions are regularly allowed. This is understandable, as it will normally take nearly the full 10 working days for the right-holder to know whether the infringer agrees to the destruction of the goods, and thus whether the simplified procedure set out in Article 11 can be applied. It is clear though that in view of Article 7 of Regulation 1891/2004 only a single extension for 10 working days (either under Article 11 or under Article 13 of the Regulation) is possible. However, no case is known in Austria where the declarant, holder or owner of the goods has asked for such an extension and the right-holder has sued in vain. It may be assumed that the declarant, holder or owner of the goods would have to pay the costs for initiating the infringement suit in such situation.

4.158   In order to show that proceedings to determine whether an intellectual property right has been infringed have been initiated, the proof issued by the relevant court, or a confirmatory letter from the right-holder's representative that the case has been filed on a certain date, has to be sent to the customs office. The latter—for keeping the term—is satisfied with a facsimile copy, however, it is wise to send the original document as well.

4.159   In the course of drafting the 2004 Austrian Law on Counterfeiting (*Produktpirateriegesetz 2004*),[81] it was debated whether a term should be set

---

[81]   *Produktpirateriegesetz 2004—PPG 2004* BGBl I 56/2004 (Law on Counterfeiting 2004).

within which a court decision should be rendered, subsequent to the commencement of Article 13 proceedings, and notified to the customs office, in order to prevent goods being detained, or their release suspended, for an unreasonably long time. However, a 'standard' term of this type which would fit any and all possible situations cannot be set, especially not when the handling of motions for preliminary injunctions often takes time, particularly when the courts apply *inter partes* proceedings. This is also true in view of the uncertainty as to whether protective measures taken in the course of pre-trial procedures in criminal cases should have been taken into account for the calculation of the term, and in view of the defendant's right of appeal. Therefore, this proposal was eventually dropped. The customs officials are content with being officially informed of the outcome of the proceedings when they are terminated.

D. Release of goods suspected of infringing certain rights on provision of a security

In the case of goods suspected of infringing design rights, patents, supplementary **4.160** protection certificates, or plant variety rights, Article 14(1) of the Regulation stipulates that the declarant, owner, importer, holder or consignee of the goods shall be able to obtain the release of the goods or an end to their detention on provision of a security, on certain conditions. One of these conditions is that customs must have been notified that proceedings have been initiated under Article 13 and on the assumption that the court did not order further detention by it in the course of their proceedings on a basis other than the Regulation (see also Article 14(1)(b) of the Regulation).

The question then arises what would happen if such goods, after being released or **4.161** their detention ended pursuant to Article 14(1), were eventually found to infringe the intellectual property right in question.

In such cases, section 5 of the Austrian 2004 Law on Counterfeiting provides that the **4.162** security referred to in Article 14(1) of the Regulation shall be subject to forfeiture in the place of the goods. In practice, however, no such decision has yet been reported.

As far as the determination of the amount of the security is concerned,[82] it is **4.163** expected—since it is usual practice with courts—that the right-holder will be allowed to put forward a sum along with a statement as to how it was calculated having regard to the price and value of the goods detained, and that such a calculation would be followed by customs if reasonable. However, the Austrian authorities generally decide on the low side of securities of any kind. The security payment itself will in principle be made by way of a bond issued by a well-known

---

[82] Cf Reg 1383/2003, Art 14(2).

Austrian bank. In some cases, a savings book will probably be deposited, together with information on the security code in order to receive interest. However, this presupposes sufficient liquidity of the debtor.

E. Storage of the goods

4.164   For the initial time period of 3, 10, and/or 20 working days provided for in Articles 11 and 13 of the Regulation, the customs office detaining, or having suspended the release of the goods keeps them on the customs premises without costs. Once the proceedings under Article 13 have been initiated, the goods will be stored by the same customs office at specialized storage places. This can prove expensive, especially if the goods are stored for a long time. The right-holder is responsible for paying all costs resulting from such storage of the goods. He can, however, arrange a different and cheaper place of storage with customs, as long as that place is considered secure by the relevant customs office.

IV. PROVISIONS APPLICABLE TO GOODS FOUND TO INFRINGE AN INTELLECTUAL PROPERTY RIGHT

4.165   Section 7 of the Austrian Law on Counterfeiting[83] clearly states that it is a financial offence to import goods found to infringe an intellectual property right at the end of the procedure provided for in Article 9 (see also Article 16) of the Regulation, to release such goods for free circulation, to remove them from the Community customs territory, to export or re-export them, and to place them under a suspensive procedure, or in a free zone or free warehouse.

4.166   More insight into the Austrian procedure is provided by the cases that resulted in the judgment rendered by the European Court of Justice on 7 January 2004 re *Rolex*.[84] These cases had their origin in Austria. In the Austrian Trade Mark Law[85] based on Article 5(3)(c) of the Harmonization Directive on trade marks,[86] only importation and exportation of counterfeit goods are listed as examples of acts constitutive of trade mark infringements. Thus, for example, the mere transit of

---

[83] Cf n 81 above.
[84] Case C-60/02 *Montres Rolex SA and others*, available on curia.eu.int.
[85] Trade Mark Law, s 10a; cf para 4.15 above.
[86] Council Reg (EC) 40/94 of 20 December 1993 on the Community Trade Mark [1994] OJ L 11/1 (14.01.1994), Art 9(3).

counterfeit goods is not explicitly considered a trade mark infringement under Austrian law. Moreover, according to Austrian criminal law, only what is clearly forbidden by law is punishable. However, the concepts of import and export on the one hand, and that of the transit of goods on the other hand, could be seen as different acts. Consequently, transit might not be punishable under Austrian criminal law (although the enumeration of forbidden acts in s 10a of the Trade Mark Law is not a finite list).

The *Rolex* case involved the external transit of counterfeit goods, originating from a non-EC Member State, and intended for another non-EC Member State. The main issue in the proceedings was whether the external transit of such goods could be considered a criminal offence under Austrian law. In the *Polo/Lauren* case,[87] the ECJ had already held that the former Regulation (3295/94)[88] applied, inter alia, to the external transit of goods. However, this decision had been made on the facts of a civil case, thus leaving it open whether the same reasoning could also be applied to criminal cases. Therefore, the Eisenstadt Regional Criminal Court (*Landesgericht Eisenstadt*) requested a preliminary ruling from the ECJ. **4.167**

The ECJ ruled that Articles 2 and 11 of Regulation 3295/94 were applicable to situations in which goods in external transit between two countries not belonging to the European Community are temporarily detained by customs in a Member State. The court also decided that the duty to interpret national law in a manner compliant with Community law could not, of itself and independently of a law adopted by a Member State, have the effect of determining or aggravating the liability in criminal law of a Member State which had failed to meet the requirements of the Regulation. **4.168**

In Austria, the Eisenstadt Regional Criminal Court decided on the legality of the detention of the goods, and confirmed that transit from a non-Member State of the European Community into another non-Member State through a Member State was covered by Austrian criminal law. In effect, it considered transit as equivalent to import into the customs area of Austria followed by export for the purpose of criminal law. By so deciding, the Eisenstadt Court construed the national law in a way which made it compliant with the requirements of the Regulation.[89] **4.169**

---

[87] Case C-383/98, *The Polo/Lauren Company LP v PT Dwidua Langgeng Pratama International Freight Forwarders*, available on curia.eu.int.

[88] Council Reg (EC) 3295/94 of 22 December 1994 laying down measures to prohibit the release for free circulation, export, re-export or entry for a suspensive procedure of counterfeit and pirated goods [1994] OJ L 341/8 (22.12.1994).

[89] The question as to whether transit is trade mark use in the territory of transit and therefore trade mark infringement was brought before the ECJ again by the German Bundesgerichtshof by its decision of 2 June 2005 in the case of Diesel jeans which were finished in Poland and then transported to Ireland through Germany. The German Bundesgerichtshof doubted that transit could be trade mark infringement; but without infringement the goods could not be rightfully detained by customs even if the Regulation so intended (see Art 1 (2) of the Regulation).

4.170 The administrative sanctions provided for independent of the right-holder in respect of goods found to infringe an intellectual property right in Austria consist mainly in fines of various levels. Forfeiture to the Republic may only be pronounced in case of wilful infringement. The law does not state what happens to the goods if they are not declared forfeited. Therefore, these administrative provisions are not entirely compliant with Article 16 of the Regulation; however, court orders on request of the right-holders will in principle always be compliant.[90]

4.171 Whenever goods are to be destroyed as a result of the simplified procedure according to Article 11 of the Regulation and section 4 of the Austrian Law on Counterfeiting,[91] respectively, section 6 of that Law provides that the destruction occurs at the cost and under the responsibility of the right-holder. Alternatively, the goods may be disposed of outside commercial channels in another way without cost to the Exchequer. Section 6(2) of the Law on Counterfeiting also envisages the possibility of using the goods for charitable purposes or otherwise utilizing them, provided that the right-holder agrees. The latter provision is consistent with Article 11 of the Regulation, which 'enables' rather than requests customs authorities to have such goods abandoned for destruction.

4.172 In fact, the reference to use of the goods for charitable purposes takes into account Article 17(1)(b) of the Regulation. Since, however, the provisions of the Customs Law Implementation Act[92] have to be borne in mind as well, there do exist bars for the 'use for charitable purposes' in so far as the use of the goods by the charitable organization remains under control of customs, which have to watch over it so as not to impair negatively competition.

4.173 In practice, a right-holder has never consented to relinquish forfeited goods to charities or allowed them to be otherwise utilized. Destruction has been pursued in all cases. This is probably because, where goods are given away to charitable trusts—possibly subject to prior removal of the counterfeit trade marks, if at all possible—it cannot be guaranteed that the goods will not reach the black market or be otherwise circulated for commercial purposes. Right-holders usually do not want similar cheap no-name products on the market. This would in fact distort competition.

4.174 In a case where a considerable number of cigarettes constituted both trade mark infringement and smuggling, the cigarettes would have been forfeited to the Exchequer under the administrative provisions concerning smuggling, and the Republic of Austria would have had the right to dispose of the cigarettes under

---

⁹⁰ Cf Part V, 'Penalties' below.

⁹¹ *Produktpirateriegesetz 2004—PPG 2004* BGBl I 56/2004 (Law on Counterfeiting 2004).

⁹² *Bundesgesetz betreffend ergänzende Regelungen zur Durchführung des Zollrechts der Europäischen Gemeinschaften (Zollrechts-Durchführungsgesetz—ZollR-DG)*—BGBl 659/1994, as amended BGBl I 26/2004 27 April 2004 (Federal Law about complementary rules for the enforcement of the customs legislation of the European Communities).

the conditions of Article 17(1)(a) or (b) of the Regulation. Giving away those cigarettes even outside commercial channels would have been unacceptable to the right-holder. Consequently, the cigarettes were eventually destroyed at the cost of the right-holder under the provisions of Article 11 of the Regulation and the equivalent provisions of the Austrian Law on Counterfeiting.

Where goods are destroyed as a result of a court order made under Article 13 of **4.175** the Regulation, the holder of the goods must pay the costs for destruction. This will be more often the case in practice in civil proceedings, where the defendant can be more easily forced to pay. In criminal proceedings (which are frequently instituted against unknown persons or against foreigners) it is often unrealistic to expect that the infringer will ever be forced to reimburse any sums, owing to a lack of personal liability of the defendants in the proceedings, or a lack of funds.

Further provisions applicable to goods found to infringe intellectual property **4.176** rights will be discussed in Part V, 'Penalties' below.

V. PENALTIES

Section 7 of the Austrian Law on Counterfeiting[93] provides that any violation of **4.177** the Regulation constitutes a financial offence, which shall be prosecuted by the financial criminal authority. In the case of an intentional offence the fine will be up to EUR 15,000, in the case of a negligent offence, up to EUR 4,000. In addition to the fine, a wilful offence will result in forfeiture of the goods under section 17 of the Austrian Financial Criminal Law.[94]

Deliberate violation of a duty of disclosure according to the Regulation[95] without **4.178** thereby committing another financial offence, constitutes a breach of financial

---

[93] Cf n 91 above.
[94] *Bundesgesetz vom 26. Juni 1958, betreffend das Finanzstrafrecht und das Finanzstrafverfahrensrecht (Finanzstrafgesetz—FinStrG.)*, BGBl I 129/1958, last amended BGBl I 57/2004). (Federal Law of 26 June 1958 relating to Financial Criminal Law, and Code of Financial Criminal Procedure.)
[95] Austrian Law on Counterfeiting, s 7(2): 'Anzeige- und Offenlegungspflicht nach der EG-Produktpiraterie-Verordnung 2004'. This term does not appear in the Regulation verbally, but refers, eg, to information that has to be included in the application for customs action pursuant to Art 5 and to the requirement pursuant to Art 8(1), second indent, according to which the right-holder shall notify the competent customs department if his right ceases to be validly registered or expires. This provision has been included in the new Austrian Law on Counterfeiting in view of the broadened scope of sanctions pursuant to Art 18 of the Regulation as compared with Art 11 of the previous Reg 3295/94.

regulations, which is punishable by a fine of up to EUR 3,625 by the financial criminal authority.

4.179 In accordance with Article 18 of the Regulation, each Member State shall introduce 'penalties' to apply in cases of violation of the Regulation. Such measures clearly should include those stated in Article 17. However, beside these 'national' sanctions, Article 16 is directly applicable, without it being necessary to implement it into national law.

4.180 Unfortunately, Article 16 forbids release of the infringing goods in any way whatsoever, but does not call for their destruction or other disposal as provided for in Article 17. That can only mean that, without suitable national sanctions, such goods would be stored at the expense of the right-holder eternally. Since this would obviously be unsatisfactory, the 'national' sanctions—which will be discussed in the following paragraphs—are of prime importance.

A. Counterfeit goods

Civil sanctions

4.181 As to trade mark infringement, the Austrian Trade Mark Law provides for the following claims under civil law:

- Claim to cease and desist from the infringement (injunction) (s 51).
- Claim to eliminate the illegal situation (s 52), that is, in particular to destroy the infringing objects and possibly existing stocks thereof (trade marked goods, business stationery, advertisement means, trade mark symbols like labels, packaging materials, etc), to render unusable tools and other equipment exclusively or predominantly designed or adapted for the manufacture of infringing objects (that is, printing plates, moulds, templates and stencils, embroidering patterns, matrices, and the like). Instead of rendering unusable infringing moulds and matrices, the court may order destruction of the same in cases where rendering the tools unusable would be more expensive than their destruction, and where there is no advance payment therefor on the part of the infringer. If there exists some other way of eliminating the illegal situation involving no, or only a minor, destruction of values, the injured party may claim such (minor) measures only. The mere removal of the counterfeit trade mark which has been affixed to the goods will only be seen as satisfactory in cases where another measure would cause undue hardship on the infringer.[96] A further alternative

---

[96] The latter provision has been introduced in s 52 of the Austrian Trade Mark Law to 'implement' Art 8 of the previous Regulation (ie Reg 3295/94) into national law. It now has to be interpreted and enforced in accordance with Art 17(1), second indent, which makes it more difficult

provided for by Austrian law is to hand over the infringing objects or tools to the injured party against an adequate compensation not exceeding the costs of manufacture.[97]

- Claim to appropriate compensation, damages, and handing over of profits (s 53): in the case of a culpable trade mark infringement, the injured party may, instead of an appropriate compensation (that is, a reasonable licence fee), claim damages, including lost profits, or the handing over of the profit made by the infringer as a result of the infringement. Irrespective of proof of damage, the injured party may claim double compensation in the case of gross negligence or wilful intent. In specific circumstances, a claim to compensation for immaterial disadvantages caused by a culpable trade mark infringement (personal grievance) may also be initiated.

- Claim to publication of the judgment and rendering of accounts (s 55, referring to ss 149 and 151 of the Patent Law[98]).

- Claim to obtain information on the provenance and distribution channels of the infringing objects (s 55a).

Criminal sanctions

The Austrian Trade Mark Law[99] also includes criminal penalties. These relate not only to registered trade marks, but also to other distinctive signs (as opposed to civil sanctions, which relate only to registered trade marks). It has, however, been pointed out that the same civil remedies are also applicable to those other distinctive signs pursuant to section 9 of the Law against Unfair Competition.[100]   **4.182**

The penalties provided for under criminal law consist in fines of up to 360 daily rates. Infringements on an industrial scale may be punished by imprisonment of up to two years (s 60).   **4.183**

Section 52 of the Trade Mark Law (elimination of the illegal situation and destruction of the infringing goods) and section 149 of the Patent Law (publication of the judgment)[101] are also applicable in criminal proceedings as well as claims for damages according to section 53 of the Trade Mark Law.   **4.184**

---

for the courts simply to order removal of the trade marks—which was common practice in Austria until 2003. It remains to be seen in how far the words 'save in exceptional cases' can be considered tantamount to the 'undue hardship' criterion provided for in s 52 of the Austrian Trade Mark Law.

[97] This could be seen as one alternative under Art 17(1)(b) of the Regulation but then the question of who pays the customs duties also has to be considered.

[98] *Patentgesetz—PatG 1970* BGBl 259/1970—WV—*Patenrechts und Gebührennovelle* 2004, BGBl I 149/2004 (Patent Law).

[99] *Markenschutzgesetz 1970 idF der Markenrechtsnov.* 1999 BGBl I 111/1999 (Trade Mark Law) and *Patentrechts- und Gebührennovelle* 2004 BGBl I 149/2004 (Patent and Fee Law Amendment).

[100] *Bundesgesetz gegen den unlauteren Wettbewerb 1984—UWG*, BGBl 448/1984 (WV) as amended BGBl I 136/2004 (Law against Unfair Competition).   [101] Cf para 4.181 above.

B. Pirated goods

Copyright infringements

Civil sanctions

4.185 The Austrian Copyright Law,[102] in common with the Austrian Trade Mark Law,[103] provides for the following claims under civil law:

- Claim to cease and desist (injunction) (s 81)
- Claim to eliminate the illegal situation (s 82)
- Claim to publication of the judgment (s 85)
- Claim to appropriate compensation (s 86)
- Claim to damages and handing over of profits (s 87)
- Claim to rendering accounts (s 87a)
- Claim to obtain information on the producer, contents, provenance and number of pirate items (s 87b).

Criminal sanctions

4.186 The Austrian Copyright Law similarly includes criminal penalties, namely imprisonment of up to six months and fines of up to 360 daily rates. Criminal offences on an industrial scale may be punished by imprisonment of up to two years. Publication of the judgment is also provided for (s 91).

4.187 Destruction of the infringing objects and rendering unusable of means exclusively or predominantly designed or adapted for the manufacture of pirated copies of the protected 'work' may also be ordered upon request of the private plaintiff (*Privatankläger*) (s 92).

Design infringements

Civil sanctions

4.188 A party whose design rights have been infringed is entitled to claim a cease and desist injunction, elimination of the infringement, publication of judgment, appropriate compensation, damages, handing over of profits, rendering of accounts, and surrendering of information on the provenance and distribution channels of the goods under section 34 of the Austrian Design Law[104] in the context of civil proceedings.

---

[102] *Bundesgesetz über das Urheberrecht an Werken der Literatur und der Kunst und über verwandte Schutzrechte (Urheberrechtsgesetz) idF der Urheberrechtsgesetz-Nov 2003* BGBl 111/1936 idF BGBl I 32/2003 (Copyright Law).   [103] Cf para 4.181 above.
[104] *Musterschutzgesetz idF der Musterschutzgesetz-Nov 2003* BGBl 497/1990 *idF* BGBl I 81/2003 and BGBl I 149/2004.

Criminal sanctions

Criminal liability for design infringement results in fines of up to 360 daily rates. Infringement on an industrial scale is punished with imprisonment of up to two years (s 35).

4.189

Sections 148 (elimination of the illegal situation), 149 (publication of the judgement), and 160 (private monetary claims) of the Patent Law[105] are also applicable in criminal proceedings (cf para 4.191 below).

4.190

C. Goods infringing a patent or a supplementary protection certificate

Patent infringements

Civil sanctions

The Austrian Patent Law[106] provides for claims to cease and desist (s 147), elimination of the illegal situation (s 148), publication of the judgment (s 149), monetary damages (s 150), rendering of accounts (s 151), and information on provenance and distribution channels (s 151a). By virtue of section 148, the injured party may demand that the infringing objects be destroyed, and that the tools and other equipment exclusively or predominantly serving for manufacturing such objects be made unusable for such purpose. In cases where rendering unusable infringing tools and similar equipment turns out to be more expensive than their destruction and where there is no advance payment for the higher costs for rendering unusable the tools for further infringement on the part of the infringer, the court may order the destruction of such tools. If there is some other way of eliminating the illegal situation involving no or only a minor destruction of values, the injured party may claim such (minor) measures only. Another alternative would be to hand over the infringing objects or infringing tools to the injured party in return for an appropriate compensation not exceeding the production costs.

4.191

Section 150 of the Austrian Patent Law sets forth that a party injured owing to unauthorized use of a patent is entitled to claim an appropriate compensation[107] from the infringing party. In the case of a culpable patent infringement,

4.192

---

[105] *Patentgesetz—PatG 1970* BGBl 259/1970—WV—*Patenrechts-und Gebührennovelle* 2004, BGBl I 149/2004 (Patent Law).

[106] *Patentgesetz—PatG 1970* BGBl 259/1970—WV—*Patenrechts-und Gebührennovelle* 2004, BGBl I 149/2004 (Patent Law).

[107] 'angemessenes Entgelt', a claim for reimbursement for unjustified enrichment derived from *Allgemeines Bürgerliches Gesetzbuch, s 1041—ABGB* (Civil Code) JGS Nr. 946/1811 and calculated licence fee.

the injured party may claim damages (*Schadenersatz*), including lost profits, or the handing over of the profits gained as a consequence of the infringement. Compensation for immaterial harm caused by a culpable infringement can also be sought. Irrespective of proof of damages, the plaintiff may claim double compensation if the patent infringement is due to gross negligence or a wilful intent.

Criminal sanctions

4.193 As to patent infringements resulting in a criminal offence, the fines range up to 360 daily rates. Infringement on an industrial scale is punished by imprisonment of up to two years (s 159).

Infringements of supplementary protection certificates

4.194 The civil and criminal sanctions provided for by the Patent Law are equally applicable to infringements of supplementary protection certificates.[108]

D. Goods infringing a plant variety right

Civil sanctions

4.195 The claims under civil law provided for in the Austrian Plant Variety Law[109] are set out in section 24. This section provides for claims to cease and desist, elimination of the illegal situation, publication of the judgment, appropriate compensation, damages, handing over of profits, and rendering of accounts.

Criminal and administrative sanctions

4.196 Infringements of plant variety rights falling within the realm of criminal jurisdiction are punishable by fines of up to 360 daily rates.

4.197 Section 26 of the Austrian Plant Variety Law provides for administrative penalties in certain cases where the activities do not constitute criminal offences within the competence of the courts, or where there are not more severe penalties applicable in accordance with other provisions. Thus, the district administrative authorities can impose fines of up to EUR 7,270 and up to EUR 36,440 in the case of repeated offences, in the following circumstances:

- where a protected plant variety has been commercialized without using the registered name;

---

[108] *Bundesgesetz betreffend ergänzende Schutzzertifikate (Schutzzertifikatsgesetz 1996)* BGBl I 11/1997 idF BGBl I 143/2001 and also BGBl I 149/2004 (Law on Supplementary Protection Certificates).
[109] *Bundesgesetz über den Schutz von Pflanzensorten (Sortenschutzgesetz 2001)* BGBl I 109/2001 and 110/2002 (Plant Variety Law).

- where the registered name of a protected variety has been used for a different variety of a similar kind;
- where a non-existent plant variety protection has been pretended.

E. Goods infringing a designation of origin or a geographical indication

Provisions on penalties for infringements of a Community designation of origin   **4.198**
or a geographical indication are set out in the Austrian Trade Mark Law.[110]
Sections 68 to 68j relate to geographical indications and designations of origin for
agricultural products and foodstuffs according to EEC Regulation 2081/92, as
amended.[111]

Civil sanctions

The measures which can be sought in civil proceedings are set out in section 68f.   **4.199**
The parties entitled to use the protected geographical indication or designation of
origin, or groups and bodies entrusted with the enhancement of relevant
economic interests, may claim a cease and desist injunction against a party violating Articles 8 or 13 of Regulation 2081/92 in the course of trade.

Provided the infringer is in possession of the relevant goods, a claim for elimina-   **4.200**
tion of the illegal situation may also be raised. Section 52 of the Austrian Trade
Mark Law is applicable in this regard.[112]

In the case of a culpable (negligible or wilful) infringement, monetary claims may   **4.201**
be initiated according to section 53 of the Trade Mark Law.[113]

Claims to publication of the judgment and rendering of accounts are also   **4.202**
provided for in the same way as in the Austrian Patent Law.[114] Also the provision
of the Trade Mark Law on information on provenance and distribution channels
is applicable.

---

[110] *Markenschutzgesetz* 1970 *idF der Markenrechtsnov.* 1999 BGBl I 111/1999 (Trade Mark Law) and *Patentrechts- und Gebührennovelle* 2004 BGBl I 149/2004 (Patent and Fee Law Amendment).

[111] Council Reg (EEC) 2081/92 of 14 July 1992 on the protection of geographical indications and designations of origin for agricultural products and foodstuffs [1992] OJ L 208/1 (24.7.1992), as amended. Cf also Council Reg (EC) 1493/1999 of 17 June 1999 on the common organization of the market in wine [1999] OJ L 179/1 (14.7.1999), as amended.

[112] *Markenschutzgesetz* 1970 *idF der Markenrechtsnov.* 1999 BGBl I 111/1999 (Trade Mark Law) and *Patentrechts- und Gebührennovelle* 2004 BGBl I 149/2004 (Patent and Fee Law Amendment).

[113] Cf para 4.181 above.

[114] *Patentgesetz—PatG 1970* BGBl 259/1970—WV—*Patenrechts-und Gebührennovelle* 2004, BGBl I 149/2004 (Patent Law) and para 4.191 above.

Criminal sanctions

4.203 Section 68h of the Austrian Trade Mark Law[115] specifies the criminal penalties applicable to infringements of a Community geographical indication or a designation of origin. It provides for fines of up to 360 daily rates. Such fines may be imposed on anyone:

- who uses a protected geographical indication or designation of origin for identifying products other than those referred to in the specification filed in respect of the relevant designation or indication, but comparable to the latter;

- who misuses, or imitates or evokes such indication or designation, even if the protected indication is translated or accompanied by an expression such as 'style', 'type', or the like;

- who uses such indication or designation in a way which makes profit of the reputation of the protected name; or

- who uses such indication or designation in another misleading manner in connection with the distribution of goods, or for identifying his enterprise.

4.204 If the above activities are carried out on an industrial scale, a jail term of up to two years is provided for.

4.205 The same penalties may also be imposed whenever goods inappropriately bearing such indications or designations are offered for sale, placed on the market, imported, exported, or possessed for these purposes.

4.206 The provisions discussed above[116] in connection with civil proceedings concerning injunction, elimination of the illegal situation, publication of the judgment and damages are also *mutatis mutandis* applicable in criminal proceedings.

VI. LIABILITY OF CUSTOMS AUTHORITIES AND RIGHT-HOLDERS

A. Liability of right-holders and sanctions

4.207 Article 12 of the Regulation provides that a right-holder receiving particulars of the names and addresses of the consignee, consignor, declarant, or holder of the goods and the origin and provenance of the goods suspected of infringing an intellectual property right may not use that information for purposes other than those

---

[115] *Markenschutzgesetz* 1970 *idF der Markenrechtsnov.* 1999 BGBl I 111/1999 (Trade Mark Law) and *Patentrechts- und Gebührennovelle* 2004 BGBl I 149/2004 (Patent and Fee Law Amendment).
[116] Cf para 4.199 above.

specified in Articles 10, 11, and 13(1) of the Regulation, that is, to establish whether an intellectual property right has been infringed under national law, and to refer this issue to the courts. Any other use, not permitted by the national legislation may, amongst others, cause the right-holder to incur civil liability.

Every notification on a new shipment as issued by the Villach customs office **4.208** includes a clear reference to the above-mentioned provisions of Article 12 of the Regulation. However, the Austrian Law on Counterfeiting[117] contains neither specific provisions on what would constitute 'non-permitted use' of information provided by customs, nor any sanctions in cases of violation of this rule.

Nevertheless, misuse of personal data (as the ones communicated by customs) will **4.209** be subject to the civil penalties set forth in the Austrian Data Protection Law[118] and criminal and administrative penalties when committed wilfully. As far as such misuse does not fall within the competence of the courts, such acts are considered administrative offences, which include the detection, processing and transmission of data without fulfilling the required duty of notification. Imprisonment of up to one year, and fines in the order of EUR 20,000 are to be anticipated. Misuse includes illicit own use, communicating to others, and publication.

Moreover, the owner, declarant or holder of the goods could also commence an **4.210** action for unfair competition against the right-holder for trying to get a commercially unfair advantage through such misuse of data.[119]

The Austrian Law on Counterfeiting[120] does not include any provisions specific **4.211** to liabilities and civil sanctions for breach of the Regulation by the right-holders in the sense of Article 19(3). Such civil sanctions according to general law in the present context consist only of damages, which always presuppose culpability. Section 394 of the specific law regulating conservatory measures and interim injunctions (*Exekutionsordnung*—Law on Execution)[121] also contains an independent claim for damages, irrespective of fault in case a preliminary injunction has been granted which is ultimately found to have been unjustified (for example, because the right was not valid, or no infringement has occurred). Then the right-holder has to pay compensation to the injured parties covering all financial loss. In the present context, this means that, if goods are detained upon an interim court order which ultimately is not upheld or converted into a permanent injunction, the right-holder shall be financially liable for the harm this may have caused.

---

[117] *Produktpirateriegesetz 2004—PPG 2004* BGBl I 56/2004 (Law on Counterfeiting 2004).
[118] Cf n 62 above; cf in particular ss 51–52.
[119] *Bundesgesetz gegen den unlauteren Wettbewerb 1984*, s 1—*UWG*, BGBl 448/1984 (WV) as amended, BGBl I 136/2004 (Law against Unfair Competition)—'acts contrary to honest practice'.
[120] *Produktpirateriegesetz 2004—PPG 2004* BGBl I 56/2004 (Law on Counterfeiting 2004).
[121] *Gesetz vom 27.5.1895 RGBl 79 über das Exekutions- und Sicherungsverfahren* (*Exekutionsordnung*), as last amended on 12 December 2003, BGBl I 112/2003 (Law on Execution).

4.212   The simplified procedure by itself normally rules out the possibility of any civil liability arising due to destruction of goods by error, since both the declarant, holder or owner of the goods and the right-holder have to agree to destruction—which agreement may in some cases be presumed. However, the declarant, holder or owner of the goods could have consented to destruction because he wanted to avoid legal proceedings, for example, because of the cost, without admitting infringement. On the other hand, the right-holder can, due to fault or negligence, request destruction without being sufficiently certain of the infringement. In this case it is clear that the declarant, holder, or owner of the goods would be entitled to damages for unjustified destruction from the right-holder because of his negligence. The limitation of action in respect of such a claim for damages is three years. It is, however, an open question as to how far the declarant, holder or owner of the goods could be considered jointly liable for the abusive destruction since he failed to object to it within the period provided for in Article 11 of the Regulation. If he was so liable, then the claim for damages would have to be reduced proportionally, or even fully set aside. This, of course, presupposes that the declarant, holder or owner of the goods was informed as to which intellectual property rights are deemed to be infringed.

4.213   Be that as it may, the liability of the right-holder is clearly defined in the declaration in accordance with Article 6 of the Regulation, which must be filed with any application for customs action. The liability which the right-holder has to accept under Article 6 is wider than that which results from the provisions of Austrian law concerning damages in all above-mentioned cases. It is not dependent on fault, and it is not restricted to cases of wrongful conservatory measures. It apparently also covers the simplified procedure.[122] However, when it can be argued on the basis of the facts that the injured party is in part responsible, together with the right-holder, for the prejudice incurred, a claim for damages will have to be lessened, if not set aside. Another issue to look at will be whether the declaration filed pursuant to Article 6 of the Regulation is binding under national law. Article 6 in itself only requires that a declaration be submitted, but does not provide for any formal requirement. Under Austrian law, this kind of document will be binding on its signatory only when personally signed or, if an electronic data interchange system is used, when accompanied by an electronically certified secure signature; where the declaration is executed on behalf of a legal person, it will only be binding on the latter provided it is signed by a (natural) person who is duly empowered to bind the company by virtue of the acts of incorporation of the company. Article 6 of the Regulation does not impose any such requirements.

---

[122] In any event, Art 11 of the Regulation provides that destruction in the context of the simplified procedure shall in all cases be carried out under the right-holder's sole responsibility, unless otherwise specified in national legislation.

B. Liability of customs authorities and sanctions

Article 19(1) of the Regulation provides that the acceptance of an application **4.214** entitles the right-holder to compensation in the event that infringing goods are not detected by customs or no action is taken to detain them, only where the law of the Member State in question permits so. Similarly, Article 19(2) states further that customs officials may only be held liable towards persons affected by an *ex officio* intervention in so far as such liability is provided by national law. The Austrian Law on Counterfeiting does not contain any specific provisions to that effect.

The national provisions that could be applicable when parties to the procedure set **4.215** out by the Regulation suffer a prejudice as a consequence of non-action or intervention by the customs officials can be found in the Public Liability Law.[123] Section 1(1) of this law provides for the opportunity to claim for damages whenever a public body (through public organs) causes harm in the context of law enforcement with fault and by an unlawful behaviour. It will be appreciated that very few decisions of interest under that heading have been published to date. One such decision[124] involved the Austrian Patent Office having failed to pass on an international trade mark application within the term prescribed. The decision makes it clear that non-compliance with deadlines to the prejudice of the parties concerned constitutes an illegal behaviour of public organs, which causes the relevant public authority to incur civil liability.

It will very often prove difficult to establish that a customs official has been at fault **4.216** in not detecting, and thus releasing, suspect goods. To do that, one would have to prove that the official did inspect the goods, checked (or ought reasonably to have checked) the application, realized that these goods matched the description contained in the application and were thus potentially infringing, and nevertheless released them. Therefore, there is little chance that the right-holder will be awarded damages under Article 19(1) of the Regulation and the Austrian Public Liability Law.

It is even less likely that a claim for damages as compensation for losses caused by **4.217** an *ex officio* customs intervention in accordance with the Regulation would ever prove successful. The Regulation itself tries to minimize unjustified losses which

---

[123] *Bundesgesetz vom 18. Dezember 1948, womit die Haftung des Bundes, der Länder, der Bezirke, der Gemeinden und der sonstigen Körperschaften und Anstalten des öffentlichen Rechts für den in Vollziehung der Gesetze zugefügten Schaden geregelt wird (Amtshaftungsgesetz—AHG) of* 18 December 1948, as amended in 1999, BGBl I 20/1949 (Public Liability Law). This Federal Law provides for the liability of the Federation, Provinces, Districts, Communities, and other bodies and institutions of public law for damages caused in enforcing laws.
[124] Case 1 Ob 95/00 b *Oberster Gerichtshof* (OGH) (Supreme Court), 25 July 2000, ÖBl 129/2001.

may result from border measures through imposing a very tight time limit on the right-holder. However, it also demands that customs officials act upon suspicion. A person aggrieved by retention of goods would need to show that the customs official took action without having 'sufficient grounds for suspecting that the goods infringe an intellectual property right'. This criterion is very flexible and will in principle very often be satisfied. Consequently, the parties involved will practically never have a chance to be granted damages under the Austrian Public Liability Law in such circumstances. However, after three working days, the relevant right-holder should have an application for action in place. If he does not fulfil this requirement, the goods will have to be released. Customs would definitely be at fault if they further detained goods without any ground after the expiry of the three-day period.

Conclusion

4.218   The Austrian national system on border measures is fully consistent with the Regulation.

4.219   The simplified procedure as it was applied prior to the entry into force of the Regulation was even more effective than the procedure set out in Article 11 of the Regulation, as the owner of the goods had only five days to oppose destruction, while the right-holder had 10 days to take legal action. With the new system, both have 10 days to react (3 when perishable goods are involved). Thus, the time period provided for under Article 11 coincides with that of Article 13, which means that in practice the right-holder will have very little time to institute court proceedings where the owner, declarant, or holder of the goods objects to destruction. Moreover, the right-holder is entitled to request an extension of time (save with respect to perishable goods) of 10 working days under Article 13 of the Regulation, but the owner, declarant, or holder of the goods can also require such an extension pursuant to Article 11(1), first indent, 'where circumstances warrant it'. The regime under the new Regulation might, therefore, necessitate the filing of an infringement action before the owner, declarant or holder of the goods has agreed to destruction or before it is clear whether he would agree at all.

4.220   Additionally, under the new Regulation one has to request information on the declarant, holder or owner and the origin of the goods, which was formerly provided right away, that is, a further complication of the proceedings.

4.221   On the whole, the majority of the cases will, as previously, be disposed of without court proceedings. Where court proceedings are to be initiated, these will generally come before the criminal courts and will lead to destruction of the goods without a final sentence being pronounced. An infringement of any of the intellectual property rights covered by the Regulation is considered a criminal offence under Austrian law, giving rise to various criminal penalties. Only very few cases will ever reach the highest courts.

The only debate which one may reasonably expect in the future relates to the **4.222** question whether pure transit (in the framework of the Regulation, *external* transit) can and/or should be covered by national intellectual property laws, which by definition prohibit infringements which occur within the jurisdiction to which they extend. However, this problem has become less significant since the enlargement of the European Union and the agreements between the Community and Switzerland, making Austria practically an inner European country.

5

BELGIUM

Olivier Vrins and Marius Schneider

Introduction

Belgium is one of the founder members of the European Communities. The first **5.01**
Community Regulation on border measures 3842/86/EEC entered into force in
the Kingdom on 1 January 1988.

However, the system of border measures in Regulation 3842/86/EEC was hardly **5.02**
applied in Belgium, as the national legislator failed to appoint the competent
authority within the meaning of Article 3 of this Regulation. As there was no
designated authority for processing applications for border measures, the system
was paralysed, with the exception of a few actions taken by particularly active
public prosecutors.[1]

It was only on 26 November 1996, nearly one and a half years after the entry into **5.03**
force on 1 July 1995 of the second generation Regulation 3295/94, that the
Belgian legislator finally deemed it necessary to adopt a Royal Decree which
proved crucial for the effective functioning of the system. The Royal Decree of 26
November 1996[2] entered into force on 14 December 1996 and is—as it has not

---

[1] The history of the application of Reg 3842/86/EEC in Belgium is described in O Vrins, 'Le
règlement (CE) n° 1383/2003 du conseil des communautés européennes du 22 juillet 2003: le droit
douanier élargit ses frontières' [2004] Intellectuele Rechten Droits Intellectuels, 101; A Braun, 'La
saisie en matière de contrefaçon: perspectives d'avenir' in F Gotzens (ed), *La saisie-contrefaçon*
(Brussels: Story-Scientia, 1991), 111.
[2] Arrêté royal du 26 novembre 1996, pris en application du Règlement (CE) n° 3295/94 du
Conseil du 22 décembre 1994 fixant des mesures en vue d'interdire la mise en libre pratique,
l'exportation, la réexportation et le placement sous un régime suspensif des marchandises de
contrefaçon et des marchandises pirates (Royal Decree of 26 November 1996 implementing Reg
(EC) No 3295/94 setting out measures to prohibit the release for free circulation, export, re-export
or entry by means of a suspensive procedure of counterfeit and pirated goods), Moniteur Belge
(Belgian State Gazette; hereinafter referred to as 'MB'), 14 December 1996.

225

yet been repeated—still in force today.[3] The Decree designates the Director General of Customs and Excise as the authority competent to process applications for customs actions.[4] It also sets out the amount of the security to be provided by the right-holder once potentially infringing goods have been discovered by customs.[5] However, this latter provision is no longer applied by Belgian Customs,[6] as Article 5(7), second indent, of Regulation 1383/2003 abolished the payment of fees and replaced it by a declaration accepting liability.[7] The Decree also specifies the amount of the security that has to be provided by the owner, importer or holder of the goods to obtain the release of the goods[8] under Article 14 of Regulation 1383/2003.[9] Finally, it makes the Director General of Customs and Excise responsible for informing customs inspectors by way of a Circular Letter of how the system of border measures is to be applied.[10] Such a Circular Letter was adopted in 1996.[11]

5.04 Another relevant provision of Belgian law, which has given rise to noteworthy case law,[12] is Article 320 of the Coordinated Laws of 18 July 1977 on Customs and Excise,[13] which imposes a duty of professional confidentiality on customs officers. On several occasions, the Belgian customs authorities have relied on this duty of confidentiality to justify their refusal to communicate the names and addresses of the persons involved in a particular case.

5.05 Following the entry into force of Regulation 1383/2003, the Belgian government presented a draft bill on the prevention of counterfeiting and piracy of intellectual

---

[3] However, the provisions conflicting with Reg 1383/2003 should no longer be applied, since the Regulation has direct effect over provisions of national law.

[4] Royal Decree of 26 November 1996, Art 1.

[5] Under Art 2 of the Royal Decree of 26 November 1996, the security to be provided by the right-holder each time suspect goods were discovered amounted to the customs value of the suspect goods, with a minimum of EUR 2,500. Fortunately, Belgian Customs had agreed that right-holders could provide a general guarantee for all customs interventions in the Kingdom.

[6] It is expected that Belgian Customs will refund the guarantee to right-holders once the customs action, under which it was paid, has been definitively closed. Right-holders who have provided a general guarantee may expect to be refunded once all actions for which the guarantee was provided have been closed.   [7] Reg 1383/2003, Art 6.

[8] Belgian Customs still apply Art 3 of the Royal Decree of 26 November 1996 to determine this amount.   [9] Compare Reg 3295/94, Art 7(2).

[10] Royal Decree of 26 November 1996, Art 4.

[11] Circulaire C.D. 593.6, Procédures Douanières, Mesures Economiques, Contrefaçon-Piraterie, Administration des Douanes et Accises, 1996 (Circular Letter C.D. 593.6, Customs Procedures, Economic Measures, Administration of Customs and Excise, Counterfeiting-Piracy, 1996), as amended on 1 July 2003 by the Circular Letter C.D. 593.80 following the implementation of EC Reg 241/1999 and 2549/1999.

[12] President of the Antwerp Court of First Instance (summary proceedings), 15 October 2002, *Koninklijke Philips International v Belgian State*, unreported, commented on in Part II of this chapter, para 5.110.

[13] Arrêté royal portant coordination des dispositions générales relatives aux douanes et accises, 18 juillet 1977, MB, 21 September 1977 (as amended). See also Loi du 6 juillet 1978 concernant les douanes et accises, MB, 12 August 1978 (as amended).

property rights.[14] This draft bill details how customs authorities may intervene under the current Regulation: including the nomination of the authority for processing applications for action, the amount of security under Article 14 of the Regulation, the simplified procedure under Article 11 of the Regulation and the criminal sanctions for violations of the Regulation. An important change is that a breach of the Regulation will, at least in some cases, be a customs offence, thus allowing customs themselves to pursue infringers. The draft law will also apply to national situations (not occurring at the borders) as it imposes criminal penalties for the violation of any intellectual property right once infringing goods are found within Belgium. The proposed measures also include a 'warning procedure' that will be applied by market inspectors specifically authorized to investigate infringements, and the possibility of settling claims with infringers. It can only be hoped that the draft bill is passed as soon as possible.

I. SUBJECT MATTER AND SCOPE OF THE NATIONAL LAW APPLYING THE REGULATION

In this Part, we will examine the circumstances in which Belgian Customs will act **5.06** against suspect goods (section A), the definition of infringing goods under Belgian law (section B) and the goods excluded from the scope of the Regulation (section C).

A. Circumstances in which Customs will act

Although Belgian Customs will in principle agree to apply border measures to **5.07** suspect goods regardless of the customs procedure, including re-exportation, external transit and transhipment, in practice statistics reveal that most of the cases opened by Belgian Customs in 2004 related to import (75 per cent), and transit (14 per cent), whereas only 10 per cent related to export.[15]

A minority of Belgian scholars argue that Regulation 1383/2003 only applies to **5.08** goods subject to a customs declaration within the meaning of Article 61 of the Community Customs Code,[16] thus excluding for example smuggled goods.[17]

---

[14] Avant-projet de loi relative à la répression de la contrefaçon et de la piraterie de droits intellectuels.

[15] European Commission (DG Taxation and Customs Union (TAXUD)), Breakdown of the number and percentages of customs procedures—EU 2004 (http://europa.eu.int/comm/taxation_customs/resources/documents/customs/customs_controls/counterfeit_piracy/statistics/counterf_comm_2004.en.pdf).

[16] Council Reg (EEC) 2913/92 of 12 October 1992 establishing the Community Customs Code [1992] OJ L302/1 (19.10.1992).

[17] C De Meyer and P Van Den Broecke, 'De douane verordening 1383/2003 en het douanebeslag' in M-C Janssens (ed), *Combattre les atteintes à la propriété intellectuelle* (Brussels: Bruylant, 2004), 83, 87–88.

This interpretation is not only contrary to the wording of the Regulation, but also to its *ratio legis*. Indeed, the Regulation not only applies to the situations where a declaration has been made under Article 61 of the Community Customs Code (which situations are defined in Article 1(1)(a) of the Regulation), but also to those situations where goods simply enter the Community customs territory in accordance with Article 37 of the Community Customs Code (referred to in Article 1(1)(b) of the Regulation).[18] In practice, this minority approach is fortunately not followed by Belgian Customs, as otherwise a significant proportion of the traffic in infringing goods would evade the application of the Regulation.[19]

B. Definition of infringing goods

5.09 According to official figures, a significant proportion of Belgian Customs' interventions in 2004—that is, 71 per cent[20]—related to goods suspected of infringing trade mark rights. Compared to infringements of other intellectual property rights, the infringement of a trade mark is fairly easy for customs to assess. We will examine the definition of counterfeit goods under Benelux law below.

5.10 Statistics also show that 28 per cent of the Belgian Customs' interventions related to pirated goods (none of them was reportedly based on a design infringement.[21] The definition of pirated goods under Belgian and Benelux law will be examined below.

5.11 A third section will deal with goods infringing other intellectual property rights. The official statistics for 2004 mention that 1 per cent of the interventions which took place in 2004 related to patents and supplementary protection certificates.

(1) Counterfeit goods

5.12 In Belgium, trade mark law is governed by the Uniform Benelux Trade Marks Law.[22] Under Article 13(A)(1) of the Uniform Benelux Trade Marks Law, which

---

[18] This principle was explicitly referred to by the Belgian legislator in the Explanatory Memorandum to the draft bill on the suppression of counterfeiting and piracy (n 14 above), 14. It is well accepted among Belgian (and international) scholars that Reg 1383/2003 covers all possible situations in which goods are likely to be intercepted by customs authorities in an EC Member State (K. Daele, 'Reg 1383/2003: A New Step in the Fight against Counterfeit and Pirated Goods at the Borders of the European Union' [2004] EIPR 214, 215).

[19] For instance, it is fair to say that at least 95% of all counterfeit cigarettes blocked by customs are smuggled goods, for which no declaration has been made under Art 61 of the Community Customs Code (n 16 above).

[20] European Commission (DG TAXUD), Breakdown of the area of law covered under Regulation (EC) 3295/94, expressed as a percentage of the number of cases—EU 2004 (n 15 above).

[21] Ibid.

[22] Loi uniforme Benelux sur les marques, MB, 14 October 1969, as last amended by the Protocol of 11 December 2001 (MB, 19 March 2003). A consolidated version of the Law is available in

is a direct result of the 'Harmonization Directive' on Trade Marks,[23] the owner of a registered Benelux trade mark has an exclusive right, without prejudice to the possible application of civil law in matters of civil liability, to prohibit third parties from doing the following without his consent:

- under Article 13(A)(1)(a), using, in the course of trade, a sign identical to the mark for identical goods or services to those for which the mark is registered;

- under subparagraph (b), using, in the course of trade, a sign for which, due to the identity or the similarity with the trade mark and due to the identity or the similarity of the products or services covered by the trade mark and the sign, there exists, in the mind of the public, a risk of confusion including the risk of associating the sign and the trade mark;

- under subparagraph (c), using, in the course of trade, a sign which is identical or similar to a trade mark for products or services which are not similar to those for which the trade mark is registered, provided this trade mark has a reputation within the Benelux territory and where the use of such sign, without due cause, takes unfair advantage of or is detrimental to the distinctive character or the reputation of the trade mark;

- under subparagraph (d), using a sign in a way other than to distinguish goods or services, where the use of such a sign, without due cause, takes unfair advantage of or is detrimental to the distinctive character or the reputation of the trade mark.

The definition of a trade mark infringement under the Uniform Benelux Trade **5.13** Marks Law is thus far broader than that of counterfeit goods under the Regulation. The latter only applies to a sign which is 'identical or which cannot be distinguished in its essential aspects' from a trade mark, and therefore certainly embraces the situations referred to in Article 13(A)(1)(a) of the Benelux Law. However, under the Benelux Law, all signs similar to the registered trade mark are infringing if a risk of confusion exists in the mind of the public (Article 13(A)(1)(b)). By way of contrast, whereas the Regulation requires that the counterfeit sign be *essentially* similar to the registered mark and that counterfeit goods be 'of the same type' as those for which the mark is registered, under Benelux law it is sufficient that the signs and the goods are similar, thus giving rise to a likelihood of confusion. Finally, the Regulation does not mention the concept of taking unfair advantage of or being detrimental to a trade mark with a reputation.

French and Dutch on the website of the Benelux Trade Marks Office www.bmb-bbm.org. The following authors examine the protection of trade marks under Benelux law in more detail: A Braun, *Précis des marques* (4th edn, Brussels: Larcier, 2004); J-J Evrard and P Peters, *La Défense de la Marque dans le Benelux* (2nd edn, Brussels: Larcier, 2000); T Van Innis, *Les Signes Distinctifs* (Brussels: Larcier, 1997).

[23] First Directive 89/104/EEC of the Council, of 21 December 1988, to Approximate the Laws of the Member States Relating to Trade Marks, [1989] OJ L 40/1 (11.2.1989).

Therefore the Regulation may not apply to the situations referred to in Article 13(A)(1)(c) and (d) of the Benelux Law.[24] This is regrettable, as many trade mark owners who are victims of counterfeiters have a trade mark with a reputation.

5.14 However, in practice, when applying the Regulation—whether at the request of the trade mark holder or in *ex officio* interventions—Belgian Customs take a broad view. They do not only act against goods that bear a trade mark that is identical to the mark on which the border measures are based, but also against goods which bear a similar trade mark leading to confusion in the consumers' mind. This includes visually and phonetically similar signs. Customs have, for example, retained goods bearing the sign NAUTIONL (instead of the word mark NATIONAL), ADIBASS (instead of ADIDAS), and VENEGRA (instead of VIAGRA). They have also taken action against goods bearing the sign in combination with an additional element (JEAN LACOSTE instead of LACOSTE) and against signs with certain elements omitted (CARDIN instead of PIERRE CARDIN). Customs are also particularly flexible when appraising whether the suspect goods fall within the list of goods (and services) referred to in the trade mark registration. Particularly in *ex officio* actions, customs block goods without applying the principle of speciality.

5.15 It is questionable whether the broad interpretation applied by Belgian Customs and the discrepancy between the Uniform Benelux Trade Marks Law and the Regulation could lead to the release of goods by a court on the grounds that the goods are infringing under trade mark law but not under the Regulation. To date there has been no decision on this particular point.

5.16 Belgian Customs do not hesitate to take measures against trade mark symbols (including logos, labels, stickers, instruction manuals or guarantee documents) and packaging material bearing a trade mark, even if presented separately. On many occasions, labels, stickers, buttons, watch faces, plastic bags, etc illegally bearing a trade mark have been blocked by customs.

5.17 It is worth recalling here that the exclusive rights of a trade mark owner do not include the right to prohibit use of the mark where it is necessary to indicate the intended purpose of a product, in particular as accessories or spare parts, provided that such use is made in accordance with honest practices in industrial or commercial matters. This important exception to the monopoly of the trade mark owner has to be kept in mind when acting against 'compatible' goods bearing a third party's trade mark. In such cases, provided the trade mark is used in small standard characters, with the preposition 'for', it will be difficult for the trade mark

---

[24] C De Meyer and P Van Den Broecke, 'De douane verordening 1383/2003 en het douanebeslag' in M-C Janssens (ed), *Combattre les atteintes à la propriété intellectuelle* (Brussels: Bruylant, 2004), 83, 89–90. On the same issue, see also, under Reg 3295/94, A Puttemans, *Droits Intellectuels et Concurrence Déloyale* (Brussels: Bruylant, 2000), 273 (n 1287).

owner to take successful action against his competitors. However, if the third party makes use of the particular script or logo used by the trade mark owner and/or if the preposition 'for' is used in smaller characters, the right-holder may take action.[25]

In Belgium, an application for action can only be based on a validly *registered* trade **5.18** mark,[26] as there is no national legislation extending the scope of the Regulation to mere trade mark applications. This may seem a burdensome requirement, as obtaining a registration certificate further to the filing of a trade mark application can sometimes prove time-consuming. However, under the Uniform Benelux Trade Marks Law, the trade mark applicant can obtain the immediate registration of the mark through an accelerated procedure.[27] Obviously the proprietor of the trade mark runs a certain risk, as his rights have not yet been examined and are open to dispute/objection. The accelerated registration procedure thus allows trade mark owners to take immediate action, which might prove a deterrent to the infringer in other countries.

(2) Pirated goods

Statistics show that almost one third of the border measures applied by Belgian **5.19** Customs in 2004 were based on a copyright, a related right, or a design infringement. Many of these interventions relate to audiovisual recordings and computer programs. This is a significant decrease compared to 2002 (56 per cent).

Article 1 of the Belgian Copyright and Neighbouring Rights Law[28] defines the **5.20** scope of protection of a copyright in Belgium. Copyright is granted for original creations which reflect the personality of the author.[29] Although a decision of the Supreme Court in March 2005 (cf n 29) may have increased it, in general the threshold for originality is not high, and even articles of everyday life, such as household goods, mobile phone accessories, watches and furniture may often be

---

[25] Uniform Benelux Trade Marks Law, Art 13(A)(7)(c). Compare First Directive 89/104/EEC (n 23 above), Art 6(1)(c), and Council Reg (EC) 40/94 of 20 December 1993 on the Community Trade Mark, OJ L 11/1 (14.01.1994) (as amended), Art 12(c). Cf also ECJ, case C-228/03 *Gillette v LA-Laboratories Ltd Oy*, 17 March 2005, not yet published.

[26] Reg 1383/2003, Art 2(1)(a)(i).   [27] Uniform Benelux Trade Marks Law, Art 6(E).

[28] Loi du 30 juin 1994 relative au droit d'auteur et aux droits voisins, MB, 27 July 1994, Corrigendum MB, 22 November 1994. This law is commented by the following scholars: F de Visscher and B Michaux, *Précis du droit d'auteur et des droits voisins*, Brussels, Bruylant, 2000; A Berenboom, *Le nouveau droit d'auteur et des droits voisins*, 3rd ed, Brussels, Larcier, 2005. Cf also the Law of 22 May 2005 implementing Directive 2001/29/EC of 22 May 2001 on the harmonization of certain aspects of copyright and related rights in the information society into Belgian law (Loi transposant en droit belge la Directive européenne 2001/29/CE du 22 mai 2001 sur l'harmonisation de certains aspects du droit d'auteur et des droits voisins dans la société de l'information), MB, 27 May 2005.

[29] Several decisions of the Belgian Supreme Court have confirmed this approach. Cf Cass 27 April 1989 [1988–1989] Arr Cass 1006; Cass 25 October 1989 [1989–1990] Arr Cass 272; Cass 11 March 2005 [2005] ECR I-2337. See also M Buydens, 'Quelques reflexions sur le contenu de la condition d'originalité', [1996] Auteurs & Médias 383.

considered as copyright protected works.[30] The protection includes, among other things, the right to reproduce or prevent the reproduction of the work in any manner or form whatsoever, the right to authorize or prohibit adaptation or translation of the work and the moral rights to the work.[31] The right is subject to many exceptions, including parody, etc.

5.21 Under Article 14 of the Uniform Benelux Design Law,[32] and without prejudice to the possible application of civil law in matters of civil liability, the owner of a design right may object to the use of a product in which the design is incorporated or to which the design is applied and which has an identical appearance to the design that has been applied for or which does not give the informed user a different overall impression. In assessing the scope of protection, the degree of freedom of the designer in developing his design is taken into consideration. Use of a product is interpreted as including the making, offering, putting on the market, selling, distributing, renting, importing, exporting, exposing, using or detaining of the product.

5.22 It appears from the above that there is again a discrepancy between the Regulation and the Belgian copyright and Benelux design laws. Whilst the Regulation uses the concept of 'copies', Belgian law defines the rights of the copyright-holders by reference to the concept of 'reproduction', which encompasses for example adaptations and translations. Under Benelux design law, all designs which have an 'identical appearance' to the registered design or 'which do not give the informed user a different overall impression' are regarded as infringing. It is therefore *a priori* difficult to agree with the point of view of some authors[33] that every copyright, neighbouring right, or design infringement as defined under Belgian copyright law or Benelux design law would be caught by the Regulation.

5.23 In practice, as for counterfeit goods, Belgian Customs take a broad approach when applying border measures to pirated goods—although their website suggests that only slavish copies will be regarded as 'pirated goods'.[34] As a rule, they will consider 'goods which are or contain copies' to include goods which are totally *or partially* similar to those protected by a copyright, a related right, or a design right.

---

[30] Benelux Court of Justice, *Screenoprint v Citroën*, 22 May 1987, [1988] RCJB 568. This liberal approach may be of strategic importance for right-holders.

[31] The scope of protection of neighbouring rights is defined in the second chapter of the law.

[32] Loi Uniforme Benelux en matière de dessins ou modèles du 25 octobre 1966, as last amended by the Protocol of 20 June 2002, approved in Belgium by the 13 March 2003 Law, MB, 14 March 2003.

[33] C De Meyer and P Van Den Broecke, 'De douane verordening 1383/2003 en het douanebeslag' in M-C Janssens (ed), *Combattre les atteintes à la propriété intellectuelle* (Brussels: Bruylant, 2004), 83, 90–91.

[34] See http://fiscus.fgov.be/interfdafr/burgers/namaak/index.htm.

(3) Goods infringing other intellectual property rights

Goods infringing a patent or a supplementary protection certificate

Official statistics for 2002 and 2003 gave no indication of Belgian Customs **5.24** actions taken on the basis of a patent or a supplementary protection certificate. This may be because the majority of cases, involving for example counterfeit medicines (such as counterfeited VIAGRA), are listed in the official statistics as trade mark infringement cases, since counterfeit pharmaceuticals often also infringe a trade mark. However, we are aware of several actions taken by Belgian Customs in the field of, for example, optical disk technology. The statistics for 2004 indicated that interventions based on patents and SPCs in Belgium amounted to 1 per cent.

Belgian Patent Law[35] states that the scope of the patent protection is determined **5.25** by the terms of the claims.[36] According to Article 27 of the Law, a patent owner has the right to prevent all third parties not having his consent:

- from making, offering, putting on the market or using a product which is the subject matter of a patent, or importing or stocking the product for those purposes;
- from using a process which is the subject matter of the patent;
- from offering, putting on the market, using or importing or stocking for those purposes the product obtained directly by a process which is the subject matter of a patent.

A patent owner can also prevent third parties from supplying or offering to supply **5.26** on Belgian territory, to a person not entitled to exploit the patented invention, an essential element for putting the invention into effect.

Certain acts such as acts done privately for non-commercial purposes and acts **5.27** done for experimental purposes are excluded from the patent protection.

The protection granted to holders of supplementary protection certificates in Belguim is governed by a law of 29 July 1994 on this subject (BS, 6 September 1994), which implements EEC Regulation 1768/92. Reference can therefore be made in this relation to Chapter 3 of this book, paras 3.152 and 3.153.

Goods infringing a national plant variety right

The protection of Belgian plant variety rights is governed by the Belgian Law of **5.28** 20 May 1975 Law.[37] Under Article 35 of this Law, the following acts amount to an infringement provided they are done knowingly and without the authorization of the holder of the plant variety right:

- the production for commercial purposes and commercialization of reproduction material of a protected variety, including ornamental plants or

---

[35] Loi sur les brevets d'invention of 28 March 1984, MB, 9 March 1985.
[36] Art 26 of the Patent Law.
[37] Loi coordonnée du 20 mai 1975 sur la protection des obtentions végétales (Law on the Protection of Plant Variety Rights), MB, 5 September 1975.

parts thereof, which are normally commercialized for purposes other than multiplication;

- the repeated use, during every reproduction cycle, of reproduction material of a protected variety, in order to produce another variety for commercial purposes.

5.29 In Belgium it is thus only possible to take action against deliberate acts of infringement where reproduction material is commercialized for the purpose of multiplication. Since under the Regulation the definition of 'goods infringing a national plant variety right' is a matter for national legislation, it can be assumed that customs actions in Belgium under this Regulation will be limited to those situations.

Goods infringing a national designation of origin or a geographical indication

5.30 The protection of designations of origin and geographical indications is governed by the Law on the designation of origin of wines and spirits of 18 April 1927[38] and the Law on unfair competition of 14 July 1991.[39] The latter Law has given rise to a series of Royal Decrees instituting Belgian designations of origin and geographical indications, such as *beurre d'Ardenne, jambon d'Ardenne, fromage de Herve.*

5.31 Belgian Customs have already received applications for action on the basis of these rights, new under the Regulation 1383/2003, and it remains to be seen how they will handle these cases in practice.

(4) Moulds and matrices

5.32 Under Article 2(3) of the Regulation, the application of border measures to 'moulds and matrices which are specifically designed or adapted for the manufacture of infringing goods' depends on the existence of a provision of national law allowing the right-holder to act against these goods.

5.33 In Belgium, the holder of a Benelux trade mark,[40] a Benelux design right,[41] a Belgian patent[42] and a copyright or a related right[43] may request that the moulds and matrices be confiscated and, in certain cases, destroyed, provided it can be proved the infringer acted in bad faith.[44]

5.34 Under criminal law, the Code of Criminal Procedure (*Code d'instruction criminelle*) provides that the public Prosecutor may seize any goods which he is

---

[38] Loi relative à la protection des appellations d'origine des vins et eaux-de-vie of 18 April 1927, MB, 28 April 1927.

[39] Loi sur les pratiques du commerce et sur l'information et la protection du consommateur of 14 July 1991, MB, 29 August 1991, cf in particular Arts 16 to 21.

[40] Uniform Benelux Trade Marks Law, Art 13bis(1). See also the Law of 1 April 1879 on Manufacture and Trade Marks (Loi sur les marques de fabrique et de commerce), MB, 3 April 1879, Art 12.   [41] Uniform Benelux Design Law, Art 14bis(1).

[42] Belgian Patent Law, Art 53.

[43] Belgian Copyright and Neighbouring Rights Law, Art 87(2)(2).

[44] For a more detailed overview of this issue, see eg M Buydens, 'La reparation du dommage en droit de la propriété intellectuelle' [1995] Revue de Droit Commercial Belge 448, 462–463.

satisfied may have served to commit an offence, thus including the infringement of an intellectual property right caught under criminal law.[45] This definition obviously covers moulds and matrices.

Customs officers should therefore retain suspected moulds and matrices, in order to allow the right-holders to demonstrate in a court action that the infringers acted in bad faith. **5.35**

C. Goods excluded by the Regulation

(1) Parallel imported goods

In Belgium, there is no national legislation allowing customs to apply border measures to parallel imported goods. **5.36**

Therefore, Belgian Customs are vigilant about not delaying the release of parallel imports. If a right-holder recognizes that the goods detained by customs are genuine goods imported from outside the European Community, he will not be entitled to seek a customs action under Regulation 1383/2003, at least under a strict interpretation of the Regulation. Likewise, as right-holders are prevented from using information provided to them by customs authorities for purposes other than those permitted by the Regulation,[46] they will in principle not be able to rely on alternative remedies under local law to act against the infringement at the borders—unless perhaps they have obtained the necessary information regarding the suspect consignment from other sources.[47] **5.37**

(2) Goods which have been manufactured under conditions other than those which have been agreed with the right-holder

There is no national legislation allowing border measures to be applied to goods which have been manufactured under conditions other than those which have **5.38**

---

[45] Cf Code of Criminal Procedure, Arts 28bis(3), 35 and 35ter. Arts 42 and 43 of the Criminal Code (*Code Penal*) also provide for the possibility for the criminal courts to order the forfeiture of moulds and matrices (see for example, Dendermende Criminal Court, 12 December 2005, Case No 20.99.5 5/00/26, not yet reported).

[46] Reg 1383/2003, Art 12; General Customs and Excise Law, Art 320 (cf para 5.98 below). As will be seen below, a violation of this rule makes the right-holder liable in civil law.

[47] There is however a recent ruling of the President of the Court of First Instance of Antwerp stating that legally obtained information—in this particular case the right-holder had filed a preventive application for action under the Regulation and was thus entitled to inspect the suspect goods and to receive the name of the consignor, consignee, declarant, or holder—may be used by the right-holder to initiate alternative procedures, such as a civil seizure of the goods. President of the Antwerp Court of First Instance (summary proceedings), 24 March 2005, *Ayezan E-Gistic LLC v Beecham Group PLC and others*, ARK n° 04/7856/A, unpublished (under appeal). This approach relies on Art 12, second indent, which suggests that any use of the above-mentioned information for purposes other than those listed in the first indent shall be permitted in accordance with national law.

been agreed upon. As with parallel imports, the right-holder may not prevent the release of such goods under the Regulation.

(3) Goods contained in travellers' personal baggage

5.39 Although Belgian Customs operate checks on travellers' personal baggage, it cannot be said that they take a particularly strict approach to any counterfeit goods found on such occasion.[48] There are no particular rules on how customs must calculate the limit of the duty free allowance of EUR 175. This is left to the discretion of the inspectors. The same applies to the appraisal of the 'non-commercial nature' of the goods. Having several items of the same kind or several sizes of the same item would certainly be taken into account when considering whether there is 'material indication of the existence of commercial traffic'.

5.40 Although customs have on several occasions been encouraged to take the value of an authentic product into consideration when calculating the limit of the duty free value, it is generally regarded as more important to raise the public's awareness of the phenomenon of counterfeiting than to control travellers' baggage for 'counterfeit knick-knacks'.[49]

II. APPLICATION FOR ACTION BY THE CUSTOMS AUTHORITIES

5.41 For many years, Belgian Customs have made extensive use of the *ex officio* procedure provided under what is now Article 4 of Regulation 1383/2003. In 2001 the overwhelming majority (90 per cent) of Belgian border measures were *ex officio* interventions, that is, interventions carried out prior to the filing of an application for action by the right-holder. In 2003 this figure dropped to 60 per cent (499 interventions), against 49 per cent in 2004 (451 interventions).[50] This indicates that right-holders have become more aware of the need to file applications for action with customs.

5.42 The so-called *ex officio* procedure will be examined in section A below, whilst the filing and processing of applications for customs action will be discussed in section B.

---

[48] In the authors' experience, it is difficult to believe the Community statistics, according to which 53% of the customs interventions made in Belgium in 2003 concerned goods found in travellers' baggage.   [49] M Schneider, Le vrai visage des faux, Le Vif, 30 July 2004.
[50] European Commission (DG TAXUD), Breakdown by Member State and type of procedure resulting in customs action (n 15 above).

A. Measures prior to an application for action by the customs authorities (*ex officio* measures)

The Belgian authorities interpret broadly the requirement of Article 4 that there **5.43** must be 'sufficient grounds for suspecting that the goods infringe an intellectual property right' for *ex officio* actions to be taken. They do not hesitate to withhold goods as soon as they have the slightest suspicion about them, in order to allow the right-holder to examine the goods and to file an application for action. The underlying idea is clearly to raise the awareness of the right-holders that their products are being counterfeited, thus putting them in a position to take the appropriate action.

Most *ex officio* interventions relate to traffic coming from, or going to countries **5.44** rated as 'high-risk countries'. As it is not possible to control the entire traffic, Belgian Customs have developed a so-called 'risk analysis', which consists of selecting the shipment that is to be physically controlled after analysing the transport documents and the place of provenance. Certain alarm signs trigger the attention of customs: incomplete addresses of the shipper and the addressee, incomplete or vague declaration of the goods contained in the shipment, unusual transportation routes, mixed shipments, etc.

When Belgian Customs uncover a suspect shipment, they retain the goods and **5.45** inform the right-holder and the declarant or holder of the goods. Very often, customs will first approach the right-holder or his Belgian representative over the telephone, informing them of the number of items and their nature. The right-holder, if he asks, will get the opportunity to inspect the goods. In many cases customs consider that the first contact with the right-holder falls within their discretionary power to ask 'the right-holder to provide them with any information they may need to confirm their suspicions'.[51] The result is that the three working days period is somewhat stretched, as the starting point is delayed by a few days, until customs *officially* notify the right-holder of their intervention. Finally, in exceptional circumstances, for example, when the right-holder is domiciled abroad or when there is a public holiday in the country where the right-holder is domiciled, customs may be more flexible in calculating the three working days deadline. It is questionable whether this flexibility is in line with Article 4 of the Regulation.

After having successfully completed an *ex officio* intervention, right-holders are **5.46** strongly advised to rely on this experience and to file a preventive application for action. By doing so they not only make available the information obtained in a specific case to all customs offices, but in addition, they are no longer bound by the short terms of the *ex officio* procedure.

---

[51] Reg 1383/2003, Art 4(2) *in fine*.

5.47 It is noteworthy that the customs post at Brussels airport (Zaventem) mainly, if not exclusively, operates on an *ex officio* basis. In certain cases customs in Zaventem do not even require the filing of an application for action *a posteriori*, once suspect goods have been retained. This rather unusual course of action developed at the time of Regulation 3842/86 and the initial version of Regulation 3295/94, which did not govern customs actions against goods placed in a free warehouse, which represented the vast majority of cases at an airport. After the amendment of Regulation 3295/94 in 1999 one would have expected that customs in Zaventem would have changed their way of working, but in fact, they have not done so.[52]

B. The lodging and processing of applications for customs action

5.48 In 2004 a total of 155 applications for action were filed with Belgian Customs, which corresponds to over 5 per cent of all applications filed in the Community during that year. This is a significant increase compared to 2002 when the figure was only 3 per cent.[53]

(1) Persons entitled to file an application for action

Definition of 'right-holders' under the Regulation

5.49 An application for action can be filed by a right-holder within the meaning of Article 2(2) of the Regulation, which includes not only the owner of the intellectual property right concerned, but also 'any other person authorised to use this right or a representative of the right-holder or authorised user'.

5.50 Some Belgian commentators believe that the definition of 'any other person authorised to use the intellectual property right' has to be applied in the broadest sense and includes (exclusive and) non-exclusive licensees and even distributors and agents.[54] Others advocate that licensees would only be entitled to file an application for action if their licence has been duly registered as required by Belgian (or Benelux) law.[55]

---

[52] L Weynants, 'Toepassing van de Piraterijverordening in België op het vlak van merkenrechten' [2000] BMM Bull 10.

[53] European Commission (DG TAXUD), Evolution of the number of applications for action per Member State, period 2002–2004 (n 15 above).

[54] C De Meyer and P Van Den Broecke, 'De douane verordening 1383/2003 en het douanebeslag' in M-C Janssens (ed), *Combattre les atteintes à la propriété intellectuelle* (Brussels: Bruylant, 2004), 83, 92–93.

[55] J-J Evrard and I Taymans, 'Défendre la marque avec l'aide des autorités douanières' in F Gotzen (ed), *Marques et concurrence* (Brussels: Bruylant, 1998), 71, n 7.

In the authors' view, Article 2(2)(b) of the Regulation raises two problems: first, **5.51** Belgian law requires that licences granted for an industrial property right be registered in order to be enforceable against third parties: this fundamental principle applies to Benelux trade marks,[56] Benelux design rights,[57] and Belgian patents.[58,59]

As the customs administration and the parties involved in a customs action (for **5.52** example, the consignee, the consignor, the declarant or the holder of the goods) are not parties to the licence, it would have to be registered in order to be enforceable against them. It may be possible to argue that the direct effect of the Regulation, which therefore prevails over national law, means that 'any other person authorised to use the intellectual property right' is entitled to request customs to intervene *irrespective* of whether the licence is registered or not—but this is questionable.

The second problem is that when an application for action by customs authorities **5.53** is filed by a 'person authorised to use the right' the infringement proceedings prolonging the customs intervention must also be brought by this authorized user: however under the Uniform Benelux Trade Marks[60] and Design[61] Laws the licensee may only initiate infringement proceedings without the right-holder if he has the authorization of the proprietor of the trade mark or the design right. Under Belgian Patent Law[62] the licensee does not have an autonomous right to commence infringement proceedings, unless he is the holder of an exclusive licence or the holder of a compulsory licence, and provided in that case that the patentee has not instituted proceedings, and he has duly notified the patentee of his actions.

For the sake of legal certainty, it is therefore recommended that persons **5.54** authorized to use the intellectual property right concerned ascertain that their licence agreement is enforceable against third parties and allows them to pursue infringers autonomously. Should this not be the case, they would be well advised to make sure that the proprietor of the intellectual property right in question agrees that they may act on his behalf.

---

[56] Art 11(C) of the Uniform Benelux Trade Marks Law provides that a licence agreement or a confirmatory declaration must be registered in order for the trade mark licence to be enforceable against third parties.

[57] Art 13(3) of the Uniform Benelux Design Law is drafted in the same terms as Art 11(C) of the Uniform Benelux Trade Marks Law. Licence agreements for a design right or a confirmatory declaration must be registered to be enforceable against third parties.

[58] It is noteworthy that under Art 23 of the Law on plant variety rights it is mandatory to register licences granted, but no sanction is provided for in the event of non-compliance with this requirement. The Law does not expressly state that licences have to be registered to be opposable but as opposability is generally dependent on the registration in most other fields of intellectual property law, this principle should presumably also apply to licences of plant variety rights.

[59] Art 45(4) of the Patent Law states that 'the granting of a licence for a patent application or for a patent (...) must be notified to the (Industrial Property) Office'. Art 45(5) provides that 'the granting of a licence (...) shall not be effective against the Office or third parties until the declaration (...) is entered in the Register and only within the limits deriving from those declarations'.

[60] Art 11(D). [61] Art 13(4). [62] Art 52(2).

5.55 In practice, Belgian Customs have seldom had to apply the broad definition of 'any other person authorised to use the intellectual property right', as almost all applications for action to date have been filed by owners of intellectual property rights or their representatives. Only a few forms have been filed by authorized users.

5.56 Under Belgian law and practice the concept of 'representative of the right-holder or authorised user' as defined in Article 2(2)(b) of the Regulation certainly includes natural and legal persons authorized to act on behalf of the right-holder such as attorneys-at-law, intellectual property right attorneys, consultants, collective management societies, and associations of right-holders. Licensees, distributors and commercial agents would also fall under this definition provided they had the authorization to act on behalf of the right owner.

Proof of entitlement to file an application for action

For right-holders stricto sensu

5.57 Under Belgian law and practice, the proprietor of an intellectual property right can prove his right for the purpose of the filing of an application for action by customs authorities using the following documents:

- For a registered trade mark, design right, patent, supplementary protection certificate, or a plant variety right, evidence that the right has been registered by the relevant office has to be submitted to customs: this includes original registration certificates or certified copies, but Belgian Customs will also accept as evidence a photocopy of the certificate or the official registration publication and printouts of official databases.[63]

- For a copyright, a related right or an unregistered Community design, any evidence establishing that the applicant for the customs measures is the actual owner of the right is sufficient. In Belgium this covers any document evidencing the ownership of the rights vested in the work. It is advisable to provide evidence with an incontestable date[64] by, for example, a notary public, the registrar of the Ministry of Finance, a bailiff, or a collecting society. However, any other evidence, such as a US copyright registration would suffice.

- For protected designations of origin, protected geographical indications, and geographical designations the applicant must prove both that he is the producer or a group of producers (association), and that the right relied upon has been registered.

5.58 In Belgium, the application for action cannot be based on a mere *application* for an industrial property right: registration is always required. Under the accelerated

---

[63] It is doubtful whether customs will accept extracts from *private* databases as evidence, with the obvious exception of private databases that contain scanned publications of the official gazette (eg www.edital.com).

[64] The 'i-dépot' is an alternative solution. This is a filing system proposed by the Benelux Trade Mark and Design Office. The author of the copyrighted work files two envelopes containing the documents evidencing the right with the administration. The latter stamps both envelopes and

registration procedure for Benelux trade mark applications the applicant will obtain a trade mark registration without delay.[65]

For persons authorized to use the right

Persons authorized to use the right within the meaning of Article 2(2)(b) of the **5.59** Regulation will have to submit as additional proof a document evidencing that the applicant is authorized to use the right in question.[66] For a copyright or a neighbouring right this would be a copy of a contract evidencing that the applicant is entitled to use the right. For an industrial property right this should be a duly registered licence agreement. As pointed out above (paras 5.49 ff), it is possible that mere distribution or agency agreements will also fulfil this requirement.

For representatives

The representative of the right-holder or any other person authorized to use the **5.60** right will have to provide customs with his authorization to act.[67] Belgian Customs accept a power of attorney form duly executed by the right-holder granting a mandate to the representative. No legalization or notarization is required. However, the original power of attorney form has to be submitted.

When an application for action is filed prior to any customs intervention a general **5.61** power of attorney may be submitted together with the application for action. If an application for action is filed as a result of an *ex officio* customs action, a specific power of attorney is required on a case-by-case basis.[68] In order to facilitate the procedure it is thus strongly recommended that a general application for action be filed prior to any customs intervention.

There is no nationality requirement for the representation before Belgian **5.62** Customs. Foreign representatives or right-holders can thus directly liaise with Belgian Customs, both in the case of national and 'Community' applications for action. Customs will however expect them to respond to customs communications without delay, and in one of the national languages (see para 5.68 below), and to be in a position to appear in person should this be required. Therefore, it is advisable to appoint a local representative.

Belgian Customs require the representative to produce the declaration referred to **5.63** in Article 6 duly executed by the right-holder.[69] Under Belgian practice, the

---

returns one of them to the author. The second envelope is held by the administration and can be produced in the event of a dispute.

[65] Cf Part 1(A)(1) of this chapter para 5.18. [66] Implementing Reg, Art 2(2).

[67] Implementing Reg, Art 2(3).

[68] This is because Belgian Customs have experienced problems with persons falsely claiming that they have been appointed as representatives of right-holders who had not taken the precaution of filing an application for action.

[69] Although the Note on Completion of the standard applications for action (cf Annexes II-A and II-B to the Implementing Regulation) provides that the undertaking under Art 6 must be signed

representative is thus, in principle, not allowed to sign the declaration on behalf of his client, although Article 2(3) of the Implementing Regulation suggests that this is possible under certain conditions.

(2) Competent customs department and formal requirements

Responsible customs department

5.64 In Belgium, the authority responsible for processing applications for action is the Director General of Customs and Excise,[70] Directorate 1 'Counterfeiting and Piracy',

SERVICE PUBLIC FEDERAL DES FINANCES
Impôts et recouvrement
Administration des Douanes et Accises
Services Gestion Groupes Cibles
Direction 1—Contrefaçon
North Galaxy—Tour A
Boulevard du Roi Albert II, 33, Bte 37
1030 Bruxelles
Tel: +32 2 336 31 38
Fax: +32 2 336 17 58
E-mail: org.contr.reg.div@minfin.fed.be
           michele.thibaut@minfin.fed.be

Form of the application for action

5.65 Under Belgian practice an application for action can be filed by facsimile or e-mail,[71] but a confirmation has to be sent by regular or registered mail. The original version of the application for action, which must be sent as a confirmation, should contain the original declaration under Article 6 of the Regulation and, if a representative has filed the application for action, the original power of attorney form.

5.66 In accordance with Article 3(3) of the Implementing Regulation, Community applications for action have to be submitted in duplicate.

5.67 In our experience it is advisable to file—together with the application for action *stricto sensu*, and the documentation described below (cf paras 5.73–5.77)—12 copies of a manual intended to be provided to the different customs inspections

---

by the applicant, ie *in casu* by the representative of the right-holder *stricto sensu*, this is inconsistent with Art 2(3) of the Implementing Regulation, which states that this undertaking must in all cases be signed by the right-holder.

[70] Cf Art 1 of the Royal Decree of 26 November 1996 (n 2 above) and Art 3 of the draft bill on the prevention of counterfeiting and piracy of intellectual property rights (n 14 above).

[71] At present, no electronic data interchange system is available.

in order to allow them to make a first risk analysis. This manual should be a concise document describing the intellectual property rights relied upon, the main characteristics of the authentic goods and the way they can be distinguished from the infringing goods and the type and pattern of the fraud.

Language requirements

According to Belgian *practice*, Belgian Customs normally require that the application for action be filed in French, Dutch, or German. However, they also seem prepared to process applications filed in another language widely used in Belgium, such as English, without any translation. **5.68**

However, a distinction should be drawn between practice and *law*. Although Article 30 of the Constitution provides that 'the use of languages which are spoken in Belgium is free', this is only true with respect to Belgium's *national* languages. In this context it has to be pointed out that Belgium is a country with three national languages, namely, French, Dutch, and German. Therefore, the use of foreign languages, including English, is excluded from the scope of the constitutional principle set out in Article 30.[72] As a consequence, under Article 30 of the Constitution, (legal and natural) persons are in principle free to use any language in their dealings with the Belgian administrations—including Customs—provided the language in question is one of the three national languages specified above. The possibility of communicating with the administrative services in foreign languages will depend on the ability and willingness of those services to understand them. **5.69**

Moreover, laws and decrees may regulate this issue in more detail. Thus, Article 3 of the 30 June 1981 Decree from the Flemish Community (*Vlaamse Gemeenschap*) provides that private individuals as well as companies domiciled or incorporated in the 'Flemish language region' (*Vlaams taalgebied*) must in principle use Dutch in their dealings with the Flemish administration—such as Flemish customs offices. This rule applies to both oral and written communications. Under Article 59 of the Decree, any communication in breach of this provision results in it being null and void. Similar rules exist concerning the use of the French language in the French language region. In the Brussels-Capital region, a choice has to be made between French and Dutch, whilst in the German language region, German should be used.[73] **5.70**

---

[72] Cf Belgian State Council (*Conseil d'Etat*), Cases Nos 38.376 and 38.377 (20.12.1991), [1994] Pasicrisie IV-27.

[73] Concerning the situation in the Brussels and German-speaking regions, cf Coordinated Laws of 18 July 1996 on the use of languages in dealings with the administration (*Lois coordonnées sur l'emploi des langues en matière administrative*, MB, 2 August 1966). The situation in the Flemish language region is governed mainly by the Decree of 30 June 1981 (Decreet houdende aanvulling van de artikelen 12 en 33 van de bij Koninklijk Besluit van 18 juli 1966 gecoördineerde wetten

5.71   In dealings with the Central Administration of Customs—which is the authority competent to process applications for action under EC Regulation 1383/2003—Belgian *private individuals* (natural persons) may use any of the three national languages. Thus, applications for action filed by *Belgian* citizens under the Regulation have to be made out in French, Dutch, or German. Although in the French and Dutch-speaking regions, *legal persons* enjoy the same right, the administration will only reply to them in the national language of the language region in which they are incorporated. Moreover, for the acts and documents imposed by law—thus including the application forms annexed to EC Regulation 1891/2004—*legal persons* incorporated in the Brussels or German-speaking regions must use the national language of the region in which they are so incorporated or in which they have exploitation seats.[74] As regards foreign individuals and companies, nothing prevents them *a priori* from using English in their dealings with the Belgian administration. But conversely, the administration is obliged to use one of Belgium's national languages—depending on the place where it is located—when issuing a legal notice or decision; any document of such a nature made out in a foreign language shall be deemed null and void.[75]

5.72   As a result of the above, it is perilous to file an application for customs action in any language other than French, Dutch (or German). The owners and authorized users of an intellectual property right should not lose sight of the (complex) laws and decrees governing the use of languages vis-à-vis the administration. Rightholders (in the broad sense) are advised to file their applications for action in the language of the region in which they are domiciled or incorporated. Similarly, a representative, whose client has elected domicile in his office, will usually make use of the language of the region in which he has his office. In any event, in order to increase the accessibility by Customs to the information and thus the efficiency of their intervention, the exhibits submitted together with an application for action should preferably be filed in one of the national languages. This ought not to give rise to any difficulty regarding registration certificates or extracts of official

---

op het gebruik van de talen in bestuurszaken wat betreft het gebruik van de talen in de betrekkingen tussen de bestuursdiensten van het Nederlands Taalgebied en de Particulieren, MB, 10 November 1981). The use of languages in the French-speaking region is dealt with in the Decree from the French Community (*Communauté française*) of 12 July 1978 (Décret sur la défense de la langue française, MB, 9 September 1978). For more information on this subject, see T De Pelsmaeker anors, *Taalgebruik in bestuurszaken* (Bruges: Die Keure, 2004), and F Depleree, *Le droit constitutionnel de la Belgique* (Brussels: Bruylant, 2002).

[74] Coordinated Laws of 18 July 1996 on the use of languages in dealings with the administration (n 73 above), Arts 41(1) and (2) and 52.

[75] Concerning the use of English by foreign legal persons in their dealings with the Belgian administration, cf Belgian Language Control Body (*Vaste Commissie Taaltoezicht*), Cases No 30.187 (22.10.1998), No 23.038–23.039 (13.6.1991), No 30.241 (10.9.1998), No 28.048/G (4.6.1996) (use of English is permitted). Concerning the use of English by the Belgian administration in their official notifications, cf M-A Flamme, *Droit administratif* (Brussels: Bruylant, 1989), I, 355, and State Council, Case No 1-012 (10.7.1951).

databases as they are always issued in one of the national languages.[76] As regards the documentation (for example, brochures and technical documents), due to Belgian Customs' flexibility, it is very likely that they will be accepted even if they are submitted in any other language widely used in Belgium, including English. Nevertheless, as for applications forms, it has to be pointed out that Belgian Customs retain the right to request a translation.

(3) Requirements regarding the content of the application for action

As to the contents of the application for action the Regulation distinguishes between mandatory information, optional information, and additional information specific to certain intellectual property rights. **5.73**

Certain right-holders are reluctant when it comes to providing customs, which is after all part of the administration of finance, with sensitive information, such as the pre-tax value of the original goods. It should however be kept in mind that the quality of information provided to customs directly conditions the result of the customs work. Therefore right-holders should supply as much information as possible when submitting an application for action. **5.74**

Mandatory information

Under Belgian law and practice there are no specific requirements for the mandatory information that has to be submitted to customs under Article 5(5) of the Regulation. It is however advisable to provide a sufficiently detailed technical description of the goods to allow customs to identify any suspect goods. The same applies to information on the type and pattern of the fraud. Belgian Customs will expect the applicant's administrative contact person to be familiar with Belgian law and the Belgian customs procedure. Therefore the administrative contact should preferably be an attorney-at-law, a patent or trade mark attorney, or an association of right-holders. The technical contact person must be familiar with the authentic goods. It is generally accepted that the administrative contact may also be the technical contact, provided he has sufficient knowledge and experience in relation to the goods. **5.75**

Optional information

Although there are also no particular requirements relating to optional information in Belgium, customs expect the right-holder to provide all information classified as optional under Article 5(5) of the Regulation in order to facilitate **5.76**

---

[76] For national industrial property rights the certificate will be issued in one of the national languages. The Benelux Trade Mark and Design Office issues certificates in French or Dutch and the Office for Harmonization in the Internal Market issues them in all official languages of the

their work. Customs authorities always retain the right to request additional information if this proves necessary.

Additional information specific to the type of intellectual property right referred to in the application

5.77   There are no specific requirements for additional information in Belgium. It is however recommended that holders of intellectual property rights with technical aspects, such as patents, plant variety rights, or geographical indications, provide specific information to customs regarding the scope of protection of their rights.

(4) Processing and acceptance of the application for action

5.78   Belgian Customs will normally process the application for action within the prescribed term of 30 working days. Should there be any open questions they will contact the right-holder to complete the application for action. We are not aware of any instance where an application for action has been refused by Belgian Customs.

5.79   Belgian law does not provide for a specific appeal procedure under Regulation 1383/2003 against decisions from the Central Customs Administration dismissing an application for action. However, a Circular Letter issued under Regulation 3295/94 explicitly stated that actions appealing such decisions could initially be taken against the Litigation Department of the Central Administration (*Division Recouvrement et Contentieux*). Subsequently, right-holders were specifically advised to initiate appeal proceedings before the national courts.[77] Most commentators advocate that the right-holder will have to bring the appeal before a civil court.[78] A minority of scholars consider that, in the absence of any specific provisions on how such decisions may be appealed, they are open to administrative review before the State Council (*Conseil d'Etat*).[79] We tend to think that, under Regulation 1383/2003, the remedy under Belgian law would be an administrative review before the State Council, although it is unlikely that a right-holder would ever have to go that far.

5.80   Normally the decision granting the application for action is valid for one year. The right-holder may however, in particular circumstances, ask customs to intervene for a shorter period, for example, to ensure expiry dates correspond with those of

---

Community. Belgian patents and European patents designating Belgium will always be issued or translated in one of the official languages of Belgium.

[77] Circular Letter C.D. 593.6, as amended by Circular Letter C.D. 593.80 (n 11 above), para 12.

[78] F De Visscher and B Michaux, *Précis du droit d'auteur et des droits voisins* (Brussels: Bruylant, 2000), 542; J-J Evrard and I Taymans, 'Défendre la marque avec l'aide des autorités douanières' in F Gotzen (ed), *Marques et concurrence* (Brussels: Bruylant, 1998), 72, n 8.

[79] T van Innis, *Les Signes Distinctifs* (Brussels: Larcier, 1997), 474.

other pending applications for action or because the intellectual property right expires before the end of the one-year term.

(5) 'Community' applications for action

Processing of 'Community' applications for action filed with Belgian Customs

There are no specific rules on the processing of 'Community' applications by Belgian Customs, who have admitted that few such applications for action have yet been filed with them.

5.81

We recommend right-holders who wish to file 'Community' applications for action with Belgian Customs to do so in one of the national languages and to provide them with the copies intended for the responsible customs authorities in the other countries, as far as possible in their respective national languages.

5.82

Processing of 'Community' applications designating Belgium

As mentioned above, Belgian Customs take a liberal approach to handling applications for action designating Belgium: generally the administration will process applications filed in languages that are understood in Belgium,[80] the administrative and technical contact need not be domiciled in Belgium, etc.

5.83

III. CONDITIONS GOVERNING ACTION BY CUSTOMS AUTHORITIES AND BY THE AUTHORITIES WITH JURISDICTION TO DETERMINE WHETHER GOODS INFRINGE AN INTELLECTUAL PROPERTY RIGHT

Once Belgian Customs declare an application for action admissible, it will monitor the traffic of goods suspected of infringing the intellectual property rights referred to in the application at the borders. We will examine below the conditions governing action by the Belgian customs authorities (section A).

5.84

Once goods suspected of infringing an intellectual property right have been intercepted by customs, the right-holders are in principle compelled to refer the case to the authorities having jurisdiction to determine whether these goods do indeed infringe an intellectual property right (section C). This procedural requirement

5.85

---

[80] Nevertheless, the above comments on the validity of such applications (see paras 5.68 ff) should be borne in mind.

proved particularly burdensome in some cases, which led the European legislator to provide for an optional simplified procedure, which the Belgian government envisages implementing (see section B). During the procedure, the goods must be stored under customs' supervision (discussed in section E), although it may in some circumstances be possible to seek the release of the goods on provision of a security (see section D).

A. Conditions governing action by customs authorities

(1) Factual background

5.86 Belgium is in the thick of the trade of counterfeited and pirated goods. At least three factors contribute to this trend: the infrastructure and the central location of Belgium within the Community, the proactive approach that Belgian Customs have recently taken towards intellectual property infringements, and the lax repression of counterfeiting and piracy by the Belgian authorities. In 2003 Belgian Customs intercepted 55,030,118 infringing articles, which corresponds to nearly 60 per cent of the goods uncovered in the whole Community! This figure drapped to 20, 395, 907 in 2004.

5.87 Pirated and counterfeit goods mainly enter Belgium through airports (82 per cent of cases in 2000 and 2001, 71 per cent in 2002, 68 per cent in 2004). By and large, however, only relatively small consignments are intercepted in airports. The customs office of Brussels International Airport (Zaventem) is obviously the authority which is the most significantly involved in this field as this airport is located at the heart of Europe; in heavy periods, the Brussels airport customs may control between 30 and 40 consignments of suspected goods a day; Bierset airport, located near Liege, close to the Luxembourg, French and German borders, also regularly encounters counterfeiting and piracy.

5.88 Although at first sight they seem to be comparatively less involved in the fight against pirated and counterfeit goods (around 15 per cent of all actions in 2001, 21 per cent in 2002, and only 7 per cent in 2004), the Antwerp customs authorities actually play an essential role in this battle. Antwerp harbour is the second largest container seaport in the Community after Rotterdam harbour, with a capacity of more than 10 million containers per year. When looking at the quantity of goods stopped, rather than at the number of interventions per year, Antwerp harbour is one of infringers' favourite platforms for the dispatching of illegal products.

5.89 While the large number of procedures allegedly commenced by Belgian Customs against passengers (at least 53 per cent of all matters in 2003, and 42 per cent in 2004, according to official statistics, although one may question whether these figures are correct) is mainly due to the intervention of the Brussels airport customs authorities, procedures relating to commercial traffic are, for the most part, initiated by the Antwerp customs officers.

Over the past few years, there have been virtually no customs actions on trains. **5.90** Actions arising from road traffic amounted to barely 1 per cent in 2003 and 2004. As for postal traffic, it represented about 25 per cent of all customs actions carried out by the Belgian customs authorities in 2003 and 2004.[81]

Orders of counterfeited goods via the Internet are an increasing phenomenon. **5.91** Under Belgian law, it is very difficult to take effective action against these goods, since the shipment of small quantities of counterfeited goods cannot easily be pursued criminally. The fact that there are no effective, proportionate and dissuasive sanctions against these violations is in breach of Article 18.[82]

In the field of interstate cooperation, it is noteworthy that the EC Commission's **5.92** plans to broaden the RALFH programme as part of the Customs 2002 Action Plan, and to create synergies between the customs authorities of the major European harbours (Rotterdam, Antwerp, Le Havre, Hamburg, and Felixstowe) and other harbour services and to create a similar programme for the main international airports, including the Brussels airport,[83] are obviously warmly welcomed.

(2) Notification of customs intervention

When a Belgian Customs office is satisfied that goods in one of the situations **5.93** referred to in Article 1(1) of Regulation 1383/2003 are suspected of infringing an intellectual property right contained in Article 2(1) of the same Regulation, it will suspend the release of those goods or detain them.

Once the right-holder concerned has filed an application for action, provided that **5.94** the application has been granted by a decision from the Central Customs Administration, the customs office will follow the procedure laid down in Article 9 of the Regulation. The customs office immediately notifies the declarant (within the meaning of Article 4(18) of the Community Customs Code) or holder of the goods (within the meaning of Article 38 of the same Code), if they are known. Although an internal Circular Letter from the Central Customs Administration

---

[81] European Commission (DG TAXUD), n 15 above.

[82] Cf paras 5.171 ff below.

[83] See the Communication from the Commission to the Council, the European Parliament and the Economic and Social Committee concerning a strategy for the Customs Union, 8 February 2001, COM(2001) 51 final, 13. See also Decision 253/2003/EC of the European Parliament and of the Council of 6 February 2003 adopting an action programme for customs in the Community (Customs 2007), OJ L 36/1 (12.2.2003), and Corrigendum in OJ L 51/23 (26.2.2003); and the Communication from the Commission to the Council, the European Parliament, and the European Economic and Social committee on a Customs response to latest trends in counterfeiting and piracy, 11 October 2005, COM (2005) 479 final.

adopted under Regulation 3295/94[84] provides that the customs office should also inform the Central Administration, which is responsible for the notification of the customs action to the right-holder, in practice the notification is often made directly by the customs office.

5.95   When the relevant right-holder has not yet filed an application, or so long as no decision has been made on an application, the customs authorities will apply Article 4 of Regulation 1383/2003. The period of three working days provided for in Article 4 of the Regulation commences on the notification to the right-holder and to the declarant or holder of the goods, during which time the customs office is allowed to suspend the release of the goods or retain them. The retention, or the suspension of the release of the goods will be confirmed when the right-holder files an application fulfilling the requirements of Article 5 of the Regulation, and provided that this application is declared admissible by the Central Customs Administration under Article 9.

5.96   In either case, the customs office will also inform the Public prosecutor in the District where the action has taken place, in accordance with Article 29 of the Belgian Criminal Prosecution Code,[85] whenever the matter is likely to fall within his jurisdiction, that is, whenever there is a suspicion that the putting into circulation of the goods constitutes or is related to a criminal offence. This will, for instance, be the case where the goods infringe trade mark rights and copyrights,[86] but not for goods infringing, for example, a design right, a supplementary protection certificate, a patent or a plant variety right, as such infringements do not constitute criminal offences under Belgian law.

5.97   All notifications are made by facsimile, as no electronic data interchange systems have so far been put in place.

5.98   The notification of a customs action by the Belgian customs authorities to the right-holder under Article 9, and *a fortiori* under Article 4, of Regulation 1383/2003 may in some circumstances prove difficult because of Article 320 of

---

[84] Circular Letter C.D. 593.6, as amended by the Circular Letter C.D. 593.80 (n 11 above). Although these Circular Letters should now be regarded as obsolete, it remains to be seen whether the customs offices will continue implicitly to rely upon them in practice, or whether the Central Administration will adopt a new Circular Letter departing from the instructions which they contain.

[85] Code d'instruction criminelle. Art 29 reads as follows: 'Any authority, state employee, civil servant or public officer who acknowledges a crime or an offence during the course of his duties, shall be obliged to immediately notify the Public prosecutor with the court of the District where this crime or offence has been committed or where the suspect is likely to be found, and to provide this magistrate with any and all information, reports and minutes relating hereto.'

[86] Although the infringement of a design right does not constitute a criminal offence under Belgian criminal law, customs will most often notify the interception of goods containing an infringement of this type to Public prosecutors, as such goods may also in some cases breach, eg, a copyright, and therefore be a crime under Belgian law.

the 18 July 1977 General Customs and Excise Law.[87] Under this provision:

> any state employee or civil servant and any other person taking part, in whatever
> capacity, in the enforcement of tax laws, or having access to the offices of the Customs
> and Excise Administration, is bound to maintain absolute silence, outside the exercise
> of his functions, about whatever he has acknowledged when carrying out his duties.

Until recently, the Central Customs Administration used to consider that Article **5.99**
320 prevented the Belgian customs authorities from notifying customs actions
to the right-holders.[88] In order to circumvent this obstacle, the Central
Administration notified all such actions to the Public prosecutors, asking them to
forward the information to the right-holder. It would seem that these directions
are, fortunately, now obsolete. Indeed, the latest Circular Letter (No 593.80) set
out by the Central Administration of Belgian Customs—which still refers to the
consolidated version of EC Regulation 3295/94—gives instruction to the customs
offices to communicate the information referred to in the Regulation, in all cases
where the latter applies, so as to enable the right-holders to institute proceedings to
determine whether an intellectual property right has been infringed under national
law. Regrettably, however, this new guidance is not applicable where, beside counterfeiting, a customs offence is being investigated by Customs.

(3) *Information to be provided by customs to the right-holder before the right-holder confirms the infringing nature of the goods*

We have seen that, under EC Regulation 1383/2003, once goods suspected of **5.100**
infringing an intellectual property right are detained by the customs authorities,
the authorities are sometimes entitled, sometimes compelled, to give certain
information to the right-holder.

As long as the right-holder has not confirmed (or denied) whether the goods **5.101**
infringe his rights, the customs office or department is *authorized* to inform
him—as well as the declarant or holder of the goods—of the actual or estimated
quantity and the actual or supposed nature of the goods the release of which has
been suspended or which have been detained. This principle applies not only in
the context of *ex officio* procedures (Article 4(2) of the Regulation) but equally in

---

[87] N 13 above. Breaches of administrative and professional secrecy are punished under Art 458 of
the Belgian Criminal Code (Code pénal), which reads as follows: 'Doctors, surgeons, health officers,
pharmacists, midwifes and any and all other persons who, by reason of his status or profession, has
secrets confided to him and who discloses such secrets will, except where called upon to testify in court
or before a Parliamentary inquiry commission and where obliged by law to disclose such secrets, be
liable to a jail term of between 8 days and 6 months and to a fine of 100 to 500 [Euros]' (cf Loi du 26
juin 2000 relative à l'introduction de l'euro dans la legislation concernant les matières visées à l'article
78 de la Constitution (Law of 26 June 2000 on the introduction of the Euro into the legislation
relating to matters referred to in Art 78 of the Constitution), MB, 29 July 2000, esp. Art 2).
[88] See the above-mentioned Circular Letters C.D. 593.6 and 593.80 (n 11 above), para 21.

the context of actions subsequent to the filing (and acceptance) of an application by the right-holder (Article 9(2) of the same Regulation).

5.102 Where customs actions take place subsequent to the acceptance of an application filed by the right-holder concerned, customs are *obliged* to inform the right-holder, at his request and if known, of the names and address of the consignee, consignor, declarant or holder of the goods and the origin or provenance of goods suspected of infringing an intellectual property right.

5.103 However, both Article 4(2) and Article 9(3) of Regulation 1383/2003 only apply in so far as they comply with the national legislation of the Member State concerned on the protection of personal data, commercial and industrial secrets and professional and administrative confidentiality.

5.104 We have already mentioned (cf para 5.98 above) that Article 320 of the General Customs and Excise Law has in certain circumstances be used by the customs authorities to justify a refusal to notify an *ex officio* intervention to intellectual property right-holders.

5.106 This provision has long been relied on by the Belgian customs authorities as a ground for denying requests for information from right-holders under Article 9(3) of Regulation 1383/2003. Even though this approach has somehow changed (cf para 5.99 above), customs still consider that Article 320 prevents them from displaying any commercial document or packaging to right-holders—unless such document or packaging is also suspected of infringing an intellectual property right falling under the scope of the Regulation. Conversely, Article 320 does not apply to the declarant or owner of the goods, who may therefore examine the goods, business documents and packaging.[89]

5.107 As for the notification to right-holders of *ex officio* actions, the Belgian customs authorities circumvent Article 320 of the General Customs and Excise Law by asking the Public prosecutors—when alerting them of their action under Article 29 of the Criminal Prosecution Code—to communicate the information detailed in Article 9(3) of the Regulation to the relevant right-holder (cf para 5.99 and n 85 above).

5.108 On the one hand, this typical 'Belgian compromise'[90] aimed at circumventing Article 320 of the General Customs and Excise Law constitutes—or at least constituted, until very recently—a significant impediment to an efficient application and enforcement of EC Regulation 1383/2003.[91] Indeed, some Public prosecutors

---

[89] As provided eg in the above-mentioned Circular Letters C.D. 593.6 and 593.80 (n 11 above), para 15, which are still applied in practice on these points.

[90] So called by L Weynants, 'Toepassing van de Piraterijverordening in België op het vlak van merkenrechten' [2000] BMM Bull 9.

[91] S Evrard, commenting on the ECJ's *Adidas* decision in Case C-223/98, n 92 below, ([1999] Ingénieur Conseil 553). See also AIPPI's report on Question Q 147 on the effectiveness of border measures after TRIPs, Belgium report, available on http://www.aippi.org/reports/q147/gr-q147-f-belgium.htm.

are not (yet) used to notifying the requested information to right-holders and, when they do, often lose sight of the stringent deadlines imposed on the right-holder under Articles 11 and 13 of the Regulation.

On the other hand, this mechanism sometimes results in the right-holder being **5.109** informed by the Public prosecutors of data which he would not have been entitled to obtain directly from customs before the filing of an application. For instance, the public prosecutors may, as the case may be, inform them about the origin or provenance of the goods or the name and address of their consignee and/or exporter, whilst Article 4(2) of the Regulation prevents customs from disclosing under an *ex officio* procedure any information other than the actual or supposed number of items and their nature.

Whatever the advantages or disadvantages, Article 320 of the General Customs **5.110** and Excise Law is clearly in breach of Article 9(3) of EC Regulation 1383/2003, like it was in breach of Article 6(1) of EC Regulation 3295/94, as interpreted by the European Court of Justice in the *Adidas* decision of 14 October 1999.[92] Belgian scholars agree that the latter ruling should be considered as applying not only to trade marks but to all intellectual property rights referred to in the Customs Regulation.[93] The President of the Antwerp Court of First Instance came to the same conclusion in a decision of 15 October 2002.[94] On the same grounds, Belgian scholars unanimously agree that Article 320 can no longer be relied upon by customs when applying Article 9(3) of Regulation 1383/2003 (and formerly Article 6(1) of Regulation 3295/94).[95]

---

[92] Case C-223/98 *Adidas AG v Kammarrätten i Stockholm* [1999] ECR I-7081.

[93] F de Visscher and B Michaux, *Précis du droit d'auteur et des droits voisins* (Brussels: Bruylant, 2000), 543, n 12.

[94] President of the Antwerp Court of First Instance (summary proceedings), *Koninklijke Philips Electronics v Belgian State*, Case No 02/939/C, unreported. In this case, the well-known company Philips had applied for and obtained action by the Antwerp customs authorities for the retention of a consignment of products suspected of infringing several of its patents. Philips subsequently requested the name and address of the exporter and consignee of the goods in question from customs under Art 6(1) of EC Reg 3295/94. The customs authorities, relying on Art 320 of the General Customs and Excise Law, refused to meet this request. Philips, which was unable to obtain the necessary information from the Public prosecutor (as patent infringements are not caught by Belgian criminal law), had no other choice but to file summary proceedings before the President of the Antwerp Court for an injunction thereby obliging the Antwerp customs immediately to provide it with the requested information. The President of the Court allowed the claim, relying on the ECJ's *Adidas* ruling and the supremacy of Community law (including Reg 3295/94) over national laws (including Art 320 of the General Customs and Excise Law) ('(. . .) [The *Adidas* decision] is binding *erga omnes* in order to ensure a uniform application of Community law in the Member States (. . .)').

[95] F de Visscher and B Michaux, *Précis du droit d'auteur et des droits voisins* (Brussels: Bruylant, 2000), 543, n 12; S Evrard, commenting on the ECJ's *Adidas* decision [1999] Ingénieur Conseil 554; E Cornu and E De Gryse, 'La contrefaçon: état des lieux à la lumière de la jurisprudence belge récente (1997–2000)' [2000] Ingénieur Conseil 3, 26.

5.111 Although not strictly necessary from a legal point of view, an amendment to Article 320 of the General Customs and Excise Law appears suitable in practice when one sees how deep-rooted its flawed application by Belgian Customs has been. The EC Commission is reportedly considering the initiation of infringement proceedings against Belgium before the ECJ in the near future.

5.112 In the meantime, right-holders who do not succeed in obtaining the information referred to in Article 9(3) from customs on an expedited basis—a situation which has, fortunately, become rare—will have no choice other than to urge Public prosecutors to forward these on to them immediately upon receipt from the customs authorities or, if this is not successful, to initiate summary proceedings against customs before the President of the Court of First Instance with proper jurisdiction.[96] Should the right-holders suffer any prejudice due to a lack of—or a late—communication of the requested data, their only recourse will be a claim for damages against customs under the general tort law provision (Article 1382 of the Civil Code).

(4) Inspection of the suspected goods

5.113 Once notified of the detention or suspension of the release of suspect goods pursuant to Article 9(2) of the Regulation, the right-holders, and more generally all persons involved, are given the opportunity by the relevant customs office to inspect those goods. However, they are under no *obligation* to carry out such an examination.

5.114 The customs office is also entitled to take representative samples of the goods at this stage. If the right-holder expressly requests this, one or more samples will be handed over or sent to him.[97] The inspection of samples will in any event be carried out under the sole responsibility of the right-holder. Strangely enough, although the last indent of Article 9(3) of the Regulation makes the handing-over of samples subject to national rules, we are not aware of customs having ever refused to provide samples to right-holders, for example, by relying on Article 320 of the General Customs and Excise Law.[98]

5.115 Although customs do not yet seem to pay much attention to this point, samples will have to be returned to the relevant customs office on completion of the technical analysis and, where applicable, before the goods are released. However, this does not always prove possible, for example where a proper analysis of the samples results in their destruction.

---

[96] On this point, see further the decision of the President of the Antwerp Court of First Instance of 15 October 2002 mentioned above (n 94).

[97] Cf Circular Letter No 593.80 (n 11 above). L Weynants, 'Toepassing van de Piraterijverordening in België op het vlak van merkenrechten' [2000] BMM Bull 9, alleges that, in practice, it would have been difficult for right-holders to obtain samples from Belgian Customs under Reg 3295/94. However, although it is true that the Regulation did not explicitly allow for this, our experience is that customs have never been particularly reluctant to hand samples over to right-holders.

[98] Compare paras 5.103 ff above.

By and large, the Belgian customs offices also agree to send digital pictures of the 5.116
goods to right-holders. However, it might be much more difficult in some cases to
assess the infringing character of certain types of goods from a photograph and
pictures may also be less effective as evidence in legal proceedings.

Although it appears from Article 9(3) of the Regulation that the inspection of the 5.117
goods and the handing over of samples are in principle only possible after the
formal notification of a customs action to the right-holder under Article 9(2), in
practice the examination of the goods or of samples is also possible in Belgium
prior to the official notification (in writing) of a customs action, subsequent to a
preliminary informal 'notification' by phone. Between this informal contact and
the formal notification, no deadline is imposed on right-holders to inspect the
goods or samples, though customs expect them to communicate the results of
their investigations within a reasonable period.

Belgian case law has not yet addressed whether samples (let alone pictures) received 5.118
from the customs offices may be used in court, or whether such use would breach the
last indent of Article 9(3) of the Regulation. However, for the reasons detailed above
in Chapter 3, paras 3.299–3.303, it is hard to see why this would not be permitted.

The inspection of the goods and the handing over of samples will allow the right- 5.119
holders to determine whether or not those goods infringe any of the intellectual
property rights referred to in their application for action. However, one should bear
in mind that, as the Belgian government rightly pointed out, '[w]hether or not
counterfeiting has taken place invariably depends on the assessment of the right-
holder invited to authenticate the goods suspected of being counterfeit or pirated
goods. However, only the judicial authority is empowered to establish whether the
industrial or intellectual property right in question has been infringed'.[99]

B. Simplified procedure allowing the destruction of the goods without the need to determine whether an intellectual property right has been infringed under national law

Article 11 of the Customs Regulation has not yet been implemented in Belgium. 5.120
To date, neither the General Customs and Excise Law nor any other piece of
legislation explicitly allows the Belgian customs authorities to apply a procedure
akin to that set out in Article 11 of Regulation 1383/2003.[100]

---

[99] Answer to the seventh question posed by Japan to the Belgian delegation to the World Trade
Organization regarding the Review of Legislation on Enforcement—Belgium, Report from the TRIPs
Council No IP/Q4/BEL/1 of 17 November 1998, available on http://www.wto.org/wto/english/
tratop_e/TRIPs_e/intel8_e.htm.
[100] Draft bill on the prevention of counterfeiting and piracy (n 14 above), Explanatory
Memorandum, comment on Art 3.

5.121   Under the Regulation 3295/94 regime, Belgian Customs were, as a rule, opposed to settlement agreements being concluded by right-holders and the importer, declarant or owner of the goods, at least when such agreements did not lead to the destruction of the goods. As already mentioned above in Chapter 3,[101] this position appeared to be in line with the provisions of Regulation 3295/94 and with point 31 of the ECJ's *Adidas* ruling. In any event, Belgian Customs fiercely object to the retrospective granting of licences by the right-holders to the owners of infringing goods which have been retained under the Customs Regulation to allow their commercialization.

5.122   Nevertheless, it remains the case that in practice, the destruction of goods detained by Belgian Customs could in most cases be easily obtained without the right-holder having to initiate (costly and lengthy) court proceedings. The filing of a criminal complaint with the Public prosecutor with proper jurisdiction has indeed often resulted in the prosecutor ordering the destruction of the goods, most of the time at the right-holder's entire risk and at his own cost, whenever the declarant, importer, owner, holder or consignee of the goods did not object, either explicitly or implicitly, to the taking of border measures by Belgian Customs.[102] It is not clear, however, to what extent this mechanism complied with EC Regulation 3295/94, let alone with the rules of national law provided in the Criminal Prosecution Code.[103]

5.123   The new draft bill on the prevention of counterfeiting and piracy seeks to implement into Belgian law the option provided to the Member States under Article 11 of Regulation 1383/2003.[104] Under Article 6(2) of the draft bill, where customs authorities have detained or suspended the release of goods which are suspected of infringing an intellectual property right falling within the scope of the Regulation, they may, 'in compliance with the deadlines and requirements provided for by Article 11(1) of the Regulation', carry out the destruction of those goods, 'at the expense and risk of the right-holder'. The destruction shall systematically be preceded by the taking of samples. It shall be subject to the prior consent in writing of the declarant, holder or owner of the goods that they abandon the goods for that purpose. This consent shall be presumed to exist when the declarant, holder or owner of the goods has not specifically opposed the destruction within the period prescribed by Article 11 of the Regulation. In all cases where the declarant,

---

[101]   Cf paras 3.333 ff.

[102]   L Weynants, 'Toepassing van de Piraterijverordening in België op het vlak van merkenrechten' [2000] BMM Bull 10.

[103]   Indeed, in principle, Public Prosecutors may not decide what happens to the goods. Such decisions should be taken by the *chambre du conseil*, ie an equivalent to the US 'Grand Jury', if not by the courts. Nevertheless, Article 216 is of the Criminal Prosecution Code empowers Public Prosecutors to conclude transactions with the authors of certain criminal offences, including counterfiting and piracy, resulting in the abandonment of the offending goods. Transactions based on 'implied consent' do not seem possible however.

[104]   N 14 above. See on this point A Puttemans, 'Quelles suites donner à la future directive en Belgique?' in M-C Janssens (ed), *Combattre les atteintes à la propriété intellectuelle* (Brussels: Bruylant, 2004), 169.

holder or owner of the goods objects to or contests the destruction of the goods, the procedure laid down in Article 13 of the Regulation will apply.[105] Although the draft bill does not explicitly provide that the right-holder's agreement to destruction is a prerequisite for commencing this simplified procedure, the words 'subject to compliance with (. . .) the requirements of the Regulation' imply that such agreement is necessary. For the same reason, one may assume that any destruction of goods will always have to be carried out under customs control.

Should this draft bill ever be adopted—as is to be hoped—it still remains to be seen how it will be applied in practice. So, for instance, it is unclear whether the simplified procedure will be handled directly by customs authorities or by the right-holders, although a glance at the proposed wording of the text, and notably the reference made there to Article 11 of the Regulation, suggests that the procedure will be initiated in the main place by right-holders. Nonetheless, the declarant, holder or owner of the goods will be entitled to give their consent to the abandonment of the goods for destruction directly to customs if customs agree. **5.124**

Article 320 of the General Customs and Excise Law will probably again impede the proper application of this simplified procedure—although the new Circular Letter of the Central Administration of Belgian Customs should normally prevent this from happening (cf para 5.99 above). Indeed, assuming that Belgian Customs were to refuse to provide the contact details of the declarant, holder and/or owner of goods detained under Regulation 1383/2003 to the right-holder, it is difficult to see how the right-holder could take any steps to commence this procedure. **5.125**

C. Conditions governing action by the authorities having jurisdiction to determine whether the goods infringe an intellectual property right

(1) Authorities having jurisdiction to determine whether the goods infringe an intellectual property right

Under Article 13(1) of Regulation 1383/2003, in order to secure border measures taken by the customs authorities, right-holders must notify the customs office referred to in Article 9(1) of the Regulation within 10 to 20 working days of receipt of the notification of suspension of release or detention of the goods, that proceedings have been initiated to determine whether an intellectual property right has been infringed under national law. As explained above, the right-holder may also, alternatively, provide this customs office with a copy of the agreement provided for in Article 11(1), where applicable. **5.126**

---

[105] Ibid, Explanatory Memorandum to Art 6(2).

The regime of EC Regulation 3295/94

5.127 Article 7(1) of the former Customs Regulation 3295/94 distinguished between the notification to the customs office by the right-holder that the matter had been referred to 'the authority competent to take a substantive decision on the case', and the notification 'that the duly empowered authority had adopted interim measures'.

5.128 It was well settled under Belgian law that a referral to the 'authority competent to take a substantive decision on the case' required the service of a writ of summons before the courts seeking a decision on the merits.[106] 'Interim measures' were those which could be obtained in *ex parte* proceedings from the presidents of the courts in summary proceedings or any kind of seizure carried out by a duly empowered authority (such as, depending on the circumstances, a criminal or a civil seizure). Although the majority of practitioners were of the view that the filing of mere criminal complaints,[107] even when not leading to a seizure under criminal law[108] ('interim measure') within the 10 (or 20) working days period, fulfilled the requirements of Article 7(1) of Regulation 3295/94, the Antwerp Court suggested that only those criminal complaints coupled with what is known under Belgian law as a 'registration as an injured party'[109] qualified as proceedings seeking 'a substantive decision on the case'.[110]

---

[106] T Van Innis, *Les Signes Distinctifs* (Brussels: Larcier, 1997), 474–476. See also the answer to the sixth question asked by Japan and the thirty-seventh question asked by the United States of America to the Belgian delegation to the World Trade Organization regarding the Review of Legislation on Enforcement—Belgium, Report from the TRIPs Council No IP/Q4/BEL/1 of 17 November 1998, n 99 above.

[107] See further eg L Weynants, 'Toepassing van de Piraterijverordening in België op het vlak van merkenrechten' [2000] BMM Bull 9; C De Meyer and P Van den Broecke, 'De douane verordening 1383/2003 en het douanebeslag' in M-C Janssens (ed), *Combattre les atteintes à la propriété intellectuelle* (Brussels: Bruylant, 2004), 83, 108.

[108] The seizure under criminal law of all goods and documents establishing the existence and scope of a criminal offence, including all infringing products, is an essential component of criminal investigations: see Criminal Prosecution Code, eg Arts 28bis, 35, 42 and 89.

[109] Constitution de partie civile. Such complaints raise civil claims for damages.

[110] Antwerp Court of First Instance, 9 March 2004, [2004] Intellectuele Rechten Droits Intellectuels, 183. The facts of this case were as follows: In December 2000 and April 2001, the Antwerp customs authorities had imposed border measures under EC Reg 3295/94 on goods suspected of infringing several of Philips' patents in CD-R and CD-RW. After examining the products, Philips confirmed that they allegedly infringed its rights and applied for action by customs. Within the 10 working days referred to in Art 7(1), Philips filed simple criminal complaints (which it had wrongly classified as 'complaints with registration as an injured party') and notified these to customs. Further to this filing, the Antwerp Public prosecutor carried out a seizure of the goods under criminal law, but after the expiry of the terms imposed by Art 7(1), and eventually lifted those measures and closed the criminal files—since patent infringements do not constitute criminal offences under Belgian law. Philips subsequently turned to the civil courts and issued proceedings on the defendants before the Antwerp Court of First Instance, far beyond the terms of Art 7(1). The Antwerp Customs also upheld the border measures taken over the goods on this basis. The consignees of the disputed products issued proceedings against the Belgian State to obtain their release. Philips intervened in these proceedings. Both defendants failed to convince the judge that the filing of mere criminal complaints, especially under patent law (infringements of which do not constitute a

In spite of the above case law, the Belgian customs authorities used to be satisfied **5.129** with the notification of the filing of a mere criminal complaint for the purposes of Article 7(1) of Regulation 3295/94.

Clearly then, the interpretation of Article 7(1) of Regulation 3295/94 in Belgium **5.130** imposed a heavy burden on right-holders, as they could not systematically limit themselves to the filing of mere criminal complaints, without registration as an injured party, to secure border measures on the goods. Whenever the matter related to a criminal offence, they either had to make sure that the Public prosecutors handling their complaint carried out a seizure under criminal law on the products within the strict time limits of this provision, which was not always easy to achieve, or they had to register as an injured party, which gave rise to burdensome administrative formalities and also often to the deposit of a financial guarantee. In all other cases, where criminal law could not be relied upon, they had to refer the matter to the courts, which was very costly and ineffective since the defendants remained in most cases difficult to trace, especially due to Article 320 of the Belgian General Customs and Excise Law (cf para 5.99 above).

The regime of the new Regulation

General

Although some Belgian officials seem to consider that Article 13(1) of the new **5.131** Regulation compels right-holders to refer all customs matters to the courts for a decision on the merits of the case,[111] this provision might actually allow the right-holders to overcome the impediments which resulted from the application of Article 7 of Regulation 3295/94. Indeed, the new provision now simply requires that procedures aimed at determining whether an intellectual property right has been infringed under national law be initiated. The nature of those proceedings is no longer relevant; only their objective is important. It no longer appears compulsory that the case be referred to the authority 'competent to take a *substantive* decision' on the case. Proceedings leading to an interlocutory decision might therefore meet the requirement of Article 13(1), provided that they seek to determine whether the goods in dispute infringe an intellectual property right.

The exact ambit of Article 13(1) of Regulation 1383/2003 will depend on how **5.132** narrowly the concept 'proceedings' is interpreted. Strictly speaking, in Belgium, legal proceedings are only properly initiated: (i) as a general rule, once a writ of summons has been served on a defendant and provided that the case has been entered on the docket of the court before the date of the introductory hearing, or

criminal offence), met the requirements of Art 7(1). The decision of the court may, however, have been different in the case of goods infringing a trade mark or a copyright, as these are caught by criminal law. Philips lodged an appeal against the above decision. The appeal proceedings are still in progress.

[111] Explanatory Memorandum of the draft bill on the prevention of counterfeiting and piracy (n 14 above), comment on Art 2, 23; comment on Arts 3 and 25.

(ii) when the law so permits, when a request is sent to the docket of the court. If it were to be understood in that way, then the concept of 'proceedings' would perhaps still preclude the filing of mere criminal complaints. Moreover, several authors are of the opinion that the filing of criminal complaints without a registration as an injured party would also be insufficient for the purpose of Article 13(1) because they are filed with the Public prosecutors, who have no jurisdiction to determine whether or not goods infringe an intellectual property right; their only role is to investigate the matter and commence criminal proceedings before the courts whenever they deem it appropriate.[112]

5.133   The authors tend to the view that the new criterion provided for in Article 13(1) of the new Regulation, in so far as it no longer requires that proceedings *on the merits* be initiated, aims to broaden the scope of the Regulation to all kinds of administrative or legal proceedings whose purpose it is to determine whether the goods infringe an intellectual right. Moreover, it is worth noting that, unlike Article 7(1) of Regulation 3295/94, Article 13(1) of Regulation 1383/2003 no longer requires that the case be referred directly to the authority competent to decide on it.

5.134   On the other hand, at least at first sight, it may seem incorrect *a priori* to state that Article 13(1) of the new Regulation is, overall, more permissive than Article 7(1) of Regulation 3295/94.[113] Indeed, while they were clearly encompassed by the latter provision, it would seem that not all 'interim measures' can be regarded as falling within the scope of the former. Thus, for example, a seizure carried out under criminal law in the absence of any criminal complaint will in principle not qualify as 'proceedings' under Article 13(1),[114] unless one considers that the 'proceedings' referred to in this provision are to be construed broadly *and* may be initiated by persons other than the right-holders.

5.135   In any event, interim decisions following the commencement of legal proceedings and giving rise to a seizure would probably satisfy the requirement of Article 13(1), provided that the aim of those interim decisions is to determine or to gather evidence of the existence of an infringement of an intellectual property right.[115]

Remedies common to all intellectual property rights covered by the new Regulation

5.136   As already mentioned, there is no doubt that, under Belgian law and practice, the filing of 'regular' proceedings on the merits[116] before the courts of proper

---

[112] See further: C De Meyer and P Van Den Broecke, 'De douane verordening 1383/2003 en het douanebeslag' in M-C Janssens (ed), *Combattre les atteintes à la propriété intellectuelle* (Brussels: Bruylant, 2004), 109.

[113] However, Art 13(1) of the Regulation might be in breach of Art 55 of TRIPs if it is interpreted as regarding mere 'interim measures' as insufficient (cf above, Chapter 3, paras 3.346 ff and in particular para 3.358).

[114] C De Meyer and P Van Den Broecke, 'De douane verordening 1383/2003 en het douanebeslag' in M-C Janssens (ed), *Combattre les atteintes à la propriété intellectuelle* (Brussels: Bruylant, 2004), 108.   [115] Ibid, 107.

[116] *Procédure au fond.*

jurisdiction[117] and relying on an intellectual property right infringement, will qualify as 'proceedings seeking to determine whether an intellectual property right has been infringed' under national law for the purposes of Article 13(1) of Regulation 1383/2003. The main inconvenience of proceedings on the merits is that the backlog of the courts in Belgium means they are very time-consuming.

For the reasons outlined above, we are of the opinion that the same applies to *intra partes* summary proceedings[118] as well as to *ex parte* summary proceedings[119] initiated before the presidents of the courts of proper jurisdiction, seeking the grant of an interim injunction based on an alleged breach of an intellectual property right. Indeed, such proceedings require at the very least a prima facie assessment of the existence and validity of the claimant's intellectual property right as well as of the existence of an infringement of it by the defendant.[120] The disadvantages of such *intra partes* summary proceedings are that they can only be used when it can be shown that the claim is urgent and that they may not prejudice the merits of the **5.137**

[117] The right-holder will have to issue proceedings against the defendant before the commercial courts for goods infringing an indication of origin (Judicial Code, Art 574(3)) and counterfeit goods (Judicial Code, Art 573(1)). However, actions based on trade marks must be initiated before the courts of first instance whenever the parties are not traders, and the claimant may also opt for this court if he is not a trader but the defendant is. Furthermore, the claim may be initiated before the Justices of the Peace provided it does not exceed EUR 1,860.

In principle, the courts of first instance have exclusive jurisdiction for all other types of intellectual property right infringements. (Under copyright law, see Judicial Code, Arts 569(7) and 590). However, when the claim does not exceed EUR 1,860, the Justices of the Peace also have jurisdiction. For software, see Judicial Code, Art 569(24) and the 30 June 1994 Law implementing European Directive 91/250 of 14 May 1991 on the Legal Protection of Computer Programs, Art 13 into Belgian law. For plant variety rights, see Judicial Code, Art 569(20) and the 20 May 1975 Plant Varieties Protection Law, Art 38. For patent litigation, see the 28 March 1984 Patent Law, Art 73.)

The territorial jurisdiction will in principle be determined on the basis of the defendant's domicile or of the District where the goods have been intercepted. There are, however, several exceptions: see, eg for infringement and invalidity claims related to Community trade marks, Judicial Code, Art 574(11) (exclusive jurisdiction of the Brussels Commercial Court. See B Daume, 'The Community Trade Mark and the Jurisdiction of the National Courts' [1999] Ingénieur Conseil 177; V von Bomhard, 'Community Trade Mark—Enforcement Issues' [1999] BMM Bull 92). For Benelux trade marks, see the Benelux Trade Marks Law, Art 37 and Benelux Court of Justice, Case A 89/8, 10 December 1990 [1990] Jurisprudence 102. For patent rights, see the Belgian Patent Law, Art 73(2). For copyright infringements relating to computer programs, see the 1994 Computer Programs Law, Art 13. In order to improve the specialization of judges having to handle intellectual property litigation, a draft bill on the civil aspects of the protection of intellectual property rights (Avant-projet de loi relative aux aspects civils de la protection de certains droits intellectuels) aims to give jurisdiction for most infringement cases exclusively to the Brussels Commercial Court. However, the Justices of the Peace and the Courts of First Instance of Antwerp, Ghent, Brussels, Mons and Liege, will continue to have jurisdiction to handle, eg, copyright infringement claims other than those related to computer programs.

For the sake of completeness, see, for international jurisdiction issues, Council Reg (EC) 44/2001 of 22 December 2000 on jurisdiction and the recognition and enforcement of judgments in civil and commercial matters [2001] OJ L12/1 (16.1.2001). [118] *Référé.*

[119] *Procédure unilatérale en extrême urgence.*

[120] See eg on this point Y Van Couter, 'De *ne bis in idem* exceptie en de *prima facie* beoordeling van een beweerde merkinbreuk door de Voorzitter zetelend in kort geding: De ene Voorzitter is de andere niet ...' [1999] Intellectuele Rechten Droits Intellectuels 161.

case (meaning that the judge having to decide on the merits is not bound in any way by the decision handed down in summary proceedings).[121] Moreover, theoretically, a decision issued in summary proceedings ceases to be enforceable if 'regular' proceedings on the merits are not initiated within a reasonable period.[122,123]

5.138   Another expedient remedy is provided for in Articles 1481ff of the Belgian Judicial Code. It allows holders of a patent, a supplementary protection certificate, copyright or neighbouring right, *sui generis* database rights and plant variety rights to file *ex parte* proceedings to obtain the authorization to gather evidence of the existence and scope of an infringement of their rights at any place where such evidence is likely to be found as well as, in clear-cut infringement cases, the effective seizure of the disputed goods. This remedy, called 'descriptive seizure',[124] is akin to the French 'saisie-contrefaçon'[125] and to the English Anton Piller Orders. As for summary proceedings, the claimant may only commence descriptive seizure proceedings if he is able to establish prima facie the existence and validity of his intellectual right and the likelihood of an infringement of this right by a third party.[126] The Seizure Judge is also obliged to weigh up the parties' respective interests when deciding whether to grant or to deny descriptive seizure measures (balance of convenience).[127]

---

[121]   Judicial Code, Art 584(1) and (2), and Art 1039.

[122]   This principle is in line with Art 50(6) of TRIPs. Although the Belgian Supreme Court (*Cour de Cassation*) considers that the TRIPs have no direct effect in Belgium (Cass, 11 May 2001 [2001] *Auteur & Media* 353), the ECJ has urged the courts of the Member States to adopt a 'TRIPs-consistent' interpretation of their national laws 'whenever possible' (see eg ECJ, Case C-53/96, *Hermès v FHT* [1998] ECR I-3603). Art 50(6) has been applied directly by eg the President of the Hasselt Court of First Instance, 24 March 2000 [2000] Intellectuele Rechten Droits Intellectuels 147.

On Belgian summary proceedings (*référé—kort geding*) see further: Lindemans, *Kort Geding* (Antwerp Kluwer: 1985); P. Taelman, 'Het kort geding. Ontwikkeling van de urgentievoorwaarde en het vereiste bij voorraad uitspraak te doen in de jaren '90 alsook enkele procedureaspecten', *P&B* 1997.

[123]   In cases of 'absolute necessity', the sealing of the goods, the appointment of a sequestrator or a judicial expert may also be obtained in *ex parte* summary proceedings (Judicial Code, Art 584(3)). 'Absolute necessity' will only be found to exist when *intra partes* proceedings would deprive the claim of any useful effect (eg because there is a risk of evidence being concealed), or when the claimant would suffer a significant harm if he were to await the outcome of such *intra partes* summary proceedings (Supreme Court, 21 May 1987 [1987] Pasicrisie I-1160; Brussels Court of Appeal, 23 December 1999 [2000], Intellectuele Rechten Droits Intellectuels 48. On *ex parte* summary proceedings see further: E Monard and D Degreef, *Het eenzijdig verzoekschrift*, Antwerp: Kluwer, 1998). However, *ex parte* proceedings may prove to be of little benefit in customs matters, where the right-holder is in principle entitled to secure the retention of the goods without having to seek such a measure from the courts.

[124]   *Saisie-description.*

[125]   P Veron anor, *Saisie-Contrefaçon*, (Paris: Dalloz, 1999).

[126]   Antwerp Court of Appeal, 10 February 1993 [1993–94] Rechtskundig Weekblad 265; Brussels Court of Appeal, 18 December 1998 [1999] Intellectuele Rechten Droits Intellectuels 65. Descriptive seizure proceedings involve the appointment of an expert by the Court, who, depending on the terms of reference, must file a report on the technical features of the goods in dispute and the scope of the alleged infringement. Descriptive seizures must in all cases be followed—or preceded (Brussels Court of First Instance, 29 January 1996 [1997] Ingénieur Conseil 92)—by proceedings on the merits, with the risk, if they are not, of the Seizure Judge's decision and the expert's report being declared void (Judicial Code, Art 1488).

[127]   Supreme Court, 3 January 2002 [2003] Rechtskundig Weekblad 1056. Claims for descriptive seizures must currently be initiated before the Seizure Judge of the place where the infringement

In the past, trade mark and design right holders often used to favour *ex parte* sum-   **5.139**
mary proceedings, as neither the law nor case law allowed them to carry out a
descriptive seizure.[128] However, given the expediency of the descriptive seizure as
a remedy, this situation will probably change following the decision of the
Arbitration Court that Article 1481 of the Judicial Code illegally discriminated
against them.[129] As a consequence of this decision, it is fair to say that 'descriptive
seizure' proceedings have now become available to trade mark holders. It is
assumed that the Arbitration Court, if it were ever asked for a preliminary ruling
on design rights, would equally rule that design right holders can also use this
remedy.[130] The aforementioned draft bill on the civil aspects of the protection of
certain intellectual property rights[131] aims to fill the gaps left by the author of the
Judicial Code and to make the 'descriptive seizure' a remedy available to all
intellectual property right holders.[132]

In spite of their obvious advantages, 'descriptive seizure' proceedings are not a   **5.140**
panacea for right-holders. As with summary proceedings, they are only a 'prelude'
to proceedings on the merits and do not allow right-holders to claim damages.
Moreover, they do not entitle them to obtain an injunction against the alleged
infringer.

Remedies specific to some intellectual property rights covered by the new Regulation

Remedies under criminal law   Criminal prosecution is also an option open to   **5.141**
right-holders whose copyrights or trade mark rights have been infringed. There

---

occurs (Judicial Code, Art 633), although there are plans to entrust the presidents of the commercial courts with such claims. For descriptive seizure proceedings, see further F Gotzen (ed), *Beslag
inzake namaak* (Brussels: Bruylant, 1994); F de Visscher, 'La saisie-description en Belgique: état des
lieux et quelques réflexions pour l'avenir' in M-C Janssens (ed), *Combattre les atteintes à la propriété
intellectuelle* (Brussels: Bruylant, 2004), 23; L Golvers, 'Investigations judiciaires en matière d'usage
illicite de programmes et/ou de données', ibid, 63; O Mignolet and D Kaesmacher 'La saisie en
matière de contrefaçon: le code judiciaire à la rencontre des droits intellectuels', [2004] Journal des
Tribunaux 57; MP Sender, 'Litiges internationaux en matière de droits de la propriété intellectuelle:
Une saisie-contrefaçon extra-territoriale?', comment on Supreme Court, 3 September 1999 [2000]
Revue de Droit Commercial Belge 128, 132.

[128]   J-J Evrard and P Peters, *La défense de la marque dans le Benelux* (2nd ed, Brussels: Larcier,
2000) 158–159 and 192; M-C Janssens, 'Overzicht van het bestaand wettelijk kader' in M-C
Janssens (ed), *Combattre les atteintes à la propriété intellectuelle* (Brussels: Bruylant, 2004), 1, 7;
President of the Liege Court of First Instance, 29 September 2000 [2001] Ingénieur Conseil 152.

[129]   Arbitration Court, 24 March 2004 [2004] Intellectuele Rechten Droits Intellectuels 138. See
also M Draps, 'Arbitragehof bevestigt: beslag inzake namaak mogelijk voor merkhouders', ibid, 142.

[130]   This remedy has sometimes been denied (President Liege Court of First Instance, 29
September 2000 [2001] Ingénieur Conseil 152), sometimes granted (President Brussels Court of
First Instance, 13 December 1996 [1997] Ingénieur Conseil 22) to design right-holders.

[131]   N 117 above.

[132]   Art 7 of the new Directive 2004/48/EC of the European Parliament and of the Council of
29 April 2004 on the Enforcement of Intellectual Property Rights seeks to impose an analogous
remedy in all Member States (OJ L 157/45 (30.4.2004). See also Recitals 20 and 21.

are no criminal penalties for design right infringements or—in contrast with the applicable legislation in the majority of the EC Member States—for patent infringements.

5.142 Article 8 of the 1 April 1879 Manufacture and Trade Marks Law classifies several types of trade mark infringements as criminal offences.[133] The following fall within the scope of this provision:

- Whoever 'counterfeits' a trade mark. The 'counterfeiting' offence requires the *reproduction* of a mark on *unlawful* products which are *put on the market* with a view to harming the right-holder.[134] In other words, only straightforward trade mark infringements are caught by Article 8 of the 1879 Law. In practice, the counterfeiting offence is quite similar to the definition of 'counterfeit goods' in EC Regulation 1383/2003.
- Whoever fraudulently uses a counterfeit trade mark.
- Whoever fraudulently affixes a trade mark belonging to a third party to his own products or other commercial devices.
- Whoever puts products on the market which they know are counterfeit.

5.143 Article 9 makes it a crime to be an accomplice to such acts.

5.144 Unlike copyright infringements, the criminal prosecution of trade mark infringements requires a criminal complaint to be filed with the Public prosecutor of proper jurisdiction. The complaint may be lodged by any party harmed by the offence,[135] who may be someone other than the trade mark holder or a licensee. In the absence of such complaints, Public prosecutors are still entitled to carry out preliminary investigations—and, as the case may be, seize the goods; however, they may not initiate criminal proceedings or entrust the matter to an investigating magistrate.[136]

5.145 It is unclear whether the provisions of the 1879 Law also apply to Community trade marks, since the Judicial Code provides that infringements of such marks fall under the exclusive jurisdiction of the Brussels Commercial Court by virtue of Article 91 of Regulation 40/94. Moreover, Article 14(1) of this Regulation provides that 'the effects of Community trade marks shall be governed solely by the provisions of this Regulation (...)'.[137] In practice, both the courts and Public

---

[133] Arts 3 and 4 of the 30 June 1969 Belgian Law approving the Benelux Product Marks Treaty (MB, 14 October 1969) provide that Arts 8 to 15 of the 1 April 1879 Law still apply to criminal prosecutions for trade mark infringements.

[134] Supreme Court, 23 May 1945 [1945] Pasicrisie I-168.

[135] Supreme Court, 18 November 1986 [1987] Journal des Tribunaux 610. See further on this point B Michaux, 'Recours à la procédure pénale' in MC Janssens (ed), *Combattre les atteintes à la propriété intellectuelle* (Brussels: Bruylant, 2004), 137.

[136] Supreme Court, 6 February 1996 [1996] Arrêts Cassation 149.

[137] M-C Janssens (ed), *Combattre les atteintes à la propriété intellectuelle* (Brussels: Bruylant, 2004), 11.

prosecutors in Belgium have agreed to apply the provisions of the 1879 Law to Community trade mark infringements, which not only appears consistent with Article 14(1), last sentence[138] and the (non-limitative) wording of Article 14(2)[139] of Regulation 40/94, but also appears necessary as a result of Article 61 of the TRIPs Agreement, to which the EC is a party.[140]

Unlike under trade mark law, the definition of a criminal offence under copyright law is very broad, encompassing any 'infringement of a copyright or neighbouring right'.[141] Likewise, the malicious or fraudulent use of the name of an author or of a holder of a neighbouring right or of any distinctive sign adopted by such person to designate his work or performance is a criminal offence.[142] It is also a criminal offence to hold, for commercial purposes or trade, devices exclusively intended for the unlawful removal or circumvention of technological anti-copying protection devices for computer programs.[143] More generally, it is a criminal offence to manufacture, distribute, import, sell, rent, or advertise for sale or rental, or hold for commercial purposes, devices, products or components, or to provide services, designed to circumvent technological measures, which are principally designed, produced, adapted, or manufactured, to prevent or restrict acts with respect to subject matter enjoying copyright or related right protection, without having obtained the rightholder's consent. The same applies to the removal or alteration of electronic rights management information.[144] However, as with trade marks, the offence must have been committed wilfully—except when it relates to the putting on the market or use of a pirated item, in which case a criminal offence is committed as soon as the offender knows about the infringing character of the product.

De lege ferenda, a new draft bill[145] aims to extend significantly the boundaries of criminal law applying to intellectual property right infringements. If this bill is passed, nearly all intellectual property right infringements in Belgium will be caught by criminal law when they are committed wilfully. Furthermore, as is already currently the case under copyright law, the filing of a criminal complaint

5.146

5.147

---

[138] '(. . .) In other respects, infringement of a Community trade mark shall be governed by the national law relating to infringement of a national trade mark in accordance with the provisions of Title X'.

[139] 'This Regulation shall not prevent action concerning a Community trade mark being brought under the law of Member States relating *in particular* to civil liability and unfair competition' (emphasis added).

[140] 'Members shall provide for criminal procedures and penalties to be applied at least in cases of wilful trade mark counterfeiting (. . .) on a commercial scale (. . .).'

[141] 30 June 1994 Copyright Law, Art 80(1).   [142] Ibid, Art 80(2).

[143] 30 June 1994 Computer Programs Law, Art 11.

[144] 30 June 1994 Copyright Law (as amended by the 22 May 2005 Law (cf n 28 above), Art 26), Art 79bis, second indent. The first indent provides that the circumvention of such protection measures and rights management information equally constitutes a criminal offence.

[145] Draft bill on the prevention of counterfeiting and piracy (n 14 above). However, infringements of designations and indications of origin will continue to fall exclusively under civil law.

will no longer be required before Public prosecutors can initiate proceedings against the infringers. Mere attempted offences will also be penalized in order to encompass every kind of offending practices used by counterfeiters.

5.148   For the reasons which we have explained above,[146] it is to be hoped that the courts will be flexible enough to regard the filing of mere criminal complaints as meeting the requirements of Article 13(1) of the Customs Regulation, since criminal actions are much more dissuasive and cheaper than civil litigation and emphasize the negative impac of counterfeiting and piracy of social welfare, and not just on the right-holder's private interests.

5.149   On the other hand, criminal actions give right-holders little or no control over the prosecution (although the fact that the Public prosecutor coordinates investigations and proceedings may be seen by some as an advantage). Moreover, except under copyright law, the lodging of a complaint will as a rule preclude the enforcement of intellectual property rights before the civil courts as long as the criminal investigations are in progress. In the field of copyright, however, where this inconvenience does not arise, the filing of a complaint will have the additional advantage of allowing more time to consider filing a civil lawsuit than under the strict deadlines of Article 13(1).

5.150   Another advantage of criminal prosecutions over civil actions is that in criminal actions, the demurrage and destruction costs will generally—but not, for example, in the Antwerp District—be classed as criminal costs, which are not charged to the right-holder, even if the goods are found not to be infringing; however, in practice, criminal files are often closed without follow-up whenever it proves impossible to apprehend the persons involved in the traffic in Belgium. In such cases, which represent the vast majority of criminal matters, the destruction of the goods will generally be at the right-holder's sole risk and at his cost.

5.151   As a rule, right-holders will only consider alternative remedies to the filing of a criminal complaint when large consignments of goods are involved and provided that they have been given sufficient information on the persons involved in the traffic.

5.152   **Remedies under civil law**   Article 87 of the Belgian Copyright Law provides for a specific remedy called a 'cease-and-desist action' (*action en cessation*).[147] This remedy, which is also available for software under the 30 June 1994 Law implementing EC Directive 91/250 into Belgian law,[148] allows not only right-holders but 'all interested persons'—for example, licensees or distributors[149]—to ask the

---

[146] Paras 5.131 ff.

[147] See eg T Heremans, 'De stakingsvordering inzake het auteursrecht' [1996] Intellectuele Rechten Droits Intellectuels 69.

[148] President of the Brussels Court of First Instance, 28 December 2000 [2002] *Auteur & Media* 150; Ibid, 30 June 2003 [2003] Intellectuele Rechten Droits Intellectuels 177.

[149] Brussels Court of Appeal, 8 October 2001 [2002] *Auteur & Média* 344.

president of the court of first instance of proper jurisdiction to prevent a defendant from further infringing a copyright or neighbouring right. These proceedings result in a decision on the merits while following the expedient procedural principles of summary proceedings. Proof of urgency is not a prerequisite to the action. In all cases, the claimant whose arguments are successful will be able to obtain an injunction against the defendant, coupled with a lump sum penalty. In some circumstances, the court will also order the publication of the decision. However, the scope of this specific cease-and-desist remedy is limited. For example, disputes based on the enforcement of a contract under copyright law do not fall within the ambit of Article 87.[150] Likewise, it is not possible to claim damages in such cease-and-desist actions.[151]

This remedy is one of the most widely used in copyright law. Its expediency and effectiveness are seen by most lawyers as outweighing its obvious disadvantages (for example, that it is not possible to claim damages).   **5.153**

A similar remedy is also available to holders of certain intellectual rights under Article 95 of the 1991 Trade Practices Law.[152] Under this provision, the presidents of the commercial courts have jurisdiction to order anyone who is found guilty of unfair trade practices to cease and desist from such practices. In other words, the judge in such proceedings does not have to determine whether an intellectual property right has been infringed, but only whether the defendant is behaving unfairly towards a competitor. Obviously, in some cases involving, for example, a trade mark infringement, the finding of an infringement will generally lead to a finding of an unfair trade practice. It remains to be seen, however, whether this 'cease-and-desist' action will be regarded by the courts as falling within the definition in Article 13(1) of Regulation 1383/2003, which refers to proceedings aiming 'to determine whether an intellectual property right has been infringed'.   **5.154**

A draft bill aiming to broaden the scope of the cease-and-desist action under Article 95 of the Trade Practices Law to all intellectual property right infringements (including infringements of plant variety rights) which also constitute an act of disloyal competition is currently before the Parliament. Should this draft   **5.155**

---

[150] President of the Brussels Court of First Instance, 22 July 2000 [2001] *Auteur & Média* 253.

[151] Liege Court of Appeal, 4 December 2000 [2001] *Auteur & Média* 363.

[152] 14 July 1991 Trade Practices and Consumer's Information and Protection Law, Art 95. Art 96 of this Law excludes from the ambit of the cease-and-desist action in Art 95 actions which rely on a patent, copyright, design right or trade mark infringement. However, the scope of this provision has been steadily narrowed by the courts, at least in so far as it sought to prevent trade mark holders from initiating cease-and-desist proceedings under Art 95 relying on an infringement of their trade marks. The Supreme Court first held that Art 96 only applied when the act of infringement relied upon by the claimant remained confined within the boundaries of the principle of speciality (Supreme Court, 3 November 1989 [1990] Revue de Droit Commercial Belge 216). The Arbitration Court subsequently declared the same provision unconstitutional (Case 2/2002, 9 January 2002 [2001–02] Rechtskundig Weekblad 1529).

bill ever be passed, the courts to which such actions are referred would be entitled, subject to the fulfilment of certain basic conditions, to order the defendant to disclose information on the counterfeiting or piracy network and to order the destruction of the goods, moulds and matrices or their removal from commercial channels, at the defendant's cost.[153]

The draft bill on the prevention of counterfeiting and piracy[154]

5.156   The draft bill on the prevention of counterfeiting and piracy significantly limits the possibilities of actions under Article 13 of Regulation 1383/2003. Indeed, if passed, it will oblige right-holders, in all cases where Article 11 does not apply, to commence specific proceedings on the merits, but in accordance with the procedural rules for summary proceedings, before the president of the court having jurisdiction to decide whether the goods infringe an intellectual property right covered by the Regulation.[155] Upon receipt of the proof that this condition has been fulfilled, the customs office involved will then communicate all information available on the suspect consignment to the president of the court, either on its own initiative, or at the court's request. The right-holder will subsequently have to notify the court decision without delay to the customs office concerned. The customs office will then inform the Customs Regional Director, who will finally initiate the prosecution proceedings in accordance with the rules set out in the General Customs and Excise Law.[156]

5.157   This overly burdensome procedure does, of course, seem to conflict with several provisions of Regulation 1383/2003, at least if one interprets it as meaning that the communication to the right-holders of the information referred to in Article 9(3) will in the future be subject to the filing of a court procedure. Indeed, Article 9(3) entitles right-holders to obtain this information directly from customs on request. Moreover, this modus operandi would be absurd, as it is precisely the purpose of such a communication to allow the right-holder to determine whether the goods fall within the scope of the Regulation or are in fact genuine (or parallel imports).

(2) *Term for notifying customs that proceedings have been started*

5.158   Under Article 13(1) of the Regulation, right-holders have 10 working days (or 3 working days for perishable goods) from the receipt of the notification by customs

---

[153] Bill on civil aspects of the protection of certain intellectual property rights (n 117 above), Art 2.

[154] N 14 above, see esp Explanatory Memorandum, comment on Art 3, 25–26.

[155] The president of the court will be allowed to seek the opinion of an independent expert to decide on the case.

[156] When the circumstances of the case indicate that the commission of the offence is the result of mere negligence or mistake, the Regional Director will be entitled to propose a settlement to the defendant (General Customs and Excise Law, Art 281), under which the defendant will voluntarily abandon the goods for destruction, agree to bear all storage and destruction costs and pay damages to the right-holder. In all other cases, he will have to refer the matter to the criminal courts (Ibid, Art 263).

of the suspension of release or of the detention of the goods to inform the customs office concerned that proceedings have been initiated to determine whether an intellectual property right has been infringed under national law.

In applying Regulation 3295/94, the Belgian courts have held that, when a right-holder had already initiated proceedings under the Regulation with respect to a specific consignment of goods, he was no longer required to commence separate proceedings for subsequent customs actions relating to the same type of goods.[157] The same principle will most likely continue to be applied under the new Regulation. **5.159**

Article 13 of Regulation 1383/2003 provides that the term of 10 working days for non-perishable goods may be extended once 'in appropriate cases'. **5.160**

In practice, the Belgian customs authorities have seldom required proof of the 'appropriateness' of an extension requested by a right-holder, but that is not to say they will never do so.[158] **5.161**

D. Release of goods suspected of infringing certain rights on provision of a security

Provided that the conditions of Article 14(1) are fulfilled, Belgian Customs consider that they are *obliged* to release the goods. They will not do so when the Public prosecutor or a civil court has imposed interim (or conservatory) measures on the goods. **5.162**

Under Article 3 of the 1996 Royal Decree, the security required by Article 14(2) is a minimum of three times the customs value of the disputed goods for non-Community goods, or the statistic value for Community goods.[159] A draft bill proposes adopting the same criteria.[160] **5.163**

---

[157] President of the Antwerp Court of First Instance, Case No 03/97/C, *Bellure v Belgian State anors*, 6 May 2003, unreported.

[158] For instance, an extension of the initial deadline may be considered appropriate where it is impossible to initiate court proceedings because of a lack of information on the natural and legal persons involved in the traffic as a result of the application of Art 320 of the General Customs and Excise Law. This extension will then allow the right-holder to obtain the necessary information from the Public prosecutors after the filing of a criminal complaint.

[159] According to L Weynants, 'Toepassing van de Piraterijverordening in België op het vlak van merkenrechten' [2000] BMM Bull 10, the concepts of 'customs value' and 'statistic value' have not been defined, giving customs the discretion to determine the amount of the security. However, these notions are defined in the Community Customs Code, Art 29. As to the concepts 'community goods' and 'non community goods', see Community Customs Code, Art 4(7) and the Belgian General Customs and Excise Law, Art 1(12). For additional information on the calculation basis of this guarantee, see the answer to the sixteenth question asked by Japan to the Belgian delegation to the World Trade Organization regarding the Review of Legislation on Enforcement—Belgium, Report from the TRIPs Council No IP/Q4/BEL/1 of 17 November 1998 (n 99 above).

[160] Bill on the prevention of counterfeiting and piracy (n 14 above), Art 4. The conditions for the deposit of the security will be contained in a new Royal Decree.

5.164 We are not aware of any situation where Belgian Customs have released goods under Article 7(2) of Regulation 3295/94 or Article 14 of the new Regulation.

E. Storage of the goods and destruction process[161]

5.165 Under Belgian law and practice, storage costs are borne by the declarant for the period prior to the expiry of the 3 or 10 (up to 20) working days period set out in Article 13(1) of Regulation 1383/2003. After expiry of this period, a distinction should be made depending on the type of proceedings initiated by the right-holder:

- Pending court proceedings, the right-holder will bear the storage costs if the declarant refuses to do so, in accordance with Article 6(1) of Regulation 1383/2003. The right-holder will then be able to claim them back from the importer, exporter, declarant and/or manufacturer of the goods, either under a settlement agreement or by filing a claim for damages before the courts.

- When a criminal complaint has been filed and followed by a criminal seizure, or interim measures issued against the goods by the duly empowered authority, the goods ought in principle to be stored with the clerk of the court's office at no cost to the right-holder. In several Districts however (such as in Antwerp, where customs very often block an entire container full of suspect goods), this is practically impossible. As a consequence, some Public prosecutors have made the right-holder's prior consent to the payment of storage costs a prerequisite to the carrying out of a seizure under criminal law. One may question whether such a course of action complies with Belgian law; yet this is probably the price to pay for an efficient enforcement policy in the field of intellectual property law.[162] An alternative solution favoured by several Public prosecutors is to agree to close the criminal file upon voluntary abandonment of the goods by the importer or exporter of the goods.[163]

5.166 Regrettably in practice, however, storage, transport and destruction costs are in a vast majority of cases systematically charged to right-holders, who have to claim them back from the persons involved in the traffic of the goods.[164]

---

[161] For a more detailed overview of this issue under Belgian law, see J-J Evrard and I Taymans, 'Défendre la marque avec l'aide des autorités douanières' in F Gotzen (ed), *Marques et concurrence* (Brussels: Bruylant, 1998), 75–77 (under EC Reg 3295/94).

[162] Indeed, Art 79 of the 28 December 1950 Legal Costs in Criminal Matters Royal Decree provides that statements of sequestrator, sealing and the like costs are forwarded by Public prosecutors to the Minister of Justice after being approved by the Investigating Magistrate.

[163] J-J Evrard and I Taymans, 'Défendre la marque avec l'aide des autorités douanières' in F Gotzen (ed), *Marques et concurrence* (Brussels: Bruylant, 1998), 76.

[164] Answer to the thirteenth question asked by Japan to the Belgian delegation to the World Trade Organization regarding the Review of Legislation on Enforcement—Belgium, Report from the TRIPs Council No IP/Q4/BEL/1 of 17 November 1998, n 99 above. Demurrage costs are calculated in accordance with para 101 of the Circular Letter 'Accountancy' No C.D. 410 of the Central Administration of Belgian Customs (Vol I).

Once the destruction of the goods is ordered by the duly empowered authority at **5.167**
the outcome of the proceedings referred to in Article 13(1) or following a settlement agreement under Article 11 of the Regulation, the destruction process is
monitored by the customs office where the goods have been blocked. As a rule, the
customs office will only consent to proceed with destruction upon notification of
a copy of a final judgment allowing this or subject to the Public prosecutor's
authorization. In either case, the customs office will also have to obtain the prior
consent of the Customs Regional Director.[165]

IV. PROVISIONS APPLICABLE TO GOODS FOUND TO INFRINGE AN INTELLECTUAL PROPERTY RIGHT

As already pointed out above, the *importation* of goods considered to infringe an **5.168**
intellectual property right under Article 2 of Regulation 1383/2003 is an act of
infringement under the various Belgian intellectual property laws.[166]

The situation is more inconsistent in the case of exportation and re-exportation.[167] **5.169**
The status of external transit, let alone that of the transhipment of goods, is even
more ambiguous. As a rule, such acts are not caught by the 1991 Trade Practices
Law, as this only applies to those acts which have been effectively committed in
Belgium and which cause harm there.[168] The intellectual property legislation is—
to say the least—unclear on this point.[169] The requirement that the illegal use of a

---

[165] Circular Letters 593.6 and 593.80 (n 11 above), para 25 (obsolete yet still applied de facto
under the new Regulation).

[166] This is the case under Art 27 of the Belgian Patent Law when the products thus imported are
intended for commercial use or sale in Belgium. For the position under trade mark law, see Uniform
Benelux Trade Marks Law, Art 13(A)(1).

[167] The Uniform Benelux Trade Marks Law explicitly prohibits the exportation of counterfeit
goods; moreover, the concept of 'exportation' includes 're-exportation' (see the Protocol of 7 August
1996 amending the Uniform Benelux Trade Marks Law, approved in Belgium by the Law of 3 June
1999, MB, 26 October 1999). The same applies under the Uniform Benelux Design Law (see the
Protocol of 7 August 1996 amending the Uniform Benelux Design Law, approved in Belgium by the
Law of 3 June 1999, MB, 26 October 1999).
By contrast, the exportation and re-exportation of goods protected by a Belgian patent are not
caught by Art 27 of the Belgian Patent Law (Explanatory Memorandum to the Belgian Patent Law,
re Art 27, 14). *Contra: Les Novelles v° Contrefaçon*, para 159.

[168] See eg President of the Antwerp Commercial Court, 6 November 2003, *Carolina Herrera Ltd
anors v Arion Perfume & Beauty Inc*, Cases No 03/5491 to 5495, 6227, 6373 to 6379, 9056 and
9057, unreported: the 1991 Law does not apply to goods coming from the United Arab Emirates
and intended for the United States of America, blocked by the Antwerp customs authorities under
EC Reg 3295/94 while in transit (point 3).

[169] In trade mark law, the Protocol of 7 August 1996 (n 167 above) included in the definition
of acts constituting a trade mark infringement the placement under a suspensive procedure, by

---

trade mark be made 'in the course of trade' to be regarded as a trade mark infringement seems to preclude trade mark holders from relying on Article 16 of the Regulation in certain circumstances, and indeed some courts have held that the transit of goods illegally bearing a trade mark would not be regarded as an act of trade mark infringement under the Uniform Benelux Trade Marks Law, despite the clear-cut wording of EC Regulation 3295/94.[170] Under patent law, scholars unanimously agree, by reference to the Explanatory Memorandum of the Patent Law, that the placement in transit of goods illegally applying a patented invention is not an act of patent infringement.[171]

5.170 However, provided that this be the actual scope of Article 16 of the Regulation,[172] the direct effect of EC Regulation 1383/2003[173] will mean that the entry into/or removal from Belgium, release for free circulation, exportation, re-exportation, placement under a suspensive procedure (including external transit and transhipment) or placement in a free zone or free warehouse of goods found to infringe an intellectual property right at the outcome of the proceedings referred to in Article 13 of this Regulation will, in principle, be prohibited by the courts of the Member States, including the Belgian courts, in accordance with Article 16 of the Regulation.[174] This Article will prevail over national legislation, which will have to be interpreted, whenever possible, consistently with the

---

reference to Art 1(1)(a) of EC Reg 3295/94. This amendment was removed by a new Protocol of 11 December 2001 (approved in Belgium by the Law of 24 December 2002, MB, 19 March 2003. The same yo-yo game was played for Benelux designs (see the Protocol of 7 August 1996 (n 167 above), withdrawn on this point by the Protocol of 20 June 2002, approved in Belgium by the Law of 13 March 2003, MB, 14 March 2003).

[170] See eg Antwerp Seizure Judge, 4 September 2002 [2003] Intellectuele Rechten Droits Intellectuels 144, 146. Please also refer to the comments made in request of case C-405/03 (ECJ) in Chapter 3 of this book, paras 3.71–3.76.

Likewise, it is unlikely that the putting on the market of moulds and matrices which are specifically designed or adapted for the manufacture of counterfeit goods will in all cases be an act of trade mark use, and therefore a trade mark infringement, under the Uniform Benelux Trade Marks Law (T Van Innis, *Les signes distinctifs* (Brussels: Larcier, 1997), 477–478).

[171] M Buydens, *Droit des Brevets d'Invention* (Brussels: Larcier, 1999), 194; A Braun and B Van Reepinghen, 'Chronique de jurisprudence—Droits intellectuels (1987–1991)' [1992] Journal des Tribunaux, 506; AC Delcorde, *La Protection des Inventions*, Story-Scientia 1985, 75–76; B Van Reepinghen and M De Brabanter, *Les Brevets d'Invention* (Brussels: Larcier, 1987), 236–237.

[172] See on this point the discussion on the actual achievements and intentions of Art 16 of EC Reg 1383/2003 in the chapter dedicated to this Regulation above, paras 3.393–3.395, 3.397, and 3.409–3.411. See also the comments on the ECJ's rulings in cases C-383/98 and C-60/02, paras 3.66–3.69.   [173] See EC Treaty (Treaty of Rome, as amended), Art 249.

[174] H Van Hees, 'De Benelux Tekeningen- en Modellenwet na de Europese Harmonisatie' [2003] Revue de Droit Commercial Belge 559, esp 632, where the author stresses that the acts classified as infringements of a Benelux design in Art 14(1)(2) of the Uniform Benelux Design Law and Art 12(1)(2) of EC Directive 98/71 are not exhaustive and would therefore encompass all acts referred to in Art 16 of EC Reg 1383/2003. See also Joint Statements of the Governments of the Benelux Countries on the Uniform Benelux Design Law, 21. It is worth emphasizing that the list of acts constituting trade mark infringements in Art 13(A)(2) of the Uniform Benelux Trade Marks Law is also purely illustrative.

Regulation.[175] Nevertheless, the ECJ recently recalled that the duty to interpret national law so as to be compatible with Regulation 3295/94 in order to achieve the aim of that Regulation cannot, of itself and independent of a law adopted by a Member State, have the effect of establishing or increasing the liability in criminal law of an entity which has failed to meet the requirements of this Regulation.[176] The same principles will obviously continue to apply under the new Customs Regulation.

In order to ensure effectiveness of Article 16 of Regulation 1383/2003 in Belgium, the Belgian legislator is considering making any breach of the prohibition set out in this provision a customs offence.[177]   **5.171**

V. PENALTIES[178]

The penalties under criminal law for fraudulent trade mark infringements are jail terms of eight days to six months and fines of EUR 143 to 11,000. The maximum penalties may be doubled when further infringements on the same grounds are committed within the five years following a first conviction. Illegally manufactured goods and devices intended for their production may also be confiscated whenever they belong to the convicted (natural or legal) person.[179]   **5.172**

The penalties for copyright infringements consist of fines of EUR 500 to 500,000, and/or jail terms from three months up to two years.[180]   **5.173**

The infringement of design rights, patents, supplementary protection certificates, plant variety rights and geographical indications is not sanctioned under criminal law.   **5.174**

Given that these penalties are not severe enough to deter international traffic, as they should pursuant to Article 18 of the Regulation a draft bill proposes to increase penalties for offences related to intellectual property rights to comply with Article 61 of the TRIPs Agreement. In substance, the criminal penalties to   **5.175**

---

[175] ECJ, Case C-60/02, *Montres Rolex SA anors v X*, 7 January 2004, unreported, point 57. See also Case C-223/98, *Adidas* (n 92 above), points 23–25. In Belgium: Brussels Court of Appeal, 29 June 2000 [2000] Ingénieur Conseil 371 (under trade mark law). See further on this point G Betlem, 'Richtlijnconforme uitleg. Interpretatieve doorwerking van EG-recht' [1994] Intellectuele Eigendomsrechten 104.
[176] ECJ, Case C-60/02, *Montres Rolex SA anors v X* (n 175 above).
[177] Draft bill on the prevention of counterfeiting and piracy (n 14 above), Art 5.
[178] For additional details on this subject, see P Maeyaert, 'Piraterij en straf- en burgerlijke sancties in de domein van de intellectuele eigendomsrechten', Biblio 1995, 173 ff and B Michau, 'Receurs à la procédure pérale' n 135 above.
[179] Law of 1 April 1879 on Manufacture and Trade Marks, Arts 8–12.
[180] See further on this point the 30 June 1994 Copyright Law, Arts 81–86, and the 30 June 1994 Computer Programs Law, Arts 10 and 11.

which they would give rise would be harmonized and vary between EUR 500 and 500,000 for fines and/or three months to three years for jail terms. These penalties may be doubled when further infringements on the same grounds are committed within the five years following a first conviction. Although it is unclear whether the penalties referred to in Article 18 of the Regulation must in all cases be *criminal* penalties—which is doubtful, given that such measures are part of the so-called 'Third Pillar' and therefore probably cannot be imposed by the EC Commission under a Regulation adopted under Article 133 of the EC Treaty—it is suggested by the ECJ and the Belgian Ministry of Economic Affairs (in charge of Intellectual Property) that they are criminal penalties.[181] The Belgian legislator has therefore recently proposed to classify as criminal offences almost all breaches of intellectual property rights which are already caught by civil law. As long as this is not the case, one may sustain that Belgian law is in breach of Article 18 of the Regulation.

5.176   In both civil and criminal law, as well as an injunction—in most cases coupled with a lump sum penalty—the claimant will in some cases also be entitled to require the judgment to be published[182] at the defendant's cost and the destruction or at least the confiscation,[183] if not the appropriation, of the infringing goods, moulds, and matrices.[184] The claimant may also in some cases be entitled to the turnover realized from the infringing goods.

5.177   In civil law, the right-holder will also be entitled to claim damages (in the context of certain types of proceedings on the merits, for example, *not* for mere cease-and-desist actions). Such claims may include reimbursement of storage and destruction costs, as well as reasonable attorneys' and experts' costs.[185] With the award of damages, the actual harm suffered by the right-holder will sometimes prove difficult to establish. In most cases, the evaluation will be made on an equitable basis (*ex aequo et bono*). This often induces courts to act with a certain avarice,[186] which is in some cases motivated by the fact that the goods have already been disposed of outside commercial channels, or is justified by blaming the right-holders for not effectively fighting counterfeiting and piracy in the upstream supply chain.[187]

---

[181] Case C-60/02, *Montres Rolex SA anors v X* (n 175 above). Cf G Bailleux, 'Quelles réponses à la contrefaçon? Les initiatives en cours et à venir', paper distributed on the occasion of the Colloquium 'Namaak en Praterij' held in Brussels on 18 May 2005, at 9.

[182] Belgian Copyright Law, Art 81; Law of 1 April 1879 on Manufacture and Trade Marks, Art 13.

[183] Belgian Copyright Law, Art 85; Law of 1 April 1879 on Manufacture and Trade Marks, Art 12.

[184] See eg the Belgian Copyright Law, Art 87(2) and the Belgian Patent Law, Art 53.

[185] Concerning specifically the issue of attorneys' costs, cf Belgian Supreme Court (*Cour de cassation*), 2 September 2004, [2004] JLMB 1320.

[186] L Weynants, 'Toepassing van de Piraterijverordening in België op het vlak van merkenrechten' [2000] BMM Bull 9. Our experience, however, is that this situation is steadily changing towards a greater severity (which is also the aim of the Enforcement Directive and of the draft bill on civil aspects of the protection of certain intellectual property rights (n 117 above).

[187] J-J Evrard and I Taymans, 'Défendre la marque avec l'aide des autorités douanières' in F Gotzen (ed), *Marques et concurrence* (Brussels: Bruylant, 1998), 76.

Some pieces of legislation are silent, however, on whether it is possible to obtain **5.178** an order for the destruction of the counterfeit or pirated goods, moulds, and matrices: this remedy is in principle not explicitly available for, for example, patent and copyright infringements. Even the confiscation of the goods may be limited for some intellectual property rights to cases of bad faith.[188] Likewise, the legislator has often failed to give the courts the ability to order infringers to disclose information to right-holders on the counterfeiting network: for example, this is not possible under patent and copyright law, except perhaps on the basis of Article 41 of the TRIPs Agreement.[189]

A draft bill aims to fill these gaps.[190] The courts will now be entitled *in all cases* to **5.179** order the destruction or the disposal of infringing goods outside commercial channels, at the infringer's, declarant's, holder's, owner's, or consignee's cost, or, when these persons cannot be identified, at the right-holder's cost. They will also be authorized to order the publication of the judgment at the defendant's cost, as well as the confiscation of all economic profits of the operation.

As long as breaches of intellectual property rights are not customs offences under **5.180** Belgian law,[191] only courts will be entitled to impose sanctions against infringers and to decide on the lot of counterfeit and pirated goods.[192]

VI. LIABILITY OF CUSTOMS AUTHORITIES AND RIGHT-HOLDERS

A. Liability of right-holders and sanctions

Under Article 1382 of the Civil Code, the general Belgian tort law provision, any **5.181** natural or legal person who suffers harm due to the fault of a third party may claim compensatory damages. This provision will govern all liability claims under Article 19(3) of Regulation 1383/2003, whether initiated by the declarant, owner, importer, exporter, holder or consignee of goods, against a right-holder who has applied the Regulation in a negligent or reckless manner.

---

[188] Belgian Patent Law, Art 53.
[189] The Ghent Court of First Instance (5 April 2000, [2000] Intellectuele Rechten Droits Intellectuels 108) applied the latter provision for that purpose.
[190] See the draft bill on civil aspects of the protection of intellectual property rights (n 117 above), Art 6.   [191] See para 5.171 above.
[192] F de Visscher and B Michaux, *Précis du droit d'auteur et des droits voisins* (Brussels: Bruylant, 2000), 544.

5.182   The same is true for any damage caused by any use of the information provided by customs to the right-holders in breach of Article 12 of the Regulation and/or of Belgian law. As Article 12 has direct effect, the Central Administration of Belgian Customs will also be entitled to suspend the right-holder's application for action for the period of validity remaining before renewal and, in the event of a further violation of Article 12, to refuse to renew the application.

B. Liability of customs authorities and sanctions

(1) Liability of the Belgian customs authorities when applying the provisions of the Regulation

5.183   Under the former Customs Regulation 3295/94, which did not address the issue of the customs authorities' liability for its application, it was generally agreed that customs would be liable under the general tort law provision of Article 1382 of the Civil Code provided that they could be shown to have applied the Regulation incorrectly, and that the right-holder had suffered harm as a result.[193] Liability claims had to be initiated against the Belgian State, represented by the Minister of Finances (who is in charge of customs policies in Belgium). This principle was confirmed in a judgment by the Antwerp Court of First Instance of 9 March 2004.[194]

5.184   It remains to be seen whether the above principles will continue to apply under Regulation 1383/2003. Indeed, Article 19(2) of the new Regulation now clearly

---

[193] Answer to the tenth question asked by Japan to the Belgian delegation to the World Trade Organization regarding the Review of Legislation on Enforcement—Belgium, Report from the TRIPs Council No IP/Q4/BEL/1 of 17 November 1998, n 99 above.

[194] Antwerp Court of First Instance, 9 March 2004, [2004] Intellectuele Rechten Droits Intellectuels 183. As already stated (n 110 above), in this case, a patentee had requested the retention of goods intercepted by the Antwerp customs authorities while in external transit. The right-holder had only filed a criminal complaint within the period referred to in Art 7(1) of Reg 3295/94 which, the Court decided, was not sufficient to secure the retention of the goods, especially because of the absence of criminal sanctions for patent infringements in Belgium. The customs authorities, which had retained the goods far beyond the 10 (and even 20) working days period, were ordered by the Court to release them. The Court agreed that, in principle, Art 1382 of the Civil Code applied to the case and that it might be possible for the consignees to claim damages from the Belgian State. However, this principle was seriously tempered by the following considerations. The Court emphasized that the claimants had not established that the customs' fault—which was not disputed—was the direct cause of the harm suffered by the consignees. The Court was of the view that it remained to be seen to what extent this fault had been induced by the right-holder, who had presumably misled the customs as to the nature of the proceedings initiated under Art 7(1) of Reg 3295/94. The Court also raised doubts as to whether the claimants had suffered real harm. It pointed out that proceedings on the merits had been commenced by the right-holder to determine whether the products in question infringed the right-holder's patents. The Court held that if the outcome of these proceedings upheld the right-holder's arguments on this point, then the alleged harm to the consignees of the goods would consist of lost sales of unlawful products, for which there can be no award of damages under Belgian law.

states that the exercise by a customs office, or by another duly empowered authority, of the powers to exercise border measures conferred on them shall not impose any liability on them to the persons involved in the situations referred to in Article 1(1) or the persons affected by the measure provided for in Article 4 for damages suffered by such persons as a result of the authority's intervention, 'except where provided for by the law of the Member State in which the application is made or, in the case of an application under Article 5(4), by the law of the Member State in which loss or damage is incurred'. It is unclear whether a general tort law provision such as Article 1382 of the Belgian Civil Code constitutes a proper ground for a liability action against the customs authorities within the meaning of Article 19(2) of Regulation 1383/2003. Indeed, if Article 19(2) is to be seen as a general rule of law having direct effect in all Member States, 'circumvention' of this general rule would only be possible if Member States adopted a provision specifically and explicitly addressing the issue of customs authorities' liability, by virtue of the principle *lex specialis generali derogat*. However, it is doubtful whether Article 19(2) can be interpreted as a general liability rule, overriding the general tort law provisions which would otherwise have applied to the situations referred to in Article 19(2).

5.185 Therefore, in our view, if the Belgian customs authorities do not comply with the provisions of the Regulation, they should, as a rule, be liable to all natural or legal persons involved in the customs action. This ought definitely to be the case where, for example, there is a breach of the strict requirements and deadlines provided for in Articles 11 and 13 of the Regulation.

(2) Liability of the Belgian customs authorities for not detecting or taking action against goods suspected of infringing an intellectual property right

Lack of action prior to the filing of an application by the relevant right-holder

5.186 As already pointed out in the comments on Regulation 1383/2003, the spirit as well as the letter of the Regulation means that customs authorities may not be held liable to *right-holders* for failing to act under Article 4 of the Regulation, that is, prior to the filing of an application for action.[195] Indeed, the application of the *ex officio* procedure is purely optional and is not binding upon the customs services of the Member States.

---

[195] C De Meyer and P Van Den Broecke, 'De douane verordening en het douane beslag' in M-C Janssens (ed), *Combattre les atteintes à la propriété intellectuelle* (Brussels: Bruylant, 2004), 83, 100–101. *Contra* (but wrongly): Answer to the eighth question asked by Japan to the Belgian delegation to the World Trade Organization regarding the Review of Legislation on Enforcement—Belgium, Report from the TRIPs Council No IP/Q4/BEL/1 of 17 November 1998, n 99 above.

5.187   On the other hand, Article 1382 of the Belgian Civil Code entitles persons, *other than the right-holders*, involved in the situations referred to in Article 1(1) or affected by the measures provided for in Article 4, to claim damages from the Belgian customs authorities for harm suffered by them as a result of the intervention of the authorities. For instance, if the Belgian customs services negligently intercept goods which ought *reasonably* not to have been suspected of infringing an intellectual property right by a normally prudent person and such detention harms the holders of the rights in the goods, the customs services could be held liable. However, only flagrant or repeated mistakes could constitute a fault within the meaning of Article 1382 of the Belgian Civil Code, and therefore be a proper ground for a liability claim. Indeed, one should not lose sight of the fact that, at the end of the day, whether or not there has been an infringement invariably depends on the assessment of the right-holder invited to authenticate the goods suspected of being counterfeit or pirated goods.

5.188   Likewise, non-compliance with the strict deadline of three working days might be a fault which, if it causes harm, may, depending on the circumstances, support a claim for damages under Article 1382 of the Civil Code.

Lack of action subsequent to the filing of an application by the relevant right-holder

5.189   Under Article 19(1) of the Regulation (which in substance mirrors Article 9(1) of Regulation 3295/94), the acceptance of an application will not entitle right-holders to compensation in the event that goods are not detected by a customs office and are released or no action is taken to detain them in accordance with Article 9(1) of the Regulation, 'save as provided by the law of the Member State in which an application is lodged or, in the case of an application under Article 5(4), by the law of the Member State in which goods infringing an intellectual property right are not detected'.

5.190   For the same reasons given under paragraphs 5.183 and 5.184, we are of the opinion that the general tort law provision in Article 1382 of the Belgian Civil Code will apply to these situations. In other words, Belgian Customs will only be liable when the failure to detain or suspend the release of goods suspected of infringing an intellectual property right harms the right-holder and when these acts amount to a 'fault' which a normally diligent and careful official would not have made.[196] The court decisions on this point will depend on the circumstances of the case. For example, a failure to detain goods will be more likely to be held to constitute a fault when the right-holder's application contained very detailed information on the goods, the detention or suspension of release of which was sought.[197]

---

[196]   Answer to the ninth question asked by Japan to the Belgian Delegation to the World Trade Organization regarding the Review of Legislation on Enforcement—Belgium, Report from the TRIPs council No 1P/Q4/BEL of 17 November 1998, 99 above.

[197]   For additional information on the application of Art 1382 of the Belgian Civil Code and the calculation of damages in the application of, among other things, border measures, please refer to

Conclusion

Belgium is certainly amongst those Member States of the European Community **5.191** where the enforcement of intellectual property rights through border measures is the most efficient. The statistics for 2003 confirm this conclusion: more than 55 million infringing articles have been uncovered in Belgium during that year alone. This represents nearly 60 per cent of all infringing goods intercepted within the Community. There can be no doubt that Belgian customs officials have developed refined techniques of risk analysis allowing them to trace infringing goods, and that their motivation to do an outstanding job is at the highest in this sector.

There are however serious obstacles that right-holders and their representatives **5.192** have to deal with in their daily practice: there is still far too much reticence amongst customs officials to communicate the information necessary for right-holders to start an action aiming to determine whether an intellectual property right has been infringed. Customs justify their attitude by invoking—often improperly—their customs secret. This is definitely a serious hurdle for every practitioner and could even soon result in a total lack of communication by customs if intellectual property right infringements were to be made a customs offence, as the Belgian legislator contemplates. The French situation is symptomatic in this respect.[198]

Furthermore, there can be little doubt that the repression of counterfeiting and **5.193** piracy is not a priority for the Belgian authorities: the laws sanctioning infringements of intellectual property rights are often outdated and the criminal penalties—where they exist at all—are neither dissuasive, nor effective.[199] When it comes to prosecuting offences the public authorities, with a few but remarkable exceptions, are often reticent to take effective action. Of course, organized crime cartels are aware of this lax approach and ship infringing products through Belgium, which is one of the European countries where they run the lowest risk.

The payment of storage costs for keeping large shipments under customs control, **5.194** together with the extensive backlog of the Belgian courts, tend to be dissuasive for many right-holders, who face the payment of significant sums just for storing goods which will one day have to be destroyed in any case. This is yet another instance, amongst others, of Belgian surrealism.

It can only be hoped that the Belgian legislator adopts the draft bill on the prevention **5.195** of counterfeiting and piracy of intellectual property rights[200] without delay—thus implementing amongst others, the 'simplified procedure' set out in Article 17 of the Regulation—and that provision will allow overcoming the current obstacles.

---

the answer to the eighteenth question asked by Japan to the Belgian delegation to the World Trade Organization on the Review of Legislation on Enforcement—Belgium, Report from the TRIPs Council No IP/Q4/BEL/1 of 17 November 1998. See also M Buydens, 'La reparation du dommage en droit de la propriété industrielle' [1995] Revue de Droit Commercial Belge 448.

[198] Cf paras 5.103 ff.   [199] Cf paras 5.177 and 5.179.   [200] Cf para 5.05.

6

CYPRUS[1]

Alecos Markides and Hermione A Markides

Introduction

The Control of Free Circulation of Counterfeit and Pirated Goods Law 2002 **6.01** ('Law 31(I) of 2002'),[2] was adopted in 2002 in order to honour an obligation undertaken by the Republic of Cyprus during negotiations to prepare for its accession to the European Union. The object of this Law was the proper incorporation into the legal order of Cyprus of the following Community Acts:

- Council Regulation (EC) 3295/94, as amended,[3]
- Commission Regulation (EC) 1367/95, as amended.[4]

Law 31(I)/2002, which came into force on 5 April 2002, is still in force today, **6.02** notwithstanding the accession of Cyprus to the EU on 1 May 2004 and the

[1] The authors are indebted to the following members and associates of Markides, Markides & Co. for their valuable contribution in collecting the necessary material and drafting the first skeleton draft of this text: Ms Maria Ioannides, Ms Niki-Anthi Teoulidou, Ms Nicky Xenofontos, Mr Nicos Makrides, and Ms Christina Matheou. Finally, the authors' special thanks go to the Director of CCED, Mrs Zeta Emilianides and her associates in the Department, especially Ms Mari Haralambous, for the valuable help and information given.
[2] Ο Περί Ελέγχου της Διακίνησης Εμπορευμάτων που Παραβιάζουν Δικαιώματα Πνευματικής Ιδιοκτησίας Νόμος 2002, Ν. 31 (I) 2002, ΕΕ Παρ. I (I) Αρ. 3592, 5.4.2002 (Official Gazette Appendix I (I) No 3592, 5.4.2002).
[3] Council Reg (EC) No 3295/94 of 22 December 1994 laying down measures concerning the entry into the Community and the export and re-export from the Community of goods infringing certain intellectual property rights (OJ L 341/8, 30.12.1994), as amended by Council Reg (EC) No 241/1999 of 25 January 1999 (OJ L 27/1, 2.2.1999) and Council Reg (EC) No 806/2003 of 14 April 2003 (OJ L 122/1, 15.5.2003).
[4] Commission Reg (EC) No 1367/95 of 15 June 1995, laying down provisions for the implementation of Council Reg (EC) No 3295/94 of 22 December 1994 laying down measures concerning the entry into the Community and the export and re-export from the Community of goods infringing certain intellectual property rights (OJ L 133/2, 17.6.1995), as amended by Commission Reg (EC) No 2549/1999 of 2 December 1999 (OJ L 308/16, 3.12.1999), and by the act concerning the conditions of accession of the Czech Republic, the Republic of Estonia,

coming into force as from 1 July 2004 of Council Regulation (EC) 1383/2003[5] and of Commission Regulation (EC) 1891/2004.[6] However, by virtue of the EC Treaty (Treaty of Rome, as amended), Article 249, EC Regulations are directly applicable in the Member States, that is, they automatically become part of their respective national legal systems, without the need for the adoption of separate national legal measures. Therefore, Council Regulation 1383/2003 and Commission Regulation 1891/2004 have, since 1 July 2004, been part of the internal legal order of Cyprus.

6.03 The nature of Council Regulation 1383/2003 is such that, in our opinion, it leaves some freedom of action to the Member States, as the wording, 'in accordance with national legislation'; 'according to the rules in force in the Member State concerned'; 'unless otherwise specified in national legislation'; 'not permitted by the national legislation of the Member State where the situation arose'; and 'each Member State shall introduce penalties to apply in cases of violation of this Regulation' suggests (see Articles 6, 9(3), 11(1), 12, 15, 17, 18, and 19(1) of Council Regulation 1383/2003).

6.04 Notwithstanding the fact that Law 31(I)/2002 is not substantially different from Council Regulation 1383/2003, there can be no doubt that Cyprus should by now have adopted new legislation, which is necessary for the efficient and proper implementation of the Council Regulation. It appears that the Cypriot authorities have recognized the problem and have begun to prepare a Bill, which, when ready, will be submitted to the Council of Ministers and, if approved, with or without amendments, will be tabled before the House of Representatives to be enacted as Law. The Bill in its present form provides for the repeal of Law 31(I)/2002 and contains provisions necessary for the proper and effective implementation of Council Regulation 1383/2003. In the meantime, until the enactment of the Bill into Law, Law 31(I)/2002 will remain in force and the administrative authorities of Cyprus are bound to enforce it. In case of conflict between Law 31(I)/2002 and Council Regulation 1383/2003, the Regulation will prevail, as being of superior force to the domestic law.[7] However, in areas in which Law 31(I)/2002 is silent and Council Regulation 1383/2003 cannot be

---

the Republic of Cyprus, the Republic of Latvia, the Republic of Lithuania, the Republic of Hungary, the Republic of Malta, the Republic of Poland, the Republic of Slovenia, and the Slovak Republic, and the adjustments to the Treaties on which the European Union is founded (OJ L 236/33, 23.9.2003).

[5] Council Reg (EC) No 1383/2003 of 22 July 2003 concerning customs action against goods suspected of infringing certain intellectual property rights and the measures to be taken against goods found to have infringed such rights (OJ L 196/7, 2.8.2003).

[6] Commission Reg (EC) No 1891/2004 of 21 October 2004 laying down provisions for the implementation of Council Reg (EC) No 1383/2003 concerning customs action against goods suspected of infringing certain intellectual property rights and the measures to be taken against goods found to have infringed such rights (OJ L 328, 30.10.2004).

[7] This principle ensues from Art 169 of the Constitution of Cyprus and the EC Treaty.

applied due to the lack of domestic implementing rules, the Cypriot authorities will face an insurmountable problem. It is to be hoped, therefore, that the new legislation will be enacted and come into force within the next few months.

Regulation 1383/2003 as well as Law 31(I)/2002 are enforced by the Department of Customs and Excise of Cyprus.   **6.05**

I. SUBJECT MATTER AND SCOPE OF THE NATIONAL LAW APPLYING THE REGULATION

This Part seeks to identify and analyse the subject matter and scope of Law 31(I)/2002, bearing in mind that in cases of conflict between Council Regulation 1383/2003 and Law 31(I)/2002 the former will be given precedence, as it is the duty of the Cypriot authorities to apply and implement the Council Regulation in so far as this is possible in the absence of implementing legislation, and taking into account that for the time being, Law 31(1)/2002 disregards this Regulation.   **6.06**

This Part is divided into three main sections: section A, the definition of the customs procedures in respect of which Cyprus Customs will take border measures against goods suspected of infringing an intellectual property right; section B, the definition of infringing goods as provided for in Council Regulation 1383/2003, Article 2, and in Law 31(I)/2002; and section C, goods that are excluded from the scope of the Regulation.   **6.07**

A. Customs procedure of the goods

Overall, the role of the Cyprus Customs and Excise Department (CCED) is closely related to the concept of *clearing of goods through customs* ('clearing') as defined in Law 31(I)/2002, section 2. This provides, inter alia, for the deposition of a customs declaration, together with the necessary documents, determined by the national customs law in force whenever goods are to be imported, exported, re-exported or put in transit, as well as when they are placed under a suspensive procedure or placed in free zones or free port areas.   **6.08**

As regards goods suspected of infringing an intellectual property right, the general provision in Law 31(I)/2002, section 3(1), stipulates that such goods must not   **6.09** be cleared, while section 11(1) provides that the clearing of goods of such nature shall be suspended and the goods confiscated.[8] Therefore, applying the aforementioned definition of clearing, the customs procedures in respect of which Cyprus Customs will take action when faced with goods suspected of infringing an intellectual property right include importation, exportation, re-exportation, transit, and other cases of placing under a suspensive procedure and zone/area allocation, but does not include transhipment. In accordance with statistics kept by the CCED during 2004 goods of a total value of CYP 176,017.00 (EUR 103,540) were confiscated and destroyed.

6.10   This approach is compatible with the provisions of the Regulation, and more specifically with Article 1(1) and Recital 3.[9] The same applies to goods entering or leaving the Community. Article 1(1) of the Regulation expressly refers to and is interpreted and/or applied in accordance with Council Regulation (EEC) 2913/92 establishing the Community Customs Code.[10] The Cyprus Customs Code Law 2004, Law 94(I) of 2004, (the 'Cyprus Customs Code')[11] has been in force in Cyprus since 30 April 2004 when it was published in the Official Gazette of Cyprus. It grants the CCED exclusive power to apply its provisions and those of the Community Customs Code.[12] Furthermore, the CCED is entitled to inspect passengers' baggage, goods and means of transport to locate any handling of pirated goods and also any customs and other infringements and criminal acts involving breaches of intellectual property.[13]

6.11   The aforementioned activities result in what is known as *customs supervision*: that is, any action aiming to enforce the provisions of the Cyprus Customs Code or other Cyprus and Community regulations granting authority, power and responsibility to the CCED in the enforcement of its provisions. This supervision applies in respect of a *customs procedure*, which is expressly defined in the Cyprus Customs Code as embracing the release for free circulation, transit, customs warehousing, inward processing, processing under customs control, temporary admission, outward processing, and exportation.[14]

---

[8] Goods are suspected of infringing an intellectual property right if there is prima facie proof of such infringement in an application to the CCED by the 'right-holder' as defined in s 2 of Law 31(I)/2002.

[9] With respect to goods, Recital 3 expressly refers to 'their introduction into the Community customs territory, including their transhipment, release for free circulation in the Community, placing under a suspensive procedure and placing in a free zone or warehouse'. As far as transhipment is concerned, the CCED applies National Legislation and in particular the Customs Code Law 2004 (Law 94(1)/2004), s 104(d).

[10] Council Reg (EEC) No 2913/92 of 12 October 1992 establishing the Community Customs Code (OJ L 302, 19.10.1992).

[11] Ο Περί Τελωνειακού Κώδικα Νόμος 2004, ΕΕ Παρ. Ι(Ι) Αρ. 3849, 30.4.2004 (Official Gazette Appendix I(I) No 3849, 30.4.2004).   [12] Cyprus Customs Code, s 4(1)(a).

[13] Ibid, s 4(2).

[14] Ibid, s 2. This is comparable and compatible with the 'Customs procedure' as defined in Art 4(16) of the Community Customs Code.

To date, there is no Cypriot case law regarding these matters. **6.12**

It is crucial to be clear that, given the continuing Turkish occupation of the **6.13**
northern part of the territory of Cyprus since 1974, Law 31(I)/2002 and any of
the other Cyprus Laws mentioned herein, though in theory in force over the
whole of the Cyprus territory, cannot be applied by reason of *force majeure* to
goods flowing onto the areas in which the Government of the Republic of Cyprus
('the Government') does not exercise any control. Moreover, in accordance with
the Treaty of Accession of Cyprus to the EU,[15] the application of the *acquis
communautaire* in the occupied part of Cyprus is suspended for the time being.
The crossing of goods from the occupied area of Cyprus to the Government-
controlled free area is governed by Council Regulation (EC) 866/2004 of 29 April
2004 under a regime outlined by Article 2 of Protocol No. 10 of the Act of
Accession[16] and Commission Regulation (EC) 1480/2004 of 10 August 2004
laying down specific rules concerning goods arriving from the areas not under
the effective control of the Government of Cyprus in the areas in which the
Government exercises effective control.[17]

Recital 1 of Commission Regulation (EC) 1480/2004 recalls in this context **6.14**
that 'Article 4 of Regulation 866/2004 provides a special regime for the treatment of goods arriving from the areas not under effective control of the
Government of the Republic of Cyprus to the areas in which the Government
exercises effective control.' Indeed, Council Regulation 866/2004, Article 4,
under Title III 'Crossing of Goods', is entitled 'Treatment of goods arriving
from the areas not under the effective control of the Government of the
Republic of Cyprus.' The Regulation provides that 'these goods shall not be
subject to customs duties or charges having equivalent effect, nor to a customs
declaration, provided that they are not eligible for export refunds or intervention measures. In order to ensure effective controls, the quantities crossing the
lines shall be registered.'

---

[15] Ο Περί της Συνθήκης Προσχώρησης της Τσεχικής Δημοκρατίας, της
Δ;ημοκρατίας της Εσθονίας, της Κυπριακής Δημοκρατίας, της Δημοκρατίας της
Λετονίας, της Δημοκρατίας της Λιθουανίας, της Δημοκρατίας της Ουγγαρίας, της
Δημοκρατίας της Μάλτας, της Δημοκρατίας της Πολωνίας, της Δημοκρατίας της
Σλοβενίας και της Σλοβακικής Δημοκρατίας στην Ευρωπαϊκή Ενωση (Κυρωτικός)
Νόμος 2003, ΕΕ Παρ. I (III) Αρ. 3740, 25.7.2003 (Treaty of Accession of the Czech Republic, the
Republic of Estonia, the Republic of Cyprus, the Republic of Latvia, the Republic of Lithuania, the
Hungarian Republic, the Republic of Malta, the Republic of Poland, the Slovenian Republic, and
the Slovak Republic into the European Union (Ratification) Law 2003, Official Gazette Appendix I
(III) No. 3740, 25.7.2003).
[16] Council Reg (EC) No 866/2004 of 29 April 2004 on a regime under Art 2 of Protocol No 10
of the Act of Accession (OJ L 161, 30.4.2004).
[17] Commission Reg (EC) No 1480/2004 of 10 August 2004 laying down specific rules concerning
goods arriving from the areas not under the effective control of the Government of Cyprus in the
areas in which the Government exercises effective control (OJ L 272, 20.8.2004).

6.15   According to Council Regulation 866/2004, Article 4(12):

> this Article shall apply immediately as from 1 May 2004 to goods wholly obtained in the areas not under the effective control of the Government of the Republic of Cyprus. In respect of other goods, the full implementation of this Article shall be subject to specific rules that take full account of the particular situation in the island of Cyprus on the basis of a Commission decision to be adopted as soon as possible and at the latest within 2 months of the adoption of this Regulation.

6.16   These specific rules, pursuant to Article 4(12), have been laid down by Commission Regulation (EC) 1480/2004, which, as stated in Recital 2 therein, implements 'the regime established by Regulation (EC) 866/2004 as regards goods other than those that are wholly obtained in the Areas'. This refers to goods manufactured or produced in the areas not under the effective control of the Government, albeit from raw material obtained from outside the Areas, or to goods imported from outside the Areas into the areas not under the effective control of the Government.

6.17   Article 1 of Commission Regulation 1480/2004 provides that 'the origin of any product to which this Regulation applies shall be determined in accordance with the provisions in force in the Community'. Article 2(1) provides that the accompanying document that must be issued by the Turkish Cypriot Chamber of Commerce to the Government of the Republic of Cyprus, as stipulated in Article 4(5) of Council Regulation 866/2004, 'shall contain all the particulars necessary for identifying the goods to which it relates'. Specifically, it must contain the names and addresses of the producer of the goods, the consignor, and the consignee. Furthermore, under Article 4(2) referring to counterfeit and pirated goods, 'the authorities of the Republic of Cyprus [. . .] shall ensure that goods crossing the line comply with the EC rules on the prohibition of the bringing in of counterfeit and pirated goods'.

6.18   The area of Cyprus north of the ceasefire line, which is not under the effective *de facto* control of the Government, is part of the Republic of Cyprus, and is recognized as such by the Treaty of Accession of Cyprus to the EU[18] as well as by the international community. Therefore, the crossing of goods through the check points from north to south and from south to north cannot be considered as import and export of goods respectively. In other words such crossing is not a border crossing. As a result Council Regulation 1383/2003 is not applicable.

6.19   The Government cannot control the import of goods from outside Cyprus to the part of Cyprus north of the ceasefire line and, consequently, Regulation 1383 cannot be implemented. On the other hand, the crossing of goods from north to south is controlled by National Legislation, namely the Trade Description Law

---

[18] N 15 above.

1987 (Law 5/1987).[19] The problems created by this situation are complex. It appears that only the solution of the Cyprus problem can normalize the whole situation.

B. Definition of infringing goods

The concept of 'goods infringing an intellectual property right' is defined in Law 31(I)/2002, section 2, which is divided into several paragraphs, each of which describes in turn the notions of *counterfeit goods*,[20] *pirated goods*,[21] *goods infringing a patent or a supplementary protection certificate as provided for in the Patent Laws of 1998 to 2000* [22] and moulds or matrices specifically designed or adapted for the manufacture of goods infringing an intellectual property right.[23]   **6.20**

Each of the above notions shall be considered below. We shall also comment on the notion of goods infringing a plant variety right and those infringing a national designation of origin and a geographical indication.   **6.21**

(1) Counterfeit goods

Law 31(I)/2002, section 2(a)(i), provides that action will be taken by the CCED in the case of infringing goods bearing a trade mark identical to another trade mark or bearing a trade mark which cannot be distinguished in its essential aspects from another trade mark. This wording, which is not as broad as that in section 6(2) of the Cyprus Trade Marks Law, Cap 268, as amended,[24] which also encompasses the use of identical or similar infringing trade marks for goods other than those for which the trade mark infringed is registered, matches the provisions of Article 2(1)(a)(i) of Council Regulation 1383/2003.   **6.22**

Considering the condition that the trade mark, on the basis of which border measures are taken, must be registered in respect of *the same type of goods* the CCED flexibly interprets this to keep pace with the provisions of Cap 268, bearing in mind that such reference is expressly provided for in Law 31(I)/2002.[25] Cap 268, section 6(2) accounts for the infringement of a registered trade mark in   **6.23**

---

[19] Ο Περί Εμπορικών Περιγραφών Νόμος 1987, Ν. 5/87, ΕΕ Παρ. Ι(Ι) Αρ. 2205, 6.2.1987 (Official Gazette Appendix I(I) No 2205, 6.2.1987).

[20] S 2, 'goods infringing intellectual property rights' para (a)(i)–(iii).   [21] Ibid, para (b).

[22] Ibid, para (c) with reference to the Patents Law 1998, Law 16(I)/98, Official Gazette Appendix I(I) No 3234, 6.4.1998 (Ο Περί Διπλωμάτων Ευρεσιτεχνίας Νόμος 1998, Ν. 16(I)/98, ΕΕ Παρ. Ι(Ι) Αρ. 3234, 6.4.1998). However, it must be noted that there have been further amendments to the Patent Law, so that reference should now be made to the Patents Laws of 1998–2002.

[23] Ibid, para (d).   [24] Ο Περί Εμπορικών Σημάτων Νόμος, Κεφ. 268.

[25] Ibid, para (a)(i).

three instances: the use of an identical mark for identical goods or services; the use of an identical or similar mark for identical or similar goods or services; and finally the use of an identical or similar trade mark for non-similar goods or services provided in the latter case that this use takes unfair advantage of, or is detrimental to, the registered trade mark. It proves more stringent than Law 31(I)/2002, in that it requires a risk of confusion in the mind of the public in the case of use of an identical or similar mark for similar respectively identical goods or services.

6.24 The CCED, in applying the provisions of Law 31(I)/2002 with reference to Cap 268, will regard as infringement any suspect goods bearing a trade mark which has been registered in respect of identical or similar goods. However, based on the provisions of Law 31(I)/2002, it will not consider as infringement the use of a sign which is identical or similar to a trade mark registered in respect of non-similar goods. This approach compared with the provisions of Cap 268 is not necessarily as restrictive and preclusive as it may seem, because the definition of *counterfeit goods* in Law 31(I)/2002 further comprehends 'any trade mark symbol'[26] as well as 'packaging materials bearing the trade marks of counterfeit goods'[27] even if these are presented separately. This widens the scope of application of border measures towards counterfeit goods.

6.25 Border measures cannot be taken regarding goods in respect of which a mere trade mark application is pending. This is due to the absence of any provisions to the contrary in the Laws of Cyprus, that is, both in Law 31(I)/2002 and Cap 268, as well as the practical difficulties involved. It is difficult to detect an infringement for registered trade marks in use to start with, let alone bring pending trade marks to the attention of the relevant customs department.

6.26 A special department has been created within the CCED for the enforcement and interpretation of the provisions in Law 31(I)/2002. Although the authorities stand firmly on the aforesaid interpretation and generally apply the provisions of Law 31(I)/2002 and Council Regulation 1383/2003 strictly, they nevertheless underline the difficulty of their task, in that it presupposes detection of the infringements. This detection ensues either from an application/complaint filed by the right-holder or by a representative of the right-holder, as will be analysed below, or from the experience of the CCED officers in tracking down infringements, or on reasonable suspicions which become more concrete as experience grows.

6.27 The CCED enforces the above provisions strictly. Instances of detection of goods infringing intellectual property rights and entering Cyprus appear in tables compiled by the CCED. As reported, during 2004 a large quantity of goods bearing well-known trade marks was retained at the borders as liable to forfeiture. In particular, the most popular trade marks include BURBERRY, NIKE, ADIDAS,

---

[26] S 2, 'goods infringing intellectual property rights', para (a)(ii).   [27] Ibid, para (a)(iii).

UMBRO, HUGO BOSS, NOKIA, WALT DISNEY, FERRARI, and LOUIS VUITTON. These were affixed on goods ranging from lighters and pens to bags and sunglasses and concerned mostly imports from Asian countries. According to CCED, in 2002, 25 border measures of goods infringing intellectual property rights were taken, in 2003, 83, and in 2004, 100.

(2) Pirated goods

'Pirated goods' are defined in Law 31(I)/2002, section 2(b), under the definition of 'goods infringing intellectual property rights' and include goods infringing a copyright, a related right or a design as is stipulated in Article 2(1)(b) of Council Regulation 1383/2003. Specifically, the definition of 'pirated goods' encompasses goods infringing a copyright, a right in a design or model registered in the Trademark Registry as provided in Cap 268, as amended, and all rights vested in any other subject matter enjoying protection in Cyprus under the relevant laws and/or regulations under these relevant laws. **6.28**

The Right in Intellectual Property Law 1976[28] protects original scientific, literary, musical, artistic, and audio-visual works, databases, transmissions and publications under the scope of 'copyright'[29] and, also, performances or renditions of works by performers under the scope of 'related rights'.[30] **6.29**

Designs are protected under the Legal Protection of Industrial Designs and Models Law 2002[31] and the regulations (secondary legislation) made thereunder.[32] Law 4(I)/2002 protects the whole or part of a product's appearance, which is inherent to the product's characteristics, especially to its outline, colours, shape, texture and/or the materials of the product and/or its decorations, if any.[33] **6.30**

The scope of implementation of Law 4(I)/2002 extends to any rights in designs and models, which have been registered or for which an application for registration is pending in the Registrar's official Record.[34] Furthermore, it extends to any rights in designs and models, which have been registered or for which an **6.31**

---

[28] Ο Περί του Δικαιώματος Πνευματικής Ιδιοκτησίας Νόμος, Ν. 59/76, ΕΕ Παρ. I(I) Αρ. 1316, 3.12.1976 (Official Gazette Appendix I(I) No 1316, 3.12.1976).
[29] Ibid s 3 (1)(a)(i)–(ix).   [30] Ibid s 3(1)(b).
[31] Ο Περί της Νομικής Προστασίας των Βιομηχανικών Σχεδίων και Υποδειγμάτων Νόμος του 2002, Ν. 4(I)/2002, ΕΕ Παρ. I(I) Αρ. 3577, 15.2.2002 (Official Gazette Appendix I(I) No 3577, 15.2.2002).
[32] Legal Protection of Industrial Designs and Models (Fees and Rights) Regulations 2002, [2002] Appendix III (I) 379 (Νομικής Προστασίας των Βιομηχανικών Σχεδίων και Υποδειγμάτων (Τέλη και Δικαιώματα) Κανονισμοί 2002, [2002] Παρ. III(I) 379); Legal Protection of Industrial Designs and Models (Applications' Particulars) Order 2003, [2003] Appendix III(I) 5597 (Νομικής Προστασίας των Βιομηχανικών Σχεδίων και Υποδειγμάτων (Λεπτομέρειες Αιτήσεων) Διάταγμα 2003, [2003] Παρ III(I) 5597).
[33] Law 59/76, s 2, definition of 'design or model'.   [34] Ibid s 3(a), (c).

application for registration is pending, which arise from international registrations designating Cyprus under the scope of international treaties enforced in Cyprus.[35]

6.32 Goods are considered as infringing a copyright, a related right or a design right under Law 31(I)/2002 when they consist of copies or contain copies produced or reproduced without the consent of the right-holder[36] or a person authorized by the right-holder in the country of production, and provided the making of those copies would constitute an infringement of that right under national (or, when applicable, Community) laws. These conditions are akin to those in Article 2(1)(b) of the Regulation.

6.33 As regards the interpretation and application of the above provision by the CCED, the latter's approach is strict, as indicated above in paragraph 6.19. However, there are fewer occurrences of entry into Cyprus of pirated goods than goods infringing a registered trade mark. The goods with respect to which copyright infringements are commonly acknowledged are CDs and GAMEBOY cartridges, although the latter may also fall within the ambit of counterfeit goods as infringing the GAMEBOY trade mark. The strict application of the provisions of the law by CCED also applies in the interpretation of the concept of 'goods which are or contain copies'. However, the scope of the provisions of the Regulation appears to be wider in that they apply to a 'right regardless of whether it is registered in national law',[37] whereas Law 31(I)/2002, expressly stipulates for 'registered design or model in the trade mark register', thus confining the application of border measures. This is therefore an instance where the CCED is bound to apply the Regulation, which is of superior force to the internal laws of Cyprus.

(3) Goods infringing other intellectual property rights

Goods infringing a patent or a supplementary protection certificate

6.34 An explicit reference to these goods is made in the general definition of 'goods infringing intellectual property rights' in Law 31(I)/2002, section 2(c). However, reference must also be made to the provisions of the Patents Law 1998–2002 in order to determine when goods must be seen as 'infringing'. Section 60(1) of the Patents Law, as amended, defines as acts of infringement:

(a) the commission of any of the acts stipulated in section 27(1), (2), and (4) of Law 16(1)/1998;

(b) by a person other than the owner of the patent;

(c) without the patentee's consent;

(d) regarding a product or a process protected by the patent.

---

[35] Law 59/76, s 3(b), (c).   [36] Ie, the holder of any of the rights referred to in para 6.20 above.
[37] Council Reg (EC) No 1383/2003, Art 2(1)(b).

The acts stipulated in section 27(1), (2), and (4), include the production, offer, **6.35** disposal, use, importation or storage of the subject matter of a patent, the use of any process which is the object of a patent and the supply of, or the offering to supply, the means allowing to apply a patented process. The inducement of another to commit any of the above activities is also explicitly referred to as constituting an act of infringement and such acts also qualify as infringements with respect to pending applications for a patent.[38]

As regards supplementary protection certificates, Law 31(I)/2002 provides that **6.36** they are included in the definition of a 'patent', according to the Patent Laws 1998–2002.[39] Accordingly, the same provisions apply for goods infringing a supplementary protection certificate as for goods infringing a patent.

As concerns the application of border measures by the CCED on goods infringing **6.37** a patent or a supplementary protection certificate, the national authority has reported no such action so far. However, in practice, if the need arises, the CCED will enforce EC Regulation 1383/2003 in respect of goods infringing a patent by reference to the aforementioned definition of infringement provided in the national Patents Law 16(I)/1998.

Goods infringing a national plant variety right

Law 31(I)/2002 contains no provision whatsoever regarding plant variety rights. **6.38** No domestic legislation exists on this point. Furthermore, the CCED has not come across such cases of infringement to date; hence the application of border measures under the provisions of Article 2(1)(c)(iii) of the Regulation has not been tested so far.

In this respect, following Cyprus accession to the European Union on 1 May **6.39** 2004, the provisions of Council Regulation 1383/2003 are directly applicable, so that, notwithstanding that there is no stipulation in national law, the provisions of the Regulation are applicable and binding. Accordingly, if the need arises, the CCED will apply the provisions of the Regulation with respect to goods infringing a Community plant variety right under EC Regulation 2100/94.

Goods infringing a national designation of origin or a geographical indication

As for plant variety rights, there exists no domestic legislation regarding **6.40** designations of origin and geographical indications in Cyprus and no instance of infringement has been reported to date. Once again, the provisions of the Regulation are directly applicable and will therefore be applied whenever necessary in the situations referred to in Article 2(1)(c)(iv).

---

[38] Law 16(I)/2002, s 60(2).   [39] 'Certificate' in Law 31(I)/2002, s 2.

(4) Moulds and matrices

6.41 Moulds and matrices relating to goods infringing any of the intellectual property rights referred to in Article 2 of Council Regulation 1383/2003 must be stopped by the CCED under Article 2(3) of this Regulation and of Law 31(I)/2002, section 3(1), since they are expressly identified therein as 'goods infringing intellectual property rights'.[40]

6.42 The conditions under which moulds or matrices can be stopped by the CCED are provided in the same provision of Law 31(I)/2002. These conditions are satisfied when a mould or a matrix is specifically designed or specifically adapted for the manufacture of any of the following:

- counterfeit trade marks
- counterfeit goods
- goods infringing a patent
- goods infringing a supplementary protection certificate
- pirated goods.

That is, all goods that have been addressed in the foregoing paragraphs and have been defined as 'goods infringing intellectual property rights'.

6.43 Such moulds and matrices can be stopped to the extent that their use infringes the rights of a right-holder in light of the Cyprus legislation in force. It is therefore necessary to identify and apply the definition of infringement relevant in each case. These definitions have been considered above, under the respective section relating to each intellectual property right. When such moulds or matrices are detected, the CCED is expressly empowered by Law 31(I)/2002, section 3(2), to detain them.

C. Goods excluded by the Regulation

6.44 Law 31(1)/2002 contains provisions identical to Article 3 of Council Regulation 1383/2003. However, because of the direct applicability of the Regulation, those provisions were strictly speaking not necessary.

(1) Parallel imported goods

6.45 In accordance with Article 3(1), first sentence, of EC Regulation 1383/2003, it has been expressly stated by the CCED in a Report of 2002 relating to Law 31(I)/2002, that:

> this Law shall not apply to parallel imported goods, that is goods which bear a trade mark with the consent of the holder of that mark or which are protected by a patent

---

[40] 'Goods infringing intellectual property rights', in Law 31(I)/2002, s 2(d).

or a supplementary protection certificate, by a copyright, a neighbouring right or by a design right and which have been manufactured with the consent of the right-holder but are introduced into the territory of Cyprus, or found during a physical examination of goods which are subject to a customs procedure or during their placement in free zones or free warehouse.[41]

(2) Goods which have been manufactured under conditions other than those which have been agreed with the right-holder

In the 2002 Report of the CCED, it also appears that Law 31(I)/2002 does not apply to goods that 'have been manufactured or bear a trade mark under conditions other than those which have been agreed with the right-holder'.[42] Consequently, Law 31(1)/2002 is consistent with the second sentence of Article 3(1) of Council Regulation 1383/2003. **6.46**

Therefore, the CCED is powerless in the circumstances referred to in paragraphs 6.36 and 6.37 above. In practice, when there is suspicion of an infringement of an intellectual property right taking place, the CCED notifies the right-holder or his representative, but, when, upon examination, it is found that the case in question concerns any of the situations addressed in Article 3(1) of the Regulation, the goods are unconditionally released. Therefore, in such cases, it is up to the right-holder to consider whether there are other legal steps available to him, such as a civil action. A plaintiff, in such a civil action, is entitled under the Civil Procedure Rules and the Law of Evidence, to subpoena the Director or any member of the CCED personnel to appear at the hearing of the action for the purpose of giving evidence and/or of adducing in evidence any document in the possession of the Department, which may be relevant to the issues in such an action. **6.47**

(3) Goods contained in travellers' personal baggage

Article 3(2) of Council Regulation 1383/2003 is mirrored in Law 31(1)/2002, section 3, which adopts a similar wording. In both cases, the general provisions on border measures of the Regulation and Cyprus Law do not apply to products or goods, which, although infringing an intellectual property right, are imported for non-commercial use (for personal use) in the travellers' personal baggage. **6.48**

Whether or not the goods are 'of a non-commercial nature' is appraised in light of Article 45 of Council (EEC) Regulation 918/83.[43] In practice, customs officers **6.49**

---

[41] 'A guide to customs procedures. The Control of the Movement of Goods Infringing Intellectual Property Rights, Law 31(1)/2002,' April 2002, Republic of Cyprus, Ministry of Finance, Department of Customs and Excise, Nicosia. Available on www.mof.gov.cy.

[42] Ibid.

[43] Council Reg (EEC) No 918/83 of 28 March 1983, setting up a Community system of reliefs from customs duty (OJ L 105, 23.4.1983).

will enquire randomly about the quantity of the goods carried by travellers. To be able to rely on Article 3(2) of the Regulation, the quantity and the nature of the goods must reflect that their movement is occasional, thus suggesting that they are intended as presents or for personal use. However, if the quantity of the goods indicates an intention to trade, the CCED can either detain them or tax them. Of course, in such cases, goods infringing intellectual property rights should be dealt with in accordance with the rules examined in this Part.

6.50 For the exemption of Article 3(2) of the Regulation to apply, the infringing products, being in the possession of a traveller and deemed to be intended for his private use, may not exceed the value of CYP 100, equivalent to approximately EUR 175. The criterion employed for the assessment of the value of the infringing goods is in general their purchase value.

6.51 However, none of the above exceptions nullifies or affects any of the powers of the CCED to inspect the baggage of travellers in cases where the CCED has reasonable grounds to suspect that the traveller in question detains anything which might constitute a threat to public security or public health. In addition, the customs officers can also inquire about the 'community character' of the products carried by a person entering the country. In such cases, the traveller is under an obligation to produce to the CCED the receipts of purchase, which must indicate the VAT number of the seller.

II. APPLICATION FOR ACTION BY THE CUSTOMS AUTHORITIES

A. Measures prior to an application for action by the customs authorities ('*ex officio* measures')

6.52 In contrast with the provisions of Article 4 of the Regulation, the legislation of Cyprus is very brief in describing the *ex officio* powers of the CCED to suspend the release of suspected goods or detain them. In practice, if the CCED becomes aware of anything prima facie suspicious, which might result in any infringement of an intellectual property right, the CCED suspends the release of the goods and detains them for a period of three working days, contacts the right-holder and forwards a sample to him, informs him of the actual or supposed number of items and their nature, and asks the right-holder to submit (if he wants to) an application for action within three working days.[44]

---

[44] Law 31(I)/2002, s 15(1)(a).

If the right-holder submits such an application for action within the three-day **6.53** period, he may then decide either to apply to the court within the next 10 working days from submitting the application for action or to follow the simplified procedure provided in Article 11 of the Regulation. In practice the right-holder may follow the simplified procedure and, if that fails to produce results in time, then file a court action. The period of 10 working days may be extended for a further 10 working days period.[45] If the affected right-holder fails to file the action within the period allowed and/or omits to communicate to the CCED the fact of having filed the action, or if within that period CCED has not received the right-holder's agreement provided for in Article 11(1) of the Regulation, the products detained will be released. There is no need for the right-holder to secure a court order in the form of interlocutory injunction (known as interim order). The timely filing of the action and the communication of that fact to CCED are by themselves sufficient to prolong the detention of the goods until its final determination.

As from 1 July 2004, the CCED applies directly Article 4 of the Regulation and **6.54** intervenes directly *ex officio*, whenever the prerequisites of its application are satisfied. Therefore, it is not necessary to discuss the differences between Article 4 and section 15(1) of Law 31(I)/2002, which was, until 30 June 2004, the source of power for the CCED to intervene *ex officio*. Article 4 empowers the CCED to intervene *ex officio*, if there are 'sufficient grounds for suspecting that the goods infringe an intellectual property right'.

The CCED retains the right to permit all interested parties to inspect the products. It **6.55** is also common practice for the CCED to provide the applicant (or the prospective applicant) with samples of the goods and as the case may be with photographs in order to allow the latter to inspect, examine and analyse the nature and quality of the goods.[46]

B. The lodging and processing of applications for customs

(1) Persons entitled to file an application for action

Definition of 'right-holders' under the Regulation and proof of entitlement to file an application for action

For right-holders stricto sensu

The 'right-holder' within the meaning of Article 2(2) of Council Regulation **6.56** 1383/2003 is primarily the person who is the holder of the right on which the

---

[45] Council Reg 1383/2003, Art 13(1).
[46] Law 31(I)/2002, s 13, which reads in translation: 'Subject to any law in force, relating to protection of personal data, industrial, commercial, professional or administrative secrets, the CCED may allow the applicant and any person involved in the clearing of the goods, to inspect the goods the clearance of which has been suspended or seized in accordance with section 11.'

application for action by customs authorities relies. The notion also encompasses any other person entitled to use the right under the relevant laws in force. The right-holder may be a legal or a natural person. As the CCED will verify the identity and capacity of the applicant, the application must include evidence of the applicant's entitlement to act, in compliance with Article 2(1) and 2(2) of Regulation 1891/2004.[47]

For persons authorized to use the right

6.57 The right-holder may grant rights of use to any other person, such as a licensee, a distributor, or a commercial agent. This person is called, if registered, 'registered user' and, if not registered, 'authorized user' of that right.

6.58 In particular, as regards trade marks, a person other than the trade mark owner may be registered as registered user under The Trade Marks Law, Cap 268, as amended, in respect of all or any of the goods or services for which the trade mark is registered. In consequence, the registered user in its broadest meaning is also authorized to file an application for action, if the relevant right of use allows him to do so. If the applicant is not a registered user, but an authorized user of the right, he is still entitled to apply, provided he produces, in addition to the documents already mentioned above,[48] a written authorization to that effect.

For representatives

6.59 A representative of the right-holder may file an application for customs action on behalf of the right-holder, provided he produces a written authorization by the latter to that effect. He has to indicate his name, full address, and the place of incorporation, if it is a company. He must also produce all documents required from the 'right-holder' and the 'authorized' or 'registered users' together with proof of his appointment as a representative, as required by Regulation 1891/2004, Article 2(3). A representative may be either a natural person or a legal entity. Any person, such as attorneys, intellectual property right agents, consultants, collective management societies etc, may be appointed by the right-holder as representatives.

(2) Formal requirements and competent customs department

Competent customs department

6.60 The CCED is the Cypriot authority having competence to process the applications for action and to enforce the relevant legislation:

Cyprus Customs and Excise Department (Customs Headquarters)
M. Karaoli
1096 Nicosia

---

[47] For further details, see www.mof.gov.cy/ce.   [48] Law 31(1)/2002, s 5(a)(i) and (ii).

P.O.B. 1440 Nicosia
Cyprus
Tel: +357 22 601652, +357 22 601858
Fax: +357 22 602769
e-mail: headquarters@customs.mof.gov.cy

This department is responsible for controlling the importation and exportation **6.61**
of goods in and out of Cyprus from every controlled and authorized port or
airport. However, the recent political developments in Cyprus and the enactment of Council Regulation 866/2004 and Commission Regulation 1480/2004
(see paragraph 6.13 above) regulating movement of goods from the northern
occupied part of Cyprus to the Government-controlled area extended the duties
of the CCED to the control of products coming from the occupied part of
Cyprus.

Form of the application of action

The application for action must be submitted to the CCED. In practice the applic- **6.62**
ation for action may be sent by fax or e-mail, but the original form with the
attached documents necessary for its support must be filed with the CCED at the
address indicated in the previous paragraph. These documents must be of a nature
to help the customs officers to distinguish the authentic goods from the infringing
ones. The application form can be obtained from any local branch of the CCED
or from the official website of the department.[49]

As from 1 July 2004, the CCED ceased to apply Law 31(1)/2002, section 10 and **6.63**
demand security or some other financial guarantee sufficient to cover any expenses
to be incurred by reason of the detention of the products, such as storage, legal fees
or damages caused to a third party as a result of error of the right-holder, if it
becomes clear that none of the products infringes any intellectual property rights.

Language requirements

Cyprus has two official languages, Greek and Turkish. The application form and **6.64**
all supporting evidence may be made out in either of those two languages. If the
originals of the supporting documents are laid down in another language, the
applicant should provide a translation. As the personnel of CCED have a very
good working knowledge of the English language and in order to help those
concerned, CCED decided to accept in practice applications and documents
made out in English.

---

[49] www.mof.gov.cy/ce

297

(3) Requirements regarding the contents of the application for action

Mandatory information

6.65 In order to comply with Article 5(5) of EC Regulation 1383/2003, the applicant must provide the CCED with the information necessary to allow the customs officers to identify the goods likely, upon a prima facie examination, to infringe his exclusive rights. The accompanying documents must contain a full description of the goods covered by the rights in question. It would be preferable if samples or photographs were provided. The applicant must also provide information as to the place where the genuine goods are produced and identify the manufacturer.[50] In the case of goods suspected of infringing an intellectual property right, the applicant must communicate, where practicable, the name and address of the consignee and of the exporter or the owner of the offending goods and a description of the goods or the consignment, so as to enable the CCED to identify them. In addition, the applicant must also provide the CCED with information of the country from which the products were dispatched, the transit method used as well as the name of the person responsible for the delivery of the goods.

Optional information

6.66 Where it is possible to do so, the applicant should also indicate the name of the manufacturer and distributor of the suspect goods. Finally, it would be very useful to inform the authorities of the possible date of arrival or departure of the allegedly offending goods, with details as to their tax classification.[51] Any document that is to be submitted to the CCED may be communicated by any means (for example, by fax), but the document itself or a certified copy of the original must simultaneously be filed with the appropriate local branch of the CCED. In summary, the applicant should provide the CCED with as much information as possible. Of course, he cannot be required to give information he does not possess.

(4) Processing and acceptance of the application for action

6.67 The applicant may request the monitoring of the borders by the CCED in view of the detention of the allegedly offending goods for a period of up to a maximum of one year. This period may be extended by a further one year, if good reasons exist in support of the relevant subsequent request.[52] The CCED is under the obligation to process the application immediately and to inform the applicant in writing of its decision.

---

[50] Law 31(I)/2002, s 5(1).   [51] Ibid, s 5 (2).   [52] Ibid, s 6(1) and (2).

If the CCED rejects the application for action, it must give to the applicant full 6.68 reasons for its refusal. The applicant is entitled to appeal this decision before the Director of the CCED. If the application for action is declared admissible, either originally, or following an appeal, the relevant decision shall be communicated to every CCED local office.

(5) *Community applications for action*

The processing of 'Community applications for action' under Article 5(4) of 6.69 Council Regulation 1383/2003, filed in Cyprus through the CCED and extending to Member States other than Cyprus, is governed by the same rules as above. In respect of applications for action filed in another EU Member State and extended to Cyprus, the Cypriot customs authorities are bound, in accordance with Council Regulation 1383/2003 and Commission Regulation 1891/2004, to provide information and assistance if requested by such other Member State's customs authorities.

III. CONDITIONS GOVERNING ACTIONS BY CUSTOMS AUTHORITIES AND BY THE AUTHORITIES COMPETENT TO DETERMINE WHETHER GOODS INFRINGE AN INTELLECTUAL PROPERTY RIGHT

A. Conditions governing action by customs authorities

(1) *Factual background*

The CCED consists mainly of two sections, which are organized in central (head- 6.70 quarters) and regional (customs stations) levels. The headquarters are in Nicosia and are entrusted with policy making and the administration of the technical operations of the Department. There are three regional customs offices, known as Collections, in Nicosia, Limassol, and Larnaca. A smaller regional office, located in Paphos, functions as a sub-unit of the Limassol customs office.

The most important customs offices involved in anti-counterfeiting in Cyprus are 6.71 located in the main harbours of Limassol and Larnaca as well as in the airports of Larnaca and Paphos.

(2) Notification of customs intervention before the right-holder
concerned has filed an application for action

6.72 According to section 15(1) of Law 31(I)/2002, if during the process of examination of goods by the customs authorities and before the submission or approval
of the application filed by the right-holder, customs are satisfied, prima facie,
that an intellectual property right has been and/or will be infringed, then they
may notify the right-holder of this fact and suspend the release of the suspected
goods in question or detain the goods for a period of three working days from the
date of notification of the right-holder, to enable the right-holder to apply for
action.

6.73 In our experience, the right-holder is notified of a customs action through his legal
representative in Cyprus, if any. To that effect, the CCED will either consult a
directory of representatives or they will call various law offices in Cyprus in order
to establish which one, if any, represents the right-holder. The CCED has access
to the Trade Marks Register, as well as to the Companies and the Patent Registries
of the Department of the Registrar of Companies.[53]

(3) Information to be provided by customs to the right-holder before the
right-holder confirms the infringing nature of the goods

6.74 Once goods suspected of infringing an intellectual property right are detained
by customs, the latter will inform the right-holder by giving him written
notice. The right-holder will then be asked to examine a sample of the goods,
which the customs officer will enclose with the written notice and to confirm
in writing that the goods infringe the intellectual property right involved.
The right-holder must give reasons as to why his right is allegedly being
infringed.

6.75 In addition to the sample of the goods that is sent to the right-holder, the latter is
usually provided with further information. In our experience, knowledge of the
quantity of the goods (even an estimated quantity) is very important to the right-
holder, as the latter often takes this information into consideration in order to
determine whether he will take action against the infringement or not. Another
consideration taken into account by the right-holder in order to determine
whether or not to take steps against the infringement is the expenses involved. As
well as the quantity of the goods, their country of origin is usually also revealed by
customs to the right-holder at this stage.

---

[53] In addition, a right-holder can pay CYP 800 per year in order for the CCED to keep a watch
over a specific trade mark. Following the passing of the proposed Bill, this method of monitoring
will be free of charge, as required by Council Reg 1383/2003.

(4) Notification of customs intervention once the right-holder concerned has filed an application for action

When a right-holder has filed an application for action, and the CCED declares **6.76** this application admissible, section 9 of Law 31(I)/2002 provides that the relevant customs office(s) must be notified of this decision.

The CCED then follows the procedure laid down in section 11 of Law 31(I)/2002. **6.77** That is, once the application for action has been allowed, and after consultation of the applicant (if necessary), release of the goods is suspended or the goods are detained.

The customs authority must also notify in writing the declarant or holder and the **6.78** applicant of the detention of the goods.

Subject to any legislation concerning the protection of personal data, industrial **6.79** and commercial secrecy, and professional or administrative confidentiality, the CCED will inform the right-holder of the name and address of the manufacturer, the consignor, the importer, the exporter, the re-exporter, and the declarant of the goods. This is to enable the right-holder to initiate proceedings before the relevant judicial authority to secure his rights, which must be done within 10 working days from the notification of the suspension of release of the goods.[54]

Personal data in Cyprus are protected under the Processing of Personal Data **6.80** (Protection of the Individual) Law, Law 138(I)/2001,[55] as amended by Law 37(I)/2003. These Laws are fully compatible with the *acquis communautaire*. In particular, they harmonized the legal system of Cyprus with EU Directive 95/46/EC on the protection of individuals with regard to the processing of personal data and the free movement of such data.[56] Cyprus has also ratified the International Convention for the Protection of Individuals from the Automatic Processing of Personal Data and its additional Protocol.[57] So far these provisions have not hindered information under Article 9(3) of the Regulation, except as regards the name of the consignor. The decision not to communicate the name of the latter is provisional, pending an Opinion in the matter by the Attorney General's Office.

---

[54] Law 31(I)/2002, s 11(5).

[55] Ο Περί Επεξεργασίας Δεδομένων Προσωπικού χαρακτήρα (Προστασία του Ατόμου) Νόμος 2001, Ν. 138(I)/2001, ΕΕ Παρ. I(I) Αρ. 3549, 23.11.2001 (Official Gazette Appendix I(I) No 3549, 23.11.2001).

[56] Directive 95/46/EC of the European Parliament and of the Council of 24 October 1995 on the protection of individuals with regard to the processing of personal data and on the free movement of such data (OJ L 281, 23.11.1995).

[57] Council of Europe, Convention for the Protection of Individuals with regard to Automatic Processing of Personal Data and its additional Protocol of 28.1.1981- see www.privacy.org/pi/agreements.html. The Convention for the Protection of Individuals with regard to Automatic Processing of Personal Data (Ratifying) Law 2001, Law 28(III)/2001, Official Gazette Appendix I(III) No 3549, 23.11.2001 (Ο Περί της Ευρωπαϊκής σύμβασης για την Προστασία του χΑτόμου από την Αυτοματοποιημένη Επεξεργασία Δεδομένων Προσωπικού

(5) Inspection of the suspected goods

6.81 Once the right-holder has confirmed in writing that his intellectual property rights have been infringed, inspection of the goods by the right-holder is allowed at the latter's specific request. The reason why an inspection is not allowed before the confirmation is that a sample of the goods in question has already been forwarded to the right-holder (which also helps the right-holder decide whether or not to submit an application for action). More generally, all persons involved enjoy the same right. However, they are under no obligation to carry out such an inspection.

6.82 As previously noted, samples and sometimes photographs of the suspected goods will be enclosed with the written notice issued by the CCED informing the right-holder of a prima facie infringement. Obviously, the right-holder usually prefers samples to photographs as samples allow for a more accurate determination of an infringement. According to Article 9(3), last indent, of Council Regulation 1383/2003, these samples should be duly returned to the CCED once the decision to take action (or not, as the case may be) has been made.

B. Simplified procedure allowing the destruction of the goods without there being any need to determine whether an intellectual property right has been infringed under national law

6.83 Article 11 of the Regulation provides:

> where customs authorities have detained or suspended the release of goods, which are suspected of infringing an intellectual property right in one of the situations covered by article 1(1), the Member States may provide, in accordance with their national legislation, for a simplified procedure, to be used with the right-holders' agreement, which enables customs authorities to have such goods abandoned for destruction under customs control, without there being any need to determine whether an intellectual property right has been infringed under national law.

6.84 In Cyprus, Law 31(I)/2002, section 16, provides that where the Director of the CCED acknowledges an offence committed under Law 31(I)/2002, the Department of Customs and Excise may:

(a) destroy, at no cost to the State, all goods that are identified as goods that infringe an intellectual property right or to dispose of these goods outside commercial channels in such a way to preclude injury to the right-holder;

χαρακτήρα (Κυρωτικός) Νόμος 2001, Ν. 28(III)/2001, ΕΕ Παρ. I(III) Αρ. 3549, 23.11.2001); Additional Protocol on the Convention for the Protection of Individuals with regard to Automatic Processing of Personal Data 1981 (Ratifying) Law 2003, Law 30(III)/2003 (Ο Περί Πρόσθετου Πρωτοκόλλου στη Σύμβαση για την Προστασία του Ατόμου από την Αυτοματοποιημένη Επεξεργασία Δεδομένων Προσωπικού χαρακτήρα του 1981 (Κυρωτικός) Νόμος 2003, Ν. 30(III)/2003).

(b) accept the abandonment of such goods to the benefit of the Republic of Cyprus, again at no cost to the State;

(c) adopt any other measures with respect to the goods depriving the persons concerned of any economic gains from the transaction.

In our opinion, the provisions of Law 31(I)/2002 cannot be considered as (satis-   **6.85** factorily) implementing the option of Article 11 of the Regulation. It is to be hoped that this will be achieved when the Bill referred to in the Introduction above becomes Law.

C. Conditions governing action by the authorities having jurisdiction to determine whether the goods infringe an intellectual property right

(1) Authorities having jurisdiction to determine whether the goods infringe an intellectual property right

Section 3(3) of Law 31(I)/2002 stipulates that independently from any other laws   **6.86** or regulations, any person who infringes an intellectual property right commits an offence. Therefore, proceedings seeking to put an end to such infringements may be either criminal or civil. (For criminal proceedings and the sentence threatened by law, see Part V, Penalties, below). Criminal proceedings for the time being can only be taken under Law 31(I)/2002. Law 31(I)/2002 treats counterfeit goods, pirated goods, goods infringing a patent or a supplementary protection certificate, goods infringing a designation of origin or a geographical indication in the same way.

Civil proceedings to protect the right-holder are also envisaged. Such civil   **6.87** proceedings may be filed either for the purpose of Article 13 of the Regulation or for another remedy recognized by law. In proceedings filed in order to satisfy the requirement of Article 13 of the Regulation, the action will be for the determination of the question whether an intellectual property right has been infringed under National Law in accordance with Article 10 of the Regulation. However, in practice further causes of action may be included in the same action, such as passing off, infringement of a registered trade mark, etc. Moreover, further claims may be added, such as a claim for an injunction restraining the defendant from infringing in the future the same right, a claim for damages, a claim for an account of profits, etc. Further, in the context of such action, the plaintiff may also apply for an interim order. The object of an interim order is to preserve matters pending the trial of the case and thus restrain the commission, continuance, or repetition of a wrongful act, until final determination of the action. It must be noted that the possibility of obtaining an interim order is not as important as it was in the past. This is due to the fact that the filing of an action for the purpose of Article 13 of the Regulation and communication of the fact of filing to CCED within the time limit of the 10 working days are by themselves sufficient to secure the retention of the allegedly offending goods until final determination of the action.

6.88   There is insufficient experience as yet to make a judgement as to the type of action preferred by right-holders. Currently, the majority of criminal proceedings end with the imposition of a fine which is perhaps the reason why offences of this kind are usually compounded. Compounding entails stricter punishment for the offender in the sense that he has to pay more than the fine usually imposed by the court. The reason why offenders accept and prefer compounding is, in our opinion, the avoidance of the social stigma that a sentence by a criminal court entails.

6.89   The advantage to right-holders of civil proceedings is that they are in full control from beginning to end. They can settle the action at any time or they can press for the action to be tried. If in the context of such proceedings an injunction is obtained, either an interim one pending the final determination of the action or a permanent one granted by the final judgment, the right-holder obtains an effective measure preventing future repetitions of the same infringement by the same person, because, if the latter disobeys the injunction, he will face certain imprisonment for contempt of court.

(2) *Term for notifying customs that proceedings have been started*

6.90   In line with Article 13 of Council Regulation 1383/2003, Law 31(I)/2002 provides that the right-holder must notify customs within 10 working days that proceedings seeking to determine whether the goods infringe an intellectual property right have been commenced. The term of 10 working days may be extended once, under section 11(5) of Law 31(I)/2002. Such requests for extension are usually not denied, particularly in cases where the right-holder is not a Cypriot national.

D. Release of goods suspected of infringing certain rights on provision of a security

6.91   In line with Article 14 of the Regulation, Law 31(I)/2002, section 12, provides that in the case of detention of goods suspected of infringing a patent, a supplementary protection certificate or a design right, the importer, holder, or consignee of the goods shall be able to obtain the release of the goods on provision of a security, the value of which will be determined by the Director of the CCED, provided that:

(a) the CCED has been informed within the time limit specified in section 11(5) of the Law 31(I)/2002 that proceedings seeking to determine whether an intellectual property right has been infringed have been initiated;
(b) the authority empowered for this purpose has not adopted interim measures before the expiry of the same time limit; and
(c) all customs formalities have been fulfilled.

The security must be sufficient to protect the interests of the right-holder and **6.92** payment of the security shall not prejudice the other legal remedies available to the right-holder.

In the case where proceedings seeking to determine whether an intellectual prop- **6.93** erty right has been infringed have been initiated by a person other than the holder of the patent, protection certificate or design right, the security will be released if the right-holder does not exercise his rights to commence legal proceedings within 30 working days from the date on which he receives notification of the suspension of release or detention.

E. Storage of the goods

Section 32 of the Cyprus Customs Code 2004,[58] governs approval of temporary **6.94** storage facilities. Section 33 of the same Code deals with public temporary storage facilities and section 34 with private temporary storage facilities. Public temporary storage facilities are under the CCED and, therefore, there is no difficulty in applying Council Regulation 1383/2003, Commission Regulation 1981/2004, and Law 31(1)/2002. Private temporary storage facilities belong to, and are operated by, private persons, hence the need for a special provision giving the CCED adequate powers. Section 34(1) of the Cyprus Customs Code provides that temporary storage in private temporary storage facilities approved under section 32(2) of goods, which are carried directly from abroad or dispatched under the transit procedure, shall be permitted on written authorization granted by the Director. CCED may, under section 34(3) carry out in such facilities all 'customs acts and procedures provided for in the customs and other legislation'. In order to understand the provision, we must look at the interpretation section (s 2 of the Code), where

---

[58] N 11 above. S 32(1) reads in translation 'the Director approves in any port or customs port or any other place, spaces for the temporary deposition of goods until these goods receive a customs destination, which spaces will be referred to in this Law as "temporary deposition storages". These storages may be temporary Public storages under the Customs Department control or temporary Private storages under the control of other natural or legal persons.'

the terms 'customs legislation' and 'other legislation' are defined. 'Customs legislation' means this Law, as may be amended from time to time, the Regulations, Orders and Notices issued under this Law and the corresponding Community Legislation, the Regulations, Orders and Notices issued for harmonization and or for the implementation of the corresponding Community Legislation, excluding the other legislation.' Consequently, goods in such temporary storage facilities are subject to the same scrutiny as that described.

IV. PROVISIONS APPLICABLE TO GOODS FOUND TO INFRINGE AN INTELLECTUAL PROPERTY RIGHT

6.95 The provisions of Cyprus national law regarding the prohibition on the free movement across the borders of goods considered as infringing an intellectual property right coincide with the provisions of Article 16 of the Regulation.

6.96 The only provision of Cyprus law which is worth mentioning in this context is section 3(5) of Law 31(I)/2002, which provides that the power to compound offences, given to the Director of CCED by the customs' legislation in force for the time being, applies, *mutatis mutandis*, to offences created by this law. Section 16 of the same Law specifies the powers given to CCED, in case an offence has been compounded in virtue of section 5(3). The powers are discretionary.

6.97 By virtue of section 16, when the CCED comes upon entry into or removal from Cyprus' customs territory, release for free circulation, exportation, re-exportation, placement under a suspending procedure, and placement in a free zone or free warehouse, of goods infringing any of the intellectual property rights referred to in Article 2 of Council Regulation 1383/2003, it is entitled, provided the offence has been compounded, to:

(a) destroy, without any cost to the State, those goods that are identified as goods that infringe intellectual property rights or to dispose the goods outside commercial channels in such a way as to preclude injury to the intellectual property right-holder;

(b) accept the abandonment of goods to the benefit of the Republic of Cyprus, without any cost to the State;

(c) adopt any other measures with respect to the goods allowing the persons concerned to be deprived of any economic gains from the transaction.

6.98 The question of who pays for the costs of destruction is answered on the basis of the declaration signed by the right-holder under Article 6 of Council Regulation

1383/2003. In that declaration the right-holder agrees, inter alia, to bear all costs incurred under the simplified procedure of Article 11. If the result of this procedure is the destruction of the goods, the costs will be borne by the right-holder, unless otherwise agreed between him and the offender. In practice the parties often agree that the offender will pay the costs of destruction. In case of an action under Article 10 of the Regulation, the costs of destruction will once again be paid by the right-holder, unless the court directs otherwise. If under the above rules the right-holder pays for the destruction, the only way for him to obtain reimbursement is to claim reimbursement in the context of a civil action. The claim can be included in an Article 10 action.

V. PENALTIES

By virtue of Law 31(I)/2002, section 3(3)(a), any person who is knowingly involved in the clearance of goods infringing an intellectual property right is guilty of a criminal offence and in case of conviction is liable to a fine not exceeding CYP 1,500,00 or imprisonment not exceeding two years or both. In case of a second or subsequent conviction, the offender is liable to a fine not exceeding CYP 2,000 or imprisonment not exceeding three years or both. However, in accordance with section 3(3)(b), any person contravening the provisions of Law 31(I)/2002, section 3, under circumstances excluding criminal liability under sub-section 3 (a), commits an offence, punishable by a fine not exceeding CYP 1,000,00. In our opinion, the provision of section 3(3)(b) is difficult to follow and it is to be hoped that the new legislation will adopt a language that will leave no room for doubt as to the meaning intended. **6.99**

The court before which proceedings are brought regarding a criminal offence in breach of the Law 31(I)/2002 may, irrespective of any conviction of the accused, order, as it may think fit, that all goods which infringe an existing intellectual property right be destroyed or handled in any other manner. The costs involved are within the court's discretion. **6.100**

VI. LIABILITY OF CUSTOMS AUTHORITIES AND RIGHT-HOLDERS

A. Liability of right-holders and sanctions

Article 12 of the Regulation provides that right-holders shall use the information, which they have been provided with by Customs under Article 9(3), first indent, **6.101** only for the purposes permitted by Articles 10, 11, and 13(1) of the Regulation. Any other use not permitted by national legislation may, on the basis of the law of the Member State where the goods are located, cause the right-holder to incur civil liability and lead to the suspension of his application for action.

6.102 Law 31(I)/2002 does not otherwise restrain use of such information; nor does it determine when its use shall be permitted. Therefore, subject to the provisions of the Processing of Personal Data (Protection of the Individual) Law, Law 138(I)/2001, as amended by Law 37(I)/2003, it is unlikely that a right-holder will ever incur civil liability for illegitimate use of information received from customs.

6.103 According to Article 19(3) of the Regulation, a right-holder's civil liability shall be governed by the law of the Member State in which the goods in question were placed in one of the situations referred to in Article 1(1) of the Regulation.

6.104 Law 31(I)/2002 does not make any specific reference to the civil liability of right-holders. We do not think that the general law of tort covers the present issue. The only basis for a civil liability is, perhaps, the Processing of Personal Data (Protection of the Individual) Law, Law 138(I)/2001 (as amended). It remains to be seen whether the proposed Bill (discussed in the Introduction above) will further regulate this question.

B. Liability of customs authorities and sanctions

6.105 In accordance with Article 19(I) of Council Regulation 1383/2003, subject to the national law of the Member State concerned, the acceptance of an application shall not entitle the right-holder to compensation in the event that goods suspected of infringing an intellectual property right are not detected by a customs office and are released, or no action is taken to detain them in accordance with Article 9(1) of the Regulation.

6.106 However, in case of a wrongful act or omission by a Government official the Republic is liable to damages in virtue of Article 172 of the Constitution which provides as follows:

> The Republic shall be liable for any wrongful act or omission causing damage committed in the exercise or purported exercise of the duties of officers or authorities of the Republic.

6.107 Nevertheless, since Law 31(I)/2002 specifically deprives intellectual property right-holders of the right to claim damages, if goods suspected of infringing their rights are not detected or are released, it remains to be seen how the courts will solve the thorny problem of reconciling the provisions of the Law with the Constitution, which is the Supreme Law of the Land. It appears that the crux of the matter is the ambit of the word 'wrongful' in Article 172 of the Constitution. The right to damages arises not only in respect of 'wrongful acts', but, also, in respect of 'wrongful omissions' 'in the exercise' or 'purported exercise' of the duties of officers or authorities of the Republic. A member of the personnel of CCED is an 'officer' within the meaning of the aforesaid term and CCED itself is an 'authority' within the meaning of the term used in Article 172. Therefore, if the act or, more interestingly, the omission is due to negligent behaviour, we would suggest that a person who suffers damage by reason of such act or omission has an arguable case to claim damages. If the act or omission in question is intentional and/or fraudulent, then we have no doubt that the victim is entitled to damages under Article 172 of the Constitution.

According to Article 19(2) of the Regulation, the exercise by a customs office or by another duly empowered authority of the powers conferred on them in order to fight against goods infringing an intellectual property right shall not render them liable towards the persons involved in the situations referred to in Article 1(1) of the Regulation, nor towards the persons affected by the measures provided for in Article 4 of the Regulation for damages suffered by them as a result of the authority's intervention, except where provided for by the law of the Member State in which the application is made or, in the case of an application under Article 5(4), by the law of the Member State in which loss or damage is incurred.   **6.108**

Section 14(1) of Law 31(I)/2002 provides that the right-holder does not have a right to damages, in cases where the goods referred to in his application are not discovered and are delivered or in cases in which reasonably no action is taken in respect of such goods.   **6.109**

The key word is 'reasonably'. If one acts reasonably, one is not guilty of negligence, and, therefore, liability for negligence is excluded. *A contrario*, the failure to act, where reasonably one ought to have acted, entails liability either for negligence or for breach of statutory duty.   **6.110**

A question of unconstitutionality by reason of Article 172 of the Constitution can only arise in respect of legislation relieving the State from the consequences of wrongful acts or omissions of its officers or authorities. There is nothing in the Constitution rendering a law relieving the officer concerned from personal liability, which such officer would have but for the relieving legislation.   **6.111**

Cyprus legislation provides a further protection shield for the customs authority. This is their entitlement to request that the applicant provides them with a guarantee, or other equal security capable of holding them harmless against a possible liability claim towards people affected by an *ex officio* action. In fact, section 10(2) of Law 31(I)/2002 provides for such security to cover possible liability towards persons who may be affected by an act or omission of the right-holder, or in case it would eventually appear that the goods in question do not infringe any intellectual property right. This provision does not refer to any liability towards the right-holder.   **6.112**

Conclusion

6.113 The negotiations for the accession of Cyprus to the EU commenced in the spring of 1998. The Accession Treaty was signed on 16 April 2003 and Cyprus became a full Member country of the EU on 1 May 2004.

6.114 During the negotiating process Cyprus made a great effort to approximate its legal system to that of the *acquis communautaire*. Law 31(I)/2002 was enacted in furtherance of this effort.

6.115 There can be no doubt that the enactment of Law 31(I)/2002 greatly improved the protection Cyprus afforded to intellectual property. Since the matters which Law 31(I)/2002 was enacted to regulate, have, since 1 July 2004, been governed by Council Regulation 1383/2003 and Commission Regulation 1891/2004, both directly applicable in all Member countries of the EU, Law 31(I)/2002 has lost much of its previous importance.

6.116 As Law 31(I)/2002 was enacted prior to the coming into force of the two said Regulations and at a time when Cyprus was not a Member of the EU, conflict or incompatibility between some of the provisions of that Law with the two Regulations or either one of them was unavoidable.

6.117 CCED took the right decision, namely to cease implementing all provisions of the Law which conflict or are incompatible with the corresponding provisions of the Regulations, as from 1 July 2004.

6.118 Though there can be no doubt about the efficacy of the CCED in implementing this decision, the situation cannot be described as satisfactory. Indeed, it is not within the normal duties of an administrative authority to judge which provisions of a law in force it is bound to apply and which provisions it is bound to disregard. This task is more akin to the nature of the judicial power than that of the executive power of the State. After all this is what the doctrine of separation of powers, which is one of the cornerstones of modern democratic norms, implies.

6.119 Therefore, the enactment of a new law to repeal and substitute Law 31(1)/2002, should now be deemed to be a matter of priority.

6.120 However, this criticism aside, nowadays Cyprus provides effective remedies to combat infringement of intellectual rights. Not only has Cyprus put in place a good national legal system, which deals with matters which the two EU Regulations left at the discretion of the Member States, but, its authorities, namely CCED, have repeatedly proved in practice that they have both the will and the ability to apply the legal system effectively, with commendable results.

7

CZECH REPUBLIC

Petra Korejzova

Introduction

Prior to the accession of the Czech Republic to the European Union on 1 May **7.02**
2004, border measures applied by customs in the field of intellectual property were
governed by the 'Act on importation, exportation, and re-exportation of goods
infringing certain intellectual property rights' (Act on Custom Actions),[1] which
was already in accordance with European legal standards as laid down in Council
Regulation 3295/94[2] and Commission Regulation 1367/95.[3] Upon the entry into
force of EC Regulation 1383/2003[4] on 1 July 2004, several amendments to the
Czech Act were adopted,[5] although no wholesale changes to the system were
required. In the Czech Republic, the national legislation on border measures has
limited itself to giving effect to EC Regulation 1383/2003 and its Implementing
Regulation 1891/2004.[6] It does not extend beyond the scope of these instruments.

---

[1] Zákon č. 191/1999 Sb., ze dne 29. července 1999 o opatřeních týkajících se dovozu, vývozu a
zpětného vývozu zboží porušujícího některá práva duševního vlastnictví a o změně některých
dalších zákonů (Law No. 191/1999 Collection of Laws ('Coll.'), 29 July 1999, governing the importation, exportation, and re-exportation of goods infringing certain intellectual property rights, and
amending certain other legislation—'Customs Action Act').

[2] Council Reg (EC) No 3295/94 of 22 December 1994 laying down measures to prohibit the release
for free circulation, export, re-export or entry for a suspensive procedure of counterfeit and pirated
goods, OJ L 341/8 (30.12.1996), as last amended by Reg (EC) No 806/2003, OJ L 122/1 (16.5.2003).

[3] Commission Reg (EC) No 1367/95 of 16 June 1995 laying down provisions for the implementation of Council Reg (EC) 3295/94, OJ L 133/2 (17.06.1995), as amended.

[4] Council Reg (EC) 1383/2003 of 22 July 2003 concerning customs action against goods
suspected of infringing certain intellectual property rights and the measures to be taken against
goods found to have infringed such rights, OJ L 196/7 (2.8.2003).

[5] The consolidated version of the Law No 191/1999 Coll. came into force on 9 June 2004,
pursuant to Law No 354/2004 Coll.

[6] Commission Reg (EC) No 1891/2004 of 21 October 2004 laying down provisions for the
implementation of Council Reg (EC) No 1383/2003 concerning customs action against goods
suspected of infringing certain intellectual property rights and the measures to be taken against
goods found to have infringed such rights 1383/2003, OJ L 328/16 (30.10.2004).

7.02 Approximation of Czech law with European law further to the entry of the Czech Republic into the European Union also encompasses substantive intellectual property law, including the area of trade mark protection.[7]

7.03 As under the former version of the Customs Actions Act, holders of intellectual property rights (including holders of trade marks, copyright or related rights, design rights, patents, supplementary protection certificates, plant variety rights, protected designations of origin, protected geographical indications, as well or any other persons authorized to use such rights, or their representatives) may thus apply for action by the Czech customs authorities to prevent infringements of these rights.

7.04 The authority of customs relating to the protection of intellectual property at the borders derives both from the legislation described above and from the Community Customs Code[8] together with its Implementation Regulation, Council Regulation 2454/93.[9]

I. SUBJECT MATTER AND SCOPE OF NATIONAL LAW IMPLEMENTING THE REGULATION

A. Customs procedure of the goods

7.05 According to the EC Regulation 1383/2003 ('the Regulation')[10] the conditions for action for all customs authorities are set when goods are suspected of infringing an intellectual property right in the situation when goods are entered for release for free circulation, export or re-export with accordance with Community Customs Code[11] or when they are found during checks on goods entering or leaving the Community customs territory. Over and above this legal framework, the national legislative states further conditions. According to the section 1, paragraph 1 of the Act on Custom Actions[12] the legal conditions for actions are set for the customs authorities against persons possessing, holding, storing, or selling goods, production

---

[7] Zákon č. 441/2003 Sb., ze dne 3.12.2004, o ochranných známkách (Law No 441/2003 Coll., of 3 December 2004, Trade Marks Act). This Act came into force on 1 April 2004.
[8] Council Reg (EC) No 2913/92 of 12 December 1992 establishing the Community Customs Code, OJ L302/1 (19.10.1992), as amended.
[9] Commission Reg (EEC) No 2454/93 of 2 July 1993 laying down provisions for the implementation of Council Reg (EEC) No 2913/92 establishing the Community Customs Code, OJ L 111/88 (29.04.1999), as amended.   [10] Reg 1383/2003, Art 1(1).
[11] Reg 245/93, Community Customs Code, Arts 37 and 183.
[12] Law No 191/1999 Coll., Customs Action Act, s 1(1) and Reg 2454/93, Community Customs Code, Art 4(13), (14).

of which the intellectual property rights were violated within the Community customs territory. It is clear that these kinds of goods must come from the third countries beyond the Community customs territory, as our customs authorities have no legal frame for taking any action against goods infringing certain intellectual property rights having been already released into the Community customs territory.

B. Definition of infringing goods

Under Article 2(1) of the Regulation 'goods infringing an intellectual property **7.06** right' means counterfeit goods, pirated goods and other goods infringing a patent, a supplementary protection certificate, a national plant variety right, designation of origin or geographical indications and geographical designations. The largest number of actions taken by the customs authorities in the Czech Republic involves counterfeit goods suspected of infringing trade mark rights. This amounts to approximately 95 per cent. There are several 'pirated goods' cases of customs actions based on rights to industrial designs, these cases create the remaining 5 per cent. There are as yet only two actions based on a patent right (and only one in the last eight years). There has never been any action based on another type of intellectual property right, such as a supplementary protection certificate, a national plant variety right, designation of origin or geographical indications, and geographical designations.

(1) Counterfeit goods

Under Article 2(1)(a)(i) of the Regulation, 'counterfeit goods' are goods, including **7.07** their packaging, bearing, without the right-holder's authorization, a designation identical to a trade mark validly registered in respect of the same type of goods, or a designation which cannot be distinguished in its essential aspects from a registered trade mark, and which thereby infringes the trade mark holder's rights under national or Community law. This relatively high degree of similarity must be obvious at first glance, even to a regular consumer.

After the application for action has been accepted by the customs authority, all the **7.08** information needed to make the goods in question readily recognizable by the customs authorities are at their disposal, in particular an accurate and detailed description of the goods, and any specific information the right-holder may have concerning the type or pattern of fraud. It is very important for the right-holder to supply the customs authority with accurate, practical details to enable them to identify quickly the goods detained (for example, photos, documents, etc). All information given in the accepted application is published in the customs on-line system and it is accessible by any custom office. The customs authorities can then compare the goods detained against this description. Right-holders are therefore well advised to lodge an application for action, even before customs have detained any counterfeit goods, and when doing so, to supply them with as much information assisting in the identification of potential counterfeits as possible. The customs authorities appreciate all help available from the right-holder in order to better their understanding of the right-holder's business activity, his production and counterfeit goods.

7.09   Once goods are suspected of infringing an intellectual property right, the customs authorities first check whether the conditions for a customs action have been met. Clearly, the customs authorities may intervene only if any of the intellectual property rights referred to in Article 2(1) of the Regulation are likely to have been infringed. Scope of the protection of trade marks is determined in detail by the Trade Mark Act, section 2,[13] which states that in the territory of the Czech Republic there is protection for trade marks registered in the Register of Trade Marks maintained by the Industrial Property Office; those registered with effect for the Czech Republic or European Union in the register maintained by the International Bureau of the World Intellectual Property Organization; and those registered in the register maintained by the Office for Harmonization in the Internal Market (trade marks and designs). The National Trade Mark Act further states in section 8 that the proprietor of the mark has an exclusive right to use the mark in relation to the goods or services covered by the trade mark. The right-holder must demonstrate the existence of a trade mark right on the basis of an official trade mark registration certificate. In cases where the original registration certificate is unavailable the customs authority requires an extract from the official database confirmed by the registration office, for example, by the stamp. The customs authorities in the Czech Republic cannot intervene solely on the basis of a trade mark *application*.

7.10   The National Trade Mark Act mentioned above also relates to the protection of the trade marks which are well known in the territory of the Czech Republic within the meaning of Article 6bis of the Paris Convention for the Protection of Industrial Property and Article 16 of the Agreement on Trade-Related Aspect of Intellectual Property Rights (TRIPs). A generally well-known trade mark is one which is in such regular usage for identical or similar goods or services provided by its owner to the relevant consumers' segment that it obtains distinctiveness despite not having been registered in the Trade Mark Register. As provided by the international treaties, such a mark is protected as a trade mark in each contractual country in which it has become well-known for identical or similar goods or products.

7.11   In order to exercise the right to a well-known mark and establish the claim, the proprietor must prove that the mark has obtained general popularity within

---

[13] Law No 441/2003 Coll, Trade Marks Act, s 2 (d).

the relevant customers' segment, for example, by submitting documents proving the sale of goods or services marked thereby, details of an advertising campaign, or results of a survey proving the level of popularity of such mark in the market.[14]

The possibility of exercising the right to a mark that has become generally well-known actually breaks the registration principle of claiming trade mark rights. However, although it is possible to ask the customs authority to pursue an action based on the right to a generally well-known mark, to date, it has not been used in practice. **7.12**

The Czech customs authorities take measures on a regular basis against violation of trade mark symbols (including logos, labels, stickers, brochures, instructions for use, or guarantee documents bearing such symbols), even if delivered separately. The same applies to packaging materials bearing counterfeit trade marks, delivered separately. **7.13**

In practice, counterfeit goods (and in particular textiles, mostly originating in China and Vietnam) have been detained mainly at market places by mobile customs groups acting in accordance with the Custom Actions Act, section 1, paragraph 1[15] against persons possessing, holding, storing, or selling goods, production of which violated the intellectual property rights. The most frequently abused trade marks are typically Adidas, Buffalo, Calvin Klein, Camel, Diesel, Esprit, Fishbone, Hugo Boss, Joop, Lacoste, Levi Strauss, Mustang, Nike, Versace, Ferrari, Puma, and Reebok, which are very often applied without their owner's authorization on textile goods, shoes, backpacks, and other products; forged trade marks of Omega, Rolex, Calvin Klein, Ferrari, and others have also been applied to watches. **7.14**

(2) Pirated goods

Under Article 2(1)(b) of the Regulation, 'pirated goods' against which the customs authorities of the Member States are to take action are those goods 'which are or contain copies made without the consent of the holder of a copyright or related right or design right, in cases where the making of those copies would constitute an infringement under national or Community law'. To date, no actions have been taken against pirated goods except those actions based on industrial design rights. A right-holder of an industrial design has to prove his right by a registration certificate or its certified copy (in the form of official restrict stamped by the office). **7.15**

A copyright-holder has to prove his right by any documents showing that the copyright to a work has been created and that the work is actually used. The **7.16**

---

[14] Law No 441/2003 Coll, Trade Marks Act, s 5.
[15] Law No 191/1999 Coll, Customs Action Act, s 1(1).

Copyright Law[16] covers a body of rights that originate upon creation of a work or its expression in any objectively perceivable form. The basic condition for granting protection pursuant to the Copyright Law is the work being a unique output of creative activity performed by a natural person, namely, the author. The importance, value, purpose, or extent of the work is insignificant.

7.17 What is understood as a work in a sense of the Copyright Law[17] may be a literary work or other work of art as well as a scientific work. It may represent particularly a work expressed by a speech or a text; a musical work, a play, a musical, a choreography or a pantomime; a photograph or a work created in form similar to photography; an audiovisual work such as a film; a visual artwork such as a painting, a graphical and/or a sculpture work; an architectural work including urban work; an applied art work; and a cartographic work. A computer program and/or a database are also considered a work pursuant to the Copyright Law provided that it is an original copy in the sense of the author's own intellectual output with respect to the form of selection or structure of the contents.

7.18 The Copyright Law, section 42 provides the duty of customs authorities to inform about any export and/or import of goods that may represent copies of a work or audio/audiovisual record of a work, or those that could serve for making such copies (unrecorded medium), or those that may represent a tool for creation of such audio or audiovisual records or printouts, or those that may represent an aid designed to remove, put out of operation, or limit the functionality of technical equipment or other means designed to protect the rights. The author is entitled to request any information from the customs authorities regarding the contents and/or extent of the export and/or import of goods that may infringe his rights within the meaning of section 42 of the Copyright Law. The provision concerned breaks the information rights embodied in the Regulation,[18] as well as those stipulated in the national Act on Customs Actions.[19] The right to receive information is supported by the right to inspect the documents,[20] which enables the author to examine the authority and/or legitimacy of such imports. The author can use this information to decide whether or not to exercise his rights pursuant to the Copyright Law, for example, whether he should file an application for action to be carried out by the customs authority.

---

[16] Zákon č. 121/2000 Sb., ze dne 7.4.2000, o právu autorském, o právech souvisejících s právem autorským a o změně některých zákonů—*autorský zákon* (Law No 121/2000 Coll of 7 April 2000, on Copyright, on interrelated laws and on amendment certain laws— 'Copyright Act').

[17] Law No 121/2000 Coll, Copyright Act, s 2.   [18] Reg 1383/2003, Art 9(3).

[19] Law No 191/1999 Customs Action Act, s 9 (1).

[20] Law No 121/2000 Copyright Act, s 42(1).

(3) Goods infringing other intellectual property rights

Goods infringing a patent or a supplementary protection certificate

Goods infringing patent rights are defined in the Czech Patent Law,[21] which **7.19** distinguishes for that purpose between direct and indirect (or contributory) infringement. A (direct) patent infringement will result, inter alia, from any importation or putting on the market of a product which is the subject matter of a patent, or products directly obtained through a patented process without the patentee's authorization. Until and unless proven otherwise, any products shall be deemed to have been obtained by a process which is the subject matter of a patent, provided that: (i) they are identical to products which are the direct result of that process; (ii) there exists a significant likelihood that the suspect products have been manufactured by using that process; and (iii) the patentee failed to identify the method of manufacture applied by the allegedly infringing products in spite of his reasonable efforts. An indirect patent infringement is constituted by any sale or offering for sale without the patentee's authorization, to any person other than those persons who have been authorized to use the patented invention, of any materials relating to the essential features of the patented invention, if it is obvious under the circumstances that those materials are suitable and have been designed for reproducing that invention. However, patentees are not allowed to prevent third parties from handling products falling under the scope of the patent if the product in question has been marketed in the Czech Republic by the patentee or with the latter's consent (national exhaustion principle).

The protection afforded to holders of supplementary protection certificates (SPCs) is **7.20** akin to that arising from the grant of the basic patent on which they rely, and is given to chemical substances or their mixtures, and micro-organisms or their mixtures, which constitute the active agents of registered preparations. The protection also extends to any use of the subject matter of the patent as a medicine or a preparation serving to protect plant(s). SPCs thus confer rights identical to those conferred by basic patents, and they are subject to the same limitations as those of basic patents.

When enforcing patent rights or SPCs under the Regulation, Czech Customs **7.21** shall not examine personally whether or not an infringement has occurred. Their decision to detain or suspend the release of goods shall rely on an application filed by the holder of the patent or SPC containing the information necessary to the identification of suspect products. Afterwards, the responsibility for the case will pass on to the right-holder, who will substantiate his allegations before the courts.

---

[21] Zákon č. 527/1990 Sb., ze dne 27. listopadu 1990, o vynálezích a zlepšovacích návrzích (Law No 527/1990 Coll. on inventions and Rationalisation Proposals). For a consolidated version, see Law No 3/2001 Coll. The acts which constitute a patent infringement are defined in ss 13 and 13(a) of this Act.

Goods infringing a national plant variety right

7.22 Protection of plant variety rights provides the holder of a breeding certificate with an exclusive right to use the protected variety. A right of protection may be granted to a variety that meets the conditions of novelty, distinctiveness, uniformity, stability and where the plant variety bears a name chosen in compliance with legal requirements. Rights of protection are dealt with at both European and national levels.

7.23 Legal protection of new plant varieties has, since 1 February 2001, been governed in the Czech Republic by the Plant Variety Rights Protection Act No 408/2000 Coll.[22]

The Czech Central Institute for Supervising and Testing in Agriculture was appointed as the authority competent for the granting and maintenance of plant variety rights in the Czech Republic. Such rights are subject to the fulfilment of the relevant statutory requirements through the approval of the name of the plant variety and the issuance of a plant-breeder's certificate.

7.24 The European protection of rights is granted on the basis of meeting all the requirements stipulated in the Council Regulation (EC) No 2100/94 of 27 July 1994 on Community plant variety rights. Examinations performed for the purpose of granting European protection of rights are organized by the Community Plant Variety Office in Angers, France. The advantage of the European protection of rights is that the rights of protection covering all EU states, including the Czech Republic, may be granted based on one application and one set of technical examinations performed according to duly defined requirements.

7.25 As yet, no case has been reported in the Czech Republic concerning an infringement claim relating to a protected plant variety, although one may reasonably expect to face such infringements in the future.

Goods infringing a national designation of origin or a geographical indication

7.26 Registered designations of origin and geographical indications are protected in the Czech Republic against any direct or indirect commercial use of these designations and indications in respect of any goods not covered by the registration if such goods are comparable to the goods registered under the designation or indication, or if such use takes profit from their goodwill.[23] Registered designations of

---

[22] Zákon č. 408/2000 Sb., ze dne 25. října 2000 o ochraně práv k odrůdám rostlin a o změně zákona č. 92/1996 Sb., o odrůdách, osivu a sadbě pěstovaných rostlin ve znění pozdějších předpisů (zákon o ochraně práv k odrůdám) (Law No 408/2000 Collection of Laws ('Coll.'), 25 October 2000, governing the plant variety rights, and amending certain other legislation—'Act on Plant Variety Rights').

[23] Zákon č. 452/2001 Sb., z 29. listopadu 2001, o ochraně označení původu a zeměpisných označení (Law No 452/2001 Coll., of 29 November 2001 on the protection of designations of origin and geographical indications), s 23(1)(a).

origin and geographical indications are also protected against any misuse, imitation or copying even where the true origin of the goods is duly mentioned on the goods or the protected designations have been translated and are accompanied by such words as 'kind', 'type', 'method', 'à la', 'imitation', or the like.[24] Protection of registered designations of origin and geographical indications further extends to any other untruthful or deceptive information as to geographical origin, nature or essential qualities of the goods indicated on their inner or outer packaging, in advertising materials or documents relating to such goods, as well as against the use of transport packaging capable of inducing false impressions as to the origin of the goods. Finally, any other conduct capable of resulting in misleading assumptions regarding the genuine origin of the goods will constitute an infringement of the geographical indication or designation of origin concerned.[25]

(4) Sui generis *database rights*

Unlike the position under the Regulation and in most EU Member States, *sui*   **7.27**
generis rights to databases are also currently protected by the Czech Customs. This has been considered by some authors as a 'surprising benefit of the Czech system', although the same authors recognize that 'this is not thought to be a major practical benefit in practice'.[26]

(5) *Moulds and matrices*

Under Article 2(3) of the Regulation, moulds and matrices specifically designed   **7.28**
or adapted for the manufacture of goods infringing an intellectual property right may be detained (or their release suspended) by customs under conditions identical to those applying to trade marks and industrial models, copyright or related rights, design rights, patents, and other intellectual property rights subjected under Article 1(1) of Regulation. In practice, customs actions have been taken only in respect of moulds and matrices infringing trade mark rights.

C. Goods excluded by the Regulation

(1) *Parallel imported goods*

If the Czech customs authorities discover suspected goods which they eventually   **7.29**
recognize as genuine but parallel imported goods, they will refrain from any

---

[24] Ibid, s 23(1)(b).   [25] Ibid, s 23(1)(c).
[26] J Rutter and M Rosinski, 'Who is the Weakest Link ?', [2004] Trademark World, 26–29.

further action under the Regulation, as such goods are excluded from the scope of this Regulation by Article 3(1), first sentence. They will not inform the right-holders concerned of this interception, as this would clearly be in breach of Article 12 of the Regulation. Customs actions may only be taken in such a context if the importer fails to document that the goods are genuine.

7.30 As regards the movement of goods across the *internal* EU borders, it should be noted in passing that the provisions on parallel imports and Community exhaustion of intellectual property rights[27] have been in force since 1 May 2004, the date of accession of the Czech Republic to the European Union.

(2) Goods which have been manufactured under conditions other than those which have been agreed with the right-holder

7.31 As for parallel imported goods, customs are not allowed to adopt border measures under the Regulation against goods, which have been manufactured under conditions other than those to which the right-holder has agreed (that is, through a licence agreement).[28] Indeed, the customs authorities are not in a position to judge whether goods comply with the terms of a licence agreement. Provided the importer proves the right-holder's consent to the manufacture and/or importation of the goods, those goods will be released for free circulation. If it appears that the goods do not comply with the conditions of a licence, it will be up to the right-holder to seek to obtain a seizure on the goods from the courts, using civil court proceedings.

(3) Goods contained in travellers' personal baggage

7.32 Travellers' personal baggage is subject only to random checks by Czech Customs. The customs officers carrying out such checks observe the provisions of the Community Customs Code and its Implementing Regulation, as well as Article 3(2) of Regulation 1383/2003. Accordingly, goods of a non-commercial nature from non-EU Member countries released for free circulation in the territory of

---

[27] As a result of this principle, 'owners of Czech [intellectual property] rights will not be able to prevent their goods from being imported into the Czech Republic from outside authorised distribution channels if such goods have already been put on the market, by the [intellectual property] right owner or with its consent, anywhere in the E[uropean] E[conomic] A[rea]. In addition, owners of [intellectual property] rights in any E[uropean] E[conomic] A[rea] country will not be able to prevent their goods being sold in the enlarged EU if they or their licensees consented to the goods being put on the market in any of the accession countries, including the Czech Republic. The potential for cheap branded and patented goods from the Czech Republic to make their way to other more expensive European markets after accession is therefore a serious issue for right owners' (J Rutter and M Rosinski, 'Who is the Weakest Link?', [2004] Trademark World, 26–29).
[28] Reg 1383/2003, Art 3(1), second sentence.

the European Union are deemed, in view of their kind and quantity, to be intended exclusively for personal use or consumption, or as gifts, and will not be detained under the Regulation.

II. APPLICATION FOR ACTION BY THE CUSTOMS AUTHORITIES

A. Measures prior to an application for action by the customs authorities ('*ex officio* measures')

The customs authorities in the Czech Republic have always been proactive in applying *ex officio* measures under Article 4 of the Regulation, meaning that they will not hesitate to act on their own initiative if they come upon suspect goods, even when the right-holder has not yet filed an application under the Regulation. The time limit of three working days imposed by Article 4 of the Regulation is strictly observed.   **7.33**

An action to be carried out by the custom authorities is further governed by the national legislation—the Custom Action Act,[29] defining terms and conditions under which a custom action may be pursued against persons that own, hold, store, or sell goods whose production or alteration violate the intellectual property rights. This provision is related the Community Custom Code[30] stipulating that what is understood by under the supervision by the custom authorities is the general activity through which the custom authorities secure observance of custom regulations and/or further legal provisions associated with the goods subject to custom supervision. Article 4 of the Customs Code then provides for what is referred to as a custom inspection, that is, performance of special actions such as goods examination, verification of the existence and authenticity of documents, inspection of accounting documents and other records, inspection of vehicles, inspection of luggage and other goods transported by persons or on persons, and, last but not least, performance of official investigations with the aim of making sure that all custom regulations and further legal provisions associated with the goods subject to custom supervisions have been met. Article 37 of the Custom Code stipulates that the goods are subject to custom supervision once they enter EU territory. The custom authorities may carry out the inspection according to the legal provisions in force only. The goods will be subject to the custom regime as long as it is necessary in order to secure their custom status.   **7.34**

---

[29] Law No 191/1999 on Customs Action, s 1 (1).
[30] Reg 2454/93—Community Customs Code, Art 4(13), (14) and (37).

7.35 If the custom authorities find out that the goods inspected are not Community goods and thus are suspected of violating intellectual property rights, they must seize the goods concerned for the period of three business days in order to enable the right-holder to file a request for action to be performed by custom authorities in accordance with Article 5 of the Regulation. Should the right-holder fail to file the request within the due date, or should the custom authority fail to issue a decision on action, the custom office must declare the decision on the goods' seizure null and void and release the goods to the person from whom the goods were seized.

7.36 Within this term the application for action has to be filed by the right-holder and accepted by the customs authority in order to enable the right-holder to ask the customs authority for information concerning the name, surname (or company name), and address of the declarant, owner or holder of the goods and, if known, on the origin and destination of the goods. Still at the right-holder's express request, they will also provide samples or digital pictures of the goods to the right-holder. The latter or his representative will even be given a chance to examine the goods in person in the customs office warehouse. In case the application for action is not accepted by the customs authority within the term of three working days, the right-holder cannot require any other information than the actual or supposed number of items and their nature in accordance to the Article 4(2) of the Regulation.

B. The lodging and processing of applications for customs action

(1) Persons entitled to file an application for action

Definition of 'right-holders' under the Regulation

7.37 By virtue of Article 2(2)(a) of the Regulation, the term 'right-holder' means in the first place, for the purpose of the Regulation, the holder of a trade mark, copyright or related right, design right, patent, supplementary protection certificate, plant variety right, protected geographical indication, protected designation of origin, and more generally, any right referred to in Article 2(1) of Regulation (right-holders *stricto sensu*).

7.38 Pursuant to Article 2(2)(b) of the Regulation, the concept of 'right-holder' also includes any other person authorized to use any of the intellectual property rights referred to in Article 2(1) on the basis of a consent issued by the right-holders *stricto sensu*. Such consent must be in writing and may be in the form of a licence agreement, or an agreement on commercial representation.

Finally, the notion of 'right-holder' also encompasses the representatives of right-holders *stricto sensu* or authorized users, that is, any natural or legal persons who are duly entitled to act on their behalf.

Proof of entitlement to file an application for action

For right-holders stricto sensu

Right-holders must provide evidence in their application for action of their **7.39** entitlement to file such an application. Holders of registered intellectual property rights must submit a certificate evidencing the registration of the right in question, issued by the appropriate registrar, or a notarized copy thereof. In case the original registration certificate is unavailable the customs authority requires an extract from the official database confirmed by the registration office, for example, by its stamp. Official databases of the Czech Industrial Property Office are available at www.upv.cz.

Extracts from private databases are not accepted as a proof of the existence of such **7.40** rights. The same applies to priority documents or any other certificates of filing an application for the registration of intellectual property rights.

Holders of a copyright or related rights must provide a certificate acknowledging **7.41** their capacity as holders of the right in question. Typically this takes the form of an agreement concluded between the author or his representative and the publisher, distributor, etc. The content of the documents, which must be legally signed, is not examined by customs.

For persons authorized to use the right

Authorization to use an intellectual property right may be proved primarily by **7.42** submitting an agreement concluded between the authorized user and the right-holder, or a declaration issued by the latter, in any form whatsoever. The document submitted must give the applicant an unequivocal right to take action for, and on behalf of, the holder of the intellectual property right concerned. Such documents need not be officially registered, but they must always be duly executed and submitted in original form, or in the form of a notarized photocopy.

In principle, Czech Customs will not verify whether the documents provided to **7.43** them are genuine, except in exceptional circumstances where they are suspicious that the documents might be fake.

Reliance on licences granted to registered holders of industrial rights (invention **7.44** patents, industrial or utility designs, trade marks, designations of origin, or geographical indications) requires prior registration with the Industrial Property Office, since in the absence of such a registration the licence cannot be enforced against third parties, including customs.

For representatives

Upon filing an application with Czech Customs under the Regulation, the repres- **7.45** entative of a right-holder *stricto sensu* or of an authorized user of the right concerned must provide a power of attorney (which may consist of a *general* power), either in original form, or in the form of a notarized copy.[31] A power of attorney may be given to all representatives, to a general designee, or to a professional representative, whose authorization is derived from national legislation.[32] Attorneys at law and foreign natural persons who are either the nationals of one of the Member States of the European Union or one of the Member States of the European Economic Area Treaty ('domestic State') and are authorized to provide legal services under the professional denomination of the domestic State pursuant to the memo issued by the Ministry of Justice published in the Collection of Codes ('European Attorney') may function as the representatives duly authorized to act on behalf of the client before all authorities and institutions as well as before courts.

7.46 In addition, the national legislation enables patent attorneys, who are either nationals or residents of some other EU or EEA Member State ('domestic State'), and as such are authorized to provide services as patent attorneys in one of the EU or EEA Member States ('foreign patent attorneys'), to provide professional aid to both natural and legal entities in matters related to industrial property, in particular to represent them before the State administration authorities and in proceedings held before courts under the conditions and within the extent provided for by the Court Proceedings Acts as well as to provide independent consulting and other services associated with the industrial property protection.[33] Both European attorneys and foreign patent attorneys may function in the Czech Republic solely within the scope of the authorization obtained in their domestic State and do so in the official language of the domestic State.

7.47 Given the fact that there are 20 different official languages currently in use within the EU, it must be stated that the national customs authorities are still not sufficiently equipped as to be able to process the requests filed in foreign languages, except for correspondence led in German and English and/or French and Italian, which is already being received in small amounts and has so far been processed quite smoothly.

7.48 Customs authorities shall communicate with any representative of a right-holder who has furnished proof of his representation, namely acceptable power of attorney. In the case of foreign representatives, translations are done outside the Czech Customs by commercial translators. At the present time customs prefer to discuss matters in the Czech language for greater convenience. Czech representatives can also be more helpful if they know the national legal system in practice.

---

[31] Czech Customs, 'Guidelines for the filing of applications for customs action in case of infringement of an intellectual property right', www.cs.mfcr.cz.
[32] Zákon č. 85/1996 Sb., ze dne 13. března 1996, o advokacii (Law No 85/1996 of the Collection of Law, of 13 March 1996, Law on Advocacy.
[33] Zákon č. 417/2004 Sb., ze dne 10. června 2004, o patentových zástupcích (Law No 417/2004 Coll. of 10 June 2004, Patent Attorneys Act).

When a representative files an application for action by fax, by e-mail or *viva voce*   **7.49**
for the records, he must supplement the application within three days by a delivery of the original documents.

(2) Competent customs department and formal requirements

Competent customs department

Pursuant to the Custom Actions Act, applications for action by customs authorities in the Czech Republic must be filed exclusively with the Customs Directorate in Hradec Králové:[34]   **7.50**

Celní ředitelství Hradec Králové (Customs Directorate Hradec Králové)
Oddělení celně právní a vymáhání
Bohuslava Martinů 1672/8a
PO BOX 88
CZ-501 01 Hradec Králové
Czech Republic
Tel.: +420-495 756 214
        +420-495 756 267
        +420-495 756 111
Fax: +420-495 756 200
E-mail: posta0601@cs.mfcr.cz
URL: www.cs.mfcr.cz

Form of the application for action

National applications for action, as well as 'Community' applications for action[35]   **7.51**
relying on a Community trade mark, a Community design, or a plant variety right, a designation of origin, or geographical indication protected by the Community, must be made out on the forms prescribed by Regulation 1891/2004.[36] The form for Community applications can be downloaded in the Czech language on the website of the Czech Customs Administration at: http://www.cs.mfcr.cz.

Even though it is currently possible to file an application for action by fax and   **7.52**
by e-mail, it is always necessary to send the originals of all relevant documents by post. Legislation on electronic signatures[37] was adopted recently in the Czech Republic, but the current technical resources of the customs authorities prevent

---

[34] Law No 191/1999, Customs Action Act, s 4(1).
[35] Such 'Community' applications may seek action by both the customs authorities in the territory of the Czech Republic and the customs authorities in one or more other Member States of the European Community.
[36] Law No 191/1999, Customs Action Act, s 4(2); Reg 1383/2003, Art 5(5).
[37] Zákon č. 227/2000 Sb., ze dne 29. června 2000, o elektronickém podpisu (Law No 227/2000 Coll, of 29 June 2000, Electronic Signature Act).

the filing of such applications solely by electronic means. However, electronic filing should be possible in the near future, though it will not be appropriate for the enclosures, the originals of which must be filed by post.

7.53 In other words, the original (or at least a certified copy) of the customs application, together with the original or certified copies of the declaration under Article 6 of the Regulation and of the documents evidencing entitlement to act as 'right-holder' must always be submitted. The Regulation laying down provisions for the implementation of Customs Regulation 1383/2003[38] stipulates that two copies of the application have to be made, one for customs and one to be retained by the right-holder.

Language requirements

7.54 Both 'national' applications for action and 'Community' applications for action, which are filed under Article 5(4) of the Regulation and designating Czech Republic, may be filed in any of the official languages of the European Community. The Czech customs authorities will then have the application (including the declaration under Article 6 of the Regulation and the exhibits enclosed with the application) translated into Czech. Pursuant to Article 6(2) of the Regulation, the applicant undertakes to pay the costs of this translation.

(3) Requirements regarding the contents of the application for action

Mandatory information

7.55 Any application for action must contain all mandatory information listed in Article 5(5), first indent, of the Regulation, in so far as it is necessary to enable customs readily to identify infringing goods. This includes an accurate and detailed technical description of the goods, any specific information the right-holder may have concerning the type and pattern of the fraud, and the name and address of a contact person appointed by the right-holder. There is no requirement for nationality of the contact person. It is more important that the contact person appointed on behalf of the right-holder can be easily contacted, preferably in the Czech language. Right-holders or their representatives must also deliver to the customs authorities any other information they have, such as the pre-tax value of the original goods on the legitimate market in the Czech Republic, the location of the goods or their intended destination, any data identifying the consignment or packages in question, the scheduled arrival or departure date of the goods, the means of transport used, the identity of the importer, exporter or holder of the goods, the country or countries of production and the routes used by traffickers. Czech Customs would also welcome any information relating to the technical differences between the genuine goods and the suspected goods, if available. All these kinds of information may help the customs to identify the goods suspected to infringe intellectual property rights.

---

[38] Reg 1891/2004, Art 3(3).

An application for action shall be accompanied by a declaration from the right-   **7.56**
holder.[39] It is necessary to file an original of the document (or its certified copy).
When filed electronically or via fax, it is necessary to submit the original
document within a term of three working days.

Optional information

Czech Customs will always be interested in having any information available about   **7.57**
previous infringements, as well as the identity of importers, exporters, or holders of
similar goods which have been detained in the past when they have been identified
afterwards. Also, should right-holders discover that certain goods marked without
their consent are to be delivered to a certain place on a certain date and time, the
right-holders are welcome to notify the customs authorities of this fact.

Additional information specific to the type of intellectual property right referred to in the application

Additional information specific to the type of intellectual property right on which   **7.58**
the application relies may also be requested by customs *a posteriori* (that is, subsequent to the filing of the application), depending on the circumstances, in
accordance with Article 5(6) of the Regulation.

(4) *Processing and acceptance of the application for action*

Prior to the entry into force of the Regulation on 1 July 2004, the processing of   **7.59**
applications for customs action in the Czech Republic was subject to a fee to cover
the administrative costs.[40] The new Regulation has abolished such fees.[41]

Under Article 5(7) of the Regulation, applications for action must be processed   **7.60**
within 30 working days of their receipt. According to the national legislation
under the Czech Administrative Code,[42] in elementary matters, especially when it
is possible to decide on the strength of documents submitted by the applicant, the
administrative organ is to make its decision without delay; in other matters
the administrative organ is obliged to make its decision in 30 days from the
initiation of the proceedings.

An application may be rejected if it fails to include the mandatory information   **7.61**
prescribed by Article 5(5). The customs directorate in Hradec Králové is entitled

---

[39] Reg 1383/2003, Art 6.
[40] J Rutter and M Rosinski, 'Who is the Weakest Link?', [2004] Trademark World, 26–29.
[41] See Reg 1383/2003, Art 5(7), second indent.
[42] Zákon č. 71/1967 Sb., z 29. června 1967, správní řád (Law. No. 71/1967 Coll, of 29 June 1967
Administrative Code), s 41(1).

to decide whether to approve or reject the application for customs action and is obliged to inform the right-holder of its decision without delay.[43] It is possible to file an appeal against a decision rejecting the customs action, however the appeal has no dilatory effect.[44] In such a case the right-holder has to file a new application meeting all formal requirements in order to have the customs action approved.

7.62 When granting an application for action, the period during which the customs authorities are to take the action shall not exceed one year. After the expiry of this period, the right-holder has to file a new application in order to extend this period for another year. The application for an extension has to appear in the form of the application for customs action according to the Article 5 of Regulation. If no new facts are known at the time of applying for the extension, the new application can refer to the original one.

7.63 As was already the case prior to the entry into force of Regulation 1383/2003, the decision allowing an application for action will cover all the customs offices in the Czech Republic.

(5) 'Community' applications for action

7.64 So far no 'Community' application for action under Article 5(4) of the Regulation has been filed through the Czech Customs. At present, only a limited number of 'Community' applications for action (in fact, less than a dozen) have designated the Czech Republic. The form and language requirements of Community applications for action have been outlined above (see paras 7.51–7.54).

III. CONDITIONS GOVERNING ACTION BY CUSTOMS AUTHORITIES AND BY THE AUTHORITIES COMPETENT TO DETERMINE WHETHER GOODS INFRINGE AN INTELLECTUAL PROPERTY RIGHT

A. Conditions governing action by customs authorities

(1) Factual background

7.65 There are more than 90 customs offices in the Czech Republic and all of them are involved in anti-counterfeiting (in the broad sense) to the same extent. Therefore,

---

[43] Law No 191/1999, Customs Action Act, s 4(1).
[44] Law No 191/1999, Customs Action Act, s 31a(1).

all customs authorities are equally important. All customs offices report to the Customs Directorate in Hradec Králové, which is competent to process applications for action and provides the customs offices with methodological instructions in the fight against piracy and counterfeiting.

Since the accession of the Czech Republic to the European Union, the Prague **7.66** Customs Directorate has accounted for the largest share of actions taken (35 per cent). One reason for this is that, apart from the international airport in Prague, the Czech Republic has no common border with any non-EU Member State, and from 1 May 2004 Czech Customs were obliged to abandon stationary customs controls at the internal EU borders (that is, at the frontiers to Poland, Germany, Austria and Slovakia).[45] Lately, the customs authorities have shifted their activities to within the country according to the Custom Code and Customs Act. Customs actions can be executed against persons, who own, keep, store, or sell goods, production or arrangement of which breaches intellectual property rights. Most of the infringements encountered by the customs relate to trade marks, nearly 95 per cent (and more specifically, to the counterfeit goods of textiles, spare parts for cars (such as for example, air conditioning, injection pumps, and car electronics), and personal computer and other electronic components). A further 5 per cent relate to pirated goods secured by virtue of design right infringement.

(2) Notification of customs intervention

Right-holders or their contact persons are notified of interventions by customs **7.67** (subsequent to the filing and acceptance of an application for action) without delay by post, e-mail, or telephone. The declarants and owners of goods are notified of the detention of the goods in the same manner.

(3) Information to be provided by customs to the right-holder before the right-holder confirms the infringing nature of the goods

In accordance with Article 9(2) of the Regulation, Czech Customs are authorized **7.68** to inform the right-holder and the declarant or holder of the goods of the actual or estimated quantity and the actual or supposed nature of goods which have been detained or whose release has been suspended on an application from the right-holder. The right-holder who has been provided with any such information is not

---

[45] Regular controls for customs and tax purposes have been kept at international airports, but not for flights from or to EU member countries (J Rutter and M Rosinski, 'Who is the Weakest Link ?', [2004] Trademark World, 26–29).

bound by such communication to notify the authority competent to take a substantive decision.

7.69   Under Article 9(3) of the Regulation, with a view to establishing whether any of their rights has been infringed, the right-holder (or his representative) will also be provided, at his request, with certain information available, including the (personal or company) name and address of the declarant, consignee, consignor or holder of the goods, if known, as well as with information as to the origin, provenance and destination of the goods.

7.70   The duty to inform is also governed by the national legislation (namely, Custom Actions Act, s 11[46]). Once the request for customs action filed by the right-holder is accepted, the customs office that holds the seized goods as requested by the right-holder must inform the holder, either by a letter or via e-mail, about the name/s, surname/s and permanent residence address or about the name of the company, place of business, or about the name of a natural person and its permanent residence address, declarant, proprietor or holder of the goods, and, if known, also the name, surname and permanent residence address or the company name and address of sender and addressee as well as the data on the place of dispatch of the goods that caused the violation of the intellectual property right so as to enable the right-holder to claim the protection of his rights before court.

7.71   The provision of the duty to inform also breaks the duty provided for by the Personal Data Protection Act, which stipulates the rights and duties of those processing personal data in order to avoid any occurrence of unauthorized privacy infringement. The Act applies to personal data being processed by government authorities (including custom authorities), municipal authorities, other public authorities as well as natural and corporate entities. Section 13 stipulates the duty imposed on persons when securing personal data in order to avoid any unauthorized or incidental access to personal data, its modification, destruction or loss, unauthorized transfers or other unauthorized processing thereto, as well as any other misuse of personal data. The obligation to maintain secrecy pursuant to the Personal Data Protection Act does not apply to the duty to inform pursuant to special laws, that is, s 9(3) of the Regulation and Customs Action Act, section 11.

(4) Inspection of the suspected goods

7.72   On being notified of the detention or suspension of the release of suspected goods, the right-holder concerned, as well as the other parties involved, are allowed to examine the goods. At the right-holder's explicit request, customs may provide

---

[46]   Zákon č. 101/2000 Sb., ze dne 4. dubna 2000, o ochraně osobních údajů (Law no. 101/2000 Coll., of 4 April 2000, on Personal Data Protection).

representative samples of the detained goods for the purposes of analysis and to facilitate the subsequent procedure. The right-holder shall then inform the customs authorities in writing (for example, by e-mail) without delay of the commencement of proceedings under Article 13 of the Regulation.

At the right-holder's request, and upon agreement with the customs authorities, **7.73** customs may take samples of the goods and hand them over or send them to the right-holder. It is up to the right-holder to decide whether to examine the goods at the place where they were detained, or on the basis of samples. The right-holder (or his representative) may also request that the competent customs office send photographs or digital pictures for the assessment of the nature and legal character of the goods. In the great majority of cases, Czech Customs accept the right-holder's choice of the method suitable for this assessment.

The customs' duty to provide right-holders with samples for the purposes of ana- **7.74** lysis is governed by section 11(2) the Custom Actions Act, which also provides, as does Article 9(3), last indent, of the Regulation, that the right-holders are to return all samples to the competent customs office on completion of the technical analysis.

B. Simplified procedure allowing the destruction of the goods without there being any need to determine whether an intellectual property right has been infringed under national law

Article 11 of the Regulation, laying down a simplified procedure allowing the **7.75** destruction of the goods without it being necessary for the right-holder to go to court to determine whether the goods infringe an intellectual property right, has been implemented in the Czech Republic through s 14(1)(a)(b)(c) of the Customs Actions Act.

The procedure leading to the destruction of goods is subject to conditions similar **7.76** to those provided for under Article 11 of the Regulation, and is always to be carried out by the customs authorities. If goods whose production or alteration violates the intellectual property holder's rights are seized by the customs office, the customs office must issue a decision on the destruction of such goods under three customs officers' supervision, where requested by the right-holder. A written goods destruction record must be made and signed by all three custom officers. It must contain the quantity and description of the goods. Further investigation of the intellectual property rights' violation may not be pursued provided that:

(a) The right-holder informs the custom office, either by letter or e-mail and within 10 business days (or within three days in the case of perishable goods) from the notification on the goods being seized by the customs office, that the goods' production and/or alteration violates his intellectual property rights.

Furthermore, the right-holder must pass to the customs office a letter of consent to the destruction of the goods granted by a declarant, owner or holder of the goods, either by post or e-mail. A declarant, owner or holder of the goods may pass the written consent directly to the customs office. Should the declarant, owner or holder of the goods fail to file opposition to the destruction within a due date, the destruction of the goods is considered approved.

(b) The 10-day time limit may be extended by another 10 days but no further extension is allowed. The three-day time limit for perishable goods may not be extended at all.

(c) Prior to the destruction of the goods, the customs office must take samples and store them in case of future court proceedings.

(d) Destruction of goods is carried out at the expense and under the liability of the declarant, owner, or holder of the goods.

All these conditions set in section 14(1) of the Law on Customs Action have to be met simultaneously.

7.77 In order to facilitate the proceedings, a time limit for lodging an action starts running along with the 10-day period in which it must be determined whether suspicious goods infringe the intellectual property rights of another person. If it is the right-holder's interest to have summary proceedings held pursuant to section 11 of the Customs Action Act but the declarant, owner, or holder of the goods fail to provide their consent within the requested deadline, or if the declarant, owner, or holder file opposition to the destruction of the goods before the deadline, the right-holder must bear in mind that, at the same time, there is a time limit to lodge an action pending idly.[47] Therefore, it is efficient to lodge the action in spite of the fact that the owner's preference is for summary proceedings leading to the goods' destruction. Once the summary proceedings are over, the right-holder may withdraw from lodging the action. In a reverse case, the right-holder has a guarantee that the customs proceedings will not be brought to an end by the expiry of the foreclosure period but will continue by proceedings duly held before court. This procedure is more easily applicable to counterfeit than pirated or other infringing goods. 'More than 50% of counterfeit goods tend to be destroyed through this process in practice.'[48]

7.78 Amicable settlements between the right-holders and the parties involved in the traffic are possible only by special arrangement. If a right-holder uses data communicated to him by the customs office for purposes other than to lodge an action in re the intellectual property rights violation, the right-holder then becomes liable towards persons participating in the customs action and must pay all costs associated with the maintenance of the goods stored under the customs'

---

[47] Law No 191/1999 on Customs Action, s 4(3) and s 9(1).
[48] J Rutter and M Rosinski, 'Who is the Weakest Link ?', [2004] Trademark World, 26–29.

supervision. Furthermore, the right-holder risks invalidating the approved customs action based on which the goods were seized, and the possibility that a new action may not be accepted pursuant to Article 12 of the Regulation. Therefore, the only amicable settlement is to compromise the action lodged at the court, which rules that the goods seized by the customs office violates the intellectual property rights of the petitioner. In this case, it is possible for the parties to define further provisions regarding the reparation for the intellectual property rights' violation consequently approved by the court. Nevertheless, the court must rule that the goods in question violate the intellectual property rights by their production or alteration. Should the court rule in favour of the right-holder, the costs incurred by persons participating in the action and those associated with maintenance of the goods under the customs' supervision shall be paid by the importer, the exporter and, in other cases, the owner or holder of the goods.

C. Conditions governing action by the authorities having jurisdiction to determine whether the goods infringe an intellectual property right

(1) Authorities having jurisdiction to determine whether the goods infringe an intellectual property right

In the event of a breach of any of the intellectual property rights covered by the Regulation, there is only one remedy available which may qualify as 'proceedings seeking to determine whether an intellectual property right has been infringed under national law' under Article 13 of the Regulation. The right-holder has to file an accusation by way of civil court proceedings in order to determine whether an intellectual property right has been infringed. It is possible to obtain an interlocutory decision[49] using this legal framework. **7.79**

The right-holder may claim damages in all types of proceedings, with the exception of proceedings seeking an interlocutory decision. Such proceedings always precede the filing of a subsequent action on the merits of the case, in which claims for damages will be asserted. Claims that the right-holder may exercise are governed by the Commercial Code within the meaning of legal remedies of protection against unfair competition pursuant to section 53, and are of property and non-property nature. It involves a right to remedy as well as a right to request that the trespasser refrain from the wrongful act and a right to remove the detrimental condition; a right-holder may further exercise a claim to appropriate **7.80**

---

[49] Zákon č. 513/1991 Sb., z 5. listopadu 1991, Obchodní zákoník (Act No 513/1991 Coll, of 5 November 1991, Commercial Code), ss 44–55.

(monetary) satisfaction and a claim to release unjust enrichment as well as a right to request publication of the court's ruling at the defendant's expense.

7.81 Besides the general legislation, the regulations provided under the intellectual property protection[50] also allow right-holders to seek additional information about the origin of the goods,[51] and/or the destruction of any moulds and matrices, which have been specifically designed or adapted for their manufacture.[52] Likewise, holders of a registered designation of origin or geographical indication are also entitled to require information about the origin of the goods on the basis of the Law on the protection of designations of origin and geographical indications.[53]

7.82 Pursuant to the general legislation,[54] a temporary adjustment (until the ruling is issued) of the state of affairs of the participants may be requested prior to the commencement of the proceedings on preliminary ruling. The current judicature supports the opinion that the court may apply the preliminary ruling whenever there is a danger of delay. The adjustment of the participants' state of affairs before the ruling is issued must be persistent, particularly if it might prevent any occurrence of damage or other detriment. The urgency of a preliminary ruling depends in principle on the circumstances of a given case. A preliminary ruling shall be issued in cases where it is clear, based on at least some evidence, that the petitioner's right has been breached. However, the preliminary ruling cannot be issued in cases where it might replace the ruling itself. The second legal reason for application of the preliminary ruling is a fear that the exercise of the court ruling might be endangered following the completion of the dispute. The court in charge of application of the preliminary ruling is the court competent to rule in the case itself.

7.83 Should a right-holder claim his rights within the aforesaid term before court, the customs office asks the right-holder to send a copy of the action form confirmed by the court, or a copy of a proposal to apply the preliminary ruling confirmed by the court in order to be able to verify whether or not it is the subject of the action/proposal to rule on violation of the rights associated with the goods seized by the customs office. Verification of the statement of claim by the customs office is decisive in ascertaining whether all the conditions have been met for the customs office to further hold the suspected goods. Should the customs office find out from the statement of claim that it is not obvious that the right-holder claims legal protection of intellectual

---

[50] Law No 191/1999 on Trade Marks, s 8(6), Law No. 207/200 on Industrial Design Protection, s 21.   [51] Trade Marks Act No 441/2003, s 8(6).

[52] Ibid, s 8(7).

[53] Law No 452/2001 on the protection of designations of origin and geographical indications, s 24(2).

[54] Zákon č. 99/1963 Sb., ze dne 4. prosince 1963, občanský soudní řád (Law No 99/1963 Coll, of 4 December 1963, Civil Procedure Code), s 74.

property, the customs office must inform the right-holder about this fact immediately.[55] If no sanction of forfeiture or protective measure by seizure of goods under offence or administrative proceedings could be applied to seized goods, or if no decision could be made over the destruction of goods during summary procedure, the goods must be returned to a person from whom they were seized.[56]

In practice, a situation may occur where an action or a proposal to apply the **7.84** preliminary ruling is lodged by the right-holder; however, the court turns the action down, for example, due to formal errors and calls on the petitioner to make corrections. The petitioner then fails to lodge a new action or a new proposal to apply the preliminary ruling at court. The law does not govern the obligation of the right-holder to inform the customs office about suspension of court proceedings; however, it would be logical to do so without any unnecessary delay. The customs office verifies and examines the status of the proceedings continuously so as to ascertain whether or not the right to hold the goods still persists.

(2) *Term for notifying Customs that proceedings have been started*

According to Article 13 of the Regulation and section 14 of the Custom Actions **7.85** Act, the right-holder shall inform the customs authorities without delay in writing or via electronic communication of the commencement of proceedings seeking to determine whether the goods infringe any of their intellectual property rights. The term of 10 working days applicable to such notification may be extended once in appropriate cases only for another 10 days. Czech Customs will usually allow a request for extension if the right-holder resides outside the Czech Republic. However, the allowance of such a request is contingent on the receipt by the customs authorities of information relating to inability on the part of the foreign right-holder to submit a certificate or any other document establishing its legal existence, together with a certified and legalized translation into Czech of these documents within the initial 10-working day term.

D. Release of goods suspected of infringing certain rights on provision of a security

Czech Customs will not release goods that have been detained, or whose release **7.86** has been suspended, until the conditions prescribed by the Regulation have

---

[55] Law No 191/1999 on Customs Action, s 4(3).
[56] Law No 191/1999 on Customs Action, s 4(3) and s 9(5).

been met. If the owner or declarant seeks to obtain the release of the goods on provision of a security under Article 14 of the Regulation, the customs authorities shall release the goods where the requirements set out in this provision are met.

7.87 When determining the amount of the security under Article 14(2) of the Regulation,[57] Czech Customs shall always take the specific circumstances of the matter into account, such as the nature of the goods, their quantity, etc. The amount of the security shall be determined by the Customs Directorate in Hradec Králové. The security can be paid in cash into the account of customs, or in the form of a bank guarantee.[58] Delivery of a cheque guaranteed by a bank shall be deemed to constitute a cash payment made into the account of customs.

E. Storage of the goods

7.88 The conditions for storage of the goods during the period of suspension of release or detention are not defined in Czech law. According to the Customs Code[59] the goods in detention by the customs authorities have a status of 'temporarily stored goods'. The selection of the most suitable procedure for storage rests with the customs office that has taken action. Goods are stored by this office and under its supervision.

7.89 Under Article 6(1) of the Regulation, right-holders must submit to Czech Customs, together with their application for customs action, a declaration of acceptance of liability, should the customs action be discontinued due to an action or failure to act by the right-holder, or should the goods in question be subsequently found not to infringe intellectual property rights. In this declaration, the right-holder must also undertake to bear all costs incurred under the Regulation in keeping goods under customs control.

7.90 A storage fee is charged for a temporary storage of goods in the customs office warehouse.[60] The costs associated with storage of seized goods are borne by the party who owns, holds, stores or sells the goods whose production or alteration violates the intellectual property rights following the court ruling. If such person is unknown or if the right-holder fails to achieve a positive court ruling, then it is the right-holder who bears all costs associated with keeping the goods under the customs supervision.[61]

---

[57] Law No 191/1999 on Customs Action, s 13(2).
[58] Law No 513/1991 Coll., Commercial Code, ss 331–332.
[59] Reg No 2913/92, Community Customs Code, Arts 50–53.
[60] Zákon č. 13/1993 Sb., ze dne 15. prosince 1992, Celní zákon (Law No 13/1993 Coll, of December 1992, Customs Act).   [61] Law No 191/1999, Customs Action Act, s 4(3).

IV. PROVISIONS APPLICABLE TO GOODS FOUND TO INFRINGE AN INTELLECTUAL PROPERTY RIGHT

Goods found to infringe an intellectual property right shall not be allowed to enter or leave the Community customs territory, to be released for free circulation, exportation, re-exportation, placement under a suspensive procedure, or placement in a free zone or free warehouse, in accordance with Article 16 of the Regulation. **7.91**

Whichever remedy (either civil or criminal) has been chosen, the procedure always results in the destruction of the goods. As an alternative to their destruction, the goods may also be disposed of outside commercial channels, in favour of charities. **7.92**

The right-holder may seek the destruction of goods infringing its rights under both Article 17 of the Regulation and section 14(2) of the Customs Actions Act. Upon a final court judgment to the effect that the goods in question infringe an intellectual property right, or in cases where the goods have been surrendered to the State, and their declarant, owner, or holder failed to destroy them themselves, the customs authorities shall secure the destruction of the goods at the expense of their declarant, owner, or holder. If the owner or holder of the goods is not known to them, customs shall secure the destruction of the goods at the expense of the right-holder. **7.93**

The conditions governing the disposal of goods in detention for humanitarian purposes are described in section 14(6) of the Custom Actions Act, as amended in 2004. Upon issuance of a final court decision ordering the forfeiture of such goods, the relevant Customs Directorate shall decide on which goods are suitable for delivery to charities, and which of those can be dispensed free of charge to their recipient organizations for humanitarian purposes under the conditions set out in the Act, namely: (i) use of the goods for humanitarian purposes will always be subject to the right-holder's prior consent, as well as (ii) to permanent marking of the goods with the word 'HUMANITA' and the removal and destruction of any elements which infringe an intellectual property right; (iii) disposal of the goods to charities' profit must be feasible in view of the nature of the goods; (iv) goods that are obviously harmful to health may not be disposed of to charities' benefit; (v) they shall be intended only for use in accordance with their purpose and having regard to the urgency for their use, taking into account the order in which applications were submitted; and (vi) detained goods designated for humanitarian purposes will only be offered to contributory organizations of the State or of territorial self-administered units (regions) or other non-profit legal entities established to **7.94** provide social care or engaged in providing health care or education, that have been providing humanitarian aid for at least two years. No other use of the goods is allowed.

7.95 We are not aware of any instance where the simple removal of the trade marks which have been affixed to counterfeit goods would have been regarded as effectively depriving the persons concerned of any economic gains from the transaction.[62] The very intention of obtaining an unjustified economic benefit constitutes a criminal offence under Czech law; actual gathering of such benefits need not be establish for such a criminal offence to take place.

V. PENALTIES

7.96 Section 16 of the Custom Actions Act defines the penalties which apply (under criminal law) in respect of offences and administrative infractions committed by a natural or legal person in connection with an intellectual property right infringement. In respect of pirated goods, counterfeit goods, goods infringing a patent or a supplementary protection certificate, a plant variety rights, a designation of origin or a geographical indication, the penalties may consist of a fine, the forfeiture or the seizure of the goods.[63]

7.97 A penalty amounting to up to CZK 100,000 (EUR 33,400) may be imposed on a natural person for an offence committed by filing a customs declaration to release goods, whose production and/or alteration violates the intellectual property rights, to free market or to export regime or to re-export, or request its placement to duty free storage.

7.98 A penalty amounting to CZK 100,000 (EUR 33,400) may be imposed on a natural person for an offence committed by failure to observe the terms and conditions for handling the goods under seizure.

7.99 Penalties listed below may be imposed on a natural person for an offence committed by breaching the customs regulations as to release of goods, whose production and/or modification violates the intellectual property rights, to free market or export regime, re-export or any regimes bearing conditional exemption from custom duty, or by placing the goods into a duty free area or duty free storage; the penalties also apply to those persons who transport, own, hold, store, or sell goods within the EU territory that evaded the customs

---

[62] Cf Reg 1383/2003, Art 17(1)(b).
[63] Law No 191/1999, Customs Action Act, s 24.

supervision and whose production or alteration violates the intellectual property rights:

(a) up to CZK 1,000,000 (EUR 33,400);
(b) up to CZK 5,000,000 (EUR 167,000), for more serious breaches of the Regulations;
(c) up to CZK 20,000,000 (EUR 670,000), if the offender has committed an extensive breach of the Regulations.

Sanction of forfeiture of goods may be imposed separately or jointly with the penalty, provided that the goods were used or were intended for committing an offence or if it were obtained through an offence, or if it were obtained for goods gained through another offence. **7.100**

VI. LIABILITY OF CUSTOMS AUTHORITIES AND RIGHT-HOLDERS

A. Liability of right-holders and sanctions

Non-permitted use of information provided to the right-holder by Czech Customs under the Regulation,[64] as well as liability for any other breach of the Regulation[65] is governed by national legislation in section 4(3) of the Customs Action Act. Where he uses the data provided by the customs office for purposes other than to initiate proceedings to determine the nature of the goods, the right-holder takes over the liability towards the action's parties involved and covers all costs associated with the placing of the goods under customs supervision in the event that he uses the data provided by the customs office for purposes other than to lodge an action or to claim summary proceedings. The Custom Directorate sends the right-holder a written notification stating the amount due. If the case of the right-holder's claim is dismissed by the court and the court refuses to consider the goods placed under customs supervision as goods which infringe his intellectual property rights, the right-holder incurs civic civil liability towards the declarant, owner, or holder of the goods in question, who may consequently institute a claim for damages before the courts. The actual damage and lost income shall be paid as compensation. Actual damage is referred to as a loss of property representing any money that had to be spent in order to return the case to its original status. The loss incurred (as an income) to the aggrieved person means that the aggrieved party's property value could not be increased due to the loss event despite the **7.101**

---

[64] Cf Reg 1383/2003, Art 12.   [65] Ibid, Art 19(3).

aggrieved party's expectations under the regular course of things. The aggrieved party must request the remedy by return of things to their original status; also, such return must be possible and effective at all.

7.102 Under Article 12 of the Regulation, any non-permitted use of the information provided to the right-holder by Czech Customs may also lead to the suspension of the application for action. The customs authority shall not accept a new action based on the prior violation of the Regulation setting the obligation to use the information provided by the customs only in the way prescribed by the law.

B. Liability of customs authorities and sanctions

7.103 The State is not liable for any prejudice suffered by the right-holder in the event that Czech Customs fail to detect (and thus release) goods infringing an intellectual property right covered by the Regulation, or in the event that no action is taken to detain them.[66]

7.104 If customs cause any harm to any of the persons involved or affected by a customs action under the Regulation,[67] the injured party may seek damages pursuant to the Act governing liability for prejudices caused by the performance of public service.[68]

Conclusion

7.105 The Czech law on customs actions in respect of goods suspected of infringing an intellectual property right has been fully harmonized with the European Union's customs legislation. However, due to the limited time the amended national legislation has been in effect and the *acquis communautaire* has been in force in the Czech Republic following the latter's accession to the European Union on 1 May 2004, no Implementing Regulation has been adopted yet under EC Regulation 1383/2003 that would facilitate its application in some specific cases. The Customs Directorate in Hradec Králové, that is, the body supervising the customs offices in the Czech Republic, has developed extensive practical experience in the application of the national legislation in force prior to 1 May 2004, as have the customs offices themselves. The number of applications for customs action (especially as regards Community-wide applications) is expected to grow in the future as a result of the new Community legal framework.

---

[66] Cf Reg 1383/2003, Art 19(1), Law No 191/1999 on Customs Action, s 14a(1).

[67] Cf, inter alia, ibid, Art 19(2).

[68] Zákon č. 82/1998 Sb., z 17. března 1998, o odpovědnosti za škodu způsobenou při výkonu veřejné moci rozhodnutím nebo nesprávným úředním postupem (Law No. 82/1998 Coll., of 17 March 1998, governing liability for prejudices caused by the performance of public service), as amended.

8

DENMARK

Mads Marstrand-Jorgensen and Bernhard Posner

Introduction

Denmark became an EC Member State as from 1 January 1973. Consequently Regulation (EEC) 3842/86, and subsequently Regulation (EC) 3295/94 as amended by Regulation (EC) 241/1999 have been applicable in Denmark from the day of their entry into force. **8.01**

Though the provisions of Regulation 3295/94 were directly applicable in Denmark, the national Danish Law[1] on Application of the Regulation set out a few supplementary provisions regarding the exercise of the powers vested in the customs authority. This Law was amended in 1999[2] following the adoption of EC Regulation 241/1999 and subsequently in 2000.[3] As a consequence of Regulation 1383/2003 the Danish Law of 1995 has been further amended in 2004[4] by a law which came into force on 1 July 2004. **8.02**

Before the system introduced by EC Regulation 3295/94 was put into practice in Denmark in 1995, the Danish system on border measures in case of intellectual **8.03**

---

[1] Lov nr. 1091 af 20. december 1995 om anvendelsen af Det Europæiske Fællesskabs forordning om foranstaltninger med henblik på at forbyde overgang til fri omsætning, udførsel, genudførsel og henførsel under en suspensionsprocedure af varemøærkeforfalskede og piratkopierede varer (Application Law no 1091 of 20 December 1995).

[2] Lov nr. 942 af 20. december 1999 om ændring af lov nr. 1091 af 20. december 1995 om anvendelsen af Det Europæiske Fællesskabs forordning om foranstaltninger med henblik på at forbyde overgang til fri omsætning, udførsel, genudførsel og henførsel under en suspensionsprocedure af varemøærkeforfalskede og piratkopierede varer (Law no 942 of 20 December 1999 amending Law no 1091).

[3] Lov nr. 1029 af 22. november 2000 ov om ændring af en række skatte- og afgiftslove (Law no 1029 of 22 November 2000 amending a number of tax laws).

[4] Lov nr. 461 af 9. juni 2004 om ændring af lov om anvendelse af Det Europæiske Føællesskabs forordning om fastsættelse af visse foranstaltninger i forbindelse med indførsel i Fællesskabet og udførsel og genudførsel fra fællesskabet af varer, der krænker visse former for intellektuel ejenomdsret (Application law no 461 of 9 June 2004).

property right infringements was not satisfactory. Until 1988, the only options available under Danish law were either to obtain help from the police in seizing counterfeit products or to try and obtain an interim injunction to prevent the marketing of counterfeits. The methods applied were not very efficient especially since the goods had usually been sold before action could be taken.

8.04 When EC Regulation 3842/86 entered into force on 1 January 1988 in Denmark, the Danish authorities erroneously appointed the Danish courts as the 'competent authority' to process applications for border measures under this Regulation, instead of customs. It appeared rather awkward that the right-holder first had to refer the case to the courts where he was not able to say if counterfeit goods were actually on their way to Denmark. The system was criticized for this state of affairs.[5]

8.05 Following the changes adopted in 1995 the system has been working satisfactorily as Danish Customs have been able to detain immediately suspicious goods on an *ex officio* basis. With the latest changes in the Regulation, the system should now be working even more smoothly.

8.06 The provisions of Danish law applicable in this field are few, and restricted to those which are absolutely necessary for the administration by customs authorities of the EC system. Prior to Regulation 1383/2003 the claiming of a fee for example necessitated a legal basis in Danish law. Another example relates to criminal provisions. By and large, however, the EC Regulation is directly applicable and requires no further legal framework.

8.07 The scope of national legislation does not extend beyond the scope of the Regulation. The Danish Law defines its scope of application by a direct reference to the terms of Regulation 1383/2003 setting out the type of intellectual property rights comprised by the Regulation. Danish domestic legislation does not in any respect convey upon customs authorities powers beyond those conveyed upon them by Community legislation and does, of course, not limit in any respect the scope of rights as set out by Regulation 1383/2003.

I. SUBJECT MATTER AND SCOPE OF THE NATIONAL LAW APPLYING THE REGULATION

8.08 In this Part, dedicated to the subject matter and scope of Danish national law applying the Regulation, we will examine under what customs procedures Danish Customs will act against suspect goods (section A), the definition of infringing

---

[5] M Marstrand-Jorgensen in UfR.1990B.208.

goods in the light of Danish law (section B) and the goods excluded from the scope of the Regulation (section C).

In the year 2003 customs carried out 290 seizures at the external borders of **8.09** Denmark. Both in respect of the number of actions carried out and the number of articles seized, clothing and accessories, audio and video recordings, and computer games were by far the most numerous. Out of 290 actions, 260 concerned these sorts of goods.

The scope of protection set out by national law does not always coincide with the **8.10** wording of the provisions of Articles 2 and 3 of Regulation 1383/2003. Where the scope and contents of protection of national law differs from the definition of counterfeit goods or pirated goods in Article 2 of the Regulation only such infringement as indicated in Article 2 of the Regulation is decisive for the power vested in customs authorities by virtue of the provisions of the Regulation. Other infringements must be pursued by action and procedures as laid down in national law.

Article 4 of the Danish Trade Mark Act[6] includes in the range of restricted acts the **8.11** use of trade marks which may create risk of confusion. Whereas the right-holder may pursue his rights through legal action, intervention by customs at the external borders of the Union would in such cases appear to be excluded.

Likewise, Danish copyright law may sanction the overly extensive use of **8.12** quotations of protected works in an independent work without the second work necessarily being a copy.

Danish law refers to the terms of the Regulation and the contents and scope of **8.13** protection according to national law is thus irrelevant for customs action. In practical terms this distinction may well be more theoretical than practical. The applicant would in his application probably refer to an infringement as defined by the terms of the Regulation and customs authorities are unlikely to challenge the applicant's interpretation.

A. Customs procedure of the goods

As noted above, the adoption of Regulation 1383/2003 in Denmark has not led **8.14** to an amendment of the customs procedures defined in local law under the regime of Regulation 3295/94, as amended in 1999. The scope of application of border measures that may be imposed by Danish Customs is thus the situation described in Article 1 of Regulation 1383/2003.

---

[6] Varemærkelov nr. 341 af 6. juni 1991 (Trade Mark Act no 341 of 6 June 1991).

B. Definition of infringing goods

(1) Counterfeit goods

8.15 Available statistics on the definition of the infringement against which customs actions are directed are subject to interpretation. Infringing goods may at the same time be counterfeit goods and pirate goods. There is reason to believe, however, that a substantial part of goods seized are 'counterfeit goods', that is, goods infringing a trade mark, defined under Danish law as goods upon which a trade mark belonging to a third party has been affixed without authorization.

8.16 Customs authorities in Denmark take action even where the goods bearing the trade mark without authorization are not entirely identical to another trade mark or which cannot be distinguished in its essential parts from another trade mark. According to the customs authorities it is very often banal details as for example a spelling error on the perfume packing or a not quite correct logo on the t-shirt which reveals that it is a fake. Such cases are considered to satisfy the requirement 'cannot be distinguished in its essential parts'.

8.17 The practical application of the provision in Article 2(1)(a)(i) of the Regulation in relation to the requirement that the suspect goods be of 'the same type' as those for which the trade mark has been registered depends to a high degree on how precisely the goods are described in the application for customs action. In the application, reference to specific goods is made by way of tariff code number as it appears from the common customs tariff code of the EU rather than reference to a class of goods under the 'Nice trade mark classification'. Right-holders of very well-known marks, producing a wide range of goods in different classes under the same trade mark may only have the mark registered in some of the classes. Should the problem arise, the custom authorities most probably would deny taking border measures with reference to court practice, according to which interim injunction may be denied in cases where the classes are different.[7]

8.18 Customs authorities will not refuse applications for action on the basis of trade mark *applications*, which have not yet been validly registered. Whether a seizure would actually take place on the basis of a mere trade mark application is another issue, however. The question has not been raised in practice and may not be particularly relevant considering that at least national trade marks in normal situations are registered within a few of months subsequent to filing.

---

[7] UfR.1983.824: *Alfred Benzon A/S v Dansk Helsekostcenter ApS.*

Under Danish law goods are seen as infringing trade mark rights not only where **8.19** the mark is identical to the trade mark but even where the suspect sign is similar to the trade mark, if a risk of confusion exists, including the risk of association. No discrepancy seems to exist between the definition of counterfeit goods under the Regulation and the definition of trade mark infringement under Danish law. Danish customs will refuse to act if it appears to be doubtful if a trade mark infringement exists.

The Danish customs authorities are entitled to take measures against trade mark **8.20** symbols even if delivered separately and the same applies to packing materials bearing the trade marks of counterfeit goods delivered separately. No cases where this has taken place have been reported as yet.

(2) Pirated goods

Intervention by Danish customs authorities is limited to reproduction of **8.21** protected material as defined under the provision of Article 2(1)(b) of the Regulation. It is not the task of customs authorities to endeavour to establish whether a work or a product, which does not claim to misappropriate in the eyes of the consumer the work or product reproduced, does nevertheless, because of similarities or use of parts of the protected product, represent an infringement of a protected work or product. Such more sophisticated assessments are to be made in the framework of legal proceedings. The infringement of a related right such as, for example, the right of the phonogram producer to authorize the reproduction of a phonogram will only be established if the phonogram has been illegally reproduced, whereas the illegal reproduction of, for example, one song from a protected album onto a different album will not be caught by the inspection of goods by customs authorities unless they have been specifically warned against this unlikely event.

The value of pirated goods both in the eyes of the pirate and the consumer is **8.22** based on the identical appearance or quality of the product. Sophisticated interpretations of intellectual property law are seldom necessary at this stage. In the eyes of customs authorities 'goods which are or contain copies' within the meaning of Article 2(1)(b) of the Regulation are goods which are recognizable as such.

The issue of whether goods suspected of infringing a copyright, a related right or **8.23** a design right under national law are, in fact, infringing such rights is not a problem for customs authorities. If they suspect products of being pirated goods they inform the right-holder of their intervention. It is up to the latter to decide whether to release the goods or pursue the infringement procedure at his own risk. Customs authorities will not release the goods against the decision of the right-holder.

(3) Goods infringing other intellectual property rights

Goods infringing a patent or a supplementary protection certificate

8.24 The application of Regulation 1383/2003 to patent rights and to the protection afforded by a supplementary protection certificate is by many quarters seen as a mere fiction. Unless informed in advance of a shipment of infringing goods customs authorities have no possibility of detecting infringements.

8.25 If patent right-holders have information on potential infringers they may inform authorities accordingly. For instance, Philips has informed customs authorities of authorized licensees in respect of its DVD patents whereas non-licensed producers are put on a 'black list'. Such information permits action, which would otherwise be excluded.

8.26 A counterfeit pharmaceutical is often detected by its packaging, which will usually show an attempted use of the original trade mark and logo, but in an erroneous manner. But neither a process patent infringement nor a product patent infringement can be detected by the inspection of goods such as that carried out by national customs authorities.

8.27 Nowadays, Danish customs authorities frequently detect shipments of medicines infringing Pfizer's patent over Viagra bought by Danish consumers on the Internet. These goods are easily detected because they are sold under the (counterfeit) Viagra trade mark. Customs action is facilitated, however, by the fact that they will block any pharmaceutical product put on the market in breach of the local legislation on the commercialization in Denmark of pharmaceutical products subject to a marketing authorization.

Goods infringing a national plant variety right

8.28 The Danish Plant Variety Protection Act[8] defines the exclusive right of the owner of a plant variety qualifying for protection as the right to authorize (or prevent) the use of the plant variety for commercial production, reproduction, treatment, storage for reproduction purposes or the offer to sell, the sale, transfer or the storage for the purpose of sale or transfer.

8.29 Any of the above restricted acts in respect of the protected plant variety will amount to an infringement.

8.30 Article 2 (1) (c) (iii) of Regulation 1383/2003 refers for plant variety rights specifically to the scope of protection as defined in national law.

---

[8] 'sortsbeskyttelsesloven' nr 145 af 1. marts 2001 som ændret ved lov nr. 967 af 4. december 2002 (Plant Variety Protection Act no. 145 of 1 March 2001 as amended by law no. 967 of 4 December 2002).

Goods infringing a national designation of origin or a geographical indication

There exists no local legislation on the protection of designation of origin or a geographical indication under Danish law. The Community Regulations relating to these intellectual property rights are directly applicable in Denmark. The restricted acts, in respect of which Danish Customs will take action at the external borders of the EC, are consequently those exclusively referred to in these Regulations. **8.31**

(4) Moulds and matrices

Moulds or matrices which are specifically designed or adapted for the manufacture of goods infringing any intellectual property right referred to in Article 2(1) of Regulation 1383/2003 may be stopped by the customs authorities, as the Danish application law makes the Regulation applicable without necessity for further national legislation. The Danish Act on Copyright, section 84 expressly states that moulds, matrices and anything else which may serve the purpose of illegal production or use may be seized, transferred to the right-holder, or destroyed. But to our knowledge, no case of seizure of moulds and matrices as described in Article 2 (1) of the Regulation has been reported. **8.32**

C. Goods excluded by the regulation

(1) Parallel imported goods

Exhaustion of rights has been claimed in Denmark in respect of trade mark rights and copyright only, not in respect of other intellectual property rights. Article 7 of the first Trade Mark Directive 89/104 (EEC) on the approximation of the laws of Member States relating to trade marks, implemented in Denmark by 'varemærkeloven'[9] No 341 of 6 June 1991 introduced Community exhaustion for trade marks. Community exhaustion has in respect of copyright and related rights been introduced by a series of Directives and is now in Denmark as in other EU Member States unchallenged as the legal principle in force in respect of all intellectual property rights. **8.33**

The principle expressed in Article 3(1) of Regulation 1383/2003 does therefore relate to the specific situation at the external borders of the European Union, but does not provide a solution for the right-holder in respect of parallel importation of goods put on the market with his consent outside the European Union. **8.34**

---

[9] Varemærkelov nr. 341 af 6. juni 1991 (Trade Mark Law no 341 of 6 June 1991).

8.35 In other words, an intellectual property right may be used to oppose the parallel importation of such goods, but the procedure does not have the character of border measures as described in Regulation 1383/2003.

8.36 In practice, however, the situation is likely to present itself in the following manner. Unless otherwise informed customs authorities will, when inspecting goods, consider parallel imported goods as counterfeit goods. They will inform the right-holder accordingly.

8.37 If the right is exhausted following the principle of Community exhaustion the right-holder will have to release the goods. If, however, the right-holder concedes that the goods are genuine but parallel imported goods from outside the EU customs must also release the goods unless the right-holder considers that he is entitled to oppose the re-importation of the goods. In that case he will instigate infringement procedures and to prevent irreparable harm obtain seizure of the goods from the courts by way of interim measures (injunction).

(2) Goods which have been manufactured under conditions other than those which have been agreed with the right-holder

8.38 Normally customs authorities will not be in a position to establish that inspected goods violate contractual obligations. However, if informed by the right-holder of the likely importation of such goods they may be in a position to act.

8.39 Danish trade mark law, in accordance with the provision of Article 7(2) of Directive 89/104 (EEC), permits the right-holder of a trade mark to oppose the marketing of goods put on the market within the EU with his consent if he has reasonable grounds for doing so, in particular if the condition of the goods has been impaired.

(3) Goods contained in travellers' personal baggage

8.40 Customs authorities carry out random spot checks of travellers' personal baggage where travellers have commenced their journey outside the EU.

8.41 Under Article 3(2) of the Regulation, the duty free allowance is computed by Danish Customs not on the basis of the value of an authentic product but rather on the basis of a rough assessment of the purchase price of the pirated product. In the absence of information to the contrary, authorities are likely to accept the information given to them by travellers in this respect.

8.42 Denmark's geographical position implies that the majority of travellers from third countries will arrive by plane. The principles set out in Article 45 of Regulation 918/83, to appraise the 'non-commercial nature' of the goods in particular in respect of the definition of personal baggage, are therefore easy to apply.

Criteria which could be considered material indication of the existence of **8.43** commercial traffic are, for example, the quantity of each item. If, say, a number of identical t-shirts in the same size and colour are found this could indicate commercial traffic. Or, if the traveller is a professional trader in the products in question, commercial traffic could be indicated.

Where suspicious goods are found customs authorities inform the right-holder. If **8.44** he chooses to pursue the matter—which often is not the case, when only minor quantities are at stake—release will not take place pending a court decision on whether the goods can be considered commercial merchandise.

II. APPLICATION FOR ACTION BY THE CUSTOMS AUTHORITIES

A. Measures prior to an application for action by the customs authorities ('*ex officio* measures')

Danish Customs apply *ex officio* measures under Article 4 to a significant extent. **8.45**

Customs apply risk analysis in order to concentrate their efforts where they have **8.46** maximum effect, and information about possible counterfeit is received among others from the International Post Centre, the Cargo Centre, the free ports, and the railroads. Danish customs have received special training in reading manifests, consignment notes and invoices and from these documents alone, they can often spot something that may be suspicious. For example, why is a container with cigarettes in transit from Indonesia intended for a textile firm in England? Also the customs keep their eye on anything new being sent to the market. If, for example, the next video production from Disney was due to be launched in October, it would immediately strike them as suspicious if they were to find it in April.

As for information to be given to the applicant, customs will normally provide **8.47** samples to the right-holder and the right-holder is allowed to examine the goods.

Customs authorities are bound by the three working days deadline of Article 4 of **8.48** the Regulation. Cases where authorities failed to comply with this deadline have been reported. However, authorities recognize that it would be extremely difficult for them should a complaint against them be made on this point.

In practice the *ex officio* procedure works very smoothly and efficiently in **8.49** Denmark. Customs operations are facilitated by an informal contact group between customs authorities and right-holders and their representatives. Within this group methods of operations are discussed and the mere existence of the group permits rapid and informal contact between authorities and interested parties.

B. The lodging and processing of applications for customs action

(1) Persons entitled to file an application for action

Definition of 'right-holders' under the Regulation

8.50 Right-holders and any other persons authorized to use the intellectual property right in question are eligible persons in respect of launching an application for customs action.

8.51 In respect of establishing authorization to use the intellectual property right in question the approach of Danish customs authorities is very pragmatic. In the absence of indications to the contrary authorities assume that applications submitted are bona fide applications, with abuse of the system not considered likely. The liability of the applicant for any damage caused by an abuse is considered to be a sufficient safeguard against such abuse.

8.52 Registration of trade mark and design licences or sub-licences and the like does not have any legal effect beyond providing certainty that the registered licensee or sub-licensee, agent, etc is informed of certain events. Accordingly, licences need not be registered for licensees to be entitled to lodge an application for action under the Regulation in Denmark.

8.53 If in doubt, Danish customs authorities contact the applicant for further information or documentation, depending on the specific circumstances of each case.

8.54 The term 'representative', as used in the Regulation, is not defined by law. Any legal or natural person may act as a representative within the meaning of Regulation 1383/2003 in Denmark.

Proof of entitlement to file an application for action

For right-holders stricto sensu

8.55 As regards intellectual property rights which come into existence by way of registration, a registration certificate is normally submitted when an application for action is lodged with Danish Customs under the Regulation. However, not all intellectual property rights come into existence by way of registration and even rights for which registration is the normal point of departure may sometimes come into existence without registration. Trade marks may thus come into existence by way of use.

Where no registration certificate can be produced—for example in respect of **8.56** recordings—the original product is submitted together with a description.

The issue of whether an application for action can be lodged on the basis of a **8.57** simple application for registration becomes an issue of secondary importance to customs authorities. Where a trade mark application is pending they would not reject the application for action on the ground that registration has not yet taken place. In view of the fact that a national registration procedure is fairly rapid they need not be concerned unless they actually have to detain or suspend the release of suspect goods while registration application is still pending before the competent authorities. Such a case would have to be decided on its specific merits.

Further, no limitations in respect of the source of documentation are known in **8.58** Danish law or practice as to the proof of ownership of an intellectual property right under the Regulation. Copies of databases, official or private, international or national, are equally suited as proving entitlement in the specific case.

For persons authorized to use the right

The authorization to use the right is normally established vis-à-vis Danish **8.59** Customs by submitting the contractual basis for the right in question. Customs authorities are not requested to verify the authenticity of the contract and no registration requirement exists.

For representatives

Attorneys-at-law, trade mark and patent attorneys are not requested to submit any **8.60** proof that they have the capacity to represent the entitled person on behalf of whom an application for customs action is lodged. As regards other persons it would appear that the answer to the question whether proof of authorization would be needed depends on the circumstances of each case. Persons established in Denmark and known to the authorities will normally not be requested to submit documentation for entitlement. The situation may be different if the applicant is established outside Denmark and unknown to the customs authorities.

The approach of the customs authorities is fairly pragmatic. No rules have been **8.61** published so far in this regard. It would appear that any documentation submitted, whether an original document, copy or fax or electronic, which would indicate legal representation is accepted. Also representatives established outside the jurisdiction of Denmark are admitted to file applications for customs action.

An important safeguard of the interest of the alleged infringer is provided by virtue **8.62** of the declaration described in Article 6 of the Regulation according to which the applicant for customs action is held responsible inter alia for compensation in case the final court decision should hold that the action was unjustified. One might think this step would be regulated by administrative decisions or customs manuals but this is not the case. Normally any declaration by any applicant will be accepted as valid. Much depends, of course, on the persons involved and on whether the alleged infringer is prepared to argue the case. However on this issue, like others, the approach of Danish customs authorities is informal and pragmatic.

(2) Competent customs department and formal requirements

Competent customs department

8.63 The competent customs department to process applications for action under Regulation 1383/2003 in Denmark is:

Central Customs and Tax Administration
Customs Control
Østbanegade 123
DK-2100 Copenhagen
Tel. +45 72379000
Fax +45 72372917
E-Mail: toldskat@toldskat.dk
Home page: www.erhverv.toldskat.dk

Form of the application for action

8.64 An application for action may be filed by e-mail, fax or letter. Filing of applications for action by electronic means is possible but not mandatory. An electronic version of the application for action will be made available to the applicants at the customs Internet homepage. An older version is available on: http://www.erhverv. toldskat.dk/ToldSkat.aspx?oID=89024&vID=0.

8.65 It is not necessary to submit more than two copies of the application; however, if the colours are crucial it would, of course, be wise to submit more than two specimens of, for example, brochures.

8.66 As to the declarations under Article 6 of the Regulation, it is worth noting that the original need not be sent to customs; sending a copy by, for example, electronic means is sufficient.

Language requirements

8.67 The application must be filed in Danish but the customs authorities also seem to accept filings in English. These language requirements are not applied differently if the application is based on a Community right under Article 5(4) in another Member State.

8.68 The declaration under Article 6 may normally be made out in Danish or English. Nevertheless, customs may request that the declaration be made in Danish.

(3) Requirements regarding the contents of the application for action

Mandatory information

The technical information relating to the goods need not be very detailed. The **8.69** Danish customs have a very practical attitude and their main concern is that it must be possible to recognize the goods in question.

Information concerning the type or pattern of fraud is not necessary but may of **8.70** course be extremely helpful.

There is no requirement as to local presence of the contact person appointed by **8.80** the right-holder but it may be most practical to have a local representative if goods have to be inspected, etc. There are no nationality requirements for the technical/ administrative contact persons.

Optional information

As already pointed out above (see para 8.55), when the application relates to an **8.81** industrial property right subject to registration, a copy of the registration certificate from the Danish Patent and Trade Marks Office or from the OHIM is expected to prove entitlement. Customs are also keen on receiving information about local companies who are authorized to import the genuine goods.

Additional information specific to the type of intellectual property right referred to in the application

In matters where specific technical knowledge is necessary to detect the fakes, the **8.82** customs authorities may request additional details under Article 5(6) of the Regulation. In a case where a mixed shipment consisting of counterfeited and parallel imported computer mice arrived, technical expertise was needed to establish which mice were counterfeited and which were not.

(4) Processing and acceptance of the application for action

If customs find that the information provided in an application for action or the **8.83** documentation submitted along with the application is insufficient they will contact the applicant and give him the opportunity to provide additional information or documentation. They will refuse the application under Article 5(8) of the Regulation only if the applicant refuses to cooperate in providing the supplementary details or documentation requested. No appeal procedure is foreseen on this point.

According to general principles of administrative law a decision of a legal **8.84** character by an administrative body dismissing a citizen's claim is subject to appeal to a higher administrative authority, the ministerial level being the highest administrative body.

8.85 The Central Danish Customs Authority is, however, its own appeal authority in respect of customs affairs. It would thus appear that the customs authority is the appeal authority for its own decisions. Customs consider any such appeals highly unlikely. However, if an applicant has cause to complain customs are likely to reconsider the application if invited to do so.

8.86 Where the application is granted it is valid for one year. Shorter periods have not been provided for.

(5) Community applications for action

8.87 Applications filed in Denmark under Article 5(4) of Regulation 1383/2003 will, as national applications, be examined to establish that they are complete to permit action to be taken, that the applicant is entitled to file an application and, as far as possible, that the intellectual property right referred to is in existence. Thereafter the applicant is informed that his application has been accepted and the application is forwarded to the competent authorities in the other EU Member States designated.

8.88 Likewise, 'Community' applications filed in other Member States are processed in much the same manner as national applications, even though some elements are likely to have been checked already, such as registration certificates and entitlement. Transmission to Danish authorities will also indicate that the application has been accepted in the country of filing, whereupon the Danish authorities will inform the sender authority of its acceptance of the application.

III. CONDITIONS GOVERNING ACTION BY CUSTOMS AUTHORITIES AND BY THE AUTHORITIES COMPETENT TO DETERMINE WHETHER GOODS INFRINGE AN INTELLECTUAL PROPERTY RIGHT

A. Conditions governing action by customs authorities

(1) Factual background

8.89 Denmark is for customs purposes divided into eight regional customs authorities, each of which exercises the powers and duties of customs authorities within their respective territorial jurisdiction. A complete list of regional authorities and regional and local offices can be found on http://www.erhverv.toldskat.dk/ToldSkat.aspx?oID=158917.

The most important regional authority is 'ToldSkat København'. The international 8.90
airport of Copenhagen and the harbour of Copenhagen are located within the
jurisdiction of this office.

By far the largest number of customs interventions take place in the Copenhagen 8.91
area and in particular in the airport of Copenhagen. While Denmark has other
international airports, Copenhagen is the only one operating intercontinental
flights. A considerable part of all customs action targets flights arriving from certain Asian countries. This trend has become stronger since the enlargement of the
European Union, when customs examination of goods arriving from the Baltic
countries ceased.

(2) Notification of customs intervention

The right-holder is informed of an intervention by customs in the most rapid and 8.92
practical manner available in the specific case. E-mail and SMS messages are
increasingly replacing other communication forms.

The declarant or the holder of the goods will be informed in writing. A standard 8.93
letter has been made out for this purpose. The notification takes place as soon as
possible, even though it is for one reason or another not regarded as a priority. Very
often the message cannot be delivered for a variety of reasons.

(3) Information to be provided by customs to the right-holder before the right-holder confirms the infringing nature of the goods

Once goods suspected of infringing an intellectual property right are detained by 8.94
customs, customs will normally inform the right-holder of the nature of the
goods, the estimated quantity, the country of origin, and destination.

Customs will also give the right-holder information about the name and address 8.95
of the consignee, consignor, declarant or holder of the goods, as well as information about their origin and provenance.

In Denmark no questions have been raised concerning the possibility of customs 8.96
providing information which would be regarded as confidential under normal
circumstances to the right-holder.

The information mentioned above will normally be provided even if the right- 8.97
holder does not request it. Information of this kind is considered indispensable if
the right-holder is going to establish whether a shipment, for example, consists of
parallel imported goods or counterfeit goods. A two-step procedure as described
in Article 9 (3) of the Regulation is seen as overly bureaucratic.

(4) Inspection of the suspected goods

8.98   The right-holder is allowed to inspect goods which have been detained immediately. Customs normally take samples of the goods and hand them over or send them to the right-holder immediately after detention.

8.99   Customs may also send digital pictures of the goods which may eventually be used for evaluation of the infringing character of the goods. The use of digital pictures as proof never has been contested before a Danish Court in a reported case.

8.100   As a rule, samples and pictures will be forwarded even when the right-holder does not so request.

8.101   There are no national provisions on the provision of samples, neither are there any specific restrictions as to their use.

8.102   In practice, samples do not have to be returned after examination, unless it appears that they are not infringing. Samples will normally be used in the context of the court proceedings.

B. Simplified procedure allowing the destruction of the goods without there being any need to determine whether an intellectual property right has been infringed under national law

8.103   Article 11 of Regulation 1383/2003 has been made explicitly applicable in Denmark.[10] There are no specific procedures laid down concerning the national procedure. In practice, however, Danish customs accept a written declaration from the owner of the infringing goods, from the declarant or from the holder to the effect that he abandons the goods in view of their destruction.

8.104   If the goods are to be disposed of outside of commercial channels, the destruction process is organized and monitored by the customs authorities.

8.105   However, the national laws of Denmark do not allow the presumption that the destruction of the infringing goods is accepted when the declarant, holder or owner of the goods does not oppose the destruction within a specific deadline. If the declarant, etc does not reply, the right-holder must initiate legal proceedings before the courts.

8.106   Amicable settlements between right-holders and owners of infringing goods are—and always have been—allowed under Danish law. Such agreements may

---

[10] Lov nr. 461 9/6 2004 om ændring af lov om anvendelse af Det Europæiske Fællesskabs forordning om fastsættelse af visse foranstaltninger i forbindelse med indførsel i Fællesskabet og udførsel og genudførsel fra Fællesskabet af varer, der krænker visse former for intellektuel ejendomsret (Application law no 461 of 9 June 2004).

contain provisions concerning reimbursement of storage and destruction costs, legal costs, cease-and-desist declarations even under conventional penalty. Customs in Denmark do not officially object to the grant of licences by the right-holders to the owner of infringing goods to allow their commercialization, but may find it odd that the owner permits infringing products to come on the market. This practice, according to which the right-holder is given full autonomy in respect of infringing goods, cannot be considered incompatible with the provisions of the Regulation. The right-holder has from the outset the right to decide whether he wishes to interfere in respect of infringing goods. He may, upon discussion with an alleged infringer, also decide whether he wishes to close his eyes in a given case. Such a decision may be unwise, but not illegal. The authors consider that customs' cooperation in the fight against counterfeit goods must be seen as a token of return for the fees paid to public bodies for the acquisition and maintenance of intellectual property rights and not as an enforcement of God-given law for its own sake.

C. Conditions governing action by the authorities having jurisdiction to determine whether the goods infringe an intellectual property right

(1) Authorities having jurisdiction to determine whether the goods infringe an intellectual property right

General introduction

Danish national proceedings seeking to determine whether an intellectual **8.107** property right has been infringed under national law are of a complex nature. There exists no general framework applicable in the same manner to all kind of intellectual property rights. Laws have come into existence at different times. Some have been amended following EC Regulations and Directives or otherwise inspired by EC legislation and other international development. Whereas civil proceedings may appear to have elements in common for most intellectual property law, criminal provisions and provisions on public prosecution of infringement are somewhat divergent.

The core of the enforcement system can in very general terms be described as follows.

Civil proceedings

Civil proceedings will be commenced in the vast majority of cases involving **8.108** Community trade mark rights and Community design rights. These cases are tried before the Copenhagen Maritime and Commercial Court which is composed in part of judges from the commercial world. Also cases involving national trade mark and design rights are tried before this court, unless the parties decide otherwise.

8.109 Patent cases and cases involving a supplementary protection certificate are tried before one of the two regional high courts with territorial jurisdiction for respectively East Denmark and West Denmark.

8.110 For copyright cases and cases involving plant variety rights, designations of origin, or geographical indications, no special jurisdiction is foreseen. These civil cases are tried before the ordinary lower courts unless they are of considerable economic importance—exceeding DKR one million (EUR 130,000)—and one of the parties requests that the trial takes place before one of the two regional high courts.

Criminal proceedings

8.111 Genuine criminal proceedings are extremely rare though criminal provisions are foreseen for infringement of trade mark and design rights, patent rights, and rights arising from supplementary protection certificates and plant variety rights. Also copyright law contains criminal provisions of a very complex character.

8.112 Infringements of intellectual property rights are normally not subject to criminal prosecution, but will be tried following the procedural remedies available for civil disputes and by the courts handling civil cases. The parties are the offended party as plaintiff and the alleged infringer as defendant.

8.113 Right-holders normally prefer to take action against counterfeiters and pirates by way of civil proceedings. The reasons for this choice are many.

8.114 First, police forces with scarce resources can not always be expected to react within a reasonable time, or at all. Further, the interest of police forces in pursuing cases where only mock penalties can be expected is fairly modest.

8.115 If enforcement agencies get involved right-holders lose control of the action. Clearly they would wish to retain control during the entire process thereby also having the opportunity to decide on possible settlements out of court.

8.116 In cases where customs authorities have taken action, the involvement of police authorities makes little sense since the goods have already been detected and retained and will continue to be blocked until a final decision has been handed down by a court.

8.117 Remedies and in particular interim measures are not dependent on the type of intellectual property at hand, but far more on what is necessary to limit the potential harm which the right-holder would incur if interim measures were not imposed.

8.118 Injunctions are frequent as interim measures in counterfeit and piracy cases because they allow marketing of the products to be prevented, which would otherwise cause the right-holder irreparable harm.

Counterfeit goods

Following the detention of goods by customs authorities the right-holder will **8.119** bring the case before the Maritime and Commercial Court to establish that an infringement has taken place and that the goods have been lawfully retained. Interim measures are not called for since the goods are in the custody of customs authorities.

The plaintiff's claims will generally include measures to prevent commercial- **8.120** ization of the goods (injunction) and a claim for damages may also be introduced.

The plaintiff will normally not seek criminal penalties, because he would then **8.121** have to prove that the infringement has been carried out intentionally or by gross negligence, which will often be difficult. Criminal sanctions hold no real advantages for the plaintiff.

The losing party will be ordered to pay the costs as computed by the court. **8.122**

Costs and damages awarded by courts in intellectual property infringement **8.123** matters are from modest to negligible. The right-holder will in no way be compensated for all costs incurred.

In many cases the right-holder chooses not to pursue the infringement, because the quantity of the counterfeit goods does not justify the costs involved. A different approach presupposes a clear policy in respect of the defence of the brand.

Pirated goods

In practice pirated goods will most often consist in computer software, **8.124** computer games, music and film recordings, and character merchandizing. Some design products are also subject to piracy, albeit the domestic production or importation of look-alikes is more widespread. Pirated literary works are rare.

From time to time the quantities of pirate goods are such that the involvement of **8.125** police and public prosecutors is warranted. This is not the case, however, when pirate goods are retained by customs authorities, because in this case the assistance of police forces to detect and seize the goods is no longer necessary. Therefore these cases too will be pursued before the civil courts.

Goods infringing a plant variety

No cases of border measures in respect of plant variety rights have been reported **8.126** yet in Denmark.

8.127 The civil proceedings described above before the ordinary courts would constitute the appropriate remedy for the purpose of Article 13 of EC Regulation 1383/2003.

Goods infringing a designation of origin or a geographical indication

8.128 No cases of border measures in respect of designations of origin or geographical indications have been reported in Denmark yet. It appears, in fact, that only a single Danish product enjoys protection in this respect, namely carrots from an area called Lammefjord ('Lammefjordsgulerødder').

8.129 The civil proceedings described above before the ordinary courts would constitute the appropriate remedy.

8.130 Many of the questions discussed in other jurisdictions, referring to the issue of whether certain steps may be considered proceedings seeking to determine whether an intellectual property right has been infringed, do not present themselves in Denmark.

8.131 Summary proceedings are unknown. Interim measures will, unless the alleged infringer dispenses with legal action and acknowledges the infringement by way of a settlement, always be followed by civil legal action aiming at establishing the fact that the interim measure has been legally carried out, which presupposes establishing an infringement.

(2) Term for notifying customs that proceedings have been started under Article 13 of the Regulation

8.132 The Danish legislation gives no information as to which sort of situations qualify for extension of the 10 working days in Article 13 of EC Regulation 1383/2003 with 10 more working days. However, permission to extend the 10-working day period is given liberally in practice.

D. Release of goods suspected of infringing certain rights on provision of a security

8.133 Provided that all conditions of Article 14(1) of the Regulation are fulfilled, customs in Denmark would no doubt consider that they are obliged to release the goods as this is the essence of Article 14(1), but no cases have yet been seen on this point. Normally the right-holder will ask the court to uphold the detention and thus prevent their release. The amount of the security according to Article 14(2) will probably be decided by the courts; no legislation or practice exists in this field.

E. Storage of the goods

In the first 10 (or 20) working days, the goods are regularly stored at the customs. **8.134** Following this, the goods will normally be stored in a store house determined by customs at the cost of the right-holder.

IV. PROVISIONS APPLICABLE TO GOODS FOUND TO INFRINGE AN INTELLECTUAL PROPERTY RIGHT

If, as a result of Article 13 proceedings, goods are found to infringe an intellectual **8.135** property right, Danish law allows the right-holder to oppose entry into/or removal from the Community customs territory, release for free circulation, exportation, re-exportation, placement under a suspensive procedure (including external transit and transhipment) and placement in a free zone or free warehouse in respect of all intellectual property rights.

Although there are no specific domestic provisions in Denmark concerning destruc- **8.136** tion of goods, disposal of goods outside commercial channels, or other measures making sure that the persons concerned be deprived of any economic gains from the transaction, the courts are entitled to order, for example, the destruction of the goods.

The remedies all depend on the claims which the right-holder wishes to make before **8.137** the court. The right-holder will in principle claim the destruction of the goods.

Goods in transit may also be destroyed by order of the court. **8.138**

The costs of the proceedings as well as destruction and storage costs must **8.139** normally be paid by the losing party, that is, the infringer. However, Danish courts seldom award damages covering the right-holder's actual expenses.

It remains to be seen whether the removal of trade marks from counterfeit goods **8.140** may lead to a situation where the goods may be released by customs. No Danish decision on this point exists. In a decision from 1994 (which did not relate to border measures)[11] a Danish company had imported a consignment of uniform jackets which had been designed for Statoil and had been furnished with Statoil's logo but had been disavowed by Statoil. The buyer had subsequently masked the logo in such a way that it was materially impossible for the logo to surface again without damaging the jackets. The court found that the buyer had not infringed Statoil's trade mark rights.

---

[11] UfR.1996.744 *Statoil A/S v A/S Heat-Net*.

V. PENALTIES

8.141   Denmark has not passed legislation dealing with the phenomena of 'counterfeiting' and 'piracy' as a whole, as is the case in Germany, for example. Instead trade mark law, design law, copyright law and patent law each introduce specific criminal penalties for cases where the infringement has been committed in an intentional way on a commercial scale. As mentioned above, however, criminal proceedings are rarely actioned.

8.142   There is no minimum and no maximum level fixed for fines. The minimum term for all prison sentences is seven days whereas the maximum term is fixed individually for the different demeanours, crimes, and contraventions.

A. Infringements of trade mark and design rights

8.143   The usual criminal penalty for intentional trade mark infringements is a fine.[12] In particular aggravating circumstances, especially if the infringement has been committed with a view to making a substantial and obviously unlawful gain, a jail term up to one year is provided.

8.144   No cases where jail terms have been applied have yet been reported.

8.145   In a case where the World Wide Nature Fund's Panda logo had been unlawfully used on a textile firm's bags and where this use could result in considerable damage to the Fund the fine was set at DKR 50,000 (EUR 7,000).[13]

8.146   Article 36 of the Danish Design Law[14] uses exactly the same language as under trade mark law. No cases where criminal penalties have been applied are known.

B. Infringements of copyright

8.147   The usual criminal penalty for copyright infringements is also a fine. In case of large scale reproduction for commercial purposes a jail term of up to one year and six months has recently been provided.

---

[12] Varemærkelov nr. 341 af 6. juni 1991 § 42 (Trade Mark Law no 341 of 6 June 1991, Art 42).
[13] UfR. 1998. 946.
[14] Designlov nr. 1259 af 20. december 2000 (Design Law no 1259 of 20 December 2000).

The very complex provisions on criminal penalties can be found in Articles 76 to 80 of the Copyright Law.[15] **8.148**

Copyright infringements are more regularly the object of criminal prosecution than infringements of other intellectual property rights, because of the public interest in safeguarding the cultural heritage (for example, enforcement of moral rights). **8.149**

Cases where jail terms have been imposed are reported, but those cases are not true piracy cases. One case concerns the production of copies of famous artists like Matisse, Miro, etc, where fakes had been sold to art collectors as genuine. This was considered a fraud case, hence the serious sanctions. **8.150**

C. Infringements of patent rights or of supplementary protection certificates

Criminal sanctions, in the form of fines, are provided in the Patent Law.[16] In particularly aggravating circumstances, especially if the infringement has been committed with a view to making a substantial and obviously unlawful gain, a prison term of up to one year is provided. **8.151**

D. Infringement of plant variety rights

Article 27 of the Plant Variety Protection Law[17] introduces criminal penalties in the shape of fines. **8.152**

No cases where fines have been applied in this field are reported. **8.153**

E. Infringements of a designation of origin or a geographical indication

No domestic legislation has been introduced under which criminal penalties can be imposed for infringements of designations of origin or geographical indications in Denmark. **8.154**

---

[15] Lovbekendtgørelse nr. 710 af 30. juni 2004; (Law publication no 710 of 30 June 2004).
[16] Patentlov nr. 479 af 20. december 1967, (Patent Law no 467 of 20 December 1967) as last amended, Arts 57 and 91.
[17] Lovbekendtgørelse nr. 145 af 1. marts 2001, (law publication no 145 of 1 March 2001).

VI. LIABILITY OF CUSTOMS AUTHORITIES AND RIGHT-HOLDERS

A. Liability of right-holders

8.155 There are no specific provisions in Danish law concerning the possibility of holding right-holders liable for non-permitted use of the information provided by customs (cf Article 12 of EC Regulation 1383/2003) or for any other breach of the Regulation (Article 19(3)). However, that is not to say that the right-holder may not be held economically liable for these acts provided that the injured party can prove that a loss has been suffered.

B. Liability of customs authorities and sanctions

8.166 Danish national law does not directly entitle right-holders to compensation in the event that goods are not detected by a customs office and are released, or in the event that no action is taken to detain them once an application has been lodged by the right-holder (cf Article 19(1) of EC Regulation 1383/2003). However, it cannot be excluded that customs may be held liable in a situation where omissions or actions performed by customs can be considered wilful or negligent.

8.167 Danish law does not directly impose liability on a customs office or another authority to the persons involved or affected by an *ex officio* procedure for damages suffered by them as a result of the authorities' intervention (cf Article 19(2) of the Regulation). No examples have yet been seen but it cannot be ruled out that customs or another authority may be held liable for obviously wrongful actions or omissions. It follows from generally accepted legal principles that economic damage caused to a party by wilful, unlawful action or by negligence may be compensated if the court so decides. This implies that the normal exercise of authority vested in customs will not entitle the offended party to damages, even if he is acquitted during infringement procedures. But under certain circumstances, for example if there is an obvious discrepancy between the importance of the infringement and the damage caused, customs may be considered to have overstepped their authority and consequently be liable for damage caused under the general principles of tort law.

8.168 That public authorities may be held liable is not unknown in Danish law in other matters. In 1993, the Danish Supreme Court held the police liable for having prevented the sale of a consignment of Iranian caviar, which they had detained,[18]

---

[18] UfR.1993.311H *E v Politimesteren i Gentofte.*

and in 1996 the High Court held customs liable for irresponsible storage of a car which customs had detained and which was damaged by flooding during storage.[19]

Conclusion

It is clear that the fight against counterfeiting and piracy in Denmark is carried out efficiently by customs in the spirit of cooperation with right-holders and with as few formalities and as little bureaucracy as the law and circumstances allow. Court procedures are also characterized by a fairly high degree of informality. **8.169**

The provisions on travellers' goods remain unclear and as long as those rules are as indulgent as is currently the case, it is very difficult to explain to ordinary citizens that counterfeiting is a serious and potentially harmful crime. **8.170**

---

[19] UfR 1997.207V *W v Told- og Skatteregion Esbjerg v Hans Christian Larsen.*

9

ESTONIA

Raivo Koitel

Introduction

Prior to the entry into force of EC Regulation 1383/2003[1] ('the Regulation'), the **9.01** Customs Code[2] and the Act on the Prevention of Import and Export of Goods Infringing Intellectual Property Rights[3] were in force in Estonia. The Customs Code was limited solely to pirated and counterfeit goods, whilst the Act on the Prevention of Import and Export of Goods Infringing Intellectual Property Rights, which came into force on 1 September 2001, also covered patents, utility models, and layout topographies of integrated circuits. The latter Act more specifically regulated the rights and obligations of right-holders and customs towards goods suspected of infringing an intellectual property right.[4] These two Acts were the basis for the fight against the entry into, or removal from, the Estonian territory of counterfeit goods (in the broad sense).

Since Estonia's accession to the European Union, the new Customs Act[5] and the **9.02** Regulation, which both entered into force on 1 May 2004, constitute the legal framework for border measures. The Customs Act is intended to regulate those issues not covered by Council Regulation (EEC) 2913/92 of 12 October 1992 establishing the Community Customs Code,[6] Commission Regulation (EEC)

---

[1] Council Reg (EC) 1383/2003 of 22 July 2003 concerning customs action against goods suspected of infringing certain intellectual property rights and the measures to be taken against goods found to have infringed such rights [2003] OJ L 196/7 (2.8.2003).

[2] Customs Code (*Tolliseadustik*) of 17 October 2001, eRT https://www.riigiteataja.ee/ert/act.jsp?id=693720 (1.7.2002).

[3] Act on Prevention of Import and Export of Goods Infringing Intellectual Property Rights (*Intellektuaalset omandit rikkuva kauba sisse- ja väljaveo tõkestamise seadus*) of 6 June 2001, eRT https://www.riigiteataja.ee/ert/act.jsp?id=693700 (1.9.2001).

[4] M Niit, Mida uut on intellektuaalse omandi kaitses tolli valdkonnas', [2001] Eesti Majanduse Teataja (Issue 9) 39–41.

[5] Customs Act (*Tolliseadus*) of 13 April 2004, eRT https://www.riigiteataja.ee/ert/act.jsp?id=740392 (1.5.2004).   [6] [1992] OJ L 302/1 (19.10.1992), as amended.

2454/93 of 2 July 1993 laying down provisions for the implementation of Council Regulation (EEC) 2913/92 establishing the Community Customs Code,[7] and other Community Regulations for the implementation of Customs Regulations.

9.03 In relation to goods infringing certain intellectual property rights, the Customs Act contains a detailed set of rules providing for, amongst other things, the possibility for right-holders to submit a written opinion on the suspected goods, the surrender of the goods to the State or their destruction, and penalties in cases of violations of the Customs Act.

9.04 It should also be pointed out that as of 1 January 2004 the two separate institutions, 'Estonian Tax Board' and 'Estonian Customs Board' were amalgamated as the 'Estonian Tax and Customs Board'.

I. SUBJECT MATTER AND SCOPE OF THE NATIONAL LAW APPLYING THE REGULATION

A. Customs procedure of the goods

9.05 In principle, Estonian Customs will apply border measures to suspect goods discovered in all customs procedures, and, more generally, in all situations listed in Article 1(1) of the Regulation. In practice however, statistics[8] reveal that most of the cases opened by the Estonian Customs relate to import (approximately 70 per cent), transit (approximately 20 per cent), and export.

9.06 To date, the largest overall shipment of pirated and counterfeited goods was discovered in March 2004: more than 90,000 items, including parts for mobile telephones and clothing, arrived from China by air freight. This was a transit shipment, as the goods were intended to be sent to Latvia and Lithuania. In September–October 2004, Estonian Customs discovered the biggest shipment of counterfeited clothing in Estonia so far: more than 51,000 items were sent from China through Russia by railway transportation to Estonia. The criminals' plan was to send the goods back to Russia (that is, to place them in transit), in order to avoid Russian import taxes. Most of the larger shipments that have been

---

[7] [1993] OJ L 253/1 (11.10.1993), as amended.
[8] Statistics received from the Chief Specialist of Customs Control Department of the Estonian Tax and Customs Board.

discovered originate from China. In August 2002 a shipment of counterfeited clothing (17,545 items) was detained: the goods had arrived by air freight from China, and were intended to be sent to Russia.[9]

B. Definition of infringing goods

(1) Counterfeit goods

The owner of a legally protected trade mark enjoys an exclusive right to the trade mark. Under the Estonian Trade Mark Act,[10] there are two ways to obtain a valid trade mark in Estonia:[11] (i) either legal protection is granted by registration, or (ii) it is protected if the trade mark is well known in Estonia within the meaning of Article 6bis of the Paris Convention for the Protection of Industrial Property.[12] **9.07**

The definition of trade mark infringement under the Estonian Trade Mark Act is far broader than the definition of counterfeit goods under Article 2(1)(a) of the Regulation. Under Article 14(1) of the Estonian Trade Mark Act the owner of a trade mark has the right to prohibit third parties from using in the course of trade: **9.08**

- any sign which is identical to the trade mark which has been granted legal protection, in respect of goods or services which are identical to those to which the protection for that trade mark extends (sub-para 1);
- any sign which is identical or similar to the trade mark which has been granted legal protection, in respect of goods or services which are identical or similar to those to which this protection extends, where, because of the identity or similarity of the goods or services covered by the trade mark and the sign, there exists a likelihood of confusion on the part of the public, which includes the likelihood of association, between the sign and the protected trade mark (sub-para 2);
- any sign which is identical to, or similar to a registered trade mark or a trade mark which is known to the majority of the Estonian population and which has been granted legal protection, where such sign is used to designate goods or services which are not similar to those for which the trade mark is registered, if use of that sign without due cause takes unfair advantage of, or is detrimental to, the distinctive character or the repute of the protected trade mark (sub-para 3).

---

[9] M Püüa, 'Venemaalt jõudis Eestisse vagunitäite kaupa võltsriideid', Postimees, 27 October 2004, 5.
[10] Trade Mark Act (*Kaubamärgiseadus*) of 22 May 2002, eRT https://www.riigiteataja.ee/ert/act.jsp?id=875611 (01.05.2004).   [11] Ibid, Art 5.
[12] 20 March 1883, Stockholm redaction as amended (14. 07. 1967), eRT https://www.riigiteataja.ee/ert/act.jsp?id=24616 (23.03.1994). Estonia initially joined the Paris Convention on 29 November 1923, and rejoined in 1994.

9.09   Under Article 14(2) of the Trade Mark Act, the following acts, inter alia, are prohibited based on the provisions of Article 14(1):

- affixing the sign to goods or to their packaging;
- offering goods for sale, or putting them on the market or stocking them for the purposes of sale under the sign;
- offering or supplying services under the sign;
- importing or exporting goods under the sign;
- using the sign on business papers, or in advertising or instruction manuals for the goods.

9.10   Estonian Customs take action against counterfeit goods not only if the trade mark used on the suspected goods is identical, but also when it is merely similar, to the protected sign.[13] Customs also check trade mark symbols (such as logos, labels, brochures, instructions for use or guarantee documents bearing such symbols), even if presented separately.[14] Obviously, the customs authorities do not independently decide whether the suspected goods infringe trade mark rights or not. This is left to the right-holder or his representative. It is also for the right-holder or his representative to decide whether the suspected goods are of the same type as those subject to the trade mark registration.[15]

9.11   State supervisory agencies protect the exclusive rights of the trade mark owners as from the date of entry of the trade mark in the Estonian Trade Mark Register (for national trade marks) or the Register of the Office for Harmonization in the Internal Market (for Community trade marks). As a result customs authorities will not take any action on the basis of mere trade mark applications.

9.12   Counterfeit goods represent the vast majority of goods that have been found by Estonian Customs to infringe intellectual property rights over the last years. Approximately 70 per cent of the goods detained by Estonian Customs are clothing, footwear and accessories bearing counterfeit trade marks.[16]

---

[13]   Under Art 2(1)(a)(i) of the Regulation, the customs authorities in the Member States are to take action against goods which infringe a trade mark under Community or national law only in the case of goods bearing without authorization a sign *identical* to a protected trade mark, *or which cannot be distinguished in its essential aspects* from such a trade mark.

[14]   Usually the brochures, instructions for use, or guarantee documents bearing such signs are sent together with the goods and if the goods are counterfeits, the enclosed documents are also counterfeit. There was a case where the packaging and the brochures of goods originating from Taiwan were labelled with the 'COMPAQ' trade mark, but the goods with the 'HUNDAI' trade marks.

[15]   Under Art 2(1)(a)(i) of the Regulation, the customs authorities in the Member States are to take action against goods which infringe a trade mark under Community or national law only in those cases where the protected trade mark is 'validly registered *in respect of the same type of goods*'.

[16]   Statistics received from the Chief Specialist of Customs Control Department of the Estonian Tax and Customs Board.

(2) Pirated goods

According to the Estonian Copyright Act,[17] copyright subsists in literary, artistic, **9.13** and scientific works. Article 4(3) of the Act contains a very extensive (but non-exhaustive) list of examples of works that may enjoy protection, including amongst others:

- written works in the fields of fiction, non-fiction, politics, education, etc;
- scientific works, or works of popular science, either written or three-dimensional (monographs, articles, reports on scientific research, plans, schemes, models, tests, etc);
- computer programs expressed in whatever form, that are to be protected as literary works;
- speeches, lectures, addresses, sermons and other works which consist of words and which are expressed orally (oral works);
- scripts and script outlines, librettos;
- dramatic and dramatico-musical works;
- musical compositions with or without words;
- choreographic works and entertainments in dumb shows;
- audiovisual works;
- works of painting, graphic arts, typography, drawing, sculpture, illustrations;
- productions and works of set design;
- architectural graphics (drawings, drafts, schemes, figures, plans, projects, etc), letters explaining the contents of a project, additional texts and programmes, architectural works of plastic art (models, etc), works of architecture and landscape architecture (buildings, constructions, parks, green areas, etc), urban developmental ensembles and complexes;
- works of applied art;
- works of design and fashion design;
- photographic works and works expressed by a process analogous to photography, slides, and slide films;
- cartographic works (topographic, geographic, geological, and the like maps, atlases, models);
- draft legislation;
- standards and draft standards;
- opinions, reviews, etc;
- derivative works, that is, translations, adaptations of original works, modifications (arrangements), and other alterations of works;
- collections of works and information (including databases);
- other creations.

---

[17] Copyright Act (*Autoriõiguse seadus*) of 11 November 1992, eRT https://www.riigiteataja.ee/ert/act.jsp?id=918060 (12.12.1992).

9.14   Under Article 13(1) of the Copyright Act an author shall enjoy the exclusive right to use the work in any manner, and to authorize or prohibit the use of the work in a similar manner by other persons.

9.15   Under Article 62(1) of the Copyright Act a performer, producer of phonograms, broadcasting organization, producer of the first fixation of a film, a person who, after the expiry of copyright protection, for the first time lawfully publishes or lawfully directs at the public a previously unpublished work, and a person who publishes a critical or scientific publication of a work not protected by copyright shall enjoy the rights in the results created by him (object of related rights). These rights are also protected by the Copyright Act.

9.16   Under Article 16 of the Estonian Industrial Design Protection Act[18] the owners of a registered industrial design have, inter alia, the following rights:

- under sub-paragraph 1, the owner of an industrial design has the exclusive right to manufacture products incorporating the industrial design, and to distribute, sell, offer for sale, import, export or stock for the aforementioned purposes products incorporating the registered industrial design;
- under sub-paragraph 2, the owner of an industrial design has the right to prohibit other persons from manufacturing without authorization products incorporating an identical or confusingly similar industrial design and from distributing, selling, offering for sale or importing, exporting or stocking for the aforementioned purposes such products.

9.17   Estonian Customs do take border measures against pirated goods.[19] According to the statistics,[20] most of the border measures applied by customs officials in Estonia on pirated goods relate to industrial designs (in particular mobile phone parts) and copyright and related rights (for example, audiovisual recordings, such as music, and movies). Again, it will be for the right-holder to confirm whether the suspected goods have been pirated.

(3)   Goods infringing other intellectual property rights

9.18   The official statistics do not mention any border measures that would have been taken in Estonia on the basis of a patent or a supplementary protection certificate, and there is no customs practice either relating to plant variety rights, geographical indications, and designations of origin. Perhaps one reason for this is the fact that the majority of goods infringing patent rights also infringe trade mark rights (for example, medicine, mobile telephones, etc, which infringe a patent are often

---

[18]   Industrial Design Protection Act (*Tööstusdisaini kaitse seadus*) of 18 November 1997, eRT https://www.riigiteataja.ee/ert/act.jsp?id=730982 (11.1.1998).
[19]   As defined in Art 2(1)(b) of the Regulation, which refers to national law for that purpose.
[20]   Statistics received from the Chief Specialist of Customs Control Department of the Estonian Tax and Customs Board.

labelled with trade marks, and therefore also violate trade mark rights). Furthermore it should be pointed out that Estonian customs authorities have not received training to assist them in identifying goods that infringe patent rights. If no prior application for action has been filed by the relevant right-holder, the customs authorities are unlikely to detect goods that infringe patent rights as there is unlikely to be sufficient information or grounds for checking the goods, or suspecting that they infringe intellectual property rights.

Goods infringing a patent or a supplementary protection certificate

Article 15 of the Estonian Patent Act[21] confers the following exclusive rights on the proprietor of a patent (and a supplementary protection certificate). During the period of validity of the patent (or a supplementary protection certificate) and without the permission of the proprietor of the patent no person shall:

9.19

- manufacture, use, distribute, sell, or offer for sale, products protected by the patent, or acquire (including by way of import) such products for the afore-mentioned purposes;
- manufacture, sell or offer for sale, components which form a significant part of the product protected by the patent, or acquire and export such components for the manufacture or preparation of the product, except if the components are other independent products;
- use, or offer for use to third persons, the patented process;
- use, distribute, sell or offer for sale, a product manufactured according to the patented process, or acquire (including by way of import) such products for the aforementioned purposes.

Goods infringing a national plant variety right

Under Article 37(1) of the Estonian Plant Variety Rights Act,[22] the holder of the plant variety right has the exclusive right to:

9.20

- produce or reproduce (multiply) for the purposes of sale;
- condition for the purpose of propagation;
- offer for sale;
- sell or transfer in any other way;
- export;
- import;
- and stock for any of the purposes specified above;

the seeds or propagating material.

---

[21] Patent Act (*Patendiseadus*) of 16 March 1994, eRT https://www.riigiteataja.ee/ert/act.jsp?id=875615 (23.05.1994).
[22] Plant Variety Rights Act (*Sordikaitseseadus*) of 25 March 1998, eRT https://www.riigiteataja.ee/ert/act.jsp?id=190200 (01.07.1998).

Goods infringing a national designation of origin or a geographical indication

9.21 Under Article 11 of the Estonian Geographical Indication Protection Act[23] the unlawful use of a geographical indication is prohibited. Under Article 11(1), the following is considered unlawful use:

- the use of a geographical indication, or a misleadingly similar indication, for identifying goods or services by a person who does not act as the producer, processor, or manufacturer, of the good specified in the registration, or as the service provider in the geographical area specified in the registration;

- the use of a geographical indication, or a misleadingly similar indication, for identifying goods or services, if the good or service lacks any quality, reputation, or other characteristic, specified in the registration;

- the use of a geographical indication, or a misleadingly similar indication, for identifying goods or services which are not covered by the registration but which are of the same kind as the goods and services covered by the registration;

- the use of a geographical indication, or a misleadingly similar indication, for identifying other goods or services which may take unfair advantage of the reputation of the geographical indication;

- the use of any misleading information about the origin, nature, or basic characteristics, of goods or services on the inner or outer packaging, advertising materials, or relevant documents;

- the use of an indication which, although literally true as to the geographical origin of the goods or services, may falsely represent to the public that the goods or services originate in another area, even if the true origin is indicated;

- other transactions which may mislead the public as to the true origin of the goods or services.

9.22 Under Article 11(3) it is also prohibited to trade goods which are unlawfully identified with a registered geographical indication, regardless of whether the distributor, vendor, or consumer, has been notified of the said specification.

(4) Moulds and matrices

9.23 Under Article 2(3) of the Regulation, the application of border measures to 'moulds and matrices which are specifically designed or adapted for the manufacture of infringing goods' depends on the existence of a provision under national law allowing the right-holder to act in respect of these goods. In Estonia, there are no provisions under national law, which relate to 'moulds and matrices which are

---

[23] Geographical Indication Protection Act (*Geograafilise tähise kaitse seadus*) of 15 December 1999, eRT https://www.riigiteataja.ee/ert/act.jsp?id=731008 (10.1.2000).

specifically designed or adapted for the manufacture of infringing goods' and there are also no applications for action filed with the customs on this matter.

According to Estonian Customs there is no actual practice relating to moulds and matrices in Estonia.

C. Goods excluded by the Regulation

(1) Parallel imported goods

In Estonia, there is no national legislation which allows customs to apply border **9.24** measures to goods defined in Article 3(1), first indent, of the Regulation. Therefore, customs do not check (genuine) parallel imported goods. The right-holder is only informed in cases where there is a suspicion that the goods infringe the right-holders' intellectual property rights.

(2) Goods which have been manufactured under conditions other than those which have been agreed with the right-holder

There is also no national legislation in Estonia which provides for the taking of **9.25** border measures in respect of goods which have been manufactured under conditions other than those which have been agreed upon with the rights owner. As with parallel imported goods, Estonian Customs do not inspect goods which, for example, do not comply with the terms of a licence agreement. Again, the relevant right-holder will be informed only in cases where there is a suspicion that the goods infringe his intellectual property rights.[24]

(3) Goods contained in travellers' personal baggage

Travellers' personal baggage is not subject to systematic control by Estonian **9.26** Customs. When applying Article 3(2) of the Regulation, it is up to the Customs Inspector to determine whether suspect goods are of a commercial nature, taking into account such considerations as whether the traveller has imported such goods in small quantities on a regular basis, or whether the imported goods are related to the registered commercial activities of the traveller.

When determining whether or not goods contained in a traveller's personal **9.27** baggage are within the limits of the duty-free allowance (that is, EUR 175), the calculation of the value of the goods differs from case to case. Usually it is

---

[24] Cf Reg 1383/2003, Art 3(1), second indent.

calculated on the basis of invoices, bills of delivery, declarations of the goods, and explanations given in the course of procedure. It is up to the Customs Inspector to decide if the value of the goods exceeds the duty-free allowance, and if such goods are for the personal use of the traveller.

9.28   Usually the goods contained in the travellers' personal luggage are not of significant quantity. Several right-holders have previously informed Estonian Customs that they are only interested in taking action if the shipment contains at least a certain number of suspect products. Under Estonian practice it is possible, for example, that a right-holder will have informed customs that he will only take action if a minimum amount of items is discovered. In some cases Estonian Customs will thus release the goods, which do not meet the minimum quantity requirements of the right-holder, although it might be obvious that the goods are for commercial purposes and directly infringe the right-holder's rights.

II. APPLICATION FOR ACTION BY THE CUSTOMS AUTHORITIES

A. Measures prior to an application for action by the customs authorities ('*ex officio* measures')

9.29   Prior to the entry into force of the Regulation most interventions by customs were taken *ex officio*. Every year, however, the number of applications for action filed by right-holders increases and, at the moment, according to a rough estimate, half of the border measures taken are based on *ex officio* interventions, and the other half of them on an application for action.

9.30   Most *ex officio* interventions relate to traffic coming from manufacturers from 'high-risk' countries, for example Russia and China. In previous years large quantities of goods infringing intellectual property rights also arrived from the Ukraine, Poland, and Lithuania. Certain 'alarm signs' trigger the attention of Estonian Customs: incomplete or vague customs declarations, unusual transport routes, incomplete contact details of the shipper and the addressee, mixed shipments, etc.

9.31   When Estonian Customs uncover a shipment containing suspect goods, they may suspend the release of the goods, or detain them. In such circumstances, they inform the right-holder or his representative (for example, his attorney-at-law, or patent or trade mark attorney) by fax or e-mail of the nature and quantity of the goods.

When suspending the release, or detaining, suspect goods *ex officio*, customs must **9.32** observe a deadline of three working days, and may later maintain such measures only if an application for action is received from the right-holder.[25]

B. The lodging and processing of applications for customs action

(1) Persons entitled to file an application for action

The total number of applications for action which have been filed with the Estonian **9.33** Customs to date[26] is 162 (including applications based on 'Community rights'[27]).

Definition of 'right-holders' under the Regulation

Applications for action under the Regulation may be filed by 'right-holders', **9.34** defined as the holders of any intellectual property right referred to in Article 2(1) of the Regulation, as well as any other persons authorized to use such rights, or representatives of the rights owner or authorized user.[28] Article 1 of the implementing Regulation 1891/2004[29] provides for useful guidance as to how to understand the concept of 'representative'. It includes both natural and legal persons, attorneys-at-law, trade mark or patent attorneys, consultants, collective management societies, associations of right-holders, etc. Licensees, distributors, and commercial agents would also fall under this definition provided they have the authorization to act on behalf of the right-holder.

Estonian legislation raises a problem for licensees. Under Estonian law licences **9.35** granted for industrial property right (certainly for trade marks,[30] industrial designs[31] and patents[32] with the exception of plant variety rights[33]) have no legal effect on third parties if they are not registered. The registration of a licence is optional, but for the sake of legal certainty, it is therefore recommended that persons authorized to use the intellectual property right concerned ascertain that the licence agreement by virtue of which they act is registered and allows them to pursue infringers, provided also that the right-holder is notified.[34]

---

[25] Reg 1383/2003, Art 4(1).
[26] Figures valid until 31 May 2005. Statistics received from the Chief Specialist of Customs Control Department of the Estonian Tax and Customs Board.
[27] Cf Reg 1383/2003, Art 5(4).   [28] Ibid, Art 2(2).
[29] Commission Reg (EC) 1891/2004 of 21 October 2004 laying down provisions for the implementation of Council Reg (EC) 1383/2003 concerning customs action against goods suspected of infringing certain intellectual property rights and the measures to be taken against goods found to have infringed such rights [2004] OJ L 328/16 (30.10.2004).   [30] N 10 above, Art 21(3).
[31] N 18 above, Art 74(4) and (6).   [32] N 21 above, Art 46(4).
[33] N 22 above, Art 46(1).
[34] N 10 above, Art 57(3); n 18 above, Art 85(2); n 21 above, Art 54(4).

9.36 In practice, all applications for action lodged with Estonian Customs under the Regulation to date have been filed by rights owners or their representatives, so that Estonian Customs authorities have never had to interpret the notion of 'authorized user'.

Proof of entitlement to file an application for action

For right-holders stricto sensu

9.37 Under Estonian law and practice, the following documents are acceptable for the proprietor of an intellectual right to prove his ownership:[35]

- For a registered trade mark, a registered industrial design, a patent or a supplementary protection certificate, a geographical indication, or a plant variety right, evidence that the right has been duly registered by the relevant office or any other authority. This includes original registration certificates or certified copies thereof, but Estonian Customs also accept a mere copy of the registration certificate or the official registration publication, or even printouts from official databases of a national, regional, or international office.[36] For example, for a trade mark, a registered industrial design, or a geographical indication, a printout from the database of the Estonian Patent Office available on-line[37] is sufficient.
- For a copyright, a related right, or an unregistered (community) design[38] right, any evidence establishing that the applicant for the customs measures is the actual owner of the right would be sufficient. It is of course recommended that evidence with an incontestable date be provided, for example, certified by a notary public, etc.

9.38 In Estonia an application for action cannot be based on a mere *application* for an industrial property right—a registration is always required. This requirement may cause delays for the filing of applications for action, taking into account the backlog at the Estonian Patent Office.

For persons authorized to use the right

9.39 The authorized user of an intellectual property right covered by the Regulation will have to submit additional documents evidencing that he is authorized to use the right in question,[39] for example a copy of a contract proving that the applicant is entitled to use a copyright, or a duly registered licence agreement for an industrial property right, etc. The licence agreement must allow the licensee to act

---

[35] Cf Reg 1891/2004, Art 2(1).   [36] Ibid, second indent.

[37] http://www.epa.ee/default.asp?id=449.

[38] It should be noted that under the Estonian Industrial Design Protection Act, protection is only provided for registered (national) industrial designs, n 18 above, Art 5(2).

[39] Reg 1891/2004, Art 2(2).

against infringers. Also, in order to avoid possible misunderstandings, the right-holder must be notified of any action to be taken on his behalf. For the sake of legal certainty, it is still recommended that the agreement of the right-holder to action taken on his behalf is ascertained.

For representatives

In cases where the application is filed by a representative, it is mandatory to submit an authorization to act on behalf of the rights owner.[40] A general power of attorney is accepted by Estonian Customs for both applications for action prior to any customs intervention and further to an *ex officio* action. The authorization has to be submitted in original. If the original power of attorney cannot be filed, a certified copy is required. The power of attorney may be sent via facsimile, provided the original or certified copy is posted later with the confirmation copy of the facsimile.   **9.40**

In Estonia, foreign representatives are authorized to appear before customs, and in practice customs are likely to accept applications filed in English. But for the sake of making the work of customs more efficient and less time consuming, it may be beneficial to appoint a local representative who is familiar with local practice and requirements.   **9.41**

Estonian Customs request that the declaration provided for under Article 6 of the Regulation, duly signed and executed by the right-holder in original, be submitted together with the application for action. The declaration may however also be signed by the representative, if he has been authorized to do so.[41]   **9.42**

(2) *Competent customs department and formal requirements*

Competent customs department

In Estonia the customs department responsible for processing applications for action pursuant to Article 5(2) of the Regulation is the headquarters of local customs: **9.43**

Estonian Tax and Customs Board (*Maksu- ja Tolliamet*)
Directorate 'Customs Control'
Narva mnt 9j
EE-15176 Tallinn
Tel: +372 683 5700
Fax: +372 683 5709
E-mail: toll@customs.ee

---

[40] Ibid, Art 2(3), first indent.   [41] Ibid, second indent.

Form of the application for action

9.44 At the moment an application for action has to be filed on paper directly by post (also by facsimile and e-mail if a confirmation follows by post). It is expected that an electronic version of the application for action will be made available to the applicant on the web page of the Estonian Tax and Customs Board, but the deadline for preparing the electronic form has not been established yet. We recommend (especially when colour copies are submitted together with the application form) filing six copies of the materials, that is, one for the headquarters, and five for the different customs offices.[42] Finally, it should be borne in mind that the original declaration under Article 6 and, where appropriate, the original power of attorney form (or a certified copy of it), must be enclosed with the application.[43]

Language requirements

9.45 In principle, an application for action has to be filed in Estonian.[44] However, generally Estonian Customs will accept the application for action, the exhibits, and the declaration under Article 6 of the Regulation if they are submitted in English. Should customs require a translation of any of the documents filed in English, they will inform the right-holder or his representative thereof. Documents in other languages must be translated, preferably directly into Estonian.

(3) Requirements regarding the content of the application for action

9.46 Under Estonian law and practice there are no specific requirements for the information to be submitted to customs under Article 5(5) of the Regulation. The application must contain all the information needed to facilitate the work of customs to enable the goods in question to be readily recognized. Technical information about the goods must be as detailed as possible, because this is the main basis for identifying suspect goods. Right-holders should likewise provide all information they have concerning the type or pattern of fraud, based on their previous experience and practice, for example, in other countries. Customs may always request additional information or details if this proves to be necessary.[45]

9.47 The contact person appointed by the right-holder need not be a local person. However, the administrative contact person should at least be familiar with Estonian law and local customs procedures. The technical contact person must be familiar with the authentic goods. The administrative contact is generally an attorney-at-law, or a patent or trade mark attorney, and normally also acts as the technical contact person. Some representatives receive special training by the

---

[42] Cf also Reg 1891/2004, Art 3(3), on this point.   [43] Cf paras 9.40 and 9.42 above.
[44] N 5 above, Art 8(1).   [45] Cf eg Reg 1383/2003, Art 5(6).

right-holder they represent in order to allow them to identify infringing goods. It is common that the administrative contact is an Estonian representative and the technical contact is the right-holder himself.

(4) *Processing and acceptance of the application for action*

Estonian Customs must process the application for action and notify the right-holder in writing of their decision within 30 working days from receipt.[46] In practice, if all the formal requirements are fulfilled, the application will be accepted within a few days. **9.48**

There is no particular provision providing for a challenge or appeal against Customs refusal to accept an application for action under Article 5(8) of the Regulation, and there is no precedent on this in Estonia. Under general law, right-holders are allowed to file a challenge before the national Tax and Customs Board[47] or under the Taxation Act[48] an appeal can be filed before Administrative Court if the challenge is not satisfied.[49] An appeal can be filed directly to the court without filing a challenge.[50] The challenge can be filed within 30 days of the date of notification of, or delivery of the administrative act.[51] Under the Code of Administrative Court Procedure[52] the appeal can be filed within 30 days of the date of notification of the administrative act.[53] **9.49**

The maximum validity period of the application for action is 12 months.[54] There are no limitations for the right-holder to determine a shorter period in the application. Also an application for single action can be filed. If there is no specific requirement for the duration of the application, the application is considered to be valid for 12 months. For 'Community' applications for action filed under Article 5(4) of the Regulation, the period during which customs are to take action shall be set at one year in all cases.[55] On expiry of the period in question, and subject to prior discharge of any debt owed by the right-holder under the Regulation, customs may, at the right-holder's request, extend that period.[56] **9.50**

(5) *'Community' applications for action*

Only a few 'Community' applications for action have been filed with Estonian Customs under Article 5(4) of the Regulation to date. In practice, no suspect **9.51**

---

[46] Ibid, Art 5(7).   [47] N 5 above, Art 7.

[48] Taxation Act (*Maksukorralduse seadus*) of 20 February 2002, eRT https://www.riigiteataja.ee/ert/act.jsp?id=901885 (1.7.2002).   [49] Ibid, Art 151(1).

[50] Ibid, Art 151(2).   [51] Ibid, Art 138(1).

[52] Code of Administrative Court Procedure (*Halduskohtumenetluse seadustik*) of 25 February 1999, eRT https://www.riigiteataja.ee/ert/act.jsp?id=782731 (1. 1. 2000).

[53] Ibid, Art 9(1).   [54] Cf eg Reg 1383/2003, Art 8(1), first indent.

[55] Ibid, Art 8(2), second indent.   [56] Ibid, Art 8(1), first indent, and 8(2), second indent.

goods have ever been detained based on a 'Community' application. Estonian Customs have informed us that they will process 'Community' applications as if they were a national application for action. Although Estonian Customs will accept 'Community' applications in English, the filing of an Estonian translation is recommended.

III. CONDITIONS GOVERNING ACTION BY CUSTOMS AUTHORITIES AND BY THE AUTHORITIES WITH JURISDICTION TO DETERMINE WHETHER GOODS INFRINGE AN INTELLECTUAL PROPERTY RIGHT

A. Conditions governing action by customs authorities

(1) Factual background

9.52 In Estonia, next to the customs department responsible for processing applications for action (cf para 9.43 above), there are five customs offices,[57] namely:

- the South-West office;
- the South-East office;
- the North-East office;
- the Tallinn office; and
- the Tartu office.

9.53 The most important customs offices involved in border measures against goods infringing intellectual property rights in Estonia are the North-East office and Tallinn office. The Tallinn office is the main office because it oversees the harbour and the airport. Pirated and counterfeit goods make their way into Estonian territory mainly through Tallinn airport (based on quantity). Most of the infringing goods discovered by the North-East office come from Russia (by railroad and by road). The other offices are of marginal importance today in relation to border measures, although before the enlargement of the European Community the other offices were also important because of the road traffic and counterfeited goods arriving for example from the Ukraine, Lithuania, and Poland.

---

[57] Regulation on Tax and Customs Board (*Maksu- ja Tolliameti põhimäärus*) of 19 January 2004, regulation No 9 of the Minister of Finance, eRT https://www.riigiteataja.ee/ert/act.jsp?id=866713 (10.05.2004), Art 31.

Each office has a customs control unit with a separate contact person for intellectual **9.54** property matters. It is the task of the contact person to orchestrate border measures in his particular area of competence. For example in the North-East office, the contact person in charge will inform the border points and moving customs groups in summary of any applications for action by e-mail. If any suspected goods are discovered, direct contact will be made with the person in charge of intellectual property matters, who will take over the further handling of the matter and contact the right-holder or his representative.

Estonian Customs and police officials have participated in training and work- **9.55** shops organized by the representatives of different right-holders, the Ministry of Culture, the Estonian Patent Office, and foreign experts where the following issues have been discussed: intellectual property protection in general, practical issues in enforcing intellectual property rights, how to determine if certain goods infringe intellectual property rights, how pirated and counterfeited goods are usually transported, methods of investigation, risk analysis, etc. Recently joint-workshops for customs and police authorities were held together with Greek experts in September and October 2004.[58,59] These two workshops were organized under the Phare programme 'Enforcement of intellectual and industrial property legislation' sponsored by the European Commission.

(2) Notification of customs intervention

Once the application for action of the right-holder is accepted, Estonian Customs **9.56** follow the procedure laid down in Article 9 of the Regulation. Where suspect goods are detected, their release is suspended or they are detained. The right-holder and the declarant or holder of the goods will be informed immediately by e-mail or fax.

In case the right-holder has not yet filed an application for action, or the applica- **9.57** tion has not yet been approved, the customs authorities will apply Article 4 of the Regulation.[60]

(3) Information to be provided by customs to the right-holder before the right-holder confirms the infringing nature of the goods

Once goods suspected of infringing intellectual property rights are detained by **9.58** Estonian Customs, the right-holder will be informed of their nature, their exact

---

[58] Seminar for Customs and Police officials on 'Prevention of counterfeiting and piracy in Estonia', Tallinn, 27–29 September 2004.
[59] Workshop 'Prevention of counterfeiting and piracy in Estonia', Tallinn, 30 September– 4 October 2004.   [60] Cf paras 9.29–9.32 above.

quantity, the country of origin and destination, and if known the country of manufacture.[61]

9.59 Once an application for action has been filed and accepted by customs, and upon the specific request of the right-holder, additional information may be provided, for example, the name of the manufacturer of the goods, consignee, consignor, declarant or holder of the goods.[62] The request for additional information can also be in verbal form—which may, however, give rise to problems of evidence.

9.60 Under Estonian law there is no provision that would preclude the disclosure of personal data in such cases. In any event, Estonian customs authorities are of the opinion that information relating to the consignee, consignor, declarant or holder of the goods does not contain any non-disclosable business secrets, and therefore disclosing such information is not problematic.

(4) Inspection of the suspected goods

9.61 On being notified of the detention or suspension of the release of suspect goods, the right-holder (or in general all persons involved, such as representatives, technical or administrative contact persons, etc) are given the opportunity to inspect the goods.[63] They are allowed to take pictures of the goods and, upon request, may even take samples. Whenever possible, Estonian Customs send digital photos of the suspect goods to the right-holder. Digital photos are generally accepted for the purpose of examining the goods, and for determining if they violate an intellectual property right.

9.62 The samples of the goods must be returned after examination. However, when the goods are destroyed during examination (for example, samples of packages of sweets, or labels of beverages) they do not have to be returned.[64]

B. Simplified procedure allowing the destruction of the goods without there being any need to determine whether an intellectual property right has been infringed under national law

9.63 Article 11 of the Regulation has not yet been implemented in Estonia and according to the Chief Specialist of Customs Control Department of the Estonian Tax and Customs Board there are no plans to implement it in the near future.

---

[61] Reg 1383/2003, Arts 4(2) and 9(2).   [62] Ibid, Art 9(3), first indent.
[63] In accordance with Reg 1383/2003, Art 9(3), second indent.
[64] Reg 1383/2003, Art 9(3), last indent, provides that samples must be returned on completion of the analysis and, where applicable, before goods are released or their detention is ended, but only 'where circumstances allow'.

Currently, neither the Estonian Customs Act,[65] nor any other Estonian law allows customs authorities to apply a simplified procedure set out in this provision.

C. Conditions governing action by the authorities having jurisdiction to determine whether the goods infringe an intellectual property right

(1) Authorities having jurisdiction to determine whether the goods infringe an intellectual property right

Under Article 13(1) of the Regulation, in order to secure border measures taken by customs, right-holders must notify the Estonian Tax and Customs Board that proceedings to determine whether an intellectual property right has been infringed under national law have been commenced within three (for perishable goods) or 10 (up to 20) working days of receipt of the notification of suspension of release or detention of the goods.[66] **9.64**

Under national legislation the authority to determine whether the goods infringe an intellectual property right of any of the goods outlined in Article 2(1) of the Regulation belongs to the right-holder himself. Under Articles 39(4) and 39(5) of the Customs Act[67] if there is doubt that certain goods could infringe intellectual property rights within the meaning of the Regulation, the right-holder shall provide, within 10 working days after being informed of the goods being detained, a written opinion on the suspected goods based on the results of examinations of samples or specimens thereof. An opinion shall set out: **9.65**

- the time and place of giving the opinion on the goods;
- the given name, surname and the official title of the person who prepared the opinion;
- a description of the samples based on which the opinion is given;
- a conclusion containing the reasoned opinion of the right-holder as to whether the goods infringe intellectual property rights or not.

The customs authorities shall immediately send a copy of an opinion received from the right-holder to the persons involved, who have the right, within 10 days of receipt of the copy of the opinion, to file written objections to the opinion to the customs authorities and provide relevant evidence.[68]

If no written opinion is received within the time limit pursuant to Article 13 of the Regulation, release of the goods shall be granted, or their detention shall be ended, as appropriate, subject to completion of all customs formalities. **9.66**

---

[65] N 5 above.   [66] Cf para 9.68 below.   [67] N 5 above.
[68] N 5 above, Art 39(6).

9.67 This procedure is the most cost-saving, quick, and simplified way of determining whether the goods infringe an intellectual property right. On the basis of the written opinion of the right-holder, the customs authorities will make their decision to take measures, such as the release of the goods or seizure and destruction or, provided the right-holder agrees, handing over to health-care or social welfare institutions after removal for example of the counterfeited trade marks. A person involved has a right to file a challenge against a decision of the customs authorities.[69]

(2) *Period for notifying customs that proceedings have been started*

9.68 Pursuant to Article 13(1) of the Regulation, the 10 working days period during which customs have to be notified that proceedings have been started may be extended by a maximum of another 10 working days 'in appropriate cases'.[70] Under Estonian practice, the 10-day period will normally be readily extended. The main reason for asking for an extension is that the right-holder is in a far-away country, or there are many intermediaries.

D. Release of goods suspected of infringing certain rights on provision of a security

9.69 There is no practice in relation to Article 14 of the Regulation in Estonia and therefore our customs authorities are unable to comment if they are obliged to release the goods. There is also no authority to set the amount of security and no Regulations governing how to determine the amount of the security.

E. Storage of the goods

9.70 Under the general principles of the Regulation, and specifically under Article 6(1), the right-holder shall agree to bear all the costs incurred in keeping the goods under customs control pursuant to Article 9 and, where applicable, Article 11. In other words, the storage of the goods shall not give rise to costs for the customs administration. Therefore, the right-holder shall bear all the costs of storing the goods. The right-holder can later claim reimbursement of the storage costs from the infringer, invoking Article 45 of the TRIPs Agreement,[71] which is also binding in Estonia.

---

[69] N 5 above, Art 7.

[70] In the case of perishable goods, this period shall be three working days, and may not be extended (Reg 1383/2003, Art 13(2)).

[71] Agreement on Trade-Related Aspects of Intellectual Property Rights (TRIPs) (*Intellektuaalomandi õiguste kaubandusaspektide leping*), Annex 1C of the Agreement establishing

IV. PROVISIONS APPLICABLE TO GOODS FOUND TO INFRINGE AN INTELLECTUAL PROPERTY RIGHT

If the goods are found to infringe an intellectual property right and they are **9.71** seized, they will be destroyed or, provided the right-holder agrees, handed over to health-care or social welfare institutions after removal of the counterfeited trade marks.

Under Articles 55 and 97(4) of the Estonian Customs Act,[72] the Regulation on **9.72** Handing Over the Goods to State Possession and also Destroying the Goods under Customs Supervision,[73] the goods found to infringe intellectual property rights shall be destroyed further to the decision of the Director General of the Tax and Customs Board, or any other person with authority, once the deadline for appealing against the decision to destroy the goods has passed. A deed in two copies is issued after the destruction, one of the copies is sent to the right-holder and the other copy is kept by customs. Under Article 97(4) of the Customs Act, the costs of destroying goods infringing intellectual property rights are to be claimed from the infringer by customs.

However, infringing goods, such as clothing and footwear, may also, under Article **9.73** 97(5) of the Customs Act, be handed over to health-care or social welfare institutions, after removal of the infringing trade marks. Under Article 3 of the Regulation on Handing Over of Seized Goods to State or Local Authority Health-Care or Social Welfare Institutions[74] the infringing goods can be handed over to such institutions only if:

- the counterfeited signs can be removed from the items without damaging them;
- at least one welfare institution has asked to receive such goods; and
- there is written consent from the right-holder for the handover of these goods to welfare institutions.

---

the World Trade Organization (Marrakesh Agreement), Estonia joined the Agreement on 13 November 1999—see http://www.epa.ee/default.asp?id=492.

[72] N 5 above.

[73] Regulation on Handing Over of the Goods to State Possession, also Destroying the Goods under Customs Supervision (*Kauba riigi omandisse ülekandmise, samuti kauba tollijärelevalve all hävitamise kord*) of 23 April 2004, regulation No 87 of the Minister of Finance, eRT https://www.riigiteataja.ee/ert/act.jsp?id=742988 (01.05.2004).

[74] Regulation on Handing Over of Seized Goods to State or Local Authority Health-Care or Social Welfare Institutions (*Konfiskeeritud võltsitud rõivaste ja jalatsite riigi või kohaliku omavalitsuse üksuse tervishoiu- või hoolekandeasutusele üleandmise kord*) of 22 April 2004, regulation No 85 of the Minister of Finance, eRT https://www.riigiteataja.ee/ert/act.jsp?id=743172 (01.05.2004).

9.74 The counterfeited trade marks will generally be removed from the goods by prisoners as part of their work programme. Both Article 46 of the TRIPs Agreement[75] and Article 17(1), second indent, of the Regulation provide that removing the trade marks which have been affixed to counterfeit goods without authorization may, 'in exceptional cases', be regarded as effectively depriving the persons concerned of any economic gains from the transaction.

9.75 Article 97(3) of the Estonian Customs Act[76] provides for the keeping of specimens of the seized goods for prevention work, to raise public awareness of intellectual property right infringements.

V. PENALTIES

9.76 As regards intellectual property infringements, civil, criminal, and misdemeanour liability will arise.

9.77 Offences in respect of intellectual property rights involve penalties consisting of fines of up to EUR 1,150 for natural persons and EUR 3,200 for legal persons for misdemeanours, and EUR 1,600 for natural persons and EUR 3,200 to the maximum penalty of EUR 16 million for legal persons for criminal offences. A jail term of up to five years is also possible. A pecuniary punishment may also be imposed on a legal person as a supplementary punishment, together with compulsory dissolution of the company. These penalties relate to all goods infringing an intellectual property right as stated in Article 2(1) of the Regulation.[77]

9.78 Right-holders may also claim compensation for damage. Damage subject to compensation may be patrimonial or non-patrimonial. Patrimonial damage includes, primarily, direct patrimonial damage and loss of profit. Non-patrimonial damage involves primarily the physical and emotional distress and suffering caused to the aggrieved person.[78]

---

[75] N 71 above.   [76] N 5 above.

[77] Cf further on this point the Copyright Act (n 17 above), Ch X¹, Penal Code *(Karistusseadustik)* of 6 June 2001, eRT https://www.riigiteataja.ee/ert/act.jsp?id=953236 (1.9.2002), Chs 3 and 14; Law of Obligations Act *(Võlaõigusseadus)* of 26 September 2001, eRT https://www. riigiteataja.ee/ert/act.jsp?id=835261 (1.7.2002), Chs 52 and 53, Customs Act (n 5 above), Ch 9.

[78] Law of Obligations Act, Art 128.

VI. LIABILITY OF CUSTOMS AUTHORITIES AND RIGHT-HOLDERS

A. Liability of right-holders and sanctions

Everyone has the right to compensation for moral and material damage caused by **9.79** the unlawful action of any person;[79] everyone, whose rights have been violated or contested or for protecting its freedom, has the right to turn to court.[80] This provision will govern all liability claims referred to under Article 19(3) of the Regulation. The same is true for any damage caused by any use of the information provided by customs to the right-holder in breach of Article 12 of the Regulation.

B. Liability of customs and sanctions

Article 19(1) excludes the right-holder from claiming compensation in the event **9.80** that possible suspect goods are not detected by a customs office and are released, or no action is taken to detain them 'save as provided by the law of the Member State in which an application is lodged or, in the case of an application under Article 5(4), by the law of the Member State in which goods infringing an intellectual property right are not detected'. There are no special provisions in national law.

It may therefore not be ruled out that customs' actions may be challenged as being **9.81** unlawful according to the State Liability Act.[81] A person whose rights are violated by the unlawful activities of a public authority in a public law relationship may claim compensation for damage caused to the person if damage could not be prevented and cannot be eliminated by the protection or restoration of rights in the manner provided in this State Liability Act. Compensation for damage caused by a failure to act may be claimed only if an administrative act is not issued in due course or a measure is not taken in due course and the rights of a person are violated thereby. Direct proprietary damage and loss of income are compensated for on the basis of the above.[82] According to Article 7 of the Customs Act a person has also a right to file a challenge against a decision of the customs authorities or an act of a customs official. Challenges shall be filed and settled pursuant to the

---

[79] The Constitution of Republic of Estonia (*Eesti Vabariigi Põhiseadus*) of 28 June 1992, eRI, https://www.riigiteataja.ee/ert/act.jsp?id=633949, Art 25.
[80] Civil Procedure Act (*Tsiviilkohtumenetluse seadustik*) of 22 April 1998, eRT https://www.riigiteataja.ee/ert/act.jsp?id=782718 (1/9/1998), Art 4(1).
[81] State Liability Act (*Riigivastutuse seadus*) of 2 May 2001, eRT https://www.riigiteataja.ee/ert/act.jsp?id=783043 (01.01.2002).   [82] N 79 above, Art 7(1)–(3).

procedure for challenges provided for in the Taxation Act—see also paragraph 9.49 above.

9.82 Similarly, it may not be ruled out that customs' actions may be challenged as being unlawful and that damages may be claimed against the Estonian customs authorities (see para 9.49) for prejudices suffered by them as a result of the *ex officio* procedure accordingly to Article 4(1) of the Regulation. It must be noted however that whether or not an infringement has taken place invariably depends on the assessment of the right-holder invited to authenticate the goods suspected of being counterfeit or pirated goods.

Conclusion

9.83 Estonian Customs are making significant progress in applying border measures against goods infringing intellectual property rights, in particular by detaining bulky shipments of counterfeit and pirated goods. A recent case involving a shipment of counterfeit clothing that had arrived from China by rail is significant on this point, for the following reasons:

- The shipment was in external transit, and thus not intended for Estonia, but for Russia. Nevertheless, it was detained by Estonian Customs, in accordance with the Regulation.
- The quantity of infringing goods was enormous.
- By applying border measures against this shipment, the Estonian customs officials showed their determination, steadfastness, and efficiency, in resolving intellectual property infringement matters.

9.84 Having said that, although there are many cases where Estonian Customs have detained suspect goods and informed right-holders accordingly under the Regulation, many right-holders are not ready to take action for a 'small' quantity of goods. Determining what is to be considered as a 'small' quantity is relative, because what may be trivial for a multinational right-holder may, in fact, prove quite significant for the Estonian market. Many of the small traffickers of counterfeit goods are private persons, who carry small quantities of goods at a time, but the whole picture must be taken into consideration: 10 people importing 25 items each carry between them a significant quantity of counterfeits. Releasing 'small' quantities often disappoints customs officials and discourages their efforts to protect right-holders.

9.85 All in all, however, there is still only limited implementation of the provisions of the Regulation in Estonian practice to date. It is likely that the actual implementation will raise additional issues, which will need further examination in the future.

10

FINLAND

Bernt Juthström and Johanna Harsu

Introduction

Finland plays a special role in the fight against counterfeiting and pirated goods **10.01** due to its geographic location at the Russian border. The territory of Finland is increasingly used for transit to infiltrate both the European and Russian markets with illegal products. The approach of the national customs authorities to anti-counterfeiting measures has been very effective and Finnish Customs is internationally recognized as an authority that is highly motivated to reduce trade in infringing goods. They were awarded the Global Anti-Counterfeiting Award in 2002 for outstanding achievement by a public organization.

Community-wide regulation on anti-counterfeiting measures at the borders has **10.02** existed as supranational legislation in Finland as of its accession to the European Community on 1 January 1995.[1] Consequently, before the entry into force of the new Regulation (EC) No 1383/2003 on 1 July 2004 (the 'Regulation')[2] Finnish Customs had already employed its European legislation-based powers for almost 10 years.

The Regulation and its predecessor, together with the cooperative attitude of the **10.03** customs authorities, have substantially improved the potential for a right-holder to have counterfeit and pirated goods detained at the border prior to their entry into the Finnish market. Finnish Customs has, as of 1995, actively employed its powers in border measure matters and the annual number of counterfeit or

---

[1] Council Reg (EC) 3295/94 laying down measures to prohibit the release for free circulation, export, re-export, or entry for a suspensive procedure of counterfeit and pirated goods [1994] OJ L 341/8 (30.12.1994), subsequently amended by Council Reg (EC) 241/1999 ([1999] OJ L 27/1 (2.2.1999)) and Council Reg (EC) 806/2003 [2003] OJ L 122/1 (16.5.2003).
[2] Council Reg (EC) 1383/2003 concerning customs action against goods suspected of infringing certain intellectual property rights and the measures to be taken against goods found to have infringed such rights [2003] OJ L 196/7 (2.8.2003).

pirated goods detained or whose release was suspended has been considerable. For example, in 2002, Finnish Customs blocked approximately 3.6 million retail packages of counterfeit or pirated goods, with a market value of over EUR 25 million. In 2004, the market value of goods detained or whose release was suspended reached EUR 34 million.[3] The bulk of the consignments blocked so far have consisted of transit goods for the Russian market. However, the number of shipments imported into Finland has also increased in recent years.

10.04   Prior to Finland's accession to the European Community in 1995, Finnish Customs could, under the Finnish Trade Mark Act,[4] suspend goods infringing registered trade mark rights. The former Chapter 6(a) of the Trade Mark Act contained specific provisions on interim measures against imported goods. However, the interim seizure of goods required a seizure order by the District Court based on the right-holder's application for an interim measure. Border measures were limited to cases where the applicant's registered right could be easily evidenced and where the trade mark infringement was clear. In practice, action could only be taken against shipments that the right-holder knew of beforehand.

10.05   Applying for an interim measure before a court of law did not provide for sufficiently rapid and adequate protection for the right-holder. Moreover, Finnish Customs were not authorized to inform the right-holder of consignments suspected of containing counterfeit goods, even though the trade mark infringement would have been evident.[5] As a consequence, interim measures and action by Finnish Customs were seldom applied for. Chapter 6(a) of the Trade Mark Act was repealed in 1995,[6] after which, EC Regulation 3295/94 has been directly applied in trade mark infringement cases. After Finland's accession to the EU, the powers of Finnish Customs were further extended to cover other intellectual property rights as well.[7] In connection with the Trade Mark Act reform it was observed that maintaining two overlapping regimes on border measures might lead to conflicts of law, therefore national provisions on border measures have been kept to the minimum in anti-counterfeiting matters.[8] The Finnish Customs Act[9] was naturally amended in connection with the accession to the EU to enable national customs authorities to inform intellectual property right-holders of counterfeit or illicitly manufactured goods.[10] The Customs Act also designates the authority competent

---

[3]   http://www.tulli.fi/fi/04_Julkaisut/05_Tulliviesti/02_Poimittua/tulliviesti2tuotevaarennys03.jsp and http://europa.eu.int/comm/taxation_customs/ resources/documents/ finl_2003_en.pdf.

[4]   *Tavaramerkkilaki* [Trade Mark Act] 7/1964.

[5]   H Salmi, P Häkkänen, R Oesch, M Tommila, *Tavaramerkki* (1st edn) 161–162.

[6]   Act amending the Trade Mark Act 1699/1995.

[7]   Reg 3295/94 and the new Reg 1383/2003 also cover other intellectual property rights whereas the former Chapter 6(a) of the Trade Mark Act only concerned trade mark rights. In its original wording Reg 3295/94 covered merely trade marks, designs and copyrights, but it was later amended by EC Reg 241/1999 to also cover patent rights and supplementary protection certificates.

[8]   Government Bill HE 181/1995.   [9]   *Tullilaki* [Customs Act] 1466/1994.

[10]   *Tullilaki* [Customs Act] 1466/1994, s 25.

in anti-counterfeiting matters. The National Board of Customs (Enforcement and Audit Unit) is the authority that makes substantive decisions in this field.[11]

As the new Regulation on border measures is directly applicable law in Finland, only a limited number of amendments[12] to the national legislation have been required to enforce the new powers of Finnish Customs under the Regulation. However, if Finland also adopts the simplified procedure introduced in Article 11 of the Regulation, more profound amendments would be required. The Finnish Anti-Counterfeiting Group has actively advocated the introduction of a simplified procedure, but the initiative has encountered initial resistance from the Ministry of Justice. Representatives of the Ministry of Justice have held that the simplified procedure might be contrary to basic principles of constitutional law such as the right to a fair trial (that is, the right to be heard) and the constitutional protection of property. However, national legislation to implement the simplified procedure is currently being prepared by the Ministry of Finance and it is anticipated that the simplified procedure will be included in the reform of the Customs Act, and will be in force by 2006 at the latest. Another issue subject to discussion relates to Article 18, which requires the Member States to guarantee efficient and proportionate penalties. It is yet to be determined whether the current section 42 of the Customs Act on customs offences sufficiently secures the requirements set forth in Article 18 of the Regulation. It is anticipated that this question will also be addressed in connection with reform of the Customs Act. **10.06**

I. SUBJECT MATTER AND SCOPE OF THE NATIONAL LAW APPLYING THE REGULATION

A. Customs procedure for goods

Finnish Customs apply border measures to goods suspected of infringing intellectual property rights defined in the Regulation regardless of the nature of the shipment, that is, regardless of whether it is an import, export, re-exportation, external transit or transhipment.[13] However, according to official statistics, the **10.07**

---

[11] In its ruling in *Salamander AG v Industria de Calcados Kissol Ltd. and Centra Anstalt*, S 96/1154, (KKO:1997:72, 30 May 1997) the Finnish Supreme Court held that a court of law does not have the power to decide upon extending or terminating the suspension of counterfeit goods that have been detained or whose release has been suspended on the grounds of Reg (EC) 3295/94 by Finnish Customs.

[12] The amendments were mainly corrections to the references to relevant EC legislation.

[13] The scope of the trade mark right protection is defined in *Tavaramerkkilaki* [Trade Mark Act] 7/1964, s 4. The relationship between the former wording of this provision and Reg (EC) 3295/94 was not clear and the question of the interpretation of the national legislation was raised on several

majority of suspensions (66 per cent of cases) have occurred in connection with transit-shipments.[14]

B. Definition of infringing goods

10.08 In Finland there are no specific laws on counterfeiting and piracy. However, various acts on different intellectual property rights such as the Trade Mark Act, the Copyright Act, the Patent Act, and the Design Right Act, as discussed below, provide a comprehensive framework for dealing with counterfeit and pirated goods.

10.09 According to official figures, a large percentage of Finnish Customs' interventions (78 per cent of cases)[15] relate to counterfeit goods, that is, goods suspected of infringing trade mark rights. Compared to other types of infringements, trade mark infringements are easier to detect and monitor than infringements of other intellectual property rights covered by the Regulation. According to statistics, the second largest type of interventions (22 per cent of cases) relate to pirated goods.[16] As official statistics indicate, the remaining types of infringements are of less significance in terms of the number of cases reported. The main reason for this is that in practice it is very difficult for Finnish Customs to assess whether the goods suspended infringe these types of rights. Moreover, risk-analysis strategies may be more difficult to apply to such shipments. Although there have been no reported border measures concerning patents or supplementary protection certificates, we are aware of some cases relating to this third category in which Finnish Customs have accepted the requested applications for customs action.

occasions in Finnish legal practice. It was unclear whether s 4 of the former Trade Mark Act covered transit consignments, where the goods shipped via Finland bore symbols allegedly infringing trade mark rights protected in Finland. The scope of the former s 4 of the Trade Mark Act was finally challenged before the Supreme Court in *Salamander AG v Industria de Calcados Kissol Ltd and Centra Anstalt* S 96/1154 (KKO:1997:72, 30 May 1997). The defendants claimed that the Finnish Trade Mark Act was not applicable as the boots and packages infringing Salamander AG's registered trade mark rights were only transited and not imported into Finland. The Supreme Court confirmed that transit cases also fall within the scope of the exclusive rights of the trade mark holder. After this case there was pressure to clarify the wording of the Trade Mark Act in this respect and, partly based on successful lobbying by the Finnish Anti-Counterfeiting Group, the Trade Mark Act was finally amended and clarified in regard to transit cases, which are now explicitly covered by the Trade Mark Act (Government Bill HE 133/1999 and Act amending the Trade Mark Act 56/2000).

[14] European Commission (DG Taxation and Customs Union, TAXUD), Breakdown by number and percentages of customs or other procedures 2003, http://europa.eu.int/comm/taxation customs/ resources/ zdocuments/counterf_comm_2003_en.pdf. In 2002 the corresponding percentage was 73%, http://europa.eu.int/comm/taxation_customs/resources/documents/statistics_en_ 2002.pdf.

[15] European Commission (DG TAXUD), Breakdown by type of right covered 2003, (above, n 14). In 2002 the corresponding figure was 77%.

[16] European Commission (DG TAXUD), Breakdown by type of right covered in 2003. There has been no change to this figure compared to 2002. (above, n 14).

(1) Counterfeit goods

The concept of counterfeit goods is used in the Regulation to refer to goods or   **10.10**
packaging bearing a trade mark without the proper authorization of the right-
holder. The Trade Mark Act[17] constitutes the main legislative framework for
taking action against counterfeiters. As a result of the Trade Marks Directive,[18]
Finnish trade mark legislation is substantially harmonized with the rest of the
European Community. Moreover, the Trade Mark Act has also been amended to
reflect Finland's adherence to the Madrid Protocol on the International
Registration of Trade Marks and EU legislation on trade marks.[19]

Under the Finnish Trade Mark Act, an exclusive right to a trade mark, whether   **10.11**
acquired by registration or through establishment (cf below, para 10.17), means
that no one other than the holder of the trade mark, without proper consent, may
use in trade for their goods a symbol likely to be confused with that trade mark,
whether on the goods or on their packaging, in advertising or business documents,
or otherwise. Under section 4 of the Trade Mark Act, the provisions of the exclusive right are applicable irrespective of whether the goods are offered or intended to
be offered for sale in Finland or abroad, or are imported into Finnish territory to be
used, kept or stored for business purposes or to be forwarded to a third country.[20]

Therefore, if a symbol is likely to be confused with a trade mark protected under   **10.12**
the Trade Mark Act, the provisions concerning infringement apply. In general,
protection against unauthorized use is available only for goods identical or similar
to those which the trade mark refers to (s 6(1) of the Trade Mark Act). Irrespective
of the aforementioned, under section 6(2) of the Trade Mark Act the likelihood of
confusion of trade marks may be invoked if a symbol is widely known in Finland
and the use of another similar symbol would result in unjustified exploitation
of the distinctive power or goodwill of the earlier mark or would be detrimental
to the distinctive character or fame of the earlier trade symbol. Therefore a mark
with a prominent reputation can enjoy protection even beyond similarity of
goods (the so-called 'well-known doctrine').[21]

The definition of trade mark infringement under the Finnish Trade Mark Act seems   **10.13**
to be broader than that of counterfeit goods under Article 2(1)(a)(i) of the Regulation.

---

[17] *Tavaramerkkilaki* [Trade Mark Act] 7/1964. The following authors examine the protection of
trade marks under Finnish law in more detail: H Salmi, P Häkkänen, R Oesch, M Tommila,
Tavaramerkki (1st edn). The Trade Mark Act was partly reformed in preparation for Finland's adherence to the EEA Agreement (1 January 1994) and Finland's accession to the EU (1 January 1995).
[18] First Council Directive (EEC) 89/104 to Approximate the Laws of the Member States
Relating to Trade Marks [1989] OJ L 40/1.
[19] Protocol relating to the Madrid Agreement concerning the International Registration of
Marks, adopted at Madrid on 27 June 1989.
[20] The scope of the *Tavaramerkkilaki* [Trade Mark Act] 7/1964, s 4, ie its applicability to transit
cases, is also discussed in n 13 above.
[21] P-L Haarmann, *Immateriaalioikeuden oppikirja* (3rd edn) 209.

The latter only applies to a sign which is 'identical to a registered trade mark or which cannot be distinguished in its essential aspects' from such a trade mark. The Article explicitly covers the situations referred to in section 6(1) of the Trade Mark Act. However, under the Trade Mark Act, all signs similar to a registered trade mark also qualify as an infringement provided that a likelihood of confusion exists. Whereas the Regulation requires that the counterfeit sign be essentially similar to the registered mark and that counterfeit goods be 'of the same type' as those for which the mark is registered, it is sufficient under section 6(1) of the Trade Mark Act for the goods to be similar. Finally, the notion of taking unfair advantage of or being detrimental to a trade mark with a reputation is not mentioned in the Regulation, therefore it does not explicitly cover the situations referred to in section 6(2) of the Trade Mark Act (extension of the trade mark rights beyond the principle of speciality).

10.14   When applying the Regulation in practice—whether upon a right-holder's request or *ex officio*—Finnish Customs interprets Article 1(a)(i) broadly to also cover all types of infringements of well-known trade marks. The customs authorities do not only act against goods bearing a trade mark identical to the mark on which the border measures are based, but also against goods affixed with signs that are deemed confusingly similar. This includes visually and phonetically similar signs. Customs have, for example, detained t-shirts bearing the sign 'Adidos' as an infringement of the Adidas trade mark. Customs are also flexible when evaluating whether the suspect goods fall within the list of goods (and services) referred to in the trade mark registration. For example, the Finnish Customs authority has suspended a shipment of shoes bearing the 'Vogue' trade mark, which in Finland is a well-known trade mark registered for tights and stockings. This interpretation and practice of Finnish Customs has not yet been tried before the courts.

10.15   Finnish Customs also take measures against trade mark symbols, including logos, labels, stickers, instruction manuals or guarantee documents, and packaging material bearing a trade mark even if they have not yet been affixed to the product itself, but have been produced without the consent of the right-holder.[22]

10.16   It is unclear as to what extent exclusive trade mark rights include the right to prohibit the use of the mark where it is necessary to indicate the intended purpose of a product, in particular, with regard to accessories or spare parts. At least in cases where the reference is contrary to fair trade practice and where the reference to the trade mark is made more prominently than needed, the right to prohibit such use prevails.[23] This spare part provision of the Trade Mark Act may in some cases cause difficulties

---

[22] For example, in 1999 the customs authorities detained a large quantity of counterfeit labels for teabags. Similarly, Finnish Customs have also taken action against 'red tabs' (which were to be affixed to jeans) that were deemed to infringe Levi Strauss' trade mark rights.

[23] *Tavaramerkkilaki* [Trade Mark Act] 7/1964, s 4(2), provides that where such reference creates the impression that the goods originate from the same company, such use may be prohibited by the right-holder.

when assessing whether or not an infringement of trade mark rights has occurred, for example, in cases where it is mentioned that the goods are 'compatible' with another manufacturer's products protected by a registered trade mark. The scope of trade mark protection in these kinds of situations is currently under review in a case pending before the Supreme Court of Finland. As the case involves the interpretation of Community law,[24] the Supreme Court has addressed this question to the European Court of Justice and requested a preliminary ruling.[25] So far it has been unclear as to what extent a spare part manufacturer may refer to another manufacturer's trade mark in connection with marketing of spare parts and accessories for the other manufacturer's products. However, unauthorized use may occur if reference is made to someone else's trade mark when marketing spare parts or other goods suited for use with someone else's goods in a manner likely to create the impression that such goods are original or that the proprietor of the trade mark has consented to the use of the mark. Examples of these types of products regularly retained by Finnish Customs are casings, batteries and other accessories for mobile phones. In these cases the right-holder normally enjoys protection against the infringing products on the basis of registered design rights but in cases where no design registration exists, the right-holder may choose to rely on his trade mark rights and the so-called spare part provision of the Trade Mark Act.

According to the exact wording of the Regulation, an action may be based on a **10.17** validly registered trade mark.[26] An application for action may, according to the current practice of Finnish Customs, also be based on a trade mark application or an unregistered trade mark protected through establishment. Under section 2(2) of the Trade Mark Act, a trade mark is deemed established if it has become generally known to the relevant business community or consumer circles in Finland as a special symbol of the proprietor's goods. Although there is no national legislation extending the scope of the Regulation to mere trade mark applications or established trade marks, the customs authorities' interpretation of the subject matter is that the application can also be based on an application or a trade mark protected through establishment.

(2) Pirated goods

According to the Regulation, pirated goods refer to goods that are or contain **10.18** copies made without the consent of the holder of a copyright or a related right or a design right. According to the statistics, the second largest category of border actions in Finland are based on a copyright or a related right (that is, 22 per cent

---

[24] Art 6(c)(i) of the Trade Mark Directive.

[25] C-228/03 *The Gillette Company and The Gillette Company Finland Oy v La Laboratories Ltd* [2003] and pending Finnish Supreme Court case S 2001 / 650, *The Gillette Company and The Gillette Company Finland Oy v La Laboratories Ltd.*   [26] Reg 1383/2003, Art 2(1)(a)(i).

of all border measures taken in 2003 on the basis of the Regulation). Many of these interventions relate to audiovisual recordings and software. Less than 1 per cent of the border measures is based on a design infringement. Most of the products retained on the basis of design rights are accessories for mobile phones.[27]

10.19   Section 2 of the Finnish Copyright Act[28] defines the scope of protection of a copyright. The rights protected under the Copyright Act can be divided into moral and economic rights. The latter include rights such as exclusive distribution and reproduction rights. These rights are defined under the Copyright Act as the rights of authors to dispose of their works by reproducing copies and making them available to the public in an unaltered or altered form, in the form of a translation or modification, or by using another production method. The author's economic rights are subject to many exceptions.

10.20   Performing artists are also given the right under the Copyright Act[29] to stop certain forms of unauthorized exploitation of their live performances, such as a concert or other live recordings. Performing artists are given rights to control the recording or broadcast of a live performance as well as rights to control the reproduction, distribution, rental and lending of copies of their performance.[30] Items such as CDs, videos, and DVDs that include unauthorized recordings of live performances may infringe the performer's performance right.

10.21   A design right is an industrial property right where the subject of protection is merely the exterior appearance of the products and not, for example, the technological elements. The Finnish Act on Design Rights[31] provides for protection of industrial designs involving functional elements, aesthetic designs, and ornaments. In contrast with copyright (where the work must be original to enjoy protection), a design right protects the appearance of a product regardless of whether the appearance is determined by aesthetic or practical considerations. Protection under the Design Right Act is obtained by registration.

10.22   Under section 5(a) of the Design Right Act, the owner of a design right may oppose the use of a product that does not differ substantially from the design or includes

---

[27] European Commission (DG TAXUD), Breakdown by type of right covered in 2003, http://europa.eu.int/comm/taxation_customs/resources/documents/counterf_comm_2003_en.pdf.
[28] *Tekijänoikeuslaki* [Copyright Act] 404/1961, as amended. The scope of sanctions set forth in the Copyright Act will be amended to criminalize certain import situations. This is stated in the Government Bill HE 28/2004 concerning the Copyright Act reform designed to implement Parliament and Council Directive (EC) 2001/29 on the harmonization of certain aspects of copyright and related rights in the information society [2001] OJ L 167/10.
[29] The scope of protection of related rights is defined in Chapter 5 of the *Tekijänoikeuslaki* [Copyright Act] 404/1961.   [30] P-L Haarmann, *Tekijänoikeus ja lähioikeudet*, (1st edn).
[31] *Mallioikeuslaki* [Design Right Act] 221/1971. The Act was originally prepared in close cooperation with the other Nordic Countries. The Design Right Act was amended on 1 August 2002 to implement Council and Parliament Directive (EC) 98/71 of 13 October 1998 on the legal protection of designs OJ L 289/28. On 1 March 2003 the Design Right Act was further amended to implement Council Reg (EC) 6/2002 on Community designs [2002] OJ L 3/1.

an element not substantially different from the design. In assessing the scope of protection and the individual character of the design, the degree of the designer's freedom to develop his design shall be taken into consideration. The design right provides for the exclusive right of the holder to exploit the design in the course of trade by manufacturing, supplying, marketing, selling, distributing, renting, importing, exporting, exposing, using or detaining the product for those purposes.

There may be a theoretical discrepancy between the explicit wording of the **10.23** Regulation and the Finnish copyright and design right legislation. The Regulation refers to the concept of 'copies', while the copyright-holder's exclusive right under national legislation includes the concept of 'reproduction' that also covers adaptations and translations. Furthermore, under the Finnish Design Right Act, all designs which have an 'identical appearance' to the registered design or 'which do not produce on the informed user a different overall impression' are regarded as infringing.[32] Accordingly, the scope of border measures under the Regulation may not cover all situations where protection against infringement may be obtained under national intellectual property legislation.

The Finnish customs authority has in practice adopted a broad approach to **10.24** border measures on pirated goods. As a rule, the definition of 'goods which are or contain copies' is considered to include goods entirely or partially similar to those protected by a copyright, related right, or design right. However, Finnish Customs may in practice consult another neutral body, such as the Copyright Council[33] when the scope of the copyright relied on is not clear.

(3) Goods infringing other intellectual property rights

Goods infringing a patent or a supplementary protection certificate

Under the Regulation, it is also possible to base an application for border measures **10.25** on patent rights, supplementary protection certificates, national plant variety rights, or national designations of origin or geographical indication. Official statistics do not mention any customs action taken on the basis of the aforementioned rights. One explanation for this is that the majority of cases involving, for example, counterfeit medicines, such as counterfeit VIAGRA, are categorized in the official statistics as trade mark infringement cases, due to the fact that counterfeit pharmaceuticals often also infringe the relevant trade mark.[34] Secondly, it

---

[32] *Mallioikeuslaki* [Design Right Act] 221/1971, s 3.

[33] The Finnish government appoints a Copyright Council every three years to assist the Ministry of Education in copyright matters and to issue opinions on the application of the Copyright Act.

[34] Eg, in 2002 Finnish Customs retained a shipment on its way to Russia containing a 34kg consignment of pharmaceutical products under the name Venegra, which were deemed to be counterfeit Viagra products.

may be more difficult in practice to target standard risk analyses at more complex products such as pharmaceuticals and, in such cases, customs actions may not be as efficient as in the case of other types of infringements. It is likely that the indicator triggering the customs action is the trade mark rather than, for example, the active ingredient of the pharmaceutical (protected by a patent or a supplementary protection certificate) indicated in the risk analysis. Moreover, these types of intellectual property rights require a higher level of expertise, which may not be available to the customs authority.

10.26   Under the Finnish Patent Act,[35] a person (or his successor in title) who has made an invention that meets the requirements of novelty and inventive step and is capable of industrial application, is entitled to obtain a patent for that invention and therefore to acquire the exclusive right to exploit it commercially. Imports of patent-protected products also fall within the scope of the exclusive rights of the proprietor.[36] A patent may also be granted under Finnish law for the product of a nutritional or medical substance.

10.27   A supplementary protection certificate ('SPC') is a certificate that can be issued to grant extended protection for patents that relate to pharmaceutical or plant protection products.[37] As patented products of this type cannot be marketed until government authorities have conducted safety tests and issued a marketing authorization, the introduction of such products can be delayed for years during which the normal 20-year term of patent protection continues to run. As this can work unfairly for the owner of such a patent, a certificate can be issued by the National Board of Patents and Registration to extend the normal 20 years of protection by an additional five years.

Goods infringing a national plant variety right

10.28   Plant variety rights are a form of registered intellectual property rights, like patents, but designed for plant varieties of which material is produced and commercialized. According to the Act on the Rights of Plant Breeders,[38] the breeder of a plant may, through registration, obtain protection against commercial exploitation through production, marketing, export and import, of a plant, if the plant meets the requirements of novelty, distinctiveness, uniformity and stability. The protection granted by registration is limited to the territory of Finland. Private use and use for non-commercial purposes (for example, experimental purposes) does not fall within the scope of protection.

---

[35] *Patenttilaki* [Patent Act] 550/1967.
[36] The scope of patent protection in Finland has recently been discussed in legal literature by R Oesch and H Pihlajamaa, *Patenttioikeus* (1st edn) 80–81.
[37] *Patenttilaki* [Patent Act] 550/1967, Chapter 9(a).
[38] *Laki kasvinjalostajanoikeudesta* [Act on the Rights of Plant Breeders] 789/1992.

Goods infringing a national designation of origin or a geographical indication

According to Article 1(a)(c)(iv) and 1(a)(c)(v) of the Regulation, it is also possible **10.29** to file an application for customs action regarding goods that are suspected of infringing a national designation of origin or a geographical indication. Protected designation of origin ('PDO') and protected geographical indication ('PGI') are classifications defined in EC legislation to protect regional food products. When a product acquires a reputation that goes beyond national borders it can find itself in a market where products purport to be the genuine article and take the same name. This unfair competition not only discourages producers but also misleads consumers. There are currently no specific national rules concerning PDOs and PGIs in Finland. We are not aware of any border measures taken by Finnish Customs, where an infringement of the aforementioned rights would have been invoked.

(4) Moulds and matrices

Under Article 2(3) of the Regulation, customs actions can be applied to moulds and **10.30** matrices that are 'specifically designed or adapted for the manufacture of infringing goods', if the relevant piece of national legislation allows the right-holder to take action against these goods. In Finland, the holder of a trade mark,[39] a design right,[40] a patent,[41] and a copyright or a related right[42] is by law entitled to demand confiscation and, in certain cases, the destruction of moulds and matrices, provided that the infringing act meets the requirements set forth in the relevant legislation.

C. Goods excluded by the Regulation

(1) Parallel imported goods

In Finland, there is no national legislation allowing customs to apply border meas- **10.31** ures to parallel imported goods. If a right-holder recognizes that the goods detained by customs are genuine goods imported from outside the European Community, it will not be entitled to apply for customs action under the Regulation. Likewise, as right-holders are prevented from using information provided to them by customs authorities for purposes other than those permitted by the Regulation,[43] they

---

[39] *Tavaramerkkilaki* [Trade Mark Act] 7/1964, s 41.
[40] *Mallioikeuslaki* [Design Right Act] 221/1971, s 5(a), which stipulates, however, that the purpose of such products must be commercial.
[41] *Patenttilaki* [Patent Act] 550/1967, s 3. However, the applicability of this provision requires the intended use to be commercial by nature.
[42] *Tekijänoikeuslaki* [Copyright Act] 404/1961, s 58.
[43] Reg 1383/2003, Art 12. This was also confirmed by the ECJ in case C-223/98 *Adidas AG v Kammarrätten I Stockholm* [1998] ECR I-7081.

would in principle also not be able to rely on alternative remedies under national law to act against such infringements at the borders unless they have obtained the necessary information regarding the suspect consignment from other sources.

(2) Goods manufactured under conditions other than those agreed with the right-holder

10.32 National legislation in Finland does not extend border measures to goods manufactured under conditions other than those agreed upon between, for example, the right-holder and a licencee. It would not be practical for the customs authorities to monitor compliance with licence terms and in any case it is not their duty to do so.

(3) Goods contained in travellers' personal baggage

10.33 Although Finnish Customs regularly check travellers' personal baggage, the main target of such investigations is rarely counterfeit goods. Carrying several items of the same kind or several sizes of the same item would certainly be taken into account when considering the 'material indication of the existence of commercial traffic' under Article 3(2) of the Regulation.[44] As a rule, right-holders are not particularly interested in small amounts of counterfeit or pirated products imported by travellers in their personal baggage. However, there are some exceptions and the music industry in particular has been relatively active in relying on customs to monitor imports of pirated CDs.

II. APPLICATION FOR ACTION BY THE CUSTOMS AUTHORITIES

A. Measures prior to an application for action by the customs authorities ('*ex officio* measures')

10.34 Finnish Customs regularly employ their *ex officio* powers provided under Article 4 of the Regulation. Already under the former regime, customs had the power to

---

[44] In case R 2001/983 (KKO 2003:136 22 December 2003), the Supreme Court of Finland deemed that the import of 80 illicitly manufactured CDs and 20 Sony PlayStation games did not fall within the scope of 'non-commercial nature' or private use. The Court stated that the quantity

act on their own initiative, if they detected goods which they deemed were infringing protected intellectual property rights. According to Regulation 3295/94 (as amended), customs could only detain goods on their own initiative if it appeared 'evident' that the goods were infringing. Now the standard has been lowered so that customs authorities can detain goods provided they have 'sufficient grounds for suspecting' that the goods are infringing. However, it is expected that this reform will not change the current practices in Finland and that the number of *ex officio* measures will continue to stay at a steady level. The authorities interpret the requirement of Article 4 broadly and goods are in practice detained by customs whenever there is merely a slight doubt about their genuine character, to give the right-holder an opportunity to examine the goods and, if necessary, to file an action.

Most *ex officio* interventions relate to traffic coming from, or going to countries **10.35** rated 'high-risk'. As it is not possible to control all traffic, Finnish Customs have developed a 'risk analysis' system[45] to concentrate actions on specific types of shipments. Certain alarm signals in transport documentation trigger the attention of the customs authorities, such as unusual transportation routes and mixed shipments. *Ex officio* measures are also typically initiated in connection with cases where the actual suspension of the whole shipment is based on a third party's application, and where the shipment is, after closer examination, also found to contain other types of products infringing other parties' intellectual property rights, of which no applications have yet been filed.

When Finnish Customs uncover a suspect shipment, they detain the goods and **10.36** inform the right-holder and the declarant or holder of the goods. Normally, customs would first notify the right-holder or his Finnish representative by telephone, fax, or e-mail about the number and characteristics of the goods and the nature of the infringement. Moreover, the authorities usually send digital pictures of a selection of the suspected goods to the right-holder. In any event, the right-holder will upon request be given an opportunity to inspect the goods, either at the customs office or based on the samples sent by customs to the right-holder or his representative. Finnish Customs have adopted a pragmatic and informal approach to informing right-holders of suspected shipments.

---

of products imported considerably exceeded what was usually regarded as 'private use'. Another argument presented by the Supreme Court related to the fact that the defendant had imported several CDs and games of a similar kind. The Court therefore deemed that it was not likely that the products were imported into Finland for the defendant's own private use, but that the defendant had imported the goods to be distributed to the public. Consequently, the defendant was found guilty of a copyright offence as defined in the Copyright Act, s 56(a).

45 This includes the electronic 'Sele'-database.

B. The lodging and processing of applications for customs action

(1) Persons entitled to file an application for action

Definition of 'right-holders' under the Regulation

10.37 According to Article 2(2) of the Regulation, an application for action can be filed by a right-holder or 'any other person authorized to use the intellectual property right or a representative of the right-holder or authorized user'. According to the present practice of the Finnish Customs authorities, persons other than the right-holder himself, such as licensees, are allowed to file an application only if they have been explicitly authorized to do so. The registration of an exclusive licence with the Trade Mark Register of the National Board of Patents and Registration does not per se entitle the licensee to file an application. In practice, Finnish Customs have never had to apply the broad definition of 'any other person authorized to use the intellectual property right', as, to date all applications for action have been filed by owners of intellectual property rights or their duly authorized representatives.

10.38 Under Finnish law and practice, the concept of 'representative of the right-holder or authorized user' as defined in Article 2(2)(b) of the Regulation includes natural and legal persons authorized to act on behalf of the right-holder such as attorneys, patent and trade mark agents and collective management societies. Licensees, distributors and commercial agents would only fall under this definition of an authorized user provided they have an explicit authorization to act on behalf of the right-holder before customs.

Proof of entitlement to file an application for action

For right-holders stricto sensu

10.39 Under Finnish law and practice, the proprietor of an intellectual property right can prove his right on the basis of the following documents:

- For a registered trade mark, design right, patent, supplementary protection certificate, or a plant variety right, written evidence that the right has been registered by the relevant office: this may include original registration certificates or certified copies, but Finnish Customs will also be satisfied merely with a copy of the certificate or the official registration publication or printouts of official databases.[46] In Finland the application for action can also be based solely on an application for an industrial property right.

- For a copyright, a related right, or an unregistered trademark or 'Community' design, any evidence establishing that the applicant for customs action is the

---

[46] The Finnish customs authorities do not accept extracts from private databases as evidence.

actual owner of the right is sufficient. In Finland this includes any document evidencing the ownership of the rights vested in the work. However, customs may want to consult a neutral third party, such as the Copyright Council in copyright matters, on the merits of the evidence submitted prior to rendering its decision on the application for border measures.

- For protected designations of origin, protected geographical indications, and geographical designations the evidence to be submitted consists of two mandatory elements, that is, proof that the applicant is either the individual producer or a group producer and proof that the right has been registered.

For persons authorized to use the right

Persons authorized to use the right within the meaning of Article 2(2)(a) of the **10.40** Regulation will also have to submit as additional proof a document evidencing such authorization. The mere registration of an exclusive licence with the trademark register kept by the Finnish National Board of Patents and Registration[47] does not suffice as evidence of an authorization to act before customs, so accordingly, the licensee needs to provide customs with a separate, explicit authorization document.

For representatives

The representative of the right-holder or any other person authorized to use the **10.41** right will have to provide customs with their authorization to act.[48] Finnish Customs accept a power of attorney form duly executed by the right-holder granting a mandate to the representative. Notarization of such a document is not required. Nonetheless, the original power of attorney document must be submitted.

There is no nationality requirement for presentation before the Finnish customs **10.42** authority. Foreign representatives or right-holders can therefore directly communicate with Finnish Customs, both in the case of national and 'Community' applications for action. However, customs will expect the representatives to respond to customs communications without delay and in one of the national languages (Finnish or Swedish) and to be in a position to appear in person if required. Therefore it is advisable to appoint a local representative. Furthermore, if civil or criminal proceedings are later instituted, it is then, for practical reasons, necessary to appoint a local representative (or at least a person with the requisite language skills and knowledge of the local legal system).

---

[47] The registration of a licence is not required by Finnish legislation and the validity of a licence is not subject to registration.
[48] Commission Reg (EC) No 1891/2004 of 21 October 2004 laying down provisions for the implementation of Council Reg (EC) No 1383/2003 concerning customs action against goods suspected of infringing certain intellectual property rights and the measures to be taken against goods found to have infringed such rights, OJ [2004] L 328/16 (30.10.2004), Art 2(3).

10.43 According to the Finnish Customs' interpretation of Article 6 of the Regulation and the wording of the Implementing Regulation 1891/2004, the representative of the right-holder may sign the declaration referred to in Article 6. Under Finnish Customs' practice, the representative is therefore, in principle, allowed to sign the declaration on behalf of his client provided that the representative has also been duly authorized to sign the declaration.

(2) Competent customs department and formal requirements

Competent customs department

10.44 In Finland the authority competent to process applications for action is the National Board of Customs (Enforcement Department).

National Board of Customs (*Tullihallitus*)
Enforcement Department (*Valvontaosasto*)
Box 512 (*PL 512*)
FI-00101 Helsinki
Tel: +358 (0)20 492 27 48
Fax: +358 (0)20 492 2669
Website: www.tulli.fi

Form of the application for action

10.45 In Finland, an application for action can, in addition to physical delivery, be filed via fax or e-mail, but a confirmation copy has to be sent by regular or registered mail in all cases, as electronic signature and data interchange systems are not yet in use in Finland. The original version of the application for action shall contain the original declaration under Article 6 of the Regulation and, if a representative files the application for action, the original power of attorney.

10.46 In accordance with Article 3(3) of the Implementing Regulation 1891/2004, the application for action must be submitted in two copies. However, in some cases it might be useful to submit several copies for the different customs offices in order to speed up the risk analysis, especially when the application contains colour pictures. It is recommended that the documents also be provided in electronic format (such as CD-R), when the application contains many exhibits or colour pictures.

Language requirements

10.47 Finland is a bilingual country with two official languages, Finnish and Swedish.[49] Finnish Customs normally require the application for action to be filed in either Finnish or Swedish. However, Finnish Customs are also prepared to process

---

[49] *Perustuslaki* [Constitution] 731/1999, s 17, and *Kielilaki* [Language Act] 731/1999, s 17.

'Community' applications for actions filed in English. Similarly, the exhibits to the application should be filed in one of the national languages. As a rule, all supporting documents provided to customs should be translated into Finnish or Swedish. However, customs often also accept enclosures (for example, brochures and technical documents) even if submitted in English.

(3) *Requirements regarding the contents of the application for action*

The quality and nature of the information disclosed directly affects the effectiveness of customs actions. For customs to be able to make the correct risk analysis and identify the relevant factors that would trigger customs actions, right-holders are advised to provide customs with the most detailed information possible on the counterfeiting problem. The sheer volume of goods that enter Finland each day means that customs can only check a small percentage of goods. Once the application has been filed, it is important to follow it up to ensure efficient monitoring of counterfeit shipments. Finnish Customs also welcome the opportunity to meet with intellectual property right-holders to receive training and further information that will help officers at borders to identify and take effective action to prevent importation of goods that infringe intellectual property rights. The right-holder is advised to be vigilant to ensure that customs notices are up to date and that customs are provided with relevant information about the activities of known counterfeiters. **10.48**

Mandatory information

Under Finnish law and practice, there are no specific requirements for the mandatory information to be submitted to customs under Article 5(5) of the Regulation. However, it is advisable for the technical description of the goods to be detailed enough to allow customs to identify suspect goods. In practice, identifying the expected customs tariff number of the consignments allegedly infringing the right-holder's protected rights, improves the allocation of border measures to the right target. The same applies to information on the type and pattern of fraud. **10.49**

Optional information

Although there are no particular requirements or rules in Finland regarding other information that may be submitted in connection with the application for action, right-holders are advised to provide all information which qualifies as optional under Article 5(5) of the Regulation in order to facilitate border control. Disclosing as much information as possible is naturally in the right-holder's interest. The right-holder is also advised to provide information on authorized and unauthorized traders, especially the Business ID numbers of known infringing companies. This is not a legal requirement, but as a practical matter this helps **10.50** customs put together a profile of infringers and target suspect goods more effectively. Moreover, the customs authorities always have the right to request additional information should the need arise.

Additional information specific to the type of intellectual property right referred to in the application

10.51   There is no specific legislation or practice on the additional information which should be provided to Finnish Customs under Article 5(6) of the Regulation. However, it is recommended that holders of intellectual property rights which involve technical aspects, such as patents, provide customs with specific information on the scope of protection of their rights for the purposes of focusing the risk analysis on the relevant characteristics of shipments likely to contain counterfeit goods.

(4)   *Processing and acceptance of the application for action*

10.52   Finnish Customs process the application for action within the term of 30 working days as set forth in the Regulation. If there are any unanswered questions, the right-holder will be requested to amend the application. The decision granting the border measure that has been applied for is usually valid for one year. The right-holder may naturally limit its application to a shorter period for any reason, except for 'Community' applications for action, where the decision is valid for at least one year in all cases.

10.53   According to Finnish Customs, no application for action has ever been refused in Finland. If Finnish Customs refuse an application for some reason, an administrative review of this type of administrative decision is possible under section 7 of the Act on Administrative Judicial Proceedings before the Administrative Court of Helsinki.[50]   A decision by the Administrative Court may be further appealed to the Supreme Administrative Court, if leave of appeal is granted.[51]

(5)   *'Community' applications for action*

Processing of 'Community' applications for action filed with Finnish Customs

10.54   There are no specific national provisions on the processing of 'Community' applications by Finnish Customs under Article 5(4) of the Regulation. It is recommended that right-holders who wish to file 'Community' applications for action

---

[50]   *Tullilaki* [Customs Act] 1466/1994, s 37.
[51]   *Hallintolainkäyttölaki* [Law on Application of Administrative Law] 586/1996, s 13.

through the Finnish Customs submit the application form either in one of the national languages or in English. For practical reasons, it is also advisable to provide the customs authorities with the relevant number of copies of the application and the exhibits to be forwarded to all the customs offices competent in the other designated countries (in English). To facilitate further processing of the documentation it may also be useful to submit these copies in electronic format (CD-R), especially if the application contains several exhibits or if they contain colour pictures.

Processing of 'Community' applications designating Finland

Finnish Customs have adopted a liberal approach to applications for action designating Finland. Essentially, Finnish Customs only execute the application in Finland and informs the local customs offices of the contents thereof. No thorough formal examination will be performed, as the admissibility of the application has already been reviewed by a competent authority in another EU Member State. Furthermore, it is unlikely that the national authorities in the designated country would even have the powers to review the original decision.   **10.55**

There are no specific language requirements regarding Community-wide applications designating Finland. The administrative and technical contact persons nominated in the application do not have to be domiciled in Finland. Finnish Customs will in practice process applications filed in English in addition to those filed in the national official languages. They may also accept the application form in any official language of the EU as the form is the same in every language. However, it is recommended that the application form be completed in English, Finnish, or Swedish. For practical reasons, the exhibits should also preferably be provided either in English, Finnish, or Swedish.   **10.56**

III. CONDITIONS GOVERNING ACTION BY CUSTOMS AUTHORITIES AND BY THE AUTHORITIES COMPETENT TO DETERMINE WHETHER GOODS INFRINGE AN INTELLECTUAL PROPERTY RIGHT

After approving the application for action, Finnish Customs will monitor the flow of goods to detect goods suspected of infringing intellectual property rights referred to in the application. If a shipment suspected of containing infringing goods is retained by Customs, the right-holder shall, according to the provisions   **10.57** of the Regulation, institute legal proceedings to have the infringement confirmed. However, in practice, the majority of customs border measure cases have, to date, been settled amicably between the parties prior to commencing (civil or criminal) proceedings. Accordingly, most of the shipments of counterfeit and pirated goods blocked by customs are destroyed on the basis of settlements between the counterfeiter and the right-holder and not on the basis of destruction orders obtained from the court.

A. Conditions governing action by customs authorities

(1) Factual background

10.58   A substantial proportion of the counterfeit and pirated goods that enter Finnish territory arrive through the customs offices located in the capital city of Helsinki, that is, (1) Helsinki-Vantaa Airport (air transport); (2) the Port of Helsinki (sea transport); and (3) Metsälä Customs (road transport). With regard to goods that are intended for transit through Finland, the most relevant customs offices are those in the cities of Kotka and Hamina, and Vaalimaa customs office at the crossing point on the Finnish-Russian border. Vaalimaa has become increasingly important mainly due to its new X-ray facilities for the scanning of trucks. Consignments from other customs offices are often sent to Vaalimaa for X-ray examinations without having to unload the shipment. Finnish Customs will soon put into use two mobile X-ray facilities which will further increase customs' ability to detect counterfeit and pirated goods.

(2) Notification of customs intervention

10.59   When a Finnish customs office encounters goods that are suspected of infringing an intellectual property right referred to in Article 2(1) of the Regulation, it suspends the release of those goods or detains them. The customs office concerned immediately notifies the declarant or the holder of the goods, if known.

10.60   If the relevant right-holder has not yet filed an application, or where no decision regarding such application has been rendered, the period of three working days set forth in Article 4 of the Regulation, during which the customs office is allowed to suspend release of the goods, is calculated from the notification to the right-holder, as provided by Article 5, second indent, of EC Regulation 1891/2004. The detention of the goods or suspension of their release will then be upheld upon filing of an application in accordance with Article 5 of the Regulation.

10.61   Finnish Customs usually notify the right-holder or his representative of the nature of the goods suspended by telephone, fax, and/or e-mail. At this point, Finnish

Customs also usually send digital pictures by e-mail of a selection of the suspected goods to the right-holder or his representative to enable preliminary assessment of the infringement.

(3) Information to be provided by customs to the right-holder before the latter confirms the infringing nature of the goods

Section 25 of the Finnish Customs Act stipulates that Finnish Customs are, as a **10.62** rule, obliged to inform the right-holder of the suspension in accordance with the provisions of the Regulation. Customs shall also under certain conditions disclose additional information to the right-holder. The new Regulation appears to have widened the scope of information to be disclosed to the right-holder at his request, (that is, the actual or estimated quantity and nature of the goods, country of origin and/or destination, and the names and addresses of the entity sending the goods and the parties to whom the goods are addressed) compared to the previous Regulation. Upon closer examination, however, the amendment of the rules on disclosure of information (Articles 4, 9(2) and 9(3) of the new Regulation) has not brought about any major changes as it was previously possible for right-holders to obtain all necessary information for the purposes of establishing whether an intellectual property right had been infringed, and, where necessary, of initiating legal proceedings. If the border measures are based on an application, Finnish Customs are able to disclose more comprehensive information to the right-holder than in *ex officio* cases. In practice, all relevant information defined in the Regulation will be disclosed by Finnish Customs to the right-holder concerned.[52] However, the right to disclosure is always subject to national provisions on the protection of personal data, commercial and industrial secrets and professional and administrative confidentiality.[53] Consequently, a commercial secret, such as pricing, is never disclosed by Finnish Customs at this stage.

(4) Inspection of the suspected goods

Once the right-holder and his representative are notified that border measures **10.63** will be taken, they are given the opportunity to inspect the goods. In practice, the 10-day period (which may be extended once) set forth in Article 13 of the

---

[52] See also case C-223/98 *Adidas AG v Kammarrätten I Stockholm* [1998] ECR I-7081, where the European Court of Justice held that Reg 3295/94 precluded a rule of national law under which the identity of declarants or consignees of imported counterfeit goods may not be disclosed to the trade mark holder whose rights have been infringed.

[53] Special provisions on the maintenance of confidentiality are included in *Tullilaki* [Customs Act] 1466/1994, s 47a and in *Laki viranomaisten toiminnan julkisuudesta* [Act on the Openness in the Activities of Public Authorities] 21.5.1999/621, s 24.

Regulation means that the investigations have to be completed rapidly in order to allow prompt commencement of the relevant proceedings under this provision. Customs officials are entitled to take representative samples of the goods and to deliver or send them to the right-holder at the latter's request. Finnish Customs officials also send digital pictures of the suspended goods upon request. The samples shall be returned to the relevant customs office on completion of the technical analysis and before the goods are released or their detention is ended. The issue of whether samples received from the customs offices may be used in court has not been addressed by Finnish case law. However, it is common practice for such samples to be used in the proceedings initiated as a result of the seizure.[54]

B. Simplified procedure allowing destruction of goods without the need to determine whether an intellectual property right has been infringed under national law

10.64 Article 11 of the Regulation providing for the so-called 'simplified procedure' has not yet been implemented in Finland. Currently, neither the Customs Act nor any other piece of legislation provides for a similar kind of procedure. As the simplified procedure would include an option for customs to destroy the goods without hearing the opposing party (based on their passivity in the matter), it is uncertain whether the provision will be implemented in Finland in its entirety as this kind of unilateral measure may conflict with the fundamental (constitutional) right to protection of property. Although national implementing legislation is currently being prepared, no major legislative steps have yet been taken.[55] Consequently, currently the only officially recognized proceedings resulting in the destruction of goods based on the passivity of the opposing party are regular court proceedings for the establishment of infringement. The court proceedings may be either civil or criminal.

10.65 However, normally, the voluntary abandonment of goods which will be destroyed will be agreed in a settlement, which will also include an undertaking by the infringer to refrain from further infringement and to compensate the intellectual property right-holder for his costs. This arrangement is time- and cost-effective since no further legal proceedings will be required. Already under the EC Regulation 3295/94 regime, Finnish Customs have agreed to the destruction of

---

[54] Although under Art 9(3), last indent, of the Regulation the samples must be returned to customs, Finnish Customs are flexible in this respect and, in practice, the samples may be in the right-holder's or his representative's possession until the examination of the merits of the case is complete.

[55] The Ministry of Finance is currently preparing the relevant legislation. The Finnish Anti-Counterfeiting Group has actively advocated the simplified procedure, which would in its view be justified and effective in cases where the infringers remain passive. The Group has prepared a draft bill on how the simplified procedure could work in practice and filed its first statement regarding the procedure to the Ministry of Finance on 10 December 2004.

counterfeit or pirated goods upon the infringer's consent. Such consent was normally given in settlements by and between the right-holder and the importer, declarant, or owner of the goods. Such agreements were filed with the Finnish Customs together with a request that they proceed with destruction. It is expected that this method of voluntary destruction of counterfeit and pirated goods will continue to be frequently used under the new regime as well. Settlement agreements usually stipulate that the infringer agrees to a voluntary destruction of the infringing goods at his own cost. The infringer also undertakes to compensate the right-holder for his legal costs and undertakes to desist from further infringing activities.

C. Conditions governing action by the authorities having jurisdiction to determine whether the goods infringe an intellectual property right

Under Article 13(1) of the Regulation, the right-holder is to notify the customs office within 10 working days of receipt of the notification of detention or suspension of release of the goods that proceedings have been initiated to determine whether an intellectual property right has been infringed. If no legal proceedings have been commenced, or the customs authorities are not provided with evidence that such proceedings have been initiated within that timeframe, the goods will be released. **10.66**

As an alternative to instituting legal proceedings, the right-holder may provide the customs office with a copy of the agreement referred to in Article 11(1) if the implementing national legislation concerning the simplified procedure has been enforced. As mentioned above, it is very common in Finland for the infringer to agree to a voluntary destruction of the goods within 10 working days. **10.67**

Article 13 of the Regulation provides for a possibility of extension of the term of 10 working days 'in appropriate cases'. Such an extension can be obtained provided the right-holder is able to give appropriate reasons why additional time is required. The Finnish customs authorities have always granted an extension if the request has been made in writing and proper grounds for the extension have been presented. The commencement of negotiations in view of a settlement has usually always been considered as constituting sufficient grounds for granting the extension. **10.68**

Remedies common to all intellectual property rights covered by the Regulation

Commencement of infringement proceedings on the merits, either civil or criminal, will qualify as 'proceedings seeking to determine whether an intellectual property right has been infringed' under national law for the purposes of **10.69**

Article 13(1) of the Regulation. It is doubtful whether the commencement of a mere interlocutory injunction would qualify as proceedings 'to determine whether an intellectual property right has been infringed under national law' as referred to in Article 13.

10.70 There are a number of options available in Finland for dealing with infringing goods that are blocked by customs. If the right-holder obtains evidence that a person is dealing in infringing goods, it is often recommended that a 'cease-and-desist' letter requesting undertakings and threatening damages be sent to the infringer.[56] In more serious cases, the right-holder may wish to institute civil or criminal proceedings without first giving the infringer an opportunity to admit liability and remedy the situation. In practice, civil proceedings may also be initiated against the freight forwarder in transit cases where the seller and purchaser of the infringing goods remain unknown. This principle is established by case law. In Finnish Supreme Court case 2002:119 the court held that in transit situations a local freight forwarder may only be summoned if the owner of the infringing goods (that is, the actual infringer) has not been identified. These proceedings against the freight forwarder may result in the destruction of the goods but the freight forwarders will not be held liable to compensate for the right-holder's legal or other costs in the matter.[57]

Remedies under criminal law

10.71 Certain serious infringements of intellectual property rights are criminalized in Finland and the infringer might in such cases face a fine or even imprisonment.[58] From the right-holder's perspective, the commencement of a criminal action may actually be a less expensive alternative to the commencement of a civil action because the case will be pursued by the Public prosecutor and the right-holder

---

[56] Sending an infringer a 'cease-and-desist' letter is often the first legal step, particularly where the number or value of the infringing items in question is relatively low and the cost of commencing legal proceedings is not justified. The aim of such a letter is to provide an opportunity for the infringer to admit liability and remedy the situation before either side has incurred significant legal costs. In practice, the higher the value of the goods in question, the less likely it is that a cease-and-desist letter will result in a quick resolution of the matter. The settlement agreement will usually stipulate inter alia that the infringer agrees to a voluntary destruction of the infringing goods at its own cost. The infringer shall also compensate the right-holder for the majority of its legal costs.

[57] Finnish Supreme Court, *Adidas Salomon AG v Scanrapid Oy and Raycom Shipping Ab* (KKO:2002:119, 20 December 2003).

[58] An offence against copyright is criminalized in *Rikoslaki* [Criminal Code] 19.12.1889/39, Chapter 49, s 1. To be regarded as an offence against copyright, the infringing act should include the intent to earn money or some other form of monetary consideration. Furthermore, the act should cause significant detriment or damage to the right-holder. Industrial property offences are criminalized in *Rikoslaki* [Criminal Code] 19.12.1889/39, Chapter 49, s 2. According to this provision an act is to be deemed an industrial property offence if it is in breach of the national Trade Mark Act, Patent Act, Design Right Act or Plant Breeders Act, and the act is also likely to cause significant financial damage to the right-holder.

does not play as active a role as in civil litigation. However, if the identity of the infringer cannot be verified or if the infringer can for other reasons not be reached for interrogation or other police investigation measures, the criminal investigations would normally be terminated. In such a case, the only option for the right-holder is to proceed by instituting a civil action. As mentioned above, Finnish territory is mainly used for transit purposes and the infringers are usually domiciled outside Finnish territory. This limits the local authorities' ability to successfully pursue criminal investigations in this type of matter.

If the right-holder chooses to institute criminal proceedings, it must provide **10.72** customs with evidence of the commencement of such proceedings in order to secure the detention of goods under Article 13 of the Regulation. This is typically done by providing customs with a copy of the request for an investigation filed with the relevant police or customs investigation authority. Once customs have received this evidence it will confirm the detention of the goods until a court decision has been obtained in the criminal proceedings. Customs will then deal with the goods in accordance with the orders made by the court.

Remedies under civil law

Individual statutory laws on intellectual property rights contain specific provisions **10.73** on infringement actions[59] Finnish courts have the power to grant injunctions and order the destruction of infringing products. They may also order the defendant to pay damages and legal costs to the right-holder. Injunctions, claims for destruction of infringing products, and damages may also be presented as civil claims in connection with criminal proceedings.

If the right-holder chooses to commence civil proceedings, Finnish Customs must **10.74** be provided with evidence that this has been undertaken in order for customs to be able to uphold the border measures (Article 13 of the Regulation). A copy of the application for summons filed with the competent District Court is usually sufficient evidence for this purpose. Once customs have received this evidence, they will continue to detain the goods until the court has rendered its decision in the matter, and will deal with the goods in accordance with the order made by the court. In most cases, the court will order the goods to be destroyed at the infringer's expense.

If the right-holder fails to prove that the products concerned infringe his rights, he **10.75** would, as a rule, be liable for the defendant's legal costs and may also be liable for any loss suffered by the importer as a result of the border measures. The dismissal of the right-holder's infringement claim would also result in the release of the goods by customs.

---

[59] *Patenttilaki* [Patent Act] 550/1967, s 57; *Tekijänoikeuslaki* [Copyright Act] 404/1961, s 57; *Tavaramerkkilaki* [Trade Mark Act] 7/1964, s 38; *Mallioikeuslaki* [Design Right Act] 221/1971, s 37; *Laki Kasvinjalostajanoikeudesta* [Act on the Rights of Plant Breeders] 789/1992, s 29.

D. Release of goods suspected of infringing certain rights on provision of security

10.76 Finnish Customs have not, to date, released any goods under Article 7(2) of Regulation 3295/94 or Article 14 of the current Regulation. The determination of the security is at the sole discretion of the customs authorities. They will in practice assess a suitable amount on a case-by-case basis so that the right-holder's interest will be sufficiently secured. It is anticipated that these situations will remain rare as the alleged infringers are usually passive or very often consent to the voluntary destruction of the goods.

E. Storage of the goods and destruction process

10.77 According to Article 15 of the Regulation, the conditions for the storage of the goods during the period of suspension of release or detention are to be determined by each Member State. There are no specific national rules in this respect under Finnish law, however. In practice Finnish Customs store the goods at the customs office where the goods have originally been stopped during the first 10-day period (which may be extended once), after which, they are usually transferred to a less extensive location for further storage. According to the current interpretation of the Regulation by Finnish Customs, right-holders can in any case be held liable for storage costs incurred during the period of the first 10 (to a maximum of 20) working days referred to in Article 13(1) of the Regulation. This liability is based on the wording of the undertaking referred to in Article 6 of the Regulation. However, because customs forward the invoices for the warehousing to the declarant/ freight forwarder (for the entire storage period), it is at the latter's discretion whether to address a claim for recourse to the right-holder in order to obtain compensation for the 'first' 10-day period (which may be extended once).

10.78 After the expiry of the 10−(+10) day period, liability is governed by national legislation. The party liable for the storage costs will depend on the type of proceedings instituted and on the claims initiated therein:

- In civil proceedings the court may, based on the claims made by the parties, decide upon all the costs incurred in the matter, including storage costs. Usually the losing party will be held liable for these costs.
- When criminal proceedings have been commenced, customs will take responsibility for the storage of the goods and will send the invoice to the declarant or the freight forwarder.

10.79 The destruction process is monitored by the customs office where the goods have been stopped. The customs officers will only proceed with the destruction after having been notified of the final court decision in the matter and having received a copy of the final judgment, or a duly signed settlement agreement to that effect. If the destruction is based on a judgment in a criminal case, the cost of destruction will be paid by the State. In civil proceedings the losing party is usually held liable for the destruction costs. If the infringing party cannot be identified or remains passive in the matter, the right-holder may be held liable to pay the destruction costs.

IV. PROVISIONS APPLICABLE TO GOODS FOUND TO INFRINGE AN INTELLECTUAL PROPERTY RIGHT

Where goods have been found to infringe intellectual property rights, the right-holder may initiate several types of claims in the infringement proceedings. First, Finnish intellectual property legislation provides for the option of obtaining an order against the defendant, prohibiting him from using the infringing products and importing, marketing, and selling same in the future.[60] **10.80**

Second, it is also possible to demand the destruction of the goods or, where appropriate, the infringing moulds and matrices.[61] Where deemed reasonable, the court may only order the goods to be altered appropriately, so that the infringement cannot be continued (for example, by removing infringing signs and marks affixed to the goods). In general, right-holders do not consider the latter measures appropriate and argue that (i) the mere removal of the infringing sign or alteration of the product does not provide sufficient means for the protection of their intellectual property rights and this type of measure would also deteriorate the quality of the products in question, and more importantly (ii) the mere removal of the trade mark or alteration of the product would not be in line with Article 17 of the Regulation, which provides that only exceptionally would such removal be considered effective enough to ensure that the infringers are deprived of any economic gain from their illicit activities. **10.81**

---

[60] *Patenttilaki* [Patent Act] 550/1967, s 57; *Tekijänoikeuslaki* [Copyright Act] 404/1961, s 57; *Tavaramerkkilaki* [Trade Mark Act] 7/1964, s 38; *Mallioikeuslaki* [Design Right Act] 221/1971, s 37; *Laki Kasvinjalostajanoikeudesta* [Act on the Rights of Plant Breeders] 789/1992, s 29.

[61] *Patenttilaki* [Patent Act] 550/1967, s 59; *Tekijänoikeuslaki* [Copyright Act] 404/1961, s 58; *Tavaramerkkilaki* [Trade Mark Act] 7/1964, s 41; *Mallioikeuslaki* [Design Right Act] 221/1971, s 37; *Laki Kasvinjalostajanoikeudesta* [Act on the Rights of Plant Breeders] 789/1992, s 32.

10.82 The third type of claim, normally presented in connection with infringement proceedings, is a claim for damages. The Finnish intellectual property laws contain several provisions on damages and fair compensation. Both can be claimed if the infringement has been caused by negligence or wilful intent. Fair compensation for the unauthorized use of the protected right may be claimed even where the infringement is not the consequence of negligence or wilful intent.

10.83 According to the Trade Mark Act, the aggrieved party is entitled to compensation from the defendant for all the damage he has suffered if the infringing act has been deliberate or negligent. Even if the defendant is not found guilty of negligence, the court may, where deemed reasonable in view of their financial and other circumstances, order that the aggrieved party provide compensation for the profits gained by such infringement during a period not exceeding the three preceding years.[62] Similarly, according to the Design Right Act, anyone who intentionally or negligently infringes the right to a design shall pay reasonable compensation for the use of the design, as well as compensation for the further damage caused by the infringement. Anyone who infringes the right to a design without intention or negligence shall pay compensation for the use of the design, in so far as such compensation may be found reasonable.[63]

10.84 Under the Finnish Patent Act,[64] compensation shall be awarded for the unauthorized use of the patented invention. In principle, such compensation will be comparable to a reasonable licence fee. Furthermore, the infringer is also liable to compensate for other damages caused by the infringement. In the case of minor negligence, the compensation may be adjusted by the court.

10.85 A copyright-holder will also be entitled to 'fair compensation', the scope of which has been determined by jurisprudence as twice the amount the infringer would have had to pay if authorization to use the right concerned had been obtained.[65] If the infringement is wilful or negligent, additional damages will also be awarded.

10.86 In practice, it is difficult to demonstrate the actual damage that the right-holder suffered due to the infringement. Therefore, the courts often exercise their powers under Chapter 17, section 6 of the Code of Judicial Procedure to estimate the amount of reasonable damages.[66] As a rule, they make their estimates cautiously, and in fact under-compensate rather than overcompensate.

---

[62] *Tavaramerkkilaki* [Trade Mark Act] 7/1964, s 38(2). If the negligence has been insignificant, the court may adjust the compensation awarded at its discretion.

[63] *Mallioikeuslaki* [Design Right Act] 221/1971, s 39(2). If the negligence is insignificant, the amount of compensation may be reduced by the court.

[64] *Patenttilaki* [Patent Act] 550/1967, s 58.

[65] 1968 II 81 [Supreme Court case, Finland], *Teosto ry v Tammelundin Liikenne Oy*.

[66] *Oikeudenkäymiskaari* [Code of Judicial Procedure].

V. PENALTIES

The Regulation imposes an obligation on the Member States regarding the **10.87** sanctions and consequences of breaches to the Regulation. Article 18 of the Regulation imposes on them an obligation to adopt penalties in such cases which must be 'effective, proportionate and dissuasive'. The content of those penalties has been left to the Member States' discretion.

The entry into force of the Regulation has not led to any legislative changes to the **10.88** penalties applicable on this point. Section 42 of the Customs Act stipulates that violation of the provisions set forth therein may be deemed a customs offence (and as such, subject to a fine) if a more severe sanction has not been imposed elsewhere in the legislation.

It is not clear whether the general provision of s 42 of the Customs Act meets the **10.89** requirements set forth in Article 18 of the Regulation. However, the most serious infringements of intellectual property rights are in any case, criminalized in the individual statutory intellectual property laws and in the Criminal Code in Finland. According to these provisions, the infringer may be punished by the imposition of a fine or even imprisoned if the infringement has been severe. The essential elements of the offences that take place in connection with border measures usually fall within the scope of these sanction provisions in specific intellectual property laws, and accordingly, the sanction provisions of the Customs Act rarely become applicable.

The most severe infringements of patent rights, trade mark rights, or design **10.90** rights are categorized as industrial property crimes and are penalized under Chapter 49 of the Criminal Code. A wilful violation of these exclusive rights may be regarded as a patent, trade mark, or design right offence if the violation is of a less serious nature and does not meet the criteria for an industrial right crime. For example, the exclusive right conferred by a patent includes the right to prevent third parties from using the invention by importing the patented products.[67] If the exclusive right is deemed to have been violated wilfully, the perpetrator may be charged a fine based on a patent offence. If the exclusive right is wilfully violated and this violation is liable to cause considerable economic loss to the right-holder, the act may be deemed an industrial property crime. According to the provisions on industrial property crime in Chapter 49 of the Criminal Code, the perpetrator could face up to two years' imprisonment or a fine. Similar references to Chapter 49 of the Criminal Code

---

[67] *Patenttilaki* [Patents Act] 550/1967, s 3.

are made in the Trade Mark Act[68] for trade mark infringements and the Design Right Act[69] as regards design right infringements and the Plant Breeders Act as regards infringements of plant variety rights.[70] As mentioned above, illegally manufactured goods and devices intended to be used for production may also be confiscated.

10.91 Criminal sanctions and liability for copyright infringements are set forth in Chapter 7 of the Copyright Act.[71] A violation of copyrights or neighbouring rights constitutes a copyright crime or a copyright offence depending on the nature and the scope of the infringement, the culpability of the infringer, and whether or not the infringement was perpetrated in the pursuit of financial gain. For instance, if a copy of a work is wilfully produced in quantity or made available in quantity to the public for economic gain, the perpetrator could face up to two years' imprisonment or a fine for copyright crimes. The same applies to commercial importation of, for example, copies of works for distribution to the public in Finland, provided the copy was produced in another country under circumstances that would have been criminally punishable if the production had been carried out in Finland. The penalties for copyright crimes are enacted in section 49(1) of the Criminal Code.[72]

10.92 If the wilful or negligent violation of a copyright or a neighbouring right was not perpetrated in the pursuit of an economic gain, the perpetrator may be fined for a copyright offence. A copyright or neighbouring right is deemed to have been violated wilfully or negligently when the perpetrator knew or should have suspected that the copy imported into Finland for distribution was produced in another country under circumstances that would have been subject to a fine had the production been carried out in Finland.[73]

10.93 According to a recent reform[74] approved by the Parliament, the provision on imports of pirated goods will be amended so that both private and commercial imports of copyright infringing goods will be punishable. The aim of the reform is to implement more effective means for controlling imports of pirated goods and block such goods prior to entering the Finnish market. This reform will enter into force on 1 January 2006.

---

[68] *Tavaramerkkilaki* [Trade Marks Act] 7/1964, s 39(2).
[69] *Mallioikeuslaki* [Design Right Act] 221/1971, s 35(2).
[70] *Laki kasvinjalostajanoikeudesta* [Act on the Rights of Plant Breeders] 789/1992, s 34.
[71] *Tekijänoikeuslaki* [Copyright Act] 404/1961.   [72] *Rikoslaki* [Criminal Code] 39/1889.
[73] These questions were assessed by the Finnish Supreme Court in the case *Oy Langh Ship Ab v Flinter Groningen B.V. and Wijnne & Barends' Cargadoors- en Agentuurkantoren B.V.*, (KKO 2003: 136, R 2001/983, 22 December 2003).   [74] Government Bill HE 28/2004.

VI. LIABILITY OF CUSTOMS AUTHORITIES AND RIGHT-HOLDERS

A. Liability of right-holders and sanctions

Pursuant to Article 12 of the Regulation a right-holder receiving information on **10.94** a shipment stopped by customs under the Regulation is only allowed to use this information for the purposes specifically defined in the Regulation. Any other use is generally not permitted, and such unauthorized use may cause the right-holder to incur civil liability or lead to the suspension of the right-holder's application for action. Furthermore, customs will also in certain circumstances be entitled to refuse to renew pending applications.

To date, customs have not been aware of any case where border measures would **10.95** have been applied for in bad faith, and where the information provided to a right-holder would have been used for purposes other than to pursue the matter. The practical reason for this is that right-holders are very aware that any misuse of the system would jeopardize the trust between the parties involved in combating piracy and counterfeiting, which would easily lead to the deterioration of the current system.

If the information were to be used for a purpose other than those defined in Article **10.96** 12 of the Regulation, the right-holder may be subject to criminal liability in certain circumstances. For example, if the information contained trade secrets, which the right-holder has taken advantage of or disclosed to a third party, such act may, in some cases, be deemed industrial espionage, or misuse or breach of trade secrets, criminalized in Chapter 30 of the Criminal Code.[75] Such illicit conduct may be subject to a fine, while, in more severe cases, the offender may incur a jail term.

The right-holder may also in certain circumstances be liable to pay damages for **10.97** misuse of the information provided by customs when this has caused harm to the other party. The same applies to any other breach of the Regulation. However, it should be noted that compensation of a purely economic loss suffered due to such misuse of information would, as a rule, require the misuse also to constitute a crime or there to be other weighty reasons for compensation. If these additional requirements are not met, a claim for damages will not be accepted.[76]

---

[75] *Rikoslaki* [Criminal Code] 39/1889.
[76] *Vahingonkorvauslaki* [Damages Act] 412/1974, s 5(1).

B. Liability of customs authorities and sanctions

(1) Liability of the Finnish customs authorities within the framework of the application of the provisions of the Regulation

10.98   There is no specific national legislation governing the liability of the Finnish customs authorities within the framework of the application of the Regulation. However, general provisions on administrative law apply in cases where the Finnish customs authorities are suspected of having acted contrary to their duties as set forth in the Customs Act or contrary to administrative practices.[77]   Claims for damages may also be filed by the injured party if actual damage has occurred and there is a causal link between such damage and the unlawful administrative action. To date, no claims have been made against Finnish Customs on the basis of the current or former Council Regulation on border measures.

(2) Liability of the Finnish customs authorities for not detecting or acting against goods suspected of infringing a right-holder's intellectual property right

10.99   Pursuant to Article 19 of the Regulation, the acceptance of an application for action by customs authorities shall not entitle the right-holder to compensation in the event that infringing goods are not detected by a customs office and are released, or no action is taken to detain them. However, if customs fail to detain or suspend the release of infringing goods due to clear negligence, they may under certain circumstances be held liable under the general provisions on the liability of public authorities set forth in the Damages Act.[78] However, it is doubtful that compensation claims would be accepted by a court of law, as the Regulation explicitly excludes such liability and it is not possible for customs to prevent all goods infringing intellectual property rights from entering Finland. Furthermore, for *ex officio* measures, liability seems ruled out, as *ex officio* actions are purely facultative, that is, customs 'may' seize the goods *ex officio* under Article 4(1).

Conclusion

10.100   Council Regulation 1383/2003 on border measures has not brought any major changes to the regulatory or administrative environment in Finland.

---

[77] *Hallintolaki* [Administrative Act] 434/2003.
[78] *Vahingonkorvauslaki* [Damages Act] 412/1974.

Consequently it is not expected that Finnish Customs' practices will alter considerably as a result of the reform.

From the right-holder's point of view, one disadvantage compared to the former **10.101** regime is that the application for action cannot be declared admissible if the applicant does not submit the declaration referred to in Article 6 of the new Regulation to customs, pursuant to which the right-holder can be held liable for the costs incurred even during the 10-day period (which may be extended once) defined in Article 13 of the Regulation. Furthermore, the right-holder is required to undertake liability for storage and destruction costs. Under the former Regulation it was unclear whether such liability existed. However, in practice it is not expected that this change will cause right-holders considerable extra costs compared to the old regime.

As pointed out above, Finland has not yet implemented the simplified procedure **10.102** referred to in Article 11 of the Regulation. Compared to this procedure, current alternatives for pursuing the matter, consisting either of commencing civil or criminal action, or settling the matter amicably with the infringer, are more time-consuming and expensive. The Finnish Anti-Counterfeiting Group has actively advocated the introduction of a simplified procedure meeting the requirements of Article 11 of the Regulation, because this would result in a greater cost-efficiency of border measures. The reform of the Finnish Customs Act is currently being looked at by the Ministry of Finance, and it is anticipated that the simplified procedure will be implemented in Finland in connection with this reform. However, it is expected that it will take some time before the legal framework for applying the simplified procedure is available in Finland.

The main challenge faced by customs is the lack of resources compared to the **10.103** increasing workload. However, Finnish Customs are motivated to reduce the trade in infringing goods and the customs officers involved in processing border measure matters under the Regulation are very proactive. Finnish Customs readily provide general advice about their services and welcome the opportunity to meet with intellectual property right-holders to receive training and further information that will help officers at the borders to identify and take efficient actions to prevent the importation of goods that infringe intellectual property rights.

The smoothness of customs procedures in Finland has been internationally **10.104** recognized. In 2002, the international management training and research centre, IMD estimated that the Finnish customs administration was the best in the world from the viewpoint of commerce and industry. Finnish Customs were awarded the Global Anti-Counterfeiting Award in 2002 for outstanding achievement by a public organization.

11

FRANCE

Juliette Biardeaud

Introduction

France is not only situated in the geographical heart of Europe, sharing land   **11.01**
borders with Belgium, Luxembourg, Germany, Italy, Spain, and a short distance
across the Channel from the United Kingdom, but it is also at the forefront of
industry, notably in the luxury goods sector. It is therefore an ideal target market
for counterfeiters, and also an interesting platform for transit purposes.

Between 2003 and 2004, the efficiency of border measures against goods infringing   **11.02**
intellectual property rights increased by almost 76 per cent, jumping from
1,987,630 items detained in 2003, to 3,495,785 items in 2004.[1]

The majority (72 per cent) of counterfeit and pirated goods crossing the French   **11.03**
borders originate from Asia, and in particular China. Although the number
originating from Turkey and Italy decreased between 2003 and 2004, the proportion of illicit goods manufactured in France has increased, and represents 6 per
cent of all products detained by customs during this period.

The share of non-authentic goods destined for the French market has increased   **11.04**
sharply from 5 per cent in 2001 to 19 per cent in 2002, 35 per cent in 2003, and
44 per cent in 2004.

Illegitimate goods in transit are increasingly destined for Africa, representing 12   **11.05**
per cent in 2002, and 20 per cent in 2003. The remainder is largely intended for
the central European market, and a small proportion for South America.

---

[1] These statistics and many more can be obtained at the *Bureau information et communication*
of the French Customs authorities (*Direction Générale des Douanes et Droits Indirects*) DGDDI,
23Bis rue de l'Université, FR-75007 PARIS, tel: +33 (0)1 44 74 49 91, fax: +33 (0)1 44 74 49 37,
or via the 2004 Customs Report, on the website http://www.douane.gouv.fr/pdf/actualite/
copebilan.pdf.

11.06   The French government has strengthened its efforts in combating counterfeit goods; checks by customs authorities have increased by 25 per cent and as a result, the number of border measures taken between 2002 and 2003 rose by 56.2 per cent, from 1,272,433 items detained in 2002 to 1,987,630 items in 2003.

11.07   Before EC Regulation 1383/2003[2] came into force, the previous Regulation 3295/94 of 22 December 1994[3]—as amended by Regulation 241/1999 of 25 January 1999[4]—and the provisions of the French Intellectual Property Code, were the relevant legislative texts governing border measures against goods infringing intellectual property rights in France.

11.08   Currently both Regulation 1383/2003 ('the Regulation') and the provisions of the Intellectual Property Code ('the IPC'), regulate these border measures. However, the IPC, only refers to trade mark rights, author rights, and related rights, and registered designs but is silent on patents or supplementary protection certificate, plant varieties rights, and designation of origins or geographical indication.

11.09   Therefore, when French Customs are confronted with goods suspected of infringing intellectual property rights protected by both the Regulation and the IPC, (trade marks, registered designs, author's rights, and related rights), they may opt to rely either on the provisions of the IPC, or on the Regulation.

11.10   In practice and when possible, customs favour use of the IPC, which provides a high level of protection for right-holders, and especially trade mark owners. In this regard, since the entry into force of the Longuet Law of 5 February 1994,[5] a trade mark infringement is considered a customs offence ('*délit douanier*').

11.11   Customs have greater experience in applying the French IPC than the EC Regulation, and most border measures are taken in reliance of the IPC provisions.

11.12   Having said that, the predominance of the IPC provisions over the Regulation could soon change, due to the involvement of the French Customs in the drafting of Regulation 1383/2003, and the fact that customs have been instructed internally to rely increasingly on the provisions of the Regulation.

---

[2] Council Reg (EC) No 1383/2003 of 22 July 2003 concerning customs action against goods suspected of infringing certain intellectual property rights and the measures to be taken against goods found to have infringed such rights [2003] OJ L 196/7.

[3] Council Reg (EEC) No 3295/94 of 22 December 1994 laying down measures to prohibit the release for free circulation, export, re-export or entry for a suspensive procedure of counterfeit and pirated goods [1996] OJ L 97/38.

[4] Council Reg (EC) No 241/1999 of 25 January 1999 [1999] OJ L 27/1.

[5] Loi N° 94-102, of 5 February 1994. This Law has been codified under Articles 414 and 432bis of the Customs Code.

I. SUBJECT MATTER AND SCOPE OF THE NATIONAL LAW APPLYING THE REGULATION

In this Part, relating to the subject matter and the scope of French national law **11.13** applying the Regulation, we will examine under which customs procedures the French customs authorities will act against suspect goods (section A), the definition of infringing goods under French law (section B), and the goods excluded from the scope of the Regulation (section C).

A. Customs procedure of the goods

(1) The French customs authorities' approach towards the various customs procedures prior to the ECJ's ruling in Commission v France

French Customs apply the provisions of the Regulation to goods in all customs **11.14** procedures specified in Article 1(1) of the Regulation.

In the context of a trade mark infringement, this approach is mirrored, for **11.15** example, by the highly protective provisions of Article L 716-9[6] of the IPC, which provides that:

> Any person who has: [. . .]
> d) Imported, under any customs procedure, or exported, goods under an infringing
>   trade mark
>   shall be punished by four years imprisonment and a fine of 400,000 Euro . . .

The other provisions of the IPC prohibiting the infringement of other intellectual **11.16** property rights do not specifically refer to 'any Customs procedure'.

Following this approach, French Customs have always considered that goods in **11.17** transit either within or outside the European Union could be the subject of customs controls and border measures.

(2) ECJ case law

This wide jurisdictional interpretation of the Community Regulations on border **11.18** controls by French customs authorities has given rise to a number of decisions by the

---

⁶ This provision originally provided for a two-year jail term and a EUR 150,000 fine, but Statute No 2004-204 of 9 March 2004 (*loi PERBEN*) stipulated that when the infringement is committed in the course of organized crime, the prison sentence shall be increased to five years, and a fine of EUR 500,000 shall apply.

European Court of Justice ('ECJ') relating to goods transiting from one Member State to another Member State, or to a country outside the European Community.

11.19 Thus, the ECJ considered twice that the French customs authorities had breached Article 28 (former Article 30) of the Treaty of Rome[7] laying down the principle of free movement of goods and services.

11.20 In the case of *Commission v France*, the French customs authorities had detained goods which had been manufactured lawfully in one Member State and were destined to be sold lawfully in another Member State, whilst in transit in France, on suspicion of an intellectual property right infringement under French national law. On 26 September 2000, the ECJ held that by implementing, pursuant to the French Intellectual Property Code, procedures for the detention by the Customs authorities of goods lawfully manufactured in a Member State of the European Community which are intended, following their transit through French territory, to be placed on the market in another Member State where they may be lawfully marketed, the French Republic has failed to fulfil its obligations under Article 30 of the EC Treaty (now, after amendment, Article 28 EC).[8]

11.21 In the more recent case of *Rioglass*, reference for a preliminary ruling had been made by the French courts to the ECJ in the context of proceedings between French Customs and two Spanish companies, Rioglass SA and Transremar SL, concerning the detention in France on suspicion of trade mark infringement, of car spare parts which had been manufactured in Spain and were in transit to a non-EC member country (Poland).

11.22 The issue to be tried in *Rioglass* was less clear cut than in the *Commission v France* case, as *Rioglass* involved intra-community trade and at the time the decision of the ECJ was handed down, Poland was not an EC Member State. The case therefore hinged on whether the provisions of the IPC could be relied upon when the final consignee of the goods was located outside the European Community.

11.23 On 23 October 2003, the ECJ considered that:

> Article 28 EC is to be interpreted as precluding the implementation, pursuant to a legislative measure of a Member State concerning intellectual property, of procedures for detention by the Customs authorities of goods lawfully manufactured in another Member State and intended, following their transit through the territory of the first Member State, to be placed on the market in a non-member country.[9]

---

[7] EC Treaty (Treaty of Rome, as amended).

[8] Case C-23/99 *Commission v France* [2000] ECR-I 7653 (operative part). This ruling has been commented on, eg, in: Propriété Industrielle—Bulletin Documentaire ('PIBD') No 711-III-01/01/2001, 18; Ch Caron [2001] Jurisclasseur Communication Commerce Electronique 17; J Vasa [2000] Revue Lamy droit des affaires (November 2000 No 32); E Arnaud, 'L'incompatibilité enfin reconnue des mesures de rétention douanière prévues dans la législation française avec le droit Communautaire' [2002] Petites Affiches (17 April 2002, No 77).

[9] Case C-115/02 *Rioglass and Transremar* [2003] ECR-I 12705 (operative part).

In addition, the Court pointed out that: **11.24**

> According to the judgment for reference, the goods in issue in the present case were
> detained on suspicion of infringement of trade mark.
>
> With respect to trade marks, it is settled case-law that the specific subject-matter of a
> trade mark is, in particular, to guarantee to the owner that he has the exclusive right
> to use that mark for the purpose of putting a product on the market for the first time
> and thus to protect him against competitors wishing to take unfair advantage of the
> status and reputation of the trade mark by selling products illegally bearing it (see, in
> particular, Case 16/74 Centrafarm [1974] ECR 1183, paragraph 8, Case 102/77
> Hoffmann-La Roche [1978] ECR 1139, paragraph 7, and Case C-349/95
> Loendersloot [1997] ECR I-6227, paragraph 22).
>
> The implementation of such protection is therefore linked to the placing on the
> market of the goods.
>
> Transit, such as that in issue in the main proceedings, which consists in transporting
> goods lawfully manufactured in a Member State to a non-member country by
> passing through one or more Member States, does not involve any marketing of the
> goods in question and is therefore not liable to infringe the specific subject matter of
> the trade mark.
>
> Furthermore, as Advocate General Mischo noted at point 45 of his Opinion, that
> conclusion holds good regardless of the final destination of the goods in transit. The
> fact that the goods are subsequently placed on the market in a non-member country
> and not in another Member State does not alter the nature of the transit operation
> which, by definition, does not constitute a placing on the market.
>
> Therefore, a measure of detention under customs control, such as that in issue in the
> main proceedings, cannot be justified on the ground of protection of industrial and
> commercial property within the meaning of Article 30 EC.[10]

(3) The approach of the French courts

The French courts have endorsed—but possibly not entirely—the above ECJ   **11.25**
precedents in two separate decisions.

In a ruling dated 3 September 2002, the Criminal Chamber of the French   **11.26**
Supreme Court (*Cour de Cassation*) was asked to determine whether a judgment
of the Aix en Provence Court of Appeal was correct in applying the principles laid
down in the *Rioglass* decision.

The Supreme Court dismissed the appeal, and considered that: **11.27**

> Whereas it results from the decision of the Court of Appeal that the Customs author-
> ities have [. . .] detained [. . .] a lorry containing, inter alia, bumpers of RENAULT
> SUPER 5, manufactured in Portugal by the Company Prasco.

---

[10] Ibid, paras 11.17-11.34. This decision has been commented on, inter alia, in J Daleau [2004] Recueil Dalloz 1239, and Ch Vilmart, 'Des pièces détachées RIOGLASS aux montres ROLEX, la Cour de Justice favorise la libre circulation des contrefaçons et limite le rôle des douanes' Revue Internationale de la Propriété Intellectuelle et Artistique ('RIPIA'), N° 215, 1er trimestre 2004, 93 (who criticizes this ruling, as well as the *Rolex* decision in case C-60/02, 7 January 2004, not yet reported). The principles set out in the *Rioglass* case will be further discussed in more detail below, when discussing the parallel importation of goods in transit.

That, after those goods were detained, the Company Renault instituted criminal proceedings [...] claiming that, by importing and having in stock on the French territory spare parts reproducing the characteristics of their designs, [the Company Prasco] had committed infringing acts and breached Renault's 'design rights'.

That to reject the claims of the injured party [the right-holder, that is, Renault], the Court of Appeal, referring to the ruling of the ECJ of 26 September 2000 [in Case C-23/99 *Commission v France*], considers that transit is not concerned with the specific subject matter of the registered designs and models in the Member States where it takes place, provided the goods have been legally manufactured in their country of origin, and are destined, after having transited through France, to another Member State where they can also be legally put on the market; That in addition, the claimant has not produced evidence that these goods have been manufactured illegally or sold in the Member States concerned.[11]

11.28   At the time where this decision was rendered, it was still unclear whether, *a contrario*, had the goods not been either lawfully marketed in the country of origin, or lawfully sold in the country of destination, the Court would also have confirmed the lawfulness of the detention procedure.

11.29   The answer to this question was given in a later ruling by the same Chamber (Criminal Chamber) of the French Supreme Court, in a case where the Dijon Court of Appeal, in a decision dated 20 November 2002,[12] had clearly referred to the ECJ ruling of 26 September 2000 in Case C-23/99, *Commission v France*, by stating that:

> Intra-community transit, which consists of the transportation of goods from one Member State to another by crossing the territories of one or several other Member States, does not involve any use of the appearance of the registered designs, and therefore does not relate to the specific subject matter of the industrial property right in the registered designs.

11.30   The Criminal Chamber of the Supreme Court overturned this decision, and held that:

> Whereas, on the one hand, in application of the ECJ decision of 26 September 2000, is to be considered as contrary to Community law, the act of detaining goods which are marketed lawfully in a Member Country of the EEA, and which are destined, after having transited through the French territory, to be placed on the market in another Member State where they can be legally sold; That in this matter, [...] Franco X had confessed that the bumpers intended for use on the Renault TWINGO model originated from a Taiwanese company Tong Yang, and had not

---

[11] Cass Crim, 3 September 2002, *Société RENAULT*, Juris data No 2002-015583, or www.legifrance.gouv.fr or PIBD No 783-III, 2003, 205, and commented on inter alia in J Vasa [2002] Revue Lamy Droit des Affaires No 55, 3, in [2002] Lamy Droit Commercial—Bulletin d'actualité No 149 (November 2002), 3. Cf also Ch Caron [2002] Jurisclasseur Communication Commerce Electronique (December 2002) 21, and PIBD No 760-III-164, 2003; A Lucas [2003] Propriétés Intellectuelles, (January 2003, No 6, 52).

[12] Extracts of this decision and further comments can be found in Décideurs Stratégie Finance Droit, No 54, 15 May–15 June 2004.

been marketed in a Member State of the European Community [...]; Whereas, on the other hand, the company Renault had emphasised [...] that the litigious spare parts could not be legally sold in Belgium, their destination country, where the selling of car spare parts reproducing the original characteristics of protected designs without the authorisation of the rights-holder is considered a copyright infringement.[13]

11.31 In this case, the spare parts of Renault were intended for sale in Belgium, and despite the fact that they had been 'legally' assembled in Italy, they were composed of spare parts fraudulently manufactured in Taiwan. Consequently, it appeared that these goods could *not* be lawfully sold in Belgium.

Eventually, the Supreme Court sent the *Rioglass* case for retrial on the facts back to the Bordeaux Court of Appeal.[14] In accordance with the ECJ decision, the latter[15] confirmed that the detention of the goods was unlawful, despite the fact that Renault had tried to prove that the marketing of the spare parts in their country of provenance (Spain) was illicit.

11.32 The French legislator took the above case law into account, and, by the Statute dated 1 August 2003,[16] inserted the following provision into the Articles L 335-10 (author's rights), L 521-7 (registered designs), and L 716-8 (trade marks) of the IPC:

> Detention mentioned in the first subparagraph does not relate to goods having a Community status, ie which have been lawfully manufactured or lawfully placed on the market in an EC Member State, and are destined, after having been placed in the Customs territory as per Article 1 of the Customs Code, to be lawfully placed on the market of another Member State.

11.33 A useful way to benefit from the approach of the French courts, as described above, is to designate France in any Community applications for action,[17] and to specify in which EC Member States the goods are considered as lawfully manufactured. This will help customs to focus on goods originating from Member States where they are not considered as lawfully manufactured.

11.34 Finally, the reaction of French scholars to the aforesaid decisions has been mixed: while some of them consider that the *Rioglass* ruling implies that the ECJ favours the free movement of counterfeit and pirated goods, and seeks to limit intervention by customs authorities in this field,[18] others consider that this case law has at last put an end to the French protectionist practice and legislation which existed

---

[13] Cass Crim, 2 December 2003, *Société RENAULT*, Juris data No 2003-021675, or www.legifrance.gouv.fr.
[14] Indeed, appeals before the Supreme Court are confined to points of law.
[15] CA Bordeaux, 21 September 2004, to be published.
[16] Loi No 2003-706 of 1 August 2003, available on www.legifrance.gouv.fr.
[17] Within the meaning of Art 5(4) of EC Reg 1383/2003.
[18] Cf Ch Vilmart (n 10 above).

previously.[19] The majority of academics seem to consider that the principle of free movement of goods should be given precedence over the safeguard of intellectual property rights, and welcome the change in tide of French case law and legislation, which are now in line with the approach taken by the ECJ.

B. Definition of infringing goods

11.35 As French Customs are highly protective of intellectual property rights, measures are taken to protect rights-holders against both counterfeit and pirated goods. Goods suspected of infringing other intellectual property rights will also be subject to border measures, as far as they can be identified.

(1) Counterfeit goods

11.36 Under the Regulation, customs are in the first place to take action against 'counterfeit goods', which are defined in Article 2(1) as goods 'bearing without authorisation a trade mark identical to the trade mark validly registered in respect of the same type of goods, or which cannot be distinguished in its essential aspects from such a trade mark', and which thereby infringes the trade mark holder's rights under national or Community law.

Identical v similar signs

11.37 The scope of the French IPC in this field is wider than the provision of Article 2(1)(a)(i) of the Regulation, which requires that the disputed sign be either identical, or essentially similar, to the registered mark, and that suspect goods be of the same type as those for which the trade mark on which the border measures rely is registered. Indeed, Articles L 713-2 and 3 of the IPC provide that any unauthorized use of an identical, *or confusingly similar*, trade mark in relation to identical *or similar* goods or services constitutes an infringement. There is no reference to a risk of association in the IPC, and therefore, the test for infringement is whether there exists a likelihood of confusion in the mind of the average consumer.

11.38 In practice, the French customs authorities take action against any suspect goods to which a sign *identical or similar* to a validly registered trade mark has been affixed. Thus, they tend to place themselves in the position of the average consumer when detaining goods on suspicion of trade mark infringement during checks on goods.

11.39 In a recent case, customs authorities detained a number of clothing items bearing a sign similar to a well-known sportswear logo consisting of concentric diamond

---

[19] E Arnaud (n 8 above).

shapes. In this case, the infringing sign comprised one instead of two diamond shapes. Upon advice from the right-holder, customs considered that this sign was confusingly similar to the earlier trade mark, and therefore seized the goods in question.

In instances where a risk of confusion is less apparent, customs tend to contact the right-holder to seek his opinion. **11.40**

The French customs authorities detained, for example, goods imitating a well-known Hip-Hop clothing brand. The registered trade mark consisted of a representation of the profile of a rhinoceros contained in an oval target shape combined with a verbal element. The suspect goods bore a similar logo representing a feline in an oval target together with a word element similar to that contained in the earlier mark. Although the logo and the word element taken separately might not have been considered to infringe the earlier mark, the combination of both elements led the trade mark proprietor to advise the customs officials that the goods were counterfeit, which resulted in their seizure. **11.41**

Further, in order to benefit from the extended protection towards trade mark infringements which constitute a customs offence ('*délit douanier*') as explained in paragraph 11.10 above, it is recommended that applications be filed for registration as a trade mark in respect of any possible subject matter, regardless of whether it is already, or could be, covered by other intellectual property rights. **11.42**

For instance, many registered designs for mobile telephone covers, which have been the subject of widespread copying, but do not bear any brand name, have been registered as three-dimensional trade marks with the French Trade Mark Registry. The level of distinctiveness required before the French Registry used to be lower than that of the Community Trade Mark Office. On the basis of this registration, the French customs authorities may seize identical or similar covers in the course of their controls as they infringe the three-dimensional trade mark obtained for the shape of the cover, as opposed to relying purely on the basis of a possible registered design infringement. **11.43**

Finally, it is noteworthy that in France, trade mark rights do not preclude use of a registered trade mark if it is necessary to indicate the intended purpose of the goods, in particular as accessories or spare parts, provided that such use does not create a risk of confusion as to the origin of the products, and that it is not 'abusive'. This provision, which is not entirely clear, is found in Article L 713-6 of the IPC,[20] the scope of which is wider than the wording of the equivalent Article **11.44**

---

[20] Art L 713-6 reads: 'A trade mark registration does not prohibit the use of an identical or similar sign as: b) the necessary reference to indicate the destination of the goods or services, notably as an accessory or a spare part, provided there is no confusion as to their origin. However, if such use violates his rights, the trade mark owner can request that the use be limited or prohibited.'

6(c) of the EC Harmonization Directive.[21] What is clear is that where the trade mark is used in large typeface and in contrast the phrase for example, 'compatible with' appears in much smaller and less prominent script on the back or underside of the packaging, it is likely that this will be considered an abusive or confusing use of the mark.

Identical v similar goods

11.45   In the same way as when determining whether or not the suspect sign can be distinguished in its essential aspects from the registered trade mark, the approach adopted by the French customs authorities to appraise whether the allegedly infringing goods are 'of the same type' as the goods listed in the trade mark registration on which the detention or seizure measures rely, is equally relatively flexible.

11.46   Indeed in practice, owing to the reference to national law in Article 2(1)(a) of the Regulation, the French customs authorities consider that they are entitled to take border measures against goods which are similar to those covered by the registered trade mark.

11.47   Furthermore, the French Fraud Repression Authorities (DGCCRF) may also take action *ex officio*, after obtaining the consent of the relevant right-holder, against any use of a trade mark for caricature purposes. Thus, for example, the slogans of a mobile telephone manufacturer and a well-known music retailer had been caricatured and printed on t-shirts intended for commercial sale. Such use was prosecuted by the DGCCRF, since the 'parody' pursued a commercial aim (that is, the selling of t-shirts), and not simply a critical aim.

11.48   In France, it is not possible to take border measures against allegedly infringing goods merely on the basis of a trade mark application, be it under the Regulation or the IPC. The mark must in all cases be registered.

11.49   Customs may also take action under the Regulation,[22] where appropriate *ex officio*, with regard to trade mark symbols (including, for example, labels and stickers), and packaging materials bearing a counterfeit trade mark, even if delivered separately from the goods in question. In practice, however, customs will require the right-holder to confirm that an infringement has occurred.

11.50   For example, it is relatively common for clothing labels bearing a counterfeit trade mark to be transported separately to be sewn onto t-shirts, for example, in Morocco. In such cases, the labels may be seized by customs.

---

[21] First Council Directive No 89/104/EEC of 21 December 1988 to approximate the laws of the Member States relating to trade marks [1989] OJ L 104/1, as amended by Council Decision No 92/10/10 of 19 December 1991 [1992] L 6/35.
[22] Cf Reg 1383/2003, Art 2(1)(a)(ii)–(iii).

(2) Pirated goods

Customs also take action against 'pirated goods', that is, goods which are or **11.51**
contain copies made without the consent of the holder of a copyright or related
right or design right, in cases where the making of those copies would constitute
an infringement of that right under national or Community law.[23]

Author's rights and related rights

Infringement of an author's rights and related rights under French law is dealt **11.52**
with under Articles L 122-4, L 335-2, L 335-3, and L 335-4 of the IPC. It should
be noted that an author's rights, as defined under French law, have a wider
scope than copyright in the common law countries. An author's rights are very
protective of the author, and include a range of additional rights, such as moral
rights.[24]

As a result, French provisions governing an author's rights are amongst the most **11.53**
protective in the world. In this respect, the threshold for enjoying protection
under French authors' rights is very low in view of the fact that according to
French case law, any work may be protected by authors' rights provided it constitutes 'an original work, which reflects its author's personality', or 'results from a
creative effort'. Thus, authors' right protection extends to a vast range of work,
including industrial products.

According to French case law, any unauthorized use of an author's right is consid- **11.54**
ered an infringement (apart from the exceptions concerning fair use listed in
Article L 122-5 of the IPC).

For instance, the making of a copy for commercial purposes for a third party,[25]
inserting a previous work into a composite one,[26] or partially copying an original
work,[27] is considered an infringement of the author's rights.

Article L 121-1 of the IPC specifically protects the author's moral rights, and **11.55**
makes it an infringement to disclose a protected work to the public for the first
time, to omit the name of the author from the work, or to modify it without the
latter's agreement.

---

[23] Ibid, Art 2(1)(b).
[24] For a comparison, cf P Sirinelli, 'Droit d'auteur et copyright: quelle opposition ?', in *Le feuilleton de la société des gens de lettres*, Numéro 11, été 2003, 17. Cf also A Strowel, *Droit d'auteur et copyright. Étude de droit comparé* (Paris: LGDJ, 1993), and JAL Sterling, *World Copyright Law* (2nd edn, London: Sweet & Maxwell, 2003).
[25] Grenoble Court of Appeal, (1st Chamber), 18 January 2001 [2001] PIBD III-423.
[26] Ibid.
[27] Supreme Court (*Cour de cassation*), Criminal Chamber, 19 March 1957 can be found on www.legifrance.gouv.fr, Bull Crim (Bulletin des arrêts de la Cour de cassation, chambres crim-inelles) 1957, 260.

11.56 The related rights are governed by the same principles as authors' rights, which means that the artist as defined by article L 212-1 of the IPC et seq and the producer of videograms or phonograms (as per articles L 214-1 and L 215-1 of the IPC et seq) can obtain the detainment of infringing goods (CDs, DVDs or videotapes) by customs. This possibility is expressly stated in Article L 335-1 of the IPC.

11.57 When goods are copies of works covered by an author's right, French Customs will stop them if they can rely on a detailed description contained in an application for action.

11.58 Regarding goods which contain copies, such as compilations, customs will in practice rarely control such goods, unless their attention is specifically drawn to them by the right-holder through an application for action.

Finally, since computer programs are also expressly covered by authors' rights protection, a custom application for action may also be lodged in respect of such goods.

Design rights

11.59 The protection of registered designs in France results from Part V of the IPC as amended by the Statute of July 25, 2001 implementing the Directive of 13 October 1998. However, provisions relating to the sanctions of designs infringement were not amended in 2001 and still derive from the Statute of 14 July 1909.

11.60 Article L 513-4 of the IPC prohibits the manufacturing, offering, placing on the market, importing, exporting, using or possession for these purposes, of a product comprising the design or model, unless authorized by the owner.

11.61 As per the Directive, a design is only valid if it is new and has an individual character. Thus, designs which do not produce on the informed observer a different overall visual impression are deemed to infringe the prior design rights.

(3) *Goods infringing other intellectual property rights*

11.62 Next to trade marks, copyright and related rights, and design rights, customs are also entitled to detain goods infringing a patent or a supplementary protection certificate, plant variety rights, a national designation of origin, or a geographical indication.[28]

Goods infringing a patent or a supplementary protection certificate

11.63 Patent infringement is dealt with by Articles L 613-3, L 613-4, and L 615-1 of the IPC.

---

[28] Reg 1383/2003, Art 2(1)(c).

Pursuant to these provisions, any use or offering for sale of a product or a process **11.64** protected by a patent, namely an invention which is considered novel, capable of industrial application and involves an inventive step, constitutes a patent infringement. Manufacturing the patented invention without the patentee's consent constitutes an act of infringement, regardless of the possible good faith of the manufacturer.[29] Repairing is an infringement if it entails reconstruction of the goods.[30] A product infringes a patent right if it performs the same function and achieves the same result by substantially the same means.[31]

In practical terms, applications for customs action on the basis of patents and/or **11.65** supplementary protection certificates are quite rare. According to the statistics compiled in 2002, such applications represented only 1 per cent of Community applications for action at that time. The small number of applications based on patents and/or supplementary protection certificates seems to result from the lack of sufficient cooperation between customs authorities and right-holders in those fields.[32]

Goods infringing a national plant variety right

Infringement of national plant varieties is dealt with under Articles L 623-4 and **11.66** L 623-25 of the IPC.

These provisions regard any use of a novel, distinct, stable, and uniform plant **11.67** variety without the right-holder's consent as an infringement, provided that a substantial characteristic of the variety is copied.[33] In addition, raising a protected variety,[34] sorting seeds in order to propagate such a variety,[35] and using seeds obtained from a protected variety,[36] also constitute acts of infringement.

Goods infringing a national designation of origin or a geographical indication

Article L 213-1 of the French Consumer Code[37] makes it a criminal offence to **11.68** mislead the public concerning the nature, type, origin, material qualities, composition, or content in terms of active ingredients, of goods, in any way whatsoever.

---

[29] Paris Court of First Instance (*Tribunal de Grande Instance*), 24 April 1986 [1986] PIBD III-331.

[30] Supreme Court (*Cour de cassation*), Criminal Chamber, 30 April 1918 [1919] Ann Prop Ind (Annales de Propriété Industrielle, Littéraire et Artistique) 55.

[31] Paris Court of Appeal (4th Chamber), 1 December 1992 [1993] PIBD 541-III-220.

[32] For further comments regarding applications for action for patents and/or supplementary protection certificates, cf the chapter of Mr W Roge of Bureau E4 of French Customs in Jurisclasseur Brevet, fasc 4635.

[33] Paris Court of First Instance (*Tribunal de Grande Instance*), 3 December 1987 [1988] PIBD 147-III-147.　　　　[34] Paris Court of Appeal, 9 December 1981 [1982] PIBD 302-III-110.

[35] Nancy Court of Appeal, 13 September 1988 [1988] PIBD 446-III-572.　　　[36] Ibid.

[37] *Code de la Consommation, partie législative*, Ch III, s I, Art L 213-1.

11.69   More specifically, Article L 115-1 of the French Consumer Code (which is cross-referred to in Article L 721-1 of the IPC) stipulates:

> A designation of origin is the denomination of a country, a region, or a town used to designate goods which are manufactured in this location, and the quality or characteristics of which derive from a specific geographical environment consisting of natural and human factors.

11.70   Thus, any use of a term which is identical or similar to a protected geographical indication in relation to products which do not originate from the protected location is prohibited. In the case of use of a similar name, a likelihood of confusion,[38] or an intention to copy, must be proved. The false indication may be affixed either to the goods themselves,[39] or to any accompanying documentation, such as delivery orders.[40]

11.71   The use of false indications of origin is also sanctioned separately as a customs offence pursuant to Articles 39 and 40 of the Customs Code.[41]

11.72   It appears that applications for action by the French customs authorities have already been filed—and accepted—in respect of Champagne and Cognac under the Regulation.

(4) Moulds and matrices

11.73   Moulds and matrices, and more generally any equipment specifically designated or adapted for the manufacture of unauthentic goods can also be detained, and subsequently destroyed, by the French customs authorities, in the context of infringements of patents, trade marks, and designs, by virtue, for example, of Article L 716-8 of the IPC.[42]

C. Goods excluded by the Regulation

11.74   Whereas the French customs authorities will not, in principle, detain, or suspend the release of goods which have been manufactured and/or marketed in breach of

---

[38] Supreme Court (*Cour de cassation*), Criminal Chamber, 18 January 1955 [1955] Bull Crim No 44; Supreme Court (*Cour de cassation*), Criminal Chamber, 12 June 1978, Bull Civ 1978, IV No 161, 138.

[39] Supreme Court (*Cour de cassation*), Criminal Chamber, 16 May 1935 [1935] Gazette du Palais 2.131.

[40] Supreme Court (*Cour de cassation*), Criminal Chamber, 17 January 1974, Bull Crim 1974 No 28, p 146.

[41] *Code des Douanes*, Ch V, s 2, *Prohibitions relatives à la protection des marques et des indications d'origines*, Arts 39 and 40.

[42] Cf Reg 1383/2003, Art 2(3). Art L 716-8 of the IPC provides that 'Officers of the judicial police may, whenever offences under Arts L 716-9 and L 716-10 have been reported, proceed

a contractual agreement with the right-holder, the same is not the case, or at least was not the case in the past, in respect of parallel imported goods.

(1) Parallel imported goods

For the reasons explained above (para 11.07), French Customs rely largely on the IPC rather than on the Regulation, and usually inform the right-holder of the movement of suspect goods, at least on an informal basis, even if they believe the goods may be genuine. **11.75**

At least in the past, border measures could be taken to prevent the circulation, *even in transit*, of (authentic) parallel goods. In this regard, French case law, and the broadly worded Article L 716-9 of the IPC defining trade mark infringement,[43] made it possible to take action against unlawful parallel imports. **11.76**

The precedents cited have not, to our knowledge, been challenged successfully. **11.77**

The Paris Court of Appeal, in two similar cases, considered, on 13 October 2000[44] and 28 November 2001,[45] that the importation, onto the French territory, of genuine goods for the purpose of shipping them back to the USA or Dubai, constituted an infringement under Article L 716-9 of the IPC. **11.78**

In the case dated 28 November 2001, the company, MTS had acquired the litigious goods (perfumes) from a Kuwaiti company for the purpose of transhipment to the USA via Paris. The goods were genuine, but MTS could not produce evidence showing that Yves Saint Laurent ('YSL') had agreed to their importation. The Court of Appeal confirmed the judgment handed down by the Court of First Instance of Créteil (having jurisdiction over border measures taken at Orly Airport). **11.79**

The Court of Appeal ruled that: **11.80**

> Considering that MTS has not proved that it had obtained the consent of YSL to bring those products onto French Territory, the infringement by way of importation, under any Customs status, as stated by Article L 716-9 of the Intellectual Property Code, is characterised by the mere transit of goods.

In the second case, goods bearing the original trade marks 'AMARIGE' and 'ANAIS ANAIS' originating from Miami and destined for Dubai had been **11.81**

---

to the seizure of goods unlawfully manufactured, imported, stocked, offered for sale, delivered, or supplied, and of any material and equipment specially designed for the purpose of such unlawful acts.'

[43] Art L 716-9 provides that 'Shall be punished by four years of prison and a fine of 400,000 Euro any person who has:[. . .]

  a) Reproduced, imitated, used, affixed, removed, or altered a trade mark [. . .] in violation of the rights conferred by the registration thereof and the prohibitions deriving therefrom;.
  b) Imported, under any customs procedure, or exported, goods under an infringing trade mark.'

[44] Paris Court of Appeal, 13 October 2000, PIBD 2001, 713-III-60.
[45] Paris Court of Appeal, 28 November 2001, PIBD 2002, 741-III-212.

blocked by the customs authorities, and infringement proceedings had been commenced by the trade mark proprietor before the Bobigny Court of First instance (having jurisdiction over border measures taken at Roissy Airport).

11.82   The Court of Appeal, in a decision dated 13 October 2000, quashed the judgment, stating that:

> With regard to Article L 716-9 of the IPC, which is relevant in this case, the fact that the litigious goods were merely in transit in France and not destined to the French market, does not prevent AL MUNIRA from being civilly liable, since it cannot prove the consent of the right-holder for this import; That, contrary to what was held by the Court of First Instance, the defendant cannot escape liability by claiming that the right of the appellant had lapsed, since it is not claimed that they would have consented to a first use in the EEA of the litigious goods.

11.83   The Court considered that the non-authorized parallel imports fell within the scope of Article L 716-9 of the IPC, even though this provision refers only to goods 'bearing an infringing trade mark'.[46]

11.84   It seems that French judges, in the context of parallel imports, still consider that the mere transit through the French territory of branded goods which, although genuine, have not been placed on the market of the EEA with the right-holder's consent constitutes a trade mark infringement. However, there are no reported decisions on this issue since the ECJ ruling in the *Rioglass* case.[47]

11.85   A definitive answer to this question will most likely be provided by the case pending before the ECJ in *Class International BV v Colgate Palmolive & Anor*,[48] which concerns the importation of toothpaste, covered by an earlier Benelux and Community trade mark, from South Africa, and detained while in transit in Rotterdam, but the final destination of which, namely within or outside the Community, was unclear.

11.86   Customs detained the goods, and following an infringement action brought by the owner of the right, the court referred a number of questions to the ECJ which may be summarized as follows: Can the exclusive right in a trade mark be relied upon to prevent the transit of goods? Does the detention of the goods in a customs office, or a bonded warehouse, constitute a 'use in the course of trade'? What is the relevance of the final destination of the goods? Who bears the onus of proof in determining the final destination of the goods?

11.87   The answer to these questions will undoubtedly prove an interesting development, and might change the course of evolving French case law on this issue.

11.88   Until the ECJ decides this matter, the highly protective stance taken by the French judiciary and customs authorities will continue to derive from the fact that the

---

[46] An exhaustive summary of all French cases dealing with parallel imports and transit can be found in PIBD 2003, 760-III-164.

[47] Cf para 11.14 above.   [48] Case C-405/03, still pending.

importation of goods which infringe trade mark rights constitutes, in addition to the criminal offence provided by the IPC, a customs offence ('*délit douanier*').[49]

This highly protective approach toward trade marks is also reflected in the fact **11.89** that the French courts consider the mere filing of a French trade mark application to be an act of infringement, which to our knowledge is unique in Europe. This principle is well established, and has recently been confirmed by several decisions.[50] However, it is questionable whether this applies only to French trade mark applications, or also to Community trade mark applications.

The connection, in our opinion, between this well-established case law principle **11.90** and the courts' attitude towards goods in transit (both unlawful or lawful parallel imports as in the *Rioglass* case), is that the French judges, in the context of trade mark infringements, are concerned neither by the lack of actual damage/use, nor by the absence of actual marketing or placing of goods on the market.

At any rate, the latest official instructions to French customs officers are to refrain **11.91** from detaining authentic parallel imports, on the basis of either the IPC or the Regulation.[51]

However, it remains possible for French Customs to take border measures against **11.92** genuine parallel imported goods when, as is often the case with goods originating from Asia, such goods are found amongst non-original goods. In this respect, Article 434 of the Customs Code provides that '[. . .] fraudulent goods may be confiscated. In addition, goods dissimulating the fraud can also be confiscated.' Accordingly, customs officers may seize unlawful parallel imports together with counterfeit goods if the genuine goods may be regarded as dissimulating the fraud.

(2) *Goods which have been manufactured under conditions other than those which have been agreed with the right-holder*

In accordance with their internal guidelines, customs do not get involved with **11.94** contractual breaches of a licence agreement by a licensee. Thus, they do not inform the right-holder when they find goods which do not comply with the terms of a licence contract. However, if the goods are of poor quality, they may detain the goods, and check with the right-holder whether they are genuine or counterfeit.

In view of the Administrative Order of 25 July 2001 implementing, inter alia, **11.95** certain provisions of the EC Directive 89/104[52] and the EC Regulation 40/94,[53]

---

[49] Cf para 11.07 and n 6 above.
[50] Cf, eg, Paris Court of Appeal, 30 January 2004, PIBD 2004, 785-III-266, and Paris Court of First Instance, 9 March 2004, PIBD 2004, 790-III-421.
[51] Indeed, the regime of the Regulation is not applicable to such goods (cf Reg 1383/2003, Art 3(1), first indent).   [52] N 21above.
[53] Council Reg (EC) No 40/94 of 20 December 1993 on the Community trade mark, [1994] OJ L 11/1, as last amended by Reg (EC) No 807/2003, [2003] OJ L 122/36.

a paragraph has been added to Article L 714-1 of the IPC (dealing with trade mark licences), which specifically provides for the possibility to act against a licensee who breaches his contractual obligations.[54]

11.96   Therefore, it is theoretically possible to request that French customs authorities detain, or suspend the release of, goods which contrave to a licence agreement concerning trade mark or authors' rights, in order to later institute proceedings, but solely on the basis of the IPC.[55]

(3) Goods contained in travellers' personal baggage

11.97   In France, travellers' personal baggage is subject to customs controls. According to the customs authorities, the limit of the duty free allowance of EUR 175 referred to in Article 3(2) of the Regulation used to be calculated by reference to the value of an authentic product, and it is now assessed on the basis of the retail value of a counterfeit or pirated product.

11.98   It is difficult for customs to evaluate the 'non-commercial nature' of goods. Upon coming across goods of a commercial nature, customs will ordinarily limit themselves to seize and destroy the goods. They may also levy a fine against the traveller, but usually they will not inform the right-holder of the measures taken, unless there are strong indications that the traveller is importing non-authentic goods on a regular basis.

11.99   In practice, customs often provide the right-holder with a summary of the seizures which have been carried out over the previous year, indicating only the dates of the seizure, and the quantities seized.

II. APPLICATION FOR ACTION BY THE CUSTOMS AUTHORITIES

11.100 In line with the heavy involvement of the French authorities in the fight against the traffic of counterfeit and pirated goods, it is relatively straightforward to be granted an application for action for customs measures under the Regulation in

---

[54] This Article reads: '[. . .] The rights deriving from a trade mark registration or application can be relied upon against the licensee who breaches the provisions of the licence regarding its term, the way the trade mark can be used, the nature of the goods or services to which it can be affixed, the territory covered, or the quality of the goods or services provided by the licensee'. This provision clarifies certain conflicting precedents which had considered that the breach of a trade mark licence only resulted in a finding of civil liability whereas in relation to authors' rights, the breach of the licence agreement also constituted an act of infringement.

[55] Indeed, the Regulation does not apply in such circumstances: cf Art 3(1), second indent.

France. Three hundred and seventy-five applications have been granted by French Customs to date, with on average, approximately, two applications being filed every month subsequent to *ex officio* procedures.

A. Measures prior to an application for action by the customs authorities ('*ex officio*' measures)

The French customs officials readily apply *ex officio* measures under Article 4 of the Regulation, in particular when large quantities of suspect goods are involved. **11.101**

Even prior to the entry into force of the current Regulation, French Customs enforced *ex officio* measures, but only when the infringement was considered blatant. **11.102**

Consequently, if the infringement appears obvious, and large quantities are involved, or where international trafficking is suspected, customs contact the right-holder or his representative (usually by accessing on-line databases to find out which representative filed the intellectual property rights in question), requesting them to file an application for action. **11.103**

The application is then processed quickly by the relevant customs department, so that the entire procedure can be handled within the time limit of three working days stipulated in Article 4(1) of the Regulation. **11.104**

Where goods are suspected of infringing a trade mark, customs are especially diligent. **11.105**

The notion of 'sufficient grounds for suspecting that the goods infringe an intellectual property right' is interpreted quite broadly by French Customs, especially when they are aware that the right-holder or his representative are cooperative, indicated by for example, their responding regularly to informal requests for information. **11.106**

The factors taken into account by the customs authorities when making the risk analysis derive from their previous experience. The country of origin of the goods in question is obviously a key factor. For example, clothing originating from Turkey and Vietnam is treated with greater vigilance than goods originating from an EC Member State. China and Dubai are also considered suspicious origins, in particular for electronic goods. **11.107**

The manner in which the goods are packaged, and the quality of the packaging also provide useful pointers to the customs officials, and of course, cases where the customs declaration does not match the goods being transported will be treated with suspicion. **11.108**

11.109 Other scenarios where, for example, several brands are being transported together, will almost certainly look suspicious.

11.110 The information provided to the right-holder by French Customs under Article 4(2) of the Regulation is essentially the nature of the goods and the country of origin as well as the country of destination.

11.111 In relation to trade marks, authors' rights and registered designs, the relevant Articles of the IPC (L 335-10, L 521-7, and L 716-8) provide that:

> for the purpose of initiating the legal proceedings stated in the above paragraph, the applicant can obtain from the Customs authorities, the names and addresses of the consignor, the importer, the recipient of the goods detained, or their retailer, as well as their quantity, notwithstanding the provisions of Article 59bis of the Customs Code relating to professional secret under which Customs officers are bound.

11.112 These Articles entitle right-holders to obtain confidential information in order to enable them to institute proceedings before either the criminal or civil courts.

11.113 Samples may only be obtained in accordance with the provisions of the Regulation as there is no provision dealing with this issue under the IPC. As a result, French Customs always refuse to provide the right-holder with samples of the goods seized if the detention has been made under the provisions of the IPC. Similarly, they will in principle refuse to hand samples over to the right-holder in the context of *ex officio* interventions under the Regulation, as long as the right-holder has not filed an application for action.[56]

11.114 A further possible way of obtaining samples in the context of *ex officio* procedures, which is more costly and time-consuming, is to request a court order authorizing the seizure of samples of the goods by relying on the relevant provisions of the IPC which permit such confiscation means (cf para 11.205 below).

11.115 However, it is now common practice to send digital pictures of the goods to the relevant right-holder, even in the context of *ex officio* procedures, before filing and acceptance of an application for action. Such pictures are often sufficient to allow the latter to determine whether the goods are genuine or infringing.

11.116 When goods are detained by customs, the right-holder is generally required formally to examine the goods, and to confirm in writing whether they are genuine.

11.117 Nonetheless, where the infringement is blatant, or can be ascertained in the course of a simple telephone conversation with the customs authorities, the right-holder may usually limit himself to confirming in writing that the goods are non-authentic, and to providing details in support of his statement on that occasion concerning, for example, the retail price for an equivalent genuine product.

---

[56] Only in this case may the right-holder rely on Art 9(3) of the Regulation.

However, customs are often cautious where, for example, the suspected trade **11.118** mark infringement concerns use of a similar, instead of an identical, sign, or if large quantities are involved. Usually in such circumstances, they will request that an official report be submitted to them in which either the right-holder or his representative confirms that the goods are illicit.

The deadline of three working days stipulated in Article 4 of the Regulation is **11.119** applied strictly by French Customs, as is the 10-day deadline of Article 13.

Generally speaking, French Customs are keen to carry out controls on goods **11.120** suspected of infringing intellectual property rights, and where they have strong grounds for suspecting that a batch of goods does indeed infringe such rights, readily act *ex officio*.

B. The lodging and processing of applications for customs action

According to customs' guidelines, an application for action can be filed by the **11.121** right-holder free of charge, either as a preventive measure, or where he has reason to believe that his intellectual property rights have been, or are likely to be, infringed.

The filing procedure for applications for action has been modified by French **11.122** Customs in September 2004, so as to match the requirements of the new Regulation.

(1) Persons entitled to file an application for action

Only 'right-holders' are entitled to file an application for action under the **11.123** Regulation. Pursuant to Article 2(2) of the Regulation, not only the owners of the intellectual property rights referred to in Article 2(1) of the Regulation qualify as such, but also the authorized users of such rights, or their representatives.

Definition of 'right-holders' under the Regulation

According to the guidelines of the French customs authorities, the right-holder **11.124** *stricto sensu* is either:

— for registered rights, or for intellectual property rights for which an application has been filed, the person who can prove title to those rights;
— for copyright, related rights and unregistered design rights, the person who can produce evidence of authorship of the status as the original owner of those rights;
— for a geographical indication, the entity which produces evidence of its entitlement to the indication.

11.125 Persons authorized to use intellectual property rights include exclusive and non-exclusive licensees, distributors, and commercial agents. They are required to file a copy of the document proving authorization to use the right in question in support of their application.

11.126 Customs do not require licensees to be recorded before relevant Industrial Property Offices in order to file a customs application, which may sometimes give rise to some problems. Indeed, in France as in some other countries, the applicability of Article 2(2)(b) of the Regulation vis-à-vis unrecorded licensees is tentative.

11.127 In this regard, under French law, licences granted for industrial property rights must be recorded with the relevant Industrial Property Offices to be enforceable against third parties. Consequently, the parties concerned by an intervention by customs (for example, the consignee, the consignor, the declarant, or the holder of the goods) being all third parties to a licence agreement, the licence would have to be recorded to be enforceable against them. The question arises whether the Regulation, which has direct effect in the national law of the Member States, 'disqualifies', so to speak, this general principle.

11.128 In addition, an unrecorded licensee will not be able to institute proceedings in his own name following a detention under national law, as infringement actions may in principle only be initiated by exclusive licensees if the right-holder decides not to act. A non-exclusive licensee can join an action in order to obtain damages covering his own loss. However, in either case, the licences will have to be recorded in order to be enforceable against third parties.

11.129 The 'representative' can be any natural or legal person whose name is mentioned in the application. It may be an attorney, an intellectual property agent, a consultant, a collective management society, or more generally, any person empowered by the right-holder to act in his name before the customs authorities.[57]

Proof of entitlement to file an application for action

For right-holders stricto sensu

11.130 The documents which have to be filed by the right-holder to prove his rights depend on whether the rights on which the application is based are registered or unregistered.[58]

11.131 For industrial property rights, such as trade marks, patents, supplementary protection certificates, plant variety rights, and registered designs, which are the subject of registration, customs request proof of such a registration with the

---

[57] Cf Commission Reg (EC) No 1891/2004 of 21 October 2004 laying down provisions for the implementation of Council Reg (EC) No 1383/2003 concerning customs action against goods suspected of infringing certain intellectual property rights and the measures to be taken against goods found to have infringed such rights [2004] OJ L 328/16, Art 1.   [58] Cf ibid, Art 2.

relevant office. Although it is permitted to provide extracts from official or commercial databases, the customs authorities prefer certified copies of the relevant registrations issued by the granting office in question.

It is noteworthy that under French law, it is possible to initiate an infringement **11.132** action (but not to file an application for action) on the basis of an application for a trade mark (Article L 716-2 of the IPC) or a patent (Article L 613-1 of the IPC), provided the application has been published, or even prior to publication in case where the application has been notified to the defendant.

For unregistered rights, such as authors' rights, related rights, or unregistered **11.133** Community designs, customs request evidence of authorship, which can be provided by any means.

Regarding designations of origin, geographical indications, and geographical **11.134** designations, customs require proof of entitlement.

For persons authorized to use the right

Individual manufacturers may also have been entitled, as 'authorized users of the **11.135** right', to submit an application for action under the Regulation.

There are no specific evidential requirements for authorized users, other than **11.136** those referred to in Article 2(2) of Regulation 1891/2004, since recording of the licence agreement does not need to be established. In this respect, customs require only a copy of the licence agreement or other contractual link between the right-holder and the authorized user.

Representatives

Representatives must submit a power of attorney together with their applica- **11.137** tions for action under the Regulation to prove that they have the capacity to represent the owner or authorized user of the right on which the application is based.

In France, attorneys-at-law (*avocats*) are considered as having the capacity *ad litem* **11.138** to represent their clients, so that no power of attorney is required for them to act before the courts. This capacity derives from Article 416 of the French New Civil Procedure Code.[59] However, although it was not their practice previously, customs now also require a power from attorneys-at-law filing an application for action under the Regulation on behalf of a client.

Customs may accept multiple applications, filed by several representatives, but in **11.139** such cases, they will require a power from each of them.

---

[59] *Nouveau Code de Procédure Civile*. Art 416 of this Code reads: 'Anyone willing to represent or assist a party must bring evidence of its mandate to do so. However, the "avocat" or the registered attorney before the Court of Appeal ("avoué") are not required to produce such proof.'

11.140 Foreign representatives not having a place of business in France may also file applications for action. However, this is often not very practical, and therefore not recommended.

11.141 Finally, the declaration referred to in Article 6 of the Regulation will have to be signed by the legal representative of the applicant.

(2) Competent customs department and formal requirements

Competent customs department

11.142 The French customs department responsible under Article 5(2) of the Regulation to process applications for action is:

Customs General Directorate (*Direction Générale des Douanes*)
Bureau E4—Intellectual Property Unit (*Section de la Propriété Intellectuelle*)
8, rue de la Tour des Dames
F-75436 Paris Cedex 09
Tel: +33 (1) 55 07 48 60
Fax: +33 (1) 55 07 48 66
marie.therese.boufares@douane.finances.gouv.fr
laurence.micheletti@douane.finances.gouv.fr
wilfrid.roge@douane.finances.gouv.fr

11.143 Details of all applications and renewals are handled by this department, which also answers questions from the relevant customs offices concerning the legality of their actions in the course of their operations.

Form of the application for action

11.144 Applications for action may be filed by e-mail, fax, or post, but original copies of the declaration under Article 6 of the Regulation and any power of attorney required must in all cases be sent by post.

11.145 In practice, customs prefer postal applications confirmed by e-mail, particularly if they can store in electronic form the enclosures detailing for example, the list of licences, and background information concerning possible counterfeits. This facilitates notification to the various offices nationwide, and enables such information to be put on the customs' intranet.

11.146 In France, it has been necessary until now to file only one copy of the application. This was particularly advantageous in cases where the genuine goods are expensive, as in such circumstances the provision of additional samples to customs can prove costly. However, it is preferable to submit digital photographs and all supporting evidence in a format which may be copied easily, to allow dissemination to all customs offices concerned.

Language requirements

There is a well-established tradition in France of using exclusively French language, particularly in matters before French administrations, since the 1539 *Edit de Villers Côteret*, and the 1994 *Loi Toubon* concerning the use of the French Language.[60] **11.147**

The working language of the French customs authorities, like all other French administrations, is French, and consequently any document which is not translated into French will be rejected. **11.148**

Therefore, a French version of the application and the declaration under Article 6 of the Regulation, together with all accompanying exhibits—also to be translated—must be submitted. In practice, bilingual versions of documents are often used. **11.149**

(3) Requirements regarding the content of the application for action

Mandatory information

The application for action must contain all the information needed to enable the goods in question to be identified easily by customs, and in particular: **11.150**

— a detailed and accurate technical description of the goods;
— any specific information the right-holder may have concerning the type or pattern of fraud;
— the name and address of the contact person appointed by the right-holder;
— the undertaking required of the applicant by Article 6 of the Regulation, and proof that the applicant is the proprietor of the intellectual property rights on which the application is based in respect of the goods in question.[61]

A detailed technical description of the goods is the key to providing a concise and effective customs application. Customs officers control massive quantities of goods, and it is therefore in the applicant's interest to provide as much information as clearly as possible in order to assist them in their task. **11.151**

The technical information provided to customs should in particular include the following: **11.152**

• the way to recognize infringing goods;
• the kind of goods or particular models which are most often copied;
• any safety labelling, such as holograms, must be enclosed with the application;
• any useful information, such as the main countries where the genuine goods are manufactured;

---

[60] *Loi Toubon* concerning use of French language No 4/8/1994, available on www.legifrance.gouv.fr.
[61] Reg 1383/2003, Art 5(5), first and second indents.

- the list of distributors and licensees;
- the main countries of origin of the counterfeits.

11.153 Failing to provide relevant material will not necessarily result in the rejection of the application, but customs will be less inclined in such cases to act for the right-holder.

11.154 There is no obligation for the right-holder to appoint a local representative, nor is there any nationality requirement for the contact person. In practice however, it is strongly recommended that a local contact be appointed.

11.155 In addition, if the administrative contact person is not informed of the technical aspects of the goods, it is important to appoint a separate contact for technical issues, as the French customs officials often have technical enquiries which require immediate assistance.

Optional information

11.156 Customs are always keen to obtain as specific and accurate information as possible to enable them to distinguish between the authentic and non-authentic goods, and more generally any information the right-holder may have concerning the suspect products (documents, pictures, etc).

11.157 Various types of information can help improve customs intelligence on specific goods and patterns of fraud.

11.158 Additional supporting details should be provided, where known, such as, for example, the pre-tax value of the authentic goods, the location of the goods or their intended destination, particulars identifying the consignment, the scheduled arrival or departure date of the goods, the means of transport used, the identity of the importer, exporter, or holder of the goods, etc.[62]

11.159 When the intellectual property right is well-known and is frequently the subject of large scale infringement, an expert will often be expected to organize a training session, where all relevant samples and documents will be exhibited, to those customs officers who often encounter counterfeit goods (that is, the customs officials active in airports and sea ports, and at the land borders).

Additional information specific to the type of intellectual property right referred to in the application

11.160 Customs may also require additional information specific to the right on which the application is based.[63] In relation to plant variety rights, for example, bulbs of the plants should preferably be filed along with the application.

---

[62] Reg 1383/2003, Art 5(5), fourth indent.   [63] Ibid, Art 5(6).

Basically, the more difficult it is to detect the counterfeit goods, the more important **11.161**
it is to file a clear and concise application, and to organize training sessions with
the major customs offices.

(4) *Processing and acceptance of the application for action*

Upon receipt of the application, the competent customs department[64] will process **11.162**
it and inform the applicant of its decision in writing within 30 working days.[65]

If customs decide to reject an application, this unilateral administrative decision **11.163**
must be based on detailed facts or points of law, which must be explained in the
refusal notification. This decision may be appealed before the Paris
Administrative Court (*Tribunal Administratif de Paris*).[66]

In practice, however, rejection notices are generally accompanied by a request to file
more detailed documentation, and are therefore, strictly speaking, not definitive.

In the case of several applications for action being filed covering the same right, for **11.164**
example by different companies within the same group, customs have no other
choice but to reject the later redundant applications.

Once the application is granted, it is valid for one year and renewable indefinitely, **11.165**
provided that renewal is requested within 45 days prior to the expiry date. However,
the right-holder may not pre-determine the renewal period in his request.

(5) *'Community' applications for action*

On receiving a 'Community' application for action filed under Article 5(4) of the **11.166**
Regulation through French Customs, the latter will send the relevant documents
to the authorities of the other Member States designated by the applicant.

However, the foreign customs authorities will often require a translation into the **11.167**
official language of the relevant country of the supporting documents, an original
of the undertaking under Article 6 of the Regulation, and preferably the appointment of a local representative in that country.

Similarly, a Community application designating France and filed in another **11.168**
Member State will have to be drafted in, or translated into, French, together with
all the supporting evidence. An original of the undertaking under Article 6 will
have to be submitted, in French. A local representative in France will also, preferably, have to be appointed by the right-holder.

Therefore, from a practical point of view, it may be as simple to file separate **11.169**
applications in each of the countries of interest as to use the Community

---

[64] Cf para 11.142 above.   [65] Reg 1383/2003, Art 5(7).
[66] Tribunal Administratif de Paris, 7 rue Jouy, 75004 Paris, Phone: +33(0)1 44 59 44 00/fax: +33
(0)1 44 59 46 46.

application route. This, at least is the strategy recommended by the French customs authorities. And indeed, in common with the customs authorities, we are of the opinion that, when France is designated in a Community application, it is advisable also to file a *national* application for action in addition to this Community application. This double application allows the right-holder to benefit from the larger scope of protection provided by the IPC, especially in the case of trade mark infringements. If the right-holder has only filed a Community application designating France, French Customs will be bound by the Regulation, and unable to rely on the more favourable provisions of the French IPC. In particular with regard to trade marks, these favourable provisions allow customs to seize infringing goods without the need for the right-holder to institute court proceedings, since trade mark infringements are considered a 'customs offence' in France.

III. CONDITIONS GOVERNING ACTION BY CUSTOMS AUTHORITIES AND BY THE AUTHORITIES WITH JURISDICTION TO DETERMINE WHETHER GOODS INFRINGE AN INTELLECTUAL PROPERTY RIGHT

11.170   Once an application for action has been accepted by French Customs, they will monitor the traffic of goods suspected of infringing the intellectual property rights referred to in the application at border posts. Section A below examines the conditions governing such actions by the French Customs authorities.

11.171   Subsequent to the interception by customs of goods suspected of infringing an intellectual property right, right-holders are in principle compelled to refer the case to the authorities having jurisdiction to determine whether these goods do indeed infringe an intellectual property right (see section C). This procedural requirement proves particularly burdensome in some cases, which led the European legislator to set out a facultative simplified procedure (discussed in section B). Following border measures, the goods must to be stored under customs' supervision (section E).

A. Conditions governing action by customs authorities

(1) Factual background

11.172   The main customs offices which can be cited as being in the forefront of the fight against counterfeit and pirated goods are located at the principal airports, such as Roissy (Charles de Gaulle airport North of Paris), Orly (Airport south of Paris).

In addition, the Lyon airport customs office has recently taken significant actions, detaining thousands of counterfeit goods. Reference can also be made to Marseille and Le Havre, as the main French seaports, as well as to the customs authorities on the Belgian border, which are all heavily involved in anti-counterfeiting.

The lion share of border measures (40 per cent in 2003, and 47 per cent in 2004) **11.173** are taken in freight controls, but there is an increasing number of counterfeits sent by post or courier which led to the seizure of 151,000 items in 2003.[67]

Customs also concentrate their surveillance on flea markets, where large numbers **11.174** of counterfeits are widely sold. When dealing with goods which are already on French territory, customs rely on the IPC, and not on the Regulation.

(2) Notification of customs intervention

The right-holder or his representative, as well as the declarant or holder of the **11.175** goods, may be notified of an intervention by customs by several means. It could be a telephone call prior to the detention of goods to check whether such goods could be infringing. It could also be a telephone call immediately after the detention of the goods, but it is more often by way of a fax or an e-mail attaching digital photographs.

The deadlines of three or 10 (up to 20) working days, referred to in Articles 4 and 13 of the Regulation, start to run from receipt of the notification by the right-holder. It is therefore imperative that the right-holder immediately acknowledges receipt of the notification which was addressed to them by the customs service, as soon as they receive such notification.

Within the framework of the Regulation and the IPC, 'working day' is defined as **11.176** not including public holidays or weekends.[68]

(3) Information to be provided by customs to the right-holder before the right-holder confirms the infringing nature of the goods

Once goods suspected of infringing intellectual property rights are detained by **11.177** customs, little information may theoretically be provided by customs to the right-holder without the latter being bound to initiate proceedings.

In the relevant provisions of the IPC, it is stated that 'for the purpose of institut- **11.178** ing legal proceedings, the plaintiff may require the Customs administration to communicate the names and addresses of the sender, the importer, the consignee or holder of the goods detained, and also the quantity thereof, notwithstanding

---

[67] See 2004 Customs Report, on the website http://www.douane.gouv.fr/pdf/actualite/copebilan.pdf.
[68] For further information on the computation of the deadlines provided for in the Regulation cf M Schneider and O Vrins, 'Reg 1383/2003', Chapter 3 in this book.

the provisions of Article 59bis of the Customs Code concerning the professional secrecy which binds all Customs officers'.[69]

11.179   Thus, any information concerning the names and addresses of the consignee, consignor, importer, declarant or holder of the goods detained, and also the quantity involved, is specifically covered by the laws of confidentiality under French customs law.

11.180   In theory therefore, customs may only give information concerning the nature of the goods, the country of origin and destination, as well as sometimes their impressions of the quality of the goods, the fact that there is only one trade mark involved, or when there are other type of goods involved in the same batch, the kind of packaging used, etc.

11.181   Whereas the confidentiality regarding the names and addresses of the parties involved is quite understandable, the confidentiality concerning the quantity of the goods is often problematic, as the numbers of counterfeit goods is of key importance in deciding whether legal action is to be commenced or not and therefore, if the confidentiality of the contact details of the various parties can be lifted. On this issue, the IPC proves to be tighter than the Regulation which, quite sensibly, allows customs to communicate the actual or estimated quantity, next to the actual or supposed nature, of the goods whose release has been suspended, or which have been detained.[70]

11.182   Despite the supremacy of Community law over national law, and in particular the fact that the Regulation has direct effect in all Member States, customs officers, when relying on the IPC (which represents the majority of cases), often refuse to reveal the quantity of goods involved.

11.183   In practical terms, information concerning the name and address of the consignee, consignor, declarant, holder of the goods is not given unless the applicant undertakes to commence legal proceedings should the goods prove to be counterfeit.[71]

11.184   Therefore, the only information which can be obtained if the right-holder is not willing to make such an undertaking is the origin of the goods and whether they are intended for the French market or in transit, and if so, towards which country.

(4) Inspection of the suspected goods

11.185   When customs suspect goods of infringing certain intellectual property rights, they contact the right-holder (either informally by telephone when no measures have been taken yet, or by a faxed notification when the goods are detained) in order to obtain confirmation of the infringement as well as the criteria for demonstrating that the goods are counterfeit, and their retail price.

---

[69] IPC, Arts L 716-8 (trade marks), L 335-10 (authors' rights) and L 521-7 (registered designs).
[70] Reg 1383/2003, Art 9(2).
[71] It is questionable, however, whether this practice is consistent with Art 9(3) of the Regulation.

Customs usually endeavour to provide the right-holder with digital **11.186** photographs, where they are equipped with a digital camera (which is not always the case), or any other information requested such as bar codes, details of the labels, etc.

The options are then as follows: **11.187**

- The inspection is made on the premises of the customs authorities, and an official report is drafted. This is the preferred option when large quantities are detained, or when the matter is particularly sensitive.
- The inspection is made on the basis of digital photos, and a formal letter is sent to customs stating that the goods are genuine or infringing together with an explanation and indicating the retail price of the genuine goods.

It should be noted that on the basis of the IPC, the French customs officials do not **11.188** provide any samples of the goods detained despite the fact this practice is at odds with Regulation 1383/2003. Even when the action is based on the Regulation, it is difficult to obtain samples which are reluctantly remitted by customs.

B. Simplified procedure allowing the destruction of the goods without there being any need to determine whether an intellectual property right has been infringed under national law

One of the principal innovations of the Regulation is the accelerated destruction **11.189** procedure set out in Article 11.

However, this provision is not compulsory and its implementation is left to the **11.190** discretion of each Member State, thereby allowing for discrepancies to develop between the practices of the different countries. This hybrid between a Directive and a Regulation is far from ideal as the provisions of Article 11, if they are ever to be implemented by Member States, will be adopted at different times and possibly in different ways.

At any rate, the implementation of Article 11 in France will most likely prove **11.191** difficult, as there is a strong tradition of protecting property under French Law.

Therefore, the idea of destroying goods, even under the responsibility of the right- **11.192** holder, if nothing is heard from the declarant, holder or owner of the goods after 10 days, would be somewhat ground breaking.

In this regard, the destruction of goods is, as matters stand, entirely at the judge's **11.193** discretion in France.

For the sake of completeness, it should be noted that a draft legislative pro- **11.194** posal suggests implementing the accelerated procedure set out in Article 11 of the Regulation, provided prior authorization from a judge is obtained in order to avoid that the *Conseil Constitutionnel* could declare such measures unconstitutional.

11.195 French Customs object to out-of-court settlements, and it was French Customs who requested and obtained the provision contained in Article 12 of the Regulation under which the use by a right-holder of the information communicated by customs, for example, to conclude a settlement with the parties involved in breach of national law might cause the right-holder to incur civil liability and lead to the suspension of the application for action.

11.196 Under French practice, only customs are entitled to enter into a settlement with the infringer, provided a fine is levied. Fines are calculated as a percentage of the estimated value of the goods, based on the retail price of genuine goods, not only of the goods subject to border measures, but also of those goods which, according to accounts and records, have been sold over the three previous years (which is the date before which legal action must be commenced for tax purposes), and the goods are destroyed.

11.197 Of course, any settlement between customs and the infringer does not preclude the right-holder from taking action against the latter.

11.198 Customs do not permit the granting of retroactive licences by the right-holder to the parties involved in the traffic of infringing goods which are being detained under either the IPC or the Regulation.

11.199 This view is similar to that of the French criminal courts which, in infringement actions where the intellectual property right is declared invalid during proceedings, nevertheless consider that the criminal intent of the infringer must be sanctioned, but do not make award for damages.[72]

C. Conditions governing action by the authorities having jurisdiction to determine whether the goods infringe an intellectual property right

11.200 Once suspect goods have been detained, the right-holder must choose a course of action, which will depend on several factual considerations, namely the kind of proof required, the nature of the infringement and of the infringer, and the remedies sought.

---

[72] In this regard, see the comments of M Marcellin in *Protection Pénale de la Propriété Intellectuelle* (Paris: Cedat, 1996) 268, and for case law: Supreme Court (Criminal Chamber), 22 November 1927 [1929] Sirey 153, and 25 May 1956 [1956] JCP (Jurisclasseur Périodique) II-9413.

(1) Authorities having jurisdiction to determine whether the goods infringe an intellectual property right

The choice of the course of action to be taken depends more on the characteristics **11.201** of the infringing acts themselves and the priorities of the right-holder, than on the type of intellectual property right infringed.

Indeed, all intellectual property rights are treated in the same way by the IPC, apart **11.202** from trade mark infringements which also constitute a customs offence ('*délit douanier*') in addition to being an infringement under the provisions of the IPC.

In practice, under criminal law, the Attorney General will be more eager to **11.203** prosecute cases *ex officio* where there are also public issues at stake such as where public health or safety are concerned.

Once the goods controlled by the customs authorities have been declared infrin- **11.204** ging by the right-holder, there are several issues to pursue, that is, first to gather evidence of the infringement, and then to obtain suitable relief.

Conservatory measures

Articles L 335-10 (for authors' rights), L 521-7 (for registered designs), and **11.205** L 716-8 (for trade marks) of the IPC provide that:

> Detention shall be lifted automatically if the plaintiff fails, within ten working days
> from the notification of the detention of the goods, to submit evidence to the
> Customs authorities:

— either that the detention measures have been decided by the President of the
   Court of First Instance;
— or that he has instituted legal proceedings, either at the civil or criminal level,
   and has deposited the required securities to cover possible liability in the event
   of infringement not being subsequently found.

Thus, in order to avoid the release of the goods, the right-holder can produce evid- **11.206** ence of conservatory measures granted by the Court of First Instance, even though it does not strictly speaking constitute proceedings.

Under French law, it is possible to obtain either a descriptive seizure, or a selection **11.207** of samples by filing a request before the court along with evidence of the rights on which the claimant is seeking to rely.[73] The court can request the payment of a retainer when an order allowing a bailiff to seize the goods is granted.

---

[73] Art L 716-7 of the IPC stipulates that:

'The owner of an application for registration, the owner of a registered mark, or the beneficiary of an exclusive right of exploitation shall be entitled, by virtue of an order issued by the President of the First Instance Court, given on request, to direct any bailiff, assisted by experts of his choice, to proceed in any place with the detailed description, with or without taking samples, or the effective

11.208 Although, in the case of infringement of authors' rights, it is theoretically possible to obtain conservatory measures carried out by a senior police constable, without any need to obtain a court order (Articles L 332-1 and 332-2 of the IPC), the provisions of the IPC dealing with detention specifically refer to 'an order granted by the Court of First Instance'. Therefore, in the case of authors' rights, the conservatory measures must be carried out as per a court order, and not by a police officer, as the Supreme Court recalled.[74]

11.209 According to some commentators, the requirement of a court order is justified, because only the courts, and not the police, can require a retainer before granting the order.[75]

Civil and criminal proceedings

11.210 Having had recourse to conservatory measures or not, the right-holder is given the choice to bring proceedings before either the civil or criminal courts.

11.211 Once the right-holder has commenced civil legal proceedings, it is no longer possible to instigate criminal proceedings. Criminal prosecution may still be instituted *ex officio* by the Attorney General, but the right-holder may not join it as a civil party in such circumstances.

11.212 Conversely, when an action is first brought before the criminal authorities, the claimant may subsequently start civil proceedings, provided such an action is commenced before a judgment is handed down in the criminal case. In such a scenario, the civil proceedings are stayed until the criminal matter is decided.

11.213 The choice of the type of proceedings will depend on the following factors:

Small quantities of goods are involved and/or the importer of the goods is a natural person

11.214 Where only small quantities of goods are involved, and/or the importer of the goods is a natural person, the right-holder will generally be well-advised to register as a civil party by way of a letter sent to the criminal court.

11.215 In this case, the right-holder has little reason to institute civil proceedings. Indeed, no substantial damages can be obtained for small quantities, and the individuals

---

seizure of the goods or services he claims are marked, offered for sale, delivered or supplied to his prejudice in infringment of his rights.

Effective seizure may be subjected by the President of the Court to the deposit of securities by the plaintiff to provide compensation for any prejudice suffered by the defendant if the infringement proceedings are subsequently held to lack merit.

If the plaintiff fails to institute legal proceedings, either by civil action or criminal action, within a period of fifteen days, the seizure shall be automatically null and void, without prejudice to any damages that may be claimed.'

[74] Supreme Court, 4 January 1984 [1984] Annales de Propriété Industrielle, Littéraire et Artistique 78 (No 75).

[75] F Greffe, *Traité des dessins et modèles* (6th edn: Paris, Litec, 2000) 520.

in question are often bankrupt. Furthermore, no useful information is likely to be recovered in the course of an investigation as the goods are often purchased from another individual, and it is unlikely that any sales invoice exists nor any trace of a wider distribution network.

11.216 In such cases, it is recommended to advise customs of the fact that the goods are infringing, explain why, and indicate the retail price of equivalent genuine goods.

11.217 If the customs procedure has been based on Article L 716-8, L 335-10, or L 521-7 of the IPC, it is important not to request any confidential information from customs, otherwise, there is an obligation to bring proceedings.[76]

11.218 When goods are detained by customs, they duly notify not only the right-holder, but also the Attorney General.

11.219 In such a case, when the right-holder informs customs that the goods infringe any of his intellectual property rights, but advises them he will refrain from instituting proceedings, customs will seize and subsequently destroy the goods, and fine the importer.

11.220 Nevertheless, the Attorney General may decide to prosecute the matter *ex officio*. In this case, the right-holder should register as a civil party in order to obtain damages. In insignificant matters, this formality may be done by sending a letter before the date of the hearing. In this respect, Article 420-1 of the Criminal Procedure Code[77] allows the victim of an infringement to register as a civil party by way of a letter by registered mail or a fax, which must be received by the court at least 24 hours before the date of the hearing.

11.221 This procedure is simple and costs little. Furthermore, there are four notable advantages which can be outlined as follows: (1) a registration as a civil party can be done by the right-holder himself, (2) it gives access to the criminal case file, (3) it allows the right-holder to recover damages, and (4) it shows customs that the right-holder is actively defending his rights.

11.222 In order to guarantee being informed of the date of the hearing, so as to be able to proceed with registration as an injured party in due time, it is advisable to inform the customs authorities from the outset that the right-holder intends to join the proceedings in this capacity. Customs may in turn duly inform the Attorney General.

11.223 Once the Attorney General has been made aware of the fact that the right-holder intends to register as a civil party, the right-holder or his representative will receive an official notification prior to the hearing. In addition, the representative of the civil party will have access to the criminal case file, which invariably proves a useful source of information.

---

[76] Cf para 11.83 above on this point.   [77] *Code de Procédure Pénale.*

*Large quantities of goods are involved and/or are addressed to a company
with offices on French territory, and the importers are either unknown, repeat
offenders, or insolvent*

11.224 A criminal action aims at protecting the general interest from counterfeit goods, and the damages awarded to the right-holder will therefore not be substantial. The commencement of criminal proceedings by way of a complaint or a *'citation directe'*—that is, through the service of summons on a defendant—are recommended when there are large quantities of goods, and/or the goods are addressed to a French or EU company, and the infringers are either repeat offenders, not identified, or insolvent.

11.225 Under the general principles of French criminal law, offences are only sanctioned if they are intentional. Therefore, bad faith on the part of the infringer is in theory a necessary prerequisite in order to show that a criminal offence has been committed. However, there is an exception in the case of intellectual property rights, such that only negligence is required, and not actual criminal intent.[78]

11.227 Description of the proceedings. Two types of criminal proceedings can be distinguished, namely a complaint against 'X' (unknown person), or a *'citation directe'*.

11.228 First, in a complaint against X, the right-holder can either file a complaint made out against 'X' or naming the infringers, but the latter option is usually not recommended as it is advisable for the investigation carried out further to the complaint to have the widest possible scope. In addition, there is more likelihood of an abusive complaint if the infringers are cited by name.

11.229 Once a complaint has been filed, it is not technically valid until the payment by the claimant of a retainer fee, the amount of which is determined by the court. The purpose of this retainer is to deter abusive complaints. If the retainer is not paid within one month of the notification, the complaint becomes void.

11.230 The question has arisen as to whether the mere filing of a complaint could interrupt the 10-day deadline referred to in Article 13 of the Regulation even if it later becomes void for non-payment. The courts answered this question positively at least in one reported cases.[79] However, some commentators[80] believe that the simple filing of a criminal complaint is not tantamount to the commencement of proceedings. Indeed, in their opinion, the wording of the Criminal Procedure Code provides that only a *'citation directe'* (cf para 11.235 below), and the actual judgment of the investigative judge before bringing the matter before the court result in the commencement of 'proceedings to determine whether an intellectual property right has been infringed' under Article 13(1) of the Regulation, and not the mere filing of a complaint.

---

[78] Supreme Court, Criminal Chamber, 13 December 1995, RIDA No 169, p. 279.
[79] Cf S Durrande, 'L'élément intentionnel de la contrefaçon et le nouveau code pénal', 1999, Recueil Dalloz 319.1 TGI Angoulême, 20 April 1995, RDPI, N 58, 55.
[80] Yves Marcellin in 'Protection pénale de la Propriété Intellectuelle', Edition CEDAT, 1996.

In our experience, French Customs will always detain, or suspend the release of the goods if a complaint has been filed, and do not make any distinction as to which type of action has been instigated by which means, provided it can be proved that a complaint has been filed. In practice, once the complaint has been filed, a copy of the first page bearing the stamp of the clerk's office must be provided to customs in order to secure detention of the goods. **11.231**

However, in the case of a particularly sensitive matter, it might be safer to opt for a '*citation directe*' to ensure that the 10-day deadline is interrupted. **11.232**

Of key importance in such a procedure is that an investigation is carried out by the investigative judge, involving police enquiries (even in other Member States of the European Community if necessary), examination of witnesses, evidence from the right-holder, etc. This investigation does not involve any costs other than the drafting and filing of the complaint, the monitoring of the case, and the pleadings before the court. **11.233**

The downside of such proceedings is that responsibility for initiating criminal proceedings lies with the claimant who can be held personally liable in case of an abusive complaint. **11.234**

Criminal proceedings may also be instigated through a so-called '*citation directe*', whereby the defendant is directly summoned before the court, without any preliminary investigation. This way, proceedings are conducted on an expedited basis. The suspected infringer is informed of the hearing date, the claims made, and the criminal acts of which he is accused, and is summoned to appear in court. **11.235**

In practice, '*citations directes*' are seldom used. Given that the case is heard directly by the court without any procedural hearings or investigations being carried out beforehand, it is only advisable if there is overwhelmingly strong incriminating evidence. **11.236**

Where there is strong supporting evidence, it is recommended that civil proceedings be instituted in view of the higher damages that may be awarded. In practical terms, a '*citation directe*' will only be recommended when the infringer is insolvent or notably a repeat offender. **11.237**

Sanctions Trade mark infringement action carries a maximum sentence, as stipulated under Article L 716-9 of the IPC, which provides for up to four years' imprisonment and a fine of up to EUR 400,000. **11.238**

Under Article L 716-12 of the IPC, the sentence is doubled in the case of two aggravating circumstances, namely in cases of repeated offences and where the infringer is/was contractually linked to the right-holder. **11.239**

This second hypothesis is specific to intellectual property rights and may arise for instance when a former licensee continues to manufacture goods without the authorization of the right-holder. **11.240**

Under Article L 716-13 of the IPC, the court may order the publication of the judgment in different newspapers, at the infringer's own expense. **11.241**

11.242 Furthermore, in accordance with the provisions of Article L 716-14 of the IPC, the court is also allowed to order the seizure of all the infringing goods together with all instruments and tools used in their manufacture. In such cases, the court can either order that these goods be relinquished to the right-holder, or that they be destroyed.

11.243 Finally, Article 132-71 of the Criminal Code[81] provides that an association of persons planning to commit an offence constitutes an aggravating circumstance.

11.244 **Time schedule** Proceedings instigated by means of a complaint as a civil party entail some investigations and the resulting procedure means that it can take up to two to three years before a judgment is issued.

11.245 However, in the case of a direct trial before the court ('*citation directe*'), the date of the hearing is set quickly, and is then communicated to the infringer who is due to appear in court without any preliminary investigations having been conducted. This type of action usually lasts less than a year.

11.246 **Damages** Awards for large amounts of damages are rare in criminal proceedings. Indeed, the victim of the infringement will need to produce evidence of the scope of the prejudice suffered; the purpose of criminal proceedings is to fine the infringer, not to recompense the right-holder. The amount of damages awarded will seldom compensate the legal costs. However, there are notable exceptions, and on several occasions, substantial damages have been awarded by the criminal courts.

11.247 Apart from the issue of damages, the very fact of being the subject of criminal proceedings can have a significant psychological impact on the infringer.

11.248 If substantial damages are sought by the right-holder, where for example, further to the investigations, it appears that the company is indeed solvent and had sold large quantities of counterfeits, it is then advised that a civil action is filed in addition to the criminal action.

Large quantities of goods are involved, and/or the goods are addressed to a company on French territory and the importer is known and solvent

11.249 In such cases, the right-holder should definitely institute civil proceedings.

11.250 **Description of the proceedings** A civil action is commenced by serving a writ of summons on the infringer claiming infringement of the plaintiff's earlier trade mark, design, patent, authors' right, plant variety right, supplementary protection certificate, or geographical indication. The case then proceeds to trial and a judgment is issued by the court, which may grant an injunction ordering the infringer to cease all infringing acts, and award damages to the right-holder.

11.251 Any civil action on the ground of trade mark infringement must be commenced within three years following the last infringing act, after which date an action will no longer be admissible.[82] For the other Intellectual Property Rights, the time limit to start proceedings is within 10 years.

---

[81] *Code Pénal.*   [82] As per Art L 716-5 of the IPC.

462

Damages The amount of damages awarded will depend on the actual **11.252** commercial damage suffered by the right-holder.

Article L 332-1 of the IPC specifically states that in the context of conservatory **11.253** seizure measures granted on the basis of possible infringement of author's rights, and only author rights, it is possible to 'seize the sums obtained from the reproduction, performance, or broadcasting, by whatever means, of a copyright work, made in breach of the author's rights'.

There are no awards for punitive damages in France, and therefore the above **11.254** provision constitutes a useful potential substitute. However, in practical terms, it is difficult to rely on this provision, as it is often difficult to determine precisely the extent of any pecuniary advantage that results from the infringing acts.

The plaintiff's prejudice is composed of two elements: the lost profits or *lucrum* **11.255** *cessans*, and the loss suffered or *damnum emergens*.

In relation to the lost profits or *lucrum cessans*, the proprietor of an intellectual **11.256** property right must be indemnified for the profits which would otherwise have been generated taking into account:

- the scope of the infringement, that is, the number of infringing goods which have been sold during the period of infringement (N);
- the proportion of actual business lost by the trade mark proprietor (X%);
- the profit margin of the trade mark proprietor for the retail of each unit (P).

The equation $(N) \times (X\%) \times (P)$ will give the amount of the lost profits of the **11.257** right proprietor.

The harm incurred or *damnum emergens* represents the depreciation of right- **11.258** holder's assets. It may include, for example, the costs for the storage and destruction of the goods.

Apart from the above peculiarity concerning damages which applies only in the **11.259** case of authors' rights infringement, damages are generally assessed on the basis of the following factors:

- Lost profits
- Breach of the property right
- Depreciation of investments
- Dilution of the goodwill in the intellectual property rights—a concept which is relatively new in French law.

In order to calculate the loss suffered, the right-holder will have to produce **11.260** evidence showing a decrease in sales and/or turnover. In addition, specific information can be used to assess the amount of profits made by the infringer:

- Prior to the trial, the conservatory seizure that is aimed at securing evidence also gives access to the accounts records of the defendant.

- After the trial, it is possible to request that an expert be appointed so as to investigate the infringer's sales, and evaluate the prejudice suffered by the plaintiff.

11.261   The defendant is not obliged in the course of the trial to reveal any information, but the courts have opined that, 'A company that refuses to justify the origin of the goods shows the unlawfulness of its supplying, and thus commits an act of unfair competition.'[83]

11.262   In addition to the issue of intellectual property rights infringement, if specific separate acts of unfair competition can be established (such as the deliberate use of model numbers which correspond to those of genuine goods—for example, in the case of mobile telephones—beside the act of copying the registered design), further damages can be obtained.

11.263   In the context of *ex parte* proceedings, the courts can allow a bailiff not only to seize the infringing goods, but also to obtain accounts information so as to calculate the amount of profits made by the infringer.

11.264   **Other sanctions**   The courts may order the seizure not only of the non-authentic goods, but also of the instruments used to manufacture them. These can either be passed to the right-holder or destroyed.

11.265   The right-holder can request the destruction of the infringing articles. Although such claims are a matter for the court's discretion, in practice, they are always granted.

11.266   The infringer can also be ordered to pay for the publication of the court decision in one or several newspapers.

11.267   Finally, the court can also order that a penalty be paid for each infringing article which would still be found on the market after a certain date, which usually coincides with the notification of the judgment.

11.268   In the event the infringer fails to comply with the court order, penalties will be charged, either at a daily rate, or per violation.

11.269   **Time schedule**   After the writ has been served on the defendant, the latter must appoint a lawyer to represent him. Thereafter, the parties all file written submissions and evidence according to a procedural timetable set by the court. Once all evidence and submissions have been filed, the court sets a date for trial.

11.270   Depending on the location of the court, and whether it is at first instance or on appeal, such proceedings, from service of the writ until a judgement is rendered, last approximately 18 to 24 months.

---

[83] *Lamy Droit Economique* No 4804. Cf also Paris Court of Appeal, 7 November 2001 [2002] Dalloz 3006, and Supreme Court (Commercial Chamber), 27 October 1997, available on www.legifrance.gouv.fr.

The term for notifying customs that proceedings have been instituted under **11.271** Article 13 of the Regulation is 10 working days of receipt of the notification of suspension of the release or of detention of the goods, except for perishable goods, where this term is three working days.

Save for perishable goods, the 10-day period referred to in Article 13(1) of the **11.272** Regulation may be extended once for another 10 working days in 'appropriate cases'. This possibility does not exist under the provisions of the IPC.

In terms of what constitutes an 'appropriate case', there are no guidelines avail- **11.273** able. In practice, requests for extension are seldom granted in France. Such an extension is exceptional and must be negotiated on a case-by-case basis. For instance, such an extension will be negotiable when there are public health or safety issues involved, or possibly when the right-holder is situated a long distance from France as this may incur delays in sending the signed original complaint for example, or in situations where confirming the authenticity of the goods proves to be difficult and requires further analysis.

Furthermore, it must be noted that such extensions are only possible if the deten- **11.274** tion measures have been taken on the basis of the Regulation, in view of the fact that the IPC provides for a 10-day term, and does not allow for any possible additional time.

D. Release of goods suspected of infringing certain rights on provision of a security

Curiously, the provisions of Article 14(1) of the Regulation allowing goods **11.275** infringing design rights, patents, supplementary protection certificates, or plant variety rights, to be released upon payment of a security, which already existed under the previous EC Regulations, have never been applied in France.

The reason for the non-application of this provision probably derives from the fact **11.276** that the goods seized or detained at the borders are almost always infringing goods, so that their owners or holders are not inclined to deposit a security. Consequently, it is difficult to anticipate what position French Customs would adopt if they were to be confronted with a request based on Article 14(1) of the Regulation.

E. Storage of the goods

The conditions of storage of the goods for the period of suspension of release or **11.277** detention in France are still unclear. According to the customs authorities, the right-holder will theoretically have to pay only the costs resulting from the storage for the first 10 (up to 20) working days, since afterwards, the goods are considered seized by customs. However, cases where the goods have been kept for long periods will need to be discussed with customs on a case-by-case basis.

11.278   Needless to say, if goods have been detained by customs, and are later released due to a mistake on the part of the right-holder, the storage costs will be charged to the latter in all cases.

IV. PROVISIONS APPLICABLE TO GOODS FOUND TO INFRINGE AN INTELLECTUAL PROPERTY RIGHT

11.279   Pursuant to Article 16, goods which have been found to infringe an intellectual property right at the end of the procedure provided for in Article 9 of the Regulation may not be allowed to enter, or to be removed from, the Community customs territory, to be released from free circulation, exported or re-exported, placed under a suspensive procedure (including external transit), or placed in a free zone or free warehouse.

11.280   However, we have already discussed in depth (see paras 11.17-11.34 above) the difficulties which arise in the case law of both the European Court of Justice and the French courts concerning the issue of goods in transit.

11.281   In France, it is not possible to dispose of goods subject to border measures, which are found to infringe an intellectual property right, outside commercial channels in any other way than destruction, which may be ordered by either a civil or criminal court.

11.282   The cost of such destruction is borne by the infringer, but if he is insolvent, the costs will be met by the right-holder. In order to save costs, the right-holder may choose to witness the destruction of the goods himself or, alternatively to authorize his representative or lawyer to do so, rather than a bailiff who usually witnesses the destruction process. Although the right-holder can obviously always try to recover any such cost incurred by way of a civil action but such actions are generally unsuccessful (due to the insolvency of the infringer).

V. PENALTIES

11.283   The basic sentence for trade mark infringement, as stipulated in Article L 716-9 of the IPC, is up to four years' imprisonment, and a fine of up to EUR 400,000.[84]

---

[84] For a complete overview of the question of both civil and criminal damages in cases of infringement, cf the article of two judges, B Brun and ME Oppelt-Reveneau, 'Améliorer le

Under Article L 716-12 of the IPC, the sentence is doubled in two aggravating **11.284**
circumstances specific to counterfeiting, namely:

- in the case of repeat offenders, or
- where the infringer is, or was, contractually linked to the right-holder.

Identical provisions apply in respect of patents under Article L 615-14 of the IPC, **11.285**
and also for authors' rights under Article L 335-4 of the same Code.

In relation to plant variety rights, Article L 623-32 of the IPC provides that **11.286**
'Any intentional breach of the right of the owner of a plant variety right, as
defined in Article L 623-4, constitutes a criminal offence punished by a fine of
2,250 Euro.'

The breach in designations of origin and geographical indications is punished by **11.287**
a fine of up to EUR 37,500 and up to two years' imprisonment.

Furthermore, in cases where an identical act was committed in the five previous **11.288**
years, the defendant may be given a six-month prison sentence.

In relation to the infringement of any intellectual property rights, the courts may **11.289**
order the publication of the judgment in several newspapers, at the infringer's
expense.

Furthermore, in accordance with the provisions of Articles L 716-14 (trade **11.290**
marks), L 615-7 (patents), L 521-3 (designs), and L 623-28 (national plant
variety right), L 335-5 (authors' rights) of the IPC, the courts may order the
seizure and forfeiture of the infringing goods, together with the instruments and
tools used in their manufacture.

Under Article 132-71 of the Criminal Code, being part of an association of **11.291**
persons planning to commit an offence constitutes an aggravating circumstance.

In addition to the general provisions of the IPC dealing with infringement of **11.292**
authors' rights, a specific provision at Article L 332-1 of the IPC, concerning conservatory seizure measures in the context of infringement of author's rights provides for the possibility to 'seize the sums obtained from the reproduction,
performance, or broadcasting, by whatever means, of a work of the mind, carried
out in violation of the author's rights'. In practice however, this provision is rarely
applied.

Finally, in the case of counterfeit goods, Article 414 of the Customs Code provides **11.293**
for up to for three years' imprisonment, the confiscation of the non-authentic
goods as well as the goods used to conceal the fraud, and a fine of up to twice the
retail value of the goods in question.

---

contentieux de la contrefaçon: du souhaitable au possible' in [2004] Propriété Industrielle 14 (June
Issue).

11.294 The charts below summarize the main criminal and civil sanctions in respect of each type of intellectual property right that may be subject to border measures under EC Regulation 1383/2003:[85]

	Criminal Sanctions	Civil Sanctions
Trade Mark Infringements (*Counterfeiting*)	*In case of imitation, detention, or selling:* • Imprisonment: 3 years • Fine: EUR 300,000 *(IPC, Art L 716-10)* *In case of import, export, or industrial production:* • Imprisonment: 4 years • Fine: EUR 400,000 *(IPC, Art L 716-9)* *In case of organized crime:* • Imprisonment: 5 years • Fine: EUR 500,000 • Partial or total closing of the company, either temporarily of permanently *(IPC, Art L 716-11-1)*	• Injunction to cease infringing acts • Confiscation of the counterfeits • Destruction of the counterfeits • Damages • Publication of the judgment
Design and Authors' Rights Infringements (*Piracy*)	• Imprisonment: 3 years • Fine: EUR 300,000 • If organized crime: 5 years' imprisonment/ EUR 500,000 fine *(IPC, Art L 335-2)* • Partial or total closing of the company, either temporarily or permanently *(IPC, Art 335-5)* • Confiscation of the profits of the infringement *(IPC, Art L 335-6)* • Billposting of the judgment at the cost of the infringer *(IPC, Art L 131-35)* • Provisions of L 335-2 × 2 if repeat offences, or if previous contract with the injured party *(IPC, Art L 335-9)*	• Transfer of the property of the means of production and seized goods to the injured party *(IPC, Art L 535-7)* • Injunction to cease infringing acts • Confiscation of the counterfeits • Destruction of the counterfeits • Damages • Publication of the judgment
Patent Infringements	• Imprisonment: 3 years • Fine: EUR 300,000 • If organized crime: 5 years' imprisonment/ EUR 500,000 fine *(IPC, Art L 715-14)* • Provisions of L 715-14 × 2 if repeat offence, or if previous contract with the injured party *(IPC, Art L 715-14-1)*	• Confiscation of the infringing goods and of the means to produce them. • Injunction prohibiting manufacture and sale of the infringing goods *(IPC, Art L 715-7)* • Damages • Publication of the judgment • Confiscation and destruction of the infringing goods
Infringements of Plant Variety Rights	• Imprisonment: 6 months if repeat offence • Fine: EUR 1,000 *(IPC, Art L 623-32)*	• Confiscation of the vegetal obtained and the production means • Injunction prohibiting manufacture and sale of the infringing goods • Damages • Publication of the judgment *(IPC, Art L 623-28)*
Infringements of Designations of Origin/ Geographic Indication	• Imprisonment: 2 years • Fine: EUR 37,500 *(Consumer Code, Art 213-1)*	• Confiscation of the infringing goods • Injunction prohibiting manufacture and sale of infringing goods • Damages

---

[85] For a detailed and up to date analysis of criminal penalties after the *Loi Perben*, cf *Dictionnaire Permanent de Droit des Affaires*, Bulletin No 626, 1 October 2004, 6535.

VI. LIABILITY OF CUSTOMS AUTHORITIES AND RIGHT-HOLDERS

A. Liability of right-holders and sanctions

11.295 As per Article 12 of the Regulation, right-holders may incur civil liability for any non-permitted use of confidential information provided by the customs authorities as per Article 1382 and 1383 of the Civil Code. This may also lead to the suspension of the application for action for the period of validity remaining before renewal, or a refusal to renew said application.

11.296 In addition, the right-holder may also be liable under civil law, again on the basis of Articles 1382 and 1383 of the Civil Code for any breach of the provisions of the Regulation, in accordance with Article 19(3) of the latter. However, no such case has been reported to date.

B. Liability of customs authorities and sanctions

11.297 Right-holders could in certain circumstances be entitled to compensation in the event that goods are not detected by French Customs and are released, or in the event that no action is taken to detain them, once an application for action has been lodged by the right-holder.[86] Customs could thus theoretically be held liable (still under the above cited Articles 1382 and 1383 of the Civil Code) for purposefully not taking the necessary steps to control certain goods. However, in practice, it would be almost impossible to prove such deliberate behaviour.

11.298 Customs could also incur civil liability to the persons involved or affected by the taking of abusive border measures *ex officio*, as Articles 401 of the Customs Code provides for liability of the customs authorities for acts committed by customs officials in the carrying out of their duties.[87]

Conclusion

11.299 The French government is highly sensitive to the proliferation of counterfeit and pirated goods. This has led to the creation of a 10-point list of measures which notably sets goals for customs to increase the quantity of goods seized by 15 per cent per year, and increase the numbers of controls by 12 per cent.[88] This

---

[86] Cf Reg 1383/2003, Art 19(1).   [87] Cf ibid, Art 19(2).

[88] This document, called 'Les 10 mesures du gouvernement pour renforcer durablement la lutte contre la contrefaçon', can be obtained from the French Industrial Property Office ('*INPI*'), Tel: +33 1 53 04 53 04.

document also provides for the creation of a national work group designed to coordinate the work of the antifraud police, the Fraud Repression authorities, and the customs authorities.

11.300 In addition, the *Loi Perben II* which entered into force on 1 October 2004 provides that infringements committed by members of criminal organizations are punished by five years' imprisonment and fines of up to EUR 500,000.

11.301 Furthermore, as this chapter has highlighted, the French customs authorities and courts are very protective of right-holders, notably in relation to trade marks.

11.302 A few other practical points should be noted: in France, legal fees are generally speaking, lower than those of the other Member States of the European Community. Therefore, the claimant is in a favourable position in view of the low cost of filing proceedings; should he be unsuccessful, the costs incurred remain within reasonable limits.

11.303 The downside is that there are no awards for punitive damages in France, and that any damages awarded by the courts are, by and large, relatively modest compared to other Member States. However, following heavy criticism on the issue of damages, it seems that the courts are not averse to the prospect of changing their practice on this. That said, the onus will still lie with the claimant to produce evidence of the loss suffered to obtain requisite damages.

11.304 In addition, the French Industrial Property Office ('INPI') has recently developed a program called 'e-mage', which allows the customs and police authorities to access a database containing details of registered intellectual property rights and characteristics of genuine goods. This programme has been launched in Roissy, Orly, and Le Havre.[89]

11.305 As a final comment, it is our strong belief that it is worthwhile to file an application for action in France, both on the grounds of EC Regulation N° 2003/1383 and on the basis of the IPC, especially for trade mark owners.

---

[89] Information concerning 'e-mage' can be obtained from ileclercq@inpi.fr or jmozziconacci@inpi.fr. Many thanks for their help to all the members of Bureau E4 of the French Customs, Philippe Loubet Del Par of the Bureau Information et Communication of Customs, and Gilles Ringeisen and Patrick Boyle of Cabinet Plasseraud for their careful reading and useful comments.

12

GERMANY

Stefanie Körber

Introduction

For some time now, the retention of goods by customs authorities has been a **12.01**
significant tool used in Germany for combating the cross-border trade of goods
infringing intellectual property rights. The tremendous rise in the practical
significance of customs retentions in Germany in recent years is demonstrated by
two sets of statistics. On the one hand, the number of applications for action filed
with the customs authorities in Germany increased from 56 in 1994 to 290 in 2004.
On the other hand, the number of cases involving the retention of goods by the customs authorities soared from 56 in 1994 to 8,564 in 2004. Germany had the largest
number of customs retentions overall in the European Communities between 1999
and 2002. In 2004, the most frequently retained groups of goods included sportswear (30.18 per cent), accessories such as bags (21.21 per cent), leisure clothing
(19.69 per cent), as well as clocks and jewellery (11.14 per cent). In 2004, the
retained goods originated, for the most part, from China (23.58 per cent) and
Thailand (23.45 per cent), often from Turkey, the United States, and Hong Kong.[1]

European customs retention regulations are not the only basis for activity by the **12.02**
German customs authorities. In fact, there have been and still are customs retention regulations in Germany that go beyond the European customs retention provisions and upon which the customs authorities may base their actions. In order
for a right-holder to benefit from these regulations, it is necessary that he file with
the customs authorities a separate application that is predicated on the national
customs retention provisions.

The regulations in effect today that concern retention by the customs authorities **12.03**
were introduced as a result of the Law for the Improvement of the Protection of

---

[1] Cf Bundesministerium der Finanzen, *Gewerblicher Rechtsschutz Jahresbericht 2004*, 29 (31).

Intellectual Property and for the Prevention of Product Piracy that came into effect on 1 July 1990, otherwise known as the 'Product Piracy Law', (*Gesetz zur Stärkung des Schutzes des geistigen Eigentums und zur Bekämpfung der Produktpiraterie 'Produktpirateriegesetz'*). German law governing retention by the customs authorities is currently derived from the following statutory provisions:

- § 146 et seq of the Law on the Protection of Trade Marks and Other Signs—'Trade Mark Law' (*Markengesetz*)
- § 142a of the Patent Law (*Patentgesetz*)
- § 111b of the Law on Copyright and Neighboring Rights—'Copyright Law' (*Urhebergesetz*)
- § 25a of the Utility Model Law (*Gebrauchsmustergesetz*)
- § 55 et seq of the Law Concerning Copyright in Industrial Designs—'Designs Law' (*Geschmacksmustergesetz*)
- § 9, para 2 of the Law on the Protection of the Topographies of Microelectronic Semiconductor Products—'Semiconductor Protection Law' (*Halbleiterschutzgesetz*)
- § 40a, para 1 of the Law on the Protection of Plant Varieties (*Sortenschutzgesetz*).

12.04 In addition to these statutory provisions, Germany is also subject to international and supranational conventions that contain provisions on retention by the customs authorities. For example, Articles 51–60 of the TRIPs Agreement (Agreement on Trade-Related Aspects of Intellectual Property Rights) that came into effect in the European Union on 1 January 1995 contains detailed provisions on retention by the customs authorities that essentially comport with the provisions of EC Regulation 3295/94. There is some controversy among German scholars as to whether the provisions of the TRIPs Agreement are directly applicable. German legislators seem to assume that the provisions of the TRIPs agreement in no way constitute directly applicable law.[2]

12.05 The need for change as a result of EC Regulation 1383/2003 (the 'Regulation') taking effect is marginal. The priority of European law must be anchored in the national legislation that deals with intellectual property rights for which retention by the customs authorities was not possible under EC Regulation 3295/94. The statutory provisions affected in particular are those in the Patent Law, the Law on the Protection of Plant Varieties, the Law on Designations of Origin and the Law on the Protection of Geographical Indications. Up until now, the German legislators have not responded with any appropriate measures.

12.06 There is no need for legislative action with regard to the intellectual property rights that have been covered for some time now by the overlapping of national and European law. In Germany, the precedence of EC law and the subsidiary function of national law have already been specifically anchored in national

---

[2] BT-Drucksache (printed matter of German parliament) 12/7655, 335 (347).

statutory provisions, for example, in § 146, para 1 and § 150 of the Trade Mark Law, § 111b, paras 1 and 8 of the Copyright Law and § 55, para 1 and § 57, para 3 of the Designs Law.

As will be discussed below, due to Article 11 of the Regulation, the German statutory provisions that govern the simplified destruction procedure will have to be adapted, at least for clarity. According to the Federal Ministry of Justice, a statutory revision is planned for the near future. **12.07**

Even where the Regulation is in effect, there are still areas that are not covered by the European provisions but are regulated by national law. Such areas include: **12.08**

- Parallel imports
- Commercial trade of goods within the European Community
- Unregistered trade marks
- Infringements of utility models and semiconductors.

If the right-holder wants to invoke action by the German customs authorities in this respect, he must file a separate application based on national law. The customs authorities have made a form available on the Internet for this purpose. **12.09**

The following provides an overview of the scope of application of the Regulation in view of the national legislation, the substantive requirements of an application for action by the customs authorities as well as the enforcement of the Regulation by the German customs authorities. **12.10**

I. SUBJECT MATTER AND SCOPE OF THE NATIONAL LAW APPLYING THE REGULATION

This first Part defines the subject matter of the Regulation and its scope of application under national law. **12.11**

A. Customs procedure of the goods

Article 1 of the Regulation first sets forth the conditions that can bring about action by the customs authorities under the Regulation. The customs authorities are afforded a broad range of powers. According to information supplied by the Central Office of Industrial Property Rights (*Zentralstelle Gewerblicher Rechtsschutz*), the German customs authorities do utilize this range of powers. They make use of their inspection powers not only in the context of customs **12.12** clearance but also at border customs stations, inland customs offices, free harbours, or by means of mobile control groups.

B. Definition of infringing goods

12.13 Article 2 of the Regulation defines the term 'goods that infringe an intellectual property right'. Such goods refer to 'counterfeit goods', 'pirated goods' as well as those goods that infringe one of the designated intellectual property rights pursuant to the laws of an individual Member State. More specifically:

(1) Counterfeit goods

12.14 The Regulation defines the term 'counterfeit goods' as follows.

12.15 It provides first that applications for action by the customs authorities can only be based on validly registered trade marks. Therefore, according to the Regulation, a mere application for a trade mark is an insufficient basis for an application for action by the customs authorities. In this regard, there is a difference between applications for action by the customs authorities under the Regulation and applications under national law. Applications for retention by the customs authorities pursuant to German national law may, under certain circumstances, be predicated on a mark or sign that has not been registered. Unlike the Regulation, the domestic statutory provisions governing retention by the customs authorities in Germany do not restrict the scope to 'validly registered' marks or signs.

12.16 According to national law, retention by the customs authorities may be predicated on unregistered marks where an unregistered trade mark right has arisen in accordance with national statutory provisions. This is the case where the requirements of § 4, para 2 or 3 or § 5 of the Trade Mark Law have been met. § 4, para 2 of the Trade Mark Law provides protection for a sign even in the absence of registration, where this sign has obtained commercial recognition as a trade mark in commerce. § 4, para 3 of the Trade Mark Law affords protection to unregistered marks by notoriety as a well-known trade mark within the meaning of Article 6bis of the Paris Convention for the Protection of Industrial Property. Finally, § 5 of the Trade Mark Law protects company symbols, such as trade names, and titles of works without the requirement of registration.

12.17 The dispositive criterion for determining a 'counterfeit good' is first the marks or signs that are affixed to the good. According to majority opinion in Germany, only those marks that are plainly recognizable as imitations are marks that cannot be distinguished from a trade mark in terms of their essential aspects. Customs authorities should not have the burden of determining the likelihood of confusion that is otherwise necessary but under certain circumstances this may be an extremely difficult issue to resolve.[3] According to majority opinion in Germany, the concept of 'counterfeit goods' is even narrower with regard to the nature of the goods. The predominant view is that counterfeit goods within the meaning of the Regulation are only those goods bearing the mark or sign that are identical to the goods that the registered trade mark right protects. Other goods, no matter how similar they may be, do not fall within the ambit of statutory protection.[4]

Another condition for goods to be considered counterfeit goods within the meaning of the Regulation is that there be an infringement of the proprietor's trade mark or sign pursuant to the Community Trade Mark Regulation[5] or—in the case of a national trade mark—pursuant to national trade mark law. § 14 of the Trade Mark Law determines whether goods that meet the aforementioned requirements under the Regulation are to be regarded as having infringed a trade mark under national law. This provision applies to international trade marks with protection for Germany by operation of § 112 and § 124 of the Trade Mark Law and to Community trade marks by operation of § 125 b of the Trade Mark Law. Pursuant to § 14 of the Trade Mark Law, a trade mark infringement exists under the following conditions: **12.18**

- existing trade mark protection
- use in the course of trade
- unlawful use
- satisfaction of one of the prerequisites for an infringing act pursuant to the provision.

The term 'use in the course of trade' can be broadly interpreted. It comprises every economic activity that allows a person to participate in gainful work through the exercise or promotion of one's own business interests or those of a third party.[6] In the case of tradesmen, there is a presumption of 'use in the course of trade'.[7] **12.19**

Following the case law of the European Court of Justice regarding the use of a trade mark,[8] the German Federal Supreme Court (*Bundesgerichtshof*) has held that for infringing use to exist, there must be a so-called 'mark-related' use. There can only be such 'mark-related use' where a significant number of persons in the **12.20**

---

[3] R Knaak 'EG-Produktpiraterie-Verordnung' in H Harte-Bavendamm (ed), *Handbuch der Markenpiraterie in Europa* (1st edn, 2000), § 4, para 16.

[4] R Knaak 'EG-Produktpiraterie-Verordnung' in H Harte-Bavendamm (ed), *Handbuch der Markenpiraterie in Europa* (1st edn, 2000), § 4, para 17.

[5] Council Reg (EC) 40/94 of 20 December 1993 on the Community trade mark.

[6] BGH GRUR 1987, 438 (440)—*Handtuchspender*; P Ströbele and F Hacker, *Markengesetz* (7th edn, 2003), § 14, para 29.

[7] P Ströbele and F Hacker, *Markengesetz* (7th edn, 2003), § 14, para 29.

[8] Cf eg ECJ Case C-63/97 *Bayerische Motorenwerke AG (BMW) v Deenik* GRUR Int 1999, 438 (440); Case C-206/01 *Arsenal v Reed* WRP 2002, 1415 (1418, 1419).

affected commercial channels associate the infringed sign with the origin of the protected product, that is, where the mark, in relation to the sale of goods or services, serves to differentiate the goods or services of one business from those of another.[9] By contrast, the use of a mark as a purely descriptive term[10] or exclusively as 'a decorative accessory or mere ornament'[11] is not regarded as 'mark-related'.

12.21 Since the Regulation provides for action by the customs authorities only where there is identity of the goods and where the marks are openly recognizable as imitations, an infringement can only be established pursuant to § 14, para 2, no 1 and 2 of the Trade Mark Law. § 14, para 2, no 1 of the Trade Mark Law provides for a trade mark infringement where a person, without the consent of the proprietor of the trade mark, uses a sign identical to the trade mark in the course of trade in relation to goods or services that are identical to those goods or services for which the trade mark is protected. For this reason, in addition to trade mark identity, identity of the products marketed under the trade mark is also necessary for an infringement to be found. § 14, para 2, no 2 of the Trade Mark Law governs cases involving a likelihood of confusion.

12.22 § 14, paras 3 and 4 of the Trade Mark Law provide examples of the prohibited use of trade marks. Pursuant to § 14, para 4, no 1 of the Trade Mark Law, prohibited use exists, in particular, where the sign is affixed to packaging, wrapping or means of marking such as labels, tags, sew-on labels, or the like. Pursuant to § 14, para 4, no 3 of the Trade Mark Law, the import or export of such objects is prohibited. Based on these provisions and on Article 2(1)(a) (ii) and (iii) of Regulation 1382/2003, German customs authorities also seize packaging, wrapping or means of marking that have not yet been physically attached to the goods and are shipped separately.

12.23 It is disputed whether the mere transit of marked goods through the territory of the Federal Republic of Germany constitutes an infringement. The decision by the European Court of Justice in *Polo/Lauren/Dwidua*[12] established that the European regulations pertaining to retention by the customs authorities apply to goods that are in transit from one third country to another via the Member States of the European Union. It is now the predominant view that European trade mark protection extends unconditionally to transit goods.[13]

---

[9] BGH GRUR 2001, 158 (160)—*3-Streifen-Kennzeichnung*; GRUR 2002, 171 (173)—*Marlboro-Dach*; GRUR 2002, 814 (815)—*Festspielhaus*.

[10] BGH GRUR 2002, 809 (811)—*Frühstücks-Drink I*, GRUR 2002, 812 (813)—*Frühstücks-Drink II*; GRUR 2002, 814—*Festspielhaus*.

[11] BGH GRUR 2002, 171 (173)—*Marlboro-Dach*; GRUR 2001, 158 (160)—*3-Streifen-Kennzeichnung*; R Ingerl and C Rohnke, *Markengesetz* (2nd edn, 2003), § 14, para 78.

[12] ECJ Case C-383/98 *The Polo/Lauren Company LP v Dwidua Langgeng Pratawa International Freight Forwarders*, GRUR Int. 2000, 748 (750).

[13] Cf Kammergericht GRUR-RR 2001, 159 (161)—*EURO-Paletten*; R Ingerl and C Rohnke, *Markengesetz* (2nd edn, 2003), § 14, para 200; P Ströbele and F Hacker, *Markengesetz* (7th edn, 2003), § 14, para 100.

(2) Pirated goods

Article 2(1)(b) of the Regulation defines 'pirated goods' as goods that infringe a **12.24** copyright or related rights or protected industrial designs. This type of infringement exists under German national law where the following prerequisites are met:

German Copyright Law governs copyright as well as neighbouring rights. **12.25**

Copyright in Germany arises by virtue of the creation of the work by the author **12.26** without any prior registration. The prerequisite is that a work of literature, science or art be created within the meaning of § 2 of the Copyright Law. Within the meaning of this provision, 'works' include, in particular, works of language, musical works, works of fine art, photographic works, and cinematographic works. Only personal intellectual creations constitute protected works. A personal intellectual creation exists where the work exhibits a certain degree of uniqueness. Comparatively, the material design must surpass average design activity.[14]

Where a copyright exists, the manufacture of copies infringes the copyright **12.27** holder's rights. In the case of a copy, § 16 of the Copyright Law provides for an infringement of the right to reproduction, that belongs exclusively to the author.

An adaptation of the work also constitutes an infringement of the copyright **12.28** holder's rights. Under § 3, § 12, § 15 et seq of the Copyright Law adaptations or other transformations of the work may only be published or exploited with the consent of the author of the work thus adapted or transformed.

There is no copyright infringement where the exploitation of the work is **12.29** permitted in the interest of the general public pursuant to §§ 45–61 of the Copyright Law.

The so-called 'related rights' or 'neighbouring rights' under the Copyright Law **12.30** also arise solely by virtue of the creation of the respective object, without there being any need for a prior registration. Related rights under the Copyright Law include:

- Rights vested in certain editions (§ 70, § 71)
- Rights to photographs (§ 72)
- Rights of performing artists (§ 73 et seq)
- The rights of a producer of audio recordings (§ 85, § 86)
- The rights of broadcasting organizations (§ 87)
- The rights of makers of a database (§ 87a et seq)
- The rights of producers of films (§ 94)
- The rights of producers of moving pictures (§ 95, § 94).

---

[14] Cf eg BGHZ 112, 264 (271)—*Betriebssystem*; BGH GRUR 1981, 267 (269)—*Dirlada*; BGH GRUR 1976, 261 (263)—*Gemäldewand*.

12.31 As is the case with copyright, it is prohibited to make copies of any protected subject matter without the prior consent of the right-holder under each of these provisions.

12.32 § 27 of the German Designs Law provides that a copyright in an industrial design may only arise by registration. From a substantive point of view, pursuant to § 2 of the same Law, statutory protection requires that the design be new and original.

12.33 The reproduction and making of copies without the design right-holder's prior consent infringes the latter's rights since § 38 of the Designs Law affords the right-holder an exclusive right to exploit the industrial design. Exploitation within the meaning of the law includes the production, offering, distribution, import, export or utilization of a product that incorporates the industrial design or uses it in conjunction with said product as well as the possession or ownership of said product for such purposes. The protection of an industrial design extends to every design that evokes in an informed user no association other than the one with the protected design.

12.34 Limitations to the rights conferred by the industrial design right are set forth in § 40 of the Designs Law. This provision states that rights in a protected design are not enforceable in particular with regard to acts done privately and for non-commercial purposes, acts done for experimental purposes, or acts of reproduction either for educational purposes or for the purpose of citation.

12.35 In the event a copyright or related right or a design right has been infringed, the customs authorities only become active where the unauthorized produced goods can be readily identified as such. Thus, action by the customs authorities does not only encompass colourable imitations but also adaptations of works protected by copyright and designs that invoke no other overall impression than that of the protected design, to the extent that the unauthorized produced goods are not too far removed from the original.

(3) Goods infringing other IP rights

12.36 The Regulation also covers those goods that infringe a patent or a supplementary protection certificate, a plant variety right, a designation of origin or a geographical indication under a Member State's law. The following section discusses the prerequisites set forth under each of the applicable statutory provisions of national law.

Goods infringing a patent or a supplementary protection certificate

12.37 Under German law, a patent is infringed where the patent is used in breach of § 9, § 10 of the Patent Law. § 9 and § 10 of the Patent Law also determine whether there has been an infringement of a supplementary protection certificate pursuant to Council Regulation (EEC) 1768/1992 concerning the creation of a supplementary protection certificate for medicinal products or under Council Regulation (EC) 1610/1996 concerning the creation of a supplementary protection certificate for plant protection products. § 16a of the Patent Law provides for the provisions to be applicable. The statutory provisions of the Patent Law provide as follows:

In the case of a product patent, third parties are prohibited from making, offering, putting on the market or either importing or storing for said designated purposes a product that is the subject matter of the patent.   **12.38**

In the case of a process patent, prohibited exploitation of the patent includes the use of the process and—under well-defined conditions—the offering of the process. Where a product has been manufactured directly from a process that is the subject matter of a patent, third parties are prohibited from offering the product, distributing the product for commercial purposes, using the product or either importing or storing the product for said purposes without the consent of the patentee.   **12.39**

§ 10 of the Patent Law also prohibits third parties from offering or supplying any means relating to an essential element of such invention for exploiting the invention. In this way, the protection of process, use and selection patents extends to situations in which the offering and supplying of means that make it possible for the supplied party to exploit the protected invention are prohibited.[15]   **12.40**

A patent infringement is excluded where the conditions set forth by §§ 11–13 of the Patent Law have not been met. § 11 of the Patent Law provides in particular that the effects of a patent do not extend to acts that are done privately and for non-commercial purposes or to acts done for experimental purposes relating to the subject matter of the patented invention. § 12 of the Patent Law provides that a prior right of use with regard to the patented invention precludes the unlawfulness of acts that exploit the patent. Finally, § 13 of the Patent Law limits the scope of protection of a patent for the public welfare and national security.   **12.41**

Exploitation of a patent is not only considered to exist where the patent is literally 'used'. § 14 of the Patent Law that governs the scope of the protection conferred by a patent provides that exploitation of a patent also constitutes an infringement where the characterizing features of a patent are realized by equivalent means (the so-called 'technically equivalent'[16]).   **12.42**

Product piracy is of great economic significance particularly with regard to patented pharmaceuticals. Customs retention can be an effective means of   **12.43**

---

[15] BGH GRUR 1992, 40 (42)—*Beheizbarer Atemluftschlauch.*
[16] Cf BGH GRUR 1987, 280 (282)—*Befestigungsvorrichtung I.*

fighting product piracy in pharmaceuticals where drug companies are able to provide the customs authorities with particular details concerning the type and time of an infringing product shipment.[17] In the absence of such concrete information, goods that infringe a patent right are generally only identified exemplarily and more as a result of happenstance. It is especially the case with pharmaceuticals that only in exceptional cases must product shipments be clearly identified in the accompanying customs documents.[18]

Goods infringing a national plant variety right

12.44 German law regards as infringement of a plant variety right any breach of the exclusive rights of the plant variety right-holder as defined under § 10 of the Law on the Protection of Plant Varieties. Under this provision, only the plant variety right-holder is entitled to place on the market for commercial purposes propagating material, that is, plants, parts of plants and seeds of the protected variety, and to produce or import such propagating material for this purpose.

Goods infringing a national designation of origin or a geographical indication

12.45 Geographical indications are protected in Germany by different statutory provisions. First, there is protection under Council Regulation (EEC) 2081/1992 for such geographical indications that are registered and protected at the Community level. Secondly, § 126 et seq of the Trade Mark Law protect geographical indications in the absence of a registration. The relationship between these statutory provisions and Council Regulation (EEC) 2081/1992 has been controversial for a long time. After the landmark decision by the European Court of Justice in *Warsteiner*,[19] it is now undisputed that national statutory provisions regarding the protection of simple geographical indications are not excluded by Council Regulation (EEC) 2081/1992. Simple geographical indications are those where there is no direct connection between the attributes of a product and its geographical origin.[20]

12.46 § 127, para 1 of the Trade Mark Law determines the existence of an infringement of a simple geographical indication within the meaning of § 126 of the same law. For there to be an infringement, the geographical indication must be used for goods or services that do not originate from the place, area, region, or country designated by the geographical indication. In addition, there must be a risk of misleading in the course of trade as to the geographical origin of the goods and services.

---

[17] B Kröger and T Bausch, '*Produktpiraterie im Patentwesen*', GRUR 1997, 321 (323).
[18] B Kröger and T Bausch, '*Produktpiraterie im Patentwesen*', GRUR 1997, 321 (323).
[19] ECJ Case C-312/98 *Schutzverband v Warsteiner* GRUR Int. 2001, 51 (54, 55).
[20] Cf BGH GRUR 2002, 160 (161)—*Warsteiner III*; GRUR 2002, 1074 (1075)—*Original Oettinger*.

Finally, even in the absence of a risk of misleading as to the geographical origin, an **12.47** infringement of a simple indication of geographical origin exists where the geographical indication enjoys a special reputation and the use of such geographical indication is likely to take unwarranted and unfair advantage of, or to be detrimental to, the reputation or the distinctive character of the geographical indication.

With regard to qualified geographical indications referred to in § 127, para 2 of **12.48** the Trade Mark Law, it remains unclear whether the protection of such indications under national law is legally viable concurrently with the protection under Council Regulation (EEC) 2081/1992. There is consensus only to the extent that national law is not applicable to those geographical indications that are registered and protected or filed at the Community level.[21] Where a geographical indication is not registered and protected at the Community level, German courts are of the opinion that there is a possibility of protecting qualified geographical indications either pursuant to the Council Regulation (EEC) 2081/1992 or by applying national statutory provisions, thus granting protection even in the absence of registration.[22] By contrast, the EU Commission takes the position of the exclusivity of protection under Community law.[23] The consequence of the latter viewpoint is that protection of qualified geographical indications can only be invoked where the indications are registered.

The issue as to whether an infringement of a geographical indication or designa- **12.49** tion of origin exists under Council Regulation (EEC) 2081/1992 is determined by § 135 of the Trade Mark Law in connection with Article 8 or 13 of Regulation 2081/1992. There is a breach of Article 8 of this Regulation where the indication g.U. (= *geschützte Ursprungsbezeichnung* = protected designation of origin), g.g.A. (= *geschützte geographische Angabe* = protected geographical indication), or equivalent indications are used for products that do not comply with Council Regulation (EEC) 2081/1992. There is a breach of Article 13 of this Regulation where the registered geographical indication is used for products of another origin.

Goods infringe a geographical indication under Council Regulation (EC) No **12.50** 1493/1999 on the common organization of the market in wine or under Council Regulation (EC) No 1576/1989 laying down general rules on the definition, description, and presentation of spirit drinks where they unlawfully bear the protected geographical indication.

---

[21] K-H Fezer, *Markenrecht* (3rd edn, 2001), Vorb 130 para 21a.
[22] BGH GRUR 1994, 307 (309)—*Mozzarella I*; BGH GRUR1995, 354 (356)—*Rügenwalder Teewurst II*; BGHZ 139 (138)—*Warsteiner I*.
[23] G Legras, '*Schutz der Bezeichnung "Mozzarella"* ', EuZW 1995, 368.

(4) Moulds and matrices

12.51 Retention by the customs authorities of moulds and matrices that have been specially designed or adapted for the manufacture of goods that infringe an intellectual property right is possible in Germany. Although the statutory provisions that set forth the scope of the respective intellectual property rights (eg § 14 of the Trade Mark Law) do not make reference to moulds or matrices, an analogous application of these provisions is favoured by legal authors with the result that the use of moulds or matrices is also regarded as an infringement of intellectual property rights.[24] However, the presumption of an infringement by moulds or matrices is conditioned on proof by the right-holder that the devices have been used or designed either exclusively or mainly for unlawful production.

12.52 § 18, para 2 of the Trade Mark Law and § 140a, para 2 of the Patent Law expressly provide right-holders with a remedy against infringers allowing to destroy or remove the devices that have been used or designed exclusively or virtually to infringe an intellectual property rights.

C. Goods excluded by the Regulation

12.53 As mentioned previously, even subsequent to the Regulation coming into effect there remain areas in which retention by the customs authorities is not possible under the Regulation. Pursuant to Article 3 of the Regulation, retentions by the customs authorities are not permissible in the case of parallel imports, goods that have been manufactured under conditions other than those agreed to by the right-holder as well as goods contained in traveller's personal baggage. As far as parallel imports and goods that have been manufactured under conditions other than those agreed to by the right-holder are concerned, the statutory provisions under national law regarding retention by the customs authorities apply, provided that all legal requirements are met.

(1) Parallel imported goods

12.54 German law basically permits retention by the customs authorities for all intellectual property rights, also in cases of so-called parallel imports from third countries (non-Member countries of the EC). With regard to just trade mark infringements, it was disputed for quite some time whether German law allowed for retention by the customs authorities in cases of parallel imports. As a result of the

---

[24] Cf for trade mark law eg K-H Fezer, *Markenrecht* (3rd edn, 2001), § 14, para 502.

decision rendered by the Federal Tax Court in the *Jockey* case on 7 October 1999,[25] it is now undisputed that the statutory provisions of national trade mark law pertaining to retention by the customs authorities also apply to parallel imports to the extent that the rights of the trade mark proprietor have not been exhausted pursuant to § 24 of the Trade Mark Law. Pursuant to § 24 of the Trade Mark Law, the rights to a trade mark are exhausted where the trade mark bearing product has been brought into commerce in the EU or another Member State to the Agreement on the European Community either by the right-holder himself or with his consent. The right-holder's consent may only be assumed if his consent refers to each specimen of the goods for which exhaustion of rights is claimed.[26]

In the opinion of the Federal Tax Court, it does not follow from § 146 of the **12.55** Trade Mark Law that this provision only applies to cases in which goods bear a mark without the prior consent of the right-holder. In the court's view, this provision is, in fact, applicable in all cases in which goods unlawfully bear a trade mark protected under the Trade Mark Law. Consequently, this provision fundamentally applies to all cases in which the trade mark rights of the right-holder are infringed by the import or export of goods bearing the trade mark. According to the court, this follows directly from the fact that § 146 of the Trade Mark Law expressly does not condition retention by the customs authorities on the goods bearing the trade mark without the consent of the proprietor of the trade mark. Rather, in a much broader manner, the provision only requires that the goods unlawfully bear a trade mark protected under the Trade Mark Law.

Commerce is impaired by a multitude of parallel imports. Therefore, it can make **12.56** sense for a right-holder to file an application for action by the customs authorities under national law as part of a global strategy to fight parallel imports in Germany. The effectiveness of an application for action by the customs authorities under national law that includes parallel imports nonetheless depends to a large extent on whether the customs authorities are provided with sufficient indications allowing them to identify the goods. Pursuant to national statutory provisions on retention by the customs authorities, the authorities will only act where the infringement is obvious. Since the identification of parallel imports is clearly more difficult than the identification of goods which are regarded as non-authentic under the intellectual property legislation, the applicant has a special duty of providing the authorities with ample information in order to ensure effective action in cases of parallel imports as well.

---

[25] Bundesfinanzgerichtshof, GRUR Int. 2000, 780 (781, 782)—*Jockey*.
[26] ECJ Case C-173/98 *Docksides v Sebago* MarkenR 1999, 240.

(2) Goods which have been manufactured under conditions other than those which have been agreed with the right-holder

12.57 Unlike under Article 3(1) of the Regulation, German law provides for retention of goods that have been manufactured under conditions other than those that have been agreed to by the right-holder. The dispositive criterion for retention by the customs authorities under German law is solely the existence of a substantive infringement. Goods that have been manufactured under conditions other than those that have been agreed with the right-holder are considered to infringe the latter's rights where the licensee significantly departs from the quality or conditioning specifications or other production requirements.[27]

12.58 However, an infringement of this type can only bring about retention by the customs authorities where it is obvious. This might only be the case where the departure is so significant that the customs authorities are able to recognize it on its face and without any doubt.[28] For this reason, the customs authorities must have precise information about the requisite quality and nature of the goods produced under licence based on the application for action by the customs authorities along with the agreements submitted. It also makes sense to provide examples of frequent discrepancies in quality which will enable the customs authorities to identify goods that have been produced in accordance with requirements other than those agreed upon by the right-holder.

(3) Goods contained in travellers' personal baggage

12.59 With regard to goods contained in traveller's personal baggage, the customs authorities adhere to the restrictions laid down by the Regulation. Consequently, the customs authorities only act where a traveller's personal baggage contains goods of a commercial nature.

12.60 The issue as to whether goods transported by a traveller are of a commercial nature is to be decided with regard to the type and quantity of the counterfeit goods, the traveller himself, as well as any other circumstances. Clear guidelines setting minimum quantities or values for determining whether goods are of a commercial nature cannot be established. For every individual transport of goods, the customs official has to make a new determination by weighing all the circumstances of the case. Should decisive factors suggest that a consignment presents a commercial

---

[27] Under trade mark law, cf R Ingerl and C Rohnke, *Markengesetz* (2nd edn, 2003), § 30, para 71; for patent law: R Busse, *Patentgesetz* (5th edn, 1999), § 15, para 65; R Schulte, *Patentgesetz* (6th edn 2001), § 15, para 40.

[28] Cf R Schulte, *Patentgesetz* (6th edn, 2001), § 142a, para 10; R Ingerl and C Rohnke, *Markengesetz* (2nd edn, 2003), § 146, para 4.

character, then the goods are retained. However, the whole consignment is stopped whenever the value of the entire transport, that is, calculated based on the wholesale price in the place of vacation, exceeds EUR 175.

II. APPLICATION FOR ACTION BY THE CUSTOMS AUTHORITIES

12.61 The second chapter of the Regulation deals with the application for action by the customs authorities. Generally, the right-holder first files an application, after which the goods in question are detained by the customs authorities. However, Article 4 of the Regulation also permits the customs authorities to act *ex officio*.

A. Measures prior to an application for action by the customs authorities ('*ex officio* measures')

12.62 The German customs authorities make use of their power to detain suspicious goods as granted to them under Article 4 of the Regulation where in the course of customs clearance or inspection they have sufficient grounds for suspecting that the goods infringe an intellectual property right. In practice, shipments frequently become conspicuous where they are part of a larger shipment containing counterfeits of a variety of trade marked products or the importer is unable to prove trade authorization.[29]

12.63 In the event that goods are detained, the customs authorities inform the right-holder by telephone, fax, or e-mail. In general, the right-holder receives information about the nature and quantity of the detained goods as well as about the origin and destination of the goods. The customs authorities also instruct the right-holder about the application requirements. They inform the right-holder that he may request samples by mail so that he can check whether the goods actually infringe his intellectual property rights. Generally, digital cameras are not available to the customs authorities so that it is not possible to send digital photographs by e-mail.

12.64 As provided by the Regulation, the right-holder must file an application for action by the customs authorities within three working days from notification. The

---

[29] K Hoffmeister and H Harte-Bavendamm 'EG-Produktpiraterie-Verordnung' in H Harte-Bavendamm (ed), *Handbuch der Markenpiraterie in Europa* (1st edn, 2000), § 5, para 209.

application can be filed either in the form of a 'global' application that is valid for one year or as an 'individual' application with regard to only one particular matter. The application process is then followed by the regular retention procedure. Applications that are received after the expiry of the three-day period are not processed by the German customs authorities, as the three-day period of time is seen as aiming to protect the declarant or holder of the retained goods.

B. The lodging and processing of applications for customs action

12.65 The Regulation contains elaborate requirements regarding the applicant's status and the form in which applications for action by the customs authorities may be filed. The following sections seek to elucidate the substantive requirements that the Central Office of Intellectual Property Rights (*Zentralstelle Gewerblicher Rechtsschutz*), with whom applications are filed, has gleaned from the requirements of the Regulation.

(1) Persons entitled to file an application for action

12.66 The persons who are entitled to file an application for action by the customs authorities under the Regulation shall be the focus here.

Definition of 'right-holders' under the Regulation

12.67 Article 5 of the Regulation provides that the right-holder is entitled to file an application. A 'right-holder' is defined more precisely in Article 2(2) of the Regulation. According to this definition, every domestic and foreign right-holder as well as any other person or representative authorized to use and/or exploit any intellectual property rights is entitled to file an application.

12.68 Persons who are authorized to use an intellectual property right include anyone who holds a right of use that has been conferred by agreement, in particular, licensees and sole distributors. Whether the license is exclusive or non-exclusive is of no consequence. In the case of an infringement of a copyright or a related right, collecting societies which have as their sole or principal purpose the management or administration of such rights are also entitled to file an application. It is precisely these societies that take legal action against infringements of intellectual property rights.[30] Also entitled to file an application are other groups or representatives who have lodged a registration application for a protected designation of

---

[30] Cf K Scherbauer, *Die Grenzbeschlagnahme von Produktpirateriewaren im Immaterialgüterrecht* (1st edn, 2000), 209.

origin or a protected geographical indication as well as plant breeders. A licensee may initiate an action for infringement within the meaning of Article 13 of the Regulation, but only with the consent of the right-holder (cf § 30, para 3 of the Trade Mark Law, § 31, para 3 of the Designs Law).

The registration of a licence is not a prerequisite for a licensee being able to file an **12.69** application for action by the customs authorities. Besides, registration of licenses in Germany is only possible in exceptional cases.

Representatives can be both legal and natural persons.[31] In particular, attorneys **12.70** and patent attorneys can act as representatives. Generally speaking, the German customs authorities prefer representation by a national attorney if the right-holder neither lives nor has his place of business in the country of filing. This ensures that action may be taken expeditiously. However, retaining a national attorney is not mandatory.

Proof of entitlement to file an application for action

For right-holders stricto sensu

In the case of intellectual property rights that can be registered, the right-holder **12.71** should submit proof of entitlement to file an application for action in the form of a certificate of registration, certified recording, or certified copies of records of the respective intellectual property rights. Database records from the official on-line databases of registration offices are also accepted. By contrast, printouts from private databases are not considered sufficient because the customs authorities cannot be sure that the record actually reflects the current status of the intellectual property right. If the application for action by the customs authorities relies on a copyright, related right, or design right that is not registered or for which an application has not been lodged, the applicant must substantiate that he is entitled to enforce the copyright. Permissible forms of substantiation include, in particular, a sworn affidavit of the author or right-holder. For protected designations of origin and protected geographical indications, the right-holder shall submit proof that he is the producer or group and that the designation or indication has been registered. The same proof shall be submitted for wines and spirits.

The intellectual property rights on which an application for action is based must **12.72** have been validly registered. Under the Regulation, an application for action by the customs authorities may not be based on a mere application for an intellectual property right. Applications for action under national law may in certain cases be based on an application (cf para 12.16, above).

---

[31] K Hoffmeister and H Harte-Bavendamm 'EG-Produktpiraterie-Verordnung' in H Harte-Bavendamm (ed), *Handbuch der Markenpiraterie in Europa* (1st edn, 2000), § 5, para 214.

For persons authorized to use the right

12.73 Where the right-holder is not himself proprietor of the rights but only authorized to use or exercise these rights, he must submit proof of such an authorization. Proof can be in the form of a simple copy of the applicable agreement. Certified copies are not required.

Representatives

12.74 Where a representative of the right-holder or of a person authorized to use the right files an application for action by the customs authorities, the representative has to submit proof of his agency. For this purpose, the representative should attach an authorization to the application. There are no special form requirements for the authorization. The customs authorities only require that the authorization expressly relates to the filing of applications for action by the customs authorities. The authorization can also provide the representative with the global power to file further applications for action as well as requests for modifications and extensions.

12.75 The authorization should be submitted in its original form along with the application. There is no certification requirement.

12.76 It is to be noted that a representative is authorized to file an application for action by the customs authorities on behalf of the right-holder or the person authorized to use the right. However, the declaration under Article 6 of the Regulation that is a mandatory part of every application filing must always bear the right-holder's own signature or the signature of the person authorized to use the right. Instead of submitting the declaration under Article 6 of the Regulation signed by the right-holder or the person authorized to use the right, the representative may submit a document authorizing him to bear any costs arising from customs action on behalf of the right-holder or the person authorized to use the right.

(2) Competent customs department and formal requirements

Competent customs department

12.77 The applicant must file the application with the

Oberfinanzdirektion Nürnberg (Nürnberg Regional Finance Office)
Zentralstelle Gewerblicher Rechtsschutz
Sophienstraße 6
D-80333 München
Tel.: (+49-89) 59 95-23 49
Fax: (+49-89) 59 95-23 17
e-mail: zgr@ofdm.bfinv.de
Internet: www.grenzbeschlagnahme.de and www.zoll-d.de

Form of the application for action

The application must be made out on a form established by the European **12.78** Commission that the Central Office of Intellectual Property Rights makes available on-line. Applicants can download it from the website located at www.zoll-d.de.(http://www.zoll-d.de/e0_downloads/b0_vordrucke/a0_ vordruckgesamtliste/index.php).

The application must be filed in original by mail. In accordance with Article 3(3) **12.79** of the Implementing Regulation, the applicant must submit two copies of his application for action. More than one duplicate is not required. In urgent cases, for example in the case of goods detained under Article 4 of the Regulation (*ex officio* actions), the application may be initially submitted by fax. At present, electronic filing is not yet possible. There are plans for establishing this type of filing procedure in the future but it is not yet known exactly when this option will become available.

Attachments to the application should, if possible, be made available in electronic **12.80** form, for example, on a disk, CD-Rom, or by e-mail. The Central Office will then put the descriptive information it receives electronically onto its intranet. This enables the local customs authorities to have access to high-quality colour images and to compare the goods they are inspecting directly with the screen image. If the attachments are stored on a data carrier, the applicant should submit one copy for every country for which the application is being filed. If the applicant is not filing the attachments electronically, then he should submit a set of exhibits for every country for which the application is being filed.

The original version of the declaration pursuant to Article 6 of the Regulation **12.81** should be filed. In urgent cases, the declaration may be sent initially by fax. Electronic submissions of declarations by themselves are not sufficient.

Language requirements

It is not mandatory that the application be filed in German. Although the official **12.82** language of the customs authorities is German pursuant to § 87 of the Tax Code (*Abgabenordnung*) and the customs authorities are entitled to require a translation of an application filed in a foreign language, the customs authorities do not require this where the application form is filed in English or French instead of in German. The same applies to the declaration under Article 6 of the Regulation.

The exhibits submitted together with the application should be filed in German. **12.83** This is especially the case where the attachments contain lengthy text. If an applicant intends to file an application for action by the customs authorities not only for Germany but also for other Member States, he should submit attachments in English or preferably in the official language of each respective country designated in the application: local customs authorities do not always have a good command of foreign languages so that effective action can only be ensured where the customs authorities are able to understand easily the information provided to them.

(3) Requirements regarding the contents of the application for action

Mandatory information

12.84   The application must identify the affected intellectual property rights and the goods the customs authorities should monitor. The application must also contain information that enables the customs authorities readily to recognize unlawful imitations. The customs authorities prefer that the information focus on the appearance of the genuine goods because the appearance of fakes changes constantly. The customs authorities request, in particular:

- a description or image of the intellectual property and an indication as to the manner in which the right-holder uses it in the course of trade;
- a description of the typical outward characteristics of an original article (for example, packaging, product insert, warranty certificate, instructions, neck labels, etc);
- indications of special safety features (for example, labels, safety threads, holograms, etc).

12.85   It is also mandatory for the applicant to provide the name of contact persons with whom the customs authorities can liaise in the event goods are retained. In the application for customs action, the applicant has to name a contact person for administrative questions as well as a contact person for technical questions. Whereas the administrative contact can be a lawyer, the technical contact should instead be an expert with regard to the goods in question. The contact persons designated for Germany need not necessarily reside in Germany. However, it is an advantage where the contact person has a command of German as this will obviously facilitate contact with the authorities. There are no other requirements relative to the contact person.

Optional information

12.86   The customs authorities are keen on receiving information on the type of shipment and shipment routes. On its website, the Central Office for Intellectual Property recommends that the applicant answer the following questions:

- Do the original goods only go through clearance at certain customs offices and, if so, which ones?
- Are the original goods cleared only following one particular procedure, for example, collective customs procedure, or for the purpose of a certain customs procedure such as storage in a free warehouse?

- Are original goods intended for import, export, or free circulation by means of a particular system of distribution, for example, only by a general customs broker or by particular shipping companies? Are any specific shipping routes followed (shipment by air, sea, ground, mail)?

- Are there any known names and addresses of companies and persons who as manufacturers, distributors, brokers, carriers, importers, consignees or exporters deal or have dealt with products infringing an intellectual property right?

- If necessary, is it possible to infer that the goods infringe an intellectual property right based on the declared low customs value, for example, since even the lowest wholesale price of a lawful product clearly exceeds the price for imitations? At which price would the limit be?

- If the products are packaged in a particular way, is there a special type of packaging and, if so, does the packaging bear any distinctive markings or attributes?

- Are unaffiliated companies authorized to deal in the trade marked products for commercial purposes? How does a licensee prove authorization? Is written authorization required for all third parties who are entitled to deal with these products commercially?

Additional information specific to the type of intellectual property right referred to in the application

With regard to intellectual property rights which are not subject to a former examination as to their merits, that is, copyright and related rights pursuant to the Copyright Law as well as industrial designs, the customs authorities require evidence of authorship or of the applicant's status of original holder in accordance with Article 2(1)(b) of the Implementing Regulation (EC) No 1891/2004. **12.87**

(4) *Processing and acceptance of the application for action*

When the Central Office of Intellectual Property Rights receives an application for action by the customs authorities, the authorities check whether the application requirements have been met and, if necessary, informally clarify with the applicant the need for any changes or additional information. In accordance with the Regulation, the authorities must process the application and render a decision within 30 working days of receipt of the application. **12.88**

In the event the authorities reject an application, the applicant may appeal from the decision in accordance with § 347 and § 348 of the Tax Code (*Abgabenordnung*). Pursuant to § 347 of the Tax Code, the customs authorities may remedy the appeal by still granting the application. If the customs authorities do not overturn their decision, § 33, para 1, no 1 of the Finance Court Procedure (*Finanzgerichtsordnung*) allows an applicant to take legal action through the **12.89** finance courts. If the finance court dismisses the action, the applicant may file an appeal with the Federal Tax Court where the finance court allows an appeal against its decision, pursuant to § 115 of the Finance Court Procedure. Generally, an appeal is to be allowed only if the case has fundamental significance or the decision serves the furtherance of justice.

12.90   If the application for action by the customs authorities is granted, it is generally valid for one year. Subsequently, the applicant can reapply as often as he chooses. At the right-holder's request, the application can also be granted for a shorter period. Such 'shortened' applications may be advantageous in different circumstances, for example, where the remaining term of the intellectual property right relied upon is less than one year. It might also be practical to obtain corresponding expiry dates for all pending applications for action.

(5) 'Community' applications for action

Processing of 'Community' applications for action filed with German Customs

12.91   Under Article 5(4) of the Regulation, if an application for action by the customs authorities relies on an intellectual property right that enjoys Community protection, the application can be filed not only with regard to the Member State in which the application is submitted but also with regard to other Member States. If the requirements have been met, the customs authorities will grant the application not only for Germany but also for the other Member States that the applicant has specified in his application. The Central Office of Intellectual Property Rights is responsible for sending notice of the decision to the central offices of the other Member States for which the application has been granted. The Central Office of Intellectual Property Rights forwards the decision to the corresponding national customs offices along with any other documents that are necessary for securing the useful effect of this decision.

Processing of 'Community' applications designating Germany

12.92   When the German Central Office of Intellectual Property Rights is notified by a central office of another Member State that an application for action by the customs authorities filed under Article 5(4) of the Regulation has been granted for Germany, this Office will receive from the notifying central office a copy of the decision and all other documents that are necessary for processing and enforcing it. If the German Central Office believes that certain documents are missing or translations are necessary, it contacts the central office of the other Member State or the right-holder. For 'Community' applications designating Germany it is not mandatory (but recommended) that the representative is domiciled in Germany.

III. CONDITIONS GOVERNING ACTION BY CUSTOMS AUTHORITIES AND BY THE AUTHORITIES COMPETENT TO DETERMINE WHETHER GOODS INFRINGE AN INTELLECTUAL PROPERTY RIGHT

A. Conditions governing action by customs authorities

The following section describes the procedure followed by the German customs authorities when retaining suspicious goods. **12.93**

(1) Factual background

The most important customs offices for retention by the customs authorities are located at the Frankfurt Airport, one of the largest freight airports in Europe, and the Port of Hamburg through which millions of containers pass into the market of the European Community every year. In addition, millions of trucks are checked annually on the occasion of border controls carried out at the borders to the central-European countries. These checks will obviously decrease now that the countries bordering the former East Germany have joined the European Union. **12.94**

(2) Notification of customs intervention

Where the customs authorities suspect that goods infringe the rights of an applicant, they suspend the release of the goods or detain them. Regularly, the right-holder and declarant or holder of the goods are notified of a suspension of release or detention of goods. Depending on the particular circumstances of the case, notice goes out by telephone, fax, or e-mail. **12.95**

(3) Information to be provided by customs to the right-holder before the right-holder confirms the infringing nature of the goods

As provided by Article 9(2) of the Regulation, the customs authorities first inform the right-holder of the quantity and nature of the goods the release of which has been suspended or that have been detained. The right-holder can also request the disclosure of further information regarding the declarant, consignor or consignee as well as the origin or provenance of the goods. However, according to **12.96** the opinion of national customs authorities expressed on their website, disclosure of this information places the right-holder under a duty to take further procedural steps in accordance with Article 13 of the Regulation, that is, to initiate legal action. If the right-holder fails to institute legal proceedings after he has received the additional information, the consequence may be that the customs authorities will not take any further measures through the expiry of the application. It is doubtful as to whether this point of view is correct legally. Article 9(3) of the Regulation indeed provides for the disclosure of additional information 'with a view to establishing whether an intellectual property right has been infringed under national law'. However, in the author's opinion, it does not follow that there is an obligation to institute legal proceedings with the purpose of determining whether an intellectual property right has been infringed. This is especially the case where the right-holder, after receiving the additional information—particularly in respect of the consignor of the goods—possibly determines that the goods being retained by customs are goods he has licensed. In this case, the right-holder cannot be forced to institute proceedings with the purpose of determining whether an intellectual property right has been infringed.

12.97 By and large, the customs authorities must take into consideration the German statutory provisions governing the protection of personal data, professional and administrative confidentiality, as well as commercial and industrial secrecy. Article 10 of the Basic Law (*Grundgesetz*, the German Constitution), in particular, is relevant in this context as it protects the secrecy of the mail and letters. § 30 of the Tax Code, that governs tax secrecy, is also applicable. With regard to retention by the customs authorities, this statutory provision concerning the protection of personal data takes precedence over the more general Federal Data Protection Law (*Bundesdatenschutzgesetz*).

12.98 However, the European Court of Justice held in its decision of 14 October 1999,[32] data protection laws may not preclude the dissemination of information specified by the Regulation. The German statutory provisions comply with these requirements first by explicitly restraining the prohibition on communication to mail and letter secrecy under Article 10 of the Basic Law. Secondly, pursuant to § 30, para 4, no 2 of the Tax Code, the dissemination of data is always permissible where expressly provided by law. Such statutory authorization is found precisely in the national laws governing retention by the customs authorities as well as in the Regulation that also has the effect of law in Germany within the meaning of § 30, para 4, no 2 of the Tax Code.[33] Therefore, the data referred to in Article 9(3) of the Regulation may be disclosed.

---

[32] ECJ Case C-223/98 WRP 1999, 1269 (1271)—*Adidas*.
[33] K Scherbauer, *Die Grenzbeschlagnahme von Produktpirateriewaren im Immaterialgüterrecht* (1st edn, 2000), 238, 239.

(4) Inspection of the suspected goods

At the request of the right-holder, the customs authorities can provide him with **12.99** samples and specimens of the detained goods. Generally, the right-holder is already informed of this option in the initial notice. Where the right-holder requests that samples and specimens be provided to him, customs will promptly send these to him by mail. Since the goods that are being sent for inspection by the right-holder are dutiable goods under the control of customs, the goods must be sent back immediately after inspection. In individual cases where it is only possible to determine an infringement of an intellectual property right by destruction of the goods, the customs authorities will accept this. However, in these cases written notification is required as to why destruction of the goods was imperative.

B. Simplified procedure allowing the destruction of the goods without there being any need to determine whether an intellectual property right has been infringed under national law

Article 11 of the Regulation allows the Member States to provide for a simplified **12.100** procedure for the destruction of goods. Under certain circumstances, retained goods can be destroyed without a judicial determination as to whether they infringe an intellectual property right.

In Germany, the simplified procedure for the destruction of retained goods sub- **12.101** ject to border measures has been employed for quite some time now in cases where there has been no judicial determination as to whether the retained goods infringe an intellectual property right. The intellectual property provisions under national law that govern action by the customs authorities consistently provide for confiscation of the goods retained by the customs authorities where the border measures have not been opposed within two weeks. Following confiscation of the goods, upon which ownership of the goods passes to the State, the goods are destroyed under customs control. Significantly, more than 75 per cent of customs procedures carried out in 2003 were concluded in this manner.[34]

The procedure laid down in Article 11 of the Regulation is inspired by existing **12.102** German law but does deviate from it with regard to the specifics. According to Article 11 of the Regulation, the simplified procedure requires the consent of the right-holder. Further, the right-holder must provide written notice within the prescribed period of time that the goods infringe an intellectual property right, whereas the national statutory provisions allow the goods to be destroyed even where the right-holder does not do so. In this case, destruction is based solely on

---

[34] Cf Bundesministerium der Finanzen, *Gewerblicher Rechtsschutz Jahresbericht* 2003, 9.

the authorities' assessment prior to the taking of border measures that the goods infringe an intellectual property right. As a rule, the Regulation also requires the written consent of all persons authorized to dispose of the goods ('authorized persons'). However, if any authorized person does not notify the right-holder or customs authorities within the prescribed two-week period, the consent can be presumed. By contrast, the consent of authorized persons is not required under national law. Authorized persons only have the right to object against the destruction of the goods.

12.103 According to the Federal Ministry of Justice, national statutory provisions on simplified procedures for the destruction of goods will soon be adapted to conform to the requirements of the Regulation.

12.104 Pursuant to the Regulation, the right-holder's consent to a simplified procedure for the destruction of goods is the only way of avoiding litigation with the infringer. The right-holder does not have the option of withdrawing his application for action by the customs authorities with regard to a particular shipment. If the right-holder chooses to settle amicably with the infringer, he must withdraw the application in its entirety. Only after a settlement has been reached in the particular matter may the right-holder resubmit an application for action by the customs authorities. This is essentially different from German law. Unlike the Regulation, the German statutory provisions on action by the customs authorities provide the right-holder with the option of withdrawing the application for action with regard to a particular shipment, cf § 147, para 2 of the Trade Mark Law, § 142a, para 4 of the Patent Law, § 111b, para 4 of the Copyright Law, § 56, para 2 of the Designs Law, § 40a, para 4 of the Law on the Protection of Plant Varieties. This provides the right-holder and the infringer with the option of entering into a settlement that does not automatically trigger the destruction of the goods. These kinds of out-of-court settlements between right-holders and infringers routinely incorporate negative covenants by the infringer to refrain from further infringements under penalty of incurring a fine. Settlement agreements also determine the future of the retained goods (destruction or clearance sale right), claims for damages as well as who bears the incurred costs, particularly storage or administrative costs.

12.105 In many instances, the Regulation does not yield satisfactory results and certainly will not do so as long as the possibility of a simplified procedure for destruction of the goods remains unavailable in Germany. It is often also opportune for the infringer to avoid the initiation of court proceedings, the costs of which he would have to bear in the end. Therefore, the infringer will often agree to the destruction of the goods. The right-holder will want to avoid withdrawing his application for action by the customs authorities altogether just to be able to reach an agreement with the infringer in exceptional cases. In these particular instances, customs law does offer one alternative outside of the Regulation. The right-holder and the infringer can agree on the infringer applying for destruction of the goods by customs authorities within the 10-day-period in accordance with § 182 of the Customs Code[35] (*Zollkodex*). Such an application by the infringer will cause the goods to be destroyed at the expense of the infringer. In this case, it is unnecessary to initiate proceedings with the purpose of determining whether an intellectual property right has been infringed.

C. Conditions governing action by the authorities having jurisdiction to determine whether the goods infringe an intellectual property right

Where the right-holder does not consent to the application of this simplified procedure for the destruction of goods pursuant to Article 11 of the Regulation, he must notify the customs office that retained the goods within the time period specified by Article 13 of the Regulation that he has initiated proceedings to determine whether an intellectual property right has been infringed. **12.106**

(1) Authorities having jurisdiction to determine whether the goods infringe an intellectual property right

The new provision of Article 13(1) of the Regulation simply demands that the right-holder initiate proceedings to determine whether an intellectual property right has been infringed under national law. The Regulation does not expressly provide for a definition of the term 'proceedings', thus leaves open the nature of the proceedings acceptable under the Regulation. Based on the plain text of the Regulation, it is not the type but the goal of the proceedings that is decisive. There is consensus that civil proceedings serve the purpose of determining whether an intellectual property right has been infringed under national law by customs authorities. By contrast it is questionable whether the filing of a criminal complaint serves the same purpose. Customs authorities take the position that the filing of a criminal complaint does not serve the purpose of determining whether an intellectual property right has been infringed. Thus, notifying customs office within the 10 working days referred to in Article 13 (1) of the Regulation that a criminal complaint has been filed will in practice lead to the release of the retained goods. **12.107**

---

[35] Council Reg (EEC) No. 2913/92 of 12 October 1992.

12.108 It is doubtful whether this point of view is correct legally. The right-holder can—in the author's opinion—also file a criminal complaint, thus initiating criminal proceedings. Wilful infringements of intellectual property rights that fall under the Regulation are punishable in Germany. The Regulation indeed does not expressly provide that criminal proceedings are to be regarded as proceedings within the meaning of Article 13(1). Nonetheless, in the author's opinion it is clear that initiating criminal proceedings is sufficient. The Regulation only requires the initiation of legal proceedings to determine whether an intellectual property right has been infringed. At the core of criminal proceedings that have been instituted based on a possible infringement of an intellectual property right is the determination as to whether there has been an infringement of an intellectual property right. Therefore, criminal proceedings must also qualify as proceedings within the meaning of Article 13 of the Regulation based on the clear purpose of criminal proceedings.

12.109 Irrespective of the author's point of view, in practice, to ensure that the goods are not being released by customs office, the right-holder should always file a civil complaint within the 10 working days.

12.110 The following sections will provide a general introduction to civil and criminal proceedings in Germany. Following these sections, there will be an explanation of the procedural particularities posed by the various intellectual property rights.

Civil proceedings

12.111 Civil proceedings first offer the possibility of preliminary injunctive relief and secondly, the possibility of the so-called main hearing or trial on the merits. It cannot be clearly inferred from the Regulation whether by itself the filing of a complaint on the merits may be regarded as 'proceedings to determine whether an intellectual property right has been infringed under national law' or whether the filing of a complaint for preliminary injunctive relief is sufficient as well. As previously mentioned, based on the plain text of the Regulation, it is not the type but the goal of the proceedings that is decisive. Even injunctive relief proceedings, in which the plaintiff only has to show an infringement prima facie and does not have to establish his case in accordance with the strictest evidentiary standard, constitute proceedings that serve the purpose of determining whether an intellectual property right has been infringed. Therefore, it would appear that both the filing of a motion seeking a preliminary injunction and the filing of a complaint on the merits of the case constitute the initiation of proceedings as provided for by Article 13 of the Regulation.

12.112 Preliminary injunctive relief has the advantage that a court decision can be rendered within a few days. This remedy constitutes a suitable precautionary measure within the meaning of Article 14(1)(b) of the Regulation. For this reason, it is beneficial for the right-holder to file a complaint for preliminary injunctive relief. A court ruling in preliminary injunction proceedings is indeed only temporary in nature. Where the defendant does not acknowledge the preliminary injunction as a permanent resolution and waives an appeal, the right-holder must file a complaint on the merits after the proceedings for injunctive relief in order to obtain a final judgment. In many instances, pursuing a trial on the merits is unnecessary because the infringer will accept the decision rendered in the preliminary injunctive proceedings as the final ruling.

Preliminary Injunctive Relief

With regard to intellectual property rights, proceedings for preliminary injunctive relief are based on the general provisions of German civil procedure, in particular, § 935 et seq of the Code of Civil Procedure. The plaintiff can request a restriction of the infringer's use (injunction) and/or impoundment (sequestration) of the suspicious goods by a bailiff. The latter makes sense because an order that prohibits use by the infringer does not prevent release of the goods. Furthermore, it is possible to claim a request for information in the motion for preliminary injunctive relief. In those cases where the infringement is obvious, the court can impose the obligation to disclose information by way of preliminary injunction (cf eg § 19, para 3 of the Trade Mark Law).   **12.113**

An order for preliminary injunctive relief requires that the plaintiff make out a prima facie case that he is proprietor of the rights. He must also prove prima facie that the defendant infringed his rights or that such an infringement is imminent (§ 920 and § 936 of the German Code of Civil Procedure). The requirement of a prima facie showing means that the plaintiff must produce evidence sufficient to satisfy the court of the facts, whereby there is a relaxed burden of proof. In addition to the usual forms of proof, the following are also permissible: **12.114**

- sworn affidavit containing the plaintiff's own statements as to the facts sought to be proved;
- attorney's affidavit regarding events that he witnessed in the exercise of his profession;
- uncertified documents.

The court weighs the evidence within its own discretion.[36]   **12.115**

Pursuant to § 937 of the German Code of Civil Procedure, preliminary injunctive relief can issue in the absence of an oral hearing where a matter of urgency is involved. The courts often make use of this option so that a decision can often be obtained within a few days. Where a court issues a preliminary injunction   **12.116**

---

[36] H Thomas and H Putzo, ZPO (Zivilprozeßordnung, 25th edn, 2003), § 294, para 1.

without an oral hearing, the disadvantage is that the decision is typically enforceable only in Germany and not in other Member States. Court orders issued on motions for preliminary injunctive relief generally qualify as rulings within the meaning of Article 32 of the Council Regulation (EC) No 44/2001 on jurisdiction and the recognition and enforcement of judgments in civil and commercial matters. However, according to the case law of the European Court of Justice, such court orders cannot be recognized where they have not issued in contradictory proceedings.[37]

Trial on the Merits

12.117 The main trial must be initiated at the outcome of proceedings for preliminary injunctive relief if the infringer does not decide to recognize the preliminary injunction as a final ruling and, therefore, does not waive the main trial. As with a motion for preliminary injunctive relief, the plaintiff first asserts a claim for injunctive relief in his writ of summons on the merits. Generally, the plaintiff will include in his motion for injunctive relief a request for disclosure of information and an accounting in order to be able to quantify the claims for damages. It is also customary to include in the same motion a request to determine the issue of liability for damages as well as a request aiming at the destruction of the infringing goods. Alternatively, the plaintiff can file a 'complaint by stages' within the meaning of § 254 of the German Code of Civil Procedure and subsequently file a motion for disclosure of information along with a claim for damages that initially does not specify any particular amount. After the disclosure of information, the plaintiff can file a motion for damages where the amount is specified.

Criminal proceedings

12.118 Where criminal proceedings are initiated as a result of a criminal complaint, the court has to decide whether the goods infringe an intellectual property right. If the court finds this to be the case, it will order the confiscation of the goods in its judgment pursuant to § 74 et seq of the German Criminal Code (*Strafgesetzbuch*). More lenient measures may be allowed in any given case. Confiscation of the goods is ordered regardless of whether the goods belong to the infringer or a third party (cf, for example, § 143, para 5 of the Trade Mark Law and § 110 of the Copyright Law, both referring to § 74a of the German Criminal Code).

12.119 It is also possible for the court to order precautionary measures in criminal proceedings within the time period provided by Article 13 of the Regulation. Pursuant to § 94 et seq of the German Code of Criminal Procedure (*Strafprozeßordnung*), a retention of goods for the purpose of preserving evidence is permissible.

---

[37] Cf ECJ Case C-125/79 *Denilauler v Couchet Frères* IPRax 1981, 95, 96.

Pursuant to § 111b et seq, the sequestration of goods that are subject to confiscation may also be envisaged. The prosecuting authorities have discretion in determining whether such measures are warranted.

Advantages and disadvantages of the different types of judicial proceedings

In both criminal and civil proceedings the result can be the destruction of the **12.120** infringing goods. The initiation of criminal proceedings has the advantage that a prima facie case does not have to be made out to prove infringement because the prosecuting authorities investigate on their own initiative. Therefore, the initiation of criminal proceedings is recommended especially where the right-holder has difficulties producing the evidence necessary for initiating civil proceedings for preliminary injunctive relief. Another advantage of initiating criminal proceedings is that criminal seizures of goods are possible where the infringing goods do not belong to the infringer. If there is uncertainty as to whether the goods belong to the infringer ascertained by customs, criminal proceedings should be initiated with the purpose of seizing the infringing goods. Further, the proceedings do not entail any costs. However, this type of proceeding has the disadvantage that the right-holder 'hands over' the remainder of the proceedings to the prosecution authorities, thus only retaining a limited influence. In practice, civil measures are more prominent. Civil proceedings have the advantage that the regional courts often have highly specialized divisions that have greater expertise for deciding infringement issues. For this reason, it is preferred to initiate civil proceedings over criminal proceedings, particularly in cases that involve difficult legal or factual issues, even if greater costs are associated with civil proceedings.[38] In addition, the civil courts often issue rulings more expeditiously than the criminal courts. Finally, only in civil proceedings can the court issue an order prohibiting the infringer from repeating the same acts of infringement and providing for a monetary fine in the event of an infringement.

The following sections are intended to clarify the particularities of the respective **12.121** intellectual property rights covered by the Regulation in civil cases:

Counterfeit goods

The regional courts have exclusive jurisdiction over cases involving counterfeit **12.122** goods with regard to both preliminary injunction proceedings and the hearings on the merits in accordance with § 140 of the Trade Mark Law for national and international trade marks with protection in Germany and § 125e of the Trade

---

[38] H Harte-Bavendamm in H Harte-Bavendamm (ed), *Handbuch der Markenpiraterie in Europa* (1st edn, 2000), § 5, para 12.

Mark Law for Community trade marks. In virtually every German State, the proper venue for trade mark disputes is determined by State regulation. The venue depends on the place of residence or domicile of the infringer (§ 12, § 13, and § 17 of the German Code of Civil Procedure) or, alternatively, the place where the infringement was committed (§ 32 of the German Code of Civil Procedure).

12.123 If goods infringe a Community trade mark, it is worth noting that preliminary injunctions issuing in the absence of an oral hearing are only enforceable in Germany. Article 99 of the Community Trade Mark Regulation expressly provides that applications for precautionary measures may be made if the issue is whether goods infringe a Community trade mark. If a court ruling issues from a Community trade mark court of proper jurisdiction as defined by Article 93(1)(4) of the Community Trade Mark Regulation, the court ruling will be applicable throughout the European Union pursuant to Article 99(2) of the Community Trade Mark Regulation. However, this rule does not apply to preliminary injunctions issuing in the absence of an oral hearing under the case law of the European Court of Justice.[39] The consequence is that such interlocutory orders issued by a Community trade mark court are not enforceable throughout the Community.

Pirated goods

12.124 The regional courts do not have exclusive jurisdiction over copyright matters. The issue as to whether the local or regional courts have jurisdiction is determined by general provisions of law and, therefore, depends on the amount in controversy. Pursuant to § 23, no 1 and § 71, para 1 of the Judicature Law (*Gerichtsverfassungsgesetz*), where the amount in dispute is up to EUR 5,000, the local courts have jurisdiction and where the amount in dispute exceeds EUR 5,000, the regional courts have jurisdiction. Where the regional courts have jurisdiction, plaintiffs must keep in mind that State regulation refers copyright disputes to certain regional courts pursuant to § 105 of the Copyright Law. As in the case of counterfeit goods, the venue depends on the place of residence or domicile of the infringer or, alternatively, the place where the infringement was committed.

12.125 Pursuant to § 52 of the Designs Law, the regional courts have exclusive jurisdiction over claims relying on a national industrial design.

12.126 In virtually every German State, the proper venue for industrial design actions is determined by State regulation. The venue depends on the place of residence or domicile of the infringer or, alternatively, the place where the infringement was committed. Pursuant to § 63 of the Designs Law, the regional courts also have

---

[39] Cf ECJ Case C-125/79 *Denilauler v Couchet Frères* IPRax 1981, 95 (96).

exclusive jurisdiction over actions relying on a Community design. In virtually every German State, the proper venue for these types of claims is also determined by State regulation. The venue in industrial design actions involving Community designs is based on the same rules applicable to cases involving national industrial designs.

With regard to motions for preliminary injunctive relief in actions involving **12.127** pirated goods, special attention must be paid to the prima facie showing of pro-prietorship. Whereas prima facie proof of proprietorship in cases involving coun-terfeit goods can be based solely on a copy of the certificate of recording, this is not possible in cases involving pirated goods. This is due to the fact that copyright and other related intellectual property rights are not recorded or registered rights under the German Copyright Law. Therefore, the right-holder does not have a certificate of recording.

The registration of an industrial design is based solely on compliance with proced- **12.128** ural requirements, regardless of any verification of compliance with the substan-tive requirements for protection. Therefore, a certificate of recording in these cases is by itself not sufficient to establish prima facie that an industrial design right exists. Where the factual and legal issues at stake in a case are complicated and the limited means of the injunction proceedings are insufficient for a ruling by the court, the preliminary injunction cannot issue if the injunctive relief sought by the plaintiff would pose a significant restriction on the defendant.[40]

Goods infringing a patent or a supplementary protection certificate

Pursuant to § 143 of the Patent Law, the regional courts have exclusive jurisdic- **12.129** tion over patent disputes. In virtually every German State, the proper venue for patent disputes is determined by State regulation. The venue depends on the place of residence or domicile of the infringer or, alternatively, the place where the infringement was committed.

Goods infringing a plant variety right

Pursuant to § 38 of the Law on the Protection of Plant Varieties, the regional **12.130** courts have exclusive jurisdiction over actions involving the protection of plant varieties. In virtually every German State, the proper venue for plant variety actions is determined by State regulation. The venue depends on the place of res-idence or domicile of the infringer or, alternatively, the place where the infringe-ment was committed.

---

[40] Oberlandesgericht Celle (Court of appeal) CR 1994, 748 (749,750).

Goods infringing a designation of origin or a geographical indication

12.131 As with actions involving counterfeit goods, § 140 of the Trade Mark Law provides the regional courts with exclusive jurisdiction in cases involving infringements of geographical indications and designations of origin.

(2) Term for notifying customs that proceedings have been started

12.132 Pursuant to Article 13 of the Regulation, the right-holder must notify the customs office detaining the goods within 10 working days that legal proceedings have been initiated to determine whether these goods infringe an intellectual property right. This deadline may be extended by a maximum of another 10 working days.

12.133 The requirements for extensions are not regulated. According to the Central Office of Intellectual Property Rights, an extension is granted where it is necessary. Generally speaking, the applicant has 10 working days to prove to the customs authorities that he has taken all necessary steps. It is conceivable that the applicant has filed a motion for injunctive relief with a civil court but has not yet received the decision. In such a case, precautionary measures within the meaning of Article 14 (1) (b) of the Regulation have not been authorized to prevent the release of the detained goods. If, for example, the applicant produces a copy of the filed motion to the customs authorities, the authorities will grant an extension under the circumstances.

D. Release of goods suspected of infringing certain rights on provision of a security

12.134 Article 14 of the Regulation allows the declarant, owner, importer, holder or consignee of the goods to obtain release of the goods, subject to fulfilment of certain conditions, by posting a security. If the conditions of Article 14 are met, the German customs authorities will consider themselves bound to release the goods. The amount of the security, the posting of which enables the release of the goods, depends heavily on the circumstances of each individual case. The customs office that has applied border measures to the goods determines the amount with the agreement of the right-holder. The security can be posted in cash (deposit) or in the form of a bank guarantee.

E. Storage of goods

12.135 Article 15 of the Regulation provides that each Member State is to determine the conditions of storage of the goods during the period of suspension of release or detention. In Germany, the storage of goods is the responsibility of the customs authorities. The goods remain under customs control until there is a final decision on the retained goods. Pursuant to § 13 of the Administrative Expenses Law (*Verwaltungskostengesetz*), the right-holder is liable for any storage fees incurred in the interim. The right-holder is the one who, as a result of filing the application, caused the detention or suspension of release of the goods by the customs authorities. According to § 178 of the German Tax Code in connection with § 10 of the Customs Cost Ordinance (*Zollkostenverordnung*), daily storage fees cost as follows:

- Shipments by mail: EUR 0.50 per package
- Parcelled freight: EUR 1.00 for each 0–100 kilograms, maximum cost EUR 25,60
- Other shipments/cargo: EUR 0.15 for each 0–1 kilogram, minimum cost EUR 6.40.

IV. PROVISIONS APPLICABLE TO GOODS FOUND TO INFRINGE AN INTELLECTUAL PROPERTY RIGHT

The fourth chapter of the Regulation deals with the procedures applicable to goods that are found to infringe an intellectual property right. **12.136**

The right-holder can prevent goods from being disposed of in breach of Article 16 of the Regulation. In civil proceedings, the right-holder must file a motion for destruction of the goods found to infringe an intellectual property right. Such a claim may rely on the following national statutory provisions: **12.137**

- § 18 of the Trade Mark Law
- § 140 a of the Patent Law
- § 98, para 1 of the Copyright Law
- § 43, para 1 of the Designs Law
- § 37a of the Law on the Protection of Plant Varieties.

In the event that destruction of goods is considered disproportionate, these provisions provide in part for more lenient measures to remedy the infringement. Under these provisions, a claim for destruction seeks destruction by the infringer with the consequence that the infringer must bear any and all costs incurred by the destruction.[41] If the goods have been previously impounded by a bailiff, it is **12.138**

---

[41] BGH GRUR 1997, 899 (902)—*Vernichtungsanspruch*.

advisable to include in the claim for relief a request for destruction by the defendant under the supervision of the bailiff.[42]

12.139 In criminal proceedings, the court orders the confiscation of the goods in its judgment. Where the goods are confiscated, they become the property of the State (§ 74e of the German Criminal Code). Since the goods cannot re-enter commercial channels, the State must arrange for the destruction of the goods.

12.140 Pursuant to Article 17 (1) (b) of the Regulation, Member States must ensure that the competent authorities are able to adopt measures that will effectively deprive concerned persons of any economic gain accruing from the transaction with the infringing goods. In Germany, this is provided for by the right-holder having a claim for damages against the infringer where the infringement was at least negligent. The right-holder has three different options for calculating damages. He can calculate the actual losses he suffered (actual damages), request the amount that the infringer would reasonably have had to pay had he asked for a licence (fictitious licensing fee), or, alternatively, ask for an amount equal to that which the defendant earned by intruding upon the right-holder's intellectual property right (so-called 'infringer profits').[43] So-called infringer profits do not constitute the entire profit which the infringer has gained by selling the goods. Rather, infringer profits are only to be regarded as a part of the profit gained, that is, the part that is derived specifically from the infringement and not from any other sales factors.[44] The court must calculate this portion by way of an appraisal.[45]

12.141 Where the right-holder does not have a claim for restitution of profits by the infringer and criminal proceedings have been opened, the criminal court can order forfeiture of the profits that have inured to the infringer from the transactions with the infringed goods pursuant to § 73 et seq of the German Criminal Code. However, this is typically precluded by the right-holder's claim for damages, § 73, para 1 of the German Criminal Code.

V. PENALTIES

12.142 Article 18 of the Regulation requires the Member States to introduce penalties for violations of the Regulation. The penalties that are applied under German law in that framework depend on the nature of the violation of the Regulation. If the

---

[42] R Ingerl and C Rohnke, *Markengesetz* (2nd edn, 2003), § 18, para 32.
[43] Cf eg BGH GRUR 1993, 55 (57)—*Tchibo/Rolex II* ibid.
[44] Cf eg BGH GRUR 2002, 532 (535)—*Unikatrahmen*.
[45] Cf eg BGH GRUR 1993, 55 (59)—*Tchibo/Rolex II* ibid.

breach results from the right-holder using information received from the customs authorities for purposes other than those specified by the Regulation, penalties are based on the administrative and criminal offence provisions of § 43 and § 44 of the Federal Data Protection Law (*Bundesdatenschutzgesetz*).

A release of goods in violation of Article 16 of the Regulation constitutes a wilful **12.143** infringement of the affected intellectual property right. This type of infringement is punishable under the statutes that govern the individual intellectual property rights, in particular:

Counterfeit goods

§ 143 and § 144 of the Trade Mark Law contain criminal provisions applicable to **12.144** trade mark infringements. In the case of commercial activities, the penalty can range from a fine to imprisonment of up to five years.

Pirated goods

The criminal provisions applicable to copyright infringements are found in § 106 **12.145** et seq of the Copyright Law. In the case of commercial activities, the penalty can range from a fine to imprisonment of up to five years.

The criminal provisions applicable to design right infringements are found in **12.146** § 51 of the Designs Law. In the case of commercial activities, the penalty can range from a fine to imprisonment of up to five years.

Goods infringing a patent or a supplementary protection certificate

The criminal provisions applicable to patent infringements are found in § 142 of **12.147** the Patent Law. In the case of commercial activities, the penalty can range from a fine to imprisonment of up to five years.

Goods infringing a plant variety right

The criminal provisions applicable to infringements of plant variety rights are **12.148** found in § 39 and § 40 of the Law on the Protection of Plant Varieties. In the case of commercial activities, the penalty can range from a fine to imprisonment of up to five years.

Goods infringing a designation of origin or a geographical indication

Under § 144 of the Trade Mark Law, the infringement of a geographical indica- **12.149** tion or designation of origin is punishable by a fine or imprisonment of up to two years.

VI. LIABILITY OF CUSTOMS AUTHORITIES AND RIGHT-HOLDERS

12.150   Articles 12 and 19 of the Regulation deal with the liability of the right-holder and provide that claims against the right-holder are governed by the laws of the respective Member States. Article 19 of the Regulation also applies to the liability of the customs authorities.

A. Liability of right-holders and sanctions

12.151   The following section discusses the conditions that give rise to a right-holder's civil liability under German national law.

12.152   Where a right-holder unlawfully uses information provided by customs, he is liable in accordance with § 7 of the Federal Data Protection Law. Under this provision, the right-holder must pay damages to the holder or owner of the disputed goods for the losses incurred as a result of the right-holder's unlawful processing, use and transmission of the data. There is a presumption of liability on the part of the right-holder. In addition, the holder or owner of the goods may assert a claim for damages based on an infringement of his right of self-determination over personal data pursuant to § 823, paras 1, 2 and § 826 of the German Civil Code (*Bürgerliches Gesetzbuch*—BGB). In contrast to § 7 of the Federal Data Protection Law, these statutory provisions also allow a plaintiff to assert intangible damages.[46]

12.153   Where the detention of goods by the customs authorities is not justified, German law provides the authorized party with a claim for damages against the right-holder. The statutory provisions that are applicable in this context are as follows:

- § 149 and § 150 of the Trade Mark Law;
- § 142a, para 5 of the Patent Law;
- § 111b, para 5 in connection with para 8 of the Copyright Law;
- § 56, para 5 and § 57, para 3 of the Designs Law;
- § 40a, para 5 of the Law on the Protection of Plant Varieties.

12.154   A person authorized to dispose of the goods may claim for damages under § 945 of the German Code of Civil Procedure, where the right-holder has unduly obtained a preliminary injunction. This provision is generally only applicable where the preliminary injunction has no substantive basis, not where it is vacated for procedural reasons.[47] For example, this is the case where it is determined in the course of the trial on the merits that a design patent is invalid.

---

[46] S Simitis, *Kommentar zum Bundesdatenschutzgesetz* (5th edn, 2003), § 7, paras 57, 65.
[47] H Thomas and H Putzo, ZPO (25th edn, 2003), § 945, para 7.

B. Liability of customs authorities and sanctions

The liability of customs authorities under national statutory provisions is determined as follows: **12.155**

Where an application for action of goods by the customs authorities is filed and a customs office fails to detect goods that infringe an intellectual property right of the right-holder and consequently releases or does not detain the goods, the customs authorities are liable to the right-holder in accordance with general principles of liability for a breach in public office or tortious governmental liability (*Amtshaftung*). **12.156**

The conditions that give rise to liability for breach of an official duty are found in § 839 of the German Civil Code in connection with Article 34 of the Basic Law and are as follows: **12.157**

- act by an official that gives rise to liability under the law
- breach of an official duty
- official duty owed to a third party
- fault
- causal relationship between act and damages
- where official acted negligently: injured party unable to obtain compensation elsewhere
- injured party has not wilfully or negligently failed to avoid damages by seeking a legal remedy.

Where the customs authorities breach their duty to take action against suspect goods, claims by right-holders against officials for breach of an official duty will typically fail where there is only negligence on the part of the customs official. In cases that only allege the negligent conduct of a customs official, the right-holder must generally seek damages from the infringer pursuant to § 839, para 1 of the German Civil Code; claims against officials for a breach of an official duty are subsidiary to claims against the infringer. **12.158**

The liability of customs authorities to persons who are affected by an *ex officio* action under Article 4 of the Regulation is also determined by the principles of liability for breach of an official duty. In this case, where there is no possibility of seeking damages elsewhere, any claims against an official for a breach of his official duty are not subsidiary. However, proving fault of the customs official involved is at best difficult. **12.159**

Conclusion

By expanding the catalogue of intellectual property rights, the Regulation has broadened the range of possibilities for action by the customs authorities. **12.160**

Nevertheless, there are still areas in which right-holders must file an application pursuant to the national statutory provisions for the taking of border measures by the customs authorities in order to obtain effective protection. This applies to parallel imports, utility models, semiconductors, and unregistered trade marks. The application can also be a practical instrument for holders of other intellectual property rights because the mobile control groups of German customs will only detain goods that infringe an intellectual property right where an application has been filed pursuant to the national statutory provisions that govern action by the customs authorities.

12.161 It is to be applauded that the new Regulation now provides for a simplified procedure for the destruction of goods that infringe an intellectual property right by the customs authorities, following the German model. In the past, most of the cases in Germany involving actions by the customs authorities have been processed by means of the simplified procedure, which is cost-effective and efficacious for right-holders. After the Regulation takes effect, national law will have to be adapted to comply with the requirements of the Regulation. However, it should not be assumed that the significance of the simplified procedure will diminish. In the end, right-holders will be able to facilitate a destruction of goods without having to put themselves through costly judicial proceedings by consenting to simplified destruction procedures, particularly in those cases where only a few infringing goods are being detained.

13

GREECE

Dimitra Georganda and Ekaterini Mouzaki

Introduction

Greece does not have a long history of fighting counterfeit and pirated goods. **13.01**
Only in recent years have the Greek authorities accepted that activities connected
with the manufacturing and marketing of counterfeit or pirated products can be
considered to have important economic consequences for the businesses
involved, and even lead to a financial crisis in a whole sector. As a result, the legal
framework in Greece surrounding the border measures to be adopted against
goods suspected of infringing an intellectual property right remains basic and the
experience of the authorities limited. During 2002, customs administrations
intercepted 23 commercial consignments containing counterfeit clothing and
accessories and five containing counterfeit cigarettes.[1] In 2003, those figures had
decreased to seven and two respectively.[2]

Before the entry into force of Council Regulation 1383/2003[3] ('the Regulation') **13.02**
and its Implementing Regulation 1891/2004[4] on 1 July 2004, border measures

---

[1] European Commission (DG Taxation and Customs Union (TAXUD)), 'Breakdown of
number of cases registered and number of articles seized by product type GREECE—2002'
(http://europa.eu.int/comm/taxation_customs/resources/documents/grec_2002_en.pdf.)
[2] European Commission (DG Taxation and Customs Union (TAXUD)), 'Breakdown of
number of cases registered and number of articles seized by product type GREECE—2003'
(http://europa.eu.int/comm/taxation_customs/resources/documents/grec_2003_en.pdf).
[3] Council Reg (EC) 1383/2003 of 22 July 2003 concerning customs action against goods suspected of infringing certain intellectual property rights and the measures to be taken against goods
found to have infringed such rights [2003] OJ L 196/7 (2.8.2003).
[4] Commission Reg (EC) 1891/2004 of 21 October 2004 laying down provisions for the implementation of Council Reg (EC) 1383/2003 concerning customs action against goods suspected of
infringing certain intellectual property rights and the measures to be taken against goods found to
have infringed such rights, OJ [2004] L 328/16 (30.10.2004).

were enforced in Greece on the basis of Regulations 3295/1994[5] and 1367/1995,[6] as amended in 1999.

13.03 In Greece, no domestic legislation has been adopted to enforce the Regulation within the national territory. However, on 29 June 2004 (two days before the entry into force of the Regulation), the Directorate General of Customs and Excise notified customs officials by Circular Letter of the provisions of this new instrument, informing them about the amended border measures.[7]

13.04 Following the entry into force of the Regulation, the Greek government also introduced guidelines for different Greek customs procedures, including those governing the repression of infringements of intellectual property rights.[8]

I. SUBJECT MATTER AND SCOPE OF THE NATIONAL LAW APPLYING THE REGULATION

13.05 In this Part, section A examines the customs procedures under which the Greek customs authorities act against goods suspected of infringing an intellectual property right, section B looks at the definition of those goods under Greek law and section C considers goods excluded from the scope of the Regulation.

A. Customs procedures

13.06 Before the entry into force of the Regulation, a claim for the destruction of goods infringing certain intellectual property rights could only be allowed in Greek case

---

[5] Council Reg (EC) 3295/94 of 22 December 1994 laying down measures to prohibit the release for free circulation, export, re-export or entry for a suspensive procedure of counterfeit and pirated goods [1994] OJ L 341/8 (22.12.1994), as amended by Council Reg 241/1999 (OJ L 27/1 (2.2.1999)) and by Council Reg (EC) 806/2003 [2003] OJ L 122/1.

[6] Commission Reg (EC) 1367/95 of 16 June 1995 laying down provisions for the implementation of Council Reg (EC) 3295/94 laying down measures concerning the entry into the Community and the export and re-export from the Community of goods infringing certain intellectual property rights [1995] OJ L 133/2 (17.6.1995), as amended by Commission Reg (EC) 2549/1999 of 2 December 1999 [1999] OJ L 308/16 (3.12.1999).

[7] Εγκύκλιος της 29ης Ιουνίου 2004 με αριθμό Πρωτοκόλλου T2620/168/AOO19, Γπουργείο Οικονομίας καί Οικονομικών, Γενική Διεύθυνση Τελωείων & Ε.Φ.Κ., Διεύθυνση 19η Τελωνείου Διαδικασιών, Κοινοποίηση Κανονισμού (ΕΚ)1383/03 (*Circular Letter No. T2620/168/AOO19/29–6-04, Greek Ministry of Economy and Finance, Directorate General of Customs and Excise, D 19 Directorate of Customs, Notification of Reg 1383/03*).

[8] Εγχειρίδιο, Γπουργείο Οικονομίας και Οικονομικών, Γενική Διεύθυνση Διοικητικής Γποστήριξης, Διεύθυνση Οργάνωσης, Τμήμα Σχέσεων Διοίκησης-Πολιτών (*Guidelines, Greek Ministry of Economy and Finance, Directorate of Administration Support, Directorate of Organization, Department of relations between the administration and the citizens, 2004*).

law provided the goods had already been released for free circulation in Greek territory.[9] Goods in external transit could not, therefore, be subject to such a claim. At that time, the legal basis for such a claim was the Unfair Competition Law,[10] according to which unfair competition can be established only when the alleged anti-competitive act takes place on Greek territory.

At present, by the terms of Article 1(1) of the Regulation, the Greek customs **13.07** authorities are bound to take action against goods suspected of infringing certain intellectual property rights which are released for free circulation, exported, re-exported, imported into, or removed from, the Community (not just the Greek) customs territory, placed under a suspensive procedure (including external transit), or are in the process of being placed in a free zone or free warehouse. In practice, however, statistics reveal that most of the cases opened in the past related to exports, imports, and transit (10 per cent, 41 per cent, and 48 per cent respectively in 2002).[11]

B. Definition of infringing goods

According to official statistics,[12] all Greek customs interventions (100 per cent) **13.08** related to goods suspected of infringing trade mark rights. In this section, we will examine the provisions of Greek law concerning the definition of counterfeit goods, pirated goods, and goods infringing other intellectual property rights.

(1) Counterfeit goods

Trade mark [JC1] infringements are governed in Greece by Law 2239/1994.[13] **13.09** According to section 4 of this Law, any use in the course of trade by a third party, without the right-holder's consent, of the following shall be considered a trade mark infringement:

(a) any sign which is identical to an earlier trade mark in respect of goods or services identical to those for which the earlier trade mark is protected;

---

[9] Commercial Court of Thessalonica, Case No 287231, *Assos INTERNATIONAL v S G LTD* (2000).
[10] Νόμος 146 της 27 Ιανοθαρί οθ 1914 *περί αθέμιτοθ ανταλφισμού* (Law 146 of 27 January 1914 relating to unfair competition).
[11] European Commission (DG Taxation and Customs Union (TAXUD)), 'Breakdown by number and percentages of customs or other procedures 2002' (http://europa.eu.int/comm/ taxation customs/customs/counterfeit_ piracy/index_en.htm).
[12] European Commission (DG TAXUD), 'Breakdown by type of right covered 2002' (See n 11 above).
[13] Νόμος 2239/1994 της 16ης Σεπτεμβρίοθ 1994 *περί σημάτφν*, ΦΕΚ Α 152/1994 (Law 2239/1994 of 16 September 1994 relating to trade marks, OJ A 152/1994).

(b) any sign where, because of its identity with, or similarity to, an earlier trade mark and the identity or similarity of the goods or services covered by the earlier trade mark and the sign, there exists a likelihood of confusion on the part of the public, including the likelihood of association between the sign and the earlier trade mark;

(c) any sign which is identical, or similar to, an earlier trade mark which has a reputation in the Greek territory, in respect of goods or services which are not similar to those for which the trade mark is registered, where use of that sign without due cause takes unfair advantage of, or is detrimental to, the distinctive character or repute of the earlier trade mark.

13.10 The Greek customs authorities are particularly strict in their interpretation of Article 2(1)(a)(i) of the Regulation, since their intervention is confined exclusively to goods bearing without authorization a sign which is identical to, or which cannot be distinguished in its essential aspects from, another trade mark. Customs have, for example, detained goods bearing the sign ADIDS (instead of the word ADIDAS) and the sign Dadoff (instead of the word Davidoff).

13.11 The Greek customs authorities have stated their determination to take measures against trade mark symbols (including logos, labels, stickers, brochures, instructions for use, or guarantee documents bearing such symbols) and packaging material bearing an infringing sign, even if delivered separately.[14] However, no such case has as yet been reported.

13.12 The Greek customs authorities do not apply border measures on the basis of simple trade mark applications, but only when the trade mark concerned has already been 'validly registered in respect of the same type of goods'.[15] However, under Greek Trade Mark Law, an application is a prerequisite to the granting by the Greek Committee of Trade Marks of a registration, and simple trade mark applications enjoy protection (in terms of priority) until the aforesaid Committee issues a decision as to their suitability for registration. By filing a trade mark application in Greece, the applicant acquires a so-called 'right of expectation'. Even if the application is rejected, the sign will still be protected as a distinctive right under Greece's Unfair Competition Law.[16]

(2) Pirated goods

13.13 According to the statistics, most border measures applied by Greek Customs are based on design infringements.

---

[14] Cf the Reg, Art 2(1)(a)(ii)–(iii).   [15] Cf ibid, Art. 2(1)(a)(i).
[16] Law 146 of 27 January 1914 relating to unfair competition (see n 10 above), Art 13.

Article 1 of the Greek Copyright and Neighbouring Rights Law[17] defines the   **13.14**
scope of protection of the copyright. The law includes amongst others the right to
reproduce the work in any manner or form whatsoever, the right to authorize
adaptation or translation of the work and the moral rights to the work. The right
is subject to many exceptions.

Under Greek Law 2417/1996 relating to designs and models,[18] goods infringe a   **13.15**
design right in the following cases:

(a) the design right is used without the prior consent of the right-holder, or

(b) a licensee exceeds the contractually permitted use of the design right or
    breaches the terms of the licence agreement in any other way.

Various pirated products can be found in the Greek market: bags, belts, t-shirts,   **13.16**
caps, shoes, jewellery (including watches) and perfumes. As has been pointed out
above (para 13.08), not one single customs action involving pirated goods has, to
date, been reported in Greece. It is therefore difficult to anticipate how the Greek
customs authorities will interpret the concept of 'goods which are or contain
copies' within the meaning of Article 2(1)(b) of the Regulation if ever they take
action in this field.

(3) Goods infringing other intellectual property rights

Goods infringing a patent or a supplementary protection certificate

According to the official statistics, Greek Customs have not yet applied border   **13.17**
measures relating to patent infringement.

Patents are protected in Greece under Law 1733/1987 relating to technology   **13.18**
transfers, inventions and technological innovation ('the Patent Law'),[19] Article 17
of which states that the acts which constitute a patent infringement have not been

---

[17] Νόμοζ 2121/1993 τηω 3^{ηω} Μαρτίοθ 1993περί πνεθματικήω ιδιοκτησίαω,
συγγενικά δικαιώματα και πολιτιστικά θέματα, ΦΕΚ 25/1993 (Law 2121/1993 of 3 March
1993 relating to intellectual property rights, related rights and other cultural subjects, OJ A
25/1993).

[18] Νόμοω 2417/1996, κύρωση τοθ Διακανονισμού τηω Χάγηω για τη διεθνή
κατάθεση των βιομηχανικών σχεδίων και θποδειγμάτων τηω 6ηω Νοεμβρίοθ 1925,
όπωω αναθεωρήθηκε στη Χάγη στιω 28 Νοεμβρίοθ 1960 και τηω Συμπληρωματικήω
Πράζηω τηω Στοκχόλμηω τηω 14ηω Ιουλίου 1967, όπωω τροποποιήθηκε στη
Στοκχόλμη στιω 28 Σεπτεμβρίου 1979, ΦΕΚ Α' 139/1996 (Law 2417/1996 on the ratification
of the Hague Agreement concerning the international registration of industrial designs of 6
November 1925, as revised at The Hague on 28 November 1967, and of the Complementary Act of
Stockholm of 14 July 1967, as amended at Stockholm on 28 September 1979, OJ A' 139/1996).

[19] Νόμοω 1733/1987 τηω 22^{ηω} Απριλίοθ 1987 σχετικά με την μεταφν;ορά τεχνολογ'''
ίαω, τιω εφν;εθρέσειω και την τεχνολογική καινοτομία, ΦΕΚ Α 171/1987 (Law 1733/1987
of 22 April 1987 relating to technology transfers, inventions and technological innovation; OJ A
171/1987).

defined. The protection of patents and supplementary protection certificates is therefore warranted only under the Greek Unfair Competition Law.[20] Specifically, section 1 of this Law applies in cases where:

- goods infringe a patent or a supplementary protection certificate,
- there is 'unfair imitation', and
- such imitation gives rise to a likelihood of confusion on the part of the relevant public.

13.19　According to Greek case law, an unfair imitation, as prohibited by the Unfair Competition Law, is one where a product is similar to the product cited in the patent claims (or directly obtained by a process recited in the claims) 'in its essential aspects, thus giving rise to confusion among consumers as to the origin of the patented invention'.[21] Such an imitation is the opposite of bona fide since the 'imitator' has not taken appropriate measures to avoid it. Consumers might in such a case be induced into believing either that the infringing product originates from the same entity as 'genuine' products of the same type, or that there is an organic economic connection between the two legal entities in question.

Goods infringing a national plant variety right

13.20　Plant variety rights are protected in Greece under Law 1564/1985.[22] As this law does not describe in detail the notion of infringement of plant variety rights, the holders of such rights may also avail themselves of the protection provided under the Unfair Competition Law.[23] Consequently, the provisions applicable to patent protection, as described in para 13.17 above apply *mutatis mutandis* to plant variety rights.

Goods infringing a national designation of origin or a geographical indication

13.21　In Greece, there is no national legislation to define national designations of origin or geographical indication. Protection is, therefore, warranted under Council Regulation 2081/1992[24] and under section 1 of the Unfair Competition Law,[25] as analysed above (cf para 13.18).

13.22　The national designations of origin that are the most often illicitly affixed to goods include 'Feta' (cheese), and 'Metaxa' and 'Ouzo' (spirits).

---

[20] See n 10 above.　　[21] Court of First Instance of Thessalonica, Case No 23598 (2003).

[22] Νόμοω 1564/1985 τηω 26ηω Σεπτεμβρίου 1985 περί οργάνωσηω παραγωγήω και εμπορίαω τοθ πολλαπλασιαστικού θλικού φν; θτικών ειδών, ΦΕΚ Α 164/1985 (Law 1564/1985 of 26 September 1985 governing the organization of the production and commercialization of plant varieties, OJ A 164/1985).　　　[23] See n 10 above.

[24] Council Reg (EEC) No. 2081/1992 of 14 July 1992 on the protection of geographical indications and designations of origin for agricultural products and foodstuffs, OJ 208, 24.7.1992, 1.

[25] Ibid.

(4) Moulds and matrices

There is no legal provision under Greek law that explicitly allows Greek Customs **13.23** to take action—under Article 2(3) of the Regulation—against moulds or matrices that have been specifically designed or adapted for the manufacture of goods that will infringe an intellectual property right. The Greek customs authorities do not often take action against such moulds or matrices. Customs officials agree, however, that suspect moulds and matrices, if found, should be detained to allow the right-holder in question to demonstrate the bad faith of the infringers within the framework of court proceedings.

C. Goods excluded by the Regulation

(1) Parallel imported goods

As there is no specific national legislation in Greece that would allow the customs **13.24** authorities to apply border measures against (genuine) parallel imported goods, Greek Customs do not take action against such goods, even where an application has been lodged by a right-holder under the terms of the Regulation. Indeed, Article 3(1), first indent, precludes such actions. Customs do not inform right-holders when they find goods which they know are parallel imported goods.

(2) Goods that have been manufactured under conditions other than those agreed with the right-holder

There is no national legislation in Greece allowing Customs to apply border **13.25** measures to such goods.

However, in practice, the Greek customs authorities inform right-holders **13.26** whenever they find goods that they suspect of non-compliance with the terms of a licence agreement, although the right-holder is responsible for having them released and for ascertaining that no use is made of the information obtained from Customs.

(3) Goods contained in travellers' personal baggage

Customs are authorized to inspect, for security reasons only, goods contained in **13.27** travellers' personal baggage. Where such goods are of a non-commercial nature and there are no material indications to suggest they are being carried for commercial purposes (in other words, where the goods are probably intended for personal use), Greek national law contains no provisions allowing the customs authorities to control whether travellers are carrying goods which may be suspected of infringing an intellectual property right.

13.28 The customs authorities therefore have to determine whether the goods contained in a traveller's personal baggage are being carried for commercial purposes before deciding whether or not to take action. Customs will also be entitled to act when the value of the goods exceeds the limits of the duty-free allowance (EUR 175). There are no specific rules to be followed in this respect. In practice, Greek customs officials do carry out random controls in order to find out if passengers are carrying more products than 'allowed' under Article 3(2) of the Regulation. Receipts and other documents can be requested to that end. Where bills of lading or other commercial documents are found, this will be considered an indication of goods comprising commercial traffic. The quantity and nature of the goods are also taken into consideration in deciding whether the goods comprise commercial traffic.

II. APPLICATION FOR ACTION BY THE CUSTOMS AUTHORITIES

13.29 In this Part, section A examines the procedures governing interventions by the customs authorities prior to an application for action ('*ex officio* measures') and section B looks at the lodging and processing of such applications under the Regulation.

A. '*Ex officio* measures'

13.30 The Greek customs authorities apply *ex officio* measures under Article 4 of the Regulation, even where the identity of the holder of the right suspected of having been infringed is unknown.

13.31 In an attempt to improve the efficiency of the *ex officio* actions performed by the Greek customs authorities under Article 4 of the Regulation, the Greek Ministry of Economy and Finance has set up a joint operation, through the conclusion in 2003 of a Memorandum of Understanding, with the TM Eye Foundation ('TM-Eye'),[26] a non-profit organization with its headquarters in Apeldoorn, in the

---

[26] The TM-Eye Foundation was established in April 2003, with the objective of fighting trade in, and production of, counterfeit products (see www.tmeye.com).

Netherlands. TM-Eye was the sole developer of the EC project, Fighting Counterfeit in Greece (FiCoG), created to fight the counterfeiting and piracy of products as efficiently and as thoroughly as possible. Approved and financed through the European Commission's AGIS 2003 programme, FiCoG is intended, on the one hand, to increase cooperation between the private and the public sectors in Greece and, on the other, to decrease the trade in counterfeited and pirated products. By the terms of the Memorandum of Understanding, TM-Eye will collaborate with the Greek authorities in the fight against infringements of intellectual property rights through the mutual supply of information. The agreement also elects TM-Eye as the only point of communication for Greek Customs regarding all issues related to the expertise and recognition of infringing products.

13.32 In order to determine whether there are 'sufficient grounds for suspecting that goods infringe an intellectual property right' under Article 4 of the Regulation, the Greek customs authorities pay special attention to the packaging of the goods, their value and the identity of the natural or legal persons involved in their importation and commercialization.

13.33 In compliance with the Memorandum of Understanding (cf para 13.31 above), the Greek customs authorities are usually able to provide TM-Eye with information regarding the importer and sender of the cargo, the quantity, nature, and estimated value of the suspected goods and, in cases where a receiver of the cargo is known, that party's details too. All this information is communicated by telephone to TM-Eye without the transmission of documents. The right-holder must subsequently file an application for action within three working days of receipt of notification of the *ex officio* intervention by Customs. However, in practice, notification under Article 4(1) of the Regulation assumes a written document.

13.34 Greek Customs undertake to provide right-holders with samples or printed (not digital) pictures of the goods. Samples must be returned to the relevant customs office, but there is no deadline for doing so. The right-holder concerned is free to decide whether or not to inspect the goods.

13.35 Where the customs authorities have sufficient grounds for suspecting that goods infringe an intellectual property right, the period of three working days from the moment of receipt of the notification by the right-holder (as provided for in Article 4(1) of the Regulation) is strictly applied. In other cases, it is subject to a degree of flexibility, that is, an extension of the deadline can be requested and will usually be granted in order to allow the right-holder to gather and provide to the authorities all the information and documents necessary to confirm their suspicions.

B. The lodging and processing of applications
for customs action

(1) Persons entitled to file an application for action

Definition of 'right-holders' under the Regulation

13.36 Pursuant to Article 2(2) of the Regulation, the owners of any of the intellectual property rights listed in Article 2(1), any other person authorized to use those rights, or their respective representatives, are all entitled to file an application for action. This includes licensees, distributors and commercial agents. Authorized users and representatives may be natural or legal persons.

13.37 Under Greek law and practice, the concept of 'representative of the right-holders or authorized user' as defined in Article 2(2) of the Regulation certainly includes the natural and legal persons authorized to act on behalf of the right-holder, for example, attorneys-at-law, associations of right-holders, licensees, distributors, and commercial agents.

Proof of entitlement to file an application for action

For right-holders stricto sensu

13.38 To prove entitlement to lodge an application for action under the Regulation, the holders of a trade mark, registered design, patent or supplementary protection certificate, plant variety, designation of origin, geographical indication or geographical designation must submit to the customs authorities a copy of the relevant registration certificate from a national or international intellectual property office evidencing their capacity as right-holders (*stricto sensu*).[27]

13.39 No specific document is requested by the customs authorities for unregistered rights such as copyright and related rights. Any evidence establishing that the applicant for customs action is the actual owner of the right is sufficient.

For persons authorized to use the right

13.40 The persons authorized to use the right on which the application is based must submit to the customs authorities a certified copy of the licensing agreement, distribution agreement, or agency agreement concluded with the owner of the right in question. The agreement must be submitted in Greek, or accompanied by an official translation into Greek. The application may not be filed in any other language.

13.41 In addition, persons authorized to use the right within the meaning of Article 2(2)(b) of the Regulation must submit a document proving that they are authorized

---

[27] Cf Reg 1891/2004, Art 2(1)(a).

to use the right in question. Under Greek law and practice, proof of authorization to use an intellectual property right consists of a contract or an invoice between the actual owner of the right and the user.

The Greek customs authorities verify whether the authorized user has the **13.42** contractual right to represent the right-holder. A certified copy of this contract must be submitted to the customs authorities together with the application form. In cases where the application for action is based on an intellectual property right, the authorization to use such right has to be registered with the appropriate intellectual property office to be enforceable, and thus accepted as evidence by, customs.

For representatives

Lawyers, agents, and all other types of representatives need to submit, along **13.43** with the application, an original or certified copy of the document by which they are empowered to represent the owner of the right or the person authorized to use it. Where the power of attorney delivered to a representative is executed by a natural person on behalf of a legal entity, this person must prove his capacity to sign the power of attorney and the declaration referred to in Article 6 of the Regulation. In Greece, such proof usually emanates from the Memorandum of Association, in which the natural persons entitled to represent the legal entity are designated.

A general power of attorney, covering all future interventions by the Greek **13.44** customs authorities, may be validly delivered and will, in principle, also specify whether the representative is entitled to execute the declaration referred to in Article 6 of the Regulation. If it does not, customs will consider that the representative is not empowered to execute this declaration, unless he is in a position to submit a separate power of attorney to that end.

It is not only Greek nationals who are authorized to appear before the customs **13.45** authorities: foreign representatives without a local presence in Greece are also so authorized. Nevertheless, it is preferable, for practical reasons, that the representative be established in Greece. Greek Customs request, in any event, that the contact person(s) designated in the application be familiar with Greek law and Greek customs procedure.

(2) Competent customs department and formal requirements

Competent customs department

In Greece, the authority competent to process applications for action **13.46** pursuant to Article 5(2) of the Regulation is the Attica Customs District (address: Ag. Nikoleou-18510 Piraeus; tel.: (+30 210) 4282461 or 4515587; fax: (+30 210) 451 10 09; website: www.e-oikonomia.gr[28]).

The application for action form

13.47   Under Greek practice, the application for action may be sent by regular or registered mail; it may not be filed by fax or e-mail. The signature on the application has to be notarized. In accordance with Article 3(3) of Regulation 1891/2004, two copies of the application have to be submitted. The Greek language version of the application for action form is available from the Attika Customs District but it is not yet available through the Greek customs authorities' website (www.-e-oikonomia.gr). *A fortiori*, it is not possible to file applications for action via electronic data interchange systems.

13.48   Under Article 6, the application for action shall be accompanied by a declaration from the right-holder. The original declaration has to be signed by the applicant. When the applicant is a legal person, the declaration has to be signed by his legal representative or his attorney. When the application for action is filed by a representative of the right-holder or the authorized user, the representative must submit a power of attorney to customs from which it appears that he is empowered to execute the declaration under Article 6 of the Regulation. If he fails to so, the declaration will be accepted only if it is executed by the owner of the right or authorized user concerned. In practice, the power of attorney may be submitted after the application has been filed.

Language requirements

13.49   The application for action, as well as all enclosures (technical documents, brochures, registration certificates, etc) and the declaration under Article 6, must be submitted in Greek, or accompanied by an official translation into Greek. The application may not be filed in any other language.

(3) Requirements regarding the contents of the application for action

Mandatory information

13.50   The Greek customs authorities strictly apply Article 5(5) of the Regulation, which lists the information which must be given in the application for action. Pursuant

---

[28] *ΠΡΟΕΔΡΙΚΟ ΔΙΑΤΑΓΜΑ ΔΙΓ ΑΡΙΘ. 13/2004 Σύσταση, κατάργηση, ενοποίηση και αναδιάρθρωση Τελωνειακών Υπηρεσιών και τροποποίηση των Π.Δ/των 284/1988 και 551/1988, ΦΕΚ Α' 8/16.01.2004* (Presidential Decree No 13/2004, constitution, abolition, consolidation and reconstitution of customs services and modification of the Presidential Decrees No 284/1988 and No 551/1988, OJ A 8/16.1.2004).

to this provision, the application must contain all the information needed to enable the goods in question to be readily recognized by customs. Reference must also be made, of course, to the intellectual property right on which the application is based (an overview of the relevant registrations relating to the Greek territory should be provided), the identity of the applicant, the capacity of the natural person executing the application and the contact persons appointed by the latter in Greece, in cases where the applicant is a foreign person.

A local presence of the contact person(s) designated by the applicant is required, **13.51** since Greek Customs assume such person's/persons' familiarity with Greek law and Greek customs procedure.

Optional information

Although there are no particular optional requirements (with regard to the **13.52** application for action) under Greek law and practice, the right-holder is expected to provide all information considered optional under Article 5(5) of the Regulation[29] in order to facilitate customs' work. In particular, the applicant will usually be asked to specify the country in which the genuine goods are produced and the regular means of transport of those goods. This information can prove very useful indeed. If, for instance, the applicant transfers the goods solely by ship, and goods similar to his are imported by train, the choice of such means of transport constitutes for the customs officials a strong indication of the non-authenticity of the goods.

Additional information specific to the type of intellectual property right referred to in the application

Customs request information other than that pertaining to the right-holder in **13.53** cases where it is not possible to ascertain exactly which party is trading in legitimate goods. In practice, Greek Customs regularly ask the applicant or his representative for more details about the intellectual property right on which the application for action is based[30]

(4) Processing and acceptance of the application for action

On receiving an application for action under the Regulation, the competent customs **13.54** department (cf para 13.46) processes it, free of charge, and notifies the applicant in writing of its decision within thirty working days of receipt of the application.[31]

---

[29] Cf Art 5(5), last indent, which lists the information that 'should' be forwarded to customs by the right-holders 'by way of indication'.   [30] Cf the Reg, Art 5(6).
[31] Cf ibid, Art 5(7).

When granting an application, the Attica Customs District forwards the decision to the other Greek customs departments and to those customs offices of the Member States likely to be concerned by the goods alleged in the application to infringe an intellectual property right.

13.55 If customs decide not to process an application for action for the reasons provided in Article 5(8) of the Regulation, the applicant has the right to appeal to the Administrative Court of First Instance.[32] As yet, however, no such appeal proceedings have been instituted on those grounds. Instead of filing an appeal, the applicant can re-submit his application, duly completed, to the competent customs department.

13.56 The right-holder cannot determine in the application the period during which the Greek customs authorities are requested to take action; the decision granting an application is valid for a maximum of one year in all cases and can be renewed on expiry of this period. When filing a request for extension under Article 8(1) of the Regulation, provided that the situation has remained as it was at the time of filing the (initial) application for action, the applicant does not have to submit any additional documents, but does have to confirm in writing that no changes have taken place. If such confirmation is not submitted before the expiry of the decision granting the application, a new application with all supportive documents will have to be submitted.

(5) 'Community' applications for action

Processing of 'Community' applications for action filed with Greek Customs

13.57 Where the applicant is the holder of a Community right listed in Article 5(4) of the Regulation, the application may, in addition to requesting action by the customs authorities of the Member State(s) in which the application is filed, request action by the customs authorities of one or more of the other Member States.

13.58 There are no specific rules governing the processing of 'Community' applications by Greek Customs.

13.59 Where such a 'Community' application for action is granted, the decision may be forwarded directly by the applicant or, with the applicant's consent, by Greek Customs, along with any other information and translations as may be necessary, to the competent customs department of the Member State(s) in which the application has requested customs action.[33]

---

[32] Άρθρο 6 τοθ Κώδικα Διοικητικής Δικονομίας, Νόμος 2717/1999 της 14ης Μαίοθ 1999, ΦΕΚ Α 97/17.5.1999 (Code of Administrative Legal Procedure, Law No 2717/1999 of 14 May 1999, ΦΕΚ Α 97/17.5.1999).   [33] Ibid, Art 8(2), third indent.

Processing of 'Community' applications designating Greece

When the application for action and the corresponding decision have been **13.60** transmitted to the Greek authorities by the respective Member State authority, a representative of the applicant has to present them in front of Greek Customs.

III. CONDITIONS GOVERNING ACTION BY CUSTOMS AUTHORITIES AND BY THE AUTHORITIES COMPETENT TO DETERMINE WHETHER GOODS INFRINGE AN INTELLECTUAL PROPERTY RIGHT

A. Conditions governing action by the customs authorities

(1) Factual background

The control of goods infringing an intellectual property right is particularly **13.61** demanding in Greece, as none of the neighbouring countries are members of the European Union. Some of those countries, such as Turkey, and various Balkan and North African countries, are rated as high-risk countries with regard to the manufacture of counterfeit and pirated goods. The landscape of Greece, with its extensive coastline and thousands of islands, makes the work of the customs authorities even harder.

The customs offices in the ports of Thessalonica, Athens, Patras, and Igoumenitsa **13.62** are confronted with the largest traffic and are therefore in the front line of the fight against counterfeit and pirated goods. Some of the smaller customs offices on islands such as Rhodes and Crete also play a very important role because of the proximity of Rhodes to Turkey, and Crete to the North African countries. On the mainland, the busiest customs offices are those at the airports of Athens and Thessalonica. Finally, the customs offices in the northern and eastern parts of the country (that is, along Greece's borders with Bulgaria and Turkey) are responsible for many of the related controls.

(2) Notification of customs intervention

When a customs office in receipt of the decision granting an application for action **13.63** suspects that goods in one of the situations referred to in Article 1(1) of the

Regulation infringe an intellectual property right covered by that decision, it proceeds as follows:

- it suspends the release of the goods or detains them, informing the authority that issued the decision on the application for action accordingly;
- it informs the right-holder and the declarant or holder of the goods of its action, the actual or estimated quantity, and the actual or supposed nature of the goods whose release has been suspended or which have been detained, without the right-holder being bound by the communication of this information to commence court proceedings aimed at determining whether the goods infringe an intellectual property right.

13.64   The relevant right-holder is informed of any eventual customs intervention by the customs authorities by telephone or in writing. On this occasion, the right-holder is invited to submit an expert report substantiating why the goods can be considered as infringing his rights.

(3) Information to be provided by customs to the right-holder before the right-holder confirms the infringing nature of the goods

13.65   Under Article 9(3) of the Regulation, the communication of the contact details of the consignee, consignor, declarant, and holder of the goods to the right-holder may only take place 'in accordance with national provisions on the protection of personal data, commercial and industrial secrecy, and professional and administrative confidentiality'.

13.66   Different national provisions[34] protect personal data, commercial and industrial secrecy, as well as professional and administrative secrecy, but do not preclude the

---

[34] Νόμος 2472/1997 τῆς 9ης Απριλίοιθ 1997, ΦΕΚ Α 50/1997 περί προστασία τοθ ατόμοθ από την επεχεργασία δεδομένων προσω πικού χαρακτήρα (Law 2472/1997 of 9 April 1997 on the legal protection of personal data, OJ A 50/1997). By the terms of s 2 of Law 2472/1997, 'personal data' is defined as 'any information referring to the subject of the data'. The contact details listed in Art 9(3) of the Regulation fall under this definition. The Unfair Competition Law does not define the notion of 'commercial and industrial secrecy', which has therefore been circumscribed by scholars. Specifically, 'commercial secrecy' refers to 'any commercial information of a confidential nature regarding an entity, such as suppliers' catalogues, advertisements and methods of price calculation', while 'industrial secrecy' refers to 'confidential information of a technical nature, such as technological methods, know-how and methods of manufacture'. Commercial and industrial secrecy is protected under ss 16 to 18 of the Unfair Competition Law. Unlawful disclosure of commercial or industrial secrets incurs criminal liability under these provisions. In addition, commercial and industrial secrecy may also be protected under the general rule laying down the obligation to behave in a 'bona fide' manner, as set out in s 1 of the Unfair Competition Law, in cases of unfair imitation. Academics have also defined the notions of 'professional and administrative confidentiality' under Greek law. 'Professional confidentiality' refers to 'any information of a confidential nature which comes to the knowledge of an employee owing to his or her professional position'. Any employee who reveals any such professional secret can

communication of the information listed in Article 9(3) to the right-holders (cf European Court of Justice, Case C-223/98).

Once goods suspected of an infringing intellectual property right are detained by Greek Customs, and before the right-holder confirms the infringing nature of the goods, detailed information is systematically provided by the customs authorities to the right-holder regarding the quantity, nature and country of origin of the goods, the names and addresses of the consignee, the consignor, the declarant and/or the holder of the goods. **13.67**

(4) Inspection of the suspected goods

After being informed of a customs intervention by the Greek customs authorities (and provided an application for action has been filed by the right-holder and accepted by customs), the right-holder and all other persons involved are given the opportunity to inspect the goods. The inspection must take place within the 10-working day period provided for in Article 13 of the Regulation. **13.68**

Customs are also entitled to take representative samples of the goods at this stage. At the right-holder's express request, one or several samples will be handed over or sent to him. The inspection of samples will in any event be carried out under the sole responsibility of the right-holder. Samples will have to be returned to the relevant customs office on completion of the technical analysis and, where applicable, before the goods are released or their detention ended. **13.69**

Contrarily, Greek Customs do not transmit digital pictures of the goods to the right-holder, although in most cases this would be the only and also the quickest way to establish whether the goods infringe an intellectual property right. However, Customs usually do send right-holders 'hard' (that is, printed) pictures of the goods. **13.70**

There is no national legislation under Greek law that would impose any restriction on right-holders with respect to the use of samples. Article 9(3) of the Regulation stipulates, however, that samples may only be used 'for the purposes of analysis and to facilitate the subsequent procedure'. The samples may thus, in principle, be used as evidence in the course of criminal and/or civil proceedings instituted against the infringer. The samples must be returned to customs on completion of the analysis and, where applicable, before goods are released or their detention ended. Where the right-holder's infringement claim is allowed by **13.71**

be punished under Art 371 of the Greek Criminal Code by a fine or a jail term of up to one year. 'Administrative secrets' include 'any information of a confidential nature which comes to the knowledge of a civil servant owing to his or her position'. Any civil servant (including customs officials) who reveals such an administrative secret incurs criminal liability under Art 252 of the Criminal Code and can be punished by a fine or a jail term of a minimum of three months.

the court, the sample(s) have to be returned in order to be destroyed along with the rest of the consignment.

B. Simplified procedure allowing the destruction of the goods without there being any need to determine whether an intellectual property right has been infringed under national law

13.72   Article 11 of the Regulation has not yet been implemented into Greek legislation. Following the Circular Letter of 29 June 2004[35] adopted by the Directorate General of Customs and Excise, Greek Customs was instructed to apply the simplified procedure set out in Article 11. The customs authorities allow destruction of goods on the basis on an expert report submitted by the right-holder ascertaining that the goods do infringe an intellectual property right. A special committee is established in order to decide on the destruction of the goods. Where it consents to destruction, the committee files a certificate of destruction. In such a case, the right-holder bears the destruction costs. In practice, the destruction of the goods is deemed to be accepted when the parties involved do not oppose destruction within a reasonable period of time.

13.73   Amicable settlements between the right-holder and the owner of the infringing goods are allowed under Greek law. The clauses that are most frequently found in such contracts provide for the payment of damages by the infringer, and the refunding by the latter of investigation, storage, and destruction costs. Customs authorities are not entitled to object to such settlements.

C. Conditions governing action by authorities having jurisdiction to determine whether goods infringe an intellectual property right

(1) Authorities having jurisdiction to determine whether goods infringe an intellectual property right

13.74   The civil courts have jurisdiction to handle claims based on the infringement of intellectual property rights in Greece.[36] Before those courts, right-holders may

---

[35] See n 7 above.
[36] For the sake of completeness, it may be useful to note that the Administrative Courts of First Instance have jurisdiction to handle appeals against administrative acts and decisions made by the customs authorities (cf eg, para 13.55).

seek either a decision on the merits of the case or the granting of interim measures. Only the criminal courts, however, have jurisdiction to process criminal complaints.

Civil proceedings

Civil proceedings against infringements of intellectual and industrial property **13.75** rights as analysed above, with respect to the unfair competition law, concern all types of rights (that is, patent rights, plant variety rights, designations of origin or geographical indications, counterfeit goods, and pirated goods). Within the framework of such proceedings, the right-holder may:

- file a motion for interim relief petitioning the temporary prohibition of use of the infringed right under penalty of a fine;
- serve a summons on the infringer on the merits of the case, and claim the cessation of the infringement and/or redress of the damage caused by such infringement.

In practice, right-holders generally prefer filing immediately for interim relief, **13.76** since such proceedings are faster than filing for a claim on the merits.

Criminal proceedings

As an alternative to the commencement of civil proceedings, right-holders often **13.77** consider criminal prosecution. Criminal proceedings are possible in all types of intellectual property infringements. The cost of instituting criminal proceedings is minimal and, in the case of a serious infringement, right-holders can expect the judicial system promptly and definitively to take the goods off the market. An additional advantage of criminal proceedings is that they do not pre-empt a civil action. Moreover, when a criminal complaint has been filed, the criminal justice system has the opportunity to investigate the matter, whereupon further information about the declarant, holder, consignor, or consignee of the goods can often be obtained. However, criminal prosecution may in practice incur delays, nullifying this advantage.

On the other hand, within the context of civil proceedings, as the investigations **13.78** have to be carried out by private investigators, right-holders have to advance the costs. However, such investigations, when carried out properly, can be much faster and more effective than a criminal enquiry, and the costs added to the claim for damages which will be subsequently initiated before the courts against the infringer(s).

In all cases concerned with an intellectual property right infringement, however, **13.79** right-holders usually opt for the immediate destruction of the goods, thus avoiding civil or criminal proceedings, which are often more costly and time-consuming.

(2) Term for notifying customs that proceedings have been started

13.80 Pursuant to Article 13(1) of the Regulation, right-holders must inform the customs authorities, within 10 working days of being notified by customs of the suspension of release or of the detention of the goods, that proceedings have been initiated to determine whether an intellectual property right has been infringed under national law. This deadline may be extended once by a further 10 working days 'in appropriate cases'. In practice, Greek Customs consider an 'appropriate case' as one where it has proved impossible to initiate court proceedings due to a lack of information on the natural and legal persons involved in the traffic. Greek Customs appraise such requests for extension strictly.

(3) Release of goods suspected of infringing certain rights on provision of a security

13.81 Provided that the conditions of Article 14(1) of the Regulation are fulfilled, Greek Customs consider that they are obliged to release the goods. The amount of the security referred to in Article 14(2) will be determined by adding to the customs duty applied to the goods an additional amount in the form of a percentage of their value.

13.82 In practice, the Greek customs authorities have not yet been confronted with the application of Article 14.

(4) Storage of the goods

13.83 When the customs authorities suspend the release of, or detain, suspect goods, those goods are stored in a customs warehouse. Once the goods have been identified as infringing goods, customs may move the cargo to another storage facility.

13.84 There are no specific conditions under Greek law governing the storage of goods subject to border measures, and the various stages of the procedure are governed by the same regime. Actual storage costs depend on the volume, weight, and place of storage of the goods. In practice, however, storage, transport, and destruction costs are in the vast majority of cases systematically charged to the right-holders, who then have to claim them back, within the framework of a settlement agreement or court proceedings, from the persons involved in the goods trafficking.

IV. PROVISIONS APPLICABLE TO GOODS FOUND TO INFRINGE AN INTELLECTUAL PROPERTY RIGHT

Greek law affords the right-holder the possibility of seeking the destruction of **13.85** goods that infringe his rights or, at the court's discretion, the removal of any counterfeit trade marks that have been affixed to the goods. In Greece, there exist companies that specialize in the destruction of goods that infringe an intellectual property right. After the goods have been destroyed, any remaining material is incinerated. The right-holder has to pay the costs of the goods being destroyed. Those costs may, nonetheless, be claimed back from the importer or the holder of the goods within the framework of a settlement agreement or court proceedings.

However, as a direct consequence of the Regulation, the entry into/removal from **13.86** Greek territory, release for free circulation, exportation, re-exportation, placement under a suspensive procedure, and placement in a free zone or free warehouse of goods found to infringe an intellectual property right will in principle be prohibited by the Greek courts in accordance with Article 16 of the Regulation.

V. PENALTIES

By and large, the penalties incurred in the case of intellectual property right **13.87** infringements are not very dissuasive under Greek law, especially when compared to the profits that can be made by selling non-authentic goods.

Pursuant to Article 157 of the Greek National Customs Code,[37] the penalties **13.88** imposed against smuggling are as follows:

- a minimum six-month jail term. If the value of the smuggled goods is not significant, or if the goods are destined for personal use, the penalty is a one-month prison sentence;
- a minimum one-year jail term if:
  a. the offender is recidivist;
  b. the offence is committed while armed or jointly with any other person or severally;
  c. the Greek State or the European Union is deprived of taxes and charges amounting to EUR 30,000 or more.

---

[37] Νόμος 2960/2001 τῆς 16ης Νοεμβρίοθ 2001, Εθνικός Τελωνειακός Κώδικας, ΦΕΚ Α 265/2001 (Law 2960/2001 of 16 November 2001, National Customs Code, OJ A 265/2001).

13.89 Attempted smuggling is punished with the same severity as actual smuggling, accomplices incurring the same penalties as the perpetrators.

13.90 Trade mark infringement is punishable under Article 28 of the Criminal Code by a minimum three-month jail term and a fine. Under Articles 26 and 27 of the Greek trade mark Law, the claimant may obtain cessation of the infringement and indemnification for damages and injunction, in most cases coupled with the forfeiture of the infringing products. Under Article 31 of that Law, the court may also order the destruction of the counterfeiting products, or, exceptionally, the removal/destruction of the counterfeit trade marks in cases of unfair imitation.

13.91 By virtue of Article 28 of Presidential Decree 259/1997 relating to designs and models, and of Article 17 of Law 1733/1987 relating to patents, right-holders can claim before the civil courts that the infringer be enjoined from further infringing their rights and be ordered to pay them damages or to surrender the benefits emanating from the unfair exploitation of the design/model.

13.92 Under Law 2121/1993 relating to intellectual property rights,[38] the injured right-holder is entitled to obtain forfeiture of the goods through injunction (Article 64), indemnification for any prejudice suffered, the condemnation of the infringer to a fine in the case of any further infringement (Article 65) and to a jail term of a minimum of one year (Article 66).

VI. LIABILITY OF CUSTOMS AUTHORITIES AND RIGHT-HOLDERS

A. Liability of right-holders and sanctions

13.93 Under the general Greek tort law provision of Article 914 of the Civil Code, any person perpetrating prejudice, illegally and expressly against another person must compensate this person for said prejudice. This provision governs all liability claims referred to in Article 19(3) of the Regulation and initiated by, for example, the declarant, owner, importer, exporter, holder, or consignee of the goods, against any right-holder who may have applied the Regulation in a neglectful or reckless manner.

13.94 To date, the Greek customs authorities have initiated no liability claims against right-holders on the grounds of non-permitted use of information provided by customs. For the customs authorities and the parties involved, the exchange of

---

[38] See n 17 above.

information is based on trust and reliability. In practice, should the applicant use the information about the infringing goods for purposes beyond the scope of the application for action, the competent authority may, at its discretion, reject any eventual application for renewal or future application for action.

B. Liability of customs authorities and sanctions

(1) Liability of the Greek customs authorities within the framework of the application of the provisions of the Regulation

13.95 Under Article 19 of the Regulation, the acceptance of an application for intervention affords the interested party the right to damages if the goods infringing the intellectual property rights have been spotted by the customs authorities and an authorization to deliver is issued or, if no seizure measures are taken under Article 9, under the conditions specified by the legislation of the Member State in which the application is submitted.

13.96 If, therefore, the application is submitted in Greece, the right to damages against the Greek state is ruled by Article 105 of the Introductory Law of the Civil Code.[39] The responsibility of the Greek state is genuine and objective, that is, the State is responsible in cases of damage, illegal act, or omission to act, for establishing the legal link between the damage and the illegal act or omission without the need to prove intent on the part of the agent that carried out the illegal act or omission. Consequently the State is responsible even if the agent is not. It suffices that the above described conditions are met.

13.97 The person that suffered the damage cannot attack the agent that carried out the illegal act or omission, since this is contrary to Article 38 of the Civil Servants' Code.[40] Only the State can attack the agent after a condemnation and compensation payment in order to obtain repair.

13.98 Article 19(2) provides for the case where an agent of the customs authority, while exercising the powers conferred upon him by the Regulation (seizure, etc) damages a third party. It states that the public authority is not responsible unless this is catered for by the national legislation of the Member State where the application was submitted or if the application was submitted according to Article 5(4), the

---

[39] Προεδρικό Διάταγμα θπ'αριθμόν 456 της 17/24 Οκτωβρίοθ 1984, Cστικός Κώδικαζ και Εισαγωγικός τοθ Νόμοζ, ΦΕΚ Α 164/1984 (Presidential Decree No 456 of 17/24 October 1984, Civil Code and Introductory Law of the Civil Code, OJ A 164/1984).

[40] Νόμοζ 2683/1999 της 5ης Φεβροθαρίοθ 1999, Κύρωση τοθ Κώδικα Κατάστασης Δημοσίων Πολιτικών Διοικητικών Υπαλλήλων και Υπαλλήλων Ν.Π.Δ.Δ. και άλλεζ διατάξειζ, ΦΕΚ Α 19/1999 (Law 2683/1999 of 5 February 1999, Approval of the Civil Servant's Code, OJ A 19/1999).

legislation of the Member State where the damage took place. If this Member State is Greece, the above article is again applied. Consequently, if, for example, seizure occurs in a situation where the conditions of the Regulation are not met, the State will be responsible regardless of whether or not the Regulation was infringed due to its agent. It suffices that the Regulation was infringed.

Conclusion

13.99   The Greek legal framework for fighting infringements of intellectual property rights at its borders is insufficient. The competent authorities do not seem to consider the issue a priority of the customs office, and customs officials still remain relatively inexperienced in the matter. At the same time, from a geographical point of view, Greece is a particularly difficult area in which to enforce such legislation. There is, however, a pressing need for a more proactive approach, since neighbouring countries such as Turkey and Bulgaria are major producers of illicit products.

13.100 The Ministry of Economy and Finance is aiming to increase the efficiency of the fight against piracy and counterfeiting. The main objectives are: enhanced information exchange with foreign customs authorities, the creation of a reliable database containing detailed information about criminal organizations, improved training for customs officials to facilitate recognition of illegitimate goods, and more efficient and prompt cargo expertise procedures, taking into consideration the three working-day term provided for under Article 4 of the Regulation for *ex officio* actions.

14

HUNGARY*

László Bérczes

Introduction

Hungary introduced the first law on border measures in respect of goods **14.01**
suspected of infringing certain intellectual property rights in 1997 in the form of
the Government Decree No 128 of 1997 ('the 1997 Decree'[1]) which entered into
force as of 1 August 1997. This law was inspired by the provisions of EC
Regulation 3295/94[2] and the TRIPs Agreement.[3] However it was applied not
only to counterfeit or pirated goods but also to parallel imports. Moreover, the
definition of the goods towards which Hungarian customs could take action was
limited to goods infringing trade mark rights, geographical indications, and
copyrights or neighbouring rights.

Under the 1997 Decree, the competent authority for processing applications for **14.02**
border measures in Hungary was the Duty and Tax Department of the National
Customs Headquarters. This department of the highest customs authority was
subsequently replaced by the Budapest No 17 Customs Office—a local office—
by a modification of the Decree that entered into force as of 1 January 2004. This
decision was strongly opposed by intellectual property practitioners.

---

* Special thanks to Captain Gyula Almási, Head of the Intellectual Property Protection
Department of the Central-Hungarian Regional Customs Headquarters for his invaluable support
for the development of this work.
    [1] Published in volume 67/1997 of the State Gazette under the name '128/1997. (VII. 24.) Korm.
rendelet a szellemi tulajdonjogok megsértésével szemben a vámigazgatási eljárásban alkalmazható
intézkedésekről' (Government Decree No 128 of 1997, issued on 24 July, on the measures applicable
in the customs administration procedure against the infringement of intellectual property rights).
    [2] Council Reg (EC) No 3295/94 of 22 December 1994 laying down measures to prohibit the
release for free circulation, export, re-export or entry for a suspensive procedure of counterfeit and
pirated goods. Official Journal L 341, 30/12/1994, 0008–0013.
    [3] The TRIPs Agreement is Annex 1C of the Marrakesh Agreement Establishing the World Trade
Organization, signed in Marrakesh, Morocco on 15 April 1994. Published in volume 17/1998 of
the State Gazette as Act No 9 of 1998.

14.03 After this flawed decision, the government came up with another strange solution when adopting the Government Decree No 98 of 2004 ('the Former 2004 Decree'[4]) which was adopted in the very last days before the date of Hungary's accession to the European Union, and came into effect on 1 May 2004. The Former 2004 Decree, which laid down provisions for the implementation of EC Regulation No 3295/94, was issued less than two months before the entry into force of EC Regulation 1383/2003[5] on 1 July 2004.

14.04 The Former 2004 Decree was partly based on the 1997 Decree, which was also applied to parallel imported goods coming from outside the European Economic Area. As the Former 2004 Decree was based on Regulation 3294/95 certain parts thereof were not in line with the provisions of Regulation 1383/2003.

14.05 Nevertheless, a significant achievement of the Former 2004 Decree was to withdraw the appointment of the Budapest No 17 Customs Office as the competent authority for processing applications for border measures. The Former 2004 Decree appointed the Central-Hungarian Regional Customs Headquarters as the competent authority for the processing of applications for customs action and to monitor and supervize the intellectual property related activities of Hungarian Customs.

14.06 In June 2004, discussions started in the Ministry of Justice in view of the adoption of a new Government Decree laying down the provisions for the implementation of EC Regulation 1383/2003 in Hungary. The new Government Decree was initially expected by 1 July 2004. However, in spite of the enthusiasm experienced in June the Hungarian government adopted it only in the very end of 2004.

14.07 The conflict created by the Former 2004 Decree was finally resolved by this new decree as the Government Decree No 371 of 2004 ('the 2004 Decree'[6]) is completely in line with the provisions of Regulation 1383/2003. The 2004 Decree came into effect on 1 January 2005 and is based not only on the provisions

---

[4] Published in volume 57/2004 of the State Gazette under the name '98/2004. (IV. 27.) Korm. rendelet az egyes szellemi tulajdonjogokat sértő áruknak a Közösségbe történő behozatalára, valamint a Közösségből történő kivitelére és újrakivitelére vonatkozó intézkedések végrehajtási szabályainak megállapításáról' (Government Decree No 98 of 2004, issued on 27 April, laying down provisions for the implementation of measures concerning the import to the Community, export and re-export from the Community of goods suspected of infringing certain intellectual property rights).

[5] Council Reg (EC) No 1383/2003 of 22 July 2003 concerning customs action against goods suspected of infringing certain intellectual property rights and the measures to be taken against goods found to have infringed such rights. Official Journal L 196, 02/08/2003, 0007–0014.

[6] Published in volume 201/2004 of the State Gazette under the name '371/2004. (XII. 26.) Korm. rendelet az egyes szellemi tulajdonjogokat sértő áruk elleni vámhatósági intézkedésekről' (Government Decree No 371 of 2004, issued on 26 December 2004, on customs action against goods infringing certain intellectual property rights).

of Regulation 1383/2003 but also on the provisions of Commission Regulation (EC) No 1891/2004.[7]

I. SUBJECT MATTER AND SCOPE OF THE NATIONAL LAW APPLYING THE REGULATION

A. Customs procedure of the goods

The customs authorities in Hungary apply the Regulation to all customs **14.08** procedures defined in Article 1(1) of Regulation 1383/2003 ('the Regulation'). In practice most of the cases initiated by Hungarian Customs relate to imports (85 per cent), with only a few cases related to exports (5 per cent) and re-exports (10 per cent).

B. Definition of infringing goods

Since 1 May 2004—that is, the date of Hungary's accession to the European **14.09** Union and of entry into force of the Former 2004 Decree—intellectual property right-holders in Hungary benefit from the uniform regime of customs protection of intellectual property rights which is applicable throughout the European Union. Since then, the scope of intellectual property rights that Hungarian Customs can help to protect has become wider as customs now have powers in relation to designs, patents, and supplementary protection certificates, which they did not previously. 'As Community trade marks and Community designs have automatically extended to the accession countries on 1 May 2004, Hungarian Customs now has powers to protect those IP rights as well.'[8]

According to official figures, 95 per cent of Hungarian Customs' interventions **14.10** relate to goods suspected of infringing trade mark rights and certain copyrights (in most cases copyrights in connection with cartoon, animation, or other film characters), while 5 per cent of all interventions relate to other kind of copyrights (such as audiovisual recordings and software). Only one intervention has been made in connection with designs, yet. According to the information of the competent

---

[7] Commission Reg (EC) No 1891/2004 of 21 October 2004 laying down provisions for the implementation of Council Reg (EC) No 1383/2003 concerning customs action against goods suspected of infringing certain intellectual property rights and the measures to be taken against goods found to have infringed such rights. Official Journal L 328, 30/10/2004, 0016–0049.

[8] J Rutter and M Rosinki, 'Who is the Weakest Link?', [2004] Trade mark World, 2629.

Customs Headquarters, since 1 May 2004 no application for action has been submitted with regard to intellectual property rights other than trade marks, copyrights and designs.

(1) Counterfeit goods

14.11 Under Article 12 of the Hungarian Trade Mark Act[9] the proprietor of a trade mark is granted an exclusive right to use the trade mark. On the basis of this exclusive right, the proprietor may initiate proceedings against any party, which, without his consent, uses in its business activities:

- a sign identical with the trade mark in connection with goods and services which are identical with those listed in the specification of goods and services for which the trade mark is registered;

- any sign that consumers may confuse with the trade mark due to the identity or similarity of the sign and the trade mark, or due to the identity or similarity of the goods or services in question;

- any sign identical or similar to the trade mark in connection with goods or services that are not listed in the specification of goods for which the trade mark is registered, to the extent that such trade mark enjoys a reputation in the domestic market, and the use of the sign without due cause would be detrimental to, or take unfair advantage, of the trade mark's distinctive character or reputation.

14.12 The definition of trade mark infringement under the Hungarian Trade Mark Act is thus broader than that of 'counterfeit goods' in Article 2(1)(a)(i) of the Regulation. Based on the national legislation and the practice of the past eight years, Hungarian Customs exercise a wide discretion to consider certain goods as suspected of infringing trade mark rights, and are not reluctant to take action in some cases even when the signs in question are not identical or can be distinguished in their essential aspects (compare Article 2(1)(a)(i) of the Regulation), provided they are confusingly similar. This practice is obviously very much appreciated by the trade mark owners. The requirement of similarity (in practice) includes visually similar signs as well. Likewise, although Article 2(1)(a)(i) of the Regulation provides that the trade mark on the basis of which border measures are taken must be 'validly registered in respect of the *same type of goods*', customs are very flexible when appraising whether the suspect goods fall within the list of goods referred to in the trade mark registration. It would, in fact, be fair to say that the list of goods in relation to which a given trade mark has been registered is not of real relevance when making the decision on customs intervention.

---

[9] Published in volume 27/1997 of the State Gazette under the name 'A védjegyek és földrajzi árujelzők oltalmáról szóló 1997. évi XI. törvény' (Act No 11 of 1997 on the protection of trademarks and geographical indications). This Act was subject to major amendments due to Hungary's accession to the European Union, which amendments entered into force on 1 May 2004.

In a few cases, Hungarian Customs took measures against trade mark **14.13** symbols (including for example, logos, labels, and stickers) and packaging material, such as paper cartons, bearing a trade mark, which had been presented separately.

An application for action can be based only on a validly *registered* trade mark, as **14.14** there is no national legislation extending the scope of the Regulation to trade mark applications. This is, of course, not favourable to owners of new brands as the registration of a national trade mark may take usually at least one to one and a half years from the filing date of the application.

(2) Pirated goods

According to the Hungarian Customs Headquarters, no application for action **14.15** by customs authorities has ever been granted in Hungary in connection with copyright or a related right apart from those few which relate to cartoon, animation, or films. During the last eight years, there have been a very small number of interventions related to audiovisual recordings and computer programs. These low figures can presumably be justified in the light of the fact that the proportion of local production exceeds 'outsider's productions'.

Article 1 of the Hungarian Copyright Act[10] defines the scope of protection **14.16** of the copyright, which includes among others classical rights such as the right to reproduce the work in any manner or form whatsoever, the right to authorize adaptation of the work, and also new rights created due to the latest tendencies of the modern economy, such as the merchandising right of the author.

Under Article 23 of the Hungarian Design Act,[11] a design infringement occurs **14.17** whenever a person uses illegally (that is, without the right-holder's authorization) a design subject to design protection.

(3) Goods infringing other intellectual property rights

Goods infringing a patent or a supplementary protection certificate

There are no records available in the official statistics on customs actions taken on **14.18** the basis of a patent or a supplementary protection certificate (SPCs) in Hungary.

---

[10] Published in volume 61/1999 of the State Gazette under the name 'A szerzői jogról szóló 1999. évi LXXVI. törvény' (Act No 76 of 1999 on copyright).
[11] Published in volume 75/2001 of the State Gazette under the name 'A formatervezési mintáról szóló 2001. évi XLVIII. törvény' (Act No 48 of 2001 on industrial design).

14.19 Under Article 35 of the Hungarian Patent Act,[12] a patent infringement occurs when a person uses illegally (that is, without the patentee's authorization) an invention which is the subject of a patent.

14.20 Under Article 22/A of the Hungarian Patent Act, all matters relating to supplementary protection certificates are basically governed by the Regulations of the European Community on this subject,[13] as well as the provisions of the Patent Act.

Goods infringing a national plant variety right

14.21 There is no record in the official statistics on customs actions taken on the basis of national plant variety rights.

14.22 The protection of plant variety rights in Hungary is governed by the Hungarian Patent Act. Article 114/C of this Act specifies what constitutes an illegal use of a protected variety and as such, results in an infringement of plant variety rights. This Article refers to the provisions of Articles 34–36 of the same Act, which define the acts which constitute a patent infringement.

Goods infringing a national designation of origin or a geographical indication

14.23 As for patents, SPCs, and plant variety rights, there are no records available disclosing the official statistics on customs actions taken on the basis of national designations of origin or geographical indications.

14.24 The protection of national designations of origin and geographical indications (both referred to below as 'geographical product markings') is governed by the Hungarian Trade Mark Act. Under Article 110 of this Act, an infringement of these rights is committed by anyone who uses a protected geographical product marking without the right-holder's authorization. Under Article 109, only the proprietor of the right may use the geographical product marking, and no licence for use may be issued to a third party.

(4) Moulds and matrices

14.25 Under Article 2(3) of the Regulation (which refers, among others, for that purpose, to the law of the Member States in which the application for action by

---

[12] Published in volume 35/1995 of the State Gazette under the name 'A találmányok szabadalmi oltalmáról szóló 1995. évi XXXIII. törvény' (Act No 33 of 1995 on the protection of inventions by patents).

[13] Council Reg (EEC) No 1768/92 of 18 June 1992 concerning the creation of a supplementary protection certificate for medicinal products and Reg (EC) No 1610/96 of the European Parliament and of the Council of 23 July 1996 concerning the creation of a supplementary protection certificate for plant protection products. Official Journal L 182, 02/07/1992, 0001–0005 and Official Journal L 198, 08/08/1996, 0030–0035, respectively.

the customs authorities is made), in Hungary, the holder of a trade mark, copyright or related right, a design, or a patent may apply for border measures (and, in the framework of subsequent court proceedings, also in certain cases the destruction) of moulds and matrices which are specifically designed or adapted for the manufacture of goods infringing their rights, *regardless of the bad or good faith* of the infringer. Under Article 2(3) of the Regulation customs are authorized to retain suspected moulds and matrices, in order to allow the right-holder to request the seizure and destruction thereof before the courts.

C. Goods excluded by the Regulation

(1) Parallel imported goods

According to the Hungarian Trade Mark, Patent and Design Acts, the holders of such rights can rely on the intervention of customs in order to prevent the import of 'infringing' goods into Hungary.[14] As the relevant provisions to that effect apply to 'infringing' goods—and not just to 'counterfeit' goods—they encompass border measures against all kinds of trade mark, patent or design infringements, thus including genuine goods, imported from outside the European Economic Area without the consent of the right-holder.   **14.26**

Although Article 3(1), first sentence, of the Regulation provides that the latter does not apply in respect of (genuine) parallel imported goods, the Hungarian customs authorities consider that they are still entitled to suspend the release of, or detain, such goods at the borders as at the time of stopping a certain shipment it is not decided, whether the suspect goods are counterfeits or 'just' parallel imported genuine products. Unless the right-holder confirms that the goods are 'just' parallel imported genuine products, the customs office—which is not expected to have the expertise to assess whether a certain product is genuine or counterfeit—has valid grounds to suspend the release of or detain such goods.   **14.27**

Several authors consider, however, that, since Hungary's accession to the European Union and the applicability of the *acquis communautaire*, 'Hungarian Customs no longer has a legal basis under the European Regulation [1383/2003] to stop parallel imported goods', even if they agree that 'it is possible that, in practice, Customs will notify intellectual property right-holders of attempted parallel imports in the future, thus enabling them to take action'.[15]   **14.28**

---

[14] Art 28 of the Hungarian Trade mark Act, Art 35/A of the Hungarian Patent Act, Art 23 of the Hungarian Industrial Design Act.

[15] J Rutter and M Rosinski, 'Who is the Weakest Link ?', [2004] Trade mark World, 26–29.

(2) Goods which have been manufactured under conditions other
than those which have been agreed with the right-holder

14.29 There is no national legislation allowing the taking of border measures in Hungary for goods which have been manufactured under conditions other than those which have been agreed with the right-holder, and such goods are clearly excluded from the scope of the Regulation by Article 3(1), second sentence.

14.30 Some authors opine that, prior to Hungary's accession to the European Union, Hungarian Customs enjoyed the power under the 1997 and the Former 2004 Decrees to stop overruns and would, since then (and due to Article 3(1) of the Regulation), have been deprived of this possibility.[16]

(3) Goods contained in travellers' personal baggage

14.31 Although Hungarian Customs check travellers' personal baggage, they do not pay special attention to the detection of counterfeit goods contained therein. The calculation of the limit of the duty free allowance at EUR 175 and the appraisal of the 'non-commercial nature' of the goods under Article 3(2) of the Regulation is left to the discretion of the customs officers.

II. APPLICATION FOR ACTION BY THE CUSTOMS AUTHORITIES

14.32 According to the statistics, in the past eight years 15 per cent of all border measures taken by Hungarian Customs were adopted prior to the filing of an application for action by the right-holder (*ex officio* actions), while the other 85 per cent of the interventions were initiated following the filing of an application for action.

A. Measures prior to an application for action by the customs authorities ('*ex officio* measures')

14.33 One cannot say that Hungarian Customs have, *overall*, initiated a large number of *ex officio* procedures in the past eight years under national law, however some 15–20 customs offices (out of the 70 offices in total) have proved extremely active in this field.

---

[16] J Rutter and M Rosinski, n 15 above.

The most proactive customs offices have interpreted the requirement of the former **14.34** national legislation (which was slightly broader than the wording of the Regulation) in a relatively permissive sense. This approach has not changed since the entry into force of the Regulation, so that it can for instance be stated that Hungarian Customs usually withhold all goods which are not imported (or exported) directly by the intellectual property right-holder, one of its subsidiaries, or a well-known licensee. In such cases, the competent customs offices immediately contact the known Hungarian representative of the right-holder, asking him to confirm or refute their suspicion. Problems may arise when a right-holder has no representative in Hungary, or when the goods are suspected of infringing, for example, a copyright since there is no official database which discloses the details of copyright holders. In these problematic cases, the taking of *ex officio* actions depends to a large extent on the diligence of the customs officers, and on whether or not they are willing to run the risk of suspending the release of the goods in question.

Naturally, most *ex officio* interventions relate to traffic coming from, or destined **14.35** for countries rated as 'high-risk countries'.

When Hungarian Customs first approach the right-holder or his representative in **14.36** Hungary over the telephone with regards to a suspect shipment, they provide information about the quantity and nature of the goods as well as the details of the parties involved in the matter (importer or exporter, consignor, shipper, consignee, etc). The right-holder is authorized to inspect the goods, take samples or pictures; if the customs office has the equipment required, it sends digital pictures of the goods to the right-holder. If the right-holder or his representative confirms that the shipment is suspicious, customs require no further information other than a written statement from the right-holder or his representative confirming that the shipment contains counterfeit goods.

Under the former regime (that is, the 1997 Decree), the right-holder was obliged **14.37** to initiate civil proceedings after having been informed of an *ex officio* intervention within 10 working days (which could be extended once by another 10 working days) as of the date of receipt of the notification.

Under the current regime, Article 4 of the Regulation imposes a deadline of three **14.38** working days subsequent to notification of an *ex officio* intervention for the filing on an application for action by the right-holder. This will then allow the right-holder to confirm and substantiate his suspicions during the additional 10 (up to 20) working days period of Article 13.

In most cases initiated on an *ex officio* basis, Hungarian Customs (apart from **14.39** letting the right-holder file an application and initiate civil proceedings) initiate a criminal prosecution. Indeed, apart from the protection available under the European Regulation, (intellectual property) right-holders may also rely on criminal law to protect their (intellectual property) rights in Hungary. If Hungarian Customs have sufficient grounds for suspecting a criminal offence in connection with the goods (for example, fraudulent designation of goods or infringement of an intellectual property right), they can seize the goods for the purposes of a criminal complaint to the competent authority. If customs do not act on their own initiative, it is still possible to report a criminal offence to customs and request that the suspect goods be seized for the purposes of criminal investigations.[17] The competent customs office will often seek to obtain an expert opinion or affidavit confirming that the goods in question are counterfeit, and, having obtained this document, will start criminal investigations. Interestingly, the expert opinion does not need to be issued by the right-holder, but may instead be rendered by any organization or expert accepted by the competent customs office.

B. The lodging and processing of applications for customs action

14.40 At the time of writing, the total number of national applications accepted by Hungarian Customs amounted to 65, while the number of Community applications handled amounts to 42.

(1) Persons entitled to file an application for action

Definition of 'right-holders' under the Regulation

14.41 Under Article 2(2) of the Regulation, applications for action by customs authorities may be lodged not only by the holder (*stricto sensu*) of the intellectual property right concerned, but also, alternatively, by any other person authorized to use it, as well as their representatives.

14.42 According to the practice of Hungarian Customs, if the application for action is not filed by the owner (*stricto sensu*) of the intellectual property right concerned, it will be accepted only if the applicant proves that he has been explicitly authorized by the right-holder to file the application. Provided that this condition is met, the recording or registration (with for example, the patent, design and trade mark registries) of the authorization to use a certain industrial property right such as a licence is not a prerequisite to the filing of an application for action.

14.43 In practice, very few applications have been filed in Hungary by persons other than the holders of the intellectual property rights on which applications rely.

14.44 In the practice of Hungarian Customs, and in line with Article 1 of EC Regulation 1891/2004, the concept of 'representative of the right-holder or authorized user'

---

[17] J Rutter and M Rosinski, 'Who is the Weakest Link ?', [2004] Trade mark World, 26–29.

as defined in Article 2(2)(b) of the Regulation may include natural and legal persons such as attorneys-at-law, patent attorneys, trade mark agents, consultants, and associations of right-holders.

Proof of entitlement to file an application for action

For right-holders stricto sensu

Although Hungarian Customs are often very flexible in several respects, they always request the presentation (not submission) of original *registration certificates or certified copies* as proof of entitlement of the applicant when the application relies on industrial property rights. **14.45**

For applications based on a copyright or other non-registered rights, any evidence establishing that the applicant for the customs measures is the actual owner of the right would be sufficient.[18] As regards copyright-based applications, the registration certificate of the United States Copyright Office is usually submitted when the right-holder holds such a registration. **14.46**

An application for action cannot rely on a mere *application* for an industrial property right: a validly *registered* right is always required. **14.47**

For persons authorized to use the right

A person authorized to use the right within the meaning of Article 2(2)(b) of the Regulation and willing to apply for customs action under the Regulation will have to prove that he is entitled to such use and has been explicitly authorized by the right-holder to file the application. Such proof can be a contract or a specific declaration signed by the right-holder, which contains an explicit authorization for filing the application. Customs usually require the documents to be submitted in the original, however in the case of contracts, a certified copy would be accepted as well. A Hungarian translation of the specific declaration or the relevant part of the contract is required in any instance. **14.48**

For representatives

The representative of the right-holder or any other person authorized to use the right will have to provide customs with his authorization to act. Such power of attorney has to be duly executed by the right-holder or the authorized user, and the authorization to file the application should be expressly stipulated. No legalization or notarization is required, however the original of the document should be submitted in a bi-lingual form or together with its Hungarian translation. Documents printed on company letter-head paper and/or the use of company seal are not required but nevertheless appreciated. **14.49**

---

[18] Reg 1891/2004, Art 2(1)(b).

14.50 A *general* power of attorney will be accepted only if it contains an authorization to file the customs application. No further specification (regarding for example, the list of the trade marks on which the application relies) is required.

14.51 There is no nationality requirement for the representation before Hungarian Customs. However, due to the fact that the Hungarian language is not widely spoken by foreign practitioners and that it is crucial that the representative should be available and able to react without delay to customs notifications under the Regulation, the right-holders generally appoint a representative in Hungary.

14.52 Hungarian Customs accept the execution of the declaration referred to in Article 6 of the Regulation by the representative of the applicant, provided the power of attorney delivered to this representative complies with the rules mentioned in paragraph 14.49 above.

(2) Competent customs department and formal requirements

Competent customs department

14.53 The authority competent to process applications for customs action under Article 5(2) of the Regulation is the Central-Hungarian Regional Customs Headquarters,[19] specifically the Intellectual Property Protection Department. This department has jurisdiction for the whole territory of Hungary.

14.54 The contact details of the department are as follows:

Vám- és Pénzügyőrség Közép-Magyarországi Regionális Parancsnoksága
Szellemi Tulajdonjog-védelmi Osztály
H-1143 Budapest, Hungária krt. 112–114., Hungary
Telephone: +361 470-41-55 and +361 470-41-00
Fax: +361 470-42-53
E-mail: sztvo.vpkmrp@mail.vpop.hu

Form of the application for action

14.55 The application for action can be filed by regular or registered mail, or by hand-delivery. The filing of the application by electronic means (at the moment only via e-mail[20]) is requested, but has no legal effect. The application for action should contain the original declaration under Article 6 of the Regulation, the original documents proving the existence of the intellectual property right, authorization to use the right as the case may be, and, where the application for action is filed by a representative, the original power of attorney form.

14.56 Two copies of the application for action must be submitted.

---

[19] 2004 Decree, Art 2.
[20] For the moment no electronic data interchange system is available.

Language requirements

The application must be filed in the Hungarian language. However, 'Community' **14.57** applications filed through another Member State under Article 5(4) of the Regulation and designating Hungary can be processed without translation, provided they are filed in English or German. Applications in other languages can also be processed, if the applicant provides Hungarian Customs with a Hungarian, English, or German translation.

The exhibits submitted together with the application for action should also be **14.58** filed in Hungarian, however registration certificates need not be translated if they are in English or German.

The declaration under Article 6 of the Regulation shall be filed in Hungarian or in **14.59** a bi-lingual form (where one of the languages is Hungarian), or a Hungarian translation should be attached.

(3) Requirements regarding the contents of the application for action

Mandatory information

Although there are no specific requirements in Hungary regarding the mandatory **14.60** information which must be submitted to customs under Article 5(5) of the Regulation, it has to be pointed out that the technical description of the goods should be as detailed as possible in order to allow customs to identify suspect goods. The same applies to the information concerning the type and pattern of fraud.

As Hungarian Customs expect the contact person designated in the application to **14.61** be available at any time and to react quickly to the authorities' requests, he should preferably be a Hungarian resident with good command of the Hungarian language. In practice, it is not necessary to distinguish between *administrative* and *technical* contact persons, as the authorities prefer contacting one single person in connection with each right-holder. Therefore, the applications filed in Hungary usually indicate one and the same person as the technical and the administrative contact person. This person is usually also the legal representative of the right-holder, who files the application.

Optional information

Right-holders are advised to enclose digital photographs of genuine and **14.62** counterfeit product samples with their applications. In addition, they are also advised to include a description of the way the genuine goods arrive in Hungary (including information such as the name of the authorized importer, the source of the authorized goods, and customs offices usually used for the clearance of these goods).

Additional information specific to the type of intellectual property right referred to in the application

14.63 Additional information specific to the type of intellectual property right on which the application relies may also be requested by Hungarian Customs *a posteriori* (that is, subsequent to the filing of the application), depending on the circumstances, in accordance with Article 5(6) of the Regulation.

(4) Processing and acceptance of the application for action

14.64 Even before the Regulation entered into force on 1 July 2004, no fees were charged by Hungarian Customs for the processing of customs monitoring applications. However, the deposit of a security (5 per cent of the value of the goods, or HUF 60, 000 per month—approximately EUR 240—if the value of the goods could not be determined at the time of filing the application[21]) was a prerequisite to accepting such applications. Further to the entry into effect of the new Regulation, this system of security deposit was abolished, as contrary to Article 5(7), second indent, of the Regulation.

14.65 Hungarian Customs usually process applications for action much faster than within the term of 30 working days prescribed by Article 5(7) of the Regulation. When they need to clarify any point in the application, the customs authorities contact the right-holder and ask him to clarify or complete the application. We are not aware of any instance where an application for action has been rejected. An applicant facing a negative decision would in any event, according to the general rules of administrative procedure,[22] be entitled to lodge an appeal before the National Customs Headquarters. If the appeal is dismissed, the applicant will be able to seek a court review of the decision.[23]

14.66 Unless a shorter period is requested by the applicant, the period of validity of the decision granting the application for action is one year.

---

[21] J Rutter and M Rosinski, 'Who is the Weakest Link ?', [2004] Trade mark World, 26–29.

[22] Entered into force on 1 October, 1957 under the name 'Az államigazgatási eljárás általános szabályairól szóló 1957. évi IV. törvény' (Act No 4 of 1957 laying down the general rules of administrative procedure).

[23] Again, we are not aware of any such any appeal having ever been filed. In any case, a right-holder whose application had been rejected would in principle be more interested in completing his application at the request of the Regional Customs Headquarters and thus obtaining a favourable decision quickly, rather than getting involved in an appeal procedure which may lead to a delay of at least half a year in the granting of the application.

(5) 'Community' applications for action

Processing of 'Community' applications for action filed through the Hungarian Customs

There are no specific rules on the processing of 'Community' applications by Hungarian Customs other than those set out in EC Regulations 1383/2003 and 1891/2004. At the time of writing, no such application had been filed with Hungarian Customs. **14.67**

Processing of 'Community' applications designating Hungary

Hungarian Customs take a liberal approach when handling applications for action designating Hungary, as they will not only process applications filed in the Hungarian language, but also those filed in English or German. At the time of writing, only 42 such applications had been processed by Hungarian Customs. **14.68**

III. CONDITIONS GOVERNING ACTION BY CUSTOMS AUTHORITIES AND BY THE AUTHORITIES COMPETENT TO DETERMINE WHETHER GOODS INFRINGE AN INTELLECTUAL PROPERTY RIGHT

A. Conditions governing action by customs authorities

(1) Factual background

With Hungary's accession to the European Union on 1 May 2004, Hungary's customs system went through a major restructuring, which caused the number and responsibilities of customs offices at the common borders with Slovakia, Austria, and Slovenia to be significantly decreased. Until 1 May 2004 approximately 15 per cent of all border measures against pirated and counterfeit goods for the last eight years were taken by customs offices located along the Slovakian border. **14.69**

A significant number of pirated and counterfeit goods (mainly small, light and relatively high-value products, such as video-games, mobile phone accessories, software, or women's underwear) arrived in the country through the Budapest International Airport (20 to 25 per cent of all interventions were made by the Airport Customs Office). **14.70**

14.71 A significant quantity of suspicious goods were intercepted in the past by customs offices at the common borders with Ukraine, Romania, and Serbia (45 to 55 per cent of all actions). However, most of the border measures were adopted by the customs offices located in Budapest and in the region of Budapest (30 to 40 per cent of all actions). The significance of the Budapest customs offices and the Budapest region is due to the capital's prominent position in the national economy. A smaller proportion of customs actions (approximately 5 to 15 per cent of all actions) were initiated by the customs offices located in Hungary's other major cities.

(2) Notification of customs intervention

14.72 When a customs office encounters suspect goods, it immediately calls the representative of the right-holder or the right-holder directly (*informal* notification). Once their suspicions are confirmed, the customs officers suspend the release of those goods or detain them by issuing a formal decision, which is sent to the right-holder or his representative (*formal* notification).

14.73 A copy of the formal decision of the customs office is delivered immediately to the declarant or holder of the goods, if known.

14.74 All (formal) notifications take place by fax first, and are followed by a confirmation copy by registered mail. The deadline of Article 13 starts from the date of delivery of the confirmation copy by registered mail.

(3) Information to be provided by customs to the right-holder before the latter confirms the infringing nature of the goods

14.75 When notifying him of an intervention under the Regulation, customs usually inform the right-holder (subsequent to acceptance of his application for action) of the actual or estimated quantity and the actual or supposed nature of the goods the release of which has been suspended or which have been detained. The right-holder is also informed about the names and addresses of the consignee, consignor, declarant, or holder of the goods and the origin, provenance, and destination of the suspect goods. This information is usually disclosed automatically to the right-holder, however should the customs office fail to disclose any of this data, it will normally be prepared to do so upon the right-holder's request.

14.76 The restrictions imposed on customs officers under national law regarding the protection of personal data, commercial and industrial secrecy and professional and administrative confidentiality, fortunately do not hinder the communication of the above information to right-holders under Article 9(3) of the Regulation in Hungary. However, pursuant to Article 16 of the Hungarian Customs Code,[24] Hungarian Customs may not disclose information not mentioned expressly in the Regulation (such as for example, the declared value of the goods in question, or copies of commercial documents). Having said that, when the right-holder initiates civil proceedings according to Articles 10 and 13 of the Regulation, the court can oblige customs to disclose further information and submit additional documents related to the suspect goods that are the subject of these proceedings.

(4) Inspection of suspect goods

The right-holder may inspect the suspect goods after having been informally **14.77** notified about the interception of the consignment. Thus in practice, Hungarian Customs make it possible for the right-holder to inspect the goods before a formal decision is made on the detention or suspension of the release of suspect goods. The reason for this flexibility is the common interest of the parties to avoid the detention (or suspension of the release) of goods, which are not infringing. Although there is no formal deadline imposed on the right-holder to inspect the goods (as notification of the intervention has *formally* not yet taken place), in practice customs expect right-holders to proceed with the inspection within 24 hours from the preliminary (that is, informal) notification. If the right-holder cannot meet this informal deadline, customs issue the formal decision on the detention or suspension of the release of the goods without waiting for the results of the right-holder's investigations. In the latter case, the right-holder is still entitled to inspect the goods within the deadline provided for in Article 13(1) of the Regulation.

The customs office is also entitled to take representative samples of the goods **14.78** which, at the right-holder's request, can be handed over or sent to him. These samples will have to be returned to the same customs office, if the release of the goods (termination of the detention) has been ordered, or when court proceedings have been initiated under Article 13 of the Regulation, upon the termination of these proceedings.

At the request of the right-holder, and in practice also upon their own initiative, **14.79** Hungarian customs offices may send digital pictures of the suspect goods, however less than 25 per cent of the customs offices have digital cameras. If the right-holder initiates legal proceedings, he would be well-advised to obtain

---

[24] Published in volume 157/2003 of the State Gazette under the name 'A Közösségi vámkódex végrehajtásáról szóló 2003. évi CXXVI. törvény' (Act No 126 of 2003 on the Implementation of the Community Customs Code).

a physical sample of the goods to provide the court with adequate evidence of the asserted infringement. Digital pictures and samples received from the customs offices may indeed be freely used by the right-holder in subsequent infringement proceedings related to the goods in question.

B. Simplified procedure allowing the destruction of the goods without there being any need to determine whether an intellectual property right has been infringed under national law

14.80 Article 11 of the Regulation has been implemented by Article 8 of the 2004 Decree. According to paragraph (2) of Article 8 of the Decree the agreement of the declarant (the holder or the owner) of the suspect goods shall be presumed to be given—thus the simplified procedure can be applied—not only in the cases specified in Article 11 of the Regulation, but also in case the delivery of the notification provided for in Article 9 of the Regulation to the declarant (the holder or the owner) of the suspect goods was not successful.

14.81 In fact, almost 50 per cent of all customs interventions in Hungary end with a settlement between the right-holder and the parties involved in the traffic, whereby the importer agrees to the destruction of the goods (in a few cases the goods are offered to charity instead of being destroyed[25]), and pays the storage and destruction costs, thus allowing the parties to save the costs of (time-consuming) court proceedings. Such amicable settlements may also contain cease and desist declarations under conventional penalty, and clauses about the payment of the legal fees and damages.

14.82 Right-holders may not, however, grant licences to the owner of infringing goods to allow their commercialization, with the exception of goods that are not actual counterfeits, but (genuine) parallel imported goods, not licensed for the territory of Hungary. In this particular case it is possible to obtain authorization for the import in consideration of the payment of a licence fee.

14.83 According to paragraph (3) of Article 8 of the 2004 Decree the destruction of the suspect goods shall be carried out at the expense of the right-holder, if the party who has consented to the destruction (including the case of 'implied consent' as mentioned in para 14.80 above) does not pay the costs of the destruction with 15 days counted from the receipt of the notification of the customs office regarding the payment of these costs.

---

[25] See further para 14.96 below on this point.

When the competent customs office or the right-holder file a criminal complaint— **14.84** a possibility afforded by the Hungarian Criminal Code and Criminal Prosecution Code[26]—the court usually orders the forfeiture and destruction of the goods, under the State's entire responsibility and at its own costs, regardless of the opposition (either explicit or implicit) of the importer, declarant, owner, holder, or consignee of the goods. However this system cannot be assimilated to a 'simplified procedure' in the sense of the Regulation as it usually takes between 6 and 18 months, depending on the county where the investigation is conducted[27] (in Budapest, such criminal procedures are lengthy, while in other parts of the country they are relatively quick).

C. Conditions governing action by the authorities having jurisdiction to determine whether the goods infringe an intellectual property right

(1) Authorities having jurisdiction to determine whether the goods infringe an intellectual property right

Remedies under civil law

In Hungary, the Budapest Metropolitan Court has an exclusive jurisdiction over **14.85** all types of industrial property right infringement claims, while copyright infringement claims can be filed with the competent county courts.[28]

Intellectual property infringement proceedings *on the merits* before the competent **14.86** civil courts undoubtedly qualify as 'proceedings seeking to determine whether an intellectual property right has been infringed' under national law for the purposes of Article 13(1) of the Regulation. These proceedings are *inter partes* proceedings, meaning that the defendant is always informed of the filing of the claim and authorized to defend himself in writing before the court issues its decision.

The main disadvantage of such proceedings is that they are very time-consuming, **14.87** taking into account the backlog of the Budapest Metropolitan Court, which has only two tribunals to deal with all industrial property infringement claims filed in Hungary.

---

[26] Art 296 (false marking of goods) and 329/A (infringement of copyrights or related rights) of Act No 4 of 1978 on the Criminal Code ['1978. évi IV. Törvény a Büntető Törvénykönyvről']; Art 195 of Act No 19 of 1998 on the Criminal Prosecution Code ['1998 évi XIX. Törvény a Büntetőeljárásról'].

[27] Territorial jurisdiction of the courts in such cases is determined on the basis of the defendant's domicile or of the place where the goods have been intercepted.

[28] Territorial jurisdiction of the county courts is determined on the basis of the defendant's domicile. However, we are not aware of any civil proceedings which would have been commenced before the county courts based on a customs intervention related to goods infringing a copyright or related right.

As a consequence of that backlog, the Metropolitan Court usually issues its interlocutory decision (interim measure) on the (court) seizure of the infringing goods whose release has been suspended by or detained by customs within 50 to 80 days from the filing of the claim, instead of the 15-day deadline provided for under national law.

14.88   The decision of the Budapest Metropolitan Court on the merits of the case is usually rendered within 8 to 12 months from the filing of the lawsuit.

14.89   This decision is subject to an appeal to the Budapest Court of Appeal, which usually issues its final judgment within four to six months from the filing of the appeal.

14.90   In the framework of trade mark infringement proceedings, the trade mark owner may claim the statement of the occurrence of a trade mark infringement by the court; the barring of the infringer from future infringements; the publication of the judgment at the expense of the infringer; the disclosure of information on the parties taking part in the manufacture and distribution of the infringing products as well as on business relationships developed for the distribution of such products; the seizure of the means/equipment used for the infringement and of the products affected by the infringement; and the destruction of those means/equipment and products. The trade mark holder may also claim the profits realized by the defendant as a result of the infringement, and compensation for damage in accordance with the general liability rules of civil law.

14.91   The holders of a copyright, design, patent, SPC, geographical indication, or designation of origin,[29] may file similar claims against the infringer to those which the trade mark holder would be able to file in trade mark infringement proceedings before the civil courts.

Remedies under criminal law

14.92   Criminal prosecution is possible in the case of *any trading activities* related to goods infringing a copyright, trade mark right, or design right, while criminal sanctions can be imposed only on the *manufacturer* of goods infringing a patent right, industrial design right, trade mark right, or geographical indication right.

14.93   The criminal complaint can be filed with the competent customs investigation office (operating in every county) either by the customs office where the suspicious goods have been declared for clearance or by the right-holder, or even by any other party harmed by the offence.

14.94   The National Headquarters of the Customs and Finance Guard has the competence to pursue criminal investigations where goods have not yet cleared Customs, and the Hungarian Police, where goods have already cleared Customs. Hungarian

---

[29] Every proprietor of a geographical indication or designation of origin may take action against an infringement independently of the others. Organizations representing the interests of the proprietors and customer protection organizations may also take action against an infringement.

Customs will often initiate criminal proceedings upon seizure of suspected infringing goods, even if Customs monitoring is in place. This offers the holder of the [intellectual property] right more options and potentially a less costly enforcement procedure.[30]

However, criminal prosecution will in principle be started only if the customs **14.95** office is provided with an expert opinion (or affidavit) confirming that the goods in question are counterfeit or pirated. This expert opinion (affidavit) can be elaborated by the right-holder or any third party accepted by customs. Hungarian Customs are relatively flexible on this point too.

As mentioned above (para 14.84), criminal prosecutions usually last for 6 to 18 **14.96** months depending on the county where the investigations are conducted. Ninety per cent of these investigations end with a decision of the competent customs investigation office or the Public prosecutor to terminate the criminal procedure, subject to forfeiture of the infringing products by the competent district court.[31] The goods thus forfeited must then be destroyed. Alternatively, according to the Act on the Charitable Use of Certain Confiscated Goods,[32] they can also be offered for charity, subject however to the right-holder's prior consent. Usually, charitable use is possible only after the infringing trade marks or characters are removed from the products. The destruction of the infringing goods or the activities related to the charitable use thereof are carried out under the State's responsibility and at the latter's own costs.

'A seizure for the purposes of criminal investigations can have a number of **14.97** advantages for right owners: it does not preclude the enforcement of [intellectual property] rights before a civil [C]ourt; it allows more time than the 10+10 business days deadline to consider filing a civil lawsuit or possibility to engage in out-of-court negotiations with the importer; and the costs of customs storage and possible destruction of the goods will qualify as criminal costs', which will not be incurred by the right-holder, 'even if the assessment of the goods as infringing proves to be incorrect'.[33] Since criminal actions are much less expensive than civil litigation (for example, storage and destruction costs are always paid by the State),

---

[30] J Rutter and M Rosinki, 'Who is the Weakest Link ?', [2004] Trade mark World, 26–29.
[31] The reason for those unfavourable (from the point of right-holders) figures is the fact that the criminal investigations are usually unsuccessful, ie they do not allow it to be proven that the importer, declarant, consignee, owner or holder of the infringing goods acted wilfully (in trade mark or design right infringement matters) or even negligently (in copyright infringement matters), so that the criminal liability of the defendant cannot be established. However, as the goods in question prove to be infringing, the public prosecutor can request their forfeiture by the competent district court following a specific procedure.
[32] Published in volume 20/2000 of the State Gazette under the name '2000. évi XIII. törvény az egyes elkobzott dolgok közérdekű felhasználásról' (Act No 13 of 2000 on the charitable use of certain forfeited goods).
[33] J Rutter and M Rosinki, 'Who is the Weakest Link ?', [2004] Trade mark World, 26–29.

in the case of consignments containing only small quantities of infringing goods, right-holders often prefer opting for criminal prosecution. Another advantage of this path is that the formalities required to initiate a criminal action are not so strict as those required in the context of civil proceedings. Thus, for example, a criminal action need not to be initiated by the right-holder but may be instituted by any other person (such as a licensee or distributor) whose economic interests could be impaired by the release into free circulation of the infringing goods.

14.98   On the other hand, criminal actions give right-holders a limited control over the proceedings.

14.99   Another strategy cherished by right-holders consists of filing a criminal complaint in order to gain time for preparing for civil proceedings, since the strict deadlines of Article 13(1) of the Regulation do not always allow in practice timely to commence action before the civil courts.

14.100   Right-holders will choose civil proceedings instead of (or alongside) a criminal complaint when large consignments of goods are involved, or the infringement is not straightforward enough (for example, the signs used on the infringing products are not exact copies of a trade mark, but rather an imitation thereof). A civil court action should certainly be favoured if the right-holder seeks to collect damages from the defendant, as in the framework of a criminal action the enforcement of a claim for damages is usually not possible.

(2) Term for notifying customs that proceedings have been started

14.101   Under Article 13(1) of the Regulation, if, within 10 working days of receipt of the notification of suspension of release or of detention, the customs office concerned has not been informed that proceedings—as defined above, see paragraphs 14.85 to 14.91—have been initiated to determine whether an intellectual property right has been infringed under national law, release of the goods shall in principle be granted, or their detention will be ended, subject to completion of all customs formalities. The 10-working day period may be extended by a maximum of another 10 working days 'in appropriate cases'.

14.102   According to the practice of Hungarian Customs an extension of the term of 10 working days provided for in Article 13(1) of the Regulation is automatically granted, if the request of the right-holder to that effect states *any* reason for the extension (the most common reason is that the right-holder cannot decide on the steps to take, or that the right-holder's representative has not been able to obtain the power of attorney required for the commencement of civil proceedings within the first 10 working days—which may indeed be particularly difficult to achieve when the right-holder is a foreign company).

D. Release of goods suspected of infringing certain rights on provision of a security

Since the entry into force of the Regulation, there has been no case in Hungary, **14.103** where Article 14(1) (which allows for the release of goods suspected of infringing certain intellectual property rights on provision of a security) could have been applied. There has been no precedent in Hungary so far regarding the interpretation and application of this, or a similar, provision.

E. Storage of the goods

The 2004 Decree obliges the right-holder *in all cases* to bear the costs incurred in **14.104** keeping goods under customs control. However, according to Article 5 of the 2004 Decree, where the right-holder fails to fulfil the requirements set out in Article 13 of the Regulation, the declarant will bear the storage costs from the third working day after the receipt of the decision on the release of the goods according to Article 13(1).

In any event, if a criminal complaint has been filed, all costs related to the storage **14.105** of the goods will be borne by the State.

The goods are usually stored by the customs office where the customs clearance **14.106** was attempted. If a criminal procedure has been initiated or an interim measure has been imposed on the goods by a civil court, the goods ought in principle to be stored with the clerk of the court's office. However, this is not feasible from a practical point of view.

Owing to these circumstances, the issue of the liability for payment of storage is a **14.107** crucial problem in Hungary, and as the storage capacity of customs is progressively reaching its limits, there is a risk that the Regulation will not (or no longer) be properly applied in Hungary due to such (merely physical) obstacles.

IV. PROVISIONS APPLICABLE TO GOODS FOUND TO INFRINGE AN INTELLECTUAL PROPERTY RIGHT

As a consequence of the direct effect of the Regulation, the entry into/or removal **14.108** from the Hungarian territory, release for free circulation, exportation, re-exportation, placement under a suspensive procedure (including external transit and transhipment), and placement in a free zone or free warehouse of goods found to infringe an intellectual property right at the outcome of the proceedings referred to in Article 13 of the Regulation are prohibited under national law in accordance with Article 16 of the Regulation.

14.109   If the Courts conclude that there has been an intellectual property right infringement in the framework of civil proceedings, as a general rule they will order the destruction of the goods in question at the expense of the defendant. As in most of the cases the defendants simply 'disappear' by the end of the proceedings, it is only possible in 10 to 20 per cent of the civil cases to execute the judgment at their expense. In the majority of the cases, the right-holder pays the costs of the destruction, even if the court ordered the defendant to bear the costs. Where these costs are paid by the right-holder, the latter may, in the course of separate proceedings, claim the reimbursement of these costs. The chances of success of such a claim are limited, however, as most defendants become insolvent by the end of the proceedings. As a consequence, several tons of infringing products are amassed in customs warehouses as most right-holders are reluctant to pay the costs of the destruction instead of the defendants.

14.110   Once the destruction of the goods is ordered by the courts[34] (in the framework of either civil or criminal proceedings) or following an amicable settlement between the parties, the destruction process is monitored by the customs office where the goods have been blocked.

14.111   As mentioned above (cf para 14.96), infringing goods which have been forfeited in the course of criminal proceedings may, as an alternative to their destruction, be offered for charity with the consent of the right-holder. This procedure is administered by the Ministry of Health, Social and Family Affairs, which will first make sure that all infringing signs (trade marks, characters, logos, etc) affixed to the infringing goods are removed. This removal process is typically carried out by organizations which employ disabled persons. Their activity is financed mostly by the State and charity organizations (for example, the Hungarian Red Cross) involved in the dispensing of the goods among the poor.

V. PENALTIES

14.112   Patent, trade mark, design, and geographical indication infringements are punished under Hungarian criminal law by jail terms of up to three years, while copyright infringements, if committed wilfully, are punished by jail terms of up to

---

[34] '[O]nly a Court can order destruction of infringing goods—Customs has no power to destroy infringing goods on its own initiative' (J Rutter and M Rosinki, 'Who is the Weakest Link?', [2004] Trade mark World, 26–29).

eight years (depending on the amount of the damage caused) or, if committed negligently, by jail terms of up to one year. However, according to case law, not one single condemnation to a jail term has ever been reported so far for such offences; the courts usually impose suspended imprisonment or fines of between EUR 200 and 1,000.

According to the Hungarian Criminal Code, illegally manufactured goods and devices (such as moulds and matrices) designed for their production may also be forfeited whenever they belong to the defendant.[35] In addition, foreign nationals found guilty of any of the above-mentioned criminal offences can be expelled from the country.

14.113

Under civil law, apart from an injunction, the right-holder of an intellectual property right is usually entitled to the publication of the judgment at the defendant's costs, the destruction of the infringing goods and moulds and matrices. Moreover, the defendant is always obliged to pay (at least partially) the legal fees of the right-holder. The courts may also order infringers to disclose information to right-holders on the counterfeiting network.[36] When the defendant's bad faith is established, the grant of damages is possible under Hungarian law, although the courts seldom allow such claims.

14.114

VI. LIABILITY OF CUSTOMS AUTHORITIES AND RIGHT-HOLDERS

A. Liability of right-holders and sanctions

Under the general Hungarian tort law provision of Article 339(1) of the Civil Code,[37] a person who causes harm to another person in violation of the law (including the provisions of the Regulation) shall be liable for such damage. This provision will govern all liability claims referred to under Article 19(3) of the Regulation, initiated by, for example, the declarant, owner, importer, exporter, holder or consignee of the goods against a right-holder who applies the Regulation in bad faith or in a negligent manner.

14.115

---

[35] Hungarian Criminal Code, Art 77.
[36] Hungarian Trade Mark Act, Art 27; Hungarian Copyright Act, Art 94; Hungarian Patent Act, Art 35.
[37] Entered into force on 1 May 1960 under the name '1959. évi IV. törvény a Polgári Törvénykönyvről' (Act No 4 of 1959 on the Civil Code).

14.116 The provision also applies in the event of a third party being prejudiced by a non-permitted use of the information provided to the right-holder by Hungarian Customs, in breach of Article 12 of the Regulation.

B. Liability of customs authorities and sanctions

(1) Liability of Hungarian Customs in the context of the application of the provisions of the Regulation

14.117 Under the general tort law provision set out in Article 349(1) of the Hungarian Civil Code, damages can in principle be claimed from customs as an authority of the State for prejudices suffered by right-holders as a result of the authority's intervention or omission. However, this provision does not constitute a proper ground for a liability action against the customs authorities within the meaning of Article 19(2) of the Regulation. Under the latter provision, 'the exercise by a Customs office or by another duly empowered authority of the powers conferred on them in order to fight against goods infringing an intellectual property right shall not render them liable towards the persons involved' in the traffic of goods suspected of infringing an intellectual property right, or the persons affected by the measures resulting from an ex officio action 'for damages suffered by them as a result of the authority's intervention', 'except where provided for by the law of the Member State in which the application is made', or, in the case of a 'Community' application for action, 'by the law of the Member State in which loss or damage is incurred'. The taking of *ex officio* actions being a mere *option* open to customs under Article 4 of the Regulation, right-holders may not be successful in procedures based on such liability claims against the customs authorities under these circumstances.

(2) Liability of Hungarian Customs for not detecting or acting against goods suspected of infringing a right-holder's intellectual property rights

14.118 As mentioned above (cf para 14.117), according to the Hungarian Civil Code, damages can be claimed from customs as an authority of the State for prejudices suffered by right-holders as a result of the authority's intervention or omission. Thus, in principle, Article 349(1) of the Civil Code might entitle right-holders to compensation in the event that goods are not detected by a customs office and are released, or in the event that no action is taken to detain them, once an application for action has been lodged by the right-holder.[38] Having said that, it is questionable whether—after filing a customs application—a right-holder, who

---

[38] Cf Reg 1383/2003, Art 19(1).

relies upon the assistance of customs on a continuous basis will sue the same authority for an unlawful intervention or omission, since a lawsuit between the same parties may have an adverse effect on their future cooperation.

Conclusion

Having recognized the increased responsibility of Hungarian Customs—since, as a result of accession, a significant part of Hungary's borders have become external borders of the European Union—to provide a strong line of defence at those borders against entry of infringing goods into the European Union, a new branch, the Department for the Protection of Intellectual Property Rights, has been set up within Hungarian Customs dedicated exclusively to dealing with customs protection of intellectual property rights.[39] Moreover, thanks to the flexibility of Hungarian Customs (especially in the processing of applications and in *ex officio* procedures), it can be said that Hungarian Customs are generally willing to cooperate with right-holders and vice versa. The Customs offices active in intellectual property protection matters are dedicated to the fight against counterfeiting and piracy and act in a very professional manner. Some of these offices are even proactive in conducting domestic market checks and are happy to seize—in the context of criminal proceedings—infringing goods, suspected of having entered Hungary in spite of a granted application for action of the right-holder concerned.   **14.119**

However, there is a significant threat to the successful operation of the border measures system in Hungary. This threat is the very limited financial resources of Hungarian Customs, which could in the short term hinder customs from taking efficient actions against goods infringing intellectual property rights. Although, under both European and international law, Hungarian Customs have been entrusted with the control of such goods for almost eight years already, they have not been granted a specific budget for the execution of this task. This may lead, among other things, to the exhaustion of storage capacity, which may eventually result in the termination of the suspension of release or detention of certain infringing goods in the future.[40]   **14.120**

---

[39] J Rutter and M Rosinski, 'Who is the Weakest Link ?', [2004] Trade mark World, 26–29.
[40] The author hopes that this chapter will be read not only by intellectual property practitioners but also politicians and responsible customs officers dedicated to the issue of intellectual property protection, who may act in order to eliminate the shortcomings of the present system so that the efficiency of the application of the Regulation can be maintained.

15

IRELAND

Patricia McGovern and Áine Matthews

Introduction

Ireland was slow to implement Council Regulation (EEC) No 3842/86 of **15.01** 1 December 1986 laying down measures to prohibit the release for free circulation of counterfeit goods ('the 1986 Regulation').[1] In fact, it was only with the implementation of the European Communities (Counterfeit Goods) Regulations 1990[2] that EC Regulation 3842/86 was, rather belatedly, given effect to in Ireland. However, failure to secure uniform implementation of the 1986 Regulation throughout the European Communities resulted in a limited operation of external border controls and undermined the functioning of this Regulation.

Criticisms and reviews[3] of the 1986 Regulation led to the introduction of **15.02** Council Regulation (EC) No 3295/94 laying down measures to prohibit the release for free circulation, export, re-export, or entry for a suspensive procedure of counterfeit and pirated goods[4] ('the 1994 Regulation') together with rules on implementation contained in Commission Regulation (EC) No 1367/95 ('the 1994 EC Implementing Regulation').[5] These European Regulations were

---

[1] Council Reg (EEC) No 3842/86 of 1 December 1986 laying down measures to prohibit the release for free circulation of counterfeit goods OJ [1986] L357/1.

[2] Statutory Instrument No 118 of 1990.

[3] Report from the Commission to the Council and the European Parliament on the functioning of the System set up by Council Reg (EEC) No 3842/86 of 1 December 1986 (Counterfeit Goods), 15 February 1991, SEC (91) 262 final.

[4] Council Reg (EC) No 3295/94 laying down measures to prohibit the release for free circulation, export, re-export or entry for a suspensive procedure of counterfeit and pirated goods, OJ [1994] L341/8.

[5] Commission Reg (EC) No 1367/95 of 16 June 1995 laying down provisions for the implementation of Council Reg (EC) No 3295/94 of 22 December 1994 laying down measures to prohibit the release for free circulation, export, re-export, or entry for a suspensive procedure of counterfeit and pirated goods, OJ [1995] L133/2.

incorporated into Irish law by the European Communities (Counterfeit and Pirated Goods) Regulations 1996[6] ('the 1996 Regulations') which introduced substantive changes to the external border control regime including the introduction of the *ex officio* procedure and the extension of protection to design rights and copyright.

15.03   Council Regulation (EC) No 241/1999 amending Council Regulation (EC) No 3295/94 laying down measures to prohibit the release for free circulation, export, re-export, or entry for a suspensive procedure of counterfeit and pirated goods[7] ('the 1999 Regulation') introduced further changes, most notably extending protection to patents and simplifying the application procedure. Ireland never introduced secondary legislation in order to implement the 1999 Regulation. However, EU Regulations are binding in their entirety and directly applicable in all Member States, therefore the provisions of the 1999 Regulation would have been applicable in Ireland.

15.04   With the introduction of Council Regulation (EC) No 1383/2003 concerning customs actions against goods suspected of infringing certain intellectual property rights and the measures to be taken against goods found to have infringed such rights[8] ('the Regulation') and Commission Regulation laying down provisions for the implementation of Council Regulation (EC) No 1383/2003 concerning customs actions against goods suspected of infringing certain intellectual property rights and the measures to be taken against goods found to have infringed such rights ('the Implementing Regulation'), (both effective from 1 July 2004) it was therefore necessary to replace the 1996 Regulations in Ireland to take account of the changes made in the Regulation and Implementing Regulation. A Statutory Instrument (which is the instrument used in Ireland to give effect to Council and Commission Regulations where it is so necessary) has recently been introduced to give effect to the Regulation and the Implementing Regulation. The Statutory Instrument is entitled the 'European Communities (Customs Action against Goods Suspected of Infringing certain Intellectual Property Rights) Regulations 2005'[9] ('the 2005 Regulations'). The 2005 Regulations set out the offences under the Regulation and the penalties for violation of these offences and, as expected, the 2005 Regulations also designate the Irish Revenue Commissioners as the competent authority in Ireland to receive and process applications for customs action as required under Article 5(2) of the Regulation. The 2005 Regulations revoked the European Communities (Customs Action Against Goods Suspected of Infringing Certain Intellectual Property Rights) Regulations 2004 (Statutory Instrument No. 181 of 2005) which was a Statutory Instrument brought in earlier in 2005 to

---

[6] Statutory Instrument No 48 of 1996.

[7] Council Reg (EC) No 241/1999 amending Reg (EC) No 3295/94 laying down measures to prohibit the release for free circulation, export, re-export or entry for a suspensive procedure of counterfeit and pirated goods, OJ [1999] L27/1.

[8] Council Reg (EC) No 1383/2003 concerning customs actions against goods suspected of infringing certain intellectual property rights and the measures to be taken against goods found to have infringed such rights, OJ [2003] L196/7.   [9] Statutory Instrument No 344 of 2005.

implement the Regulation and Implementing Regulation. The 2005 Regulations now govern the implementation of the Regulation and Implementing Regulation. As an aside, the European Communities (Customs Action Against Goods Suspected of Infringing Certain Intellectual Property Rights) Regulations 2004 also revoked the 1996 Regulations. However, for the purposes of this chapter, we will proceed on the basis that the 2005 Regulations revoked the 1996 Regulations.

I. SUBJECT MATTER AND SCOPE OF THE NATIONAL LAW APPLYING THE REGULATION

This Part examines under which custom regimes, Customs and Excise will act against   **15.05** suspect goods (section A), the definition of infringing goods under Irish law (section B) and the goods excluded from the Regulation (section C). Customs and Excise is a branch of the Irish Revenue Commissioners and the Irish Revenue Commissioners is the competent authority designated in Ireland to receive and process applications for customs action. Customs and Excise will be referred to hereinafter as 'Irish Customs'.

A. Customs procedure of the goods

Irish Customs apply the Regulation to all customs procedures defined in Article   **15.06** 1(1) of the Regulation, namely goods entered for release for free circulation, export, or re-export in accordance with Article 61 of the Community Customs Code;[10] goods found during checks on goods entering or leaving the Community customs territory in accordance with Articles 37 and 183 of the Community Customs Code; goods placed under a suspensive procedure within the meaning of Article 84(1)(a) of the Community Customs Code; goods re-exported subject to notification under Article 182(2) of the Community Customs Code; and goods placed in a free zone or warehouse within the meaning of Article 166 of the Community Customs Code. Irish Customs also apply the terms of the Regulation to goods in external transit which are goods passing through Community customs territory from one non-Member State to another non-Member State.

B. Definition of infringing goods

Statistics would suggest that Irish Customs find it relatively easier to identify   **15.07** counterfeit and pirated goods in relation to copyright and related rights (such as database rights, for example) rather than goods protected by design rights, patent

---

[10] Council Reg (EC) No 2913/92 of 12 October 1992 establishing the Community Customs Code.

rights, or Supplementary Protection Certificates ('SPCs'). Official figures highlight this position in that in 2002, 38 per cent of cases related to trade mark rights and 60 per cent of cases related to copyright and related rights.[11] In 2003, 76 per cent of cases related to trade mark rights and 24 per cent of cases related to copyright and related rights.[12] No figures are available for designs, patents, or SPCs. An obvious difficulty exists for Irish Customs, as indeed for other customs authorities, in determining whether goods infringe a patent or an SPC in that it is difficult to ascertain whether goods fall within the claims of a registered patent. We examine the definition of counterfeit goods, pirated goods, and other intellectual property rights below.

(1) Counterfeit goods

15.08 Trade marks in Ireland are governed at common law by the action for passing off, and by the Trade Marks Act 1996 ('the TMA 1996') and the Trade Marks Rules 1996. The TMA 1996, which implements the European Community (EC) Directive on the Approximation of the Laws of the European Union (EU) Member States relating to Trade Marks,[13] contains provisions in connection with the EC Council Regulation on the Community Trade Mark and gives effect to the Madrid Protocol and to certain provisions of the Paris Convention.

15.09 Section 14 of the TMA 1996 provides that a person infringes a registered trade mark if he uses, in the course of trade:

- an identical mark on identical goods or services;
- an identical mark on similar goods or services or a similar mark on identical or similar goods or services and there exists a likelihood of confusion on the part of the public (including a likelihood of association).

15.10 A person also infringes a registered trade mark if he uses, in the course of trade, a mark which is identical with or similar to the registered trade mark in relation to goods or services which are not similar to those for which the trade mark is registered, where the trade mark has a reputation in Ireland and the use of the mark is without due cause and takes unfair advantage of or is detrimental to the distinctive character or reputation of the registered trade mark. In Ireland, a person may use a registered trade mark for the purposes of identifying goods or

---

[11] European Commission (DG Taxation and Customs Union (TAXUD), Breakdown of type of right covered 2002 (http://europa.eu.int/comm/taxation_customs/customs/counterfeit_piracy/index_en.htm).

[12] European Commission (DG Taxation and Customs Union (TAXUD), Breakdown of type of right covered 2003 (http://europa.eu.int/comm/taxation_customs/customs/counterfeit_piracy/index_en.htm).

[13] First Directive 89/104/EEC of the Council, of 21 December 1988, to Approximate the Laws of the Member States Relating to Trade Marks, [1989] OJ L40/1 (11.2.1989).

services as those of the proprietor or licensee of the registered trade mark where such use is in accordance with honest practices and without taking unfair advantage of or being detrimental to the distinctive character or reputation of the trade mark.[14] Therefore, this provision effectively allows a person to engage in comparative advertising and allows the use of another person's registered trade mark for the purposes of identifying the goods or services of the proprietor of the registered trade mark or the licensee.

15.11 It is important to note that use for infringement purposes includes marking goods or their packaging with the trade mark, offering goods or services under the trade mark, importing or exporting under the trade mark, or using the trade mark on business papers or in advertising.[15]

15.12 The definition of trade mark infringement under the TMA 1996, in terms of identity and the notion of similarity resulting in a likelihood of confusion which includes the likelihood of association, is much broader than that of the definition of counterfeit goods under the Regulation which only applies to a sign which is 'identical . . . or which cannot be distinguished in its essential aspects . . .' from such a trade mark. The Regulation further requires that the counterfeit goods be 'of the same type' whereas the TMA 1996 applies to both identical and confusingly similar goods. Furthermore, the concept of dilution exists under the TMA 1996, a concept which is, unfortunately, not provided for in the Regulation.

15.13 In practice, Irish Customs only take action in the case of goods bearing, without authorization, a trade mark identical to another trade mark or which is substantially indistinguishable from the registered trade mark mentioned in the application for action. Irish Customs have informed us that they apply the legislation in full and act in accordance with the provisions of the Regulation. Whist Irish Customs are careful not to make pronouncements on their interpretation of the Regulation, it is fair to say that they would probably act against both identical and confusingly similar trade marks (within the parameters of 'substantially indistinguishable') applied to goods whether it be in an *ex officio* intervention or upon the request of the trade mark holder. However, the trade mark must be registered in respect of the same type of goods.

15.14 The question has been raised by other authors in this publication[16] as to whether the discrepancy between national trade mark legislation and the Regulation (in that national trade mark legislation tends to be broader in its scope than the Regulation) could lead to the release of goods by a court. This situation has not yet be decided upon by the Irish courts but the criteria of 'substantially indistinguishable' can really only be judged on a case-by-case basis.

---

[14] Trade Marks Act 1996, s 14(6).   [15] Trade Marks Act 1996, s 14(4).
[16] Olivier Vrins and Marius Schneider—Belgium (Chapter 5).

15.15 In terms of the extent to which it is possible to take border measures on the basis of an application we would comment as follows. Prior to the implementation of the 2005 Regulations it appeared, in the case of a right that was registered or for which an application had been lodged, proof of registration with the relevant office or proof that the application had been lodged was required. Once the application for action was approved by Irish Customs, border measures could then be taken. Therefore, before the implementation of the 2005 Regulations it appeared that action in Ireland could be based on a trade mark application. This position derived from the 1996 Regulations. However, the 1996 Regulations have been revoked by the 2004 Regulations and the 2005 Regulations make no reference to the type of documentation to be lodged. It is helpful to look at the 1996 Regulations and section 4(4) of the 1996 Regulations which provided as follows:

Where the holder of the right applies on his own behalf he shall also submit:

(a) In the case of a right, being a trade mark or design right, that is registered or for which an application has for the time being lodged:
   (i) the certificate of registration (or a copy thereof) issued by the Controller in respect of the right specified in the application and where appropriate, the certificate of renewal issued by the Controller for the time being in force, or a copy thereof; or
   (ii) a statement in writing signed by the Controller or an officer duly authorised by him in that behalf giving such information in relation to the said right as may be specified by the Revenue Commissioners.

15.16 However, as stated above, the 1996 Regulations are no longer in force and, for further guidance, we must look to the Implementing Regulation and, in particular, Article 2(1)(a). Whilst there is no reference to, for example, trade mark applications in the Regulation, Article 2(1)(a) of the Implementing Regulation provides that the necessary proof in an application for border measures shall be 'in the case of a right that is registered or for which an application has been lodged, proof of registration with the relevant office or proof that the application has been lodged'. However, section 7 of the 2005 Regulations refer to 'registered trade mark mentioned in the application'. There is some debate as to whether the Regulation should be applied to trade mark and design applications and on the basis of the wording in section 7 of the 2005 Regulations, it would appear that border measures may only be taken on the basis of a registered mark. However, the wording of the Implementing Regulation leaves room for debate.

15.17 With regard to trade mark symbols and packaging materials, Irish Customs act in accordance with the provisions of Article 2(1)(a)(ii) and (iii) of the Regulation and take measures with regard to trade mark symbols (including logos, labels, stickers, brochures, instructions for use, or guarantee documents) and packaging material bearing a trade mark even presented separately. These provisions prevent counterfeiters from evading border measures by importing unmarked goods separately from their labelling, packaging and other accompanying materials and then arranging for the goods to be labeled and packaged after importation. The fact that these materials are classified as counterfeit in their own right assists trade mark holders in combating the trade in labelling and packaging materials. In one particular case, Irish Customs, working with Dublin airport staff, seized 150,000 buttons. All of the buttons were branded with major brand marks. The attempted importation of buttons indicates that a factory may exist where the garments are put together. The scenario in such cases would be that blank garments, labels, logos, etc are smuggled and the garments are made up on a 'just in time' basis which is dependent on the market activity at any given time. Therefore, it is certainly advisable that separate trade mark registrations are secured for labelling and packaging materials, for example, it would be prudent for a clothing manufacturer to secure registration of its trade mark not only in Class 25 for clothing but also in Class 24 for labels and Class 26 for buttons. Certain clothing manufacturers also apply their trade marks not only to the clothing itself but also to the clothing's labels and buttons, thereby necessitating the need for registration in respect of all goods to which its mark is applied. The same can also be said for cosmetic manufacturers that would normally register in Class 3 for cosmetics. However, registration should also be secured in at the very least Class 16 for packaging.

(2) Pirated goods

The majority (60 per cent) of interventions by Irish Customs in 2002 related to copyright and related rights in relation to, in particular, CDs (audio, games, software, etc), DVDs and cassettes.[17] In 2003, this figure fell to 24 per cent.[18] Such interventions are of paramount importance considering that Ireland exports significant amounts of computer hardware and software and the technology industry is critical to Ireland's economic well-being. **15.18**

In Ireland, copyright is governed by the Copyright and Related Rights Act 2000 ('the CRRA 2000'). The CRRA 2000 consolidated previous legislation in Ireland in relation to computer programs and the duration of copyright and, for the first time, introduced performers' rights and moral rights into Irish copyright law. Copyright is defined in the CRRA 2000 as a property right whereby the owner of copyright in any work may undertake or authorize other persons in relation to **15.19**

---

[17] European Commission (DG Taxation and Customs Union (TAXUD), Breakdown of type of right covered 2002 (http://europa.eu.int/comm/taxation_customs/customs/ counterfeit_piracy/ index_en.htm).
[18] European Commission (DG Taxation and Customs Union (TAXUD), Breakdown of type of right covered 2003 (http://europa.eu.int/comm/taxation_customs/customs/ counterfeit_piracy/ index_en.htm).

that work to undertake certain acts in Ireland being acts which are designated by the CRRA 2000 as acts restricted by copyright in works of that description.

15.20   Section 37 of the CRRA 2000 provides that copyright in a work is infringed by the following:

- copying the work;
- making available the work to the public;
- issuing copies of a work to the public; or
- making an adaptation of a work.

15.21   Section 45 of the CRRA 2000 defines secondary infringement of copyright as where a person without the licence of the copyright owner and in relation to a copy of the work which is or which he knows or has reason to believe is an infringing copy of the work:

- sells, rents, lends, or offers or exposes it for sale, rent, or loan;
- imports it into Ireland otherwise than for his private and domestic use;
- in the course of a business, trade, or profession, has it in his possession, custody, or control or makes it available to the public; and
- other than in the course of business, trade, or profession, makes it available to the public to such an extent as to prejudice the interest of the owner of the copyright.

15.22   Section 147(1) of the CRRA 2000 provides that the owner of a copyright work may give notice to the Irish Revenue Commissioners (meaning Irish Customs) to treat as prohibited goods:

- copies of the work which are infringing copies;
- articles specifically designed or adapted or used for making infringing copies of the work; or
- protection-defeating devices.

15.23   Prohibited goods under the CRRA 2000 are defined as meaning counterfeit or pirated goods within the meaning of the 1996 Regulations. The period specified in any such notice given shall not exceed five years and in any case shall not extend beyond the period for which copyright is to subsist. This period of five years is in conflict with the period of one year as outlined in the Regulation. However, given the direct effect of EU Regulations, it is certainly arguable that the Regulation should take precedence over this particular provision of section 147. Section 147(3) of the CRRA 2000 further provides that the owner of a copyright work may give notice to the Irish Revenue Commissioners (meaning Irish Customs) that infringing copies, articles, or devices are expected to arrive in the State at a time and place specified in the notice and that he requests the Revenue Commissioners to treat those copies, articles, or devices as prohibited goods.

Irish registered designs are governed by the Industrial Designs Act 2001 ('the IDA **15.24** 2001'). 'Design' is defined in the IDA 2001 as meaning 'the appearance of the whole or a part of a product resulting from the features of, in particular, the lines, contours, colour, shape, texture or material for the product itself or its ornamentation'.

Section 42 of the IDA 2001 provides that the design right entitles the owner to the **15.25** exclusive right to use the design and to authorize others to use it, including the right to make, offer, put on the market, import, export, or use a product in which the design is incorporated or to which it is applied, or to stock such a product for those purposes. The design right is therefore infringed by a person who, without the licence of the registered proprietor of the design and while the design right is in force, undertakes or authorizes another to undertake any act which is the exclusive right of the registered proprietor.[19]

A person also infringes the design right where he, without the licence of the regis- **15.26** tered proprietor of the design and while the design right is in force, sells, rents or offers or exposes for sale or rent, imports into Ireland otherwise than for his private and domestic use, or in the course of a business, trade, or profession has in his possession, custody, or control a product which is and which he knows or has reason to believe is an infringing product.[20]

Section 73 of the IDA 2001 set out similar provisions to those set out in section **15.27** 147(1) of the CRRA 2000 for the treatment of infringing goods as prohibited goods and section 147(3) to prevent the importation of prohibited goods.

Ireland's copyright and design legislation is very up to date and is drafted in such **15.28** a way as to be technologically neutral. Therefore, it would appear that the Regulation, with its use of the term 'copies', is consistent with the CRRA 2000 and the IDA 2001 and no apparent conflict emerges. Irish Customs are very active in respect of pirated goods and are open minded in their interpretation of 'goods which are or contain copies' considering the importance of the information technology sector to Ireland.

(3) Goods infringing other intellectual property rights

Goods infringing a patent, a supplementary protection certificate or a plant variety right

Patents in Ireland are governed by the Patents Act 1992 ('the PA 1992') and Patents **15.29** Rules 1992. Essentially a patent confers on its proprietor the right to prevent all third parties not having his consent from supplying in Ireland a product subject

---

[19] Industrial Designs Act 2001, s 51(1).   [20] Industrial Designs Act 2001, s 52.

to the patent, a process subject to the patent, or a product of the process subject to the patent. It is important to note that if the subject matter of the alleged infringement is the same product, then the defendant must prove non-infringement. Otherwise the plaintiff must prove infringement.

15.30 Section 40 of the PA 1992 allows the proprietor of a patent to prevent all third parties from doing in Ireland the following acts without his consent:

- making, offering, putting on the market or using a product, which is the subject matter of the patent, or importing or stocking the product for those purposes;
- using a process which is the subject matter of the patent or, when the third party knows or it is obvious to a reasonable person in the circumstances, that the use of the process is prohibited without the consent of the proprietor of the patent, offering the process for use in Ireland; or
- offering, putting on the market, using or importing or stocking for those purposes, the product obtained directly by a process that is the subject matter of the patent.

15.31 Other relevant patent legislation includes the European Communities (Supplementary Protection Certificates) (SPCs) Regulations 1993[21] which implemented Council Regulation (EEC) No 1768/92 concerning the creation of SPCs for medicinal products.[22] The SPC recognizes that the period of time between filing a patent application and obtaining regulatory approval to market a new medicinal product can mean that the effective period of patent protection is very much reduced. Once an SPC has been granted, it will not take effect until the end of the term of the basic patent. The period of protection conferred is equal to the period which elapsed between the date of filing of the application for the basic patent and the date of the first marketing authorization in the EU reduced by a period of five years. The duration of an SPC in Ireland is not to exceed five years.

15.32 A similar system of SPCs for plant protection products was introduced by Council Regulation (EC) No 1610/96.[23] No implementing legislation was required to bring into effect this Regulation in Ireland as the European Communities (Supplementary Protection Certificates) Regulations 1993 referred to above was considered sufficient.

15.33 Ireland is also bound by Council Regulation (EC) No 2100/94 (as amended) on Community Plant Variety Rights[24] which was implemented into Irish law by the

---

[21] Statutory Instrument No 125 of 1993.

[22] Council Reg (EEC) No 1768/92 of 18 June 1992 concerning the creation of a supplementary protection certificate for medicinal products.

[23] Council Reg (EC) No 1610/96 concerning the creation of a supplementary protection certificate for plant protection products, OJ [1996] L 198.

[24] Council Reg (EC) No 2100/94 (as amended) on Community Plant Variety Rights, OJ [1994] L 227/1.

Plant Varieties (Proprietary Rights) (Amendment) Acts 1980 and 1998. Plant breeders' rights means all proprietary rights in relation to any variety of any plant genus or species which has been independently bred or discovered and developed. Where plant breeders rights are granted, section 4 affords the exclusive right, subject to other restrictions in the Plant Varieties (Proprietary Rights) (Amendment) Acts 1980 and 1998 to:

- produce, for the purposes of its being commercially marketed, reproductive material of the plant variety to which the grant relates;
- to sell or offer such material for sale or to export or import it;
- in case the plant variety is an ornamental plant variety, to propagate the variety in the course of commercially producing ornamental plants or cut flowers;
- to authorize any other person to do all or any of the aforesaid things;

and infringements of such plant breeders' rights are actionable at the suit of the holder of such rights.

Irish Customs act in accordance with the provisions of the legislation mentioned **15.34** above in respect of patents, SPCs, and plant variety rights. Official statistics are silent on the success or otherwise of Irish Customs in this area. It is, not surprisingly, difficult for Irish Customs to ascertain whether the goods come within the parameters of the very specialized and technical claims. In addition, the capture of counterfeit medicines, in any event, may generally be accounted for in the trade mark infringement statistics.

Goods infringing a designation of origin or a geographical indication

Council Regulation (EEC) No 2081/92 of 14 July 1992 as amended by Council **15.35** Regulation (EC) No 535/97 of 17 March 1997 on the protection of geographical indications and designations of origin for agricultural products and foodstuffs governs the treatment of national designations and geographical indications in Ireland.[25] In the EU, more than 600 traditional and quality products are protected as 'geographical indications' and 'designations of origin'. Of these, Ireland has just three: Clare Island Salmon, Imokilly Regato, and Timoleague Brown Pudding. The aforementioned Regulations offer protection for geographical denominations of foodstuffs by prohibiting:

- any direct or indirect commercial use of the protected name;
- any misuse, imitation, or evocation, even if the true origin of the product is indicated, or if the protected name is translated or accompanied by

---

[25] Implemented in Ireland by European Communities (Protection of Geographical Indications and Designations of Origin for Agricultural Products and Foodstuffs) Regulations, 1995 (Statutory Instrument No 148/1995 and European Communities (Protection of Geographical Indications and Designations of Origin for Agricultural Products and Foodstuffs) (Amendment) Regulations, 1995 (Statutory Instrument No 275/1999).

an expression such as 'style', 'type', 'method', 'as produced in', 'imitation' or similar;

- any other false or misleading indication as to the provenance, origin, nature, or essential qualities of the product;
- any other practice liable to mislead the public as to the true origin of the product.

15.36 Irish whiskey and Irish cream liqueur are protected under parallel rules for the protection of wines and spirits.[26]

15.37 Irish Customs act in accordance with the provisions of Council Regulation (EEC) No 2081/92 and (EC) No 1493/99. In addition to the above, there are also national laws which address issues such as consumer protection guarding against false or misleading descriptions.[27]

15.38 However, some of the most important legislation dealing with customs offences in Ireland is contained in the Customs Consolidation Act 1876 (which is normally used in relation to the smuggling of non-excisable goods), the Customs Act 1956 and the Customs and Excise (Miscellaneous Provisions) Act 1988. In brief, the Customs Consolidation Act 1876 contains the primary enforcement legislation for dealing with customs offences arising from the importation into Ireland from a third country or, in the case of goods subject to restriction or prohibition, from any country.

15.39 Section 186 of the Customs Consolidation Act 1876 provides that a person shall not:

- import, bring in, or be concerned in the importing/bringing in to Ireland of goods contrary to prohibitions or restrictions or on which duties have not been paid or secured;
- be knowingly concerned with the importing, bringing in, harbouring, or concealing of prohibited, restricted, or uncustomed goods;
- be knowingly concerned in dealing with any such goods.

15.40 The Customs Act 1956 contains the primary enforcement legislation relating to exportation. Section 3 of the Customs Act 1956 sets out the offences in relation to the exportation of any goods in contravention of any enactment or statutory instrument.

15.41 The Finance Act 2001[28] deals with the smuggling of excisable products such as cigarettes and alcohol and such matters are outside the scope of this Chapter.

---

[26] Council Reg (EC) No 1493/99 of 17 May 1999 (OJ L 179, 14.7.1999) brings together a number of earlier Regulations in relation to the protection of wine names and covers the protection of geographical indications and 'traditional terms' and Council Reg (EC) No 1576/89 sets out similar provisions for the protection of spirit names.   [27] Consumer Information Act 1978.
[28] Finance Act 2001, ss 119 and 140–143.

(4) Moulds and matrices

Article 1(3) of the Regulation provides that any mould or matrix which is specifically designed or adapted for the manufacture of goods infringing an intellectual property right shall be treated as goods of that kind if the use of such moulds or matrices infringes the right-holder's rights under Community law or the law of the Member State. **15.42**

There are specific references to moulds and matrices in Ireland's national intellectual property legislation, in particular, the CRRA 2000 and the IDA 2001. However, it must be borne in mind that the majority of equipment used to produce counterfeit and pirated goods also has other legitimate uses. Article 1(3) is restricted to equipment 'specifically designed or adapted for the manufacture of goods infringing an intellectual property right'. **15.43**

Section 20 of the TMA 1996 provides for the delivery up of, inter alia, 'infringing articles' in relation to a registered trade mark which means articles which are specifically designed or adapted for making copies of a sign identical or similar to the registered trade mark and which are in the possession, custody, or control of a person who knows or has reason to believe that they have been or are used to produce infringing goods or material. **15.44**

It appears that the PA 1992 does not contain specific references to moulds and matrices. However, section 41 of the PA 1992 could be of assistance in that it sets out the provisions in relation to the prevention of the indirect use of the invention. Section 41 provides that the proprietor of a patent has the right to prevent all third parties not having his consent from supplying or offering to supply in Ireland, a person, other than a person entitled to exploit the patented invention, with means, relating to an essential element of that invention for putting into effect therein, when the third party knows or it is obvious in the circumstances to a reasonable person that the said means are suitable and intended for putting that invention into effect. **15.45**

Section 140(3)(d) of the CRRA 2000 provides that it is an infringement of the copyright in a work to have in one's possession, custody, or control an article specifically designed or adapted for making copies of a work without the licence of the copyright owner, knowing or having reason to believe that it has been or is to be used to make infringing copies. **15.46**

Section 53 of the IDA 2001 provides that a person infringes a design right where he, without the licence of the registered proprietor of the design, has in his possession, custody, or control an article specifically designed or adapted for applying to or incorporating in a product the design, knowing or having reason to believe **15.47** that it has or is to be used to make infringing products. A product is an 'infringing product' in relation to a registered design where:

- the application of the design to or the incorporation of the design in the product is an infringement of the design right in the design;
- the product has been or is proposed to be imported into Ireland and the application of the design to or incorporation of the design in the product in Ireland would constitute an infringement of the design right in the design; or
- the use of the product in any other way infringes the design right.[29]

C. Goods excluded by the Regulation

(1) Parallel imported goods

15.48 The Regulation does not apply to genuine parallel goods imported into Ireland. Where the importation of goods give rise to a breach of the Regulation then action will be taken by Irish Customs in accordance with the offence committed. Irish Customs are not entitled to take border measures against genuine parallel goods under Irish domestic law. Irish Customs will not inform the right-holder of the importation of such goods.

(2) Goods which have been manufactured under conditions other than those which have been agreed with the right-holder

15.49 In Ireland, Irish Customs do not inform the right-holder if they detect goods which do not comply with the terms of a licence agreement nor will they take action against such goods.

(3) Goods contained in travellers' personal baggage

15.50 Travellers' personal baggage is controlled by Irish Customs. The legislation governing the control of baggage of persons arriving in or departing the EU is contained in Article 41 of Council Regulation (EEC) No 2913/92 (The Community Customs Code) and Articles 190 to 197, 225, 226 and 230 to 234 of Commission Regulation (EEC) No 2454/93 (Customs Code implementing Provisions). The duty free allowance applies to travellers coming into any EU country from third countries. There exist set duty free allowances for tobacco products, alcoholic drinks, perfumes and other goods including beer, gifts, and souvenirs. Irish

---

[29] Industrial Designs Act 2001, s 54.

Customs take into account the purchase value of the imported goods and the non-commercial nature is decided by means of the value and quantity thereof.

II. APPLICATION FOR ACTION BY THE CUSTOMS AUTHORITIES

In 2002, the number of *ex officio* actions taken by Irish Customs amounted to 11 whereas 281 actions were taken on the basis of an application for action by a right-holder.[30] The small number of *ex officio* actions in Ireland is rather alarming and such figures emphasize the need for right-holders to be ever vigilant and lodge applications for action. In 2003, the figures were nine and 338 respectively.[31]

15.51

We now propose to examine the *ex officio* action in section A and the processing of an application for customs action in section B below.

15.52

A. Measures prior to an application for action by the customs authorities ('*ex officio* measures')

Irish Customs act in accordance with the provisions laid down under Article 4 of the Regulation which provides that where the customs authorities, in the course of action in one of the situations referred to in Article 1(1) and before an application has been lodged by a right-holder or granted, have sufficient grounds for suspecting that goods infringe an intellectual property right, they may suspend the release of the goods or detain them for a period of three working days from the moment of receipt of the notification by the right-holder and by the declarant or holder of the goods, if the latter is known, in order to enable the right-holder to submit an application for action in accordance with Article 5.

15.53

Irish Customs, if they have sufficient grounds for suspecting that the goods infringe an intellectual property right, make use of their *ex officio* powers granted under Article 4 of the Regulation. However, the number of *ex officio* actions in Ireland in 2002 and 2003 were 11 and 9 respectively. As stated above, these figures are alarming and greater use must be made of these powers. However, it

15.54

---

[30] European Commission (DG Taxation and Customs Union (TAXUD), Breakdown by Member State and by type of procedure resulting in customs action 2002 (http://europa.eu.int/comm/taxation_customs/customs/ counterfeit_piracy/index_en.htm).

[31] European Commission (DG Taxation and Customs Union (TAXUD), Breakdown by Member State and by type of procedure resulting in customs action 2003 (http://europa.eu.int/comm/taxation_customs/customs/ counterfeit_piracy/index_en.htm).

appears that *ex officio* powers are used as the exception rather than the rule. In the meantime, right-holders need to lodge applications for action if their intellectual property rights are to be protected.

15.55   Irish Customs are aided, in particular, by Article 4(2) of the Regulation which provides that customs may, without divulging any information other than the actual or supposed number of items and their nature and before informing the right-holder of the possible infringement, ask the right-holder to provide them with any information they may need to confirm their suspicions. Contact with the right-holder is made by whatever means open to Irish Customs, including telephonic and electronic means, in order to request information from the right-holder as quickly as possible. Inevitably, the right-holder then requests the opportunity to inspect the goods. However, the right-holder may only inspect the goods under Article 9 of the Regulation after having filed an application for action and that application has been granted. In *ex officio* actions, Irish Customs may only inform the right-holder of the nature and quantity of the goods intercepted. In the event that the right-holder requests more information or wishes to inspect the goods, the right-holder must secure the grant of the application for action.

15.56   As stated above, Article 4 of the Regulation permits Irish Customs to act of their own violation 'in circumstances where they have sufficient grounds' to suggest that goods infringe an intellectual property right within the terms of Article 2(1) of the Regulation (*ex officio* actions). Article 4 also applies to situations where an application for action under Article 5 has been filed but has not yet been granted. The right-holder is notified of the detention of the goods and invited to make an application under Article 5. The declarant or holder of the goods is also notified. Inevitably, the right-holder must make an application (known as a Post Importation Application) if he wishes Irish Customs to take action as the period of detention or suspension is limited to three days in the framework of *ex officio* actions. In the absence of an application, Irish Customs are obliged to release the goods. Certain right-holders may have already lodged an application with Irish Customs. This is known as a Pre-Importation Application and lasts for a period of 12 months.

15.57   Whilst one may well argue that Article 4 of the Regulation facilitates a fishing expedition by Irish Customs and other customs authorities throughout the European Community, it is most certainly a necessary evil as Article 4 is an invaluable tool in the customs authority's arsenal in the fight against infringing goods under the Regulation. The increasing importance of intellectual property to commercial entities mandates the existence of such powers. As always, however, the availability of sufficient resources is of paramount importance as there is little point in giving rights to the customs authorities only to be defeated by the lack of personnel in enforcing such rights. Irish Customs avail themselves of all procedures open to them under the Regulation. No official pronouncements have been made in respect of 'risk analysis' or interpretation of Article 4. Indeed Irish Customs would be careful not to engage in such formal and written interpretations as such interpretation falls with the ambit of the Irish courts or the European Court of Justice. Furthermore, Irish Customs may be wary of disclosing 'trade secrets' as it were as to the form of 'risk analysis' it engages in order to seize counterfeit and pirated goods. However, it is difficult to see how Irish Customs would differ from other customs authorities and they most probably have their own list of 'high risk countries' and keep a close eye on the completeness or otherwise of documentation in order to detect suspect goods.

15.58 Article 4 provides that where customs authorities have sufficient grounds for suspecting that goods infringe an intellectual property right, 'they may suspend the release of the goods or detain then for a period of three working days from the moment of receipt of the notification by the right-holder and by the declarant or holder of the goods, if the latter are known, in order to enable the right-holder to submit an application for action in accordance with Article 5'. Article 5 of the Implementing Regulation further provides that the time limit of three working days shall only start running from the time the right-holder is notified. In the event that an application for action is lodged by the right-holder before the expiry of the three working days time limit, the time limits referred to in Articles 11 and 13 of the Regulation shall be counted only from the day after the application is received. Irish Customs are not flexible in their application of the three-day rule, as any such flexibility would invite a legal challenge from a party who was adversely affected by the decision to extend the three-day period.

B. The lodging and processing of applications for customs action

15.59 In 2002, 281 applications for action were filed with Irish Customs. When this figure is compared with the number of *ex officio* actions of 11, it is evident that Irish Customs are much more active in taking action on the basis of a granted application for action.[32] In 2003, the figures were similar with 338 applications for action and nine *ex officio* applications.[33]

---

[32] European Commission (DG Taxation and Customs Union (TAXUD), Breakdown by Member State and by type of procedure resulting in customs action 2002 (http://europa.eu.int/comm/taxation_customs/customs/ counterfeit_piracy/index_en.htm).

[33] European Commission (DG Taxation and Customs Union (TAXUD), Breakdown by Member State and by type of procedure resulting in customs action 2003 (http://europa.eu.int/comm/taxation_customs/customs/ counterfeit_piracy/index_en.htm).

(1) Persons entitled to file an application for action

Definition of 'right-holders' under the Regulation

15.60 In Ireland, an application for action can be filed by a right-holder within the meaning of Article 2(2) of the Regulation, which includes not only the owner of the intellectual property right concerned but also 'any other person authorized to use this right or a representative of the right-holder or authorized user'. Any other person authorized under Article 2(2)(b) is a person who must provide documentary proof from the right-holder that the person is authorized to use the right in question.

15.61 According to Irish Customs, exclusive licensees, non-exclusive licensees, distributors, commercial agents, etc may be authorized to file an application for action provided that they:

- are right-holders' representatives; or
- are authorized to use the right; or
- are representatives of an authorized user.

15.62 Documentary proof of authorization to use any right is required by Irish Customs. Proof of registration of this authorization is not required. Irish Customs will not normally verify whether the authorized user is entitled under the contract with the right-holder to represent him but will require evidence.

15.63 In Ireland, the position in respect of Article 2(2)(b) of the Regulation which deals with authorized users is not exactly clear-cut. In order to explain the situation more clearly it is necessary to look at Ireland's national intellectual property laws in order to ascertain the national position in relation to licences and the recording thereof.

15.64 Section 84 of the PA 1992 provides that details of, inter alia, all licences must be entered in the Register of Patents. Pursuant to section 85 of the PA 1992, where a person becomes entitled by licence to an interest in a published patent application or a patent, he must apply to the Controller of Patents ('the Controller') for registration of his interest in the Register of Patents. An application for registration may also be made by the licensor. When the Controller is satisfied as to title, he will register the interest of the licensee. It is important for a licensee to ensure that his interest is entered in the Register of Patents as a document in respect of which no entry has been made may only be admitted in court as evidence of the title of any person to a patent application or a registered patent if the court so directs.[34]

15.65 In relation to trade marks, it should be noted that the grant of a licence of a registered trade mark is a registerable transaction.[35] Until an application is made for

---

[34] Patents Act 1992, s 85(7).   [35] Trade Marks Act 1996, s 29.

the registration of the prescribed particulars of a registerable transaction, the transaction is ineffective as against a person acquiring a conflicting interest in or under the registered trade mark in ignorance of it and a person claiming to be a licensee by virtue of the transaction will not have the protection of section 34 of the TMA 1996 (which deals with the rights of licensees in infringement proceedings) and section 35 of the TMA 1996 (which deals with rights of an exclusive licensee). Unless an application for registration of the prescribed particulars of the transaction is made before the end of the period of six months beginning with the date of the transaction or the court is satisfied that it was not practicable for such an application to be made before the end of that period and that an application was made as soon as practicable thereafter, that person will not be entitled to damages or an account of profits in respect of any infringement of the registered trade mark occurring after the date of the transaction and before application for registration is made. In addition, a licensee who neglects to register a licence agreement runs the risk of a later assignee, mortgagee, or licensee, who is ignorant of the earlier transaction, securing priority through earlier registration.

Section 78 of the IDA 2001 sets out the provisions in respect of the recording of **15.66** licences. It provides that until an application has been made for registration of a licence, the transaction shall be ineffective as against a person acquiring a conflicting interest in or under the registered design in ignorance of it and, more importantly, a person claiming to be a licensee by virtue of the transaction shall not be entitled to the rights and remedies conferred by section 63 (which deals with rights and remedies of exclusive licensees) of the IDA 2001 and section 65 (which deals with rights and remedies of licensees).

Unlike patents, trade marks, and designs, no system exists for the registration of **15.67** copyright. However, copyright is transmissible by assignment, by testamentary disposition, or by operation of law as personal or moveable property.[36] There is therefore nothing to prevent copyright being licensed. A licence granted by a copyright owner is binding on every successor in title to his interest in the copyright, except a purchaser in good faith for valuable consideration and without notice (actual or constructive) of the licence or a person deriving title from such a purchaser.[37]

Therefore, in Ireland, in respect of patents, it is necessary to record with the **15.68** Controller the licence before taking any action before an Irish court, unless the court directs otherwise. In the case of trade marks, damages or an account of profits will not be awarded by a court in respect of any infringement occurring after the date of the transaction and before application for registration is made.

---

[36] Copyright and Related Rights Act 2000, s 120(1).
[37] Copyright and Related Rights Act 2000, s 120(4).

Furthermore the right of a licensee to take action is severely hampered by non-recording of the licence, particularly in the case of designs and trade marks. Nevertheless, as stated above, proof of registration is not required by Irish Customs.

15.69   In respect of representation within the meaning of Article 2(2)(b) of Regulation, natural persons or companies can act as representatives of the right-holder. A representative can be an attorney, intellectual property right agents, consultants, or collective management societies.

Proof of entitlement to file an application for action

For right-holders stricto sensu

15.70   In accordance with the Implementing Regulation, Irish Customs require the following documentation from the right-holder to prove his intellectual property right. In the case of a right that is registered, proof of registration with the Patents Office must be provided. For protected designations of origin and protected geographical indications, proof shall consist of two mandatory elements: proof that the person concerned is the producer or group and proof that the designation or indication has been registered.

15.71   In the case of a right that is not subject to registration (such as a copyright) or for which an application has not been lodged (such as an unregistered design), any evidence of authorship or of the applicant's status as original holder will suffice. As stated above in paragraph 15.15, it is open to question whether Irish Customs are willing to take border measures on the basis of trade mark and design applications.

15.72   A copy of a registration from the database of a national or international office may be deemed proof of registration but not if it is from a private database.

For persons authorized to use the right

15.73   In accordance with the provisions of Article 2(2)(b) of the Regulation, the onus is on the persons authorized to use the right to provide documentary proof of this authorization such as the licence agreement. In contrast, as pointed out above, Irish Customs will, in principle, not verify whether these persons are so entitled under an agreement to represent the right-holder, nor will they request proof of registration of the agreement (where relevant).

For representatives

15.74   The representatives of the right-holder or of 'other persons authorized to use the right' will have to provide to Irish Customs documentary proof of the represent-atives' authorization to represent and of the authorization to use the right.

The authorization may be submitted in original, electronic, facsimile, or other copy form. It is not possible to give a general power and specific documents are required in each case.

In Ireland, no nationality requirements exist in this area and foreign represent- **15.75** atives are authorized to appear before Irish Customs in respect of national and Community applications for actions. However, all communications must be in English, or alternatively in one of the other official languages of the European Union, in which case an English translation must be provided.

In relation to any special requirements concerning the entitlement to sign the **15.76** declaration referred to in Article 6 of the Regulation, Irish Customs have informed us that no special requirements exist. However, Article 2(3) of the Implementing Regulation provides that the undertaking under Article 6 must be signed by the right-holder unless the representative can produce a document authorizing the representative to bear any costs arising from customs action.

(2) Competent customs department and formal requirements

Competent customs department

In Ireland, the competent authority designated to process applications for action **15.77** is the Customs Branch of the Office of the Revenue Commissioners whose details are as follows:

Office of the Revenue Commissioners
Customs Branch
Unit 2
Government Offices
Nenagh
Co Tipperary
Tel.: (353 67 63238)
Fax: (353 67 32381)
e-mail: tariff@revenue.ie
Internet: www.revenue.ie

Form of the application for action

The 2005 Regulations provide that 'an application, in either written or electronic **15.78** form, to the Revenue Commissioners by a right-holder for action in respect of goods suspected of infringing property rights shall be in accordance with Articles 5 and 6 of the Council Regulation'. Therefore, Irish Customs will accept an original, faxed, or e-mailed application. In Ireland, applicants are increasingly encouraged to submit their application electronically. An electronic version of the application will be made available on the website referred to above in the near future. However, it must be noted that an original version of the declaration under Article 6 of the Regulation must be provided.

15.79 In accordance with Article 3(3) of the Implementing Regulation, two copies of the application must be submitted.

Language requirements

15.80 In terms of language requirements, the application must be in one of the official languages of the EU and a translation provided when the application is in a language other than English. Whilst Irish is the first official language of the 26 counties comprised in the Irish Republic under the Irish Constitution, the English language prevails as the working language of the island and is widely spoken and effectively treated as a first language. Therefore, at national level, the majority of applications for action, exhibits submitted with the application and the necessary declaration under Article 6 are submitted in English. Applications for action, exhibits and the Article 6 declaration can also be submitted in any other of the official languages of the EU provided that the documentation is accompanied by a translation. It is difficult to see how national applications could create difficulties with Irish Customs considering that all supporting documentation would be in English for example, all documentation issued from the Irish Patents Office is in English. However, Community applications in a language other than English are required to be translated.

(3) Requirements regarding the contents of the application for action

15.81 The Regulation distinguishes between mandatory information, optional information, and additional information specific to certain intellectual property rights.

Mandatory information

15.82 There is no national legislation to extend the scope of Article 5(5) of the Regulation. In general, the technical description of the goods must be detailed enough for customs to be able to identify the goods in question together with any information that would be considered beneficial to customs in assisting to identify the goods in question. In addition, a local contact person is not necessarily required. However, both administrative and technical contacts should be easily contactable and therefore it would be advisable to instruct a solicitor, patent/trade mark agent, consultant, or collective management society in this jurisdiction. As stated above, no nationality requirements exist.

Optional information

In relation to optional information, no specific requirements exist although the **15.83**
right-holder should provide all information set out as optional under Article 5(5)
in order to facilitate the work of Irish Customs.

Additional information specific to the type of intellectual property right referred to in the application

Whilst no specific requirements exist, it is nevertheless important to give Irish **15.84**
Customs as much information as possible to deal with the specific rights protected
where patents, SPCs, plant variety rights, and geographic indications are involved.
As is the case with most applications, each individual case is considered on its
merit. Nonetheless, we are instructed by Irish Customs that, to date, there have
been no instances where Irish Customs have requested additional details under
Article 5(6) of the Regulation.

(4) *Processing and acceptance of the application for action*

Irish Customs will process the application for action within the prescribed term of **15.85**
30 working days and will contact the right-holder should any issue arise.

In the event that the application for action is refused, the right-holder can appeal **15.86**
in writing to the Irish Revenue Commissioners. This appeal will then be forwarded up the line within the Irish Revenue Commissioners and will be examined
by an impartial person. It is unfortunate that this procedure was not more clearly
defined in the 2005 Regulations.

In relation to duration of action, Irish Customs take action for a period of one **15.87**
year. The right-holder may not determine what the period is.

(5) *'Community' applications for action*

Processing of 'Community' applications for action filed with Irish Customs

In Ireland, there are no national guidelines on the processing of Community **15.88**
applications.

Processing of 'Community' applications designating Ireland

Irish Customs accept and process all applications that have been filed in other **15.89**
Member States and extended to Ireland.

III. CONDITIONS GOVERNING ACTION BY CUSTOMS AUTHORITIES AND BY THE AUTHORITIES COMPETENT TO DETERMINE WHETHER GOODS INFRINGE AN INTELLECTUAL PROPERTY RIGHT

15.90 Once an application for action has been declared admissible by Irish Customs, the latter will monitor the traffic of goods suspected of infringing the intellectual property rights referred to in the application at the borders. We will examine below the conditions governing action by the Irish Customs and the simplified procedure. Subsequent to the interception by Irish Customs of goods suspected of infringing an intellectual property right, the right-holder is, in principle, compelled to refer the case to the authorities having jurisdiction to determine that these goods do indeed infringe an intellectual property right. We will also briefly look at security for the release of the goods and storage.

A. Conditions governing action by customs authorities

(1) Factual background

15.91 According to statistics, counterfeit and pirated goods made their way into Ireland in 2002 through airports (42 per cent), sea (1 per cent) and post (57 per cent).[38] In 2003, the figures were airports (20 per cent), sea (2 per cent) and post (78 per cent).[39] Irish Customs are careful not to detail which ports experience the most traffic. However, Rosslare Harbour encounters a lot of activity which is not reflected in the figure of 1 per cent from 2002 or 2 per cent from 2003. The national postal service (An Post) main sorting office would also encounter a lot of traffic of counterfeit and pirated goods and other goods infringing intellectual property rights.

---

[38] European Commission (DG Taxation and Customs Union (TAXUD), Breakdown by means of transport used for the cases examined by Customs administration of the EU—2002 (http://europa.eu.int/comm/taxation_customs/customs/ counterfeit_piracy/index_en.htm).

[39] European Commission (DG Taxation and Customs Union (TAXUD), Breakdown by means of transport used for the cases examined by Customs administration of the EU—2003 (http://europa.eu.int/comm/taxation_customs/customs/ counterfeit_piracy/index_en.htm).

(2) Notification of customs intervention

In accordance with the provisions of Article 1(1) of the Regulation, Irish Customs **15.92** will detain or suspend the release of goods suspected of infringing an intellectual property right within the meaning of Article 2(1) of the Regulation.[40]

In circumstances where the right-holder's application for action has been accepted **15.93** under Article 5, Irish Customs will then follow the procedure laid down in Article 9 of the Regulation. Irish Customs must then not only inform the right-holder but must also notify the declarant (within the meaning of Article 4(18) of the Community Customs Code[41]) or holder of the goods (within the meaning of Article 38 of same) of the interception of the goods.

Irish Customs will usually notify the relevant parties by fax. It is hoped that elec- **15.94** tronic communication methods will soon be introduced and the Irish Revenue Commissioners have been very proactive in their use of information technology in all areas of their work.

(3) Information to be provided by customs to the right-holder before the latter confirms the infringing nature of the goods

Articles 4(2), 9(2), and 9(3), of the Regulation sets out the parameters of the informa- **15.95** tion that may be provided by customs to right-holders. Article 4(2) governs the extent of disclosure permissible prior to an application for action and is limited to informing the right-holder of the actual or supposed number and nature of the goods. Article 4 allows customs to seek further information from the right-holder to confirm their suspicions. However, the right-holder must not be informed of the possible infringement.

Articles 9(2) and 9(3) allow the disclosure of more extensive information to the right-holder after the application for action has been accepted. Irish Customs are therefore obliged, if the right-holder so requests, to inform the right-holder of details (if known) relating to the names and addresses of the consignee, the consignor, the declarant, or holder of the goods and the origin and provenance of goods suspected of infringing an intellectual property right. The provisions in relation to disclosure are, however, dependent on national provisions relating to the protection of personal data, commercial and industrial secrecy, and professional and administrative confidentiality. Such provisions could include legislation pertaining to data protection[42] or official secrets.[43] However, Irish Customs

---

[40] Customs and Excise (Miscellaneous Provisions) Act 1988, s 7(1).
[41] Council Regulation (EEC) 2913/92 of 12 October 1992 establishing the Community Customs Code [1992] OJ L 302/1 (19.10.1992).   [42] Data Protection Acts, 1988 to 2003.
[43] Official Secrets Act, 1963.

have not encountered much resistance in these areas. One could imagine that a declarant could seek court protection to prevent disclosure by Irish Customs of goods subject to patent protection. However, it would be up to the declarant to seek court protection in any scenario whereby he sought the non-disclosure of information by Irish Customs.

(4) Inspection of the suspected goods

15.96 Once an application for action has been accepted, Article 9(3) provides that the applicant (right-holder) and any person known to be involved in the import or export of the goods are entitled to inspect the goods whose release has been suspended or which have been detained. At the right-holder's request, Irish Customs, in accordance with their obligations under Article 9(4), would facilitate the inspection of the goods by sending the right-holder a sample of the goods in question. All samples must, however, be returned on completion of the analysis and before the goods are released or their detention has ended. In the event that the right-holder requires the sample of goods for court proceedings, it would be necessary to call an official of Irish Customs as a witness who would also bring the sample of goods in question.

15.97 The right-holder must then confirm in writing whether the goods detained actually infringe its intellectual property rights. In the event that Irish Customs are satisfied that the goods infringe an intellectual property right protected by the Regulation, they will then seize the goods by means of a 'Notice of Seizure'.[44] A Notice of Seizure should in all cases be given to the owner, suspected owner, or to the person in whose control the goods lie. The notice must specify clearly the goods to which it relates and the grounds upon which they have been seized.

B. Simplified procedure allowing the destruction of the goods without there being any need to determine whether an intellectual property right has been infringed under national law

15.98 The simplified procedure envisaged by Article 11 of the Regulation has not yet been implemented in Ireland and the 2005 Regulations contain no measures in relation to the simplified procedure. However, as discussed below, Ireland has, in fact, for the past few years operated a form of simplified procedure.

15.99 It should be noted as an aside that no provisions exist under Irish law for the recognition of amicable settlements between the relevant parties.

---

[44] Customs Consolidation Act 1876, s 202.

In Ireland, the decision to seize the goods is taken by Irish Customs. In the event **15.100** that seizure is uncontested, the goods will be destroyed without there being any need to determine whether an intellectual property right has been infringed. Whilst, this procedure is beneficial to the right-holder in that the infringing goods are destroyed, the procedure is not fully compliant with the parameters of Article 11 in that no provision is made for the written agreement of the declarant, the holder, or owner of the goods to abandon the goods for destruction. The declarant, the holder, or owner of the goods must lodge a claim (known as a valid claim) if seizure is contested. If no valid claim is lodged, the silence of the declarant, holder, or owner of the goods is taken as a form of consent. Unfortunately, the 2005 Regulations have made no attempt to clarify the situation in Ireland in relation to Article 11. If seizure is contested and a valid claim entered by the holder of the goods, condemnation proceedings must be instituted before the Irish courts. Condemnation proceedings are proceedings whereby the Irish courts determine whether the goods infringe an intellectual property right in accordance with the parameters of the Regulation. If no valid claim is received within the statutory period of one month,[45] the goods are automatically deemed to have been condemned as forfeited. In Ireland, in instances where the seizure is contested and a valid claim lodged, the claim is inevitably withdrawn or not followed up by the holder of the goods. Before destruction takes place, the right-holder will be informed and Irish Customs will liaise with the right-holder to determine the most appropriate method and means of destruction. In normal circumstances, the right-holder bears the costs of destruction.

C. Conditions governing action by the authorities having jurisdiction to determine whether the goods infringe an intellectual property right

(1) Authorities having jurisdiction to determine whether the goods infringe an intellectual property right

Under Article 13(1) of the Regulation, in order to secure border measures taken **15.101** by the customs authorities, right-holders must notify the customs office referred to in Article 9(1) of the Regulation within 10 (which may be extended up to 20) working days of receipt of the notification of suspension of release or detention of the goods, that proceedings have been initiated to determine whether an intellectual property right has been infringed under national law. As stated above, this may not be necessary in the event that a valid claim has not been entered by the

---

[45] Customs and Excise (Miscellaneous Provisions) Act 1988, s 7(3).

declarant, holder and/or owner of the goods as in those cases the goods are automatically deemed to have been condemned as forfeited.

The regime of EC Regulation 3295/94

15.102   The 1994 Regulation set out broad provisions for determining whether goods were counterfeit or pirated. In Ireland, section 5 of the 1996 Regulations (which implemented the 1994 Regulation) provided that the Revenue Commissioners may supply the applicant with, or request the applicant to examine, a sample of goods taken from a consignment entered for free circulation, export, re-export, or for a suspensive procedure which appears to them to correspond to the description of goods contained in an application granted under Article 3(5) of the 1994 Regulation and which, in the case of counterfeit goods, appears to bear a trade mark identical to or substantially indistinguishable from the registered trade mark mentioned in the application and the applicant must, within 24 hours of being requested by the Revenue Commissioners (or within such further time as they may allow), confirm to them in writing whether or not in his opinion the sample is counterfeit or pirated, giving his reasons, by reference to characteristics of the sample or its packaging or otherwise. Pursuant to the 2005 Regulations counterfeit or pirated goods prohibited from being released for free circulation, exported, re-exported or entered for a suspensive procedure are deemed to be so prohibited for the purposes of the Customs Consolidation Act 1876,[46] the Customs Act 1956[47] and the Customs and Excise (Miscellaneous Provisions) Act 1988.[48]

15.103   Article 7 of the 1994 Regulation envisaged that in situations where goods are initially detained by customs because they correspond to the description of the goods contained in the decision under Article 3, the matter is then referred to an 'authority competent to take a substantive decision' to determine whether the goods so detained are in fact counterfeit or pirated. In Ireland, as discussed above, if Irish Customs are satisfied that the goods are counterfeit or pirated, it will not release the goods and treat them as prohibited goods within the meaning of the Regulation. If such actions of Irish Customs are contested by the owner of the seized goods as set out above, Irish Customs are then bound to institute condemnation proceedings.

The regime of the new Regulation

15.104   In Ireland, the position under the new Regulation will not alter substantially and it is always open to the right-holder to refer the matter to the Irish courts.

---

[46]   Customs Consolidation Act 1876, ss 42, 178, 202, 207 and 208.
[47]   Customs Act 1956, ss 3 and 5.
[48]   Customs and Excise (Miscellaneous Provisions) Act 1988, ss 6, 7, and 9.

Remedies common to all intellectual property rights covered by the new Regulation

As set out above, Irish Customs will, following the entry of a valid claim, institute **15.105** condemnation proceedings. However, we propose to set out hereunder the other remedies available to the right-holder under Irish law. The actions of Irish Customs are without prejudice to the right-holder's right to commence proceedings before the Irish courts himself, for example, to claim damages or to seek to obtain an injunction. However, it should be borne in mind that it is a rather expensive process in order to initiate proceedings in order to claim damages, therefore whether the right-holder takes action himself is likely to be influenced by the quantity of the counterfeit goods.

In Ireland, both civil proceedings and criminal prosecutions may be taken in **15.106** relation to goods infringing an intellectual property right. However, the civil law/criminal law dichotomy in Irish law must be borne in mind. Consequently, the decision to take a criminal prosecution is a matter for adjudication by an independent officer—the Director of Public Prosecutions ('DPP'). Irish Customs will send a file to the DPP in order for the DPP to decide whether to prosecute. In Ireland, there has been only one successful case taken by the DPP under the 1996 Regulations (*DPP v McCarthy*[49]) which was a case decided in the Irish District Court. The case was decided under section 10 of the 1996 Regulations.[50]

In respect of civil proceedings, a *quia timet* or interlocutory injunction is usually **15.107** the remedy sought when there is an infringement of intellectual property rights. It is an equitable remedy granted at the courts discretion. On application, which may be *ex parte* or on notice, the plaintiff will be required to give an undertaking as to damages to the court so that in the event that the plaintiff is not successful at the full hearing of the action, he will be obliged to pay to the defendant damages for the loss the defendant sustained. To obtain an interlocutory injunction, the plaintiff must show that there is a fair question to be tried, that the balance of convenience lies in favour of granting the injunction and that damages would not be an adequate remedy.[51] A perpetual injunction is considered at the close of the actual hearing on the merits of the dispute between the parties.

Anton Piller orders are a tool often used by right-holders in the fight against counter- **15.108** feiters. Anton Piller orders are available in circumstances where it is important to ensure that evidence in the defendant's possession is not removed or destroyed

---

[49] *DPP v McCarthy*, Cork District Court, September 2004, still unreported.
[50] S 10 (1) of the 1996 Regulations provides 'Any person who makes a false declaration for the release for free circulation, for export or for re-export or for placing under a suspensive procedure, in respect of goods found to be counterfeit or pirated shall, without prejudice to any other penalty to which he may be liable, be guilty of an offence and shall be liable on summary conviction thereof to a fine not exceeding €1,270.'
[51] This test was adopted by the Irish courts in *Campus Oil v Minister for Industry and Energy (No1)* 1983 ILRM 258.

so as deliberately to deprive a plaintiff of evidence required to prove his case. Therefore, a court, in granting an Anton Piller order, effectively orders the detention, custody, or preservation of the goods which are the subject matter of an action, as well as the inspection of any goods which are in the possession of any of the parties to the action. Anton Piller orders are, however, only of assistance where Irish Customs have not taken action. To obtain an Anton Piller order, the plaintiff must establish:

- that there is a strong prima facie case for infringement;
- the actual or potential damage to him is very serious;
- the defendant has infringing articles or documents or incriminating documents in his possession; and
- there is a real possibility that these articles or documents will be destroyed and that an application will be made on notice to the defendant for an interlocutory injunction.

15.109 If a defendant refuses access to his premises the plaintiff will have to return to court and seek an order for contempt.

15.110 A Mareva injunction is also available whereby the defendant is restrained from disposing of moneys or moving the subject matter of the action out of the jurisdiction until trial or further order.

15.111 Of particular importance in cases of counterfeiting is the option of a *quia timet* injunction. This is available if there is a well-founded apprehension of injury namely proof of actual and real danger, a strong probability almost to a moral certainty. This is an injunction prohibiting the defendant from carrying out a threatened act in violation of the plaintiff's rights.

15.112 Ireland has recently introduced the option of proceeding through the Commercial Court instead of the normal courts. New Commercial Court rules define the type of commercial proceedings that can be brought before this court. While, in general, all proceedings (other than personal injuries proceedings) where the value of the claim or counterclaim is not less than EUR 1,000,000 are eligible to be admitted to the Commercial Court, of particular interest is that the definition of commercial proceedings includes proceedings for remedies in respect of intellectual property rights whether under the various statutes governing patents, trade mark, copyright and related rights and industrial designs and also the common law remedy of passing off, regardless of the value of such claims. Matters proceeding though the Commercial Courts will move at a much faster pace than the normal courts which may be of great benefit to the right-holder.

Remedies specific to some intellectual property rights covered by the new Regulation

15.113 **Trade marks**   Perhaps the most effective remedies available in Irish law are those contained within sections 19, 20, 23, and 25 of the TMA 1996. Section 19 of the

TMA 1996 gives the Irish High Court the power to order an offending sign to be erased, removed, or obliterated from infringing goods, materials, or articles or, if this is not practical, for the goods, materials, or articles to be destroyed. Section 20 of the TMA 1996 permits a trade mark owner with a validly registered trade mark to apply to the Circuit Court or to the High Court for an order directing that infringing goods be delivered up to the trade mark proprietor or such other person as the court may direct. The goods must be in the possession, custody, or control of the person in the course of business or otherwise for the purpose of dealing in any way. The provision also relates to machinery specially adapted for making infringing goods as well as materials used for making the goods. Application must be made within six years of the date on which the trade mark was applied to the goods, their packaging or the material or in the case of articles the date on which they were made. However, no order will be made unless the court also makes, or it appears to the court that there are grounds for making, an order as to disposal of the infringing goods, materials, or articles. If such an order is not made the person to whom the goods, materials, or articles are delivered up to shall retain them pending the making of such an order or the decision not to make such an order.

15.114 When the goods are delivered up, the proprietor of the trade mark to whom the goods have been delivered has to return to the Circuit Court or High Court with the goods and prove to the court that the goods are, in fact, counterfeit and are infringing the registered trade mark. The Circuit Court or High Court may then make several possible orders. Section 23 gives the High Court and Circuit Court the power to order the destruction or forfeiture of goods, which have been seized under section 20. The court may order that the goods be dealt with in any manner that the court thinks fit. Provision may be made by Rules of Court as to the service of notice on anyone having an interest in the goods, materials, or articles and they shall be entitled to appear whether or not they have been served and to appeal against any order made whether or not they appeared. The order will not take effect until the notice period has expired or an appeal has been heard. If the court decides to make no order, the goods, materials, or articles must be returned to the person from whom they were taken.

15.115 In respect of the District Court, if a District Court is satisfied by evidence that there is reasonable grounds for believing that infringing goods, materials, or articles are in the possession, custody, or control of any person in the course of business or otherwise for the purpose of dealing in any way, the District Courts are given the power to authorize a member of the Garda Siochana (the Irish police force) to seize infringing goods, materials, or articles without warrant and bring them before the court.[52] Search warrants may also be granted to enter premises, if need be, by force.

---

[52] Trade Marks Act 1996, s 25.

15.116 On proof to the District Court that any goods, materials or articles brought before them are infringing goods, materials or articles, the court may order them to be delivered up to the proprietor of the registered trade mark concerned, or order them to be destroyed or forfeited to such person as the court thinks fit, or order them to be dealt with in such other way as the court thinks fit. The relevant District Court for the purpose of these provisions is the District Court for the district in which the goods, materials, or articles are for the time being.

15.117 There is a very real possibility of criminal prosecution for counterfeiting where the counterfeiting activity contravenes section 92 of the TMA 1996. Section 92 makes it an offence:

- to apply a mark identical to or nearly resembling a registered trade mark to goods or material used or intended to be used for labelling, packaging, or advertising goods;
- to sell, let for hire, offer or expose for sale or hire, or distribute goods bearing such a mark or material bearing such a mark;
- to use material bearing such a mark in the course of a business, for labelling, packaging or advertising goods;
- to possess in the course of a business, goods or materials bearing such a mark with a view to doing any of those things mentioned hereabove.

15.118 **Patents** The relief available for infringement of a patent (including SPCs) is set out in section 47 of the PA 1992, which provides that the following relief may be sought:

- an injunction to restrain further infringement;
- delivery of or destruction of infringing products;
- damages;
- account of profits; and
- a declaration of validity.

15.119 The damages awarded may be determined on the basis of the normal commercial royalty that would have been charged to the defendant had he obtained a licence under the patent. Alternatively, the damages may be based on the loss of profits having gone to the defendant instead of to the plaintiff.

15.120 **Copyright** In terms of remedies available to the copyright-holder, both civil and criminal remedies exist. An action for infringement of copyright may be commenced and heard in the District Court, Circuit Court, or High Court. Each court has a specific monetary jurisdiction. Damages up to EUR 6,348 may be obtained in the District Court and up to EUR 38,092 in the Circuit Court. The High Court has unlimited monetary jurisdiction. While proceedings in the District Court are relatively inexpensive, costs in the Circuit and High Court are progressively more expensive.

The copyright owner may also seek an injunction—either an interlocutory or **15.121** permanent injunction. The District Court may make an order for the seizure and confiscation of infringing articles if it is satisfied that there are reasonable grounds for believing that infringing copies of the work or articles or protection-defeating devices are being hawked, carried about, or marketed. The court may make an order authorizing the Garda Siochana (Irish police force) to seize the copies, articles or devices. The seized items will be brought before the District Court and if proven to be infringements of copyright, will be destroyed or delivered up to the copyright owner as the court thinks fit. There is also provision in section 133 of the CRRA 2000 for seizure of infringing articles and detention by the copyright owner where the articles are found to be hawked, carried about, or marketed and where it would be impracticable for the copyright owner to apply to the District Court.

Under sections 132 and 133 of the CRRA 2000, the copyright owner may apply **15.122** to the District Court for an order that infringing articles be seized and confiscated. The standard again is one of reasonable grounds, that is, the court must be satisfied that infringing copies of the work or articles are being hawked, carried about, or marketed. The court may make an order authorizing the Garda Siochana (Irish police force) to seize the copies, articles, or devices.[53] The seized items will be brought before the District Court and, if proven to be infringements of copyright, will be destroyed or delivered up to the copyright owner as the court thinks fit. The court will admit hearsay evidence to the extent that the witness or deponent believes that the infringing material may be found in a particular location and the witness or deponent cannot be obliged to furnish the source of his information.[54]

Other offences under the CRRA 2000 relate to possession of articles specifically **15.123** designed or adapted for making copies of a work knowing or having reason to believe that it has been or is to be used to make infringing copies. The circumvention of rights protection measures is also an offence.

The remedies available under the IDA 2001 are very similar to those offered under **15.124** the CRRA 2000. Section 57(3) of the IDA 2001 provides that in an action for the infringement of a design all relief by way of damages, injunction, account of profits, or otherwise is available to the plaintiff.

Section 21 of the Plant Varieties (Propriety Rights) (Amendment) Act 1998 pro- **15.125** vides that an infringement of plant breeder's rights shall be actionable at the suit of the holder and in any proceedings for such infringement all such relief, by way of damages, injunction, account or otherwise, as is available in any corresponding proceedings in respect of any other proprietary rights shall be available.

---

[53] Copyright and Related Rights Act 2000, s 132(1).
[54] Copyright and Related Rights Act 2000, s 132.

15.126 In respect of the remedies available under Council Regulation (EC) No 2081/92 of 14 July 1992 as amended by Council Regulation (EC) No 535/97 of 17 March 1997 on the protection of geographical indications and designations of origin for agricultural products and foodstuffs, the remedies are set out in the Statutory Instruments governing the implementation of the aforementioned Regulations namely European Communities (Protection of Geographical Indications and Designations of Origin for Agricultural Products and Foodstuffs) Regulations, 1995[55] and European Communities (Protection of Geographical Indications and Designations of Origin for Agricultural Products and Foodstuffs) (Amendment) Regulations, 1999.[56] Section 7 of the European Communities (Protection of Geographical Indications and Designations of Origin for Agricultural Products and Foodstuffs) Regulations, 1995 provides that a person guilty of an offence shall be liable on summary conviction to a fine not exceeding EUR 1,900 or imprisonment for a term not exceeding 12 months or both. Furthermore, where a person has been convicted of an offence, the District Court may order the forfeiture to the Minister of anything used for the purposes of committing such offence.

15.127 Mention should also be made of the remedy of passing off. Passing off is a remedy in tort and the essential elements in passing off have been summarized over the years in various cases as follows:

- a misrepresentation;
- made by a trader in the course of trade;
- to prospective customers of his or ultimate consumers of goods or services supplied by him;
- which is calculated to injure the business or goodwill of another trader (in the sense that it is a reasonably foreseeable consequence);
- which causes actual damage to a business or goodwill of a trader by whom the action is brought or (in a *quia timet* action) will probably do so.

15.128 To establish the tort of passing off it is necessary for the plaintiff to show that it has some goodwill or reputation. If it does so, the plaintiff can apply to the court for injunctive relief to prevent the sale and marketing of goods or services with a get-up so similar to the original goods or services that the public are likely to be deceived into believing that they are being produced by one and the same person. Passing off can be used in situations where the products were not counterfeit but are sufficiently similar to cause confusion in the minds of consumers. Furthermore, passing off is also of assistance in situations where the plaintiff does not have the protection of registration intellectual property and must instead rely on common law rights.

---

[55] Statutory Instrument No 148/1995.   [56] Statutory Instrument No 275/1999.

Irish intellectual property laws provide many remedies for infringements of its **15.129** rights. However, these remedies will only be necessary in the event that Irish Customs do not seize or release the goods. It is possible for the right-holder to commence proceedings before the Irish courts himself, for example, to claim damages or to seek to obtain an injunction. If counterfeit goods pass through Irish Customs undetected or are released, right-holders will then have to avail themselves of the remedies available under legislation. In such a case, right-holders would normally institute injunctive proceedings with a view to seeking an order for delivery up of the goods and to obtain the disclosure of all documentation available in order to trace the source of the goods. In counterfeiting cases, right-holders are frequently more interested in tracing the source of the goods. Depending on the circumstances of each particular case, a letter known as a 'cease and desist' letter may be sent to the holder of the goods before injunctive proceedings are issued requesting that the sale of the counterfeit goods be stopped and seeking the delivery up of the goods and the disclosure of all relevant information. Right-holders are often concerned that, following the receipt of a cease and desist letter, the goods and all relevant documentation will be destroyed and hence be unavailable for handover. On the other hand, a court may not grant an injunction or award damages where the right-holder has failed to send a cease and desist letter. Each case must be judged on its own merits and carefully considered.

(2) *Term for notifying customs that proceedings have been started*

Article 13 of the Regulation provides that the right-holder must inform the **15.130** customs authorities within 10 working days (or 3 working days in the case of perishable goods) that proceedings have been initiated. Except for perishable goods, this 10-day period may be extended by another maximum of 10 working days in appropriate cases. Irish Customs have offered no guidance on what an appropriate case would be. In the event that the right-holder fails to notify Irish Customs within the deadline, customs will be obliged to release the goods subject to the completion of customs formalities.

D. Release of goods suspected of infringing certain rights on provision of a security

In the event that the conditions of Article 14(1) of the Regulation are fulfilled, **15.131** Irish Customs will release the goods. However, such goods will not be released in the event that an Irish court has granted interim measures such as an interim injunction.

E. Storage of the goods and destruction process

15.132 Article 15 of the Regulation states that it is up to each Member State to determine the conditions of storage of goods detained but such storage costs shall not give rise to costs for customs administrations. Ireland has made no provisions in relation to Article 15 in the 2005 Regulations. Currently, all goods are stored in the State Warehouse at the State's expense.

IV. PROVISIONS APPLICABLE TO GOODS FOUND TO INFRINGE AN INTELLECTUAL PROPERTY RIGHT

15.133 Article 16 of the Regulation will govern the situation in relation to goods found to infringe an intellectual property right as a result of Article 13 proceedings and the direct effect of the Regulation will prevail over any inconsistencies in Irish national legislation.

15.134 In cases where goods are found to infringe an intellectual property right, the Irish courts will make orders that are in accordance with the Regulation in the event that the case is brought by Irish Customs in response to the filing of a valid claim. The 2005 Regulations provide that 'the Revenue Commissioners may take such measures as they consider necessary in respect of goods found to infringe an intellectual property right in accordance with Article 17 of the Council Regulation'. However, if it is the case that the right-holder brings a separate action, Irish courts will be bound by the provisions of Irish intellectual property legislation such as the TMA 1996, PA 1992, CRRA 2000, and the IDA 2001.

15.135 As stated above in paragraph 15.114, section 23 of the TMA 1996 gives the High Court and Circuit Court the power to order the destruction or forfeiture of goods, which have been seized under section 20. The court may order that the goods be dealt with in any manner that the court thinks fit. If the court decides to make no order, the goods, materials or articles must be returned to the person from whom they were taken. It is also within the courts power to award damages and/or an account of profits to the right-holder. Section 19 of the TMA 1996 gives the Irish High Court the power to order an offending sign to be erased, removed, or obliterated from infringing goods, materials, or articles or if this is not practical for the goods, materials, or articles to be destroyed. The fact that the trade mark has been removed from the goods effectively circumvents the economic gain of the counterfeiter. In respect of the remaining intellectual property rights, as set out above, similar provisions in terms of destruction, damages, and an account of profits are also provided for in the PA 1992, CRRA 2000, and the IDA 2001.

In terms of costs, it is open to the court to decide to award the costs in favour of **15.136** the right-holder. In Ireland, costs normally follow the event, however it does depend on the particular circumstances of the case.

V. PENALTIES

The 2005 Regulations sets out the offences and penalties applicable for a **15.137** contravention of the Regulation. It provides as follows:

- a person who gives, in an application for action, details which he knows are false or misleading is guilty of an offence;
- a person who makes a false declaration for the purposes of Article 9 of the Regulation is guilty of an offence;
- a person who contravenes Article 16 of the Regulation is guilty of an offence and a person who aids and abets him is also guilty of an offence; and
- where an offence under the 2005 Regulations is committed by a body corporate and is proved to have been so committed with the consent, connivance, or approval of, or to be attributable to any neglect on the part of a person being a director, manager, secretary, or other officer of the body corporate, or any other person who was acting or purporting to act in any such capacity, that person, as well as the body corporate is guilty of an offence and is liable to be proceeded against and punished as if he were guilty of the first mentioned offence.

The 2005 Regulations provide that a person guilty of an offence under the 2005 **15.138** Regulations is liable on summary conviction to a fine not exceeding EUR 5,000.

Various penalties also exist under the Customs Consolidation Act 1876. Penalties **15.139** for the illegal importation of goods under section 186 is EUR 1,900 on summary conviction and/or up to 12 months' imprisonment or EUR 12,695 on indictment or a fine of treble the duty paid value (whichever is the greater) and/or up to five years' imprisonment. Section 177 also provides for forfeiture.

We will now briefly examine the penalties under the TMA 1996, the CRRA 2000, **15.140** and the IDA 2001.

Under the TMA 1996, a person who contravenes section 92 is guilty of an offence **15.141** only if he acts with a view to gain for himself or another with the intent to cause a loss to another. It is a defence for a person to show that he believed on reasonable grounds that he was entitled to use the marks. The seriousness with which a breach of s 92 is treated is evidenced by the penalties in operation for breach of the section namely upon summary conviction, a fine of EUR 1,270 or six months' imprisonment and on conviction on indictment, a fine of EUR 127,000 and or five years' imprisonment.

15.142 Under section 4 of the Criminal Law Act 1997, an indictable offence under section 92 of the 1996 Act is an arrestable offence. This effectively means that a person may be arrested by An Garda Siochana (Irish Police Force) on suspicion that they have committed this offence.

15.143 Under the CRRA 2000, various penalties exist. In particular section 140(7) provides that a person guilty of an offence shall be liable on summary conviction, to a fine not exceeding EUR 1,905 in respect of each infringing copy, article, or device, or to imprisonment for a term not exceeding 12 months, or both, or on conviction on indictment, to a fine not exceeding EUR 127,000, or to imprisonment for a term not exceeding five years or both.

15.144 Sections 66 to 70 of the IDA 2001 deal with criminal offences. A person guilty of an offence is liable on summary conviction to a fine not exceeding EUR 1,905 in respect of each infringing product or article or to imprisonment for a term not exceeding 12 months or both or on conviction on indictment, to a fine not exceeding EUR 127,000 or to imprisonment for a term not exceeding five years, or both.

15.145 In conjunction with criminal remedies, civil remedies also exist as set out in paragraphs 15.105 to 15.125 above and for the most part comprise, inter alia, injunctive relief, damages, delivery up, and account of profits.

VI. LIABILITY OF CUSTOMS AUTHORITIES AND RIGHT-HOLDERS

A. Liability of right-holders and sanctions

15.146 Section 8 of the 1996 Regulations provided that an application for action shall have no effect, or where a decision to grant an application has already been made, that decision shall cease to have effect, without prejudice to the validity of anything already done where the applicant for action (that is, the right-holder) has failed to comply with any of the requirements of the 1996 Regulations or any change, following the making of the application, which takes place in the ownership or authorized use or in the registration of the right specified in the application, is not communicated in writing to Irish Customs. The 2004

Regulations contain no similar provisions. Therefore, as regards the position under the 1996 Regulations, should a right-holder not have complied with the Regulation, its rights of action were effectively removed. Although, the 2005 Regulations contain no similar provision, it is expected that the situation will remain the same. In terms of civil liability, Ireland is a common law jurisdiction and general tort law will govern all actions initiated by the holder of the goods against the right-holder. It will, of course, be necessary to prove, inter alia, that the right-holder was negligent in its actions resulting in damage.

There is no specific mention of mis-use of information in the 1996 Regulations as set out in Article 12 of the Regulation. The 2005 Regulations do not remedy that omission and do not take account of the provisions relating to the mis-use of information provided to the right-holder under the terms of Article 9(3) of the Regulation. However, as the Regulation has direct effect, consequently the application for action may be suspended or renewal of the application refused in certain circumstances. Separate civil proceedings could also be taken by an injured party. **15.147**

B. Liability of customs authorities and sanctions

(1) *Liability of Irish Customs in the framework of the application of the provisions of the Regulation*

Section 9(2) of the Customs & Excise (Miscellaneous Provisions) Act 1988 applies to any proceedings relating to any goods seized under the Customs Acts and brought against either the State, the Attorney General, the Revenue Commissioners, the Revenue Solicitor, and/or an officer of Customs and Excise. It provides that where any question arises as to the place from which any goods have been brought or as to compliance with any probation or restriction on the importation or exportation of goods or as to whether: **15.148**

- the goods were lawfully imported on payment or securement of duties payable thereon, or
- the goods were lawfully imported or lawfully unshipped or unladen from any ship or boat or from any aircraft, train or vehicle, or
- the goods were lawfully brought to, sent to or kept at any place for the purpose of exportation, or
- the goods were lawfully dealt with in any other manner for the purpose of exportation,
  in every such case the onus of proof in relation to any such question shall lie upon the person bringing the proceedings.

The above-mentioned provision deals with the burden of proof in proceedings relating to goods seized under the Customs Acts and the said provision is equally applicable to holders of goods as well as to right-holders. **15.149**

15.150 Section 7 of the 1996 Regulations provided that an applicant for action shall give to the Revenue Commissioners such security within such time and in such manner as they may require against all actions, proceedings, claims, and demands whatsoever which may be taken or made against, or costs and expenses which may be incurred by them in consequence if the detention of, or anything done in relation to, any goods to which the application relates. In addition, the applicant was also required (regardless of whether or not security has been provided) to keep the Revenue Commissioners indemnified against all such liability and expenses. Strangely, the 2005 Regulations are silent on this area and only time will reveal the consequences of such omission.

(2) Liability of Irish Customs for not detecting or acting against goods suspected of infringing a right-holder's intellectual property right or where an application for action has been lodged

15.151 In terms of the liability of Irish Customs for failing to detect prohibited goods after an application is lodged, the 1996 Regulations made no reference to liability and the 2005 Regulations are, again, silent on this matter. Instead, Article 19(1) of the Regulation will have direct effect so that the acceptance of an application will not entitle a right-holder to compensation in the event that prohibited goods are not detected by Irish Customs. As an overall point, the Irish State is vicariously liable for the torts of servants of the State committed in the course of their employment. Therefore, the argument could be made that the omission of Irish Customs in not detecting the prohibited goods resulted in damage to the right-holder which is actionable by the right-holder. However, such actions could only be judged on a case-by-case basis and one would imagine that only a small minority of cases would have any chance of success. Take, for example, counterfeit goods. It is becoming increasing difficult for even the right-holder to determine at first glance whether a product is genuine or counterfeit and often detailed analysis must be carried out to determine the matter conclusively. Therefore, it is not surprising that such goods could potentially pass through Irish Customs without being detected. Therefore, there will be circumstances where Irish Customs will be acting in good faith and not be in any way negligent. However, there may be circumstances where Irish Customs could potentially act outside of their powers such as extending deadlines where no such power exists. Procedural matters are taken very seriously by Irish Courts and Irish Customs are readily aware of the potential for legal challenges.

Lack of action prior to the filing of an application by the relevant right-holder

15.152 No liability is imposed in respect of situations where infringing goods are not detected. *Ex officio* proceedings are merely extra powers conferred on Irish Customs and Irish Customs are under no obligation to use them.

Conclusion

Irish Customs procedures may not substantially change under the Regulation. **15.153** However, the fact that the legislation in this area is constantly being reassessed and re-designed is certainly to be welcome. Counterfeit and pirated goods and goods infringing other intellectual property rights caught by the Regulation not only affect the right-holder but also have significant implications for the economy. Whilst the number of *ex officio* actions in Ireland may be low, the number of actions taken on the basis of granted applications is increasing. Consequently, right-holders must not rely on the *ex officio* procedure to detect counterfeit goods and other goods infringing an intellectual property right and instead be vigilant and lodge applications for action in order to defend their intellectual property rights.

16

ITALY

Raffaella Barbuto and Raffaella Arista

Introduction

As a Member State of the European Union, Italy must apply the European Community legislation. **16.01**

In the past, the Italian legislator failed to adopt immediately provisions necessary to put in practice the first generation of Community Regulations on border measures[1], that is, Regulations (EEC) No 3842/86[2] and 3077/87.[3] **16.02**

In fact, these Regulations became applicable by the Italian customs authorities as late as 1991, when Article 35 of Law No 428 of 29 December 1990[4] appointed the *Direzione Generale delle Dogane e Imposte Indirette* (General Directorate of Customs and Indirect Taxes), a section of the Ministry of Finance, as the Italian administrative body competent to process applications for action by customs authorities under the Regulations. The same provision also stipulated that applicants for customs interventions were liable for any occasional damage caused to the importers and/or third parties involved. In addition, the applicants had to bear all the costs of the procedure, and the costs for storage of the goods.

---

[1] M Ricolfi, 'Le Misure Doganali a tutela della Proprietà Intellettuale', in *Studio di Diritto Industriale in onore di Adriano Vanzetti*, [2004] Giuffrè 1241.

[2] Council Reg (EEC) No 3842/86 of 1 December 1986 laying down measures to prohibit the release for free circulation of counterfeit goods [1986] OJ L 357/1 (18.12.1986); Corr. [1987] OJ L 33/18 (4.2.1987).

[3] Commission Reg (EEC) No 3077/87 of 14 October 1987 laying down provisions for the implementation of Council Reg (EEC) No 3842/86 laying down measures to prohibit the release for free circulation of counterfeit goods [1987] OJ L 291/19 (15.10.1987).

[4] 'Law No 428 of 29 December 1990 laying down provisions for fulfilment of obligations arising from Italy's accession to the European Communities', *Italian State Gazette*, 12 January 1991, 10. This Law is known as Legge Comunitaria 1991, because it established the implementation 'in bulk' of a number of Community Regulations and Directives in Italy.

16.03 The Community system on border measures was amended by the second and third generations of Community Regulations, namely Regulations (EC) No 3295/94[5] and 1367/95[6] (second generation) and Regulations (EC) No 241/1999[7] and 2549/1999[8] (third generation).

16.04 Regulations (EC) No 1383/2003 ('the Regulation') and 1891/2004 ('the Implementing Regulation')[9] have been given effect in Italy through two Circulars[10] issued by the Customs Agency, namely Circular No 32/D of 23 June 2004 ('First Circular') entitled 'Guidelines on new community and national measures for customs authorities to take action against goods suspected of infringing certain intellectual property rights' and Circular No 74/D of December 3, 2004 ('Second Circular'), concerning additional implementing instructions.

16.05 Both Circulars are addressed to the local offices of customs and they merely contain the operational instructions, guidelines, and procedures to be followed by the customs authorities for correct application of the provisions of the Community Regulations in force and an efficient pursuit of the objectives set by the Community legislator. The Circulars are also very useful for intellectual property right-holders or for the persons authorized to use such rights and their representatives, when lodging an application for customs action, since they contain procedures to be followed by the authorities.

---

[5] Council Reg (EC) 3295/94 of 22 December 1994 laying down measures to prohibit the release for free circulation, export, re-export or entry for a suspensive procedure of counterfeit and pirated goods [1994] OJ L 341/8 (22.12.1994).

[6] Commission Reg (EC) No 1367/95 of 16 June 1995 laying down provisions for the implementation of Council Reg (EC) No 3295/94 laying down measures to prohibit the release for free circulation, export, re-export or entry for a suspensive procedure of counterfeit and pirated goods [1995] OJ L 133/2 (17.6.1995).

[7] Council Reg (EC) No 241/1999 of 25 January 1999 amending Reg (EC) No 3295/94 laying down measures to prohibit the release for free circulation, export, re-export or entry for a suspensive procedure of counterfeit and pirated goods [1999] OJ L 27/1 (2.2.1999).

[8] Commission Reg (EC) No 2549/1999 of 2 December 1999 amending Reg (EC) No 1367/95 laying down provisions for the implementation of Council Reg (EC) No 3295/94 laying down measures to prohibit the release for free circulation, export, re-export or entry for a suspensive procedure of counterfeit and pirated goods [1999] OJ L 308/16 (3.12.1999).

[9] Commission Reg (EC) 1891/2004 of 21 October 2004 laying down provisions for the implementation of Council Reg (EC) 1383/2003 concerning customs action against goods suspected of infringing certain intellectual property rights and the measures to be taken against goods found to have infringed such rights [2004] OJ L 328/16 (30.10.2004).

[10] The Italian and English text of the Circulars are published on the website of the Custom Agency at the following address: http://www.agenziadogane.it/italiano/dcsd/normativa-contraffazione.htm. According to Italian practice, some Circulars issued by public authorities, when addressed to public offices providing merely operational instructions with internal relevance, shall not be published in the *Italian State Gazette*.

I. SUBJECT MATTER AND SCOPE OF THE NATIONAL LAW APPLYING THE REGULATION

In this Part, we examine the scope of Italian national law applying the Regulation.   **16.06**

On 19 March, 2005, the Industrial Property Code ('the IP Code') came into force   **16.07**
in Italy, with Legislative Decree No 30 of 10 February, 2005[11] which sets out in a
unitary, harmonized, and clear manner the regulations on industrial property
matters, enabling companies, both Italian and foreign companies, operating in
Italy, to have much easier recourse to the instruments guaranteed by Italian law in
matters of protection of industrial property rights.

In particular, the IP Code contains the regulations in matters of trade marks,   **16.08**
geographical indications, industrial designs, invention patents, utility models,
topographies of integrated circuits, protection of undisclosed information,
and plant varieties. Copyright and related rights are excluded from the ambit of
the IP Code.

The pre-existing regulations in matters of industrial property rights and their   **16.09**
protection have remained substantially unchanged, except for civil court actions,
for which a new shortened procedure has been brought in, already in effect for
company law.[12]

The IP Code does not, however, represent merely the unification and
reorganization of these matters under a single Act; it is also the re-arrangement
and coordination of all the provisions within the national, international, and
Community regulatory framework.

One of the main principles stated by the IP Code is the distinction between   **16.10**
Registered Rights and Unregistered Rights. Registered Rights are those

---

[11] Codice della Proprietà Industriale 'IP Code', *Italian State Gazette* 4 March 2005, 52. The IP
Code contains 246 Articles, articulated in eight sections concerning, respectively: 1) General provisions concerning the fundamental principles, such as the scope of application of the laws, objectives,
rules applicable to foreigners, and provisions regarding priority and expiry of rights; 2) substantial
provisions concerning each of the intellectual property rights, subdivided into sections dealing,
respectively, with trade marks, geographical indications, industrial designs, invention patents, utility
models, topographies of integrated circuits, protection of undisclosed information, and plant
varieties; 3) Rules of jurisdictional protection codifying in one single text the numerous rules set out
by the various special statutes in force to date; 4) The conditions and the procedures for acquiring
and maintaining validity of intellectual property titles, among which the procedure for opposing the
registration of trade marks; 5) special procedures, such as expropriation, confiscation, seizure, etc;
6) regulations regarding professionals; 7) management of services rendered by the Italian Patent and
Trade Mark Office; 8) transitional provisions.
[12] N 85 below.

subject to registration and patenting, namely registered trade marks, patents, utility models, designs, models, new vegetable varieties, and semiconductor product topographies. Unregistered Rights are those which arise without patenting or registration, but having recourse to legal assumptions they are also protected by IP Code regulations. They are mainly unregistered trade marks, confidential company information, guarantees of origin, and geographical indications.

Article 2 of the IP Code in fact sets out that:

1. Industrial property rights are acquired by means of patenting, by registration and / or in the other ways stipulated in this code. Patenting and registration give rise to industrial property titles.
2. The subject of patenting are inventions, utility models and new vegetable varieties.
3. Subject of registration are trademarks, designs and models and semiconductor product topographies.
4. With recourse to legal premises, distinctive signs different from the registered trademark, confidential company information, geographical indications and guarantees of origin, are protected.
5. The patenting and registration administrative proceeding is by nature that of constitutional assessment and gives rise to titles subject to a special system of nullity and lapse on the basis of the regulations contained in this Code.

16.11   The extension of the industrial property regulations to include expressly also Unregistered Rights is an innovation of particular importance in the Italian legal system, that could also have repercussions in matters of legal actions for fighting infringement. The holder of an Unregistered Right could, in fact, by showing the validity of his rights, act against any infringements, on the basis of the IP Code regulations and not only on the basis of the residual regulations in matters of unfair competition (passing-off actions).

16.12   We cannot exclude the possibility that applications of intervention of custom authorities could also be filed on the basis of an Unregistered Right, like distinctive signs and trade marks, provided there is evidence of their continuing use.

A. Customs procedure of the goods

16.13   Italian customs authorities have to adopt border measures towards goods subject to the customs procedures defined in Article 1 of the Regulation, for example, when goods are declared for release for free circulation, export, or re-export, or have been discovered on the occasion of a control carried out on goods entering or leaving the Community customs territory, placed under a suspensive procedure,[13] in the process of being re-exported subject to notification, or placed in a free zone or free warehouse.

According to information provided by the Italian customs authorities, during **16.14** 2004 there were 1,133 interventions concerning counterfeit and pirated goods (that is, violation of trade marks and designs) and only 57 concerning violation of other IP rights (that is, patents).

B. Definition of infringing goods

(1) Counterfeit goods

The definition of 'counterfeit goods' contained in Article 2(1)(a) of the **16.15** Regulation has been entirely taken over by the First Circular. Consequently, the Italian customs authorities consider as counterfeit any goods, including packaging thereof, bearing, without the right-holder's authorization:

- a sign identical to a trade mark validly registered with respect to the same type of goods; or
- a sign that cannot be distinguished in its essential aspects from such a trade mark,

and which thereby infringes the trade mark-holder's rights under Community law,[14] or under Italian trade mark law, now the IP Code.[15]

Furthermore, goods to which a trade mark symbol (including a logo, label, **16.16** sticker, brochure, instructions for use, or guarantee document bearing such a symbol) has been affixed, as well as packaging materials, even if presented separately, which infringe the trade mark-holder's rights, are also considered counterfeit.

The First Circular specifies that the term 'trade mark' generally means 'any sign **16.17** capable of graphical reproduction which is used to distinguish the products forming the subject matter of the activity of a natural or legal person'. Accordingly, 'a trade mark can consist, inter alia, of names presented under any form, such as words, set of words, patronymic names, pseudonyms, letters, digits, acronyms, symbols, etc'.

---

[13] Thus, the customs authorities also detain, or suspend the release of goods in external transit, where they are suspected of infringing an intellectual property right. The harbour of Gioa Tauro, eg, frequently faces such situations.

[14] Reg (EC) No 40/94 of 20 December 1993 on the Community Trade Mark [1994] OJ L 11/1 (14.1.1994), as amended.   [15] Italian IP Code, cf para 16.07 above.

16.18   This definition is more or less identical to the definition of signs that are suscepti-ble to registration as trade marks contained in Article 7 of the IP Code, which states as follows:

> All signs liable to be represented graphically, in particular words, including the names of people, drawings, letters, figures, sounds, the shape of the product and its packaging, colours combinations and tones, may be the subject of registration, pro-vided that they are capable of distinguishing the products or services of a company from those of another company.

16.19   Article 20 of the IP Code provides that a registered trade mark shall confer on its proprietor the exclusive right to prevent any third parties not having his consent from using, in the course of trade:

- any sign which is identical to the trade mark in relation to goods or services which are identical to those for which the trade mark is registered;
- any sign where, because of its identity with, or similarity to, the trade mark, and the identity or similarity of the goods or services covered by the trade mark and the sign, there is a likelihood of confusion on the part of the public. The likeli-hood of confusion includes the likelihood of association between the sign and the trade mark;
- any sign which is identical, or similar, to the trade mark in relation to goods or services which are not similar to those for which the trade mark is registered, where the latter has a reputation in the country, and where use of that sign with-out due cause takes unfair advantage of, or is detrimental to, the distinctive character or the repute of the trade mark.

16.20   Consequently, trade mark owners may prohibit third parties, inter alia, to:

- affix the sign to the goods, or to the packaging thereof;
- offer the goods, put them on the market, or stock them for these purposes, or offer or supply services, under that sign;
- import or export the goods under that sign;
- use that sign on business papers and in advertising.

16.21   Under the provisions of the IP Code, a trade mark infringement occurs not only in the case of goods bearing a trade mark identical to another trade mark, or which cannot be distinguished in its essential aspects from another trade mark, but also in those cases where a *similar* trade mark is being used, provided that such use gives rise to a likelihood of confusion. Likewise, the protection conferred on trade mark holders in Italy does not only extend to the use of a conflicting sign for goods which are identical to the goods listed in the trade mark registration, but also to goods which are confusingly similar.

16.22   It is clear that the definition of trade mark infringement under the IP Code is thus far broader that that of counterfeit goods under the Regulation. The latter only applies to a sign which is 'identical or which cannot be distinguished in its essential aspects' from such a trade mark, and therefore certainly embraces the situations referred to in Article 20 of the IP Code. However, the Italian Law also regards as infringing all signs similar to the registered trade mark, provided a risk of confusion exists in the mind of the public.

By way of contrast, whereas the Regulation requires that the counterfeit sign be **16.23** *essentially* similar to the registered mark and that counterfeit goods be 'of the same type' as those for which the mark is registered, under Italian law it is sufficient that the goods be similar.

Finally, the notion of taking unfair advantage of or being detrimental to a **16.24** trade mark with a reputation is not mentioned in the Regulation, which might in other words not explicitly cover the situations referred to in Article 20 of IP Code.

This explains why, in practice, the definition of 'counterfeit goods' under Article **16.25** 2(1)(a) of the Regulation is substantially different from the definition of the scope of protection conferred on trade mark owners by the IP Code. In fact, the definition adopted by the Regulation only covers clear-cut trade mark infringement cases. However, the aim of the Regulation is clearly to allow the customs authorities of the Member States to take action whenever they have good reason to believe, on a prima facie examination, that the goods infringe a validly registered trade mark.

However, even if the Italian customs authorities are not competent, as a tribunal **16.26** could be, to ascertain similarity between the suspect sign and the registered trade mark, and/or the affinity between the goods, their aim is to stop any suspected products.

Some recent examples[16] will illustrate the way in which Italian Customs interpret **16.27** the concept of 'counterfeit goods' in practice.

- On 27 September 2004, the Bologna customs office suspended the release of 116 covers for mobile telephone bearing the 'NOKIA' and 'SIEMENS' trade marks (use of signs identical to validly registered trade marks in respect of goods identical to those listed in the trade mark registration certificate).
- On 2 October 2003, the La Spezia customs office suspended the release of bags bearing a logo 'XL', which appeared very similar to the 'LV' (Louis Vuitton) trade mark as to its graphics and overall presentation (use of a sign similar to a validly registered trade mark in respect of goods identical to those listed in the trade mark registration certificate).

---

[16] Cf the website of the Italian Custom Authorities www.agenziadogane.it. All border measures taken by Italian Customs are published on this site.

- On 20 September 2004, the Gioia Tauro customs office suspended the release of 35,000 backpacks bearing the trade mark and the image of the 'BARBIE' doll.
- On 9 September 2004, the Naples customs officers suspended the release of 52,000 t-shirts bearing the 'NIKE' figurative trade mark.

16.28 According to the First Circular, the Italian customs authorities have to take action on the basis of the following.

— Any national (that is, Italian) trade mark. The Circular provides that the holder of an Italian trade mark must enclose a copy of the relevant registration certificate with his application for action by the customs authorities. It seems possible to apply for customs action on the basis of a mere Italian trade mark application.

— Any registered Community trade mark. Again, the Circular states that a copy of the registration certificate concerned must be enclosed with the application form.

— Any registered international trade mark having effect in Italy. A copy of the registration certificate must be enclosed with the application.

16.29 Finally, it is questionable whether the Italian customs authorities may act on the basis of a trade mark which has neither been applied for, nor registered.[17] The cited Article 2 of the IP Code does grant protection to certain unregistered trade marks, provided that the owner of the sign can demonstrate and prove continuous and widespread use of the sign as a trade mark in the Italian territory. So, it could be possible that the owner of an unregistered trade mark could base an application for action thereupon. This approach can be considered inconsistent with Article 2(1)(a) of the Regulation, which requires a 'validly registered' trade mark as basis of an application of customs intervention. However, we are not aware of any application for action based on a non-registered trade mark having ever been lodged—and accepted—in Italy to date.

(2) Pirated goods

16.30 The definition of 'pirated goods' provided by the First Italian Circular is identical to that provided by Article 2(1)(b) of the Regulation and covers goods which are or contain copies made without the consent of the holder of a copyright or related right or design right, regardless of whether it is registered in national law, or of a person authorized by the right-holder in the country of production, in cases where

---

[17] M. Venturello '*La Tutela dei Diritti di proprietà Industriale e intellettuale alle frontiere. La nuova normativa dell'Unione Europea: il Regolamento (CE) n. 1383/2003*', in *Contratto e Impresa / Europa*, Cedam—Padova, 2003, 2, 1331.

the making of those copies would constitute an infringement of that right under Council Regulation (EC) 6/2002,[18] or under the Italian provisions governing copyright, related rights, and design rights.

In practice, for the purpose of determining whether products can be suspected of being 'pirated goods', the Italian customs authorities adopt the same flexibility as with counterfeit goods. As a rule, they consider 'goods which are or contain copies' any goods that are totally or partially similar to goods protected by a copyright, a related right, or a design right. **16.31**

In order to determine whether such 'copies' can be seen as infringing a copyright, related right, or design right under Italian law, regard should be had to the relevant pieces of legislation. The following paragraphs provide an overview of the legal framework dealing with this issue. **16.32**

Scope of protection of copyright

Article 1 of the Copyright Law[19] confers copyright protection on any original works in the field of literature, music, figurative arts, architecture, theatre, and cinematography, expressed in any manner and by any means. The holder of a copyright (that is, the creator of the work) enjoys the right to prohibit publication, reproduction, transcription, execution, representation, recitation, distribution, translation, and modification of his work, or any substantial part of it, without his prior consent. It is generally recommended that the creator register his work with the SIAE (*Società Italiana Autori e Editori*). Such a registration will serve as proof of the date of creation of the work, and of the contents of the same. **16.33**

Software enjoys copyright protection in Italy under Legislative Decree No 518 of 29 December 1992[20] and Decree No 244 of 3 January 1994,[21] both **16.34**

---

[18] Council Reg (EC) 6/2002 of 12 December 2001 on Community designs [2002] OJ L 3/1 (5.1.2002), as amended.

[19] As said (cf para 16.07 above) the IP Code contains no regulations on matters of copyright. Therefore, to date Italy still has in force Legge sulla Protezione del diritto d'autore e di altri diritti connessi al suo esercizio, 'Copyright Law', *Italian State Gazette*, 16 July 1941, 166, amended by Legislative Decree No 68 of 9 April 2003 implementing EC Directive No 29/2001, *Italian State Gazette*, 14 April 2003, 68, and by Law No 43 of 31 March 2005, Conversione in legge, con modificazioni, del decreto-legge 31 gennaio 2005, n. 7, recante disposizioni urgenti per l'università e la ricerca, per i beni e le attività culturali, per il completamento di grandi opere strategiche, per la mobilità dei pubblici dipendenti, nonché per semplificare gli adempimenti relativi a imposte di bollo e tasse di concessione, 'Urgent measures for university, research, cultural activities', *Italian State Gazette*, 1 April 2005, 75.

[20] Attuazione della Direttiva 91/250/CEE relative alla tutela giuridica dei programmi per elaboratore 'Software Law' Legislative Decree No 518 of 29 December 1992, *Italian State Gazette*, 31 December 1992, 306.

[21] Regolamento concernente il Registro Pubblico Speciale per I programmi per elaboratore, 'Regulation on public register of software', *Italian State Gazette* 22 April 1994, 93.

implementing Directive 91/250/EEC of 14 May 1991.[22] Those pieces of legislation have brought some changes to the Italian Copyright Law. Application for the registration of computer programs may be filed with the Special Public Register at the OLAF Section of the SIAE by the right-holder in question, or his professional agents, by submitting a special form and an optical support containing the computer program for which registration is sought. The registration serves as proof of the date of the creation of the software, and of other data contained in the relevant file(s), such as authorship, title, and date of publication. The exclusive rights on software comprise the right to the economic exploitation of the program, as well as the right to carry out, or authorize, any form of reproduction, translation, adaptation, transformation, modification, and/or distribution of the software.

Scope of protection of design rights

16.35   The scope of protection of design rights under national law is determined by section III of the Italian IP Code (Articles from 31 to 44).

16.36   Article 41.3 of the IP Code states that the holder of a design right may oppose the use of a product in which the design is incorporated or applied, and which has an identical appearance to the design that has been applied for, or which does not produce on the informed user a different overall impression. The degree of freedom of the designer in developing his design is taken into consideration when assessing the scope of protection of such intellectual right. In particular, Article 41.1 and 41.2 states that the registration of a design allows the holder the exclusive right to use the product and to prohibit its use by third parties without his consent. Use of a product is interpreted as including, amongst others, the making, offering, putting on the market, selling, distributing, renting, importing, exporting, exposing, using, or detaining the product for those purposes.

(3) Goods infringing other intellectual property rights

16.37   According to the information provided by Italian custom authorities, there were only 57 cases concerning patent infringement in 2004. The reason for the small number is that to ascertain the infringement of rights with technical aspects is, in practice, very difficult. However, it is probable that some cases may be considered trade mark counterfeiting and not patent infringement, when the name of the product is reproduced.

---

[22] Council Directive 91/250/EEC of 14 May 1991 on the legal protection of computer programs [1991] OJ L 122/42 (17.5.1991).

Goods infringing a patent or a supplementary protection certificate

The scope of protection of patent rights under Italian law is determined by section IV (Inventions) and section V (Utility Models) of the IP Code. **16.38**

Pursuant to Article 66 of IP Code the holder of a patent has the right to prevent any third party not having his consent from exploiting his invention. More specifically, the patent confers the following rights on its proprietor: **16.39**

- if the subject of the patent is a product, the right to prohibit third parties, unless with the holder's consent, from producing, using, marketing, selling or importing for these purposes the product in question;
- if the subject of the patent is a procedure, the right to prohibit third parties, unless with the holder's consent, from applying the procedure, and also using, marketing, selling or importing for these purposes the product directly obtained with the procedure in question.

As far as supplementary protection certificates are concerned, Article 61 of the IP Code states that they have the same effect as the patent referred to, limited to the part or parts thereof relating to the medicine that is the subject of the marketing licence. **16.40**

The effects of the supplementary protection certificate come into force from the moment the patent reaches the end of its legal term and extend for a period equal to that which elapses between the date of placement of the patent application and the date of the decree whereby the first marketing licence for the medicine is granted. The term of the supplementary protection certificate cannot in any case be longer than 18 years from the date whereon the patent reaches the end of its legal term. **16.41**

Goods infringing a national plant variety right

The scope of protection of plant variety right under Italian law is determined by section VIII of the IP Code. In Italy plant variety rights are protected by means of a registration. **16.42**

Article 107 of the IP Code states that the rights arising from the granting of a registration for a plant variety include the right to produce and reproduce the protected variety. In particular, the following acts in relation to reproductive or vegetative propagating material of the protected variety shall require the breeder's consent: **16.43**

— production or reproduction;
— processing for the purpose of propagation;
— offering for sale, selling, or any other form of marketing;
— exporting or importing;
— stocking for any of the above purposes.

The breeder's authorization shall be required for any of the above-mentioned acts with respect to harvested material, including whole plants and parts of plants obtained though unauthorized use of propagating material of the protected variety, unless the breeder has had reasonable opportunity to exercise his right in relation to the said propagating material. Use shall be presumed unauthorized in the absence of proof to the contrary.

Goods infringing a national designation of origin or a geographical indication

16.44 The scope of protection of geographical indications is now provided for by section II of the IP Italian Code.

16.45 Article 29 states:

> Geographical indications and guarantees of origin identifying a country, a region or a town are protected, when they are used to designate a product that originates therefrom, and whose qualities, reputation and features are due exclusively or essentially to the geographical environment of origin, including natural, human and traditional factors.

16.46 Furthermore, Article 30 expressly states that it is forbidden, for the purposes of deceiving the public, to use geographical indications and guarantees of origin, as well as the use of any means in the designation or presentation of a product, that state or suggest that the product itself comes from a location other than the true place of origin, or that the product has the qualities that are those of the products that come from a location designated by a specific geographical indication.

16.47 According to the information provided by customs authorities, to date there have been no cases of intervention based on violation of geographical indications.

(4) Moulds and matrices

16.48 According to the First Circular, which on this point mirrors Article 2(3) of the Regulation, any mould or matrix which is specifically designed or adapted for the manufacture of goods infringing an intellectual property right shall be treated in the same manner as the infringing goods themselves, if the use of such moulds or matrices infringes the right-holder's rights under Community or Italian legislation.

16.49 Italian legislation, like that of the Community, entitles the right-holder to obtain seizure of means intended for the manufacture of goods infringing his right (Article 129 of IP Code). Furthermore, where there has been infringement, the order may be given, for the specific means that are used solely to produce the infringing goods to be assigned in ownership to the right-holder himself, without prejudice to his right of compensation for damages. The judge is also authorized, at the request of the owner of these means of production, having taken account of the residual duration of the right, or of the particular circumstances of the case, to order the seizure, at the expense of the perpetrator of the infringement, until the right expires, of the means of production. In the latter case, the right-holder may request that the objects seized are allocated at the price that, in the event of lack of agreement between the parties, is set by the enforcing judge, after consultation, if necessary, with an expert (Article 124 (4)(5) of the IP Code).

The same is true under criminal law.[23] For example, under Article 171 of the **16.50** Copyright Law[24] the order is always given for confiscation of the instruments and materials used or intended to commit the offences as set out in Articles 171bis, 171ter and 171quater of the Regulations.

C. Goods excluded by the Regulation

(1) Parallel imported goods

According to Article 3(1), first indent, of the Regulation, border measures cannot **16.51** be taken under the Regulation against goods bearing a trade mark, a protected designation of origin or geographical indication, or which are protected by a patent, a supplementary protection certificate, a copyright, related right, design right, or plant variety right, and which have been manufactured with the consent of the right-holder, but are placed under any of the customs procedures referred to in Article 1(1) of the Regulation without the right-holder's consent.

The Circular reaffirms the application of this principle in Italy. More specifically, **16.52** it recalls that the aim of the provision is to prevent the application of the Regulation to 'possible disputes of private law between the right-holder and the importer and, in particular, to the so-called "parallel" selling [sic] [. . .]. This selling commonly concerns products of original trade marks [. . .] by distributors [. . .] outside the official distribution chain required by the manufacturers to protect their commercial interests (so-called "grey market").'

However, according to recent Community[25] and Italian case law,[26] the **16.53** parallel trade in products addressed to non-Community markets without

---

[23] Codice Penale, 'Criminal Code', *Italian State Gazette*, 26 October 1930, 251.
[24] Para 16.159 below.
[25] Case C-355/96 *Silhouette International Schmied GmbH & Co. KG v Hartlauer Handelsgesellschaft mbH* [1996] ECR 1998 Page I-04799; Case C-173/98 *Sebago Inc. And Ancienne Maison Dubois et Fils SA v. GB Unic SA* [1999] ECR 1999 Page I-04103.
[26] Civil Court of First Instance of Bologna, 28 February 2002, *Giurisprudenza Annotata di Diritto Industriale* [2002]; Civil Court of First Instance of Milan, 17 March 2001, *Giurisprudenza Annotata di Diritto Industriale* [2001].

the right-holder's consent, is generally deemed a counterfeiting activity which can be pursued under civil law. Therefore, the holder of an intellectual property right may always ask the Italian civil courts for interim measures aimed at obtaining, for example, the seizure of goods, and a prohibition to sell them within the Italian territory. However, such measures are not to be confused with border measures under the Regulation, and may thus not be applied by customs.

(2) Goods which have been manufactured under conditions other than those which have been agreed with the right-holder

16.54 Border measures may not be taken with respect to goods manufactured under conditions other than those which were agreed upon by the right-holder, as set forth by Article 3(1), second indent, of the Regulation. The Circular reiterates this principle.

16.55 Again, the right-holder concerned is, in principle, entitled under Italian intellectual property law and/or contract law, to file a motion before the civil courts aimed at obtaining, for example the seizure of the goods, an injunctive relief with effect throughout the Italian territory, and/or the payment of damages. However, such remedies are not to be confused with border measures, which may not be adopted by customs.

(3) Goods contained in travellers' personal baggage

16.56 Italian Customs will perform checks only on travellers' personal baggage originating in countries which are not a party to the Schengen Agreement.[27]

16.57 Article 3(2) of the Regulation prevents the detention, or suspension of release of, goods of a non-commercial nature contained in travellers' personal baggage within the limits of the duty-free allowance, unless there are material indications to suggest they are part of a commercial traffic.

---

[27] Cf, inter alia, Agreement of 14 June 1985 between the Governments of the States of the Benelux Economic Union, the Federal Republic of Germany and the French Republic on the Gradual Abolition of Checks at their Common Borders; Convention of 19 June 1990 Implementing the Schengen Agreement of 14 June 1985 between the Governments of the States of the Benelux Economic Union, the Federal Republic of Germany and the French Republic on the Gradual Abolition of Checks at their Common Borders (Convention Implementing the Schengen Agreement); and Treaty of Amsterdam of 2 October 1997.

Parties to the Schengen Agreement are: Austria, Belgium, Denmark, Finland, France, Germany, Greece, Iceland, Italy, Luxemburg, the Netherlands, Norway, Portugal, Spain, and Sweden. Discussions are currently ongoing as to the future accession of Switzerland to the Agreement.

Circular No 22/D adopted by the Italian Customs Agency on 5 May 2004[28] **16.58**
recalls in this context that the duty-free allowance applies to goods whose final
value does not exceed EUR 175. This amount is lowered to EUR 90 for travellers
under 16. Alcoholic products, perfumes, tobaccos, tea, and coffee, are excluded
from the duty free allowance, pursuant to Ministerial Decree No 500/98.[29]

For the purpose of calculating the limit of the duty free allowance, the Italian cus- **16.59**
toms authorities have, in principle, regard to the purchase value of the infringing
products.

When assessing the 'non-commercial nature' of the goods, and the existence of **16.60**
'material indications' of the existence of a 'commercial traffic', Italian Customs
apply Article 45(2)(b) of Council Regulation (EEC) No 918/83.[30] In particular,
according to the European Court of Justice:[31]

> The question whether an importation of goods is non-commercial [. . .], must be **16.61**
> examined case by case on the basis of an overall assessment of the circumstances,
> taking into account the nature of the importation and the quantity of goods
> involved, the frequency with which those goods are imported by the traveller
> concerned, but also, where appropriate, taking account the traveller's lifestyle and
> habits or of his family environment.

In practice, the quantity of goods and the existence of commercial documents **16.62**
relating to the purchase of the goods, such as invoices, are particularly significant
in determining whether the goods are part of a commercial traffic.

II. APPLICATION FOR ACTION BY
THE CUSTOMS AUTHORITIES

The Regulation stipulates two different intervention procedures by customs: the **16.63**
so-called *ex officio* procedure, according to which customs make interventions

---

[28] The Italian and English text of the Circular is published on the website of the Customs Agency
at the following address: http://www.agenziadogane.it/italiano/dcsd/normativa-contraffazione.
htm. According to Italian practice, some Circulars issued by public authorities, when addressed to
public offices providing merely operational instructions with internal relevance, shall not be
published in the *Italian State Gazette*.

[29] Regolamento recante norme per l'esenzione dai diritti doganali per gli oggetti ed i generi di
consumo importati a seguito dei viaggiatori, *Italian State Gazette*, 29 January 1999, 23.

[30] Council Reg (EEC) No 918/83 of 28 March 1983 setting up a Community system of reliefs
from customs duty [1983] OJ L 105/3 (23.4.1983), as amended. Art 45(2)(b) of this Regulation is discussed in the contribution by M Schneider and O Vrins relating to EC Reg 1383/2003 in this book.

[31] Case C-99/00, Criminal proceedings against Kenny Roland Lyckeskog [2002] ECR 2002
Page I-04839.

prior to the filing of an application for action by the right-holder (Article 4); and the procedure of intervention following the filing of an application for action (Article 5).

A. Measures prior to an application for action by the customs authorities ('*ex officio* measures')

16.64 According to information provided by Italian Customs, the customs agencies make abundant use of the *ex officio* procedure. This happens either because the intellectual property right-holders are not aware of the existence of counterfeit procedures to the detriment of their own rights, or because intellectual property right-holders are not aware of the existence of the procedures stipulated by the Regulation and, as a result, do not implement the relevant supervisory procedure.

16.65 In any case, on being notified of the potential infringement of their intellectual property rights in the framework of an *ex officio* intervention, right-holders apply for customs' action under Article 5 of the Regulation in the vast majority of cases.

16.66 In accordance with Article 4(1) of the Regulation, the Italian customs authorities take *ex officio* measures whenever they have 'sufficient grounds for suspecting that the goods infringe an intellectual property right'. However, for practical reasons, the authorities are not in a position to inspect all goods brought into the Italian customs territory. Therefore, they select shipments according to a computerized system of risk analysis following methods of control of customs declarations, as provided for in Articles 68 and 71 of Regulation No 2913/1992.[32]

16.67 This risk analysis is based on multiple items of information gathered from previous customs actions and from trade and industry associations, with which Italian Customs have signed specific memoranda of understanding. In particular, the First Circular has emphasized that the contribution and support of those associations has proved to be positive and effective in identifying specific risk indicators, and useful for the prevention and repression of fraudulent situations.

16.68 The risk analysis takes into account the categories of products which are most frequently subject to infringements, and the importers who have

---

[32] Council Reg (EEC) No 2913/92 of 12 October 1992 establishing the Community Customs Code [1992] L 302/1 (19.10.1992), as amended.

already been involved in fraudulent activities. Based on these consolidated principles, since 1999 the Italian Customs Administration has been using an automated customs circuit procedure for the selection of shipments which are to be subject to a physical check, whose provisions for the relevant sectors were updated by the Italian Circular No 74/D of 18 December 2004.[33]

When any of the Italian customs offices has sufficient grounds for suspecting that **16.69** goods infringe an intellectual property right, they may suspend the release of the goods, or detain them, for a period of three working days following notification of such action to the right-holder, in order to enable the latter to submit an application for action pursuant to Article 5 of the Regulation.[34] The notification to the right-holder will normally be sent by fax. The term of three working days is strictly observed by Italian Customs.

Under Italian practice, although this approach might conflict with Article 4(2) of the Regulation, the right-holder is not only informed about the actual or supposed number of infringing items and their nature,[35] but is also allowed at this stage to examine the goods, thus allowing him to decide whether to file the application for action.

B. The lodging and processing of applications for customs action

In accordance with Article 5 of the Regulation, right-holders may file an applica- **16.70** tion for action by the customs authorities in writing with the competent customs department in Italy when goods suspected of infringing his rights have been found, or are likely to be apprehended in the future.

According to information provided by Italian custom authorities, the number of **16.71** applications of customs actions filed in the last five years is as follows:

Year 2000: 77 applications
Year 2001: 79 applications
Year 2002: 107 applications
Year 2003: 151 applications
Year 2004: 203 applications
Year 2005 (from January to April): 250 applications

The number of applications for intervention has increased considerably **16.72** over the years. Of particular note is how in the first four months of 2005

---

[33] Cf para 16.04 above.   [34] Reg 1383/2003, Art 4(1).   [35] Ibid, Art 4(2).

more requests were submitted than during the whole of the 12 months of 2004. Certainly the Community Regulation coming into force has helped publicize this instrument for fighting counterfeiting, with a quicker and clearer procedure. Also, in the last year the customs authorities themselves have sought to encourage the use of this instrument, instilling confidence in entrepreneurs, who have finally understood its effectiveness and importance for protecting their own intellectual property rights, including by means of customs supervision.

(1) Persons entitled to file an application for action

Definition of 'right-holders' under the Regulation

16.73   The First Circular confirms that the following persons qualify as 'right-holder' under Article 2(2) of the Regulation, and may, in this capacity, lodge an application for action under Article 5:

- the holder of a trade mark, copyright or related right, design right, patent, supplementary protection certificate, plant variety right, protected designation of origin, protected geographical indication and, more generally, any right referred to in Article 2(1)(c) of the Regulation;
- any other legal or natural person authorized to use any of these intellectual property rights; and
- the representatives of the right owner or authorized user.

16.74   According to the First Circular, the 'person authorized to use' one of the rights listed in Article 2(1) of the Regulation means any natural or legal person that is authorized to use such a right by virtue of an agreement or contract. Thus, as far as licensees (whether exclusive or non-exclusive), distributors, and commercial agents, for example, are concerned, their entitlement to file an application for action depends on the terms of their agreement with the right-holder *stricto sensu*: if the licence, agency, or distribution agreement also entitles them to apply for customs action, such licensees, agents, and distributors may file an application for action under the Regulation.

16.75   The First Circular provides that 'representative' of the right-holder or authorized user means the natural or legal person with the power to act on behalf and on account of the right-holder or authorized user. This includes, for example, law firms, intellectual property counsels, collecting societies whose only or main purpose is the management of copyrights or related rights, and the associations referred to in Article 5 of Regulation No 2081/92 on the protection of geographical indications and designations of origin for agricultural products and foodstuffs.

Proof of entitlement to file an application for action

For right-holders stricto sensu

A right-holder *stricto sensu* should submit proof of his title to the intellectual property right claimed when he files an application for action by the customs authorities.   **16.76**

The Circulars[36] provide the following requisites on this point.

Trade mark rights   The holders of Italian trade marks enclose a photocopy of the trade mark registration issued by the Italian Patent and Trade Mark Office, or a photocopy of the application for registration of the trade mark, with their application for action. Holders of Community trade marks must provide a photocopy of the certificate of registration of the Community trade mark, issued by the Office for Harmonization in the Internal Market ('OHIM'). Holders of international trade marks must enclose a photocopy of the International Registration certificate issued by the World Intellectual Property Organization ('WIPO').   **16.77**

As provided for by Article 2 of Regulation 1891/2004, a photocopy of registration from the database of a national or international office may be considered a suitable document.   **16.78**

As has been pointed out above,[37] it is questionable whether an application for action may be filed on the basis of non-registered trade marks or other distinctive signs, such as company names or domain names used in the course of trade as trade marks. The IP Code protects unregistered signs and trade marks, provided that the owner submits the evidence of his right,[38] namely extensive and continuous use in the Italian territory. The protection is granted for the specific goods in respect of which the mark has been used and the territory where use has been established. We believe that the customs agency would accept an application for action filed by the owner of a non-registered trade mark, provided the applicant provides sufficient proof of entitlement to the sign.   **16.79**

Such proof may consist, for example, for the owner of a company name in a document issued by the Register of Companies certifying the date of incorporation of the company. Owners of a domain name may submit a copy of the receipt of registration with the relevant registration authority. However, since these documents show only the first date of use but not continuous and extensive use, additional evidence should be required.   **16.80**

According to the information provided by custom authorities, to date there are no cases of application of intervention based on unregistered signs.   **16.81**

---

[36] Cf para 16.04 above.   [37] Cf paras 16.10–16.12 above.
[38] Art 2 of the IP Code, cited at para 16.10 above.

16.82 **Design rights** The Circulars[39] do not list the documents to be enclosed with applications for action based on (registered or unregistered) design rights. As a general rule, as regards registered designs, proof of the registration or filing with the relevant office (that is, the Italian Patent and Trade Mark Office for Italian designs, or the OHIM for Community Designs) must be enclosed with the application form. Proof of right in a non-registered design can be provided by any means and in any form, such as documents attesting the first use, first exhibition, first selling, etc of the product embodying the protected design.

16.83 **Copyrights and related rights** The Circulars do not require any specific documents to be attached to the application for action with respect to copyrights and related rights. However, Article 2(1)(b) of Regulation 1891/2004 stipulates that, in the case of copyright, related goods or design which are not registered or for which an application has not been filed, the application for intervention should be filed on the basis of any evidence of authorship or of the applicant's status as original holder.

16.84 So, in principle, in Italy if the author has applied for copyright protection of this work, proof of the filing certificate with the corresponding office (that is, the SIAE—*Società Italiana Autori ed Editori*) must be enclosed with the application for action. Title to a non-registered copyright (or related right) may be evidenced by any means, such as through documents attesting the first use, first exhibition, first selling, and first publication of the protected subject matter.

16.85 **Patents and supplementary protection certificates** The Circulars do not provide for any guidelines in this respect either. As a general rule and also provided by Article 2 of Regulation 1981/2004, a proof of the registration of the title with the corresponding office must be submitted together with the application for action.

16.86 **Plant variety rights** The holder of a plant variety right shall present a certificate issued by the relevant office (that is, the Community or National Plant Variety Office) certifying the existence of such right.

16.87 **Designations of origin, geographical indications, geographical designations** In accordance with Article 2(1), third indent, of the Regulation 1981/2004, proof of entitlement consists of two mandatory elements, namely, proof that the person in question is the manufacturer or the association managing the right, and proof that the designation or indication has been registered. The same applies to wines and spirits.[40]

---

[39] Cf para 16.04 above.

[40] For any further information, the Circular refers to the website of the European Communities: http://europa.eu.int/comm/agriculture/foodqual/quali1_it.htm.

For persons authorized to use the right

With regard to applications for action lodged by persons authorized to use the right, the applicant is required to submit any useful documents attesting this capacity, such as a copy of the agreement concluded with the owner of the right, or a separate authorization. **16.88**

The Italian customs authorities carry out a thorough control of the capacity of licensees, agents, and distributors, and make sure they are entitled to act in the name and on behalf of the right owner. **16.89**

In addition, the person authorized to use the right must provide all the evidence normally required from right-holders *stricto sensu*. **16.90**

For representatives

The representative of the owner or authorized user of the right must provide a proxy or a power of attorney attesting his capacity and power to act in their name and on their behalf. The proxy or power of attorney should be signed in the original document by the grantor. If a copy is submitted, Italian Customs may at any time ask the representative, to produce the original document. A general power of attorney covering all customs actions is accepted. **16.91**

As stated by Article 2.3 of Regulation 1981/2004, the representative must also submit the declaration required under Article 6 of the Basic Regulation, signed respectively by the owner of the right or authorized user of the right. He shall also be required to present the document authorizing him to incur all costs resulting from the customs action, under Article 6(2) of the Regulation. **16.92**

The Second Circular[41] expressly stated that this Regulation is justified, taking into account the consequences that arise from this signing: in fact, by signing the declaration stated in Article 6 of the basic Regulation, the signatory undertakes on his own to bear all the costs arising from the customs intervention. **16.93**

General comments on the documents to be submitted to evidence the entitlement to file an application for action

The documents required as proof of the existence of the rights on which applications for action filed under the Regulation are based may be produced in copy. However, the customs authorities may ask the party concerned to produce originals of the documents at any time. **16.94**

---

[41] Cf para 16.04 above.

Printouts of registration certificates from private databases (that is, databases not maintained by the official national, regional, or international intellectual property offices) are not acceptable.

16.95 The First Circular[42] also addresses the issue of the validity of the legalizations affixed to documents established abroad. In particular:

- Documents made in foreign countries where specific International Agreements are in force do not require any further formalities and, therefore, are immediately and directly valid in Italy.
- Legalizations made within countries which are signatories of the International Convention of The Hague of 5 October 1961 (Apostille Convention) are valid in Italy, provided they bear the Apostille.
- For documents made abroad in countries other than the above-mentioned, the legalization of the signature of the certifying public official is required. In this case the provisions of Article 33(2) of the DPR No 445/2000[43] shall apply. Pursuant to this Decree, the signatures on documents executed abroad by foreign authorities require, to be valid in Italy, to be legalized by the diplomatic or consular representation of the Italian government in the relevant country. Signatures on documents executed by the competent bodies of the Italian diplomatic and consular representations, or by officials acting on their behalf, do not require legalization.

16.96 Any document laid down in a foreign language must be accompanied by a translation into Italian, certified as a true copy by the competent diplomatic and consular representation, or by an official translator.

(2) Competent customs department and formal requirements

Competent customs department

16.97 The national customs department entitled to receive and process applications for action filed by rights-holders under Article 5(2) of the Regulation in Italy is the *Agenzia Della Dogane* (Customs Agency), *Ufficio Antifrode Centrale* (Central Antifraud Office) located via Mario Carucci 71 in I-00144 Roma. The telephone numbers are +39 (0)6 50 24 20 81 or +39 (0)6 50 24 65 96, the fax numbers are +39 (0)6 50 95 73 00 or 50 24 20 21. E-mails may be sent to dogane.antifrode@agenziadogane.it. The URL of the website

---

[42] Ibid.

[43] Testo Unico delle disposizioni legislative e regolamentari in materia di documentazione amministrativa, 'Unified Text about Administrative Documents requirements', *Italian State Gazette* 20 February 2001, 42.

administered by Italian Customs is http://www.agenziadogane.gov.it/italiano/dcsd/contraffazione.htm.

Form of the application for action

At present, applications for action still have to be filed by letter using the application forms available on the Internet site of the Italian customs authorities.[44] The declaration provided for in Article 6 of the Regulation must be enclosed in the original with the application. However, in practice, the Central Antifraud Office allows copies of the application to be sent by fax in the first place, together with all the relevant documentation, so that the office can start examining it immediately. A confirmation letter containing the originals must follow. **16.98**

The Central Antifraud Office requires that the application (and related documentation) be filed in the original, together with a further 14 copies. The copies are forwarded, shortly after the application is accepted, to the 14 Regional Directorates of the Customs authority (namely, Ancona, Bari, Naples, Bologna, Trento, Rome, Genoa, Milan, Turin, Cagliari, Palermo, Florence, Bolzano, and Venice). **16.99**

In order to strengthen the tools for fighting infringements of intellectual property rights, Article 4(54) of the Financial Law 2004[45] provides for the future implementation of a multimedia database containing all the specific data allowing for the identification of rights and products to be protected. The Custom Director's Decision No 282/UD of 28 February 2004[46] established that the database would be placed in the premises of the Customs Agency and fed with data contained in the applications for action submitted by the intellectual property right-holders. Once this tool is set up, the applications in question shall be submitted electronically in accordance with the provisions governing the conditions and technical procedures for the presentation of customs documents through the Electronic Data Interchange System (EDI). **16.100**

Language requirements

The applications for action and the exhibits enclosed (for example, technical documents, brochures, certificates of registration, etc) should always be submitted in **16.101**

---

[44] The national application for action is published under http://www.agenziadogane. gov.it/italiano/dcagp/circolari_2004/circ_32d/allegato1_circ32d.pdf; the Community application for action may be found under http://www.agenziadogane.gov.it/italiano/dcagp/circolari_2004/ circ_32d/allegato2_circ32d.pdf. Other useful information is available under http://www.agenziadogane.gov.it/italiano/dcsd/modelli-contraffazione.htm.

[45] Law 24 December 2003, No 350 Disposizioni per la formazione del bilancio annuale e pluriennale dello Stato (legge finanziaria 2004), 'Financial Law 2004', *Official State Gazette* 27 December 2003, 299.

[46] Communication of the Custom Agency Director 28 February 2004, Rif. 282/UD, published in http://www.agenziadogane.it/italiano/dcsd/normativa-contraffazione.htm.

the Italian language. The same applies to the declaration under Article 6 of the Regulation. Any document written in a foreign language must be accompanied by a translation into Italian, certified as a true copy by the competent diplomatic and consular representation, or by an official translator.

16.102   In practice and according to the information unofficially provided by custom authorities, Community applications for action filed through foreign Customs authorities[47] are, in 90 per cent of cases, filed in English; the remaining 10 per cent are filed in French or German. The Italian customs authorities will always require a translation of such applications.

(3) Requirements regarding the contents of the application for action

Mandatory information

16.103   In line with Article 5(5) of the Regulation, the First Circular[48] reaffirms that both national and Community applications for action must contain the following mandatory information:

- an accurate and detailed technical description of the goods;
- any specific information the right-holder may have concerning the type or pattern of fraud; and
- the name and address of the contact person(s) appointed by the right-holder. Indication of local presence for the technical and administrative matters is required.

Optional information

16.104   Furthermore, by way of indication and where known, right-holders should also forward any other information they may have, such as:

- the pre-tax value of the original goods on the legitimate market in the country in which the application for action is lodged;
- the location of the goods or their intended destination;
- particulars identifying the consignment or packages;
- the scheduled arrival or departure date of the goods;
- the means of transport used;
- the identity of the importer, exporter, or holder of the goods;
- the country or countries of production and the routes used by traffickers;
- the technical differences, if known, between the authentic and the suspect goods.

---

[47]   Cf Reg 1383/2003, Art 5(6).   [48]   Cf para 16.04 above.

Additional information specific to the type of intellectual property right referred to in the application

Details may also be required which are specific to the type of intellectual property right referred to in the application for action.[49] For instance, photographs, pictures, catalogues, and any information about the technical details of the products are very much appreciated by customs. **16.105**

(4) *Processing and acceptance of the application for action*

On receiving an application for action, the Central Antifraud Office controls whether that application is presented by the entitled person and contains all the mandatory elements and documents listed in Article 5(5) of the Regulation. It notifies the applicant in writing of its decision within 30 working days of receipt of the application. **16.106**

Italian Customs will reject any application for action that does not contain all the mandatory information required in Article 5(5) of the Regulation. The decision to dismiss an application is set out in writing and provides the reasons for such rejection. It is formally notified to the applicant by registered letter with return receipt. Such a decision is final, and there can be no administrative appeal against it. However, the applicant may appeal the decision before the Latium Regional Court of proper jurisdiction. The legislation in force concerning appeals lodged before an administrative court shall apply. Rejected applications may be re-submitted when duly completed. **16.107**

Once accepted, the Central Antifraud Office forwards the application for action, together with the documents, to the 14 Regional Directorates of the Customs Agency. **16.108**

The duration of application, both Italian and community, is one year and it is renewable.

(5) *'Community' applications for action*

Where the applicant is the holder of a Community trade mark or a design right, a Community plant variety right, a designation of origin, a geographical indication, or a geographical designation protected under Community law, the application for action may seek action not only by the customs authorities of the Member State where the application is submitted, but also by the customs **16.109**

---

[49] Ibid, Art 5(6).

authorities of other Member States.[50] Such 'Community' applications for action shall indicate the Member State(s) in which customs action is requested, and the names and addresses of the right-holder in each of the Member States concerned.[51]

16.110 Community applications for action shall be made out in English. The same formal requirements and information as those requested for national applications for action are required when filing Community applications for action in Italy. The Italian customs authorities conduct similar thorough verifications as with national applications. However, when a Community application is filed in another Member State and extends to Italy, the Italian authorities trust that such verifications have already been conducted. So, normally they do not require to be provided with the documents attesting ownership and entitlement.

16.111 According to information provided by the customs authorities, from January to April 2005, 250 applications for intervention have been filed: 192 of them are national applications and 58 of them are Community applications.

III. CONDITIONS GOVERNING ACTION BY CUSTOMS AUTHORITIES AND BY THE AUTHORITIES WITH JURISDICTION TO DETERMINE WHETHER GOODS INFRINGE AN INTELLECTUAL PROPERTY RIGHT

16.112 Once the application for action, according to the Regulation, has been accepted, the customs offices are asked to control the borders and stop those goods which appear to infringe intellectual property rights. However, once pirated and counterfeit goods are intercepted, and therefore their release is suspended, customs are obliged to inform the right-holder and under some conditions the competent administrative and judicial authorities, having jurisdiction to determine whether these goods infringe an intellectual property right. Finally, a decision by such authorities is required to confirm seizure of infringing goods and, under some conditions, their final destruction.

---

[50] Cf para 16.04 above, Art 5(4).   [51] Ibid, Art 5(5), third indent.

A. Conditions governing action by customs authorities

(1) Factual background

Customs actions against goods suspected of infringing intellectual pro- **16.113** perty rights in Italy is mainly concentrated in the harbours of Genoa, La Spezia, and Naples (in particular as far as products coming from Asian countries are concerned). The customs offices located in the airports of Fiumicino (Rome II) and Malpensa (Milan II) are equally deeply involved in this field. In other words, the most important customs offices involved in anti-counterfeiting are the Regional Directorates of Rome, Milan, Genoa and Naples.

(2) Notification of customs intervention

The right-holder is immediately notified of a customs intervention by the cus- **16.114** toms authorities, who will liaise to that effect with the contact person[52] indicated in the application for action, and will instruct the right-holder to appoint a technical expert to examine the goods suspected of infringing an intellectual property right and conduct a survey thereon. Customs will, simultaneously, inform the declarant or holder of the goods of the detention, or suspension of release, of the goods in question.

(3) Information to be provided by customs to the right-holder before the right-holder confirms the infringing nature of the goods

Where goods suspected of infringing an intellectual property right are detained, **16.115** or their release suspended, by Italian Customs, the latter—without the right-holder being bound by the communication of such information to notify the authority having jurisdiction to determine whether the goods infringe an intellectual property right[53]—shall inform the right-holder of the actual or estimated quantity and the nature of the goods.

In practice, the customs authority may also supply additional information (such as a general description of the products, their packaging, and the country of origin).

---

[52] Cf ibid, Art 5(5), first indent, (iii).   [53] Ibid, Art 9(2).

16.116 Furthermore, according to Article 9(3) of the Regulation, Italian Customs shall provide the right-holder, at the latter's request and if known, with all information useful to establish whether an intellectual property right has been infringed under Italian law. This may, in particular, include the name and address of the consignee, consignor, declarant, or holder of the goods, the country of origin and provenance of the products, as well as a detailed description of the goods supplemented, as the case may be, by digital photographs.

16.117 Although the Italian legislation contains several provisions on the protection of personal data,[54] commercial and industrial secrecy,[55] and professional and administrative confidentiality,[56] within the meaning of Article 9(3) of the Regulation, in practice, Italian Customs take into account the decision of the European Court of Justice in case C-223/98,[57] and normally are not reluctant to communicate, at the right-holder's request, the identity of the declarant or consignee of goods which the right-holder has found to be infringing his intellectual property rights.

(4) Inspection of the suspected goods

16.118 Once the right-holder is informed of the taking of border measures, and subject to acceptance of his application for action, he must be given the opportunity to inspect the suspect consignment.[58] Right-holders are strongly advised to do so if they do not want to incur civil liability within the meaning of Article 6 of the Regulation.

16.119 The next step in the procedure is for the right-holder to confirm whether the suspect goods infringe his intellectual property rights. For this purpose, according to the Circular, the right-holder is required formally to appoint an expert to examine the goods, and to determine whether an infringement has occurred.[59]

16.120 The expert report may be based on digital pictures of the suspect goods taken by the relevant customs office, thus facilitating the identification. Obviously, the

---

[54] Codice in material di protezione dei dati personali 'Personal Data Protection Code', *Italian State Gazette* 29 July 2003, 174.

[55] Art 2598 of Codice Civile 'Civil Code', *Italian State Gazette*, 4 April 1942, 79; Arts 98 and 99 of the IP Code.

[56] Arts 622 and 623 of the Criminal Code.

[57] Case C-223/98 *Adidas AG* [1999] ECR 1999 Page I-07081.

[58] Reg 1383/2003, Art 9(3), second indent.

[59] Cf para 16.127 below.

right-holder shall bear the responsibility for his choice to identify the goods only by way of digital photographs, and will accept the possible consequences of this choice.

The customs office may also send samples of the products to the right-holder, or hand them over to the latter. However, the expert appointed by the right-holder will normally prefer to inspect the products and be supplied with samples in person. **16.121**

Use of samples is limited strictly for the purposes of conducting a technical analysis. In principle, samples must be returned on completion of the examination.[60] In practice, customs will only be stringent on this point when the samples have a significant economic value. **16.122**

On the basis of the results of the examination, the right-holder must provide an analytical report of all the investigations and tests conducted over the samples to the customs authorities. **16.123**

B. Simplified procedure allowing the destruction of the goods without there being any need to determine whether an intellectual property right has been infringed under national law

The simplified procedure laid down in Article 11 of the Regulation, whereby goods suspected of infringing an intellectual property right may be destroyed, without the need to establish whether an infringement of the said right has occurred, is not currently applied in Italy. **16.124**

However, Italian legislation has introduced, by Financial Law 2004,[61] Article 4 (80), a different proceeding concerning destruction of goods according to which: **16.125**

> [i]f the administrative authority ascertains, either at the time of importation or exportation, or during the commercialisation or distribution of goods, the violation of any intellectual property right, such an authority may, also on their own initiative, subject to the prior consent of the judicial authority of proper jurisdiction, seize the infringing goods and, after three months, destroy them, whilst charging the destruction costs to the counterfeiter wherever possible. Samples of the goods shall be kept for judicial purposes.

---

[60] Reg 1383/2003, Art 9(3), second indent.   [61] N 45 above.

C. Conditions governing action by the authorities having jurisdiction to determine whether the goods infringe an intellectual property right

(1) Authorities having jurisdiction to determine whether the goods infringe an intellectual property right

16.126　According to Article 13 of the Regulation, within 10 working days (3 working days in the case of perishable goods) of receipt of the notification of suspension of release or of detention of the goods, the right-holder—and under some conditions the intervening customs[62]—is required to bring the appropriate civil or criminal actions before the courts of proper jurisdiction to determine whether an intellectual property right has been infringed under national law. If the customs authorities are not informed of the commencement of such proceedings in due time, release of the goods shall be granted, or their detention shall be ended, as appropriate, subject to completion of all customs formalities.

Criminal action

16.127　Pursuant to the First Circular, once the expert appointed by the right-holder, according to Article 348 of the Criminal Procedure Code,[63] has confirmed the existence of an infringement of an intellectual property right, and provided such an infringement constitutes a possible criminal offence under Articles 473, 474, 517, and 648 of Criminal Code[64] and Articles from 171 to 171quater of the Copyright Law,[65] the intervening customs office shall, regardless of the right-holder's initiative, according to Article 347 of the Criminal Procedure Code, inform the judicial authority having jurisdiction thereof by filing a complaint with the Public Prosecutor's Office.[66]

However, we would point out that, even in these cases the right-holder is, in any case, entitled to file an independent compliant under Articles 330ff of the Criminal Procedure Code.

---

[62]　Cf para 16.127 below.

[63]　Codice di Procedura Penale 'Criminal Procedure Code', *Italian State Gazette* 24 October 1988, 250.

[64]　For detailed examination of these criminal cases, cf nn 80 and 88 below.

[65]　For detailed examination of these criminal cases, cf n 86 below.

[66]　Art 347 of Criminal Procedure Code states 'Obligation to report the offender's information— 1. Having obtained the offender's information, the judicial police, without delay, reports to the public prosecutor, in writing, on the essential items of the case and other items so far collected, stating the sources of evidence and the activities carried out, sending the relevant documents thereof. 2. They also send, as soon as possible, the general details, address and any other relevant information for identification of the person who is being investigated, the victim and those who are able to report on important circumstances for reconstructing the events (. . .).'

On the other hand, the right-holder is the only person entitled to file the **16.128** complaint under Articles 336 and 337 of the Criminal Procedure Code, in the case of violation of Article 127 of the IP Code.[67]

In both cases, once the criminal action has been brought, the judicial authority **16.129** should impose, under Article 354(2) of the Criminal Procedure Code, the immediate seizure of counterfeiting products and the articles belonging thereto, thus confirming the previous customs' decision to suspend the realization of goods. Seizure of the goods is, in such a case, almost immediate and, when applied to goods protected by any of the intellectual property rights described in Article 14(1) of the Regulation, cannot be revoked by the payment of a security.[68]

Furthermore, it is possible for the right-holder to file a complaint as the injured **16.130** party in the criminal proceedings, according to Articles 76 to 78 of Criminal Procedure Code, and to claim compensation for damages.

Finally, when the criminal courts confirm the existence of an intellectual **16.131** property right infringement, they order the forfeiture and destruction of the goods under seizure (according to Article 334 of the Criminal Code and Article 171sexies of the Copyright Law),[69] the forfeiture and destruction of moulds and matrices,[70] and also, under the terms of Article 475 of the Criminal Code and Article 171ter of the Copyright Law, the publication of the sentence.[71]

According to the First Circular, it is recommended that right-holders draft their **16.132** expert report under Article 348 of the Criminal Procedure Code in such a way as to outline the presumed criminal offence, establish the required link between the presumed offence and the precautionary measure (that is, the seizure) to be taken, and clearly point out the aim of these measures (for example, to prevent the holder of the goods disposing of them, thus precluding further investigation concerning the goods).

In fact, for the purposes of preventing the terms described in Article 13 of the **16.133** Regulation from lapsing, the customs authorities acknowledge a 'key role' for the expert report. By sending the expert report to customs, the right-holder confirms his serious interest in ascertaining whether there has been an infringement of his rights and preventing the counterfeit products from being realized within the internal market. This will ensure that, after the expert report has been sent, customs will not release the infringing products. In any case, it will then be

---

[67] Cf nn 83, 88, 90, 92, 94, 103 and 113 below.   [68] Cf n 97 below.
[69] N 97 below.   [70] Cf n 25 above.
[71] Art 475, Additional penalty—Conviction for any of the offences stipulated by the previous two articles entails publication of the sentence.

necessary for the judicial authority to confirm customs' decision by the precautionary measure of seizure, under Article 354(2) of the Criminal Procedure Code.[72]

Civil action

16.134   Once customs have suspended the release of goods suspected of infringing an intellectual property right, the right-holder is always entitled to bring an ordinary civil action (proceedings on the merits), according to the Civil Procedure Code[73] and the specific statutory provisions relating to intellectual property,[74] addressed to ascertain the violation of the right-holder's right and, therefore, to obtain, according to the IP Code and Copyright Law, the seizure of goods, the banning of manufacture, marketing and use of what constitutes infringement of the right (injunction),[75] and publication of the court decision, in full or in summary form, taking into account the seriousness of the actions, in one or more daily newspapers, at the expense of the losing party.[76]

16.135   According to Article 121 of the IP Code, if the right-holder has provided material evidence to substantiate his petitions, and has determined documents, items, or information held by the opposing party that confirm this evidence, he can ask the judge to order documents to be submitted by, or request information from, the opposing party. He may also ask the judge to order the provision of items to identify the individuals involved in the production and distribution of products that infringe intellectual property rights. In making these arrangements, the judge takes the correct steps to ensure that confidential information is protected, after consultation with the opposing party.

16.136   When pronouncing the ban, the judge may set a sum due for each infringement or non-observance subsequently recorded and for each delay in implementing the measure.[77]

16.137   Furthermore the right-holder may claim damages as compensation for loss incurred as a result of the infringement. Loss of earnings is assessed by the judge, in particular, also taking into account the profits made in infringement of the right and the fees the infringing party would have had to pay if he had obtained a licence from the right-holder.[78]

---

[72] Cf para 16.129 above.
[73] Codice di Procedura Civile 'Code of Civil Procedure', *Italian State Gazette* 28 October 1940, 253.
[74] Arts 117–134 of the IP Code and Arts 156–167 of the Copyright Law.
[75] Art 124(1) of the IP Code and Art 156 of the Copyright Law.
[76] Art 126 of the IP Code and Art 166 of the Copyright Law.
[77] Art 124(2) of the IP Code.
[78] Art 125 (1) of the IP Code and Art 158 of the Copyright Law.

The sentence that is pronounced on compensation for damages may, at the **16.138** request of one party, order settlement in one overall sum established on the basis of the documents of the case and on the presumptions arising therefrom.[79]

In serious cases, in addition to prohibiting the manufacture, sale, and use of the **16.139** infringing objects, the decision may also provide for the seizure and transfer to the right-holder of the infringing goods and manufacturing facilities.[80]

Finally, where the infringement of an industrial property right is ascertained, the **16.140** destruction of all the items constituting the infringement may be ordered.[81]

Seizure of products suspected of infringing an intellectual property right[82] and a **16.141** ban on their manufacture, marketing and use,[83] can be obtained by the right-holder, in a few weeks by summary proceedings.[84] However, in this case it is quite difficult to obtain publication of the court decision. Such proceedings can be started either before introducing the ordinary proceedings or during the course of the action.

Summary proceedings may be instituted under Articles 669bis of the Civil **16.142** Procedure Code, with the purpose of ensuring effective legal protection by counteracting any prejudice or damage to the claimant which may be incurred pending the proceedings on the merits.

By seizure of counterfeit products, the judicial authority may confirm the previ- **16.143** ous customs' decision to suspend realization of the goods.

It is necessary to consider whether the request for seizure (and prevention) filed **16.144** before ordinary proceedings are brought, can be considered 'proceedings to determine whether an intellectual property right has been infringed' under Article 13 of the Regulation. It appears that it is possible to answer 'yes' to this question, in particular in the light of the recently introduced IP Code.

Before the effective date of the IP Code, summary proceedings were considered to **16.145** be provisional (and instrumental) measures compared with ordinary proceedings. In fact, under the terms of Article 669octies of the Civil Procedure Code, the right-holder was obliged, once the seizure of the goods has been obtained, to bring ordinary proceedings designed to ascertain the violation of his right and to confirm the efficacy of the provisional measures already obtained. Failure to start ordinary proceedings led to the definite loss of efficacy of the provisional measure.

---

[79] Art 125(2) of the IP Code.
[80] Art 124(4), (5) of the IP Code and Art 159 of the Copyright Law.
[81] Art 124(3) of the IP Code and Arts 158–160 of the Copyright Law.
[82] Art 129(3) of the IP Code and Art 161 of the Copyright Law.
[83] Art 131 of the IP Code and Art 163 of the Copyright Law.
[84] Art 129 (3) of the IP Code.

16.146 Today, Article 134 of the IP Code stipulates that the new procedural rules described by Legislative Decree No 5, of 17 January 2003[85] apply to summary proceedings. Pursuant to these new provisions,[86] interim measures do not cease to be effective if ordinary proceedings on the merits are not subsequently initiated. These measures may, therefore, guarantee some 'stability' towards the parties in whose favour they have been issued,[87] and may even, ultimately, remain the only effective remedies in place to jugulate the infringement of the right-holder's rights. Consequently, it seems fair to conclude that such interim measures should be deemed to fulfil the requirements set out in Article 13 of the Regulation. However, such a rule appears to be in clear contrast to Article 50(6) of the TRIPs Agreement. Finally, it is noteworthy that it does not apply to copyright.

16.147 In practice, when suspect goods are detained, or their release suspended under the Regulation, we advise right-holders to file a criminal action, since it is a quick action (seizure under Article 354(2) of the Criminal Procedure Code is almost immediate) and incisive, both from the point of view of the responsibility of the person investigated and that of the penalties applied.

16.148 It should, however, be remembered that it is easier (and faster) to obtain damages in the context of civil proceedings. Therefore, provided there is a possibility of recovering damages, our advice is to file both criminal and civil actions.

16.149 We examine below the specific types of action, both criminal and civil, that the right-holder is entitled to bring in the event of violation of each single intellectual property right.

Counterfeit goods

16.150 In the case of the counterfeiting of goods, it is possible to bring criminal actions under Article 473 of Criminal Code ('Counterfeiting, pirating or using of trade-marks of engineering works or industrial products'),[88] Article 474 of Criminal

---

[85] Definizione dei procedimenti in materia di diritto societario e di intermediazione finanziaria nonchè in materia bancaria e creditizia, in attuazione dell'art. 12 delle legge 3 ottobre 2001, n. 266, *Italian State Gazette* 22 January 2003, 17.

[86] Art 23 (1) of Legislative Decree No 5 of 17 January, 2003 (n 85 above).

[87] In any case, it should be taken into account that, according to Art 23(3) of cited Legislative Decree No 5 of 17 January, 2003 (cf n 85 above), the measures in question may be changed or revoked in the case where changes in circumstances occur, to be understood also as previous circumstances which become known subsequent to the cautionary measure.

[88] Art 473 of the Criminal Code—'Anyone who counterfeits trade marks or brands of national or foreign engineering works or industrial products, or without participating in the actual counterfeiting, makes use of these counterfeit trade marks or brands, will be liable to prosecution, imprisonment of up to 3 years and a fine of up to 2,065.86 Euros.

Anyone counterfeiting of forging national or foreign patents or industrial drawings or patterns, or without actually participating in the counterfeiting or forging of these foreign patents or industrial drawings or patterns makes use of them, is equally liable to prosecution and the same punishment.(. . .).'

Code ('Introducing products bearing false trademarks into the country for commercial reasons')[89] and Article 517 of Criminal Code ('Selling of industrial products bearing false trademarks').[90,91]

With regard to interpretation of these Regulations in Italian case law, we set out below some decisions of particular significance.   **16.151**

The Italian Supreme Court, after an initial judgment that excluded the existence of the criminal case as set out in Article 474 of the Criminal Code in the case of 'serious forgery', subsequently corrected interpretation of the Regulation, opining in this respect that: **16.152**

> The judicial interest protected by arts. 473 and 474 of the Criminal Code is the public trust in an objective sense, understood as the public's trust in the trademarks or distinguishing signs that characterise intellectual works or industrial products and guarantee their circulation, and not the trust of the individual, so that, in order to include the offence, it is not necessary for a situation to arise in order to persuade the customer in error with regard to the product's authenticity. On the contrary, the offence may exist, if the counterfeiting is carried out objectively, even if the purchaser has been made aware by the vendor himself of the lack of authenticity of the trade mark.[92]

In more general terms, the Supreme Court has given clarification that the offence under Article 474 is a 'dangerous offence, for whose configuration it is not necessary for the deception to have taken place'.[93]   **16.153**

From this point of view, there is a clear difference between the cases included in Article 474 of the Criminal Code and those described under Article 517 of the Criminal Code. The two cases are differentiated by the protected judicial value,   **16.154**

---

[89] Art 474 of the Criminal Code—'Apart from the cases covered in the preceding article, anyone introducing counterfeited or imitations of national or foreign engineering works or industrial products bearing trademarks or brand names into this country for commercial reasons, for holding in stock for later sale, or for putting on the market, will be subject to prosecution and imprisonment of up to 2 years or a fine of up to 2,065.86 Euros.'

[90] Art 517 of the Criminal Code—'Anyone who sells or circulates engineering works or industrial products bearing national or foreign names, brands or trademarks which may deceive the purchaser about the origin or the quality of the product is subject, in case the act is not provided for as a crime by another provision of the law, to prosecution of up to one year or a fine up to 20,000.00 Euros.'

[91] Then there are other criminal Regulations that may incidentally concern acts of infringement of the trade mark Regulations: Art 514 of the Criminal Code ('Cases of fraud against national industries'); Art 515 of the Criminal Code ('Cases of fraud in commercial activity'); as well as Art 648 of the Criminal Code ('Receiving stolen property') and Art 712 of the Criminal Code ('Purchase of articles of suspect origin').

[92] Supreme Court, Criminal Section, 21 February 2002, in *Giurisprudenza Annotata di Diritto Industriale*,. [2002], 4335). The same principle can be found in Supreme Court, Criminal Section, 2 February 2001, *Cassazione Penale*, [2002], 3768.

[93] Supreme Court, 14 December 2000, in *Rivista Penale*, [2001], 161.

namely that in the case of Article 474 of the Criminal Code it is the public trust which is being protected, whereas in the case of Article 517 of Criminal Code it is the economic order.

16.155　Finally, with regard to the moment when the actual offence is carried out, as described in Article 517 of Criminal Code, we note that Article 4(49) of the Financial Law 2004, has also made clear that ' the import and export for marketing purposes' (presentation in customs of goods with false signs) includes the case of the actual offence carried out as stipulated by Article 517.

16.156　Furthermore, the offence of receiving can also be concurrent to the cases described, in accordance with Article 648 of the Criminal Code ('Receiving of counterfeit goods').[94]

16.157　Finally, the IP Code has introduced, under Article 127, a new provision concerning 'Criminal and administrative penalties'[95] which has a residual application with regard to Articles 473, 474, and 517 of Criminal Code. With regard to application of this case—which applies to all intellectual property rights (with the exception of copyright as excluded from the IP Code)—we note that it should oblige investigation by the judicial authority of the validity of the right infringed. Of course, this decision will have efficacy solely *inter partes*, since, under Italian legislation, the action addressed to ascertain the final nullity of an intellectual property right is filed by civil or administrative proceedings.

16.158　On the other hand, the right-holder can start civil proceedings on grounds of violation of Articles 20 and 21 of IP Code.[96]

---

[94] 'With the exception of cases of criminal complicity, anyone who, with the aim of financial gain for himself or for others, buys, receives, or conceals money or items deriving from any crime whatsoever, or contributes to having them bought, received or concealed, shall be subject to prosecution, two to eight years' imprisonment, and a fine ranging from EUR 516,46 to EUR 10.329,14. For less serious cases, the maximums are six years' imprisonment, and a fine of EUR 516,46.

These provisions apply regardless of whether the perpetrator of the offence is not indictable or not punishable.

[95] Art 127 of the IP Code, '1. Without prejudice to application of articles 473, 474 and 517 of the criminal code, anyone who manufactures, sells, exhibits, uses for industrial purposes or brings into the State objects in infringement of a valid industrial property right, under the terms of the regulations of this code, is punished, by legal action, with the fine of up to 1,032.91 Euros.

2. Anyone who affixes on an object words or directions that are not true, leading to the belief that the object is protected by patent, design or model, or topography, or to the belief that the trade mark distinguishing it has been registered, is punished with the administrative penalty of from 51.65 Euros to 516.46 Euros.

3. Unless the action constitues an offence, anyone who makes use of a registered trademark, after the said registration has been declared null and void, when the cause of nullity leads to the illegality of the use of the trademark, or removes the trademark of the producer or trader from whom he has received the rights or the goods for commercial purposes, is punished with the administrative penalty of up to 2,065.83 Euros, even when there has been no damage to the third party.'

[96] Cf paras 16.19–16.20 above.

Pirated goods

In situations involving the infringement of a copyright or related rights, it is **16.159** possible to bring criminal actions under Articles 171, 171bis-nonies, 172, 173, 174, and 174bis-quinquies of the Copyright Law.[97]

> **Article 171** Without prejudice to the provisions of Article 171bis and Article 171ter, any person who, without having the right thereto, and for any purpose and in any form:
>
> (a) reproduces, transcribes, recites in public, disseminates, sells or offers for sale, or otherwise commercially distributes the work of another person, or reveals the contents of such work before it is made public, or introduces or circulates within the territory of the State copies produced abroad contrary to Italian law;
>
> (b) performs or recites in public or disseminates, with or without variations or additions, the work of another person intended for public performance, or a musical composition. Performance includes the public showing of a cinematographic work, the performance in public of musical compositions included in cinematographic works, and broadcasting by means of a loudspeaker operated in public;
>
> (c) commits the acts referred to in the preceding subparagraphs by means of any form of transformation referred to in this Law;
>
> (d) reproduces copies or gives performances in excess of the number which he has the right to reproduce or perform;
>
> (e) [repealed]
>
> (f) in violation of Article 79, retransmits by wire or by radio, or records on phonograph records or other like devices radiophonic transmissions or retransmissions, or sells the unlawfully recorded phonograph records or other devices;
>
> shall be liable to a fine of between Euro 51,00 and Euro 2065,00.
>
> The penalty shall be imprisonment of up to one year or a fine of not less than Euro 516,00 if the acts referred to above are committed in relation to a work of another person which is not intended for public disclosure or by usurpation of the authorship of the work or with deformation, mutilation or other modification of the work and such acts constitute an offense against the honor or reputation of the author.
>
> Violation of the provisions of the third and fourth paragraphs of Article 68 shall cause the photocopying or xerocopying activity or comparable system of reproduction to be suspended for a period of six months to one year, and a fine of between Euro 1032,00 and Euro 5164,00 to be imposed.
>
> **171bis.**-(1) Any person who unlawfully duplicates computer programs for profit-making purposes or who imports, distributes, sells, holds for commercial or business purposes or rents programs embodied in media not bearing the mark of the SIAE shall be liable to a prison term of between six months and three years and to a fine of between Euro 2580,00 and Euro 15483,00. The same penalty shall apply if the act involves any means intended solely to permit or facilitate the unauthorized removal or circumvention of any technical device applied to protect a computer program. For

---

[97] Such a criminal legislation on copyright infringements (including unauthorized reproduction or use of software and databases) has recently been implemented (n 19 above). We are here reporting the main articles concerning violation of copyright under the Regulation, as translated by WIPO in website http://www.wipo.int/clea/docs_new/en/it/it099en.html.

a serious offense, the penalty shall be a prison term of not less than two years and a fine of Euro 15483,00.

(2) Any person who, for profit-making purposes, using media not bearing the mark of the SIAE, reproduces, transfers to another medium, distributes, communicates, presents or demonstrates in public the contents of a data bank in breach of the provisions of Articles 64quinquies and 64sexies, or extracts or re-uses material from a data bank in breach of the provisions of Articles 102bis and 102ter, or who distributes, sells or rents a data bank, shall be liable to a prison term of between six months and three years and to a fine of between Euro 2582,00 and Euro 15493,00. The penalty shall be a prison term of not less than two years and a fine of Euro 15483,00 if the offense is serious.

171ter.-(1) A prison term of six months to three years and a fine of Euro 2582,00 and Euro 15493,00 shall be imposed, if the act is committed for other than personal use, on any person who, with gainful intent:

(a) unlawfully duplicates, reproduces, transmits or broadcasts in public by whatever means, in whole or in part, an intellectual work intended for television or cinema use, through sale or hire, or discs, tapes or similar media or any other media containing phonograms or videograms of comparable musical, cinematographic or audiovisual works or sequences of moving images;

(b) unlawfully reproduces, transmits or broadcasts in public, by whatever means, works or parts of works of literary, dramatic, scientific or educational, musical or dramatico-musical character, as well as multimedia works, even when included in collective or composite works or data banks;

(c) without having participated in the duplication or reproduction, brings into the territory of the State, holds for sale or distribution, distributes, places on sale, rents or releases for any reason, shows in public or broadcasts on television by whatever means, transmits by radio, or causes to be heard in public, the unlawful duplications or reproductions referred to in subparagraphs (a) and (b);

(d) holds for sale or distribution, places on sale, sells, rents, releases for any reason, shows in public or broadcasts by television or radio by whatever means videocassettes, music cassettes, any medium containing phonograms or videograms of musical, cinematographic or audiovisual works or sequences of moving images, or any other medium to which, in accordance with this Law, the SIAE is required to affix its mark, either without such a mark or with a counterfeit or altered mark, or produces, uses, imports, places on sale, rents or releases for any reason equipment capable of circumventing, decoding or removing measures designed to protect copyright or related rights;

(e) in the absence of an agreement with the lawful distributor, transmits or broadcasts, by any means, an encrypted service received by apparatus or parts of apparatus capable of decoding transmissions subject to restricted access;

(f) brings into the territory of the State, holds for sale or distribution, distributes, sells, rents, releases for any reason, advertises for commercial purposes or installs special decoding devices or components that afford access to an encrypted service without payment of the necessary fee;

f bis) manufactures, imports, distributes, sells, hires, assigns to any title, advertises for sale or hore, or holds for commercial purposes, equipment, products or component parts, or provides services, whose main aim or commercial use is to evade effective technological measures, as set out in art.102-quater, or are mainly designed, produced, adapted or made with the aim of making possible or helping the evasion of the aforesaid measures. Included in the technological measures are those applied, or that remain, following removal of the same measures as a result of voluntary initiative by the right-holders and by agreement between the latter and the beneficiaries of exceptions, or following execution of measures by the administrativel or jurisdictional authority;

h) unlawfully removes or alters electronic information as set out in art. 102-quinquies, or distributes, imports for distribution purposes, broadcasts on radio or television, notifies or makes available to the public, protected works or other materials from which the electronic information itself has been removed.

(2) Any person who:

(a) unlawfully reproduces, duplicates, transmits or broadcasts, sells or otherwise places on the market, releases for any reason or imports unlawfully more than 50 copies or originals of works protected by copyright or by related rights;

(b) in the course of a business activity involving the reproduction, distribution, sale, marketing or importation of works protected by copyright or related rights, renders himself guilty of the offenses referred to in paragraph (1);

(c) promotes or organizes the unlawful activities referred to in paragraph (1);

shall be liable to a prison term of between one and four years and to a fine of between Euro 2582,00 and Euro 15493,00. (3) The penalty shall be reduced if the evidence of the offense is particularly tenuous.

(4) Conviction for one of the offenses referred to in paragraph (1) shall include:

(a) the application of the subsidiary penalties provided for in Articles 30 and 32bis of the Criminal Code;

(b) publication of the sentence in one or more daily newspapers, including at least one in national circulation, and in one or more specialized reviews;

(c) suspension for one year of the radio or television broadcasting license or authorization with respect to the exercise of the production or business activity.

(5) Income deriving from the imposition of the fines provided for in the preceding paragraphs shall be paid to the National Provident and Assistance Agency for Painters and Sculptors, Musicians, Writers and Playwrights [Ente nazionale di previdenza ed assistenza per i pittori e scultori, musicisti, scrittori ed autori drammatici].

171quater. Any person who, without being authorized to do so and with gainful intent:

(a) rents or in any manner permits the use, for whatever purpose, of original specimens or of copies or of media, obtained lawfully, of copyrighted works;

(b) records the performances referred to in Article 80 on audio, video or audiovisual media;

shall be liable, except where the act amounts to a more serious offense, to imprisonment of up to one year or a fine of between Euro 516,00 and Euro 5164,00.

171quinquies.-(1) For the purposes of the provisions of this Law, sale with a repurchase option or rescission clause shall be deemed equivalent to renting if provision is made for the seller, in the event of repurchase invocation of the clause, to repay a sum lower than that paid, or if the purchaser, at the time of delivery, makes provision for payment of a sum as a deposit or otherwise on account which is in any event lower than the sale price.

171sexies.-(1) If the seized material, owing to its size, is difficult to store, the judicial authority may order its destruction under the provisions of Article 83 of the implementing, coordinating and transitional provisions of the Criminal Procedure Code, approved by Legislative Decree No. 271 of July 28, 1989.

(2) Provision shall always be made for the confiscation of instruments and materials used or intended for committing the offenses referred to in Articles 171bis, 171ter and 171quater, and of videocassettes or other audiovisual, phonographic, data processing or multimedia material unlawfully duplicated, reproduced, released, traded, held or brought into the national territory, or which either do not bear the mark of the SIAE where required or bear an SIAE mark that is counterfeit, altered or intended for a different work. Confiscation shall also be ordered in the event of enforcement of a penalty on a request made by the parties under Article 444 of the Criminal Procedure Code.

(3) The provisions of the previous paragraphs shall also apply if the goods belong to a different legal person in whose interests one of the parties to the offense has acted.

171septies.-(1) The penalty referred to in Article 171ter(1) shall also apply:

(a) to producers or importers of media not subject to marking under Article 181bis who fail to provide the SIAE with data permitting unambiguous identification of the said media within 30 days of the date of their becoming available for sale on the national territory or being imported;

(b) to any person who falsely declares fulfillment of his obligations under Article 181bis(2) of this Law, except where the act does not constitute a more serious offense.

171octies.-(1) If the act does not constitute a more serious offense, any person who with fraudulent intent produces, offers for sale, imports, advertises, installs or modifies, or makes public or private use of, devices or parts of devices capable of decoding audiovisual transmissions subject to special conditions of access and effected on the air, by satellite or by cable, in analog or digital form, shall be liable to a prison term of between six months and three years and a fine of between Euro 2582,00 and Euro 25822,00. Such special conditions of access shall be understood to be those whereby all audiovisual signals transmitted by Italian or foreign broadcasters are in a form that renders them perceivable only by closed groups of users selected by the broadcaster of the signals, whether or not a fee is payable for such a service to be enjoyed.

(2) For a serious offense, the penalty shall not be less than a prison term of two years and a fine of Euro 15493,00.

171nonies.-(1) The main penalty for the offenses referred to in Articles 171bis, 171ter and 171quater shall be reduced by one-third to a half, and the subsidiary penalties shall not apply, in the case of a person who, prior to being charged individually with a violation by the judicial authority, either reports it spontaneously or, by providing all the information in his possession, facilitates the identification of a promoter or organizer of the unlawful activity referred to in Articles 171ter and 171quater or of another duplicator or distributor, or who facilitates the seizure of substantial quantities of audiovisual or phonographic media or of instruments or materials used or intended for the commission of such offenses.

(2) The provisions of this Article shall not apply to a promoter or organizer of unlawful activities under 171bis(1) and Article 171ter(1).

Article 172. If the acts referred to in Article 171 are committed by negligence, the penalty shall be a fine of up to Euro 1032,00.

Any person who

(a) acts as an intermediary in violation of Articles 180 and 183,

(b) fails to carry out the obligations set out in Articles 153 and 154,

(c) violates the provisions of Articles 175 and 176,

shall be liable to the same penalty.

Article 173. The penalties set out in the preceding Articles shall apply in all instances where the acts in question do not constitute a more serious offense under the Penal Code or other laws.

Article 174. In penal proceedings governed by this Section, a party, who sues for civil injury, may at any time request the penal court to apply the measures and penalties set out in Articles 159 and 160.

Article 174bis.-(1) Without prejudice to the applicable penal sanctions, violation of the provisions set out in this Section shall be punished with an administrative fine equivalent to double the market price of the work or medium to which the violation relates, and in any case not less than €103,00. If the price is not easily ascertainable, the violation shall be punished with an administrative fine of between 103,00 and 1032,00. The administrative penalty shall be applied in the prescribed amount for each violation and for each unlawfully duplicated or reproduced item.

Articles from 174ter to 174quinquies (omissis).

One of the greatest difficulties our jurisprudence found in applying the Regulations in question concerns concurrence among the offences described in Article 171ter of the Copyright Law and Article 648 of the Criminal Code.[98]   **16.160**

At present, the strict guidelines of the Supreme Court remain in place. In very many findings the Court has confirmed the possibility of configuring in concurrence the criminal cases by someone who, while not being involved in duplication, but knowing the illegal origin, has purchased or holds for sale music cassettes that have been reproduced without authorization.[99] These guidelines are, however, subject to a great deal of criticism by our doctrine.[100]   **16.161**

The right-holder can start civil proceedings on grounds of violation of rights of economic use, according to Article 156 of the Copyright Act.   **16.162**

Finally Articles 473 (2) and 648 of the Criminal Code and Article 127 of the IP Code can be applied in the case of violation of a design right.   **16.163**

With regard to the application of Article 473 (2) of the Criminal Code, up until the late nineties, doctrine and jurisprudence interpreted the Regulations in such as way as to consider them applicable to the more material falsifications carried out on the certificate of the right being granted.[101] The Supreme Court, aligning   **16.164**

---

[98] N 94 above.

[99] Supreme Court, Criminal Section, 10 February 1998, in *Rivista Penale* 1998, 1133, Supreme Court, Criminal Section, 6 May 1993, in *Rivista Penale*, 1994, 33; Supreme Court, Criminal Section, 17 November 1992, in *Foro Italiano*, 1993, II, 564.

[100] Alessandri, in *Ubertazzi, La legge sul software* (Giuffrè), 243.

[101] Di Cataldo (*I brevetti per invenzione e per modello cit.* 2000, 59, Vanzetti, Di Cataldo (*Manuale di diritto industriale cit.* [2003], 411; Pretura of Lodi, 28.6.1985, in *Giurisprudenza Annotata di Diritto Industriale*, [1986], 232.

itself with a single precedent of 1993[102] has subsequently found, in a significant decision in 1999,[103] on the matter of models concerning headgear, that:

> The offence of counterfeiting of ornamental designs or models, stipulated by Article 473 of Criminal Code can be configured whenever the product has the shape and colours that may lead the public to identify it as coming from a certain company, regardless of the situation where it is provided with trademarks showing the different and actual origin.

16.165   In its finding, the Supreme Court also gave clarification to the effect that: 'The assessment of the offence stipulated in Article 473(2) of Criminal Code requires interpretation of the communicative meaning of the counterfeited model in order to check the latter's ability to cause a false representation of the product's origin.'[104]

16.166   Finally, the right-holder may start civil proceedings on grounds of violation of Article 41 of the IP Code.[105]

Goods infringing a patent or a supplementary protection certificate

16.167   In the case of goods infringing a patent or a supplementary protection certificate, it is possible to bring criminal actions under Articles 473 (2) and 648 of the Criminal Code and Article 127 of the IP Code.

16.168   The right-holder may start civil proceedings on grounds of violation of Articles 66 and 67 of the IP Code.[106]

Goods infringing a plant variety right

16.169   In the case of goods infringing a plant variety right, it is possible to bring criminal actions under Articles 473 (2) and 648 of the Criminal Code and Article 127 of the IP Code.

16.170   The right-holder may start civil proceedings on grounds of violation of Article 107 of the IP Code.[107]

---

[102]   Supreme Court, Criminal Section, 9 December 1993, in *Giustizia Penale* [1994], II, 551.

[103]   Supreme Court, Criminal Section, 22 June 1999, in *Rivista Penale* [1999], 991.

[104]   Similar principles have been expressed: in decision no 6418 of the Supreme Court, Criminal Section, on 26 March, 1998, *Cassazione Pen*ale [2000], 49, concerning a case of counterfeiting a patent for an ornamental model for gold bracelets and in decision no 552 of the Supreme Court, of 14 April 1998, *Cassazione Penale*, [2000], 869), concerning a case of counterfeiting a patent for an ornamental model relating to industrial goods.

[105]   Cf paras 16.35–16.36 above.   [106]   Cf paras 16.38–16.41 above.

[107]   Cf paras 16.42–16.43 above.

Goods infringing a designation of origin or a geographical indication

In the case of goods infringing a designation of origin or a geographical indica- **16.171**
tion, it is possible to bring criminal actions under Articles 517 and 648 of the
Criminal Code and Article 127 of the IP Code.

The right-holder may start civil proceedings on grounds of violation of Article 30 **16.172**
of the IP Code[108] and Article 2598 of the Civil Code by relying on an act of unfair
competition.

(2) *Term for notifying customs that proceedings have been started*

Article 13 of the Regulation provides that the term of 10 working days may be **16.173**
extended once by another 10 working days 'in appropriate cases'. Italian Customs
are relatively flexible on this point, and consider as 'appropriate cases', for
instance, the time (often exceeding 10 working days) necessary to complete
the expertise of the goods, and, therefore, to ascertain the infringement of an
intellectual property right. This applies, in particular, to the infringement of software, patents, plant variety rights, etc which often involve complex technical
considerations.

D. Release of goods suspected of infringing certain rights on provision of a security

Provided that the conditions of Article 14(1) of the Regulation are observed, the **16.174**
Italian customs authorities consider that they are obliged to release the goods,
unless the infringing products are under seizure pursuant to the Criminal
Procedure Code (which happens in the overwhelming majority of cases),[109] in
which case the goods cannot be released.

For the purpose of determining the amount of security provided for in Article **16.175**
14(2) of the Regulation, the commercial value of the products should be taken
into account. The amount will be set by the authority called upon to ascertain the
infringement of intellectual property rights.

In any case, we note that this instrument is not normally used very much, **16.176**
particularly by the civil courts.

---

[108] Cf paras 16.44–16.45 above.
[109] Cf para 16.129 above.

E. Storage of the goods

16.177 During the period of suspension of release or detention, the goods are kept in 'terminals for temporary charge'. Storage costs are initially borne by the right-holder until the dispute has been finally adjudicated by the courts. Where a final court decision confirms the infringement of an intellectual property right, the right-holder is entitled to ask the court to order the infringer to bear the storage costs.

IV. PROVISIONS APPLICABLE TO GOODS FOUND TO INFRINGE AN INTELLECTUAL PROPERTY RIGHT

16.178 If, as a result of the proceedings referred to in Article 13 of the Regulation, goods are found to infringe an intellectual property right, Italian law allows the right-holder to oppose entry into or removal from the Community customs territory, release for free circulation, exportation, re-exportation, placement under a suspensive procedure (including external transit and transhipment), and placement in a free zone or free warehouse of such goods, in accordance with Article 16 of the Regulation.

16.179 This principle should also apply to infringing goods that are only in transit in the Italian territory and, therefore, not intended for the national market.

16.180 As has been pointed out above, the right-holder may seek the destruction of goods which have been found by a court to infringe any of his rights.[110]

16.181 Finally Article 4(80) of the Financial Law 2004 is applicable.[111]

16.182 Therefore, it will usually be the case that where the courts conclude there has been an infringement of an intellectual property right, they will order the forfeiture and destruction of the goods.

16.183 The Italian authorities have sought alternative measures to remove the infringing goods from the commercial channels, and thus preclude injury to the right-holder. However, customs' experience in this field has always proven negative. In particular, products which had been relinquished to charities have been found again on the market some time later. Consequently, the authorities no longer consent to the application of such alternative measures.

---

[110] Cf para 16.131 above.   [111] Cf para 16.125 above.

Similarly, under the current Italian legislation, simply removing the trade marks **16.184** that have been affixed to counterfeit goods is not considered effective enough to deprive the persons concerned of any economic gains from the transaction.

V. PENALTIES

When intellectual property rights are infringed, the infringer may have criminal **16.185** penalties imposed on him. He may also be ordered to pay damages to the right-holder to compensate him for any loss he has incurred.

We have examined above the Regulations, both criminal and civil, to which the **16.186** right-holder has recourse in the case of infringement of each individual right included in the Regulation, and the relevant penalties. We will go on to summarize them below in outline, referring to the paragraphs above for a fuller examination.

Counterfeit goods

Trade mark infringements are punished under criminal law by imprisonment of **16.187** up to three years and a fine of up to EUR 20,000.00.[112] In a case which also includes the offence of receiving stolen property, those infringements may be punished by between two and eight years' imprisonment, and a fine ranging from EUR 516.46 to EUR 10,329.14. For less serious cases, the maximum penalties are six years' imprisonment, and a fine of EUR 516.46.[113] Lastly, where these penalties are not applicable, Article 127 of the IP Code imposes payment of a fine of up to EUR 1,032.91.[114]

2. Furthermore, it is possible for the right-holder to claim compensation for damages,[115] the forfeiture and destruction of the goods under seizure,[116] the forfeiture and destruction of moulds and matrices,[117] as well as publication of the finding.[118]

Under civil law, according to the Civil Procedure Code and the specific statutory **16.188** provisions relating to intellectual property,[119] the claimant may obtain: seizure of counterfeit goods, the ban on manufacture, marketing and use of what constitutes infringement of the right (injunction)[120] and publication of the court decision, in

---

[112] Arts 473, 474, and 517 of the Criminal Code (cf. paras 16.150 ff above).
[113] Art 648 of the Criminal Code (cf. para 16.156 above).
[114] Cf para 16.157 above.   [115] Cf n 67 above.   [116] Cf para 16.131 above.
[117] Cf n 25 above.   [118] Cf n 68 above.
[119] Arts 117–134 of the IP Code (cf para 16.134 above).
[120] Art 124(1) of the IP Code.

full or in summary form, in one or more daily newspapers at the expense of the losing party.[121] When pronouncing the ban, the judge may set a sum due for each infringement or non-observance subsequently recorded and for each delay in implementing the measure.[122] In serious cases, in addition to banning manufacture, sale, and use of the infringing objects, the decision may also provide for seizure and transfer to the right-holder of the infringing goods and manufacturing facilities.[123] Finally, with the decision ascertaining the infringement of an industrial property right, the destruction of all the items constituting the infringement may be ordered.[124] Furthermore, the right-holder may claim damages as compensation for the loss incurred as a result of the infringement.[125]

Pirated goods

16.189   Copyright infringements are punished under criminal law by imprisonment of between six months and four years and to a fine of between EUR 2582,00 and EUR 15,493.00. For a serious offence, the penalty shall be a prison term of not less than two years and a fine of EUR 15,493.00.[126] If the acts referred to in Article 171 are committed due to negligence, the penalty shall be a fine of up to EUR 1,033.00.[127]

16.190   Finally, without prejudice to the applicable penal sanctions, violation of copyrights shall be punished with an administrative fine equivalent to double the market price of the work or medium to which the violation relates, and in any case not less than EUR 103.00. If the price is not easily ascertainable, the violation shall be punished with an administrative fine of between EUR 103.00 and EUR 1,030.00. The administrative penalty shall be applied in the prescribed amount for each violation and for each unlawfully duplicated or reproduced item.[128]

16.191   Furthermore, it is possible for the right-holder to claim compensation for damages,[129] the forfeiture and destruction of the goods under seizure,[130] the forfeiture and destruction of moulds and matrices,[131] as well as publication of the finding.[132]

16.192   Under civil law, according to the Civil Procedure Code and the specific statutory provisions relating to intellectual property,[133] the claimant may obtain: seizure of goods, the ban on the manufacture, marketing and use of what constitutes infringement of the right (injunction)[134] and publication of the court

---

[121] Art 126 of the IP Code.   [122] Art 124 (2) of the IP Code.
[123] Art 124(4), (5) of the IP Code.   [124] Art 124(3) of the IP Code.
[125] Art 125(2) of the IP Code.   [126] Arts 171–171ter of the Copyright Law.
[127] Art 172 of the Copyright Law.   [128] Art 174bis of the Copyright Law.
[129] Cf n 67 above.   [130] Art 171sexies of the Copyright Law.
[131] Cf n 25 above.   [132] Art 171ter of the Copyright Law.
[133] Arts 156–167 of the Copyright Law.   [134] Art 156 of the Copyright Law.

decision, in full or in summary form, in one or more daily newspapers, at the expense of the losing party.[135] Furthermore, the right-holder may claim damages as compensation for the loss incurred as a result of the infringement. Loss of earnings is assessed by the judge, in particular, also taking into account the profits made in infringement of the right and the fees the infringing party would have had to pay if he had obtained a licence from the right-holder.[136] In serious cases, in addition to banning the manufacture, sale, and use of the infringing objects, the decision may also provide for seizure and transfer to the right-holder of the infringing goods and manufacturing facilities.[137] Finally, with the decision ascertaining the infringement of an industrial property right, the destruction of all the items constituting the infringement may be ordered.[138]

Design right infringements are punished under criminal law by imprisonment of up to two years and a fine of up to EUR 20,000.00.[139] In the case where there are also items of the offence of receiving stolen property, those infringements may be punished by between two and eight years' imprisonment, and a fine ranging from EUR 516.46 to EUR 10,329.14. For less serious cases, the maximum penalties are six years' imprisonment, and a fine of EUR 516.46.[140] Lastly, in the case where these penalties are not applicable, Article 127 of the IP Code imposes payment of a fine of up to EUR 1,032.91.[141] **16.193**

Furthermore, it is possible for the right-holder to claim compensation for damages,[142] the forfeiture and destruction of the goods under seizure,[143] the forfeiture and destruction of moulds and matrices,[144] as well as publication of the finding.[145] **16.194**

Under civil law, see paragraph 16.188 above. **16.195**

Goods infringing a patent or a supplementary protection certificate

See paragraphs 16.193 to 16.195 above. **16.196**

Goods infringing a plant variety right

See paragraphs 16.193 to 16.195 above. **16.197**

---

[135] Art 166 of the Copyright Law.   [136] Art 158 of the Copyright Law.
[137] Art 159 of the Copyright Law.   [138] Arts 158–160 of the Copyright Law.
[139] Arts 474 and 517 of the Criminal Code (cf paras 16.150 ff above).
[140] Art 648 of the Criminal Code (cf para 16.156 above).
[141] Cf para 16.157 above.   [142] Cf n 67 above.   [143] Cf para 16.131 above.
[144] Cf n 25 above.   [145] Cf nn 70 ff above.

Goods infringing a designation of origin or a geographical indication

16.198 Designation of origin or a geographical indication infringements are punished under criminal law by imprisonment of up to one year or a fine up to EUR 20,000.00.[146] In the case where there are also items of the offence of receiving stolen property, those infringements may be punished by between two and eight years' imprisonment, and a fine ranging from EUR 516.46 to EUR 10,329. For less serious cases, the maximum penalties are six years' imprisonment, and a fine of EUR 516.46.[147] Lastly, in the case where these penalties are not applicable, Article 127 of the IP Code nevertheless imposes payment of a fine of up to EUR 1,032.91.[148]

16.199 Furthermore, it is possible for the right-holder to claim compensation for damages,[149] the forfeiture and destruction of the goods under seizure,[150] the forfeiture and destruction of moulds and matrices.[151]

16.200 Under civil law, see paragraph 16.188 above.

VI. LIABILITY OF CUSTOMS AUTHORITIES AND RIGHT-HOLDERS

A. Liability of right-holders and sanctions

16.201 Article 12 of the Regulation provides that right-holders may not use the information obtained from customs under the Regulation for purposes other than to determine if the suspect goods infringe an intellectual property right and, therefore, to initiate the relevant actions before the courts.

16.202 If a right-holder uses such information for any other purpose, he could be held liable under Italian unfair competition law where the information appears to have been used in order to damage a competitor. In particular, Article 2598 of Italian Civil Code provides that:

> Notwithstanding the application of the rules concerning the protection of distinctive signs and patent rights, a person shall be liable for unfair competition who: 1) [. . .]; 2) spreads information and appreciation about a competitor's products

---

[146] Art 517 of the Criminal Code (cf paras 16.150 ff above).
[147] Art 648 of the Criminal Code (cf para 16.156 above).
[148] Cf para 16.157 above.   [149] Cf n 67 above.   [150] Cf n 68 above.
[151] Cf n 25 above.

or activities, which could impair that competitor's reputation, or ascribes to himself qualities belonging to a competitor's products or a competitor's enterprise; or 3) directly or un directly uses any other means of unfair competition in order to damage enterprises belonging to competitors.

Moreover, the right-holder could be held liable under Personal Data Protection Code and on commercial and industrial secrecy.[152]   **16.203**

Apart from liability for non-permitted use of information obtained from the Customs authorities, right-holders can be held liable under Italian law if a procedure initiated pursuant to Article 1(1) of the Regulation is discontinued owing to an act or omission by the right-holder, and in the event that the suspect goods are subsequently found not to infringe an intellectual property right.[153] Such liability is regulated by Article 2043 of the Italian Civil Code on non-contractual responsibility. According to this provision: 'any fraudulent or culpable fact that causes harm to a third party, renders its author liable to compensate the third party for the prejudice thus incurred'.   **16.204**

B. Liability of customs authorities and sanctions

As already explained,[154] the selection of goods to be examined by the customs offices is done by means of a computerized system of risk analysis recognized at Community level. The current system already contains the appropriate risk profiles dynamically calibrated for the sector, which is subjected to periodic examination. Therefore the First Circular provides that customs should be considered liable (and therefore the right-holder entitled to obtain compensation for damages) in the case where goods were selected for physical control by the customs control circuit or the physical control was decided autonomously on grounds of specific information provided by the right-holder, but no action was taken to detain them.[155] In such a case, the customs authorities could be held liable by the right-holder under Article 2043 of Italian Civil Code.   **16.205**

Finally, when the persons involved in or affected by an *ex officio* customs action suffer prejudice as a result of the authorities' intervention, within the meaning of Article 19(2) of the Regulation, the customs office may be held liable under Article 2043 of Italian Civil Code if it is possible to prove negligence or malpractice in the examination of the suspect goods, and/or in the evaluation of the existence of an infringement of an intellectual property rights The latter elements are, in any case, relatively difficult to establish.   **16.206**

---

[152] Cf para 16.117 above.   [153] Cf Reg 1383/2003, Arts 6(1) and 19(3).
[154] Cf paras 16.67–16.68 above.   [155] Cf ibid, Art 19(1).

Conclusion

16.207 Although Italy has not yet enacted any statutory provisions to ensure enforceability of EC Regulation 1383/2003, the system of border measures set up by this Regulation can be considered wholly operative in Italy. The Regulation and the Circular adopted recently by the Italian Customs administration are, in fact, wholly sufficient in this context.

16.208 Italian Customs are very active in the fight against intellectual property infringements. However, the whole structure cannot be entirely expedient if right-holders do not provide them with as much information as possible regarding the flow of non-authentic goods and the probable provenance of such products. To that effect, the customs authorities have built up an informal and direct relationship with the holders of intellectual property rights and their representatives, which has proven to be very constructive and fruitful.

17

LATVIA

Mara Uzulena and Gatis Merzvinskis

Introduction

Since 1991, Latvia has undergone profound political, social, and economical **17.01** changes, including the transition from a centrally planned to a market economy. Having started from scratch, Latvia has established an efficient legislative system in all fields of social life, including intellectual property. Shortly after regaining independence in 1991, appropriate legislation governing intellectual property rights as well as their protection was adopted in Latvia.

In 1997, the Latvian legislator adopted a new Customs Law, containing provi- **17.02** sions on Customs control.[1] The Customs Law required the Cabinet of Ministers of the Republic of Latvia to determine the procedures for customs control measures in view of the protection of intellectual property rights (inter alia through a prohibition on release for free circulation, exportation, re-exportation, placement in a free zone or free warehouse, and placement under a suspensive procedure (including inward processing, inward processing under customs control, temporary admission, re-importation, importation to a duty-free shop, outward processing, transit and abandonment for the benefit of the State) of goods infringing an intellectual property right. In 1999, the Cabinet of Ministers adopted Cabinet Regulation No 43 of 9 February 1999 on Customs Control Measures for the Protection of Intellectual Property.[2] This instrument was repealed with effect from

---

[1] Muitas likums (*Customs Law*). Adopted on 11 June 1997 and published in the Official State Gazette 'Latvijas Republikas Saeimas un Ministru Kabineta Ziņotājs', 1997, No. 15. This law was in force from 1 July 1997 till Latvia's accession to the European Community on 1 May 2004.

[2] Noteikumi par muitas kontroles pasākumiem intelektuālā īpašuma aizsardzībai (*Regulation on Customs Control Measures for the Protection of Intellectual Property*). Adopted on 9 February 1999 and published in the Official State Gazette 'Latvijas Vēstnesis' on 12 February 1999. These Regulations were in force from 1 July 1999 till 28 July 2001.

28 July 2001 further to the entry into force of a more detailed instrument, namely, Cabinet Regulation No 325 of 24 July 2001 laying down the Procedures for the Adoption of Customs Control Measures for the Protection of Intellectual Property.[3] With a view to harmonizing Latvian national law with the requirements of the international agreements in force in Latvia (such as TRIPs),[4] and taking into account the local and other countries' customs practice, the Cabinet of Ministers replaced the latter Regulation by a new Regulation No 420 of 10 September 2002.[5]

17.03 It is fair to say that these statutory provisions on border measures did allow for the adequate protection of intellectual property rights. The pre-existing Latvian national system on border measures was entirely TRIPs compliant.

17.04 The Republic of Latvia became a Member State of the European Community on 1 May 2004, and consequently, both the Cabinet Regulation No 420 of 10 September 2002 and the 1997 Latvian Customs Law were repealed. On 18 March 2004, the Parliament adopted a new Customs Law[6] in line with European law (*acquis communautaire*). During the two month period running from 1 May 2004 to the date on which EC Regulation 1383/2003[7] came into effect, the Latvian customs authorities applied EC Regulation 3295/94.[8]

---

[3] Kārtība, kādā veicami muitas kontroles pasākumi intelektuālā īpašuma aizsardzībai (*Procedures for the Adoption of Customs Control Measures for the Protection of Intellectual Property*). Adopted on July 24 2001 and published in the Official State Gazette 'Latvijas Vēstnesis' 27 July 2001. These Regulations were in force from 28 July 2001 till 12 October 2002.

[4] The Agreement on Trade-Related Aspects of Intellectual Property Rights entered into force in Latvia on 10 February 1999. It is noteworthy that Latvian law applies the doctrine of direct effect, ie the provisions of those international agreements which have been ratified by the *Saeima* (the Parliament of the Republic of Latvia), are directly applicable, without the need of any implementing law or regulations.

[5] Kārtība, kādā veicami muitas kontroles pasākumi intelektuālā īpašuma aizsardzībai (*Procedures for the Adoption of Customs Control Measures for the Protection of Intellectual Property*). Adopted on 10 September 2002 and published in the Official State Gazette 'Latvijas Vēstnesis' 11 October 2002. This law was in force from 12 October 2002 till 28 July 2001.

[6] Muitas likums (Customs Law). Adopted on 24 March 2004 and published in the Official State Gazette 'Latvijas Vēstnesis' on 6 April 2004. This Law came into effect on 1 May 2004, and is still in force today.

[7] Council Reg (EC) 1383/2003 of 22 July 2003 concerning customs action against goods suspected of infringing certain intellectual property rights and the measures to be taken against goods found to have infringed such rights [2003] OJ L 196/7 (2.8.2003).

[8] Council Reg (EC) 3295/94 of 22 December 1994 laying down measures to prohibit the release for free circulation, export, re-export or entry for a suspensive procedure of counterfeit and pirated goods [1994] OJ L 341/8 (22.12.1994), as amended by Council Reg 241/1999 [1999] OJ L 27/1 (2.2.1999), and by Council Reg (EC) 806/2003 [2003] OJ L 122/1. Cf also Commission Reg (EC) 1367/95 of 16 June 1995 laying down provisions for the implementation of Council Reg (EC) 3295/94 laying down measures concerning the entry into the Community and the export and re-export from the Community of goods infringing certain intellectual property rights [1995] OJ L 133/2 (17.6.1995), as amended by Commission Reg (EC) 2549/1999 of 2 December 1999 [1999] OJ L 308/16 (3.12.1999).

Current practice shows that the entry into force of Regulation 1383/2003 ('the **17.05** Regulation') and of Regulation 1891/2004 ('the Implementing Regulation')[9] gave rise to some problems, which might be due to a lack of consistency between these Community instruments and the Latvian national legislation, and more particularly the statutory provisions governing the respective intellectual property rights as well as the administrative procedures in the field of customs actions. Latvian Customs have tried to solve these problems by issuing Instructions on Procedures for the Adoption of Customs Control Measures for the Protection of Intellectual Property Rights.[10] However some problems still exist. We will comment on these problems below. The future will tell whether—and if it is so to what extent— Latvian national law should be amended so as to bring it into line with the current EC Regulations on border measures towards goods suspected of infringing an intellectual property right.

The Regulation covers more intellectual property rights than the Latvian Cabinet **17.06** Regulations, which had been in force in Latvia prior to the latter's accession to the European Community. Specifically, these national regulations did not relate to national plant varieties, designations of origin, and geographical indications. Today, the situation is exactly the opposite: next to the intellectual property rights listed in the Community Regulation, the national legislation also protects additional rights, that is, intellectual property vested in topographies of semiconductor products.[11]

I. SUBJECT MATTER AND SCOPE OF THE NATIONAL LAW APPLYING THE REGULATION

A. Customs procedure of the goods

The Latvian customs authorities have announced that they will apply Regulation **17.07** 1383/2003 to all customs procedures defined in Article 1(1) of the Regulation, including re-exportation, external transit, and transhipment.

---

[9] Commission Reg (EC) 1891/2004 of 21 October 2004 laying down provisions for the implementation of Council Reg (EC) 1383/2003 concerning customs action against goods suspected of infringing certain intellectual property rights and the measures to be taken against goods found to have infringed such rights [2004] OJ L 328/16 (30.10.2004).

[10] Kārtība, kādā veicami muitas kontroles pasākumi intelektuālā īpašuma aizsardzībai (*Procedures for the Adoption of Customs Control Measures for the Protection of Intellectual Property*). Adopted on 11 February 2005 and published in the Official State Gazette 'Latvijas Vēstnesis' 18 February 2005.

[11] Muitas likums (*Customs Law*). Adopted on 24 March 2004 and published in the Official State Gazette 'Latvijas Vēstnesis' on 6 April 2004. This Law came into effect on 1 May 2004, and is still in force today.

Customs control actions can be carried out at border checkpoints, border posts, and customs checkpoints, on customs territories, in free warehouses, free zones, and in any places where goods subject to customs procedures are stored or processed.

B. Definition of infringing goods

17.08 In this section, we will examine the definition of infringing goods which are subject to border measures as provided for by the Regulation, and how this definition contrasts with the scope of the protection granted by different intellectual property rights under Latvian law.

(1) Counterfeit goods

17.09 It should be pointed out here that the vast majority of infringing goods apprehended by Latvian Customs are counterfeit goods, including for example counterfeit clothing, footwear, tobacco products, and household electrical appliances. Since 1 May 2004 Latvian Customs have confiscated clothing and footwear (29 cases), vehicle spare parts (three cases), electronic equipments (two cases), cigarettes (four cases), audio/video recordings (three cases), other goods (one case).

17.10 Latvian trade mark law is governed by the Law on Trade Marks and Indications of Geographical Origin[12] (the Latvian Trade Mark Law/99). Under this Law, the holder of a validly registered trade mark, the person in whose name the trade mark has been registered, enjoys the exclusive right to prohibit other persons not having his consent from using, in the course of trade:

— any sign which is identical to the trade mark in relation to goods or services which are identical to those for which the trade mark is registered;

— any sign where, because of its identity or similarity to the trade mark and the identity or similarity of the goods or services for which the trade mark is registered and for which the sign is used, there exists a likelihood of confusion, including the likelihood of association between the sign and the trade mark, on the part of the relevant consumers.[13]

---

[12] Likums 'Par preču zīmēm un ģeogrāfiskās izcelsmes norādēm' (Law on Trademarks and Indications of Geographical Origin). Adopted on 16 June 1999 and published in the Official State Gazette 'Latvijas Vēstnesis' on 1 July 1999. This Law entered into effect on 15 July 1999, and was amended on 8 November 2001 and 10 October 2004.   [13] Trade Mark Law/99, Art 4(6).

In addition, the Latvian Trade Mark Law/99 provides that the owner of a well-known trade mark enjoying a reputation in Latvia is also entitled to prevent the use, in the course of trade, of any sign in relation to goods which are *not* similar to those for which that trade mark is registered, provided that consumers may perceive the use of such a sign as suggesting a connection between these goods and the owner of the trade mark.[14] However, the question whether a trade mark is well-known has to be resolved by an official institution of Latvia, that is, by the Court or the Patent Office of the Republic of Latvia.

17.11

Under the Latvian Competition Law,[15] the following actions are also prohibited:

17.12

— the use or imitation by any trader of a firm name, distinctive sign, or the like features, which have been legally used earlier on by another market participant, if such use is likely to mislead the consumers as regards the identity of the trader;

— the imitation by a trader of the trade mark, external appearance, labelling, or packaging of goods produced or sold by another market participant, or the use of distinctive signs, provided such imitation or use may be misleading as regards the origin of the goods.

Article 2(1)(a)(i) of the Regulation provides for a definition of 'counterfeit goods' which is far more restrictive than the definition of the acts prohibited under the national law. Indeed, as it has been pointed out in the previous paragraph, Article 4(6) of the Trade Mark Law/99 provides protection against the use of *any* similar sign for *similar* goods, which is likely to cause confusion between the sign and the protected trade mark on the part of relevant consumers, whilst Article 8(2) even extends the scope of protection for well-known trade marks beyond the principle of speciality, thus allowing the owners of such marks to oppose the use of a conflicting sign in respect of dissimilar goods. By contrast, Article 2(1)(a)(i) of the Regulation suggests that customs are only entitled to take action against goods bearing without authorization a sign which is *identical* to, or cannot be distinguished in its essential aspects from, a validly registered trade mark. Moreover, this provision requires that the trade mark on the basis of which border measures are taken be registered for the *same type of goods*.

17.13

Taking into account the insufficient practical experience of Latvian Customs in the application of EC Regulation 3295/94 and the new Regulation 1383/2003, it

17.14

---

[14] Ibid, Art 8(2).
[15] Konkurences likums (*Competition Law*). Adopted on 4 October 2001 and published in the Official State Gazette 'Latvijas Vēstnesis' on 23 October 2001, Art 18(3)1, 2. This Law entered into effect on 1 January 2002 and was amended on 22 April 2004.

is hard to determine how broad Latvian customs officials interpret the notion of 'essential aspects' when assessing whether the goods are likely to be 'counterfeit', and whether this notion embraces, in practice, any confusingly similar trade marks. The majority of the cases which we have come across in our practice relate to goods on which signs had been affixed were identical or almost identical to a registered trade mark. For example, customs took action against goods bearing the semi-figurative device sign 'Diodora' on the basis of an application for action which relied on the word mark 'Diadora'. In this case the sign differed from the registered trade mark in one letter. Another good example is a case which involved pharmaceutical preparations marked 'Validols', 'Validolum', 'Validol', 'Validol (in Cyrillic)' and 'Validols-Uvi'; all these goods were deemed by customs to infringe the trade mark 'Validols', and were therefore detained as 'counterfeit goods', although the respective packaging designs of the suspected products and the genuine medicines were completely different.

17.15 In Latvia, border measures will be taken by the customs authorities only against goods which are covered by the trade mark registration on which the application for action is based. Following this approach, jeans marked with a well-known trade mark registered for vehicles were released by Latvian Customs for free circulation. Under Latvian Trade Mark Law/99, however, one may question whether such goods could not be seen as an infringement.

17.16 The Latvian customs authorities have announced that, in accordance with Article 2(1)(a) of the Regulation, they are eager to take measures against trade mark symbols, including for example, brochures, instructions for use or any other documents, even if delivered separately. The same applies to the packaging materials bearing the trade marks of counterfeit goods, delivered separately. However, actions of this type have not yet been reported in Latvia.

17.17 It is not possible to file an application for action in Latvia on the basis of a simple trade mark application, since in principle trade mark protection under Latvian Trade Mark Law/99 only arises from registration. This solution is consistent with Article 2(1)(a) of the Regulation, which requires that the trade mark must be 'validly registered'.

(2) Pirated goods

17.18 Under Latvian Copyright Law,[16] any reproduction or adaptation of an original work qualifying for copyright protection without the right-holder's consent will

---

[16] Autortiesību likums (Copyright Law). Adopted on 6 April 2000 and published in the Official State Gazette 'Latvijas Vēstnesis' on 27 April 2000. The Copyright Law came into force on 11 May 2000, and was subsequently amended on 6 March 2003 and 22 April 2004.

cause such copies to be considered (infringing) pirated. Copyright applies to works of literature, science, art and other works, also unfinished works, regardless of the purpose of the work and the value, form, or type of expression. Neighbouring rights are the rights of performers, phonogram producers, film producers, and of broadcasting organizations. The objects of neighbouring rights are performances, and their fixations, phonograms, films, and broadcasts. The right-holders are performers, phonogram producers, film producers, and broadcasting organizations or their successors in title, and heirs. Copyright and neighbouring rights objects protected in Latvia which have been imported from countries where such works are not protected by copyright or where the term of protection has expired are also deemed to be infringing copies. The scope of protection derived from the design patent is determined by the external appearance of the industrial design, as a whole. Exclusive rights to industrial design use allow the patent owner to forbid the utilization of industrial design to other persons. Exclusive rights take effect on the date the design patent is granted. The manufacture, use, offering for sale of the articles in which the patented industrial design is used, or their storage, import or export from Latvia for these purposes, as well as other actions of introducing such articles into economic circulation without the consent of the patent owner is considered as an infringement of the rights of the patent owner.

Latvian Customs interpret the concept of 'copies' in a relatively broad sense, as **17.19** covering any goods, which embody a protected subject matter (that is, either an original work, an original performance, or a design, and which have been manufactured and distributed without the permission of the right-holder). In compliance with the definition provided in Article 2(1)(b) of the Regulation, as far as designs are concerned, customs will take action regardless of whether the protected design is registered in Latvia (copyrights and related rights are never subject to registration in Latvia).

(3) Goods infringing other intellectual property rights

Goods infringing a patent or a supplementary protection certificate

Goods will be considered to infringe a patent or a supplementary protection **17.20** certificate under the Latvian Patent Law[17]—and therefore subject to customs intervention under the Regulation—if any of the exclusive rights conferred by the patent on its owner relating to the exploitation of the protected invention are

---

[17] Patentu likums (Patent Law). Adopted on 30 March 1995 and published in the Official State Gazette 'Latvijas Vēstnesis' on 19 April 1995. This Law entered into effect on 20 April 1995 and was amended on 22 April 2004.

directly or indirectly violated. A *direct* patent infringement arises when, without consent of the patent owner, and within the period of validity of the patent or supplementary protection certificate, a product falling within the patent claims, or a product which has been directly obtained by using a process recited in the claims, has been manufactured, offered on the market, put into circulation for commercial purposes, used, or imported or stocked for these purposes. An *indirect* patent infringement occurs when a third party not having obtained the right-holder's consent supplies essential elements of the patented invention (except where the components in question are widely known in trade).

Goods infringing a national plant variety right

17.21   Goods will be considered to infringe plant variety rights protected in Latvia— and therefore subject to border measures under the Regulation—pursuant to the Plant Varieties Protection Law[18] if a person turns a protected variety into a source of income without the permission of the holder of the breeder's right. Such permission is required if third persons wish to produce, propagate, process in conformity with the sowing requirements to multiply the variety, offer for sale, sell or market in any other way, export, import, or stock the propagating material of a protected plant variety. In addition, goods will also infringe a national plant variety right when they are essentially derived from such a variety.

Goods infringing a national designation of origin or a geographical indication

17.22   Goods will be held as infringing a designation of origin or a geographical indication under the national Trade Mark Law,[19] where false indications of geographical origin or any other such geographical names or designations of geographical nature, or similar signs, are used in the course of trade, provided that such use is likely to mislead consumers as to the geographical origin of the goods. False use of such signs in the course of trade will also be deemed an act of unfair competition, subject to the sanctions provided for in the Latvian Competition Law.[20]

Goods infringing a topography of semiconductor products

17.23   Next to the intellectual property rights listed in the Community Regulation, the national legislation on border measures also ensures protection at the borders to

---

[18] Augu aizsardzības likums (Plant Varieties Protection Law). Adopted on 2 May 2002 and published in the Official State Gazette 'Latvijas Vēstnesis' on 17 May 2002. This Law entered into effect on 31 May 2002.   [19] N 12 above, Arts 40–43.
[20] N 15 above, Art 18.

additional rights, that is, intellectual property vested in topographies of semiconductor products.[21]

(4) Moulds and matrices

17.24 The statutory protection conferred on trade marks, copyrights and related rights, designs, and patents under Latvian law applies *mutatis mutandis* to any mould and matrix which is specially designed or adapted for the manufacture of counterfeit or pirated goods, or goods infringing a patent or a supplementary protection certificate. Such goods shall be treated by the Latvian customs authorities in the same way as infringing goods.

C. Goods excluded by the Regulation

(1) Parallel imported goods

17.25 The Latvian statutory provisions concerning these intellectual property rights do not prohibit the cross-border movement of goods, which have been put on the market on the territory of the Republic of Latvia with the permission of the holder of the intellectual property rights ('grey market goods') in Latvia. Customs will therefore not take action where such goods are for example, declared for exportation.

17.26 In accordance with Article 3(1), first indent, of the Regulation, customs will also not take action against genuine goods which have been put on the market abroad by the right-holder or with his permission, and are subsequently placed under one of the customs procedures defined in Article 1(1) of the Regulation, even though in such case this may result in an infringement of an intellectual property right under national or Community law.

17.27 However, when the goods have been impaired, or their quality changed, after being put on the market, the right-holder has legitimate grounds to prohibit further commercialization of the goods in all cases, and customs may consider taking action.[22]

---

[21] Pusvadītāju izstrādājumu topogrāfiju aizsardzības likums (Law on Protection of Topographies of Semiconductor Products). Adopted on 12 March 1998 and published in the Official State Gazette 'Latvijas Vēstnesis' on 31 March 1998. This Law entered into effect on 30 April 1998.

[22] N 11 above, Art 5 (2), (3).

*(2) Goods, which have been manufactured under
conditions other than those which have been
agreed with the right-holder*

17.28 There is no national legislation in Latvia that would allow customs to take action against goods, which have been manufactured with the consent of the right-holder, but under conditions other than those agreed with the latter. Latvian Customs will therefore not detain, or suspend the release of, such goods, in accordance with Article 3(1), second indent, of the Regulation.

(3) Goods contained in travellers' personal baggage

17.29 The provisions of Article 3(2) of the Regulation regarding goods contained in travellers' personal baggage are implemented into Latvian national legislation (although such 'implementation' was not necessary, owing to the direct effect of the Regulation). Article 15–18 of the Customs Law also regards inspection of travellers' baggage as an exceptional form of customs control. However, if there are sufficient grounds to believe that a person crossing the border carries for commercial purposes goods, which can be suspected of infringing an intellectual property right, inspection may be performed. Similarly, goods the value of which exceeds the limits of the duty-free allowance, or which are of a commercial nature, are—rightly—considered by Latvian Customs to fall under the scope of the Regulation.

17.30 When appraising the 'non-commercial nature' of suspect goods contained in a traveller's personal baggage under Article 3(2) of the Regulation, Latvian customs officers will take into account the value and quantity of the goods, whether the goods are similar or identical as to their structure, characteristics, and quality, whether they have the same commercial origin, etc. If there is only one single suspect item in a traveller's personal baggage, and there are grounds to believe that it is not intended for commercial purposes, it will be allowed entry.

17.31 The controls carried out by Latvian Customs on travellers' baggage prove very efficient, as there is a large 'ant-traffic' of fake goods between the Baltic States and the countries of the Former Soviet Union.[23]

---

[23] When checking travellers' personal baggage, the Latvian customs authorities have eg apprehended large quantities of pirated CDs and DVDs hidden in thermos flasks (2002).

II. APPLICATION FOR ACTION BY THE CUSTOMS AUTHORITIES

A. Measures prior to an application for action by the customs authorities ('*ex officio* measures')

Latvian Customs frequently apply *ex officio* measures under Article 4 of the
Regulation. If during the course of customs control, goods suspected of infringing an intellectual property right listed in Article 2 of the Regulation are discovered, they will notify the right-holder or his representative. When assessing
whether the goods are suspect, Latvian Customs take into account the quality
(appearance) of the goods, the form of packaging, information mentioned on the
labels, the exporting country, etc. Latvian customs officials will take action
ex officio where, for example, the quality of the goods is evidently doubtful, the
goods are not adequately packed but simply put in large boxes or sacks, the labels
do not include essential information with regard to the producer or product
itself, and of course when the labels do not correspond with the product to which
they are affixed. Latvian Customs have for example, apprehended *ex officio* a shirt
bearing the 'Esprit' trade mark to which a label which was suitable only for jeans
had been affixed. Cases have also been reported in which the imported goods (for
example, 'DKNY' sport suits) lacked any labelling. The documentation accompanying the suspected goods is often incorrect, or contains typographical errors.
Generally, *ex officio* procedures in Latvia relate to counterfeit goods bearing well-
known trade marks, often consisting of commodity goods which are commonly
used by the public at large (for example, 'Nike', 'Adidas', and other well-known
sport brands, 'Nokia' mobile phones, etc).

17.32

In the framework of an *ex officio* action, Latvian customs officials provide the right-
holder concerned with information available regarding the nature of the suspected
goods, their quantity and their country of origin. Samples and/or digital pictures
of the goods are forwarded to the right-holder together with the notification about
the possible infringement. If he confirms customs' suspicions, the right-holder
must file an application for action within three working days as from this notification. Failure to do so will cause the goods to be released. Customs strictly observe
all deadlines as concerns submission of a notification. If the application for action
has been already granted the notification must be submitted within 10 working
days. Depending on the circumstances of the case, customs may be rather more
flexible when applying the deadline to submissions of additional documents.

17.33

Additional information, including the names and addresses of the consignee, the
consignor, the declarant or the holder of the goods, as well as information

17.34

regarding the precise origin and provenance of the goods, are provided only after a written application for action has been filed.

17.35 In practice, in order to expedite the procedure and to meet the deadline of three working days, Latvian Customs usually contact the right-holder over the telephone and inform him about the possible infringement. The right-holder will thereupon go in person to the relevant customs office where he will be provided with the samples and photos of the suspected products. However the deadline for submission of notification is counted from the date when the official letter is received from customs.

B. The lodging and processing of applications for customs action

(1) Persons entitled to file an application for action

Definition of 'right-holders' under the Regulation

17.36 Under Article 2(2) of the Regulation, the following may lodge an application for action: the owners of any of the intellectual property rights listed in Article 2(1) of the Regulation; any person authorized to use such a right; or their respective representatives.

17.37 The notion of 'any other person authorized to use' an intellectual property right referred to in Article 2(2)(a) is interpreted by Latvian Customs as including any natural or legal person (for example, a licensee, distributor, commercial agent, etc) who is officially authorized by the right-holder (i) to use the right concerned *and* (ii) who has the authorization to defend and maintain this right. When the application for action is based on a trade mark or a design right which has been licensed to the applicant, the latter needs not prove that the licence has been recorded with the relevant industrial property office. As far as patents, trade marks, and designs are concerned, however, a licence agreement is enforceable against third parties (including customs) once it has been registered with the Latvian Patent Office. Where an application for action is based on a patent, trade mark, or design and filed by a licensee, and where the licence agreement is not registered with the Patent Office, the applicant has to submit to customs a document confirming that he has been duly authorized by the right-holder to enforce the rights and to represent the latter before customs.

17.38 Right-holders may appoint a representative who is entitled, with respect to the customs authorities, to perform any such acts and fulfil any such formalities as may be necessary when applying the Regulation. Representatives of any natural or legal person could include a law firm, collecting society, patent attorney, or an intellectual property right agent. Representatives must notify customs when they are acting on behalf of a right-holder. The customs authorities require the representative to submit a power of attorney.

Theoretically, foreign representatives without an office (or domicile) in Latvia **17.39** may appear before the Latvian customs authorities, however, in practice language problems may arise in such case.

Proof of entitlement to file an application for action

For right-holders stricto sensu

Right-holders have to submit to Latvian customs authorities any official docu- **17.40** ment establishing their legitimate rights to the intellectual property right concerned. In trade mark, designations of origin, and geographical indication matters it is mandatory to submit an extract from the Latvian State Trade Mark Register certified by the Patent Office of Latvia (for Latvian registrations), a certified copy of the trade mark registration certificate issued by WIPO or OHIM or a printout from the relevant trade mark database. For designs, patents, and supplementary protection certificates, or breeders' rights protected in Latvia, it is necessary to submit a certified copy of the registration certificate, or a certified extract from the State Patent or Design or Protected Plant Varieties Registers. As to copyright and related rights, any kind of proof establishing the capacity of an author or original holder of the rights must be submitted.

In Latvia, an application for action under the Regulation cannot be filed on the **17.41** basis of a mere application for an intellectual property right. Exclusive rights to industrial property only arise from effective registration of the industrial property rights with the Patent Office of the Republic of Latvia, or from registration effected pursuant to the provisions of the regulations on international registration of such rights, which are in force in Latvia.

For persons authorized to use the right

Regarding a licence, the 'authorization to use the right' can be evidenced by submit- **17.42** ting a certified extract from the Register of the relevant industrial property office, provided the licence agreement has been recorded with that office. In the absence of such a recording, it is necessary to provide customs with a certified copy of the licence agreement or any other agreement authorizing the applicant for customs action to use and defend the rights on which the application is based. Customs are entitled to verify the scope of the authorization granted to the user of the right in question.

For representatives

When filing an application for action, the representative of the owner of the right **17.43** or authorized user must submit the original, or a certified copy, of the power of attorney form duly signed by the person he represents, notarized and certified with the *Apostille*. If the document is drawn up in a country which has joined the Hague Convention Abolishing the Requirement of Legalizations for Foreign Public Documents of 1961,[24] its authenticity should be certified with an *Apostille* by the competent institution of the relevant state according to provisions of the Convention. The document bearing an *Apostille* is not subject to any other confirmation by Latvian diplomatic/consular missions.

17.44 The owner of the right or authorized user may issue a general power (for all matters) or a special power (just regarding a specific trade mark or patent, etc Latvian Customs will accept both forms).

17.45 The declaration referred to in Article 6 of the Regulation must be signed by the right-holder or the authorized user, notarized and certified with the *Apostille*. Foreign public documents made within the countries signatories of the Hague Convention Abolishing the Requirement of Legalisation for Foreign Public Documents of 5 October 1961 are only valid in Latvia if they bear the *Apostille*.

17.46 It should be noted that the notarization and certification with the *Apostille* of the declaration under Article 6 and the power of attorney is very time-consuming and rather complicated. Therefore, in practice, only copies of the subject documents notarized in Latvia are submitted to customs authorities, whilst the originals are kept in the representative's files.

(2) Competent customs department and formal requirements

Competent customs department

17.47 The Latvian customs department in charge of processing applications for action under Article 5(2) of the Regulation is the following:

Intellectual Property Rights Subdivision
Enforcement Division
National Customs Board
State Revenue Service of the Republic of Latvia
Kr. Valdemara Street 1a, Riga, LV-1841, LATVIA
Tel.: +371 7047400, +371 7047442
Fax: +371 7047440
e-mail: customs@dep.vid.gov.lv
Internet: www.vid.gov.lv

---

[24] Par Hāgas konvenciju par ārvalstu publisko dokumentu legalizācijas prasības atcelšanu (the Hague Convention Abolishing the Requirement of Legalisation for Foreign Public Documents) adopted in Latvia on 9 February 1995 and published in the Official State Gazette 'Latvijas Vēstnesis' on 18 February 1995.

Form of the application for action

Pursuant to the national legislation currently in force, an application for action **17.48** shall be filed using an official form. It is also possible to send the application for action by fax but submission of the original is required. It is envisaged that in the very near future applications for action filed by electronic means will be accepted. The electronic version of the application for action both for CTM and national intellectual property right enforcement is available for applicants.

The filing of an application for action by electronic means is not yet possible in Latvia.

Two copies of the application for action have to be submitted with the cus- **17.49** toms authorities: one is intended for the Central Customs Board competent to process applications for action under the Regulation (cf para 17.47 above). The other copy is returned when the application for action is granted or refused.

Language requirements

The national application for action must be filed in the Latvian language. If the **17.50** application form is filed in any other official language of the European Union, the Latvian customs authorities will request the right-holder to provide a Latvian translation at his own cost. The same applies to the declaration referred to in Article 6 of the Regulation. If customs consider that the information provided in the exhibits submitted together with the application is difficult to understand, they will request the right-holder to provide a Latvian translation of these documents as well.

(3) Requirements regarding the contents of the application for action

Mandatory information

Pursuant to Article 5(5) of the Regulation, the following information has to be **17.51** mentioned in the application for action: (i) a technical description of the goods so as to enable the customs authorities readily to recognize them; (ii) any specific information the right-holder may have concerning the type or pattern of fraud; and (iii) the name and address of a local contact person appointed by the applicant, who is in a position to confirm on an expedited basis whether the goods are authentic or fake. Of particular importance are also (if known) the actual or presumed locations of the suspect goods, or the customs territory on which those goods can be found. It is advised to pass on all available information regarding the genuine and, if available, suspect goods. The application must also be accompanied by proof that the applicant is the holder of the intellectual property rights on which the application is based.

Optional information

17.52 The communication to customs of any other useful information is desirable and expected. In addition, Latvian Customs may request the right-holder to provide any additional information at any time pursuant to Article 5(6) of the Regulation.

(4) Processing and acceptance of the application for action

17.53 By virtue of Article 5(7) of the Regulation, an application for action filed with Latvian Customs must be processed within 30 working days. In the event that the Director of the Central Customs Board of the State Revenue Service rejects the application, an appeal may be filed within 30 days of the receipt of the decision with the General Director of the State Revenue Service. In accordance with the Latvian Administrative Process Law,[25] the Decision of the General Director of the State Revenue Service can, in turn, be appealed filing an application to the Administrative District Court within one month from the date when it becomes valid.

17.54 Once the application is granted, Latvian Customs will take action for a period not exceeding one year (at the request of the right-holder, they may provide for a period shorter than one year). However, this period shall always be set at one year in the case of a 'Community' application filed under Article 5(4) of the Regulation.[26] The right-holder can request a renewal of the application for action at the expiry of the decision granting the application.

(5) 'Community' applications for action

Processing of 'Community' applications for action filed with Latvian Customs

17.55 By now, more than 39 'Community' applications for action have been filed through Latvian Customs. These applications are processed in the same way as

---

[25] Administratīvā procesa likums (Administrative Process Law). Adopted on 25 October 2001 and published in the Official State Gazette 'Latvijas Vēstnesis' on 14 November 2001. This Law entered into effect on 1 February 2004, and was amended on 12 June 2003 and 15 January 2004.
[26] Reg 1383/2003, Art 8(1), first indent; Art 8(2), second indent.

national applications, with the exception that it is an additional requirement for the right-holder to provide a translation of the form, and all the necessary documents and information.

Processing of 'Community' applications for action filed abroad and designating Latvia

The Latvian customs authorities have received several 'Community' applications **17.56** for customs action filed in other Member States and extended to Latvia. In such cases after suspension of infringing goods the Latvian customs officials will directly communicate with the applicant's representative (contact person) in the Member State of filing, or with the customs department through which the application was filed.

III. CONDITIONS GOVERNING ACTION BY CUSTOMS AUTHORITIES AND BY THE AUTHORITIES COMPETENT TO DETERMINE WHETHER GOODS INFRINGE AN INTELLECTUAL PROPERTY RIGHT

A. Conditions governing action by customs authorities

(1) Factual background

In Latvia the following authorities are involved in border measures: the Central **17.57** Customs Board of the State Revenue Service, the Customs Criminal Department of the State Revenue Service, the Riga Regional Customs Office, and four other regional customs offices in the different districts of Latvia (Latgales Regional Customs Office, Zemgales Regional Customs Office, Vidzemes Regional Customs Office, Kurzemes Regional Customs Office). The actions of these different authorities are coordinated by the Intellectual Property Rights Division of the Central Customs Board.

(2) Notification of customs intervention

17.58 The right-holder, or his Latvian representative, is usually notified of the border measures by the relevant Regional office. In most cases, the customs officials contact the right-holder or his representative directly—first by phone, and afterwards by post with a request to confirm whether the detained goods infringe his rights. The declarant or the holders of the goods are also immediately notified of the customs action.

(3) Information to be provided by customs to the right-holder before the latter confirms the infringing nature of the goods

17.59 Once suspect goods are detained by Latvian Customs, the right-holder is informed of their quantity, their nature, and the exporting country. At the right-holder's written request, customs also inform the right-holder of the names and addresses of the consignee, consignor, declarant, and/or holder of the goods, as well as the origin and provenance of goods (if known).

17.60 The national Latvian legislation on the protection of personal data, trade and industrial secrecy, administrative and professional confidentiality does not preclude Latvian Customs from providing the right-holder with this information. The customs officials must warrant the confidentiality of data regarding tax payments, as the Latvian Law on Taxes and Fees prohibits making public any information regarding the taxpayer.[27] However, they are permitted to inform investigation institutions and courts, as well as the competent offices of the European Community in all cases provided by the national and European Community legislative acts. The exception is that it is not permissible to provide the name of the declarant (taxpayer).

(4) Inspection of the suspected goods

17.61 The right-holder is allowed to inspect the suspect goods once customs have informed him about the possible infringement. Whenever possible, customs provide the right-holder with samples or digital pictures of the goods. The sending of pictures or samples is automatic, that is, the right-holder does not have to request this. Our experience shows that the sending of digital pictures is in most

---

[27] Likums 'Par nodokļiem un nodevām' (Law on Taxes and Fees). Adopted on 2 February 1995 and published in the Official State Gazette 'Latvijas Vēstnesis' on 18 February 1995. This Law entered into effect on 1 April 1995, Art 22.

cases (where the presumed infringement relates to the appearance of the goods) sufficient to enable the right-holder to confirm the infringing character of the goods.

The samples can only be used for the purpose of examination and must be returned on completion of the technical analysis and, where applicable, before the goods are released or their termination is ended. **17.62**

B. Simplified procedure allowing the destruction of the goods without there being any need to determine whether an intellectual property right has been infringed under national law

Article 11 of the Regulation has been implemented in Latvia through the Administrative Process Law providing procedure of issue of administrative acts and the Administrative Penalty Code.[28] In those cases where the infringement of intellectual property rights is obvious, Latvian Customs may confiscate the infringing goods subject to border measure when the offender cannot be identified or has not reacted to the decision ordering the destruction of goods within a month. Customs will then arrange the destruction of the goods. **17.63**

If the declarant, holder, consignor, or consignee of the goods contests the infringing character of the goods, the simplified procedure does not apply, but the right-holder may obviously file an action with the civil court to have it confirm the existence of an infringement and oblige customs to destroy the goods. **17.64**

The right-holder and the owner of the infringing goods may also enter into a settlement agreement regarding the goods. It will then be up to the parties to decide on the clauses to be inserted into such agreements. Latvian Customs do not object to the conclusion of an amicable settlement by the parties. However, the grant of a licence by the right-holder to the owner of the infringing goods to allow their commercialization contradicts the very concept of intellectual property protection. Nevertheless under Latvian law it is permissible to grant such licences under which the goods would be released. **17.65**

---

[28] Administratīvo pārkāpumu kodeks (Administrative Penalty Code). Adopted on 7 December 1984 and entered into effect on 1 July 1985. The Law was amended numerous times, Art 201.

C. Conditions governing action by the authorities having jurisdiction to determine whether the goods infringe an intellectual property right

(1) Authorities having jurisdiction to determine whether the goods infringe an intellectual property right

Remedies specific to some intellectual property rights covered by the Regulation

17.66 Under Latvian law, it is possible to initiate both criminal and civil proceedings in order to determine whether an intellectual property right has been infringed. If the right-holder wishes to obtain a decision determining whether an intellectual property right has been infringed, and ordering customs to destroy the infringing goods, allocating damages and recovery of expenses and losses, it is advisable to initiate an action under the Civil Process Law.[29] At first instance a civil action will most likely be decided within a period of six months to one year.

17.67 If the infringement is obvious and serious, the right-holder may request, or customs may initiate, criminal proceeding under the Criminal Process Law.[30] In this case, adjudication of the matter may be completed in a shorter period of time than in the framework of civil proceedings.

Remedies under civil law

Counterfeit goods

17.68 In cases where the goods which have been detained or their release suspended under the Regulation, bear a sign which is not identical to the trade mark on which the application for action is based, the right-holder has to obtain a declaration from the courts of proper jurisdiction, confirming that he has the right to prohibit use of the sign because a risk of confusion with the registered trade mark exists. It is not only the word element of the trade mark, but also any figurative elements that will be taken into account in determining whether a likelihood of confusion may arise on the part of the relevant public.

---

[29] Civil procesa likums (Civil Process Law). Adopted on 14 October 1998 and published in the Official State Gazette 'Latvijas Vēstnesis' on 3 November 1998. This Law entered into effect on 1 March 1999 and was amended numerous times.

[30] Kriminālprocesa likums (Criminal Process Law). Adopted on 21 April 2005 and published in the Official State Gazette 'Latvijas Vēstnesis' on 11 May 2005. This Law will enter into effect on 1 October 2005. Currently in force is the old Criminal Process Code, adopted on 6 January 1961 and amended uncountable times.

Pursuant to the Latvian Trade Mark Law,[31] the owner of a trade mark may bring **17.69** an action in the Regional Court of Riga for unlawful use of the trade mark. The burden of proof of the existence of an infringement lies with the aggrieved party. The Court will adjudicate such civil case on the merits (seizure is not applicable while the Court has not determined whether an intellectual property right has been infringed or not). If the infringement is established, and depending upon the degree of fault, the injured party may request the Court to order the following measures: (i) the cessation of the unlawful use of the trade mark; (ii) the payment of damages redressing the prejudice arising from the unlawful use of the trade mark, including lost profits; (iii) the recovery of court costs, including the litigation expenses as prescribed by law, and the fees paid to the plaintiff's representative. The Court may, in its judgment, provide for measures to prevent further infringement of the trade mark, including imposing the obligation to destroy the goods with the unlawful marking, or to convey those goods at cost price to the owner of the trade mark or a licensee if they so agree, or to relinquish the goods for use for charitable purposes.

Pirated goods

Pursuant to the Latvian Copyright Law,[32] the holder of a copyright or related **17.70** right may initiate court proceedings if any of their moral or economic rights have been infringed, including their right to prohibit the fixation, publication, reproduction, or distribution in any form of a protected subject matter. The holders of a copyright or related rights, as well as collecting societies and other representatives, have the right to prevent the use of the protected works or performances, and to obtain compensation for the losses incurred owing to the infringement, including lost profits. Finally the right-holder can obtain an order that the infringing copies be destroyed. It is worth pointing out that the above principles apply regardless of whether the infringement, which is the object of the proceedings, presents an economic character.

Goods infringing design rights

Any use of an industrial design that contradicts the Industrial Design Law of **17.71** Latvia is considered a patent infringement.[33] Under this Law industrial design use is the introduction into economic circulation of an article, which has been manufactured in accordance with a patented industrial design. Disputes associated with industrial designs are reviewed by court in the procedure set by civil legislation.

---

[31] N 12 above, Art 28.   [32] N 16 above, Art 69.

[33] Dizainparaugu likums (Industrial Design Law). Adopted on 28 October 2004 and published in the Official State Gazette 'Latvijas Vēstnesis' on 17 November 2004. This Law entered into effect on 18 November 2004, Art 48.

Also under the jurisdiction of the Riga Regional Court is the infringement of the exclusive and property rights of design patent owners. Depending on the nature and effects of the infringement, the court may, simultaneously, have the infringer compensate for losses and impose a fine on him, as well as ordering the confiscation, destruction, or detainment of the illegal articles and the equipment used in their manufacture, and demand that they be sold at cost to the patent owner or that they be transferred to use for charitable purposes.

Goods infringing a patent

17.72   Under the Latvian Patent Law,[34] patentees enjoy the same remedies as copyright owners. Within the period of the provisional legal protection from the grant up to the expiry of the patent (or supplementary protection certificate), the patent owner may initiate a patent infringement claim before the civil courts. Where the patent infringement is established, the court may, on the plaintiff's motion, order the following measures, depending on the degree of seriousness of the infringer's fault: (i) the termination of the use of the invention; (ii) the seizure of the articles falling under the scope of protection of the patent, or of all devices of which such articles form part; as well as (iii) the surrendering of these articles to the aggrieved party; and (iv) the redress of any injury caused as a result of the infringement, including the reimbursement of undue profits, and payment of the costs of the proceedings.

Goods infringing a plant variety right

17.73   Under the Latvian Plant Variety Law if a third party utilizes a propagating material of a variety, responsibility for the infringement of the breeder's right is applied from the day of publication of the application.[35] A person who has infringed the breeder's right shall compensate, for the utilization of a variety, any losses to the owner of the breeder's right which have resulted from the infringer's non-compliance with this Law.

Goods infringing a designation of origin or a geographical indication

17.74   Any unfair or misleading use of a designation of origin or a geographical indication on goods results in an infringement of these rights pursuant to the provisions of the Latvian Trade Mark Law protecting use of such signs in the course of trade.[36] Any infringement will be considered as an act of unfair competition, and shall therefore be subject to the sanctions laid down in the statutory unfair competition provisions, for instance, the Latvian Competition Law.[37] The civil action may be brought before the Regional Court of Riga by any interested persons, including

---

[34] N 17 above, Arts 40–45.   [35] N 18 above, Arts 38, 39, 40.
[36] N 12 above, Arts 41, 42, 43.   [37] N 15 above, Art 18.

professional associations and associations of manufacturers, traders, or service providers, whose Articles of Association provide for the protection of the economic interests of their associates, as well as by organizations and authorities whose purpose, under their articles of association, relates to consumer protection.

Remedies under criminal law

In cases where the infringement of an intellectual property right has been **17.75** committed deliberately or with malicious intent, the persons responsible may also be called to administrative or criminal liability. Further to the filing of a complaint by the right-holder, or by customs (in cases of serious crimes when losses are very high), the police, public prosecutor, or court of proper jurisdiction may initiate investigations under the Criminal Process Law. Criminal prosecution may be initiated provided a substantial harm is caused to the rights and interests of a person protected by law. Criminal proceedings may, in particular, be initiated where the offender has committed repeated infringements, or where the infringement constitutive of a criminal offence has been perpetrated by a group of persons, either pursuant to a premeditated agreement, or on a large scale.

Civil or criminal?

If there is a dispute as to whether or not the intellectual property rights have been **17.76** infringed, the best first step would be to request that the court initiate an action under civil process. If the infringement is obvious and the right-holder has suffered significantly and the amount of imported goods is very large, there should be no hesitation in asking the official institutions to initiate an action under criminal law. Civil claims for compensation of financial loss or moral injury in criminal matters may be brought in accordance with the procedures prescribed by the Criminal Process Law.[38] If a civil claim has not been submitted or adjudicated in a criminal matter, an action may be brought in accordance with the procedures prescribed by the Civil Process Law.[39]

(2) Term for notifying customs that proceedings have been started

Under Article 13(1) of the Regulation, the term of 10 working days for notifying **17.77** customs that proceedings have been commenced may be extended by a maximum of another 10 working days, at the right-holder's request. By virtue of this provision, however, an extension may only be granted 'in appropriate cases'.

---

[38] N 30 above.   [39] N 29 above.

In practice, Latvian Customs will allow such requests provided that they are grounded on sufficient reasons. 'Sufficient reasons' may be that time for filing an action has been too short, later receipt of official documents required for the court, etc. In fact, Latvian Customs will be flexible in this matter. The concept of 'appropriate cases' is analysed on the indicated facts.

D. Release of goods suspected of infringing certain rights on provision of a security

17.78   No cases have been reported in Latvia so far where goods suspected of infringing any of the intellectual property rights referred to in Article 14 of the Regulation would have been released. In Latvia the civil court may determine or the parties may agree on the applicable amount of security.

E. Storage of the goods

17.79   During the period of suspension of release or detention, the goods are initially stored in the place under customs' control. As soon as the right-holder confirms that, in his opinion, the goods infringe any of his intellectual property rights, the goods are forwarded to a customs warehouse designed for that purpose, where they stay until their destruction or release is ordered by customs (in those cases where the simplified procedure is applied) or by the courts (in the opposite event). The storage costs have to be borne by the right-holder in the first place, who will however be able to recover some from the infringer(s), either in the framework of the court proceedings, or pursuant to the terms of a settlement agreement entered into in application of the simplified procedure.

IV. PROVISIONS APPLICABLE TO GOODS FOUND TO INFRINGE AN INTELLECTUAL PROPERTY RIGHT

17.80   The Latvian Customs Law allows the infringer to abandon the goods to the Exchequer, in which case they will be destroyed.[40] The owner of infringing goods

---

[40] N 11 above, Arts, 19, 20, 21, 22.

may file an application to customs asking that the infringing goods be destroyed. Such a request may be substantiated in accordance with the decision of the customs office. The destruction of the goods may also result from a court decision or a settlement agreement concluded in the framework of the application of the 'simplified procedure'.[41] The courts may order the destruction of the goods in all cases where it has been requested by the right-holder and the goods are found to infringe an intellectual property right. The costs related to the destruction of the goods are to be covered by the right-holder. In order to obtain reimbursement of these costs, he has to bring an action against the declarant, holder or owner of the goods according to the procedure provided by the Latvian Civil Process Law. The right-holder may seek reimbursement of financial loss or moral injury in criminal matters also.

Latvian law permits the giving of infringing goods to charities. However, this is an issue of great debate, which has been properly discussed both by judges and right-holders in Latvia. Taking into account the fact that the confiscated goods are not genuine and the right-holder cannot take any responsibility for the quality of these goods, the right-holders, especially those from America tend more towards the destruction of such goods. In addition, if the trade mark of the right-holder is on the infringing goods and these goods are of poor quality, such use of the mark may be detrimental to the distinctive character or the reputation of the trade mark. The judges take the view that from an economic standpoint, donating infringing goods to for example, retirement communities, asylums, or orphanages, may be more reasonable. **17.81**

V. PENALTIES

Under the Latvian Criminal Law and Administrative Penalty Code, administrative and criminal sanctions are applied to infringers of intellectual property rights. Civil sanctions have been discussed in paragraphs 17.80 and 17.81 above. **17.82**

A. Administrative sanctions

For unlawful use of a trade mark that is registered under established procedure the administrative sanctions consist in fines (which range from LATS 50 to LATS 100 (EUR 72 to EUR 144), and the forfeiture of the counterfeit goods. For obtaining **17.83**

---

[41] Cf paras 17.63 to 17.65 above.

for realization, storage or hiding of published, reproduced or in any other way using objects of copyrights and related rights, the sanctions consist in fines ranging from LATS 100 up to LATS 250 (EUR 144 to EUR 356), and the forfeiture of the pirated goods and their carriers. If border measures are applied to any counterfeited and pirated goods or such goods are temporarily stored, a fine may be imposed: for natural persons from LATS 50 to LATS 250 (EUR 72 to EUR 356) and for legal persons from LATS 500 to LATS 5,000 (EUR 712 to EUR 7,114), and the forfeiture of the goods may also be pronounced in this case.[42] There are no special administrative sanctions for other types of intellectual property rights infringement. Regarding design infringement, administrative sanctions for copyrights infringement may be applied.

B. Criminal sanctions

17.84 The Latvian Criminal Law provides for penalties in case of wilful unauthorized use of trade marks, other distinctive signs, and designs. The applicable sanctions consist either of a jail term not exceeding one year, custodial arrest, community service, or a fine not exceeding the sum of 100 times the minimum monthly wage, with or without confiscation of property. Where the same offence has been committed repeatedly, or where substantial harm is caused thereby to a third party's rights and interests, the penalties consist of a jail term not exceeding five years, or a fine not exceeding the sum of 200 times the minimum monthly wage, with or without confiscation of property.[43]

17.85 The authors of wilful infringements of a copyright or related neighbouring right incur a custodial arrest, community service, or a fine not exceeding the sum of 100 times the minimum monthly wage, with or without confiscation of property. Where the same offence of this nature has been committed repeatedly by its author, or has been committed premeditatedly by a group of persons, the penalties consist of a jail term not exceeding two years, custodial arrest, or a fine not exceeding the sum of 150 times the minimum monthly wage, with or without confiscation of property. Any person who obtains goods infringing a copyright or neighbouring rights for the purpose of selling, storing, or concealing such goods repeatedly during a period of one year, incurs a custodial arrest, a community service penalty, or a fine not exceeding the sum of 100 times the minimum monthly wage, with or without confiscation of property.[44]

17.86 Any person who commits an appropriation of authorship or compel of joint authorship of a patented invention or a protected design incurs a jail term not

---

[42] Administrative Penalty Code, Arts 155[8], 166[17], and 201[12].
[43] Krimināllikums (Criminal Law), Art 206.   [44] Ibid, Arts 148–149.

exceeding three years, custodial arrest, or a fine not exceeding the sum of 200 times the minimum monthly wages, with or without forfeiture of property.[45]

No specific penalties regarding goods infringing a plant variety right, a designation of origin, or a geographical indication, are provided by the Administrative Penalty Code or the Criminal Law.

VI. LIABILITY OF CUSTOMS AUTHORITIES AND RIGHT-HOLDERS

A. Liability of right-holders and sanctions

The right-holder is liable for any breach of the Regulation (Article 19 (3)) pursuant to the civil law prescribing civil liability.[46] For non-permitted use of the information provided by customs (cf Article 12) the right-holder may be held also liable under the civil law as well as or criminal law of Latvia prescribing sanctions for such breaches of law. If, due to illegal disclosure of restricted access information, harm has been caused to its owner or another person, or his legal interests have been materially infringed, these persons have the right to bring an action against the person at fault for damages for the harm done, or for restoration of the rights infringed.[47] **17.87**

B. Liability of customs authorities and sanctions

(1) Liability of the customs authorities for not detecting or acting against goods suspected of infringing an intellectual property right

If the right-holder has substantial grounds to consider that a Latvian customs office has intentionally failed to detect goods suspected of infringing his intellectual property rights whilst the right-holder had lodged an application to that effect which had been duly accepted by the competent customs department, he may claim compensation for the harm incurred owing to such an omission. Indeed, the Latvian customs officials are liable for damages caused by their **17.88**

---

[45] Ibid, Art 147.

[46] Civillikums (Civil Law). Adopted on 28 January 1937 and in force since regaining of independence (1991).

[47] Informacijas atklatibas likums (Freedom of Information Law). Adopted on 29 October 1998 and published in the Official State Gazette 'Latvijas Vēstnesis' on 6 November 1998, Art 16(2).

unlawful decisions, acts, or omissions. Losses incurred by a legal or natural person (also to the third parties) as a result of an illegitimate action, or inexcusable mistake, from the State Revenue Service (including customs) officials shall be reimbursed from the state budget—furthermore, the refundable amount may be increased according to the refinancing rate established by the Bank of Latvia during the relevant period.[48]

Conclusion

17.89 When evaluating the application of Regulation 1383/2003 in Latvia, one can conclude that the approach adopted by this instrument is not entirely in line with the provisions of national, international and Community legislation defining the acts which are to be considered an infringement of the intellectual property rights referred to in the Regulation. For instance, it is not clear whether all acts defined as a trade mark infringement under the Trade Mark Directive and Community Trade Mark Regulation are caught by the definition of Article 2(1)(a) of Regulation 1383/2003. In addition, the Latvian customs officials should receive further training to help them readily recognize infringements of patents, designs, plant varieties, designations of origin, and geographical indications.

---

[48] Likums par Valsts ieņēmumu dienestu (State Revenue Service Law). Adopted on 28 October 1993 and published in the Official State Gazette 'Latvijas Vēstnesis' on 17 November 1993, Art 23.

18

LITHUANIA

Asta Lukošiūtė

Introduction

The effective fight against counterfeiting and piracy in Lithuania started in the **18.01** spring of 2000 and was considerably strengthened with the adoption on 21 December 2001 of the Law on the protection of intellectual property rights upon importation and exportation of goods ('the Intellectual Property Law').[1] This Law entered into force on 1 January 2001 and was already in line with Council Regulation (EC) 3295/94,[2] but more importantly, it anticipated the draft document that became Council Regulation (EC) 1383/2003.[3] The Intellectual Property Law applied to a similar range of intellectual property rights, and provided for very similar procedures. Therefore, the entry into force of Council Regulation (EC) 1383/2003 did not substantially change the previously existing procedures and practice in Lithuania with regard to border measures.

The Intellectual Property Law was repealed on 1 May 2004, that is, the date on **18.02** which Lithuania joined the European Union. Since then, Council Regulation (EC) 3295/94 has directly applied in Lithuania.

As of 1 July 2004, the new Council Regulation (EC) 1383/2003 has been applied **18.03** in Lithuania along with its implementing Commission Regulation (EC)

---

[1] LR No IX-117 lektinės nuosavybės apsaugos importuojant ir eksportuojant prekes įstatymas of 21 December 2000 [2000] Valstybės Žinios (State news) No 113-3611, repealed as of 1 May 2004.
[2] Council Reg (EC) 3295/94 of 22 December 1994 laying down measures to prohibit the release for free circulation, export, re-export or entry for a suspensive procedure of counterfeit and pirated goods [1994] OJ L 341/8, as amended by Council Reg (EC) No 241/1999 of 25 January 1999 amending Reg (EC) No 3295/94 laying down measures to prohibit the release for free circulation, export, re-export or entry for a suspensive procedure of counterfeit and pirated goods [1999] OJ L 27/1.
[3] Council Reg (EC) 1383/2003 of 22 July 2003 concerning customs action against goods suspected of infringing certain intellectual property rights and the measures to be taken against goods found to have infringed such rights [2003] OJ L 196/7.

1891/2004[4] and the national statutory provisions on the same subject. The main national pieces of legislation which are currently in force in Lithuania in the sphere of border measures are the following:

— the Customs Law of 2004 (in particular Articles 80–87);[5]
— the Order of the Director of the Customs Department setting out the regulation on the provision of information concerning actions against goods suspected of infringing intellectual property rights 2004;[6]
— the Order of the Director of the Customs Department setting out the regulation on the suspension of release, detention, storage, inspection, and the taking of samples of goods suspected of infringing intellectual property rights in 2004;[7]
— the Order of the Director of the Customs Department setting out the regulation on the deposit of securities in relation to the protection of certain intellectual property rights in 2004;[8]
— the Order of the Director of the Customs Department setting out the regulation on the destruction of goods under the customs supervision in 2004;[9]
— the Order of the Director of the Customs Department setting out the regulation on the destruction of the detained or not released by the customs goods suspected of infringing intellectual property rights in 2005.[10]

18.04 In Lithuania, the experience to date in the field of border measures against goods suspected of infringing intellectual property rights is relatively limited. The reason for this limited practice is probably that the first legislative measures concerning

---

[4] Commission Reg (EC) 1891/2004 of 21 October 2004 laying down provisions for the implementation of Council Reg (EC) 1383/2003 concerning customs action against goods suspected of infringing certain intellectual property rights and the measures to be taken against goods found to have infringed such rights [2004] OJ L 328/16 (30.10.2004).

[5] LR No IX-2183 Muitinės įstatymas of 27 April 2004, [2004] VŽ No 73-2517.

[6] Muitinės departamento prie LR Finansų ministerijos generalinio direktoriaus įsakymas dėl informavimo apie veiksmus su prekėmis, laikytinomis pagamintomis pažeidžiant intelektinės nuosavybės teises, taisyklių patvirtinimo No 1B-622 of 9 June 2004, [2004] VŽ No 94-3472.

[7] Muitinės departamento prie LR Finansų ministerijos generalinio direktoriaus įsakymas dėl prekių, laikytinų pagamintomis pažeidžiant intelektinės nuosavybės teises, neišleidimo, sulaikymo, saugojimo, apžiūros ir pavyzdžių ėmimo taisyklių patvirtinimo No 1B-549 of 24 May 2004, [2004] VŽ No 86-3160, as amended.

[8] Muitinės departamento prie LR Finansų ministerijos generalinio direktoriaus įsakymas dėl garantijų, susijusių su tam tikrų intelektinės nuosavybės teisių apsauga, pateikimo No 1B-550 of 24 May 2004, [2004] VŽ No 86-3159.

[9] Muitinės departamento prie LR Finansų ministerijos generalinio direktoriaus įsakymas dėl muitinės prižiūrimų prekių sunaikinimo taisyklių patvirtinimo No 1B-1180 of 24 December 2004, [2004] VŽ No 186-6951.

[10] Muitinės departamento prie LR Finansų ministerijos generalinio direktoriaus įsakymas dėl muitinės neišleistų arba sulaikytų prekių, kurios, kaip įtariama, pagamintos pažeidžiant intelektinės nuosavybės teises, sunaikinimo taisyklių patvirtinimo No 1B-288 of 15 April 2005, [2005] VŽ No 51-1731.

the fight against counterfeiting and piracy only became effective as of 2001. Since then, only a few applications for action have been filed, most of them relating to trade marks rights.[11] None of these concerns copyright or patent rights, whilst one single application relates to design rights.

Since the Intellectual Property Law was repealed, some questions are no longer **18.05** regulated and some notions need to be clarified. The practice under Council Regulation (EC) 1383/2003 is still evolving and cannot be generalized yet. Consequently, it is often necessary to turn to the practice under the former Intellectual Property Law to try to infer how certain questions shall be solved. Therefore, in this chapter, in addition to analysing the current situation, we will refer to the previous practice, as it existed before the entry into force of Council Regulation (EC) 1383/2003.

I. SUBJECT MATTER AND SCOPE OF THE NATIONAL LAW APPLYING THE REGULATION

In Lithuania there is no specific piece of legislation defining the scope of applica- **18.06** tion of Council Regulation (EC) 1383/2003. The exact scope of application, definition of the goods infringing intellectual property rights and related issues shall be dealt with by consulting specific legislation on particular intellectual property rights or case law of the courts, which admittedly is rather limited.

A. Customs procedure of goods

Already prior to the entry into force of Council Regulation (EC) 1383/2003, the **18.07** Lithuanian Intellectual Property Law[12] provided that the Lithuanian customs authorities were to take action against goods suspected of infringing an intellectual property rights, irrespective of their customs procedure, including, among others, import, transit, export, release for free circulation, re-export, and placing in free zones or free warehouses. Although the Intellectual Property Law has been repealed, the Regulation clearly provides that it applies to all types of customs

---

[11] According to the data provided by Lithuanian Customs department (available at www.cust.lt/lt/rubric?rubricID = 562) on 7 November 2005, 169 applications had been filed.
[12] LR Intellectual Property Law 2000, Art 5 (n 1 above).

procedures.[13] In practice, most of the customs measures are taken against imported goods, goods in transit being in a second location.[14]

18.08   The Lithuanian Supreme Court in case No 3-K-3-160 '*Mita*'[15] was called upon to give its interpretation of Article 9(4) of the Paris Convention,[16] in particular whether the lower courts deciding the case correctly upheld the application of customs measures against the counterfeit goods in transit. In its decision of 17 November 2003, the Supreme Court maintained that Article 9(4) of the Paris Convention did not impose any obligation on the Member States but on the contrary, left to their discretion the issue of whether to impose border measures against counterfeit goods in transit. Thus, Intellectual Property Law allowing the taking of customs actions against counterfeit goods in transit did not contradict the provisions of the Paris Convention and was correctly applied. The decision of the Supreme Court upheld this point regarding the rulings rendered by the Vilnius District Court and the Court of Appeals.

B. Definition of infringing goods

18.09   Under the Council Regulation (EC) 1383/2003, Lithuanian Customs are to take border measures against infringements of a large number of intellectual and industrial property rights. This was already the case since 2001 under the former Intellectual Property Law. However, most of the border measures taken by Lithuanian Customs relate to trade mark infringements.[17] So far, only one application for action has been filed by the design owners and no applications by the owners of other intellectual property rights has been filed yet. No *ex officio* action has ever been taken with regard to such rights, except when pirated copies of CDs or DVDs were confiscated several times as being smuggled or infringing other administrative law provisions.

---

[13] Council Reg 1383/2003, Art 1(1).

[14] In 2004 customs took 22 actions against imported goods, seven actions against goods in transit and one seizure of exported goods (data provided by the Customs department).

[15] Lithuanian Supreme Court decision of 17 November 2003, civil case No 3K-3-1060/2003 *The H.D. Lee Company Inc v UAB Mita* (available at http://ovada.tic.lt/lat/nutartis.aspx?id = 25312).

[16] Paris Convention for the Protection of the Industrial Property (Paris Convention) of 20 March 1883 as revised and amended. Art 9 'Marks, Trade Names: *Seizure, on Importation, etc., of Goods Unlawfully Bearing a Mark or Trade Name*': (4) The authorities shall not be bound to effect seizure of goods in transit.

[17] In 2004 in Lithuania more than 500,000 items of goods infringing trade mark rights were seized, compared to about 660 seized items of goods infringing copyrights and related rights. There were no seizures of goods infringing other intellectual property rights (data provided by the customs department).

(1) Counterfeit goods

According to Article 2(1)(a)(i) of the Council Regulation (EC) 1383/2003, **18.10**
'counterfeit goods' shall mean goods, bearing without authorization a sign identical to a trade mark validly registered in respect of the same type of goods, or which cannot be distinguished in its essential aspects from such trade mark and which thereby infringes the trade mark holder's rights under Community law or national law.

Under Article 38 of the Lithuanian Law on Trade Marks[18] ('the Trade Mark Law'), **18.11**
the proprietor of a registered trade mark shall have the exclusive right to prevent any third persons not having his consent from using in the course of trade, any sign:

- which is identical with the registered mark in relation to goods and/or services which are identical with those for which the mark is registered;

- where, because of its identity with or similarity to the registered mark covering identical or similar goods and/or services, there exists a likelihood of confusion on the part of the public, including the likelihood of association between the sign and the mark;

- which is identical with or similar to the registered mark in relation to goods and/or services which are not similar to those for which the mark is registered, where the latter has a reputation in the Republic of Lithuania, and where use of that sign without due cause takes unfair advantage of, or is detrimental to, the distinctive character or the repute of the mark.

When evaluating the risk of confusion, the Lithuanian courts will not only take **18.12**
into account Community legislation[19] and case law, but also the methodical guidelines on the examination of the similarity of trade marks and goods effective as of 1996[20] adopted by the Lithuanian State Patent Office. It is evident from the above that the scope of protection—especially with regard to use of similar marks for similar or even dissimilar goods—afforded under Lithuanian law is broader than the definition contained in Council Regulation (EC) 1383/2003.

---

[18] LR Prekių ženklų įstatymas No VIII-1981 of 10 October 2000, [2000] VŽ No 92-2844, as last amended on 19 February 2004, [2004] VŽ No 39-1272.

[19] Cf First Council Directive 89/104/EEC of 21 December 1988 to approximate the laws of the Member States relating to trade marks [1989] L 40/1, as amended; Reg (EC) No 40/94 of 20 December 1993 on the Community Trade Mark [1994] OJ L 11/1, as amended.

[20] Metodiniai nurodymai dėl prekių ir paslaugų ženklų tapatumo ir panašumo nustatymo, patvirtinti LR Valstybinio patentų biuro įsakymu No 28 of 11 July 1996.

18.13 The proprietor of a trade mark may, in particular, prohibit the following acts:[21]

- affixing a sign to goods, or to the packaging thereof;
- offering the goods or putting them on the market, or stocking, renting, lending, or disposing of them in any other form for these purposes or offering or supplying services under the conflicting sign;
- importing or exporting goods under that sign;
- using such signs on business papers and in advertising;
- manufacturing such signs or keeping specimens thereof for the purpose of performing any of the actions specified above.

18.14 The counterfeit goods, which are apprehended in customs' daily practice in Lithuania, seldom consist of goods bearing signs that are completely identical to the trade mark they are copying. Instead, in most cases, such goods bear a confusing imitation of that trade mark. One can find, for example, marks bearing the name '7th Avenue', '15th Avenue', or '55th Avenue' perfumes, 'SQNY' or 'PANASONIK' car radios, 'CANEL' handbags, and other clear-cut imitations of the same type. Perfumes and cosmetics, in addition to similar brands, usually use the same or similar shapes, typewriting, or logos as the original products. It is also common to affix trade marks with a reputation to products for which the mark is not normally used, for example, MARLBORO for t-shirts, FERRARI for caps, etc. Thus, in order to be effective, broader measures should not only be applied to signs which are identical to a trade mark validly registered for the same type of goods, but also to imitations and confusingly similar marks or products, which under Lithuanian law, would be considered as infringing.

18.15 It may be questioned whether the seemingly broader protection accorded by Lithuanian Trade Mark Law is consistent with Article 2(1)(a) of the Council Regulation (EC) 1383/2003. However Recital 8 of the Regulation expressly provides that 'proceedings initiated to determine whether an intellectual property right has been infringed under national law will be conducted with reference to the criteria used to establish whether goods produced in that Member State infringe intellectual property rights'. In Lithuania, those criteria include not only identity of the signs and products, but also their confusing similarity.

18.16 In practice, the Lithuanian customs authorities do not engage in a thorough legal evaluation whether the sign affixed to the suspect goods is confusingly similar to the registered trade mark according to the provisions of the law and case law. They leave it to the court to decide on this point at a later stage of the procedure. The customs officers usually trust their common sense and examine whether the suspect goods are likely to infringe the rights of the trade mark owner. When they are in the presence of what they consider a clear imitation of a protected trade mark,

---

[21] LR Trade Mark Law 2004, Art 38(2) (n 18 above).

customs officials habitually inform the right-holder or their representative of the possible infringement. Thus, Lithuanian Customs adopted border measures for example, on sandals bearing the sign 'ANMANI' instead of 'ARMANI', or perfumes 'GOSHI PUSH' imitating 'GUCCI RUSH'. In the latter case, the imitation also included the use of a very similar shape of the perfume bottle.[22]

In general, in Lithuania the customs officers, before taking action against suspicious **18.17** goods, usually ask the trade mark owner or their representative to confirm that the goods are most probably non-authentic and that the trade marks are at least confusingly similar. They also enquire whether the trade mark owner would be interested in pursuing the presumed infringement. This practice is convenient both for customs and for the trade mark owners and ultimately, for the importers of goods.

Such informal communication between customs and trade mark owners helps to **18.18** avoid a waste of resources and time in applying legal measures against the goods if the trade mark owner is not interested in pursuing a case or considers that the goods are not infringing his rights. Such communication also avoids creating unnecessary obstacles for the importers of goods because they are not constrained even for a short period in their actions.

The Council Regulation (EC) 1383/2003 also applies to any trade mark symbols **18.19** or packaging materials bearing the trade marks of counterfeit goods, even if presented separately.[23] In practice, we are not aware of any case where such symbols or packaging materials would have been subject to border measures in Lithuania.

Article 38 of the Lithuanian Trade Mark Law states that the trade mark owner may **18.20** rely on his exclusive rights only once their trade mark is validly registered or is recognized by the court as a well-known mark. The requirement of registration is in line with Article 2(1)(a)(i) of the Council Regulation (EC) 1383/2003, which also provides that counterfeit goods are those which bear without authorization, a sign identical to a trade mark which has been 'validly registered'. However, the Regulation is silent on the question of the protection of non-registered and well-known marks. In our opinion, since all EU Member States are also signatories of the Paris Convention, and are thus bound by its provisions, including an obligation to protect well-known marks, the Council Regulation (EC) 1383/2003 shall also apply to such marks. In Lithuania, previous Intellectual Property Law applies as non-registered, but is recognized by the court as a well-known mark.[24]

---

[22] The owners of the suspect goods voluntarily agreed to destroy the goods, and both matters were settled out of court. There is thus unfortunately no case law on these interesting matters.

[23] Council Reg 1383/2003, Art 2(1)(a)(ii)–(iii). The same provisions were contained in Art 2(7) of the Intellectual Property Law (n 1 above), which allowed the customs authorities to take action against logos, labels, stickers, instructions for use, brochures, or other trade mark symbols, and packaging materials, even if presented separately.

[24] LR Intellectual Property Law 2000, Art 2.

(2) *Pirated goods*

18.21   To date, not a single case of border measures taken against pirated goods either applying the EC Regulations or previous Intellectual Property Law has ever been reported in Lithuania.

18.22   Article 73 of the Lithuanian Law on Copyright and Related Rights of 1999[25] ('the Copyright Law') defines the scope of protection of copyrights and related rights. The Law considers as infringing goods any copy of a work, the subject matter of a related right or *sui generis* right,[26] produced in, or imported into, the Republic of Lithuania without the consent of the right-holder or a person duly authorized by the latter (that is, either in the absence of an agreement with the right-holder, or upon violating the terms and conditions set out in such an agreement). The Law provides for several exceptions, where the protected subject matter may be reproduced without the right-owner's prior authorization. Any copy of a work or protected material in which rights-management information, or any other anti-copying technological protection device has been removed or altered without the permission of the owner of the rights, shall also infringe the latter's copyright, related right, or *sui generis* right.

18.23   Until now, goods suspected of infringing a copyright or a related right, have never been detained or their release suspended by the Lithuanian customs authorities subsequent to the filing of an application for action, but always due to those goods being detected following smuggling controls. In most instances, the goods infringing a copyright or a related right have been CDs or DVDs, which were imported into Lithuania separately or without cases and covers. If they had covers, the printing was of poor quality or they were simply photocopied. It is thus often easy for customs to identify them as pirated goods. When it comes to determining whether goods infringe a copyright or a related right, the customs authorities regularly contact the Lithuanian copyright protection association LATGA-A, the Lithuanian related rights association AGATA, the Lithuanian musical industry association or the Lithuanian phonogram producers and distributors association for preliminary expertise and opinion concerning the products. Most of the cases involving pirated goods usually end up being resolved under criminal or administrative court proceedings for smuggling and because the goods are also found to infringe an intellectual property right, they are eventually destroyed.

18.24   Under Article 36 of the Lithuanian Law on Designs of 2002[27] ('the Design Law'), the owner of a registered design enjoys the exclusive right to use, to allow or

---

[25]   LR Autorių teisių ir gretutinių teisių įstatymas No VIII-1185 of 18 May 1999, [1999] VŽ No 50-1598, as last amended on 21 March 2003, [2003] VŽ No 28-1125.

[26]   Right of a database producer.

[27]   LR Dizaino įstatymas No IX-118 of 17 November 2002, [2002] VŽ No 112-4980, as last amended on 29 April 2004, [2004] VŽ No 73-2538.

prohibit others without its consent from manufacturing, offering for sale, selling, marketing, importing, exporting, stocking and using any goods the design of which does not create on an informed user an overall impression different from the registered design. This provision defining the scope of protection of a design is phrased, interpreted and applied in compliance with Council Directive (EC) 98/71[28] and Council Regulation (EC) 6/2002.[29]

18.25 There is no practice in Lithuania on border measures in relation to goods infringing design rights and the case law on design right protection is also very limited. Therefore, right-holders should be aware that, unless the infringing copies of the design are almost identical to the protected design, the court proceedings in this field may be lengthy and complex, requiring public opinion surveys on the perception of the design by users, experts opinions, etc.

18.26 Under the Lithuanian Design Law, the rights to the design are vested in the right-holder only after registration.[30] Therefore, in order to be able to rely on those national rights in court, the owner must submit evidence of the design registration. Consequently, an application for action under the Regulation may only be filed on the basis of a registered design right, as otherwise, the right-holder will not be in a position to enforce their rights before the courts or take any other action against the infringers. It is not clear how this requirement of Lithuanian Design Law shall be reconciled with the clear indication in Article 2(1)(b) of the Council Regulation (EC) 1383/2003 that the design right need not be registered. However, as mentioned above, under Lithuanian law there is no design right without registration.[31] This is, of course, without prejudice to the protection accorded by Council Regulation (EC) 6/2002 to the unregistered Community design.[32]

(3) Goods infringing other intellectual property rights

Goods infringing a patent or a supplementary protection certificate

18.27 The Lithuanian Patent Law 1994[33] regulates the protection of inventions in Lithuania under patents and supplementary protection certificates. According to

---

[28] Directive 98/71/EC of the European Parliament and of the Council of 13 October 1998 on the legal protection of designs [1998] OJ L 289/28.
[29] Council Reg (EC) No 6/2002 of 12 December 2001 on Community Designs [2002] OJ L 3/1.　　　　　　　　　　　　　　　[30] LR Design Law 2002, Art 36 (n 27 above).
[31] Such an unregistered design may be protected on the basis of copyright laws, which do not foresee any registration.　　　　　[32] Council Reg 6/2002, Art 1(2)(a), Art 11, Art 19(2).
[33] LR Patentų įstatymas No I-327 of 18 January 1994, [1994] VŽ No 8-120, as last amended on 30 June 2005, [2005] VŽ No 85-3135.

Article 26 of the Law, the rights of the owner of a patent include the exclusive right to prevent third parties of not having their consent in the following cases:

- where the subject matter of the patent is a product, making, using, offering for sale, selling, importing, or exporting that product;
- where the subject matter of the patent is a process, using that process, and using, offering for sale, selling, importing, or exporting a product obtained directly by that process;
- supplying or offering to supply essential elements of the patented invention with the exception of those which are widely known in trade if the supply of such elements is necessary for performing any of the acts provided above.

18.28 It shall be noted that the Lithuanian State Patent Office, before granting a patent, does not examine whether the invention is new or involves an inventive step. In patent infringement cases, it is therefore likely that the accused infringer will file a counterclaim pertaining to the validity of the patent that makes any litigation related to patents very cumbersome and complex, requiring technical expertise and in-depth novelty and non-obviousness searches and analysis. Right-holders should be aware of this.

18.29 The Lithuanian Patent Law provides that the patentee may only enforce his rights on the basis of a registered patent or a published patent application.[34] Consequently, applications for actions under the Regulation in Lithuania may also be based on a published patent application because such a title affords provisional legal protection to its owner and may be relied on in legal proceedings aimed at the enforcement of the patent rights.

18.30 As mentioned above, in Lithuania, no application for action has ever been filed by patent owners to date. While *ex officio* actions concerning suspected patent infringements are very unlikely, owing to the fact that such infringements, unlike other intellectual property right violations, require extensive technical knowledge and expertise in order to be detected, let alone the fact that the customs officials, in the vast majority of cases, are not in a position to determine the object and scope of the protection of patents.

Goods infringing a national plant variety right

18.31 The Lithuanian Law on Plant Variety Rights 2001[35] is relatively recent and the possibility of filing an application for action by customs authorities for protected plant varieties did not exist before the entry into the force of Council Regulation (EC) 1383/2003.

---

[34] LR Patent Law (n 33 above), Art 41.
[35] LR Augalų veislių apsaugos įstatymas No IX-618 of 22 November 2001, [2001] VŽ No 104-3701.

Under Article 26 of the Law on Plant Variety Rights, the breeder has the right to **18.32** authorize, with respect to the propagating material of the protected variety, its production and reproduction, conditioning for the purpose of propagation, offering for sale, selling or any other form of marketing, exporting, importing, or stocking for any of the above-mentioned purposes. The breeder's rights also extend to:

- varieties which are essentially derived from those that are initially protected, provided they are not themselves an essentially derived variety;
- varieties which are not clearly distinguishable from the protected variety;
- varieties whose production requires only the repeated use of the protected variety.

The Law on Plant Variety Rights contains provisions on the exhaustion of rights **18.33** that are arguably at odds with Community law. Indeed it provides that the 'breeder's rights shall not extend to acts concerning any propagating or plant material of the protected variety, which has been sold or otherwise marketed by the breeder or with his consent in the territory of a member state of the International Union for the Protection of New Varieties of Plants (UPOV)[36] or any material derived from the material unless such acts involve further production of the propagating and plant material of the variety in question or involve the exportation of the propagating and plant material of the variety to a country which does not protect varieties of the plant genus or species to which the variety belongs, except where the exported plant material is for final consumption purposes.[37] This provision does not limit exhaustion of plant variety rights solely to the territory of the European Community, but extends beyond to other member countries of UPOV. On the other hand, several Member States of the European Community are not yet members of UPOV and it seems that the exhaustion of plant variety rights should not apply towards their territories under Lithuanian Law.

The owner of plant variety rights is granted protection for their variety from the **18.34** moment of registration of the variety in the list of protected plant varieties.[38] A certificate is issued upon effective registration of the variety. The right-holder can only enforce his rights pursuant to such registrations. Therefore, an application for action under the Council Regulation (EC) 1383/2003 may only be filed in Lithuania on the basis of a registered variety.

---

[36] Cf The International Convention for the Protection of New Varieties of Plants (UPOV Convention) of 2 December 1961, as revised at Geneva on 10 November 1972, on 23 October 1978, and on 19 March 1991.   [37] LR Law on Plant Variety Rights 2001, Art 29.
[38] Id, Art 20.

Goods infringing a national designation of origin or a geographical indication

18.35 The only national legislation in Lithuania on the protection of geographical indications or designations of origin is the Regulation on the protection of geographical indications and designations of origin for agricultural products and foodstuffs of 2002[39] which was, in fact adopted with the view of implementation of Community Regulations referred to in Article 2(1)(c)(iv) of the Council Regulation (EC) 1383/2003.[40] As these Regulations came into force in Lithuania only after Lithuania's accession to the European Union on 1 May 2004, there have been almost no cases or disputes relating to the protection of geographical indications or designations of origin.[41]

(4) Moulds and matrices

18.36 The Lithuanian Trade Mark Law provides that the manufacturing or keeping of specimens of a trade mark with a view to performing any acts which may infringe a trade mark owner's rights shall be considered an infringement.[42] Furthermore, in trade mark infringement proceedings, the right-holder may ask the court to order the destruction, not only of the goods bearing the counterfeit trade mark, but also of any devices and equipment used for the production of such trade marks. Similarly, Lithuanian Design Law and Copyright Law foresee that in design or copyright infringement proceedings respectively, the court may order the confiscation or destruction of the devices, tools, and equipment used to produce the infringing design or copies of work protected under copyright, related right, or *sui generis* rights.[43]

18.37 Therefore, concerning trade marks, designs and copyrights, Lithuanian law does allow the right-holder to request customs action against moulds and matrices, which are specifically designed or adapted for the manufacture of goods infringing an intellectual property right, in accordance with Article 2(3) of the Council

---

[39] LR Žemės ūkio ministro įsakymas dėl žemės ūkio ir maisto produktų kilmės vietos nuorodų ir geografinių nuorodų apsaugos taisyklių patvirtinimo No 499 of 20 December 2002, [2003] VŽ No 1-12, as revised on 26 April 2004, VŽ [2004] No 65-2316.

[40] Council Reg (EEC) No 2081/92 of 14 July 1992 on the protection of geographical indications and designations of origin for agricultural products and foodstuffs [1992] OJ L 208/1, as amended; Council Reg (EC) No 1493/1999 of 17 May 1999 on the common organization of the market in wine [1999] OJ L 179/1, as amended; Council Reg (EEC) No 1576/89 of 29 May 1989 laying down general rules on the definition, description and presentation of spirit drinks [1989] OJ L 160/1, as amended.

[41] There were some cases under the Trade Mark Law, ie disputes concerning registration of geographical indication as a trade marks   [42] LR Trade Mark Law 2004, Art 38.

[43] LR Design Law 2002, Art 47; LR Copyright law 2003, Art 77.

Regulation (EC) 1383/2003. However, no such action has been reported to date.

Lithuanian Patent Law, on the other hand, has no explicit provision allowing for taking action against devices and equipment used to produce patented products or performing patented processes. However, it is provided that the rights of the patent holder extend to the main elements of the patented invention unless they are commonly known.[44] **18.38**

C. Goods excluded by the Regulation

(1) Parallel imported goods

Lithuania, in common with the other Member States of the European Union, applies Community-wide exhaustion of intellectual property rights (except for plant variety rights as mentioned above, cf para 18.33). This being said, there is no legal act in Lithuania which would entitle Lithuanian Customs to take border measures against parallel imported goods originating in non-member countries.[45] Therefore, as this possibility is also ruled out under the Council Regulation (EC) 1383/2003 by virtue of Article 3(1), first indent, right-holders may not request customs actions in these situations. **18.39**

In practice, the customs authorities contact the relevant right-holder or his representative when they discover goods which might be genuine, but whose importer or exporter is not indicated in the right-holder's application for action as being authorized or licensed to trade in such goods. Typically, the customs officers informally ask the right-holder to confirm that the goods are genuine. The pragmatic attitude of customs in this context can only be welcomed, since it allows validating that 'good-quality copies' are confused with parallel imports of genuine goods. **18.40**

(2) Goods which have been manufactured under conditions other than those which have been agreed with the right-holder

In accordance with Article 3(1), second indent, of the Council Regulation (EC) 1383/2003, Lithuanian Customs will not apply border measures towards goods which have been manufactured with the consent of, or under a licence from, the **18.41**

---

[44] LR Patent Law 2001, Art 26.
[45] It is interesting to point out that Art 4 of the Intellectual Property Law (n 1 above) explicitly provided that border measures could not be taken against parallel imports.

right-holder, but under conditions other than those agreed upon. Indeed customs are not in a position to determine, in the light of an application for action filed under the Regulation, whether goods comply with the terms of an agreement concluded with the right-holder. Traditionally, such applications for action only contain a list of authorized users of the right in question, or licensees, and do not provide for the terms and conditions of the licence. Therefore, it is unlikely that the right-holder will be contacted by customs in such cases, even informally, unless, for example, a particular licensee was not mentioned in the application for action because the term of their licence contained a prohibition to import the goods into Lithuania. In such cases, it is possible that the customs authorities would contact the right-holder or his representative to clarify the situation. As with parallel imports, right-holders may not request customs action in this context.

18.42 However, under these circumstances, that is, when the goods were manufactured under conditions other than those agreed with, the right-holder concerned may initiated civil proceedings and file a motion for a preliminary injunction before the courts. Nevertheless, as they are precluded from relying on the Regulation, customs have no right to detain the goods pending these proceedings.

(3) Goods contained in travellers' personal baggage

18.43 Lithuanian Customs inspect the personal baggage of a traveller if they suspect that it contains smuggled goods. Counterfeit goods have been found in these circumstances on a number of occasions, for example, the customs authorities detained 28 sport suits, 20 t-shirts, and 7 women's sports trousers bearing the 'NIKE' trade mark, brought into the Lithuanian territory by four travellers.[46] The main criterion which the Lithuanian customs authorities take into consideration when deciding whether or not to act against such type of infringements under Article 3(2) of the Council Regulation (EC) 1383/2003 is whether there are material indications to suggest that the goods are part of commercial traffic. Whether or not the goods are within the limits of the duty-free allowance is not deemed relevant in practice. One or two pairs of shoes may be for personal use, but 10 pairs of identical shoes will raise suspicion. Recently, customs authorities detained 20 counterfeit watches bearing the mark 'ROLEX' in the process of being imported into Lithuania in private baggage. It would be difficult to believe that a person would bring such a quantity of goods as gifts to friends or relatives.

---

[46] Vilnius District Court decision of 19 March 2004, civil case No 2³⁵—221/2004 *Nike International Ltd. v Tamara Tolmaciova and ors.*

II. APPLICATION FOR ACTION BY THE CUSTOMS AUTHORITIES

A. Measures prior to an application for action by the customs authorities ('*ex officio* measures')

The Intellectual Property Law already provided a legal basis for the Lithuanian customs authorities to act *ex officio* and detain, for three working days, goods that were suspected of infringing intellectual property rights, in order to allow the right-holder to file an application for action.[47] It is noted that Lithuanian Customs did make use of this provision and on numerous occasions detained infringing goods *ex officio*—since 2001, 19 cases have been reported. **18.44**

Usually, customs are alerted when suspect goods, for which no application for action has been filed, are imported alongside suspect goods for which an application has been filed. It is then presumed by customs that the entire cargo contains infringing products and the whole shipment is detained. In other cases, the goods immediately give the impression of being of poor quality, are declared at an exceedingly low price, have a suspicious origin (Seychelles, Vietnam, China, Turkey, etc), further making customs hesitant as to their genuine nature. The Lithuanian customs officials also take into consideration before taking *ex officio* action, for example, whether the intellectual property right in question enjoys protection in Lithuania, and whether the right-holder's representative may be easily identified and contacted. **18.45**

In 2003, the Lithuanian customs authorities detained on their own initiative, a large shipment containing 66,499 t-shirts bearing the trade marks 'DIESEL' without the consent of the right-holder. This was the fourth *ex officio* detention of counterfeit goods bearing this trade mark. Customs were alerted to the fact that the transport documents stated that the consignee of the goods was a company from the British Virgin Islands and the consignor was a company established in Seychelles, while the goods were transported by a Russian individual. Normally, Lithuanian customs authorities are, for obvious reasons, very cautious when detaining large shipments on an *ex officio* basis. In this particular case, the customs authorities did not hesitate to detain such a large shipment (with an approximate value of EUR 280,000) because the owner of the 'DIESEL' trade mark had already acted promptly in the framework of previous *ex officio* interventions. **18.46**

---

[47] LR Intellectual Property Law 2000, Art 12.

18.47 The Lithuanian Customs Law[48] and the Lithuanian Regulation on the provision of information[49] provide that the customs authorities in the framework of *ex officio* actions, before informing the right-holder of any suspected infringement of his rights, may ask him to provide additional information necessary to confirm their suspicions.[50] Thus, once suspicious goods are detained following an *ex officio* intervention by customs, the right-holder is provided with information on the date and place of the action and the actual or supposed nature and quantity of the goods. The Lithuanian Regulation on the provision of information also provides that the notification shall be accompanied by digital photographs of the suspected goods if available. In practice, digital photographs are taken in most cases and made available to the right-holder or his representative without the need for a specific request. Notifications are sent by fax or e-mail, the latter being a more prevalent means of communication. However, a first warning is usually made by phone.

18.48 The right-holder or his representative shall immediately, but not later than within one working day, confirm the receipt of customs notification informing of *ex officio* action. Such confirmation shall be done by fax after signing the relevant field in the notification form. If no confirmation is received by the customs within the prescribed term, the goods are released.[51]

18.49 The goods detained following *ex officio* action are also released if, within three working days, the right-holder does not file with the Customs Department an application for the customs measures.[52]

B. The lodging and processing of applications for customs actions

(1) Persons entitled to file an application for action

18.50 An application for action under the Regulation may be filed by any 'right-holder' of an intellectual property right referred to in Article 2(1) of the Council Regulation (EC) 1383/2003. Article 2(2) of the Regulation specifies that the concept of 'right-holder' shall, in addition to the owner of the intellectual property right *stricto sensu*, also include any person authorized to use that right or a representative of the owner or authorized user of that right.

---

[48] LR Customs Law 2004, Art 80(4).
[49] LR Regulation on the provision of information 2004, point 6 (n 6 above).
[50] Those principles comply with Art 4 of the Council Regulation (EC) 1383/2003.
[51] LR Regulation on the provision of information 2004 (n 6 above) points 7, 8.1.
[52] Id, point 8.2.

Definition of 'right-holders' under the Regulation

The notions of 'representative' and 'right-holder' were defined in the Intellectual Property Law,[53] but since this Law has been repealed, there is no statutory provision in Lithuania any longer which would help clarify these notions. This being said, one may reasonably assume that the definitions provided under the Intellectual Property Law may still be taken into account to interpret the concepts of the 'right-holder' and 'representative' under the Regulation.

18.51

Thus, the right-holder *stricto sensu* or his successor in title or assignee would be the owner of the rights.

18.52

The former Intellectual Property Law provided that the notion of 'representative of a right-owner or authorized user' was to be understood as covering any natural or legal person, for example, a patent or trade mark attorney, an attorney-at-law, or an association for the collective management of copyright and related rights. In substance, anyone holding a power of attorney may act as representative of the owner or authorized user of the right. As the law made no reference to the nationality of the representative, one may assume that a foreign national or legal person could act in this capacity. This is exactly the practice of the Lithuanian Customs Department today. Furthermore, the Customs Department does not even require the provision of a local contact person. However, as all communications subsequent to the initial notification with the local customs authorities and the courts will be in the Lithuanian language, foreign representatives at a certain point, would have to appoint a local contact person.

18.53

Proof of entitlement to file an application for action

For right-holders stricto sensu

When filing an application for action, the owner of the intellectual property right in question must prove entitlement to this right. The former Intellectual Property Law specified what documents were to be considered as proper evidence of such entitlements by the customs authorities,[54] while at the moment, this question is not regulated.

18.54

In practice, the Customs Department accepts simple copies of registration certificates or extracts from official databases as proof of ownership. As far as national rights are concerned, the only available official database in Lithuania concerns trade marks. However, as mentioned above (cf para 18.04 above), for the moment in Lithuania, applications for customs actions have only been filed with regard to trade marks and one concerning design so it is not clear what documents would

18.55

---

[53] LR Intellectual Property Law 2000, Art 2.   [54] Id, Art 7(2).

be required to prove the ownership of other intellectual property rights. We would consider that a simple copy of a registration certificate or a copy of a publication of a particular right in an official bulletin should be sufficient.

For persons authorized to use the right

18.56 'Authorized users' (that is, licensees) who wish to file an application for action should note that under Lithuanian law,[55] trade mark, design, and patent licences are only enforceable against third parties (including customs), provided they are registered with the State Patent Office. Licences for plant variety rights should also be registered with the Registrar of Plant Varieties in order to be enforceable.[56] Therefore, if the holder of a licence for any of these intellectual property rights wants to file an application for action, he must make sure that his licence has been registered with a relevant institution. Proof of such records will have to be provided together with the application. If this is not the case, the owner of the suspect goods may dispute that the application for action was filed by a duly entitled person, which could lead to the goods being released.

18.57 Licences for copyright and related rights do not have to be registered to be enforceable against third parties. They have effect from the date provided in the agreement. However, such licence agreements should be concluded in writing and fulfil the requirements set out by the Copyright Law[57] to be enforceable.

18.58 Customs authorities will not carry out any thorough examination to ascertain whether the licensee has a right under the agreement to file an application for action, since under Lithuanian practice, it is sufficient for licensees of a registered (that is, industrial property) right to provide an extract from the relevant register attesting that the agreement is registered. The full text of the agreement does not

---

[55] LR Trade Mark Law 2000, Art 34(5), 44(5); LR Design Law 2002, Art 41(5); LR Patent Law 2001, Art 34.
[56] LR Law on Plant Variety Rights 2001, Art 33.
[57] LR Copyright Law 2003, s 6. The copyright licence agreement shall include the following provisions:
- the title of a work,
- the licensed rights (mode of exploitiation of a work. If modes of use are not stipulated it shall be considered that the agreements is concluded only for those modes of use which are necessary for the parties to achieve the purpose which is the reason of the conclusion of the agreement) and type of the licence (exclusive or not),
- the territory covered (if no territory is indicated the agreement covers only Lithuania),
- the term of validity (if no term is indicated the agreement may be terminated by either of the parties informing the other in writing one year in advance),
- the amount of remuneration and terms of payment,
- dispute settlement procedure and liability of the parties,
- other conditions.

have to be submitted. Entitlement to file an application with customs for licensees is presumed and any disputes concerning this matter are to be resolved between the parties to the licence agreement.

For representatives

A representative filing an application for action on behalf of the owner or an authorized user of the right concerned must provide an original power of attorney which empowers him to act accordingly.   **18.59**

There are no *specific* requirements provided under Lithuanian law regarding the   **18.60**
form of the power of attorney. However, it must comply with the general civil law requirements, that is, any power of attorney delivered by a foreign person must fulfil all validity requirements provided under the law of the country where it was issued to be accepted in Lithuania. Nevertheless, if the term of validity is not provided in the power of attorney, then it is determined according to the laws of the country where the representative acts. The same law also applies to the rights and obligations of the representative and the mutual liability in addition to liability against third parties of a representative and the person giving the power.[58] Consequently, Lithuanian law would apply these issues when the power of attorney empowers a representative to take action in the right-holder's name in Lithuania. It is important to note that under the rules of the Lithuanian Civil Code, a power of attorney failing to indicate the term of validity shall be valid for one year from the date of its issuance.[59] In addition, the power of attorney must be notarized and foreseen with an *Apostille* under the 1961 Hague Convention,[60] provided it is issued in a member state of the said convention, or legalized if the place of issuance of the power is not within a Member State of the convention. In certain instances, when there is an agreement on legal cooperation between the country where the power is issued and the Lithuanian Republic, notarization of the document is sufficient.[61]

The power of attorney may be either limited to a single matter or cover all future   **18.61**
interventions. In any case, it should preferably mention all possible acts the representative may accomplish in the name of the right-holder in order to avoid problems of interpretation as to its scope.

---

[58] LR Civilinis kodeksas (LR Civil Code) No VIII-1864 of 18 July 2000, [2000] VŽ No 74-2262, Art 1(40).   [59] Id, Art 2(142).

[60] Convention Abolishing the Requirement of Legalisation for Foreign Public Documents, concluded in the Hague on 5 October 1961, available on http://hcch.e-vision.nl/.

[61] On 7 November 2005, such countries included Armenia, Azerbaijan, Byelorussia, Estonia, Kazakhstan, China, Latvia, Poland, Moldova, Russia, Ukraine, and Uzbekistan. The full list is available on http://www.urm.lt/index.php?-729455731.

(2) *Competent customs department and formal requirements*

Competent customs department

18.62 In Lithuania, the Customs Department responsible for the processing of applications for action under the Regulation is the 'Customs Department under the Ministry of Finance of the Republic of Lithuania':

Muitinės Departamentas
Prie Lietuvos Respublikos Finansų Ministerijos
A. Jakšto g. 1/25
LT-01105 Vilnius
Lietuva (Lithuania)
Tel: +370 5 2666111/ info in English +370 5 2617158
Fax: + 370 5 2666005

18.63 The website of the Customs Department is www.cust.lt. This contains the texts of the legal acts related to customs actions as well as the list of intellectual property rights for which applications for action have been filed. It is also possible to download the forms of national and Community applications for customs actions (www.cust.lt/lt/rubric?rubricID=563). Regretfully, this information is only available on the Lithuanian version of the website.

Form of the application for action

18.64 The applications for action and the declaration under Article 6 of the Council Regulation (EC) 1383/2003 must be filed using an original, either by delivering it to the Customs Department or by sending it by mail. The Lithuanian Customs Law provides that in certain situations and in accordance with the rules adopted by the director of the Customs Department, the application for action and the declaration under Article 6 may be filed electronically.[62] However, no provisions have been adopted so far allowing for the electronic filing of such applications, that is, the system is not functional yet and there are no concrete plans for its implementation. The main obstacle for this is the fact that in Lithuania, the system of electronic signatures is not yet operative.

18.65 Pursuant to Article 3(3) of the implementing Commission Regulation (EC) 1891/2004, two formal copies of the application should be filed with customs. However, in order to facilitate the work of the customs authorities, it is preferable to submit five copies of coloured exhibits, as there are five territorial customs offices in Lithuania. If the exhibits are in digital form, they may be sent to the customs authorities by e-mail or filed alongside with the application on an electronic data carrier.

---

[62] LR Customs Law 2004, Art 80(2).

Language requirements

Not all documents which are filed with the Lithuanian Customs Department **18.66**
need to be translated into the Lithuanian language. This is so in relation to the certificates of trade mark registrations, as Customs Departments have access to the databases and may check the related data. Furthermore, translation is not needed for European Community applications. However, translation is required for the submission of powers of attorney.

(3) Requirements regarding the content of the application for action

There are no national provisions detailing the requirements regarding the manda- **18.67**
tory or optional information to be submitted to customs under Article 5(5) of the Council Regulation (EC) 1383/2003 in Lithuania. The information must be sufficient to enable the customs officials to detect and recognize infringing goods. Lithuanian Customs accept applications for action even without much detail and exhaustive information on the technical description of the goods or the type and pattern of the fraud. The latter information is usually not known to the rightholder, as there are numerous trafficking routes for goods to be brought into Lithuania. The above-mentioned example of the DIESEL t-shirts case (cf para 18.46 above) shows that in at least three instances where counterfeits had been detained, they were carried to Lithuania by different persons from different countries and had different destinations. Obviously, the type and range of information necessary to provide with the application may vary depending on the intellectual property right on which the application relies.

There are no particular rules in Lithuania concerning the contact person referred **18.68**
to in Article 5(5)(iii) of the Regulation. The appointed contact person shall, however, be available on call from the Customs Department to answer questions and requests, inspect the goods, and perform any other actions necessary without delay. The contact person should speak Lithuanian because all the contact that takes place and all the information received from customs, is in this language. Thus, even though there are no formal requirements on the nationality or residence of the contact persons, in practice, he shall have a local presence in Lithuania.

(4) Processing and acceptance of the application for action

Pursuant to Article 5(7) of the Regulation, applications for action must be **18.69**
processed by the Customs Department identified above (para 18.62) within 30 working days from its receipt. In the event that no decision is handed down within this term or the application is refused, the applicant may lodge an appeal within

one month from the date of receipt of the negative decision or respectively from the date on which the time period to process the application has expired.[63] Such an appeal may be filed either with the Supreme Administrative Disputes Commission ('Vyriausioji administracinių ginčų komisija'), or the administrative courts.

18.70   Lithuanian national law does not define the period during which customs are to take action once the application is granted. Under the former Intellectual Property Law, this period was one year in all cases. The same approach is applied under Council Regulation (EC) 1383/2003 irrespective of the protected intellectual property right.

(5) 'Community' applications for action

18.71   There are no specific provisions in Lithuania on the processing of applications for action based on a 'Community right' referred to in Article 5(4) of the Regulation rather than on a national intellectual property right. Neither are there any particular rules on how such applications should be dealt with when they are filed in other member states and extended to Lithuania.

Processing of 'Community' applications for action filed with Lithuanian Customs

18.72   Lithuanian legislation does not provide any particular rules for the processing of 'Community' applications filed with Lithuanian Customs. The customs law only provides that when 'Community' applications are filed through Lithuanian Customs and designate other Member States, the right-holder shall personally inform the relevant customs authorities in the respective Member States of the decision regarding the Lithuanian Customs Department granting the application.[64]

Processing of 'Community' applications filed abroad and designating Lithuania

18.73   When an application based on a 'Community right' listed in Article 5(4) of the Regulation is filed in another Member State and designates Lithuania, the Lithuanian customs authorities may ask to be provided with a translation of the application into the Lithuanian language. Such a translation might not be required for those sections of the application containing only numbers, names and addresses or other data available to the customs authorities (para 18.66), because due to the use of the unified application forms annexed to Commission

---

[63]   LR Customs Law 2004, Art 90.
[64]   Compare Council Reg 1383/2003, Art 8(2), third indent.

Regulation 1891/2004, these sections may be easily understood. For other sections of the application, as well as some additional documents, a translation might be required.

III. CONDITIONS GOVERNING ACTION BY CUSTOMS AUTHORITIES AND BY THE AUTHORITIES HAVING JURISDICTION TO DETERMINE WHETHER GOODS INFRINGE AN INTELLECTUAL PROPERTY RIGHT

A. Conditions governing action by customs authorities

(1) Factual background

In Lithuania, there are five territorial customs and they are all involved in more or less equal terms in the fight against counterfeiting and piracy. They are located in the five largest Lithuanian cities, namely, Vilnius, Kaunas, Klaipeda, Panevezys, and Siauliai. **18.74**

(2) Notification of customs intervention

Where suspect goods are detained or their release suspended, by a customs office under Article 9(1) of the Council Regulation (EC) 1383/2003, the latter informs the Customs Department which processed the application, as well as the right-holder or his representative. Even before proceeding with the 'official' detention or suspension of release of the goods, the customs officials informally contact the right-holder or his representative in order to enquire whether the goods infringe an intellectual property right and whether the right-holder would be interested in taking action against the goods. Indeed, it often happens in practice that the goods are genuine—but parallel imported or in a quantity so small that the right-holder is not interested in pursuing the matter. In this case, no action is formally taken, and the importer of goods will not usually be informed of customs suspicions.[65] Where the right-holder confirms or suspects that the goods may be bogus, the formal detention/suspension takes place and official notifications occur. **18.75**

---

[65] In most cases, the right-holder may quickly appraise whether the goods are likely to violate any of his rights. Therefore, informal communication between customs and right-holders helps to avoid

18.76 Official notifications are usually sent by fax or e-mail. The original confirmation copy may be sent by post at a later time.

(3) Information to be provided by customs to the right-holder before the right-holder confirms the infringing nature of the goods

18.77 The provision of information to the right-holder in respect of goods which are being detained or the release of which has been suspended under Council Regulation (EC) 1383/2003, is regulated by the Order of the director of the Lithuanian Customs Department setting out the Regulation on the provision of information concerning actions against goods suspected of infringing intellectual property rights.[66] The following information is provided to the right-holder in such circumstances: information on when the customs intervention took place, where the goods are being detained and the nature and quantity of the goods.[67] After acknowledging the receipt of the notification of the customs action made under Article 9(1) of the Regulation (which must be done immediately but not later than within one working day), the right-holder may request the customs authorities to provide additional information on the shipment.[68] Thereupon, a supplementary notification is sent to the right-holder containing a detailed description of the goods, the countries of origin and provenance, the value of the goods and of course, information (name, address, and other contact details) on who declares the goods in Lithuania, consignor, consignee, or holder. The order on the provision of information also provides that notification shall be accompanied by digital photographs of the suspect goods, if available, without any specific request to this regard. In practice, digital photographs are almost always communicated to the right-holder or his representative. The above information will be provided to the right-holder by fax or e-mail.

18.78 All information provided by the Lithuanian customs authorities may only be used by the right-holder for the purpose of determining whether the suspect goods

---

a waste of resources and time in applying border measures against goods if the right-holder is not interested in pursuing the case or considers that the goods do not infringe his rights. This does not create any inconvenience to the declarant or holder of the goods either, because they are not constrained in their actions. Furthermore, the practice of informally notifying right-holders before taking any formal step under Art 9(1) of the Regulation has proved to be very efficient because customs procedures such as the import of goods usually takes time which is enough for a right-holder to make a decision as to whether he would be interested in pursuing the matter. In any case, if the right-holder has doubts, the option provided by the Regulation for the goods to be detained for 10 working days, during which the right-holder may make a decision, negotiate with the importer to voluntarily abandon the goods for destruction, or take any other action which he considers necessary, is not pre-empted by such informal notifications.

[66] LR Regulation on the provision of information 2004.
[67] Id, annex 3; Compare Council Reg 1383/2003, Art 9(2).   [68] Id, points 14 and 17.

infringe his rights and for the enforcement of such rights.[69] Otherwise the right-holder may be liable for any damages resulting from his actions. He may also be fined an administrative fine for up to 1,000 Litas (about EUR 300) for the infringement of the personal data protection rules.[70]

(4) Inspection of the suspected goods

Once suspect goods are detained or their release suspended, the right-holder may inspect the goods at their place of storage. The inspection of the goods and the taking of samples is regulated by the Order of the director of the Lithuanian Customs Department setting out the Regulation on suspension of release, detention, storage, inspection, the taking of samples and of goods suspected of infringing intellectual property rights.[71] During the inspection of goods, a customs officer, as well as a person responsible for the storage of goods, shall be present. The presence of the owner of the goods in person is not required. On the occasion of the examination, the goods may be unpacked, opened or otherwise taken out of their packaging, even if the latter is destroyed, without, however, damaging the goods themselves. The goods may also be photographed and filmed during their inspection. **18.79**

The right-holder or his representative may request that samples of the suspect goods be provided for examination purposes. To that effect, the right-holder must present a written request to the customs office where the goods have officially been detained. Such a request shall include the following information: **18.80**

* name and address of the right-holder;
* name and address of his representative;
* date and number of the customs notification on the detention of goods;
* nature and quantity of the requested samples;
* date and time on which the person (that is, the representative) or courier company appointed by the right-holder will arrive to take the samples (sending of samples via courier service shall be organized on request and all costs are borne by the right-holder);
* name of the person or courier company to which the samples will have to be remitted;
* declaration that the samples will be returned if required.[72]

---

[69] LR Customs Law 2004, Art 87.
[70] Administracinių teisės pažeidimų kodeksas (Administrative Penalties Code) of 13 December 1984, [1985] VŽ No 1-1, as amended Art 214(16).
[71] LR Regulation on the suspension of release, detention, storage, inspection, and the taking of samples, of goods 2004.   [72] Id, point 23.

18.81 The samples shall be returned to the person responsible for the storage of the goods in the following instances:

- where customs authorities have not been provided within the term of three or 10 or even up to 20 working days referred to in Article 13 of the Council Regulation (EC) 1383/2003 with a document proving that the right-holder has initiated proceedings with the courts;
- where the right-holder has informed the customs authorities that the goods may be released;
- where a court decision rejecting the right-holder's infringement claim has become final.[73]

B. Simplified procedure allowing the destruction of goods without there being any need to determine whether an intellectual property right has been infringed under national law

18.82 The destruction of goods following a simplified procedure is regulated by the Regulation on the destruction of goods which have been detained or the release of which has been suspended by customs on suspicion of an intellectual property right infringement.[74]

18.83 The right-holder or his representative wishing to benefit from a simplified procedure for the destruction of goods foreseen in Article 11 of Council Regulation (EC) 1383/2003, shall file an application with the territorial customs where the goods were detained or their release was suspended. Such applications shall be accompanied with:

- confirmation that the goods do infringe intellectual property rights;
- agreement of the declarant or the owner of the goods to destroy the goods or documents, proving that either of those persons was informed by the registered mail about the foreseen destruction of the goods.[75]

18.84 The application shall indicate the date of commencement of the destruction of goods. The term between the date when the right-holder was notified by the customs authorities that the goods suspected of infringing their intellectual property rights being detained and the commencement of the destruction of the goods shall be no shorter than 10 working days (3 working days in the case of perishable goods) and no longer than the maximum term foreseen in Council Regulation (EC) 1383/2003 for the detention of goods. In case the destruction of goods is foreseen before the expiry of the 10-day limit, the explicit agreement of the declarant or the owner of goods to destroy them shall be provided.[76]

---

[73] Compare Council Reg 1383/2003, Art 9(3), last indent.
[74] LR Regulation on the destruction of goods 2004, LR Regulation on the destruction of the detained or not released by the customs goods 2005.   [75] Id, point 5.
[76] Id, point 6.

The application for a simplified destruction procedure shall be filed within 10 **18.85** working days from the date when the right-holder was notified by the customs authorities that the goods suspected of infringing his intellectual property rights were detained[77] or his application following *ex officio* action was accepted.[78] In case of perishable goods, the application shall be filed within three working days. The right-holder may ask for an extension of these time limits. In practice, such extensions are usually granted.

The declarant or the owner of goods objecting to the destruction of the goods fol- **18.86** lowing a simplified procedure shall inform accordingly the territorial customs within 10 working days (3 days in the case of perishable goods) from the detention of the goods. Failure to state the objection within the prescribed time limit is considered as an agreement to the destruction of the goods following the simplified procedure.[79]

The right-holder is responsible for organizing the destruction of the goods which **18.87** shall take place at the time indicated in the application. The right-holder shall also cover all costs related to the destruction of the goods.

Under the former intellectual property law, it was customary for the importer of **18.88** goods infringing an intellectual property right to agree voluntarily to their destruction. In practice, this proved to be a very common procedure, which was relied on more frequently than the commencement of court proceedings aimed at the destruction of goods. This is still the case today. Indeed, where the cargo concerned is of a reasonably small size, the importer of suspect goods after being informed of the status of the law, a cost estimate, and his financial liability usually agrees on a voluntary basis to have the goods destroyed. Moreover, in most cases, the existence of an infringement is not disputed by the parties involved in such matters.

Lithuanian law does not provide for any explicit prohibition or acceptance of the **18.89** settlement agreements between the right-holder and the owner of the goods. According to the general civil proceedings rules, the parties may at any time come to an agreement during the proceedings, thus ending the case.[80] The same presumably would apply for an agreement entered between the parties during a customs procedure phase before the proceedings in the court had started.

The only limit imposed by law to the settlement agreement is that it shall not con- **18.90** tradict the imperative norms of the law or public interest.[81] There are no cases, as

---

[77] Council Reg 1383/2003, Art 9(2).   [78] Id, Art 4.
[79] LR Regulation on the destruction of the detained or not released by the customs goods 2004, point 8.
[80] Civilinio proceso kodeksas (Civil Proceedings Code) No IX-743 of 28 February 2002, [2002] VŽ No 36-1340, Art 140 (3).   [81] Id, Art 42(2).

yet where the right-holder and the owner of counterfeit goods would have entered into a settlement agreement. Therefore, it is not clear whether such an agreement would be accepted by the court or would be considered as contrary to the public interest. On the other hand, it is for the right-holder to confirm that the detained goods infringe his rights and are counterfeit. Thus, should he want to enter into agreement with the owner of the goods or issue a licence to the owner, he may simply state that the goods do not infringe his rights. Alternatively, he may not file a claim with the court within the time limits, may withdraw his claim, or not ask for the enforcement of the judgment.

C. Conditions governing action by the authorities having jurisdiction to determine whether the goods infringe an intellectual property right

(1) Authorities having jurisdiction to determine whether the goods infringe an intellectual property right

18.91 In Lithuania, the right-holder may initiate only civil proceedings for the enforcement of intellectual property rights. Criminal prosecution may be officially initiated only by State officials and in practice, takes place only in cases of smuggling. In practical terms. the remedies available in the civil proceedings do not differ depending on the intellectual property right on which the claims are based. In all cases, the general rules governing civil proceedings will be applied.

18.92 According to Lithuanian civil procedure law, all claims concerning the protection and enforcement of patents, supplementary protection certificates, trade marks and designs are dealt with by the Vilnius District Court.[82] In all other cases, the jurisdiction of the courts will be determined in the light of the general rules governing civil proceedings: if the object of the claim exceeds 100,000 Litas (approximately EUR 30,000) or concerns moral rights arising out of copyright, it will be dealt with in district courts; in the opposite event, it will be handled by the regional courts.[83]

18.93 The right-holder, when filing a claim before the courts aimed at the protection and enforcement of his rights, may ask for a preliminary injunction, whereby the defendant is enjoined from any further infringement of the plaintiff's rights. In fact, preliminary injunctions may be requested even before the filing of a claim on the merits of the case or at any stage in the course of such proceedings on their merits. When the request for interim measures is presented before filing the claim, the latter shall be filed within 14 days.[84]

---

[82] Civil Proceedings Code (n 80 above), Part IV.   [83] Id.   [84] Id, Art 148.

Before deciding on a claim for an interim injunction, the court may require the **18.94** deposit of a guarantee by the plaintiff, ensuring that they will be able to cover potential expenses related to the injunction or compensate the defendant for any harm caused by such a measure. Note that when an application for action by customs authorities is filed, such a guarantee must already be provided by the rightholder under Article 6 of the Council Regulation (EC) 1383/2003. One may expect that the courts having to handle an infringement claim further to the taking of border measures under the Regulation will not require any additional security. However, to our knowledge, there has been no case decided on this particular question as yet.

The decision on the claim for a preliminary injunction shall be rendered not later **18.95** than within three days from the filing of such a claim.[85] The defendant is normally informed of the plaintiff's request for a preliminary injunction. However, if there is a real threat that after informing the defendant, the application of interim measures becomes excessively difficult or impossible, the decision on a preliminary injunction may be taken without advance warning of the defendant.

Claims for an interim injunction are considered as 'proceedings to determine **18.96** whether an intellectual property right has been infringed' within the meaning of Article 13 of the Regulation. However, according to Customs Law, the suspended goods are released unless the claim of the infringed rights of the trade mark owner is received. It is questionable whether the court will accept a claim for interim injunction as the goods are already suspended at customs. In practice, customs had never exercised the court's decision on interim injunctions.

Proceedings on the merits before the courts of the first instance are handled as fol- **18.97** lows: before the oral hearings of the case are set, the parties may exchange their pleas and arguments twice. At this stage, both parties have to provide all evidence and arguments concerning their claims; the court may reject them if provided at a later time. The court always sets strict deadlines for a party to provide its answer to the opposing party's claims and the terms do not normally exceed 14 days from receipt of the opposing party's submissions. If the case is well substantiated, however, the deadlines may be extended. Strict adherence to deadlines means that the case is processed relatively fast and the pleadings are usually set within two to three months from the date of service of the writ of summons. It shall be noted that when instituting civil proceedings, the right-holder has to ask for a decision in absence for cases where the defendant would not react to the writ and shows no interest in the case.

In the framework of legal proceedings, the court may take a decision in the **18.98** absence of one of the parties—usually the defendant if the latter does not appear

---

[85] Id, Art 148.

in court in person and failed to appoint a representative. In such cases, the court performs only a formal examination of the evidence, that is, makes sure that there would be grounds for a decision allowing the claims if the content of the evidence submitted to it would prove to be true. Decisions handed down in absence, may not be appealed by the party (or parties) who failed to attend the hearings. The non- attending party may only ask within 20 days of issuance of the ruling for its review if it justifies its absence appropriately.

18.99   In other instances, the case is heard in oral proceedings in the course of which all evidence is examined and the court renders its decision based on an in-depth assessment of the matter. Decisions handed down in such proceedings may be appealed within 30 days.

18.100   The decision of the court and the measures ordered by it depend on the remedies prescribed by the piece(s) of legislation related to the intellectual property rights in question, as well as on the general provisions regulating civil proceedings.

18.101   The Trade Mark Law provides[86] that with the aim of protecting their rights, the proprietor of a trade mark shall be entitled to apply to a court, in accordance with the procedure prescribed by law, which may decide on claims seeking:

- recognition of the plaintiff's rights;
- the granting of an injunction ordering the defendant to cease and desist from all actions which infringe or are likely to infringe the plaintiff's rights;
- examples such as the granting of damages as compensation for harm (including lost profits, expenses, and moral prejudice) caused to the trade mark owner owing to the infringement;
- the seizure and where necessary, the destruction of the unlawfully used trade marks, devices, or equipment for the production thereof, as well as the goods as a whole when it proves impossible to remove the marks unlawfully affixed to them, as well as other devices and equipment used for the infringement of the rights conferred by the Trade Mark Law.

18.102   At the request of the trade mark owner, the court may also oblige the defendant to provide information on the origin and distribution channels of the goods infringing its rights.[87]

18.103   Identical rights are provided for the owner of the design by the Design Law.[88]

18.104   Patent Law[89] also provides that the patent owner may turn to the court asking it to grant an injunction ordering the defendant to cease and desist from all actions which infringe or are likely to infringe their rights. They also may ask for damages.

---

[86] LR Trade Mark Law 2000, Art 50.   [87] Id.   [88] LR Design Law 2004, Art 47.
[89] LR Patent Law 2001, Art 41.

The Copyright Law[90] provides that the owners of copyright, related rights, or *sui generis* rights shall be entitled to apply to a court seeking for: **18.105**

- recognition of rights;
- injunction to terminate unlawful acts;
- injunction against the acts which may actually infringed the rights or may cause damage;
- redressing of the infringed moral rights (injunction to make appropriate amendments, to announce the infringement in the press, or any other way);
- exaction of unpaid remuneration for unlawful use of objects of copyright, related rights, or *sui generis* rights;
- compensation for property damage, including lost income and other expenses, and non-pecuniary damage, as well;
- payment of compensation;
- seizure and, after a final court's decision, withdrawal from a circulation in a way that no damage is made to the right-holder and protection of their rights is ensured (for example, reprocess), transfer to the aggrieved at his request or destruction at the expense of the offender of infringing copies of works, computer programs, carriers of audiovisual works (films) and phonograms possessed by the said offender and the devices or equipment used for the manufacture or duplication of infringing copies intended for distribution.

The offenders who reproduce or distribute infringing copies of works or other   **18.106**
objects, violating the rights of owners of copyright, related rights or *sui generis* rights, must, upon the order of the court, immediately furnish all information about the origin of such copies, especially the identity (names and surnames) and addresses of producers, suppliers (distributors), clients, channels of distribution of infringing copies of works, amount of produced, submitted, received or ordered infringing copies.[91]

(2) *Term for notifying customs that proceedings have been started*

On being notified of the suspension of release or of the detention of goods by the   **18.107**
customs authorities, the right-holder has 10 working days (3 working days in the case of perishable goods) to submit evidence to customs that proceedings have been instituted in view of determining whether an intellectual property right has been infringed. Failure to do so will result in the release of the goods. Except in the case of perishable goods, the above term may be extended once by a maximum of 10 working days 'in appropriate cases'.[92] In practice, the customs authorities are

---

90 LR Copyright Law 2003, Art 77.   91 Cf also Part IV below, on this point.
92 Council Reg 1383/2003, Art 13.

eager to grant such an extension typically where negotiations are in progress between the parties concerning the voluntary destruction of goods.[93]

D. Release of goods suspected of infringing certain rights on the provision of a security

18.108   The Lithuanian Customs Law[94] provides that goods which have been detained, or the release of which has been suspended, under Council Regulation (EC) 1383/2003 shall be released on provision by the owner of the goods, the declarant, consigner, or consignee of a security, provided the conditions of Article 14 of the Regulation are fulfilled and the right-holder has not notified the customs authorities of a court decision authorizing precautionary measures (such as a preliminary injunction) before the time limit laid down in Article 13.

18.109   The Order of the director of Lithuanian customs setting out the Regulation on the deposit of securities in relation to the protection of certain intellectual property rights[95] provides that the declarant, owner, holder, or consignee of goods suspected of infringing a patent, supplementary protection certificate, plant variety rights, or design rights, when requesting the release of the goods under Article 14 of the Council Regulation (EC) 1383/2003, shall provide a security in an amount equal to twice the customs value of the goods to protect the right-holder's interests. The provision of this security does not exonerate the owner, consignee, declarant, and/or holder of the goods from their obligation to provide additional guarantees securing their commitments and responsibilities towards customs.

E. Storage of the goods

18.110   The conditions of storage of goods which have been detained, or the release of which has been suspended, by Lithuanian Customs under Council Regulation (EC) 1383/2003, are governed by the Order of the director of Lithuanian customs setting out the Regulation on the suspension of release, detention, storage, inspection, and the taking of samples of goods suspected of infringing intellectual property rights.[96] According to the provisions of this order, the goods whose *release has been suspended*, continue to be stored in customs warehouses or places of temporary storage, whilst goods which have been *detained* are stored in specific

---

[93] Compare Council Reg 1891/2004, Art 7(1).   [94] LR Customs Law 2004, Art 85.
[95] LR Regulation on the deposit of securities 2004.
[96] LR Regulation on the suspension of release, detention, storage, inspection, and the taking of samples, of goods 2004.

warehouses for detained goods or other places which are deemed acceptable for customs.

The costs for transporting goods to storage rooms, storage costs, and the costs for **18.111** the destruction of the goods shall be borne by the right-holder, unless the declarant or the holder, owner, or consignee of the goods are held liable for such costs. In the event that the goods were detained or their release suspended, following an *ex officio* action, the right-holder is immune from paying the above-mentioned costs, if he is not interested in pursuing the matter and does not file an application for customs measures.

IV. PROVISIONS APPLICABLE TO GOODS FOUND TO INFRINGE AN INTELLECTUAL PROPERTY RIGHT

The Lithuanian Customs Law[97] provides that the courts, when concluding that **18.112** the goods infringe an intellectual property right, may:

- authorize the defendant to use (for example, reprocess, etc) the goods without putting them on the market, provided that the right-holder's rights are secured and the state does not incur any costs in relation to such use;
- apply any other measures (such as, for example, the relinquishing of the goods to the right-holder or any other persons indicated by them) having as a consequence effectively to deprive the persons concerned (including the owner of the goods) of any economic gains from the transaction. If the goods are surrendered to persons other than the right-holder, the court may oblige them to remove all infringing trade marks;
- order the destruction of the goods at the expense of the person who declares them, the holder, owner, or consignee.

The scope and nature of the decision handed down by the court will depend on **18.113** the right-holder's claims. In practice, the right-holder almost always requests the destruction of all infringing goods. Usually, such claims are granted in practice.

In a ruling of 24 November 2003 in civil case No 3K-3-1069/2003, *Diesel Spa v* **18.114** *Mita*,[98] the Lithuanian Supreme Court spelled out an educational provision,

---

[97] LR Customs Law 2004, Art 86.
[98] Lithuanian Supreme Court decision of 24 November 2003, civil case No 3K-3-1069/2003 *Diesel S.p.A./UAB Mita* (available at http://ovada.tic.lt/lat/nutartis.aspx?id = 25312 [cf yy-mm-dd]), commented on in [2004] World Trade marks Law Report (4 February 2004).

suggesting that the lower courts, when confronted with intellectual property rights infringements, should play a more active role and suggest to the plaintiff to make use of other ways for enforcing his rights than systematically to destroy the goods in their entirety. According to the Supreme Court, once the infringing labels and trade marks have been removed from the goods, and provided the goods still have a material value, the goods could be used for the plaintiff's or third parties' interests. We are of the opinion that this practice is not contrary to the provisions of Article 17(1), second indent, of Council Regulation (EC) 1383/2003[99] because the Supreme Court does not recommend that the goods should be returned to their owner, but proposes that the plaintiff use them, for example, by donating them to underprivileged people.

18.115 Similarly, the same court, in a decision of 18 February 2004, in case No 3K-3-*Euroimport Rudorfer GmbH v UAB 'Filipopolis'*,[100] held that the lower courts, before ordering the destruction of 2,700 bottles of wine bearing a label infringing the plaintiff's trade mark rights, should have first examined whether the right-holder's interests could have been protected by removing the labels without destroying the wine. Such an assessment appeared even more necessary taking into account that the right-holder had not specifically requested the destruction of the goods and the defendant had on their side, raised objections against the destruction. Upon return of the case to the lower court, it was decided that the labels were to be removed and the goods released.

18.116 In all cases where goods are found to infringe an intellectual property right and at the right-holder's request, liability for the expenses related to the case for example, the costs for the detention, storage, and destruction of the goods, the costs of the court proceedings, etc are imposed on the defendant (namely, the declarant, holder, owner, or consignee of the infringing goods). Of course, in practice, the actual reimbursement of the costs is not always guaranteed, as the defendant may be insolvent and objectively unable to pay. In any case, the recovery of such costs is a matter dealt with under the general provisions governing civil proceedings.

18.117 The destruction of the goods following the ruling of the court is regulated by the same Regulations on the destruction of goods which have been detained or the release of which has been suspended by customs on suspicion of an intellectual property right infringement,[101] as the destruction of the goods following a simplified

---

[99] This provision stipulates that simply removing the trade marks which have been affixed to counterfeit goods without authorization shall not be regarded as effectively depriving the persons concerned of any economic gains from the transaction, 'save in exceptional cases'.

[100] Lithuanian Supreme Court decision of 18 February 2004, civil case No 3K-3-81/2004 *Euroimport Rudorfer GmbH/UAB Filipopolis* (available at http://ovada.tic.lt/lat/nutartis.aspx?id=25312).

[101] LR Regulation on the destruction of goods, 2004; LR Regulation on the destruction of goods which have been detained or the release of which has been suspended by customs, 2005.

procedure (cf paras 18.82–18.90). The decision to destroy the goods, specifying the place, time, and mode of destruction, is made by the head of the territorial customs involved. The right-holder or his representative, as well as a customs officer and a representative of the company destroying the goods shall attend the destruction process. The presence of the declarant, holder, owner, or consignee of the goods is not required, but in practice they will always make sure to monitor the process. The costs resulting from the transportation of the goods to the place of destruction, as well as the costs of their destruction are normally adjudicated by the decision of the court to the declarant, holder, owner, or consignee of the goods. Otherwise they shall be borne by the right-holder. In most cases, the destruction takes place on the customs premises or in the warehouse where the goods are stored by cutting, chopping, shredding, breaking, incinerating, or otherwise making the goods unusable.

V. PENALTIES

Despite explicit obligations imposed on the Member States by Article 18 of the Council Regulation (EC) 1383/2003 to provide for effective, proportionate, and dissuasive penalties in cases of violation of this Regulation, there were no specific provisions adopted in this regard in Lithuania. However, the breach of certain specific provisions of the Council Regulation (EC) 1383/2003 may, besides civil liability, also result in administrative or criminal liability (cf Part VI below). The Administrative Penalties Code also provides for penalties for the breach of general customs rules, for example, provision of false data in customs declaration, failure to export the goods after export procedure is performed, smuggling, etc.[102]   **18.118**

The Administrative Penalties Code provides for administrative liability for the infringement of copyright and related right. It provides that such infringement is subject to a fine of up to 2,000 Litas (about EUR 600) and confiscation of all illegal copies and equipment for their production.[103] However, it is silent on the infringements of trade mark, design, and other intellectual property rights.   **18.119**

The Lithuanian Criminal Code provides for criminal liability in cases of illegal use of someone else's trade mark when the damage is caused or infringement of patent and design rights. The penalty depends on the seriousness of the crime and may amount to imprisonment of up to two years, prohibition to undertake certain activity, or a fine.[104] The same criminal liability is also foreseen for the infringement   **18.120**

---

[102] LR Administrative Penalties Code 1985.   [103] Id, Art 214(10).
[104] LR Baudžiamasis Kodeksas (Criminal Code) No VIII-1968 of 26 September 2000, [2000] VŽ No 89-2741, as last amended on 22 December 2004, [2004] VŽ No 188-6995, Arts 195, 204.

of copyright and related rights, as well as for the illegal removal of the protection devices from the copyright or related right protected works.[105]

VI. LIABILITY OF CUSTOMS AUTHORITIES AND RIGHT-HOLDERS

A. Liability of right-holders and sanctions

18.121 Right-holders using the information provided by customs for purposes other than those permitted under Council Regulation (EC) 1383/2003 may be held liable for the violation of Lithuanian laws on the legal protection of personal data,[106] State and public service confidentiality,[107] and the Civil Code,[108] providing for the protection of trade secrets. In the event of a breach of any of these laws, the right-holder, besides the sanctions provided for in Article 12 of the Regulation, may incur civil, administrative, and/or criminal liability. The breach of laws on the legal protection of personal data may result in an administrative fine of up to 1,000 Litas (about EUR 300).[109] A fine of up to 4,000 Litas (about EUR 1, 200) may be imposed in the case of loss or destruction of a public service secret when it was confided following the laws.[110]

18.122 Similarly, the declarant, holder, owner, or consignee of the detained goods may claim compensation for losses or damages incurred owing to the use by the right-holder of the information received from the customs authorities for purposes other than the enforcement of his intellectual property rights. Any profit made by the right-holder as a result of such non-permitted use of the information communicated by customs is considered an ungrounded enrichment and shall be subject to redress.

18.123 In addition to civil liability, the infringement of the national provisions on the protection of personal data protection may incur administrative liability, which is normally sanctioned by a fine. The disclosure of commercial, public service, or state secrets may also result in criminal sanctions.

---

[105] Criminal Code (n 104 above), chapter XXIX.
[106] LR Asmens duomenų teisinės apsaugos įstatymas No I-1374 of 11 June 1996, [1996] VŽ No 63-1479, as last amended on 13 April 2004, [2004] VŽ No 60-2120.
[107] Valstybės ir tarnybos paslapčių įstatymas No VIII-1443 of 25 November 1999, [1999] VŽ No 105-3019, as last amended on 13 January 2004, [2004] VŽ No 116-4322.
[108] LR Civil Code 2000, Art 1.116.
[109] LR Administrative Penalties Code 1985, Art 214(16).   [110] Id, Art 214(18).

There are no specific provisions in Lithuanian law on liability of the right-holder **18.124** for the breach of Council Regulation (EC) 1383/2003. In all cases, general civil law provisions apply and the right-holder may be liable for any damage and loss caused by his actions.

B. Liability of customs authorities and sanctions

Under Lithuanian Customs Law, the right-holder is not entitled to any compen- **18.125** sation if the customs authorities failed to detect or recognize goods infringing his intellectual property rights, after an application for action has been filed and accepted.[111]

Similarly, Lithuanian law does not impose any liability on customs towards the **18.126** persons involved in, or affected by, *ex officio* actions under Article 4 of Council Regulation (EC) 1383/2003.[112] Damages may only be claimed if the customs' action proved to be illegal.

Conclusion

Although it may reasonably be regarded as user-friendly, the practical approach to **18.127** Council Regulation (EC) 1383/2003 in Lithuania still needs to be further improved, as the legal regime has to be consolidated by the adoption of additional provisions. Many issues in relation to border measures against goods suspected of infringing (and eventually found to infringe) an intellectual property right were previously addressed in Lithuania by Intellectual Property Law. Since this Law has been repealed, a gap in the legal framework has appeared. On the other hand, with the recent adoption of the bill relating to the simplified procedure for the destruction of goods, most of the national rules necessary for the implementation of the Regulation are considered by the customs authorities to be in place and we are not aware of any pending proposal which could fill remaining gaps. However, it may be anticipated that the Lithuanian customs authorities' practice will remain inspired by the principles previously laid down in the Intellectual Property Law and indeed, the first cases decided under the new version of Council Regulation (EC) 1383/2003 seem to confirm this analysis.

As a final remark, we would like to point out that Lithuanian Customs are very **18.128** eager to assist right-holders in their fight against intellectual property thefts.

---

[111] LR Customs Law 2004, Art 87(2), Cf Council Reg 1383/2003, Art 19(1).
[112] Cf Council Reg 1383/2003, Art 19(2).

Besides their official actions, they keep constant unofficial contact with right-holders or their representatives in this context. Both sides exchange views, provide advice to each other, organize seminars on a regular basis, and thus, strive for better protection of intellectual property rights, which ultimately results in the strengthening of consumer protection.

19

LUXEMBOURG[1]

Gary Cywie

Introduction

Council Regulation (EEC) 3842/86 of 1 December 1986 laying down **19.01** measures to prohibit the release for free circulation of counterfeit goods[2] entered into force in Luxembourg on 1 January 1988. Considering that the provisions of this Regulation were directly applicable in Luxembourg as of the day of its publication in the Official Journal of the European Communities,[3] the Luxembourg authorities satisfied themselves with adopting a Decree on 29 June 1988 relating to the application of Regulation 3842/86, which specified the competent authority referred to in Article 3 of this Regulation.[4]

This Regulation was replaced by Regulation 3295/94 of 22 December 1994 lay- **19.02** ing down measures to prohibit the release for free circulation, export, re-export, or entry for a suspensive procedure of counterfeit and pirated goods, which entered into force on 1 July 1995.[5]

---

[1] Any reference made hereunder to 'Luxembourg' should be construed as designating the Grand Duchy of Luxembourg.

[2] [1986] OJ L 357/1 (18.12.1986); Corr [1987] L 33/18 (4.2.1987).

[3] Reg 3842/86, Art 12.

[4] Règlement grand-ducal du 29 juin 1988 relatif aux modalités d'application du Règlement du Conseil des communautés européennes n° 3842 du 1er décembre 1986 fixant les mesures en vue d'interdire la mise en libre pratique des marchandises de contrefaçon (*Grand-ducal Decree of 29 June 1988 relating to application modalities of European communities Council Reg No 3842 of 1 December 1986 laying down measures to prohibit the release for free circulation of counterfeit goods*), [1988] Mémorial 679 (The Mémorial is the Luxembourg Official State Gazette).

[5] [1994] OJ L 341/8 (30.12.1994).

19.03 After a few amendments in 1999[6] as well as in 2003,[7] the latter was finally replaced by Regulation 1383/2003[8] which will be examined further below, which entered into effect on 1 July 2004.

19.04 Apart from the Decree of 29 June 1988[9] specifying the authority having jurisdiction to process applications for action by the Luxembourg customs authorities under the above Regulations, the Community Regulations on border measures have not given rise to any national legislation to date in Luxembourg. It should be noted that, generally speaking, Luxembourg Customs usually adhere to the provisions of European Regulations on this subject, and that they are very likely to continue to do so in the future.

I. SUBJECT MATTER AND SCOPE OF THE NATIONAL LAW APPLYING THE REGULATION

19.05 This Part describes the customs procedures under which suspect goods may be subject to border measures (section A), the definition of infringing goods (section B), and the goods which are excluded from the scope of the Regulation (section C).

A. Customs procedure of the goods

19.06 Luxembourg Customs apply border measures under EC Regulation 1383/2003 ('the Regulation') irrespective of the type of customs procedure under which the suspect goods are placed, whether importation, exportation, re-exportation (for example, after inward processing), transit (including *external* transit), or transhipment.

19.07 However, it should be noted that the majority of suspect goods apprehended in the past by Luxembourg Customs were discovered whilst being imported to Luxembourg or in transit to be made available for consumption in the European Community.[10] Nevertheless, several cases have been reported where suspected goods shipped by air were in *external* transit, or subject to transhipment, predominantly

---

[6] Cf Council Reg (EC) No 241/1999 of 25 January 1999 [1999] OJ L 27/1 (2.2.1999).

[7] Cf Council Reg (EC) No 806/2003 of 14 April 2003 [2003] OJ L 122/1 (16.5.2003).

[8] Council Reg (EC) 1383/2003 of 22 July 2003 concerning customs action against goods suspected of infringing certain intellectual property rights and the measures to be taken against goods found to have infringed such rights [2003] OJ L 196/7 (2.8.2003).   [9] N 4 above.

[10] More generally, according to the Direction of the Customs Administration, about 95 per cent of goods transiting through Luxembourg are directed to another Member State.

originating in the Far East and mainly directed to Mexico, the African continent, and the United States of America. Only one case of re-exported suspect goods has occurred in recent years. Luxembourg Customs have never found suspect goods exported from Luxembourg.

B. Definition of infringing goods

According to the official figures,[11] which only take into account cases were the non-authentic nature of the goods has been finally confirmed through information given by the right-holder, 93 per cent of Luxembourg Customs' interventions as regards infringements upon intellectual property rights have related to trade marks. The definition of counterfeit goods in Article 2(1)(a) of the Regulation and its application in Luxembourg Customs will be examined below. **19.08**

The remaining 7 per cent of customs' interventions have related to designs. The definition of pirated goods in Article 2(1)(b) of the Regulation and its application by Luxembourg Customs will be examined below. **19.09**

No practical examples of goods infringing other industrial or intellectual property rights have been dealt with by the Luxembourg customs authorities, or have come to our knowledge, apart from one patent infringement. However, for the sake of completeness, we will address the scope of these 'other' rights under Luxembourg law. **19.10**

(1) Counterfeit goods

Trade mark law is governed in Luxembourg by the Uniform Benelux Law on Marks.[12] **19.11**

For the purpose of the present section, we will consider that the trade marks referred to are rightful, valid, and lawful registrations which are not challenged, and made prior to any other identical registration covering the Benelux territory. **19.12**

Article 13(A)(1) of the Uniform Benelux Law on Marks gives the holder of a trade mark a series of exclusive rights. It is divided into four parts ((a)–(d)). **19.13**

Article 13(A)(1)(a) gives the holder the right to oppose any use, in the course of trade, of the trade mark in relation with goods for which this trade mark was registered. **19.14**

---

[11] European Commission, DG Taxation and Customs Union (TAXUD), Breakdown by type of right covered, 2003 (http://europa.eu.int/comm/taxation_customs/resources/documents/counterf_comm_2003_en.pdf).

[12] *Loi uniforme Benelux sur les marques* [1966] Mémorial 1153, as amended. This Law is examined in detail in J-J Evrard and P Peters, *La Défense de la Marque dans le Benelux* (2nd edn, Brussels: Larcier, 2000).

19.15 Under this provision, identical goods and services designated by an identical sign, *stricto sensu*, are counterfeit. The sign may be a mark, registered or not, or a designation of origin.

19.16 Article 13(A)(1)(b) confers on the holder the right to oppose any use, in the course of trade, of the trade mark or a similar sign in relation with goods for which this trade mark was registered, or similar goods, if a risk of confusion between the sign and the mark exists on the part of the public.

19.17 This provision aims at protecting the holder of a trade mark against the use of an identical or similar trade mark in relation with identical or similar goods or services, to the extent that such use creates confusion in the public's mind.

19.18 With regard to Article 13(A)(1)(b), it was ruled by the Luxembourg Court of Appeal that even when a certain number of differences exist between the trade mark and the sign appearing on the goods alleged to be counterfeit, it is sufficient for the sign to be considered as counterfeit if a great impression of resemblance exists so that there is a risk of confusion about the origin of the product in the consumers' mind.[13]

19.19 Pursuant to Article 13(A)(1)(c), the trade mark holder has the right to oppose any unjustified use, in the course of trade, of a trade mark which has a reputation in the Benelux territory, or a similar sign, in relation with goods not similar to those for which the trade mark was registered, to the extent that such sign takes unfair advantage of, or is detrimental to, the distinctive character or the repute of the trade mark.

19.20 Thus, greater protection is granted in relation to dissimilar products and services if the trade mark enjoys a reputation among a certain public, to be determined according to the situation.

19.21 Finally, Article 13(A)(1)(d) grants the holder the right to oppose any unjustified use, in the course of trade, of a trade mark or a similar sign otherwise than for distinguishing goods, to the extent that such sign takes unfair advantage of, or is detrimental to, the distinctive character or the repute of the trade mark.

19.22 This provision may apply even if the trade mark does not have a reputation, as it aims at protecting the trade mark against any use in bad faith.

19.23 When applying the Regulation, Luxembourg Customs take measures whenever there is a likelihood that the goods under consideration are 'counterfeit', regardless of whether the sign affixed to the suspect goods is identical or only *similar* to the trade mark, to the extent there is a risk of confusion in the consumers' mind.

---

[13] Luxembourg Court of Appeal, 7 March 1986, Case No 127/86 (*Campari*), not published; Luxembourg Court of Appeal (commercial section), 20 March 2002, [2003] Pasicrisie Luxembourgeoise 239.

Errors or inaccuracy in the signs, whether intentional or not, are not deemed **19.24**
relevant to determine whether a risk of confusion exists. For example, Luxembourg
Customs detained NETCAFÉ branded goods, considering the risk of confusion
with the well-known NESCAFÉ trade mark registered by NESTLÉ SA. A case has
also been reported where the CONNECTING PEOPLE trade mark was used
alongside the mark of mobile phones other than Nokia's.

Therefore, it should be noted that interventions of Luxembourg Customs may **19.25**
extend beyond the scope defined in Article 2(1)(a) of the Regulation, and this is
in accordance with the interpretation given to 'counterfeiting' under the Uniform
Benelux Law on Marks. Indeed, the definition of 'counterfeit goods' provided for
in Article 2(1)(a) of the Regulation only covers marks which are identical to, or
which cannot be distinguished in their essential aspects from, a trade mark registered in relation with the same type of goods. On the contrary, under certain conditions mentioned above, the Uniform Benelux Law on Marks is not limited to
this kind of infringement but also prohibits use of similar trade marks registered
in relation with similar goods or services.

Also, according to the facts, Luxembourg Customs do not automatically take into **19.26**
account the principle of speciality. For example, the Luxembourg Customs officers blocked *ex officio* a container with COCA-COLA labelled caps embedded
within a small radio receiving set.

However, Luxembourg Customs only take action on the grounds of registered, **19.27**
not challenged and, when applicable, duly renewed trade marks. No interventions, whether *ex offico* or upon the filing of an application for customs action, will
be undertaken on the grounds of a simple trade mark application, or a trade mark
against which an opposition has been filed.

Luxembourg Customs readily undertake actions against trade mark symbols **19.28**
(including logos, labels, stickers, brochures, and instruction manuals bearing such
symbols), and packaging material bearing a trade mark, even if presented separately. For example, a shipment of small crocodiles, probably destined to be sewn
onto polo shirts, was detained by Luxembourg Customs. According to the
customs representatives, this often occurs with respect to clothing.

(2) Pirated goods

For interpreting the concept of 'pirated goods', that is, 'goods which are or contain **19.29**
copies' of works enjoying protection under the law of copyright, related rights, or
designs, under the Regulation,[14] Luxembourg Customs look at the overall picture
and consider the goods as a whole.

---

[14] Reg 1383/2003, Art 2(1)(b).

19.30 According to the official figures,[15] no practical example of goods suspected of infringing industrial or intellectual property rights others than trade marks have been encountered by Luxembourg Customs, save with respect to designs (4 per cent).

19.31 In Luxembourg, designs are protected under the Uniform Benelux Law on Designs.[16]

19.32 Article 14 of the Law gives the holder of a design, without prejudice to the potential application of the law of torts, the exclusive right to oppose the use of a product in which the design is incorporated, or to which it is applied, and having an identical appearance in comparison to the design as it has been applied for with the Benelux Design Office, or which does not produce on the informed user an overall different impression, taking into account the designer's level of freedom in the development of the design. Use shall be construed as referring, in particular, to manufacturing, offering, marketing, selling, delivering, leasing, importing, exporting, using, or holding for one of these purposes, such products.

19.33 Therefore, it should be noted that, where the Regulation only refers to 'made/making',[17] Benelux law provides for a larger range of actions according to which goods may be considered as pirated.

19.34 Moreover, it may be questioned whether the concept of 'copies' referred to in the Regulation also covers all cases where the overall impression produced by the alleged 'copy' on the informed user does not differ from that of the 'authentic' product.

19.35 Only a very small quantity of goods suspected of infringing a copyright has been apprehended by Luxembourg Customs in the recent years. Such rights are protected under the Law on Copyrights, Related Rights and Databases.[18]

19.36 The Law on Copyrights, Related Rights and Databases grants the author the exclusive right to authorize or prevent reproduction of his original artistic and literary works, of any type or form of expression, including photographs, databases, and computer programs. The right of reproduction includes the right to oppose adaptation, arrangement, translation, integration in, or extraction from, a database, renting and lending of original or copies of the works, and communication to the public by any means, including wire and wireless transmission, by radio, satellite, cable, or network.

---

[15] European Commission, DG TAXUD, Breakdown by type of right covered, 2003 (n 11 above).

[16] *Loi Uniforme Benelux en matière de dessins ou modèles* [1973] Mémorial 1046, as amended.

[17] Cf Reg 1383/2003, Art 2(1)(b).

[18] *Loi du 18 avril 2001 sur les droits d'auteur, les droits voisins et les bases de données* [2001] Mémorial 1042, as recently amended ([2004] Mémorial 942).

Several exceptions to the author's copyright are provided under certain conditions **19.37** by the Law on Copyrights, Related Rights and Databases, for among other things short quotations, education purposes, private use, caching, and parody.

Other so-called related rights are provided, mainly as regards to artists and per- **19.38** formers as well as to artists, performers, and producers of phonograms and first recordings of motion-picture films. Databases are also protected as such.

(3) Goods infringing other intellectual property rights

No border measures have yet been taken in Luxembourg under EC Regulations **19.39** No 241/1999 and No 1383/2003 in relation to patents (except in one case, which is curently pending before the Luxembourg courts), supplementary protection certificates, national plant variety rights, national designations of origin, or geographical indications. We will, however, describe very briefly the scope of protection of these intellectual property rights under Luxembourg law below.

Goods infringing a patent or a supplementary protection certificate

Notwithstanding the international conventions to which Luxembourg is party **19.40** (including the European Patent Convention), patents are governed by the Law Modifying the Patents Regime.[19]

A national patent gives its holder the right to prohibit any direct use of the invention **19.41** without his consent. This right includes the right to prevent any third party from:

* manufacturing, offering, marketing, using, or importing or holding for these purposes, products covered by the patent;
* using a process covered by the patent or, to the extent the third party knows, or the circumstances make obvious, that the use of such process is forbidden without the patentee's consent, offering it for use on Luxembourg territory;
* offering, marketing, or using, or importing or holding for the purposes mentioned above, any product obtained directly from the process covered by the patent.

The holder of a patent may also, under certain conditions, forbid indirect **19.42** exploitation of the patent.

As regards supplementary protection certificates, Luxembourg's regulation[20] referring to European Council Regulation (EEC) No 1768/92 of 18 June 1992

---

[19] *Loi du 22 juillet 1992 portant modification du régime des brevets d'invention* [1992] Mémorial 1529.
[20] *Règlement grand-ducal du 17 novembre 1997 concernant la procédure et les formalités administratives en matière de brevets d'invention, en exécution de la loi du 20 juillet 1992 portant modification du régime des brevets d'invention et du règlement (CEE) No 1768/92 du Conseil du 18 juin 1992*

concerning the creation of a supplementary protection certificate for medicinal products[21] provides the rules and process for obtaining such certificate in Luxembourg on the basis of an existing patent.

Goods infringing a national plant variety right, a national designation of origin, or a geographical indication

19.43 Luxembourg has signed the Paris Convention of 20 March 1883 for the Protection of Industrial Property specifically applying not only to actual industry and commerce, but likewise to agricultural and extractive industries, and to all manufactured or natural products, as well as to designations of origin or geographical indications.[22] This Convention ensures, inter alia, an equivalence of treatment between nationals of its signatory countries.

19.44 However, it should be noted that the Law Modifying the Patents Regime[23] specifically excludes from patentability plant varieties and processes for obtaining plants essentially by biological means (except for microbiological processes). Moreover, Luxembourg is not a member of the International Convention for the Protection of New Varieties of Plants (1961), as revised at Geneva (1972, 1978 and 1991). Therefore, there is no specific protection in Luxembourg for plant variety rights.

19.45 Several laws apply to designations of origin. Among others, we can mention:

- the Law of 24 July 1909 on the regime of wines and similar beverages,[24] forbidding the use of controlled appellations like 'Cognac', 'Eau-de-vie de Cognac', 'Eau-de-vie des Charentes', 'Fine Champagne', and 'Armagnac', protected under French law;
- the Ministerial Decree of 30 March 1937 relating to appellations of origin for Luxemburg wines;[25]
- the Ministerial Decree of 25 October 1949 relating to the protection of appellations of origin for Luxemburg wines;[26] and
- the Government in Council Decree of 30 October 1987 creating an appellation of quality for Luxembourg butter.[27]

---

concernant la création d'un certificat complémentaire de protection pour les médicaments, [1997] Mémorial, 2946.
    [21] [1992] OJ L 182/1 (2.7.1992)   [22] Paris Convention, Art 1.   [23] N 19 above.
    [24] *Loi du 24 juillet 1909 sur le régime des vins et boissons similaires*, [1909] Mémorial 745.
    [25] *Arrêté ministériel du 30 mars 1937 concernant la protection des appellations d'origine pour les vins luxembourgeois*, [1937] Mémorial 175.
    [26] *Arrêté ministériel du 25 octobre 1949 concernant la protection des appellations d'origine pour les vins luxembourgeois*, [1949] Mémorial 1057.
    [27] *Règlement du Gouvernement en Conseil du 30 octobre 1987 portant création d'une appellation de qualité pour le beurre luxembourgeois*, [1987] Mémorial 2051.

(4) *Moulds and matrices*

At least in the recent years, Luxembourg Customs have never stopped any moulds   **19.46**
or matrices designed or adapted for the manufacture of counterfeit or pirated
goods, as defined above.

National law does not *specifically* set out such intervention. However, several   **19.47**
pieces of legislation mentioned above provide, under certain conditions, for the
transfer of property to the holder, or the confiscation and destruction of moulds
and matrices or any other tool specifically designed or adapted for the manufacture of goods found to infringe specific intellectual property rights. Thus, the
holder of a Benelux registered trade mark,[28] a Benelux registered design,[29] a copyright or related right,[30] or a Luxembourg patent,[31] may ask for their forfeiture or
destruction to be ordered. Therefore, it can be maintained that Luxembourg
Customs are entitled, under Article 2(3) of the Regulation, to take action against
such moulds and matrices.

C. Goods excluded by the Regulation

(1) *Parallel imported goods*

There is no specific legislation about parallel importation of goods in Luxembourg.   **19.48**

Therefore, in accordance with Article 3(1), first indent, of the Regulation,   **19.49**
Luxembourg Customs would not take action or inform right-holders if such
goods were found.

(2) *Goods which have been manufactured under conditions other*
than those which have been agreed with the right-holder

There is no specific legislation in Luxembourg about goods manufactured under   **19.50**
conditions other than those which have been agreed between a licensee and the
right-holder.

Therefore, in accordance with Article 3(1), second indent, of the Regulation,   **19.51**
Luxembourg Customs would not take action or inform right-holders if such
goods were found. For example, in general, customs do not consider overruns as
counterfeits. However, decisions are always taken on a case-by-case basis and it

---

[28] Uniform Benelux Law on Marks (n 12 above), Art 13bis(1).
[29] Uniform Benelux Law on Design (n 16 above), Art 14bis(1).
[30] Law on Copyrights, Related Rights and Databases (n 18 above), Art 83.
[31] Law Modifying the Patents Regime (n 19 above), Art 81.

may occur that, considering the facts of a particular case, customs suspend release of the goods and, provided an application for action is filed by the right-holder, information about the goods is conveyed to the latter.

(3) *Goods contained in travellers' personal baggage*

19.52   Even though Luxembourg Customs do check travellers' personal baggage, it cannot be said that they take a very strict view regarding suspect goods they may find in them. More than ever, in this matter, examination on a case-by-case basis is carried out.

19.53   To the extent they feel that no commercial use of the goods contained in travellers' personal baggage is intended, Luxembourg customs inspectors will take no action. They are free to evaluate the situation according to two non-cumulative factors, namely the EUR 175 'duty-free allowance' and 'material indication of the existence of a commercial traffic' referred to in Article 3(2) of the Regulation.

19.54   As regards the calculation of the customs value of the goods, on the basis of which customs are to determine whether goods contained in a traveller's baggage are within the limits of the duty-free allowance, a sales slip should be taken into consideration. However, it is easy to imagine that in numerous cases, the value indicated on the sales slip, if any, is far from the reality.

19.55   In considering the existence of a commercial traffic, bringing back from vacation one or two purses would seem acceptable. Carrying 10 would probably attract the inspectors' attention.

II. APPLICATION FOR ACTION BY THE CUSTOMS AUTHORITIES

19.56   This Part will describe how Luxembourg Customs deal with *ex officio* procedures under the Regulation (section A), and applications for actions by right-holders (section B).

19.57   According to the official statistics, out of the 71 customs interventions recorded in 2003 in Luxembourg under the Regulation, 30 *ex officio* procedures were undertaken by Luxembourg Customs. 41 applications for action were filed and 58 per cent of border measures resulted from an application for action.[32]

---

[32] European Commission, DG TAXUD, Number of applications for action, 2003 (n 11 above).

A. Measures prior to an application for action by the customs authorities ('*ex officio*' measures)

Luxembourg Customs are eager to apply *ex officio* measures and this has occurred quite often in recent years. **19.58**

Before taking any *ex officio* measures, and because it is obviously impossible to control physically all and any shipments transiting via Luxembourg, customs take into account several criteria for assessing whether the goods are suspect or not. **19.59**

The criteria to determine the level of suspicion are revealed from the examination of the transportation documents accompanying the goods. Customs therefore analyse beforehand all available shipping documents (bill of lading, invoice, guarantee certificates, which are frequently false in the case of goods infringing an intellectual property right), to check their completeness and accuracy. **19.60**

The major criteria are as follows: bad craftsmanship of the goods, bad quality of the packaging, multi-brand shipments (this criterion is very significant according to customs), place of origin and destination, and place of production of the goods as well as shipper details (that is, lack of information about the shipper, perhaps on the bill of lading, is in general a good indication of risk). **19.61**

Should there be any doubt in the mind of customs officers about the genuine nature of the goods, they would prefer to suspend their release and give the opportunity to the right-holder to file an application for action. **19.62**

After taking *ex officio* measures in relation with suspect goods, customs transmit to the right-holder information on the quantity of the goods, and a description of their nature, generally with digital pictures of them. They would not give other information about the shipper or the declarant, nor send samples of the goods, at least until an application for action is filed by the right-holder.[33] **19.63**

The three working days deadline for retaining suspect goods under the *ex officio* procedure is very strictly applied by the Luxembourg customs authorities, which consider that during this time, the goods are retained under their responsibility. Computing of this timeframe is calculated on the basis of Regulation No 1182/71 of the Council of 3 June 1971 determining the rules applicable to periods, dates, and time limits.[34] According to this Regulation, only holidays in the country where the act is to be carried out should be taken into account. In addition, Saturdays and Sundays are not counted as working days. The first day of the period starts to run on the first hour of the following day to be considered (that is, the day on which notification has been received by the right-holder), and ends on **19.64**

---

[33] Cf Reg 1383/2003, Art 4(2).   [34] [1971] OJ L 124/1 (8.6.1971).

the last hour of the last day of the period. Customs strictly stick to these rules, although some departments are open seven days a week, 24 hours a day.

B. The lodging and processing of applications for customs action

(1) Persons entitled to file an application for action

19.65   In defining who is entitled to file an application for action, Luxembourg Customs do not deviate from the provisions of the Regulation.

Definition of 'right-holders' under the Regulation

19.66   For Luxembourg Customs, and as provided by the Regulation,[35] it is not only the owner of the intellectual property right in question who is entitled to file an application for action under the Regulation, but also any other person authorized to use such right (such as exclusive or non-exclusive licensees),[36] or representatives of such right owner or authorized user, whether natural or legal persons (such as attorneys, intellectual property right agents, consultants, collective management societies, etc).[37] Customs will verify, according to the documents that must be provided in such case together with the application for action,[38] that these persons are entitled under the contract with the right-holder to represent him.

Proof of entitlement to file an application for action

For right-holders stricto sensu

19.67   As stated above, according to the 2003 official figures, 93 per cent of Luxembourg Customs interventions are related to trade marks, and the remaining 7 per cent to registered designs.[39] For these cases, Luxembourg Customs require evidence that the trade mark or design is duly registered. A mere application would not be sufficient.

19.68   With respect to documents that should be provided by applicants for customs action in relation with other intellectual property rights, Luxembourg Customs

---

[35]   Reg 1383/2003, Art 2(2)(b).
[36]   This is in line with the provisions of Art 13bis of the Uniform Benelux Law on Marks (n 12 above) and Art 14bis of the Uniform Benelux Law on Designs (n 16 above).
[37]   Commission Reg (EC) 1891/2004 of 21 October 2004 laying down provisions for the implementation of Council Reg (EC) 1383/2003 concerning customs action against goods suspected of infringing certain intellectual property rights and the measures to be taken against goods found to have infringed such rights [2004] OJ L 328/16 (30.10.2004), Art 1.
[38]   Cf paras 19.67–19.72 below.   [39]   Para 19.08 above.

are not too demanding, taking into account that anyway the applicant also files a declaration covering potential liability.[40] However, with respect to patents, customs also require proof of a duly registered patent.[41]

Copies of certificates from official databases of a national or international office **19.69** may be submitted.[42] However, only certificates originating from databases to which customs have access (that is, among others, WIPO,[43] OHIM,[44] or BTO[45] databases) may be filed, so that they can verify the reliability of the documents submitted. Certificates from private databases are acceptable to the extent customs can verify their trustworthiness.

For persons authorized to use the right

Persons authorized to use the right subject of the application for action must pro- **19.70** vide a licence agreement to evidence such an authorization. Generally, a copy will be sufficient. Customs will however not check the content of such agreement or if the authorization has been registered with the relevant industrial property office (where required by law).

For representatives

Although mandatory pursuant to EC Regulation 1891/2004,[46] no particular **19.71** proof of the power of the representative is required by Luxembourg Customs. Nevertheless, a duly executed proxy will be required each time the declaration referred to in Article 6 of the Regulation is not signed by the right-holder in person.[47] If copies are provided at the first place, originals will have to be sent by regular mail.

Foreign representatives are authorized to appear before customs, even if they do **19.72** not have an office in Luxembourg.

(2) Competent customs department and formal requirements

Competent customs department

The Luxembourg customs department entrusted with the processing of applica- **19.73** tions for action filed under the Regulation[48] is the 'Department of Customs and

---

[40] Reg 1383/2003, Art 6.   [41] Cf also Reg 1891/2004 (n 37 above), Art 2(1).
[42] Ibid, Art 2(1), second indent.
[43] World Intellectual Property Organization, www.wipo.org.
[44] Office for Harmonization in the Internal Market, www.oami.eu.int.
[45] Benelux Trade mark Office, www.bmb-bbm.org.
[46] N 37 above, Art 2(3), first indent.   [47] Ibid, second indent.
[48] Cf Reg 1383/2003, Art 5(2).

Excise'.[49] To contact this authority, address any correspondence to:

Direction des douanes et accises
Division 'Attributions Sécuritaires'
B.P. 1605
L-1016 Luxembourg
Tel: +352 29 01 91
Fax: +352 49 87 90
E-mail: douanes@do.etat.lu

Form of the application for action

19.74 Applications for action may be filed in whatever form available to the Luxembourg customs authorities. This includes letter, fax, e-mail, and CD-ROM. E-mails are much appreciated, if not recommended, in practice.[50]

19.75 However, any document addressed to customs must be confirmed with originals sent by regular mail in two copies (especially after *ex officio* measures).

19.76 In the near future, Luxembourg Customs intend to put in place on their Internet site a web form for filing applications. Information about such on-line filing will probably be made available on the customs' current website, http://www.do.etat.lu.

19.77 If colour or large documents (for example, brochures or manuals), or materials of which copies cannot easily be made, are provided to support an application for action, it is recommended to file six copies with the Department of Customs and Excise, which will then forward them to all customs offices concerned.

19.78 Generally, Luxembourg Customs are digitally oriented and encourage the use of scanned documents which can be sent electronically. Therefore, CD-ROMs containing the application for action and all mandatory and supporting documents are welcome thanks to the fact they can easily be consulted by all the customs' divisions and offices involved. In such cases, one CD-ROM is sufficient, as its content will be uploaded on customs' intranet. A confirmation copy must however be sent by post.

Language requirements

19.79 The application as well as all mandatory and supporting documents may be filed in any of the following languages: German, French or English.

---

[49] Decree of 29 June 1988 relating to application of Reg No 3842 of 1 December 1986 (n 4 above). This Decree, even though it refers to a Regulation which is no longer in force, is still valid as references made to a replaced Regulation must be construed as referring to the new Regulation having the same object. Cf eg Reg 1383/2003, Art 24, and the Joint Practical Guide for persons involved in the drafting of legislation within the Community institutions, s 16 (References), n 12 (http://europa.eu.int/eur-lex/en/about/techleg/guide/16_en.htm).

[50] Cf Reg 1383/2003, Art 5(3).

(3) Requirements regarding the contents of the application for action

Mandatory information

Pursuant to Article 5(5) of the Regulation, applications for action must be made out on the forms established under Regulation 1891/2004,[51] and contain all the information needed to enable the goods in question to be readily identified by customs. **19.80**

Information to be provided includes, in particular, a technical description of the goods. The content of the description will obviously depend on the nature of the relevant goods. Generally, a broad description of the goods would be sufficient for Luxembourg Customs. **19.81**

Although under the Regulation, right-holders *must* also provide any specific information concerning the type or pattern of fraud,[52] such information is not considered mandatory in practice by Luxembourg Customs. **19.82**

Finally, the right-holder must indicate in his application the name and address of a contact person.[53] This person need not have a local presence in Luxembourg, although this may of course facilitate the identification of suspect goods. **19.83**

Optional information

Where known, customs consider that providing information on the identity of the shipper or the manufacturer, or on the destination of the goods, is useful, although not essential. The Regulation also encourages right-holders to submit any other useful information they may have, by way of indication.[54] **19.84**

Additional information specific to the type of intellectual property right referred to in the application

Customs rarely request additional information as per Article 5(6) of the Regulation. However, as pointed out in the previous paragraph, any additional information which can help customs to make a decision in relation with the application for action is always welcome. **19.85**

(4) Processing and acceptance of the application for action

There is no *specific* appeal procedure in case the right-holder wishes to challenge a customs decision about an application for action, whether because customs failed to make a decision (or failed to make a decision within 30 working days of its **19.86**

---

[51] N 37 above.   [52] Reg 1383/2003, Art 5(5), first indent, (ii).
[53] Ibid, Art 5(5), first indent, (iii).   [54] Ibid, Art 5(5), last indent.

receipt, as required by the Regulation[55]), or because the decision seems to rely on false grounds, or is in any way unsatisfactory to the right-holder.[56]

19.87   Therefore, 'regular' national procedures for challenging administrative acts of the State may be followed.

19.88   In the first place, an administrative appeal[57] is always possible against any administrative decision. There are five situations where cancellation of the decision may be expected, namely where the authority which issued the decision (i) had no jurisdiction to do so, (ii) committed an abuse of power, (iii) made a fraudulent use of authority, (iv) committed a breach of law, or (v) a breach of procedures destined to protect private interests. In these cases, the administrative tribunal[58] weighs the legality of the act.[59]

19.89   The law of 1 December 1978 regulating non-contentious administrative proceedings[60] is set out to maintain the respect of the rights of the citizens by trying to associate the latter, to the greatest extent possible, to the administrative decision process. Against this background, the citizens have the right to be heard and to obtain from the administration information about the administrative operation processes. The above-mentioned law requires the administration to provide reasons for its decisions. Before any trial with the judicial authority, it is possible to appeal the decision with the authority which has taken the decision. Thereafter, the authority will take a new decision, which may be the same as the previous but based on other grounds.

19.90   Actions of customs following acceptance of an application filed by the right-holder may last up to one year. This period may however be extended for one more year at the right-holder's request and under the conditions provided by Article 8(1) of the Regulation.

(5) 'Community' applications for action

19.91   The conditions for processing 'Community' applications for action filed under Article 5(4) of the Regulation are exactly the same as for national applications, should they be filed in Luxembourg, or in another Member State and request action in Luxembourg.

---

[55] Reg 1383/2003, Art 5(7), first indent.
[56] Eg where customs decide not to process the application for action because they consider that it does not contain the mandatory information listed in Art 5(5) of the Regulation (Ibid, Art 5(8)).
[57] '*Recours administratif*'.   [58] '*Tribunal Administratif*'.
[59] G Ravarani, *La responsabilité civile des personnes privées et publiques* (Luxembourg: Saint Paul, 2000, 74).
[60] *Loi du 1er décembre 1978 réglant la procédure administrative non contentieuse*, [1978] Mémorial 2486.

The only potential issue relates to the language used by the applicant. There is no **19.92** particular difficulty if the application is in German, French, or English. If they are in other languages, applications for action and supporting documents must be translated in one of the three aforementioned languages.

III. CONDITIONS GOVERNING ACTION BY CUSTOMS AUTHORITIES AND BY THE AUTHORITIES COMPETENT TO DETERMINE WHETHER GOODS INFRINGE AN INTELLECTUAL PROPERTY RIGHT

If an application for action is accepted by Customs, and suspect goods are found, **19.93** notification of such discovery will be given, information will be conveyed to the right-holder, and the opportunity will be given to the latter to analyse the goods to determine whether they infringe any of his intellectual property rights.

The Regulation provides for a simplified procedure to allow destruction of the **19.94** goods afterwards without the need to have a Court determine whether an intellectual property right has been infringed under national law. However, it is the opinion of the Luxembourg authorities that such a procedure needs to be implemented in national law to be applicable, and this is not yet the case in Luxembourg.

Therefore, in order for the goods to be retained by Customs, right-holders will **19.95** have to evidence commencement of proceedings aiming at determining whether the goods infringe an intellectual property right.

It is sometimes possible under the Regulation to have goods suspected of infring- **19.96** ing certain rights released on provision of a security. However, this has not happened in the recent years in Luxembourg.

Pending the above procedure, the goods have to be stored. The conditions of their **19.97** warehousing will be examined below.

A. Conditions governing action by customs authorities

(1) Factual background

It should be noted that, although Luxembourg is a small country, mainly well- **19.98** known for its expertise in financial services, transportation also constitutes one of the country's most dynamic sectors. Two main air transport sector companies are based at Luxembourg airport, namely 'Luxair' (for passenger transport) and 'Cargolux' (for air freight transport). The latter, carrying more than a half million tons per year and serving 50 destinations, is among the largest air freight common carriers in the world.[61]

19.99   Therefore, the *Bureau des Douanes Aéroport*[62] is without doubt the most important office involved in anti-counterfeiting (in the broad sense). Actually, according to the official statistics, in 2003, 76 per cent of the cases examined by Luxembourg Customs have arisen in relation to goods shipped by air and 24 per cent in relation to goods shipped by regular post.[63]

19.100   If the official figures can be relied on, no customs interventions have been made in Luxembourg over goods transported or shipped by train, boat (the *Moselle* River, with more than ten million items transported per year, is nonetheless considered as a large load profile waterway[64]), or road. However, we have been informed that a few cases occurred where goods were shipped by road.

19.101   While undertaking interventions according to an application for action, Luxembourg Customs strictly stick to the provisions of the Regulation, more specifically Article 9 (cf paras 19.102 ff below).

(2) Notification of customs intervention

19.102   Where a Luxembourg customs office detains, or suspends release of, goods suspected of infringing an intellectual property right, it informs the right-holder concerned of its action.[65] In general, Luxembourg Customs will liaise with the right-holder, or his representative or contact person, by the same telecommunications means used for filing the application for action, if any.[66] In *ex officio* procedures, customs will prefer to use the right-holder's e-mail, where known.

19.103   Customs interventions are normally notified to the declarant or holder of the goods at the same time as the right-holder. Interventions are always notified to the forwarding agents of the customs agency involved in the transportation of the suspect goods.

---

[61]   Ministry of Economic Affairs, Central Service for Statistics and Economic Studies, STATEC (http://www.portrait.public.lu/structures_economiques/structure/coups_de_projecteur/transport_comm/). [62]   Airport Customs Office.
[63]   European Commission, DG TAXUD, Breakdown by means of transport used for the cases examined by Customs, 2003 (n 11 above).
[64]   Cf Voies navigables de France (http://www.transports.equipement.gouv.fr/dttdocs/fich_vn_presentation_VN_2003.pdf). [65]   Reg 1383/2003, Art 9(2).
[66]   Cf para 19.71 above.

(3) Information to be provided by customs to the right-holder before the right-holder confirms the infringing nature of the goods

Once an application for action has been filed and accepted, customs commu- **19.104**
nicate to the right-holder the available details of the consignee, the shipper, the
declarant or holder of the goods, and information about the origin and provenance of the suspect goods.[67] These details and information are sometimes automatically provided, depending on the particulars of the case. Specific requests
from the right-holder for such information are generally accepted. Other
information, such as actual or estimated quantity, or nature of the goods is also
communicated to the right-holder.

The Law on the protection of individuals with regard to the processing of personal **19.105**
data[68] normally applies to such communications. This Law may have been impeding customs from disclosing information about the persons involved in the transport of the goods. However, customs still have in mind the '*Adidas*'[69] ruling, in
connection with former Regulation 3295/94,[70] in which the European Court of
Justice stressed that the Regulation 'precludes a rule of national law under which
the identity of declarants or consignees of imported goods which the trade mark
owner has found to be counterfeit may not be disclosed to him'. This decision
applies *mutatis mutandis* in the context of Article 9(3) of Regulation 1383/2003.

(4) Inspection of the suspected goods

Once the detention, or the suspension of release, of the goods has been decided, **19.106**
the right-holder is allowed to inspect the goods, having thus the opportunity to
evaluate their infringing character.

For that purpose, digital pictures will be sent to the right-holder. Depending on
the merits of the case, samples may also be provided to the right-holder upon
request. The quantity and nature of the goods may determine whether samples
will be provided or not. For example, if customs retain only one or two items of
the suspect goods, as it is often the case for prestigious brands of watches like
'Rolex', no sample will be provided to the right-holder. Instead, customs will ask
for a local accredited expert to examine the goods on customs' premises.

In principle, samples must be returned to customs after examination. However, **19.107**
this is not always the case and depends, in practice, on the value and nature of the
goods. In this respect, perfume samples need not be returned to customs as, in any

---

[67] Cf Reg 1383/2003, Art 9(3).
[68] *Loi du 2 août 2002 sur la protection des personnes à l'égard du traitement de données à caractère personnel*, [2002] Mémorial 1836.
[69] ECJ, Case C-223/98 Adidas AG, [1999] ECR I-7081. [70] N 5 above.

event, once opened, the bottle cannot be used anymore. In the same way, customs will not pursue one or two samples of low value goods.

B. Simplified procedure allowing the destruction of the goods without there being any need to determine whether an intellectual property right has been infringed under national law

19.108   Currently, Article 11 of the Regulation has not been implemented in Luxembourg law. As this provision specifically refers to procedures set out by national legislation, customs will not take any measure referred to in relation with the simplified procedure, at least until such legislation is adopted. Although customs would like to instigate discussions with the legislative power to specify the necessary national provisions for setting out a simplified procedure, there is for the time being no possibility for such a procedure to be initiated by customs for the suspect goods to be abandoned and destroyed under their supervision. Therefore, it is not possible to assess whether the applicant, holder, or owner of the goods is deemed to accept their destruction if no objection is raised within a specific deadline.

19.109   However, in propitious cases and under particular conditions, customs will take in consideration amicable settlements between right-holders and owners of suspect goods, to the extent they consider they do not have the power to oppose such contractual agreements.

19.110   Nonetheless, customs would not accept licences being granted by the right-holder to the owner of suspect goods to allow their marketing. The following fictional maxim gives a good picture of customs' views in this respect: 'Infringing goods may not become lawful.'

C. Conditions governing action by the authorities having jurisdiction to determine whether the goods infringe an intellectual property right

(1) Authorities having jurisdiction to determine whether the goods infringe an intellectual property right

General principle

19.111   After border measures have been undertaken by customs, and in the absence of any simplified procedure or amicable settlement, the right-holder must inform and provide customs within 10 working days (which can be extended to 20 working days in total[71]) with the evidence that proceedings have been initiated by the right-holder aiming at determining if an intellectual property right has actually been infringed according to the national legislation. If such evidence is not provided, the goods will be released.[72]

Different sorts of proceedings (summary proceedings and/or proceedings on the merits) may be initiated by the right-holder before the judges sitting in civil, commercial, or criminal matters, and different remedies may be claimed,[73] depending on the type of right under consideration (some remedies apply regardless of the type of right involved). However, as stated above,[74] only trade marks (principally) and design rights infringements are significant for the purpose of the application of the Regulation in Luxembourg. We will thus only focus our attention on trade mark infringements, after first giving a broad view of the common regimes governing other intellectual property rights infringements.   **19.112**

Civil proceedings

Summary proceedings

Regardless of the type of right considered, preliminary injunctions may be issued by the president of the District Tribunal[75] having jurisdiction, at the request of the right-holder, by serving on the defendant a writ of summons for summary proceedings. Such *inter partes* proceedings[76] will however be admissible, and thus lead to a preliminary injunction, only if the applicant (that is, the right-holder) is able to demonstrate, in addition to an alleged clear-cut breach of intellectual property rights, that the case requires celerity. Celerity is a question of fact that must be addressed by the president of the tribunal.[77] Moreover, preliminary injunctions may only provide for interim relief—whereby the defendant is ordered to cease and desist from actions alleged to be in breach of the claimant's rights[78]—which do not bind the judge who will rule on the merits of the case. In our view, such summary proceedings may be considered as 'proceedings to determine whether an intellectual property right has been infringed' within the meaning of Article 13 of the Regulation.   **19.113**

---

[71] In the case of perishable goods, however, this period shall be three working days, and may not be extended (Reg 1383/2003, Art 13(2)). Cf para 19.122 below.   [72] Ibid, Art 13(1).

[73] Essentially civil remedies, save for infringement to copyrights and, under certain conditions, to trade marks.   [74] Cf para 19.08 above.

[75] 'Président du Tribunal d'Arrondissement' (Luxembourg and Diekirch).

[76] 'Référé ordinaire sur assignation' (Art 932 of the New Code for Civil Proceedings, *Nouveau code de procédure civile*).

[77] Luxembourg Court of Appeal, 14 March 1966, *Pasicrisie Luxembourgeoise* 20, 90.

[78] 'Cessation provisoire'.

Seizures and Anton Piller Orders

19.114   As regards copyright or patent infringements, proceedings may be commenced intending to obtain a descriptive seizure[79] of the goods alleged to infringe the copyright owner's or patentee's rights, allowing the possibility of collecting evidence about the existence and scope of the infringement (the Luxembourg 'descriptive seizure' proceedings can thus be compared to the Anton Piller Orders in the United Kingdom, or the discovery procedure in the United States). Such a remedy is generally productive thanks to the surprise effect it causes. In copyright matters, these proceedings may also be used to obtain a conservatory seizure[80] leading to the confiscation of the profits generated by the illicit operation.[81] In patent matters, they can be used to obtain the physical seizure[82] of the goods alleged to infringe the patent. Such *ex parte* proceedings[83] are commenced by lodging a petition with the judge of adequate jurisdiction.[84] Such proceedings may be considered as 'proceedings to determine whether an intellectual property right has been infringed' within the meaning of Article 13 of the Regulation.

Proceedings on the merits

19.115   As damages may only be claimed in proceedings on the merits of the case, and the retention of the suspected goods is already warranted under the Regulation in customs matters, preliminary injunctions and 'civil' seizures can often be viewed as worthless in such situations.

19.116   Civil proceedings on the merits may be commenced after or aside from summary proceedings by serving a writ of summons to the defendant to have him appear before the judge of proper jurisdiction. The *ratione materiae* jurisdiction of the judge depends on the type of right alleged to be infringed. The plaintiff can claim for damages, recovery (ie surrendering of property right) of the infringing goods, and destruction of such goods. However, it should be noted that Luxembourg courts are quite timorous when granting damages for infringements to intellectual property rights. For example, in the case *Chemise Lacoste v Hosencenter*,[85] the Luxembourg Court of Appeal granted damages in an amount of approximately EUR 1,130 Euro to the right-holder in consideration of the sale of about 80 counterfeit shirts.

---

[79] '*Saisie-description*' referred to in Art 72 of the Law on Copyrights, Related Rights and Databases (n 18 above), and in Art 79(1) of the Law Modifying the Patents Regime (n 19 above).
[80] '*Saisie conservatoire*' referred to in Art 72 of the Law on Copyrights, Related Rights and Databases (n 18 above).
[81] Upon the request of the right-holder, the judge may order the infringer to convey all information about its accounts (invoices, sales slip, etc).
[82] '*Saisie contrefaçon*' referred to in Art 79(2) of the Law Modifying the Patents Regime (n 19 above).   [83] '*Référé sur requête unilatérale*'.
[84] The President of the District Court of the place of counterfeiting sitting in civil matters.
[85] Luxembourg Court of Appeal, 30 May 1984, Case No 7328, not published.

Criminal prosecution

We consider that Regulation 1383/2003, by replacing the Regulation,[86] principally **19.117** intends to improve the right-holders' position. Therefore, we are of the view that the concept of 'proceedings' should be interpreted in a broad sense, and thus also encompasses criminal complaints, although one may question whether the filing of such complaints results in the effective 'commencement' of criminal proceedings in the proper sense. Of course this view is limited to infringements to rights in relation with which a criminal offence is provided by law. It seems that Luxembourg Customs take the same view, as they accept copies of complaints as sufficiently demonstrating that proceedings have been initiated aiming at determining if an intellectual property right has been infringed. This was also the case under the previous Regulation, although it was more burdensome as Article 7(1) of this Regulation provided that the right-holder had to inform customs that proceedings with the authority having jurisdiction 'to take a substantive decision on the case' had been commenced. The public prosecutor,[87] in charge of the processing of such criminal complaints, could nonetheless not be considered as an authority having jurisdiction to take substantive decisions about intellectual property rights infringements, should the latter constitute a criminal offence.

Our view may be confirmed by the fact that the Regulation no longer mentions **19.118** the need to refer the case to a body which may take a decision, but only that proceedings to that effect have been commenced.

Injurious or fraudulent infringements to rights protected under the Law on **19.119** Copyrights, Related Rights and Databases[88] constitute a criminal offence. The same offence applies to those who knowingly sell, market, import, export, attach, reproduce, convey, transmit, make available to the public, or more generally circulate, for free or for money, a protected work without the consent of the right-holder.

With respect to trade marks, Article 191 of the Criminal Code must be taken into **19.120** consideration. It provides that 'whoever has affixed or made someone affix, by addition, deletion or any alteration, to manufactured goods, the name of a manufacturer other than that of the author, or the commercial name of a manufacturer other than that of the actual manufacturer, will be punished (. . .)'. The same applies to any merchant, dealer or trader who knowingly sells, imports, or circulates, goods to which supposed or altered names have been affixed. Prosecuting such infringements requires the filing of a criminal complaint with the public prosecutor. The prosecutor may start investigations with the assistance of the police. However, it seems that Luxembourg's examining magistrates do not often

---

[86] N 5 above.   [87] '*Procureur d'Etat*'.
[88] N 18 above. This includes protection of copyrights, related rights, databases and computer programs (Art 82).

follow up criminal complaints in intellectual property matters. It is however possible for the right-holder to overcome the prosecutor's decision not to prosecute the offence by appearing as an injured party.[89]

19.121 Due to the criminal penalties, that is large criminal fines, that may be incurred by the defendant losing the case, opting for criminal proceedings may create a dissuasive effect on intellectual property rights infringements and, hopefully, contribute to their reduction.

(2) *Term for notifying customs that proceedings have been started*

19.122 Luxembourg Customs are not extremely strict as regards the interpretation of the concept of 'appropriate cases' referred to in Article 13 of the Regulation, in which the term of 10 working days during which right-holders are to inform customs that proceedings have been commenced may be extended by another 10 working days upon the request of the right-holder.[90] In general, if the application for action is complete and the file compliant with the rules set out in the Regulation, customs have no reason to refuse such extension. However, we have been informed of one case where such an extension was refused. It occurred in relation to a right-holder who systematically filed requests for extensions, but never initiated any proceedings aiming at determining whether the goods infringe an intellectual property right.

19.123 Moreover, it has to be noted that the filing of the application for action interrupts the three working days referred to in Article 4 of the Regulation for retaining suspect goods under the *ex officio* procedure. The part of the 3 working day period already elapsed does not count for the 10-working day period, nor do Saturdays and Sundays.

D. Release of goods suspected of infringing certain rights on provision of a security

19.124 Article 14(1) of the Regulation provides for the possibility of obtaining the release of goods suspected of infringing design rights, patents, supplementary protection certificates, or plant variety rights, on provision of a security. To the extent the conditions set out in this provision are fulfilled, Luxembourg Customs will consider themselves obliged to release the suspect goods. However, no such case has been reported in the recent years.

---

[89] 'Constitution de partie civile'.   [90] Cf para 19.111 above.

E. Storage of the goods

There is no national provision setting out the regime under which goods suspected **19.125** of infringing an intellectual property right should be stored once being detained by Luxembourg Customs under the Regulation. In practice, they are stored in airport warehouses belonging to the companies 'Luxair S.A.' and 'Swissport Cargo Services Luxembourg S.A.' The storage and demurrage costs, if any (often, handling costs are the only costs incurred) are borne by the right-holder. To the best of our knowledge, there is no case law to date from which it would be possible to determine if the right-holder is entitled to claim reimbursement of these costs in the framework of court proceedings. However, judges would be entitled, if requested to do so under Article 240 of the New Code for Civil Proceedings,[91] to put such costs at the charge of the infringing party. It would also be possible to provide for such reimbursement in the framework of a settlement agreement.

IV. PROVISIONS APPLICABLE TO GOODS FOUND TO INFRINGE AN INTELLECTUAL PROPERTY RIGHT

Generally, Luxembourg national law prohibits the *importation* of goods infring- **19.126** ing any type of intellectual property right covered by the Regulation. *Exportation*, including re-exportation, is also a situation under which the national law allows the right-holder to intervene to protect his rights, more specifically in the context of trade mark counterfeiting.[92] It is less clear whether other customs procedures, such as external transit or transhipment, are comprised within the cases in which intervention is possible under the Luxembourg law. However, we have seen that Luxembourg Customs are eager to take actions whatever the regime under which the suspect goods are found.[93] As a direct consequence of the Regulation, which is directly applicable on the national territories of the Member States, it is more than likely that the courts will prohibit the movement of goods found to infringe an intellectual property right under national (or Community) law, irrespective of the customs procedure under which those goods were found, and regardless of whether they are intended for the Luxembourg market.[94]

---

[91] This provision allows the judge to condemn a party to pay the other party an amount it determines if it is found that it would be inequitable to leave such expenses at the latter party's costs.
[92] The Uniform Benelux Law on Marks (n 12 above) explicitly prohibits the exportation of counterfeit goods and specifically refers to re-exportation.   [93] Cf para 19.06 above.
[94] Cf Reg 1383/2003, Art 16.

19.127   As per the national legislation, destruction of the goods is possible in case of infringement to any of the following intellectual property rights: copyrights,[95] trade marks,[96] designs rights,[97] and patents.[98] Recovery is provided in relation with infringement to trade marks[99] and design rights.[100] Confiscation is permitted for copyright[101] and patent[102] infringements, and surrendering of profits in connection with trade marks[103] and designs rights[104] is also possible.

19.128   Moreover, Article 240 of the New Code for Civil Proceedings allows the judge to condemn a party to pay the other party an amount it determines if it is found that it would be inequitable to leave such expenses at the latter party's costs.

V. PENALTIES

19.129   Copyright and related rights infringements are subject to a criminal fine ranging from EUR 251 to EUR 250,000, to confiscation of all pirated works, as well as the moulds and matrices which were used for committing the infringement (regardless to whom they belong), or any other tool used to copy, digitize or upload the works on networks. Destruction of the latter may be ordered by the judge, as well as closing of the premises exploited by the losing party, or publication of the judgment, and granting of damages.[105]

19.130   Trade mark infringements are subject to imprisonment of one to six months and/or criminal fine ranging from EUR 251 to EUR 5,000.[106] Right-holders of trade marks and design rights may claim for recovery[107] or destruction,[108] of the counterfeit or pirated goods, and for surrendering of the profits presumed to arise

---

[95]   Law on Copyrights, Related Rights and Databases (n 18 above), Arts 83 and 84.
[96]   Uniform Benelux Law on Marks (n 12 above), Art 13bis.
[97]   Uniform Benelux Law on Design (n 16 above), Art 14bis.
[98]   Law Modifying the Patents Regime (n 19 above), Art 81(3).
[99]   Uniform Benelux Law on Marks (n 12 above), Art 13bis.
[100]   Uniform Benelux Law on Design (n 16 above), Art 14bis.
[101]   Law on Copyrights, Related Rights and Databases (n 18 above), Arts 83 and 84.
[102]   Law Modifying the Patents Regime (n 19 above), Art 81(3).
[103]   Uniform Benelux Law on Marks (n 12 above), Art 13(A)(2)(5).
[104]   Uniform Benelux Law on Design (n 16 above), Art 14(3).
[105]   Law on Copyrights, Related Rights and Databases (n 18 above), Art 83.
[106]   Criminal Code, Art 191.
[107]   Uniform Benelux Law on Marks (n 12 above), Art 13bis and Uniform Benelux Law on Design (n 16 above), Art 14bis.
[108]   Uniform Benelux Law on Marks (n 12 above), Art 13bis and Uniform Benelux Law on Design (n 16 above), Art 14bis.

from the illicit activities, to the extent it can be proved that the infringement was committed in bad faith.[109]

Patent Infringements are subject, upon request of the right-holder to the judge, to damages, and publication of the judgment in newspapers at the defendant's costs. The right-holder may also ask for the destruction of the infringing goods.[110]   **19.131**

Infringements to the Law of 24 July 1909 on the regime of wines and similar beverages and to the Ministerial Decree of 25 October 1949 relating to the protection of appellations of origin for Luxemburg wines[111] are principally subject to imprisonment of six to eight months and/or a criminal fine of EUR 251 to EUR 15,000.[112]   **19.132**

VI. LIABILITY OF CUSTOMS AUTHORITIES AND RIGHT-HOLDERS

A. Liability of right-holders and sanctions

Non-permitted use of any information provided by customs to the right-holder under the Regulation, within the meaning of Articles 12 and/or 19(3) of the Regulation, and causing harm to a third party, entitles the latter to claim for damages, according to the law of torts.[113]   **19.133**

This is the only general rule that may apply in such a case under Luxembourg law, as the use of information regarding one or two persons would probably not be considered as the processing of personal data according to the Law on the protection of individuals with regard to the processing of personal data.[114] There is no specific provision in national legislation prohibiting any use of such information provided by customs to the right-holder under the Regulation.   **19.134**

Cases in which right-holders may be held liable under Article 19(3) of the Regulation would be dealt with under Article 1382 of the Civil Code, according to which any person causing harm to a third party must redress such prejudice.   **19.135**

---

[109] Uniform Benelux Law on Marks (n 12 above), Art 13(A)(2)(5)and Uniform Benelux Law on Design (n 16 above), Art 14(3).

[110] Law Modifying the Patents Regime (n 19 above), Arts 80 and 81.

[111] *Arrêté ministériel du 25 octobre 1949 concernant la protection des appellations d'origine pour les vins luxembourgeois* (n 26 above).

[112] *Loi du 24 juillet 1909 sur le régime des vins et boissons similaires* (n 24 above), Art 26.

[113] Civil Code, Art 1382.   [114] N 68 above.

B. Liability of customs authorities and sanctions

19.136 In our view, and unless Articles 19(1) and 19(2) of the Regulation can be considered as meaning that only a provision *specifically* aimed at governing the liability of customs in case of action, failure or omission to take action—which interpretation we reject—the Law of 1 September 1988 relating to the civil liability of the State and local authorities[115] applies to customs, inter alia, if a prejudice is caused to a person affected by an *ex officio* measure under Article 4 of the Regulation,[116] or to a right-holder owing to a failure or omission to take action after the filing of an application for action.[117] This Law renders the State and other public corporations liable under Article 1382 of the Civil Code,[118] according to which any person causing harm to a third party must redress such prejudice. In this context, only the civil courts have jurisdiction. The majority of the case law admits that the cancellation or reformation by a judge of an individual administrative decision points to a fault of the State. However, even though the judicial courts accept jurisdiction for examining the legality of decisions and managing activities of the public authorities, they refuse to control their suitability.

19.137 As a consequence, if a fault of customs causes a prejudice to a third party, whether to right-holders or other third parties, in case of failure to detect goods after an application for action has been filed, these persons should be entitled to claim for damages before the civil courts.

Conclusion

19.138 One of the main advantages of the border measures system as it is applied in Luxembourg is that customs adopt border measures irrespective of the type of customs procedure under which the suspect goods are placed. The Luxembourg customs officers also embrace a broad view of what constitutes piracy, and in particular, trade mark counterfeiting, thus enabling right-holders to bring their case before the courts in numerous situations involving an intellectual property right infringement.

19.139 Although there is no national legislation in Luxembourg concerning border measures in matters involving intellectual property right infringements, the Regulation plays its intended role perfectly, and customs adhere to its provisions as far as possible.

---

[115] *Loi du 1er septembre 1988 relative à la responsabilité civile de l'Etat et des collectivités publiques,* [1988] Mémorial 1000.　　　　[116] Cf Reg 1383/2003, Art 19(2).
[117] Cf ibid, Art 19(1).　　　[118] '*Code Civil*'.

However, there is still a gap to fill with regard to Article 11 of the Regulation, and the intervention of the legislator would therefore be needed before customs may undertake any action with respect to a simplified procedure. **19.140**

More generally speaking, Luxembourg Customs are very approachable and open-minded, and a quick response may often be expected from them. These qualities render easier the fight against infringements of intellectual property rights in Luxembourg, at least in the field. The airfield, should we say, as nearly all traffic in non-authentic goods in Luxembourg pass through the Luxembourg Airport. **19.141**

20

MALTA

David Tonna and Antoine Camilleri

Introduction

The regulation of border measures under Maltese law, in the fight against **20.01** counterfeiting, commenced back in the year 2000 with the promulgation by the Maltese Parliament of a law entitled Intellectual Property Rights (Cross-Border Measures) Law.[1] The scope behind this Law was that of establishing measures relating to the importation into Malta, and exportation and re-exportation from Malta, of goods in contravention of intellectual property rights.[2]

As a background to intellectual property law in Malta, it is interesting to note that the **20.02** years 2000 to 2004 will undoubtedly be remembered as the period in which Maltese legislation experienced its most radical developments in the field of intellectual property law. This fact is easily evidenced by the coming into force not only of the Intellectual Property Rights (Cross-Border Measures) Law but also of other intellectual property law-related legislation dealing with trade marks, copyright, designs, patents and supplementary protection certificates. The titles of this legislation are as follows: the Copyright Law[3], the Trade Marks Law,[4] and the Patents and Designs Law.[5]

---

[1] Law VIII of 2000, reported in Chapter 414 of The Laws Of Malta, brought into force on 29 February 2000.   [2] As described in the short title to the Law itself.

[3] Law XIII of 2000 of 25 April 2000, reported in Chapter 415 of The Laws Of Malta, brought into force by Legal Notice No 155 of 2000 whereby it was established that Parts I to X and XII to XIII of the Copyright Law 2000 were to become effective as from 24 August 2000 whilst that Part XI, dealing with 'Collective Administration of Rights', became effective as from 1st January 2001. This Law has repealed the 1967 Copyright Law, (Act VI of 1967, Chapter 196 of The Laws Of Malta).

[4] Law XVI of 2000 of 23 June 2000, reported in Chapter 416 of The Laws of Malta, brought into force by Legal Notice No 282 of 2000 whereby all the contents and provisions of the Trade Marks Law 2000 were made effective as from 1 January 2001. This Law has repealed Part III of the Industrial Property (Protection) Ordinance and every reference to trade marks in Parts IV and V of this Law.

[5] Law XVII of 2000 of 11 July 2000, reported in Chapter 417 of The Laws Of Malta, brought into force on 1 July 2002. This Law has repealed Part I and Part II of the Industrial Property

20.03 This legislation has essentially been the result of Malta's obligations subsequent to signing the World Trade Agreement in 1995 which incorporated the TRIPs Agreement.[6] However, it is to be noted from the outset that all of the intellectual property laws which were promulgated by the Maltese Parliament have gone beyond TRIPs. This point can be easily ascertained from the legislation itself where one may note the quite extensive influence of European Community law notions in all of the above-mentioned Laws. Given that the level of protection for intellectual property rights provided by EC legislation is greater than that provided in the TRIPs Agreement, and in line with Malta's intention at that time to proceed with EU accession,[7] it was decided back in 2000 that Malta's new intellectual property laws should not only be TRIPs-compliant but also in line with the *Acquis Communautaire.*

20.04 The Intellectual Property Rights (Cross-Border Measures) Law (the 'Cross-Border Measures Law') was essentially structured on the wording utilized by EC Regulation 3295/94.[8] The reason for this is because the Cross-Border Measures Law was promulgated in the year 2000 when the EC Regulation was still into force.

20.05 Subsequent to the entry into force of EC Regulation 1383/2003[9] (the 'Regulation'), the Cross-Border Measures Law remained in effect and was not amended to bring it in line with the changes brought about by the Regulation. In addition, it is interesting to note that there are no known present high-level discussions in the Maltese Government considering the repeal or the amendment of the Cross-Border Measures Law. Given the fact that this Law has been drafted along the lines of EC Regulation 3295/94, and considering the fact that EC Regulation 1383/2003 has brought about a number of developments in the field of EC intellectual property law, the Maltese legal situation is currently somewhat unclear on a number of legal aspects. At present, the policy adopted by Maltese Customs is that of applying the provisions of both the Cross-Border Measures Law and of the Regulation. In those situations where a conflict or a doubt arises between these two pieces of legislation, the Regulation is being

---

(Protection) Ordinance and every reference to patents and to designs in Parts IV, V, and VI of this Law.

[6] Agreement on Trade-Related Aspects of Intellectual Property Rights, Including Trade in Counterfeit Goods, 1 January 1995.

[7] Malta became a Member State of the EU in its recent enlargement of 1 May 2004.

[8] Council Reg (EC) No 3295/94 of 22 December 1994 laying down measures to prohibit the release for free circulation, export, re-export or entry for a suspensive procedure of counterfeit and pirated goods OJ L 341/8, 30.12.1994.

[9] Council Reg (EC) No 1383/2003 of 22 July 2003 concerning customs action against goods suspected of infringing certain intellectual property rights and the measures to be taken against goods found to have infringed such rights, OJ L 196/7, 2.8.2003.

given precedence and is the law that is being observed on the basis of the principle of direct effect.

I. SUBJECT MATTER AND SCOPE OF THE NATIONAL LAW APPLYING THE REGULATION

Throughout this Part which is dedicated to the subject matter and the scope of **20.06** Maltese law applying the Regulation, we will examine under what customs procedures Maltese Customs will act against suspect goods (section A), the definition of infringing goods in the light of Maltese law (section B) and the goods excluded from the scope of the Regulation (section C).

A. Customs procedure of the goods

The Regulation applies to various customs procedures as outlined by the **20.07** Regulation itself in Article 1(1). Maltese Customs observe the application of the Regulation in all such scenarios and, on this point, it is worth referring to Article 4 of the Cross-Border Measures Law which states that:

> The entry into Malta, export or re-export, release for free circulation, temporary importation, placing in a free zone or free warehouse of goods found to be goods infringing an intellectual property right shall be prohibited.

Besides instances of importation, export or re-exportation of goods which are **20.08** clear, customs also act where goods are placed in a 'free-zone or free warehouse'. The latter situations involve instances of transhipments of goods. The only instance where goods are not checked by Maltese Customs is when the goods enter Malta while 'in transit', that is, when the goods, though on the Maltese territory, remain on board the vessel which is carrying them.

On this provision of the law it is important to keep in mind that Malta is a small **20.09** country;[10] however, the strategic location of Malta in the centre of the Mediterranean Sea has given rise to extensive commercial shipping activities to and from the island, in particular in the transhipment of goods in containers.

---

[10] (1) Geography: The area of the country is 316 square kilometres. It consists of an archipelago: Malta, Gozo, and Comino and three other smaller uninhabited islets. The country lies at the centre of the Mediterranean Sea, 93km south of Sicily and 288km north of Africa. (2) Population: In the year 2002 population was 397,500. Density is of 1,249 inhabitants per square kilometre. (3) Languages: Malta has two official languages: Maltese and English.

B. Definition of infringing goods

(1) Counterfeit goods

20.10 Article 2(1)(a) of the Cross-Border Measures Law is substantially identical to Article 2(1)(a) of the Regulation with the exception that the Maltese law does not make reference to Council Regulation (EC) No 40/94 of 20 December 1993 on the Community Trade Mark.[11] However, Maltese Customs take cognizance of Community Trade Marks which are registered under the regime provided by Regulation 40/94 and apply the Cross-Border Measures Law and Regulation 1383/2003 in respect of trade marks which are registered locally or with the Office for Harmonization in the Internal Market.

20.11 Maltese Customs apply a relatively wide interpretation of Article 2(1)(a) of both the Cross-Border Measures Law and of the Regulation since action has been taken not only in respect of those goods bearing without authorization a trade mark which is identical to another trade mark or which cannot be distinguished in its essential aspects from such trade mark. For instance, Maltese Customs have been known to detain under the provisions of the Cross-Border Measures Law consignments of goods bearing the mark 'NIKELINE' since these goods were clearly in violation of the Maltese registered trade mark 'NIKE'.

20.12 However, in all probability, Maltese Customs would have difficulty in detaining consignments of goods bearing without authorization a trade mark in respect of goods which are different from those for which the trade mark is registered. This does not mean that Maltese Customs would automatically release any such consignment since they would, most probably, first prefer to hear what the right-holder or his representative would have to say on this point. It is therefore possible that customs would decide to detain the consignment and then leave it up to the right-holder to take responsibility as to whether to file legal proceedings against the consignee and to secure the seizure of the consignment. The question is particularly sensitive in respect of goods which, though not being identical to those covered by the registered trade mark, may be considered to be similar or which could be considered substitutable or interchangeable by consumers. The reputation in Malta of the trade mark in question would also be of particular relevance.

20.13 Maltese Customs would also be willing to detain consignments of goods on the basis of trade marks which have still not been validly registered as such under Regulation 40/94 or under the Maltese Trade Marks Law.[12] Again the issue of the

---

[11] OJ L 11, 14.01.1994, p.1. Reg last amended by Reg (EC) No 807/2003.

[12] Art 5(3) of the Cross-Border Measures Law, dealing with the application for action by customs authorities, makes it clear that the proof to be submitted by the holder of a right may consist in documentary evidence showing the filing of an application for the registration of a trade mark, patent, or design right.

reputation in Malta of the trade mark in question would play an important role. In addition, it is to be noted that, once registered, a trade mark would have effect as from the filing date of the trade mark application. Therefore, it is conceivable for Maltese Customs to agree to the detention of goods which bear a mark which has significant reputation in Malta especially if such a mark is awaiting registration as a trade mark with the Maltese or the EU's authorities.

In determining whether goods can be seen as infringing a trade mark holder's **20.14** rights under Maltese law, Maltese Customs would also have recourse to the relevant provisions in the Maltese Trade Marks Law. However, any such recourse would be made within the ambits of the provisions of Article 2(1)(a) of the Cross-Border Measures Law and of the Regulation, as discussed above.

Article 10 of the Maltese Trade Marks Law lists the instances whereby a trade mark **20.15** is infringed. Thus, a registered trade mark is infringed where a person uses,[13] in the course of trade, a sign which is identical with the trade mark in relation to goods or services which are identical to those for which the first mark is registered.[14] In addition, a person also infringes a registered trade mark if he uses a sign in the course of trade where, because this sign is identical with the trade mark and is used in relation to goods or services similar to those for which the trade mark is registered, or this sign is similar to the trade mark and is used in relation to goods or services identical with or similar to those for which the trade mark is registered, there exists a likelihood of confusion on the part of the public, including the likelihood of association with the trade mark. It is to be noted that the mere association without a likelihood of confusion would not be considered as constituting an infringement of the registered trade mark.[15] These provisions of the Trade Marks Law could be easily invoked within the ambits of application of Article 2(1)(a) of the Cross-Border Measures Law and of the Regulation.

To date, only a few civil proceedings dealing with issues of cross-border measures **20.16** have been fully determined by the Maltese courts. A number of other proceedings[16] are presently pending and are being heard in front of the courts. The judgments that have been delivered have been based on Article 2(1)(a) of the Cross-Border Measures Law dealing with counterfeit goods. In *Dr David Tonna*

---

[13] For the purposes of Art 10 of the Maltese Trade Marks Law, Art 10(4) states that a person is considered to use a sign if he (a) affixes it to goods or the packaging thereof; (b) offers or exposes goods for sale, puts them on the market or stocks them for those purposes under the sign, or offers or supplies services under the sign; (c) imports or exports goods under this sign; or (d) uses the sign on business papers or in advertising. In Art 10(5), the Law also specifies that a person who applies a registered trade mark to material intended to be used for labelling or packaging goods, as a business paper, or for advertising goods or services, shall be treated as a party to any use of the material which infringes the registered trade mark if when he applied the mark he knew or had reason to believe that the application of the mark was not duly authorized by the proprietor or a licensee.

[14] Maltese Trade Marks Law, Art 10(1). [15] Ibid, Art 10(2).

[16] Approximately 30 other civil proceedings in all.

noe v Dr Richard Sladden et noe,[17] the First Hall of the Civil Court found in favour of the plaintiff Philip Morris Products SA and ordered the Comptroller of Customs to destroy a container-load of counterfeit 'Marlboro' branded cigarettes since these cigarettes were found to infringe the plaintiff's rights in its Maltese registered trade marks. An identical judgment was obtained in *Dr David Tonna noe v Dr Mark Busuttil et noe*[18] where a large consignment of counterfeit sports shoes bearing the registered trade marks of the plaintiff Nike International Limited was destroyed by the Comptroller of Customs after these sports shoes were declared by the court to be counterfeit goods.

20.17   As noted above, the situation would be different in respect of goods which are different from those for which the trade mark is registered. In fact the Trade Marks Law contemplates such a scenario and outlines another ground of infringement of a registered trade mark in situations where a person uses in the course of trade a sign which is identical with or similar to the trade mark in relation to goods or services which are not similar to those for which the trade mark is registered where the trade mark in question has reputation in Malta and the use, of the sign, without due cause, takes unfair advantage of, or is detrimental to, the distinctive character or the repute of the trade mark.[19] It is still a moot point whether this provision might be successfully invoked within the ambits of cross-border measures legislation before the Maltese courts.

20.18   Though there is probably no precedent for taking any such measures, Maltese Customs would definitely take the required action against trade mark symbols (including logos, labels, stickers, brochures, instructions for use, or guarantee documents bearing such symbols), even if these were delivered separately from the goods. The same applies in respect of packaging materials bearing the trade marks of counterfeit goods, delivered separately. Customs would take action in both instances according to Article 2(1)(a) of the Cross-Border Measures Law and of the Regulation. In any such circumstance, it might be of assistance establishing a link for any such symbols and packaging material with the goods being consigned separately. If this cannot be done, action may be taken by the right-holder where it is clear that any such symbols and packaging materials are to be affixed or used in conjunction with goods as understood by Article 2(1)(a)(i) of the Regulation.

(2) *Pirated goods*

20.19   Application of the Cross-Border Measures Law within the ambits of 'pirated goods' has not been a frequent occurrence in Malta. However, nothing will

---

[17] [599/02], 17 November 2003, decided by the First Hall of the Civil Court.
[18] [1102/02], 1 December 2003, decided by the First Hall of the Civil Court.
[19] Maltese Trade Marks Law, Art 10(3).

preclude customs from taking action against copies which infringe copyright, neighbouring rights and design rights under Maltese law. Difficulties would probably arise in those situations where goods embody or contain copies which infringe any of the above rights since Maltese Customs would probably ask for sufficient evidence from the right-holder that the goods clearly violate the right-holder's exclusive rights according to law.

In applying these provisions of the Cross-Border Measures Law, customs would **20.20** have recourse to the Maltese Copyright Law and the Maltese Patents And Designs Law. As far as copyright is concerned, the right-holder would need to show Maltese Customs that the alleged pirated goods infringe its exclusive reproduction right (that is, the right against unauthorized copying of the work) outlined by Article 7 of the Copyright Law. It is interesting to note that presently there are two civil proceedings in front of the Maltese courts which have been initiated by a leading European satellite broadcasting organization against two different consignees who tried to import into Malta a number of blank decoder cards. The point being raised by the plaintiff in these proceedings is that these decoder cards cannot be put to any use in Malta other than to copy thereon the codes of satellite broadcasting agencies in violation of their copyright in their encrypted codes. The proceedings are based on the circumvention of the technological measures (in this case the scrambling and encryption processes) that are put in place by such broadcasting organizations in their satellite transmissions and in their genuine decoder cards, which circumventing activity would take place by the defendants once they used the decoder cards containing pirated codes. Such circumventing act would constitute a copyright infringement under the Copyright Law.[20] The question being considered by the courts is whether such an activity amounts to a violation of copyright. Essentially, the courts are being asked to determine that the only use which these decoder cards may be put to is that of circumventing an effective technological measure, that is, amounting to the infringement of copyright of the broadcasting organizations. If this violation is established, then the courts should be in a position to determine that the imported decoder cards are pirated goods and that they should be destroyed according to the provisions of the Cross-Border Measures Act, as requested by the plaintiff.

(3) Goods infringing other intellectual property rights

Regarding designs and patents, recourse would need to be made to the Patents and **20.21** Designs Law. To date, no action has ever been taken by any right-holder with Maltese Customs for an infringement of a patent or of a design. It is important to note that plant varieties are recognized by the Malta Patents and Designs Law and

---

[20] According to the Copyright Law, Art 42(1).

may be registered as a patent under the provisions of the same Law. As for trade mark and copyright law, reference would be made to the alleged infringing act of the consignee to the detriment of the right-holder's exclusive rights as recognized by the Patents and Designs Law. Next to patent protection, supplementary certificates for plant varieties and medicinal products may be obtained according to Maltese law and this by virtue of two pieces of subsidiary legislation which have been issued under the provisions of the Maltese Patents and Designs Law.[21] To date, no action has ever been taken by any right-holder with Maltese Customs in respect of any infringement of a patent, supplementary protection certificate, designation of origin, or geographical indication under Maltese law.

20.22 The Cross-Border Measures Law does not recognize infringements of intellectual property rights other than those stated above. Therefore, the provisions of the Regulation would need to be directly invoked by right-holders, where this is possible. It is to be noted that there is presently no national legislation dealing with designations of origin or geographical indications under Maltese law. Therefore the principles emanating from Council Regulations (EEC) 1576/89,[22] (EEC) 2081/92,[23] and (EC) 1493/1999[24] would need to be relied upon in situations which require the invocation of rights associated with designations of origin or geographical indications, where this is possible.

(4) Moulds and matrices

20.23 Article 2(2) of the Cross-Border Measures Law states that materials and implements, the predominant use of which has been for the manufacture of a counterfeit trade mark or of goods bearing such a trade mark, for the manufacture of goods infringing a patent or for the manufacture of pirated goods shall be treated as goods infringing an intellectual property right, provided that the use of such materials and implements infringes the rights of the holder of the right in question under Maltese law. It should be noted that the scope of equivalent provision in Article 2(3) of the Regulation is more extensive. In addition, the text of the Regulation does not refer to materials and implements but to a 'mould or matrix'. More significantly, whilst the prohibitive act under the Cross-Border Measures Law is tied up to 'the predominant use' of materials and implements, the Regulation is stricter in application since the moulds or matrices must have been 'specifically designed or adapted' for the manufacture of goods infringing an intellectual property right.

---

[21] Patents (Plant Protection Products) Regulations, 2002—issued by Legal Notice 260 of 2002—and Patents (Medicinal Products) Regulations, 2002—issued by Legal Notice 261 of 2002.

[22] OJ L 160/1, 12.6.1989,1 as last amended by Reg (EC) 3378/94 of the European Parliament and of the Council (OJ L 366/1, 31.12.1994).

[23] OJ L 208/1, 24.7.1992, as last amended by Reg (EC) 806/2003.

[24] OJ L 179/1, 14.7.1999, as last amended by Reg (EC) 806/2003.

The application of the above-mentioned Maltese and EC provisions could be **20.24**
quite tricky under Maltese law since, with the exception of a limited application
of the rule within the ambit of the application of the provisions in the Maltese
Copyright Law prohibiting the use of devices circumventing effective technological measures, these provisions may in practice prove difficult to apply under any
other national intellectual property rights legislation.

C. Goods excluded by the Regulation

(1) Parallel imported goods

Article 3 of the Cross-Border Measures Law is almost identical to Article 3 of the **20.25**
Regulation. To date, there is no knowledge of any action taken at cross-border
level in Malta in respect of parallel imported genuine goods.

In the event that genuine parallel imported goods are imported into Malta and the **20.26**
right-holder gets to know of any such consignment through Maltese Customs, it
would then be up to the right-holder to decide whether to take appropriate action
under any of the domestic intellectual property legislation. However, the goods
would first need to be *released* by Maltese Customs. The reason for this is because
the Cross-Border Measures Law does not contemplate the detention of parallel
imported genuine goods.[25]

(2) Goods which have been manufactured under conditions other than those which have been agreed with the right-holder

The same principles discussed above would apply in respect of goods which have **20.27**
been manufactured under conditions other than those agreed with the right-
holder. Thus, these goods will be released by Maltese Customs and it would then
be up to the right-holder to take any action it deems fit under any provision of
domestic intellectual property legislation.

---

[25] As a matter of interest Art 12 of the Maltese Trade Marks Law reflects the doctrine of exhaustion which is presently being observed throughout the EU. Art 12 states as follows:
   '(1) A trade mark shall not entitle the proprietor to prohibit its use in relation to goods bearing
      that trade mark which have been put on the market by the proprietor or with his consent.
   (2) The provisions of subarticle (1) shall not apply where there are legitimate reasons for the pro-
      prietor to oppose further commercialization of the goods particularly where the condition of
      the goods is changed or impaired after they have been put on the market.
   (3) For the purpose of this article "market" means the market in Malta and as from 1 May 2004,
      the market in any member State.'

(3) Goods contained in travellers' personal baggage

20.28 Maltese Customs tend to interpret Article 3(2) of the Regulation and its counter-part found in Article 3(3) of the Cross-Border Measures Law very narrowly. Prior to May 2004 when Malta joined the EU, Maltese Customs had always blocked importations of small quantities of goods which appeared to them to be goods infringing an intellectual property right. For instance, on various occasions Malta prevented importation of goods found in traveller's baggage where this consisted of a few garments or of a handful of counterfeit watches. Presently traveller's baggage is still controlled by customs though, since Malta's accession to the EU, the controls on the baggage of travellers originating from within the EU has substantially decreased. Customs do not place much importance on the duty free allowance of EUR 175 and tend to take into account the value of the counterfeit or pirated products instead of that of a genuine product. In ascertaining whether the goods imported have a non-commercial nature as is contemplated by Article 3(2) of the Regulation, Maltese Customs consider the quantities imported and the regularity of similar importations by the same individuals. This helps in ascertaining whether the importations in question form part of commercial traffic, in which case the goods would definitely be detained by Maltese Customs. However, as stated above, customs tend to adopt a very stringent approach when applying the above-mentioned provisions of the Cross-Border Measures Law and of the Regulation and, in most cases, any amount of goods being imported which may qualify as infringing an intellectual property right would be almost certainly detained. Though this might not be altogether in line with the provisions of the Regulation, it is suggested that the fact that customs are detaining small quantities of goods forming part of a traveller's baggage may eliminate any such traveller's future prospects of importing larger consignments of the same goods where these are counterfeit. It is to be noted that a number of travellers tend to 'test' the reaction of Maltese Customs when they are confronted with the importation of goods of a particular brand. Clearly, customs action in this regard has definitely yielded its fruits.

II. APPLICATION FOR ACTION BY THE CUSTOMS AUTHORITIES

20.29 The so called *ex officio* procedure will be examined in section A, whilst the lodging and processing of applications for customs action will be discussed in section B.

A. Measures prior to an application for action by the customs authorities ('*ex officio* measures')

The majority of border measures to date which have been taken with the inter- **20.30** vention of Maltese Customs, have actually been the result of *ex officio* procedures which have been initiated under the provisions of the Cross-Border Measures Law.[26] Customs have utilized the *ex officio* action only in situations where they have had sufficient grounds to believe and to suspect that the goods in question actually infringe an intellectual property right. Various factors are used by Maltese Customs in addressing this question. For instance, a number of border measures in respect of counterfeit tobacco products have been taken in the framework of *ex officio* actions. The factors which led customs to suspect that the goods were counterfeit were various, such as the origin of the goods, their destination, certain suspicious markings on the products,[27] the details of the consignees, false declarations on the bill of lading, and other related factors.

The strategy developed by customs with right-holders is as follows. First of all, **20.31** they would do their utmost to get in contact with the right-holder himself or with his legal or intellectual property representative in Malta. Once this is done, it is in the interest of the right-holder to communicate immediately to Maltese Customs his request to be provided with samples via his representative in Malta. In turn, this would allow the representative to examine the samples and to take digital pictures of them which are then forwarded to the right-holder. In most cases, the above procedure would not take any more than one or two working days and, on the basis of the digital pictures, the right-holder should be able to determine whether the goods in question are actually counterfeit or not. In addition to the samples, customs would usually give other information relating to the quantity of goods and the manner of transportation being utilized (that is, whether by air or sea-freight).

The deadline of three working days is strictly applied by customs since otherwise, **20.32** any eventual civil proceedings commenced by the right-holder against the consignee could be challenged on the non-observance of this time period. However, if the above procedure is effectively observed by Maltese Customs, the right-holder, and his legal representative, the time period of three working days should not pose any particular difficulties especially where this period happens to be

---

[26] The *ex officio* action is outlined in Art 6 of this Law.
[27] For instance, a consignment of counterfeit cigarettes was detected on the basis of a number of spelling mistakes in the health warnings on the packaging of the master cases and outercases of the cigarettes. Another cigarette consignment had duty free tags on the outercases of the cigarettes which tags looked counterfeit. This was ascertained by Maltese Customs once they contacted the customs authorities of the country for which the goods were destined.

'extended' by non-working days (for example, a Saturday and a Sunday). Having stated this, it is interesting to note that prior to the application of the provisions of the Regulation by Maltese Customs in the context of *ex officio* measures, Article 6 of the Cross-Border Measures Law allowed a longer period of five working days which was almost always 'extended' by an intervening weekend.

20.33   Overall, from experience the time period of three working days has only in isolated instances posed a problem to Maltese Customs to enable the right-holder to take cross-border measures action. Most of these isolated circumstances were actually not the result of this tight deadline but more due to the lack of interest shown by certain right-holders in taking the required action.

B. The lodging and processing of applications for customs action

(1) Persons entitled to file an application for action

Definition of 'right-holders' under the Regulation

20.34   The persons entitled to file an application for action with customs are defined in Article 2 of Regulation 1383/2003. Paragraph (a) of this provision is pretty clear in that it outlines and identifies by name those right-holders which may directly file any such application with customs.

20.35   However, paragraph (1)(b) of Article 2 is somewhat vague in that it allows any other person authorized to use any of the intellectual property rights mentioned in paragraph (1)(a), or a representative of the right-holder or authorized user to file the application. One of the difficulties raised by this provision relates to the fact that it does not distinguish between exclusive and non-exclusive users or licensees of a particular intellectual property right. Moreover, in Malta one could have different exclusive users for certain geographic areas of the country. Who would be entitled to file such an application?

20.36   To date, the authors have no knowledge of any action that would have been taken by any such authorized users. Most probably, the persons least likely to face difficulties are exclusive licensees for all of the territory of Malta, especially exclusive trade mark licensees, since the Maltese Trade Marks Law specifically indicates that exclusive licensees have the same rights of the proprietor in respect of infringement of the registered trade mark in question.[28] Certain exclusive licensees may even be given the same rights as an assignee of the registered trade mark, that is, such licensees would have the same rights as the owner of the registered trade mark.[29] To a certain extent, the same may be said of patents, registered designs, and

---

[28] Trade Marks Law, Arts 24 to 29.   [29] Ibid, Art 29.

copyrights since the Maltese Patents and Designs Law and the Maltese Copyright Law recognize the notion of licensing of these intellectual property rights.[30]

The matter gets more complicated where a distributor, a commercial agent or any **20.37** other person who has interest in the particular intellectual property right decides to file an application for action with Maltese Customs. In these latter situations, most probably, Maltese Customs would require such an entity or person to either (a) request the direct intervention of the right-holder in the lodging of the application in which case the application would be directly in the name of the right-holder, or (b) request any such a person to obtain documentary evidence which authorizes the latter to file any such application with customs.

In accordance with the Implementing Regulation,[31] Maltese Customs would **20.38** similarly allow an application submitted by legal representatives, an intellectual property right agent, or a collecting society. The term 'representative' as stated by Article 1, first indent, of Regulation 1891/2004 is taken to include both natural and legal persons. On this point, it is interesting to note that the definition given to the term 'holder of a right' in Article 2 of the Cross-Border Measures Law makes it clear that the holder of a right or any other person authorized to use the right may be represented by a natural or legal person. In addition, this provision states that this notion shall include a collecting society, which has as its sole or principal purpose the management, or administration of copyright or neighbouring rights.

Proof of entitlement to file an application for action

For right-holders stricto sensu

In proving their entitlement over the intellectual property which is sought to be **20.39** registered with Maltese Customs when submitting an application for action, right-holders for now need not submit any documentary evidence to customs. It would be sufficient to identify clearly the intellectual property right concerned in the application. That said, with the exception of certain trade marks and copyrights, it might be very difficult, if not impossible, to define precisely the intellectual property right in question in the application. Therefore, it would be in the interest of right-holders to provide Maltese Customs with documentary evidence which shows their entitlement over the right concerned. For instance, such evidence could consist in copies of registration certificates for any trade mark, design,

---

[30] Patents and Designs Law, Arts 35 to 38 and 82 to 87; Copyright Act, Art 24.
[31] Commission Reg (EC) No 1891/2004 of 21 October 2004 laying down provisions for the implementation of Council Reg (EC) No 1383/2003 concerning action against goods suspected of infringing certain intellectual property rights and the measures to be taken against goods found to have infringed such rights, OJ L 328, 30.10.2004.

or patent and supplementary protection certificates where any such registration has effect for Malta.[32]

20.40   As far as copyright is concerned, since there is no copyright registration system in Malta, documentary evidence could subsist in submitting copies of copyright registration certificates where these have been obtained abroad and which may be conferred some effects for Malta under the provisions of the Maltese Copyright Law.[33]

20.41   One may therefore submit that the present practice of Maltese Customs is not exactly in line with the Implementing Regulation since the way Article 2(1) is drafted makes it a burden on the right-holder to provide the required proof by means of any of a number of documents mentioned in the same provision. Thus, if the right being invoked is a registered trade mark, then Article 2(1) of the Implementing Regulation would require that extracts or copies of the national trade marks or of the Community Trade Mark in the name of the right-holder would need to be provided to customs authorities.

20.42   It is questionable whether such proof could be submitted in the form of copies obtained from a private database. Much would depend on the type of private database from which the copies or extracts are obtained and the type of intellectual property in question. In any such case, it would be in the discretion of Maltese Customs whether to accept any such evidence and whether they would still ask the right-holder to provide documentary evidence of a more official nature. In all probability, Maltese Customs would allow documentary evidence obtained from EU institutions or from other official bodies, such as from the CTM-Online database for Community Trade Marks, in line with Article 2(1), last paragraph, of the Implementing Regulation.

20.43   Difficulties could arise in respect of designations of origin, geographical indications or designations since, as remarked above, such intellectual property rights are not explicitly recognized by any Maltese domestic legislation. The right-holder might decide to submit documentary evidence of registration of any such rights obtained in any Member State of the European Union and request that Maltese Customs detain any consignment which might appear to infringe these rights. In any case, it would be extremely difficult for the right-holder to enforce such rights in Malta before the courts. Having stated the above, Maltese Customs would rely on the provisions of Article 2(1) of the Implementing Regulation

---

[32] For instance, taking the example of trade marks, a right-holder might decide to submit copies of the registration certificate for a Maltese registered trade mark or for a Community Trade Mark.

[33] Such certificates may for instance help to substantiate entitlement to copyright protection either on the basis of authorship or by reference to the country where the work was created or published, in line with Arts 4 and 5 of the Copyright Law.

which requires proof consisting of two mandatory elements: proof that the person concerned is the producer or group and proof that the designation of origin or geographical indication has been registered.

The Cross-Border Measures Law offers a number of examples relating to the proof **20.44** which the right-holder might decide to give to Maltese Customs when filing an application. In those instances where the application is submitted by the right-holder itself, and where the right is capable of registration such as in the case of a trade mark, patent or design right, the proof could consist in the registration certificate or at least in an official document ascertaining that an application for registration of this right has been lodged with the relevant office. In the case of a copyright, a neighbouring right, or a design right that is unregistered or for which an application has not been lodged, proof could consist in showing evidence of authorship or the person's status as original holder.[34]

For persons authorized to use the right

As yet there is no hard and fast rule which needs to be observed by persons author- **20.45** ized to use the right in question when they submit their application for action with Maltese Customs. Therefore, much would depend on the type of authority the applicant would have over the intellectual property right concerned.

It is not clear whether Maltese Customs would require an applicant to provide **20.46** evidence of their contractual relationship with the right-holder. However, exclusive or non-exclusive licensees of trade marks, patents, or designs, especially those who have registered their interest in the intellectual property[35] with the Malta Industrial Property Registrations Directorate,[36] would be well-advised to submit a copy of their licensing agreement with the right-holder to Maltese Customs together with the application for action. Of course, if would be important for any such licensing agreement to recognize the licensee's right to file any such applications with Maltese Customs for cross-border measures actions. This would facilitate the job of Maltese Customs and would increase the chances of the licensee in having his application granted.

As pointed out above, the agreement establishing the relationship between the **20.47** authorized user and the right-holder should preferably be presented to customs. Except in the case of exclusive licensees which have the rights mentioned above

---

[34] Cross-Border Measures Law, Art 5(3)(a).

[35] Such as in the case of trade marks where the trade mark licensee will have rights as a licensee in Malta (according to a number of provisions in the same Trademarks Law) only once he is recorded as such with the Malta Industrial Property Registrations Directorate.

[36] This Directorate forms part of the Commerce Division situated in Valletta, Malta and falls within the portfolio of the Maltese Minister responsible for the protection of industrial and intellectual property.

from domestic legislation to represent the interests of the right-holder in Malta, it would be advisable for all other authorized users to present documentary evidence to Maltese Customs which not only shows their entitlement to use the intellectual property right in question but also to take all required action at the borders with customs authorities. On this point, the Cross-Border Measures Law states that where the application is made by any other person authorized to use an intellectual property right, in addition to the proof requested from right-holders when they directly submit an application for action, the document by virtue of which the person is authorized to use the right in question has also to be produced or sufficiently quoted.[37] This will enable customs to grant the application for action. This is also in line with Article 2(2) of the Implementing Regulation.

20.48   In all probability, customs will not determine or question the veracity of such documents and it would be the responsibility of the applicant immediately to inform customs of any changes in its relationship with the right-holder. Where an application is based on an industrial property right such as a trade mark, patent, or design against which a licensee may be registered as a registered user with the Malta Industrial Property Registrations Directorate, for the moment the applicant need not file with customs any documentary evidence which shows its registered user status against the industrial property in question.

For representatives

20.49   As far as representatives of the right-holder are concerned, in all cases Maltese Customs would require proof of authority from the right-holder that is granted to any such person which authorizes him to lodge such an application.[38] This authorization would take the form of a Power of Attorney issued in favour of the representative by the right-holder. According to Maltese laws of civil procedure relating to the execution of documents by persons who are not domiciled or established in Malta, the signatures on the Power of Attorney would need to be first duly notarized and then subsequently duly legalized by the *Apostille* procedure according to the provisions of the 1961 Hague Convention Abolishing the Requirement of Legalization for Foreign Public Documents.[39] In practice, it would suffice if a certified copy of such document is submitted with Maltese Customs by post. Maltese Customs would not insist on a general authority and it would therefore be at the discretion of the right-holder whether to limit the authority to be given to its representative to one or several matters. Given the tight deadline of three working days within such documentation should be provided, Maltese Customs would be

---

[37] Cross-Border Measures Law, Art 5(3)(b).
[38] Ibid, Art 5(3)(c).
[39] Signed on 5 October 1961.

prepared to continue to detain the goods if at least a copy of a signed authorization of Power of Attorney is sent to them. A certified notarized and legalized copy of the Power of Attorney could then be submitted to Maltese Customs later in the proceedings.

Foreign representatives who do not have an office or a legal seat in Malta are not **20.50** authorized to appear before customs. In any case, given the timeframes of the Cross-Border Measures Law, the Regulation and the necessity to initiate civil proceedings before a Maltese court wherever this is necessary, it is always advisable for a right-holder to be represented in Malta by a person or an entity who is established in the country itself.

Presently there are no known special requirements imposed by Maltese Customs **20.51** concerning the entitlement to sign the declaration referred to in Article 6 of the Regulation. Maltese Customs have recently started to require the execution of the standard national application form for action.[40] Until December 2004, the policy adopted by customs was that of requiring the issue of a security in the form of a bank guarantee in favour of the Comptroller of Customs on behalf of the Maltese Customs Department, which security would be in an amount determined by customs and would cover any possible costs which customs might become liable to in the event that a procedure initiated pursuant to Article 9(1) of the Regulation would be discontinued owing to an act or omission of the right-holder or in the event that the goods in question are subsequently found not to infringe an intellectual property right. As of January 2005, Maltese customs officials have required the execution of the standard forms promulgated by the EC Commission which are systematically required in which case the declarations attached to these forms in line with Article 6 of the Regulation would also be required. The declaration would also be required in order to cover any possible payment of costs incurred in accordance with the Cross-Border Measures Law, in particular in keeping the goods under customs control. This new policy has brought Maltese Customs in line with the requirements of Article 3(3) of the Implementing Regulation.

(2) Competent customs department and formal requirements

Competent customs department

The particulars of the Maltese Customs Department which is competent under **20.52** Article 5(2) of EC Regulation 1383/2003 to process applications for customs

---

[40] Ie the National AA application form annexed to the Implementing Regulation, and comprising the standard declaration form under Art 6 of the Basic Reg.

action are as follows:

Malta Customs Department
Customs House
Valletta CMR 02
Malta
Telephone: 00356 2568 5100
Facsimile: 00356 2568 5230
e-mail: iro.galea@gov.mt
website: www.maltacustoms.gov.mt

Form of the application for action

20.53   An application for action with Maltese Customs may be filed by letter or by fax. To date, there is no system in place to accept applications for action by electronic data interchange. Although it is possible for an applicant to file an application via e-mail, Maltese Customs would still require the receipt of the same application via fax or letter. An electronic version of the application for action has been made available.

20.54   It would suffice if the applicant files at least two copies of the application for action. However, it is advisable for the applicant to file not less than four copies of the same application in particular where it contains colour exhibits. Since a copy of the exhibits or other important documentary evidence accompanying the application would be circulated amongst the various customs offices around Malta, the applicant would be well-advised to have a clear copy of its documents in the hands of customs officials posted in all of these offices.

20.55   Presently, it is not clear whether an original declaration or a copy would be required by Maltese Customs under Article 6 of Regulation 1383/2003. Most probably, it would suffice if a certified copy of such a declaration is filed with Maltese Customs.

Language requirements

20.56   As far as language requirements are concerned, Malta has two official languages: Maltese and English. Therefore, it would suffice if the application form filed with Maltese Customs is made out in either the Maltese or the English language. Should an application be based on Article 5(4) of the Regulation, that is, rely on a Community Trade Mark or a Community Design right, a Community plant variety right or a designation of origin or geographical indication or a geographical designation protected by Community law and extend to several Member States, it would be well-considered for the right-holder to file with Maltese Customs at least a certified translation of any documentation in the Maltese or English language.

As to the declaration under Article 6 of the Regulation, it would suffice if it is filed in the Maltese or the English language. If the declaration is filed in another language, it must be accompanied with a certified translation in the Maltese or English language.

(3) *Requirements regarding the contents of the application for action*

Mandatory information

There is no generic hard and fast rule which is applied by Maltese Customs on the information that needs to be submitted with the application for action. Customs would require the right-holder to observe the requisites of paragraphs (i) to (iii) of Article 5(5) of the Regulation. In all probability, Maltese Customs would apply these paragraphs together with equivalent though more detailed provisions found in the Cross-Border Measures Law in Article 5(2)(3)(4)(5).[41] In addition, the description of the goods must be sufficiently detailed as to enable Maltese Customs to recognize and identify them. In addition, Article 5(2)(ii) of the Cross-Border Measures Law requires the application to establish, on a prima facie basis, that the goods infringe the right in question.

20.57

The information that the applicant would need to give to customs in showing the type or pattern of fraud in question should relate to the features which the goods should bear and which would identify them as goods infringing an intellectual property right. The name and address of the contact person for Maltese Customs should preferably be Maltese and have an office or reside in Malta. This person could be either an expert in the field of the right or the legal representative of the right-holder who should be based in Malta.

20.58

Optional information

All other optional information outlined by Article 5(5) of the Regulation, if in the possession of the applicant, should be submitted to Maltese Customs in order for it to be in a position to identify and detain the goods in a faster and more effective manner. Maltese Customs would, in particular, ask for the expected date of arrival of the goods, the means of transport used and any possible identity of the importer, exporter, or holder of the goods.

20.59

---

[41] Art 5(2) requiring a detailed description of the goods and proof of entitlement of the right for the goods in question; Art 5(3) requiring documentary evidence showing the intellectual property right being invoked, or proof of authorship, or proof of authorization of the licensee or of the representative of the holder of the right; Art 5(4) requiring the holder of the right to provide all pertinent information to customs to take a decision on the facts; Art 5(5) requiring the submission of certain specific information in the case of pirated goods or goods infringing a patent.

Additional information specific to the type of intellectual property right referred to in the application

20.60 Since goods infringing an intellectual property right could consist of all sorts of goods, Maltese Customs could ask the applicant to provide specific and unequivocal information concerning the type of intellectual property right being referred to in the application for action and show the manner in which this right is being infringed by its use in connection with the goods.

(4) *Processing and acceptance of the application for action*

20.61 Should customs decide not to process the application for action under Article 5(8) of the Regulation, the applicant has the right under the Cross-Border Measures Law to appeal to the Maltese Minister responsible for customs. Such an appeal would have to be lodged within three working days from the service to the applicant of the notice of the refusal.[42] Such an appeal must be made in writing and must contain a brief statement of the facts and state the reasons for the appeal. In addition, it must be notified as well to the Comptroller of Customs who is required to reply within three working days from receipt of the appeal.

20.62 As yet, Maltese Customs have not set down a period during which they will take action once an application is granted. It is therefore at the discretion of the Comptroller of Customs to decide on the period during which Maltese Customs would suspend the release of or detain suspect goods. Therefore, it would be in the interest of the right-holder to propose a period to the Comptroller in his application. However, having stated this, it is envisaged that Maltese Customs will at least make sure that this period will not exceed one year, in line with the provisions of Article 8(1) of the Regulation.

20.63 As far as pirated goods or goods infringing patents are concerned, the Cross-Border Measures Law states that the information to be provided in the application, where possible, should include by way of indication: (i) the place where the goods are situated or their intended destination; (ii) particulars identifying the consignment or packages; (iii) the scheduled date of arrival or departure of the goods; (iv) the means of transport used; and (v) the identity of the importer, exporter, or holder.

(5) *'Community' applications for action*

Processing of 'Community' applications for action filed with Maltese Customs

20.64 As yet, Maltese Customs still have not received a single 'Community' application which is filed under Article 5(4) of the Regulation where this is filed directly in

---

[42] Cross-Border Measures Law, Art 5(10).

Malta. However, where any such applications are filed, Maltese Customs would follow the provisions of the Implementing Regulation. At present Maltese Customs are in the process of devising a way of converting applications for action which had been filed with them over the last recent years so as to bring them in line with the regime brought about by the Regulation and in accordance with the provisions of the Implementing Regulation. It is likely that all of the applications that had been filed with Maltese Customs would need to be re-filed afresh in line with the Regulation and Implementing Regulation.

Processing of 'Community' applications designating Malta

Where a Community application is filed in another Member State and is made to extend to Malta, customs would register the application on their alert list. When customs decide to take cross-border action on this application, they would start by making contact with the legal representative of the right-holder in Malta who would be mentioned in the application. In addition, customs might decide to make contact directly with the right-holder. **20.65**

III. CONDITIONS GOVERNING ACTION BY CUSTOMS AUTHORITIES AND BY THE AUTHORITIES COMPETENT TO DETERMINE WHETHER GOODS INFRINGE AN INTELLECTUAL PROPERTY RIGHT

A. Conditions governing action by customs authorities

(1) Factual background

The most important customs offices in Malta are situated in Valletta. These offices constitute the premises of the Maltese Customs Department from which all central customs activities are handled. A number of other important customs posts are found over the island, namely the Hal-Luqa Freight Shed and the Hal-Far Groupage Bond. There is also the Customs Bonded Stores in Marsa and the Arrivals Section in the Malta International Airport at Hal-Luqa. All of these offices are front-line offices which deal with anti-counterfeiting. Other offices include the Customs Intelligence Section which is based in Hal-Luqa and the Container Monitoring Unit which is set up at the Malta Freeports Terminal. This Terminal, found in Kalafrana Birzebbuga, is extremely important since it handles **20.66** a total of 1.3 million TEUs[43] every year. Presently there are plans nearly to double this amount to 2.3 million TEUs each year. To date, the Container Monitoring Unit at the Malta Freeports Terminal in conjunction with the Customs central offices in Valletta have been extremely successful in their application of the Cross-Border Measures Law and of the Regulation, in particular in respect of consignments of counterfeit goods that are found in containers which are set to be transhipped via Malta to other destinations.

20.67 The following is some statistical information that has been obtained by customs for action taken under the provisions of the Cross-Border Measures Act as from the year 2001 up to February 2005:

	2001	2002	2003	2004	February 2005
Cigarettes	7,230,000	49,440,000	11,500,000	86,120,000	9,390,000
Garments	9,283	4,458	1,008	38,297	8,179
Sports Shoes	4,000	4,306	3,908	77,714	12,512
Wrist-Watches	600	390	7	10,222	Nil

These figures show that the detention of goods by customs is on the increase, in particular in light of the figures shown above for the year 2004 and up to February 2005.

(2) Notification of customs intervention

20.68 In most cases, the legal representative of the right-holder is notified by Maltese Customs of an intervention by means of a telephone call which is then immediately followed up by an e-mail which is sent directly to the legal representative who normally handles the right-holder's legal interest with customs. Where no legal representative has been appointed, Maltese Customs would notify the right-holder directly by means of an e-mail and/or fax.

20.69 The declarant or holder of the goods is immediately informed of the detention of the goods. In situations where the goods detained are in transhipment, the shipping agent is informed and has the right to be present during the verifications made on the contents of the consignment by customs, by the right-holder or his legal representative, or by any other person who may be appointed by the right-holder to inspect the goods and who is approved by Maltese Customs (see para 20.72 below).

---

[43] TEU is an abbreviation for 'twenty feet equivalent unit'.

(3) *Information to be provided by customs to the right-holder before the latter confirms the infringing nature of the goods*

Once goods suspected of infringing an intellectual property right are detained by   **20.70**
Maltese Customs, certain information will be given to the right-holder under
Article 9(2) of the Regulation. This information would specify the estimated
quantity of the goods. Where the quantity is difficult to ascertain, customs would
inform the right-holder that they would be instructing their officials to carry out
the required checks on the consignment in order to ascertain the precise quantities. In addition, information relating to the country of origin, country of destination and other details relating to the shipment of the goods would be given to the
right-holder. This latter information would usually include information relating
to the consignee, consignor, declarant, or holder of the goods in question.

In order to establish whether an intellectual property right has been infringed,   **20.71**
customs would be prepared to provide the right-holder with every type of information in their possession, as long as this does not breach domestic legislation on personal data, commercial and industrial secrecy, and professional and
administrative confidentiality.[44] For instance, Maltese Customs would be prepared to provide the right-holder with any information they might have obtained
from other foreign customs authorities as long as this information may be
divulged. Thus, thanks to the authority which the Comptroller of Customs is
given by Article 9 of the Data Protection Act,[45] he is allowed to divulge a lot of
information which is related to the shipment and which the right-holder requires
in order to be in a position to take the required action under the Cross-Border
Measures Law. Any other personal data which the right-holder does not require in
order to take action according to law would not be divulged or disclosed to him.

(4) *Inspection of the suspected goods*

In exercising his rights under Article 9(3) of the Regulation, the right-holder will   **20.72**
be given the opportunity to inspect the goods. Where a small consignment is
detained by customs, the latter would usually provide the right-holder with a few
digital pictures of some samples that are taken from the consignment. In such
cases, the right-holder would in principle not require a physical examination of

---

[44] Issues which may arise would be under the Maltese Data Protection Law (Chapter 440 of The
Laws Of Malta) and related secondary and subsidiary legislation.
[45] Art 9(b) entitles the processing of personal data where this is necessary for compliance with a
legal obligation to which the controller is subject; and Art 9(e) entitles the processing of personal
data where this is carried out in the exercise of official authority vested in the controller to whom the
data is disclosed.

the goods since he would generally be able to ascertain, on the basis of the photographs, whether the goods are genuine or not.

20.73 In situations where large suspected consignments enter Malta, customs have regularly allowed right-holders to send their own technical experts to analyse various samples taken at random from the consignment.

20.74 In ascertaining the nature of the goods, customs frequently release into the possession of representatives of the right-holder a few samples so that these may be sent directly to the right-holder for verification purposes. All of the above is mostly done at the initial stage of the proceedings when the right-holder is still verifying the genuine or counterfeit nature of the goods.

20.75 The right-holder would be entitled to perform all the required verifications on the samples which, in certain instances, may result in their destruction. Customs would allow this where it is essential for the right-holder to check whether the goods are genuine or not. The right-holder would be allowed to retain a sample of the goods in those instances where it is found that the goods are counterfeit and where the right-holder has proceeded with the required action under the Regulation. Where the goods are found to be genuine, the right-holder would be asked to return the samples to customs.

B. Simplified procedure allowing the destruction of the goods without there being any need to determine whether an intellectual property right has been infringed under national law

20.76 Article 11 of the Regulation, allowing for the destruction of goods without there being a need to first determine whether an intellectual property right has been infringed under Maltese law, has still not been implemented in the Cross-Border Measures Law. Having stated this, given that the Cross-Border Measures Law does not rule out the destruction of any such goods on the basis of an amicable out-of-court settlement between the parties, it has been a practice for right-holders and consignees of goods to resolve cross-border issues by means of private agreements. Such agreements have become popular in Malta in particular in the case of small consignments of goods which the right-holder determines to be counterfeit. As in most cases, the goods would not have been purchased by the consignee at a high price, it would be in the interest of both the right-holder and of the consignee to resolve the issue out-of-court and as expediently as possible.

20.77 Such procedures are usually handled by both customs and the right-holder. The right-holder would inform the consignee that unless the latter surrenders the detained goods to him for destruction purposes, the consignee would be taken to court. Where the consignee agrees to the surrender of the goods, this would be made on the basis of a private agreement. The parties would therefore meet at Maltese Customs where a contract would be signed between the right-holder (or his legal representative) and the consignee. The agreement would oblige the right-holder to instruct customs to release the goods into the possession of the consignee. In turn, the latter would have undertaken in the agreement immediately to pass the goods into the possession of the right-holder so that the same goods may be destroyed under the supervision of Maltese Customs.

The transactional agreements mentioned above would be regulated by ordinary Maltese obligations law, the same legislation which is observed for basic civil law issues of contract. Thus, the parties are free to draw up the settlement agreement in the way they deem fit as long as this is in line with Maltese civil and commercial law. Thus, clauses relating to reimbursement of destruction costs, storage costs, legal costs, punitive damages, pre-liquidated damages in respect of future infringing consignments, etc, may be specified in the agreement. The above may be considered to be in line with the Regulation principally due to the fact that Member States have discretion under this provision as to whether to implement or not the simplified procedure contemplated by Article 11. As yet no decision has been taken by the Maltese Government as to whether the Cross-Border Measures Law will be amended so as to incorporate the simplified procedure.   **20.78**

Customs would not look favourably on the granting of licences by right-holders to the owners of the infringing goods to allow for their commercialization. Customs would prefer that the parties agree to the destruction of the goods where this is done under their supervision, as this is also the only possibility left open by Article 11 of the Regulation.   **20.79**

C. Conditions governing action by the authorities having jurisdiction to determine whether the goods infringe an intellectual property right

(1) Authorities having jurisdiction to determine whether the goods infringe an intellectual property right

According to the Cross-Border Measures Law, the proceedings that need to be taken in order to determine whether an intellectual property right has been infringed must be civil judicial proceedings. These proceedings must be of such nature as to lead to a substantive decision on the merits of the case.[46]   **20.80**

---

[46] Cross-Border Measures Law, Art 7(4).

20.81   The fact that the Cross-Border Measures Act requires civil proceedings to be taken has its merits, though also some drawbacks. The main advantage of pursuing a civil action in matters relating to cross-border measures would be having the opportunity to make any form of demand before the civil courts as is allowed for all other ordinary civil actions. Thus, the right-holder would be in a position to ask the court to order the defendant in the proceedings to the payment of damages in favour of the former. These proceedings would also be the best means to obtain a quick determination of the merits of the case, in particular in situations where the goods are not claimed by anyone, such as in the case of transhipments which are detained by Maltese Customs. In these cases, a curator would normally be appointed by the court to represent the absentee defendant's interests. If the curator fails to make contact with the owners or with the person having a title to the goods (that is, the actual defendant), the action would remain uncontested and it would be relatively straightforward for the plaintiff right-holder to obtain a favourable judgment on the merits of the case. Such proceedings usually do not take longer than 18 months until judgment is delivered.

20.82   The matter might be more complicated where the cause is fiercely contested by the parties since the proceedings could then take a few years until they are determined by a civil court. Another disadvantage with civil proceedings lies in the fact that these tend to be costly, especially when one considers that in cases where the goods remain unclaimed, all court costs, including plaintiff, defendant and Court Registry costs, have to be borne by the right-holder.

20.83   Civil proceedings need to be taken in respect of all types of intellectual property rights contemplated in Article 2(1) of the Regulation. Each particular intellectual property right would be considered in the light of the relevant legislation. For instance, where goods are detained on the basis that they are counterfeit goods, the Trade Marks Law would be invoked. Where the issue relates to pirated goods, the Copyright Law would apply for works that are protected by copyright and the Patents and Designs Law for designs. The latter Law would also be invoked for an alleged violation of a patent or of a supplementary protection certificate. As pointed out above, difficulties would arise for goods infringing a designation of origin or a geographical indication since there is no ad hoc Maltese legislation regulating these intellectual property rights.

20.84   In civil proceedings, in particular where the case is heavily fought by the parties, a Maltese civil court would in most cases appoint a legal expert on intellectual property. This legal expert would be required to collect the evidence from the parties, to hold hearings and to question witnesses. The expert would then prepare a report which would contain his findings and include his opinion as to whether the plaintiff's demands should be upheld or not by the court. In addition to a legal expert, the parties could also ask the court to appoint a technical expert, in particular where the intellectual property relates to information technology or to scientific and technical matters.

(2) *Term for notifying customs that proceedings have been started*

Article 13 of the Regulation allows customs to extend the term of 10 working days **20.85** within which the right-holder must initiate proceedings aimed at determining whether the goods infringe an intellectual property right to secure the detention of these goods. Maltese Customs have always been prepared to extend this term by a further 10 working days as long as the right-holder confirms to customs that he is still interested with filing the required civil proceedings in court within the extended term.

D. Release of goods suspected of infringing certain rights on provision of a security

The way Article 14(1) of Regulation 1383/2003 is worded suggests that **20.86** customs would have no option but to release the goods to their declarant, owner, importer, holder, or consignee whenever the conditions of this provision are observed. To date, this provision has not been applied by Maltese Customs since all border measures that have been taken under the Cross-Border Measures Law related exclusively to counterfeit goods and goods infringing copyright. In such matters, customs have always detained the goods until a civil court issues a decision on the merits of the case that would have been initiated by the right-holder.

E. Storage of the goods and destruction process

During the period of suspension of release, the goods would be kept under cus- **20.87** toms control. Depending on the type of goods and the quantity involved, customs would prefer to keep the goods under lock and key in their warehouses. The goods would be kept there until the matter is decided by a Maltese civil court. The storage costs would be paid by the party which ends up losing the proceedings in court since the court, in its judgment, would usually order the losing party to bear all costs related to the action. However, where the proceedings are initiated against curators representing an absentee defendant, all costs including storage costs would be at the charge of the plaintiff right-holder.

IV. PROVISIONS APPLICABLE TO GOODS FOUND TO INFRINGE AN INTELLECTUAL PROPERTY RIGHT

20.88 When goods are found by a court to infringe an intellectual property right, the remedies at the disposal of the right-holder are those outlined by Article 17 of the Regulation. Article 8 of the Cross-Border Measures Law requests the court, as a general rule, to order the Comptroller of Customs to dispose of the goods outside the channels of commerce in such a way as to preclude injury to the right-holder. Alternatively, the court may order customs to destroy the goods, in any case without compensation of any sort to and, at the cost of, the importer, exporter, or owner of the goods.[47] A third option at the disposal of the court is that of ordering the Comptroller of Customs to take any other measures having the effect of effectively depriving the persons concerned of the economic benefits of the transaction.[48] In line with Article 17 of the Regulation, the Cross-Border Measures Law continues by stating that simply removing the trade marks, which have been affixed to the counterfeit goods without authorization, shall not be considered as having this effect.

20.89 To date, in all proceedings that have been instituted on the basis of the Cross-Border Measures Law and the Regulation, the claim raised by the right-holder to the court in the writ of summons has been that of ordering the destruction of the goods. At the same time, this has been the course of action preferred by Maltese courts in that, until today, the few judgments that have been delivered for those actions that have been instituted under the provisions of the Cross-Border Measures Law have always opted for the destruction of the infringing goods. Such a solution has been preferred over the not too clear concept of entrusting customs with the task of finding a way of depriving the persons concerned of any economic gains from the transaction.

20.90 As stated above, costs of civil proceedings are usually paid by the party against which the court judgment is delivered. The court would also be prepared to instruct the losing party to pay the other costs associated with the storage of the goods, their transportation, customs handling costs, destruction costs and any costs incurred in the issue of any security which might be required from customs according to the Cross-Border Measures Law and/or the Regulation. As has been stated above in respect of storage costs, in proceedings initiated by right-holders against curators representing an absentee defendant, even where the right-holder obtains a favourable judgment he would be responsible towards the payment of all costs.

---

[47] Cross-Border Measures Law, Art 8(1)(a).   [48] Ibid, Art 8(1)(b).

V. PENALTIES

The penalties afforded under national legislation for a breach of the Regulation **20.91**
arise from the Cross-Border Measures Law and from each individual piece of
intellectual property legislation.

Article 11 of the Cross-Border Measures Law states that if any person imports or **20.92**
causes to be imported any goods infringing an intellectual property right, such
person shall be liable for every such offence to a fine (*multa*) equivalent to twice
the value of the goods. This provision has never been applied and to date, the
actions that have been taken under the provisions of the Cross-Border Measures
Law have fallen short of the criminal remedy.

An infringement of an intellectual property right under the Regulation would **20.93**
entitle the right-holder to the remedies found in the Trade Marks Law, the
Copyright Law and the Patents and Designs Law. In addition, the right-holder
would be entitled to the payment of damages that he might have suffered as a
result of the infringement.

Thus, where a trade mark is infringed by counterfeit goods, a right-holder, in **20.94**
addition to the remedies found under the Cross-Border Measures Law, may invoke
the provisions of the Trade Marks Law and request a civil court to order the erasure,
removal or obliteration of the offending sign.[49] The right-holder may also request
that the court orders in his favour the delivery up of infringing goods, material, or
articles.[50] The court is always empowered by the Trade Marks Law to order itself the
destruction of goods, material, or articles which infringe a registered trade mark.

In the case of pirated goods were a copyright is infringed, the right-holder may **20.95**
rely on the provisions of the Copyright Law and request a civil court to order the
defendant to pay the plaintiff a sum equal to the restitution of all profit that might
have been derived from the infringement of the copyright.[51] In addition, a civil
court may in an action for copyright infringement, having regard to all the circumstances of the case and in particular to the flagrancy of the infringement and
any benefit accruing to the defendant by reason of the infringement, award such
additional damages as it may deem to be reasonably justifiable.[52] The court may,
moreover, on the application of the plaintiff, order that all infringing articles in
the possession of the defendant be surrendered to the plaintiff.[53] However, given
that in cross-border measures related actions, the possession of the articles would
be entrusted to Maltese Customs, it is questionable whether this latter remedy
may be availed of by the right-holder.

---

[49] Trade Marks Law, Art 15.   [50] Ibid, Art 16.   [51] Copyright Law, Art 43(1).
[52] Ibid, Art 43(2).   [53] Ibid, Art 43(3).

20.96 Where pirated goods infringe a registered design, the right-holder would be entitled to a number of remedies under the Patents and Designs Law. He would first be entitled to request a civil court to order the delivery up to him of all infringing machinery, products, or materials.[54] In addition, he may request that the court orders that the infringing goods be destroyed or forfeited to such person as the court may deem fit.[55]

20.97 Goods infringing a patent, a supplementary protection certificate, or a plant variety right are all actionable under the provisions of the Patents and Designs Law. The right-holder may in these cases ask a civil court to order that the machinery, or any other industrial means or contrivances used in contravention of the patent, the infringing articles, and the apparatus devised for their production, be forfeited, wholly or partially, and delivered up to the right-holder.[56]

20.98 Since there is no Maltese legislation dealing with designations of origin or geographical indications, the remedies of right-holders are limited in the sense that they may only resort to the remedies provided for under the Cross-Border Measures Law.

VI. LIABILITY OF CUSTOMS AUTHORITIES AND RIGHT-HOLDERS

A. Liability of right-holders and sanctions

20.99 Should right-holders be in breach of any provision of the Regulation to the detriment of third parties, though there are no specific national provisions which provide a remedy for any such event, these third parties could always avail themselves of the Maltese Civil Code[57] provisions under tort law[58] and file proceedings against the right-holder to claim damages compensating the prejudice which they may have suffered.

B. Liability of customs authorities and sanctions

20.100 On the other hand, the right-holder is not entitled to compensation where goods are not detected by Customs and are released or where no action has been taken to

---

[54] Patents and Designs Law, Art 114(1).   [55] Ibid, Art 115(1).   [56] Ibid, Art 47(3).
[57] Chapter 16 of The Laws Of Malta.
[58] Such as the rule that any person shall be liable for the damage which occurs through his fault—Art 1032 of the Civil Code.

detain them or to withhold release thereof. The Cross-Border Measures Law states that the exercise by the Comptroller of Customs of the powers conferred to him with regards to counterfeit or pirated goods shall not render him liable towards any person, in the event of their suffering loss or damage as a result of their action.[59] The Law remains silent in respect of goods infringing intellectual property rights other than trade marks, copyrights or design rights, as to whether the right-holder or any other person might actually have some sort of remedy against the Comptroller of Customs.

Conclusion

The Cross-Border Measures Law can be regarded as an important piece of legislation in that numerous border measures have been taken in Malta which have put Maltese Customs to the forefront amongst the Member States of the EU in the fight against intellectual property rights infringements.   **20.101**

That said, a number of legal practitioners in Malta feel that the Cross-Border Measures Law needs revision in order to bring its provisions more in line with those of Regulation 1383/2003, in particular in amending the definition of 'goods infringing an intellectual property right', introducing provisions putting into practice the simplified procedure allowing for the destruction of the goods without the need of taking court action, and introducing tougher penalties against those persons who infringe an intellectual property right.   **20.102**

---

[59] Cross-Border Measures Law, Art 9.

21

THE NETHERLANDS

Christine Noordzij, Marchien Maks, Frits Mutsaerts, and Maaike Grondman

Introduction

Before Council Regulation (EC) No 1383/2003[1] (the 'Regulation') came into force on 1 July 2004, the Netherlands, being a founding Member State of the European Community, already actively enforced the previous Council Regulations No 3842/86 and No 3295/94 (the 'Previous Regulations').[2]   **21.01**

Through the years national law has been amended in the Netherlands to ensure consistency with these Previous Regulations. Since the Regulation is based on its predecessors, no additional amendments were required. However, the internal guidelines for the Dutch customs authorities ('Dutch Customs') are currently undergoing a few changes. On the basis of the Regulation and the Implementing Council Regulation 1891/2004[3] (the 'Implementing Regulation'), the Dutch Ministry of Economic Affairs has prepared draft rules on customs' tasks concerning the infringement of intellectual property rights[4] for the implementation of the Regulation and the Implementing Regulation in the Netherlands (the 'Draft Rules'). These Draft Rules still need to be formally approved by the Ministry of   **21.02**

---

[1] Council Reg (EC) 1383/2003 of 22 July 2003 concerning customs action against goods suspected of infringing certain intellectual property rights and the measures to be taken against goods found to have infringed such rights [2003] OJ L 196/7.

[2] Council Reg (EEC) No 3842/86 of 1 December 1986 laying down measures to prohibit the release for free circulation of counterfeit goods [1986] OJ L 357/1, and Council Reg (EEC) No 3295/94 of 22 December 1994 laying down measures to prohibit the release for free circulation, export, re-export or entry for a suspensive procedure of counterfeit and pirated goods [1996] OJ L 97/38.

[3] Commission Reg (EC) No 1891/2004 of 21 October 2004 laying down provisions for the implementation of Council Reg (EC) No 1383/2003 concerning customs action against goods suspected of infringing certain intellectual property rights and the measures to be taken against goods found to have infringed such rights [2004] OJ L 328/16.

[4] 'Draft rules on customs' tasks concerning the infringement of intellectual property rights' [2004] 4 ('*Concept Voorschrift douanetaak inbreuk intellectuele eigendomsrechten*' [2004] 4).

Economic Affairs.[5] They have, however, already become part of Dutch Customs practice.

I. SUBJECT MATTER AND SCOPE OF THE NATIONAL LAW APPLYING THE REGULATION

21.03 Articles 1(1) and 2(1) of the Regulation define the scope of its application. Next to the Regulation, there is additional legislation that may be used to protect intellectual property rights at the borders in the Netherlands.

A. Customs procedure of the goods

21.04 Articles 5 and 11 of the Dutch Customs Act regulate the authority of Dutch Customs to control and search for instance shipments and warehouses.[6] Article 5 of this Act regulates a declaration for border measures by Dutch Customs and Article 11 regulates the authority of Dutch Customs to search transit warehouses, vehicles, etc. Action by Dutch Customs based on the Regulation is allowed if, during a customs control (within the meaning of Articles 5 and 11 of the Dutch Customs Act), goods are traced which are:

- in one of the situations referred to in Article 1(1) of the Regulation; and
- suspected of infringing an intellectual property right listed in Article 2(1) of the Regulation.

21.05 Dutch Customs are thus entitled to, and in effect *do*, impose border measures where suspected goods are entered for release for free circulation, export, or re-export, are found during checks on entering or leaving the Community customs territory, placed under a suspensive procedure, in the process of being re-exported subject to notification, or placed in a free zone or free warehouse. Border measures are frequently taken in the Netherlands under the Regulation against suspect goods that are placed in transit,[7] or are in the process of being

---

[5] The Ministry of Economic Affairs has approved the draft Regulation beginning 2005. However, the Regulation has not yet (end of May 2005) been published.

[6] Customs Act *(Douane wet: wet van 2 november 1995 tot herziening van de douane wetgeving) Staatsblad* [Official State Gazette] [1995] 55, Arts 5 and 11.

[7] In *Spirits International v Antra Trading*, the Rotterdam District Court (Civil law Section) decided, on 18 July 2003, that goods in transit did already fall under the scope of EC Reg 3295/94 (see n 2 above). This ruling is consistent with the case law of the European Court of Justice, which has already been extensively referred to in Chapter 3 of this book dealing with Reg 1383/2003.

transhipped.[8] In the year 2003, Dutch Customs intercepted a total of 3,258,120 articles and in 2004, Dutch Customs intercepted 74,452,395 articles.[9]

B. Definition of infringing goods

This section looks at the circumstances in which infringement takes place accord- **21.06**
ing to the applicable national law. It will cover piracy as well as each intellectual property right mentioned in the Regulation.

(1) Counterfeit goods

Dutch Customs are very proactive and often apply border measures to goods **21.07**
that—in their opinion—can be suspected of infringing intellectual property rights. If they have a suspicion, the products will be detained and the case will be reported to the Central Customs Administration, that is, Customs North (Groningen) (the 'Dutch Central Customs Administration').[10] According to the statistics reported on the website of the European Commission, in 2003 Dutch Customs detained a total of 1,307,258 articles. In 2002 the number of articles detained was an even greater 5,920,768.[11] The statistics on detained articles in 2004 were not yet available at the time of writing.

Dutch Customs are very well informed and often have knowledge about new **21.08**
products, rightful owners, manufacturers, and distribution routes. The officers receive training, for example, from right-holders on the appearance of products and on so-called 'risk' countries. Therefore, they are usually very well able to recognize counterfeit products.

The Uniform Benelux Law on Marks[12] governs trade mark law in the **21.09**
Netherlands, Belgium, and Luxembourg. Pursuant to Article 13 of this Law, goods can be seen as infringing the exclusive rights of a trade mark owner when they bear a sign that is:

- identical to the registered trade mark and used in the course of trade in respect of identical goods for which the trade mark is registered;[13]

---

[8] The transhipment of goods constitutes the main type of traffic at the Dutch airports—such as the Schiphol International Airport—and seaports, such as the Rotterdam Port.

[9] See http://europa.eu.int/comm/taxation_customs/customs/customs_controls/counterfeit_piracy/statistics/index_en.htm (website of the TAXUD Directorate General of the EC Commission).

[10] For more information on this point see below, para 21.75.

[11] See n 9 above.

[12] Uniform Benelux Law on Marks, as last amended by the Protocol of 11 December 2001, Art 6(E) *(Eenvormige Beneluxwet op de merken (Tractatenblad)* [Bulletin of Acts and Decrees] *1962, 58, BIE 1969, p 242, zoals laatst gewijzigd bij Protocol van 11 december 2001, Art 6(E))*.

[13] Ibid, Art 13(A)(1)(a).

- identical or similar to the registered trade mark, and used in the course of trade in respect of identical or similar goods, where there exists a likelihood of confusion in the public's mind, comprising a risk of association between the sign and the trade mark;[14]

- identical or similar to the registered trade mark, and used in the course of trade for goods that are dissimilar to those for which the trade mark is registered, provided that this trade mark has a reputation in the Benelux and use of this sign, without due cause, takes unfair advantage of, or is detrimental to, the distinctive character or the reputation of the trade mark;[15]

- used for purposes other than to distinguish goods, where use of this sign, without due cause, takes unfair advantage of, or is detrimental to, the distinctive character or the reputation of the trade mark.[16]

21.10 The definition of 'counterfeit goods' provided for in Article 2(1)(a)(i) of the Regulation does not encompass all situations referred to in Article 13 of the Uniform Benelux Law on Marks. Under the Regulation, Dutch Customs are entitled to take action only against goods bearing a trade mark identical to another (registered) trade mark, or which cannot be distinguished in its essential aspects from another trade mark, without authorization of the trade mark owner.[17] The definition of infringing goods seems to be broader under Benelux Law. As can be noticed from Article 13 of the Uniform Benelux Law on Marks, similarity between goods is sufficient. Moreover, the Regulation mentions the possibility of a sign taking unfair advantage of, or being detrimental to, a trade mark with a certain reputation.

21.11 In practice, however, Dutch Customs are eager to take action whenever they feel that the goods involved may cause confusion in the consumers' mind as to their origin. Dutch Customs may thus intervene in cases where some characters of a word mark have been altered (for example 'CARON' instead of 'CANON'), or the colour of a device or design has been modified. According to the Draft Rules,[18] similarity may be determined at different levels, that is, auditory, visual, and conceptual. Similarity at one level is enough for Dutch Customs to assume that the goods are likely to be counterfeit.

21.12 According to Article 2(1)(a)(i) of the Regulation, the trade mark on the basis of which border measures are taken must be 'validly registered in respect of the same type of goods'. Therefore, it is not possible to file an application for action under the Regulation on the basis of a simple trade mark application, which has not yet matured in an effective registration. However, under the Uniform Benelux Law on Marks it is possible to obtain immediate registration by using the so-called

---

[14] Uniform Benelux Law on Marks, as last amended by the Protocol of 11 December 2001, Art 13(A)(1)(b).   [15] Ibid, Art 13(A)(1)(c).
[16] Ibid, Art 13(A)(1)(d).   [17] Cf Reg 1383/2003, Art 2(1)(a)(i).   [18] See n 4 above.

'accelerated procedure'. In practice, Dutch Customs will check the status of the trade mark in question to ensure it has been registered in the relevant register.

Trade mark protection in the Benelux is based on the 'principle of speciality',   **21.13** which means that a trade mark is only protected for the goods as claimed or for similar goods. The Regulation is stricter, since it uses the term 'same kind of goods'.[19] In practice, when checking for possible counterfeit products, Dutch Customs usually do not look at the goods as listed in the trade mark registration concerned. They will only verify whether the trade mark on which the intervention is based is in effect. In the affirmative matter they will inform the right-holder or representative.

For example, Dutch Customs once agreed to detain products bearing the trade   **21.14** mark of a famous toy dog, while this trade mark had not been registered for the same type of goods in the Benelux. Although the suspect products sold under the trade mark consisted of toy dogs, books, clothing, etc, the Benelux trade mark registration only covered the class containing milk products. However, being confronted with a famous trade mark, Dutch Customs assumed that these goods found bearing this famous trade mark and being of a poor quality, probably had to be considered counterfeit.

In most cases, the owner of the infringing goods will abandon these goods after   **21.15** being contacted by (a representative of) the trade mark owner. Obviously, when Dutch Customs detain (or suspend the release of) products not being covered by the trade mark registration on which their intervention is based while the conflict has not been settled between parties, the judge has to decide on the dispute by having regard to the description of the goods referred to in the trade mark registration. Because Dutch Customs do not explicitly have regard to the goods listed in the trade mark registration certificate when applying the Regulation, problems may arise in the event the matter is brought before a national court where the suspect products are not of the same type as the goods for which the trade mark has been registered. For example, if the toy dogs mentioned above had not enjoyed a significant reputation, this matter could have been decided against the trade mark owner, if the case had been brought before the court.

Another example that is worth mentioning in this context concerns a porcelain   **21.16** service bearing the symbol of a figure from Greek mythology, which is often used by a famous designer, and is protected as a trade mark. The trade mark holder had authorized a German porcelain manufacturer to produce china decorated with his trade mark. However, when Dutch Customs detained a container originating from Turkey filled with porcelain bearing the above sign, it appeared that the trade mark in question did not extend to porcelain. Nevertheless, Dutch Customs did

---

[19] See n 17 above.

uphold the detention of the porcelain because it was worked in a way that was identical to the goods as commercialized by the trade mark owner, and because of the inferior quality of the suspect porcelain. Eventually, the addressee cooperated with the right-holder, and Dutch Customs destroyed the goods.

21.17 Similarly, Dutch Customs detained several consignments of games, sunshades and caps decorated with the trade mark of a famous Dutch brewery. Because such products do not form part of the trade mark owner's core business, they were not protected by any trade mark registration. However, again, the addressee agreed to collaborate with the right-holder, and the goods were destroyed.

21.20 Apart from taking border measures against goods suspected of being counterfeit, Dutch Customs will also take such measures when they notice possible infringing use of trade marks on, for example, logos, labels, stickers, brochures, manuals, and packaging materials. Action will also be taken in the event the above materials are delivered separately from the goods for which they are intended.

21.21 In the year 2003 and 2004, 45 per cent of the counterfeit cases in which Dutch Customs were involved were about trade marks.[20]

(2) Pirated goods

21.22 Under Article 2(1)(b) of the Regulation, customs in the Member States of the European Union are also to take action against pirated goods that are defined as 'goods which are or contain copies made without the consent of the holder of a copyright or related right or design right, regardless of whether it is registered in national law, or of a person authorized by the right-holder in the country of production, in cases where the making of those copies would constitute an infringement of that right under Council Regulation (EC) No 6/2002 of 12 December 2001 on Community Designs[21] or the law of the Member State in which the application for customs action is made'.

21.23 Dutch Customs interpret the concept of 'goods that are or contain copies' very broadly. The inspected product does not have to be an exact copy of the genuine product. For instance, CDs have an IFPI number that indicates their authenticity. If this number is missing, customs will assume they are counterfeit.

21.24 In the case where customs are aware of the regular distribution route of genuine products, or know in which country they are produced, and come across goods crossing the border which do not originate from that specific country or have not been delivered exactly through that distribution route, Dutch Customs assume that the goods concerned are pirated goods. In those cases, they will assume the

---

[20] See n 9 above.   [21] OJ L 3/1.

products involved are not genuine and inform the right-holder. This is particularly the case if the goods originate from countries like China and Taiwan, which are traditionally rated as high-risk countries.

Furthermore, Dutch Customs make sure that they are well informed about the **21.25**
trends within society. Thus, over the last year, many collectors' cards, other 'Pokémon' products, and many so-called 'Bey Blades' (which are battle-spinning tops for children) were detained by Dutch Customs. Information about these trends and the specific products are all docketed and published on customs' intranet.

As pointed out above, Dutch Customs also act on the basis of intuition and **21.26**
experience. Most of the piracy cases in the Netherlands are related to products that can be used in the fields of sound and image. Therefore, Dutch Customs always pay particular attention to these products. Moreover, Dutch Customs have a list noting the 'top 10' of pirated goods. This list is updated every month with information about detained products, information provided by right-holders, and data supplied by customs in other countries. In the light of the information thus docketed, Dutch Customs are able to make a risk analysis, based on which they decide whether or not to take action.

The 1912 Dutch Copyright Law governs Dutch copyright law.[22] Under Article 1 **21.27**
of this Law, goods may infringe a copyright where they consist of the reproduction of a protected work without the right-holder's consent,[23] and are made available to the public.[24] However, there are many exceptions, for example, a parody is not always regarded as an illicit reproduction.[25]

Pursuant to Article 2 of the Dutch Related Rights Law,[26] performing artists have **21.28**
the exclusive right to authorize or prohibit any of the following activities:

- any recording of a performance;[27]
- any reproduction of a recording of a performance;[28]
- the selling, renting, lending, delivering, or otherwise putting into trade, of a performance, recording of a performance, or a reproduction thereof, or importing, offering, or having in stock, of a recording of a performance, for any of the above-mentioned purposes;[29]
- any transmission or re-transmission of a performance or recording of a performance, or a reproduction thereof, or making the same available to the public by any other means.[30]

---

[22] 1912 Dutch Copyright Law *(Auteurswet 1912) Staatsblad* [Official State Gazette] [1912] 308.
[23] Ibid, Art 13.   [24] Ibid, Art 12.
[25] See *Suske en Wiske*, Supreme Court 13 April 1984, NJ 1984, 524.
[26] Dutch Related Rights Law (*Wet op de naburige rechten*) *Staatsblad* [Official State Gazette] [1990] 303, 304.   [27] Ibid, Art 2(1)(a).
[28] Ibid, Art 2(1)(b).   [29] Ibid, Art 2(1)(c).   [30] Ibid, Art 2(1)(d).

21.29 According to Article 1(f) of the Related Rights Law, the term 'reproduction' means the 'manufacture of one or more duplicates of a recording of a performance, or a part thereof'. The reproduction of a protected subject matter will even be caught by this Law where the original performance has undergone modifications, provided the personal input of the performer has been copied.[31]

21.30 In the period between 1 October 2003 and 30 September 2004, Dutch Customs took action in 330 cases involving suspicions of an infringement of related rights.[32] Dutch Customs detained 466,696 CDs, DVDs, and audio cassettes in 2003, and 5,445,378 articles in 2004.[33] Apart from pre-recorded performances, most of the pirated products consist of video games, software, etc. The huge amount of products detained by Dutch Customs indicates the importance of the artists' ability to claim protection for their performances.

21.31 As the Regulation requires, Dutch Customs will also take action when design rights are infringed. According to Article 14 of the Uniform Benelux Design Law,[34] goods can be seen as infringing a design right if they are products with the same or a similar appearance as the design as registered in the Benelux Register, and are brought on the market. Protection may also be claimed based on a registered or unregistered Community design.

21.32 Customs are regularly informed by right-holders about their new designs. Furthermore, Dutch Customs know from experience what kind of designs are often subject to piracy. For instance, Nokia updates the Dutch Customs regularly on their new designs for changeable covers for mobile phones. Both Nokia and Siemens products are often subject to design right infringements. Therefore, Dutch Customs pay extra attention to goods that embody any of their registered designs, and/or show resemblance to their products. However, although Dutch Customs have up to date knowledge about designs, in 2003 only 7 per cent of the counterfeit cases in which they were involved concerned designs.[35] The figures for 2004 have not yet been published.

21.33 Another example is the case of a consignment of toy cars showing resemblance with the appearance of toy cars manufactured by a very famous car producer. Dutch Customs were alerted by the too low purchase price and the inferior quality of the goods, but most of all by the fact that the suspect cars did not bear a consent

---

[31] Gielen and Verkade, 'Tekst & Commentaar Intellectuele Eigendom' (*'Tekst and Comment Intellectual Property Law'*) [1998] ISBN 90 268 2829 2103, Kluwer, Deventer.

[32] Information provided by the head officer of the Central Customs Administration, Department IPR.   [33] Ibid, and see n 9 above.

[34] 1975 Uniform Benelux Design Law (as last amended by the Protocol of June 20 2002, Bulletin of Acts and Decrees [2002] 129) (*Eenvormige Beneluxwet inzake tekeningen en modellen*) *Tractatenblad zoals gewijzigd bij Protocol van 20 juni 2002, Tractatenblad 2002, 129* Art 14.

[35] See n 9 above.

declaration from the right-holder, which Dutch Customs knew that all toy cars produced in the name of the right-holder should bear.

(3) Goods infringing other intellectual property rights

Goods infringing a patent or a supplementary protection certificate

A few applications for customs action based on patents or supplementary **21.34** protection certificates have been filed to date with Dutch Customs. The filing of applications for action by customs in these fields proves very important in practice. Indeed, Dutch Customs will in principle never act *ex officio* in matters like these, as they are usually not in a position, owing to a lack of technical expertise, to decide whether or not goods infringe such rights.

The essence of patent protection according to Dutch patent law, which is **21.35** enshrined in the 1995 Patent Law,[36] consists in the right to prevent any use of the patented invention by parties other than the patentee without the latter's consent. However, this exclusive right is subject to a few exceptions, listed in Articles 54 to 60 of the Patent Law.

In case of a product patent, Article 53(1)(a) of the Patent Law confers on its owner **21.36** the exclusive right to produce, use, market, sell, rent, deliver or otherwise trade in, offer, import, or store the protected product.

In case of a patent protection for a method or process, Article 53(1)(b) of the **21.37** same Law gives the patentee the exclusive right to use this method or process, or to use, market, sell, rent, deliver or otherwise trade in, offer, import, or store any product directly obtained by using the protected method or process, provided said method or process is subject to patent protection under Article 3 of the Patent Law.

A patentee seeking action by the Dutch customs authorities on the basis of **21.38** his patent rights will have to supply customs with very specific information. All relevant details will be published on customs' intranet. On this website, all prior applications for action, as well as additional information provided by right-holders over the past few years, can be found. When the information thus provided is sufficiently detailed, Dutch Customs are in a position to make an effective risk analysis and, on that basis, to impose border measures on possibly infringing products.

In the period between 1 October 2003 and 30 September 2004, Dutch Customs **21.39** registered 30 interventions based on suspicions of a patent infringement.[37]

---

[36] 1995 Patent Law *(Rijksoctrooiwet 1995) Staatsblad* [Official State Gazette] [1995] 51.
[37] See n 31 above.

Goods infringing a national plant variety right

21.40 Under Article 2(1)(c)(iii) of the Regulation, Dutch Customs may also take action against goods that are suspected of infringing plant variety rights. In practice, no *ex officio* action will be taken on that basis by Dutch Customs, for the same reason as for patents and supplementary protection certificates.

21.41 Pursuant to Article 40 of the Dutch Seeds and Planting Materials Law,[38] any reproduction, marketing, sale, exportation, or storage of breeding material of a particular plant variety without permission from the owner of the breeder's right constitutes an infringement. Article 40(2), (3), and (4) of the Law list the exceptions to this principle.

21.42 The owner of protected plant variety rights seeking action by Dutch Customs will therefore have to file an application for action under Article 5 of the Regulation, and will be required on that occasion to supply Dutch Customs with very specific information concerning the scope of his rights. This will be published on customs' intranet. As with applications based on a patent or a supplementary protection certificate, if the information received by customs is specific enough, it will enable them to carry out an efficient risk analysis and, on that basis, to block goods suspected of infringing the relevant breeder's rights under Dutch Law.

Goods infringing a national designation of origin or a geographical indication

21.43 Whilst Regulation (EEC) No 2081/92[39] made it possible to register designations of origin and geographical indications at the EC level, at the Dutch national level this possibility was set forth in the Agriculture Quality Decree concerning designations of origin, geographical indications, and certificates of special character.[40] Under Articles 2(1) and 2(2) of the Decree, any use of a protected designation of origin or geographical indication in the course of trade or in advertisements, as well as of markings that suggest that the products concerned originate from a protected geographical area, is strictly forbidden. In addition, protection may also be claimed under the general provisions relating to tort law and misleading

---

[38] Seeds and Planting Materials Law *(Zaaizaad- en Plantgoed wet) Staatsblad* [Offical State Gazette] [1996] 398, Art 40.

[39] Council Reg (EEC) No 2081/92 on the protection of geographical indications and designations of origin for agricultural products and foodstuffs [1992] OJ L 208/1. Cf also Council Reg (EC) No 1493/1999 on the common organization of the market in wine [1999] OJ L 179/1.

[40] Decree of 16 December 1993 laying down the agriculture quality concerning designations of origin, geographical indications and certificates of special character *(Landbouwkwaliteitsbesluit geografische aanduidingen, oorsprongsbenamingen en specifiteitscertificering, besluit van 16 december 1993, Staatsblad 1994, 37, laatstelijk gewijzigd bij besluit van 8 december 1997, Staatsblad 142).*

advertising,[41] where use of a designation of origin or geographical indication is likely to deceive the public or to be considered a wrongdoing.

The possibility of having designations of origin and geographical indications **21.44** registered was not well promoted within the Netherlands, and as a result not many applications were filed. Dutch Customs are not very familiar with designations of origin and geographical indications, and therefore are not eager to act *ex officio* in this sector. To meet this concern, holders of such rights will be well-advised to file an application for action under Article 5 of the Regulation. Upon receipt of the first application on that ground, Dutch Customs will determine how to proceed practically, what additional information is needed, and how to inform their officers.

(4) Moulds and matrices

Under Article 2(3) of the Regulation, in the event a mould or matrix is specifically **21.45** designed or adapted for the manufacture of goods infringing an intellectual property right, it must be treated as goods of that kind if the use of such moulds or matrices infringes the right-holder's rights under Community law or the law of the Member State in which the application for action by the customs authorities is made.

Under Dutch copyright law,[42] moulds and matrices are considered as reproduc- **21.46** tions because they are used to produce identical copies of a work. If the work of which duplication with the mould or matrix concerned is sought is itself subject to copyright protection, use of such moulds and matrices for that purpose with the right-holder's consent results in a copyright infringement.[43] Moulds and matrices of that type are therefore subject to border measures.

In practice, it is almost impossible for Dutch Customs to take action *ex officio* **21.47** against moulds and matrices that are specifically designed or adapted to manufacture goods that infringe intellectual property rights, as it will not always be clear from a mould or matrix what the final product will be, and what it will look like.

It is possible to file an application for action to that effect. However, as with **21.48** applications based on patent rights, supplementary protection certificates, and plant variety rights, the right-holder should, in such case, make sure to provide Dutch Customs with extensive information substantiating his suspicions. In the case of moulds and matrices, it is even more important to provide such information to customs, owing to that fact that customs have seldom the opportunity to come across such products, and therefore their experience in this field is limited.

---

[41] Dutch Civil Code (*Burgerlijk Wetboek*), Book 6, Arts 192 and 194.
[42] Dutch Copyright Law (n 22 above), Art 13.   [43] Ibid, Art 1.

C. Goods excluded by the Regulation

(1) Parallel imported goods

21.49 The Regulation does not apply to goods bearing a trade mark with the consent of the holder of the trade mark, or to goods bearing a protected designation of origin or a protected geographical indication, or which are protected by a patent or a supplementary protection certificate, by a copyright or related right, or by a design right or a plant variety right, and which have been manufactured with the right-holder's consent but are put into circulation without the right-holder's authorization.[44] Neither is there any alternative provision under national law that would allow Dutch Customs to take action under such circumstances.

21.50 Moreover, Dutch Customs do not consider it their job to act in such matters, thus they will not even inform the right-holder when coming across parallel imported goods to enable the latter to take the appropriate steps before the courts.

(2) Goods which have been manufactured under conditions other than those which have been agreed with the right-holder

21.51 Likewise, goods that have been manufactured under conditions other than those that have been agreed with the right-holder may not be subject to border measures under the Regulation.[45] Furthermore, customs are of the opinion that it is impossible for them to control whether or not the conditions agreed on between parties have been fulfilled. Moreover, Dutch Customs do not consider it their task to monitor whether or not the terms and conditions imposed on third parties by the right-holders have been complied with. This is the responsibility of the parties involved.

(3) Goods contained in travellers' personal baggage

21.52 Even though the Regulation is not applicable where travellers' baggage contains suspect goods of a non-commercial nature within the limits of the duty-free allowance of EUR 175 and there are no indications to suggest that the goods are part of commercial traffic,[46] Dutch Customs are allowed to check personal luggage based on Article 13 of the Community Customs Code.[47] This provision allows Dutch Customs to take (under certain conditions) all measures that they deem necessary to the correct enforcement of the customs legislation.

21.53 In practice, Dutch Customs do carry out controls on travellers' personal baggage, either at random, or by means of so-called '100 per cent actions'. A '100 per cent

---

[44] Reg 1383/2003, Art 3(1), first indent.   [45] Ibid, Art 3 (1), second indent.
[46] Ibid, Art 3(2).   [47] Council Reg (EEC) No 2913/92, see n 7 above.

action' will be conducted where a flight originates from a so-called 'risk-rated' country. In the case of a '100 per cent action', all luggage having that origin will be checked.

The second condition mentioned in Article 3.2 of the Regulation is that there are **21.54** no indications to suggest that the goods are part of commercial traffic. On a European level, this condition has already been dealt with in Council Regulation No 918/83 setting up a Community system of reliefs from customs duty, and more specifically, in Article 45 of this Regulation.[48] Based on this Regulation, Dutch Customs have prepared tables which indicate exactly how many items of a certain product per traveller will be considered as non-commercial.[49] For example, Dutch Customs consider two watches and 250 ml of perfume as 'a few items for personal use' and therefore as non-commercial. However, there are exceptions. If those were, for instance, counterfeit products, customs would take action *ex officio*.[50]

Whether the duty-free allowance has been exceeded will be decided on experi- **21.55** ence, statistics, the value of an authentic product, and the regulations based on the Community Customs Code as laid down in Part C, Section II, No 9.00.00 of the Dutch Customs Handbook.[51] When customs suspect that a product infringes an intellectual property right based on the (often too low) amount paid for the product, they will ask for additional information from the traveller concerned. If the product involved is, for example, a 'Louis Vuitton' bag and the receipt divulges a price in an amount of, say, EUR 55, customs will assume that the value of the product will exceed the limits of the duty-free allowance of EUR 175. By now, every customs officer in the Netherlands is probably aware of the fact that a 'Louis Vuitton' bag could never have been bought for EUR 55 (unless it were counterfeit).

The table below discloses the figures on non-authentic goods published by **21.56** Dutch Customs and the FIOD-ECD (that is, the investigation department of the Public Prosecution Service in charge of combating intellectual property right infringements) which were confiscated from travellers' personal baggage at the Schiphol Airport in 2002 and 2003 (the numbers confiscated in 2004 have not yet been published, but will in total amount to 40,937 articles,

---

[48] Council Reg No 918/83 of March 28, 2983 setting up a Community system of reliefs from customs duty [1983] OJ L 105/1-37, Art 45.   [49] See n 4 above, 58/59.
[50] Ibid, 58.
[51] Customs Handbook for Import and Export, Part C, Section II, No 9.00.00 (*Douane Handboek voor In- en Uitvoer, Deel C: Algemene douane- en aanverwante wetgeving, sectie II, no. 9.00.00*) ISBN 9054046589, SDU Uitgevers B.V., Den Haag. This handbook for Customs officers handles with customs affairs and explains all regulations and legislation important for Customs officers. Furthermore, arrangements between the Netherlands and third countries concerning trade are discussed.

according to oral information supplied by Dutch Customs; this denotes a real decrease):[52]

	2003	2002
Toys and games	1,694	574
Cosmetics	72	85
Clothing and accessories	10,789	7,255
CDs and DVDs	37,058	19,755
Electrical goods	6	22
Computers and accessories	0	0
Watches and jewellery	2,405	9,639
Miscellaneous	9,600	18,888
Total	61,624	56,224

II. APPLICATION FOR ACTION BY THE CUSTOMS AUTHORITIES

A. Measures prior to an application for action by the Customs authorities ('*ex officio*' measures)

21.57 Dutch Customs are very proactive in combating piracy and counterfeiting. This means that they will often act '*ex officio*' in accordance with Article 4 of the Regulation. In the year 2003, the Dutch Customs started 620 *ex officio* procedures.[53] For 2004, statistics have not yet been published, but at a rough guess, they will probably show an increase of *ex officio* procedures.

21.58 Dutch Customs are very well informed about the latest 'trends' in those fields, and are regularly updated on special courses. Right-holders or their representatives often attend such training sessions to gather additional information. Information about details of products is also published on the customs' intranet. In addition, several customs officers are specifically trained in the field of intellectual property, and these officers will assist their colleagues in determining whether or not *ex officio* action should be taken.

21.59 However, Dutch Customs are reticent to intervene *ex officio* in cases involving a technical assessment, as is the case, for example in the field of patents, supplementary protection certificates, and plant variety rights. Holders of such rights are therefore well-advised to file an application for action under Article 5 of the Regulation.

---

[52] See n 9 above.   [53] See n 10 above.

When deciding whether or not to take action *ex officio* under the Regulation, **21.60** Dutch Customs take into account, among other things, the country of origin of the goods, their quality, and the usual distribution channels of the genuine products. They will thus make a so-called 'risk analysis'. This risk analysis is based on a check-list on how to recognize counterfeit products, which is continuously updated with product information and additional data from previous customs actions. This list is also updated with information provided by right-holders. All this information is obviously kept secret in order to prevent counterfeiters benefiting from it.

If Dutch Customs cannot decide whether or not to take action *ex officio*, they may **21.61** ask the right-holder to confirm their suspicions. In these cases, the Dutch Central Customs Administration may inform the right-holder in accordance with Article 4(2) of the Regulation about the actual or estimated quantity of the goods, and their nature.[54]

When notifying the right-holder concerned of a possible infringement, the Dutch **21.62** Central Customs Administration will also inform the latter of the three-day period provided for in Article 4 of the Regulation within which the right-holder should lodge an application for action. The starting date of this term depends on the first contact between the right-holder (or his representative) and the Central Customs Administration. This term is applied very strictly by Dutch Customs. However, in the event of administrative errors on their side, they will extend the relevant period if necessary.

In most cases in which *ex officio* action is taken, the Dutch Central Customs **21.63** Administration will first contact the right-holder or its representative by e-mail or by phone. Thereafter, the Dutch Central Customs Administration will send the official notification (referring to the three-day period) by fax and by regular mail.[55]

B. The lodging and processing of applications for customs action

(1) Persons entitled to file an application for action

Definition of 'right-holders' under the Regulation

Persons entitled to file an application for action under the Regulation are defined **21.64** as 'right-holders' in Article 2(2) of the Regulation, and include:

- the holder of a trade mark, copyright or related right, design right, patent, supplementary protection certificate, plant variety right, protected designation

---

[54] Reg 1383/2003, Art 4(2).
[55] As to the information which may be provided by customs to the right-holder in the context of *ex officio* procedures, see Reg 1383/2003, Art 4(2), and para 21.103 below.

of origin, protected geographical indication and, more generally, any right referred to in Article 2(1) of the Regulation;

- any other person authorized to use any of the intellectual property rights mentioned above, or a representative of the right-holder or authorized user.

21.65 The definition of 'any person authorized to use the right'[56] is applied by Dutch Customs in the broadest sense. Any original contract, such as a licence agreement, evidencing the authorization to use the right will be accepted, provided however that such authorization is unmistakably mentioned in the contract. This means that even a distributor or a commercial agent could be considered as 'an authorized user', as long as they are able to provide clear and unmistakable proof thereof.

21.66 A representative may be either a natural person or a company.[57] Foreign representatives without an office in the Netherlands are also allowed to file an application for action on the same conditions as a representative located in the Netherlands.

Proof of entitlement to file an application for action

21.67 In accordance with Article 5(5), second indent, of the Regulation, any application for action must always contain proof that the applicant holds the rights on which said application is based for the goods in question. In application of this provision, Dutch Customs always request evidence of ownership. Where appropriate, they will also require proof of the authorization to use the right, and empowerment of the applicant to act on behalf of the right owner or authorized user. They will carefully examine the evidence thus submitted.

For right-holders stricto sensu

21.68 When filing an application for action based on a registered right (such as a patent, trade mark, registered design, plant variety right, designation of origin, or geographical indication), the right-holder must submit a copy of the registration certificate, or a printout of the certificate from the relevant on-line register.[58] Moreover, it is not possible to base an application for action on an application for a registered right; the right has to be actually registered.

21.69 In case of an unregistered right (that is, a copyright, related right, or unregistered design right), the right-holder is required to submit the proof to Dutch Customs, by any means, that he is the author of the protected work or the initial owner of

---

[56] Cf Reg 1891/2004, Art 2(2). [57] Cf on this point Reg 1891/2004, Art 1.
[58] Ibid, Art 2(1), first indent, (a). Cf also Art 2(1), second indent.

the right.[59] He will thus have to establish, on the basis of materials and documents, that the creation of which he claims to be the author was completed on an incontestable date, which is earlier in time than the date on which the alleged pirate product has been conceived. An incontestable date may be obtained from the Dutch tax authorities or a notary public.[60]

Additionally, it is possible to register a copyright in some countries, for instance in **21.70** the United States. When a copyright has been registered in another country, Dutch Customs will also accept (a copy of) the certificate of registration of the copyright outside the Netherlands.

For persons authorized to use the right

Where an application for action is filed by an 'authorized user of the right' **21.71** according to Article 2(2)(b) of the Regulation, Dutch Customs shall require to be supplied with an original contract, such as a licence agreement, evidencing the authorization to use the right.[61] Provided such authorization is clearly and unmistakably mentioned in the contract, customs will accept it.

In addition, it should be pointed out that under Dutch law it is not mandatory to **21.72** register the authorization to use a right with the relevant industrial property office, that is, a license is also valid if not recorded. However, if not recorded, the contract is not enforceable against third parties like the consignee, the consignor, or the holder of the goods. Dutch Customs' practice shows that they only examine the contract in which the authorization to use the right has been given. In the light of the above, it seems that Dutch Customs will agree to take action on the basis of an application for action filed by any 'authorized user', whether the contract has been registered or not.

For representatives

In the case of a representative according to Article 2(2)(b) of the Regulation, **21.73** customs will always accept a general power of attorney as evidence of the applicant's capacity as representative of the owner or authorized user of the right. Note that an original document should be filed.

If no document evidencing the authorization to act has been submitted by the **21.74** applicant, Dutch Customs will require such evidence.[62] In general, they will grant the application in advance, while awaiting the power of attorney or any additional document they may need.

---

[59] Ibid, Art 2(1), first indent, (b).
[60] However, this is not a legal requirement. In practice, it means that the document evidencing the work or creation will receive a date stamp, which makes it easier to prove its existence on a certain date. This stamped document will also be accepted by customs as proof of the existence of a copyright.   [61] Cf Reg 1891/2004, Art 2(2).
[62] Cf ibid, Art 2(3).

(2) Competent customs department and formal requirements

Competent customs department

21.75   Applications for action by the Dutch Customs should be filed with the Dutch Central Customs Administration, which is the department responsible under Article 5(2) of the Regulation to process such applications:

Douane Noord, kantoor Groningen (*Customs North, Groningen office*)
Afdeling IER (*Department IPR*)
P.O. Box 380
NL-9700 AJ Groningen
The Netherlands
T.: + 31 50 523 21 75
F.: + 31 50 523 21 76
douane.hier@tiscalimail.nl
www.douane.nl

Form of the application for action

21.76   The application for action may be filed electronically or by fax. However, additionally a copy of the original application form needs to be filed by regular mail together with the originally executed power of attorney, and the originally executed liability declaration referred to in Article 6 of the Regulation. The website of Dutch Customs[63] contains a digital version of Regulation No 1891/2004, which includes an application for action. Moreover, Dutch Customs are always willing to forward an application for action, if requested.

21.77   According to Article 5(5) of the Regulation, the applicant should execute the Article 6 Declaration. On the other hand, according to Article 6 of the Regulation, an application for action shall be accompanied by a Declaration from the right-holder. Based on the above, the Regulation is not completely clear which person, in the case of a representative filing the application, should execute the Article 6 Declaration. Since not every representative is willing to accept the possible implications of signing the Declaration (liability), Dutch Customs also accept the Declaration executed by the right-holder only. Therefore, it is up to the representative and the right-holder to decide who will execute the Declaration.

21.78   Subsequent to the filing and acceptance of the application, customs prefer to receive additional information regarding, for example, a technical description of suspect products and changes in the distribution channels by e-mail, which makes it easier for them to distribute this information within their own administration.

---

[63]   See www.douane.nl.

Dutch Customs have their own intranet, on which this kind of information is made available.

According to Article 3(3) of the Implementing Regulation,[64] two copies of the application for action should be filed with customs. In addition, as mentioned in the previous paragraph, additional information can be provided by e-mail at any time. **21.79**

Language requirements

Dutch Customs and the Dutch Public Prosecutors Department have agreed that an application under Article 5(1) of the Regulation should preferably be filed in the Dutch language. However, in practice, it is also possible to submit the application in English. Nonetheless, customs prefer receiving 'Community' applications for action filed under Article 5(4) in English, as this makes it easier for them to forward these applications to the relevant customs in the other Member States concerned. **21.80**

Although there are no special requirements concerning the exhibits accompanying the application form, Dutch Customs must be able to understand them. Therefore, the exhibits should preferably be in the following languages: Dutch, English, and/or German. However, the Article 6 liability Declaration should preferably be in Dutch. Customs are prepared to accept such declarations in another language, yet in that case they should be accompanied by a certified Dutch translation. **21.81**

(3) Requirements regarding the content of the application for action

There is no special requirement, other than that referred to in Article 5(5) of the Regulation, concerning the information to be provided to Dutch Customs when filing an application. All the information given should be as detailed as possible, and holders of 'technical' rights (such as patents) should be as accurate and specific as possible when describing the scope of protection of their rights. Information about the genuine products and the type or pattern of fraud should contain, if known, the countries of origin and countries of production of the authentic and suspect goods, distribution channels, original packaging, original logos, etc. Article 5(5) of the Regulation also requires the right-holder to provide the name and address of a contact person. Dutch Customs prefer to have a contact person in the Netherlands; however, this is not mandatory. **21.82**

Situations may arise in which Dutch Customs request additional information or details.[65] For example, in the case of Russian vodka of which a shipment was detained, customs wanted to know the particulars of the rightful distributors, **21.83**

---

[64] See n 3 above. [65] Cf Reg 1383/2003, Art 5(6).

and whether there was already prior knowledge about the manufacturers of the counterfeit products. In this case it was not clear who the rightful owner of the trade mark was. The original owner of the trade mark had assigned it. However, in Russia the transfer of companies and their property should also be registered with a special government organization. Therefore, the transfer of the trade mark had to be registered in the Trademark Register and in a special government register. Unfortunately, the transfer of one of the trade marks had not been duly registered with the government organization. A competitor (a government enterprise) had started producing vodka under an identical trade mark, claiming that the mark was part of the public domain, as it had not been properly registered. It was therefore difficult for customs determine who was entitled to the trade mark and they required additional information from the applicant for customs action to help them with this.

(4) Processing and acceptance of the application for action

21.84 When Dutch Customs decide not to process an application for action pursuant to Article 5(8) of the Regulation, they issue an administrative decision based on the General Administrative Law.[66] Under this Law, an opposition against a decision rendered by customs may be lodged before the same authority within six weeks.[67] If the decision rendered on opposition upholds the rejection of the application, an appeal may be filed with the civil courts.[68] The term for filing the appeal is also six weeks.

21.85 The period during which Dutch Customs are to take action when an application is granted shall not exceed one year.[69] There is no minimum period. It is even possible to file an application for action concerning for instance a special shipment. If the right-holder is aware for instance of a shipment consisting of counterfeit goods that will cross the border in the near future or on a certain date, customs will still accept an application for action concerning this one-time shipment. However, when a 'Community' application for action is granted under Article 5(4) of the Regulation, this period shall be set at one year in all cases.[70] On expiry of the period in question, an extension can be obtained for another year,[71] and there is no limitation as to the number of extension.

(5) 'Community' applications for action

21.86 When a 'Community' application for action designating the Netherlands has been filed in another Member State under Article 5(4) of the Regulation, the

---

[66] General Administrative Law *(Algemene wet bestuursrecht), Staatsblad* [Official State Gazette] [2002] 148, s 1:5. [67] Ibid, s 6:7.
[68] Ibid, s 6:7. [69] Reg 1383/2003, Art 8(1), first indent.
[70] Ibid, Art 8(2), second indent. [71] Ibid, Art 8(1), first indent, and 8(2), second indent.

formalities will already have been checked by the relevant customs department in that State when the application reaches Dutch Customs and therefore there will be no further examination in the Netherlands on this point.

If a 'Community' application is lodged through Dutch Customs, the latter will **21.87** check whether all formalities imposed by the Regulation have been fulfilled before forwarding the application to the other European countries concerned.

The number of applications for action has increased by 21 per cent over the period **21.88** 2001–2003. In the year 2001, 135 applications were filed, in 2002, there were 151 applications, and in 2003 that number had increased to 183.[72] Information regarding the number of applications in 2004 has not yet been published.

III. CONDITIONS GOVERNING ACTION BY CUSTOMS AUTHORITIES AND BY THE AUTHORITIES COMPETENT TO DETERMINE WHETHER GOODS INFRINGE AN INTELLECTUAL PROPERTY RIGHT

Once customs grant an application for action, the traffic of goods suspected of **21.89** infringing the intellectual property rights referred to in this application will be monitored at the borders. We examine below the conditions governing action by Dutch Customs.

A. Conditions governing action by customs authorities

(1) Factual background

The Customs Office at the Amsterdam International Airport (Schiphol) is **21.90** obviously the most significantly involved authority in the war against pirated and counterfeit goods, because of its size and location at the heart of Europe. The Rotterdam Port Customs also play an essential role in this field, as this port constitutes the largest container seaport in the European Community. As stated, Dutch Central Customs Administration (Groningen) is responsible for all intellectual property issues and coordinates these issues. All matters related to suspicions of intellectual property infringements have to be reported to this

---

[72] See n 10 above.

department. In 2001, a total of 34,502,462 articles suspected of violating an intellectual property right were intercepted in the Netherlands, 5,920,768 in 2002, 3.258.120 in 2003 and 8,646,029 in 2004.[73]

21.91   Because of the Netherlands' geographical position (and in particular its direct access to the sea and the European hinterland), the country has traditionally been a transit country. A huge volume of products find their way to the end-user through the Netherlands. The Port of Rotterdam and the Schiphol Airport process the biggest flows of goods. Many unauthentic goods that are destined for the Dutch or European market are imported through these logistical hubs.

21.92   As far as non-authentic luxury goods are concerned, the Netherlands can be regarded as an importing and transit country. The vast majority of goods of this nature that are intercepted by customs and other law enforcement authorities engaged in combating counterfeit and pirated goods have not been produced in the Netherlands. Most of them come from Asia, and China in particular.

21.93   On the basis that, 'just one won't hurt' and 'the producers of luxury goods earn enough as it is', many Dutch nationals do not mind buying and using counterfeit luxury goods. The producers of these types of goods, such as Rolex, Cartier, Chanel, Walt Disney, Armani, D&G, etc do not publish any figures on the losses they suffer because of such illegal trade, but it is clear that such losses run into hundreds of millions of Euros.

21.94   With regard to software piracy and illegal copies of sound recordings and audio-visual works, the Netherlands is both an importing country and a producing country. Although substantial numbers of pirate CDs, DVDs, and CD-ROMS are imported from abroad, it cannot be denied that disks with software or film and music files are produced on a large scale in the Netherlands. Many Dutch citizens have a computer at home which they use to copy music or software. Unfortunately, such infringing activities are generally tolerated in Dutch society; few are ashamed to play illegally copied music, or to use pirated software.

21.95   Besides these 'home copiers', there are also those who trade on a professional or business basis in illegal copies of software and sound recordings or audiovisual works. Large quantities of illegal collection albums are produced in the Netherlands under fictitious brand names (labels), containing a selection of the most popular music of the moment. These illegal albums are pressed by professionals on to CDs or DVDs. The DVD has been gaining ground over the last few years thanks to its storage capacity. The external appearance of these

---

[73]   K Daele, 'Reg 1383/2003: A New Step in the Fight against Counterfeit and Pirated Goods at the Borders of the European Union' [2004] EIPR 214–224. See also http://europa.eu.int/comm/taxation_customs/customs/customs_controls/counterfeit_piracy/statistics/index_en.htm (website of the TAXUD Directorate General of the EC Commission).

albums is usually of a very high quality. Illegal software is also produced and distributed on a large scale in the Netherlands.

The information technology sector and the music and film industry suffer substantial **21.96** losses as a result of such activities. The music and film sectors too suffer considerable losses from the illegal copying of sound recordings and audiovisual works.

The holders of intellectual property rights who are confronted on a large scale **21.97** with the trade in unauthentic goods do not publish any figures on the quantity of such goods confiscated.

The distribution of these goods is largely carried out in the Netherlands by small **21.98** traders. Many of them are sold in markets, by street vendors, in pubs and bars, at schools, and at other small-scale locations. There are no large public sales outlets where non-original goods are offered for sale. Nor is this possible, because the government does not tolerate such large-scale sale of counterfeit goods. The government turns a blind eye to small-scale trading of illegitimate goods, provided that there are no risks to public health. The reason why the government does not take action against such small-scale trade has to do with capacity problems. The Dutch government takes the view that it should use its enforcement resources primarily for tracking 'big fish'. The holders of intellectual property rights are therefore forced to combat the trade in non-authentic goods through civil action.

If there is large-scale trade in counterfeit goods, and it proves impossible for the **21.99** holder of an intellectual property right to prevent its rights from being infringed through civil actions, the public prosecution service will generally initiate an investigation and criminal proceedings against the parties involved.[74]

(2) Notification of customs intervention

When Dutch Customs are satisfied, after consulting the right-holder, that goods **21.100** in one of the situations referred to in Article 1(1) of the Regulation are suspected of infringing an intellectual property right recited in Article 2(1), they suspend the release of those goods, or detain them.

Where the right-holder has filed an application for action, and this application **21.101** has been granted, the Central Customs Administration, once informed of the customs intervention by the relevant Dutch Customs office, follows the procedure laid down in Article 9 of the Regulation. It immediately[75] notifies the

---

[74] For more details, see Part V.
[75] With regard to Council Reg (EEC) No 3295/94, see the answer to question 4 asked by Japan to the Dutch delegation to the World Trade Organization regarding the Review of Legislation on Enforcement—the Netherlands, Report from the TRIPs Council No IP/Q4/NLD/1 of 17 November 1998, available on-line at: www.wto.org: 'Reg 3295/94 does not provide for any precise

right-holder in question, as well as the declarant (within the meaning of Article 4(18) of the Customs Act[76]) or holder of the goods (within the meaning of Article 38 of the same Act) in writing, either by fax or e-mail.

21.102   Where the right-holder has not yet filed an application, or as long as no decision has been rendered concerning this application, the Central Customs Administration will apply Article 4 of the Regulation. This means customs will suspend the release of the goods, or detain them, for three working days, and will notify the right-holder and the declarant or holder of the goods of their intervention. The detention or the suspension of the release of the goods will be upheld upon filing of an application by the right-holder.[77]

(3)   *Information to be provided by customs to the right-holder before the right-holder confirms the infringing nature of the goods*

21.103   Where goods suspected of infringing an intellectual property right are detained, or their release suspended, by Dutch Customs, the Dutch Central Customs Administration is in some cases entitled, in some cases compelled, to provide specific information to the relevant right-holder.

21.104   As long as the right-holder has not filed an application for action in accordance with Article 5 of the Regulation, and this application has not been granted, the Central Customs Administration is *authorized* to inform him about the actual or estimated quantity of the goods, and their nature.[78] In practice, the Central Customs Administration also divulges information regarding the country of origin and/or destination of the goods.

21.105   Regarding customs actions taking place (or upheld) subsequent to the filing of an application by the right-holder, customs are also *authorized* to provide the right-holder—and the declarant or holder of the goods—with this information.[79]

21.106   In addition, in such cases, they are *compelled* to inform him, at his request, of the names and addresses of the consignee, consignor, declarant or holder, and the origin or provenance, of the goods suspected of infringing his intellectual property rights, so as to enable him to establish whether such an infringement has occurred.[80]

21.107   However, the communication of the above information as provided for under both Article 4(2) and Article 9(3) of the Regulation is subject to compliance with the national provisions of each Member State on the protection of personal

---

period. Art 3(5) of this Regulation stipulates that the competent authority shall forthwith notify the applicant in writing of this decision.'

[76] See n 6 above.

[77] This application must fulfil the requirements of Art 5(5) of the Regulation. See more about the application of the *ex officio* procedure of Art 4 of the Regulation in the Netherlands above, paras 21.57–21.63.

[78] Reg 1383/2003, Art 4(2).   [79] Ibid, Art 9(2).   [80] Ibid, Art 9(3).

data, commercial and industrial secrecy, and professional and administrative confidentiality.

Contrary to, for example, Belgium,[81] in the Netherlands there is no legal **21.108** provision or customs practice that would be conflicting with the application of Articles 4(2) and/or 9(3) of the Regulation. The Central Customs Administration immediately arranges for supplying the information referred to above to the right-holders.[82] Nevertheless, section 67 of the Dutch State Tax Law,[83] concerning civil service secrecy, precludes the communication of any *additional* information to the right-holders as long as no legal decision is rendered as to whether an intellectual property infringement has occurred.[84]

(4) Inspection of the suspected goods

Once notified of the detention or suspension of the release of suspect goods pursuant **21.109** to Article 9(2) of the Regulation, the Central Customs Administration gives the right-holder and the other persons involved the opportunity[85] to inspect those goods.[86]

Customs are also entitled to take representative samples of the goods at this stage. **21.110** At the request of the right-holder, one or several samples will be handed over or sent to him. If possible, the Central Customs Administration will send digital pictures of those samples to the right-holder first. On the basis of these pictures a right-holder will sometimes be able to determine whether or not the suspected goods are counterfeit goods.

The inspection of samples will be carried out under the sole responsibility of the **21.111** right-holder. The samples will have to be returned to the relevant customs office on completion of the technical analysis and, where applicable, before the goods are released or their detention is ended.[87]

As mentioned, if possible the Central Customs Administration requests the relevant **21.112** customs office to send digital pictures. The Central Customs Administration (as coordinating medium) then sends these digital pictures of the (samples of the) goods to the right-holder. However, it might be more difficult in some cases to determine

---

[81] Cf the Belgian General Customs and Excise Law, Art 320 (see Chapter 5, para 5.98).
[82] This is in line with the interpretation of former Reg (EC) 3295/94, cf European Court of Justice, Case C-223/98 *Adidas v Kammarrätten I Stockholm* [1999] ECR I-7081.
[83] The General State Tax Law (*Algemene Wet Rijksbelastingen*), s 67.
[84] Cf the answer to questions 12 and 13 asked by Japan to the Dutch delegation to the World Trade Organization regarding the Review of Legislation on Enforcement—the Netherlands, under the regime of Reg 3295/94: 'Art 6(1) of the Regulation gives the Dutch competent authority the possibility to inform the right-holder. However, because of national rules concerning civil service secrecy, the competent authority does not provide information other than name and address unless there is certainty about the infringement through a decision on the merits of the case by judicial authorities.'
[85] The right-holder has no obligation to inspect the goods, and there is no deadline for doing so.
[86] Reg 1383/2003, Art 9(3), second indent.   [87] Ibid, Art 9(3), last indent.

the infringing character of certain types of goods on that basis. More importantly, pictures may be less suitable to serve as evidence in the framework of legal proceedings. In such circumstances, the right-holder is advised to request samples.

21.113　The samples may be used only 'for the purposes of analysis and to facilitate the subsequent procedure'.[88] In our opinion, they may therefore also be used in the context of legal proceedings before the courts.[89] However, the Regulation is not clear about this. In practice, at the outcome of the proceedings, samples will occasionally be used by Dutch Customs for educational purposes and trainings (obviously with the right-holder's prior consent).

B. Simplified procedure allowing the destruction of the goods without there being any need to determine whether an intellectual property right has been infringed under national law

21.114　Article 11 of the Regulation has not yet been implemented in the Netherlands. In practice, however, the Article 11 procedure is being applied already, including the presumption that the destruction of the goods is deemed to be accepted when the declarant, the holder, or the owner of the goods has not explicitly opposed the destruction within a specific period (the 'Implied Consent theory'). Such *de facto* application is, strictly speaking, not allowed under the Regulation, since the wording of this provision reads: 'the Member States may provide, in accordance with their national legislation, for a simplified procedure (. . .)'. The practical application however is not (yet) in accordance with Dutch national legislation.

21.115　The simplified procedure is handled by the right-holder. Typically, the right-holder will send a cease and desist letter to the declarant, the holder, and/or the owner of the goods, in which he must (i) give information and provide details on the Implied Consent theory, and (ii) mention the specific period of time applying to this procedure. If the declarant, the holder, or the owner of the goods objects to, or contests, the destruction of the goods, the procedure laid down in Article 13 of the Regulation will apply.

21.116　Another way for the right-holder to seek the destruction of the goods in an expedited manner is to summon their addressee to have him agree *expressly* with this destruction. To that effect, the right-holder will send a cease and desist letter to the consignee of the goods, on the basis of the information communicated to him by the Central Customs Administration under Article 9(3) of the Regulation.

---

[88]　Reg 1383/2003, Art 9(3), last indent.

[89]　See Dutch Customs Act, Art 16, and *Handboek Douane, deel 3: Monsterneming en monsteronderzoek* (Customs Handbook, part 3: Sampling and examination of samples).

However, it will often prove more efficient to request the declarant or holder of the goods to abandon them. In practice, such a written request is not even necessary, since the declarant or holder of the goods usually surrenders them automatically when he receives no instructions from the infringer/addressee. Dutch transporters usually have clauses in the transportation agreement which allow them to abandon goods, containing a stipulation in case the transporter receives a cease and desist letter from a right-holder. This letter will usually be forwarded to the transports' client. In case this client does not reply, the clause in the contract reads the transporter is free to abandon the goods. Sometimes a right-holder requests the transporter to send a waiver to his client. This waiver, which contains clauses regarding renouncement of goods and/or rights, penalties, and/or damages has to be signed and returned to the right-holder. In practice, the methods and way of acting of transporters vary highly.

Under the regime of Council Regulation (EEC) No 3295/94, Dutch Customs **21.117** usually opposed the conclusion of settlement agreements concluded by right-holders with the importer, declarant, or owner of the goods, at least when such agreements did not lead to the destruction of the goods.[90] One may expect customs to adopt the same approach under the (new) Regulation, and thus to disregard settlement agreements which do not have the destruction of the products as a consequence. In any event, the Central Customs Administration fiercely objects to the granting of *a posteriori* licences by the right-holder to the owner of infringing goods to (still) allow them to be marketed.

C. Conditions governing action by the authorities having jurisdiction to determine whether the goods infringe an intellectual property right

(1) Authorities having jurisdiction to determine whether the goods infringe an intellectual property right

Under Article 13(1) of the Regulation, to secure border measures taken by **21.118** customs, right-holders are obliged to notify[91] the relevant customs office[92] that

---

[90] This position appeared consistent with the provisions of Reg 3295/94 and with the *Adidas* ruling (see n 82 above). In practice however, the right-holder could in most cases obtain the destruction of goods detained by Dutch Customs without having to initiate (costly and lengthy) proceedings before the courts. Indeed, the filing of a simple criminal complaint often resulted in the destruction of the products. However, filing of such criminal complaint does not suffice anymore. The right-holder will have to serve a writ of (civil) sequestration.

[91] Within 10 (up to 20) working days of receipt of the notification of suspension of release or detention of the goods (Reg 1383/2003, Art 13(1)). In the case of perishable goods, however, this period shall be three working days, and may not be extended (Ibid, Art 13(2)).

[92] Referred to in Art 9(1) of the Regulation.

specific 'proceedings'[93] have been initiated. As explained above, the right-holder may also provide the customs office that took action with a copy of the agreement provided for in Article 11(1), or a request to apply 'the Implied Consent theory' in accordance with the same provision. In the event that the owner, declarant, and holder of the goods do not agree to an amicable settlement, or contest the infringing nature of the goods, the right-holder needs to commence legal proceedings in order (inter alia) to seek their destruction.

21.119 Article 13(1) of the Regulation requires the right-holder to initiate proceedings aimed at determining whether an intellectual property right has been infringed under national law. The *nature* of those proceedings is no longer[94] relevant; only their *aim* is of importance. Proceedings leading to an interlocutory decision might therefore meet the requirement of Article 13(1), provided that they seek to determine whether the goods in dispute infringe an intellectual property right. The exact ambit of Article 13(1) of the Regulation will depend on the interpretation of the word 'proceedings' by the courts—and ultimately the European Court of Justice—in the future.

21.120 The Netherlands provides an extensive and varied legal system.[95] There is no doubt that, under Dutch law and practice, the commencement of proceedings *on the merits of the case*[96] will qualify as 'proceedings seeking to determine whether an intellectual property right has been infringed' under national law within the meaning of Article 13(1) of the Regulation. The main disadvantage of proceedings on the merits is that they are very time-consuming, and may sometimes be expensive.

21.121 *Interlocutory (or summary) proceedings*[97] seeking the granting of an interim injunction based on an alleged breach of an intellectual property right could also qualify as proceedings seeking 'to determine whether an intellectual property right has been infringed'. Such proceedings require the proof of the urgency of the claim, and do not prejudice the merits of the case (meaning that the judge having to decide on the merits is not bound in any way by the decision pronounced in

---

[93] More specifically, 'proceedings to determine whether an intellectual property right has been infringed under national law'.

[94] Art 7(1) of EC Reg 3295/94 required the right-holder to notify customs that the matter had been referred to the 'authority competent to take a substantive decision on the case', or that the 'duly empowered authority had adopted interim measures'.

[95] Cf, eg, the answer to question 5 asked by Japan to the Dutch delegation to the World Trade Organization regarding the Review of Legislation on Enforcement—the Netherlands. For a more detailed overview of this subject, cf Hugenholtz and Heemskerk, 'Hoofdlijnen van Nederlands Burgerlijk Procesrecht' (*Outlines of Civil Procedural Law*) [2002] ISBN 90574994495, Elsevier Bedrijfsinformatie BV, The Hague, and HJ Ssnijders, M Yzonides, and GJ Meijer in 'Nederlands Burgerlijk Procesrecht' (*Dutch Civil Procedural Law*), Deventer, 2002, ISBN 9027152160.

[96] The so-called '*bodemprocedure*' (cf Dutch Code of Civil Procedure, Art 11).

[97] The so-called '*kort geding*' (cf Ibid, Art 254).

summary proceedings). The decision rendered in summary proceedings is immediately enforceable, and does not affect the proceedings on the merits of the case.[98] Interlocutory proceedings are very popular in intellectual property cases in the Netherlands.

Another option open to, for example, trade mark and copyright holders whose **21.122** intellectual property rights have been infringed is to institute *criminal proceedings*. Hopefully (but it is not to be expected) the Dutch Customs authorities will be flexible enough to regard the filing of criminal complaints as meeting the requirements of Article 13(1) of the Customs Regulation, since criminal actions are much less expensive than civil proceedings.[99] Another advantage of criminal prosecution over civil actions is that the demurrage and destruction costs will in principle qualify as criminal costs, which will not be charged to the right-holder but rather to the Dutch state. However, in practice criminal files are often closed without follow-up whenever it proves impossible to apprehend the persons involved in the traffic in the Netherlands. Therefore, the filing of a criminal complaint can be regarded mainly as a measure *complementary* to the commencement of civil proceedings.

The remedies and penalties available under Dutch law in the context of intellec-   **21.123** tual property right infringements will be set out in Part V below.

(2) *Term for notifying customs that proceedings have been started*

According to Article 13(1) of the Regulation, right-holders have 10 working days **21.124** from the receipt of the notification of the suspension of release or of the detention of the goods by customs to inform the latter that proceedings have been initiated to determine whether an intellectual property right has been infringed under national law. This period may be extended once 'in appropriate cases'. In practice, the Dutch customs authorities have seldom required the proof of the 'appropriate' character of an extension requested by a right-holder. However, a right-holder seeking an extension of the term referred to in Article 13(1) must in any case be able to prove that he did not remain passive (for example, that he sent a cease and desist letter in the meantime to the persons involved in the traffic), and show that he is not to blame for the late notification. Where Article 11 (2) of the Regulation applies, the right-holder shall notify customs that proceedings have been initiated to determine whether, under national law, an intellectual property right has been infringed. Except in the case of perishable goods, if insufficient time remains to apply for such proceedings before expiry of the time-limit laid down in the first

---

[98] Dutch Civil Code (*Burgerlijk Wetboek*), Art 257.
[99] On the other hand, as already stated, eg in the Belgian Chapter of this book, criminal actions give right-holders no control over the prosecution.

sub-paragraph of Article 13 (1) of the Regulation, the situation may be deemed an appropriate case within the meaning of the second sub-paragraph of that provision.[100]

21.125   It should be noted that, in the case of perishable goods, the period within which the right-holder must notify customs of the commencement of proceedings is three working days, and this may not be extended.[101]

D. Release of goods suspected of infringing certain rights on provision of a security

21.126   Article 14(1) of the Regulation allows the declarant, owner, importer, holder, or consignee of goods suspected of infringing certain rights, to obtain the release of these goods, on provision of a security. This possibility is limited to goods suspected of infringing patents, supplementary protection certificates, plant variety rights and design rights, as for these rights it is often more complicated to establish whether an infringement occurs. Where the conditions set out in Article 14(1) are fulfilled, Dutch Customs are obliged[102] to release the products. However, this will not be possible where the authority empowered for this purpose has authorized precautionary measures, such as a seizure of the goods.

21.127   The security must be sufficient to protect the interests of the right-holder, and will generally be calculated on the basis of the value of the suspect goods.[103]

21.128   The amount of security provided for in Article 14(2) of the Regulation may be determined jointly by the right-holder and the alleged infringer. The right-holder must inform the Central Customs Administration of the amount of security.

E. Storage of the goods and destruction process[104]

21.129   Under Dutch law and practice, storage costs should be borne by the declarant for the period prior to the expiry of the first 3 or 10 (up to 20) working days set out in Article 13(1) of the Regulation. After the expiry of this term, a distinction

---

[100] See Art 7(1) of Reg 1891/2004.   [101] Reg 1383/2003, Art 13(2).

[102] At least, a strict interpretation of this provision obliges the Central Customs Administration to do so.

[103] See eg K Daele, 'Reg 1383/2003: A New Step in the Fight Against Counterfeit and Pirated Goods at the Borders of the European Union' [2004] EIPR 221.

[104] Regarding the process for the destruction of infringing goods in the Netherlands see eg R Brohm, 'Praktische uitwerking toepassing EU Vo 3295/94 in Nederland' ('*Practical impact of the application of EU Vo 3295/94 in the Netherlands*') [2000/1] BMM Bulletin 2 (Thematic Issue on Piracy ('*Piraterij*')).

ought to be made depending on the type of proceedings initiated by the right-holder:

— pending civil proceedings, the right-holder will bear the storage costs if the declarant refuses to do so, in accordance with Article 6(1) of the Regulation;
— pending criminal proceedings, if a complaint has been filed or interim (precautionary) measures have been imposed on the goods by the 'duly empowered authority', the goods will be stored at the court's office at no cost to the right-holder.

IV. PROVISIONS APPLICABLE TO GOODS FOUND TO INFRINGE AN INTELLECTUAL PROPERTY RIGHT

In accordance with Article 16 of the Regulation, the Dutch courts will (have to) prohibit the entry into/or removal from the Community customs territory (including transhipment), release for free circulation, exportation, re-exportation, placement under a suspensive procedure (including external transit), and placement in a free zone or free warehouse, of goods found to infringe an intellectual property right.   **21.130**

The Dutch Civil Code[105] contains a general provision laying down the so-called unlawful (that is, tortuous) acts. Protection based on this section may be claimed in addition to specific laws in the field of intellectual property, or if the specific intellectual property laws are not applicable.   **21.131**

Pursuant to the Dutch Criminal Code[106] it is illegal to import deliberately, ship goods in transit, export, sell, offer for sale, deliver, distribute, or having in stock, pirated, counterfeit or illegally manufactured trade marks, models, and designs. In those cases that affect the public interest, the Public prosecutor is entitled to start criminal proceedings.   **21.132**

The *importation* (that is, the release for free circulation) of goods considered as infringing an intellectual property right under Article 2(1) of the Regulation is explicitly considered an act of infringement under the various intellectual property laws in the Netherlands.[107]   **21.133**

---

[105] Dutch Civil Code (*Burgerlijk Wetboek*), Art 6:162.
[106] Dutch Criminal Code (*Wetboek van Strafrecht*), Art 337.
[107] This is the case under Art 53 of the Dutch Patent Law when the products thus imported are intended for commercial use or for sale in the Netherlands. Under trade mark law, cf Art 13(A)(1) of the Uniform Benelux Law on Marks. Under copyright law, cf Art 31(a) of the Dutch Copyright Law (cf also *Staatsblad* [Official State Gazette] [1999] 110).

21.134   The Dutch national legal framework is less consistent with Article 16 of the Regulation for the cases of *exportation* and *re-exportation*,[108] as well as *external transit*.[109]

21.135   Indeed, to be regarded as a trade mark infringement, the illegal use of a trade mark must be made 'in the course of trade'. The issue whether goods in transit fulfil this requirement is still heavily debated.[110]

21.136   Under patent law, the placement in transit of goods illegally applying a patented invention cannot be considered a patent infringement.[111]

21.137   The destruction of the goods can in principle be claimed in respect of all goods mentioned in Article 2(1) of the Regulation, including the moulds and matrices.[112] For some intellectual property rights, the confiscation of the goods may be limited to the case of bad faith.[113] In practice, goods are destroyed and if possible, recycled. The right-holder has to file an application for destruction at the relevant customs office. The goods will (have to) be destroyed under customs' supervision, for the risk and account of the right-holder, who will also have to pay the destruction costs.

---

[108] The Uniform Benelux Law on Marks prohibits the exportation and re-exportation of counterfeit goods (see the Protocol of 7 August 1996 amending the Uniform Benelux Law on Marks). The same applies under the Uniform Benelux Act on Designs and Models (see the Protocol of 7 August 1996 amending the Uniform Benelux Design Law). Cf *MAC v Nokia*, Haarlem District Court, 28 December 2001, BIE 2002,51, where the court decided (in a complicated way) that this re-exportation causes infringement. By contrast, the exportation and re-exportation of counterfeit goods under patent law are not prohibited under national law, cf the 1995 Dutch Patent Law, Art 53.

[109] See *Adidas v Hapag-Lloyd*, President of the Rotterdam District Court, 7 January 2000, IER 2000,33, in particular point 5.3 (the question here was whether or not the goods, which circulated in transit, could be considered as having been brought into the Dutch territory).

[110] This issue (with regard to trade marks) is currently pending before the Benelux Court of Justice. See eg *Comercial Iberica Exclusives Deportivas / Nike International*, President of the Haarlem District Court, 8 September 2000, BIE 2001/14. In which case was decided that transit goods which may be used in the course of trade in Spain, but not in the Netherlands (because of trade mark infringement) do not infringe the trade mark rights of Nike. See M. De Cock Buning, 'De Nieuwe Antipiraterij Verordening', (2004) Bijblad Industriele Eigendom para 3.2.1, 237.

[111] 1995 Dutch Patent Law, Art 53.

[112] Cf eg Copyright Law, Art 27(a); Patent Law, Art 70; Uniform Benelux Law on Marks, Art 13(A)(4); Uniform Benelux Design Law, Art 14(3). For a more detailed overview, cf T Cohen Jehoram, 'Schadevergoeding naast winstafdracht (in de Aw, WNR, ROW 1995, BMW en BTMW)' ['*Damages besides surrender of profits*'] [2000] BMM Bull 9 (Thematic Issue Enforcement ('*Rechtshandhaving*')).

[113] Cf eg F Bus, 'Het recht op (beslag tot) afgifte in het merkenrecht en gebruik in het economisch verkeer' ['*The right of (attachment for the purpose of) surrender in trade mark law and use in the course of trade*'] [2000] BMM Bulletin 9.

V. PENALTIES

Pursuant to Article 17 of the Regulation, every Member State must provide effective, **21.138** proportionate, and dissuasive remedies and penalties to apply in cases of a violation of its provisions. As today enforcement still varies between the Member States, the Netherlands is severe and effective in combating counterfeiting and piracy.

A. Civil sanctions

Various remedies are available to right-holders in intellectual property cases, **21.139** which depend on the facts of the case and the nature of the infringement. Commonly, the following remedies are sought:

• declaratory judgments (wrongful act or, sometimes, legality of certain action demanded by a claimant who fears postponed action plus substantive claim for damages afterwards);
• a court order to abstain from certain activities,[114] usually reinforced by conditional damages in case of non-compliance;
• a court order to act, such as recalling illegally published books, official correction of unjust allegations, publication of court decision in newspaper or magazine;
• the recall of illegal copies for destruction;
• the provision of information about suppliers or buyers;
• a claim on, or even destruction of, production equipment used for the production of infringing goods.[115]

Several Dutch intellectual property laws lay down a possibility for the courts to **21.140** order infringers to disclose information to right-holders about the counterfeiting network.[116]

---

[114] Concerning jurisdictions and cross-boarder measures and injunctions related to patent infringement in a case where the goods were deemed to be produced in the Netherlands (on the basis of the so-called 'Interlas-fiction': cf *Hoge Raad* (Dutch Supreme Court) 24 November 1989, NJ 1992, 404, r.o. 4.2.4 ('Interlas') and *Hoge Raad* (Dutch Supreme Court) 21 February 1992, NJ 1993, 164 ('Barbie')), the Dutch Supreme Court rendered an interesting judgment in 2004. See *Hoge Raad* (Dutch Supreme Court) 19 March 2004, IER 2004 / 50: Philips/Postech.

[115] Cf, eg, the answer to question 5 asked by Japan to the Dutch delegation to the World Trade Organization regarding the Review of Legislation on Enforcement—the Netherlands.

[116] With regard to trade mark law, cf Ch Gielen, 'Artikel 13bis BMW ofwel, de strijd tegen namaak' ['*Art 13 Uniform Benelux Law on Marks, or the Fight Against Counterfeiting*'] in *1/4 eeuw Benelux Merkenrecht*, Benelux trade mark Office, 1996, 165. Cf also the *Chloé* case, Dutch Supreme Court (*Hoge Raad*), 27 November 1987, NJ 1988, 722, where it was held that a refusal to mention the names of third persons involved in a trade mark infringement could be considered a tortious act. Cf also Uniform Benelux Law on Marks, Art 13(B)(5) and the *Jack Daniel's* case, Dutch Supreme Court (*Hoge Raad*), 15 February 2002, NJ 2002, 464.

21.141 On demand, measures can be ordered provisionally enforceable, meaning that appeal does not preclude the winning party from enforcing the judgment. In such cases, the losing party is entitled to demand that the party enforcing the decision provide a bank guarantee to cover costs, etc in case of reversal.

21.142 Injunctive relief can be sought in ordinary proceedings, but one might also want to revert to interlocutory proceedings for that purpose. In Dutch procedural law, interlocutory proceedings originally intended to offer the plaintiffs a provisional remedy only, but over the years they established themselves as an excellent way to settle a dispute quickly through the courts. Such proceedings follow the service by the plaintiffs of a writ of summons on the defendant, which will contain the grounds of the claim. The defendant is then given an opportunity to respond to the summons before the court.

21.143 Where necessary, judges may hear cases at short notice or at weekends. It is up to the claimant to see to it that the defendant is duly summoned, in conformity with the court's orders, which will state the ultimate date for such summons to be served.

21.144 The criteria for use of any of the remedies are extensive, varied, and highly dependent on the facts and circumstances of the case. They are found in general statutes (for example, the Civil Code) as well as specific pieces of legislation, such as the Copyright Law. In jurisprudence, the statutory provisions have been refined and elaborated upon by the *Hoge Raad* (Supreme Court).

21.145 The nature and extent of the infringement, the good or bad faith of the infringer, questions of reasonableness and fairness, legitimate expectations, and other general principles of law will all have an impact on the court's decision.

21.146 Any intellectual property right infringement may cause the infringer to incur civil liability, and thus to be condemned to the surrender of profits as well as damages.[117] The claimant may also in some cases obtain the handing over of the turnover realized from the infringing goods.

21.147 The general provisions on damages are set out in Articles 95–96 and 110 of Book 6 of the Dutch Civil Code. Damages can be awarded based on the factual method (actual loss incurred) or abstract method whereby the costs of repair are awarded irrespective of whether the claimant does in fact make such repair. The court may also decide *ex aequo et bono* (that is, in equity) on this point. Regarding the grant of damages, the actual harm suffered by the right-holder will in practice sometimes prove difficult to establish. In most cases, evaluation

---

[117] Copyright Law, Art 27–27(a); Related Rights Law, Art 16; Patent Law, Art 70(4); Uniform Benelux Law on Marks, Art 13(A)(4); Uniform Benelux Design Law, Art 14(3).

will take place *ex aequo et bono*. Actual or abstract damages can be mitigated by the court.[118]

Immaterial damages can be awarded pursuant to Article 106 of Book 6 of the Dutch Civil Code. Damages in case of non-compliance with a court order are governed by Articles 611(a)–611(i) of the Dutch Code of Civil Procedure.

B. Criminal sanctions

Under Dutch criminal law, trade mark infringements are punished by prison sentences of one year and fines to a maximum of EUR 45,000. In the case of professional trade, the jail term may be extended to four years.[119] An exception is made for a person's own use of 'a few products'. **21.148**

Copyright and other intellectual property rights infringements involve penalties consisting of fines to a maximum of EUR 11,200, and/or prison sentences of six months.[120] **21.149**

Since 1 June 2002, a so-called instruction within the meaning of section 130 of the Judiciary (Organisation) Act has been in effect. This instruction, from the Board of Procurators General and addressed to the heads of the Public Prosecutions Departments, contains rules for investigation, prosecution, and provision of information in the event of the violation of intellectual property rights, more particularly Article 337 of the Criminal Code (trade mark fraud) and Articles 31–33 of the Copyright Act. **21.150**

In the policy pursued thus far in the event of such violations, the various Public Prosecution Departments (associated with just as many districts, namely 19) have applied different criteria. Furthermore, some districts were frequently confronted with such counterfeit, for example Haarlem (that has jurisdiction over Schiphol) and the Rotterdam District Court (in connection with the harbour there), while other districts hardly had any experience with it. **21.151**

The (very general) policy pursued was that in case of serious violations, the Public Prosecutions Department was prepared to act, provided the owner of the trade **21.152**

---

[118] Should all data allowing for the assessment of the right-holder's prejudice not yet be available at the time of the decision, damages can be claimed in a separate follow-up procedure for the determination of damages following Arts 612–615b of the Code of Civil Procedure.

[119] Dutch Criminal Code, Art 337.

[120] Dutch Copyright Law, Art 31(a). For a more detailed overview, cf the answer to question 21 asked by Japan to the Dutch delegation to the World Trade Organization regarding the Review of Legislation on Enforcement—the Netherlands.

mark or copyright could prove that it had also taken civil steps such as levying attachment and instituting interlocutory proceedings. If the owner was unable to demonstrate its own initiatives, the Public Prosecutions Department was also reserved in its actions.

21.153   As mentioned, as from 1 June 2002 there has been a major change: there is now a uniform policy for all 19 'parketten' (synonym for Public Prosecution Department). This instruction pertains to the violation of Article 337 of the Criminal Code (trade mark fraud) criminal provisions of the Copyright Act and the Neighbouring Rights Act, including the illegal copying of image and sound carriers such as music cassettes, CDs, videotapes, and CD-ROMs, and very important computer software and Internet productions, illegal copies of business software and also violations relating to 'character licensing', in other words where violation is concerned of a name, pictorial representation or logo protected by copyright to be used on an article produced by a third party.

21.154   Civil action is the first matter of importance, but when the general interest is at stake, such as public health, danger to society and the professional commission of intellectual property fraud, criminal action is taken. To determine a uniform approach in tracing a few goods for own use, a model has been developed in which several types of goods are mentioned in as well as the permissible (maximum) quantity for one's own use.

21.155   Article 337(2) of the Criminal Code gives as a ground for exemption from criminal liability having a few goods, parts of them or trade marks as described in subsection 1 in stock for one's own use. From the viewpoint of efficiency, standards for 'own use' have been set. The quantities mentioned below are in keeping with the violations ascertained in practice.

Type of goods	Quantity for own use
All types of goods except watches, perfumes and image and sound carriers	15 pieces/pairs
Watches	2 pieces
Perfumes	250 millilitres
Image and sound carriers except master(s)	5 pieces (different titles)
Goods that could be dangerous to consumers	None > always prosecute

21.156   Other standards await those who make a profession or business out of committing crimes relating to intellectual property. First of all, police custody and pre-trial detention are possible. Secondly, a much stricter, uniform new regime applies here:

Type of goods	Small batches for which a settlement can be offered by means of a waiver up to and including a quantity of:	Criminal or civil action, at the discretion of the Public Prosecutions Department
All types of goods except watches, perfumes, image and sound carriers	15–50 pieces/pairs/units (regardless of the brand)	> 50 pieces (regardless of the brand)
Watches	1–2 pieces (regardless of the brand)	> 2 pieces (regardless of the brand)
Perfumes	250 ml (regardless of the brand)	> 250 ml (regardless of the brand)
Image and sound carriers	5–25 pieces except master(s)	> 25 pieces and for masters
Goods that could be dangerous to consumers	N/A	Always prosecute

With these uniform and toughened rules, justice is done to the interests of the holders of intellectual property (rights). **21.157**

Intellectual property interests have been taken ever more seriously in the past few years, by both politicians and the Public Prosecutions Department, which need not surprise anyone: the loss to the national economy, particularly from the large-scale form of intellectual property fraud, seriously disrupts the market, in addition to the damage done to the private interest of the trade mark owner when the reputation and exclusivity of trade marks and/or works protected by copyright are impaired. This more energetic action from the Public Prosecutions Departments makes an important contribution to this positive development. There are good relations between the owners of intellectual property rights and the investigation service and this contributes to an effective combating of the trade in counterfeit products. Even so, the owner of an intellectual property right should choose in most cases for enforcement in civil proceedings. **21.158**

VI. LIABILITY OF CUSTOMS AUTHORITIES AND RIGHT-HOLDERS

A. Liability of right-holders and sanctions

Under Article 162 of Book 6 of the Dutch Civil Code any natural or legal person having suffered a prejudice due to the fault committed by a third party may claim damages compensating this prejudice. This provision will govern all liability claims **21.159** referred to in Article 19(3) of the Regulation, initiated by the declarant, owner, importer, exporter, holder, or consignee of the goods, against a right-holder who would have applied the Regulation in a neglectful or reckless manner.[121]

21.160   The same applies as to damage caused by any use of the information provided by Dutch Customs to a right-holder in breach of Article 12 of the Regulation. Due to the direct effect of this provision, the Central Customs Administration will also be entitled to suspend or refuse to renew the right-holder's application(s) for action.

B. Liability of customs authorities and sanctions

(1) Liability of the Dutch customs authorities when applying the provisions of the Regulation

21.161   Article 19(2) of the Regulation stipulates that the exercise by a customs office, or another duly empowered authority, of the powers conferred on them in combating goods infringing an intellectual property right does not render them liable towards the persons involved in the situations referred to in Article 1(1) or the persons affected by the measure provided for in Article 4 for damages suffered by them as a result of the authority's intervention, 'except where provided for by the law of the Member State in which the application is made or, in the case of an application under Article 5(4), by the law of the Member State in which loss or damage is incurred'.

21.162   It is unclear whether a general provision such as the one contained in Article 162 of Book 6 of the Dutch Civil Code constitutes a proper ground for a liability action against Dutch Customs within the meaning of Article 19(2) of the Regulation. If Article 19(2) is to be seen as a general rule of law having direct effect in all Member States, only a more specific provision could 'overrule' this provision. However, it is doubtful whether Article 19(2) can be interpreted as a generally applicable liability rule, 'disqualifying' the application of the general tort law provisions which would otherwise have been regarded as applying to the situations referred to in this Article 19(2).

(2) Liability of the Dutch customs authorities for not detecting or acting against goods suspected of infringing a right-holder's intellectual property right

21.163   The Dutch Customs may not be held liable towards right-holders for failing to act under Article 4 of the Regulation, that is, prior to the filing of an application for

---

[121] Cf the answer to question 9 asked by Japan to the Dutch delegation to the World Trade Organization regarding the Review of Legislation on Enforcement—the Netherlands.

action, since the application of the *ex officio* procedure is purely optional, and is not binding on the customs of the Member States.

Under Article 19(1) of the Regulation, the fact that an application has been **21.164** accepted does not mean that the right-holder is entitled to compensation in the event that goods are not detected by a customs office, and are therefore released, or no action is taken to detain suspect goods in accordance with Article 9(1) of the Regulation, 'save as provided by the law of the Member State in which an application is lodged or, in the case of an application under Article 5(4), by the law of the Member State in which goods infringing an intellectual property right are not detected'.

The provisions of Article 162 of Book 6 of the Dutch Civil Code might apply to **21.165** these situations, provided the lack of detection (of the release of goods suspected of infringing a right-holder's intellectual property right) has caused harm to the right-holder, and customs' omission can be seen as a 'fault' which a normally diligent and careful official would not have made. Whether or not the courts will retain customs' liability in such circumstances will depend on the circumstances of the case. It goes without saying that a lack of detection will more likely be held to constitute a fault when the right-holder's application contained very detailed information as to the goods the detention or suspension of release of which was sought.[122]

Conclusion

The sale and distribution of counterfeit and pirated goods has considerable **21.166** negative social and economic implications. Such goods may mislead consumers and may cause harm to the holders of the intellectual property right(s) infringed. Their profitability, reputation, attractiveness, and exclusiveness are reduced. Given the often clandestine, and sometimes even criminal, nature of counterfeiting and piracy, it is difficult to estimate the actual extent of their impact.

Mindful of the importance of the fight against counterfeiting and piracy, the **21.167** European Community has adopted several specific provisions, amongst others in the field of border measures. On 1 July 2004, Regulation 3295/94 was replaced by Regulation 1383/2003. Article 11 of the Regulation provides for a possibility for the Member State to implement a so-called 'simplified procedure', whereby right-holders may request that customs destroy suspect goods, without the need to have a court determine whether or not an intellectual property right has been infringed. This option constitutes an important change to the former regime.

---

[122] Cf the answer to questions 9, 10, and 11 asked by Japan to the Dutch delegation to the World Trade Organization regarding the Review of Legislation on Enforcement—the Netherlands.

Despite the fact that this procedure has not yet been implemented by way of a specific statute into Dutch law, it is already being applied in the Netherlands.

21.168 However, where the declarant, holder, or owner of the goods objects to their destruction, the 'regular' procedure of Article 13 will apply. If, at the end of the court proceedings initiated under this provision, the suspect goods are found to infringe any of the intellectual property rights listed in Article 2(1) of the Regulation, the goods will be destroyed.

21.169 Cooperation between right-holders and declarants, holders, or owners of suspect goods, as well as collaboration between the same and customs, is of great importance. At a European level, cooperation between Member States and the Customs Union is essential. In the Customs Action Plan[123] such cooperation has been set out with respect to the major European ports (which includes obviously the Rotterdam harbour) and airports (including the Schiphol Airport).

21.170 The provisions aimed at policing the external frontiers of the European Union so as to prevent counterfeit and pirated goods from entering or leaving the Community customs territory are particularly important in the fight to stop the production of such goods at source. It is to be hoped that the scope of the EC anti-counterfeiting and anti-piracy system will systematically keep on extending over the years.

21.171 As for the Netherlands, these provisions will certainly prove of great help in the war against counterfeiting. Because of the Netherlands' geographical position (and in particular its direct access to the sea and the European hinterland), the country has traditionally been a transit country. A huge volume of products find their way to the end-user through the Netherlands. The Port of Rotterdam and the Schiphol Airport process the biggest flows of goods.

21.172 The holders of intellectual property rights who are confronted on a large scale with the trade in unauthentic goods do not publish any figures on the quantity of such goods confiscated.

21.173 The distribution of these goods is largely carried out in the Netherlands by small traders. Many of them are sold in markets, by street vendors, in pubs and bars, at schools, and at other small-scale locations. There are no large public sales outlets where non-original goods are offered for sale. Nor is this possible, because the government does not tolerate such large-scale sale of counterfeit goods.

21.174 The government turns a blind eye to small-scale trading of illegitimate goods, provided that there are no risks to public health. The reason why the government

---

[123] Communication from the Commission to the Council, the European Parliament, and the Economic and Social Committee, concerning a strategy for the Customs Union of 8 February 2001, COM(2001) 51 final (8.2.2001).

does not take action against such small-scale trade has to do with capacity problems. The Dutch government takes the view that it should use its enforcement resources primarily for tracking 'big fish'. The holders of intellectual property rights are therefore forced to combat the trade in non-authentic goods through civil action.

If there is large-scale trade in counterfeit goods, and it proves impossible for the **21.175** holder of an intellectual property right to prevent its rights from being infringed through civil actions, the public prosecution service will generally initiate an investigation and criminal proceedings against the parties involved.

When bearing in mind the radiography of the Dutch counterfeiting market **21.176** described above,[124] it becomes evident that the Regulation is of great importance in preventing the movement of illicit goods in the Netherlands. The way to manage the application and scope of sanctions at a national level is another (equally crucial) issue, together with the fact that copying music or software and buying counterfeit luxury goods are still considered a commonly accepted practice. Hopefully there will be a change of mind in the near future. To that effect, it is essential that Dutch consumers be informed of the negative social, economic, and legal consequences of counterfeiting and piracy.

---

[124] Cf para 21.90–21.99 above: factual background.

22

POLAND

Dorota Rzążewska and Zofia Senda

Introduction

Poland's accession to the European Union—on 1 May 2004—is an important **22.01** turning point in the transition from national legislation on border measures to the Regulations of European Law.

Until 30 April 2004, proceedings conducted by Polish customs authorities in **22.02** the case of suspected entry into the Polish customs area of infringed goods were based on national law. The main legislation was the Law of 9 January 1997— the Customs Code[1] and its implementing regulation, namely the Regulation of the Council of Ministers of 5 February 2002, on the subject of the method and course of procedure of customs authorities in the case of detention or suspension of release of goods suspected of infringement of intellectual property rights.[2]

Article 57(1) to (3) of the Customs Code previously in force constituted the basis **22.03** for the procedures of customs authorities, as it provided for actions *ex officio* or resulting from a motion filed, consisting of detention or suspension of release of goods in cases of suspected infringement of intellectual property rights. Detailed proceedings conducted by customs authorities, the course of filing with customs authorities of applications for action at the border and the granting of the protection were provided for in the above Regulation.

In general, these provisions tended to be similar to the legal regulations in force **22.04** within the Community, since during earlier accession negotiations the national

---

[1] Ustawa z dnia 9 stycznia, 1997 r. Kodeks Celny, consolidated text: Dz.U. of 2001, No 75, item 802 with subsequent amendments.

[2] Rozporządzenie Rady Ministrów z dnia 5 lutego 2002 r. w sprawie sposobu i trybu postępowania organów celnych przy zatrzymaniu towarów w wypadkach podejrzenia naruszenia przepisów dotyczacych własności intelektualnej, Dz.U.of 2002, No 12, item 112.

legislation had to be harmonized with the European law in order to ensure the same level of protection of intellectual property rights.

22.05 Inauguration of Poland's membership of the European Union, on 1 May 2004 was simultaneously the day on which legislation of the European Union came into force. On that day Polish regulations in the form of the Customs Code and its implementing rules were revoked. Instead, the following legislation came into force: Council Regulation (EEC) No 2913/92 of 12 October 1992, establishing the Community Customs Code[3] and Council Regulation (EC) No 3295/94 of 22 December 1994, laying down measures concerning the entry into the Community and the export and re-export from the Community of goods infringing certain intellectual property rights[4] and Commission Regulation (EC) No 1367/95 of 19 June 1995, laying down provisions for the implementation of Council Regulation (EC) No 3295/94, as amended in 1999.[5]

22.06 To ensure a coherent enforcement of the Council Regulation and to maintain continuity of decisions issued under the provisions formerly applicable in Poland with regard to the protection of intellectual property rights at the borders, two regulations on the matter were adopted on 19 March 2004, namely the Customs Law[6] and the Provisions Introducing the Customs Law.[7]

22.07 On the basis of Article 25 of the Provisions Introducing the Customs Law, the Customs Code of 9 January 1997 was revoked along with its implementing rules, except in so far as they were replaced by provisional regulations. The national Regulation of the Council of Ministers concerning protection of intellectual property rights was revoked. As a result, on the date of Poland's accession, only the provisions of Community law, that is, Council Regulation No 3295/94 of 22 December 1994 (as amended in 1999) were applicable with respect to protection against entry into the Community territory and the export and re-export beyond the Community borders of goods infringing certain intellectual property rights, and Commission Regulation No 1367/95 establishing secondary legislation for the basic Regulation No 3295/94.

---

[3] OJ L 302 (19.10.1992).

[4] OJ L 341 (30.12.1994), as amended by Council Reg (EC) No 241/1999 of 25 January 1999, OJ L 27/1 (2.2.1999). See also Council Reg (EC) No 806/2003 of 14 April 2003, OJ L 122/1 (16.5.2003).

[5] OJ L 133 (17.6.1995), as amended by Commission Reg (EC) No 2549/1999 of 2 December 1999, OJ L 308/16 (3.12.1999) and by the Law concerning the conditions of accession of the Czech Republic, the Republic of Estonia, the Republic of Cyprus, the Republic of Latvia, the Republic of Lithuania, the Republic of Hungary, the Reg of Malta, the Republic of Poland, the Republic of Slovenia and the Slovak Republic and the adjustments to the Treaties on which the European Union is founded, OJ L 236/33 (23.9.2003).

[6] Ustawa z dnia 19 marca, 2004 r. Prawo celne, Dz.U. of 2004, No 68, item 622, as amended.

[7] Ustawa z dnia 19 marca, 2004 r. Przepisy wprowadzajace ustawę—Prawo Celne, Dz.U. of 2004, No 68, item 623.

Pursuant to Article 3(8) of Regulation No 3295/94, within the structure of its **22.08** customs bodies, Poland appointed customs authorities competent to examine and accept applications for action in the case of suspicion that situations had occurred which are identified in the Regulation relating to goods infringing certain intellectual property rights (for instance release for free circulation, export, and re-export). In Poland, the authority competent to consider such applications is the Director of the Customs Chamber in Warsaw. The powers of this body are established under the national Regulation of Minister of Finance of 22 April 2004 concerning the appointment of the Director of the Customs Chamber in Warsaw to manage certain customs matters,[8] which was based on Article 70(3) of the Customs Law of 19 March 2004

On 1 July 2004, the provisions of the new Council Regulation No 1383/2003 **22.09** concerning customs action against goods suspected of infringing certain intellectual property rights and the measures to be taken against goods found to have infringed such rights,[9] as well as Commission Regulation No 1891/2004 of 21 October 2004 laying down provisions for the implementation of Regulation No 1383/2003,[10] came into force in the European Union including Poland. Owing to their direct effect, the provisions of Council Regulation No 1383/2003 concerning border measures do not require any implementation measures. The national law provides only for the issues which are beyond the scope of the Regulation, but are necessary to enforce provisions of Community law, such as provisions on administrative procedure before customs authorities. As such, procedural issues are subject to the national laws of the Member States. In Poland, according to the Customs Law (Article 73) the provisions of Article 12 and Part IV (Tax proceedings) of the 29 August 1997 Tax Ordinance,[11] as amended, are accordingly applied.

Pursuant to the above, the only provisions effective in Poland regarding border **22.10** measures are those of Council Regulation No 1383/2003. There is no national legislation that would permit application of the rules laid down in the above Regulation to other intellectual property rights.

The subjective scope of the application of the Regulation is significant from a **22.11** practical point of view since, in the regulatory environment prior to 1 May 2004; decisions were issued on the protection of exclusive rights that are no longer covered by Regulation 1383/2003. These rights included, for instance, an exclusive right for production and sale of a specific product in the Republic of Poland. This

---

[8] Rozporządzenie Ministra Finansów z dnia 22 kwietnia 2004 r. w sprawie wyznaczenia Dyrektora Izby Celnej w Warszawie do prowadzenia niektórych spraw celnych, Dz.U. of 2004 No 87, item 830. [9] OJ WE L 196 (2.8.2003).
[10] OJ L 328 (30.10.2004).
[11] Ustawa z dnia 29 sierpnia 1997 r.—Ordynacja podatkowa, Dz.U. of 1997, No 137, item 926 with amendments.

right was granted by a decision of the President of the Patent Office of the Republic of Poland on the basis of the regulations formerly in force concerning inventive activity, namely the Law on Inventive Activity, as amended by the Law on Inventive Activity of the 30 October 1992 and the Law on the Patent Office of the Republic of Poland.[12] These laws were introduced in the implementation of the Treaty on Commercial and Economic Relations concluded between the Republic of Poland and The United States of America[13] and constituted a transitional stage pending integration of measures to protect pharmaceuticals into the Law on Inventive Activity of 19 October 1972,[14] which is no longer in force. Thus, by virtue of the legislation effective prior to EU accession, border measures could be applied to other exclusive rights, categorized by academics as industrial property rights. This, however, is no longer possible. Furthermore, Polish legislation lacks provisions enabling application of border measures to issues other than those covered by Regulation 1383/2003, such as parallel import.

22.12　Among introductory issues, it is also necessary to elaborate on the problem of decisions to protect intellectual property rights that were granted prior to the coming into force of Council Regulation No 1383/2003, even before the date of Poland's accession to the European Union, that is, by virtue of national legislation effective until 30 April 2004. Pursuant to transitional legislation,[15] such decisions will be valid until the end of the period for which they have been issued, provided that they are applied in accordance with the conditions laid down in the provisions of the Customs Law effective after Poland's accession to the European Union.

I. SUBJECT MATTER AND SCOPE OF THE NATIONAL LAW APPLYING THE REGULATION

A. Customs procedure of the goods

22.13　In Poland, Council Regulation (EC) No 1383/2003 is applied to all customs procedures defined in Article 1(1) of the Regulation (release for free circulation, export, or re-export) as well as those mentioned in Article 1(2).

---

[12] Ustawa z dnia 30 października 1992 r. o zmianie ustawy o wynalazczości i ustawy o Urzędzie Patentowym RP, Dz.U. of 1993, No 4, item 14.

[13] Traktat o stosunkach handlowych i gospodarczych między Rzeczpospolitą Polską a Stanami Zjednoczonymi Ameryki, M.P. of 1991, No 27, item 191.

[14] Ustawa z dnia 19 października 1972 r. o wynalazczości, Dz.U. of 1993, No 26, item 117 with subsequent amendments.

[15] Transitional provision in the form of Art 32 in conjunction with Art 27 (1–3) of the Regs Introducing the Customs Law. Ustawa z dnia 19 marca, 2004 r. Prawo celne (Dz.U. of 2004, No 68, item 622, as amended)

Nonetheless, our experience is that a majority of goods suspected of infringement **22.14** of intellectual property rights are detained during import and export. Furthermore, many actions, in particular those undertaken by customs *ex officio*, relate to tax procedures in respect of smuggling, especially if goods suspected of infringing intellectual property rights were not the subject of a customs declaration, and the persons attempting to introduce such goods were charged with understating the value of the customs duty. Recently, this situation has mostly pertained to attempts to import cosmetics marked with counterfeit trade marks.

B. Definition of infringing goods

Polish Customs do not have the power to take action in respect of all intellectual **22.15** property rights that exist in Poland (for example, they cannot adopt border measures in respect of unregistered trade marks). When intercepting suspected goods, customs will first make sure they comply with the definitions contained in Article 2 of the Regulation before taking action.

(1) Counterfeit goods

Pursuant to Article 2(1)(a)(i) of Regulation 1383/2003, counterfeit goods are **22.16** goods, including their packaging, bearing without authorization, a trade mark identical to another mark or which cannot be distinguished in its essential aspects from a registered trade mark when the trade mark in question is registered for the same type of goods, provided that such goods infringe the right-holder's right under Community law or the national law of the Member State in which the application for action was filed.

The following prerequisites must be fulfilled for goods to be considered as coun- **22.17** terfeit goods within the meaning of Council Regulation No 1383/2003: identical or similar trade mark, identical goods, resulting in an infringement of the right of protection for a trade mark. The above definition is narrower than that provided under Polish law, which classifies as infringement, not only an unlawful use of a trade mark identical or similar to a trade mark registered for the same type of goods, but also an infringement of the right to a renowned trade mark, which may occur beyond the principle of speciality or the right to a well-known mark within the meaning of Article 6bis of the Paris Convention.

In Poland the issue of trade marks, patents and supplementary protection certifi- **22.18** cates, utility models and industrial designs, geographical indications of origin (with the exception of geographical indications and designations of origin for agricultural products specified in Annex I to the Treaty establishing the European

Community and agricultural products and foodstuffs specified in the Annexes to Council Regulation (EEC) No 2081/92 of 14 July 1992 on the protection of geographical indications and designations of origin for agricultural products and foodstuffs) and topographies of integrated circuits are governed by the Law on Industrial Property of 30 June 2000[16] ('the IPL'). Under Article 120(3)(3) of the IPL, counterfeit trade mark refers to an identical trade mark unlawfully used or to a trade mark which in the course of trade cannot be distinguished from the trade mark registered for the goods covered by the certificate of protection.

22.19   The definition of counterfeit goods in the IPL covers all situations referred to in Article 2(1)(a)(i) of Council Regulation No 1383/2003. However, the IPL contains a broader definition of infringement in respect of trade mark rights.

22.20   Under Article 296(2) of the IPL, infringement of a trade mark consists of unlawful use in the course of trade of:

- a trade mark identical to a trade mark registered in respect of identical goods,
- a trade mark identical or similar to a trade mark registered in respect of identical or similar goods, if a likelihood exists of misleading the public, including in particular a risk of associating the trade mark with a registered trade mark;
- a trade mark identical or similar to a renowned trade mark registered for any kind of goods, if such use without due cause would take unfair advantage of or be detrimental to the distinctive character or the repute of the earlier trade mark.

22.21   When assessing the existence of a trade mark infringement within the meaning of Regulation 1383/2003 it should be stated that, according to the provisions of the IPL, the use of a trade mark identical to a registered trade mark as well as the use of a trade mark that cannot be distinguished from a trade mark registered in the course of trade, when unlawfully used for goods similar to the goods for which the trade mark has been registered, does not constitute an infringement. Indeed, Article 2(1)(a)(i) provides that the goods must be 'of the same type' as those referred to in the trade mark registration. Moreover, while Regulation 1383/2003 contains references to trade mark infringements under Community or national laws, it does not provide grounds for considering a trade mark identical or similar to a renowned trade mark to be a counterfeit trade mark in the situations where it is used on goods other than those for which a renowned trade mark is registered.

22.22   Fortunately, Polish customs authorities view the issue of how to qualify goods as 'counterfeit' in a broader context since they assess it in the light of the definition of what constitutes a trade mark infringement under Article 296 of the IPL. On the basis of the IPL, customs also consider goods to be counterfeit if they are marked with a trade mark identical or similar to the trade mark registered for the

---

[16]   Ustawa z dnia 30 czerwca 2000 r. Prawo własności przemysłowej, consolidated text: Dz.U. of 2001, No 49, item 508 as amended.

same or similar goods. Furthermore, in the case of renowned trade marks, goods are considered counterfeit if such a trade mark is unlawfully used on any goods. In accordance with Polish law, renowned trade marks are protected beyond the principle of speciality and the proof of a risk of confusion is not required. Their protection also covers situations of trade mark's unjustified use for any goods, which may result in gaining unjustified benefits or be detrimental to the distinctive character or the repute of the registered trade mark.

In practice, a broader interpretation of the concept 'counterfeit goods' allows **22.23** action to be taken if goods are marked with signs which have been phonetically or graphically modified (for example by exchange of letters: Odidas or Abidas instead of Adidas, by letter transposition: Neki instead of Nike, Chalin instead of Chanel, Slazengers or Slazeenger instead of Slazenger). Polish Customs also take action when an element of a trade mark composed of several parts has been omitted or a word or graphic distinction has been added.

Moreover, when they are faced with a similar mark and different goods, customs **22.24** do not hesitate to act *ex officio* if they suspect an infringement has occurred.

The notion of 'counterfeit goods' embraces not only goods marked with a trade **22.25** mark but also all kinds of products bearing a trade mark symbol such as a logo, label, or sticker, including brochures, instructions for use or guarantee documents even presented separately. Counterfeit goods also comprise packaging materials bearing the trade marks of counterfeit goods, presented separately, under the same conditions as the goods referred to in Article 2(1)(a)(i) of Regulation 1383/2003.

Actions are also initiated by Polish customs authorities in the event of an **22.26** attempted release for free circulation of goods marked with infringing trade marks, such as pendants, ballpoint pens, spectacle frames, sun glasses, disposable and non-disposable bags, note-books, or sandals.

Practice shows that customs also scrutinize all sorts of packaging and boxes, bear- **22.27** ing trade mark symbols. Sometimes, even original packaging or boxes are detained, when transported separately from the contents. For instance, customs detained a shipment of empty metal boxes bearing the 'STR.8' trade mark that were intended as containers for toilet water.

Polish law does not permit initiation of customs action to protect a trade mark **22.28** whose application for registration is still pending. Due to the lack of alternative legislation at the national level, it is not possible to extend the scope of Council Regulation No 1383/2003 to cover applications for trade mark registrations.

(2) Pirated goods

Pursuant to the definition laid down in Article 2(1)(b) of Council Regulation **22.29** 1383/2003, 'pirated goods' are goods which are or contain copies made without the consent of the holder of a copyright or related right or design right, regardless of whether it was registered under national law, or of a person authorized by the right-holder in the country of production, in cases where the making of those copies would constitute an infringement of that right under Council Regulation (EC) No 6/2002 of 12 December 2001 on Community designs[17] or under the law of the Member State in which the application for customs action is made.

22.30 Polish Copyright Law[18] ('the Copyright Law'), deals with copyrights and related rights. This Law does not contain a definition of pirated goods or goods which are or contain copies. Therefore, Polish national law does not provide any guidelines on how to interpret these concepts.

22.31 Nonetheless, the Copyright Law contains a definition of 'reproduction of works',[19] which covers production of copies of a work with the use of a specific technology, the said production being part of the author's economic rights. Under Article 17 of the Copyright Law, the author's economic rights also include the exclusive right to use the work, to dispose of its use throughout all fields of exploitation, and to receive remuneration for the use of the work. Accordingly, the reproduction of a work (that is, the production of copies of a work) without the author's consent, irrespective of the type of technology used, constitutes a copyright infringement. Furthermore, copies produced without the author's consent or exceeding his consent are illegal copies, whose release for free circulation or other use is in breach of law and gives rise to civil[20] and criminal liability.[21] The adjective 'pirated' in colloquial language is understood as relating to illegally produced copies of a work.

22.32 The Copyright Law provides for the following categories of related rights: rights in artistic performances,[22] rights in phonograms and videograms,[23] rights to programme broadcasts,[24] rights to first editions and scientific and critical editions.[25] The differences existing as to the ambit of these specific rights are of little significance for the application of border measures. To interpret the phrase 'pirated goods, namely goods which are or contain copies made without the consent of the holder of a related right', the most important issue relates to the authorization of the right-holder as to the use and disposal of the subject matter of a related right following its fixing, reproduction, and introduction into trade. The right-holder's authorization is a prerequisite to the lawful exercise of all related rights protected in Poland.[26] Therefore, reproduction, of the subject matter of a related right (for instance an artistic performance, a phonogram, radio, or television programme broadcasts) without the consent of the right-holder shall constitute an infringement.

---

[17] OJ L 3 (5.1.2002).
[18] Ustawa z dnia 4 lutego 1994 r. o prawie autorskim i prawach pokrewnych, consolidated text: Dz.U. of 2000, No 80, item 904, as amended. [19] Ibid, Art 50.
[20] Ibid, Art 79. [21] Ibid, Arts 115–123. [22] Ibid, Arts 85–93.
[23] Ibid, Arts 94–96. [24] Ibid, Arts 97–99. [25] Ibid, Art 99(1)–(4).
[26] Ibid, Art 86(1)(2)(a) and (b); Art 94(4)(1) and (2); Art 97(2) and (5); Art 99(1).

Customs authorities, acting on the basis of Regulation No 1383/2003 in respect   **22.33**
of pirated goods, focus not only on the definition of Article 2(1)(b), but also on
the definition of infringement of copyright or related rights arising under national
law. Therefore, any reproduction of a work or of the subject matter of a related
right without the consent of the right-holder is considered by customs as an illegal
(pirated) good.

In the case of industrial designs registered in accordance with the IPL,[27] by obtain-   **22.34**
ing the right of registration, the holder acquires the exclusive right to exploit the
industrial design for commercial or professional purposes throughout the territory of the Republic of Poland.[28] Moreover, the right-holder shall enjoy the right
to prevent any third party from making, offering, putting on the market, importing, exporting, or using a product in which the design is incorporated or to which
it is applied, or stocking such a product for those purposes.[29] Furthermore, the
rights deriving from a registered design extend to any design which does not produce on the informed user a different overall impression.[30] Hence, under the laws
of Poland, among other things, import and export not only of a product in which
the registered design is incorporated, but also of a product which does not produce on the informed user a different overall impression than the registered
design, if it is used for products for which that design was registered, shall constitute an infringement.

Under Polish law, provisions on industrial designs are laid down in the Industrial   **22.35**
Property Law (Articles 102–119) of 30 June 2000. The appearance of the whole
or part of a product resulting from the features of, in particular, the lines, colours,
shape, texture, or materials of the product and its ornamentation shall qualify for
protection as an industrial design,[31] provided that it is new and has an individual
character. Any industrial or handicraft item, including, in particular, packaging,
graphic symbols and typographic typefaces, but excluding computer programs,
shall be considered to be 'a product'.[32] Furthermore, complex products and their
components if they may be the subject of commercialization or remain visible
during normal use shall also constitute a product.

As regards the legal situation of industrial designs in Poland, much depends on   **22.36**
whether a design is registered or not.

Those designs which are not registered and, therefore, do not fall within the   **22.37**
protection under the IPL, may be protected under the Copyright Law, provided
they possess the characteristics of a work within the meaning of that Law.

In light of the aforementioned definitions of infringements of copyrights, related   **22.38**
rights, and registered design rights, it should be acknowledged that any attempt to

---

[27] Ibid, Art 105(1).   [28] Ibid, Art 105(2).   [29] Ibid, Art 105(3).
[30] Ibid, Art 105(4).   [31] IPL, Art 102(1).   [32] Ibid, Art 102(2).

introduce into the Community territory goods that embody any of these rights and are produced without the right-holder's consent shall be subject to the provisions of Regulation No 1383/2003.

(3) Goods infringing other intellectual property rights

Goods infringing a patent or a supplementary protection certificate

22.39   A patent confers on its owner the exclusive right to exploit the invention, for commercial or professional purposes, throughout the territory of the Republic of Poland.[33]

22.40   Under Article 66 of the IPL, the patent holder has the right to prevent any third party, not having his consent, from exploiting his invention for commercial or professional purposes by:

- making, using, offering, putting on the market a product that is the subject matter of the invention, or importing the product for such purposes, or
- using a process that is the subject matter of the invention, as well as using, offering, putting on the market or importing for such purposes the product directly obtained by that process.

22.41   Polish law provides for patent protection with respect to inventions which consist either of a product or of a process and, in which case, products directly obtained by means of that process are also protected. In the light of Regulation No 1383/2003, goods which are the subject matter of a product patent as well as those manufactured by means of a patented process may be seen as infringing a patent.

22.42   It is also worth emphasizing that pursuant to Article 64(2) of the IPL, in cases where a patented process results in the manufacture of a new product, or where the right-holder proves that he was unable through reasonable efforts to identify the process of manufacture actually used by the alleged infringer, the product which may be obtained by means of the patented process shall be deemed to have been obtained by that process, unless proven otherwise.

22.43   Polish national legislation regarding supplementary protection certificates is entirely compatible with the system of protection of medicinal products and plant protection products as laid down in Council Regulation (EEC) No 1768/92 of 18 June 1992 concerning the creation of a supplementary protection certificate for medicinal products[34] and Regulation (EC) No 1610/96 of the European Parliament and of the Council of 23 July 1996 concerning the creation of

---

[33] Ibid, Art 63.   [34] OJ L 182 (2.7.1992).

a supplementary protection certificate for plant protection products.[35] Polish industrial property law provides that, subject to the conditions specified in the provisions relating to supplementary protection certificates for medicinal products and plant protection products in the European Union, supplementary protection rights are granted for the territory of the Republic of Poland.[36]

As the EC Regulations are directly applicable, goods infringing a supplementary **22.44** protection certificate shall include the goods infringing the basic patent, but only in respect of products covered by the authorization to place the corresponding medicinal product on the market.[37] This also applies to plant protection products.

Goods infringing a national plant variety right

Protection of plant varieties under Polish national law is regulated by the Law on **22.45** the Legal Protection of Plant Variety Rights of 26 June 2003.[38] In accordance with the provisions of this Law, the breeder's exclusive right to a protected plant variety covers the following methods of using seed material of a protected plant variety: production, breeding, preparation for breeding, offering for sale, sale, or other forms of disposal, export, import, and/or storage.

Apart from the above, in addition to seed material, the breeder's exclusive right **22.46** covers the following:[39]

- crop material and products manufactured therefrom, provided the breeder could not rely on the exclusive right concerning seed material of a protected variety;
- seed material of decorative or fruit plants, if used again for commercial purposes:
  - reproductive material for the production of decorative plants, or
  - cut flowers, or
  - seed material of trees, shrubs or perennials;
- varieties:
  - derivative varieties, discovered or produced from the protected mother variety, not being a derivative variety,
  - varieties that cannot be clearly distinguished from the protected variety, and
  - varieties that require repeated use of the variety protected by the exclusive right in respect of their seed material.

Taking into account the scope of the exclusive rights to a plant variety, seed **22.47** material produced or reproduced without the consent of the authorized breeder, seed material which illegally bears the name of a protected plant variety, or seed material placed on the market without the right-holder's consent will infringe the

---

[35] OJ L 198 (8.8.1996).   [36] IPL, Art 75(1).   [37] Council Reg No 1768/92, Art 4.
[38] Ustawa z dnia 26 czerwca 2003 r. o ochronie prawnej odmian roślin, Dz.U. of 2003, No 137, item 1300.   [39] Ibid, Art 22.

latter's rights. Under the 26 June 2003 Law, the last category covers the offering for sale, sale, or other forms of disposal, export, and import of such seed materials.

22.48 To date, customs authorities have not undertaken any action against goods infringing a national plant variety right.

Goods infringing a national designation of origin or a geographical indication

22.49 Geographical indications and designations of origin are protected in Poland on the basis of the provisions of the IPL and of the Suppression of Unfair Competition Law of 16 April 1993[40] whereas geographical indications and designations of origins of agricultural products specified in Annex I to the Treaty establishing the European Community and agricultural products and foodstuffs referred to in the Annexes to Council Regulation (EEC) No 2081/92,[41] are protected in accordance with the provisions of Council Regulation (EEC) No 2081/92 of 14 July 1992 on the protection of geographical indications and designations of origin for agricultural products and foodstuffs and the Law of 17 December 2004 on the registration and protection of names and designations of agricultural products and foodstuffs and on traditional products[42] which came into force on 17 February 2005.

22.50 Articles 175 to 195 of the IPL, which form the Chapter on Geographical Indications, distinguish between two types of geographical indications, namely, the names of regions and designations of origin. The latter are designations used to describe products originating in a specific territory, and the properties of which are essentially or exclusively due to a particular geographical environment with its inherent natural and human factors, and the production or processing of which takes place in that territory.[43] Names of regions relate to products originating in a specific territory, and the properties or other characteristics of which are essentially attributable to their geographical origin, that is the territory where they are produced or processed.[44]

22.51 Moreover, geographical indications shall also mean designations used to describe products made of raw materials or intermediate products coming from a defined area larger that the production or processing area, provided that special conditions for the preparation of the raw materials or intermediate products exist and there are inspection arrangements in place to ensure that those conditions are adhered to.[45]

---

[40] Ustawa z dnia 16 kwietnia 1993 r. o zwalczaniu nieuczciwej konkurencji, Dz.U. of 2003, No 153, item 1503, as amended.

[41] Council Reg (EEC) No 2081/92, OJ L 208 of 24.7.1992.

[42] Ustawa z dnia 17 grudnia 2004 r. o rejestracji i ochronie nazw i oznaczeń produktów rolnych i środków spożywczych oraz o produktach tradycyjnych, Dz. U. of 2005, No 10, item 68.

[43] IPL, Art 175(1), first indent.　　　　[44] Ibid, Art 175(1), second indent.

[45] Ibid, Art 175(2).

Furthermore, the IPL specifies that geographical indications shall also include geographical designations which do not correspond to the true place in which the product originates, or other traditional designations, if they are normally used in respect of goods originating in a given area.[46]

Taking into account these definitions of geographical indications, any goods **22.52** unlawfully marked with the indications in question, that is, not originating in the relevant territory, and deprived of the properties or other characteristics which are decisive to be entitled to mark the goods with the geographical indication, infringe the rights deriving from geographical indications. This results from Article 185 of the IPL, which relates to infringements of a geographical indication. Pursuant to this provision, a registered geographical indication may not be used on the territory of the Republic of Poland by anyone, whose products do not satisfy the requirements for the grant of such a right. The same applies even if such use is not intended to designate the geographical origin of the products or where the true place of production of the product is indicated. A geographical indication may not be used either in the above circumstances even if accompanied by expressions indicating the kind of the product, such as 'imitation', 'type', or 'process'. The prohibition referred to shall cover geographical indications in their original wording, in translations or in other related forms.

Pursuant to Article 174(3) of the IPL, the regulations on the protection of **22.53** geographical indications laid down in the IPL are not applicable to foodstuffs specified in Annex I to the Treaty establishing the European Community and agricultural products and foodstuffs specified in the Annexes to Council Regulation (EEC) No 2081/92 of 14 July 1992 on the protection of geographical indications and designations of origin for agricultural products and foodstuffs.

The rules governing the protection of designations of origin and geographical **22.54** indications are laid down in Council Regulation (EEC) No 2081/92[47] and the Law of 17 December 2004 on the registration and protection of names and designations of agricultural products and foodstuffs and on traditional products,[48] in force from 17 February 2005.

The provisions of Council Regulation (EEC) No 2081/92 are directly applicable **22.55** in Poland, therefore the scope of protection of the designations registered under that Regulation is specified in this instrument.

Beside detailed provisions on the prosecution of applications for registration of **22.56** geographical indications and designations of origin, the Polish Law also contains regulations on temporary protection under national law, to which designations of

---

[46] Ibid, Art 175(3). [47] Council Reg (EEC) No 2081/92, OJ L 208 of 24.7.1992.
[48] Ustawa z dnia 17 grudnia 2004 r. o rejestracji i ochronie nazw i oznaczeń produktów rolnych i środków spożywczych oraz o produktach tradycyjnych, Dz. U. of 2005, No 10, item 68.

origin and geographical indications of agricultural products are entitled from the date of the decision issued by the Minister responsible for agricultural market issues, subject to compliance of the application with the requirements specified in Council Regulation (EEC) No 2081/92.

22.57　In accordance with Article 35(2) of the Law of 17 December 2004 on the registration and protection of names and designations of agricultural products and foodstuffs and on traditional products, designations of origin and geographical indications enjoying temporary protection are entered in the List kept by the Minister responsible for agricultural market issues. The List is an open list.

22.58　Temporary national protection expires on the date of the recording of a designation of origin or a geographical indication in the Register of protected designations of origin and geographical indications conducted in accordance with Council Regulation (EEC) No 2081/92, or on the date on which such a recording is refused.

22.59　The entity which produces, in accordance with the requirements included in the specification, an agricultural product or a foodstuff the designation of origin or geographical indication of which has been entered in the List referred to in Article 35 (2) of the Law of 17 December 2004, has the right to use the name entered in that List in the course of trade.

22.60　In summary, any goods on which a geographical indication has been unlawfully affixed in the aforesaid manner may be considered as goods infringing an intellectual property right in the understanding of Council Regulation 1383/2003. The same is also true for geographical indications protected under Community law.

22.61　The provisions of the Suppression of Unfair Competition Law of 16 April 1993[49] (Articles 8[50] and 9[51]) do not affect the definition of goods infringing a geographical indication. Indeed, this Law does not deal with geographical indications, but only with the responsibility for committing acts of unfair competition.

(4) Moulds and matrices

22.62　Under Article 2(3) of EC Regulation 1383/2003, any moulds or matrices which are specifically designed or adapted for the manufacture of goods infringing

---

[49]　Dz.U. of 2003 No 153 item 1503, as amended.

[50]　Pursuant to Art 8 of the Suppression of Unfair Competition Law, labelling goods or services with a false or fraudulent geographical designation indicating directly or indirectly a country, a region or a place or origin, or using such designation in trade, advertising, commercial correspondence, invoices or other documents, shall be considered an act of unfair competition.

[51]　Pursuant to Art 9 of the Suppression of Unfair Competition Law, if goods or services benefit from protection in the place of origin, and their special characteristics or properties are connected with origin from a specific region or locality, then false or fraudulent use of such geographic regional designations, even with the added words 'variety of', 'type of', 'method' or synonyms thereof, shall be considered an act of unfair competition.

an intellectual property right shall be treated as goods of that kind if the use of such moulds or matrices infringes the right-holder's rights.

In the light of Article 2(3), the use of these moulds or matrices must result in **22.63** infringement of the right-holder's exclusive right. The use of such moulds or matrices may infringe the following intellectual property rights protected in Poland:

- trade mark rights, if the matrix enables the reproduction of a counterfeit trade mark (for example, a word or device trade mark applied to a container or the container itself if its shape has been registered as a three-dimensional trade mark);
- an industrial design right, if the design can be reproduced with the use of the mould;
- a copyright, if the matrix is designed for the manufacture of illegal copies of a work.

Possession of a matrix by an unauthorized person which is an image of the goods **22.64** or its packaging with an exposed trade mark is an action constituting a threat to infringe the right of protection. Therefore, the right-holder of the trade mark may demand that such actions cease in accordance with Article 285 of the IPL.

Each mould or matrix enabling the manufacture of goods infringing the above **22.65** intellectual property rights will therefore be considered as infringing those rights under Article 2(3) of Regulation 1383/2003.

In practice, Polish Customs often detain moulds used for the production of coun- **22.66** terfeit goods (within the meaning of Article 2(1)(a)(i) of the Regulation).

C. Goods excluded by the Regulation

(1) Parallel imported goods

In Poland, there is no national legislation permitting the application of border **22.67** measures to parallel imported (genuine) goods. Regulation 1383/2003 is the only piece of legislation in force in Poland to be considered when addressing this issue. In light of the above, when goods not originating from the Community and suspected of infringing an intellectual property right are intercepted at the borders, the customs authorities contact the right-holder to verify whether the goods are genuine. If it appears that they come from an entity authorized to use the industrial property rights concerned (and can therefore be considered authentic), then, despite the fact that the goods are introduced into trade within the European Union without the right-holder's consent, the procedures laid down in the Regulation are not applicable, owing to the fact that Article 3(1), first sentence, of the Regulation excludes application of the border procedure to parallel imported goods.

(2) Goods which have been manufactured under conditions other than those which have been agreed with the right-holder

22.68   If goods have been manufactured under conditions other than those which have been agreed with the holder of an intellectual property right and his contractor, the right-holder cannot apply for action by customs authorities aimed at the detention or suspension of release of the goods, since there is no alternative national legislation to Regulation 1383/2003 on this point.

22.69   However, Article 3(1) of Regulation 1383/2003 does not prejudice the right of the holder of the intellectual property right concerned to seek discontinuation of, or the grant of damages for the infringement of his right or breach of contract, on legal grounds not relying on the Regulation.

(3) Goods contained in travellers' personal baggage

22.70   In general, a travellers' personal baggage may be subject to customs inspection if it gives rise to suspicions following a risk analysis conducted by customs authorities. Its content is also inspected to check for potential infringements of intellectual property rights. When performing a baggage check, customs authorities are guided first and foremost by Article 3 (2) of the Regulation, the provisions of Council Regulation 918/83 of 28 March 1983, setting up a Community system of relief's from customs duty[52] and the provisions of the International Convention Concerning Customs Facilities for Touring, signed in New York on 4 June 1954 (known as the 'New York Convention').

22.71   Having said that, we must stress that, when carrying out baggage checks, Polish customs authorities apply the duty-free allowance of EUR 175 under Article 3(2) of Regulation 1383/2003. There are no provisions detailing the method of evaluation of the limit of the duty-free allowance. Neither does Polish national law specify how to appraise the non-commercial nature of goods. In practice, these issues are left to the discretion of the customs officials performing the check. Depending on the circumstances, the quantity of the respective goods, their identical style, differences in size if the baggage belongs to one person and individual packaging will be indications to be taken into account when appraising the commercial nature of the goods.

22.72   In our experience, when a travellers' baggage contains several identical items of clothing bearing suspicious trade marks customs will be inclined to apply Regulation 1383/2003 although in general such quantity would not exceed the limit of the duty-free allowance, which, in accordance with Article 3(2) of the Regulation, provides a basis for deciding whether or not to apply the procedure of Regulation 1383/2003.

---

[52] OJ L 105 (23.4.1983).

II. APPLICATION FOR ACTION BY THE CUSTOMS AUTHORITIES

A. Measures prior to an application for action by the customs authorities ('*ex officio* measures')

Polish customs authorities never hesitate to take action on an *ex officio* basis, **22.73** as they are entitled to under Article 4 of EC Regulation 1383/2003. Under this provision, the existence of 'sufficient grounds for suspecting that the goods infringe an intellectual property right' is a prerequisite to any *ex officio* action. Suspicions will have to be confirmed by the holder of the intellectual property right, any (legal or natural) person authorized to use it, or their representative(s). To identify them, Polish Customs makes use of the database of intellectual property rights protected in Poland and the database of the Patent Office of the Republic of Poland containing data on right-holders and representatives.

Polish customs authorities could already initiate *ex officio* actions prior to Poland's **22.74** accession to the European Union. As pointed out in the Introduction, Polish customoms authorities were entitled to act on their own initiative under national law since 1998. Therefore, *ex officio* actions have a long history in Poland and have proved very effective.

Polish national law does not contain any provisions indicating how strict the **22.75** notion of 'sufficient grounds for suspecting that goods infringe an intellectual property right' should be interpreted. It is difficult to specify thoroughly the prerequisites considered by customs authorities while inspecting shipments of goods. In general, it may be assumed that the results of risk analysis for the goods concerned provide grounds for action. Among others, the following criteria are taken into account in a risk analysis: the country of origin (shipments from some 'sensitive' countries are subject to particular attention from customs authorities), lack of detailed data on the consignor, non-standard means of transportation, wide diversification of the range of goods, packaging, etc).

Customs authorities keep their methods of selecting high-risk shipments secret as **22.76** widespread knowledge of the risk assessment process by customs would make it easier for entities intending to transport goods infringing intellectual property rights to avoid customs control.

Following detection of a suspected infringement of an intellectual property right **22.77** and after contacting the right-holder or his representative, customs authorities suspend, on an *ex officio* basis, the release for free circulation of the goods or detain them for three working days. Contact with the right-holder is usually made by telephone or fax, although customs authorities may also communicate via e-mail. By using e-mail, it is possible to provide information immediately, including photographs of samples of the suspected goods, which in some circumstances is helpful to check the genuine or infringing nature of the goods.

22.78 The three-day deadline referred to in Article 4 of the Regulation is applied very strictly.

22.79 At the request of the right-holder or his representative, prior to filing of an application for action under Article 5, customs authorities usually supply information to the right-holder regarding the actual or estimated quantity and nature of the goods suspected of infringing the intellectual property right in question, in accordance with Article 4(2) of the Regulation.

22.80 When taking *ex officio* actions customs authorities primarily request the right-holder or his representative to provide confirmation of the infringing character of the goods concerned; if necessary, they may also ask him to provide a sample of a genuine product in which the intellectual property right in question is vested. For that purpose, they accept the supply of digital photographs of suspected goods to the right-holder or his representative.

B. The lodging and processing of applications for customs action

(1) Persons entitled to file an application for action

Definition of 'right-holders' under the Regulation

22.81 Under Article 5 of Regulation 1383/2003, an application for action by customs authorities may be lodged by a right-holder, that is, any holder of an intellectual property right to which the Regulation applies.

22.82 The concept of 'right-holder' is defined in Article 2(2) of the Regulation as any person holding the exclusive rights specified in that article, that is, the holder of a trade mark, copyright or related right, design right, patent, supplementary protection certificate, plant variety right, protected designation of origin, protected geographical indication, or geographical designation.

22.83 Another category of persons entitled to lodge an application for action by customs authorities comprises persons authorized to use any of the intellectual property rights mentioned in Article 2(2)(a) of the Regulation. Who exactly qualifies as an 'authorized user' will depend on the type of right to which the application refers. The differences result, above all, from the fact that some of the intellectual property rights are subject to registration (industrial property rights) while others, such as copyrights and related rights, cannot be registered. Accordingly, the requirements relating to the registration of certain intellectual property rights of the beneficiaries of licences with respect to such rights, influence the definition of the concept of 'authorized users' entitled to appear before customs authorities in their own name for the purpose of protecting the rights which they exploit with the consent of the actual right-holder.

Hence, in the case of trade marks, persons authorized to file an application in their own name as 'right-holders' include exclusive licensees recorded in the trade mark register, unless the provisions of the licence agreement deprive them of this right. In accordance with Articles 76(6) and 163 of the IPL, the beneficiary of an exclusive licence recorded in the register may, to the same extent as the holder of the trade mark rights, enforce his claims in the event of an infringement unless the license agreement stipulates otherwise. In such case, the licensee is entitled to act in his own name.

22.84

However, exclusive licensees who are not recorded in the trade mark register as well as non-exclusive licensees may also qualify as 'authorized users' under Article 2(2)(a) of the Regulation in some cases. The licence agreement (or another additional agreement concluded between the licensee and the trade mark owner) may authorize the licensee to take action to enforce his rights. However, as opposed to exclusive licensees, such licensees will always have to act in the name and on behalf of the right-holder (that is the licensor), and their actions will stem from an order to take specific actions included in the authorization granted by the licensor. Therefore, both exclusive or non-exclusive licensees who are not registered in the trade mark register may act as representatives of the right-holder based on an explicit authorization to take action, in this case, to file an application for action by the customs authorities.

22.85

Consequently, in the aforesaid circumstances, Polish customs authorities are obliged to accept applications for action lodged by licensees. However, they will require the applicant to produce a licence agreement in order to make sure that the applicant is authorized to act under Article 2(2)(a) of the Regulation.

22.86

The rationale behind such requirement is twofold. First, it may follow from an exclusive licence agreement[53] that, in spite of a record of the licence in the trade mark register, the licensee is not authorized to take any preventive steps with respect to the trade mark. Secondly, and conversely, non-exclusive licence agreements may grant authorization to enforce the trade mark to the licensee, or indeed even order him to take such action. The licensee may also be entitled to undertake such actions under a separate agreement. Therefore, in each case the nature of the legal relationship between the right-holder and the licensee will determine whether the latter can file an application for action by customs authorities.

22.87

---

[53] Under Art 76(6) of the IPL, the licence agreement may pre-empt authorization to enforce the trade mark object of the licence.

22.88 Similar remarks are also pertinent for other 'authorized users', such as commercial agents and exclusive commercial distributors. The designations under which such 'users' operate and the scope of their territorial activity, exclusivity or lack thereof within a specific territory, are not the most significant criteria to look at when assessing whether they may apply for action before customs authorities. Instead, the authorization granted to them to act in the name of the right-holder is of key importance. Practice seems to demonstrate that if an agent or distributor is properly authorized to enforce an exclusive right in a customs procedure (for example, by filing an application for action), he will be considered by customs as entitled to rely on Regulation 1383/2003 under Article 2(2)(a) of that Regulation.

22.89 The rules applicable to the licensees of a trade mark are applicable respectively to patent licensees, to whom Article 76(6) of the IPL directly applies, licensees of a supplementary protection certificate[54] and licensees of a registered industrial design.[55]

22.90 As provided in Article 1, second indent, of EC Regulation 1891/2004, the entity authorized to file geographical indication or designation of origin under national law is entitled to file an application for border measures with customs authorities aimed at the protection of such rights. Pursuant to Article 176(2–4) of the IPL, the aforementioned entity is an organization authorized to represent interests of producers operating within a specified territory, a governmental body or a territorial self-government competent within the territory to which the geographical indication applies.

22.91 All legal and natural persons entitled by law to use a geographical indication should also be considered authorized to take action before customs authorities. Pursuant to Article 187(1) of the IPL a party, whose products satisfy the conditions for use of the geographical indication, may request the Polish Patent Office to be entered into its Register in accordance with Article 184(2) of the IPL as a party authorized to use that indication.

22.92 As to the designations entered in the List of designations of origin and geographical indications which are subject to temporary national protection in accordance with the Law of 17 December 2004 on the registration and protection of names and designations of agricultural products and foodstuffs and on traditional products, the entities entered in the List as well as the groups which produce an agricultural product or a foodstuff in compliance with the requirements contained in the specification should be treated as authorized to file applications for action with customs authorities.

---

[54] Pursuant to Art 75(9) of the IPL, the provisions governing the grant of licences and assignment of patent rights apply *mutatis mutandis* to supplementary protection certificates.
[55] IPL, Art 118(1).

As regards geographical indications to which the provisions of Community law **22.93** apply, that is, Council Regulation (EEC) No 2081/92 of 14 July 1993 on protection of geographical indications and designations of origin of agricultural products and foodstuffs,[56] the entities entitled to file an application for registration of a protected designation of origin or a protected geographical indication are authorized to file applications for action with customs authorities. To date, however, no application for action has ever been lodged on that basis in Poland.

In the absence of any precedent, the issue of the definition of persons authorized **22.94** to act before customs authorities on the basis of plant variety rights remains equally academic. No application for protection of such rights has been lodged to date with border officials. Nor are we aware of any *ex officio* actions in this respect. Nonetheless, to present a comprehensive analysis of the question of persons entitled to file an application for customs action under Article 5 of Regulation 1383/2003, this issue must be taken into consideration. At the national level, the protection of plant varieties is dealt with in the Law on Protection of Plant Variety Rights of 26 June 2003.[57] Holders of an exclusive right to a protected plant variety are authorized to take action before customs authorities. Pursuant to the provisions of the Law, such entities may be growers,[58] persons who acquired rights from a grower under a written contract to a plant variety grown or discovered and introduced by the grower,[59] and licensees of an exclusive right[60] to a protected plant variety, who can be regarded as authorized users within the meaning of Article 2(2)(b) of Regulation 1383/2003.

New plant varieties are protected in Poland, not only under national law, but also **22.95** under Community legislation (namely, Council Regulation (EC) No 2100/94[61]).

Persons entitled to file a motion for protection of the copyright and related rights **22.96** would be persons originally entitled to these rights (authors,[62] producers of audio-visual works,[63] artistic performers,[64] producers of phonograms or videograms,[65] publishers[66]) and those other persons who acquired an author's economic rights or related rights as a result of an act of law.

In practice, applications for customs action are typically filed by representatives **22.97** of the right-holder *sensu stricto* rather than by right-holders themselves. In the case of copyrights and related rights, these representatives are typically collective

---

[56] OJ L 208/1 (24.7.1992). Reg as last amended by Reg (EC) No 806/2003.
[57] Ustawa z dnia 26 czerwca 2003 r. o ochronie prawnej odmian roślin, Dz.U. of 2003, No 137, item 1300.   [58] Ibid, Art 4(1).
[59] Ibid, Art 4(2).   [60] Ibid, Art 30.
[61] OJ L 227/1 (1.9.1994). Reg as last amended by Reg (EC) No 807/2003.
[62] Copyright Law, Art 8 (Ustawa z dnia 4 lutego, 1994 r. o prawie autorskim i prawach pokrewnych, cosolidated text: Dz.U. of 2000, No 80, item 904, as amended.
[63] Ibid, Art 15 and 70.   [64] Ibid, Art 86.   [65] Ibid, Art 94.   [66] Ibid, Art 99(1).

management societies, explicitly regarded as entitled to file such applications for action in Article 1, second indent, of the implementing Regulation.

22.98   Finally, the issue who will qualify as 'representative' of the right-holder *sensu stricto* or of an authorized user Article 2(2)(b) of Regulation 1383/2003 and Article 1 of Regulation 1891/2004, requires some consideration.

22.99   In accordance with Article 5 of Council Regulation (EEC) No 2913/92 establishing the Community Customs Code, any person may appoint a representative in his dealings with the customs authorities. All natural or legal persons having their domicile or registered office in Community territory may act in this capacity.

22.100   Polish law does not depart in any way from this rule. Therefore, attorneys-at-law, legal counsel, patent attorneys, agents, or collecting societies administering copyrights and related rights, may all act as authorized representatives before customs authorities. The only provisions restricting the participation of foreign representatives in this framework are contained in the national legislation relating to legal assistance provided by foreign lawyers. However, they only apply to lawyers and attorneys-at-law, not to patent attorneys. This issue will be further discussed below in relation to formalities surrounding the filing of an application for action under Regulation 1383/2003.

(2) Proof of entitlement to file an application for action

For right-holders *stricto sensu*

Trade mark rights

22.101   The holder of a trade mark is obliged under Article 5(5) of Regulation 1383/2003 and Article 2(1)(a) of Regulation 1891/2004 to provide evidence of his entitlement to this mark. Certificate of protection, registration decisions, or extracts from the Polish Trade Mark Register are all accepted by Polish customs authorities as proof of entitlement to trade mark rights. If the right-holder is not in possession of the aforementioned evidence upon filing of the application, he may submit a printout from the official Internet database of the Patent Office of the Republic of Poland.[67] In the course of the handling of the application, he will nevertheless be called upon by customs authorities to produce any one of the above-mentioned documents.

22.102   When the right relied upon consists of an international trade mark protected in Poland, the right-holder must produce an extract from the Trade Register administered by the World Intellectual Property Organization (WIPO) and proof of acceptance of the protection of the trade mark concerned in Poland as published

---

[67] http://www.uprp.pl.

in the Patent Office Journal (Wiadomości Urzędu Patentowego). An extract from the on-line WIPO database may be informally submitted at a first stage as in the case of national marks. Eventually, however, it will not be accepted as sufficient evidence and formal deficiencies will have to be remedied in due course.

As regards Community trade marks, the right-holder must produce an extract **22.103** from the Register of Community Trade Marks as proof of his rights. An extract from the Internet database of the Office for the Harmonization in the Internal Market may be submitted in the first place together with the application, subject, however, to the filing of an official extract from the Register at a later stage.

The Director of the Customs Chamber in Warsaw, who is the authority compe- **22.104** tent to process applications for action by customs authorities in Poland, usually allows seven days for formal deficiencies to be remedied. If the deficiencies are not remedied within that time limit, the application will be disregarded.

A practice newly adopted by customs authorities following the coming into force **22.105** of Commission Regulation 1891/2004 will put to the test the above remarks regarding the filing of entitlement to apply for border measures under those Regulations. Indeed, pursuant to Article 2 (1), second indent, of the Implementing Regulation, a copy from the databases of national or international offices may be regarded as a proof of entitlement to a right subject to registration. This new piece of legislation will undoubtedly make life much easier for right-holders in this context.

Design rights

Turning to design rights, extracts from the Register of Industrial Designs admin- **22.106** istered by the Patent Office of the Republic of Poland will constitute satisfactory evidence of one's entitlement to such rights. As for trade marks, a decision on granting of a registered design right may equally constitute sufficient proof. The right may also be evidenced by means of a certificate of protection. As in the case of trade marks, a printout from the database of the Patent Office of the Republic of Poland[68] may be filed at a preliminary phase, subject to the subsequent filing of an official extract from the Register.

As far as Community designs are concerned, an extract from the Register of **22.107** Community Designs will be held to prove entitlement to such rights.

With reference to the rights deriving from the registration of industrial designs, **22.108** Article 2(1) of Regulation 1891/2004 applies accordingly.

---

[68] http://www.uprp.pl.

Copyrights and related rights

22.109   Under Polish Copyright Law, copyright protection arises from the creation of the work. An author enjoys copyright protection regardless of any formalities.[69] As a consequence, there is no copyright register in Poland, and the protection of an original work commences as soon as it is created in a form that allows it to be perceived by third parties.

22.110   Under Article 8 (2) of Polish Copyright Law, the author of a work is presumed to be the person whose name has been indicated as the author's on copies of that work, or whose capacity as author has been disclosed to the public in any other manner in connection with the dissemination of the work. Therefore, if an application for action by customs authorities is filed by the author of a work enjoying copyright protection, the author-applicant will in principle be able to establish entitlement by reference to the indication of his name on the original work. Other acceptable evidence may also consist of, for example, publication about the work concerned and ascertaining that the person filing the application is the author. In this case, an official identification document (that is, identity card or passport) will usefully complement the above indications.

22.111   A different situation arises when the legal or natural person in whose name the application for action by customs authorities is filed is not the author but an assignee of the author's economic rights. Such assignment may result from a contract or from an acquisition by means of inheritance. In such a situation, proof of the transfer of the author's economic rights will be established from the assignment agreement ascertaining the assignee's entitlement to these rights to the extent to which he intends to apply for action by the customs authorities. In the case of acquisition of rights by way of inheritance, a court decision evidencing the acquisition of inheritance for example, will constitute proper evidence of entitlement.

22.112   In addition, it should be pointed out that Polish customs authorities recognize copyright registration certificates filed in foreign countries as prima facie evidence of entitlement. If the right-holder made use of the possibility offered by other legal systems allowing for copyright registration and obtained a certificate of protection in his own name, a copy of the certificate of registration with the US Copyright Office, for instance, may be submitted as evidence in support of entitlement to the copyright vested in the work. Polish customs authorities accept such documents as evidence, provided, however, they are presented with a certified translation.

22.113   Specific provisions concerning some work categories, such as collective works, employee's work or audiovisual works, are significant for the purposes of evidence. Indeed, under Polish Copyright Law, an author's economic rights to these

---

[69]   Copyright Law, Art 1(3) and (4) (Ustawa z dnia 4 lutego, 1994 r. o prawie autorskim i prawach pokrewnych, cosolidated text: Dz.U.of 2000, No 80, item 904, as amended).

categories of works are vested in entities other than the author. For that reason, in the case of the aforementioned works, it is necessary to supply evidence to the customs authorities specifying which entity is a publisher, a producer, or an employer. Contracts concluded between authors and producers or employers will of course constitute the most appropriate evidence material, aside from evidence of the production of the work concerned (information indicated on the work).

Regarding related rights, as in the case of copyrights, any documents (such as contracts) indicating that a person is entitled to seek protection of related rights will be admitted as evidence to that effect. **22.114**

Patents and supplementary protection certificates

Patents and supplementary protection certificates are registered rights. Therefore, as in the case of other registered rights, the evidence of entitlement to these rights appears from extracts from the Register administered by the Patent Office of the Republic of Poland, decisions on granting patent protection and patent documents. In line with Regulation 1891/2004, copies from the official database[70] of the Polish Patent Office should also be accepted as a proof. **22.115**

A certificate of protection, registration decisions, and extracts from the Patent Register are all accepted by Polish customs authorities as proof of entitlement to the rights concerned. **22.116**

Plant variety rights

To prove entitlement to an exclusive plant variety right, a decision on granting of Plant Breeders' Right and the entering thereof in the Register of Plant Varieties should be produced. The decisions in question are issued by the Director of COBORU (Research Centre for Cultivar Testing).[71] Protected plant varieties are entered in the national register (the Register of Varieties protected by Plant Breeders' Rights), administered by COBORU.[72] An extract from the Polish Gazette for Plant Breeders' Rights and National List (COBORU Diariusz), in which the authority concerned publishes entries in the Register of Varieties protected by Plant Breeders' Rights, will also be deemed to constitute proper evidence of entitlement to plant variety rights. **22.117**

Designations of origin

A decision on the grant of a geographical indication,[73] and an extract from the Register of Geographical Indications administered by the Polish Patent Office **22.118**

---

[70] http://www.uprp.pl.
[71] Law on Legal Protection of Plant Variety Rights (Dz.U. of 2003 No 137 item 1300), Art 20 (Ustawa z dnia 26 czerwca 2003 r. o ochronie prawnej odmian roślin, Dz.U. of 2003, No 137, item 1300).
[72] Ibid, Art 36.   [73] IPL, Art 182.

serve as evidence of ownership of a right deriving from the registration of a geographical indication. Article 2(1), second indent, of Commission Regulation 1891/2004, pursuant to which a copy from an official database shall be regarded as proof of a registered right, is also applicable in this context.

22.119   When an application for action by customs authorities relies on a geographical indication or a designation of origin protected under Community law, the applicant must produce the evidence that he is a producer authorized to use the designation concerned or that he belongs to a group which is so authorized. Moreover, he must provide proof of registration of the designation in accordance with the provisions of Community law.

22.120   As to the designations entered in the List of designations of origin and geographical indications enjoying temporary national protection, in accordance with the Law of 17 December 2004 on the registration and protection of names and designations of agricultural products and foodstuffs and on traditional products, the applicant must produce the evidence that he is a producer authorized to use the designation concerned or that he belongs to a group which is so authorized. Moreover, he must provide the proof that the designation of origin or the geographical indication enjoys temporary national protection.

For persons authorized to use the right

22.121   Persons authorized to use an intellectual property right covered by EC Regulation 1383/2003 and willing to file an application for action must provide additional proof of such authorization. The evidence required will depend on the type of authorization and right relied upon.

22.122   When the intellectual property which is the basis of an application for action by Polish customs authorities is subject to registration, and provided the legislation in force allows the grant of licenses of such a right (as, for example, for trade marks and patents), the licensee may act as an 'authorized person'. Evidence of the licensee's authorization will consist of an extract from the Register of the Patent Office of the Republic of Poland (if the licence is registered), or the licence agreement. In the case of unregistered rights, any types of contracts concluded with the intellectual property right-holder, containing an authorization, granted to the applicant for border measures, to use the right in question, shall be considered as meeting the standard of proof. The aforementioned contracts include licence agreements, distribution agreements, and agency contracts.

For representatives

The representative of the right-holder *sensu stricto* or of the 'person authorized to use the right' must provide customs with proof of his authorization to act in the name of the right-holder or authorized user.

22.123

The original or a certified copy of a power of attorney will have to be submitted to satisfy this requirement. If an attorney-at-law or patent attorney acts as a representative, he may certify the copy himself. In other cases, the copy should be notarized. The power of attorney must be presented in Polish and if it is in a foreign language, it will have to be translated into Polish by a certified translator.

22.124

A general power of attorney may be provided for these purposes and, therefore, a separate document is not required for each action.

22.125

Both natural and legal persons domiciled or having their registered office in the European Community may act as 'representatives' in the context of actions taken by Polish Customs. This principle also applies to professional representatives. Hence, a foreign lawyer may also act as a representative.

22.126

Pursuant to Article 35(1) of the Law on the Provision by Foreign Lawyers of Legal Assistance in the Republic of Poland of 5 July 2002,[74] foreign lawyers from a Member State of the European Union are entitled to render legal services in Poland and shall be entitled to provide cross-border services using the professional title conferred in their home state, expressed in the official language of that state, with the designation of the home state's professional organization of which they are a member or of the court before which they are entitled to practise in accordance with the laws of that state.

22.127

Under Article 39 of the same Law, foreign lawyers established in the European Union countries and representing a client in proceedings before the courts or other public authorities in Poland must identify to the court or authority conducting the proceedings, a person for service of documents and proceedings in the Republic of Poland. Failure to do so will cause all documents destined for those lawyers to be served on their client if they are domiciled or otherwise established in Poland. If the client has no known domicile or office in Poland, the documents shall be left in the case files and deemed to have been served.

22.128

Additionally, taking into account the requirement that all proceedings before Polish courts and authorities are to be conducted in Polish, and considering the strict deadlines imposed by Regulation 1383/2003 the right-holders and 'authorized users' will be well-advised to appoint a local representative in all cases.

22.129

---

[74] Ustawa z dnia 5 lipca 2002 o świadczeniu przez prawników zagranicznych pomocy prawnej w Rzeczypospolitej Polskiej, Dz.U. of 2002, No 126, item 1069, as amended.

(3) Formal requirements and competent customs department

Competent customs department

22.130 In Poland, the authority competent to process applications for customs action is the Director of the Customs Chamber in Warsaw.[75] The powers of this body are established by the Regulation of the Minister of Finance of 22 April 2004, appointing the Director of the Customs Chamber in Warsaw to manage customs matters, issued on the basis of Article 70(3) of the Customs Law of 19 March 2004.

22.131 The contact details of this department are as follows:

Izba Celna w Warszawie (The Customs Chamber in Warsaw)
ul. Modlińska 4
PL-03216 Warszawa
Tel.: +48 22 510 46 11
Fax: +48 22 811 57 45
IC440000@war.mofnet.gov.pl
www.icwarszawa.internetdsl.pl

Form of the application for action

22.132 An application for action under the EC Regulation 1383/2003 may be filed with Polish Customs by mail, fax, or e-mail. However, when sending by fax or e-mail it should always be followed by a written confirmation in the form of a 'traditional' letter.

22.133 This requirement arises from legislation concerning acknowledgement of the authenticity and originality of a signature. An application submitted by fax or e-mail does not enjoy the status of an original document.

22.134 All applications sent by e-mail must also be confirmed by a letter containing an original signature. Public authorities are not prepared to rely on electronic signatures delivered by certification service providers. However, the Electronic Signature Law of 18 September 2001[76] provides that within a period of four years from the coming into force of that Law, (that is, in 2006), public authorities will have to make it possible for certification service providers to submit applications and requests as well as other acts or deeds in electronic form, whenever the law requires that they be made in a specific form or according to a specific template. Therefore, one may assume that the filing of applications for border measures by

---

[75] The basis for this statement can be found in the legal provisions that are referred to above under n 8.

[76] Ustawa z dnia 18 września 2001 r. o podpisie elektronicznym; Dz.U. of 2001, No 130, item 1450, as amended.

e-mail will be regarded as fully admissible and equivalent to an original document in Poland as from 2006.

The declaration referred to in Article 6 of Regulation 1383/2003 must be filed either as an original or in the form of a certified copy. Attorneys-at-law or patent attorneys may certify the copy themselves provided they act as representatives of the right-holder *sensu stricto* or of an 'authorized user' within the meaning of Article 2(2) of the Regulation. In other cases, the copy ought to be notarized. **22.135**

Language requirements

An application for action by Polish Customs under EC Regulation 1383/2003 must be filed in Polish. This obligation arises from the Law on the Polish Language of 7 October 1999.[77] In accordance with Article 4 of this Law, Polish is the official language admissible before public authorities. **22.136**

This requirement also applies to all documents enclosed with the application (that is, technical documentation, description of the goods, extracts from registers). Consequently, if an original document is in a foreign language, it must be filed with Polish Customs along with a certified translation. **22.137**

The declaration filed on the basis of Article 6 of Regulation 1383/2003 must fulfil the same requirements. It must be submitted in Polish. In practice, the declaration filed by a foreign entity may therefore be produced in two ways: either in a bilingual version, or in a foreign language version accompanied by a certified translation into Polish. **22.138**

(4) Requirements regarding the contents of the application for action

Mandatory information

Polish national law does not provide for any requirements in respect of information and materials which must be contained in or enclosed with the application for action by the customs authorities. **22.139**

The technical description of the goods must be detailed enough to allow the customs authorities to distinguish the original goods from the infringing ones. Particularly useful are technical descriptions containing photographs or drawings highlighting the characteristics of the genuine products which are usually not copied by the infringers due to the lack of technical instruments or knowledge of these characteristics. **22.140**

---

[77] Ustawa z dnia 7 października 1999 r. o języku polskim, Dz.U. of 1999, No 90, item 999, as amended.

22.141 If the applicant is aware of the method of infringement and the characteristics of the infringing products, it is particularly useful to mention them. Photographs of typical infringing goods are often enclosed with the application to help customs distinguish between genuine and fake items.

22.142 In practice, a representative appointed by the right-holder or the persons authorized to use the right will act as the administrative contact person. Given that knowledge in the field of the relevant law (both Community and national) and rules of procedure is essential in this situation, the right-holder will in most cases be well-advised to appoint a legal professional, such as an attorney-at-law, a patent or trade mark agent, or any other legal counsel as the administrative contact person vis-à-vis customs.

22.143 The technical contact person appointed in the application ought to be familiar with genuine products, and have sufficient knowledge and skills to allow him to distinguish unequivocally between authentic and infringing goods.

22.144 There are no specific requirements under Polish national law concerning the nationality of persons appointed as administrative or technical representatives (except under the aforementioned legislation on the scope of the legal assistance provided by foreign lawyers). Nonetheless, for practical reasons, it is advisable to appoint in this capacity persons having their domicile in the Republic of Poland, so that they can meet with customs and inspect the goods whenever appropriate.

Optional information

22.145 Polish law does not provide for any additional requirements relating to the contents of the application. Practice demonstrates that Polish customs authorities may require information aimed at facilitating the decision process regarding the risk analysis. The effectiveness and appropriateness of actions taken by customs primarily depend on the minuteness of detailed information supplied by the right-holder.

Additional information specific to the type of intellectual property right referred to in the application

22.146 Under Article 5(6) of EC Regulation 1383/2003, Polish Customs are also entitled to request additional information specific to the type of intellectual property right relied on in the application.

(5) Processing and acceptance of the application for action

22.147 Polish Customs process the application for action within 30 working days from filing thereof, as required by the Regulation. In the meantime, if the need arises, explanatory proceedings (concerning the completion of mandatory materials, for instance original documents or certified copies, translation of documents filed in a foreign language, etc) are carried out.

The Stamp Duty Law of 9 September 2000[78] does not provide for any fees for **22.148** filing an application beside a stamp duty of the amount of PLN 5 for an application and PLN 0.5 per enclosure.[79] These are not of administrative character and, therefore, presumably do not infringe the provisions of Regulation 1383/2003.

Acceptance of the application is acknowledged in a decision of the Director of the **22.149** Customs Chamber in Warsaw, issued on the basis of Article 207(1) of the 29 August 1997 Tax Ordinance, in conjunction with Article 5(1) of Regulation 1383/2003. In this decision, the Director specifies the subject matter of the protection, indicating the type of right concerned and the protection period. Usually, protection is granted for the maximum length allowed by the Regulation, that is, 12 months, and has effect as of the day of issue. However, at the applicant's request, customs may grant a shorter protection period, except when the application relies on a 'Community-wide' intellectual property right under Article 5(4) of the Regulation.

When Polish Customs decide not to process an application for action under Article **22.150** 5(8) of the Regulation, the applicant may file an appeal against the decision of the Director of the Customs Chamber in Warsaw to the same authority.[80] Legal grounds for appeal are detailed in the provisions of the Tax Ordinance[81] which, among other things, lays down provisions regarding appeal proceedings before customs authorities.[82] The appeal must be filed within 14 days from the date of receipt of the decision, via the authority which issued that decision.[83] It must set forth the grounds for appeal against the decision, specify the essence and scope of the claims being the subject of the appeal, and produce evidence of those claims.[84]

(6) 'Community' applications for action

Polish law does not contain specific rules on the processing of applications **22.151** concerning the protection of 'Community-wide' intellectual property rights.

The provisions of Community law, that is, Council Regulation 1383/2003 and **22.152** Commission Regulation 1891/2004 are self-sufficient on this point and Polish Customs apply them carefully.

---

[78] Ustawa z dnia 9 września 2000 r. o opłacie skarbowej, Dz.U. of 2000, No 86, item 960, as amended.

[79] Stamp Duty Law, Art 1(1)(1)(a), in conjunction with Art 9 (Ustawa z dnia 9 września 2000 r. o opłacie skarbowej, Dz.U. of 2000, No 86, item 960, as amended).

[80] Tax Ordinance, Art 221 (Ustawa z dnia 29 sierpnia 1997 r.—Ordynacja podatkowa, Dz.U. of 1997 No 137 item 923, as amended). [81] See above n 11.

[82] Ibid, Arts 220–235. [83] Ibid Art 223. [84] Ibid, Art 222.

22.153   From the practical point of view and to speed up the procedure, it is recommended that the original application filed under Article 5(4) of Regulation 1383/2003 be accompanied by a translation into the official languages of the countries in which protection of the right is sought.

III. CONDITIONS GOVERNING ACTION BY CUSTOMS AUTHORITIES AND BY THE AUTHORITIES COMPETENT TO DETERMINE WHETHER GOODS INFRINGE AN INTELLECTUAL PROPERTY RIGHT

A. Conditions governing action by customs authorities

(1) Factual background

22.154   Regulation 1383/2003 has been in force in Poland for only a short time and Poland only became a Member of the European Union on 1 May 2004. However, experience gained prior to Poland's accession to the European Union and subsequent to the coming into force of the Regulation, allows us to state that most border measures taken in respect of goods suspected of infringing an intellectual property right are by the customs offices located on the eastern border of Poland as well as in the airports (especially in Warsaw), and the ports (eg Gdynia, Gdańsk, and Szczecin).

22.155   The eastern Polish border sees the entry of pirated goods produced in Russia or other countries which were previously part of the Soviet Union and also originating in Asian countries. However, in the case of goods coming from China or Korea, air transport is more and more frequently used.

22.156   Over the last few years, there has been an increase in cases where natural persons are involved in the entry of pirated goods into Poland. Wrongdoers usually make sure not to carry more than a dozen pirated items, so that they can claim, in the case of a customs check, that these goods constitute their personal belongings and hope, that because of the insignificant number of the goods, the holder of the relevant intellectual property rights will refrain from taking action.

22.157   Likewise, under Polish law, the small number of goods may often result in the discontinuation of criminal proceedings, since in such matters the danger to 'public order' is considered minimal.

(2) Notification of customs intervention

When the customs authorities suspect that goods entering Poland infringe an **22.158** intellectual property right, the right-holder or his representative is immediately notified of the detention of the goods by fax or e-mail (and in some cases also by telephone, but then always followed by confirmation with a fax or e-mail).

The customs authorities derive the information as to Polish attorneys of foreign **22.159** right-holders from the registers containing the records of the granted intellectual property rights. It regards patents, additional certificates of protection, industrial designs, trade marks, designations or origin, geographical indications, and protected plant varieties.

It is, therefore, essential to note the changes of the attorneys in the offices keeping **22.160** particular registers of the exclusive rights so that they contain current data. In that way, the customs authorities can quickly contact the right entity in view of institution of further actions.

A more difficult situation occurs in the case of pirated goods infringing the copy- **22.161** right of third parties. Obtaining the copyright does not depend on its registration since there is no register of copyrights which are protected in Poland. In such a situation, information regarding the holder of such rights might be provided by the organizations of collective management of copyrights. They conclude relevant civil law agreements with the authors and thereby obtain authorization to take action with the intention to protect against infringement.

(3) Information to be provided by customs to the right-holder before the right-holder confirms the infringing nature of the goods

When notifying the right-holder of the detention of suspect goods, the customs **22.162** authorities inform him or his representative of the nature of the goods (for example, perfumes, CDs, clothes, bags, etc), their estimated quantity and the nature of the suspected designation together with its name (such as a trade mark—TINY GIRL—, a character—SHREK—, etc). When notifying the right-holder or his representative of the detention of goods, the customs authorities also more and more frequently send a picture of the goods.

Once notified of an *ex officio* action by customs, in situations where the above infor- **22.163** mation is not sufficient to confirm the existence of an infringement of his intellectual property rights, the right-holder or his representative, on condition of filing an application for action under Article 5 of EC Regulation 1383/2003, with the customs authorities, may lodge a motion for obtaining additional data regarding:

- the particulars of the holder of the goods including his name, address, and in the case of a business entity, its company name and place of establishment;

- the particulars of the consignor of the goods, including his name, address, and in case of a business entity, its company name and place of establishment;
- the particulars of the consignee and/or declarant of the detained goods, including their names, addresses, and in case of business entities, their company names and places of establishment;
- the country of origin of the goods;
- the country of destination of the goods;
- pictures of the detained goods if they were not sent previously, together with notification of the detention of the goods;
- samples of the goods.

22.164 At first sight, it may seem difficult to reconcile the above with the provisions of Polish law on the protection of personal data.

22.165 Taking into account the hierarchy of the legal acts having effect in Poland and the direct applicability of the provisions contained in the EC Regulations and, in particular Article 9(3) of Regulation 1383/2003, the customs authorities of the Member States, when detaining at the borders goods suspected of infringing an intellectual property right, are obliged to disclose the aforesaid information to the right-holder when he is entitled to it under the Regulation. Refusal to reveal such data cannot be justified by the provisions of national law relating to the protection of personal data.

22.166 The Law on Protection of Personal Data of 29 August 1997[85] regulating the conditions of protection, use, and disclosure of personal data allows the disclosure of personal data to persons or entities authorized to obtain them by law and to persons and entities who can reasonably justify such disclosure.

22.167 Therefore, in light of the above, there are no obstacles to the customs authorities revealing to the holder of an intellectual property right or his representative, the information contained in customs documents relating to goods suspected of infringing such a right.

(4) Inspection of the suspected goods

22.168 As indicated above, once an application has been filed by the right-holder or his representative under Article 5 of Regulation 1383/2003, the customs authorities take samples of the detained goods and hand them over to the right-holder with a view to determining whether the goods infringe his rights.

22.169 Although the customs authorities endeavour to send such samples without delay, because of the lack of national provisions regarding the conditions and procedure

---

[85] Ustawa z dnia 29 sierpnia 1997 r. o ochronie danych osobowych, Dz.U. of 2002, No 101, item 926, as amended.

for the submission of samples, they usually reach the right-holder or his representative so late that it is not possible to comply with the 10-working day period for providing customs with documents confirming the commencement of proceedings intended to determine whether the goods infringe intellectual property rights under Article 13 of the Regulation, which leads to the necessity of requesting an extension of that period.

Both the digital pictures and samples of the goods provided by customs may be used by the right-holder in order to determine whether his rights have been infringed. **22.170**

The samples of the goods must be returned to the customs authorities after examination. **22.171**

B. Simplified procedure allowing the destruction of the goods without there being any need to determine whether an intellectual property right has been infringed under national law

The simplified procedure laid down in Article 11 of Council Regulation 1383/2003 has not been implemented in Polish law. Although we have been advised that inter-departmental works aimed at implementation of this provision are under way, as of now, no official Bill which could be the basis for a detailed review of the method and conditions of such implementation has been filed. Polish law does not permit the destruction of the goods as long as a court has not so ordered. **22.172**

Nonetheless, common practice demonstrates that the infringer of an intellectual property right usually concludes a settlement with the right-holder to resolve the dispute in order to avoid time-consuming and expensive court proceedings. **22.173**

In such event, it will normally be one of the conditions of the settlement that the infringer undertakes to destroy the goods at his own cost or (if this is technically possible), to remove the signs or features resulting in an intellectual property right infringement, for example through permanently removing the unlawful trade mark and donating the goods to charity. **22.174**

A settlement made between the right-holder and an infringer has the character of a civil law agreement and, in consequence, in the light of the provisions binding in Poland, the parties enjoy the right to decide freely about the provisions of such a settlement. Therefore, it is possible to include therein, besides the above mentioned provisions regarding the destruction of counterfeit goods, provisions referring to an infringer's obligation to redress the damage, pay damages or **22.175** a declaration undertaking to refrain from infringing in future the exclusive rights of the right-holder.

22.176   However, experience shows that in the case of including provisions in a settlement regarding an obligation to pay damages, the sum which Polish infringers are ready to pay in that respect bears no resemblance to the real amount of the damage suffered, and is more symbolic.

22.177   The above results from the fact that infringers are aware that in the case of the institution of court proceedings, in order to demand payment of damages, the right-holder would be obliged to prove that he has suffered loss as a result of the infringement of his exclusive rights.. In addition, it should be noted that this procedure is quite complicated under Polish law and often involves the necessity of conducting long and tiresome proceedings to produce evidence to prove the claim. To make matters even worse, after the completion of such proceedings, it frequently turns out that the infringer does not possess sufficient assets to enforce payment of the damages awarded by the court.

22.178   However, in the cases of criminal proceedings being brought against the infringer, the goods will be retained as evidence of the offence. In later proceedings in the matter, they have the status of goods originating from the offence. Therefore upon passing sentence, discontinuance of proceedings, or conditional discontinuance of the proceedings the court usually orders the forfeiture of the goods to the State Treasury which results in the destruction of the goods in question.

C. Conditions governing action by the authorities having jurisdiction to determine whether the goods infringe an intellectual property right

22.179   Article 13(1) of Regulation 1383/2003 imposes on right-holders the duty to notify the customs authorities within 10 working days from the date of receipt of the notification of suspension of release or detention of the goods that proceedings have been initiated to determine whether an intellectual property right has been infringed. Under the provisions which were in force prior to Poland's accession to the European Union, right-holders were required to submit to the customs authorities a decision issued by a prosecutor on commencement of criminal proceedings or securing of evidence, or to provide them with a decision of a civil court granting an interim injunction.

22.180   Under Article 13(1) of Regulation 1383/2003, the right-holder will have to show that civil or criminal proceedings have been commenced. He will no longer be required—as was previously the case—to submit a substantive decision from the competent authorities (namely, a court or public prosecutor),[86] within 10 working days from the date of suspension of release, or detention of the goods.

Appropriate evidence of the commencement of proceedings will be:　　　　　**22.181**

- a copy of a motion for a temporary injunction or a writ of summons together with proof of its delivery to the court in civil proceedings;
- a copy of a notification on commission of an offence with a motion for prosecution, together with proof of its delivery to the public prosecutor's office or the police station in criminal proceedings.

However, practice reveals, that despite the provision of Article 13 of Regulation 　**22.182** 1383/2003, the customs authorities do not find it sufficient to be notified only of the instigation of criminal or civil proceedings but require to be provided with a copy of the above documents. They do not treat even this as meeting the requirement defined in that Article. In addition they require evidence either of an interim injunction issued by a court (in the case of civil proceedings), or an order on the institution of investigations or on seizure of the goods (in the case of criminal proceedings).

Under Polish law, whether an intellectual property right has been infringed may 　**22.183** be determined in the course of either civil or criminal proceedings. It should be noted that court proceedings, both civil and criminal, may last for a long time, and it can take years before proceedings are concluded. When comparing both these proceedings, it should be mentioned that the civil proceedings are relatively more expensive than criminal ones. The latter is faster than the first and ensures that the right-holder has less opportunities of influencing it than in civil proceedings. This results from the fact that in criminal proceedings, a bill of indictment is prepared and lodged by the prosecutor and the right-holder may only cooperate as an auxiliary prosecutor by supporting the charges made in the bill of indictment.

In the course of civil proceedings, it is the right-holder who prepares the case and, 　**22.184** therefore, he enjoys the freedom to formulate claims and accusations and present arguments in their support as well as to choose the evidence by which he is going to prove the grounds for his demands.[87]

---

[86] Prior to the entry into force of Reg 1383/2003, in order to have infringing goods detained by Polish Customs, a right-holder had to provide customs with either evidence that criminal proceedings had been commenced, or a decision granting an injunction or a decision regarding the seizure of the goods for the purpose of evidence in criminal proceedings. Such requirements obviously made it difficult to justify taking action in those cases where the consignment of goods concerned was of little significance.
[87] J Rutter and M Rosinski, 'Who is the Weakest Link?', [2004] Trade Mark World, 26–29.

(1) Civil proceedings

General remarks

22.185 Civil proceedings may be instituted by the right-holder by:

- filing a motion for a preliminary (or interim) injunction; or
- filing a suit on the merits.

22.186 A motion for an interim injunction may be filed during civil proceedings or, in accordance with Article 734 of the Code of Civil Procedure,[88] prior to the commencement of such proceedings. In the latter event, the holder of the intellectual property right in question is subject to a time limit for the commencement of a civil action against the alleged infringer. This time limit may not exceed 14 days from the date of service of an order in which the Court secured the claims. Failure to observe this rule—which arises directly under Article 733 of the Code of Civil Procedure, as well as Article 50(6) of the TRIPs Agreement—results in the loss of the interim relief.

22.187 In light of Article 730 of the Code of Civil Procedure the courts may issue an interim injunction if the claimant's claim is credible upon a prima facie examination and when the claimant has presented evidence for possessing a legal interest in being granted such an injunction.

22.188 Legal interest in granting an interim injunction occurs when lack of injunction will prevent or seriously impede in carrying out a verdict or if it in any way prevents or seriously impedes in accomplishing the objective of the proceedings in the case.

22.189 These formal requirements are confirmed by Article 736[89] of the Code of Civil Procedure which states that a motion for a preliminary injunction should present the circumstances which justify such a claim and make them credible.

22.190 The court accepts a motion for granting a preliminary injunction within its jurisdiction, and considers the evidence produced in the motion as the basis for its decision. In the event it decides that the motion does not fulfill the requirements provided for in Article 736, the motion is returned to the right-holder without inviting him to amend it.

22.191 The Court may issue an interim injunction provided it *deems it appropriate in the circumstances*. In the case of goods which infringe an intellectual property right in

---

[88] Ustawa z dnia 17 listopada, 1964 r. Kodeks postępowania cywilnego, Dz.U. of 1974, No 24, item 142.

[89] Ibid, Art 736(1) The motion for granting an injunction shall meet the requirements of a pleading. Furthermore, it should contain: (a) indication of the method of injunction, in the cases of pecuniary claims also an indication of the injunction amount; (b) substantiation of the circumstances justifying the motion;

Art 736(2) If a motion for granting an injunction was filed prior to institution of proceeding, in addition to the above, the case should be presented in as concise form as possible.

the meaning of Regulation 1383/2003, the injunction may result for example, in the seizure of the goods for the duration of the proceedings.

The main feature of proceedings seeking interim relief is their speed. Article 737 **22.192** of the Code of Civil Procedure provides that a motion for an interim injunction should be considered without delay, and in any event, not later than within one week from the date of filing unless some special provision states otherwise.

The Polish Law on Copyright and Neighbouring Rights provides for even shorter **22.193** terms, stating that such motions should be considered no later that within three days[90] of the date of filing.

In practice, however, this term is longer and lasts from one to three months. **22.194**

In principle, court costs are borne by the party that loses the proceedings. This **22.195** means in practice that upon winning the case the right-holder may claim reimbursement of such costs from the infringer.

Practice shows, however, that when awarding reimbursement of the costs of the **22.196** proceedings, the courts are often unwilling to order the losing party to reimburse the entirety of the attorneys' fees incurred by the other party. Rather, they assess such costs on an equitable basis after taking into consideration the complexity of the case and having regard to the rates applied as minimal remuneration by professional attorneys in civil cases that result from the binding regulations in this respect.

Counterfeit goods

In the case of counterfeit goods, the trade mark owner may seek: (i) an order from **22.197** the Courts on the basis of Article 296(1) of the IPL[91] requiring the defendant to refrain from further infringement of its rights; (ii) the destruction of the goods; (iii) the publication of a specific statement in the press at the defendant's expense; and (iv) the surrendering of profits and the award of damages pursuant to the provisions of the Civil Code.

When deciding on an intellectual property infringement case, the courts may, on **22.198** the right-holder's motion, decide on the further disposal of the infringing goods and/or the means which were used for their production or marking. In the case of counterfeit goods,[92] Article 17(1)(b), second indent, of the Regulation stipulates

---

Art 736(3) The injunction amount specified in (1) cannot exceed the pursued claim with interest calculated from the day of issuing a decision on granting an injunction and the costs of execution of the injunction. The amount may also include anticipated costs of the proceedings.

Art 736(4) If, with regard to the provision of the injunction, the obligated party pays the security amount, the sum referred to ought to be paid into the court's deposit account, unless a specific reg provides otherwise. The provision of Art 752 should be applied accordingly

[90] Copyright Law, Art 75 (Ustawa z dnia 4 lutego, 1994 r. o prawie autorskim i prawach pokrewnych, consolidated text: Dz.U. of 2000, No 80, item 904, as amended).

[91] See above, n 16.   [92] IPL, Art 286.

that the court may only decide 'in exceptional cases' that the simple removal of the infringing signs from the goods is sufficient effectively to deprive the persons concerned of any financial gains from the transaction and therefore to allow the release of the goods for free circulation.

22.199 In relation to trade mark infringement proceedings before the civil courts, the right-holder may also file a motion for an interim injunction.

22.200 Article 310 of the Code of Civil Procedure also allows trade mark holders to file a motion for securing evidence in the case where a risk exists that it might otherwise become impossible or unreasonably difficult to produce such evidence. A motion for securing evidence may prove very helpful especially in the context of customs actions under the Regulation, owing to the stringent deadlines imposed on right-holders by the latter.

Pirated goods

22.201 The provisions of the Copyright Law[93] provide that in the event of a breach of his rights, the copyright owner may seek: (i) an injunction in respect of future infringements against the defendant; (ii) the surrendering of the turnover or the imposition of a penalty amounting to the payment of twice or three times the profits made from the pirated goods if the infringement was committed in bad faith. A claim for damages may also be initiated on the same condition.

22.202 The Copyright Law also contains a few provisions regarding claims for the securing of evidence. Under these provisions,[94] the courts established in the locality where the alleged infringer carries on business or where his/her property is located, shall also consider, before the filing of proceedings on the merits, motions from any interested parties within three days as from the date of filing, aimed at:

- securing evidence;
- ordering the alleged infringer to provide information and access to any documentation indicated by the court which would prove substantial for the protecting of the claimant's copyrights;
- the granting of an interim injunction.

The courts may make the grant of such claims conditional upon the provision of some security.[95]

22.203 It seems that because of Regulation 1383/2003, a motion ordering the alleged infringer to provide further information may in practice prove particularly useful, since it could allow the right-holder to obtain the information and documents

---

[93] Copyright Law, Art 79 (Ustawa z dnia 4 lutego, 1994 r. o prawie autorskim i prawach pokrewnych.   [94] Ibid, Art 80(1).
[95] Ibid, Art 80(2).

which would enable him to file proceedings on the merits and to establish not only the infringement of his rights but also the scope of his loss and damages.

In the case of goods infringing a registered design, the right-holder may seek: (i) an injunction preventing the infringer from further infringing its rights, (ii) the destruction of the goods; (iii) the surrendering of the profits unlawfully gained from the infringement; and (iv) the award of damages. The right-holder may also request that the infringer be ordered to publish an appropriate statement in the press.[96] **22.204**

It should be also remembered that pursuant to Article 116 of the IPL after expiration of rights from registration of a design, protection of author's economic rights provided for in the Copyright Law, does not apply to products manufactured in accordance with an industrial design and put on the market after the lapse of the right in registration granted for such a design. **22.205**

Goods infringing a patent or a supplementary protection certificate

The IPL provides that in the case of a patent infringement, the relevant patentee, or any other person enjoying the same status under the Law (such as for example, a licensee recorded in the Patent Register)[97] may require the cessation of the infringement, the redress of its consequences, the surrender of the unlawfully obtained profits and compensation for the loss incurred in accordance with the general principles of law. At the patentee's request, the infringer may also be ordered to publish an appropriate statement in the press and, if he had acted intentionally, to pay an adequate amount of money to a social organization which encourages inventive activity in its range of activities.[98] **22.206**

The holder of a supplementary protection certificate may initiate similar claims under Article 291(1) of the IPL. **22.207**

Goods infringing a plant variety right

The provisions of the Law on the Protection of Plant Variety Rights do not include any regulations that would give the right-holder the right to initiate civil proceedings. **22.208**

Under this Law that the only remedy open to holders of plant variety rights in the case of an infringement of their rights consists in initiating a liability claim on the basis of the Code of Misdemeanours Procedure of the 24 August 2001[99] which will be discussed later in the context of criminal proceedings. **22.209**

---

[96] IPL, Art 105(2).   [97] Ibid, Art 76(6).   [98] Ibid Art 287.
[99] Ustawa z dnia 24 sierpnia, 2001 r. Kodeks postępowania w sprawach o wykroczenia Dz.U. of 2001 No 106, item 1148, as amended.

Goods infringing a designation of origin or a geographical indication

22.210 Pursuant to Article 302(1) of the IPL, subject to Article 186,[100] the provisions regarding the protection of trade marks apply *mutatis mutandis* to geographical indications, enjoying protection on the basis of the provisions of the IPL.

22.211 Accordingly, the holder of a geographical indication may, in the case of an infringement of his rights, initiate the same claims as a trade mark holder (see above, paras 22.197–22.200). Any party entered in the Patent Register and entitled to the use of a given geographical indication may also make such claims.

22.212 Under Article 286, the courts may, at the holder's request, order the disposal of unlawfully manufactured or marked products and of the means used for manufacturing or marking those goods.

22.213 The Law of 17 December 2004 on registration and protection of names and designations of agricultural products, foodstuffs, and traditional products provides in Article 38 that the names of origin or the geographical indications entered in the List of names of origin and geographical indications enjoying temporary national protection cannot be used in the course of trade on the territory of the Republic of Poland if the agricultural products or foodstuffs to which they relate do not fulfil the requirements for such a name to be entered on that List, even where:

1) such a use is not aimed at indicating the geographical origin of the agricultural products or foodstuffs and where the real place of production of the agricultural product or foodstuff is indicated;
2) expressions such as 'in the style of', 'variety of', 'using the method of', 'as produced in', 'imitation of' or 'similar to', are used;
3) the protected designation is used in an original wording or in translation;
4) the protected designation is used together with another misleading or false reference to a place of origin, qualities or basic characteristics of the product on the inner or outer packaging, in the advertising materials or in documents referring to a particular product;
5) the protected designation is used in the context of other practices which might be misleading as to a true origin of a product.

22.214 The regulations in force in Poland also provide for the possibility of claiming protection on the basis of the Suppression of Unfair Competition Law which

---

[100] 'Any party who, while operating on a given territory, earlier used a geographical indication in good faith, and whose products do not fulfill the requirements for the grant of a right in registration, may continue to use that indication for the maximum one year as from the date of the grant of the right to registration.'

contains a definition of an act of unfair competition in respect of geographical indications and designations of origin in Articles 8[101] and 9.[102]

(2) Criminal proceedings

General remarks

The provisions regarding criminal liability in the case of infringements of intel- **22.215**
lectual property rights are found in Laws concerning special provisions. They
define the acts which constitute a criminal offence and determine the penalties to
which they give rise. The Criminal Code of 6 June 1997[103] applies in respect of all
issues which are not regulated by the above-mentioned laws.

The conduct of criminal proceedings is dealt with by the provisions of the Code **22.216**
of Criminal Procedure of 6 June 1997.[104]

One of the mains features of criminal offences resulting from an intellectual prop- **22.217**
erty right infringement is that they are only prosecuted upon the motion of the
injured party. This means that in order to institute criminal proceedings, it is
necessary for the injured party to file a complaint at a police station or with the
prosecutor's office. The filing of such complaints is free of charge in Poland. The
injured person can be a natural or a legal person. In case of offences to intellectual
property rights, the injured party may be either the right-holder or an authorized
user whose exploitation right (for example, a licence) is recorded in the relevant
Register. Without a motion of the injured party, neither the police nor the
prosecutor is entitled to institute and conduct criminal proceedings *ex officio*.

Under Polish law, not only the offender, but also co-offenders and all persons **22.218**
having wilfully taken part in an offence committed by another, as well as instiga-
tors and agents, will incur criminal liability.

It should also be pointed out that the Polish Criminal Code provides for criminal **22.219**
liability not only upon committing an offence, but also upon attempting to

---

[101] Pursuant to Art 8 of the Suppression of Unfair Competition Law, labelling goods or services with a false or fraudulent geographical designation indicating directly or indirectly a country, a region or a locality of origin, or using such designation in commercial activity, advertising, commercial correspondence, invoices or other documents shall be considered an act of unfair competition.
[102] Pursuant to Art 9 of the Suppression of Unfair Competition Law, if goods or services benefit from protection in the place of origin, and their special characteristics or properties are connected with origin from a specific region or locality, then false or fraudulent use of such geographic regional designations, even with the added words 'variety of', 'type of', 'method', or synonyms thereof, shall be considered an act of unfair competition.
[103] Ustawa z dnia 6 czerwca 1997 r. Kodeks karny, Dz.U. of 1997, No 88, item 553, as amended.
[104] Ustawa z dnia 6 czerwca 1997 r. Kodeks postępowania karnego, Dz.U. of 1997, No 89, item 555, as amended.

commit the same. Pursuant to Article 13(1) of the Polish Criminal Code any person who wilfully attempts to commit a criminal offence but effectively fails to commit it, shall be held criminally liable for this act.

22.220 The above provision in many cases offers an appropriate basis for requesting the commencement of criminal proceedings in situations where the goods infringing an intellectual property right have been intercepted before being actually placed on the market.

22.221 After being notified of an offence and receiving a motion for prosecution, the prosecution authorities take all steps necessary to gather evidence of the offence. When these are successful, the authorities prepare a bill of indictment which is directed to the Criminal Court before which the proceedings, based on the provisions of the Code of Criminal Procedure, are to be conducted.

22.222 In the course of the court proceedings, the injured person may participate in it in a role of an auxiliary prosecutor and cooperate with the prosecutor. The court proceedings conclude with a verdict in which the court finds whether an offence has been committed. The court also imposes, as it deems fit, a penalty and adjudicates on the disposal of property connected with the offence.

22.223 In the course of criminal proceedings, the injured party (that is, in the present context the holder of the intellectual property rights whose rights have been infringed as a result of the offence) may also file a civil motion in which he can claim damages.

22.224 However, the Criminal Court before which the criminal proceedings have been initiated may also consider a claim for damages despite the fact that such claims are of a civil nature.

22.225 Conversely, the Criminal Court may rule out from the criminal proceedings such claims for damages and direct them to the Civil Court of proper jurisdiction, as happens in practice in the vast majority of cases.

22.226 Finally, it is worth pointing out that Article 17(1)(1) of the Code of Criminal Procedure provides that no criminal prosecution shall take place when the offence does not significantly impact on public order. This situation is not unusual in practice, and is indeed often deemed to exist when it comes to the import into Poland of a small quantity of goods infringing an intellectual property right.

Counterfeit goods

22.227 In accordance with Article 305 of the IPL, the placing on the market of goods bearing a counterfeit trade mark constitutes a criminal offence. Under Article 120(2)(3) of this Law, a counterfeit trade mark is a trade mark identical to a(n earlier) registered trade mark used without the right-holder's consent in the course of trade, or a trade mark which in normal conditions of trade cannot be distinguished from that registered trade mark in respect of the goods which are covered by the registration certificate.

Therefore, Article 305 may constitute the grounds for instituting criminal proceedings when border measures are taken by the customs authorities against goods suspected of infringing a trade mark. **22.228**

Pirated goods

With regard to pirated goods, Article 116 of the Copyright Law provides that dissemination of someone else's work without authorization or against the terms and conditions of a licence agreement, in the original or a derivative version, constitutes a criminal offence. 'Dissemination of a work' is understood as any activity which is aimed at making a work available to third parties, which may thus include also the sale or other forms of dissemination of a work, for example, import or export. **22.229**

Article 116 of the Copyright Law distinguishes between two qualified forms of criminal offences in the case of a copyright infringement. The first occurs when the offender commits the above-specified act in order to gain material benefits. Such offences are punishable by an imprisonment for up to three years. The second occurs when the offender commits the offence described above as a regular source of income or organizes or manages a criminal activity. In this case, the court may impose a penalty of imprisonment for a term of between six months and five years. **22.230**

Under the IPL, which contains the basic regulations regarding industrial designs, infringements of a design right do not constitute criminal offences. Therefore, in the case of a detention or suspension of the release by the customs authorities of goods infringing a registered design right, it is not possible to institute criminal proceedings. **22.231**

Having said that, if the design qualifies as an original work under the Copyright Law, it is possible to seek criminal prosecution under the criminal provisions contained in that Law. **22.232**

Moreover, Article 307 of the IPL makes it a criminal offence for anyone to knowingly place on the market goods to which a false designation has been affixed suggesting that these goods are protected by a registered design, whereas this is not the case. **22.233**

Article 24 of the Suppression of Unfair Competition Law[105] provides that any person, who, with the aid of technical reproduction means, copies the external **22.234**

---

[105] See n 40 above.

appearance of a product or introduces the product copied on the market, thus giving rise to a risk of confusion in the customers' mind as to the identity of the manufacturer of the product, and which results in substantial damage to a business entity, shall be held criminally liable for such an act.

Goods infringing a patent or a supplementary protection certificate

22.235 The IPL does not explicitly state that the import of goods infringing a patent without the patentee's authorization would constitute a criminal offence.

22.236 Nevertheless, this does not mean that Polish criminal law affords no legal basis for the criminal prosecution of such infringements.

22.237 For instance, Article 303 of the IPL makes it a criminal offence to usurp another's authorship, mislead a third party as to the authorship of another's invention, or otherwise infringe rights of the author of an invention. It seems that the general expression 'or otherwise infringe rights' in this provision enable patentees to file a criminal complaint in some specific cases.

22.238 Moreover, Article 307 of the IPL makes it a criminal offence, subject to a fine or a term of imprisonment, to mark goods which are not protected by a patent or a supplementary protection certificate, for the purpose of placing them on the market, with statements or signs aimed at inducing the consumers into believing that the goods do enjoy such protection.

Goods infringing a national plant variety right

22.239 The provisions of the Law on the Protection of Plant Variety Rights regard as criminal offences a significant number of acts. For instance, Article 37(1) of this Law provides for criminal liability in the case of an infringement of the exclusive right to a protected plant variety (including for example, the right to offer for sale, sell or otherwise market, import or export protected plant varieties). Likewise, the marking of the seeds obtained from a crop of another or unknown variety with the name of a variety which is protected by the exclusive right constitutes a criminal offence. The authors of such offences are liable to a fine.

22.240 The proceedings in the above cases are conducted on the basis of the Code of Misdemeanours Procedure. The principles which are binding in the course of such proceedings relate to the principles resulting from the provisions of the Code of Criminal Procedure.

22.241 As in criminal proceedings, in order to initiate the proceedings regarding the offences mentioned in Article 24 of the Law on the Protection of Plant Variety Right, a motion of the injured party is required for the prosecution of the offender.

The proceedings regarding the offences are generally conducted by the police who **22.242** act as the public prosecutor. After the evidence is collected, in the course of ascertaining that the offence has been committed, a motion for prosecution of the offender is directed to the court. The injured party, who is the owner of the exclusive rights to the protected name of a plant in the cases indicated in Article 24 of the Law, may cooperate with the Police by acting as an auxiliary prosecutor and supporting a motion for prosecution of the offender.

Adjudications are made in the form of judgments or decisions issued at the trials **22.243** or closed sittings when the courts find the offender guilty of the alleged offence and decide on the sentence to be imposed.

The provisions of the Code of Misdemeanours Procedure include a number of **22.244** regulations (for example, Articles 58,[106] 64,[107] 93[108]) that, in cases that do not raise any doubts as to the identity of the offender, his guilt and the circumstances of committing the offence, enable the courts to issue a verdict without the necessity to hold a hearing. In such cases, materials attached to the motion for punishment of the offender are considered as evidence.

Goods infringing a designation of origin or a geographical indication

Under the IPL, the import or export of goods infringing a designation of origin or **22.245** a geographical indication are not defined as criminal offences.

---

[106] The Code of Misdemeanours Procedure, Art 58(1)
With the consent of the defendant who has been previously heard in the course of explanatory acts under Art 54(6), the public prosecutor may file in the motion for punishment, a motion for conviction of the person charged with the act without conducting a trial, and for imposing a specified penalty or penal measure, or for non-imposition of punishment or penal measure.
    Art 58(1)
The motion for conviction referred to in § 1 may be filed only if, in view of the evidence, the statement of the defendant and the circumstances of committing the misdemeanor do not raise doubts, and the aims of the proceedings have been achieved despite the fact that the trial has not been conducted.

[107] Art 64(1)
While recognizing the motion of the defendant filed before the commencement of a trial, for convicting him in a specified manner without conducting a trial, the court applies Art 63 accordingly.
    Art 64(2)
The court may accept the motion referred to, provided that neither the public prosecutor nor the auxiliary prosecutor (if he appears in the case) has objected to it, and only when the circumstances of the committed act and the defendant's statement do not raise doubts in view of the evidence.

[108] Art 93(1)
In misdemeanour cases, the court may issue a judgment in the form of an order, in which it is sufficient to give a reprimand, impose a fine or a penalty of restricted freedom. The court issues a verdict and sentence without the participation of the parties.
    Art 93(2)
The verdict and sentence may be issued in the form of an order if the circumstances of the committed act and the guilt of the defendant do not raise doubts. Upon issuing a sentence, the court considers the evidence filed with the motion for punishment.

22.246 However, Article 307 of the IPL makes it a criminal offence for any person to knowingly place on the market goods bearing an indication falsely suggesting that these goods are protected by a geographical indication.

22.247 This provision may be applied, although probably only to a very limited extent due to the specific definition of the prohibited act, with regard to goods detained at the border by the customs authorities.

22.248 The Law of 17 December 2004 on registration and protection of names and designations of agricultural products, foodstuffs, and traditional products[109] introduced the provisions regarding criminal liability for infringement of the names of origin and geographical indications entered into the Register of protected names of origin and geographical indications and also the names entered into the List of geographical indications and names of origin enjoying the temporary national protection.

22.249 In accordance with Article 57 of this Law, any entity who, whilst not being entitled to use a name entered into the Register of protected names of origin and geographical indications or a name entered into the List of geographical indications and names of origin enjoying the temporary national protection, introduces onto the market agricultural products or foodstuffs designated with such a name, shall incur criminal liability.

22.250 Similarly, any entity which uses in the course of trade a name of origin or a geographical indication infringing Article 13.1 of the Council Regulation No 2081/92 or uses in the course of trade a name entered into the List of agricultural products and foodstuffs enjoying the temporary national protection in breach of the requirements specified in Article 38[110] of the Law of 17 December 2004 on registration and protection of names and designations of agricultural products, foodstuffs, and traditional products, is also liable for criminal proceedings.

22.251 An entity who makes preparations to commit any of the above-mentioned prohibited acts will also face criminal liability.

22.252 This Law provides also for criminal liability for graded forms of the aforesaid offences where the offender has made such prohibited acts his permanent source of income or commits such offences with respect to agricultural products or foodstuffs of a considerable value.

---

[109] Ustawa z dnia 17 grudnia 2004 r. o rejestracji i ochronie nazw i oznaczeń produktów rolnych i środków spożywczych oraz o produktach tradycyjnych, Dz. U. of 2005, No 10, item 68.

[110] Cf para 22.208 above.

Pursuant to Article 58 of the Law of 17 December 2004, a person failing to fulfil **22.253** the conditions defined in the specification, introduces in the course of trade an agricultural product or a foodstuff and places on this product or a foodstuff or a packaging thereof or use in another way:

1) a name entered into the List, or
2) a name entered into the Register of protected names of origin and geographical indications, or
3) a name entered into the Register of certificates of a specific character if an applicant requested its protection in a motion for registration, or
4) a symbol of a protected name of origin, a protected geographical indication or a certificate of a specific character,

is subject to a fine not lower than PLN 4,000.

D. Release of goods suspected of infringing certain rights on provision of a security

The release of goods suspected of infringing a design right, a patent, a supple- **22.254** mentary protection certificate, or a plant variety right may be requested by their declarant, owner, importer, holder, or consignee on provision of a security, subject to the fulfilment of the conditions set out in Article 14 of Regulation 1383/2003.

However, in accordance with this provision, Polish Customs will refuse to release **22.255** the goods where the authority empowered for that purpose (that is, a court in the context of civil proceeding, or the Public prosecutor in criminal proceeding) has authorized precautionary measures (that is, has issued an interim injunction or a decision securing evidence) before the expiry of the 10 (up to 20) working days time limit laid down in Article 13(1) of the Regulation.

Polish law does not contain any specific provision on this point. It is therefore **22.256** difficult to predict, for example, how the amount of the security provided for in Article 14(2) of the Regulation will be calculated in practice. The security must, in any event, be sufficient to protect the right-holder's interest. It should therefore be determined by taking due account of the specific circumstances of the case, such as in the first place the extent of the suspected infringement, the extent of the potential prejudice suffered by the right-holder, and the value of the goods. The amount of the security ought to be determined by the Head of the Customs Department responsible for the detention or suspension of release of the goods.

To our knowledge, the possibility afforded by Article 14 of the Regulation has **22.257** never been applied in Poland.

E. Storage of the goods

22.258 Where customs authorities detain or suspend the release of goods suspected of infringing an intellectual property right, these goods are stored on deposit by the customs office. The holder of the goods may be obliged to wrap them in packaging which would guarantee proper storage of the goods and preserve their identity.

22.259 The customs authorities acknowledge acceptance of the detained goods for deposit by issuing a delivery receipt which must be returned on recovering the goods.

22.260 In accordance with the Decree of the Minister of Finance of 19 July 2004 on Deposits of the Customs Authorities,[111] the duration of the storage of goods which have been detained, or whose release has been suspended, depends on the decision of the relevant authorities.

22.261 Depending on the steps which the holder of the intellectual property right concerned will take after being notified of the detention of goods suspected of infringing his rights, several situations may be distinguished regarding the conditions for storage of the goods. The most common situations are as follows:

- The first situation refers to the case where the right-holder enters into a *settlement agreement* with the parties involved in the traffic which leads to the release of the detained goods before the expiry of the time limit provided for under Article 13(1) of the Regulation (that is, within which the right-holder is obliged to notify customs that proceedings have been initiated to determine whether an intellectual property right has been infringed). In such a case, Polish Customs will normally consent to the release of the goods on being provided with a copy of the settlement agreement. Under the principle of freedom of contract, the parties may stipulate that the infringer will be liable for the payment of the costs of the storage of the detained goods.

- The second situation relates to cases where the holder of the intellectual property right concerned has initiated *criminal* proceedings to determine whether his right has been infringed and required the Public prosecutor to seize the goods detained by the customs authorities. If the prosecutor acts accordingly, the goods will fall under his control and he will be responsible for the proper storage of the goods pending the proceedings. In such a case, the fate of the goods (for example, forfeiture) will be determined by the final judgment of the court.

- In a third situation, the intellectual property right-holder has initiated *civil* proceedings aimed at determining whether his rights have been violated and filed a motion for an interim injunction resulting in the seizure of the goods detained by customs pending the proceedings. In such a case, the right-holder must bear the storage costs.

---

[111] Rozporządzenie Ministra Finansów w sprawie depozytu urzędu celnego, Dz.U. of 2004 No 169, item 1771.

IV. PROVISIONS APPLICABLE TO GOODS FOUND TO INFRINGE AN INTELLECTUAL PROPERTY RIGHT

Further to the adoption of border measures by the customs authorities under the **22.262** Regulation, the (civil or criminal) courts will determine whether the goods infringe an intellectual property right.

In such proceedings, right-holders are entitled to seek the destruction of the goods **22.263** and/or of the moulds and matrices which were specifically adapted or designed for their manufacture, their disposal outside commercial channels—thus preventing the placement of such goods and devices on the market—or 'in exceptional cases', the removal from the goods of all elements which infringe an intellectual property right. The right-holder may also claim that the defendant be ordered to pay all costs relating to the enforcement of such measures.

Where the destruction of goods detained by customs has been ordered by the **22.264** courts, the destruction process is set out in the Decree of the Minister of Finance of 12 July 2004 laying down the conditions and procedures applying to the destruction of the goods and the forfeiture of the goods to the State Treasury.[112] The destruction of the goods is monitored by the customs authorities, unless the goods are destroyed by authorized entities specifically appointed to take care of the destruction of particular kinds of goods. The destruction process is reported, in due course, in a certificate of destruction.

According to Article 6 of the Decree, the costs entailed in the destruction process, **22.265** inclusive of transport, storage and destruction are borne by the person who obtained the consent. Therefore, if the court decision fails to impose liability for the payment of such costs on the infringer, these will be borne by the right-holder.

It should also be pointed out that in the course of the court proceedings, it is possible **22.266** to conclude an agreement which would contain provisions regarding the goods detained by customs. In other words, the parties to the proceedings may decide who will be responsible for the costs of storage of the goods, whether the goods should be destroyed or relinquished to social organizations—subject in that case, to the prior removal of all signs and designations which infringe an intellectual property right— and who shall bear the costs incurred as a result of such measures.

Polish criminal law also entitles the holders of intellectual property rights to prevent **22.267** the placement on the market of the goods detained by the customs authorities under

---

[112] Rozporządzenie Ministra Finansów z dnia 12 lipca 2004 r. w sprawie szczegółowych warunków I trybu postępowania przy zniszczeniu towarów I zrzeczeniu się towaru na rzecz Skarbu Państwa, Dz.U. of 2004, No 167, item 1748.

the Regulation. Typically, the criminal court will declare the goods forfeited to the state treasury. The goods will then be destroyed in accordance with the procedure set out in the above-mentioned Decree of the Minister of Finance. However, the state treasury may ask the holder of the intellectual property right concerned for his consent to the placement on the market of the goods whose forfeiture has been ordered, or to the offering of these goods to charities. In practice, whether or not the right-holder will allow such requests will depend on the fulfilment of the conditions which, from his point of view, are of such a nature as to secure his rights—such as the prior removal of the infringing signs which have been affixed to the goods.

V. PENALTIES

A. General remarks

22.268 The Polish Criminal Code provides for three types of criminal penalties, namely, deprivation of liberty, restriction of liberty, and a fine.[113] Deprivations of liberty and restrictions of liberty are calculated in months, and the lower threshold is set at one month.[114] As regards fines, the courts calculate them in daily rates and determine the number and the amount of such rates. Unless provided otherwise under a specific piece of legislation, the lowest number of rates is 10 and the highest 360.[115] When determining a daily rate, the court takes into account the income of the offender, his personal and family circumstances, financial state, and profit-making possibilities. A daily rate cannot be lower than PLN 10 or higher than PLN 2,000.

22.269 In imposing a penalty for a criminal offence, the courts act at their own discretion. However, in the light of the Criminal Code,[116] they should take into account the degree of danger of an offence to the public order. Moreover, as is also provided in Article 18 of the Regulation, such penalties must be effective, dissuasive, and proportionate to the guilt.

22.270 In particular, the courts will have regard to the motivation behind the offender's behaviour, the kind, and extent of the negative consequences of his acts, his lifestyle before he committed them, and the manner in which he behaved afterwards, that is, whether or not he attempted to redress the damage. In deciding on the appropriate penalty, the courts also take into account the positive results of the mediation conducted between the injured party and the offender, or the settlement

---

[113] Criminal Code, Art 32 (Ustawa z dnia 6 czerwca 1997 r.—Kodeks karny, Dz.U. of 1997, No 88, item 553 as amended).   [114] Ibid, Arts 34 and 36.
[115] Ibid, Art 33.   [116] Ibid, Art 53.

which they might have been concluded in the course of the proceedings. The Polish Criminal Code also provides for the possible extraordinary mitigation of a sentence[117] in cases where the court finds that the lowest punishment applied with reference to a particular offence would prove much too stringent, especially in those cases where the injured party reconciled with the offender, the latter has redressed the loss, or the injured party and the offender have agreed on a method to redress it.

22.271 The Criminal Code also enables the criminal courts to declare the goods forfeited, to order the offender to redress the damage, or to order the publication of the judgment.[118]

B. Counterfeit goods

22.272 The criminal offences defined in Article 305(1) of the IPL[119] are subject to a fine, restriction of liberty or deprivation of liberty of up to two years. Where these offences are of a more significant seriousness, the offender can incur a term of imprisonment of six months to five years.[120] In contrast, when the offence proves of a minor nature, the offender will only be liable to a fine.

22.273 When dealing with counterfeit goods, the courts will, in addition, always declare the infringing goods, moulds and matrices forfeited to the state treasury, even if they do not belong to the offender. However, to obtain the forfeiture of such products, it is necessary to file a specific motion for that purpose, except where the trade mark infringement proves particularly serious.

C. Pirated goods

22.274 The criminal offences defined in Articles 116(1)[121] and 117(1)[122] of the Copyright Law are punishable by a fine, restriction of liberty, or deprivation of

---

[117] Ibid, Art 53.   [118] Ibid, Art 39.

[119] 'Any person who affixes a counterfeit trade mark to goods for the purpose of placing them on the market, or who does place goods bearing such trade mark on the market, shall be liable to a fine, restriction of liberty or deprivation of liberty for a period of up to two years.'

[120] IPL, Art 305(3) ('Any person who has made the offence referred to in Art 305(1) his continuing source of profits or commits that offence in respect of goods of handsome value shall be liable to a jail term of six months to five years.')

[121] Copyright Law, Art 116(1) 'Whoever, without authorization or against the terms and conditions of a contract, disseminates someone else's work, artistic performance, sound recording, audiovisual recording or broadcast, in the original or a derivative version shall be liable to a fine, restriction of liberty or deprivation of liberty of up to two years.'

[122] Copyright Law, Art 117(1) 'Whoever, without authorization or against the terms and conditions of a contract, and for the purposes of dissemination, fixes or reproduces someone else's work, artistic performance, sound recording, audiovisual recording or broadcast, in the original or a derivative

liberty. The upper limit of the latter, depending on the seriousness of the offence, ranges from one to three years.

22.275 The penalties may be more stringent; however, when the offence has been committed for the purpose of gaining material benefits, or making it a regular source of income.[123] In such cases, the penalty may consist of a term of imprisonment of three to five years.

22.276 It should be pointed out that in the case of a conviction for any of the above offences, the criminal court is *obliged* to declare the goods forfeited, even if they are not in the offender's possession. Optionally, the court may also order the forfeiture of the devices (including the moulds and matrices) which have been used in the committing of the offence, even if they do not belong to the offender.[124] The court's decision on this point will depend on the specific circumstances of the case and on the filing of a motion by the injured party for that purpose.

22.277 As indicated above, the criminal provisions contained in the Suppression of Unfair Competition Law may also be applied with reference to pirated goods but to a limited extent. The criminal offence referred to in Article 24 of this Law[125] is subject to a fine, restriction of liberty, or a term of imprisonment of up to two years.

D. Goods infringing a patent or a supplementary protection certificate

22.278 The criminal offence defined in Article 303(1) of the IPL[126] incurs liability to a fine, restriction of liberty, or term of imprisonment of up to one year. Where the offence is particularly grave, the term of imprisonment can be up to two years.[127] The perpetrators of the offence defined in Article 307 of the IPL[128] incur the

---

version, and gives his/her consent to its dissemination, shall be liable to a fine, restriction of liberty or deprivation of liberty of up to two years.'

[123] Copyright Law, Arts 116(2), (3) and 117(2).   [124] Ibid, Art 121(2).

[125] Supression of Unfair Competition Law, Art 24.

'Any person, who, with the aid of technical reproduction means, copies the lay-out of a product or introduces a product thus copied onto the market, therefore giving rise to a risk of confusion in the consumers' mind as to the identity of the producer of the product, and hereby causes substantial harm to a business entity shall incur criminal liability.'

[126] IPL, Art 303(1) 'A person who usurps another's authorship or misleads a third party as to the authorship of another's invention, or otherwise infringes rights of the creator of an invention, shall be liable to a fine, restriction of liberty or term of imprisonment for a period not exceeding one year.'

[127] IPL, Art 303(2) 'Any person who committing the offence referred to in Art 303(1) for the purpose of making material profits or personal economic gains shall be liable to a fine, restriction of liberty or term of imprisonment for a period up to two years.'

[128] IPL, Art 307 'Any person marking goods which are not protected by a patent, a utility model or a registered design, a topography of an integrated circuit, or a geographical indication, with statements or signs aiming at suggesting that the goods do enjoy such protection, shall be liable to a fine or a term of imprisonment.'

liability of a fine or a term of imprisonment. The same penalties apply to those persons who place on the market goods on which an indication has been affixed to the effect of wrongly suggesting that these goods are protected by a patent or a supplementary protection certificate, while knowing that they are not.

E. Goods infringing a national plant variety right

Infringements of plant variety rights in Poland are only punishable by a fine **22.279** ranging from PLN 20 to PLN 5,000.[129]

By virtue of Article 307 of the IPL, infringements of a designation of origin or a **22.280** geographical indication constitute criminal offences. The authors of such offences are liable to a fine or a term of imprisonment The same penalties apply to those persons who, place on the market goods on which a statement has been affixed to the effect of wrongly suggesting that the goods are protected by a geographical indication, while knowing that this is not the case.[130]

As regards names of origin or geographical indications regulated by the provisions of **22.281** the Law of 17 December 2004 on registration and protection of names and designations of agricultural products, foodstuffs, and traditional products,[131] the penalty for committing a prohibited act referred to in Article 57(1)[132] or Article 57(2)[133] of this Law is a fine, restriction of liberty, or deprivation of liberty of up to two years.

The same penalty is provided with reference to anyone who only makes prepara- **22.282** tions for committing any of the prohibited acts defined in Article 57(1) or (2).

In the event of graded forms of offences when the offender makes any of the pro- **22.283** hibited acts defined in Article 57(1) or (2) his permanent source of income or when he commits them or makes preparations to commit such offences with respect to agricultural products or foodstuffs of a considerable value, the Law[134] provides for a higher penalty, that is deprivation of liberty from six months up to five years.

---

[129] Law on the Protection of Plant Variety Rights, Art 37 (Ustawa z dnia 26 czerwca 2003 r. o ochronie prawnej odmian roślin, Dz.U. of 2003, No 137, item 1300).   [130] IPL, Art 307(2).

[131] Dz. U. of 2005, No 10, item 68

[132] 'A person who not being authorized to use a name entered into the List referred to in Art 35(2), a name entered into the Register of protected names of origin and geographical indications, a protected name entered into the Register of certificates of a specific character, a symbol of a protected name of origin, a protected geographical indication or a certificate of a specific character carries on trade in agricultural products or foodstuffs designated with such a name or a symbol is subject to a fine, restriction of liberty or deprivation of liberty of up to 2 years.'

[133] 'A person who uses in turnover a name entered into the List referred to in Art 35(2) infringing the conditions specified in Art 38 or a name of origin or a geographical indication infringing Art 13(1) of Reg No. 2081/92 is subject to the same penalty.'

[134] 'In a situation when the offender has made committing an offence defined in Art 57(1) or Art 57(2) his permanent source of income or when he commits the offences defined in Art 57(1–3)

22.284   As regards the prohibited acts referred to in Article 58[135] of the Law on registration and protection of names and designations of agricultural products, foodstuffs, and traditional products, the regulations provide for a fine not lower than PLN 4,000.

VI. LIABILITY OF CUSTOMS AUTHORITIES AND RIGHT-HOLDERS

A. Liability of right-holders and sanctions

22.285   Under the general law of Tort and the provisions of Article 415 of the Polish Civil Code,[136] 'whoever by his fault caused damage to another person shall be obliged to redress it'.

22.286   Polish law does not contain any provision specifically addressing the issue of the right-holder's civil liability for harm caused in the context of the application of Regulation 1383/2003.[137] Liability claims may be initiated, however, on the basis of Article 415 of the Civil Code. For that purpose, the injured party will have to prove that he has suffered loss which is the immediate result of a wrongdoing committed by the right-holder. Subject to the fulfilment of these conditions and to the proof of the extent of the loss, the claimant will be entitled to compensation for both lost profits (*lucrum cessans*) and actual harm (*damnum emergens*).

22.287   It should be recalled that under Article 6 of the Regulation, the right-holder must enclose with his motion for action a declaration whereby he accepts liability towards the other persons in the event that proceedings are discontinued owing to an act or omission by the right-holder, or in the event that the goods in question are subsequently found not to infringe an intellectual property right.

22.288   Liability claims may also rely on Article 415 of the Civil Code, subject to the circumstances of the case concerned, in the event of non-permitted use by the right-holder of information obtained from customs authorities under Article 9(3) of the Regulation. Moreover, Article 12 of the Regulation provides that such unauthorized use may also lead to the suspension of the motion for action, for the period of validity remaining before renewal, in the Member State in which the events have

---

with respect to agricultural products or foodstuffs of a considerable value, is subject to deprivation of liberty from 6 months up to 5 years.'

[135] 'A person who, whilst failing to fulfill the conditions defined in the specification, introduces in trade an agricultural product or a foodstuff and places on this product or foodstuff or a packaging thereof or otherwise uses a name entered into the List is subject to a fine not lower than 4000 PLN.'

[136] Ustawa z dnia 23 kwietnia 1964 r. Kodeks Cywilny, Dz.U. of 1964, No 16, item 93, as amended.   [137] Cf Reg 1383/2003, Art 19(3).

taken place. Moreover, any unauthorized use of the information listed in Article 9(3) of the Regulation may also cause the right-holder to incur civil liability under Article 14(1) of the Suppression of Unfair Competition Law.[138] Pursuant to this provision, dissemination of untrue or misleading information about one's own or another business entity or enterprise in order to benefit from it or to cause harm shall be considered an act of unfair competition and may, as such, cause the perpetrator of such an act to incur civil liability. In accordance with Article 14(2)(4) of the Law, the information referred to in Article 14(1) may consist in particular of information on an economic or legal situation. The particulars cited in the first indent of Article 9(3) of the Regulation may be considered as falling under this category.

Finally, in the event of the use by the right-holder of the above information in a manner that may threaten or impair the interest of a third party undertaking, in accordance with Article 18 of the Suppression of Unfair Competition Law, the injured party may claim the cessation of such acts, the elimination of their consequences, the publication of specific statements, redress of the loss incurred according to the general principles of the Law of Tort (under Article 415 of the Civil Code), and/or the surrendering of all undue profits. **22.289**

B. Liability of customs authorities and sanctions

Under Article 417 of the Polish Civil Code, the State Treasury shall be liable for any damages caused by a State official (including employees of State authorities, State administration authorities, and State economic organizations) in the course of carrying out his duties. Customs officers qualify as State officials, which means that the State Treasury shall be liable for their actions in breach of the law, and thus for compensation for any loss which they may have caused. **22.290**

However, in accordance with Article 421 of the Civil Code, the provisions on the liability of the State Treasury for the losses caused by State officials do not apply if that liability is the object of any specific provisions under a separate piece of legislation. **22.291**

The provisions of Article 12 and Part IV (tax proceedings) of the 29 August 1997 Tax Ordinance,[139] as amended, are particularly relevant in this context. Chapter 21 of Part IV of the Tax Ordinance deals with the issue of liability of customs officials, which implies that, by virtue of Article 421 of the Civil Code, the provisions **22.292**

---

[138] See above n 40.
[139] Ustawa z dnia 29 sierpnia 1997 r.—Ordynacja podatkowa, Dz.U. of 1997 No 137, item 926 as amended.

of Article 417 of this Code will not be applicable to customs authorities. Pursuant to Article 260 of the Tax Ordinance, any person who suffers loss as a result of a decision issued and subsequently withdrawn owing to a resumption of the procedure, or subsequently found invalid, shall be entitled to compensation for this loss, unless the withdrawal or cancellation of the decision in question was caused by the injured party's own fault.

22.293   Therefore, to be successful in its claim against customs, the injured party must submit a decision on the resumption of the proceedings[140] or a decision confirming annulment of a decision[141] whose issue and enforcement resulted in damage.

22.294   The indemnity may be claimed from the authority which has issued the decision in breach of the law. An application for indemnity shall be filed with the said authority, while the decision on the indemnity will be issued by the tax authority, which annulled the decision or decided its invalidity.

22.295   Where the claim for damages against the authority is dismissed (in whole or in part), the injured party may file a motion before the common courts within 30 days from the day of service of the decision.[142] Failure to issue a decision within two months from the day of filing of the claim shall be considered as a rejection of the claim. In this latter situation, a motion to the common courts may be filed at any time.

---

[140]   Cf Tax Ordinance, Art 240(1): 'Where a case has been closed by a final decision, the procedure shall be resumed if:

    1)   the evidence upon which the factual circumstances relevant to the case were established appears to be false;
    2)   the decision was issued as a result of an offence;
    3)   the decision was issued by an employee of the tax authority subject to exclusion under Arts 130 to 132;
    4)   the party does not take part in the procedure through no fault of that party;
    5)   new factual circumstances relevant to the case or new evidence is revealed, which already existed on the day of issuing the decision but were unknown to the authority which issued it;
    6)   the decision was issued without obtaining an opinion of another authority required by law;
    7)   the decision was issued on the grounds of another decision or a court decision which was subsequently revoked or amended in a way which might affect the content of the decision issued;
    8)   the decision was issued pursuant to a provision whose incompatibility with the Constitution of the Republic of Poland, a statute or a ratified international agreement has been pronounced by the Constitutional Tribunal.'

[141]   Cf ibid, Art 247(1). The tax authority shall pronounce the invalidity of a final decision:

    1)   which was issued in breach of the provisions on jurisdiction;
    2)   which was issued without legal basis;
    3)   which was issued through gross violation of law;
    4)   which relates to a case which had already been resolved by another final decision;
    5)   which was addressed to a person who was not a party in that case;
    6)   which was non-enforceable on the day on which it was issued and has since then become permanently non-enforceable;
    7)   which is affected by a defect resulting in its invalidity by virtue of a clear provision of law;
    8)   whose enforcement would lead to the commission of a punishable act.

[142]   Ibid, Art 261(4).

Article 260(3) of the Tax Ordinance contains an exception to the general rules **22.296** indicated above. If the occurrence of the fact which led to the withdrawal of the decision further to the resumption of the proceedings, or to the invalidation of the decision, has been caused by the fault of another party involved in the proceedings, the injured party may claim compensation directly against that party before the common courts.

As pointed out above, liability claims relying on Article 260(1) of the Tax **22.297** Ordinance are subject to proof of loss caused by a decision issued by the customs authorities. This is not the case, however, under Article 417 of the Civil Code, which is the only legal basis for liability claims against customs where the alleged loss has been caused by an omission of the latter.

In the light of the provisions contained in Chapter 21, Part IV of the Tax **22.298** Ordinance and Article 421 of the Civil Code, it seems that right-holders are entitled, under Article 417 of the Civil Code, to claim compensation in the event that goods are not detected by a customs office and are released, or in the event that no action is taken to detain them, once an application has been lodged by the relevant right-holder. Indeed, an omission to take action when this was regarded as obligatory under the provisions in force in Poland (thus including the provisions of the Regulation) might be regarded as a fault, which may cause customs to incur civil liability.[143] However, the burden of proof of the existence of such a fault and of loss caused by this fault lies with the claimant.

Conclusion

As of 1 May 2004, the Polish border became the eastern border of the EU, and Polish Customs offices become the first firewall against the import of [infringing] goods. This triggered a great organizational and financial effort of the Polish Customs administration prior to accession. Approximately 2000 Customs personnel have been relocated to Poland's Eastern borders in recognition of the importance of those borders and substantial training of Customs officers is underway.[144]

Council Regulation (EC) 1383/2003 has been in force in Poland for such a short **22.299** period of time (since 1 July 2004), that one cannot say, yet, that Polish Customs have adopted a consistent and uniform approach in the context of its application. The lack of uniformity in practice in this respect also results from the delay in adopting the Implementing Regulation 1891/2004, which was done as late as 1 October 2004. We trust that, on the basis of this Regulation, Polish Customs will soon be in a position to harmonize their procedures to establish an even more efficient protection of intellectual property rights.

---

[143] Cf Reg 1383/2003, Art 19(1).
[144] J Rutter and M Rosinski, 'Who is the Weakest Link?', [2004] Trade mark World, 26–29.

22.300   The Practice of Polish Customs demonstrates, in any case, that '[t]he effectiveness of Poland's Customs administration has improved in the last few years', particularly as regards *ex officio* actions. However Poland was listed in the Special 501 Report published on 1 May 2003 by the US Trade Department as a 'country with a substantial copyright piracy and trade mark counterfeiting problem'.[145] Unfortunately, the backlog of the criminal and civil courts dealing with proceedings aimed at determining whether an intellectual property right has been infringed, subsequent to taking of actions by customs under the Regulation undermines such initiatives. Indeed, owing to the length of court proceedings, many cases concerning intellectual property right infringements initiated as a result of customs actions do not lead to any ruling, but are eventually settled between the parties to save storage costs, for example.

---

[145]   J Rutter and M Rosinski, 'Who is the Weakest Link?', [2004] Trade mark World, 26–29.

23

PORTUGAL

Gonçalo Moreira Rato and Nuno Cruz

Introduction

A. The laws on intellectual property

Portugal traditionally follows the legislative system of codification. It is therefore **23.01**
no surprise that Portuguese national legislation in the field of intellectual property
is included in only two codes, as well as a few other individual laws governing
specific aspects of copyright.

This is the case particularly of the industrial property legislation, which is totally **23.02**
compiled into a single law, known as the *Código da Propriedade Industrial*
('Industrial Property Code').

It is interesting to note that in Portugal the industrial property legislation has **23.03**
maintained a unified structure since the Law of 21 May 1896, known as the *Carta
de Lei de 1896* ('Charter of 1896'). This Law was substituted by the Industrial
Property Code of 1940,[1] which was followed by the Industrial Property Code of
1995.[2] The latter was replaced by the Industrial Property Code of 2003,[3] which
entered into force on 1 July of that year.[4]

The current Industrial Property Code consists of five parts. Part II contains the **23.04**
specific provisions relating to each of the industrial property rights,[5] including the
formalities and procedure for obtaining protection (patents and registrations), as
well as the contents of these rights. Part III contains the provisions relating to

---

[1] Approved by Decree-Law 30 679 of 24 August 1940.
[2] Approved by Decree-Law 16/95 of 24 January 1995. This Code entered into force on 1 June
1995.   [3] Approved by Decree-Law 36/2003 of 5 March 2003.
[4] On the historical development of industrial property legislation in Portugal, cf Jorge Cruz,
Código da Propriedade Industrial (Lisbon, 2003).   [5] Cf paras 23.24–23.26 below.

unfair competition, as well as enforcement of the various industrial property rights, including border measures.[6]

23.05 As far as copyright is concerned, the main Portuguese national law is the *Código do Direito de Autor e dos Direitos Conexos* ('Copyright and Neighbouring Rights Code').

23.06 The first copyright law in Portugal dates back to 1851[7] and was substituted a few years later by a chapter included in the Civil Code of 1867.[8] This regulation remained in force for six decades, until 1927 when a new separate regulation covering copyright came into force,[9] which was in turn replaced by the Copyright Code of 1966.[10] The current Copyright Code entered into force on 14 March 1985.[11]

23.07 The Copyright Code of 1985 is divided into six parts. Part I contains the general rules regarding the categories of works that are protected, as well as the content of copyright. Part IV contains the provisions relating to copyright infringement and enforcement.

23.08 Beside the Copyright Code, there are other individual laws relating to this subject. These laws include in particular the 1991 Law on Computer Criminality,[12] the 1994 Law on the Legal Protection of Computer Programs,[13] and the 2000 Law on the Legal Protection of Databases.[14]

23.09 In addition to the above-mentioned specific industrial property and copyright legislation, other general national laws are also applicable.

23.10 First of all, the Civil Code is important in defining the content of intellectual property rights as property rights.[15] This Code is also relevant to various other aspects of intellectual property law, such as the regulating of evidence in judicial proceedings and the rules governing damages.

23.11 As far as intellectual property infringements and litigation are concerned, the Criminal Code, as well as the Code of Civil Procedure and the Code of Criminal Procedure, are fundamental. Also subsidiarily applicable are the Law on a General

---

[6] Cf paras 23.22–23.28 below.

[7] Published in *Diário do Governo* on 18 July 1851.

[8] The *Código Civil Português*, approved by the Charter of 1 July 1867, which was the first civil code in Portugal.

[9] Law on Literary, Scientific and Artistic Property, approved by Decree 13 725 of 3 June 1927.

[10] *Código do Direito de Autor* (1966), approved by Decree-Law 46 980 of 27 April 1966.

[11] On the historical development of copyright law in Portugal, cf L F Rebello, *Código do Direito de Autor e dos Direitos Conexos Anotado* (2nd edn, November 1998).

[12] Law 109/91 of 17 August 1991 on Computer Criminality (*Lei da Criminalidade Informática*).

[13] Decree-Law 252/94 of 20 October 1994, which implemented Council Directive 91/250/EEC of 14 May 1991 on the legal protection of computer programs ([1991] OJ L 122/42 (17.5.1991)).

[14] Decree-Law 122/2000 of 4 July 2000, which implemented Directive 96/9/EC of the European Parliament and of the Council of 11 March 1996 on the legal protection of databases ([1996] OJ L 77/20 (27.3.1996)).   [15] Cf para 23.38 and n. 53 below.

System for Counter-Ordinances,[16] and the Law on Anti-Economic and Public Health Infringements.[17]

B. Legislation on border measures

Portugal joined the EEC in 1986, and has therefore been a Member State when all the Community Regulations on border measures have taken effect under its legal system, going back to Regulation (EEC) 3842/86.[18]   **23.12**

This first Regulation entered into force on 1 January 1988, and shortly afterwards the Portuguese national law containing the administrative rules necessary for implementing the Regulation was published.[19] In particular, the *Direcção Geral das Alfândegas* ('General Directorate of Customs') was designated as the entity responsible for receiving and processing applications for customs intervention by trade mark right-holders. This law also established that the Portuguese Industrial Property Office[20] would provide technical assistance with regard to industrial property matters at the request of the General Directorate of Customs.   **23.13**

With regard to Regulation (EC) 3295/94,[21] it was only in January 1999 that the respective Portuguese national implementing law[22] was published, which substituted the Law of 1988. The new Law maintained the General Directorate of Customs as the entity responsible for receiving and processing applications for customs intervention. It also regulated a few aspects relating to the provision of guarantees provided under Article 6 of the Regulation.[23] As regards the technical support furnished to customs, the new Law maintained the role of the Portuguese Industrial Property Office for this purpose and provided for the intervention of other entities in respect of these functions, namely the *Sociedade Portuguesa de*   **23.14**

---

[16] Decree-Law 433/82 of 27 October 1982, which was amended by successive laws, the latest one being Decree-Law 244/95 of 14 September 1995. On infringements of this nature, cf paras 23.291–23.295 below.   [17] Decree-Law 28/84 of 20 January 1984.

[18] Council Reg (EEC) 3842/86 of 1 December 1986 laying down measures to prohibit the release for free circulation of counterfeit goods [1986] OJ L 357/1 (18.12.1986).

[19] Decree-Law 160/88 of 13 May 1988, with retroactive effect dating back to 1 January of that year.

[20] In Portuguese, *Instituto Nacional da Propriedade Industrial*.

[21] Council Reg (EC) 3295/94 of 22 December 1994 laying down measures to prohibit the release for free circulation, export, re-export or entry for a suspensive procedure of counterfeit and pirated goods [1994] OJ L 341/8 (22.12.1994), as amended by Council Reg (EC) 241/1999 (OJ L 27/1 (2.2.1999)) and Council Reg (EC) 806/2003 [2003] OJ L 122/1 (16.5.2003).

[22] Decree-Law 20/99 of 28 January 1999, which is still in force today.

[23] Ibid, Art 2. Para 1 of this national law provision states that the applicant may be required to provide a guarantee '(...) at the moment when the customs intervention occurs (...)', and para 2 stipulates that 'The amount of the guarantee shall be calculated taking account of the elements contained in the application for customs intervention, the value of the merchandise, as well as any other elements which the Customs authorities may consider to be relevant for this purpose.'

Autores[24] ('Portuguese Association of Authors') in the field of copyright, as well as '(...) any other entity technically qualified in the field of intellectual property rights (...)'. The Law also established exemption from civil liability on the part of customs before declarants or holders of goods in cases of *ex officio* actions[25] and, finally, it created a penal sanction for the acts provided in the Regulation involving counterfeit or pirated goods.[26]

23.15 As in the case of many other Member States, it may be said that the Community system of border measures only truly started to function in Portugal with the implementation of Regulation (EC) 3295/94. In fact, it was while this second Regulation was in force that Portuguese Customs started to detain suspect goods on a fairly regular basis.

23.16 No national legislation on border measures has ever existed in Portugal relating specifically to the protection of copyrights or neighbouring rights. However, as far as industrial property is concerned, Portugal has for a long time had its own system of customs actions through border measures.

23.17 The first border measures were governed under Portuguese law by the Charter of 4 June 1883.[27] This Law provided for the seizure by customs of goods of foreign origin that displayed, without the authorization of the right-holder, trade marks or trade names of commercial or industrial companies that were established in Portugal.

23.18 The following Law, the Charter of 1896, also contained measures for the detention by customs of goods manufactured in foreign countries. The provisions of this Law, however, focused more on preventing situations of 'false indications of origin' in respect of imported goods than protecting trade mark rights per se.

23.19 The Industrial Property Code of 1940 introduced in Portugal a system of border measures by customs that is basically the same as the system that is now in force under the current national law. Article 229 of that Code ordered the detention of goods under the following circumstances: '(...) during the act of importation or exportation of any goods or merchandise that directly or indirectly display false indications of origin or appellations of origin, trade marks or names that are illicitly used or applied or in any other way constitute an offence against industrial property rights'.

---

[24] The *Sociedade Portuguesa de Autores* is a limited liability cooperative founded in 1925 for the management of copyrights in accordance with Portuguese national legislation. It represents in all areas of literature and the arts Portuguese authors, their successors and assignees who are registered with the association, as well as the authors, successors and assignees registered with the 170 sister associations existing in 90 countries in all the continents, with which the *Sociedade Portuguesa de Autores* maintains reciprocal contractual relations.

[25] Decree-Law 20/99 (n 22 above), Art 3.

[26] In the opinion of the authors of this work, the legislative technique used for this purpose was, however, rather erroneous (cf para 23.279 below).

[27] This Charter became known as the first trade mark law in Portugal.

Thus, Portuguese law has been providing for a fully comprehensive border measures **23.20** system since 1940. Such measures covered infringements of all categories of industrial property rights and acts of importation *and* exportation, and were applicable *ex officio*.

The Industrial Property Code of 1995, in its Article 274, maintained the above- **23.21** mentioned provision of the Industrial Property Code of 1940 with exactly the same wording.

The border measures that currently exist under Portuguese national law still only **23.22** refer to industrial property rights and they directly succeeded those that were pro- vided under the two previous Industrial Property Codes of 1940 and 1995, now being contained in Article 319 of the Industrial Property Code of 2003.

This Article, entitled 'Seizures by Customs', states as follows: **23.23**

1—Any goods or merchandise which directly or indirectly bear false indications of origin or appellations of origin, trade marks or names that are illegally used or applied, or display evidence of an offence stipulated in this Code, shall be seized by Customs during the act of importation or exportation.

2—In a case of clear infringement, the seizure shall be made on the initiative of the Customs authorities, which shall immediately notify the interested party, allowing the latter to remedy the subject of the preventive seizure, notwithstanding any liabilities that may already have been incurred.

3—The seizure may also be carried out at the request of any interested party.

4—The seizure shall lapse if, within 10 working days of the right-holder being notified, its confirmation is not requested in Court by the Public Prosecutor or by the injured party.

5—The term stipulated in the preceding subsection can be extended for an identical period in duly justified cases.

In accordance with this provision of Portuguese national law, border measures are **23.24** applicable to *any infringement* as defined in the Industrial Property Code. This Code governs the following industrial property rights: patents, utility models, topographies of semiconductor products, designs or models, trade marks, awards,[28] names and emblems of establishment,[29] logos,[30] appellations of origin, and geographical indications.

---

[28] 'Awards' correspond to decorations, medals, certificates of analysis, supplier certificates or any other prizes or demonstrations of preference of an official nature awarded to products. Portuguese law provides for the possibility of registering these awards at the Industrial Property Office (under Arts 271–281 of the Industrial Property Code). They have existed as such since the Charter of 1896 (cf para 23.03 above) and remain as an archaism (and certainly a peculiarity) of Portuguese law, it being highly doubtful that they correspond to an industrial property right in the true sense of the concept.

[29] The distinctive signs of the actual premises ('establishments') where goods are manufactured and/or commercialized, or where services are rendered.

[30] Known in Portuguese as *logótipos*, being distinctive signs of the actual company.

23.25 Next to the enforcement of the 'private industrial property rights' mentioned above, the Industrial Property Code also regulates as infringements the various acts of unfair competition,[31] including the 'Protection of undisclosed information'.[32]

23.26 Thus, within the scope of industrial property, Portuguese national legislation provides for border measures in respect of more categories of industrial property rights than the EC Regulation currently in force on the same subject.[33]

23.27 As far as customs procedures are concerned, Portuguese national law provides for border measures against goods suspected of infringing an intellectual property right which are in the process of *'importation* or *exportation'*—thus using the same terminology in this regard as the corresponding provision (Article 229) of the old Industrial Property Code of 1940. When this provision was originally drafted in 1940, it was certainly intended to cover *all* possible customs procedures. However, the fact is that technically the expression 'importation or exportation' does not cover all the regimes defined in the current customs legislation and provided for as such in the new EC Regulation 1383/2003[34] ('the Regulation'). Therefore, with regard to this aspect, Portuguese law will be narrower in scope than the EC Regulation—although this will have a few or no practical repercussions in relation to the action of the customs authorities under Article 319 of the Industrial Property Code.

23.28 Finally, it is interesting to note that Portuguese law provides for the possibility of customs intervention at intra-Community borders. However, in reality this is almost only a *theoretical* possibility, since in practice there is no longer any customs control at the borders within the European Union.[35]

23.29 Owing to the progressive broadening of the scope of the successive EC Regulations on this subject,[36] Portuguese national legislation on border measures has an increasingly residual function. The most important practical effect of Article 319 of the Industrial Property Code is probably the possibility of customs intervention in respect of infringements of intellectual property rights that are not covered by the current Regulation. This is the case for utility models, topographies

---

[31] Industrial Property Code of 2003, Art 317.

[32] Ibid, Art 318, which is based directly on the TRIPs Agreement (Agreement on the Trade-Related Aspects of Intellectual Property Rights), Art 39.

[33] This difference in scope between EC and Portuguese legislation was of course more obvious while Reg (EEC) 3842/86 (n 18 above) and even Reg (EC) 3295/94 (n 21 above) were in force, especially before the latter was amended by Reg (EC) 241/1999 (n 21 above).

[34] Council Reg (EC) 1383/2003 of 22 July 2003 concerning customs action against goods suspected of infringing certain intellectual property rights and the measures to be taken against goods found to have infringed such rights [2003] OJ L 196/7 (2.8.2003).

[35] Exceptional situations may arise when, for example, intra-Community borders are temporarily subject to checks, namely for reasons of domestic security—as happened in Portugal during the 2004 European Football Championship.   [36] Cf nn 18, 21 and 34 above.

of semiconductor products, and (in certain situations) the distinctive signs specific to Portuguese law.[37] Another (interesting) additional category of intellectual property rights, not covered by the Regulation, is the category of trade marks with a reputation, in the sense of Article 5(2) of the Trade Mark Directive,[38] the infringement of which in Portugal is prohibited as a criminal offence.[39]

In any case, in formal terms, the provisions of the Regulation and Article 319 of the **23.30** Industrial Property Code are still autonomous of each other. In view of this, and also because there are no discrepancies or contradictions between the Community legislation and the above-mentioned provision of Portuguese national law, it should not be necessary to make any significant alterations to the latter.[40]

Obviously, a new national law for implementing certain aspects of the Regulation **23.31** is expected, which will replace the one that is currently in force.[41] One of the most relevant alterations that will in principle be made by the future law are the rules required for implementing Article 11 of the new Regulation,[42] as well as Article 14(1) thereof.[43]

In addition to the implementing law, Portuguese Customs have also issued, in **23.32** respect of the successive EC Regulations, circulars with instructions for their application. As far as Regulation 1383/2003 is concerned, the customs authorities issued on 2 August 2004 Circular 78/2004 containing the 'Instructions for Application' of this Regulation, and on 13 September of the same year, Circular 91/2004 was issued, setting out the 'Criminal Procedural Formalities relating to Infringement and other Merchandise suspected of infringing certain Intellectual Property rights'.

I. SUBJECT MATTER AND SCOPE OF THE NATIONAL LAW APPLYING THE REGULATION

A. Customs status of the goods

Portuguese Customs apply the Regulation to all situations and customs **23.33** procedures defined in Article 1(1) thereof. This is the practice that had already

---

[37] Namely, names and emblems of establishments and logos.
[38] First Council Directive (EEC) 89/104 of 21 December 1988 to Approximate the Laws of the Member States Relating to Trade Marks [1989] OJ L 40/1 (11.2.1989). This Directive was implemented into Portuguese national law by the Industrial Property Code of 1995.
[39] Cf paras 23.50–23.52 below. The protection granted to such trade marks extends to use in respect of dissimilar goods, which cannot be considered as 'counterfeit goods' under Art 2(1)(a)(i) of the Regulation.
[40] With the exception perhaps of a few inaccuracies in the current text of the legal provision, as mentioned in para 23.27 above. [41] Decree-Law 20/99 (n 22 above).
[42] Cf paras 23.198–23.215 below. [43] Cf paras 23.257–23.264.

been adopted in accordance with the national industrial property legislation on border measures long before the entry into force of the first Community Regulation[44] in 1988.

23.34   Item II[45] of Circular 78/2004[46] provides that the Regulation '(...) is intended to combat the introduction into the Community customs territory, including transhipment, of goods suspected of infringing certain intellectual property rights'. The Circular also expressly clarifies that '(...) customs intervention covers exchanges with third countries and involves suspending the release (that is, the clearance process) of [infringing] goods (...) when declared for free circulation, export or re-export under an economic regime, or detaining such merchandise in the case of goods introduced into the Community customs territory and placed under a suspensive procedure[47] (for example, external transit regime), or in the case of goods that are in the process of being re-exported subject to notification or placed in a free zone or free warehouse, when they are found during customs checks'.

23.35   The statistics disclosed by the European Commission reveal, however, that in practice almost all customs interventions in Portugal related to imports. This is the case, at least, in the light of the data reported for the year 2003, according to which 98 per cent of the customs procedures instituted under the Regulation in Portugal concerned acts of *importation*, whereas 2 per cent (that is, one case) concerned the 'customs warehousing' regime.[48]

B. Definition of infringing goods

23.36   In accordance with the wording of the Regulation itself, the acts that constitute infringements of each intellectual property right are defined either in the respective EC Regulations in the case of Community rights or, in the case of national rights, by the '(...) law of the Member State in which the application for action by the Customs authorities is made'. An identical reference to 'Community legislation or the legislation of the Member State' is made in Circular 78/2004.[49]

---

[44] N 18 above.   [45] This item mirrors Recital 3 of the Regulation.
[46] Para 23.32 above.
[47] The Circular clarifies in a footnote that suspensive procedures, within the meaning of Art 84(1)(a) of the Community Customs Code (Council Reg (EEC) 2913/92 of 12 October 1992 establishing the Community Customs Code [1992] OJ L 302/1 (19.10.1992), as amended), are the following: external transit, customs warehousing, inward processing under a suspension system, processing under customs control, and temporary importation.
[48] DG TAXUD, Annual report on the activities of the Community customs in the fight against counterfeiting and piracy (2003)—Breakdown by number and percentage of customs and other procedures (http://europa.eu.int/comm/taxation_customs/resources/documents/counterf_comm_2003_en.pdf).   [49] Para 23.32 above.

The provisions of substantive law setting out the content of each of the relevant **23.37** intellectual property rights are contained in the Industrial Property Code[50] as far as industrial property rights are concerned, and, in the case of copyrights, in the Copyright Code[51]—with the exception of software, the protection of which is regulated under a separate law.[52]

With regard to the nature of the various intellectual property rights, Portuguese **23.38** law contains a few provisions which are common to all rights and are fundamental for defining not only the nature and scope of protection of the rights, but also the judicial means available for enforcing them.[53]

According to the statistics provided by the European Commission,[54] in 2003 **23.39** 70 per cent of the customs procedures instituted in Portugal concerned counterfeit goods (trade mark infringements), whereas the remaining 30 per cent involved the infringement of copyrights.[55] The statistics do not mention any intervention by Portuguese Customs in respect of other types of rights covered by the Regulation in 2003,[56] namely patents, supplementary protection certificates, geographical indications, and designations of origin.[57]

---

[50] The Industrial Property Code of 2003, paras 23.03–23.04 above.
[51] The Copyright and Neighbouring Rights Code of 1985, paras 23.05–23.07 above.
[52] N 13 above.
[53] One of the basic provisions is Art 1303 of the Civil Code, entitled 'Intellectual Property.' Para 1 of this article states that 'Copyright and industrial property are subject to special legislation.' Para 2 clarifies, however, that 'The provisions [of the Civil Code] are nevertheless subsidiarily applicable to copyright and industrial property when they are in accordance with the nature of those rights and do not contradict the special regime applicable thereto.' As far as industrial property rights are concerned, the above-mentioned provision of the Civil Code is reinforced and complemented by Art 316 of the Industrial Property Code, which states that 'Industrial property enjoys the guarantees provided for by law for property in general, and shall be specially protected in accordance with the terms of [the Industrial Property Code] and other legislation and conventions that are in force.' This provision already existed, with the same wording, in the Industrial Property Code of 1995, Art 257, and in the earlier Industrial Property Code of 1940, Art 211. Regarding the 'guarantees established by law for property in general', Art 1305 of the Civil Code is also of particular relevance, stating that 'The proprietor shall fully and exclusively enjoy the rights of use, enjoyment and possession of the property that belongs to him, within the limits of the law and in accordance with the restrictions imposed thereby.' These provisions constitute the legal basis for the enforcement of IP rights against certain forms of infringement which are not expressly governed by the respective special statutes (that is, the Industrial Property Code, the Copyright Code, and the other statutes referred to in paras 23.03–23.08 above), and which are known as '*indirect* infringements'. They are acts which do not constitute direct infringements of intellectual property rights (the *direct* infringements provided for under Portuguese law will be described below in respect of each of the intellectual property rights in the subsequent paragraphs of this section B), but are nevertheless liable to prejudice these rights, in particular their economic value—eg, in the case of trade marks, acts of dilution (Cf, as representing all Portuguese authors, C Olavo, *Propriedade Industrial* (2nd edn, Almedina, 2005) 134.
[54] N 48 above, breakdown by type of right covered.
[55] The statistics actually report that 30% of the cases concerned goods suspected of infringing *design* rights, but this is certainly an error.
[56] At that time, Reg (EC) 3295/94 (n 21 above).
[57] In this regard, the data reported in the statistics compiled by the EC Commission is in accordance with the professional experience of the authors of this contribution.

23.40 As regards more recent data, it is interesting to highlight an intervention that the customs reported, carried out in February 2005 by the Lisbon Airport office, of 35,600 roses coming from Brazil and imported by a Portuguese company, which were suspected of infringing plant variety rights.[58]

23.41 The statistics do not mention any intervention by Portuguese Customs in respect of other types of rights covered by the Regulation in 2003,[59] namely patents, supplementary protection certificates, geographical indications, and designations of origin.[60]

(1) Counterfeit goods

23.42 Article 224 of the Industrial Property Code stipulates that the registration of a trade mark 'shall confer on its owner the ownership of the trade mark and exclusive rights therein for the goods and services that it designates'. In line with Article 5(1) of the Trade Mark Directive,[61] the scope of the exclusive trade mark rights is defined in Article 258 of the same Code as '(. . .) confer[ring] on the owner the right to prevent third parties not having his consent from using in the course of trade any sign which is *identical or similar* in relation to goods or services which *are identical or have an affinity* with those for which the trade mark is registered, or any sign which, because of the *similarity* of the signs and the *affinity* between the goods or services, may create a *risk of confusion* or *association* in the mind of the consumer'.

23.43 Portuguese law has always provided for the protection of trade marks against the use or registration not only of *identical* signs, but also of *confusingly similar* signs.[62] In the case of the former, the expressions used in Portuguese legal terminology are 'trade mark *reproduction*' or 'trade mark *counterfeiting*', whereas in the case of the latter, the term used is 'trade mark *imitation*'.[63]

23.44 Likewise, the legal protection of trade marks covers not only the *same* goods as those for which they are (validly) registered ('identical products'), but also goods that are *similar* thereto ('similar products').

23.45 The scope of protection of trade marks in Portugal is defined in Article 245(1) of the Industrial Property Code, with reference to the legal concept of 'trade mark

---

[58] Information bulletin issued by the Portuguese Customs on 11 February 2005. This bulletin refers to roses 'protected by rights belonging to *trade mark* owners', but this case actually involved exclusively plant variety rights.   [59] At that time, Reg (EC) 3295/94 (n 21 above).

[60] In this regard, the data reported in the statistics compiled by the EC Commission is in accordance with the professional experience of the authors of this chapter.   [61] N 38 above.

[62] This distinction was already made in the first Portuguese Trade Mark Law of 1883, Art 5.

[63] In other words, in Portugal 'The reproduction or servile copying of a trade mark is generally known as counterfeiting; when a trade mark is similar to another to the extent that they may be confused, it is said that there is imitation': Justino Cruz, commenting on the Industrial Property Code of 1940 in *Código da Propriedade Industrial* (2nd edn, Coimbra, 1985) 203.

imitation' and the notions of identity and similarity of goods and marks. Pursuant to this provision, the concept of imitation requires a comparison to be made between the trade mark and the sign in question, and implies that both of them:[64]

- 'are intended to designate goods or services which are identical or have affinity';
- 'display graphic, figurative, phonetic, or another type of, similarity which is likely to mislead or confuse consumers, or which may cause a risk of association with an earlier registered trade mark, so that consumers would only be able to distinguish them by means of a careful examination or comparison'.

Portuguese law prohibits and punishes all trade mark infringements on exactly the same terms, whether they consist of the *reproduction* (or *counterfeiting*) of a trade mark (identical signs), or the *imitation* of a trade mark (confusingly similar signs). This identical legal treatment of both types of trade mark infringement is contained in Article 323 of the Industrial Property Code, entitled 'Counterfeiting, imitation, and illegal use of a trade mark', which punishes such infringements as criminal offences.   **23.46**

As examples of older Portuguese jurisprudence,[65] we may cite the following decisions, which all considered the registered trade mark and the disputed sign as confusingly similar: **23.47**

CIGANO / CINZANO (TRL,[66] 25 January 1947)
SUEPE / SCHWEPPES (JCL,[67] 21 November 1960)
ALCOTEX / ALCOTEST (JCL, 1 July 1965)
TOTOCOLA / COCA-COLA (TRL, 7 January 1966)
AMALIUM / VALIUM (JCL, 12 July 1966)
ONE UP / SEVEN UP and 7 UP (STJ,[68] 1 July 1969)
PANTELMIN / PANTERGIN (STJ, 18 November 1975)
AEROCROM / AERO-OM (JCL, 12 February 1980)
NUCITA / NUXINA (JCL, 13 March 1981).

Examples from more recent case law[69] are the following decisions: **23.48**

KNUFFI / GUFFI (STJ, 24 May 1990)
BARRI / BALLY (STJ, 2 October 1990)
FERMAIPAM / FERMIPAN (TRP,[70] 8 July 1991)

---

[64] It should be noted in this respect that the questions emerging from the legal concept of 'trade mark imitation' are undoubtedly the ones that dominate the Portuguese courts, and are those that produce the greatest volume of case law—which is not always uniform, and can even be contradictory.

[65] Cited by Justino Cruz, n 63 above, at 231–239.

[66] Abbrevation for *Tribunal da Relação de Lisboa*—the Lisbon Court of second instance.

[67] Abbreviation for *Juízo Cível de Lisboa*—the Lisbon civil Court of first instance.

[68] Abbreviation for *Supremo Tribunal de Justiça*—the Portuguese Supreme Court.

[69] Cited by L M Couto Gonçalves in *Direito de Marcas* (2nd edn, 2003), at 130, and A Dias Pereira in *Propriedade Industrial II/Código da Propriedade Industrial* (2003), at 93–110.

[70] Abbreviation for *Tribunal da Relação do Porto*—the Oporto Court of second instance.

PEPE DIAS PARAMO / PEPE and PEPE JEANS (STJ, 18 May 1999)
DE LUCIA / SANTA LUCIA (STJ, 3 May 2001)
SALUSTAR / SALUTAR (Coimbra Court of first instance, 11 October 2001).

23.49 The following examples all relate to decisions which considered that the earlier trade mark and the sign in dispute were similar:[71]

FLOMEX / FLUDEX (JCL, 1 March 2001)
FRUTIN / FRUCTINEST (T Com L,[72] 12 March 2002)
BIORIGINE / BIOREGIME (T Com L, 29 June 2004)
JUMEN / JUMEX (TRL, 17 July 2004).

23.50 Regarding the acts that specifically constitute trade mark infringements, Article 323 of the Industrial Property Code considers the following to be criminal offences:

- *counterfeiting* or *imitation* of registered trade marks—in the sense of materially reproducing or imitating the protected signs (on labels, embroidered labels, packaging, etc);
- *use* of counterfeit or imitated trade marks;
- use, counterfeiting, or imitation, of *well-known* trade marks or trade marks *with a reputation*.

23.51 In turn, Article 324 of the same Code classifies as a criminal offence the *offering for sale* or the *placing into circulation* or *concealing* of goods with counterfeit or imitated trade marks.

23.52 Finally, Article 335 classifies as counter-ordinances[73] the *preparatory acts* relating to the above-mentioned crimes, namely manufacturing, importing, acquiring or storing signs that are protected as registered trade marks.

23.53 For the purpose of the application of Article 2(1)(a) of the Regulation, customs should naturally follow the criteria resulting from the jurisprudence produced by the courts, and define the limits of their interventions by having regard to the degree of similarity of the marks in line with this jurisprudence. The same applies to the interpretation of the condition provided for in Article 2(1)(a)(i) that the trade mark on the basis of which border measures are taken must be validly registered 'in respect of the same type of goods'.

---

[71] These examples were taken from the first three 2005 issues of the Industrial Property Bulletin (*Boletim da Propriedade Industrial*, published on a monthly basis under the responsibility of the Portuguese Industrial Property Office).
[72] Abbreviation for *Tribunal de Comércio de Lisboa* (Lisbon Court of Commerce), being the Court having jurisdiction at first instance to deal with, inter alia, industrial property cases, created in 1990 and meanwhile also designated as a 'Community Court' for the purpose of the Community Trade Mark and Design Regulations.
[73] Counter-ordinances are *administrative* infringements, punishable by pecuniary sanctions; they are not criminal in nature: cf paras 23.290–23.292 below.

Thus, the Portuguese customs authorities should certainly take action not only in **23.54** the case of goods bearing without authorization a trade mark identical to a registered trade mark, but also in the case of goods bearing signs considered to be confusingly similar to (or an imitation of) a registered trade mark.

Although the legal scope of the intervention of the customs authorities is duly **23.55** defined in the law, difficulties may obviously arise as far as this aspect is concerned in *specific situations*, more precisely when assessing whether or not a certain (non-identical) sign which has been affixed to goods detected by customs constitutes an imitation of the registered trade mark. The same difficulties may arise when assessing whether or not the goods detected by customs are similar to the goods for which the trade mark is registered.[74]

Under the Portuguese legal system, registration is *constitutive* of industrial pro- **23.56** perty rights.[75] This is particularly so in the case of trade marks (and the other distinctive signs), in accordance with Article 224(1) of the Industrial Property Code, which provides that 'The registration shall *confer* on its owner the ownership of the trade mark and exclusive rights therein (...)'.

This basic principle of Portuguese law has been repeatedly upheld in the case law, **23.57** and confirmed by the Supreme Court of Justice which considered that: 'The Industrial Property Code adopted the system whereby registration confers ownership, [and] until registration has been effected no right exists to prohibit the use of the trade mark (...)'.[76] A trade mark '(...) can only have legal protection after the date of its registration, and not during the period that elapses between the date on which registration was requested and the date on which it was granted, at least not in order to prevent another from using the same mark during this period'.[77]

As far as trade marks are concerned under Portuguese law, use is only relevant **23.58** when defining the trade mark holder's rights in that it confers a right of *priority*, provided that no more than six months elapse between the date of the first use and the filing of the application.[78] As other exceptions to the 'first to register' rule, Portuguese law expressly recognises the status of well-known trade marks, and trade marks filed by an agent or representative (in the sense of Articles 6bis and

---

[74] In any case, in practical terms these questions have not really been reflected in the actions of the customs authorities. At least, there is no record of situations where customs encountered problems in determining whether the trade marks in question were confusingly similar, or whether the goods were similar.

[75] Contrary to what happens in the case of copyright, which, in accordance with the Copyright Code, Arts 11 and 12, 'belongs to the intellectual author of the work' and is 'recognised *irrespective* of registration, deposit, or any other formality'.   [76] STJ (n 68 above), 31 January 1991.

[77] STJ (n 68 above), 24 January 1995.

[78] This is an old principle, which existed already under the first Portuguese trade mark law of 1883, and is currently contained in the Industrial Property Code, Art 227.

6septies of the Paris Convention[79]), and, more generally, prohibits unfair competition.[80]

23.59 The understanding that a trade mark *application* only confers on the applicant a *priority* right and does not allow him to prevent the use by third parties of identical or confusingly similar marks was not essentially altered with the entry into force of the current Industrial Property Code of 2003, in spite of the introduction of the concept of 'provisional protection', as provided in Article 5 for applications for industrial property rights.[81] Although the Portuguese courts have already recognized the possibility of ordering provisional measures defending a trade mark application in civil injunction proceedings,[82] there is no doubt that this enforcement cannot be invoked in criminal proceedings, or even in civil actions on the merits.[83]

23.60 In view of the above, Portuguese Customs do not grant applications for customs intervention, nor (in principle) do they, take border measures, on the basis of simple trade mark *applications*.

23.61 However, since the use of an unregistered mark by a third party can, under certain circumstances, constitute an act of unfair competition, and such acts result in an infringement provided for in the Industrial Property Code, it may not be inappropriate to envisage the possibility of customs intervention, on the basis of Article 319 of this Code, in cases of importation of goods branded with unregistered marks, when they involve unfair competition.

23.62 This scenario of possible intervention, however, would certainly seem to be rather 'out of the ordinary' to the customs authorities. In any case, such interventions

---

[79] Paris Convention for the Protection of Industrial Property of 20 March 1883, as revised in Stockholm on 14 July 1967.

[80] The use of an unregistered trade mark can constitute an act of unfair competition when such use results in an act that is 'contrary to fair trade practices and usage in any field of economic activity' and, in particular, is 'liable to create confusion with (...) the goods or services of competitors' or consists in the use of 'unauthorized indications or references (...) [to] a name, establishment, or trade mark of another': Industrial Property Code, Art 317(a) and (c), which mirrors in part Paris Convention (n 79 above), Art 10*bis*. This does not correspond to any objective form of protection of the trade mark as an intellectual property right per se. In these situations the law (indirectly) protects the trade mark, but only in so far as the use thereof by another may give rise to unfair competition: cf, among other Portuguese authors, JP Paúl, *Concorrência Desleal* (Coimbra Editora, 1965), A Ferrer Correia, *Lições de Direito Comercial* (Volume I, University of Coimbra, 1973), Justino Cruz, n 63 above, and J de Oliveira Ascensão, *Concorrência Desleal* (Almedina, 2002).

[81] This 'provisional protection' was already provided in the previous Industrial Property Code of 1995 (Art 62) in respect of patents, utility models, and designs, in line with the European Patent Convention, Art 67.

[82] As happened in a recent decision of the Lisbon Court of Commerce dated 9 March 2005 (unreported).

[83] The Industrial Property Code, Art 5(3), stipulates that '[Final] Judicial decisions relating to actions lodged on the basis of provisional protection cannot be given before the final grant or refusal of the (...) registration.'

would only be viable in certain sporadic situations, through applications requesting the authorities to act in particular specific cases (bearing in mind that an application for customs intervention in principle cannot be filed on the basis of an unregistered trade mark).

The mere material *execution of signs* that reproduce or imitate registered trade **23.63** marks (on labels, packaging materials, etc) is a crime under Portuguese law, irrespective of their actual affixation to, and/or use on, goods.[84] The *importation* or *acquisition* of material bearing these signs is also illegal.

Thus, the Portuguese customs authorities do not hesitate to detain such trade **23.64** mark symbols and materials, even if delivered separately,[85] exactly as they do in respect of other types of counterfeit goods, whenever they detect them during customs checks.

(2) *Pirated goods*

Goods infringing a design right

Designs are governed in Portugal by Articles 173 to 221 of the Industrial Property **23.65** Code,[86] which implement into Portuguese law the Design Directive.[87]

The scope of protection of designs is defined in Article 199(1) of the Industrial **23.66** Property Code as covering '(. . .) any designs or models which do not produce on the informed user a *different overall impression*'. Paragraph 2 of the same provision specifies that 'In determining the scope of protection, the degree of freedom of the creator in developing the design or model shall be taken into consideration.'[88]

Furthermore, as regards the enforcement of design rights, Article 322(a) of the **23.67** Industrial Property Code prohibits and punishes as a criminal offence the reproduction *or imitation*, as a whole or *in respect of some of its characteristic parts*, of a registered model or design.

Portuguese law therefore protects registered designs not only against any **23.68** unauthorized reproduction thereof, but also against any use of designs that do not produce a *different overall impression*, that is, that are *imitations* of registered designs—thus applying a concept equivalent to trade mark imitation.[89]

---

[84] Industrial Property Code, Art 324.   [85] Cf Reg 1383/2003, Art 2(1)(a)(ii)–(iii).

[86] These provisions constitute Chapter III of Part II of the Industrial Property Code, entitled 'Designs or models'.

[87] Directive 98/71/EC of the European Parliament and of the Council of 13 October 1998 on the legal protection of designs [1998] OJ L 289/28 (18.10.1998).

[88] This provision corresponds to Art 5 of the Design Directive (n 87 above).

[89] Cf paras 23.42–23.49 above. Similarly, under the earlier Industrial Property Code of 1940 it was considered that '(. . .) not only is the copying *in full* of models or designs belonging to others prohibited, but also the copying of the characteristic parts thereof, ie the elements that confer on the

23.69 Article 203(1) of the Industrial Property Code defines the scope of the exclusive rights in a design as conferring on their owner the exclusive right to use it and to prevent third parties from using it. Paragraph 2 of the same provision specifies that this use '(...) shall cover, in particular, the manufacturing, offering, placing on the market, importing, exporting, or using, of a product in which the design or model is incorporated, or to which it is applied, or stocking such a product for those purposes'.

23.70 Under criminal law, Article 322 of the Industrial Property Code punishes as a criminal offence the following acts, when they are carried out without the consent of the right-holder:

- the *reproduction* or *imitation*, as a whole or in respect of some of its characteristic parts, of a registered design;
- the *working* of a registered design belonging to another;
- the *importation* or *distribution* of designs obtained by any of the above-mentioned means.

Goods infringing a copyright or a related right

23.71 In the 'Instructions for Application' of the Regulation contained in Circular 78/2004, it is stated that when determining what should be considered as 'pirated goods', reference should be made to the provisions of the Copyright Code.

23.72 Article 9 of the Copyright Code defines the content of copyright as covering '(...) rights of a *patrimonial* nature, and rights of a personal nature (...)' (*moral rights*). Regarding patrimonial rights, paragraph 2 of the same provision specifies that they include '(...) the exclusive right to *possess, enjoy* and *use* the work or *authorize* the enjoyment or use thereof by third parties (...)', whereas in the case of moral rights, paragraph 3 states that 'Irrespective of patrimonial rights (...)', the author shall always be able to '(...) assert the right of *paternity* [in respect of his work], and ensure the *genuineness* and *integrity* thereof'.

23.73 As far as neighbouring (or 'related') rights are concerned, Article 178 of the Copyright Code basically establishes that performing artists or performers shall have the exclusive right to undertake or authorize the broadcasting and communication to the public, fixation, reproduction and making available to the public of their performances.

23.74 In terms of criminal liability, the acts that constitute infringements of copyrights and neighbouring rights are defined in Part IV of the Copyright Code.

23.75 Article 195 stipulates as the crime of 'usurpation' the unauthorized *use*[90] of a protected work or performance, whereas Article 196 defines as 'counterfeiting' the

---

whole its own physiognomy. Likewise, total imitation and partial imitation are both prohibited, but such imitation must refer to one of the characteristic parts of the model or design': Justino Cruz (n 63 above), commenting on the Industrial Property Code of 1940, at 398.

[90] 'Use' obviously in the sense of economic working.

unauthorized use as one's own creation or performance of a work or performance '(...) which is merely a total or partial *reproduction* of a work or performance belonging to another (...), or which is so *similar* that it does not have its own individuality'.

Article 198 relates to the crime of 'infringement of moral rights'. **23.76**

Finally (and very importantly), Article 199 provides for and punishes the crime of **23.77** 'use of a counterfeit or usurped work', which corresponds to the *sale, offering for sale, import, export* or *distribution* of a usurped or counterfeit work or an unauthorized copy of a sound or video recording, whether the respective copies were produced in Portugal or abroad.

In the particular case of software, Article 14 of the law on the legal protection of **23.78** computer programs[91] states that 'computer software shall enjoy *criminal protection* against unauthorized reproduction'. However, the content of this criminal offence is legally defined by reference to another law[92] as covering any *reproduction, disclosure*, or *communication to the public*, of a computer program protected by law.

Also regarding the scope of the legal protection of copyrights and neighbouring **23.79** rights, it should be pointed out that as in the case of the other intellectual property rights, protection is conferred by Portuguese law in a broad sense, in view of the fact that it is not limited to cases involving the reproduction of the protected work or performance. This appears, in particular, from the aforementioned Article 196(1) of the Copyright Code, pursuant to which infringement of these rights also exists when there is 'similarity' to the extent that the reproduction does not have its 'own individuality'.

In terms of the intervention of the customs authorities, difficulties may arise in **23.80** practice when they are required to assess in specific cases whether or not the goods in question infringe the above rights. For this purpose, next to the assistance of the right-holder, customs often request the support of experts from an authority known as the *Inspecção Geral das Actividades Culturais* (the IGAC).[93] In the particular case of video recordings, the customs authorities are also assisted by a private right-holders' association, namely, the *Federação de Editores de Videogramas* ('Federation of Video Recording Producers', or FEVIP), namely for the purpose of conducting expert examinations.

---

[91] N 13 above.   [92] Law 109/91 on Computer Criminality (n 12 above), Art 9.

[93] The IGAC ('Department of Cultural Activities'), created by Decree-Law 80/97 of 8 April 1997, is the Portuguese body, depending on the Ministry of Culture, which is responsible for ensuring the development of legislation in the field of culture through the disclosure of the relevant laws and inspection actions. One of its functions is to enforce copyrights and neighbouring rights, including overseeing the production, *importation* or *exportation*, distribution, and sale, of sound and video recordings.

(3) Goods infringing other intellectual property rights

Goods infringing a patent or a supplementary protection certificate

23.81 Patent rights are governed under Articles 51 to 114 of the Industrial Property Code.[94] Next to granting national patents, Portugal is also a member of the European Patent Convention ('EPC'), with effect from 1 January 1992, as well as the Patent Cooperation Treaty ('PCT'), which Portugal joined on 14 November of the same year.

23.82 Article 97(1) of the Industrial Property Code states that the scope of protection conferred by a patent is '(. . .) determined by the contents of the claims, the description and drawings being used to interpret the claims'. Furthermore, paragraph 2 of the same provision specifies that 'If the subject matter of the patent is a process, the rights conferred by the patent shall extend to the products directly obtained by the patented process.'

23.83 The specifics of biotechnological patents are governed by paragraphs 3 to 6 of Article 97, resulting from the implementation of Directive 98/44/EC of 6 July 1998.[95]

23.84 In accordance with Article 101(1), 'The patent shall confer the exclusive right to work the invention in any part of Portuguese territory.' Paragraph 2 of this provision states that 'The patent shall also confer on its owner the right to prevent third parties not having his consent from manufacturing, offering, storing, offering for sale, or using, the patented product, and from importing or possessing such product for any of the abovementioned purposes.'

23.85 As to the scope of protection of patents, Article 101(4) of the Industrial Property Code provides that 'The rights conferred by a patent *may not exceed* the scope defined by the claims.' A *literal* interpretation of this provision could lead to the conclusion that only an *exact* reproduction of the invention would constitute an infringement of the patent.

23.86 However, the general understanding among Portuguese authors is that in order for patent infringement to exist '(. . .) there does not have to be a total or complete reproduction of the subject matter of the invention (. . .); it is essential to consider in detail what constitutes the characteristic and fundamental subject matter of the invention, disregarding minor modifications, which are very often made to disguise the infringement. In order for infringement of the patentee's right to exist (. . .) the patent does not have to be imitated in its entirety, it must simply be imitated in respect of its essential and constitutive parts. (. . .) It would be inadmissible not to consider imitation as infringement. Servile reproduction is rare.'[96]

---

[94] These provisions are contained in Chapter I of Part II of the Industrial Property Code.
[95] Directive 98/44/EC of the European Parliament and of the Council of 6 July 1998 on the legal protection of biotechnological inventions [1998] OJ L 213/13 (30.7.1998).
[96] Justino Cruz, quoting the eminent French authors, P Roubier and P Mathély, in his comments on the Industrial Property Code of 1940 (n 63 above) at 392.

When analysing the possible existence of a patent infringement, the well-known **23.87** doctrine of equivalents is also of particular relevance. This theory has been discussed by several Portuguese authors,[97] and our country's case law[98] considers that it is perfectly applicable within the Portuguese legal system.

In terms of penal liability, Article 321 of the Industrial Property Code classifies as **23.88** criminal offences the following acts when carried out without the consent of the right-holder:

- the *manufacture* of artefacts or products constituting the subject matter of the patent;
- the *use* or *application of the means or processes* constituting the subject matter of the patent;
- the *importation* or *distribution* of products obtained by using any of the above-mentioned means.

Supplementary protection certificates ('SPCs') were implemented into the **23.89** Portuguese legal system through Community legislation, and have never been provided for as a type of national intellectual property right. The relevant Community Regulations, namely, Regulations (EEC) 1768/92[99] and (EC) 1610/96[100] only entered into force in Portugal on 2 January 1998.

The scope of protection of these rights is therefore comprehensively defined in **23.90** the above-mentioned Regulations. The provisions contained in Part II of the Industrial Property Code relating to supplementary protection certificates (Articles 115 and 116) only concern the formalities for the application and the examination procedure before the Portuguese Industrial Property Office.

In view of the above, in order to determine whether there is infringement of a **23.91** supplementary protection certificate, the customs authorities will have to consider essentially the provisions of the respective Regulations concerning the subject matter of protection, according to which protection shall extend only to the product covered by the authorization to place the corresponding medicinal product (or plant protection product) on the market, and for any use of the product as a medicinal product (or as a plant protection product) that has been authorized before the expiry of the certificate.[101]

---

[97] Cf A da Silva Carvalho, *O Objecto da Invenção* (Coimbra, 1970), at 73, and Justino Cruz, ibidem, commenting on the Industrial Property Code of 1940, at 393.

[98] Decisions of the TRL (n 66 above), dated 24 May 1974 (published in *Boletim do Ministério da Justiça* No 237, 297) and 26 June 1974 (ibid, at 277).

[99] Council Reg (EEC) 1768/92 of 18 June 1992 concerning the creation of a supplementary protection certificate for medicinal products [1992] OJ L 182/1 (2.7.1992).

[100] Reg (EC) 1610/96 of the European Parliament and of the Council of 23 July 1996 concerning the creation of a supplementary protection certificate for plant protection products [1996] OJ L 198/30 (8.8.1996).

[101] Reg 1768/92 (n 99 above), Art 4; Reg 1610/96 (n 100 above), Art 4.

23.92 Criminal liability for infringement of the rights conferred by a supplementary protection certificate is provided for under the provisions of the Industrial Property Code that relates to patents (more specifically, Article 321) with regard to the same acts as mentioned in paragraph 23.88 above.

Goods infringing a national plant variety right

23.93 Plant varieties are conferred protection under Portuguese national law by Decree-Law 213/1990 of 28 June 1990 and the Administrative Order 940/1990 of 4 October 1990.

23.94 Under these pieces of legislation, 'The breeder's right in a plant variety shall confer on its owner the exclusive right to produce and market plants of that variety, or the corresponding reproductive or vegetative propagating material.' However, this right '(. . .) shall not prevent the use of the protected plant variety as initial or basic material for the production of other varieties, except where its repeated or systematic use is necessary'.

23.95 Article 7 of Decree-Law 213/1990 provides for and punishes the infringement of plant variety rights as a counter-ordinance.[102] Infringements include, in particular, the '*production*, *marketing*, and *use*, of plant varieties'. Acts of negligence are also punishable.

23.96 It may be considered that this Article 7 is also applicable to infringements in Portugal of Community plant variety rights, by virtue of Article 22(1) of Regulation (EC) 2100/94,[103] which states that this type of Community right as an object of property is to be regarded in all respects, and for the entire territory of the Community, as a corresponding property right in the Member States.[104]

Goods infringing a national designation of origin or a geographical indication

23.97 Under Portuguese national law, designations of origin and geographical indications are currently governed by Articles 305 to 315 of the Industrial Property Code.

23.98 These intellectual property rights are traditionally very important in Portugal, being a country that produces quite a number of products designated by these distinctive signs, some of which are world famous—including in particular the fortified wines *Porto* and *Madeira*, the table wine *Vinho Verde*, and the cheese *Queijo Serra da Estrela*.

---

[102] Cf paras 23.09–23.11 and n 16 above, and of more relevance, paras 23.291–23.293 below.
[103] Council Reg (EC) 2100/94 of 27 July 1994 on Community plant variety rights [1994] OJ L 227/1 (1.9.1994), as amended.
[104] The same principle is applicable to other Community rights, such as Community trade marks and designs.

Portugal is a founder member of the Madrid Agreement of 14 April 1891 for the **23.99** Repression of False or Deceptive Indications of Source on Goods and the Lisbon Agreement for the Protection of Appellations of Origin and their International Registration (Lisbon Union) of 31 October 1958. Furthermore, appellations of origin have been protected under Portuguese national law since the Industrial Property Code of 1940, irrespective of the corresponding Community legislation.

In the current Industrial Property Code (of 2003), the scope of protection of **23.100** designations of origin ('DO') and geographical indications ('GI') is defined in Article 312, which stipulates that the registration of these signs confers the right to prevent:

- any use by third parties of any means in the designation or presentation of a product that indicates or suggests that the product in question originates in a geographical region other than its true place of origin;
- any use which constitutes an act of unfair competition within the meaning of Article 10bis of the Paris Convention;
- any use of the DO or GI without the authorization of the right-holder.

The same provision specifies that the wording contained in a DO or a GI '(...) **23.101** shall not be used in any way (...)' in or on tags, labels, advertising, or any documents, relating to products that do not originate in the respective demarcated regions. It further states that this prohibition of the use of DOs or GIs is also applicable even if the true origin of the products is indicated, or if the wording belonging to the DO or GI is accompanied by qualifiers such as 'kind', 'type', 'quality', or the like.

It is important to mention that the law prohibits not only the use of wording that **23.102** is *identical* to that of DOs or GIs, but also the use of '(...) any expression, presentation, or graphic combination, *liable to mislead or confuse the consumer*'— a concept equivalent to trade mark imitation.[105]

Finally, Portuguese law also recognizes (as in the case of trade marks) the category **23.103** of DOs or GIs *with a reputation* in Portugal or in the European Community, prohibiting the use thereof '(...) for products which are not identical, or do not have affinity, where the use thereof without due cause would take unfair advantage of, or could be detrimental to, the distinctive character or the reputation of the earlier registered designation of origin or geographical indication'.

Infringement of a DO or a GI is punishable as a criminal offence under Article **23.104** 325 of the Industrial Property Code, which considers as such the following acts:

- the *reproduction* or *imitation*, in whole or in part, of a protected DO or GI;
- the *use*, without the right or authorization to do so, of signs which constitute a reproduction, imitation, or translation thereof.

---

[105] Cf paras 23.42–23.49 above.

(4) Moulds and matrices

23.105 There are various legal provisions under Portuguese national law which refer to the seizure of moulds, matrices and, in general, any instruments used essentially for committing a crime, including infringements of intellectual property rights.

23.106 Under *criminal* law, the basic provision relating to these seizures is Article 178 of the Code of Criminal Procedure, which states that 'Objects which have been used, or are intended to be used, for committing a crime shall be seized (...)'. This provision specifies that 'The seized objects shall be attached to the proceedings when possible, or, if not, they shall be handed over to the judicial officer responsible for the proceedings, or to a depositary (...)'. Still pursuant to the same provision, such seizures shall be '(...) authorized, ordered, or validated by a decision of the judicial authority'.

23.107 Regarding the moment when these seizures are carried out, Article 249(2)(c)[106] of the same Code stipulates that the criminal police bodies should take the appropriate action even *before* being ordered to do so by the judicial authority.[107]

23.108 Article 178 of the Code of Criminal Procedure is reinforced, for the purpose of criminal proceedings for infringement of industrial property rights, by Article 342 of the Industrial Property Code, which sets forth that even before the beginning of the inquiry phase, the criminal police bodies shall carry out the necessary inspections and take any preventive measures *ex officio*. The same provision states that within the scope of these measures 'Articles which display evidence of a crime provided under this Code, as well as all materials or instruments that were mainly used to commit the crime, shall always be seized.'

23.109 Still under criminal law, but now with regard to copyright infringement, Article 201(1) of the Copyright Code also provides that 'Articles or copies of usurped or pirated works (...), as well as the respective packaging materials, machines, or other instruments or documents suspected of having been used or of being intended for committing the infringement, shall always be seized.' This provision seems to confer even broader seizure powers than those that apply to infringements of industrial property rights, as they refer in general terms to the instruments used in committing the crime, and not just those that were mainly used for this purpose.

23.110 Under *civil* law, in the context of industrial property infringements, Article 340 of the Industrial Property Code expressly provides for *ex parte* proceedings[108] for the seizure of the goods and '(...) the instruments which can only be used for carrying

---

[106] This Article is entitled 'Preventive measures in respect of evidence.'
[107] The term 'judicial authority' is understood to mean judges, or the public prosecutor.
[108] Known in Portuguese as an *arresto*. On this type of civil proceedings, cf paras 23.241–23.242 below.

out these illicit acts'. This particular measure is, however, limited to infringements of registered designs, trade marks, and other distinctive signs.

In the light of the legal framework described above, it may be concluded that the   **23.111**
Portuguese Customs have the powers required for proceeding with the seizure of moulds, matrices, and any other instruments, which are specifically or mainly designed or adapted for the manufacture of goods infringing an intellectual property right.[109]

C. Goods excluded by the Regulation

(1) Parallel imported goods

Portuguese Customs do *not* take action against (genuine) parallel imported   **23.112**
merchandise. This position is clearly confirmed in the instructions for application of the Regulation contained in Circular 78/2004, issued by the customs authorities.

In legislative terms, there is no provision expressly referring to parallel imports in   **23.113**
Portugal, other than the provisions relating to the exhaustion of the various intellectual property rights.

As far as trade marks are concerned, Article 259(1) of the Industrial Property   **23.114**
Code[110] stipulates that 'The rights conferred by the registration shall not allow the owner to prohibit the use of the trade mark in relation to goods commercialised in the European Economic Area by the owner or with his consent.'

The same principle applies to patents, pursuant to Article 103 of the Industrial   **23.115**
Property Code, which provides that 'The rights conferred by the patent shall not allow its owner to prohibit acts in relation to the products that it protects after they have been commercialised in the European Economic Area by the owner or with his consent.'[111]

Similar provisions exist in the Industrial Property Code also in respect of designs   **23.116**
(Article 205) and utility models (Article 146).

The question of whether or not, in the light of the provisions of the Industrial   **23.117**
Property Code, parallel imports constitute an infringement of industrial property

---

[109] Cf Reg 1383/2003, Art 2(3).

[110] This provision is the direct 'successor' of Art 208(1) of the previous Industrial Property Code of 1995, which in turn implemented the Trade Mark Directive (n 38 above), Art 7(1).

[111] The same provision was also included in the Industrial Property Code of 1995, Art 99, although this provision did not result from the implementation of any Community or international legislation (although the existence of an equivalent provision in the European Patent Convention of 1973 (Art 67) may have constituted an indirect basis and additional justification for the inclusion of this provision into Portuguese national law).

rights is still controversial in Portugal. Some authors claim that they are not.[112] Others consider that, as a rule, parallel imports do constitute an infringement, albeit of a civil nature (a tort) and not a criminal offence[113] as it is not expressly classified as such under Portuguese law.[114]

23.118 Assuming that parallel imports do constitute an infringement of intellectual property rights, Portuguese national law does in principle give the customs authorities the necessary powers for intervening against such acts. Indeed, Article 319 of the Industrial Property Code provides that 'Any goods or merchandise which (...) display evidence of an offence stipulated in this Code, shall be seized by Customs during the act of importation or exportation.'

23.119 Portuguese law therefore seems to provide customs measures with regard to the infringement of *any type* of intellectual right by any means, with no exceptions.

23.120 However, Portuguese Customs do not take a stance against parallel imports. With regard to this aspect of customs intervention (as well as all other aspects in general), they circumscribe the scope of their action by having regard to the limits imposed by the Regulation,[115] even in those cases where Portuguese national legislation confers wider powers.

23.121 Of course, it may well happen (and does indeed happen) that the customs authorities inform the right-holder of parallel imported goods, but their reason for doing so is because they believe that the goods are, or may be, counterfeit.

(2) Goods which have been manufactured under conditions other than those which have been agreed with the right-holder

23.122 For Portuguese Customs, goods that infringe contractual obligations are in a situation identical to that of parallel imported goods, particularly in the case of trade mark rights.

23.123 In fact, as far as trade marks are concerned, Article 264 of the Industrial Property Code states that 'The owner of a trade mark registration may invoke the rights conferred by the registration against a licensee who infringes any clause or provision of a licence agreement, in particular those relating to its duration, the identity of the trade mark, the nature of the goods or services for which the

---

[112] Eg, namely in the field of trade marks, P Sousa e Silva, *Direito Comunitário e Propriedade Industrial* (Coimbra Editora, 1996) and A da Silva Carvalho, *Direito de Marcas* (Coimbra Editora, 2004).

[113] Eg, C Olavo, in an article entitled 'Importações Paralelas e Esgotamento de Direitos' in *Revista da Ordem dos Advogados* (December 2001).

[114] Contrary to what happens, eg, in Spain, where parallel imports are punishable as criminal offences.   [115] In this case, Art 3(1), first indent.

licence is granted, the demarcation of the area or territory, or the quality of the goods manufactured or of the services provided by the licensee.'[116]

Thus, the importation of goods that infringe Article 264 of the Industrial **23.124** Property Code also constitutes an illicit act, albeit of a merely civil nature. This means that Portuguese Customs would also have powers to intervene in those cases under Article 319 of the Industrial Property Code, on the same terms as described in paragraphs 23.112 ff above.

However, these situations, together with parallel imports, have been one of the **23.125** 'taboos' of the Portuguese customs authorities, whose practice has for a long time been *not* to intervene in such cases.[117] With regard to both situations, the instructions for application of the Regulation contained in Circular 78/2004 state that '(. . .) the merchandise concerned may (and as a rule does) consist of *genuine* goods (as opposed to counterfeit goods), which are the subject of commercial operations that have not been authorized by the owner of the protected right. These cases involve *private right conflicts* between the right-holder and the international trader, who introduces the goods into a circuit parallel to the authorized distribution networks without the consent of the right-holder.'

(3) Goods contained in travellers' personal baggage

Portuguese Customs control travellers' personal baggage on a regular basis, and **23.126** right-holders are often requested to examine goods seized during such checks.[118]

The useful criteria for the assessment of the fulfilment of the requirements set out **23.127** in Article 3(2) of the Regulation are detailed in Circular 78/2004, in the part relating to the Community Customs Code.

Thus, 'personal baggage' is understood to mean 'all the objects transported by **23.128** a traveller, irrespective of the means of transportation'. 'Merchandise of a non-commercial nature' are goods '(. . .) which are occasionally subject to the customs procedure in question and which, by virtue of their nature and quantity, are reserved for private or family use on the part of the consignees or the persons transporting them, or which are intended as gifts'. Finally, the limits of the duty-free allowance are set at EUR 175, or EUR 90 for children under the age of 15, and are calculated by taking into account the value of equivalent genuine products.

---

[116] This provision implements the Trade Mark Directive (n 38 above), Art 8(2).

[117] Owing to Reg 1383/2003, Art 3(1), second indent.

[118] This statement relies mainly on the professional experience of the authors of this chapter, and is corroborated by information obtained through contacts with customs officials, even though the statistics furnished by the European Commission for 2003 do not mention any procedure arising from customs controls on travellers (Cf DG TAXUD, Annual report on the activities of the Community customs in the fight against counterfeiting and piracy (2003) (n 48 above), at 13).

23.129 The customs authorities appraise the possible commercial nature of the goods, as well as the existence of a commercial traffic, by using criteria based essentially on common sense, having regard to the circumstances of the specific case. To that effect, they consider, among other aspects, the relationship between the nature and number of goods in question.

II. APPLICATION FOR ACTION BY THE CUSTOMS AUTHORITIES

A. Measures prior to an application for action by the Customs authorities ('*ex officio* measures')

23.130 Portuguese Customs have for many years made use of the *ex officio* procedure provided under Article 4 of Regulation 1383/2003.[119] In this regard, the statistics furnished by the European Commission reveal that in 2003 the *ex officio* procedures represented 24 per cent of the total number of customs interventions in Portugal.[120] According to our experience, the customs office at Lisbon Airport mainly operates on an *ex officio* basis.

23.131 The authorities interpret in a broad sense the requirement of Article 4, according to which there must be 'sufficient grounds for suspecting that the goods infringe an intellectual property right' to take *ex officio* action. They do not hesitate to detain or suspend the release of goods as soon as they have any suspicions, in order to allow the right-holder to examine the goods and file an application for action within the deadline established by law.

23.132 Most *ex officio* interventions relate to traffic coming from, or going to, countries rated as 'high-risk countries'.[121] As it is not possible to control the entire traffic, Portuguese Customs have developed a system of 'risk analysis', as happens in many other countries, which consists of selecting the shipment that is to be physically controlled after the analysis of the transport documents and the place of origin. Certain alarm signals alert the attention of customs: place of origin of the merchandise, incomplete identification of the consignor and the consignee, the type of goods contained in the shipment, unusual transportation routes, mixed shipments, kind of packaging, etc.

---

[119] Formerly, Reg 3295/94, as amended (n 21 above), Art 4.

[120] DG TAXUD, Annual report on the activities of the Community customs in the fight against counterfeiting and piracy (2003) (n 48 above), at 15.

[121] The 2003 report of the DG TAXUD (ibid) reveals that during this period the goods which gave rise to the greatest number of customs procedures originated in the following countries: China (56%), Malaysia (8%), Hong Kong (6%), USA (6%), Morocco (2%), Taiwan (2%), and the Netherlands (2%).

When Portuguese Customs uncover a suspect shipment, they retain the goods and **23.133** should immediately inform either the declarant or holder of the goods and the right-holder[122] of their intervention.

The information which customs furnish to the right-holder at this stage concer- **23.134** ning an intervention may vary a little depending on the office providing it.[123] However, this information basically consists of the identification of the manufac- turer and/or exporter in the country of origin, the declarant and the importer, as well as a brief description of the merchandise (type and quantity) and the intel- lectual property right suspected of being infringed. Any other information (including samples of the goods or photographs thereof) will only be provided to right-holders after they have filed an application under Article 5 of the Regulation.

In general terms, the Portuguese authorities apply strictly the deadline of three **23.135** working days provided for in Article 4 (1) of the Regulation.

B. The lodging and processing of applications for customs action

(1) Persons entitled to file an application for action

Definition of 'right-holders' under the Regulation

An application for action can be filed by a right-holder within the meaning of **23.136** Article 2(2) of the Regulation, which includes not only the owner of the intellect- ual property right concerned, but also 'any other person authorized to use [this right] (...), or a representative of the right-holder or authorized user'.

In Portugal, the definition of 'any other person authorized to use the intellectual **23.137** property right' includes exclusive and non-exclusive licensees.

However, it is considered that licensees would only be permitted to file an applica- **23.138** tion for action if their licence has been duly registered with the Portuguese Industrial Property Office, and if the licence agreement expressly allows such action in order to protect the intellectual property rights in question.

It is therefore recommended that licensees ascertain, before taking action, that the **23.139** licence agreement is enforceable against third parties, and allows them to pursue infringers autonomously.

---

[122] As confirmed in item 5.2. of Customs Circular 78/2004 (cf para 23.32 above).
[123] There are no instructions regarding this specific aspect in either of the customs Circulars (cf para 23.32 above). The details of the information provided, as described below in the body of this article, are based on the professional experience of the authors of this work.

23.140 However, Portuguese Customs have never had to apply the broad definition of 'any other person authorized to use any of the intellectual property rights', as to date all applications for action have been filed by owners of intellectual property rights or their representatives.

23.141 Under Portuguese law and practice, the concept of 'representative of the right-holder or authorized user' as defined in Article 2(2)(b) of the Regulation includes natural and legal persons authorized to act on behalf of the right-holder,[124] such as lawyers, intellectual property attorneys, consultants, collective management societies, and associations of right-holders. Licensees, distributors, and commercial agents would also fall under this definition, provided they are authorized to act on behalf of the right-holder.

Proof of entitlement to file an application for action

For right-holders stricto sensu

23.142 In accordance with Portuguese law and practice, the following documents are acceptable for the proprietor of an intellectual property right to prove his right:[125]

- For a registered trade mark, design, patent, supplementary protection certificate, or a plant variety right, evidence that the right has been registered by the relevant office has to be submitted to customs. This includes original registration certificates or certified copies, but Portuguese Customs will *not* accept as evidence a mere copy of the certificate or publication of the official registration, or printouts from official databases.[126]

- For a copyright, a related right, or an unregistered Community design, any evidence establishing that the applicant for the customs measures is the actual owner of the right would be sufficient.

- For protected designations of origin, geographical indications, and geographical designations, the evidence to be submitted consists of two mandatory elements,

---

[124] Cf Commission Reg (EC) 1891/2004 of 21 October 2004 laying down provisions for the implementation of Council Reg (EC) 1383/2003 concerning customs action against goods suspected of infringing certain intellectual property rights and the measures to be taken against goods found to have infringed such rights [2004] OJ L 328/16 (30.10.2004), Art 1.

[125] Cf ibid, Art 2(1).

[126] This stringency with regard to the proof of all industrial property rights is in accordance with the principle which has been expressly included in Portuguese law at least since the Industrial Property Code of 1940 (cf para 23.03 above). In fact, Art 7 of the current Industrial Property Code states that the proof of these rights shall be made by means of the respective certificates or by certified copies thereof (this has even been confirmed by the jurisprudence of the higher Portuguese courts, in the sense that these certificates or certified copies cannot be substituted by other means of proof—for example, witnesses). Portuguese Customs do *not* use the possibility provided in Art 2(1), last indent, of Reg 1891/2004, and on the contrary have reaffirmed the general principle of the law

namely, proof that the applicant is a producer, and proof that the right has been registered.

In Portugal, the application for action cannot be based on a mere *application* for **23.143** an industrial property right, and must always be based on a registration.

For persons authorized to use the right

Persons authorized to use the right within the meaning of Article 2(2)(b) of the **23.144** Regulation will have to submit as additional proof any document evidencing that they are indeed authorized to use the right in question.[127] For a copyright or a neighbouring right, this would be a copy of a contract evidencing that the applicant is entitled to use the right. For an industrial property right, this should be a duly registered licence agreement. It is possible that distribution or agency agreements would also be accepted.

For representatives

The representative of the right-holder or any other person authorized to use the **23.145** right will have to provide customs with his authorization to act.[128] Portuguese Customs accept a power of attorney duly executed by the right-holder granting a mandate to the representative. No notarization or legalization is required. However, the original power of attorney will have to be submitted.

When an application for action is filed prior to any customs intervention, a **23.146** general power of attorney may be submitted together with the application for action. If an application for action is filed further to an *ex officio* customs action, a specific power of attorney is required on a case-by-case basis.

Neither the implementing law[129] nor the Regulation nor any of the various **23.147** customs Circulars contain any provisions or instructions relating to the nationality or domicile of the legal representatives. Thus, the general principles contained in Portuguese national law and Community law are applicable in this regard.

Entitlement to sign the declaration referred to in Article 6 of the Regulation can **23.148** be granted by the right-holder to his representative.

---

with regard to the proof of these rights in their Circular 78/2004, item 4.5.(a), by requesting '(...) the document attesting to the registration or deposit issued by the competent body (...)' in the form of a title or certificate. Even if the law is changed in the future in line with the Regulation, it seems clear that copies taken from official or private databases could only be valid for the purpose of applications for customs intervention, in view of the fact that any further actions (eg the judicial proceedings provided under Art 13 of the Regulation) will have to be documented with the means of proof required under Portuguese law.

[127] Ibid, Art 2(2).   [128] Cf ibid, Art 2(3).
[129] Currently, Decree-Law 20/99, cf para 23.14 and n 22 above.

(2) Competent customs department and formal requirements

Competent customs department

23.149 In Portugal, the authority responsible under Article 5(2) of the Regulation to process applications for customs action is the following:

Ministério das Finanças
Direcção-Geral das Alfândegas e dos Impostos Especiais sobre o Consumo
(*General Directorate of Customs*)
Direcção de Serviços de Regulação Aduaneira
Rua da Alfândega, 5 R/C
P-1149-006 Lisbon
Portugal
Tel: +351 218813890
Fax: +351 218813984
E-mail: dsra@dgaiec.min-financas.pt
Website: www.dgaiec.min-financas.pt

Form of the application for action

23.150 According to Portuguese practice, an application for action can be filed by fax or e-mail, among other means, but confirmation has to be sent by regular or registered mail. However, it is the date of the first filing (by fax or e-mail) that is taken into account for meeting the deadline provided under Article 4(1) of the Regulation. The original version of the application for action, which is to be sent as confirmation, should contain the original declaration as per Article 6 of the Regulation and, if the application for action is filed by a representative, an original power of attorney.[130]

Language requirements

23.151 In Portugal, the application for action can only be filed in Portuguese.

23.152 The exhibits, such as brochures and technical documents, submitted together with an application for action, if in a foreign language, should be translated into Portuguese.

(3) Requirements regarding the contents of the application for action

Mandatory information

23.153 In accordance with Portuguese law and practice, there are no specific requirements for the mandatory information that has to be submitted to customs under

---

[130] Cf para 23.145 above.

Article 5(5)(i)–(ii) of the Regulation. Right-holders should bear in mind that the technical description of the goods must be detailed enough to allow customs to identify the suspect goods. The same applies to the information concerning the type and pattern of fraud.

As regards the *administrative* contact person to be appointed by the right-holder,[131] it is advisable to choose a local representative, namely because customs will expect them to respond without delay to customs communications, and to be in a position to appear in person should this be required. **23.154**

The *technical* contact person must be familiar with the authentic goods. **23.155**

It is generally accepted that the administrative contact can also be the technical contact, provided that he has sufficient knowledge and experience in relation to the goods. **23.156**

Optional information

The right-holder is expected to provide all information deemed to be optional under Article 5(5) of the Regulation in order to facilitate the work of customs. The customs authorities may always request additional information if this proves to be necessary. **23.157**

Additional information specific to the type of intellectual property right referred to in the application

No specific requirements exist in this respect.[132] However, it is recommended that holders of intellectual property rights which involve technical aspects, such as patents, plant variety rights, or geographical indications, provide specific information to Customs regarding the scope of protection of their rights. **23.158**

(4) Processing and acceptance of the application for action

In accordance with the internal instructions of the customs for the application of the Regulation,[133] 'Whenever the application does not contain the elements considered to be compulsory (...) the competent entity may decide *not to analyse the application*, in which case it must justify its decision and provide the information necessary for an appeal procedure.' **23.159**

Although this is not expressly mentioned in the implementing law or the customs Circulars, there will certainly be nothing to prevent the right-holder from filing a **23.160**

---

[131] Cf Reg 1383/2003, Art 5(5)(iii).   [132] Cf ibid, Art 5(6).
[133] Circular 78/2004, item 4.6.1.

new application at the customs or amending the one that was originally filed, instead of lodging an appeal. The right-holder may, however, opt to appeal against the decision of refusal issued by the customs.

23.161 Portuguese law does not provide for a specific appeal procedure against a decision of the General Directorate of Customs dismissing an application for action under Article 5(8) of the Regulation. The general rules governing appeals against decisions of the Portuguese public administrative authorities, as provided for under the Code of Administrative Procedure, are applicable.

23.162 Under these circumstances, an appeal may be filed to the hierarchically superior body, which is the Minister of Finance. The decision of the Minister of Finance can be appealed to the *Tribunal Administrativo e Fiscal de Lisboa* ('Administrative and Fiscal Court of Lisbon'), whose decision may in turn be appealed to the *Tribunal Central Administrativo do Sul* ('Southern Central Administrative Court'). A final appeal may be lodged at the *Supremo Tribunal de Justiça* ('Supreme Court of Justice'). During the proceedings, both parties submit their written arguments, meaning that the customs are always heard in the several appeals.

23.163 Portuguese Customs will normally process the application for action within the prescribed period of 30 working days.[134]

23.164 The period of validity of an application for customs intervention is one year.[135] Portuguese Customs will not in principle accept applications for shorter periods, even at the request of the applicant, although in reality there is nothing in the implementing law or the internal Circulars which expressly prevents this possibility.[136]

(5) 'Community' applications for action

23.165 There are no specific rules for the processing by Portuguese Customs of 'Community' applications for action filed under Article 5(4) of the Regulation.

23.166 Such applications are processed exactly as if they related to national rights.

---

[134] Reg 1383/2003, Art 5(7).

[135] Since 1 July 2004, with the entry into force of the Regulation (previously, the period of validity was six months). In the case of 'Community' applications for action filed under Art 5(4) of the Regulation, the period of validity is obviously always one year: ibid, Art 8(2), second indent.

[136] In this respect, item 4.6.1. of Circular 78/2004 simply repeats Art 8(1), second indent, of the Regulation, stipulating that 'That period shall not exceed one year.'

III. CONDITIONS GOVERNING ACTION BY CUSTOMS AUTHORITIES AND BY THE AUTHORITIES HAVING JURISDICTION TO DETERMINE WHETHER GOODS INFRINGE AN INTELLECTUAL PROPERTY RIGHT

A. Conditions governing action by customs authorities

(1) Factual background

Portugal's only land borders are with another country of the European Union, namely, Spain. Thus, the extra-Community traffic of merchandise is handled mainly through the airport and seaport customs authorities. **23.167**

Land customs offices do exist, the main ones being Alcântara-Norte, Alverca and Jardim do Tabaco (in Lisbon), Freixieiro (in Oporto), Braga and Viana do Castelo (northern Portugal), Aveiro (northern central Portugal), Peniche (central Portugal), Setúbal and Faro (southern Portugal).[137] However, for the reasons given above, the volume of merchandise coming from outside the Community that is cleared through these customs offices is relatively low. **23.168**

The main seaport customs offices are situated in the cities of Lisbon (Lisbon Seaport Customs), Oporto (Leixões Customs), Viana do Castelo, Aveiro, Setúbal, and Faro. **23.169**

As far as the airport customs are concerned, they are situated at Lisbon, Oporto, and Faro airports. **23.170**

There are also airport and seaport customs offices on the archipelagos of Madeira (Funchal Customs) and the Azores (Ponta Delgada Customs). **23.171**

The most active customs offices involved in anti-counterfeiting so far have without a doubt been the Lisbon Seaport Customs, Leixões Customs, Lisbon Airport Customs, and Oporto Airport Customs. Significantly, the statistics for 2003[138] reveal that 57 per cent of the customs interventions were carried out in respect of merchandise transported by air, while the remaining 43 per cent involved merchandise transported by boat. **23.172**

---

[137] As we will see in the next paragraph, some of these offices have land departments (for road and/or railway checks) and also maritime departments.

[138] DG TAXUD, Annual report on the activities of the Community customs in the fight against counterfeiting and piracy (2003) (n 48 above), at 14.

(2) Notification of customs intervention

23.173   After an intervention by customs, which may (depending on the case) consist of *suspending clearance* of the goods, by not authorizing their release, or *detaining* the goods,[139] the customs office involved will immediately notify the right-holder and the holder of the goods (depending on the case) of this intervention.[140] At the same time, the customs office will notify these facts by fax to the General Directorate of Customs, which is the department responsible for the processing of customs applications under the Regulation.[141]

23.174   Communications with the right-holder or with his legal representative[142] are made by fax or e-mail. In certain more urgent situations, customs may make an initial contact by telephone or they may even make a personal notification (inviting the person in question to appear at the customs office). In either of the latter two cases, the notification must be confirmed in writing, though the date of the first telephone or personal contact shall be considered.

(3) Information to be provided by customs to the right-holder before
the right-holder confirms the infringing nature of the goods

23.175   The content of the information provided by customs in their *first* communication to the right-holder has not been totally uniform.[143] In fact, the type of information contained in these communications has varied considerably, depending on the situation and, in particular, the customs office providing it.

23.176   Generally, the first communication is very complete, indicating the *nature* and *quantity* of the goods, their *origin* (through the complete identification of the exporter or simply the country), and also the *importer* and/or the *declarant* or *holder* of the goods. When notifications are made by e-mail, digital pictures of the suspected goods are frequently sent.[144]

23.177   Sometimes however, though more rarely, the first communication is fairly brief (simply revealing, for example, the nature of the goods and, of course, the infringed right).

23.178   In accordance with the regulations on customs procedures contained in Circular 91/2004, issued by the customs authorities on 13 September 2004,[145] the contents of the first notification to the right-holder should be standardized and, as

---

[139] Reg 1383/2003, Art 9(1), first indent.   [140] Ibid, Art 9(2).
[141] Cf para 23.149 above. Ibid, Art 9(1), second indent.
[142] As stipulated in item III A 1.1. of Circular 91/2004 of the customs (cf para 23.32 above): '(. . .) these notifications shall be made by the *quickest means of communication* (. . .)'.
[143] This statement relies solely on the basis of the professional experience of the authors of this contribution resulting from the cases of customs intervention that they have handled.
[144] Cf paras 23.191–23.192 below.   [145] Cf para 23.32 above.

may be seen from the draft notification attached to the Circular, should only indicate the nature of the goods and the type of suspected infringement that they involve.[146] This notification should also inform the right-holder that the merchandise concerned is available for examination in order to meet the deadlines stipulated in Article 13 of the Regulation.

It is still not certain whether these instructions for procedure will actually alter the **23.179** practice previously followed by the various customs offices with regard to the first notification to the right-holder, or whether they will continue to provide in these notifications more information than is strictly required in accordance with the instructions contained in the above-mentioned Circular and Article 9(2) of the Regulation.

Nevertheless, at the request of the right-holder, the customs authorities will fur- **23.180** nish all the information stipulated in Article 9(2) and (3) of the Regulation. This possibility of providing such information is fully confirmed in item 5.1.3. of Circular 78/2004 of the Customs authorities,[147] which states that 'The head of the customs office involved shall inform the applicant [right-holder], at his request, of the names and addresses of the consignee, the consignor, the declarant or the holder of the goods, if known, and the origin and provenance of the goods suspected of infringing an intellectual property right.'

Portuguese law provides for and protects several forms of secrecy in the laws gov- **23.181** erning various economic and professional activities. However, the protection of these secrets would not seem to be capable of truly preventing or even interfering with the provision by Portuguese Customs of the information referred to in Article 9.[148]

What *could* in reality interfere with the communication of this information is the **23.182** *in camera* requirement imposed by the Portuguese criminal laws. In accordance with Article 86(1) and (3) of the Code of Criminal Procedure, this requirement of secrecy must be scrupulously observed by anyone who, for any reason, has access to facts relating to criminal proceedings, and it covers the whole of the initial phase of such proceedings (that is, until a decision of accusation is issued by the public prosecutor or, if relevant, an indictment is issued by the Inquiring Judge).

This *in camera* requirement has been interpreted very stringently by the courts, although there has not yet been any real experience of how this could affect the intervention of the customs authorities in the earlier phase of the proceedings.

---

[146] Compare Reg 1383/2003, Art 9(2).   [147] Ibid.
[148] Pursuant to Reg 1383/2003, Art 9(3), communication of the information listed in this provision is permitted only 'in accordance with national provisions on the protection of personal data, commercial and industrial secrecy and professional and administrative confidentiality'.

(4) Inspection of the suspected goods

23.183   The provision of proof that the goods do in fact constitute an infringement of an intellectual property right is an indispensable part of the proceedings that follow the customs interventions. This proof will almost invariably be made by means of an *expert examination* of the goods, with a view to demonstrating that they were not in fact produced by the right-holder or by someone with a licence or consent. As will be mentioned below in paragraphs 23.231–23.234, in the case of criminal proceedings this expert examination might even be the *only* action required by law of the right-holder with a view to convicting the defendants or, at least, securing the destruction of the infringing goods without any penalty to the infringer (depending on whether the case concerns a public crime or a semi-public crime[149]).

23.184   The conducting of an expert examination is subject to certain formalities, which are laid down in the Code of Civil Procedure in respect of civil actions, and in the Code of Criminal Procedure with regard to criminal proceedings.

23.185   As mentioned above in paragraphs 23.173 ff, the right-holder is immediately informed, in an initial notification sent by customs after an intervention, that the suspected goods are available for examination (in accordance with the second paragraph of Article 9(3) of the Regulation).

23.186   In this connection, Circular 91/2004 of customs states that the right-holder '(. . .) shall have ten working days, which may be extended by a maximum of another ten working days[150] counted from the date of notification of the detention (. . .), to make a statement *in the expert examination report* with regard to the nature of the merchandise (. . .)' (or obviously three non-extendible working days in the case of perishable goods). This implies that, in accordance with the understanding of Portuguese Customs, the right-holder must provide complete and definitive proof that the suspected goods infringe his rights within the deadlines stipulated in Article 13 of the Regulation.

23.187   This, however, would seem to be a rather over-stringent interpretation of the law, since both the Regulation and the Industrial Property Code simply provide that the right-holder must have initiated *proceedings* within the stipulated deadlines to determine whether an intellectual property right has been infringed under national law, without stipulating that *full proof* of the infringement must have been submitted—and in accordance with the applicable procedure laws, this proof can be submitted at a later stage in the proceedings.

23.188   In any case, the commencement of proceedings by the right-holder naturally requires on his part at least the basic knowledge that the goods are infringing

---

[149]   Regarding the distinction between the nature of these crimes, cf paras 23.219–23.224 below.
[150]   In a footnote regarding these deadlines, the Circular refers to both Art 13(1) of the Regulation and Art 319(4) and (5) of the Industrial Property Code.

products and why. It has therefore been the practice of the customs authorities to request that the right-holder examines the goods[151] within the deadline for the purpose of initiating the action stipulated under Article 13 of the Regulation, and to submit together with the action an expert examination report, or at least to give a brief demonstration in the action of the infringing nature of the goods (in which case adequate proof must be submitted at a later date).

Item 5.1.2. of Circular 78/2004 of customs states that when examining the goods, **23.189** '(…) the Customs authorities may take samples of the suspected goods, with a view to facilitating the documentation of the proceedings'. It further states that 'In practice, the taking of samples shall be made *at the request of the applicant* and in accordance with the conditions laid down in the general customs regulations,[152] which provide for the attendance of the declarant at this operation, mentioning the number of samples taken.'

As a consequence of this Circular, therefore, customs will only provide samples at **23.190** the specific request of the right-holder. However, these samples may be provided to the right-holder at any stage of the procedure, either immediately for the filing of the action provided for under Article 13 of the Regulation, or at a later date.

The customs offices have been sending digital pictures of the goods to right-hold- **23.191** ers (or, of course, to their legal representatives), provided that the offices in question are equipped with the necessary means to that effect. Generally, these digital pictures are sent on the initiative of customs together with the initial notification made to the right-holder after an intervention, but if this is not the case, they can also be sent at a later stage, at the specific request of the right-holder.

Very often (if not in most cases), the digital pictures make it possible to clearly **23.192** confirm that the suspected goods are indeed not genuine. When this happens, these pictures will be sufficient at least to demonstrate that the goods in question are infringing products for the purpose of filing the action provided for under Article 13 of the Regulation—although in these cases it is necessary to submit at a later date a report on an expert examination conducted with a direct observation of the goods.[153]

The goods detained by customs constitute both the *result* of an infringement and **23.193** the actual *evidence* of this infringement. Consequently, in terms of national legislation, namely in the field of criminal law, these goods will be subject to the general rules laid down in the Criminal Code[154] governing the loss of products of this nature, and also those contained in the Code of Criminal Procedure[155] governing evidence and means of obtaining evidence.

---

[151] At least through photographs, as we will see in paras 23.191–23.192 below.
[152] Basically, the Community Customs Code (n 47 above).
[153] Cf paras 23.183–23.188 above.   [154] Criminal Code, Arts 109 and 112.
[155] In particular, Code of Criminal Procedure, Arts 161 and 178.

23.194 As will be described in more detail in paragraph 23.285–23.287 below, these goods will be declared to have been '*lost* in favour of the State' if it is confirmed that they are not in fact genuine (that is, that they are infringing goods), which generally leads to the destruction of the goods in question. However, this only occurs with the decision to be given by the judge at the *end* of the proceedings.

23.195 Meanwhile, the goods must remain in storage and (whenever possible) sealed, upon the order of the court. The law even stipulates that when the seals are removed, it is necessary to '(...) verify whether the seals were violated or any other alteration was made to the seized objects'.[156] If, for example, it becomes necessary to carry out an expert examination of these goods which might cause damage or destruction to them, the authorization of the judge responsible for the proceedings must be obtained, in which case photographs of the goods will remain on file.[157]

23.196 It may therefore be concluded that the destination of goods which have been detained, or the release of which has been suspended, by customs, is regulated fairly strictly under Portuguese law, in the sense that they must be retained until the end of the proceedings, and cannot be removed or damaged without an order from a judicial authority.

23.197 In accordance with the general provisions of Portuguese law, the samples must therefore be *returned* after they have been examined. This is also laid down in Article 69 of the Community Customs Code as well as in Article 9(3) of the Regulation, and further confirmed in the instructions for application of the Regulation contained in item 5.1.2. of Circular 78/2004 of customs.

B. Simplified procedure allowing the destruction of the goods without there being any need to determine whether an intellectual property right has been infringed under national law

23.198 No national legislation has yet been enacted with a view to implementing Article 11 of the Regulation. The text of a law is apparently being drawn up for this purpose, though no draft has been disclosed so far, and it is therefore not known what the solutions of the future law will be with regard to the aspects that the Regulation requires to be defined by the Member States.

23.199 Notwithstanding the absence of an implementing law, both of the customs Circulars[158] already refer to the possibility of using the simplified procedure. In particular, Circular 78/2004 states in item 5.1.2. (final paragraphs) that the parties can opt immediately for this procedure, for which purpose the right-holder

---

[156] In particular, Code of Criminal Procedure, Art 184.
[157] Ibid, Art 161. There is also a provision equivalent in scope contained in Art 583(2) and (3) of the Code of Civil Procedure.   [158] Cf para 23.32 above.

must confirm within a term of 10 working days (or three working days, in the case of perishable goods) the infringing nature of the suspected goods and provide customs with the written agreement of the declarant, holder, or owner of those goods.

The wording of the customs Circular may give the impression that this simplified **23.200** procedure has already been implemented under Portuguese law and that it is therefore already applicable in Portugal as such, which *is not* the case.

Of course, agreements and extrajudicial solutions in these situations are already **23.201** possible, but only within the limits imposed by the general rules of Portuguese law (in particular the penal and penal procedure laws), irrespective of any implementation of Article 11 of the Regulation. Within these limits, agreements between the parties are currently available (including along the lines of Article 11 of the Regulation), but only in the case of certain infringements. In other cases, the use in Portugal of the system provided under Article 11 of the Regulation will require adaptations to be made to national law.

The problem lies in cases involving what are considered to be *public crimes*.[159] This **23.202** is the case of most copyright infringements.

In the case of public crimes it is *compulsory* for criminal proceedings to be **23.203** instituted on the part of the public prosecutor, irrespective of the wishes of the possible interested parties or the position that they take. The right-holder has absolutely no power to *avoid* such proceedings, or to *terminate* the proceedings after it has begun.

Furthermore, the Code of Criminal Procedure establishes the general rule that the **23.204** police authorities and all State officials are required to report to the public prosecutor any crime of which they become aware.[160] This duty thus applies to customs officials when they detect any merchandise suspected of infringing an intellectual property right. It is therefore clear from the above that a simplified procedure as described in Article 11 of the Regulation is simply not possible in Portugal in cases of copyright infringement, in the light of the general principles of criminal law. Since it is unlikely that these infringements will cease to be considered as public crimes, any future implementation of Article 11 of the Regulation will imply (at least) the creation of a regime of exception for this purpose to the existing national law on copyright.

The situation in this respect is different with regard to the other infringements **23.205** provided under the Regulation involving industrial property rights, which under Portuguese law are classified as *semi-public crimes*.[161]

---

[159] Regarding the distinction between *public* crimes and *semi-public* crimes, and the respective practical repercussions in the enforcement of the corresponding intellectual property rights, cf in more detail paras 23.219–23.225 below.
[160] This is the system of what is termed the 'compulsory denunciation'. Cf para 23.222 below.
[161] Cf para 23.224 below.

23.206 As far as these infringements are concerned, criminal proceedings only take place *upon a complaint* filed by someone with legal capacity, and the *withdrawal* of this complaint is admissible by law, thus bringing an end to the proceedings. Thus, in the case of industrial property rights, the existing national law permits amicable settlements between the parties, in line with the provisions of Article 11 of the Regulation.

23.207 Agreements between the parties are in fact possible, within the scope of both criminal proceedings (only, of course, when the case concerns a semi-public crime) and civil actions.

23.208 In civil actions, agreements can be reached *within* the scope of the actual proceedings,[162] whereby the parties declare that they wish to bring an end to the proceedings and establish the clauses that they mutually undertake to observe. These agreements are ratified by the court, which orders the parties to fulfil the undertakings made therein, and the respective agreement is deemed equivalent to a judicial decision.

23.209 In the case of criminal proceedings, however, agreements between right-holders and defendants are necessarily acts that take place *outside* the scope of the judicial proceeding, drawn up in private documents between the interested parties. In formal terms, the only action that can be taken during the proceeding is the *withdrawal of the complaint* by the injured party, which will then be validated by the judge.

23.210 Normally, the clauses included in such agreements contain an undertaking to respect the infringed rights in the future (which can be made under conventional penalty), to pay costs (expenses incurred in the storage and destruction of the goods, attorney fees, or other expenses) and/or compensation, as well as to settle judicial costs.

23.211 In general terms, these agreements can validly contain any clauses that the interested parties may wish to include therein,[163] provided that they do not relate to non-disposable rights.[164]

23.212 Within the scope of a civil action, the right-holder can, in principle, freely authorize the reintroduction of the infringing goods onto the market, and can even sign an agreement with the owner of the goods for this purpose. In the context of criminal proceedings, this consent on the part of the right-holder is only possible

---

[162] These agreements are known as 'judicial transactions': Code of Civil Procedure, Arts 287 onwards.

[163] It is nevertheless considered that a judicial transaction should be limited to the object of the action.

[164] Non-disposable rights are rights which cannot be disposed of by their owner, ie rights regarding which the wishes of the owner are invalid for the purpose of assigning or extinguishing them. Under Portuguese intellectual property law, an example of such rights relates to moral rights in copyrights.

in cases of the infringement of industrial property rights[165] (as they are semi-public crimes), but not in cases of copyright infringement (which is a public crime).

In any case, it is a known fact that customs officials consider (and in our opinion **23.213** quite rightly so) authorizing the commercialization of infringing goods against payment of compensation to be a very negative practice. The customs authorities strive to intervene actively in the fight against counterfeiting, not only in defence of the private interests of right-holders, but also because counterfeiting is an extremely damaging phenomenon in economic and social terms, which also affects important interests of a public nature. Allowing the infringing goods to be commercialized against payment of compensation would totally defeat the objective of the action of the customs authorities, who would furthermore feel like they had been used to attend to the doubtful private interests of the right-holder.

As will be explained in more detail below,[166] only a judge can decide on the **23.214** destination of the suspected goods and this decision will, in principle, only be taken at the end of the proceedings. The goods will be declared as 'lost in favour of the State', which will normally lead to the destruction thereof, provided obviously that the proceedings contain proof that they actually infringe an intellectual property right.

Outside this framework, particularly before any judicial proceedings have been **23.215** instituted with a view to determining whether or not there is infringement of an intellectual property right, only the owner of the suspected goods, or someone having his consent, can take any measures with regard to those goods. This consent must be *express*, and cannot be tacitly presumed by virtue of the mere silence of the owner.[167]

C. Conditions governing action by the authorities having jurisdiction to determine whether the goods infringe an intellectual property right

(1) Authorities having jurisdiction to determine whether the goods infringe an intellectual property right

Portuguese law basically provides the same measures and remedies for the enforce- **23.216** ment of the various rights covered by the Regulation. In addition, of course, to

---

[165] This possibility is expressly permitted under Art 330(1) of the current Industrial Property Code, which entered into force on 1 July 2003 (cf para 23.03 above). However, this provision now seems openly to contradict Arts 16 and 17(1)(b) of the Regulation.

[166] Cf paras 23.285–23.287 below.

[167] In other words, the presumption provided for in Art 11 of the Regulation according to which the destruction of the goods is deemed to be accepted when the declarant, holder, and owner of the goods do not oppose the destruction within a specific time period does not apply in Portugal.

border measures, right-holders can also use both the criminal and civil proceedings regulated by the respective general laws, the same procedural rules being applicable to the various cases of infringement.

23.217   The exception (still with regard to the rights included under the Regulation) are plant variety rights, regarding which infringements are dealt with by means of counter-ordinance[168] proceedings rather than criminal proceedings. There is also a special civil injunction proceeding, which is only applicable to some intellectual property rights, that is, trade marks and designs.

Criminal actions

23.218   The lodging of criminal proceedings in Portugal is the exclusive competence of the Public prosecutor. The Public prosecutor (as an entity) is a State body constituted by a hierarchical organization of magistrates (without any relationship of subordination or dependency in relation to the judges, collectively known as the 'judicial magistracy'), upon whom it is incumbent to represent, inter alia, the State before the courts. In criminal proceedings, as well as exercising penal action, the Public prosecutor has the duty to assist the court in discovering the truth, and all his interventions must be governed by strict objectivity. In particular, the Public prosecutor has the function in these proceedings of receiving denunciations and complaints, assessing them and following them up, conducting the initial phase of the proceedings known as the 'inquiry phase', drawing up (when this is the case) the accusation, and upholding it throughout the proceedings, as well as lodging appeals and executing penalties.[169]

23.219   As far as criminal proceedings are concerned, an important distinction must be made with regard to the nature of the various intellectual property right infringements, which has some relevant implications in the enforcement thereof. This is the distinction between public and semi-public crimes.[170]

23.220   As regards these two types of crimes, it is the Public prosecutor who has legal capacity to instigate criminal proceedings. Also, irrespective of the nature of the crimes, it is incumbent upon the Public prosecutor to proceed *ex officio* with 'any measures which are deemed to be essential for discovering the truth and which fall within his jurisdiction (...)'.[171]

23.221   However, as far as *semi-public* crimes are concerned, the Public prosecutor only instigates proceedings when a *complaint* is filed by the injured party.[172]

---

[168] Cf paras 23.291–23.293 below.   [169] Code of Criminal Procedure, Arts 48 and 53.
[170] In this respect, Portuguese criminal law also provides for what are known as *private* crimes, but this category is not relevant to intellectual property right infringements.
[171] Code of Criminal Procedure, Art 50(2).
[172] Ibid, Art 49; Criminal Code, Art 113. This principle does not prejudice the duty of the Public prosecutor and/or the authorities to take certain urgent or even definitive measures on an *ex officio* basis, as in the case of products that infringe industrial property rights.

Furthermore, the right to lodge such criminal complaints lapses six months after the date on which the injured party learns of the infringement.[173] The injured party can withdraw its complaint up until the publication of the decision of the court of first instance,[174] provided that there is no express opposition to this on the part of the defendant.[175]

With regard to *public* crimes, the proceedings do not require any complaint or initiative on the part of the injured party. On the contrary, the Public prosecutor *must* pursue the proceedings irrespective of the position taken by the possible interested parties, as soon as he is informed of the infringement. In turn, notification of this infringement may come from any police or administrative authority (in which case notification is *compulsory*[176]), or from *any person* who may have learned of the infringement.[177] Furthermore, in the case of public crimes, the injured party cannot withdraw or renounce to the proceedings.[178] **23.222**

As concerns intellectual property rights, in Portugal public crimes are all the copyright infringements[179] referred to in Article 2(1)(c) of the Regulation, including software infringements, with the exception of infringements relating exclusively to moral rights.[180] **23.223**

However, infringements of industrial property rights are now considered to be *semi-public* crimes under the Industrial Property Code of 2003. In fact, in accordance with this Code, criminal proceedings for the infringement of industrial property rights depend on the filing of a complaint[181] by the injured party. **23.224**

---

[173] Criminal Code, Art 115.
[174] Ibid, Art 116(2).
[175] Ibid, Art 116(2); Code of Criminal Procedure, Art 51(3).
[176] What the law designates as a 'compulsory denunciation', which must be made in respect of crimes of any nature: Code of Criminal Procedure, Art 242.
[177] Notification known as an 'optional denunciation', which is only valid in the case of public crimes: Ibid, Art 244.
[178] As far as public crimes are concerned, it is not even appropriate to talk of 'withdrawal', since in such cases the proceedings do not depend on a *complaint* in the technical sense.
[179] Cf paras 23.74–23.78 above.
[180] Copyright Code, Art 200(1).
[181] Industrial Property Code, Art 329. This was in fact one of the most relevant amendments included in the Industrial Property Code of 2003 with regard to the enforcement of industrial property rights. Previously, infringements of these rights were also public crimes.
Notwithstanding the need for this complaint, Art 342(1) of the Industrial Property Code clearly provides that 'Even before the beginning of the inquiry phase (. . .), the criminal police bodies shall carry out the necessary inspections and take any preventive measures in an ex officio capacity.' It is further clarified in para 2 that 'Articles which display evidence of a crime provided under this Code, as well as the materials or instruments that were mainly used to commit the crime, *shall always be seized*.' In addition, Art 342(3) also expressly states that 'Irrespective of whether or not a complaint is filed (. . .), the judicial authority shall order an expert examination of the seized objects mentioned in the preceding paragraph, whenever this is necessary for determining whether or not they are manufactured or commercialised by the right-holder or by a party having his authorization.' In the event that the objects seized are in fact infringing goods, the law stipulates that they will be destroyed,

23.225 The legal requirements for the occurrence of a proceeding vary according to the nature of the crime concerned,[182] and this *should* have practical consequences for the purpose of the fulfilment of Article 13 of the Regulation. In particular, in the case of copyright infringements (which are *public* crimes), the simple denunciation of the infringement that the customs make *ex officio* to the public prosecutor should be sufficient, without the need for any future action on the part of the right-holder.

23.226 Circular 91/2004 of customs states that criminal complaints (always directed, of course, to the Public prosecutor) can be delivered to the customs offices that carried out the seizure of the goods, and these offices must always subsequently forward them to the Public prosecutor. The standard procedure, however, is to file the complaint at the actual Department of Public Prosecution, in which case either this entity or the right-holder must inform customs that the complaint was filed within the term of 10 working days stipulated in Article 13 of the Regulation.[183]

23.227 The procedural stages in a criminal action are the same in all cases,[184] irrespective of the intellectual property right involved.

23.228 If the right-holder opts to institute criminal proceedings following a customs intervention, any claim for damages must also be filed *within* the scope of those proceedings and be assessed by the criminal court—with the exception of certain situations stipulated in the law.[185] However, this claim[186] will only have to be filed at a later stage in the proceedings, that is within 20 days of the defendant being formally accused or indicted[187] of the crimes.[188]

23.229 The trying of a criminal case and the decision given at the end of the proceedings will naturally imply on the part of the court a decision as to 'whether an intellectual property has been infringed under [Portuguese] national law',[189] as required in accordance with the Regulation.

---

unless the right-holder '(...) expressly authorizes the reintroduction of such objects into commercial circuits or the taking of any other measures in respect thereof': Industrial Property Code, Art 330(1). In view of the above, it may be concluded that with regard to infringements against industrial property rights, the semi-public nature of these crimes is mitigated by the important principle that irrespective of whether or not a complaint is filed, *ex officio* measures will always be taken in respect of the infringing goods and the instruments that are mainly used for manufacturing them, with a view to their being destroyed.

[182] Cf paras 23.219–23.224 above.

[183] This is confirmed in Customs Circular 78/2004, item 5.1.4.(b), and in Customs Circular 91/2004 (para 23.32 above), item III 1.3.

[184] This is known as the 'common proceeding', regulated under the Code of Criminal Procedure, Arts 262–380.

[185] This is known as the 'principle of adhesion', established in the Code of Criminal Procedure, Art 71.   [186] The 'civil claim for damages'.

[187] By the public prosecutor or the Inquiring Judge respectively, depending on the stage of the proceedings when this occurs.   [188] Code of Criminal Procedure, Art 77.

[189] Unless the criminal proceeding is meanwhile considered to have been *extinguished*, by virtue of factors such as amnesties, lapsing of proceedings or others, which unfortunately is not exactly a rare occurrence in Portugal, in view of the length of criminal proceedings.

If the court rules the accusation as admissible, it will impose on the defendants the **23.230** penalties that it deems to be appropriate.[190] In the same decision, the court will also rule on the civil claim for damages, if applicable. Irrespective of whether or not any penalty is imposed on the defendant, in its decision the court should always take a position in relation to the seized goods.[191]

Still on the subject of criminal proceedings, although this only applies to indus- **23.231** trial property infringements, it is interesting to note that the law provides for the possibility of taking measures solely in respect of the seized (infringing) goods, without the need for instituting a 'full' proceeding leading to the trial of the infringers and the application of penalties against them.[192]

The first legal basis for this solution is a legal provision contained in Article 109 of **23.232** the Penal Code, according to which the infringing goods[193] 'are to be declared as lost in favour of the State',[194] which means as a rule that they will be 'totally or partially destroyed or withdrawn from the commercial circuit'.[195] The above-mentioned provision states that this will be the case even if no one can actually be punished for the crime committed.

More specifically with regard to the infringement of industrial property rights, **23.233** Article 342(3) of the Industrial Property Code states that 'Irrespective of whether or not a complaint is filed by the injured party, the judicial authority shall order an expert examination of the seized objects mentioned in the preceding paragraph, whenever this is necessary for determining whether or not they are manufactured or commercialised by the right-holder or by a party having his authorization.' In turn, Article 330 of the same Code confirms the above-mentioned provision of the Penal Code (Article 109) according to which the infringing goods and instruments are (in principle) to be destroyed.

In these cases, all the right-holder will have to do is confirm that the suspected **23.234** goods do indeed infringe his intellectual property rights, providing (on his initiative or at the request of the judicial authority) an expert examination for this purpose. In Circular 91/2004 of customs (item III 2.1.) it is confirmed that this procedure will be sufficient to comply with the Regulation.

Only one of the rights covered by the Regulation is not enforceable through criminal **23.235** proceedings. As mentioned previously,[196] infringements of plant variety rights are

---

[190] Regarding the penalties in criminal proceedings, cf paras 23.288–23.290 and 23.296–23.307 below.

[191] Regarding this aspect, cf paras 23.285–23.287 below.

[192] This is a solution applicable to the enforcement of industrial property in general, which is independent of (and existed before) the 'simplified procedure' proposed in Art 11 of the Regulation.

[193] Including the instruments mainly used to commit the crime—on this point, cf paras 23.105–23.109 above.

[194] Literal translation of the expression used in the Portuguese law.

[195] Cf paras 23.284–23.285.   [196] Cf para 23.217.

resolved by means of administrative counter-ordinance proceedings.[197] For this purpose, the legislation applicable is the special law that governs these rights, namely, Decree-Law 213/1990 of 28 June 1990,[198] as well as the general law on counter-ordinance proceedings, Decree-Law 433/82 of 27 October 1982.[199]

23.236 The proceedings relating to counter-ordinances and the application of fines are processed by the same administrative authority as is responsible for all the legal formalities relating to plant variety rights (for example, receiving and deciding applications for the protection of these rights). This is the National Centre for the Registration of Protected Plant Variety Rights,[200] known by the acronym CENARVE, which in turn functions under the aegis of another entity called the National Institute of Agrarian Research[201] (abbreviated to INIA).

23.237 The decision given by CENARVE in counter-ordinance proceedings also implies a pronouncement as to whether or not a plant variety right was infringed. It is nevertheless interesting to note that the decisions of the above-named authority can be the subject of a *judicial* appeal.[202]

Civil actions

23.238 Civil actions also follow the same procedural rules,[203] irrespective of the intellectual property right infringed.

23.239 These actions[204] must be filed at the courts, in accordance with the rules of territorial jurisdiction defined in the Code of Civil Procedure.[205] For the simple enforcement of intellectual property rights, actions known in Portuguese law as 'declaratory[206] actions of conviction'[207] are in principle used, following the format of 'ordinary proceedings'.[208]

23.240 Typically, in these actions right-holders request the courts to order the defendants (infringers) to:

- definitively cease the infringing acts;
- pay damages[209] to them;

---

[197] Cf paras 23.291–23.295 below. [198] Para 23.93 above.
[199] Para 23.11 and n 16 above.
[200] In Portuguese, *Centro Nacional de Registo de Variedades Vegetais Protegidas*.
[201] In Portuguese, *Instituto Nacional de Investigação Agrária*.
[202] Decree-Law 433/82 (para 23.11 and n 16 above), Arts 59 and 61.
[203] Contained in the Code of Civil Procedure.
[204] On the merits, also commonly termed 'main actions', in reference to the preliminary or interlocutory injunctions (provisional measures), when these proceedings are used.
[205] Or, when applicable, in Title X of the Community Trade Mark Regulation—Council Reg (EC) 40/94 of 20 December 1993 on the Community trade mark.
[206] Totally different from what in English are known as 'declaratory judgments'.
[207] In Portuguese, *acções declarativas de condenação*.
[208] Regulated under Articles 467 to 675 of the Code of Civil Procedure.
[209] Or a sum of money as reimbursement for unfair profits (in Portuguese, *enriquecimento sem causa*).

- pay for the destruction of the infringing goods;
- pay conventional damages[210] in the event of non-compliance with the decision;
- pay for the final decision to be published in the press;
- pay the judicial costs incurred in the proceedings.[211]

Also in respect of civil proceedings, Portuguese law provides for the filing of **23.241** preliminary injunctions. These proceedings can be lodged either before or during a main action and they are processed separately from the main action[212] (although they are dependent thereupon). Through these proceedings, right-holders can request that the court decrees certain measures of an urgent nature, such as (typically) an order to the infringer to cease the illegal activity, the seizure of the infringing goods, or both.

These injunctions are fairly widely used in Portugal within the scope of the **23.242** enforcement of intellectual property rights (of any kind) through the civil jurisdiction. However, in the specific case of judicial actions following customs interventions, these injunctions would not seem to have much scope for practical application, in view of the fact that the necessary urgent measures will (in principle) already have been taken by the customs authorities.

Criminal or civil proceedings: how to decide?

In general terms, criminal proceedings are preferred in straightforward cases of **23.243** trade mark infringement, and they are actually the most effective means to combat certain types of infringement, in particular those resulting from bad faith infringers, illegal traders, or organized fraud groups. These proceedings play a crucial role in the enforcement of intellectual property rights in Portugal, especially due to the concerted actions of some of the police authorities,[213] which periodically, and very often on their own initiative, organize seizure actions at the more notorious points of sale[214] of counterfeit goods, as well as, whenever possible, at the actual factories[215] where the goods are produced.

Criminal proceedings, in relation to civil actions, constitute enforcement options **23.244** that are much less costly, and generally produce more rapid results on terms of urgent measures.

---

[210] Known in Portuguese as *sanções pecuniárias compulsórias*.

[211] This does not include attorney fees and other costs borne by the other party (except in extreme cases of bad faith litigation).

[212] Contrary to what happens in other countries, where the court can be requested to grant injunctions and other urgent reliefs in the same brief as the main action.

[213] Of these police authorities, we would highlight in particular the *Inspecção Geral das Actividades Económicas* ('General Bureau of Trade Inspection')–IGAE–and the *Brigada Fiscal* ('Fiscal Brigade') of the *Guarda Nacional Republicana* ('National Republican Guard')—BF/GNR.

[214] Not only the well-known weekly markets held all over the country where travelling vendors sell their goods, but also some border towns where many counterfeit goods are sold and purchased by a large number of Portuguese and Spanish consumers.

[215] Including the textile and footwear factories situated in the north of Portugal.

23.245   However, proceedings of this nature can be very lengthy through the various stages until a decision is given by the court of first instance, and there is also the disadvantage of the parties almost completely 'losing' control of the development of the proceedings.[216] They are furthermore not the most appropriate type of proceedings in cases where one of the main priorities of the right-holders is to obtain the best compensation possible.

23.246   Civil actions are also very important in the enforcement of intellectual property rights in Portugal. They are normally more appropriate in cases of more 'sophisticated' infringement, or in disputes between companies with a good reputation. For certain types of intellectual property right infringements, they are normally the only viable means, as in the case of patent litigation.

23.247   As a rule, civil proceedings are nevertheless considerably more costly than criminal proceedings. Regarding the urgent measures in these actions, although injunction proceedings are generally efficient, they also tend to take rather longer to be resolved.

23.248   In order to comply with Article 13 of the Regulation, after a customs intervention, right-holders can use either criminal proceedings[217] or a civil action, depending on the options and objectives that they consider to be most relevant in each case.

23.249   In reality, however, criminal proceedings are the ones that have invariably been used in these situations. In fact, there is no record[218] of a single civil action having been filed following a customs intervention.

23.250   In this connection, it is significant to note that the customs Circulars only refer to criminal actions,[219] which could imply that these are the only adequate judicial proceedings for complying with Article 13 of the Regulation. However, this is certainly not the case, since Portuguese national law permits the use of civil actions[220] in these situations.

23.251   In any case, the systematic use of criminal proceedings following the customs interventions can be justified in practice by various factors.

23.252   First of all, criminal proceedings are habitually considered in Portugal to be the 'natural option' for the enforcement (in general terms) of the infringements which

---

[216] Although in this respect criminal proceedings against the infringement of industrial property rights have become more flexible, as a result of the alteration of their nature to semi-public crimes with the entry into force of the Industrial Property Code of 2003 (cf paras 23.219–23.224 above). In particular, right-holders can now put an end to these proceedings and reach agreements with the infringers.

[217] Except, of course, in the case of plant variety rights, regarding which counter-ordinance proceedings must be used instead of criminal proceedings: cf para 23.217 above.

[218] In accordance with unofficial information obtained from customs by the authors of this contribution.

[219] In particular, Circular 91/2004 (para 23.32 above).

[220] Although it may also be said that copyright infringements (public crimes) should strictly always give rise to criminal proceedings: cf paras 23.222–23.223 above.

have been mainly detected by customs—that is, trade mark and copyright infringements. Furthermore, criminal proceedings are much less costly than civil actions, and can also be pursued to completion with a minimum level of intervention of the part of the right-holder. These are undoubtedly important aspects, especially for the right-holder who is most greatly affected by the infringement of intellectual property rights, and thus have to handle a large number of judicial proceedings (which can sometimes reach several dozen a year).

It still remains to be seen what option will be taken in the future by right-holders in cases of the detention or suspension of the release by customs of goods suspected of infringing other types of rights, such as patents or SPCs, as there has been no experience to date of situations of this kind. In our opinion, this could depend on whether or not the right-holder has sufficient prima facie evidence that a certain import or export of goods involves an infringement of their patent or SPC rights. If so, criminal proceedings could also be appropriate for dealing with these cases (or, if not, the goods would probably not be detected by customs anyway . . .). **23.253**

(2) *Term for notifying customs that proceedings have been started*

Both of the customs Circulars[221] only make brief references to the term mentioned in Article 13 of the Regulation. **23.254**

Item II 5.2. of Circular 78/2004 specifies that 'When, within the scope of an ex officio procedure, the application for customs intervention is filed before the end of the term of three working days [stipulated in Article 4(1) of the Regulation], the term of ten working days (plus an extension when permitted) (. . .) is counted from the date on which the application for customs intervention is lodged (. . .)'.[222] **23.255**

With regard to the possibility of extending the term of 10 working days, as provided under Article 13 of the Regulation, item III 1.3. of Circular 91/2004 simply states that the term can be extended '(. . .) provided that the [request for] extension is duly justified'. No experience really exists as to what would constitute 'due justification' (or, as in the English version of the Regulation, an 'appropriate case'), but we suppose that Portuguese Customs would not be too stringent in the application of this concept, especially in cases where they are not being pressured by the declarant or holder of the goods. **23.256**

---

[221] Para 23.32 above.
[222] There seems to be a discrepancy between this item of the customs Circular and Art 5 of Reg 1891/2004, which stipulates that the time limit in question shall be counted from the *day after* the application for customs action is received. This will depend on what, in accordance with the directive, is supposed to be the *first day* of the 10-day term at issue. As currently stated in the text of the customs Circular, it is considered in Portugal that the first day of this term is actually the day after the day when the application is filed, which, according to the general rule for calculating deadlines, is not included in the respective term (this is the principle of *dies a quo non computatur in termino*, as laid down in Art 279(b) of the Civil Code).

D. Release of goods suspected of infringing certain rights on provision of a security

23.257   As regards the application of Article 14(1) of the Regulation, the instructions contained in Circular 78/2004 of customs include an item which basically parrots this provision.[223] A footnote to the item in question clarifies that the application to lift the suspension of customs clearance or to end the detention of the merchandise '(. . .) shall be lodged with the head of the customs office involved'.

23.258   Even though this provision already existed under the previous Regulation,[224] the fact is that the customs authorities have no experience of the application thereof.

23.259   In any case, if such a situation ever arises, Portuguese Customs will very probably make a literal application of this provision. In other words, although they will not necessarily consider that they are *obliged* to release the goods, they will probably not raise any obstacles to this release.

23.260   The problem, however, concerns the actual legal powers of customs to take measures in respect of goods suspected of infringement without receiving an order to do so from the judicial authority, in the light of the general rules of the substantive and procedural criminal laws in force in Portugal. This is actually the same question as raised in paragraphs 23.202–23.203 above with respect to the proposed simplified procedure and it is, in fact, rather doubtful that customs would be able to take any measures regarding the suspected goods without a judicial decision authorizing them to do so, especially in cases involving crimes that are designated as 'public crimes'[225] (that is, copyright infringements), even if they have the consent of the injured party.

23.261   This is therefore another provision of the Regulation which will certainly require a few adaptations to be made to national law.

23.262   Likewise, no experience exists in the depositing or calculation of the security provided for under Article 14(2) of the Regulation, nor have any guidelines been drawn up for this purpose (either in the Circulars issued by the customs authorities, or in any other format). Furthermore, Portuguese Customs have almost no practical experience at all with regard to the provision of securities of any kind— and this was the case even when securities were provided for under the previous Regulations for the purpose of the actual applications for customs action.[226]

23.263   One situation that Portuguese law regulates with aspects similar to Article 14 of the Regulation concerns the preliminary injunctions provided for in the Code of

---

[223] Circular 78/2004 (para 23.32 above), item 5.1.4.(b), 2nd paragraph.
[224] Reg 3295/94, as amended by Reg 241/1999 (n 21 above), Art 7(2).
[225] Cf paras 23.219–23.224 above.
[226] Reg 3842/86 (n 18 above), Art 3(3); Reg (EC) 3295/94 (n 21 above), Art 3(6).

Civil Procedure.[227] Article 387(3) of this Code allows a provisional measure ordered by the court to be '(. . .) substituted by an *adequate security*, at the request of the defendant, provided that the security offered, after the plaintiff has been heard, is *sufficient to prevent the damage or to repair it in full*'.[228]

An equivalent criterion, based on the provision of an amount sufficient for **23.264** *preventing* or *repairing in full* the damage caused to the right-holder, would seem to be adequate for the application of the provision of the Regulation and for fulfilling the condition laid down in Article 14(2), in the sense that the security must be sufficient to protect the interests of the right-holder. This amount could in turn be calculated on the basis of the loss of profits sustained by the right-holder due to the introduction of the infringing goods onto the Portuguese market or, subsidiarily, on the basis of the unfair profits that the holder of the goods would obtain through the sale thereof on the market.

E. Storage of the goods

As has been the case since the first Regulation,[229] Article 15 of Regulation (EC) **23.265** 1383/2003 stipulates that the *conditions* of storage of the suspected goods are to be determined by each Member State, now with the additional clarification that this shall not give rise to any costs for the customs authorities.

However, the new Regulation has introduced a relevant alteration which should **23.266** considerably affect the practice followed in Portugal with regard to storage costs. This is, of course, the alteration contained in the second indent of Article 6(1), which states that the right-holder shall agree to bear all costs incurred in keeping the merchandise under customs control.

In this respect, Regulation 3295/94 had already established the principle that the **23.267** Member States *could* require the provision of a security intended (also) to ensure payment of the costs incurred in the storage of the goods.[230] However, although this provision was implemented in Portugal,[231] the customs authorities never actually requested right-holders to provide a security for this purpose.

Moreover, Portuguese law does not contain any general provisions relating to the **23.268** storage of goods. In criminal proceedings, the seized goods are retained until they are destroyed at the end of the proceedings, at facilities belonging to the State

---

[227] Code of Civil Procedure, Arts 381–392. Cf paras 23.238–23.242 above.

[228] Another situation that is also regulated by the Code of Civil Procedure (Art 692) is the possibility of obtaining, with the filing of an appeal, the *suspensive* effect of a decision of the Court of first instance, if the defendant-appellant invokes that the execution of the decision would cause considerable harm and offers to pay a security.　　　　　　　　　　　　　　　　　[229] N 18 above.

[230] Reg 3295/94 (n 21 above), Art 3(6).

[231] Through Decree-Law 20/99 (cf para 23.14 above), Art 2.

(usually court or police premises), with no costs being attributed or incurred for this purpose. In civil proceedings, the seized goods are entrusted to someone appointed by the court,[232] who in practice is very often the actual defendant, or even the plaintiff (if any costs are incurred in storing the goods, they are borne by the appointed person or entity).

23.269   In the case of Portuguese Customs, however, they do not have any warehouses or other premises suitable for storing the goods—nor even, as mentioned above, are they supposed to incur any costs in connection with the storage of the goods.

23.270   What has happened in Portugal is that the seized goods have been stored at the actual premises of the private cargo transport companies operating at the ports and airports.

23.271   For example, at the port zone of Lisbon, several companies hold concessions to operate the various container terminals, where they carry out various port operation activities (docking, loading and unloading, transhipment, packing and unpacking containers, storage and shipment of merchandise, etc). At the port of Leixões (Oporto), there are basically three companies operating as customs agents with similar functions, who have warehouses (with areas of between 2,500 and 5,000 m² which, although they are operated economically by these companies, are under the permanent control of customs.

23.272   At the airports there are companies with equivalent functions with regard to the traffic of cargo transported by air, who have an area reserved for the storage of seized goods in accordance with an agreement signed with the customs authorities. As far as parcels sent by air are concerned, the post offices situated at the airports function in a separate area allotted for this purpose.

23.273   Customs frequently check the merchandise transported by all the above-mentioned companies, and when any suspected goods are detected, they are duly sealed and stored at the respective premises. Some port operators in Lisbon (where apparently the interior warehouses are considerably smaller, especially in comparison with those existing in Oporto) opt to store the seized goods in sealed containers situated in the exterior areas belonging to their concessionary zones.

23.274   The companies that provide transportation services involving what are considered as high-risk countries are naturally more affected by this phenomenon. One of these companies has reported that it currently has in its storage area a total of ten containers full of seized goods.

23.275   Furthermore, the merchandise has to be retained until the end of the proceedings, and can only be moved by means of a court order. This can actually mean a very

---

[232] Known as a 'loyal depositary'.

long time, especially in the case of criminal proceedings.[233] Some of these companies have merchandise that has been stored under these conditions for around three or four years!

Finally, another (unsolved) problem regarding the storage of the goods is the pay- **23.276** ment of the costs incurred therewith. The customs agents, in particular the port operators, have been trying to obtain the payment of these costs from the importers of the seized goods, on the rare occasions that they are required to go to the agent's premises to destroy the merchandise or take any other measures stipulated in a judicial decision. Not surprisingly, the vast majority of payments are not made,[234] and even when they are, they take a very long time to be settled.

It can be seen from the above that the burden of storing the goods lies almost **23.277** totally with the customs agents and operators, who do not receive the compensation that is due to them (not even in the long term). In addition, while it seems inevitable that these companies will continue to be involved in the storage of the goods, it is still uncertain when their situation with regard to the payment of the respective costs will be altered in the light of the new rules laid down in the Regulation.

IV. PROVISIONS APPLICABLE TO GOODS FOUND TO INFRINGE AN INTELLECTUAL PROPERTY RIGHT

The various intellectual property laws in Portugal, namely the Industrial Property **23.278** Code (Articles 319, 321, and 322) and the Copyright Code (Article 201), explicitly provide that the importation and exportation of goods infringing an intellectual property right are considered to be an act of infringement.

The actual implementing law[235] for Regulation (EC) 3295/94 reinforced the **23.279** penal sanctions for these illicit acts of importation, by adding the penal provision relating to such acts in the (already existing) Article 23 of Decree-Law 28/84 relating to the Law on Anti-Economic and Public Health Infringements.[236] However, this legislative option was not in our opinion totally correct, not only because these acts were already duly penalized in the laws that regulated the respective

---

[233] In Portugal, criminal proceedings have so far been the only type of proceedings used by rightholders following a customs intervention (cf paras 23.243 and 23.248–23.252 above).

[234] One of the most greatly affected companies estimates that around 90% (or maybe more) of these payments are still outstanding.   [235] Cf para 23.14 and n 22.

[236] Cf para 23.11.

intellectual property rights,[237] but also because the above-mentioned Decree-Law 28/84 relates to infringements against the economy, whose nature and legal requirements are different from intellectual property right infringements.

23.280 In the field of intellectual property law, the wording of Portuguese law contains a particularity which is susceptible of interfering with the *criminal* prosecution after a customs intervention in respect of an act of *importation* of counterfeit goods. Articles 323 and 324 of the Industrial Property Code[238] refer to the acts of counterfeiting or imitating registered trade marks, or of using counterfeit or imitated trade marks, as well as the acts of distributing, selling or concealing goods with these marks, but none of these provisions specifically mentions the *importation* of such merchandise.

23.281 This situation is more obvious if we compare the above-mentioned provisions (in respect of trade mark infringements) with the corresponding provisions of the same Code in respect of patents (Article 321) and designs (Article 322), both of which expressly state that the act of importation of infringing goods constitutes a crime.[239]

23.282 Although it is certainly compulsory for the Customs authorities to detain or suspend the release of counterfeit goods,[240] and notwithstanding the fact that it is undoubtedly an illicit act of a civil nature (tort), the above-mentioned omission in the law could lead to the conclusion that the act of *importing* counterfeit goods is not per se a criminal offence under Portuguese law, in view of the fact that no criminal provision exists to that effect. This understanding has already been shared by a few public prosecutors when assessing cases referred to them following a customs seizure. In these cases, the public prosecutors considered that the imported counterfeit goods *objectively* constituted a crime of trade mark counterfeiting as provided under Article 323 of the Industrial Property Code, but a crime *committed abroad*, meaning that the Portuguese courts had no jurisdiction to handle such cases. They also considered that these cases did not involve the crime provided under Article 324 (distribution, sale, or concealing, of counterfeit goods), since the goods never actually came into the defendant's possession, and therefore proposed the closure of the proceedings.[241] Fortunately, this has in no way been the dominant position on the part of the judicial authorities, as most criminal cases based on the importation of counterfeit goods have been prosecuted successfully without this question having been raised.[242]

---

[237] With only a few reservations specifically relating to trade marks, as will be explained in paras 23.280–23.282. [238] Cf paras 23.50–23.51 above.

[239] Cf paras 23.70 and 23.88 above.

[240] As required by the Industrial Property Code, Art 319(1).

[241] As in the case of a decision rendered by the Public prosecutor with the Lisbon criminal courts dated 14 July 2004 (unreported).

[242] One case has recently been reported (decision of the 4th Chamber of the Lisbon Court of Criminal Investigation, 15 February 2005 (unreported) where the defendant cited the above-mentioned argument in his defence, but the judicial authority rejected it, and considered that '(. . .)

As regards the situations of re-exportation, external transit, and transhipment of goods, they are not expressly provided for under these laws, which gives rise to doubt as to whether they can be applicable. **23.283**

However, as a consequence of the direct effect of Regulation 1383/2003, the entry into/or removal from Portuguese territory, release for free circulation, exportation, re-exportation, placement under a suspensive procedure (including external transit and transhipment) and placement in a free zone or free warehouse of goods found to infringe an intellectual property right at the outcome of the proceedings referred to in Article 13 of this Regulation, will in principle be prohibited by the courts of the Member States, including the Portuguese courts, in accordance with Article 16 of the Regulation. **23.284**

In Portugal, the Industrial Property Code (Article 330) and the Copyright Code (Article 201(2)) expressly provide for the possibility of destroying the counterfeit goods. **23.285**

However, as an alternative, the judge in his decision may also order that the goods, for example, articles of clothing, be handed over to charitable institutions, provided that the right-holder gives his consent to that effect. The goods will thus be placed outside commercial channels in such a way as to preclude any possible injury to the right-holder, in accordance with Article 17(1)(a) of the Regulation. **23.286**

The costs of destruction will be paid by the infringer, or by the Portuguese authorities if the infringer is unknown or does not have any establishment in Portugal. **23.287**

V. PENALTIES

The penalties for criminal offences in the field of intellectual property are mainly provided for in the Industrial Property Code in respect of industrial property rights and in the Copyright Code with regard to copyrights. **23.288**

The penalties for infringements of plant variety rights are provided for separately under the law that governs these rights, Decree-Law 213/1990.[243] **23.289**

Regarding the infringement of industrial property rights, the accessory penalties provided for under Decree-Law 28/84[244] are applicable. **23.290**

---

even though the defendant did not actually sell [the imported] goods or offer them for sale, *it was at his request that the goods in question were placed in circulation with a view to being sold* (...), meaning that (...) the defendant's conduct does fall within [the provision] of the Industrial Property Code'. The latter interpretation of Art 324 of the Industrial Property Code does in fact seem to be the most correct, although some clarification on the part of the legislator would be welcome.

[243] Cf paras 23.93–23.96.   [244] Cf para 23.11 and n 17 above, and para 23.303 below.

23.291   Some intellectual property infringements are punishable in Portugal under a branch of law which can be translated literally into English as the *law on mere social order*.[245]

23.292   This branch of law falls within a criminal policy characterized by a tendency towards decriminalization, which emerged in various European countries during the second half of the twentieth century. This decriminalization movement resulted in the creation of a distinction between acts considered to be relevant (and sanctionable) in terms of their ethico-social classification, and acts considered as being *neutral* in ethico-social terms, regarding which the respective offence is merely *prohibited*. The former illicit acts were maintained within the scope of criminal law, whereas the latter (ethico-socially neutral acts) were excluded from the scope of criminal law, and formed the new branch of the law on mere social order.[246, 247]

23.293   It should be pointed out that these infringements are *administrative* and not criminal in nature. Consequently, the corresponding proceedings are examined and decided by the competent administrative authorities, and not by the judicial courts.[248] These infringements are designated as *counter-ordinances*[249] and are punishable by pecuniary sanctions.[250]

23.294   As already discussed, plant variety rights are the only rights included in Regulation (EC) 1383/2003 the infringement of which under Portuguese law is primarily provided for and punishable as a counter-ordinance.[251] The other infringements provided for under the Regulation which are punishable as counter-ordinances are the *preparatory acts* relating to infringements of industrial property rights.[252]

23.295   There are also other categories of infringements provided for in the Industrial Property Code which are *not* included under the Regulation and are punishable as counter-ordinances. This is the case, for example, of unfair competition (Articles 317, 318, and 331 of the Industrial Property Code), infringements of names or emblems of establishment (Article 333) and logos (Article 334), the use of trade marks with false indications (Article 336), or the undue use of registration notices, such as the symbol ® (Article 338).

---

[245] In Portuguese, *direito de mera ordenação social*.

[246] The first country to create this category of infringements was the Federal Republic of Germany in 1949, followed by Switzerland (1974), Austria, Portugal (1979), and Italy (1981).

[247] Regarding this question, cf J de Figueiredo Dias, *Direito Penal* (Volume I, Coimbra Editora, 2004).

[248] Except in the case of an infringement of this nature *committed at the same time* as a crime, in which case the criminal Courts have jurisdiction to handle both offences.

[249] This is a free translation of the Portuguese term *contra-ordenação*. The corresponding original German expression is *Ordnungswidrigkeiten*.

[250] This type of sanction may be designated in English as a 'fine', though in Portuguese the term used (*coima*) is different from the term used to designate the equivalent criminal sanction (*multa*).

[251] Cf paras 23.95–23.96 above.

[252] Industrial Property Code, Art 335. Cf para 23.52 above and para 23.307 below.

In the field of criminal law, of the various types of penalties provided for under the **23.296** Portuguese criminal system, those that are mainly applicable in the case of infringements of intellectual property rights are prison sentences and fines.

In Portugal, prison sentences are of a minimum term of one month and a **23.297** maximum of 20 years. In the case of various concurrent prison sentences, the maximum term is 25 years, which can never be exceeded.[253]

In turn, fines are set in terms of the number of 'days' (for example, '*x* day fine'). As **23.298** a rule, the minimum number of days is 10 and the maximum 360. Each 'day-fine' corresponds to an amount between EUR 1 and EUR 498.80, which the courts set in accordance with the economic and financial situation of the convicted party and his personal outgoings.[254]

The Industrial Property Code punishes with the same degree of penalty the **23.299** infringements against the various industrial property rights, which are, for the purpose of the Regulation, patents (Article 321), designs (Article 322), trade marks (Article 323), and designations of origin and geographical indications (Article 325). This penalty is a prison sentence of up to three years, or a fine of up to 360 days.

However, our law distinguishes between the acts of *manufacturing* the infringing **23.300** products, which is punishable by the above-mentioned penalty, and the acts of *selling, placing into circulation* or *concealing* these products (Article 324), which are punishable by a lesser penalty of a one-year prison sentence or a fine of up to 120 days.

In Article 335 of the Industrial Property Code, the law also provides for, and **23.301** punishes separately, the *preparatory* acts relating to the above-mentioned infringements. These preparatory acts are classified as counter-ordinances and are punishable by fines of between EUR 3,000 and EUR 30,000 if the infringer is a corporate body, and between EUR 750 and EUR 7,500 if the infringer is a natural person.

Also regarding the infringement of industrial property rights, it is possible by **23.302** virtue of Article 320 of the Industrial Property Code to apply the accessory penalties provided in the Law on anti-economic and public health infringements, namely, Decree-Law 28/84 of 20 January 1984.[255]

The accessory penalties are listed in Article 8 of the above-mentioned Law, and are **23.303** specifically provided for under Articles 9 to 19. These penalties are the following:

- Loss of goods—Article 8(a)—which '(...) covers illicit gains obtained by the infringer' (Article 9(1));
- Privation of the right to subsidies or grants awarded by public bodies or departments—Article 8(f) and Article 14;

---

[253] Criminal Code, Art 41.   [254] Ibid, Art 47.   [255] Cf para 23.11 and n 17 above.

- Prohibition against participating in fairs or markets—Article 8(g)—when the infringement '(. . .) was committed by a party legally authorized to participate as a seller in fairs or markets (. . .) for a minimum period of two months and a maximum of two years' (Article 15(1)).

- Temporary closure of an establishment—Article 8(i)—for '(. . .) a minimum period of one month and a maximum of one year' (Article 17(1)).

- Definitive closure of the establishment—Article 8(j)—in the case of a re-offence when the infringer 'was previously condemned to the penalty of temporary closure of the same or another establishment' (Article 18).

- Publication of the decision—Article 8(l)—'(. . .) at the expense of the infringer, in a periodical publication (. . .), as well as through the affixation of a public notice for a minimum period of 30 days at the commercial or industrial establishment in question or at the place where the activity is carried out', or 'in particularly serious cases (. . .) in *Diário da República,*[256] Series II, or by any other means' (Article 19(1) and (2)).

23.304   It is interesting to note that these accessory penalties, which have been applicable in cases of offences against industrial property since 1995, correspond essentially to some of the measures recommended in the original draft of what was to become Directive 2004/48/EC.[257]

23.305   The acts of copyright infringement stipulated in the Copyright Code, that is, 'counterfeiting' (Article 196), 'usurpation' (Article 195) and 'use' of a pirated or usurped work, are all punishable by a prison sentence of up to three years and a fine of between 150 and 250 days. If these crimes are committed through negligence, they are punishable by a fine of between 50 and 150 days.

23.306   In the particular case of software, copyright infringement is punishable by a prison sentence of up to three years and a fine (the limits of which are not defined by the law).[258]

23.307   Finally, infringements of plant variety rights are classified under Article 7 of Decree-Law 213/90 as counter-ordinances,[259] and are punishable by fines of between EUR 100 and EUR 2,500 if the infringer is an individual person. If the infringer is a corporate body, the fines are increased to EUR 30,000 in the case of wilful acts and EUR 15,000 in the case of negligent acts.

---

[256] The official journal in Portugal.

[257] Directive 2004/48/EC of the European Parliament and of the Council of 29 April 2004 on the enforcement of intellectual property rights [2004] OJ L 157/45 (30.4.2004). These penalties were included among the criminal measures that were excluded from the final version of the Directive.

[258] Penalty stipulated under Art 9(1) of Law 109/91 on Computer Criminality (n 12 above), applicable by virtue of Art 14 of Decree-Law 252/94 on the Legal Protection of Software (n 13 above).

[259] Cf paras 23.291–23.293 above.

VI. LIABILITY OF CUSTOMS AUTHORITIES AND RIGHT-HOLDERS

A. Liability of right-holders and sanctions

In Portugal, Article 483 of the Civil Code establishes that any natural or legal person who has suffered damages due to a fault committed by a third party may claim compensation for such damages. **23.308**

This provision will govern all liability claims provided for under Article 19(3) of the Regulation, initiated for example, by the owner, importer, exporter, holder, or consignee of the goods, against a right-holder who may have applied the Regulation in a negligent or irresponsible manner. **23.309**

The same applies to any damages caused by use of the information provided by customs to the right-holder in breach of Article 12 of the Regulation and/or of Portuguese law. **23.310**

Due to the direct effect of Article 12, the General Directorate of Customs will also be entitled to suspend the right-holder's application for action for the period of validity remaining before renewal and, in the event of a further violation of Article 12, to refuse to renew the application. **23.311**

B. Liability of customs authorities and sanctions

Under Article 19(1) of the Regulation, the acceptance of an application for action will not entitle the right-holder to compensation in the event that goods are not detected by a customs office and are released, or no action is taken to detain them in accordance with Article 9(1) of the Regulation, 'Save as provided by the law of the Member State in which an application is lodged or, in the case of an application under Article 5(4), by the law of the Member State in which goods infringing an intellectual property right are not detected (. . .)'. **23.312**

Article 19(2) of the Regulation states that the exercise by a customs office or by another duly empowered authority of the powers conferred on them in order to fight against goods infringing an intellectual property right shall not render them liable towards the persons involved in the situations referred to in Article 1(1) or the persons affected by the measure provided for in Article 4 for damages suffered by them as a result of the authority's intervention, '(. . .) except where provided for by the law of the Member State in which the application is made or, in the case of an application under Article 5(4), by the law of the Member State in which loss or damage is incurred'. **23.313**

23.314   In our opinion, the general provision of Article 483 of the Civil Code could be relied upon against customs, provided that fault could be attributed to them within the context of the application of the Regulation and the right-holder had suffered harm as a result of this fault.

23.315   Liability claims have to be initiated against the Portuguese State, represented by the Minister of Finance (who is in charge of customs policies in Portugal).

23.316   In accordance with the general framework, the customs authorities cannot be held liable vis-à-vis *right-holders* for failing to act under Article 4 of the Regulation, that is, prior to the filing of an application for action. Indeed, the application of the *ex officio* procedure is purely optional and is not binding upon the customs authorities of the Member States.

23.317   On the other hand, Article 483 of the Civil Code entitles persons *other than the right-holders* who are involved in the situations referred to in Article 1(1) or affected by the measures provided for in Article 4 to claim compensation against the Portuguese customs authorities for damages suffered as a result of the intervention of these authorities. For instance, it cannot be ruled out that Portuguese Customs, having negligently intercepted goods which ought *reasonably* not to have been regarded as suspected of infringing an intellectual property right by a normally careful person, could be held liable if such negligent detention would have caused damages to the holders of the rights in respect of the goods. However, only flagrant or repeated erroneous assessments can possibly be held to constitute a fault within the meaning of Article 483 of the Civil Code and as such qualify as proper grounds for a liability claim.

23.318   We are of the opinion that the general provision of Article 483 of the Civil Code will apply to these situations. This means that the liability of Portuguese Customs will only exist when the non-detection and release of goods suspected of infringing a right-holder's intellectual property right has caused damages to the right-holder, and these acts qualify as a 'fault' which a normally diligent and careful official would not have committed.

Conclusion

23.319   Border measures in Portugal are a good example of when a strong law is very often not in itself sufficient for ensuring the defence of rights. In fact, as mentioned at the beginning of this chapter, since as far back as 1940, Portugal has had a national system providing for the complete protection of all industrial property rights at the borders, giving full powers to customs to intervene (including in an *ex officio* capacity) in all situations. However, it was only while the second EC Regulation[260]

---

[260]   Ie Reg 3295/94 (n 21 above).

was in force that the system of border measures truly began to function in Portugal.

Community legislation in this area started with a rather 'timid' approach to the protection of intellectual property rights at customs level. This degree of protection evolved considerably under the second[261] and third[262] Regulations and, with the entry into force of the latest Regulation,[263] an adequate level of protection has been achieved. In this respect, it should be pointed out that Regulation 1383/2003 does not simply provide strong protection to (almost) all intellectual property rights, applicable to all customs procedures, as in the case of the Portuguese national system. More than this, the Regulation governs and resolves certain procedural aspects, thereby ensuring that in practice it can be successfully applied. **23.320**

However, in our opinion, the increasing success of the system of border measures is not simply due to the existence of adequate legislation. In order to achieve this success, a fundamental factor has also been the growing awareness on the part of the customs authorities of the seriousness of the problem of counterfeiting and of the importance of their intervention in the fight against this phenomenon. In this regard, the European Commission has played a decisive role, first of all by making this function of the customs authorities a priority within the Member States, and also by coordinating and motivating these authorities to take action. **23.321**

Another factor which we believe has been very relevant to the smooth functioning of the system is the organization of the various national customs authorities as a substantially homogenous and cohesive organization, namely through the World Customs Organization, which has existed as such for many years. Indeed, the various national customs will certainly be the enforcement agencies with by far the most highly coordinated collective functioning. **23.322**

As far as Portugal is concerned, its national customs are highly motivated to apply the Regulation and to combat counterfeiting in general, and they strongly endeavour to carry out this task, in spite of the fact that they suffer from a certain lack of resources and staff available to fulfil these functions.[264] **23.323**

As for the future, there will probably still be room for alterations and improvements to the Regulation, even though the existing version is already very satisfactory in terms of statutory law. One of the issues that may be examined in a future revision of the Regulation is the question of parallel imports, in the event that the EU countries should all agree to opt for the Community exhaustion of rights. **23.324**

---

[261] Ibid.   [262] Ie Reg 241/1999 (n 21 above).   [263] Ie Reg 1383/2003 (n 34 above).
[264] The authors of this chapter would like to take this opportunity to thank warmly for their kind assistance the various officials at Portuguese Customs, in particular Mrs Margarida Osório (of the General Directorate of Customs) and Mr Mário Silva (of the Lisbon Airport Customs).

23.325 It will be very important to adequately implement Article 11 of the Regulation, as well as to encourage the use of the procedure that it provides, in order to expedite the judicial proceedings and contribute towards easing the serious problem of the storage of goods.

23.326 The European Commission must continue in and, if possible, increase its role in motivating and providing training for the customs authorities. Another key point would be to improve the system of checking and controlling merchandise by customs, in order to cover the greatest possible volume of traffic, though without hindering the free movement of goods.[265]

---

[265] The authors of this work would also like to express their thanks for the valuable assistance provided by Ms Fiona Underhill, who was responsible for the revision of the English-language version of this work, and who actually translated a large part of the text from the original Portuguese.

24

SLOVAK REPUBLIC

Jan Hák

Introduction

National legislation on border measures in respect of goods suspected of **24.01** infringing an intellectual property right already existed in the Slovak Republic prior to the entry into force of EC Regulation No 1383/2003[1] ('the Regulation') in the form of Law No 271/2001 Coll.

Further to the adoption of the new Regulation and its Implementing **24.02** Regulation,[2] this Law was replaced by Law No 200/2004 Coll, 'laying down the measures to be taken against imported, exported and parallel imported goods which infringe an intellectual property right'[3] ('the 2004 Law'). This new law, which was published on 10 March 2004 and came into force on the same day as the new Regulation (that is, on 1 July 2004), governs border measures against goods suspected of infringing an industrial property right, copyright or related rights.

---

[1] Council Reg (EC) No 1383/2003 of 22 July 2003 concerning customs action against goods suspected of infringing certain intellectual property rights and the measures to be taken against goods found to have infringed such rights, [2003] OJ L 196/7 (2.8.2003).

[2] Commission Reg (EC) No 1891/2004 of 21 October 2004 laying down provisions for the implementation of Council Reg (EC) No 1383/2003 concerning customs action against goods suspected of infringing certain intellectual property rights and the measures to be taken against goods found to have infringed such rights, [2004] OJ L 328/16 (30.10.2004).

[3] Zákon o opatreniach proti porušovaniu práv duševného vlastníctva pri dovoze, vývoze a spatnom vývoze tovaru.

I. SUBJECT MATTER AND SCOPE OF THE NATIONAL LAW APPLYING THE REGULATION

A. Customs procedure of the goods

24.03 The customs authorities in the Slovak Republic apply the Regulation to all customs procedures defined in Article 1(1) of the Regulation, including entry for release for free circulation and exportation. The actions taken by Slovak Customs in those situations rely on both Article 1(1) of the Regulation (which has direct effect in all of the Member States of the European Union), and section 1 of the 2004 Law.

B. Definition of infringing goods

(1) Counterfeit goods

24.04 Pursuant to Article 2(1)(a) of the Regulation, the customs authorities of the Member States are to take action against 'counterfeit goods', which are defined as:

- goods, including packaging, bearing without authorization a trade mark identical to the trade mark validly registered in respect of the same type of goods, or which cannot be distinguished in its essential aspects from such a trade mark, and which thereby infringes the trade mark-holder's rights under Community law, as provided for by Council Regulation (EC) No 40/94 of 20 December 1993 on the Community Trade Mark[4] or the law of the Member State in which the application for action by customs authorities is made;

- any trade mark symbol (including a logo, label, sticker, brochure, instructions for use or guarantee document bearing such a symbol), even if presented separately, on the same conditions as the goods referred to here above first bullet point; and

- packaging materials bearing the trade marks of counterfeited goods, presented separately, again on the same conditions as the goods referred to here above first bullet point.

---

[4] [1994] OJ L 11/1 (14.1.1994).

Slovak Customs are therefore entitled under the Regulation, and also under **24.05** section 6 of the 2004 Law, to take action in the case of goods, symbols, and packaging materials which, basically, bear without authorization a trade mark identical to another trade mark, or which cannot be distinguished in its essential aspects from another trade mark. The latter category of goods is deemed by Slovak Customs to encompass any goods to which a trade mark has been affixed which can be seen as *confusingly similar* to another registered trade mark, within the meaning of Article 5(1)(b) of the Trade Marks Directive.[5]

In accordance with Article 2(1)(a) of the Regulation, under section 2 of the 2004 **24.06** Law, the trade mark on the basis of which border measures are taken must be validly registered in respect of the same or similar type of goods. However, the trade mark relied upon must have been 'validly registered', which implies that it is not possible to take border measures under the Regulation or the 2004 Law on the basis of simple trade mark *applications.*

Both Article 2(1)(a) of the Regulation and Article 25 of the Slovak Trade Marks **24.07** Law[6] allow Slovak Customs to detain or suspend the release of trade mark symbols and packaging materials bearing the trade marks of counterfeit goods, even if delivered separately, on the same conditions as for those goods themselves.

(2) Pirated goods

Under Article 2(1)(b) of EC Regulation 1383/2003, the customs authorities in **24.08** the Member States of the European Union are also to take action against pirated goods, which are defined as 'goods which are or contain copies made without the consent of the holder of a copyright or related right or design right, regardless of whether it is registered in national law, or of a person authorised by the right-holder in the country of production in cases where the making of those copies would constitute an infringement of that right under Council Regulation (EC) No 6/2002 of 12 December 2001 on Community Designs[7] or the 2004 law of the Member State in which the application for customs action is made'.

Slovak Customs interpret strictly the concept of 'goods which are or contain **24.09** copies'. As in the case of trade marks, they are usually prepared to act against goods which cannot—or contain components which cannot—be distinguished in their essential aspects, from a protected work or design.

---

[5] First Council Directive No 89/104 of 21 December 1988 to approximate the laws of the Member States relating to trade marks, [1989] OJ L 40/1 (11.2.1989).
[6] Law No 55/1997 (Zákon o ochranných známkach). This Law came into force on 1 March 1997.
[7] [2002] OJ L 3/1 (5.1.2002).

(3) Goods infringing other intellectual property rights

24.10   Pursuant to Article 2(1)(c) of the Regulation, the Slovak customs authorities also take actions in the case of goods which infringe, under Slovak law, a patent or a supplementary protection certificate,[8] a plant variety right,[9] a designation of origin or a geographical indication.[10]

(4) Moulds and matrices

24.11   Moulds and matrices which are specifically designated or adapted for the manufacture of goods infringing any of the above intellectual property rights can be stopped by Slovak Customs.

C. Goods excluded by the Regulation

(1) Parallel imported goods

24.12   Article 3(1), first indent, of the Regulation excludes genuine parallel imported goods from border measures. Although Slovak Customs are thus not entitled to detain or suspend release of (genuine) parallel imported goods, they will in practice inform the right-holder when they find such goods, even when they know that the goods are authentic.

(2) Goods which have been manufactured under conditions other than those which have been agreed with the right-holder

24.13   By virtue of Article 3(1), second indent, of the Regulation, the latter does not apply either to goods which have been manufactured under conditions other than those agreed with the right-holder and are subsequently discovered at the external borders of the Community. Accordingly, in the absence of any (alternative) domestic provisions allowing them to act otherwise, Slovak Customs will not take action in these situations.

(3) Goods contained in travellers' personal baggage

24.14   Under Article 3(2) of the Regulation, customs authorities from the Member States are not entitled to act against goods of a non-commercial nature contained in

---

[8] Cf Law No 435/2001 Coll on patents and supplementary protection certificates (Zákon o patentoch a dodatkových osvečeniach).

[9] Law No 291/1996 Coll on plant varieties and seeds (Zákon o odrodach a osivách).

[10] Law No 469/2003 Coll on designations of origin and geographical indications (Zákon o označení puovodu a zemepisných označeniach).

travellers' personal baggage, within the limits of the duty-free allowance, unless there are material indications to suggest that these goods are part of a commercial traffic.

Slovak Customs carry out random checks of travellers' personal baggage. In **24.15** order to determine whether the value of the goods exceed the limit of the duty-free allowance (that is, EUR 175) and thus to decide whether or not they should take action against goods which are contained in a traveller's personal baggage under Article 3(2) of the Regulation, the customs officers take into account the value of an authentic product or the purchase value of a counterfeit or pirated product. Usually, they appraise the (non-)commercial nature and the presence of material indications of the existence of a commercial traffic in the light of the features and quantity of the goods. Customs will also be guided by the provisions of Article 45 of EC Regulation 918/83.[11]

II. APPLICATION FOR ACTION BY THE CUSTOMS AUTHORITIES

A. Measures prior to an application for action by the customs authorities ('*ex officio* measures')

Both Article 4 of the Regulation and the 2004 Law allow Customs in the Slovak **24.16** Republic to act '*ex officio*' (that is, before an application for that purpose has been lodged by the holder of the right concerned or granted yet) against goods which they can reasonably suspect of infringing any of the intellectual property rights listed in Article 2 of the Regulation. Where they are sufficient grounds to presume that the goods are indeed infringing, Slovak Customs will ask the right-holder to provide them with any information they may need to confirm their suspicions. The declarant, owner or holder of the goods may require to be provided with a copy of the written decision of the customs authorities within the three-working day period of time provided for in Article 4(1) of the Regulation. As far as he is concerned, the right-holder must submit an application for action in accordance with Article 5 of the Regulation within this period. Failure to do so will lead to the release of the goods.

---

[11] Council Reg (EEC) No 918/83 of 28 March 1983 setting up a Community system of reliefs from customs duty, [1983] OJ L 105/1 (23.4.1983), as amended. Reference is made on this point to Chapter 3 of this book dealing specifically with EC Reg 1383/2003.

B. The lodging and processing of applications for customs action

(1) Persons entitled to file an application for action

Definition of 'right-holders' under the Regulation

24.17   Persons entitled to file an application for action under the Regulation are defined in Article 2(2) of the Regulation.

24.18   Licensees will obviously qualify as 'authorized users', and will therefore be in a position, in this capacity, to file an application for action by the customs authorities in the Slovak Republic. However, when the application relies on an industrial property right, the licence must be registered with the relevant Industrial Property Office (or the Office for the Harmonization in the National Market in the case of a licence of a Community trade mark), otherwise the licence will not be enforceable against third parties (including customs).

24.19   'Representatives' of the right-holder *stricto sensu* or an authorized user include patent and trade mark attorneys, attorneys-at-law, and any other natural and legal persons to whom the right-holder or authorized user granted a duly executed power of attorney.[12]

Proof of entitlement to file an application for action

For right-holders stricto sensu

24.20   When filing an application for action under Article 5 of the Regulation, the right-holder must submit evidence to customs that he holds the intellectual property right on which the application relies for the goods in question.[13] For that purpose, the application must contain a certificate of grant from the Industrial Property Office when it is based on a patent or a supplementary protection certificate, or a registration certificate from the Register maintained by that Office, when it is based on a utility model, an industrial design, a designation of origin, a geographical indication, or a plant variety right.[14]

24.21   For protected designations of origin and protected geographical indications, the proof required shall, in addition, consist in proof that the right-holder is the producer or group and proof that the designation or indication has been registered.[15]

24.22   In the case of a copyright, related right, or design right which is not registered or for which an application has not been lodged, any evidence of authorship or of the applicant's status as original holder shall be deemed sufficient.[16]

---

[12] Cf Reg 1891/2004 (n 2 above), Art 1.   [13] Reg 1383/2003, Art 5(5), second indent.
[14] Cf Reg 1891/2004 (n 2 above), Art 2(1), first indent, sub (a).
[15] Ibid, Art 2(1), last indent.   [16] Ibid, Art 2(1), first indent, sub (b).

Non-certified copies from an official database or the relevant (national, regional, **24.23** or international) Intellectual (or Industrial) Property Office may be submitted to customs and ought in such case be considered sufficient evidence. However, in practice, Slovak Customs will only accept such documents when they may have access to the database concerned. *A fortiori*, extracts from private databases will, as a general rule, not be admitted.

As mentioned above, a mere application (such as for example, a trade mark application) will not constitute an acceptable basis for the filing of an application for action by customs authorities, if the right in question has not yet been registered.

For persons authorized to use the right

In order to prove his capacity as 'authorized user' under Article 2(2)(b) of the **24.24** Regulation, the applicant must provide, in addition to the proof required from right-holders *stricto sensu*, a copy of his licence agreement with the right-holder to Slovak Customs.[17] Submission of such a document will be deemed satisfactory, and customs will therefore not verify whether the licensee is entitled under the terms of the contract to represent the right-holder before customs and to act on the latter's behalf. As has been pointed out above, when the application is based on an industrial property right, the authorization to use (that is, the licence) has to be registered with the relevant Industrial Property Office if it is to be declared enforceable against third parties, and thus to be accepted as proof of entitlement to act by customs.

For representatives

Where the application for action is lodged by a representative of the right-holder **24.25** or of any other person authorized to use one of the rights covered by the Regulation, in addition to the proof required respectively from right-holders (*stricto sensu*) and authorized users, consist in his authorization to act.[18] In other words, the representatives must add the proof in the application that they have the capacity to represent the right-holder, or the person authorized to use the right. This proof will consist in an original or certified copy of a duly executed power of attorney. General powers-of-attorney, valid for all customs action regarding the same intellectual property right, are accepted.

It should be stressed that foreign representatives without an office (or domicile) in **24.26** the Slovak Republic are *not* authorized to appear before Slovak Customs. One may question whether such a pre-emption complies with the European Community's well-established principle of freedom of services.

A representative must produce the declaration required pursuant to Article 6 of **24.27** the Regulation, signed by the right-holder (*stricto sensu*) or authorized user, or

---

[17] Ibid, Art 2(2).   [18] Ibid, Art 2(3), first indent.

a document authorizing him to bear any costs arising from customs action on their behalf in accordance with this provision.[19]

(2) *Competent customs department and formal requirements*

Competent customs department

24.28 The customs department competent under Article 5(2) of the Regulation to process applications for action is:

Colné riaditelstvo Slovenskej republiky (Customs Directorate of the Slovak Republic)
Mierova 23
SK-815 11 Bratislava
Slovakia
Tel: + 421 248 273 101
Fax: + 421 243 336 448
miccr@colnasprava.sk
Internet: www.colnasprava.sk

Form of the application for action

24.29 According to section 3 of the 2004 Law, an application for action can be filed either by letter, fax, or e-mail (miccr@colnasprava.sk). In the case of electronic filing, however, the applicant is obliged to submit a hard copy of the application within three days.

24.30 Two copies of the application for action should be submitted to customs.

The declaration under Article 6 may be submitted either in writing or by electronic means.[20] In the case of electronic filing, the applicant is obliged to submit the original of the declaration by post, together with the hard copy of the application, within three days.

Language requirements

24.31 The application form as well as the declaration under Article 6 of the Regulation must be filed in the Slovak language. If they are filed in another language, the applicant will be required to submit an authorized translation into Slovak. This language requirement applies regardless of whether the application consists of a

---

[19] Cf Reg 1891/2004 (n 2 above), Art 2(3), second indent.
[20] Reference can be made in this context to Art 5(3) of the Regulation, which provides that, where an electronic data interchange systems exist, the Member States shall encourage right-holders to lodge applications electronically. As can be acknowledged in this book, the Slovak Republic is one of the few member countries where electronic filing has been made possible to date.

'national' application, or a 'Community' application under Article 5(4) of the Regulation (that is, an application based on a Community right). When such a 'Community' application has been lodged through customs authorities in another Member State of the European Union and designates the Slovak Republic amongst the countries where the applicant seeks to have customs act, Slovak Customs will, in principle, require a translation of the application form into Slovak.

The language requirements in relation to the exhibits submitted together with the **24.33** application, (for example, technical documents and brochures, proof of entitlement to file the application, etc) are fortunately not applied as strictly as for the application form itself. The necessity to have such documents translated will depend on their nature and the language in which they are set up.

(3) Requirements regarding the contents of the application for action

Mandatory information

Pursuant to Article 5(5) of the Regulation, the application for action must be **24.34** made out on the forms attached to Implementing Regulation 1891/2004, and must contain all the information needed to enable the goods in question to be readily recognized by the customs authorities. In particular, it should contain an accurate and detailed technical description of the goods, any specific information the right-holder may have concerning the type or pattern of fraud, and the name and address of the contact person appointed by the right-holder. Although those contact persons do not have to be established or domiciled in the Slovak Republic, a local presence in the country is preferred for practical reasons.

The application for action must also contain the declaration required of the applic- **24.35** ant by Article 6 of the Regulation, and proof that the latter holds the rights for the goods in question.

Optional information

By way of indication and where known, the right-holder should, moreover, for- **24.36** ward in the application any other information he may have, such as the pre-tax value of the original goods on the legitimate market in the country in which the application for action is lodged, the location of the goods or their intended destination, particulars identifying the consignment or packages, the scheduled arrival or departure date of the goods, the means of transport used, the identity of the importer, exporter, or holder of the goods, the country or countries of production and the routes used by traffickers, and the technical differences between the genuine and suspect goods.[21]

---

[21] Reg 1383/2003, Art 5(5), last indent.

Additional information specific to the type of intellectual property right referred to in the application

24.37 Details may also be required by Slovak Customs which are specific to the type of intellectual property right referred to in the application for action, by virtue of Article 5(6) of the Regulation. Slovak Customs will most often not rely on this possibility, except where the specific circumstances of the case and nature of the goods require so.

(4) Processing and acceptance of the application for action

24.38 Pursuant to Article 5(7) of the Regulation, Slovak Customs must process applications for action and notify the applicants in writing of their decision within 30 working days of its receipt.

24.39 If the competent customs department decides not to process an application for action under Article 5(8) of the Regulation—because it does not contain the mandatory information listed in Article 5(5)—, the applicant may, within 15 days of notification of customs decision, appeal to the Ministry of Finance of the Slovak Republic in Bratislava.

24.40 When an application for action is granted, the period during which the Slovak customs authorities are to take action will usually be six months, except when the application relates to any of the 'Community-wide' intellectual property right listed in Article 5(4) of the Regulation, in which case the period for which customs will take action will be set at one year.[22] On expiry of the period in question, and subject to prior discharge of any debt owed by the right-holder under the Regulation, the customs department which processed the initial application shall, at the right-holder's request, extend that period.[23]

(5) 'Community' applications for action

24.41 Under Article 5(4) of the Regulation, where the applicant is the right-holder of a Community trade mark, a Community design right, a Community plant variety, or a designation of origin or geographical indication or a geographical designation protected by the Community, he may, in addition to requesting action by the customs authorities of the Member State in which it is lodged, request action by the customs authorities of one or more other Member States. Such 'Community' applications for action may therefore be filed through Slovak Customs and extend to other Member States, or be filed through the competent customs department in another Member State and designate, for example, the Slovak Republic as one

---

[22] Reg 1383/2003, Art 8(2), second indent.   [23] Ibid, Art 8(1).

of the member countries in which customs action is requested. The application must in such cases indicate the countries in which customs monitoring is sought, as well as the names and addresses of the right-holder (or authorized user, or their representatives) in each of the Member States concerned.[24]

III. CONDITIONS GOVERNING ACTION BY CUSTOMS AUTHORITIES AND BY THE AUTHORITIES COMPETENT TO DETERMINE WHETHER GOODS INFRINGE AN INTELLECTUAL PROPERTY RIGHT

A. Conditions governing action by customs authorities

(1) Factual background

The most important customs office in the Slovak Republic is *Colné riaditelstvo*   **24.42**
Slovenskej republiky (Customs Directorate of the Slovak Republic) in Bratislava, which is also the customs department competent to process applications for action under the Regulation in the Slovak Republic. The contact details of this department have already been indicated above.[25]

(2) Notification of customs intervention

Right-holders, and declarants and holders of suspected goods are usually notified   **24.43**
of a customs intervention under the Regulation by letter, fax, or e-mail.

(3) Information to be provided by customs to the right-holder before the right-holder confirms the infringing nature of the goods

Once goods suspected of infringing an intellectual property right are detained by   **24.44**
Slovak Customs, the relevant customs office shall inform the right-holder and the declarant or holder of the goods of its action as indicated in the previous paragraph, and is authorized to inform them of the actual or estimated quantity, the actual or supposed nature, and country of origin or destination of the goods whose release has been suspended or which have been detained, without the right-holder being bound by the communication of that information to notify

---

[24] Ibid, Art 5 (5), third indent.   [25] Para 24. 28 above.

the authority competent to take a substantive decision under Article 13 of the Regulation.[26]

24.45 Slovak Customs will inform the right-holder, at his request and if known, of the names and address of the consignee, the consignor, the declarant, or the holder of the goods, and the origin and provenance of goods suspected of infringing an intellectual property right.[27] The communication of the above information is subject to compliance 'with national provisions on the protection of personal data, commercial and industrial secrecy, and professional and administrative confidentiality',[28] which are contained, under Slovak law, in Law No 428/2002 Coll on the protection of personal data and commercial secrecy, as well as in the Commercial Law No 513/1991 Coll. However, in accordance with the case law of the European Court of Justice,[29] the provisions of these Laws do not preclude disclosure of the above information by Slovak Customs to the right-holder.

(4) Inspection of the suspected goods

24.46 Upon acceptance of his application for action by customs authorities, the right-holder will usually immediately be given the opportunity to inspect the goods whose release has been suspended or which have been detained. All persons involved enjoy the same right.[30] The Slovak customs offices may also hand over or send samples of the goods to the right-holder at his express request, for the purposes of analysis and to facilitate the subsequent procedure.[31] No rule in force in the Slovak Republic precludes this possibility.

B. Simplified procedure allowing the destruction of the goods without there being any need to determine whether an intellectual property right has been infringed under national law

24.47 The simplified procedure set out in Article 11 of the Regulation has not yet been implemented in the Slovak Republic, and one may fear that it will not be. Indeed, the 2004 Law, which was adopted subsequent to the Regulation, provides that the destruction of goods which are suspected of infringing an intellectual property right and have, as such, been detained by Slovak Customs, may only take place on the basis of a court decision concluding to the existence of such an infringement under national law, in the framework of proceedings initiated by the relevant right-holder under Article 13 of the Regulation.

---

[26] Reg 1383/2003, Art 9(2).   [27] Ibid, Art 9(3).   [28] Ibid.
[29] Cf, eg, ECJ, Case C-223–98, *Adidas v Kammarrätten i Stockholm*, [1999] ECR 7081.
[30] Reg 1383/2003, Art 9(3), second indent.   [31] Ibid, Art 9(3), third indent.

Slovak national law does not apply the presumption set out in Article 11 of the Regulation, that the destruction of the goods is deemed to be accepted when the declarant, holder or owner of the goods do not oppose the destruction within a specific deadline.

Having said that, it is important to point out that the 2004 Law does not preclude **24.49** the conclusion of settlement agreements concluded between the right-holder and the owner, declarant and/or holder of the goods. Pursuant to the Commercial Law and the various pieces of legislations dealing with intellectual property in the Slovak Republic, such contracts may be entered into in all phases of the proceedings. In practice, the right-holder and the owner, declarant and/or holder of the goods are therefore authorized to enter into such agreements, whereby the destruction of the goods is accepted on a voluntary basis. Although one may question whether this is allowed under Article 11 of the Regulation (which provides that the suspect goods must be destroyed in all cases), in practice, licensing agreements may also be concluded subsequent to a customs action in the Slovak Republic, whereby the release of the goods is authorized in view of their further commercialization.

C. Conditions governing action by the authorities having jurisdiction to determine whether the goods infringe an intellectual property right

(1) Authorities having jurisdiction to determine whether the goods infringe an intellectual property right

The courts are the only authorities having jurisdiction to determine whether **24.50** goods infringe an intellectual property right, within the meaning of Article 13 of the Regulation, in the Slovak Republic.

In the case of counterfeit goods, the right-holder's claims will rely on the Slovak **24.51** Trade Mark Law No 55/1997 Coll on Trade Marks, as amended by the Trade Mark Law No 577/2001 Coll so as to take into consideration Council Regulation (EC) No 40/94 on the Community Trade Mark.[32]

In the case of pirated goods, the right-holder's claims will rely on the Design Law **24.52** No 444/2002 Coll, on the Business Law No 513/1991 Coll, as well as on Council Regulation (EC) 6/2002 on Community Designs.[33]

In matters regarding patent infringements and infringements of a supplement- **24.53** ary protection certificate, the courts will handle the case of the basis of Law

---

[32] Cf n 4 above.　　　[33] Cf n 7 above.

No 435/2001 Coll on patents and supplementary protection certificates, and/or of Council Regulations (EC) No 1768/92[34] and No 1610/96.[35]

As to goods infringing a plant variety right, the right-holder's claims will be dealt with by the courts under Law No 291/96 Coll on plant varieties and seeds, and/or under Council Regulation (EC) No 2100/94.[36]

24.54 Goods infringing a designation of origin or a geographical indication are dealt with under Law No 469/2003 Coll on designations of origin and geographical indications, and/or Council Regulations (EEC) No 2081/92,[37] No 1576/89,[38] and No 1493/1999.[39]

(2) *Term for notifying customs that proceeding have been started*

24.55 Pursuant to Article 13 of the Regulation, the term of 10 working days provided for in this provision, within which customs must have been notified by the right-holder of the commencement of proceedings aimed at determining whether the goods infringe an intellectual property right, may be extended once 'in appropriate cases'. In practice, Slovak Customs will judge upon the appropriateness of an extension in the light of the circumstances put forward by the right-holder in his request for term extension.

D. Release of goods suspected of infringing certain rights on provision of a security

24.56 In accordance with Article 14 of the Regulation, Slovak Customs will release the goods, provided that the relevant customs office or department has not been notified within a period of 10 working days that proceedings have been initiated before the courts to establish whether an intellectual property right has been infringed under national law, that the authority empowered for this purpose has not authorized precautionary measures before the expiry of the time limit laid

---

[34] Council Reg (EEC) No 1768/92 of 18 June 1992 concerning the creation of a supplementary protection certificate for medicinal products, OJ L 182/1 (2.7.1992).

[35] Reg (EC) No 1610/96 of the European Parliament and of the Council of 23 July 1996 concerning the creation of a supplementary protection certificate for plant protection products, [1996] OJ L 198/30 (8.8.1996).

[36] Council Reg (EC) No 2100/94 of 27 July 1994 on Community plant variety rights, [994] OJ L 227/1 (1.9.1994).

[37] Council Reg (EEC) No 2081/92 of 14 July 1992 on the protection of geographical indications and designations of origin for agricultural products and foodstuffs, [1992] OJ L 208/1 (24.7.1992).

[38] Council Reg (EEC) No 1576/89 of 29 May 1989 laying down general rules on the definition, description and presentation of spirit drinks, [1989] OJ L 160/1 (12.6.1989).

[39] Council Reg (EC) No 1493/1999 of 17 May 1999 on the common organization of the market in wine, [1999] OJ L 179/1 (14.7.1999).

down in Article 13(1) of the Regulation, and that all customs formalities have been completed.

E. Storage of the goods

The conditions for storage of the goods during the period of suspension of release **24.57**
or detention of the goods are regulated by section 7 of the 2004 Law, which mirrors the provisions of Article 50 ff of the Community Customs Code[40] Such goods 'in temporary storage' will only be stored as approved by customs and under their supervision.

As regards the issue of costs, it should be recalled that applications for action under **24.58**
the Regulation must be accompanied by a declaration from the applicant that he agrees to bear all costs incurred in keeping goods under customs control,[41] which includes storage costs.

IV. PROVISIONS APPLICABLE TO GOODS FOUND TO INFRINGE AN INTELLECTUAL PROPERTY RIGHT

If, as a result of Article 13 proceedings, goods are, on the basis of a court decision, **24.59**
found to infringe an intellectual property right, the relevant customs office issues a decision to the effect that the goods shall not be allowed to enter or leave the Community customs territory, be released for free circulation, exported, re-exported, placed under a suspensive procedure, or placed in a free zone or a free warehouse.[42]

Under section 10 of the 2004 Law, the right-holder concerned may in such cases ask **24.60**
customs to take care of the destruction of all infringing goods, or to make sure that these goods be disposed of outside commercial channels.[43] The holder of the goods will most often be condemned by the courts to bear the costs for the destruction of the goods. If the holder of the goods has not been identified and has therefore not been brought before the courts, the destruction costs will be borne by customs.

In exceptional cases, and subject to the right-holder's prior consent in writing, **24.61**
the relevant customs office may relinquish counterfeit goods free of charge to charities (for humanitarian purposes), after having removed the trade marks which have

---

[40] Council Reg (EEC) No 2913/92 of 12 October 1992 establishing the Community Customs Code, [1992] OJ L 302/1 (19.10.1992). [41] Reg 1383/2003, Art 6(1), second indent.
[42] Cf Ibid, Art 16. [43] Cf Ibid, Art 17 (1), first indent.

been affixed to the goods.[44] In such a case, the goods may be surrendered to social services organizations, health establishments, and non-profit organizations only.

V. PENALTIES

24.62 In addition to the destruction of the goods, or the disposal thereof outside commercial channels in such a way as to preclude injury to the right-holder,[45] the Slovak customs authorities are entitled under the 2004 Law to apply administrative penalties consisting in fines.

VI. LIABILITY OF CUSTOMS AUTHORITIES AND RIGHT-HOLDERS

A. Liability of right-holders and sanctions

24.63 Under section 4 of the 2004 Law and Article 6 of the Regulation, the right-holder must enclose with his application for action by Slovak customs authorities a declaration whereby he accepts liability towards the persons involved in the event that a procedure initiated by customs, on an application from the right-holder, is discontinued owing to an act or omission by the right-holder, or in the event that the goods in question are subsequently found not to infringe an intellectual property right. Under Article 19(3) of the Regulation, such liability claims shall be governed by the law of the Slovak Republic.

B. Liability of customs authorities and sanctions

24.64 Slovak national law does not contain any provision on compensation to the right-holder in the event that goods are not detected by a customs office and are released, or in the event that no action is taken to detain them.

Conclusion

24.65 Further to the adoption of the new Regulation and its Implementing Regulation, the Slovak legislator adopted Law No 200/2004 Coll, 'laying down the measures

---

[44] Cf Reg 1383/2003, Art 17 (1), second indent.   [45] Cf paras 24.60–24.61 above.

to be taken against imported, exported and parallel imported goods which infringe an intellectual property right'. This new Law, which came into force on 1 July 2004, allows Slovak Customs to enforce in an efficient way the provisions of the new Regulation in respect of goods suspected of infringing an industrial property right, or a copyright, or related right. This new legal framework will be subject to amendments in the light of the experience gathered in the application of the Regulation and, more generally, of the *acquis communautaire* further to accession to the European Union.

25

SLOVENIA[1]

Gregor Maček and Andrej Bukovnik

Introduction

Prior to Slovenia's entry into the European Union on 1 May 2004, border   **25.01**
measures were regulated by the Customs Code[2] and the Law on Customs
Measures Relating to Infringements of Intellectual Property Rights.[3] Both pieces
of legislation were in line with the *acquis communautaire* on border measures, and
the Slovenian customs authorities enforced them effectively.

On 1 May 2004, both the Customs Code and the Law on customs measures were   **25.02**
repealed and replaced by EC Regulation 3295/94[4] and the Law on the
Implementation of the European Union Regulations on Customs Measures ('the
Customs Measures Law').[5] Since 1 July 2004, border measures against goods
suspected of infringing an intellectual property right are regulated by EC
Regulation 1383/2003[6] ('the Regulation'), the Implementing Regulation

---

[1] In this chapter, 'Slovenia' shall be used to mean the Republic of Slovenia.
[2] Carinski zakon, Official Journal of the Republic of Slovenia ('OJ RS') No 1-3/1995, as
amended on 26 May 1995, OJ RS 28-1288/1995; on 6 May 1999, OJ RS 32-1515/1999; on
28 May 1999, OJ RS 40-1/1999, and on 5 July 2002, OJ RS 59-283/2002.
[3] Zakon o carinskih ukrepih pri krsitvah pravic intelektualne lastnine, OJ RS No 30/2001.
[4] Council Reg (EC) 3295/94 of 22 December 1994 laying down measures to prohibit the release
for free circulation, export, re-export or entry for a suspensive procedure of counterfeit and pirated
goods [1994] OJ L 341/8 (22. 12. 1994), as amended by Council Reg 241/1999 (OJ L 27/1 (2. 2.
1999)) and by Council Reg (EC) 806/2003 [2003] OJ L 122/1. Cf also Commission Reg (EC)
1367/95 of 16 June 1995 laying down provisions for the implementation of Council Reg (EC)
3295/94 laying down measures concerning the entry into the Community and the export and
re-export from the Community of goods infringing certain intellectual property rights [1995] OJ L
133/2 (17. 6. 1995), as amended by Commission Reg (EC) 2549/1999 of 2 December 1999 [1999]
OJ L 308/16 (3. 12. 1999).
[5] Zakon o izvajanju carinskih predpisov Evropske skupnosti, OJ RS No 25-1064/2004.
[6] Council Reg (EC) 1383/2003 of 22 July 2003 concerning customs action against goods
suspected of infringing certain intellectual property rights and the measures to be taken against
goods found to have infringed such rights [2003] OJ L 196/7 (02. 08. 2003).

1891/2004 ('the Implementing Regulation'),[7] and the above-mentioned implementation Law.

25.03 The Customs Measures Law is an implementation law, and therefore it does not extend beyond the scope of the Regulation. This Law also contains a few transitional provisions dealing with the period between Slovenia's accession to the European Union and the entry into force of the Regulation.

25.04 Unlike the 2001 Customs Measures Law, EC Regulation 1383/2003 provides for the simplified procedure, that is, under certain circumstances allows the destruction of counterfeits without the judgment of the Civil Court. Furthermore, EC Regulation 1383/2003 provides for the handing over of the samples by the customs to the right-holder for further analysis. Another important difference is that under the 2001 Customs Measures Law the right-holder had to provide customs with a bank guarantee which was realized to cover the storage costs in case the customs measures proved to be unjustified.

I. SUBJECT MATTER AND SCOPE OF THE NATIONAL LAW APPLYING THE REGULATION

A. Customs procedure of the goods

25.05 Slovenian Customs apply the Regulation 1383/2003 directly, and without any restrictions or limitations with regard to the customs procedure of the goods. This means that the Slovenian Customs take action against suspected goods in any of the situations referred to in Article 1(1) of the Regulation, including for example, export and re-export, external transit and transhipment.

B. Definition of infringing goods

(1) Counterfeit goods

25.06 Slovenian Customs will take action (where appropriate even *ex officio*) against goods bearing without authorization a sign identical to, or which cannot be

---

[7] Commission Reg (EC) 1891/2004 of 21 October 2004 laying down provisions for the implementation of Council Reg (EC) 1383/2003 concerning customs action against goods suspected of infringing certain intellectual property rights and the measures to be taken against goods found to have infringed such rights [2004] OJ L 328/16 (30. 10. 2004).

distinguished in its essential aspect from, a registered trade mark. Customs will therefore take action against goods defined as counterfeit under Article 2(1)(a) of the Regulation, even where the trade mark affixed to the goods is not completely identical to the (earlier) registered trade mark: both signs need only be substantially similar.

Where the relevant trade mark holder has filed an application for action **25.07** under Article 5 of the Regulation, customs are also prepared to detain or suspend the release of goods even if the sign affixed on those goods is only slightly similar to the trade mark on which the application for action is based. The final determination of whether the goods infringe trade mark rights will be resolved by the courts in the infringement action proceedings. Therefore, in practice, Slovenian Customs will seldom refuse to detain or suspend the release of alleged counterfeit goods upon the trade mark holder's explicit request.

The same approach will be adopted as regards the definition of the type of **25.08** goods against which action will be taken. That is, Slovenian Customs will prove reasonably flexible when determining whether the suspect sign is affixed to goods 'of the same type' as those for which the trade mark concerned has been registered, provided that the holder of that trade mark has lodged an application for action under Article 5 of the Regulation. In certain circumstances, customs agree to detain or suspend the release of goods which are not covered by the trade mark registration, provided however they are very similar to those for which the trade mark is registered, or provided the trade mark in question is considered by the respective customs officer as a 'well known' trade mark (for example, customs would probably be eager to block a shipment of t-shirts bearing without authorization a well-known trade mark for mobile phones). For obvious reasons, the customs authorities will be more reluctant to adopt border measures *ex officio* against goods which are only slightly similar to those for which the trade mark is registered, as in such cases their civil liability might be at stake.

As provided by Article 2(1)(a) of the Regulation, however, Slovenian Customs **25.09** will only agree to take action on the basis of a 'validly registered trade mark', and thus not on the basis of simple trade mark applications.

Finally, having regard to the definition of 'counterfeit goods' under Article **25.10** 2(1)(a) of the Regulation, Slovenian Customs will also take measures against trade mark symbols (including logos, labels, stickers, brochures, instructions for use, or guarantee documents bearing such symbols), as well as against packaging materials, bearing a counterfeit trade mark, even if they are delivered separately.

25.11   According to Article 47 of the Slovenian Industrial Property Law[8] the holder of a trade mark has the right to prevent others from using without his consent:

(a)   any sign identical to the trade mark in relation to goods or services identical to those for which the trade mark is registered;

(b)   any sign where, because of its identity with or similarity to the trade mark and the identity or similarity of the goods or services covered by the trade mark and the sign, there exists a likelihood of confusion on the part of the public, which includes the likelihood of association between the sign and the trade mark;

(c)   any sign which is identical or similar to the trade mark in relation to goods and services which are not similar to those for which the trade mark is registered, where the mark has a reputation in the Republic of Slovenia, and where the use without due cause of the sign would take unfair advantage of, or be detrimental to, the distinctive character or the repute of the trade mark.

25.12   The definition of trade mark infringement under Slovenian Industrial Property Law extends beyond the definition of 'counterfeit goods' under the Regulation. In practice this means that when customs are deciding whether to detain or suspend the release of the goods, they will take into consideration the narrow definition of the Regulation. The courts, however will establish the infringement based on the provisions of the Industrial Property Law.

25.13   The following forms of use of the above-mentioned signs are inter alia considered as an infringement of the trade mark according to the Industrial Property Law:

(a)   affixing the sign to the goods or to the packaging thereof;

(b)   offering or putting the goods on the market under that sign or offering or supplying services under that sign, or stocking the goods for these purposes;

(c)   importing or exporting the goods under that sign;

(d)   using the sign on business papers and in advertising.

25.14   Under Article 16 of the Regulation, the transit, re-export, transhipment, and placement in a free zone or free warehouse of counterfeit goods are also considered as trade mark infringements in Slovenia.

(2)   Pirated goods

25.15   Slovenian Customs are careful when it comes to detecting goods suspected of infringing a copyright, related right or design right, as it is often difficult to determine which goods are, or contain, unauthorized copies of a protected subject

---

[8]   Zakon o industrijski lastnini, OJ RS No 45-2547/2001, as amended on 14 November 2002, OJ RS 96-4798/2002 and on 15 April 2004, OJ RS 37-1601/2004.

matter. Therefore, customs seldom act *ex officio* against such types of (suspected) intellectual property infringements in Slovenia.

However, where the right-holder explicitly claims that a particular shipment **25.16** contains pirated goods, the customs authorities will detain, or suspend release of, this consignment, without assessing in detail whether the goods are, or contain, *identical* copies or simply a *similar* version of the genuine products.

Under the Copyright and Related Rights Law[9] a product infringes a copyright or **25.17** related right in Slovenia, among others, when it consists of an unauthorized reproduction or adaptation of the original work or performance, or is distributed without the right-holder's consent.

Pursuant to Article 37 of the Industrial Property Law, a design is infringed under **25.18** Slovenian law by producing, offering, putting on the market, importing, exporting, or using of a product to which the protected design is applied, or storing such a product for these purposes. Under Slovenian law, a product infringes a design when its appearance is identical or similar to the design to such an extent that it does not make a different overall impression on the informed consumer.

The definition of the design infringement and infringement of copyright or a **25.19** related right according to the Regulation is narrower than the one under the Industrial Property Law and Copyright and Related Rights Law. In practice this means that when customs are deciding whether to detain or suspend the release of the goods, they will take into consideration the narrow definition of the Regulation. The courts, however will establish the infringement based on the provisions of the Industrial Property Law and Copyright and Related Rights Law.

(3) Goods infringing other intellectual property rights

Goods infringing a patent or a supplementary protection certificate

According to Article 18 of the Industrial Property Law, a patent or a supplement- **25.20** ary protection certificate are infringed when third parties, not having the right-holder's consent: (i) produce, use, offer for sale, sell, or import products covered by the patent, or (ii) use the process recited in the patent, and/or offer for sale, sell, or import products obtained directly from that process.

The Regulation refers to the Member States' national legislations to define which **25.21** goods infringe patents or supplementary protection certificates, so customs will decide based on the definitions under the Industrial Property Law.

---

[9] Zakon o avtorskih in sorodnih pravicah, OJ RS No 21-958/1995, as amended on 9 February 2001, OJ RS 9-531/2001, and on 26 April 2004, OJ 43-1927/2004.

Goods infringing a national plant variety right

25.22 By virtue of Article 15 of the Plant Variety Protection Law[10] a plant variety right is infringed in Slovenia when the protected plant variety is used, without the holder's consent, for: (i) production and reproduction of propagating material; (ii) conditioning for the purpose of propagating; (iii) marketing, including import and export of propagating material; and (iv) stocking of the material of the protected variety.

25.23 The Regulation refers to the Member States' national legislations to define which goods infringe plant variety right, so customs will decide based on the definitions under the Plant Variety Protection Law.

Goods infringing a national designation of origin or a geographical indication

25.24 Pursuant to Article 58 of the Industrial Property Law and Articles 49–50 of the Agriculture Law[11] national designations of origin and geographical indications are infringed where:

— they are used by an unauthorized person,
— the goods do not originate in the place indicated by the designation of origin or the geographical indication, even if the true origin of the goods is indicated, or
— the designation of origin or the geographical indication is used by an unauthorized person in translation or accompanied by expressions such as 'kind', 'type', 'style', 'imitation', or the like.

25.25 The Regulation refers to the Member States' national legislations to define which goods infringe designations of origin and geographical indications, so customs will decide based on the definitions under the Industrial Property Law and Agriculture Law.

(4) Moulds and matrices

25.26 Under Article 2(3) of the Regulation, Slovenian Customs are also to take border measures against moulds or matrices which are specifically designed or adapted for manufacturing goods that infringe any of the above intellectual property rights, since their use results in an infringement of those rights under Slovenian law. Indeed, by virtue of Article 121 of the Industrial Property Law and Article 167 of the Copyright and Related Rights Law, the right-holders may request the destruction of such moulds or matrices.

---

[10] Zakon o varstvu novih sort rastlin, OJ RS No. 86/1998.
[11] Zakon o kmetijstvu, OJ RS No. 54-2497/2000 as amended on April 29, 2004, OJ RS 45 2131/2004.

C. Goods excluded by the Regulation

(1) Parallel imported goods

Since the customs authorities of the Member States of the European Union are **25.27**
not entitled to detain or suspend the release of (genuine) parallel imported goods
under the Regulation,[12] and since there is no national legislation in Slovenia
allowing customs to act accordingly, such goods cannot be apprehended by
Slovenian Customs. The latter will, of course, inform the right-holder when they
are not sure whether the goods are non-authentic or genuine. However, where
there is no doubt that the goods are authentic, the relevant right-holder will not
be informed about the importation.

(2) Goods which have been manufactured under conditions other than those which have been agreed with the right-holder

Like with parallel imported goods, border measures cannot be taken under the **25.28**
Regulation against goods which have been manufactured under conditions other
than those agreed to with the right-holder. Neither does any alternative (national)
legislation allow Slovenian Customs to detain, or suspend the release, of such
goods on that ground alone.

(3) Goods contained in travellers' personal baggage

Travellers' personal baggage may be controlled by Slovenian Customs. However, **25.29**
in accordance with Article 3(2) of the Regulation, goods of a non-commercial
nature found in a traveller's personal baggage, the value of which does not exceed
the limits of the duty-free allowance (EUR 175), will not be subject to border
measures under the Regulation, unless there are material indications to suggest
they are part of commercial traffic. The decision whether or not to control a
baggage is at the discretion of customs officers.

When determining whether goods contained in a traveller's personal baggage are **25.30**
within the limits of the duty-free allowance, their value may be estimated in different ways, the most common method being to take into account their purchase
value.

The commercial or non-commercial nature of the goods will be appraised having **25.31**
regard to the quantity and purpose of the goods. Goods of a non-commercial nature
should be intended for personal, individual, or family use. The determination of

---

[12] Cf Reg 1383/2003, Art 3 (1), first indent.

whether the goods are of a non-commercial nature is within the discretion of the customs officers, and depends on the circumstances of each case.

II APPLICATION FOR ACTION BY THE CUSTOMS AUTHORITIES

A. Measures prior to an application for action by the customs authorities ('*ex officio* measures')

25.32 Slovenian Customs regularly take action *ex officio* under Article 4 of the Regulation. In compliance with this provision, they will detain or suspend the release of any suspected goods for three working days, during which the right-holder may file an application for action. This initial three day-period is applied very strictly.

25.33 The customs authorities will act *ex officio* if they have sufficient grounds for suspecting that the goods infringe an intellectual property right. The quality of the goods and their packaging, their origin, their declared value in relation to market value, the identity of the consignor or consignee, etc are taken into consideration when carrying out the risk analysis. The success of the assessment will obviously strongly depend on the customs officers' experience.

25.34 During the three-working day period provided for in Article 4(1) of the Regulation, customs will inform the right-holder or his representative of the detention or suspension of release of the goods, and will usually send digital photographs of the goods to the right-holder concerned. If available, they will also provide information regarding the names and addresses of the consignee, the consignor, the declarant, or the owner of the suspected goods, as well as their origin, destination, and quantity. Although customs are not obliged to provide the right-holder or his representative with the digital photographs and available information during the three working day-period, customs in practice will usually do so.

25.35 In the framework of *ex officio* actions, it is essential for customs to be able to identify the relevant right-holder or his representative in Slovenia. To that end, the customs officers will sometimes look for distributors of the genuine products in Slovenia, or the right-holder's legal representatives, whose contact details can in some cases be found, for example, in the databases available on the Internet (such as the trade mark or patent databases). In practice, unfortunately, customs will not bother with the shipment if they cannot trace those persons. This emphasizes the obvious advantage for right-holders of lodging an application for action under Article 5 of the Regulation with the Slovenian customs authorities.

B. The lodging and processing of applications for customs action

(1) Persons entitled to file an application for action

Definition of 'right-holders' under the Regulation

An application for action under the Regulation may be filed either by the actual **25.36** owner of any of the intellectual property rights listed in Article 2 of the Regulation, by any other persons authorized to use such rights, or by their respective representatives. The category 'authorized users' includes exclusive licensees (as they may sue for infringement before the civil courts), as well as any other persons having the right to use any of the following collective rights: (i) a collective trade mark, (ii) a designation of origin, and (iii) a geographical indication. To date there have been no applications for action filed by exclusive licensees or other 'authorized users'.

Non-exclusive licensees, commercial agents, distributors, etc will in principle not **25.37** qualify as 'authorized users' under Article 2(2) of the Regulation, as they are not allowed by law to initiate infringement claims under Slovenian intellectual property law. They may, however, file an application for action in the name of the persons defined in the previous paragraph, as 'representatives', in which case they must submit a power.

Both natural and legal persons may act as representatives of the owner or autho- **25.38** rized user of the right in question. There are no specific requirements under Slovenian law on this point, except that a valid power must be provided.

Proof of entitlement to file an application for action

For right-holders stricto sensu

In order to prove entitlement to the intellectual property right on which his **25.39** application for action is based, the right-holder (in the narrow sense) must demonstrate that he is the owner of either:

— trade mark rights, by providing a copy or a printout from the relevant trade mark register, or from the trade mark database maintained by the office in question (which may be either the Slovenian Intellectual Property Office (for national trade mark registrations),[13] the World Intellectual Property

---

[13] http://www.uil-sipo.si/.

Organization ('WIPO') (for international trade mark registrations), or the Office for Harmonization in the Internal Market ('OHIM') (for Community trade marks));

— registered design rights, by providing a copy or a printout from the register of designs, or from the design database maintained by the office in question (which may be either the Slovenian Intellectual Property Office (for international design registrations), WIPO (for international registrations), or OHIM (for Community designs));

— copyrights or related rights, by providing a certificate of registration where available, or a sample of the genuine goods or a contract evidencing that the applicant for customs action holds such rights. Although the registration of the copyrights and related rights in Slovenia is optional, it is nevertheless useful to obtain it for it is much easier to prove the existence of the right to customs.

— patent rights, or rights arising from a supplementary protection certificate, by providing a copy or a printout from the patent register, or a printout from the patent database maintained by the office in question (for example, the Slovenian Intellectual Property Office or the European Patent Office);

— plant variety rights, by providing a copy of the certificate of registration;

— a designation of origin, or a geographical indication, by providing a copy of the certificate of registration.

25.40 An application for action may be based only on validly registered or granted right(s). An application for action based on a simple *application* for a particular intellectual property right will therefore be rejected. Copyrights, related rights and unregistered Community designs are the only exceptions to this principle, because their coming into existence is not subject to registration.

For persons authorized to use the right

25.41 As well as the documents referred to in the previous section (paras 25.39–25.40), authorized users must submit proof of their authorization to use the right concerned. In the case of a collective trade mark, the applicant must provide proof of its registration, the regulations governing use and evidence of compliance with the regulation requirements. For designations of origin and geographical indications, the applicant must show that he originates from the respective area, and that all other requirements for using the respective right have been complied with. An exclusive licensee must provide a copy of the licence agreement pursuant to which he enjoys this capacity.

25.42 Customs will usually not verify in detail the presented documents, unless there is obvious uncertainty as to whether they entitle the person to use the intellectual property right on which the application for action is based. In such circumstances, the customs authorities will request additional documentation.

Under Slovenian law, an authorization to use an industrial property right (arising, **25.43** for example, from a licence agreement) need not be registered to be enforceable against third parties (including the customs authorities).

For representatives

In addition to the above evidential material, any legal or natural person representing **25.44** the owner or authorized user of the right in question before the Slovenian customs authorities must submit a power of attorney duly executed by the right-holder or authorized user. The details of the owner or authorized user of the intellectual property right, as mentioned in the power of attorney, must match those indicated in the relevant registration certificates or other documents proving the existence of that right. The power of attorney must be submitted in the original, but need not be notarized or legalized. The general power of attorney concerning all customs actions may be delivered to customs.

Although a local presence in Slovenia is not imposed on representatives under **25.45** Slovenian law, in practice, Slovenian Customs will agree to liaise only with those representatives who have a domicile or office in Slovenia.

The declaration referred to in Article 6 of the Regulation must in principle always **25.46** be signed by the right-holder. A representative of the right-holder cannot sign the declaration in the name of the right-holder, unless he has been explicitly empowered to do so.

(2) Competent customs department and formal requirements

Competent customs department

The contact details of the customs department competent to process applications **25.47** for action pursuant to Article 5(2) of the Regulation are as follows:

Carinska uprava Republike Slovenije (*Customs Administration of the Republic of Slovenia*)

Generalni carinski urad (*General Customs Directorate*)
Šmartinska 55
SLO-1523 Ljubljana
Slovenia
Tel.: + 386 1 478 38 00
Fax: + 386 1 478 39 00
E-mail: ipr.curs@gov.si
Website: http://carina.gov.si/angl/index.htm

Form of the application for action

25.48 Any application for action under the Regulation must be handed over or sent by mail to the customs department competent to process it, namely, the General Customs Directorate in Slovenia (cf para 25.47 above). Filing by electronic means is not accepted. However, Slovenian Customs will accept an application sent by fax initially, provided an original copy follows by mail. The original may be submitted after expiry of the deadline set out in Article 4 of the Regulation, provided that the fax has been sent in time.

25.49 Until the entry into force of Implementing Regulation 1891/2004 on 30 October 2004, it was considered sufficient to submit one single copy of the application. Since that date, however, Article 3(3) of this Regulation provides that applications for action must be filed in duplicate.

25.50 As to the declaration referred to in Article 6 of the Regulation, it must be signed and submitted in the original. However, it does not have to be notarized or legalized.

Language requirements

25.51 According to Slovenian Customs' current practice and General Administrative Procedure Law,[14] the application for action must be filed in Slovenian. Applications lodged in other languages will not be accepted. Where the application for action is based on a Community right under Article 5(4) of the Regulation and is lodged through the Slovenian customs authorities, it must be filed both in Slovenian and English. Customs will then forward the English version of the application to the customs authorities in the other Member States concerned.

25.52 Evidence and additional documentation submitted together with the application for action may be in any language as long as the basic information which is being given to customs is evident or easily understood by the officers (for example, a brochure showing the appearance of the original product may be in any language, as the relevant part is the picture).

25.53 Slovenian Customs also accept certificates and printouts of international or Community trade marks or designs in French or in English.

25.54 The rule remains, however, that if a document cannot be understood by customs officers, they may request a translation.

25.55 The declaration referred to in Article 6 of the Regulation must be filed in Slovenian. Customs will, however, also accept a bilingual declaration (in

---

[14] *Zakon o splosnem upravnem postopku*, OJ RS No. 80/1999 as last amended on July 5, 2004, OJ RS 73/2004.

Slovenian and one other language), or a declaration in a foreign language accompanied by a certified translation into Slovenian.

(3) Requirements regarding the contents of the application for action

Mandatory information

Pursuant to Article 5(5) of the Regulation, the application must contain all the information needed to enable customs readily to recognize the goods in question, in particular a technical description of the goods, any specific information the applicant may have about the type or pattern of fraud, and the name and address of the contact person(s) appointed by the applicant. The application for action must also contain the declaration referred to in Article 6 of the Regulation, and proof that the applicant holds the right for the goods in question. In practice, the applicant must make sure to provide information concerning the right on which the application is based, and specify to which goods this right refers. **25.56**

It goes without saying that the more details and additional information on how to detect and recognize the infringing goods are provided, the better the chances are that customs will find suspected goods. **25.57**

Although there are no explicit provisions on this issue, Slovenian Customs agree to liaise only with representatives and contact persons domiciled in Slovenia. All communications will take place in the Slovenian language. **25.58**

Optional information

The applicant should also submit, by way of indication, any useful additional information, such as for example, the designation and packaging of the infringing goods, and any other visual characteristics of the infringing goods or markings on these goods, if known. The same applies to information concerning shipment(s) of suspect goods which are expected or have already arrived in Slovenia, and the features of the genuine products, and the identity of all distributors, licensees, and importers of such goods. **25.59**

Additional information specific to the type of intellectual property right referred to in the application

In accordance with Article 5(6) of the Regulation, Slovenian Customs may (and will at times) request additional details where appropriate, in particular in relation to goods which are protected by an intellectual property right involving technical considerations. This might for instance help them determine the scope of protection of the right on which the application for action relies, when doubts arise on this point. **25.60**

(4) Processing and acceptance of the application for action

25.61 Applications for action are usually processed by Slovenian Customs within a relatively short period of time, that is, between 5 to 10 days, provided it is complete. If the application is incomplete, the General Customs Directorate contacts the applicant to clarify any matters before granting the application. If customs decide not to process an application for action pursuant to Article 5(8) of the Regulation, the applicant may initiate administrative proceedings before the Administrative Court of proper jurisdiction to challenge this decision in accordance with Article 70 of the Customs Measures Law.

25.62 Once the application is granted, the Slovenian customs offices will take action against any suspect goods for a maximum period of one year. Save for Community applications for action, the applicant may request that this period be shorter than one year.

(5) 'Community' applications for action

25.63 Slovenia joined the European Union on 1 May 2004. Customs' practice regarding 'Community' applications for action under Article 5(4) of the Regulation is still in development.

Processing of 'Community' applications for action filed with Slovenian Customs

25.64 As pointed out above (para 25.51), the 'Community' applications for action filed through the Slovenian customs authorities must be made out in both Slovenian and English, and must designate the Member States in which the right-holder requests action by customs. Slovenian Customs will subsequently forward the English version of the application to the competent customs departments in those Member States.

Processing of 'Community' applications for action filed in other Member States and designating Slovenia

25.65 Where a 'Community' application for action is lodged in another Member State of the European Union, and Slovenia is designated in that application as one of the countries in which the right-holder seeks action by the customs authorities, the application form will be forwarded to Slovenian Customs, together with the enclosed documents. Usually, a CD containing the relevant information is enclosed with the application. Next, Slovenian Customs acknowledge receipt of the application and inform all local customs offices in Slovenia of it. Customs will not request the 'Community' application to be translated into Slovenian.

III. CONDITIONS GOVERNING ACTION BY CUSTOMS AUTHORITIES AND BY THE AUTHORITIES COMPETENT TO DETERMINE WHETHER GOODS INFRINGE AN INTELLECTUAL PROPERTY RIGHT

A. Conditions governing action by customs authorities

(1) Factual background

The most important customs office dealing with anti-counterfeiting (in the broad **25.66** sense) in Slovenia is the Koper Customs Office (Vojkovo nabrezje 36, SLO-6000 Koper/Capodistria). This office controls the port of Koper, which is the main harbour in Slovenia, and also one of the most important ones in the northern Adriatic Sea. This office also controls the southern part of the Slovenian border with Croatia.

(2) Notification of customs intervention

Where Slovenian Customs are satisfied that goods are suspected of infringing an **25.67** intellectual property right covered by the decision granting the application, they suspend the release of the goods or detain them, and inform the right-holder. This notification is made in writing in the form of a formal decision. Given the short terms imposed by the Regulation, customs will in principle, whenever possible, send their decision initially by fax, followed by a confirmation by mail. Where customs have been provided with the telephone number of the contact person designated in the application for action, they will also often contact him even before issuing a formal decision on detention or suspension of release of the goods, in order to consult him, and thus establish whether he confirms their suspicions. This might result in the avoidance of genuine goods being unduly detained (or their release suspended).

The declarant or holder of the goods will be informed of the detention or suspens- **25.68** ion of release of the goods at the same time as the right-holder. In most cases, the customs authorities will liaise with the forwarding agent, who is considered to be a declarant or his representative.

(3) Information to be provided by customs to the right-holder before the
right-holder confirms the infringing nature of the goods

25.69 Once goods suspected of infringing an intellectual property right are officially detained, or their release suspended, customs will provide the right-holder with all available information concerning:

— the actual or estimated quantity and the nature of the goods (including a basic description of the characteristics of the goods),
— their declared value,
— the names and addresses of the declarant, holder, consignor, and/or consignee of the goods,
— their country of origin and/or destination of the goods.

25.70 Where, on the basis of the aforesaid information, the right-holder notifies customs that the goods do not infringe his rights, the latter will release the goods, or their detention will be ended.

25.71 Occasionally, customs will provide some of the above-mentioned information to the right-holder even prior to officially detaining or suspending release of the goods. In such cases, however, the information supplied will usually be limited.

25.72 There are no limitations under Slovenian law as to the extent to which the above information may be divulged to the right-holder, provided that this information is intended to enable the right-holder to enforce his intellectual property rights.

(4) Inspection of the suspected goods

25.73 The right-holder is given the opportunity to inspect the suspect goods at any time during the procedure—after being notified of a customs intervention, and subsequent to acceptance of his application for action. At the right-holder's request, customs will send or hand samples of the goods over to him for the purposes of analysis. In practice, the samples are seldom returned to the customs authorities on completion of the technical analysis, although Article 9(3) of the Regulation explicitly requires so. Customs are also eager to provide digital photographs of the goods upon the right-holder's request.

B. Simplified procedure allowing the destruction of the goods without there being any need to determine whether an intellectual property right has been infringed under national law

25.74 The simplified procedure laid down in Article 11 of the Regulation has been implemented in Slovenia through the Customs Measures Law, with effect as of 1 May 2004.

Under Articles 71 and 72 of the Customs Measures Law, the suspect goods will be **25.75** destroyed at the right-holder's expense, without there being any need for him to initiate court proceedings, in the following cases:

1. Where the right-holder submits to Slovenian Customs, within 10 working days, which may be extended by a further 10 working days where circumstances warrant it (or 3 working days in the case of perishable goods—term not extendible) of receipt of the notification of the detention, or suspension of release, of the goods, a notarized agreement concluded between the right-holder, and the declarant, owner, or holder of the goods, stipulating that the latter abandon the goods for destruction, or

2. Where the owner, the declarant, and the holder of the goods fail to oppose destruction within the same period as prescribed above under 1, by sustaining that the goods do not infringe the intellectual property right in question.

The owner, the declarant, and/or the holder of the goods will be informed about **25.76** this simplified procedure when being informed by customs of the detention, or suspension of release, of the goods.

Under Slovenian law, amicable settlements between a right-holder and the **25.77** declarant, holder and/or owner of the suspect goods are thus permitted at any time during the 10- (or 3-) working day period. Such settlements remain permitted afterwards as well, that is, pending the proceedings referred to in Article 13(1) of the Regulation. They may comprise clauses determining who will bear the storage, destruction, and legal costs, provide for punitive damages, contain an undertaking whereby the infringer commits itself to cease and desist from any further infringement, and/or contractual penalties in the case of a breach of the terms of the settlement agreement. Slovenian Customs will not object to the grant of licences by the right-holders to the owner of the goods to allow their commercialization.

C. Conditions governing action by the authorities having jurisdiction to determine whether the goods infringe an intellectual property right

(1) Authorities having jurisdiction to determine whether the goods infringe an intellectual property right

In Slovenia, the question of whether or not an intellectual property right men- **25.78** tioned in Article 2(1) of the Regulation has been infringed can only be resolved in the course of civil proceedings before the civil courts in accordance with the Article 71 of the Customs Measures Law.

25.79 In the framework of civil proceedings, the right-holder may claim a declaration that the goods do indeed infringe his intellectual property rights, the grant of damages, an injunction, the destruction of the infringing goods, and the prohibition of any future infringements, Upon the right-holder's request, the court may also order the defendant to disclose additional information on the distribution network of the goods, the scope of the infringement, and other useful details, although there is no effective sanction if the defendant refuses to divulge this information.

(2) *Term for notifying customs that proceedings have been started*

25.80 The period of 10 working days provided for in Article 13(1) of the Regulation, during which the right-holder must notify customs that a lawsuit has been filed against the infringer(s), can be extended once 'in appropriate cases' by another 10 working days. It is difficult to anticipate in which cases and for what reasons such an extension will be deemed 'appropriate' by customs. However, in practice, the Slovenian Customs authorities almost always grant the extension when it is requested. In some cases, customs will extend the initial period of 10 working days by an additional period of less than 10 working days.

D. Release of goods suspected of infringing certain rights on provision of a security

25.81 According to Slovenian Customs, no request for release of goods whose release had been suspended, or which had been detained, under the Regulation (or its predecessor, EC Regulation 3295/94) on provision of a security has ever been made in Slovenia. If the conditions set by the Regulation are met, the Slovenian customs authorities will release the goods upon payment of a security. However, neither the Regulation, nor the national legislation, allow Slovenian Customs to release goods suspected of infringing a trade mark, a copyright or related right, a designation of origin, or a geographical indication on provision of a security.

25.82 The amount of the security referred to in Article 14(2) of the Regulation is determined by the General Customs Directorate of the Republic of Slovenia by having regard to the right-holder's estimation of the amount of possible damages, and the declared value of the goods. The security is provided by depositing the requested amount of money, or by issuing a bank guarantee which should be valid for a period of no less than one year and 45 days. If the court proceedings have not yet come to an end by the expiry of this period, the bank guarantee must be extended.[15]

---

[15] Based on the 'Rules on the method of payment of security, the criteria for determining its amount and the method of its release or exercise in the event of application of customs measures for infringement of intellectual property rights', OJ RS 70/2004.

E. Storage of the goods

The goods towards which border measures have been adopted under the **25.83** Regulation will be stored in customs warehouses under the conditions set out by Customs Measures Law. Customs storehouses are not necessarily on the customs property, but they are under their constant supervision.

The goods are stored under the same regime from the day of their detention, or of **25.84** the suspension of their release, until the day of their destruction or release. The costs for storing the goods under customs' supervision will initially be borne by customs. However, once proceedings have been instituted by the right-holder to determine whether the goods infringe an intellectual property right, the storage costs will be charged by customs to the defendant in these proceedings, that is, the alleged infringer. The party losing the lawsuit will be liable for the payment of all storage and destruction costs. Notwithstanding this general rule, in practice, the right-holder must always bear the storage costs incurred by customs between the first 10 (up to 20) working days referred to in Article 13(1) of the Regulation, if such costs cannot be refunded by the infringer.

IV. PROVISIONS APPLICABLE TO GOODS FOUND TO INFRINGE AN INTELLECTUAL PROPERTY RIGHT

It is still unclear under Slovenian law whether the right-holder who seeks to have **25.85** goods which infringe his rights destroyed must explicitly request the destruction in the framework of the court proceedings, or whether it is sufficient to request that the court establishes and declares that the goods infringe the plaintiff's rights (in which case customs would presumably be entitled to proceed '*ex officio*' with the destruction of the goods). The difference is essential as, pursuant to the Slovenian Industrial Property Law (which covers patents, designs, trade marks, and partly also geographical indications), the plaintiff is entitled to destruction of infringing goods only if there is no other way to dispose effectively of the goods outside commercial channels. In the framework of border measures, the Customs Measures Law defines the destruction of the goods as the only option of dealing with infringing goods. In practice, the right-holder will make sure, for the sake of certainty, to claim both a declaratory judgment concluding to the infringing character of the goods, and the destruction of those goods, in the context of the court proceedings.

The right-holder may also claim damages from the infringer, although the **25.86** chances of being awarded damages are usually insignificant, as the defendant will most often successfully claim that no actual damage occurred since the goods were apprehended prior to being released into the market. If the plaintiff is successful in the lawsuit, the defendant will have to bear the plaintiff's litigation costs. The losing party must cover the costs of storage and maintenance of the goods, as well as the destruction costs.

V. PENALTIES

25.87   In Slovenia, the following sanctions apply where there has been a violation of an intellectual property right:

- Patents, supplementary protection certificates, trade marks, and designs
  Civil sanctions:
  — Disposal of the goods outside commercial channels, ie seizure and destruction of the goods,[16]
  — Damages,[17] including reimbursement of the litigation costs,[18]
  — Prohibition of future infringements (injunction),[19]
  — Publication of the judgment.[20]
  Criminal sanctions:[21]
  — Seizure and destruction of the goods,
  — Jail term of up to three years.

- Copyright and related rights
  Civil sanctions:
  — Disposal of the goods outside commercial channels, that is, seizure and destruction of the goods,[22]
  — Damages[23] (including reimbursement of the litigation costs),[24] and punitive damages,[25]
  — Prohibition of future infringements,[26]
  — Publication of the judgment.[27]
  Criminal sanctions:
  — Seizure and destruction of the goods,[28]

---

[16] Art 121 of the Industrial Property Law.   [17] Art 168 of the Obligation Code.
[18] Art 154 of the Zakon o pravdnem postopku (*Civil Procedure Law*), OJ 26/1999.
[19] Art 121 of the Industrial Property Law.   [20] Art 121 of the Industrial Property Law.
[21] Art 238 of the Kazenski zakonik (*Penal Code*), OJ 63-2167/1994.
[22] Art 167 of the Copyright and Related Rights Law.
[23] Art 168 of the Obligation Code.   [24] Art 154 of the Civil Procedure Law.
[25] Art 168 of the Copyright and Related Rights Law.
[26] Art 167 of the Copyright and Related Rights Law.
[27] Art 167 of the Copyright and Related Rights Law.   [28] Art 158–160 of the Penal Code.

— Imposition of a fine (at least 400,000 Slovenian Tolars),[29]
— Jail term of up to eight years.[30]

• Plant variety rights
  Civil sanctions:
  — Disposal of the goods outside commercial channels, ie seizure and destruction of the goods,[31]
  — Damages,[32] including reimbursement of the litigation costs,[33]
  — Prohibition of future infringements (injunction).[34]
  Criminal sanction:
  — Imposition of a fine (at least 500,000 Slovenian Tolars).[35]

• Designations of origin, and geographical indications
  Civil sanctions:
  — Seizure and destruction of the goods,[36]
  — Damages,[37] including reimbursement of the litigation costs,[38]
  — Prohibition of future infringements (injunction).[39]
  Criminal sanction:
  — Imposition of a fine (up to 1,200,000 Slovenian Tolars).[40]

It is worth pointing out in this context that criminal penalties apply only when the **25.88** infringement has been committed wilfully. In practice, such sanctions are extremely rare.

VI. LIABILITY OF CUSTOMS AUTHORITIES AND RIGHT-HOLDERS

A. Liability of right-holders and sanctions

Under Slovenian law, the right-holder cannot incur any civil liability if he uses the **25.89** information provided by customs only for the purposes of enforcing his intellectual property rights.

A right-holder will be held liable for the storage and maintenance costs, **25.90** and, where applicable, the costs for the destruction of the goods, as well as

---

[29] Art 184 of the Copyright and Related Rights Law.   [30] Arts 158–160 of the Penal Code.
[31] Art 47 of the Plant Variety Protection Law.   [32] Art 168 of the Obligation Code.
[33] Art 154 of the Civil Procedure Law.   [34] Art 47 of the Plant Variety Protection Law.
[35] Art 51 of the Plant Variety Protection Law.   [36] Art 121 of the Industrial Property Act.
[37] Art 168 of the Obligation Code.   [38] Art 154 of the Civil Procedure Law.
[39] Art 121 of the Industrial Property Act.   [40] Art 122 of the Agriculture Law.

additional damages as may prove appropriate in the circumstances, in the event that:

- the goods must be released or their detention terminated owing to an act or omission by the right-holder (for example, if he fails to commence proceedings to determine whether the goods infringe an intellectual property right in accordance with Article 13 of the Regulation within the timeframe prescribed in this provision, after he declares to customs that the goods infringe his rights,

- he loses the infringement lawsuit before the courts, or

- customs cannot collect these costs from a person that is primarily liable to pay them.

25.91 By virtue of the general tort law clause and provisions on damages,[41] the right-holder will also be liable to redress any harm caused by his own fault to the persons involved, in the event that it later turns out that the border measures requested by the right-holder did not rely on valid grounds, for example, if the goods are eventually found by the courts not to infringe an intellectual property right.

B. Liability of customs authorities and sanctions

25.92 There are no provisions under Slovenian law that would entitle the right-holder to claim compensation from customs in the event that goods are not detected by a customs office and are released, or if no action is taken to detain them.

25.93 Nonetheless, Slovenian Customs, as any or other State authorities, are liable for damage caused to third parties by their actions, where such actions contravene the law (including the Regulation).

Conclusion

25.94 Slovenian Customs are proactive in searching for goods which infringe intellectual property rights, and will often detain such goods, or suspend their release, on their own initiative ('*ex officio*'). The customs authorities in Slovenia will take border measures under the new EC Regulation 1383/2003 even where the suspect goods are in transit, are being transhipped, or are in the process of being placed in a free zone or free warehouse or re-exported. The Slovenian legislator has implemented the simplified procedure set out in Article 11 of the

---

[41] Obligacijski zakonik (*Obligation Code*), OJ RS No 83-4287/2001.

Regulation. Therefore, since 1 May 2004 it is possible to obtain the destruction of the goods without the right-holder having to commence (time-consuming and costly) proceedings, provided that the owner, the holder, and the declarant of the goods—expressly or impliedly—agree with the destruction. If the litigation is initiated and the defendant fails to respond to the writ of summons, he will also automatically lose the case. Overall, the Slovenian customs procedure can be seen as an effective and relatively inexpensive way of protecting intellectual property rights.

26

SPAIN

Luis H Larramendi and Ignacio Diez de Rivera Elzaburu

Introduction

Spain joined the European Community in 1986 and applied the system of border **26.01** measures set out by the European legislator since the entry into force of Community Regulation No 3842/86 on 1 January 1988.[1]

The border measures system in Spain[2] has from the very beginning been applied **26.02** directly from EC Regulations 3842/86 and 3295/94.[3] Border measures were applied timidly at first but the number of applications for action and effective actions by Spanish Customs and the efficacy of the Spanish customs authorities has gradually increased.[4] Spain has not developed national legislation adapted to

---

[1] Council Reg (EEC) 3842/86 of 1 December 1986 laying down measures to prohibit the release for free circulation of counterfeit goods [1987] OJ L 357/1 (18.12.1986); Corrigendum: [1986] OJ L 33/18 (4.2.1987).

[2] For the history of border measures in Spain, cf M Arean Lalin, La lucha de las aduanas contra la piratería de marcas, en Estudios Jurídicos en homenaje al Profesor Aurelio Menéndez, [Customs' fight against trade mark counterfeiting, in *Legal Studies in honour of Prof. Aurelio Menéndez*] Madrid Civitas 1996 671; M Arean Lalin Nuevas perspectivas de la protección aduanera de la propiedad industrial e intelectual en la Unión Europea [*New horizons for Customs protection of industrial and intellectual property in the European Union*], ADI Madrid Marcial Pons 1994–1995 935, Botana Agra El Reglamento (CE) 2549/1999, de lucha contra la piratería en materia de Propiedad Intelectual [*Reg (EC) 2549/1999 and the fight against the pirating of intellectual property*], ADI Madrid Marcial Pons 1999 1454 and F Lois Bastida El Reglamento (CE) 1383/2003, de lucha contra la piratería en materia de Propiedad Intelectual, Madrid ADI, Marcial Pons 2003 1125–1235.

[3] Council Reg (EC) 3295/94 laying down measures to prohibit the release for free circulation, export, re-export or entry for a suspensive procedure of counterfeit and pirated goods [1994] OJ L 341/8 (30.12.1994), subsequently amended by Council Reg (EC) 241/1999 ([1999] OJ L 27/1 (2.2.1999)) and Council Reg (EC) 806/2003 [2003] OJ L 122/1 (16.5.2003).

[4] According to the EC Commission Report to the Council and Parliament of 15 February 1991 regarding the functioning of the system in its first three years of existence, until 1990 only four Member States had detained or suspended the release of counterfeit merchandise at the borders (ie 452 cases in Great Britain, 148 in Germany, 126 in France, and 9 in Spain). Cf A Garcia Vidal,

the Community Regulations.[5] Relying on the direct applicability of such inst-ruments, Spanish lawmakers did not consider it necessary to enact any other legislation to expand upon it. This approach has been partially modified under the new Regulation in this field, namely, EC Regulation 1383/2003.[6] For the first time the Spanish customs authorities are currently preparing a Ministerial Order (Orden Ministerial) to implement certain aspects of the Regulation.[7]

26.03   The creation of a Spanish Inter-Ministerial Commission[8] to act against the infringements of intellectual and industrial property rights in the year 2000 has been of extraordinary importance in the fight against counterfeiting in Spain. The objective of the Commission is threefold: the study and proposal of guidelines to act against violations of industrial and intellectual property rights; the coordina-tion, surveillance, and control of the activity of the bodies in charge of combating this form of delinquency; and training and dissemination activities.[9] The initiat-ive reveals the extent to which the Spanish government is committed to the fight against commercial counterfeiting—in the broad sense.

I. SUBJECT MATTER AND SCOPE OF THE NATIONAL LAW APPLYING THE REGULATION

A. Customs procedure of the goods

26.04   In accordance with Article 16 of Regulation 1383/2003 (the 'Regulation'), border measures can be applied under all customs procedures, including importation,

---

'El tránsito por el territorio de la Unión Europea de mercancías que vulneran un derecho de propiedad industrial o intellectual (Comentario a la sentencia del TJCE de 6 de abril de 2000, "The Polo/Lauren Company LP y PT. Dwidua Langgeng Pratama International Freight Forwarders")' in *Actas de Derecho Industrial Marcial Pons*, 2001 469–487).

[5] To begin with, certain lesser practical aspects have been dealt with in the Orden del Ministerio de relaciones con las Cortes y de Secretaria de Gobierno of 12 July 1988. BOE of 19 July 1998 [Ministerial Order on relations with Parliament and the General Secretariat of the Government of 12 July 1988, *Official State Gazette* of 19 July 1998].

[6] Council Reg (EC) 1383/2003 concerning customs action against goods suspected of infring-ing certain intellectual property rights and the measures to be taken against goods found to have infringed such rights [2003] OJ L 196/7 (2.8.2003).

[7] The content of which is not yet known as no draft has been made public to date.

[8] Real Decreto 114/2000 de 28 de enero, por el que se crea y regula la Comisión Interministerial para actuar contra las actividades vulneradoras de los derechos de propiedad Intelectual e Industrial (Royal Decree 114/2000 creating the Interministerial Commission) BOE 8 February 2000 5704–5706.

[9] The annual reports of the Commission are made public in the web page of the Spanish Patent and Trademark Office (http://www.oepm.es/internet/infgral/primera.htm).

release for free circulation, exportation, re-exportation, placement under a suspensive procedure, or placement in a free zone or free warehouse. In practice the majority of border measures in Spain involve merchandise that has been imported into the country (73.9 per cent in 2003), with less number of cases relating to transit (25.3 per cent) or export (1 per cent).[10]

The issue of compatibility of Spanish national law with the Regulation as to whether the external transit of goods could be considered damaging to the right-holder under criminal law is not absolutely clear. Criminal legislation dealing with piracy all prohibit the *import* of counterfeit or pirated goods, leaving undecided whether transit through Spanish territory can strictly be deemed to be importing, but criminal laws tend to be strictly constructed. This issue has not yet been finally decided by the Spanish Supreme Court.[11] **26.05**

B. Definition of infringing goods

According to official statistics,[12] the vast majority of actions taken by Spanish Customs involve trade mark infringements (91 per cent in 2003). Only a small percentage involve infringements of designs and copyrights (9 per cent in 2003), and there are practically no actions taken against goods suspected of infringing patents or other intellectual property rights. **26.06**

The reason why the majority of customs measures are applied to goods that are suspected of infringing trade mark rights is twofold: in the first place because the majority of applications for action refer to trade marks, and in the second place because it is easier for customs officials to identify merchandise bearing a counterfeit trade mark than merchandise that would infringe, for example, a design, patent or plant variety right. **26.07**

---

[10] European Commission, (DG TAXUD), Breakdown by number and % of customs or other procedures. 2003 (http://europa.eu.int/comm/taxation_customs/customs/customs_controls/counterfeit_piracy/statistics/index_en.htm).
[11] A judgment in the affirmative was handed down by the Court of Justice of the European Communities on 6 April 2000 in the Polo Lauren Company case (Case C-383/98, *The Polo/Lauren Company LP v PT Dwidua Langgeng Pratama International Freight Forwarders*, [2000] ECR I-2519), although in its subsequent judgment of 7 January 2004 in the Rolex case (Case C-60/02, Criminal proceedings against X, [2004] ECR I-651), this Court qualified that the obligation to interpret national law in accordance with Community law could not create or aggravate the criminal liability of whomever breaches the provisions of the Community Regulation. In the latter case, Austrian law did not prohibit the movement of goods infringing an intellectual property right originating in non-EC Member countries.
[12] European Commission, (DG TAXUD), Breakdown by type of right covered 2003 (n 10 above).

(1) Counterfeit goods

26.08 In Spain trade marks are governed by the Trade Mark Law,[13] which came into force on 31 July 2002.

26.09 Article 40 of this Law entitles the owner of a trade mark to institute civil or criminal actions against those who infringe his rights. The Trade Mark Law governs civil actions filed by the owner of a trade mark, whereas criminal actions are dealt with by the Criminal Code.[14]

26.10 The prosecution of counterfeiting activities usually focuses on criminal rather than civil actions. Trade mark counterfeiting has traditionally been considered to form part of trade mark infringement (*infracción de marcas*). Trade mark counterfeiting is considered particularly serious in that it involves an element of fraudulent intent which makes it the subject of criminal prosecution. Protection from such intentional conduct may however also be obtained on the basis of civil or private law. In the case of criminal action, priority is given to the defence of the public interest, through repressive instruments that seek to protect the legally protected asset from a social perspective, whereas under civil law it is private interests that are protected according to the principle of availability of the parties.

26.11 Article 34 of the Spanish Trade Mark Law,[15] which is in line with the Community Directive on Harmonization of Trade Marks,[16] sets out the *'ius prohibendi'* that entitles the owner of a registered trade mark to prohibit the use in the course of trade:

- under Article 34(2)(a): of any sign identical to the mark in respect of goods or services identical to those for which the trade mark has been registered;
- under Article 34(2)(b): of any sign which, because of its identity with, or similarity to, the trade mark and the identity or similarity of the goods or services covered by the trade mark and the sign, gives rise to a likelihood of confusion on the part of the public. The likelihood of confusion includes the likelihood of association between the sign and the trade mark.

---

[13] Ley 17/2001, de 7 de diciembre, de marcas (Spanish Trade Mark Law) BOE 8 December 2001.

[14] Last amended by Ley orgánica 15/2003 de 25 de noviembre, por la que se modifica la Ley Orgánica 10/1995, de 23 de noviembre, del Código Penal (Criminal Code) BOE 26 November 2003. The new reform of the Criminal Code came into force on 1 October 2004.

[15] Cf C Fernández Novoa, Tratado de Derecho de Marcas (*Trade Mark Law Treaty*) Madrid, Marcial Pons 2001 and C Gonzalez Bueno, Comentarios a la Ley y al Reglamento de marcas (*Comments on the Trade Mark Law and Regulation*) Madrid, Civitas 2003.

[16] First Council Directive 89/104 /CEE of 21 December 1988 to approximate the laws of the Member States relating to trade marks, OJ [1989] L 40/1 (11.2.1989).

- under Article 34(2)(c): of any identical or similar sign used in respect of goods or services which are not similar to those for which the trade mark has been registered, where the latter is well-known or enjoys a reputation in Spain, and where use of that sign without due cause could indicate a connection between the said goods or services and the trade mark owner or, more generally, where such use takes unfair advantage of, or is detrimental to, the distinctive character or the repute of the registered trade mark.

Under criminal law, it is Article 274 of the Criminal Code that governs trade mark **26.12** counterfeiting, since it punishes whoever

> for industrial or commercial purposes, without the consent from the proprietor of an industrial property right registered under trade mark law, and knowing of the registration, reproduces, imitates, modifies or otherwise uses a distinctive sign identical or confusingly similar to that right to distinguish products, services, activities or establishments identical or similar to those for which the industrial property right is registered.

As can be seen, the definitions set out in the Spanish Trade Mark Law and **26.13** Criminal Code are much broader than the definition of 'counterfeit goods' in Article 2(1)(a) of the Regulation. Indeed, the criterion adopted to define the infringement under Spanish civil and criminal law relates to the identical *or confusingly similar* character of the signs to distinguish the same *or similar* goods and services. The application of the Regulation has indeed given rise to some problems in interpretation since the definition of counterfeiting in Article 2(1)(a) is unduly limited. The Regulation refers to goods bearing without authorization a sign which is 'identical' to, *or* 'which cannot be distinguished in its essential aspects' from, a registered trade mark. This definition is clearly much more limited than that of the Spanish Trade Mark Law, and, as a matter of fact, of the Trade Mark Directive, which relies primarily on a confusion of the signs.

As regards the goods to which the signs are affixed, the Regulation provides that to **26.14** be entitled to take action, the goods controlled by customs must consist of the 'same type' of goods as those which are covered in the trade mark registration. Customs actions against goods which are only 'similar' would therefore seem precluded under the Regulation. In our view, the definition under the Spanish Criminal Code is more appropriate than the definition adopted in the Regulation, which is unquestionably insufficient to tackle the phenomenon of counterfeiting. In any case, the Regulation has direct effect in Spain, and hence in our view penalization is not inherent to its nature, and in consequence its definition of counterfeit and pirated products only affects the scope of the Regulation as it relates to application of the administrative procedure on border measures, without putting in place any conditions on the scope of application of national provisions regarding penalties for infringement of rights defined separately under national law.

26.15 It is worth mentioning, however, that in Spain, the customs authorities have wisely adopted a broad interpretation of the concept of 'counterfeit goods' when taking border measures against goods which are suspected of infringing a trade mark and are perfectly distinguishable from genuine ones. In other words, even though Article 2(1)(a) of the Regulation refers to 'identical' trade marks, or marks 'which cannot be distinguished in their essential aspects' from the genuine mark, Spanish Customs consider counterfeit goods to include goods to which marks have been affixed with a name which *differs* from the genuine mark, but which nonetheless reveal this element of intent or fraud entailed by counterfeiting. When making this assessment they have regard not only to the identity between the trade marks, but also to other elements of the product, such as its presentation, the packaging or design, which would clearly show the fraudulent intent of the infringer.

26.16 Spanish Customs follow the same approach when considering the comparison of the goods that are suspected of being counterfeit and those which are covered by the relevant trade mark registration. Spanish Customs will detain, or suspend the release of, any goods that they believe to be infringing, even when the goods involved are not 'of the same type' as those for which the mark is registered, in particular in the case of trade marks with a reputation and well-known marks (including the merchandising of well-known marks in a specific sector, for example, disposable cameras bearing a well-known drinks brand, or clothing bearing a famous automobile brand). In our opinion, it is appropriate to consider as counterfeit or pirated goods not only those covered by a trade mark registration but also others that infringe rights for commercial gain and thus defraud consumers, as in the case of merchandising products.

26.17 In accordance with Article 2(1)(a) of the Regulation, in Spain, applications for action under the Regulation may only rely—in respect of counterfeit goods—on a 'validly registered' trade mark. Therefore, when a right-holder wishes to have Spanish Customs take border measures against counterfeit goods, he must rely on a trade mark registration when filing his application for action. This is also an indispensable condition for the prosecution of trade mark counterfeiting. It is thus not sufficient to lay claim to a mere trade mark *application*.

(2) Pirated goods

26.18 As with trade marks, there is a special law on copyright infringement in Spain,[17] even though the concept of 'pirated goods' *stricto sensu* is dealt with exclusively

---

[17] Real Decreto Legislativo 1/1996, texto refundido de la Ley de Propiedad Intelectual (Intellectual Property Law), of 12 April, BOE 22 April 1996.

from the standpoint of criminal law under Article 270 onwards of the Spanish Criminal Code. Those provisions define piracy as an intellectual property offence, and punish whoever

> with gainful intent and to the detriment of a third party, reproduces, plagiarises, distributes or makes publicly available, in whole or in part, a literary, artistic or scientific work, or an artistic adaptation, interpretation or performance of such a work, on any type of media, without authorisation from the owners of the corresponding intellectual property rights or their assignees.

Under Article 17 of the Spanish Intellectual Property Act the exclusive right to exploitation includes reproduction, distribution, communication to the public, and alteration, which may not be exercised without the author's consent. Related rights are governed by this same Act. Articles 138 to 141 of the Act regulate infringement of intellectual property rights that involve unlawful exploitation, without specifically defining the nature of infringing activity. In contrast, Article 270 of the Criminal Code goes into quite some detail and may be somewhat redundant in listing such activities (reproduction, plagiarism, distribution, public disclosure). In any event, no conflict between the wording of Article 2.1.b) of the Regulation and the relevant national legislation has yet surfaced. It should be noted that the number of actions by customs in defence of copyrights has been negligible.   **26.19**

Turning now to designs, Article 45 in the 2003 Spanish Act[18] prohibits use of registered designs by third parties, use being defined as the manufacture, offering, marketing, importing and exporting as well as use of products incorporating the design, including stocking for those purposes. All designs that do not cause informed users to have a different overall impression fall within the scope of protection. Similarly, Article 273 of the Criminal Code prohibits the manufacture, importing, possession, use, offering, or placing in trade of goods protected by a design right. The new legislation on designs is fully in keeping with the Community Directive on harmonization.[19]   **26.20**

(3) Goods infringing other intellectual property rights

As mentioned above (cf para 26.06), there are practically no cases of border measures adopted by Spanish Customs that have affected intellectual property rights other than trade mark rights, copyrights, and design rights.   **26.21**

---

[18] Ley 20/2003 de protección jurídica del diseño industrial (Law on industrial design) of 7 July BOE 8 July 2003.
[19] Directive 98/71/EEC of the European Parliament and the Council, of 13 October 1998, on the legal protection of designs [1998] OJ L 289 (28. 10. 1998).

Goods infringing a patent or a supplementary protection certificate

26.22   Patent protection including supplementary protection certificates in Spain is governed by the Patent Law.[20] Articles 62 onwards govern the corresponding actions that may be brought against patent infringement. Article 50 of this Law defines the following acts constitutive of a patent infringement:

- manufacturing, offering for sale, putting on the market, or using the product that is the subject matter of the patent or importing or possessing the product for one of the above-mentioned purposes;

- making use of a process that is the subject matter of a patent or offering such use when the third party is aware, or the circumstances make it obvious, that use of the process without the consent of the patent's owner is prohibited;

- offering for sale, putting on the market, or using the product directly obtained by the process that is the subject matter of the patent or importing or possessing the said product for any of the above-mentioned purposes.

26.23   Under criminal law, the prosecution of infringement of patents or supplementary protection certificates is dealt with by Article 273 of the Criminal Code, which prohibits the manufacture, importing, possession, use, offering, or placing in trade of goods protected by a patent.

Goods infringing a national plant variety right

26.24   There have been no known customs actions involving plant variety rights. Spanish legislation on plant varieties is found in Law 3/2000 on Plant Varieties.[21] The Criminal Code punishes, under Article 274(3), whoever

> for agricultural or commercial purposes, without the consent of the owner of a plant variety certificate, and while knowing of the registration, produces, reproduces, modifies with a view to producing or reproducing, offers for sale, sells or markets in any other way, exports or imports, or possesses for those same purposes, any plant material that has been reproduced or obtained from a protected plant variety in accordance with legislation on the protection of plant varieties.

Goods infringing a national designation of origin or a geographical indication

26.25   Infringement of designations of origin or geographical indications is regulated in Spain through several Royal Decrees, which mainly refer to agricultural foodstuffs

---

[20]   Ley de Patentes 11/1986 (Patent Law) of 20 March 1986 BOE 26 March 2003.
[21]   Ley 3-2000 de régimen jurídico de las obtenciones vegetales (Plant Varieties) of 7 January 2000, BOE 10 January 2000.

and wines.[22] Community Regulations 2081/92,[23] 1576/89,[24] and 1493/1999[25] on this subject are also directly applicable. The Criminal Code imposes punishments in this regard in Article 275.

(4) Moulds and matrices

In practice, Spanish Customs rarely stop moulds and matrices. Spanish criminal **26.26** procedure does allow right-holders to take action against moulds and matrices, including the confiscation and destruction thereof.[26] Seizure, attribution of ownership, and destruction of the means used for production or carrying out the patented process area available in civil proceedings involving patents.[27] They are likewise available in cases involving copyright.[28] While the law does not prescribe this specifically in the case of trade marks and designs, it is deemed feasible under the general entitlement to cessation of the infringing acts and destruction of infringing goods.[29]

C. Goods excluded by the Regulation

(1) Parallel imported goods

In accordance with Article 3(1), first indent, of the Regulation, Spanish Customs **26.27** do not apply the Regulation if they know that the goods are (genuine) parallel imports. Neither do they inform the right-holder concerned when they uncover

---

[22] Real Decreto 728/1988, por el que se establece la normativa a que deben ajustarse las denominaciones de origen, específicas o genéricas de productos agroalimentarios no vínicos (Designations of Origin for Agricultural Products and Foodstuffs), of 8 July, BOE 12 July 1988; Real Decreto 157/1988, por el que se establece la normativa a la que deben ajustarse las denominaciones de origen y las denominaciones de origen calificadas de vinos y sus respectivos Reglamentos (Designations of Origin for Wines), of 22 February, BOE 24 February 1988. Real Decreto 1573/1985, por el que se regulan las denominaciones genéricas y específicas de productos alimentarios (Designations of Origin for Agricultural Products and Foodstuffs), of 1 August, BOE 6 September 1985; REAL DECRETO 1126/2003, por el que se establecen las reglas generales de utilización de las indicaciones geográficas y de la mención tradicional «vino de la tierra» en la designación de los vinos.(Use of Geographical Indications and the term 'vino de la tierra') of 5 September, BOE 23 September 2003.
[23] Council Reg (EEC) 2081/92 of 14 July 1992 on the protection of geographical indications and designations of origin for agricultural products and foodstuffs, OJ L 208/1 (24.7.1992), as amended.
[24] Council Reg (EEC) 1576/89 of 29 May 1989 laying down general rules on the definition, description and presentation of spirit drinks, OJ L 160/1 (12.6.1989), as amended.
[25] Council Reg (EC) 1493/1999 of 17 May 1999 on the common organization of the market in wine, OJ L 179/1 (14.7.1999), as amended.
[26] Spanish Law on Criminal Procedural Art 338.   [27] Spanish Patent Law Art 63.
[28] Spanish Copyright Law, Art 139.
[29] Spanish Trademark Law, Art 41, and Spanish Design Law, Art 53.

such goods.[30] To date, Spanish Customs have always released the consignments as soon as they receive confirmation that the goods involve parallel imports, except in those cases where the goods also infringe other laws (for example, smuggled goods,[31] or goods harming public health).

26.28   Under Article 274(1), of the Spanish Criminal Code the wilful importation of goods without the consent of their owner, *whether they have a licit or illicit origin in their country of origin*,[32] is considered an offence. As of today, it is difficult to predict how the courts will interpret this provision which appears to consider the unauthorized parallel importation of genuine goods as a criminal offence. Neither is it possible to anticipate how Spanish Customs will behave in practice in the light of this provision. Even though they are not authorized to prevent the entry of parallel goods under the provisions of the Regulation, they are obliged as a public duty to report any criminal offence of which they have aware, considered as such in the Criminal Code. In line with its latest practice, Spanish Customs displays a propensity not to detain parallel goods, since the Regulation contains no provision for this and since ultimately it tends to be difficult to establish whether the right-holder has furnished consent.

(2) Goods which have been manufactured under conditions other than those which have been agreed with the right-holder

26.29   For the same reasons as for parallel imported goods, and in accordance with Article 3(1), second indent, of the Regulation, Spanish Customs do not act against goods which have been manufactured in breach of a licence agreement (for example, 'overruns'). Neither will they inform the right-holder concerned about the clearance of such goods.

26.30   Under Article 274(1) of the Spanish criminal law,[33] there must be a lack of consent by the owner of the right for an offence to be committed owing to the importation of the goods. Consent is considered to exist within the framework of a manufacturing agreement. However, non-compliance with the terms of such an agreement will result in an infringement of the licensor's rights. From a practical point of view, the biggest problem with this subject is the production of evidence

---

[30] A Castan, 'Las Medidas en Frontera como medio de lucha contra la piratería comercial. La experiencia española' (Border measures as a means to fight commercial piracy. The Spanish experience') 1er. Forum Iberoamericano sobre Inovación, Propiedad Industrial e Intellectual y Desarrollo (Records of the 1st Ibero-American Forum on Innovation, Industrial and Intellectual Property and Development), Madrid, 2000, 320–330.

[31] Cf on this point Ley Orgánica 12/1995 of 12 December 1995 represión del contrabando (the suppression of smuggling).

[32] New wording of Art 274(1) of the Criminal Code, as amended by Organic Law 15/2003, with effect as of 1 October 2004.   [33] Cf above, para 26.28.

in the proceedings, because the merchandise that has been authorized for manufacture or marketing by the right-holder usually cannot be distinguished from unauthorized goods.

(3) Goods contained in travellers' personal baggage

A significant number of border measures adopted by Spanish Customs over the last few years were applied towards travellers. According to statistics of 2003[34] 184 Spanish customs interventions (that is, 24 per cent of the cases) relate to passenger traffic. The other 577 interventions (76 per cent of the cases) are commercial traffic.[35] Although the Spanish Customs' priority in the surveillance of travellers is centred on drug trafficking, weapons, protected species, or cultural assets, infringements of trade marks and other intellectual property rights are also subject to special monitoring. **26.31**

The limit of the duty-free allowance set out in Article 4 of the Regulation is not often conferred a decisive role in this context. Indeed, when deciding whether or not to take border measures towards goods found in travellers' personal baggage, customs officials evaluate on a case-by-case basis whether the goods can be suspected of forming part of a commercial traffic. For that purpose, Spanish Customs will pay attention not only to the value of the goods but to other factors, such as their quantity, for example. **26.32**

II. APPLICATION FOR ACTION BY THE CUSTOMS AUTHORITIES

A. Measures prior to an application for action by the customs authorities ('ex officio measures')

Spanish Customs act *ex officio*, under Article 4 of the Regulation, and enjoy an appropriate training in the detection of suspect goods. The customs offices also benefit from a Risk Analysis Department, which will normally have acquired **26.33**

---

[34] European Commission (DG TAXUD) Breakdown by Member State and type of procedure resulting in Customs action 2003 (n 10 above).
[35] European Commission (DG TAXUD) Breakdown by type of traffic resulting in Customs action 2003 (n 10 above). Customs searches in respect of travellers in the field of intellectual property infringements often prove successful, but the number of illicit items found in travellers' personal baggage is usually small.

adequate experience in this sector and may be expected to yield good results. Logically, most of the cases detected on an *ex officio* basis relate to trade marks that are well-known to the public in general. In Spain the prestigious police body, named *Guardia Civil* cooperates very effectively with customs officials. According to statistics of 2003[36] 60 Spanish customs interventions (that is, 8 per cent of the cases) have been taken *ex officio* by the customs authorities. The other 700 interventions (92 per cent of the cases) have been taken following the filing of an application for action by the right-holder.

26.34 Spanish Customs adhere strictly to the provision of Article 4 of the Regulation, and thus grant the right-holder a maximum of three working days as of the detention or suspension of release of the goods to file an application for action. However, in view of the practical difficulties which are often entailed in obtaining the documentation required for the filing of such an application (power of attorney, proof of entitlement, undertaking under Article 6 of the Regulation, etc), Spanish Customs have hitherto tended to take a flexible approach and, therefore, have deemed the application valid although lodged without all the necessary supporting documentation, subject to submission of the latter as soon as possible.

26.35 As regards the information provided by Spanish Customs to the right-holder in practice in the context of *ex officio* actions, see paragraph 26.64 below.

B. The lodging and processing of applications for customs action

26.36 In the year 2003, according to official statistics, a total of 92 applications for action were lodged under the Regulation with Spanish Customs. This represents 3 per cent of all applications filed in the Community during that year.[37]

(1) Persons entitled to file an application for action

Definition of 'right-holders' under the Regulation

26.37 The holders of any right referred to in Article 2(1) of the Regulation, and any persons authorized to use any of those rights, as well as their representatives, are all, in their capacity as 'right-holders' (in the broad sense), entitled to file an application for action under the Regulation.[38]

---

[36] European Commission (DG TAXUD) Breakdown by Member State and type of procedure resulting in Customs action 2003 (n 10 above).
[37] European Commission, (DG TAXUD), Breakdown by request for intervention 2003 (n 10 above).   [38] Cf Reg 1383/2003, Art 2(2).

In those cases where the right is acquired through registration (that is, trade **26.38** marks, designs, patents, plant varieties, designations of origin, and geographical indications), the identity of the right-holder *stricto sensu* will in principle appear from the registration certificate. In the case of unregistered rights (for example, a copyright or related right), the right-holder will normally be the author of the protected work or performance, or the party to whom the author may have assigned the right to exploit same.

On the same footing as right-holders *stricto sensu* are persons authorized to make **26.39** use of the rights listed in Article 2(1) of the Regulation (such as licensees, assignees, etc) and authorized representatives. In practice, however, in almost all cases, it is the owner of the right, rather than a person authorized to use it, who lodges the application for customs action in Spain, while representatives act as such in the name of the owner of the right, but not in the capacity of applicant in the latter's place.

In Spain, the term, 'representative' means any natural person with capacity to act. **26.40** The only requirement is a notarized power of representation. In practice representation is usually granted to *abogados* (attorneys).

Proof of entitlement to file an application for action

For right-holders stricto sensu

Prior to the entry into force of the new Regulation, Spanish Customs used to **26.41** require an official certificate of ownership as proof of entitlement of the right-holder *stricto sensu* to lodge an application for customs action, in the case of rights arising out of a registration. In the case of a copyright that had been registered at the copyright office, it was sufficient to submit the copyright certificate issued by the Copyright Office of the country of origin of the holder of the right.

Since the new Regulation and its Implementing Regulation 1891/2004[39] came **26.42** into force, it is understood that it is no longer necessary to submit original certificates or certified copies, which can take time and prove costly to obtain, and that an extract from the registration certificate obtained from the database of the corresponding national or international industrial property office will be sufficient.[40] The official database of the Spanish Patent and Trade Mark Office, which displays the relevant details of the status of industrial property rights and certificates processed by that Office, is called Sitadex, and may be accessed via www.oepm.es.

---

[39] Commission Reg (EC) 1891/2004 of 21 October 2004 laying down provisions for the implementation of Council Reg (EC) 1383/2003 concerning customs action against goods suspected of infringing certain intellectual property rights and the measures to be taken against goods found to have infringed such rights, OJ [2004] L 328/16 (30.10.2004). Cf in particular Art 2(1).

[40] Cf Reg 1891/04, Art 2(1), second indent.

For persons authorized to use the right

26.43   Proof of entitlement of authorized users to file an application for action by the Spanish customs authorities under the Regulation will normally consist of the document whereby the owner of the right authorizes the other party to use it. That can be a licence agreement, a franchise agreement, etc. Such agreements must, in all case, be accompanied by evidence of the ownership and current status of the right along the lines indicated in the preceding paragraph.[41] When the application is based on an industrial property right, the authorization to use does not have to be registered with the relevant industrial property office to be accepted by customs as proof of entitlement.

For representatives

26.44   Proof of entitlement to represent a right-holder or authorized user for the purpose of filing an application for action with Spanish Customs under the Regulation will in principle consist in a notarized power of representation, which, when granted to lawyers, is known in Spain as a general power of attorney for litigation. It may define broadly the authority of the attorney to represent the right-holder in administrative and court proceedings. It is not necessary that it specify the precise administrative body before which action must be taken. It is mandatory, however, that the document be executed before a notary public. Customs demand that the original document be submitted, although it can subsequently be returned once a copy has been taken. Should the right-holder so desire, he may instead execute a power of attorney authorizing the representative to act solely before customs. In that event, however, problems of representation may arise if proceedings of a judicial or other nature, not covered by the power of attorney, subsequently ensue.

26.45   As previously mentioned (para 26.39), the representative usually acts in the name, not in the place, of the right-holder. Thus, the undertaking to cover liabilities required by Article 6 of the Regulation, for example, is normally executed by the right-holder, and not by his representative.

26.46   Spanish Customs recommend that a local representative, whom they may contact whenever necessary, be designated in the application form. Problems tend to arise when a local contact person has not been designated, as may sometimes happen in cases of Community applications for action filed through the customs authorities from another Member State. In such cases, Spanish Customs may contact the right-holder via a postal or e-mail address or fax number indicated in the application to acknowledge receipt of the application. Subsequently, however, they prefer being provided with the details of a local contact person, and of course communicate in Spanish language.

---

[41]   Cf Reg 1891/04 Art 2(2).

(2) Competent customs department and formal requirements

Competent customs department

The competent authority under Article 5(2) of the Regulation for processing **26.47** applications for action by customs is currently the following:

Departamento de Aduanas e Impuestos Especiales
Subdirección General de Gestión Aduanera
Avenida del Llano Castellano, 17, Edificio A
2ª Planta,
E-28034 Madrid
Tel: +34 91 728 98 54
Fax: +34 91 729 12 00

The Spanish Customs Department is in turn subdivided into 56 customs offices **26.48** distributed throughout the whole of Spanish territory.

Form of the application for action

Until recently it was common practice to file the application for action with **26.49** Spanish Customs in the form of a brief containing all the necessary information, together with the documents required. Following the entry into force of the new Regulation, the new forms, as set out in the Implementing Regulation 1891/2004 must be used for that purpose.

For the time being, the application for action must be submitted in the form of a **26.50** signed original. A second copy for the applicant must also be submitted. Electronic filing is currently under study but is not possible at this time. The original signed declaration under Article 6 also has to be submitted. The person who signs the declaration should be the same person who signs the authorization appointing the representative, because on occasion customs has required proof of the signer's identity.

Language requirements

Any written submission to the Spanish administration must be made out in **26.51** Spanish, which is the official State language.[42] This language requirement will therefore apply to applications for action lodged with Spanish Customs under the Regulation. The documentation enclosed with the application

---

[42] Ley 30/1992 de Régimen jurídico de las Administraciones Públicas y del procedimiento Administrativo Común (Legal System of the Public Administration and Common Administrative Procedure Act) as modified by Law 4/1999 of 13 January, BOE 14 January 1999, Art 36.

form must equally have been translated into Spanish in order to be valid. It is possible to use the official local languages of certain of Spain's autonomous communities, but even in that case all submissions must be accompanied by a Spanish translation.

(3) Requirements regarding the contents of the application for action

Mandatory information

26.52 The mandatory information to be mentioned in, or enclosed with, the application for action consists in the first place of the applicant's particulars, evidence of the ownership of the right and entitlement to apply for action, the declaration of liability under Article 6 of the Regulation, and, where appropriate, a power of representation evidencing entitlement to act on behalf of the right-holder *stricto sensu* or authorized user. The application must also contain all the information needed to enable customs readily to recognize the goods in question, and in particular an accurate and detailed technical description of the goods to be monitored, any specific information the right-holder may have concerning the type or pattern of fraud, and the name and address of the contact person(s) appointed by the applicant.[43] Customs also request the sending of electronic files in jpg or pdf format containing images of the rights and which could help to detect fake products, in order to incorporate them to customs' internal database accessible to all local customs offices.

Optional information

26.53 Spanish Customs also urge that the application for action be accompanied, by way of indication and where known, by a technical analysis allowing customs to distinguish between genuine and suspect goods.[44] It is most advisable to submit photographs of the goods in question and, if available, a manual containing guidelines for authenticating the products, including, for example, a list of authorized Spanish distributors or a list of persons suspected of having infringed the right-holder's rights in the past.

---

[43] Cf Reg 1383/2003, Art 5(5), first and second indents. Cf also above, para 26.44, regarding the requirements relating to contact persons appointed by the applicant.

[44] Right-holders should also forward, where known, any other information they may have, such as the pre-tax value of the original goods on the legitimate market in Spain, the location of the goods or their intended destination, particulars identifying the consignment or packages, the scheduled arrival or departure date of the goods, the means of transport used, the identity of the importer, exporter or holder of the goods, the country or countries of production, and the routes used by traffickers (Ibid, Art 5(5), last indent).

Additional information specific to the type of intellectual property right referred to in the application

Should the product have technical characteristics requiring a detailed description, **26.54** such a description should be submitted. In this context, Spanish Customs will not hesitate to require an overview of all details which could be specific to the type of intellectual property right referred to in the application for action, pursuant to Article 5(6) of the Regulation.

(4) Processing and acceptance of the application for action

Spanish Customs are ordinarily able to process applications for action filed under **26.55** the Regulation within 30 working days, as required by Article 5(7) of the Regulation. When the application is granted, the duplicate copy of the application is returned to the applicant with the notification of the decision, stating the annual period of validity of the granted application.

If some defect is observed (that is, when the application does not contain the **26.56** mandatory information listed in Article 5(5)), the competent customs department will notify the right-holder or his representative so as to allow remedy of the defect and re-submission of the application, duly completed. If customs decide not to process an application, an administrative appeal procedure (*recurso de alzada*) can be filed under the Common Administrative Procedure Act.[45]

In those cases where a right-holder files two applications for action referring to **25.57** different rights, Spanish Customs usually require that they be 'consolidated' in order to avoid difficulties in administrative processing. In the same manner, if one single right is protected by a Community application and a national application, the right-holder will in principle be required to select one application or the other. Therefore, Spanish Customs do not accept the double protection of rights.

(5) 'Community' applications for action

To date, very few 'Community' application are known to have been filed in Spain. **26.58** On the other hand, 'Community' applications filed through the competent customs departments in other Member States and requesting protection on the Spanish territory are more numerous.

---

[45] Ley 30/1992 de Régimen jurídico de las Administraciones Públicas y del procedimiento Administrativo Común (Legal System of the Public Administration and Common Administrative Procedure Act), Art 107.

26.59 In the case of 'Community' applications (lodged under Article 5(4) of the Regulation), Spanish Customs usually require the right-holder to appoint a duly authorized local representative to facilitate communication.[46] In any event, Spanish Customs will always address all decisions and notifications to foreign applicants in the Spanish language, and will only attend to communications received in Spanish.[47]

III. CONDITIONS GOVERNING ACTION BY CUSTOMS AUTHORITIES AND BY THE AUTHORITIES COMPETENT TO DETERMINE WHETHER GOODS INFRINGE AN INTELLECTUAL PROPERTY RIGHT

26.60 Once an application for action has been accepted, the central customs administration forwards the information concerning the application to the 56 local offices located throughout the Spanish territory. At this point of time the monitoring begins.

26.61 Spanish Customs have recently implemented a programme allowing the basic information in applications for action to be processed through a database. To date, the programme includes the basic details of the application along with graphic files which allow the genuine products to be identified and distinguished from the infringing one. The programme is currently undergoing improvement.

A. Conditions governing action by customs authorities

(1) Factual background

26.62 Spanish Customs control the traffic of merchandise through borders with countries not belonging to the Internal Market through airports, ports, railroads, and roads. Most border measures are taken at ports and airports. The busiest Spanish ports are those of Barcelona, Valencia, Algeciras, Las Palmas, and Málaga. Customs at Madrid airport are also very active.

---

[46] Cf also above, para 26.46.   [47] Cf also above, para 26.51, on this point.

(2) Notification of customs intervention

The detention or suspension of release of suspicious merchandise by local   **26.63**
customs offices is immediately reported to the central customs administration in
Madrid. As mentioned above,[48] the specific body is the Department of Customs
and Special Taxes (*Departamento de Aduanas e Impuestos Especiales*), which notifies
the right-holder (or his representative), as well as the declarant or holder of the
goods, of the customs intervention, usually by fax.[49]

(3) Information to be provided by customs to the right-holder before the right-holder confirms the infringing nature of the goods

The Spanish customs authorities supply different information to the right-holder,   **26.64**
depending on whether the intervention takes place *ex officio* or is the result of an
application for action.

When they act *ex officio*, as a general rule, customs simply notify the right-holder   **26.65**
that there has been an intervention at a certain customs office. They also inform
the right-holder of the right they suspect has been infringed, and request that an
application for action be filed within three days, as provided by Article 4 of the
Regulation, but it provides no further information at this stage.

Once an application for action has been filed by the right-holder and accepted by the   **26.66**
competent customs department, upon request of the applicant, the customs authorities divulge the information referred to in Article 9.3 of the Regulation, that is, the
volume, the nature and the origin and/or destination of the goods, without the right-
holder being bound by the communication of that information to notify the authority competent to take a substantive decision under Article 13 of the Regulation.[50]

Both Articles 9 (3) and 4(2) of the Regulation are subject to national provisions   **26.67**
on the protection of personal data,[51] commercial and industrial secrets[52] and professional and administrative confidentiality.

(4) Inspection of the suspected goods

Until the entry into force of the new Regulation, Spanish Customs required the   **26.68**
goods to be inspected in person by the right-holder. It was not possible to send

---

[48] Cf para 26.47.   [49] Cf Reg 1383/2003, Art 9(2).
[50] Cf Reg 1383/2003, Art 9(3).
[51] Ley Orgánica 15/1999, de 13 de diciembre, de Protección de Datos de Carácter Personal (Law
on the protection of personal data) BOE 14 December 1999.
[52] Spanish Criminal Code, Art 278.

samples or even photographs for analysis. Due to the size of the Spanish territory and the difficulties involved in travelling to certain locations (for example, the Canary Islands or Algeciras), making a journey for the inspection proved too expensive unless the right-holder had a representative in the place where the initial inspection had taken place, particularly when the quantity of goods detained was not very significant.

26.69   The entry into force of the new Regulation 1383/2003 has radically altered the previous state of affairs in that Spanish Customs have begun to apply Article 9(3) of the Regulation and are prepared to hand over or send samples of the products to the right-holder at his request, usually by post or express courier, for analysis and expert opinion, although without covering any of the expense.

26.70   Customs will send samples upon submission of the representative's credentials and a declaration of liability, which can be done electronically (via fax or e-mail).

B. Simplified procedure allowing the destruction of the goods without there being any need to determine whether an intellectual property right has been infringed under national law

26.71   The implementation of the simplified procedure set out in Article 11 of the Regulation in Spain has brought about a radical change in the way detentions by customs are carried out, as it allows for the possibility of the goods being destroyed immediately without the need for a complaint to be filed or court proceedings to be instituted, provided that an agreement to abandon and destroy the goods is reached between their holder, declarant, or owner, and the right-holder, either by means of an express (written) agreement sent to the customs authorities, or tacit consent if the holder, declarant, and owner of the goods do not object to the destruction requested by the right-holder. After some initial hesitation on how to apply this provision, the Spanish customs authorities are currently preparing a Ministerial Order (Orden Ministerial) to implement this procedure. For the moment, customs will only proceed with destruction if express agreement to abandonment and destruction of the goods is obtained from the importer or holder. Although Article 11 stipulates that 'the Member States may provide . . .' for application of this simplified procedure, in fact what is currently being done (abandonment for destruction) was already permitted under the Community Customs Code.

26.72   In practice, once the goods have been inspected and their illicit nature has been confirmed, customs forward the contact details of the importer or holder of the goods,[53] and the right-holder may thus contact the infringer and request him to consent to the abandonment and destruction of the goods and accept liability for any costs arising from the destruction. On many occasions, there is a problem with the importer's contact details, either because the information is false, or because they conceal the person responsible for the goods by means of intermediaries or contact telephone numbers that cannot be reached (for example, mobile telephones with restricted access or anonymous postcodes). On other occasions, the difficulty in contacting the person responsible is due to his poor understanding of Spanish and the Spanish legal system, as these persons may be illegal immigrants who disappear when an attempt is made to contact them.

Tacit consent is deemed to occur where a request has been made for the destruc- **26.73** tion of the goods within the legal term provided for in Article 11 of the Regulation (that is, 10 working days—which may be extended once for an equal period of time 'where circumstances warrant it'—or 3 working days in the case of perishable goods, as from the notification of a customs intervention under Article 9), and the declarant, the holder, or the owner of the goods has not expressly contested said destruction.

C. Conditions governing action by the authorities having jurisdiction to determine whether the goods infringe an intellectual property right

(1) Authorities having jurisdiction to determine whether the goods infringe an intellectual property right

After being notified of the suspension of release or of the detention of suspect **26.74** goods, and within the term of 10 working days prescribed by Article 13 of the Regulation (which can be extended once for an extra term of 10 working days 'in appropriate cases'), the right-holder must prove that he has commenced proceedings with a view to determining whether an infringement has occurred. The practice in Spain is to bring criminal proceedings, which commence with the filing of a complaint.[54] In reality, the extremely short timeframe rules out the institution of civil proceedings, which are subject to greater formalities regarding the filing of the initial brief of complaint and the evidence to be submitted with that brief.

---

[53] Cf Reg 1383/2003, Art 9(3), and above, para 26.66.
[54] The acts constitutive of a criminal offence in the field of intellectual property under Spanish criminal law have been defined above, in Part I, section B, in this chapter.

26.75 It should be pointed out that until the entry into force of the reform of the Criminal Code on 1 October 2004, offences against intellectual property required a complaint to be filed by the injured party and could not be prosecuted *ex officio*. The situation has changed, and the right-holder will no longer have to file a criminal complaint for the offence to be prosecuted, as they are now defined as public offences that can be prosecuted *ex officio*.

26.76 The court taking receipt of the complaint will first review whether it has jurisdiction to handle the matter and will then open the preliminary inquiries in the criminal proceedings as appropriate to prepare the action, disclose the facts, establish that a criminal offence has been committed, and elucidate all circumstances that may have a bearing on the charges and the guilt of the offenders, as well as ensure that the offenders are at the disposal of the court and secure coverage for any financial liabilities.

26.77 As a first step, the court may invite the complainant to intervene in the proceedings, though it does not always do so. This involves notifying the complainant that he may enter a formal appearance in the proceedings and bring the pertinent civil and criminal actions.

26.78 Once the complaint has been filed, there are two alternatives:

- Not to intervene in the criminal proceedings, leaving the court to proceed *ex officio*, with the Public Prosecutor's Office, should it choose to do so, being responsible directly for filing the indictment and requesting damages pursuant to the offence. Obviously, the Office's concerns may differ from those of the complainant. The only involvement of the injured party would then be to attend to any summonses issued by the court.

- To intervene in the action as a private party to the prosecution, represented by a counsel and by a court procurator, with a view to pressing charges and actively following the proceedings and being entitled to petition for and participate in the performance of inquiries. Naturally, this entails higher costs.

26.79 To decide on one or the other of the alternatives, the right-holder should evaluate the circumstances of the case (for example, the importance of the matter; whether the goods were detained from a manufacturer or a distributor; the nationality, domicile, and assets of the importer; whether the matter involves a location especially important from the standpoint of tourism or an area where counterfeiting is common, etc). Intervention as a private party is recommended when it appears to be warranted by the circumstances, restricting the action to merely filing the complaint in other, less important matters.

26.80 The introduction of the new simplified procedure under Article 11 of the Regulation could affect the practice used up to now, in that for practical and financial reasons, the right-holder may now try to reach an agreement to abandon and destroy the detained goods without bringing the corresponding court action, particularly where the financial value of said goods is not significant. Nevertheless, the effect of court actions as preventive measures and warnings against future infringements should be taken into consideration.

26.81 From a practical standpoint, and as already mentioned, a criminal complaint is the remedy normally available to the right-holder. This applies to all kinds of rights. Under Article 13 of the Regulation, the 'proceedings to determine whether an intellectual property right has been infringed' also include civil proceedings, but in practice it is extremely difficult to prepare a civil action, which is more complicated and expensive, in the short space of time available, since all the documents on which a party's claim is based have to be filed when the action is lodged, with no deferments available.[55] An option that is sometimes used is to file an immediate petition for interlocutory measures in order to maintain the suspension of release of the goods, after which a civil action must be filed within 20 days after the measures have been granted.

(2) *Term for notifying customs that proceedings have been started*

26.82 The term for notifying customs that a legal action has been taken against the infringing goods is 10 working days from receipt of the notice of detention or suspension of release of the goods, which can be extended once for a further 10 working days 'in appropriate cases'.[56]

26.83 In practice, Spanish Customs tend to grant the 10-day extension upon receipt of a written request from the applicant.

D. Release of goods suspected of infringing certain rights on provision of a security

26.84 There has been no known case in Spain of suspected goods being released on provision of a security by their holder. In fact, Article 14 of the Regulation only applies to those goods suspected of infringing rights in designs, patents, supplementary protection certificates, or plant varieties. As we previously mentioned (cf above, para 26.06), the practice of detaining or suspending the release of goods on suspicion that they infringe rights of this kind is virtually nonexistent in Spain.

---

[55] Cf Art 270 of the Spanish Law on Civil Procedure regarding exceptions to this rule.
[56] Cf Reg 1383/2003, Art 13(1).

E. Storage of the goods

26.85 While the suspicious goods are being detained or their release suspended for the period provided for in Article 13 of the Regulation, no special storage conditions apply. That is, the goods are stored in a warehouse, which may belong to the company that handled transport arrangements, or at the customs facilities themselves. In any case, the goods are under the control of customs and cannot be moved without permission. If the goods are released at the end of the period prescribed in Article 13, customs do not usually pass any charge for storage on to the right-holder.

26.86 Once proceedings aimed at determining whether an intellectual property right has been infringed have been initiated under Article 13 of the Regulation, the goods will be in the custody of the court and their fate will be determined by the latter. According to new Article 6(1) of Regulation 1383/2003, the right-holder should bear the storage costs if the declarant refuses to do so. Until now it was not usual practice to charge the right-holder with these costs. Storage costs were ordinarily borne by the declarant. At the end all is subject to what the court may finally order in its decision on the merits. If the right-holder's infringement claim is dismissed, the declarant will probably request that the right-holder pays for the cost incurred.

IV. PROVISIONS APPLICABLE TO GOODS FOUND TO INFRINGE AN INTELLECTUAL PROPERTY RIGHT

26.87 Spain's Criminal Code penalizes marketing, including importation, of goods which infringe an intellectual property right.[57] In contrast, where a customs procedure other than importation is applicable to the goods, the picture is not so clear, as will be explained below.

26.88 In the case of importation of goods bearing a counterfeit trade mark, the infringer often alleges in his defence that since the merchandise has been intercepted before its effective material possession and before its effective sale in the Spanish market, the owner has not suffered any harm at all, and that therefore the offence has not been perpetrated. The infringer thus requests acquittal or at least that the offence

---

[57] Spanish Criminal Code, Arts 270 and 274.

be prosecuted as an attempted offence. The majority of case law rejects this view and considers that the mediate or immediate holding of the goods is sufficient to consider that an offence has been perpetrated.[58]

As regards destruction of the goods, Article 338 in the Spanish Law on Criminal Procedure[59] establishes that goods seized in relation to industrial and intellectual property offences at the enquiry stage should be destroyed. This provision also states that an inventory, an expert opinion, and sufficient samples should be kept before a decision is issued on the merits of the case. Strangely, Articles 271 and 276, which dealt with the possible temporary or permanent closure of the plant or establishment in the most serious offences against industrial and intellectual property, were deleted from the recent revision of the Criminal Code. **26.89**

V. PENALTIES

Jail terms and fines are the basic criminal penalties for intellectual property infringements provided for under the Criminal Code.[60] Fines are measured by a fines per-day system that ranges from EUR 2 to EUR 400 per day. Penalties vary according to whether or not any aggravating circumstances apply to the basic case. Other penalties include banning from professional practice relating to the criminal offence committed in cases of trade mark counterfeiting. **26.90**

---

[58] Case law regarding the perpetration of an offence in the case of importation of goods bearing a counterfeit trade mark includes eg several decisions rendered by the Provincial Court of Appeal of Madrid on 26 November 2003 *Octavio v Loewe SA.* Case number 444/2002, JUR 2003\110811, 11 July 2003 *Time Warner Entertainment Company, L.P. y Warner Bros Consumer Products, S.A., v Intervell Electrónica, S.L.* Case number 345/2002, ARP 2003\783, 2 February 2001 *Gora G v Louis Vuitton Malletier S.A.* Case number 343/2000, JUR 2001\133923, 10 July 2001 Sporloisirs S.A., *The Polo Lauren Company S.P., Reebok, Adidas v Félix Miguel F.* Case Number 203/2001, JUR 2001\308189, a decision by the Provincial Court of Appeal of Santa Cruz de Tenerife of 21 May 2004 *D./Dña Enrique y Emilia v The Polo Lauren Company y Hugo Boss AG* Case number 161/2004, JUR 2004\205176 , and a decision by the Provincial Court of Appeal of Cantabria of 27 September 1999 *Loewe, S.A v D José Antonio E. R. y Dª Asunción V. R.* Case number 137/1999, ARP 1999\4408. Case law regarding the consideration of the importation of counterfeit merchandise as an attempted offence can be found in a decision issued by the Provincial Court of Appeal of Valencia on 3 May 2002 *Bandai España, S.A. v Gope G.K.* Case number 270/2002, ARP 2002\638, or a decision by the Provincial Court of Appeal of Barcelona of 2 May 2001 *Pernod Ricard, S.A. v Teichenne, S.A.*, Case number 1017/1999, AC 2001\1038.
[59] Ley 38/2002 de reforma parcial de la Ley de Enjuiciamiento Criminal, sobre procedimiento para el enjuiciamiento rápido e inmediato de determinados delitos y faltas, y de modificación del procedimiento abreviado. (*Reform of the Criminal Procedure Law.*) of 24 October, BOE 28 October 2002.
[60] The acts constitutive of a criminal offence in the field of intellectual property under Spanish criminal law have been defined above, in Part I, section B, of this chapter.

26.91 The penalty for counterfeiting of distinctive signs (trade marks and trade names) provided for by the Criminal Code is a prison term of from six months to two years, and a fine of from 12 to 24 months.[61]

26.92 For pirating a literary, artistic, or scientific work or an alteration, interpretation, or artistic rendering thereof, the Criminal Code provides for a penalty comprising a prison term of from six months to two years, and a fine of from 12 to 24 months.[62]

26.93 The penalty for infringing a patent, or an industrial or artistic design, provided for by the Criminal Code is a prison term of from six months to two years, and a fine of from 12 to 24 months.[63]

26.94 For infringing a protected plant variety, the Criminal Code provides for a penalty comprising a prison term of from six months to two years and a fine of from 12 to 24 months.[64]

26.95 The penalty for infringing a designation of origin or a geographical indication provided for by the Criminal Code is a prison term of from six months to two years and a fine of from 12 to 24 months.[65]

VI. LIABILITY OF CUSTOMS AUTHORITIES AND RIGHT-HOLDERS

A. Liability of right-holders and sanctions

26.96 Article 1092 of the Spanish Civil Code[66] lays down a definition of civil liability in the event of tort by providing that 'whoever, through fault or negligence, causes injury to another shall be obligated to remedy the injury suffered'. Pursuant to Article 19(3) of the Regulation, the right-holders' civil liability in the case of a breach of the Regulation shall be governed, under Spanish law, by the general tort law provision of Article 1092 of the Civil Code.

26.97 Liability as referred to in Article 12 of the Regulation (that is, in the case of non-permitted use of the information provided by customs to the right-holder) may arise from different causes, and has to be considered in light of the general clause on civil liability in the event of tort referred to in the preceding paragraph. First, it needs to be noted that the Regulation is of course intended to curb the

---

[61] Criminal Code, Art 274.   [62] Ibid, Art 270.   [63] Ibid, Art 273.
[64] Ibid, Art 274(3).   [65] Ibid, Art 275.   [66] Código Civil Español de 1889.

infringements of intellectual property rights at the Internal Market's borders. Fraudulent use or use for other purposes not in keeping with the primary purpose of the Regulation shall be liable to sanction. Another reason why customs may raise a claim for liability against right-holders in such cases is that actions by customs in their capacity as part of the public administration are intended to safeguard interests that cannot be subordinated to the right-holders' private interests where there is conspicuous abuse of law. This is a controversial subject, particularly where it comes to concluding private agreements between the parties outside the procedures provided for by the Regulation. In this respect Spanish Customs have raised objections in the past to private agreements between the parties, thus obviating the corresponding legal actions, considering that customs were used simply as a supplier of business information. Currently, the simplified procedure allows the goods to be abandoned for destruction as a way to conclude the proceedings without any actual need for instituting a civil or criminal action. To our mind there is no conflict between the right-holder being able to try to achieve a practical outcome satisfactory to his own private interests, including, for example, reaching agreement with the infringer as to compensation for damages, and the public administration's being able, if it so chooses, to defend the public interest by instituting criminal proceedings where it deems it appropriate to do so, especially now that a complaint by the right-holder is no longer a requirement for criminal proceedings.

B. Liability of customs authorities and sanctions

Article 19(1) of the Regulation stipulates that the right-holder is not entitled to claim compensation from customs where a customs office has failed to detect infringing goods. There is no problem with this, inasmuch as services provided by customs cannot be made subject to a pre-established outcome. In reference to the possible exception that may be provided for under the national law of a Member State, it should be noted that Article 106(2) of Spain's Constitution does lay down the principle of financial liability by the administration where an individual suffers injury as a consequence of improper operation of public services, except in cases of *force majeure*.[67] There is a large body of case law on this subject, though none dealing with customs action in the framework of the powers conferred under the Regulation.

26.98

---

[67] Cf also Ley 4/1999 de modificación de la Ley 30/1992, de Régimen jurídico de las Administraciones Públicas y del procedimeinto Administrativo Común) (Legal System of the Public Administration and Common Administrative Procedure Act) of 13 January, BOE 14 January 1999.

26.99 The exemption from liability provided for in Article 19(2) of the Regulation is more debatable. This Article stipulates that the exercise by customs of the powers conferred on them in order to fight *ex officio* against goods infringing intellectual property rights shall incur no liability, 'except where provided for by the law of the Member State' concerned. In this connection, the same comment made in the preceding paragraph concerning the exception in Article 19(1) and to the principle of financial liability by the administration set out in Article 106(2) of Spain's Constitution is also applicable to the case contemplated in Article 19(2).

Conclusion

26.100 Entry into force of new Regulation 1383/2003 represents a significant enhancement of the procedures relating to border measures against infringements of industrial and intellectual property rights which have been employed in Spain up to now. Procedures have now been expedited and are less burdensome to rightholders. A particularly significant aspect is the improvement to the procedure for detaining and inspecting goods, in which provision is now made for delivering samples for analysis and inspection, thereby eliminating the need to carry out inspection in person. Another very interesting feature is the simplified procedure, in which the procedure can be terminated on an expedited basis by abandonment and subsequent destruction of infringing goods with the infringer's consent, although the effect of implementation of the Ministerial Order that has been announced remains to be seen. Lastly, in the specific case of Spain, the increased use of electronic means of communication, basically e-mail and fax, has considerably simplified the performance of procedures before the Spanish customs authorities.[68]

---

[68] The authors express their gratitude to the European Commission for its ongoing initiatives in the fight against counterfeiting and piracy and its efforts and sensitivity to this major problem, which undermines the economies of the Member States of the European Union and causes incalculable losses to private enterprise. In recent years Spanish Customs, too, have made exceptional efforts to apply the Regulation effectively in full cooperation with right-holders, achieving significant positive results.

27

SWEDEN

Bengt Eliasson and Helena Wassén Öström

Introduction

Before Sweden's entry into the European Union in 1995, border measures against **27.01** counterfeit and pirated goods were rather unusual. It was more common that action was taken against the goods after they had entered the country.

At the time of Sweden's entry into the European Union, a new Customs Act was **27.02** introduced.[1] This Customs Act was a supplement to the Community legislation concerning border measures, Regulation (EEC) No 3842/86.[2] Since the Swedish Customs Act that was introduced in 1995 was rushed in order to be finalized before entry into the European Union, a new Customs Act was introduced in 2001.[3] In Chapter 7 of this new Act, reference is made to EC Regulation No 3295/94.[4]

Since their entry into force on 1 July 2004, the new EC Regulation Nos **27.03** 1383/2003[5] and 1891/2004[6] are being applied by Swedish Customs. However, so far the Swedish legislator has not proposed any amendments to the Swedish Customs Act considering EC Regulation Nos 1383/2003 and 1891/2004.

---

[1] Customs Act (*Tullagen 1994:1550*). This Act came into force on 1 January 1995.
[2] Council Reg (EEC) No 3842/86 of 1 December 1986 laying down measures to prohibit the release for free circulation of counterfeit goods [1986] OJ L 357/1.
[3] Customs Act (*Tullagen 2000:1281*).
[4] Council Reg (EC) No 3295/94 of 22 December 1994 laying down measures to prohibit the release for free circulation, export, re-export or entry for a suspensive procedure of counterfeit and pirated goods [1994] OJ L 341/8.
[5] Council Reg (EC) No 1383/2003 of 22 July 2003 concerning customs action against goods suspected of infringing certain intellectual property rights and the measures to be taken against goods found to have infringed such rights [2003] OJ L 196/7.
[6] Commission Reg (EC) No 1891/2004 of 21 October 2004 laying down provisions for the implementation of Council Reg (EC) No 1383/2003 concerning customs action against goods suspected of infringing certain intellectual property rights and the measures to be taken against goods found to have infringed such rights [2004] OJ L 328/16.

According to the Swedish legislator they are planning to present a proposal for amendments of the Swedish Customs Act during 2006.

27.04 Following Sweden's accession to the European Union and the enlargement of the European Union, the country's customs have fewer tasks to carry out. In view of this and due also to a tighter budget, Swedish Customs were reorganized and in July 2004, a new structure was introduced. Instead of being divided into regional offices, Swedish customs now work in different competence departments responsible for different tasks. In the new organization the department with national specialists responsible for intellectual property, the handling of applications for action, and other general questions concerning border measures were increased from two to three specialists. These national specialists also became responsible for questions concerning product safety and generic drugs imported to Sweden. In the new organization each customs office around the country should have one or more officers responsible for border measures concerning intellectual property. In the first few months following the reorganization, there was a significant reduction in customs activities. Thereafter, however, customs actions have increased and the total seizures in relation to intellectual property for 2004 exceeded the amount of seizures for 2003.[7] The reduction was probably due to the fact that new officers working with these questions lacked experience and competence. In addition, the personnel with experience had other tasks to handle besides the border measures concerning intellectual property.

27.05 As background, it should be noted that earlier border measures against counterfeit and pirated goods were not politically prioritized in Sweden. One reason for this was probably that Swedish rights-holders were not subject to counterfeit or piracy crimes as often as for example French fashion goods.

27.06 In preparing this chapter, we have consulted Swedish Customs' national specialists responsible for handling applications for customs action under EC Regulation Nos 1383/2003 and 1891/2004 (see para 27.93 below).

I. SUBJECT MATTER AND SCOPE OF THE NATIONAL LAW APPLYING THE REGULATION

27.07 This Part clarifies under which customs procedures Swedish Customs will act against suspected goods (section A), the definition of the infringing goods towards

---

[7] There were 470 seizures in 2004, compared to 396 in 2003, cf para 27. 71.

which they will take action (section B), and the goods excluded from the scope of the Regulation (section C).

A. Customs procedure of the goods

In principle, Swedish Customs will apply the Regulation to all customs **27.08** procedures mentioned in Article 1(1) of the Regulation, thus including entry into or removal from the Community customs territory, release for free circulation, exportation, re-exportation, placement under a suspensive procedure (for example, external transit), and placement in a free zone or free warehouse.

B. Definition of infringing goods

(1) Counterfeit goods

Article 2(1)(a)(i) of EC Regulation 1383/2003 defines 'counterfeit goods' against **27.09** which customs may take action as 'goods, including packaging, bearing without authorization a trademark identical to the trademark validly registered in respect of the same type of goods, or which cannot be distinguished in its essential aspects from such a trademark, and which thereby infringes the trademark-holder's rights under Community law, as provided for by Council Regulation (EC) No 40/94 of 20 December 1993 on the Community trademark[8] or the law of the Member State in which the application for action by the customs authorities is made'. Under Articles 2(1)(a)(ii) and 2(1)(a)(iii), also considered as counterfeit goods, on the same conditions are: '(ii) any trademark symbol (including a logo, label, sticker, brochure, instructions for use or guarantee document bearing such a symbol), even if presented separately'; and '(iii) packaging materials bearing the trademarks of counterfeited goods, presented separately'.

Identical trade marks and trade marks which cannot be distinguished in their essential aspect from the trade mark as registered

Under the Swedish Customs Act, which makes reference to EC Regulation No **27.10** 3295/94, Swedish customs authorities have acted both against goods bearing without authorization a trade mark *identical* to and trade marks that are only *similar* to (that is, which cannot be distinguished in their essential aspects from) a registered trade mark. This approach has remained unchanged subsequent to the entry into force of EC Regulation No 1383/2003. Our experience is that Swedish Customs act against goods when the customs officer suspects that the goods could infringe a trade mark under national or community trade mark law. However,

---

8 [1994] OJ L 11/1. Regulation as last amended by Reg (EC) No 807/2003 [2003] OJ L 122/36.

before customs take any decision to detain or suspend release of the goods, they notify the right-holder and ask him to confirm whether or not the goods are in his view considered as 'counterfeit goods'.

27.11 The border measures are often taken against identical or almost identical marks, but sometimes border measures are also taken against goods that bear similar marks. The formulation 'cannot be distinguished' has in such cases been interpreted broadly by the Swedish Customs. Customs application of the EC Regulation No 1383/2003 in principle corresponds to the Swedish courts' evaluation of what constitutes a trade mark infringement. In view of this, Swedish Customs' application of the Regulation might be considered to be broader than the definition in Article 2(1)(a)(i).

Validly registered in respect of the same type of goods

27.12 Swedish Customs will only act against goods that are covered in the relevant trade mark registration. If it is unclear whether or not the goods in a suspected shipment are covered in the registration, it is up to the individual customs officer to decide whether or not to take action. The officer sometimes also checks with the right-holder whether or not he considers the goods to be covered by the registration.

27.13 If only some of the goods in a registration have been included in the customs application, customs will, if they find a suspected shipment with goods covered by the registration, but not by the customs application, contact the right-holder in order to give him the possibility to supplement the customs application.

Trade mark applications as a basis for application for action

27.14 In Sweden, it is not possible to rely on a trade mark application as a basis for an application for action to the customs authorities.

Trade mark infringement

27.15 According to Article 4 of the Swedish Trade Marks Act[9] the right in a trade symbol granted under Article 1 (registered rights), Article 2 (right established through use), or Article 3 (right to use family name, etc, as a trade symbol):

> shall imply that no person other than the owner is entitled to use, in the course of business activities, a symbol which is confusingly similar to the protected one for his goods, whether on the goods or on their packages, in advertising or on business documents or in any other way, including also oral use thereof. This shall apply regardless of whether the goods are offered for sale or intended to be offered for sale in this country or abroad or are imported here.

---

[9] *Varumärkeslag (1960:644).*

When evaluating whether or not two trade symbols are confusingly similar, the **27.16** symbols and the goods concerned are compared. The more similarity there is between the symbols (trade marks), the less similarity there has to be between the goods, or vice versa, in order to give rise to a trade mark infringement.

As mentioned in paragraph 27.10 above Swedish Customs act against both **27.17** identical and similar trade marks. Swedish Customs' application of EC Regulation No 1383/2003 is in principle similar to the evaluation concerning risk of confusion that the Swedish courts conduct in an infringement case in accordance with the Trade Mark Act.

There have been several cases where Swedish Customs have suspended the release **27.18** of goods to which a sign had been affixed which is 'identical to' or which 'cannot be distinguished in its essential aspects from' a protected trade mark and which, thereafter, have been found by the appropriate court as infringing the rightholder's rights. In one case, Customs in Borås had suspended the release of 400 t-shirts marked with BATMAN and SUPERMAN. The importer was a private company that did not respond to the writ of summons. The court ruled that an infringement had been committed and ordered the importer to pay legal costs and damages in an amount of SEK 85,000.[10,11]

In another case concerning mobile phone covers, 1,000 pirate copies of NOKIA **27.19** covers were found in a shipment containing 7,000 covers. In the course of the proceedings, the importer claimed that he had acted in good faith and that he had told his buyer, who had travelled to Bangkok to buy the goods, that the goods should not have any trade marks on them. Nokia claimed both trade mark and design infringement. In the decision, the court stated that the importer has a far-reaching duty to examine the nature of the goods. In view of the fact that the covers had been bought at a low price and not from one of Nokia's retailers, the examination duty was not limited. The importer had acted negligently by not investigating the origin of the goods. The court ordered the importer to pay damages amounting to SEK 50,000, legal costs of SEK 80,000, and storage costs of SEK 56,000.[12]

Trade mark symbols and packaging materials

Swedish Customs also take measures against trade mark symbols, such as logos, **27.20** labels, stickers, brochures, instructions for use, or guarantee documents bearing a counterfeit trade mark, even if delivered separately. They will also act against packaging materials bearing such a trade mark, even if delivered separately.

---

[10] SEK 1, 000 equals approximately EUR 110.
[11] *DC Comics v Mats Delin*. (District Court of Stockholm, Case No T-9086-02, 11 October 2002).
[12] *Nokia Corporation v Muzasser Cavdarlar*. (Ibid, Case No T-18766-01, 21 October 2002).

27.21   For instance, customs have suspended the release of labels for football shirts which had been imported separately. Note, however, that protected trade marks could be legally used on goods to indicate the intended purpose of a product, for instance on printer ink cartridges. In order to be considered acceptable use, the reference to the trade mark should be made discreetly with the trade mark in small standard characters (not logo or device mark) with, for instance, the preposition 'for'. In a recent case the Swedish Supreme Court has decided that spare parts to Volvo cars packed in packages marked with the importer's name and logo and with the statements 'Rod Volvo' and 'Stabilizer link Volvo' in standard letters should be released by customs since the markings were considered necessary.[13]

27.22   In another case, customs suspended the release of a shipment that contained guarantee certificates and seals marked with the trade mark ROLEX. The right-holder sued the importer. The latter did not respond to the allegations and the court ruled in favour of the right-holder. The importer was sentenced to pay SEK 140,000 in damages and legal costs and the goods were destroyed.[14]

(2) Pirated goods

27.23   Under Article 2(1)(b) of EC Regulation 1383/2003, the customs authorities in the Member States of the European Union are also competent to take action against pirated goods, which are defined as 'goods which are or contain copies made without the consent of the holder of a copyright or related right or design right, regardless of whether it is registered in national law, or of a person authorized by the right-holder in the country of production in cases where the making of those copies would constitute an infringement of that right under Council Regulation (EC) No 6/2002 of 12 December 2001 on Community designs[15] or the law of the Member State in which the application for customs action is made'.

27.24   As mentioned above regarding counterfeit goods, the customs officers will, if they suspect that a shipment contains goods that are or contain unauthorized copies, inform the right-holder of the goods concerned and ask him to confirm whether or not he considers the goods to be pirated. The customs officers will not suspend the release of the goods until they have received a confirmation from the relevant right-holder that the goods should indeed be considered to be infringing.

---

[13] *Scan-Tech USA/Sweden AB v Volvo Personvagnar Aktiebolag*. (Swedish Supreme Court, Case No Ö 4188-04, 1 April 2005). In the case the Court made reference to Case C-63/97 *BMW v Deenik*. [1999] ECR I-0000.
[14] *Rolex S.A. v Word Wide Workers Import och Bemanning AB i konkurs*. (District Court of Stockholm, Case No T-17143-02, 13 January 2003).   [15] [2002] OJ L 3/1.

Copyright infringement and infringement of related rights

According to Article 2 of the Swedish Copyright Act:[16] **27.25**

[a] copyright shall include the exclusive right to control the work by reproducing it and by making it available to the public, be it in the original or an altered form, in translation or adaptation, in another literary or artistic form, or by other technical means. As a production of copies shall also be considered the recording of a work on a material support by means of which it can be reproduced. A work is made available to the public by public performance, or by having copies of it placed on sale, leased, lent, or otherwise distributed to the public or publicly exhibited. As a public performance shall also be deemed a performance which takes place within the framework of commercial activities for a comparatively large closed group of persons.

The Act includes limitations of these rights, such as reproductions for private **27.26** purposes, reproductions within educational activities, hospitals and certain archives and libraries, reproduction for visually handicapped persons, etc, composite works for use in educational activities, distribution and exhibition of copies, public performance, quotations, use of works of fine art and buildings under certain circumstances, information on current events, public debates, public documents and alteration of buildings and useful articles. There are also special provisions concerning sound radio and television, computer programs and extended collective agreement licences.

Protection for related rights enjoyed by performing artists, producers of sound or **27.27** audiovisual recordings, broadcasting organizations, producers of catalogues, etc, and photographers, is dealt with in Chapter 5 of the Swedish Copyright Act.

Following the EC Copyright Directive 2001/29/EC about harmonization of **27.28** certain aspects of copyright and related rights in the Information Society,[17] the Swedish Justice Department has drawn up a communication[18] in view of implementing the Directive into the Swedish Copyright Act. The suggested amendments came into force on 1 July 2005.

Article 2 of the Swedish Copyright Act has long been considered vague in certain **27.29** aspects, especially concerning what should be considered 'exhibition of copies' and what should be considered 'public performance' within the digital environment. Through the proposed amendments, the copyright-holders' exclusive rights will hopefully be made more clear. Article 3 of the Copyright Directive states that 'Member States shall provide authors with the exclusive right to authorize or prohibit any communication to the public of their works [. . .].' This includes, for instance, when the work is made available to the public in a way that makes it possible for individuals to access the work at any time they choose

---

[16] *Lag 1960:729 om upphovsrätt till litterära och konstnärliga verk.*
[17] [2001] OJ L 167/1.   [18] *Ds 2003:35.*

('on-demand' reproduction). This has a large impact on works that have been made available on the Internet. In Sweden, making works available on the Internet has often been considered as exhibition of copies or public performance, which, under certain circumstances, has been exempted from the exclusive rights of the right-holder.

27.30   In the proposed amendment, it is made clear that the right-holder's exclusive right includes all forms of making the works available to the public, including on the Internet.

27.31   What should be considered as production of copies has also been a problem in Sweden. According to Article 2 of the Copyright Act, 'production of copies shall also encompass the recording of a work on a material support by means of which it can be reproduced'. In the proposed amendment, it is made clear that production of copies should include any direct or indirect, temporary or permanent production of copies of the work, regardless of in which form or by which means this is done, and regardless of whether it is done partly or as a whole.

27.32   In the amendment, the exemption of 'reproductions for private purposes' in Article 12 of the Copyright Act is limited. Through the amendment, copies made from an original that has been made available to the public without the consent of the copyright-holder will not be considered legitimate. Still according to Article 12, 'Anyone is entitled to make, for private purposes, single copies of works [...].' In the past, 'single copies' has been interpreted quite generously for the public, which has, of course, been criticized by right-holders. In order to be consistent with the Directive, the proposed amendment makes clear that this exception should be circumscribed to a few copies for private use. Through this amendment, it should, for instance, be understood that reproduction at the workplace is not included in this exemption, and that the number of copies allowed should be very limited.

27.33   The proposed amendments to the Copyright Act (cf para 27.25 above) include a proposal also to strengthen the scope of related rights.

27.34   As mentioned in paragraphs 27.10 and 27.17 above in relation to counterfeit goods, the Swedish Customs seem to have taken quite a broad approach on the application of EC Regulation No 1383/2003 for copyright. Although the majority of cases have concerned copies, it is not just copies that have been seized. Goods similar to or with markings similar to copyright protected goods or characters/marks have occasionally been seized as well. However there have not been many cases which have included copyright and/or related rights. During 2004 only 10 per cent of the seizures taken by Swedish Customs related to copyright or design rights (cf para 27.38 below).

Design right infringement

According to Article 5 of the Swedish Design Act,[19] a design right shall 'imply that no **27.35** other person may exploit the design without the authorization by the holder of the design rights (the design-holder). The prohibition against exploitation comprises, in particular, the manufacture, offering for sale, marketing, importation into and exportation from Sweden, or the use of any product of which the design forms part or to which it is applied, or to keep in stock such a product for the purposes mentioned.' The design rights are limited through Article 7 (that is, when the use is made for private non-commercial purposes or for experimental purposes, or when the design is reproduced for the purposes of quotation or teaching), Article 7a (that is, when the design forms part of an equipment—such as a spare part— on ships and aircraft belonging to another State), and Article 7b (that is, products put on the market within the European Economic Area ('EEA') by the design-holder or with his consent—so-called 'exhaustion of rights' principle).

Design right protection shall extend to any design which, although not identical **27.36** to the design as registered, does not produce on the informed user a different overall impression than that of the registered design. In assessing the scope of protection of design rights, the degree of freedom of the designer in developing his design shall be taken into consideration.

Whether or not a design constitutes an infringement is decided through **27.37** comparing the suspected design and the registered design as the latter is shown in the pictures or drawings filed together with the application for protection. For the purposes of this assessment, it is thus the registered design and not the design as it is being used that is compared with the suspected infringing design.

The customs border measures against design rights has so far been rather limited **27.38** in number (cf para 27.34 above) and it is therefore difficult to evaluate whether or not the Regulation is being applied broadly by Swedish Customs.

(3) *Goods infringing other intellectual property rights*

Goods infringing a patent or a supplementary protection certificate

According to Article 39 of the Swedish Patent Act,[20] '[t]he scope of patent **27.39** protection shall be determined by the patent claims. For the construction of the patent claims the description could be taken into account.'

The supplementary protection certificate (SPC) shall confer the same legal effects **27.40** as the patent.

---

[19] Swedish Design Act (*Mönsterskyddslag 1970:485*).
[20] Swedish Patent Act (*Patentlagen 1967:837*).

27.41 Under Article 3 of the Swedish Patent Act, a patent (and an SPC) confers on its owner the exclusive right to prohibit others not having his consent from:

- making, offering, putting on the market or using a product protected by the patent, or importing or storing such product for these purposes;
- using a process that is protected by the patent or, while knowing, or it being obvious from the circumstances, that the use of the process is prohibited without the consent of the patentee, offering the process for use in Sweden;
- offering, putting on the market, or using products directly obtained by a process protected by the patent, or importing or storing such product for these purposes.

27.42 The offering or supplying of means that relate to an essential element of the invention for carrying out the invention to a person who is not entitled to exploit in Sweden can also, on certain conditions, result in a patent infringement.

27.43 Under Article 3(3) of the Patents Act, the patentee's exclusive rights do not include non-commercial use of the patented invention, the further commercialization of products which have been put on the market within the EEA by the patentee or with his consent, use of the invention for experiments that relate to the object of the invention itself, or preparation in a pharmacy (in individual cases).

27.44 Swedish Customs have handled some limited cases concerning patent rights. However these cases have also included infringement of trade mark and/or design rights. In view of the very limited amount of seizures concerning patent and SPC rights it is not possible to draw any conclusion as to whether customs apply EC Regulation No 1383/2003 broadly or not.

Goods infringing a national plant variety

27.45 According to Chapter 2, Article 2, of the Swedish Plant Variety Act,[21] plant variety rights gives plant breeders the right to prohibit, without their authorization, commercial exploitation of the plant variety concerned through:

- producing or reproducing breeding material of the variety,
- arranging breeding material of the variety for reproduction purposes,
- offering for sale breeding material of the variety,
- selling or in any other manner making available breeding material of the variety,
- exporting breeding material of the variety from Sweden,
- importing breeding material of the variety into Sweden, or
- keeping in stock breeding material for any of the purposes mentioned here above.

27.46 The plant breeder's rights do not include exploitation for personal or non-commercial purposes, exploitation for experimental purposes, or exploitation for

---

[21] Swedish Plant Variety Act (*Växtförädlarrättslag 1997:306*).

the production of new plant varieties.[22] Nor do they extend, in principle, to plant varieties that have been placed on the market within the EEA by the owner of the plant breeder's rights, or with his consent.[23]

To our knowledge, Swedish Customs have not detained or suspended the release of goods suspected of infringing a plant variety right to date. **27.47**

Goods infringing a national designation of origin or a geographical indication

Sweden is a party to the 1883 Paris Convention, the Madrid Protocol and the TRIPs Agreement,[24] that came into force in 1996. Furthermore, Sweden is, of course, bound by the EC Regulations concerning national designations of origin and geographical indications.[25] **27.48**

From a historical and political point of view geographical indications and designations of origin have had low priority in Sweden. One reason for this could be that questions concerning designation of origin and geographical indications have not been culturally and politically prioritized. Until now, Sweden only has two geographical indications, namely 'Svecia'[26] and 'Skånsk spettekaka'[27] and one traditional speciality, namely 'Falukorv'[28] registered. **27.49**

This might explain why Sweden lacks a *sui generis* protection for national designations of origin and geographical indications. Instead, protection is conferred on these titles through general laws such as the Trade Marks Act[29] and the Marketing Act.[30] Thus, the general clause set out in Article 4 of the Marketing Act, which prohibits unfair competition, and Article 6 of the Marketing Act, which prohibits misleading advertising, could be seen as conferring a general protection on designations of origin and geographical indications. For example, these provisions prohibit any misleading information concerning a product's geographical and commercial origin or a product's nature and character. Other provisions from the Marketing Act that might also be relevant for the protection of designations of origin and geographical indications are Article 8, relating to misleading imitations, and Article 8a, dealing with comparative advertising.

---

[22] Ibid, Ch 2, Art 3.   [23] Ibid, Ch 2, Art 4.
[24] Paris Convention for the Protection of Industrial Property as last amended on 28 September 1979, Protocol Relating to the Madrid Agreement Concerning the International Registration of Marks (as signed 1989) and Agreement on Trade-Related Aspects of Intellectual Property Rights (1995).
[25] Council Reg (EEC) No 2081/92 of 14 July 1992 on the protection of geographical indications and designations of origin for agricultural products and foodstuffs [1992] OJ L 208/1. As last amended by Commission Reg (EC) No 1215/2004 of 30 June 2004 [2004] OJ L 232/21. Council Reg (EEC) No 2082/92 of 14 July 1992 on certificates of specific character for agricultural products and foodstuffs [1992] OJ L 208/9. As last amended by Council Reg (EC) No 806/2003 of 14 April 2003 [2003] OJ L *122/1*.   [26] Protected Geographical Indication for a Swedish cheese.
[27] Protected Geographical Indication for a pastry from the south of Sweden.
[28] Traditional Specialties Guaranteed for the sausage 'Falukorv'.
[29] *Varumärkeslag (1960:644)*.   [30] *Marknadsföringslag (1995:450)*.

27.50   Most cases concerning violations of the Swedish Marketing Act are handled by the Swedish Market Court. Some rulings made under the Marketing Act are, however, brought before the District Court of Stockholm (cf para 27.140 below). It is up to the manufacturer using the questioned indication to prove that the advertisement is accurate. In principle, protection only accrues to advertisements concerning similar and/or competing products. However, it may also be possible to act against other products where the protected indication has a reputation.

27.51   In 2002, the Swedish Market Court ruled[31] against a manufacturer that had been marketing yoghurt to which the statement 'champagne taste' was affixed. The manufacturer was forbidden, under penalty of a fine, to use this statement or any other phrase with reference to 'champagne'. The use of the wording 'champagne taste' in respect of yoghurt was considered as sponging on the reputation of the designation of origin 'champagne'. However, its use was not considered misleading as to the geographical origin of the product, since yoghurt and champagne, according to the court, are essentially different in their nature.

27.52   Due to lack of resources and knowledge about designations of origin and geographical indications there is a great risk that Swedish Customs would not recognize goods infringing designations of origin and geographical indications and act *ex officio*. So far Swedish Customs have not received any applications concerning designations of origin and geographical indications.

27.53   The Swedish Trade Marks Act also provides general protection for designations of origin and geographical indications, since by virtue of this Act, geographical names may not be registered as trade marks or form part of a registered trade mark.[32] The reason for this is that geographical indications and indications of origin lack distinctiveness. A geographical name might also be considered misleading.[33] If a trade mark has been registered in spite of these provisions, it is subject to cancellation in accordance with Article 25 of the Swedish Trade Marks Act.

27.54   In 2003, the Market Court ruled[34] that a crisp-bread manufactured in the province of Värmland could not be called Mora, which is a town in the province of Dalarna. The indication was considered as misleading as to the geographical origin of the product, notwithstanding the fact that the manufacturer had been using the indication since the 1970s.

---

[31] *Institut National des Appelations d'Origine (INAO), Comité Interprofessionel du Vin de Champagne (CIVC), Veuve Clicquot Ponsardin and Pierre Cheval v Arla Foods AB* (Swedish Market Court, Case No C 33/99, 29 August 2002).

[32] Swedish Trade Marks Act, Arts 1(2) and 13(1).   [33] Ibid, Art 14.

[34] *Leksandsbröd Aktiebolag v Wasabröd Aktiebolag.* (Swedish Market Court, Case No C 4/01, 29 April 2003).

If a designation of origin or a geographical indication has become protected as a **27.55**
trade mark through extensive use, the normal regulations concerning trade marks
and trade mark infringement could be used.[35]

Other Swedish pieces of legislation that contain provisions pertaining to the **27.56**
protection for designations of origin and geographical indications include, for
instance, the Collective Trade Marks Act,[36] the Act on the Protection of
Designations on Agricultural Products and Provisions,[37] and the Alcohol Act.[38]

To our knowledge, customs have never taken border measures against any desig- **27.57**
nations of origin or geographical indications.

(4) Moulds and matrices

Pursuant to Article 2(3) of EC Regulation 1383/2003, the customs authorities of **27.58**
the Member States are also to take action against '[a]ny moulds or matrix which is
specifically designed or adapted for the manufacture of goods infringing an
intellectual property right', provided however that 'the use of such moulds or
matrices infringes the right-holder's rights under Community law or the law of
the Member State in which the application for action by the customs authorities
is made'.

It could be argued that under Swedish law the import of moulds or matrices **27.59**
should be considered as an attempt or preparation to commit infringement of an
intellectual property right. Furthermore, under the Swedish Patent Act Article 3
the right-holder has a right to prevent third parties not having the right-holder's
consent from supplying or offering to supply in Sweden a person not entitled with
means relating to an essential element of the invention, when the third party
knows or it is obvious in the circumstances that these means are suitable and
intended for putting the invention into effect.

In infringement matters the patent-holder can claim that an object which, if used, **27.60**
could constitute a patent infringement should be altered, detained for the remainder of the term of patent or destroyed.[39] The same kind of claims could be put forward in design and trademark infringement cases.[40] Under Swedish Copyright
the court may, at the request of the author or his successor in title, in accordance
with what is considered reasonable, order that type matter, printing blocks,
moulds, or other similar devices which can be used only for the production

---

[35] Swedish Trade Marks Act, Art 6(1) and (2).   [36] *Kollektivmärkeslag (1960:645).*
[37] *Lag (1995:1336) om skydd för beteckningar på jordbruksprodukter och livsmedel, m.m.*
Supplementing Council Reg (EEC) No 2081/92 and Council Reg (EEC) No 2082/92.
[38] *Alkohollag (1994:1738).*   [39] Swedish Patent Act, Art 59.
[40] Swedish Design Act, Art. 37; Swedish Trade Mark Act, Art. 41.

of infringing goods shall be destroyed or altered in specific ways or that other measures shall be taken to prevent unauthorized use.[41]

27.61 There is a great risk that customs would not be able to detect and recognize moulds and matrices which could be used for the production of infringing goods, at least without very specific information from the right-holder.

27.62 To our knowledge, Swedish Customs have not yet acted against any moulds or matrices.

C. Goods excluded by the Regulation

(1) Parallel imported goods

27.63 In accordance with Article 3(1), first indent, of EC Regulation 1383/2003, and absent any alternative provision for that purpose under national law, customs authorities in Sweden may not and *will* not initiate border measures against (genuine) parallel imported goods. If customs are certain that the goods are genuine (but parallel imported) goods, they will not inform the right-holder when they find such goods. However, in most cases, they will first check with the right-holder whether the goods are genuine. Customs will not take the responsibility of deciding whether a shipment contains infringing or genuine goods. They will instead require written confirmation from the right-holder that the goods have to be considered suspect of infringing an intellectual property right, before deciding to detain or suspend the release of the goods. If the right-holder is unable to inform customs why a shipment should be thought to contain non-authentic goods, this will suggest that the goods could be genuine parallel imported goods. The goods will be released if no acceptable explanation is provided by the right-holder on this point.

(2) Goods which have been manufactured under conditions other than those which have been agreed with the right-holder

27.64 By virtue of Article 3(1), second indent, of EC Regulation 1383/2003, the Regulation does not apply to genuine goods which have been manufactured under conditions other than those agreed with the right-holder and are subsequently parallel imported into the European Community (or placed under another customs procedure at the external borders of the Community).

27.65 Accordingly, in principle, Swedish Customs will not take action in the above-mentioned situation. This can be justified by the fact that, in principle, customs are not informed about the content of the licence agreements concluded by right-holders.

---

[41] Swedish Copyright Act, Art. 55.

Even where they are informed thereof, they are not willing to take the responsibility of deciding whether or not the consignment complies with the terms of such an agreement. In customs' view, it is not possible for them to check this.

(3) *Goods contained in travellers' personal baggage*

Under Article 3(2) of EC Regulation 1383/2003, action of the customs author- **27.66** ities from the Member States on the basis of the Regulation is precluded where a traveller's personal baggage contains goods of a non-commercial nature within the limits of the duty-free allowance (EUR 175), and there are no material indications to suggest that the goods are part of a commercial traffic.

Travellers' personal baggage is not controlled by Swedish Customs unless they **27.67** have reason to suspect that they contain unauthorized goods falling within the scope of Regulation 1383/2003.

In order not to be the object of a customs action under the Regulation, the value of the **27.68** goods contained in a traveller's personal baggage has to be less than EUR 175, and it should be obvious in the circumstances that the nature of the goods is non-commercial. For that purpose, Swedish Customs make an overall assessment of the amount of goods, their purchase value, etc. If they have no information about the value of the goods, they estimate their value reasonably, and may, where appropriate, rely on trade statistics for that purpose. In difficult cases, an expert may be called upon.

For example, if a traveller's personal baggage contains 100 t-shirts bought in **27.69** Thailand for EUR 1.7 each, the nature of the goods will probably be considered to be commercial. If a traveller's baggage contains a relatively high quantity of t-shirts of different sizes, this could also indicate that these goods are not intended for personal use.

II. APPLICATION FOR ACTION BY THE CUSTOMS AUTHORITIES

Part II reviews the '*ex officio*' customs measures and the formal requirements for **27.70** the filing and processing of applications for action by the customs authorities.

In 2004 Swedish Customs made 470 seizures. These seizures included about **27.71** 125,000 articles of different kinds. The market value of the corresponding amount of original goods was about SEK 29 million.[42]

---

[42] Information from Swedish Customs.

A. Measures prior to an application for action by the customs authorities ('*ex officio* measures')

(1) General remarks

27.72 Pursuant to Article 4 of EC Regulation 1383/2003, where the customs authorities of the Member States, before an application for action has been lodged by the relevant right-holder, have sufficient grounds for suspecting that goods infringe an intellectual property right, they may suspend the release of the goods or detain them for a period of three working days from the moment of receipt of the notification by the right-holder and by the declarant or holder of the goods, if the latter are known, in order to enable the right-holder to submit an application for action.

27.73 Under this provision, Swedish Customs are willing to act *ex officio* and take border measures when they find goods that they suspect of infringing an intellectual property right. However, the monitoring of goods suspected of infringing an intellectual property right which is the object of an application for action lodged under Article 5 of the Regulation are prioritized. Indeed, the fact that an application has been filed testifies to the right-holder's interest in having customs take action to monitor and protect his rights.

27.74 Quite a lot of *ex officio* measures have been taken by Swedish Customs in the past[43] when the consignments have contained large quantities of suspected goods. Right-holders who, in spite of having been informed by customs of suspected shipments, repeatedly refrain from filing an application for action, run the risk that customs will see this as an indication that they are not interested in having their rights monitored. This could give a wrong signal to customs officers, so that the next time a consignment with suspected goods is found, they will not contact the right-holder again.

Assessment of the existence of sufficient grounds for suspecting that the goods infringe an intellectual property right

27.75 When deciding whether goods are suspicious or not, Swedish Customs make an overall assessment of, for example, the value of the shipment, export country, country of origin, previous shipments, etc. It is up to the customs officers to make this assessment individually and if they suspect goods of infringing an intellectual property right, they will contact the right-holder and ask for a written statement as to whether or not the right-holder considers the goods to infringe his rights. Only on being provided with such a written statement, will customs decide to suspend the release of the goods or detain them.[44]

---

[43] Of the 470 seizures conducted in 2004, 50 were *ex officio* actions.
[44] Cf paras 27.77 and 27.79–27.80.

Information provided by customs to the right-holder

In order for the right-holder to evaluate whether the goods infringe any of his **27.76** intellectual property rights, Swedish Customs are always prepared to send digital pictures of the suspected goods for their attention. It is also possible for the right-holder to request that samples of the goods be handed over to him. However, customs prefer that only digital pictures are used. The right-holder is in any case not obliged to examine the goods, provided that he is in a position to confirm that the goods infringe his rights without physically examining them. At this point of the process the right-holder does not get any information about the importer, the origin of the goods etc.

For customs it is important that the right-holder explains why the suspected **27.77** goods are considered to be infringing his rights and how this could be decided. According to Swedish Customs it is impossible for them to know when the goods are infringing a certain trade mark. Sometimes it is very difficult to decide whether or not the goods are infringing goods and customs do not consider themselves to be in a position where they can recognize when, for instance, that a label is not in accordance with the right-holder's manual and therefore could be counterfeit.

Even if the right-holder provide customs with comprehensive information on how to decide whether or not imported goods are counterfeit or pirated goods Swedish Customs have taken the approach of always asking for a confirmation from the right-holder before they decide whether or not to seize the goods.[45]

The deadline of three working days

The deadline of three working days provided for in Article 4(1) of the Regulation **27.78** is in principle applied strictly by Swedish Customs. After a formal decision to detain or suspend the release of the goods has been taken, the right-holder is informed of the deadline for filing an application for action. If the application is lodged after the deadline has expired, it will be considered too late, and the goods will be released.

In *ex officio* cases, customs will, as mentioned in paras 27.76–27.77 above, contact **27.79** the right-holder directly, or through his registered representative, when they find a suspicious shipment. Where goods are suspected of infringing a registered intellectual property right, customs check the official registers to ascertain the owner of this right and his representative. On finding a shipment containing suspicious goods, customs often initially phone the right-holder's representative to check if he still represents the right-holder and, if so, to notify him of the suspected goods. Thereafter, customs normally send digital pictures of the goods and ask the right-holder to confirm as soon as possible (within one or two days) whether or not they

---

[45] Cf below, para 27.80.

should be considered as infringing his rights, and whether or not the right-holder wishes to take action against them. After the right-holder has confirmed that he wishes to act against the goods, customs take an *ex officio* decision to suspend release of the goods for three working days. In practice this means that the right-holder has more than three working days to act.

27.80 This approach might be considered as contrary to Article 4 of EC Regulation 1383/2003 since the term of three working days should start 'from the moment of receipt of the notification by the right-holder . . .'. The approach of Swedish Customs could be explained as customs not considering that they 'have sufficient grounds for suspecting that the goods infringe an intellectual property right' before they have received a confirmation from the right-holder. This is also considered by customs as a way to protect the importer since the importer's name and address is not revealed until the right-holder has actually confirmed that the goods are considered as infringing his right and that he would like to act against the goods.

27.81 Further, Article 4(2) of EC Regulation No 1383/2003 provides that customs 'may, without divulging any information other than the actual or supposed number of items and their nature and before informing the right-holder of the possible infringement, ask the right-holder to provide them with any information they may need to confirm their suspicions'. In some cases customs have taken the opportunity to ask for information in order to confirm or rule out suspicions, but in most cases customs simply ask the right-holder for confirmation.

B. The lodging and processing of applications for customs action

(1) Persons entitled to file an application for action

Definition of 'right-holders' under the Regulation

27.82 Under Article 2(2) of EC Regulation 1383/2003, 'right-holders' shall mean, for the purposes of the Regulation:

(a) the holder of a trade mark, copyright or related right, design right, patent, supplementary protection certificate, plant variety right, protected designation of origin, protected geographical indication and, more generally, any right referred to in Article 2(1) of the Regulation;

(b) any other person authorized to use any of the intellectual property rights mentioned in point (a), or a representative of the right-holder or authorized user.

27.83 An application for action under the Regulation may therefore be filed either by the right-holder *stricto sensu*, authorized users (such as licensees), or their representatives.

So far Swedish Customs have only received applications from right-holders and **27.84**
have thus not yet evaluated how they would interpret 'any other person
authorized [...]'.[46] An exclusive licence would be accepted. If a licence is limited
to certain kind of goods the licensee would probably only be able to file an
application for the goods for which he has a licence.

The concept of 'representative' is interpreted quite broadly in Sweden. In principle, **27.85**
anyone with a power of attorney from a right-holder (*stricto sensu*) or an
authorized user may act in this capacity before customs or any other authorities
(including the courts).

Proof of entitlement to file an application for action

For right-holders stricto sensu

In order to prove entitlement to a registered trade mark right, a design right, a **27.86**
patent right, a plant variety right or designation of origin, geographical indication
and geographical designation in Sweden, the right-holder must file a registration
certificate with customs or provide them with copies from an official database
(that is, databases maintained by a national,[47] regional, or international industrial
property office)[48] establishing the existence of the registered right. For copyright
and related rights, the right-holder may submit a simple declaration in which the
right-holder declares in writing that he is the rightful owner of the copyright. The
document should be accompanied by pictures and/or examples of the copyright
protected goods. This document does not need to be notarized or legalized, but
the original document should be filed.

A customs application cannot be granted on the basis of a mere application for **27.87**
registration of an intellectual property right. An application could, of course, be
filed to draw customs' attention to the fact that a shipment with suspicious goods
is expected, for example. However, customs cannot grant an application lodged
under Article 5 of the Regulation or act *ex officio* merely on the basis of an
application for registration of an intellectual property right.

For persons authorized to use the right

If a licensee wishes to file an application for action with Swedish Customs under **27.88**
the Regulation, he must file a copy of the licence agreement together with the
application. If the licensee should also act as representative of the right-holder, he
also needs a power of attorney. The licence agreement should mention the rights

---

[46] See also paras 27.88–27.89.   [47] www.prv.se/vmi/.
[48] Swedish Customs only accept copies of registration certificates or extracts from *official* databases. However, extracts from private databases are normally also accepted if it could be shown that
the information in the database is collected from the official registers.

that have been licensed.[49] Furthermore, the registration certificates or extracts from a database for the registered rights that have been licensed should be enclosed with the application. Originals of the documents (except the power of attorney) are not required, nor need they be notarized or legalized.

27.89 Swedish Customs would probably not request that the licence is registered for industrial property rights since this is not obligatory under the Swedish industrial rights laws. When an application is filed customs will evaluate whether or not the applicant is authorized under the EC Regulation 1383/2003.

For representatives

27.90 The representatives should file, before or together with their customs application, a power of attorney establishing that they are authoriced to represent the right-holder or authorized user. A simple copy of the power of attorney is accepted in matters of urgency, but the original should be filed as soon as possible after lodging the customs application. A general power of attorney, in respect of *all* customs actions, is also accepted by Swedish Customs. If a general power of attorney is filed, however, customs appreciate being provided with a copy of this document in future cases. Swedish Customs do not register powers-of-attorney centrally.

27.91 Swedish Customs cannot deny foreign representatives (that is, representatives without an office/domicile in Sweden) the right to act before them. However, they prefer a Swedish representative who is familiar with the Swedish customs system, Swedish geography and the Swedish language.

27.92 The declaration referred to in Article 6 of the Regulation should be signed either by the right-holder *stricto sensu* or the authorized user. Swedish Customs would probably, despite the wording of Art 2(3) of EC Regulation No 1891/2004, also accept a declaration signed by the representative. Customs do not recommend however that the representative signs the declaration since they would then be personally liable for all costs. This does of course presuppose that the representative is authorized by the right-holder or the authorized user to bear any costs.

(2) Competent customs department and formal requirements

Competent customs department

27.93 As mentioned above (para 27.04) Swedish Customs were reorganized in July 2004. Many of the officers who had worked with customs actions in the field of intellectual property protection were transferred to other positions or were entrusted with other duties in addition to border measures concerning intellectual property.

---

[49] Cf para 27.84.

The contact details of the department with national specialists responsible for **27.94** handling applications for customs action under EC Regulation 1383/2003 are as follows:

Tullverket Effektiv Handel
Box 12854
S-112 98 Stockholm
Tel: (46) 771 520 520
Fax: (46-8) 405 05 50
www.tullverket.se
tullverket@tullverket.se

This department employs three national specialists. **27.95**

When an application for action is filed under the aforesaid Regulation, it is **27.96** processed by one of these three specialists. After the application is granted, the applicant is notified about the decision and the deadline for renewing the application.

Swedish Customs estimate that they handle about 200 active applications at the **27.97** moment.[50] Approximately 260 applications have been filed in total, but some have not been renewed and are therefore considered inactive.

Form of the application for action

An application for action by customs authorities under EC Regulation **27.98** 1383/2003 may, in matters of urgency, be filed by fax, but the original must be filed afterwards. The application itself may *not* be lodged through an electronic data interchange system or by e-mail. The form for the application can be found on the customs homepage, www.tullverket.se. The application is handled internally by customs, and no electronic version of the application form is made available to the applicant or his representative.

Swedish Customs would appreciate several copies of, for instance, brochures, **27.99** being filed since these could then be kept in several customs offices. Such material and, for example, pictures of original goods and suspected goods may be (and are preferably) sent electronically to customs by e-mail to tullverket@tullverket.se, www.tullverket.se as well as being sent in 'hard copies' together with the application.

The declaration mentioned in Article 6 of the Regulation has to be filed in **27.100** original, but in matters of urgency may also be filed by fax. The original must then be sent afterwards, however.

---

[50] Information from Swedish Customs, March 2005. The number of active applications changes all the time since new applications are constantly filed and old applications become inactive if they are not renewed.

Language requirements

27.101   The application, any material enclosed with the application (exhibits), the declaration under Article 6 and the power of attorney may be filed in either Swedish, English, or both. Customs prefer Swedish, however.

(3) *Requirements regarding the contents of the application for action*

27.102   As a general rule, a right-holder lodging an application for action under Article 5 of EC Regulation 1383/2003 is advised to provide customs with as much information as possible, as this will enable the customs officers to monitor more accurately possible infringements of the intellectual property rights concerned. Information about authorized users, shipping routes, suspected importers and exporters, etc could prove very helpful in this context.

27.103   All information provided to Swedish Customs will be analysed and included in the database from which the customs officers who carry out controls get their information. For example, when information about suspected importers and exporters is provided, customs can put an electronic block on these companies or individuals. Such a block means that the customs offices will automatically be notified that the company in question is suspected of infringing intellectual property rights, which should facilitate the taking of actions under the Regulation on an expedited manner when this company tries to clear a shipment through customs control. This could thus help the customs officers decide if a physical control should be made on a given consignment.

27.104   It is also recommended that customs be informed of all authorized, respectively unauthorized/suspected importers and/or exporters who are known to the right-holder. This will make it easier for customs to check whether a shipment may be considered suspicious.

Mandatory information

Technical information

27.105   Information which must be mentioned in the application pursuant to Article 5(5) of EC Regulation 1383/2003 includes, in the first place, a technical description of the goods. Although the above provision requires that the description be 'accurate and detailed', in practice, it can be quite general. Reference is often made for that purpose to the registration certificate of the intellectual property right concerned (for example, a trade mark certificate listing the goods for which the trade mark has been registered, a copy of the patent specification and the patent claims, etc). Needless to say that the more information provided to customs, the more efficient will their monitoring be.

Type or pattern of fraud

Under Article 5(5) of the Regulation, an applicant for customs actions is also **27.106** required to provide customs with any specific information he may have concerning the type or pattern of fraud. This will also help to improve customs' monitoring of the rights on which the applicants rely. It is therefore in the applicant's own interest that customs be provided with all the information available to be able to guarantee an efficient watch on the applicant's intellectual property.

Since the entry into force of EC Regulation No 1383/2003 Swedish Customs **27.107** have become more active in requesting further information from right-holders, especially concerning the pattern of fraud.

Contact persons

The application forms prescribed by EC Regulation 1891/2004 ask the right- **27.108** holder to provide the particulars of the applicant's contact person(s) for dealing with administrative and technical matters. Swedish Customs do not require a local presence of these contact person(s), but prefer liaising with a Swedish person, for practical reasons.

Other

The application for action must also contain the declaration required of the applic- **27.109** ant under Article 6 of the Regulation, and the proof that the applicant holds the right for the goods in question. When the application consists of a 'Community' application for action under Article 5(4) of the Regulation, it must also indicate the Member State(s) in which customs action is required as well as the names and addresses of the right-holder in each of the Member States concerned.[51]

Optional information

Any additional information that makes it easier for customs to identify infringing **27.110** goods, avoid suspending the release of genuine goods, evaluate suspected goods and determine whether or not goods are infringing or genuine will of course be welcomed by customs. This includes the pre-tax value of the original goods on the legitimate market in the country in which the application for action is lodged, the location of the goods or their intended destination, particulars identifying the consignment or packages, the scheduled arrival or departure date of the goods, the means of transport used, the identity of the importer, exporter, or holder of the goods, the country or countries of production and the routes used by traffickers, and the technical differences between the genuine and suspect goods.[52] Lists of authorized licensees and/or suspected companies can prove particularly helpful.

---

[51] Reg 1383/2003, Art 5(5).   [52] Ibid.

Additional information specific to the type of intellectual property right referred to in the application

27.111   Pursuant to Article 5(6) of EC Regulation 1383/2003, details which are specific to the type of intellectual property right referred to in the application for action may also be required by customs. We are not aware of any case where Swedish Customs have made use of this option to date.

(4) Processing and acceptance of the application for action

Term for the processing of an application for action

27.112   On receiving an application for action, the competent customs department must process the application and notify the applicant in writing of its decision within 30 working days of its receipt.[53]

Appeal of the customs authority decision

27.113   A decision by the customs authority to reject or not process an application for action under the Regulation can be appealed before the administrative courts.[54] When an application does not contain the required information, the officer handling it will however in principle simply request additional details.[55] If the application is not supplemented with the requested information the application will be rejected in accordance with Article 5(8) of Regulation No 1383/2003.

Period during which customs are to take action once an application is accepted

27.114   By virtue of Article 8(1) of Regulation No 1383/2003, an application can be granted for a maximum of 12 months. Thereafter, it has to be renewed. Save in the case of Community applications for action, which are always granted for one year, the applicant can request a shorter period of time during which he would like his rights to be monitored.

(5) 'Community' applications for action

27.115   Community applications for action filed through Swedish Customs under Article 5(4) of Regulation 1383/2003 will be processed as any other (that is, national) application. The customs authorities in those countries in which the applicant would like his rights to be monitored will be notified of such an application by Swedish Customs. In these notifications, Swedish Customs will enclose a response

---

[53] Reg 1383/2003, Art 5(7).   [54] Swedish Customs Act (*Tullagen 2000:1281*), Ch 9, Art 2.
[55] Cf on this point Reg 1383/2003, Art 5(8).

envelope in which the receiving customs authority can return a confirmation of receipt to Swedish Customs.

Conversely, when a Community application for action has been filed in another **27.116** Member State of the European Union, and the applicant has indicated that he would like his rights to be monitored in Sweden, Swedish Customs will be notified by the authorities in the Member State where the application has been filed. Swedish Customs will then acknowledge receipt of this notification and thereafter handle the application as a normal (that is, national) application valid for Sweden. As mentioned above, Swedish Customs will prefer that a contact person be appointed in Sweden for the Swedish part of the Community application for action.

III. CONDITIONS GOVERNING ACTION BY CUSTOMS AUTHORITIES AND BY THE AUTHORITIES COMPETENT TO DETERMINE WHETHER GOODS INFRINGE AN INTELLECTUAL PROPERTY RIGHT

A. Conditions governing action by customs authorities

(1) Factual background

Since Swedish Customs were reorganized in July 2004, the customs offices in **27.117** Sweden are no longer divided into regions, but into competence departments with different responsibilities. Each customs office should in principle comprise at least one officer responsible for the protection of intellectual property rights at the borders.

Subsequent to the reorganization, there was a noticeable decline in the taking of **27.118** border measures in Sweden, which led to criticism.[56] According to customs, the reason for this decline was that several of the new officers handling border measures in the beginning were inexperienced in these types of matters. In addition, the experienced officers who are still responsible for this kind of measures were also entrusted with other tasks as well.

Historically, the customs offices in Gothenburg and at the Arlanda Airport in **27.119** Stockholm have been the most important ones, or at least the most active, in

---

[56] For instance from the Swedish Anti Counterfeiting Group, www.sacg.org.

taking border measures. According to Swedish Customs, the reason for this is that a lot of goods are cleared through these offices, and that the personnel have been engaged for dealing with—and show a particular interest in—matters concerning border measures in the field of intellectual property.

(2) *Notification of customs intervention*

27.120   The right-holder is notified of a customs action under Regulation 1383/2003 by customs, either directly, or through his registered representative. Customs normally phone the right-holder or representative and inform them that they have found suspicious goods in a shipment. Thereafter, customs usually send digital pictures of the suspected goods for examination by the right-holder or his representative.

27.121   When deciding to detain or suspend the release of suspected goods, Customs also inform the declarant or holder of the goods at the same time as the right-holder. Before customs have taken an official decision regarding the goods in question, their declarant or holder will in principle only be told that an investigation is ongoing concerning the goods if they seek to have them released.

27.122   When taking a decision to detain or suspend the release of suspected goods Swedish Customs have to consider the principle of proportionality[57] which means that the reasons for action have to outweigh the interference in or detriment to the persons affected by the action.

(3) *Information to be provided by customs to the right-holder before the right-holder confirms the infringing nature of the goods*

27.123   Once customs have decided to detain or suspend the release of goods suspected of infringing an intellectual property right, the right-holder concerned will be notified of the nature of the goods, the actual or estimated quantity of the goods,[58] and the name and address of the importer, the consignee, the holder of the goods, and the declarant. This information will in principle be provided in writing, together with the notification of the detention or suspension of release of the goods. The right-holder may also receive information about the countries of origin and destination. If known customs would also inform the right-holder, upon his request, about the name and address of the consignor.

27.124   The Swedish Act on the Protection of Trade Secrets[59] applies to unwarranted infringements of trade secrets. However, as an unwarranted infringement is not to

---

[57] Swedish Customs Act, Ch 6 Art 1.

[58] Before EC Reg 1383/2003 came into force, customs were not allowed to reveal the quantity of goods included in a suspected shipment, which gave rise to some problems in Sweden.

[59] *Lag (1990:409) om skydd för företagshemligheter.*

be considered the fact that someone acquires, exploits, or divulges what is a trade secret of a person conducting business or industrial activities in order to make available to the public or before a public authority something that may be an offence for which imprisonment may be adjudicated, or which may be considered to be another serious incongruity in the business or industrial activity of a person conducting such activities. Furthermore an unwarranted infringement is not considered the fact that someone exploits or divulges a trade secret which he or someone before him acquired knowledge of in good faith.

Other Swedish legislation which should be observed in this connection is the Act **27.125** concerning personal data,[60] the Press Act[61] and Secrets Act.[62] However as concluded in ECJ Case C-233/98,[63] the Regulation[64] 'precludes a rule of national law under which the identity of declarants or consignees of imported goods which the trade mark owner has found to be counterfeit may not be disclosed to him'. After this decision the Swedish Secrets Act Chapter 9, Articles 1 and 2 were amended[65] and now make reference to the exceptions under the EC Regulation No 3295/94. The practice of Swedish Customs has changed accordingly.

(4) Inspection of the suspected goods

The right-holder is allowed (but not obliged) to inspect the goods at any time after **27.126** he has been informed by customs of their detention or the suspension of their release. The right-holder can also request that samples of the goods be handed over or sent to him at any time. Customs may be prepared to send samples, but generally prefer that they be collected at the customs premises.

Instead of inspecting or taking samples of the goods, the most common way for **27.127** the right-holder to get information about the goods is through digital pictures provided by customs. The effective examination of the goods or the taking of samples may be seen as useful alternatives in those cases where the right-holder is not able to evaluate whether or not the goods infringe his rights solely by reviewing digital pictures.

Digital pictures of the goods are always provided to the right-holder by customs **27.128** prior to their taking any decision to detain or suspend the release of the goods. Before any decision is taken, customs request that the right-holder confirms that the goods are likely to infringe intellectual property rights and substantiate why

---

[60] *Personuppgiftslag (1998:204).* [61] *Tryckfrihetsförordning (1949:105).*
[62] *Sekretesslag (1980:100).*
[63] Case C-223/98 Adidas AG Reference for a preliminary ruling [1999] ECR I-7081.
[64] Council Reg (EC) No 3295/94 of 22 December 1994 laying down measures to prohibit the release for circulation, export, re-export or entry for suspensive procedure of counterfeit and pirated goods. [65] *Lag om ändring i Sekretesslagen (1980:100) SFS 2002:1124.*

they can be considered as such. In this regard customs apply the same procedure as in matters where they act *ex officio* (cf paras 27.75, 27.77 and 27.79–27.80 above).

27.129 Samples will only be provided at the right-holder's express request. The samples thus sent or handed over to the right-holder may be used in any way necessary in order to establish whether the goods infringe an intellectual property right, including before the courts.

B. Simplified procedure allowing the destruction of the goods without there being any need to determine whether an intellectual property right has been infringed under national law

27.130 Swedish Customs apply Article 11 of EC Regulation No 1383/2003, as they already did in practice before this Regulation came into force. Swedish Customs have taken the position that they cannot detain goods after the right-holder has decided that he will not file a writ of summons against the owner, declarant, or holder of the goods. If the right-holder and the owner, declarant, or the holder of the goods agree that the goods are to be destroyed and the owner, declarant, or holder of the goods file a request for destruction of goods Swedish Customs are not in a position to keep a suspension of release on the goods.

27.131 The procedure set out in Article 11 allows the right-holder and the owner, declarant, and holder of the goods to agree on their abandonment for destruction under customs control. It is up to the parties (including the right-holder) to try to find an amicable settlement if they wish to avoid court proceedings. In practice, the owner, declarant, or holder of the suspected goods will, as a minimum, have to agree to the destruction of the goods at his own expense to find the right-holder prepared to settle the matter. The right-holder often requires that the owner (or declarant or holder) of the goods sign a declaration under which he agrees to the relinquishment and/or destruction of the goods at his own costs, undertakes to pay any storage costs incurred, and to refrain from further infringing the intellectual property rights concerned in the future. The owner (or declarant or holder) of the goods will in principle also be required to pay some kind of additional damages to the right-holder as a compensation for the infringement.

27.132 If the right-holder and the owner (or declarant or holder) of the goods agree on the place where the goods are to be destroyed, customs will monitor the process of destruction of the goods and confirm to the right-holder when they have been destroyed.

Customs will release goods for destruction under customs control only after a   **27.133**
request for destruction has been filed. Such a request may be filed by the
owner, declarant, or holder of the goods or the right-holder if the owner,
declarant, and holder of the goods have accepted to assign the goods to the
right-holder. If the right-holder requests the destruction of the goods, a copy of
the settlement agreement must be filed with customs before or together with the
request.

By contrast with Article 11 of EC Regulation 1383/2003, Swedish Customs   **27.134**
refuse to assume that the destruction of the goods is deemed to be accepted when
the declarant, holder, or owner of the goods have not opposed such destruction
within the deadline or 10 working days (or three working days in the case of perishable goods) provided for in this provision.

Customs will not interfere in negotiations between the right-holder and the   **27.135**
owner, holder, and declarant of the suspected goods, and will not object to any
clauses concerning for example, the reimbursement of the destruction, storage
and legal costs, the grant of punitive damages, or cease and desist declarations.

C. Conditions governing action by the authorities having jurisdiction to determine whether the goods infringe an intellectual property right

(1) Authorities having jurisdiction to determine whether the goods infringe an intellectual property right

If the right-holder is not interested in reaching, or is not able to reach, an   **27.136**
amicable settlement with the owner, declarant, and holder of the suspected
goods within the maximum of 3, respectively 10 (up to 20) working days, as
provided in Articles 11 and 13 of the Regulation, proceedings aiming at
determining whether an intellectual property right has been infringed under
national law must be initiated to secure the detention or suspension of the release
of the goods.

In Part 1, section B, (1) to (3) above, we have already explained under what   **27.137**
conditions goods are considered as infringing trade mark rights, copyrights,
design rights, patent rights and supplementary protection certificates, national
plant variety rights, and national designations or geographical indications in
Sweden. We will now go through the rules which apply to determine the proper
forums under the different intellectual property laws in Sweden, the different
remedies available, as well as the advantages and disadvantages of the different
types of proceedings available.

Choice of the proper forum

27.138 The proper forum for handling cases concerning trade mark, design, and copyright infringements in both civil and criminal proceedings is, in the first place, the District Court in the place where the defendant has his place of business or residence. For patent infringements and cases concerning infringement of Community trade marks, the District Court in Stockholm is the exclusive forum in both criminal and civil proceedings. The same has also been suggested for cases that concern Community designs.

27.139 The decisions rendered at first instance may be appealed to the Court of Appeal of proper jurisdiction (second instance) and thereafter, under leave to appeal, to the Supreme Court (third and final instance).

27.140 For infringements of designations of origin or geographical indications where claims for injunction are brought in a civil action under the Swedish Marketing Act,[66] the Market Court in Stockholm is the appropriate forum. Decisions by the Market Court cannot be appealed against. Claims for damages under the Market Act should be initiated before the District Court in Stockholm, whose decisions can be appealed to the Market Court.

Remedies common to all intellectual property rights covered by the Regulation

27.141 In principle, all intellectual property rights covered by the Regulation could be tried either through civil or criminal action. The right-holder can thus choose whether to file a writ of summons on his own or to try to have the Public prosecutor initiate a criminal complaint and bring the case to Court.

27.142 The possibilities to have an indictment brought by the Public prosecutor differ somewhat between the different intellectual property rights and will therefore be handled separately below.

27.143 Through a civil action, the right-holder can claim prohibition, interlocutory injunction (under special circumstances), damages, and alteration or destruction of the goods/material.

27.144 For a more detailed overview of the remedies available to intellectual property right-holders in Sweden, please refer to Part V below.

Interlocutory injunction

27.145 If the right-holder shows reasonable grounds that an act implying an infringement or a violation of his rights is taking place, and if it can be reasonably expected that

---

[66] Cf paras 27.49–27.50.

the alleged infringer, through continuing the act, is diminishing the value of the intellectual property rights, the court may issue an injunction for the time until the case has been finally adjudicated or is decided otherwise. It could be requested that the injunction should be issued under penalty of a fine.

An additional condition for the issuance of an interlocutory injunction is that the **27.146** right-holder deposits a security with the court for the damage that may be caused to the defendant. It is, under certain circumstances, possible for the court to liberate the right-holder from this obligation. Often, this security is made in the form of a bank guarantee. If a security has been deposited, the court will examine it if the defendant has not accepted it.

In principle, the defendant should have an opportunity to respond before an **27.147** interlocutory decision is taken by the court. However, the right-holder could request that this rule should not apply if the delay that this would lead to entails a risk for further damages.

When the case is finally adjudicated, the court should decide if the injunction **27.148** should continue to apply.

Seizure

Under the Trade Marks Act, Design Act, Patent Act, Copyright Act, and Plant **27.149** Variety Act, goods can be seized if it can reasonably be assumed that an infringement has been committed. Under the Market Act, seizure is only available to secure a claim for market disruption fee.[67] A seizure of the goods can be sought in the course of both criminal and civil proceedings.

Criminal actions

Under the Swedish Trade Marks Act, Patent Act, Design Act, and Plant Variety **27.150** Act, an indictment for the offence[68] may be brought by the Public prosecutor only at the instance of the aggrieved party, *and* provided that such prosecution is deemed justified in the public interest.

Under the Copyright Act, on the other hand, '[a] criminal action [...] may be **27.151** instituted by a Public Prosecutor only if there is a complaint from the injured party *or* if such an action is called for in the public interest'.[69] The Public prosecutor has to start a criminal action if the right-holder files a complaint, even if he does not find it called for in the public interest.

---

[67] For seizures, Chapter 15 of the Code of Judicial Procedure applies.
[68] The acts constitutive of a criminal offence in the field of intellectual property law will be defined in Part V below.   [69] Swedish Copyright Act, Art 59. Emphasis added.

27.152   An action concerning breach of the Swedish Market Act cannot be brought by a Public prosecutor. Instead, the Swedish Consumer Ombudsman could bring actions under the Swedish Market Act.

Infringement investigation

27.153   Under the Trade Marks Act, Design Act, Copyright Act, Plant Variety Act, and Patent Act, the court may, under certain circumstances and if it can be reasonably assumed that an infringement has been committed, in order to secure evidence concerning the infringement, decide that an infringement investigation be conducted.

27.154   By virtue of Article 13(1) of Regulation 1383/2003, in order to have the detention or suspension of the release of the goods upheld by customs, the right-holder must notify them within 10 (up to 20) working days of receipt of the notification of the relevant customs action, that 'proceedings have been initiated to determine whether an intellectual property right has been infringed under national law' (unless of course the matter has been settled on the basis of Article 11).

27.155   Customs consider proceedings to determine whether or not goods are infringing an intellectual property right to have been initiated upon the filing of a writ of summons concerning infringement of the intellectual property at the proper court. A copy of the writ of summons together with information about the appointed Court Case No is sufficient as evidence that a proceeding has been initiated.

27.156   The filing of a writ of summons concerning breach against the Swedish Marketing Act at the Market Court would probably not be accepted by customs as evidence that proceedings to determine whether or not goods are infringing the intellectual property right since a case before the Market Court would not decide whether an intellectual property has been infringed or not.

27.157   If the public prosecutor acts against the consignment customs seizure has to be replaced by a decision of the public prosecutor that the goods are to be seized.

Advantages and disadvantages of the different remedies available

27.158   In view of limited public resources, and the fact that trade mark infringements have not been prioritized by Public prosecutors, most matters are today handled as civil cases on the motion of the right-holder. Criminal actions have so far only been initiated when it was evident that the importer was continuously importing infringing goods and/or was importing large amounts of infringing goods.

27.159   One advantage with the civil proceedings is that the right-holder is in charge of the proceedings and can pursue the matter in his own way. In a criminal action, on the other hand, the right-holder is dependent on the Public prosecutor and most of the Public prosecutors in Sweden are very unfamiliar with handling intellectual property cases. Since civil actions are also the most common, courts are equally unfamiliar with handling intellectual property cases under criminal law.

Another advantage with the civil proceedings is the possibility to reach an amicable settlement at any time during the proceedings. **27.160**

Advantages with criminal proceedings are that public resources and experience concerning investigation could be used, and that they perhaps have a greater deterrent effect than a civil action. **27.161**

(2) *Term for notifying customs that proceedings have been started*

As already pointed out above, pursuant to Article 13(1) of EC Regulation 1383/2003, within 10 working days of receipt of the notification of suspension of release or of detention of the goods, the right-holder must notify customs that proceedings have been started to determine whether an intellectual property right has been infringed, or, alternatively, that the matter has been amicably settled. Should the right-holder fail to act accordingly, the goods will be release or their detention ended, subject to completion of all customs formalities. **27.162**

In the case of perishable goods detention should be ended within three working days if the right-holder has not initiated any action to determine whether an intellectual property right has been infringed. It is important to check that the deadline given in the notice from customs is correct in order not to risk losing the possibility of bringing an action. **27.163**

The term of 10 working days (except for perishable goods) may be extended by another 10 working days 'in appropriate cases'. Swedish Customs will grant an extension if the right-holder has not been able to get in contact with the owner of the goods, or when they are negotiating and it might still be possible to settle the matter amicably. Being on holiday has not been accepted as a ground for extension. **27.164**

D. Release of goods suspected of infringing certain rights on provision of a security

Swedish Customs have no practice concerning the application of Article 14(1) of Regulation 1383/2003, which allows the declarant, owner, importer, holder, or consignee of the goods to obtain the release of goods suspected of infringing design rights, patents, supplementary protection certificates or plant variety rights, on provision of a security, and subject to the fulfilment of several other conditions. Today, customs will not release goods after a civil action has been initiated, or after the Public prosecutor has imposed interim measures (seizure) over **27.165** the goods. If a security is provided after civil action has been initiated customs would probably await a decision from the court before the goods are released. If the court decides that the goods could be released after provision of a security customs would most probably release the goods.

27.166　Hopefully the application of Article 14(1) of the Regulation and the determination of the security under Article 14(2) will soon be dealt with in a new Swedish Customs Act following the coming into force of the EC Regulation 1383/2003. A proposition for a new Customs Act is expected to be presented in spring 2005.

E. Storage of the goods

27.167　Normally, the suspected goods are stored in warehouses belonging to private storage companies. It is possible for the right-holder to request transfer of the goods to another storage room in order, for instance, to keep the costs as low as possible (as warehouses where the goods are initially stored are often quite expensive). The right-holder is responsible for the storage costs, but will usually request that the owner of the goods pay the costs. If a request to transfer the goods to a new storage room is filed with the private storage company, customs will be notified of the transfer so that the goods can always be traced when the time for their destruction (or release) comes.

27.168　In those cases where court proceedings are initiated, the right-holder can claim compensation for storage costs against the defendant in the framework of such proceedings.

IV. PROVISIONS APPLICABLE TO GOODS FOUND TO INFRINGE AN INTELLECTUAL PROPERTY RIGHT

27.169　In view of the fact that EC Regulation 1383/2003 has a direct effect in Sweden, the right-holder could, in accordance with Article 16 of the Regulation, oppose entry into or removal from the Community customs territory, release for free circulation, exportation, re-exportation, placement under a suspensive procedure, and placement in a free zone or free warehouse of all goods that are found to infringe an intellectual property right referred to in Article 2.

27.170　The national provisions allowing the right-holder to claim destruction of the goods (which can indeed be requested in most cases, cf paras 27.180–27.181,

27.190–27.192, 27.199 and 27.201–27.203 below), or their disposal outside commercial channels in such a way as to preclude injury to the right-holder, as well as any other measures allowing the persons concerned to be deprived of any economic gains from the transaction, in accordance with Article 17 of the Regulation, will be discussed below in Part V.

In court proceedings in Sweden, the losing party will, as a general rule, be ordered to bear the costs of the winning party, as well as any possible damages. **27.171**

V. PENALTIES

Most of the Swedish intellectual property laws have been more or less harmonized concerning penalties imposed in the case of infringements. For example the same grounds for calculation of damages are used in most cases. In view of this, the material below might sometimes appear repetitive. **27.172**

(1) Counterfeit goods

Fines and imprisonment

A trade mark infringement can, if committed wilfully or with gross negligence, be punished under criminal law by fines or imprisonment for not more than two years.[70] Attempts to commit an infringement as well as the preparation of such acts are punishable according to the provisions of Chapter 23 of the Swedish Criminal Code.[71] **27.173**

Injunctions (including interlocutory decisions)

Under Article 38 of the Swedish Trade Marks Act, the court may, on the request of the right-holder or an authorized user in civil proceedings, issue an injunction prohibiting, under penalty of a fine, a person who has committed an act constituting an infringement continuing that act. **27.174**

It is also possible for the right-holder or the authorized user, under the same provision, to seek an interlocutory injunction. An interlocutory injunction may be issued if the plaintiff can show a probable case that an act constituting an infringement takes place and that it can be reasonably assumed that the defendant, through continuing the act, diminishes the value of the exclusive right in the trade symbol. In cases of a claim for an interlocutory injunction, the court will always **27.175**

---

[70] Swedish Trade Marks Act, Art 37.   [71] *Brottsbalk (1962:700)*.

give the defendant an opportunity to respond, unless a delay would entail a risk of injury. In principle, an injunction will not be issued unless the plaintiff deposits a security with the court for the injury that may be caused to the defendant.

27.176 The Swedish Supreme Court has however ruled that the right-holder or the authorized user do not have to claim any interlocutory injunction in an infringement case initiated after customs have decided to seize goods.[72]

Damages

27.177 Besides fines, imprisonment, and injunctions, damages could be claimed for an infringement. Damages could be claimed either in a civil action or as a separate part of the criminal action. Article 38[73] states that:

> [a]nyone who wilfully or with negligence commits a trade mark infringement shall pay an equitable compensation for the use of the trade mark and compensation for the further damage caused by the infringement. When determining the amount of the compensation also the right owner's interest that a trade mark infringement not be committed and circumstances of other than purely economic importance shall be taken into account. Anyone who without intention or negligence commits a trade mark infringement shall pay a compensation for the use of the trade mark, if and to the extent that this is considered reasonable.

27.178 Damages may in principle only be awarded for injuries suffered during the five years immediately preceding the action being brought.[74]

27.179 Compared to other countries the damages awarded in Swedish court cases are often considered quite low.

Removal, alteration, or destruction of the infringing goods or trade symbols

27.180 The Public prosecutor in a criminal action or right-holders or authorized users in a civil action may claim that a trade symbol on an infringing product should be removed or altered. Destruction or surrender of the goods could also be claimed.[75]

27.181 The EC Regulation No 1383/2003 only mentions destruction of goods and disposal outside commercial channels.[76] Normally the right-holder in an infringement action claims that the goods are to be destroyed. However if a court would rule that removal or alteration of the trade symbol on an infringing product should be considered enough customs would not object to such a judgment. Furthermore there have been a few cases where the right-holder and the owner, holder, or declarant of the infringing goods have amicably agreed that the goods could be released after removal/alteration of the trade symbol and customs have not objected to such agreement between the parties involved. To our knowledge the only objection

---

[72] *Scan-Tech USA/Sweden AB v Volvo Personvagnar Aktiebolag* (n 13 above).
[73] Swedish Trade Marks Act.   [74] Swedish Trade Marks Act, Art 40.
[75] Ibid, Art 41.   [76] Reg 1383/2003, Art 17(1)b.

customs have had against this procedure is that they do not have the resources to monitor the removal/alteration of the goods if the consignment contains a lot of goods and that it is up to the right-holder and the owner, holder or declarant to agree how removal/alteration should be monitored/safeguarded.

Seizure

If necessary, seizure of the goods may be claimed in a criminal or civil action.[77] Goods may be seized when it can reasonably be assumed that a violation has been committed.   **27.182**

(2) Pirated goods

Fines and imprisonment

Design or copyright infringements can also, if committed wilfully or with gross negligence, be punished in a criminal action by fines or a jail term of not more than two years.[78] Attempts to commit an infringement as well as the preparation of such acts are punishable as well according to the provisions of Chapter 23 of the Swedish Criminal Code.   **27.183**

For copyright infringements, there is a special regulation concerning infringements in the form of sale, lease or offer for sale or possession for sale, lease or other commercial purposes, of devices intended solely for facilitating the unauthorized removal or circumvention of a device placed in order to protect a computer program against unauthorized reproduction. Such infringements are punished, under criminal law, by fines or imprisonment for not more than six months.[79]   **27.184**

Injunctions (including interlocutory decisions)

For design and copyright infringements, it is also possible for the right-holder or authorized user to claim, in a civil case, an injunction prohibition under penalty of a fine and interlocutory injunction. The same rules apply on this point as for trade mark infringements.[80]   **27.185**

Damages

Regulations concerning damages for design infringement are the same as for trade mark infringements.[81]   **27.186**

---

[77] Regulations concerning seizure are to be found in the Swedish Code of Judicial Procedure.
[78] Swedish Copyright Act, Art 53; Swedish Design Act, Art 35.
[79] Swedish Copyright Act, Art 57 a.
[80] Swedish Copyright Act, Art 53 a; Swedish Design Act, Art 35 a. Compare with Swedish Trade Marks Act, Art 35. Cf paras 27.174–27.176.
[81] Swedish Design Act, Art 36. Compare with Swedish Trade Marks Act, Art 38. Cf paras 27.177–27.179.

27.187 Anyone committing a copyright infringement shall pay such compensation to the author or copyright owner as will constitute a reasonable remuneration for the exploitation or the protected work.[82]

27.188 If the infringement has been carried out wilfully or with gross negligence, compensation shall also be paid for losses other than lost royalties as well as for moral harm and for other injury. The wilful or negligent infringer shall also pay to the author or his successor in title compensation for losses, mental suffering, or other injury caused by the act.[83]

27.189 The damages awarded in copyright and design right infringement matters in Sweden are comparatively low.

Removal, alteration, or destruction of the infringing goods or components

27.190 Any person who has suffered injury from a design infringement may claim that the infringing goods should be altered in a specified manner or be taken into custody for the remainder of the term of protection, or be destroyed or, as regards goods which have been manufactured without authorization in, or imported into, Sweden, be surrendered, against payment of a stamp fee, to the injured party.[84] This does not apply if a person has acquired the property or a specific right in the goods in good faith and who has himself not committed a design infringement.

27.191 The court may, however, decide on request that the owner of the infringing goods may have the right to use the goods for the remainder of the term of protection, or part of that term, against an equitable compensation and subject to other reasonable conditions.[85] There is a risk that this provision would be considered contrary to Article 17(1)b of the EC Regulation No 1383/2003 under which the measures taken by the competent authority should deprive 'the persons concerned of any economic gains from the transaction'. If the goods could be used after payment of compensation the owner of the goods might be able to profit from the goods. It should however be noted that this provision should only apply in extraordinary cases.

27.192 According to Article 55 of the Copyright Act, a copyright infringer should 'surrender to the author or his successor in title, as compensation, the property involved in the infringement or the violation. The same shall apply to typographical material, printing blocks, moulds or other similar devices which can only be used for the production of property of the kind now mentioned'. The right-holder may also claim destruction or alteration or, under certain circumstances, surrender of the

---

[82] It is to be noted that negligence or willfulness is not a prerequisite to the granting of this kind of compensation. [83] Swedish Copyright Act, Art 54.

[84] As far as we know, the provision that the goods could be surrendered to the injured party against the payment of a stamp fee has not had any practical significance in Sweden.

[85] Swedish Design Act, Art 37.

goods. This shall not apply in respect of persons who have in good faith acquired the property or a right in the goods, nor in cases involving the construction of a work of architecture.[86]

Under certain circumstances, the court may also, after payment of a fair remuneration to the author or his successor in title, rule that the copies should be made available to the public or otherwise used for their intended purpose.[87]   **27.193**

Seizure

In accordance with Article 59 of the Copyright Act and Article 37 of the Design Act, goods may be seized when it can reasonably be assumed that they infringe a copyright, a related right or a design right.   **27.194**

(3) Goods infringing a patent or a supplementary protection certificate

Fines and imprisonment

Patent infringements committed wilfully or with gross negligence can be punished, in criminal proceedings, by fines or a jail term of not more than two years. Any attempt or preparation to offend a patent shall also be deemed a criminal offence.[88]   **27.195**

Injunctions (including interlocutory decisions)

As for trade mark, design, and copyright infringements, it is possible for a patentee or the authorized users of a patented invention to claim, in the framework of a civil patent infringement case, an injunction prohibition under penalty of a fine, and an interlocutory injunction.[89]   **27.196**

Damages

The rules concerning damages for patent infringements are the same as for trade mark infringements (see paras 27.177–27.179 above).[90]   **27.197**

As for other intellectual property rights the damages awarded in patent infringement cases in Sweden are often quite low.   **27.198**

Removal, alteration, or destruction of the infringing goods or components

The courts may rule that the infringing products should be modified or surrendered for safekeeping for the remainder of the period of patent protection, or be   **27.199**

---

[86] Swedish Copyright Act, Art 55.   [87] Ibid, Art 56.
[88] Swedish Patent Act, Art 57; Swedish Criminal Code, Ch 23.
[89] Swedish Patent Act, Art 57 a. Cf above paras 27.174 ff.
[90] Ibid, Art 58. Compare with Swedish Trade Marks Act, Art 38.

destroyed or, under certain circumstances, be surrendered, against payment of a stamp fee, to the injured person.[91] The foregoing does not apply to those persons who have acquired the property or a special right to the goods in good faith and who has himself not infringed a patent. If there are special reasons, it may be decided that the patent infringer shall enjoy the use of the property for the remainder of, or a part of, the period of the patent protection against a reasonable consideration and on reasonable terms in other respects.[92]

Seizure

27.200   If appropriate, seizure of the goods may also be claimed.[93] Goods may be seized when it can reasonably be assumed that they infringe a patent right.

(4) Goods infringing a plant variety right

27.201   For plant variety rights in general, the same rules concerning fines, jail terms, injunctions, damages, removal, alteration or destruction and seizure apply as for trade mark infringements (see paras 27.173–27.182 above).[94]

(5) Goods infringing a designation of origin or a geographical indication

27.202   See above (paras 27.173–27.182) for actions against infringements of a designation of origin or geographical indication under the Swedish Trade Marks Act.

27.203   As regards actions against infringements of a designation of origin or geographical indication under the Swedish Market Act, prohibition injunctions (including injunctions under penalty of a fine and interlocutory decisions), an information order, damages and destruction of the goods could be claimed by any trader affected by their being marketed, or by the Consumer Ombudsman.[95] The Consumer Ombudsman may also, subject to the injured trader's consent, issue an injunction under penalty of a fine or order the infringer, under penalty of a fine, to provide whatever information or technical aid necessary.[96] Marketing disorder fees may also be claimed by the Consumer Ombudsman or, if the Consumer Ombudsman refrains from acting, any trade affected by the disputed marketing activities.[97]

---

[91] Cf n 84 above.
[92] Swedish Patent Act, Art 59. As mentioned in paras 27.190–27.191 above there is a risk that the fact that the infringer could under certain extraordinary circumstances be able to use the infringing goods might be considered contrary to Reg 1383/2003, Art 17(1)b.
[93] Ibid. Regulations concerning seizure are to be found in the Swedish Code of Judicial Procedure.
[94] Swedish Plant Variety Act, Ch 9, Arts 1 to 8.
[95] Swedish Marketing Act, Arts 14, 15, 16a, 17, 29 and 38.   [96] Ibid, Art 21.
[97] Ibid, Arts 22 and 39.

Note also that some of the remedies are to be claimed before the Marketing Court, **27.204**
while others, such as damages, have to be claimed before the District Court of
Stockholm, at first instance. It is therefore important to evaluate what the
right-holder wishes to accomplish through the action before actions are started.

VI. LIABILITY OF CUSTOMS AUTHORITIES AND RIGHT-HOLDERS

A. Liability of right-holders and sanctions

Under Article 12 of the EC Regulation 1383/2003 customs could suspend the **27.205**
application for action for the period of validity remaining before renewal, or, in
the event of a further breach of this provision, refuse to renew it, in the event of
any non-permitted use (that is, any use other than for the purposes specified in
Articles 10, 11, and 13(1) and prohibited by the national legislation) by the right-
holder of the particulars cited in the first indent of Article 9(3).

The information received from customs could not be used for instance to state in **27.206**
commercial activities that the owner, holder, or declarant are in fact infringing the
right-holder's rights before it has been confirmed by court that an infringement
has taken place. In Sweden the sending of cease and desist letters to the customers
of alleged infringers have been considered as a commercial activity and have under
certain circumstances been considered contrary to the Swedish Marketing Act.

B. Liability of customs authorities and sanctions

Swedish law does not entitle right-holders to compensation in the event that **27.207**
infringing goods are not detected by customs, or in the event that no action is
taken to detain suspected goods after an application has been filed.[98] Neither does
Swedish law impose liability on customs nor any other authority towards the persons involved in, or affected by an *ex officio* procedure.[99]

Conclusion

Although the Swedish legislator has, regrettably, failed to amend the Swedish **27.208**
Customs Act to put it in line with EC Regulation 1383/2003 so far, fortunately,

---

[98] Cf Reg 1383/2003, Art 19(1).   [99] Cf Ibid, Art 19(2).

Swedish Customs have not waited for this to be done before applying this new instrument efficiently. Indeed, the lack of amendment has had little impact in practice, since the Regulation has direct effect in the Member States of the European Union. Nevertheless, in our view, it would be beneficial for all the provisions of the Regulation to be reviewed and evaluated by the legislator from a Swedish point of view. An amendment to the Customs Act is on its way and it is hoped that a proposal will be presented in autumn 2005.

27.209 The new Regulation is in most respects being applied smoothly by Swedish customs officers, but there is still a lot of work that could be done to improve the customs watching of intellectual property rights in Sweden and the process concerning actions taken against suspicious goods. From time to time discussions are held between right-holders, various associations, and Customs in order to exchange knowledge.

27.210 Compared to Regulation 3295/94, the new Regulation 1383/2003 has made it clear that customs are allowed, for example, to reveal the amount of goods imported to the right-holder when taking action (even on an *ex officio* basis). The fact that the previous Regulation contained no legal basis for that measure gave rise to some problems in Sweden, since the quantity of the goods can affect the right-holder's decision as to what measures to take against an infringement.

28

UNITED KINGDOM

Alison Firth and Jeremy Phillips

Introduction

A. Border measures in the UK prior to Regulation 1383/2003

The United Kingdom has a long history of national measures to discourage the **28.01** entry of infringing goods from abroad. Clark[1] cites an Act for General Regulation of Customs as long ago as 1845. The United Kingdom was a founder member of the Paris Convention for the Protection of Industrial Property of 1883. Since the Convention's entry into force on 7 July 1884, therefore, the United Kingdom has had an international obligation to provide for seizure of imports bearing protected marks.[2] However, international treaties are not self-executing in the UK. They require implementation by national legislation. The Merchandise Marks Act of 1887, section 16, achieved this, at least in theory. This was a criminal statute and did not confer civil rights of action upon aggrieved traders; section 16 does not appear to have been much used.[3]

Article 16 of the Berne Convention for the Protection of Literary and Artistic **28.02** Works also contemplates seizure of infringing copies upon importation; again this has to take effect in the UK by way of domestic legislation, and not directly. The WTO Agreement on Trade-Related Aspects of Intellectual Property Rights ('TRIPs'), Article 51(2), requires special customs measures for the detention of

---

[1] A Clark, 'The Use of Border Measures to Prevent International Trade in Counterfeit and Pirated Goods: Implementation and Proposed Reform of Council Reg 3295/94' [1998] EIPR 414.

[2] Under Art 9 of the Paris Convention.

[3] There is reference to a presumed seizure under s 16 in *Niblett v Confectioners' Materials Co* [1921] 3 KB 387.

'counterfeit trade mark' or 'pirated copyright' goods,[4] subject to latitude for parallel imports.

28.03   The Merchandise Marks Act 1887 was repealed by the Trade Descriptions Act 1968, which also placed customs seizure provisions in the trade marks legislation.[5] Similar national legislation continues to enable customs to seize imports as 'prohibited' if they are infringing copies of copyright works or contravene trade mark legislation. The chief provisions are section 111 of the Copyright, Designs and Patents Act 1988, and section 89 of the Trade Marks Act 1994.[6]

28.04   These remain in force.[7] However, they were amended by the Copyright (EC Measures relating to Counterfeit Goods) Regulations 1995[8] and the Trade Marks (EC Measures Relating to Pirated Goods and the Abolition of Restrictions on the Import of Goods) Regulations 1995[9] to exclude situations covered by Articles 1(1) and 5(1) of EC Regulation 3295/94, and again to make them mutually exclusive with Regulation 1383/2003.[10,11] In the UK, a number of statutory instruments[12] were promulgated to give effect to Regulation 3295/94 and its amending Regulation 241/1999:[13]

---

[4]   This phraseology is reflected in the EC and national legislation; TRIPs, Art 51, n 14 provides the following definitions:

'For the purposes of this Agreement:

(a) "counterfeit trademark goods" shall mean any goods, including packaging, bearing without authorization a trademark which is identical to the trademark validly registered in respect of such goods, or which cannot be distinguished in its essential aspects from such a trademark, and which thereby infringes the rights of the owner of the trademark in question under the law of the country of importation;

(b) "pirated copyright goods" shall mean any goods which are copies made without the consent of the right-holder or person duly authorized by the right-holder in the country of production and which are made directly or indirectly from an article where the making of that copy would have constituted an infringement of copyright or a related right under the law of the country of importation.'

[5]   By inserting a new s 64A into the Trade Marks Act 1938.

[6]   Accompanied by the Trade Marks (Customs) Regulations 1994, SI 1994 No 2625.

[7]   As amended. A Clark, 'The Use of Border Measures to Prevent International Trade in Counterfeit and Pirated Goods: Implementation and Proposed Reform of Council Reg 3295/94' [1998] EIPR 414 at n 8, has pointed out that these provisions, with secondary legislation in the form of the Trade Marks (Customs) Regulations 1994, SI 1994 No 2625 and Copyright (Customs) Regulation 1989, SI 1989 No 1178 were rarely used.   [8]   SI 1995 No 1445.

[9]   SI 1995 No 1444.

[10]   Council Reg (EC) 1383/2003 of 22 July 2003 concerning customs action against goods suspected of infringing certain intellectual property rights and the measures to be taken against goods found to have infringed such rights [2003] OJ L 196/7 (2.8.2003).

[11]   For the current legal position, see Part I below.

[12]   Secondary legislation under the European Communities Act 1972.

[13]   Council Reg (EC) 3295/94 of 22 December 1994 laying down measures to prohibit the release for free circulation, export, re-export or entry for a suspensive procedure of counterfeit and pirated goods [1994] OJ L 341/8 (22.12.1994), as amended by Council Reg 241/1999 (OJ L 27/1 (2.2.1999)) and Council Reg (EC) 806/2003 [2003] OJ L 122/1.

- The Counterfeit and Pirated Goods (Customs) Regulations 1995[14]
- The Counterfeit and Pirated Goods (Consequential Provisions) Regulations 1995[15] and later
- The Goods Infringing Intellectual Property Rights (Customs) Regulations 1999[16]
- The Goods Infringing Intellectual Property Rights (Consequential Provisions) Regulations 1999[17]

In 2003 fees for notifications to customs were abolished by: **28.05**

- The Goods Infringing Intellectual Property Rights (Customs) Regulation 2003[18]

Thus, in situations covered by EC Regulation 3295/94, that Regulation was given   **28.06**
full effect in the UK by statutory instrument. The *vires* of this legislation were
challenged in *Pointing v Commissioners of Customs and Excise*[19] but the Customs
Regulations were held to have been validly promulgated under powers in the
European Communities Act 1972. More recently, in *Levi Strauss v Tesco Stores*,[20]
the English High Court emphasized the consistency between Regulation
3295/94 and Article 7 of the Trade Marks Harmonization Directive, 89/104.[21]

Other than items for travellers' own private and domestic use,[22] by 1999 all the   **28.07**
following were subject to border measures: (i) 'counterfeit goods', including packaging
and trade mark symbols, goods that infringed registrations of the same, or indistinguishable trade marks for the same goods or type of goods, (ii) 'pirated goods'
infringing copyright[23] or related rights,[24] or design rights (registered or unregistered), and (iii) goods infringing patents and supplementary protection certificates.

Customs officials could detain or suspend the release of suspect goods pursuant to   **28.08**
a request from the right-holder or on their own initiative,[25] with a period of three
days during which the right-holder could lodge a request. After consulting with
the right-holder, customs could seize the goods and apply to the court for an order
that the goods were counterfeit or infringing, and therefore should be condemned
as liable to forfeiture[26]—so-called 'condemnation' proceedings.

---

[14] SI 1995 No 1430.
[15] SI 1995 No 1447.   [16] SI 1999 No 1601.   [17] SI 1999 No 1618.
[18] SI 2003 No 1316.   [19] [1999] FSR 394 (Ch D).
[20] [2002] ETMR 95; [2003] RPC 18.
[21] First Council Directive (EEC) 89/104 of 21 December 1988 to Approximate the Laws of the
Member States Relating to Trade Marks [1989] OJ L 40/1 (11.2.1989).
[22] A number of cases have been decided on the limits of this in relation to alcohol and cigarettes.
Cf eg *David Lishman Young v HM Customs and Excise, The Crown Court at Durham* [2004] EWCA
Civ 1519 CA (Civ Div).
[23] The 'neighbouring' rights of broadcasters, producers of phonograms, etc are referred to below
as 'copyright'.
[24] Such as rights in performances. See R Fry 'Copyright Infringement and Collective Enforcement'
[2002] EIPR 516.   [25] *Pointing v Commissioners of Customs and Excise* (n 19 above).
[26] In *Pointing* (n 19 above) Customs' application was heard together with the goods owners'
application for release.

B. The courts' interpretation of measures
under Regulation 3295/94

28.09 The body of case law is small, but establishes at least the following:

> *(a) Customs procedures are distinct from civil proceedings and remedies for infringe-*
> *ment, or declarations of non-infringement; the burdens of proof differ.*

28.10 This had been emphasized by Falconer J in *CBS Inc v Blue Suede Music.*[27] In that case, the defendant in infringement proceedings had asked the court to order the claimant to withdraw the notice under which customs had seized some guitars. The judge refused on the basis that challenge should be brought under the customs procedures themselves.

28.11 In customs cases the burden falls upon the person seeking release of the goods to show that they do not infringe.[28] In infringement proceedings the burden of proof falls upon the claimant to show that the goods infringe.

> *(b) However, the consignee of the goods can seek a declaration of non-infringement*
> *from the court; customs may also ask the court to rule on infringing status. In either*
> *case the court's decision will be given due weight in condemnation proceedings.*

28.12 In *Commissioners for Customs and Excise v Top High Development,*[29] the respondent to condemnation proceedings had obtained a declaration of non-infringement in the English High Court. Mr Inigo Bing, the magistrate hearing proceedings for condemnation of the goods, gave great weight to the High Court's findings and to the evidence upon which they were based.[30]

28.13 In *Pointing v Commissioners of Customs and Excise*[31] the High Court heard parallel proceedings for release (at the suit of the goods owner) and condemnation (applications by customs). The judge, having decided that the goods were liable to forfeiture, ordered their condemnation. He further held that although the court was the 'authority competent to take a substantive decision', customs themselves were a duly empowered authority under Article 7(2) of Regulation 3295/94 as regards interim measures, such as seizing the goods, pending the court's decision on their status.

> *(c) Where registered rights are concerned, actual registration is required, not just an*
> *application to register.*

---

[27] [1982] RPC 523.
[28] Eg para 4(2) of the Counterfeit and Pirated Goods (Consequential Provisions) Regulations 1995 (n 15 above), applied in *Commissioners of Customs and Excise v Top High Development* [1998] FSR 464 (MC).   [29] N 28 above.
[30] Although as the parties were not identical, there was no estoppel on the issues.
[31] N 19 above.

This follows from the fact that, under substantive UK law, industrial property   **28.14**
rights need to be registered before they can be litigated.[32] In *Commissioners for*
Customs and Excise v Top High Development,[33] customs had relied upon a trade
mark application; this was held to be incorrect. Furthermore, where packaging is
to be seized separately from goods, it appears that customs require registration of
the mark for the packaging itself.[34]

C. Rights for which there were no border measures

Neither the Plant Varieties Act 1997 nor the EC-based Customs Regulations   **28.15**
provided border measures to protect the interests of plant variety right-holders.
Nor were geographical indications subject to border measures, unless they were
registered as Certification or Collective marks, in which case they would be
treated as other registered trade marks.[35] Passing off rights do not give rise to
remedies under any of the border measures legislation.[36] Nor is there provision in
the event that unlicensed confidential information has been used to make the
imported products. Although the Olympic Symbols, etc, Protection Act 1995
gave power to the Secretary of State to extend a number of trade mark remedies to
the 'Olympic association right'[37] conferred by the Act (such as erasure of offending signs, delivery up of infringing goods, materials or articles), those powers do
not extend to customs measures. Well-known marks which are not registered with
effect in the UK[38] did not seem to enjoy protection either under section 89 of the
Trade Marks Act or under the EC-based regime.

The United Kingdom does not recognize a general doctrine of international   **28.16**
exhaustion of rights,[39] so in principle parallel imports from countries outside the
European Economic Area ('EEA') were and are subject to the procedures under

---

[32] Patents Act 1977, s 69(2); Registered Designs Act 1949 (as amended) s 7A(6); Trade Marks
Act 1994, s 9(2)(a).   [33] N 28 above.
[34] A Clark, 'The Use of Border Measures to Prevent International Trade in Counterfeit and
Pirated Goods: Implementation and Proposed Reform of Council Reg 3295/94' [1998] EIPR 414
at 422. Cf also para 28.27 below.
[35] Trade Marks Act 1994, s 50 and Sched 2, para 1 (general provisions of the Trade Marks Act
apply to certification marks); Trade Marks Act 1994, s 49 and sched 1, para 1 (general provisions of
the Trade Marks Act apply to collective marks).
[36] Passing off has been used in the UK courts to protect the denomination 'Swiss' for chocolate
in *Chocosuisse Union des Fabricants Suisses de Chocolat v Cadbury Ltd* [1999] RPC 826.
[37] Protecting the five-ring Olympic symbol, the motto '*Citius, altius, fortius*' and various words
derived from 'Olympic'.
[38] Whether as national registrations, as international registrations under the Madrid Protocol, or
as Community Trade Marks.
[39] *Levi Strauss & Co v Tesco Stores Limited*, [2002] 3 CMLR 11; [2003] RPC 18; [2002]
ETMR 95.

section 89 of the Trade Marks Act 1994 and section 111 of the Copyright, Designs and Patents Act 1988. However, as pointed out by Clark, customs seizures of any kind under these provisions have been rare.[40]

28.17   As explained in Part I below, UK legislation had to be amended following the entry into force of Regulation 1383/2003. This was achieved by another Statutory Instrument in 2004, revoking the earlier provisions.[41] Statistics for the new regime are not yet available, but those for 2003 show a 49 per cent increase in articles seized, compared to 2002.[42]

I. SUBJECT MATTER AND SCOPE OF THE NATIONAL LAW APPLYING THE REGULATION

28.18   This Part will examine the customs procedures in which Her Majesty's Customs will act against suspect goods (section A), the definition of infringing goods under UK law (section B), and the goods excluded from the scope of the Regulation (section C).

A. Customs procedure of the goods

28.19   Regulation 1383/2003 was given effect in the UK by the Goods Infringing Intellectual Property Rights (Customs) Regulations 2004.[43] Regulation 3 of this instrument declares that goods infringing an intellectual property right which correspond to the description of goods contained in a decision shall be liable to forfeiture in *any* of the situations mentioned in Article 1(1) of the Council Regulation. All the customs procedures are therefore covered. Other specific Regulations, such as the Trade Marks (Customs) Regulations 1994 and the Copyright (Customs) Regulations 1989 remain in force with appropriate amendments.

28.20   In relation to all that follows, it must be borne in mind that customs officials scrutinizing consignments of goods will have in mind not only the provisions of Regulation 1383/2003 and any information furnished by the rights owner, but also the other tasks with which customs are charged.[44] Such other tasks include

---

[40]   A Clark, 'Parallel Imports: A New Job For Customs' [1999] EIPR 1.
[41]   SI 2004 No 1473. Regs 12, 13, 14 and Schedule revoke the earlier legislation.
[42]   http://europa.eu.int/comm/taxation_customs/resources/documents/uk_2003_en.pdf.
[43]   SI 2004 No 1473.
[44]   SI 2004 No 1473 reg 10 expressly preserves other powers of customs and the courts.

determining the customs value of imported goods under the Community Customs Code[45] and investigating VAT fraud. For example, if goods invoiced at a low price bear 'luxury' trade marks, suggesting that they will be sold at a substantial premium over the price for basic goods, customs may well decide to detain the goods for further inquiry as to their valuation. Even with genuine goods, there may be questions as to the royalty component of value for duty or VAT purposes.[46] In these situations, factors such as declared value and the addresses of origin and destination may weigh in the decision, as well as the resemblance of marks and goods. Furthermore, customs may be assisted by information from other law enforcement agencies, from industry bodies, or from the UK Patent Office. The decision in *Commissioners for Customs and Excise v Top High Development*,[47] for example, refers to assistance from the Patent Office. In June 2001, a Memorandum of Understanding was concluded between customs, police and other enforcement bodies, and industry groups formed to combat counterfeiting and piracy.[48] REACT UK,[49] a branch of the European Anti-Counterfeiting Network, is said[50] to maintain computer databases and an information system to provide data on behalf of rights owners to enforcement agencies in the UK and Ireland, and (via the European Network) to other European countries. Notes on completion of customs form C1340, at Annex IA(iv), show that customs officials use risk analysis principles to identify suspect consignments.

B. Definition of infringing goods

Regulation 2 of the Goods Infringing Intellectual Property Rights (Customs) Regulations 2004[51] defines 'goods infringing an intellectual property right' in terms of Article 2(1) of Council Regulation 1383/2003. The definitions therefore coincide exactly. **28.21**

---

[45] Council Reg (EEC) 2913/92 of 12 October 1992 establishing the Community Customs Code ([1992] OJ L 302/1 (19.10.1992), as amended) and Commission Reg (EEC) 2454/93 of 2 July 1993 laying down provisions for the implementation of Council Reg (EEC) 2913/92 establishing the Community Customs Code ([1993] OJ L 253/1 (11.10.1993). For proposed revisions, see http://europa.eu.int/comm/taxation_customs/customs/consultations/458rev.pdf.

[46] Cf Notice 252 'Valuation of imported goods for customs purposes, VAT and trade statistics', available on the HM customs and excise web site at www.hmrc.gov.uk. Cf also Articles 157–161 of Commission Reg 2454/93 (n 45 above) on the treatment of royalties and licence fees under the Community Customs Code. [47] N 28 above.

[48] Memorandum Of Understanding on Co-operation in the Field of the Detection, Investigation and Prosecution of Intellectual Property Rights Offences. The text of this memorandum is available at http://www.acpo.police.uk/asp/policies/Data/property_rights_offences_mou.doc.

[49] REACT UK, Portal Business Centre, Dallam Court, Dallam Lane, Warrington, WA2 7LT Tel: + 44 (0)1494 449192; E-mail: enquiries@react.uk.net.

[50] http://www.intellectual-property.gov.uk/std/resources/ip_organisations/reactuk.htm.

[51] SI 2004 No 1473.

(1) Counterfeit goods

28.22 Article 2(1)(a)(i) of EC Regulation 1383/2003 defines 'counterfeit goods' against which customs may take action as 'goods, including packaging, bearing without authorisation a trade mark identical to the trade mark validly registered in respect of the same type of goods, or which cannot be distinguished in its essential aspects from such a trade mark, and which thereby infringes the trade mark-holder's rights under Community law, as provided for by Council Regulation (EC) No 40/94 of 20 December 1993 on the Community Trade Mark[52] or the law of the Member State in which the application for action by customs authorities is made'. Article 2(1)(a)(ii) and (iii), also consider as such: '(ii) any trade mark symbol (including a logo, label, sticker, brochure, instructions for use or guarantee document bearing such a symbol), even if presented separately'; and '(iii) packaging materials bearing the trade marks of counterfeited goods, presented separately'.

'A trade mark identical to another trade mark . . . or which cannot be distinguished in its essential aspects from such a trade mark'

28.23 In considering whether a mark is identical or indistinguishable,[53] officials may have regard to any special features of the registration. For example, a 'Lacoste' type crocodile which is pointing in the wrong direction might be distinguished by an official from a crocodile positioned as registered. However, factors relevant to the official's other powers (cf para 28.20 above) may influence the decision to take some kind of action in such a case. Similar phraseology to the above, 'likely to be mistaken for' a registered trade mark is contained in the Trade Marks Act 1994, sections 92 and 103. In *R v Keane*,[54] a case involving imitation designer apparel, the Court of Appeal upheld the judge's decision to leave the question of resemblance of marks to the jury. This suggests that a common sense approach to the customs provisions would be approved.

'Validly registered in respect of the same type of goods'

28.24 In comparing goods, a customs official is again likely to use his common sense and take an overall view as to whether goods are 'of the same type' as the regsitration.

Trade mark applications (which have not yet been validly registered)

28.25 As mentioned in the Introduction,[55] actual registration is required, not just an application to register. In *Commissioners for Customs and Excise v Top High*

---

[52] [1994] OJ L 11/1 (14.1.1994). Regulation as last amended by Reg (EC) No 807/2003 ([2003] OJ L 122/36 (16.5.2003)).

[53] The European Court of Justice has held these criteria synonymous in case 291/00 *LCJ Diffusion v SABAS Vertbaudet* [2003] ECR I-2799; [2003] ETMR 83 (ARTHUR ET FELICIE).

[54] [2001] FSR 7 CA (Crim Div).   [55] Cf para 28.14 above.

Development,[56] reliance by customs upon a trade mark application was held inappropriate. Despite a reference to lodging of trade mark applications in Annex I-A to form 1340, it is submitted that this is still good law.

Infringing a trade mark-holder's rights under UK law

The Goods Infringing Intellectual Property Rights (Customs) Regulations 2004 **28.26** SI No 1473 Regulation 2 defines 'goods infringing an intellectual property right' in terms of Article 2(1) of the Council Regulation. By contrast, the Trade Marks Act 1994, sections 9 and 10 as amended, give a wider definition of infringement. Use of a mark in the course of trade, or use of a similar mark, may infringe if the goods are identical, similar, or dissimilar. For identical marks and products, the protection is absolute.[57] In other cases, infringement depends upon the likelihood of confusion,[58] unless the mark has a reputation and use without due cause would take unfair advantage of, or be detrimental to, the distinctive character or repute of the mark.[59] Defences available under sections 11 and 12 of the Trade Marks Act 1994 include honest use of the defendant's own name and address, of descriptive indicators, and use to indicate ancillary goods or services.

Material delivered separately

Where packaging is to be seized separately from goods, it appears that customs **28.27** require registration of the mark for the packaging itself.[60] The domestic infringement provisions of the UK Trade Marks Act 1994, section 10(5), make a label manufacturer responsible for any infringing use of the label subsequently made in the UK. The logic behind this section appears to be that the mischief is done when the signs on the labels are used in such a way as to undermine the trade mark registration. Where labels are imported, however, section 10(5) probably does not apply. It would be helpful to rights owners were UK Customs to interpret their powers broadly, to reflect the fact that Article 2(1)(a)(ii) and (iii) also consider as counterfeits, on the same conditions as the goods themselves: '(ii) any trade mark symbol (including a logo, label, sticker, brochure, instructions for use or guarantee document bearing such a symbol), even if presented separately'; and '(iii) packaging materials bearing the trade marks of counterfeited goods, presented separately'. Possibly the European legislator meant to treat logos, labels, and packaging as

---

[56] N 28 above.
[57] Requiring no proof of confusion, etc: Trade Marks Act, s 10(1).
[58] Trade Marks Act, s 10(2).
[59] Trade Marks Act 1994, s 10(3), as amended. An unofficial consolidation of the Trade Marks Act 1994 and subsequent amendments may be consulted on the website of the UK Patent Office, http://www.patent.gov.uk/tm/legal/tmact94.pdf.
[60] Cf para 28.14 above, and A Clark, 'The Use of Border Measures to Prevent International Trade in Counterfeit and Pirated Goods: Implementation and Proposed Reform of Council Reg 3295/94' [1998] EIPR 414 at 422.

infringing even if there was no valid registration in classes 16 (paper) and 26 (buttons). However, the difficulty with this approach is that in the absence of any goods for which the mark is registered, or other evidence, it is impossible for customs to form a view as to what may be done with the labels. For example, the labels might be used by a licensee in relation to other goods, or by someone who has concurrent rights in the word on the label.

(2) *Pirated goods*

28.28   Under Article 2(1)(b) of EC Regulation 1383/2003, the customs authorities in the Member States of the European Union are also competent to take action against pirated goods, which are defined as 'goods which are or contain copies made without the consent of the holder of a copyright or related right or design right, regardless of whether it is registered in national law, or of a person authorized by the right-holder in the country of production in cases where the making of those copies would constitute an infringement of that right under Council Regulation (EC) No 6/2002 of 12 December 2001 on Community Designs[61] or the law of the Member State in which the application for customs action is made'.

'Goods which are or contain copies'

28.29   As mentioned above,[62] strictness of interpretation may be tempered by other factors.

Infringing a copyright, related right, or design right

28.30   Infringement may involve the reproduction of the whole or a substantial part of a copyright work: section 16(3)(a) of the Copyright, Designs and Patents Act 1988. Infringing goods are defined in section 27 of the Copyright, Designs and Patents Act 1988. Imported goods will be regarded as infringing under section 27(3) if their making in the United Kingdom would have constituted an infringement of copyright or a breach of an exclusive licence agreement. Parallel imports from outside the EEA may therefore be infringing goods. A number of exceptions to infringement or 'permitted acts' are established by sections 28–76 of the 1988 Act.[63] Similar forms of infringement apply to the rights of performers (ss 188–190) and design rights (ss 226–228). Note that there are criminal offences under copyright (ss 107–110) and performers' right (ss 198–202), and certain other activities such as circumvention of copy protection (ss 296–296ZG) are also criminal offences.

---

[61]   [2002] OJ L 3/1 (5.1.2002).   [62]   Cf para 28.20 above.
[63]   An unofficial consolidation of the 1988 Act and subsequent amendments may be consulted on the website of the UK Patent office at www.patent.gov.uk/copy/legislation/legislation.pdf.

Registered designs are protected under sections 7 and 7A of the Registered **28.31**
Designs Act 1949, as amended to comply with Directive 98/71/EC,[64] or under the
Community Design Regulation 6/2002.[65] Note that unregistered Community
designs are also protected for three years after being made available to the public.

(3) *Goods infringing other intellectual property rights*

Goods infringing a patent or a supplementary protection certificate

Goods infringe a patent or supplementary protection certificate by virtue of **28.32**
section 60(1)(a) and (c) of the Patents Act 1977. Sub-section (a) provides that
product claims will be infringed by making, disposal, offering to dispose, use,
import or keeping of a product which falls within the claims. Sub-section (c) makes
similar provision for products obtained directly[66] from the use of a patented
process. As well as applying to products and processes which fall literally within
the patent's claims, non-literal infringement is also possible, as envisaged by the
Protocol to Article 69 of the European Patent Convention ('EPC').[67] The UK
House of Lords has recently ruled on non-literal infringement in the case of
Kirin-Amgen Inc v Hoechst Marion Roussel Limited.[68] Defences to infringement
under section 60(5) include private and non-commercial use of an invention,
experimental use relating to the subject matter of the invention, extemporaneous
preparation of medicine to a prescription, certain acts on ships, aircraft and other
vessels temporarily or accidentally within UK territorial waters, and use of farm-
saved seed or animal reproductive material by a farmer who obtained precursor
plant or animal matter from a licensed source.[69]

Goods infringing a national plant variety right

This is governed by the Plant Varieties Act 1997, section 6.[70] As well as applying to **28.33**
the protected variety, the rights extend to harvested material obtained through use of

---

[64] Directive 98/71/EC of the European Parliament and of the Council of 13 October 1998 on
the legal protection of designs [1998] OJ L 289/28 (28.10.1998). An unofficial consolidation of
UK registered designs legislation may be viewed at the web site of the UK Patent Office
http://www.patent.gov.uk/design/legal/act.pdf.

[65] N 61 above. For a consolidated version of the regulation and amendments, see the website of the
Office for Harmonisation in the Internal Market http://oami.eu.int/EN/design/pdf/reg2002_6.pdf.

[66] This is a strict requirement, cf *Pioneer Electronics Capital Inc v Warner Music Manufacturing
Europe GmbH* [1997] RPC 757.

[67] Cf http://www.european-patent-office.org/legal/epc/e/ar69.html.

[68] [2004] UKHL 46.

[69] An unofficial consolidation of the Patents Act 1977 and amendments may be consulted at the
website of the UK Patents Office www.patent.gov.uk/patent/legal/consolidation.pdf.

[70] Guidance on the application of the Plant Variety rights Act 1997 and the Community Plant
Variety Rights Regulation can be found on the website of the UK Department for the Environment,
Food and Rural Affairs www.defra.gov.uk/planth/pvs/pbrguide.htm and the Community plant
variety office www.cpvo.eu.int.

the protected variety,[71] and may extend further to certain products made from such harvests.[72] Section 8 of the 1997 Act provides general exceptions similar to those for patents, and section 9 allows for farm saved seed to be used without infringement in certain circumstances.

Goods infringing a national designation of origin or a geographical indication

28.34 Where a geographical indication is protected under EC Regulation, the courts may give direct effect to the relevant Regulation, and award an injunction to protect consumers from confusion, as in *Taittinger SA v Allbev Ltd*,[73] a case involving restraint on the term 'Elderflower Champagne'. Otherwise, the tort of passing off can be invoked, as in *Chocosuisse Union des Fabricants Suisses de Chocolat v Cadbury Ltd*,[74] where use of 'Swiss Chalet' for chocolate made in the UK was concerned.

(4) Moulds and matrices

28.35 Pursuant to Article 2(3) of EC Regulation 1383/2003, the customs authorities of the Member States are also to take action against '[a]ny mould or matrix which is specifically designed or adapted for the manufacture of goods infringing an intellectual property right', provided however that 'the use of such moulds or matrices infringes the right-holder's rights under Community law or the law of the Member State in which the application for action by the customs authorities is made'.

28.36 As far as UK legislation in relation to moulds or matrices is concerned, some but not all of the statutes refer to such items. Section 24 of the Copyright, Designs and Patents Act 1988 establishes infringement where an article 'specifically designed or adapted for making copies' of a copyright work is imported by someone who knows or has reason to believe that it will be used for making infringing copies. Similar provision appears in section 230 regarding articles specifically designed or adapted to make copies of a design protected by a UK unregistered design right. Section 92(3) of the Trade Marks Act 1994 creates a criminal offence of making or possessing an article 'designed or adapted for making copies of signs identical to or likely to be mistaken for certain registered trade marks'. In *R v Davies*,[75] the accused pleaded guilty to such an offence by possession of computer discs.

---

[71] S 6(3).   [72] S 6(4),(5).

[73] [1993] FSR 641: Council Reg (EEC) 823/87 of 16 March 1987 laying down special provisions relating to quality wines produced in specified regions ([1987] OJ L 84/59 (27.3.1987)) is directly applicable where there is risk of confusion.

[74] N 36 above. In this case the Court of Appeal held that the relevant trade association lacked standing to sue in passing off.   [75] [2004] FSR 24.

C. Goods excluded by the Regulation

(1) Parallel imported goods

Since 'grey goods' are not subject to customs' powers under Regulation **28.37**
1383/2003,[76] it is unlikely that parallel imports would be detained. However, where
parallel imports from outside the EEA involve the use of a protected mark or copyright work, they would fall within the scope of a notice under section 89 of the Trade
Marks Act 1994 and section 111 of the Copyright, Designs and Patents Act 1988,
as outlined above.[77] These sections require a prior notice from the rights owner.

(2) Goods which have been manufactured under conditions other than those which have been agreed with the right-holder

In principle these, too, may be the subject of a notice under the Trade Marks Act **28.38**
1994, section 89 or the Copyright, Designs and Patents Act 1988, section 111.[78]
Again they would be detained only in accordance with a notice duly submitted by the
right-holder as they are formally excluded from the scope of Regulation 1383/2003.[79]

(3) Goods contained in travellers' personal baggage

Under Article 3(2) of EC Regulation 1383/2003, action of the customs author- **28.39**
ities from the Member States on the basis of the Regulation is precluded where a
traveller's personal baggage contains goods of a non-commercial nature within the
limits of the duty-free allowance (that is, EUR 175), and there are no material
indications to suggest that the goods are part of a commercial operation.

Travellers' personal baggage is not systematically controlled by UK Customs. At **28.40**
ports and airports there are three channels—a red channel for 'goods to declare', a
green channel for 'nothing to declare' (that is, within the current duty-free limits
from non-EU countries), and a blue channel for travellers from other EU countries. The blue and green channels may be subject to spot checks. These are carried
out under powers conferred by the Customs and Excise Management Act 1979,
section 78, and sections 163 and 163A for tobacco and alcohol.[80] Travellers with
merchandise in their baggage are required to use the red channel.[81]

---

[76] Reg 1383/2003, Art 3(1), first indent.
[77] Please see Introduction (in particular paras 28.01 and 28.05 above) for details of these
provisions.   [78] Cf para 28.37 above.
[79] Reg 1383/2003, Art 3(1), second indent.
[80] Cf HMCE Reference: Leaflet number: 02/CD/013, 'Entering the UK from another EU
Country: Customs Rules Fact and Fiction', available on www.hmrc.gov.uk.
[81] Customs Notice 6, 'Merchandise in baggage' available on www.hmrc.gov.uk.

28.41 The distinction between items of a non-commercial nature and merchandise arises most frequently in connection with duty paid cigarettes and alcohol purchased in other EU countries, where duty rates are much lower than in the UK. In its guidance to travellers bringing such items into the UK,[82] HM Customs & Excise warns that the customs officers could check or question a traveller as to:

- the type and quantity of goods;[83]
- why the traveller bought them;
- how the traveller paid for the goods;
- whether all the goods were openly displayed or concealed;
- how often the person travels;
- how much they normally smoke or drink;
- any other relevant circumstances.

28.42 The guidance goes on to state:

> The Officer will take into account all the factors of the situation and your explanation. If you are unable or you refuse to provide a satisfactory explanation the Officer may well conclude that those goods are for commercial purposes[84] and not for your own use.

28.43 The purchase price in the place of origin is likely to be the default calculation for the duty-free allowance; this is the basis for calculation of customs or import duty. However, form C1340, Appendix I-A-IV refers to 'the pre-tax value of the legal goods' whilst Customs Notice 34, 'Intellectual property rights' refers to 'the pre-tax value of the original goods on the legitimate market of the country in which the application for action is lodged',[85] both in the context of an application for customs measures. If such information is available, it may be possible for customs to take it into account when assessing a traveller's baggage items.

28.44 Right-holders would be prudent to inform UK Customs of the pre-tax value of the authentic goods on the UK market.[86] Where the value of even a single import exceeds the duty-free allowance of EUR 175, customs may take action, at least in the absence of a purchase receipt.

---

[82] HMCE Reference: Leaflet number: 02/CD/009, 'Shopping across the Channel? Bringing back Cigarettes or Alcohol?', available on www.hmrc.gov.uk.

[83] On which see also *Elder v Crowe* [1996] SCCR 38, a Scots case under the Trade Descriptions Act 1968, in which 300 bottles of counterfeit perfume were held to be evidence of commercial activity.

[84] Also in issue in *Lindsay v Commissioners of Customs and Excise* [2002] EWCA Civ 267 CA.

[85] HM Customs and Excise Notice 34: 'Intellectual Property Rights' (July 2004) ('Notice 34'). Cf also Reg 1383/2003, Art 5(5).   [86] Cf Reg 1383/2003, Art 5(5).

II. APPLICATION FOR ACTION BY THE CUSTOMS AUTHORITIES

A. Measures prior to an application for action by the customs authorities ('*ex officio* measures')

(1) Ex officio *measures under Article 4 of the Regulation*

The Commissioners of Customs & Excise need not wait for an application under   **28.45**
Article 1(1) of the Regulation to be made or granted before taking action. If, in the
course of checks carried out in relation to goods in one of the situations mentioned in that Article, the Commissioners have sufficient grounds for suspicion
that those goods infringe intellectual property rights, they may, in accordance
with Article 4 of that Regulation:

(a) notify the right-holder of the nature and quantity of goods and ask in return
    for such information as they need in order to confirm their suspicion that
    those goods indeed infringe;
(b) notify the right-holder and the declarant of possible infringement;
(c) detain those goods or suspend their release;
(d) invite the intellectual property owner to make an application within three
    working days of the notification of suspension or detention.[87]

What constitutes 'sufficient grounds for suspecting that the goods infringe an intellectual property right'?

In the absence of authoritative case law it is not possible to define with confidence the   **28.46**
standard by which 'sufficient grounds for suspecting that the goods infringe an intellectual property right' must be measured. However, it is reasonable to suppose that
grounds for suspecting infringement will be taken to be a far wider term than grounds
for establishing liability. The fact that a suspected infringer may have a defence under
civil law to an action for infringement may exonerate him from both civil and criminal liability[88] but will not prevent his actions from being prima facie suspicious.

It is understood that customs are not bound by any formal rules or guidance in   **28.47**
assessing whether goods infringe an intellectual property right, but will exercise
their discretion in the light of their own knowledge, of information received by
them, and the circumstances before them.[89]

---

[87] Goods Infringing Intellectual Property Rights (Customs) Regs 2004 (SI 2004 No 1473),
Reg 4(1).   [88] Cf *R v Johnstone* [2003] UKHL 28, [2003] ETMR 1.
[89] SI 2004 No 1473, Reg 4(1)(a).

Notification by customs

28.48 The Commissioners are empowered to notify a right-holder of (i) the nature of items suspected, and (ii) their actual or supposed number.[90] The word 'nature' is susceptible of different interpretations, and may refer to one or more of the following: their physical description (for example, what is their appearance, and what is the language of their labelling and packaging?); their generic description (that is, what sort of goods are they?); their contextual description (for example, how are they packaged, with what other goods have they been found?); and their commercial description (for example, are they in good condition, have their bar codes been obliterated, has the 'sell-by' date expired?).

28.49 The transmission of digital or analogue photographs of the suspected goods would appear to fall within the plain meaning of the words '[notification] of the nature of the items'.

Provision of information to the Commissioners to confirm their suspicions

28.50 Further, a right-holder may be asked to provide any information that customs may need in order to confirm their suspicions that the goods before them infringe intellectual property rights. There is no indication, in the implementing Regulations, in case law or in any guidance from the Commissioners, as to what form that information might take, or as to what its probative value must be. Presumably this information may consist of such items as copies of trade mark, design, patent registration certificates, information concerning security devices and product codes, whether encrypted or otherwise, as well as information concerning the marketing of the product itself (for example, information to establish that DVDs of a kind suspected of being counterfeit have not yet been lawfully placed on the market at all).

Examination of the information contained in the notification

28.51 The notification procedure with regard to suspected infringing goods would appear to be optional, at the discretion of the Commissioners who *may*[91] furnish information to right-holders but are not obliged to do so. Once in possession of the information so furnished, the right-holder is not required to respond to the notification, although it will normally be in his interest to do so.

The 'three working days' deadline

28.52 The term 'working days' is computed by excluding from the count the day on which the notification has been received.[92] The implementing Regulations do not

---

[90] Ibid. Cf also Reg 1383/2003, Art 4(2).   [91] SI 2004 No 1473, Reg 4(1).
[92] Applying Council Reg (EEC, Euratom) 1182/1971 determining the rules applicable to periods, dates and time limits ([1971] OJ L 124/1 (8.6.1971)), Art 3(1).

appear to allow for any latitude, and Notice 34 states: 'This deadline cannot be extended.'

B. The lodging and processing of applications for customs action

(1) Persons entitled to file an application for action

Definition of 'right-holder' under the Regulation

An application for action under the Regulation may be made by a 'right-holder', **28.53** that is (i) the holder of the relevant intellectual property right, or (ii) 'any other person authorized to use any of the intellectual property rights', or (iii) a representative of either of the two persons mentioned previously.[93]

The United Kingdom courts have not yet construed the meaning of the term **28.54** 'right-holder' in the context of Council Regulation 1383/2003, and it is unlikely that, when they do so, they would give it a meaning that was not consistent with the very broad definition contained in that provision. Accordingly, although they are not specifically mentioned, licensees, distributors and commercial agents would appear to fall within the categories of persons entitled to make an application as 'authorized users'. In the context of products which are suspected of infringing a patent, this category would include compulsory licensees and licensees under a licence of right.[94]

There is no legal requirement that the Commissioners verify the identity or the **28.55** entitlement of the right-holder. Where the right-holder is an assignee or an authorised user under a registered intellectual property right, it would not in many instances be feasible to require proof of entitlement in the form of certification from the Patent Office, Design Registry, or Trade Mark Registry, because there is often a considerable lapse of time between the third party becoming entitled and that entitlement to an assigned or licensed right being recorded.

'Representative', in this context, means both a legal and a natural person.[95] The term **28.56** appears to include any legal, commercial or other representative, without limitation.

---

[93] SI 2004 No 1473, Reg 2(1), implementing Council Reg 1383/2003/EC concerning customs action against goods suspected of infringing certain intellectual property rights and the measures to be taken against goods found to have infringed such rights, Art 2(2).

[94] See Patents Act 1977, ss 46, 48, and 48B.

[95] Interpretation Act 1978, Sched 1. Compare Commission Reg (EC) 1891/2004 of 21 October 2004 laying down provisions for the implementation of Council Reg (EC) 1383/2003 concerning customs action against goods suspected of infringing certain intellectual property rights and the measures to be taken against goods found to have infringed such rights [2004] OJ L 328/16 (30.10.2004), Art 1.

Proof of entitlement to file an application for action

For right-holders stricto sensu

28.57   Implementing Regulation 1891/2004 makes provision as to what a person claiming to be a right-holder must furnish as proof of entitlement to file an application: existence and interest in the right under which the application is being submitted. Considering that (i) the rights that may be asserted by the right-holder include registered and unregistered rights, (ii) even in respect of registered rights the interest of the right-holder may not have been recorded in the relevant register, and (iii) time may be of the essence when an application is made, for example in respect of allegedly infringing counterfeit pharmaceutical or safety products, it might be considered unreasonable to require any proof as a condition precedent for the filing of an application other than a statement on the part of the applicant that he is indeed the owner of a relevant intellectual property right. The applicant is however required to provide proof as follows:

- For registered trade mark and design rights: proof of registration. This is most conveniently furnished by way of a certified copy of the entry on the register. This will show the current state of the register, including any interests such as licences which have been notified to the Registry. The UK registry will provide such a copy upon submission of the relevant form—TM31R for trade marks[96] and DF23 for registered designs[97]—and fee.
- For copyright, rights in performances, and unregistered design rights: evidence of authorship of status as right-holder.
- For patents and SPCs: proof that the patent or SPC has been granted and is still in force: again copies of the entry on the register may be obtained from the Patent Office.[98]
- For plant varieties, protected designations of origin, and protected geographical indications: evidence of the right to exercise such a right.[99]

28.58   There is no suggestion that an application for customs action may be based upon evidence of an application to register an intellectual property right, in the absence of evidence of effective registration or grant: see *Commissioners for Customs and Excise v Top High Development*.[100]

---

[96] http://www.patent.gov.uk/tm/forms/tm31r.pdf; for Community trade marks, see the form at http://oami.eu.int/pdf/forms/Inspectionform-EN.pdf.

[97] http://www.patent.gov.uk/design/forms/design/df23.pdf; for Community designs, see the form at http://oami.eu.int/pdf/forms/Inspectionform-EN.pdf.

[98] http://www.patent.gov.uk/patent/forms/ukpatsupp.htm.

[99] Notice 34 (n 85 above), para 3.2; Annex I-A to form 1340. Compare Reg 1891/2004 (n 95 above), Art 2(1).   [100] N 28 above.

For persons authorized to use the right

28.59 An application by an authorized user must provide proof of his authority to use that right.[101] There is no explicit requirement that the authorization be registered with the relevant authority, although if it is, the copy entry from the register will refer to it.

For representatives

28.60 An application by a representative must provide proof of his authority to act on behalf of either the right owner or an authorized user.[102] No specific requirements are laid down as to the form in which such documentary evidence may be submitted. Accordingly it is submitted that any document which provides evidence of prima facie authorization will be accepted by the competent authority, regardless of whether it would be admissible as evidence of authorization in a court of law. Box 2 of customs form 1340 contains only the postal address for submission of the application, but refers to full contact details in Annex 1-C, which include a fax number. However, sending or delivering documents to the postal address will reduce the need to furnish further documents for use in court.

28.61 There is no limitation as to the extent of authorization to which a submitted document gives evidence. Accordingly a power of attorney may be general (for all future cases of border measures) or specific to one particular matter. Nor is there any express limitation or requirement that relates to the nationality, domicile, or other legal incidents of foreign or non-resident representatives.

(2) Competent customs department and formal requirements

Competent customs department

28.62 According to Notice 34, the competent authority for processing all applications and for dealing with all issues arising out of border measures taken against suspected goods is:

HM Customs and Excise[103]
Customs International Trade Operations ('CITOPs') 1st Floor West, Alexander House, 21 Victoria Avenue
Southend-on-Sea, Essex SS99 1AA
Tel: +44 1702 367221
Fax: +44 1702 366825
www.hmrc.gov.uk

---

[101] Ibid.   [102] Ibid.
[103] HM Customs and Excise and the UK Inland Revenue Services merged on 28 April 2005 into a new body, HM Revenue and Customs. Commissioners for Revenue and Customs Act 2005.

Form of the application for action

28.63   Two forms are provided for the making of an application. Form 1340 is designed for an application made in respect of a right arising under national law, while Form 1340A is designed for an application made in respect of a Community right.[104]

28.64   Applicants are invited to send a single completed application to the competent authority, but neither the implementing provisions nor Notice 34 specify the means of doing so. Since the forms are not adapted for electronic completion and transmission, it might be assumed that applications may be sent by post, or fax, or may be delivered by hand. The forms themselves contain a rubric that suggests that they are intended to be completed and transmitted either electronically or manually.[105]

28.65   The application must be accompanied by a completed form,[106] in compliance with Article 6 of the Council Regulation 1383/2003, in which the applicant undertakes to assume liability in the event that (i) any procedure initiated by him should be discontinued through his own action or omission or (ii) the goods are subsequently found not to infringe an intellectual property right. In the absence of any specific guidance, it may be assumed that the requirements applicable to the sending of an application apply equally to the sending in of this form. In keeping with Article 6(2) of the Regulation, an applicant in respect of intellectual property rights arising under a Community law must agree to bear any translation costs that are 'required'.[107]

Language requirements

28.66   The sole language in which an application may be filed in the United Kingdom is the English language, whether the application is based on a right arising under the law of the United Kingdom or on a right arising under Community law. Both versions of the application form are in the English language, though assistance to Welsh language speakers is available.[108]

---

[104]   Both forms are accessible from the Customs and Excise website at http://www.hmrc.gov.uk. They actually duplicate the forms annexed to Reg 1891/2004. This is important to assure consistency with Art 5(5), first indent, of Reg 1383/2003.

[105]   'The application for action can be transmitted electronically if an electronic data exchange system is available. In all other cases, the form is to be completed by mechanical means or in legible handwriting and must not contain erasures or overwriting'; Forms 1340 and 1340A, Annex I-A, ii.

[106]   This form may be found at Annex I-B to Form 1340 and at Annex II-B to Form 1340A.

[107]   Form 1340A, Annex II-B, bullet-point 2: the wording of the text does not specify by whom the translation may be required. Also, Art 6 of Council Reg 1383/2003 refers to costs which are 'necessary'; since the words 'necessary' and 'required' are not synonymous, an unsuccessful applicant may face translation costs that fell outside the contemplation of the legislator.

[108]   This assistance is available from the National Advice Service on +44 (0) 845 010 0300.

(3) Requirements regarding the contents of the application for action

Mandatory information

The core information which the applicant is obliged to provide is that which **28.67**
identifies (i) the intellectual property right, (ii) his standing to make the application,
whether as right owner, right user, or representative, (iii) contact details of a person
appointed by the applicant, and (iv) 'essential data on the authentic goods'.[109]

Where available, specific information concerning the 'type or pattern of fraud' **28.68**
practised by the manufacturer, importer, or other person involved in the
suspected unlawful importation must be furnished.[110]

There is no apparent minimum or maximum limit to the degree of detail in which **28.69**
information may be furnished.

While Notice 34 refers to only a single contact person,[111] the forms both require **28.70**
an applicant to furnish details of two such persons: a contact for administrative
matters, and a contact for technical matters.[112] There is nothing to preclude the
same person from serving as both the administrative contact and the technical
one. In the case of an application arising out of a Community right the applicant
is requested to nominate both an administrative contact and a technical contact
in each country in which action is sought.[113]

From the context it is implicit that each of these contact persons is a live **28.71**
individual rather than a purely legal entity; he must also be capable of being
contacted at short notice.[114] Indeed, in the case of an application arising out
of a Community right the applicant is prompted to nominate, in the case of an
administrative contact, a 'lawyer' and, in the case of a technical contact,
an 'expert'.[115] It seems that the physical presence of a contact person within the
jurisdiction is not required, since the contact details required of him include his
name and his various telecommunication coordinates and e-mail address as well
as postal address.

Further optional information

All other information is merely 'additional'. Any other intelligence, however **28.72**
trivial, should be provided in order to assist in the interception of goods.[116] This

---

[109] Form 1340, Box 8; Form 1340A, Box 7.
[110] Reg 1383/2003, Art 5(5)(ii); Notice 34 (n 85 above), para 3.2.
[111] Compare Reg 1383/2003, Art 5(5)(iii).
[112] The same is true for the forms annexed to Reg 1891/2004.
[113] Form 1340A, Boxes 11 and 12.   [114] Forms 1340 and 1340A, Annex I-A, iv.
[115] Form 1340A, Boxes 11 and 12.
[116] Notice 34 (n 85 above), para 33. Compare Reg 1383/2003, Art 5(5), last indent.

'additional' information, which should be included 'wherever possible', includes:

- the location of the goods and their intended destination;
- particulars identifying the consignment or packages;
- the expected date of arrival or departure of the goods;
- the means of transport;
- the identity (including VAT registration number) of the importer or exporter;
- the country or countries of production and the routes used by traffickers;
- the technical differences, if known, between the authentic and the suspected goods; and
- the pre-tax value of the original goods on the legitimate market in the country in which the application for action is lodged.

Additional information specific to the type of intellectual property right referred to in the application

28.73 Council Regulation 1383/2003, Article 5(6) permits the customs authorities to require further information which is specific to the type of intellectual property right referred to in the application for action. The United Kingdom's implementing provisions make no special reference to such information and no boxes are designated for it in either of the application form templates.

(4) Processing and acceptance of the application for action

28.74 In the event that the customs authorities decline to process an application for action under Article 5(8) of the Regulation, there is no specific appeal provision. A general two-stage appeal procedure was established by the Finance Act 1994 as amended; with further appeal matters being added under the Customs Reviews and Appeals (Tariff and Origin) Regulations 1997.[117] First, a request must be made for a Departmental Review of a decision. The outcome of this can then be appealed to the Tribunal responsible for VAT appeals. In the event that the decision is considered to fall outside these procedures, an applicant who believes that the authorities have erred in failing to act upon the information contained in the application may apply to the High Court for a judicial review of the manner in which HM Customs and Excise, as a branch of the executive, has carried out its functions.[118]

---

[117] Cf Notice 990 issued March 2003, update 1 issued June 2004, available at www.hmrc.gov.uk.
[118] For a recent and accessible account of judicial review see Hilaire Barnett, *Constitutional & Administrative Law* (Cavendish Publishing, 5th edn, 2004), at 707 to 783.

Neither the implementing provisions nor Notice 34 make any express **28.75** statement as to the period during which the customs authorities may or must act upon information once the application for action is received. This will occur once the application has been processed. Article 5(7) of Regulation 1383/2003 allows 30 working days for customs to notify the applicant of their decision. Where a decision is made to grant an application, it will cease to have effect in the event that (i) a change takes place in relationship to the ownership or authorized use of the intellectual property right which is not communicated to the customs authorities, or (ii) the intellectual property right specified in the application expires.[119] In any event, the currency of a granted application for action in the United Kingdom is 12 months. It is not clear whether this 12-month period runs from the date upon which the application is made, received, or approved.

The 12-month period may be extended by the right-holder if he writes to **28.76** the customs authorities prior to the expiry date.[120] No form is provided for this purpose, a request and continuation of indemnity on company headed notepaper is recommended. If a request for extension reaches customs after that date it will be of no effect, and the right-holder will have to lodge a fresh application.

An applicant may amend details of the information contained in the initial **28.77** application at any time during its currency by writing to the customs authorities. Again, no form is provided for this purpose.

(5) Applications for action in respect of Community rights

The procedure for processing applications for action in respect of Community **28.78** rights is the same as that for the processing of applications arising from national rights, subject to the very few and minor differences recorded above.

At the time of writing this chapter, there is no publicly available information as to **28.79** how applications for action in respect of Community rights, having been filed in other countries, are processed in the United Kingdom. With the necessary exception of issues arising from the translation into the English language of information and certification which has been filed in another European Union language, it is believed that such applications would be processed in exactly the same manner as applications originating in the United Kingdom.

---

[119] SI 2004 No 1473, Reg 5.
[120] Notice 34 (n 85 above), para 36(a). Customs' practice is to send out reminders about four weeks before expiry.

III. CONDITIONS GOVERNING ACTION BY CUSTOMS AUTHORITIES AND BY THE AUTHORITIES COMPETENT TO DETERMINE WHETHER GOODS INFRINGE AN INTELLECTUAL PROPERTY RIGHT

A. Conditions governing action by customs authorities

(1) Factual background

28.80   The office at Southend-on-Sea mentioned in the previous Part (para 26.62 above) deals with the receipt of notices under Regulation 1383/2003. There is a head office of Customs and Excise at Queen's Dock, Liverpool. However, customs operations are carried out at major airports, such as London, Manchester, Prestwick, lesser airports, sea ports, and at the terminus of the Channel Tunnel. UK Customs operate a national telephone advice service.[121]

28.81   The Customs and Excise Management Act 1979 confers generic powers under which officials carry out their day-to-day tasks. Goods infringing intellectual property rights should be seen in the context of 'prohibited goods' generally, which may be detained or seized as liable to forfeiture. Section 139(1) of the 1979 Act states:

> Any thing liable to forfeiture under the Customs and Excise Acts may be seized or detained by any officer or constable or any member of Her Majesty's armed forces or coastguard.

28.82   Where detained by non-customs personnel, the goods should be delivered to the nearest customs office,[122] unless they need to be kept at a police station in connection with criminal proceedings. Section 139(7) imposes criminal penalties on non-(customs) officers who seize or detain goods and fail to comply with the Act or with customs directions.

28.83   There is a default procedure, whereby a declarant who has been notified of detention has one month in which to lodge his claim that the goods are not liable to forfeiture.[123] In the absence of such a claim, the goods can be condemned as

---

[121]   +44 (0) 845 010 9000, open from 8am–8pm Monday to Friday.

[122]   Customs and Excise Management Act 1979, s 139(2)(a), or described in writing if delivery is not practicable: s 139(2)(b). Customs must also be notified if the articles are kept at a police station pending criminal proceedings.

[123]   Customs and Excise Management Act 1979, Sched 3, para 3. The Act does not specify any particular form of notice; it may be lodged at any customs office.

forfeit and destroyed or disposed of without further ado. Where a notice has been received, customs must begin condemnation proceedings in court, usually the local[124] Magistrates Court (England & Wales), Sheriff Court (Scotland), or other court of summary jurisdiction (Northern Ireland). As was seen in the introduction, the High Courts (England & Wales, Northern Ireland) and Court of Session (Scotland) also have jurisdiction under section 152 of the 1979 Act. Thereafter, the Commissioners of Customs and Excise have wide discretion to release goods and to stay condemnation proceedings and return goods under section 152 of the 1979 Act.

28.84 In some cases the vehicle used to import prohibited goods may also be detained and liable to forfeiture, providing this is proportionate.[125]

28.85 The non-EC provisions of section 89 of the Trade Marks Act 1994 and section 111 of the Copyright, Designs and Patents Act 1988 enable infringing goods, materials or articles to be treated as prohibited goods within the meaning of the Customs and Excise Management Act 1979. A number of the procedural provisions of the 1979 Act are applied by the UK Regulations implementing Regulation 1383/2003.[126]

(2) Notification of customs intervention

28.86 The *right-holder* will be notified of customs intervention using the contact details specified in the notice. Notification may be by letter, fax, e-mail, or by telephone with written confirmation.[127]

28.87 Whether the *declarant or holder of the goods* (within the meaning of Article 38 of Regulation (EEC) No 2913/92[128]) need be notified depends on the circumstances in which the goods were detained. If they were detained in the presence of the person whose offence or suspected offence occasioned seizure, or an owner of the goods, or his servant or agent, or the master or commander of the ship or aircraft in which the goods arrived, notice need not be given.[129] In these circumstances, there will be actual knowledge by a relevant person. Otherwise, customs will attempt to notify the owner, declarant or holder in writing in person, at their last known address or registered office (if a company). Where the address is unknown, customs will place a notice in the official Gazette.[130]

---

[124] Customs and Excise Management Act 1979, Sched 3, para 8.
[125] Eg *Young v Customs and Excise Commissioners* [2004] EWCA Civ 1519 (car used to transport cigarettes); *Customs and Excise Commissioners v Air Canada* [1991] 2 QB 446 (aircraft on which cannabis cargo had entered the UK).   [126] SI 2004 No 1473, Regs 7, 8(5) and (6).
[127] Notice 34 (n 85 above), para 5.2.   [128] N 45 above.
[129] Customs and Excise Management Act 1979, Sched 3, para 1(2).
[130] Ibid, Sched 3, para 2.

(3) Information to be provided by customs to the
right-holder before the right-holder confirms the
infringing nature of the goods

Information provided

28.88   When goods are suspected of infringing a trade mark, copyright or performer's
right[131] they may be scrutinized under more than one regime, provided they are
covered by a valid application or notice. When intercepted or detained by
customs, they will be dealt with according to the relevant EC or UK legislation.[132]
Information will be furnished as to:

- the actual or estimated quantity, and
- the nature of the goods.

28.89   Where Regulation 1382/2003 applies, and a valid application is in force in relation
to one of the intellectual property rights referred to in the Regulation, customs will
on request, also supply (in so far as known) the name and address of the:

- consignee
- consignor
- declarant
- importer or exporter
- manufacturer, and
- holder of the goods.[133]

**Protection of personal data, commercial and industrial secrecy, and
professional and administrative confidentiality**

28.90   In the UK, where confidential information is given for a specific purpose,
use for a different purpose will amount to breach of confidence, actionable
by the injured party as a matter of private law.[134] This applies to drawings
or objects embodying confidential information as well as documentary
information; in *Saltman* the information was embodied in drawings for leather
punches.

28.91   Notice 34 states that information supplied by customs is provided only for the
right-holder to determine if goods infringe and for no other purpose, and refers to
sanctions including suspension or non-renewal of the application.[135]

---

[131] Notice 34 (n 85 above), para 5.2(a).   [132] Ibid, para 5.2.   [133] Ibid, para 3.8.
[134] *Saltman Engineering Co Ltd v Campbell Engineering Co Ltd* [1948] 65 RPC 203 and many
subsequent cases.   [135] Under Art 12 of Reg 1383/2003 and reg 11 of SI 2004 No 1473.

(4) Inspection of the suspect goods

Once the goods have been detained or suspended from release, customs will **28.92**
arrange for the right-holder to examine a sample.[136] It appears[137] that standard
procedure is for customs to send the sample to the right-holder; however, there
will doubtless be cases in which it is more appropriate for the right-holder's representative to inspect the goods *in situ*. Customs will follow the EC procedure
where it applies; this means that the return of samples is governed by the
provisions of Article 9(3) of Council Regulation 1383/2003.

B. Simplified procedure allowing the destruction of the goods without there being any need to determine whether an intellectual property right has been infringed under national law

What happens after notification depends on the rights infringed. In the case of **28.93**
'counterfeit and pirated' goods—those infringing trade marks, copyright, design
right and performers' rights *only*—a simplified procedure is available. The right-
holder will be asked to respond within 10 working days with a reasoned, written
opinion as to whether the goods infringe. The right-holder may apply, with
reasons, to extend this period once by a maximum of 10 further working days. For
perishable goods, the period of time is three working days and may not be
extended.

In the case of other rights, the relevant court must be asked to determine the status **28.94**
of the goods, the right-holder being given a similar period to initiate proceedings
for infringement.

Simplified procedure

In the case of 'counterfeit and pirated' goods—those infringing trade marks, **28.95**
copyright and performers' rights—where customs are satisfied, on the basis of the
right-holder's written opinion, that the goods are liable to forfeiture, they will
seize the goods. If an appeal against seizure is received, customs will commence
condemnation proceedings within one month and the goods owner may appear
to show why the goods are not liable to forfeiture.[138] For these proceedings

---

[136] Notice 34 (n 85 above), para 5.2. SI 2004 1473, Reg 6, refers to samples being made
available.

[137] See, eg, *Pointing v Commissioners of Customs and Excise* [1999] FSR 394 (Ch D) referring to
the Counterfeit and Pirated Goods Customs Regs 1995.

[138] The burden is upon the party so alleging: SI 2004 No 1473, Reg 7(2); Customs and Excise
Management Act 1979, Sched 3.

customs may call upon the right-holder to provide witness statements and attend the condemnation hearing.[139] The right-holder may also be liable for costs.[140]

28.96   Thus for these rights, Article 11 has been implemented by assimilation to the national procedure for goods liable to forfeiture.[141] Article 11 is a permissive provision and makes clear (twice) that the simplified procedure is to be in accordance with national law. Articles 11 and 13 of Regulation 1383/2003 envisage three possibilities once customs receives notice that the goods are infringing and the rights holder wishes them to be 'abandoned for destruction under Customs control':

(a) the declarant, holder, or owner of the goods agrees in writing to abandon the goods for destruction. This harmonious situation is straightforward but rare;

(b) the declarant, holder, and owner of the goods are presumed to consent to destruction because they have not specifically opposed it within the prescribed period. This period is not defined in Article 11, so it must be the period prescribed under relevant national law—one month;

(c) the declarant, holder, or owner of the goods objects to destruction. In this case, Article 13 comes into play and ensures that where customs have not been notified that proceedings have been initiated to determine the infringing status of the goods, the goods shall be released or detention ended, 'subject to completion of all Customs formalities'.

28.97   In the first two situations, customs seizure and destruction may go ahead, subject to preservation of samples by way of evidence as envisaged in Article 11(1), second indent. In the third situation, the correspondence between Article 11 and the national procedure for 'goods liable to forfeiture' is more subtle. This is because condemnation proceedings, which are triggered by an appeal against seizure, are themselves court proceedings in which the status of the goods is determined. This can be seen from the cases outlined in paragraph 28.08 above, specifically *Commissioners for Customs and Excise v Top High Development*[142] and *Pointing v Commissioners of Customs and Excise*.[143]

28.98   If seizure is not contested within one month, or if condemnation is ordered, customs will arrange for goods to be destroyed at the right-holder's expense, although they may discuss other options such as destruction by the right-holder, use as training or educational aids, or disposal to charity. This appears to accord with

---

[139] Notice 34 (n 85 above), para 5.2. Cf also para 28.81 above.

[140] Notice 34, paras 3.7, 4.5, and 5.3.

[141] Customs and Excise Management Act 1979, Sched 3. Trade Marks Act 1994, s 89, and Copyright, Designs and Patents Act 1988, s 111, achieve a similar effect with respect to infringing goods, parallel imports, and over-runs from outside the EEA which are not covered by Reg 1383/2003.   [142] N 28 above.

[143] N 19 above.

the spirit of Regulation 1383/2003, Article 17, which allows disposal outside commercial channels in such a way as to preclude injury to the right-holder. Discussion with the right-holder is a sensible way to ascertain how this may be achieved.

Note that condemnation proceedings are usually heard by local, non-specialist **28.99** Magistrates' Courts, although the High Courts also have jurisdiction.[144]

Amicable settlements

These may be reached at a number of stages. For goods other than counterfeit or **28.100** pirated goods (as defined in para 28.95 above), instead of giving an opinion on infringement, a right-holder may notify customs of waiver of its rights.[145] Customs will thereafter treat the goods as non-infringing.[146] In these circumstances there are no restrictions on the terms on which such a waiver might be issued. Customs also have discretion not to pursue condemnation proceedings[147] and to restore goods, subject to such conditions as they think fit.[148] Although this statutory discretion is broad, any decision to exercise it must be reasonable.[149] In the event where a settlement between the right-holder and importer was annexed to a court decision, Customs would no doubt give it effect. In other cases, Article 17 of the Regulation could provide useful guidance on the exercise of discretion by customs.

C. Conditions governing action by the authorities having jurisdiction to determine whether the goods infringe an intellectual property right

Where goods infringe rights other than trade marks, copyright, or performers' **28.101** rights, the full procedure is applicable[150] (unless the other rights are waived).

---

[144] See *Pointing v Commissioners of Customs and Excise* (n 19 above).

[145] The period is 10 working days, or three for perishable goods—SI 2004 No 1473, Reg 8(2)&(3); Reg 1383/2003, Art 11.

[146] Goods Infringing Intellectual Property Rights (Customs) Regs, SI 2004 No 1473, Reg 8(4).

[147] They may 'stay, sist or compound' the proceedings: Customs and Excise Management Act 1979, s 152(a) and return. [148] Customs and Excise Management Act 1979, s 152(b).

[149] *Associated Provincial Picture Houses Ltd v Wednesbury Corp* [1948] 1 KB 223 (CA). For comment on the modern application of the test for reasonableness laid down in this case, and its relationship to the concept of proportionality in EU law, see Gale, 'Unreasonableness and Proportionality: Recent Developments in Judicial Review' [2005] SLT 23.

[150] SI 2004 No 1473, Reg 8(1)—patents, supplementary protection certificates, Community designs, plant breeders' rights, Community plant variety rights, designations of origin, geographical indications, or geographical designations, *whether or not* they also appear to infringe any other intellectual property right.

*(1) Authorities having jurisdiction to determine whether
the goods infringe an intellectual property right*

**Proceedings to determine whether an intellectual property right has
been infringed**

28.102   In respect of each of these intellectual property rights,[151] 'initiation of proceedings
to determine whether an intellectual property right has been infringed' can only
be achieved by commencing and serving due process, 'alleging that the goods
infringe an intellectual property right of his and seeking relief which that Court
has the power to grant after a finding of such infringement', that is, seeking final
relief in civil proceedings.[152] In practice proceedings have to be commenced to
gain conservatory measures and served at least when those measures take effect.
Commencement and due service are also necessary for summary judgment. The
'relevant Courts' and originating processes are:[153]

- England and Wales, the High Court, Chancery Division, or the Patents
  County Court (proceedings commenced by claim form)
- Northern Ireland, the High Court (writ)
- Scotland, the Court of Session (summons and proceedings signeted).

28.103   Evidence must be furnished to customs that proceedings have been duly issued
and served, and that the proceedings relate to the goods detained by customs.
Customs Notice 34 stresses that they need to be satisfied not only that proceedings have been issued but also that they are being actively pursued.[154] Customs
may contact the right-holder to check the state of play.

28.104   The Patents County Court was created[155] as a lower cost alternative to the Patents
Court. However, procedures in the English High Court have been simplified, so
that distinctions are not so pronounced as when the Patents County Court was
conceived.[156] In the Patents County Court a patent agent or solicitor can represent the rights owner and act as advocate, which may reduce the costs. Certain
patent agents may litigate in the High Court, and certain trade mark attorneys in
the High and County Courts. In all of these courts the full range of remedies is
available: an inquiry as to damages is available as of right as a final remedy upon

---

[151] Ie those listed in Article 2(d) of Regulation 1383/2003; for copyright, perfomers' rights, and
trade marks, the simplified procedure applies (cf para 28.93 above).

[152] SI 2004 No 1473, Reg 9(1),(2).

[153] Ibid, Reg 9(4)–(6). County Courts also have copyright and some have trade mark jurisdiction.

[154] Notice 34 (n 85 above), para 5.2(b). From SI 2004 No 1473, Reg 9(3), it is clear that customs
may release goods if they are not satisfied, or cease to be satisfied, that proceedings have been commenced, or that the proceedings have been withdrawn, or otherwise terminated without issue of
other such proceedings.

[155] By order under s 287 of the Copyright, Designs and Patents Act 1988.

[156] Lambert, 'IP Litigation after Woolf' [1999] EIPR 427 and 'IP Litigation after Woolf
Revisited' [2003] EIPR 406.

proof of infringement. Discretionary remedies include accounts of profits (final remedy), interim and final injunctions[157] to restrain infringement, 'search and seize' or 'Anton Piller' orders to preserve evidence; 'discovery and inspection of documents' (whereby relevant documents in the other party's possession must be revealed and produced, subject to legal privilege), freezing orders to ensure that assets are not spirited away to defeat justice. Summary judgment is available where the claimant's case is so strong that there is no effective defence, or the defendant fails to appear or file a defence. A defendant may apply to strike out a hopeless case.

Advantages and disadvantages

Counterfeit goods

For these goods, the simplified procedure applies.[158] This will obviously be attractive to right-holders on grounds of comparatively low cost and the reversed burden of proof, but the only remedy in customs proceedings is forfeiture, condemnation, or destruction of the goods. However, importation is not expressly classified as an act of trade mark infringement under the Trade Marks Act 1994,[159] so the customs procedures enable damage to be minimized by keeping the counterfeit goods off the UK market. The simplified procedure is not available where other rights such as patents are also infringed.[160] However, these other rights may be waived in relation to particular consignments of goods under Regulation 8(2)–(4); the effect of waiver is that goods can then revert to the simplified procedure.[161] Customs Notice 34 outlines the choices available to the right-holder.[162]   **28.105**

Pirated goods

For these goods, the simplified procedure again applies.[163] This will be attractive to right-holders on grounds of comparatively low cost and the reversed burden of proof, but the only remedy in customs proceedings is forfeiture, condemnation, or destruction of the goods. Importation is not classified as an act of primary infringement of copyright or performer's rights under the Copyright, Designs and Patents Act 1988[164] although there are forms of 'secondary' infringement by knowing importation of infringing copies.[165] The simplified procedure is not available where other rights such as patents are also infringed.[166] However, these other rights may be waived in relation to particular consignments of goods under   **28.106**

---

[157] In Scotland, 'interdict'.   [158] See para 28.95 above.
[159] Ss 9 and 10 do not refer to importation.
[160] SI 2004 No 1473, Reg 8(1). Cf paras 28.95 and 28.101 above.
[161] Ibid, Reg 9(4)(a).
[162] At para 5.2(c)—use the simplified procedure only, pursuing no further action under the other rights, deal with all rights under the full procedure, or deal only with patents, etc, under the full, procedure (a logical but unlikely alternative).   [163] Para 28.95 above.
[164] S 16.   [165] S 22.   [166] SI 2004 No 1473, Reg 8(1). Cf paras 28.95 and 28.101 above.

Regulation 8(2)–(4); the effect of waiver is that goods can then revert to the simplified procedure.[167]

Goods infringing a patent or a supplementary protection certificate

28.107 For these goods the simplified procedure does not apply, and proceedings must be commenced in the relevant High Court, Court of Session, or Patents County Court, before customs will seize the goods as liable to forfeiture.

Goods infringing a plant variety right

28.108 For these goods the simplified procedure does not apply, and proceedings must be commenced in the relevant High Court, Court of Session, or Patents County Court, before customs will seize the goods as liable to forfeiture.

Goods infringing a designation of origin or a geographical indication

28.109 For these goods the simplified procedure does not apply, and proceedings must be commenced in the relevant High Court, or Court of Session before customs will seize the goods as liable to forfeiture.

(2) *Term for notifying customs that proceedings have been started*

28.110 Article 13 of Regulation 1383/2003 provides that the term of 10 working days may be extended once 'in appropriate cases'. In order to obtain an extension, a reasoned application must be submitted within the initial 10-day period.[168] There appears to be no case law on what constitutes 'appropriate cases'. In *Pointing v Her Majesty's Commissioners of Customs and Excise*,[169] the propriety of time limits was challenged. It was held that there was an implicit extension of the time for the right-holder to give an opinion on the status of the goods, in view of the time limits set by customs. This suggests that the courts take a common-sense view of the issue of extensions of time, so customs will be entitled to do the same.

D. Release of goods suspected of infringing certain rights on provision of a security

28.111 Customs Notice 34[170] warns that, provided that the conditions of Article 14(1) of Regulation 1383/2003 are fulfilled, the owner, importer, or consignee has the *right* to take delivery of the goods against a security. In order to ensure that such security is adequate, customs will ask the right-holder for a 'realistic estimate', with supporting evidence, of the level required to protect their interests. Customs

---

[167] SI 2004 No 1473, Reg 9(4)(a).   [168] N 85 above, para 5.2(b).
[169] N 19 above.   [170] Para 5.2(b) under 'security'.

may also seek corresponding advice from the owner, importer, or consignee. A prudent right-holder should consider asking the court for an order restraining release.

E. Storage of the goods

Customs appear to take a pragmatic view of storage; where the nature or quantity **28.112** of goods requires it, they may use commercial storage facilities. The right-holder is liable to indemnify customs for all costs and liabilities incurred under Regulation 1383/2003. Customs Notice 34[171], paragraph 3.7, gives the following examples:

— storage charges where correctly detained goods were subsequently found not to be infringing;
— storage charges where goods have been detained or seized, a claim has been issued from the court and the outcome is awaited;
— storage charges for correctly detained and seized goods where commercial facilities have proved necessary.

IV. PROVISIONS APPLICABLE TO GOODS FOUND TO INFRINGE AN INTELLECTUAL PROPERTY RIGHT

The national law of the United Kingdom provides for an intellectual property **28.113** right-holder to oppose the entry into the Community customs territory of infringing goods or their exportation from it, to oppose the release of infringing goods for free circulation, exportation, or re-exportation, to oppose their placement under a suspensive procedure, and to oppose their placement in a free zone or free warehouse.[172]

Even where goods which infringe a national or Community trade mark right are **28.114** in transit and are not therefore intended for the national market, English law provides that they constitute infringing goods in respect of which legal relief may be ordered.[173] This decision has been referred to with approval in a patent case, *Sabaf SpA v MFI Furniture Centres Ltd*.[174]

---

[171] N 85 above.
[172] SI 2004 No 1473, Reg 9; Trade Marks Act 1994, s 89; Copyright, Designs and Patents Act 1988, s 111(3B).   [173] *Waterford Wedgwood plc v David Nagli Ltd* [1998] FSR 92.
[174] [2005] RPC 10; [2004] UKHL 45 HL.

28.115   The destruction of infringing goods may be ordered in respect of products that infringe copyright, trade mark, and patent rights. There is however no specific provision for the disposal of goods outside commercial channels in such a way as to preclude damage to the right-holder.[175]

28.116   Where the infringing party has committed a criminal offence under United Kingdom law his assets may in certain circumstances be confiscated.[176] Assets which are confiscated are not however distributed to the victim of the crime. There is a separate provision whereby payment of compensation may be ordered in favour of victims of criminal offences.[177] This provision has not, to the authors' knowledge, been applied to any situation in which a criminal offence has been perpetrated against an intellectual property right-holder.

28.117   Where, in result of an application for action, the action is dealt with through the exercise by the customs authorities of their executive functions alone, there is no provision for the payment of costs, and each party will therefore pay its own, subject to the payment by the applicant for action of any costs necessarily incurred in result of the withdrawal or failure of his application.[178] In the event that an application results in legal proceedings, costs will be allocated between the parties in accordance with normal principles of law in England and Wales,[179] Scotland,[180] or Northern Ireland,[181] as the case may be.

28.118   The authors are not aware of any situations in which the removal of trade marks which have been affixed to counterfeit goods has been viewed as depriving the persons concerned of any economic gains that they might otherwise have derived from any transaction.[182]

---

[175] Cf the Agreement on Trade-Related Aspects of Intellectual Property Rights (TRIPs), Art 46, which provides that the judicial authorities of Members (which include the United Kingdom) shall have the authority to dispose of infringing goods in this manner. Compare Reg 1383/2003, Art 17(1)(a).

[176] Proceeds of Crime Act 2002, s 6, Crown Court. The court may exercise its powers where the convicted person has benefited from a criminal lifestyle in general as well as from particular conduct.

[177] Powers of Criminal Courts (Sentencing) Act 2000, s 130. In making a compensation order, the court must take account of any confiscation order, although it is possible to make both. R Fry 'Copyright Infringement and Collective Enforcement' [2002] EIPR 516 comments on judicial reluctance to be drawn into compensation orders in copyright cases.

[178] Para 28.122 below. Compare Reg 1383/2003, Art 6.

[179] Cf the Law Society website at http://www.lawsociety.org.uk/choosingandusing/payingforservices/faqs.law.

[180] Cf the Law Society of Scotland website at http://www.lawscot.org.uk/legalcosts/legal.html.

[181] Cf the Northern Ireland Court Service website (http://www.courtsni.gov.uk/courtsni/).

[182] Compare Reg 1383/2003, Art 17(1)(b).

V. PENALTIES

The only penalty for breach of the Regulation, or indeed under section 89 of the   **28.119**
Trade Marks Act 1994 and section 111 of the Copyright, Designs and Patents Act
1988, is forfeiture of the goods in question. However, other provisions create
criminal offences which attract further penalties, such as fines, imprisonment,
and confiscation[183] of the proceeds of crime under the Criminal Justice Act 1988,
as amended, or latterly the Proceeds of Crime Act 2002.

A. Counterfeit goods

Section 92 of the Trade Marks Act 1994 creates a number of criminal offences   **28.120**
where there has been application or use of 'a sign identical to, or likely to be mistaken for, a registered trade mark'.[184] There is an element of 'mens rea'—that the
accused acted 'with a view to gain for himself or another, or with intent to cause
loss to another'.[185] Although importation is not listed as one of the criminal activities,
possession and distribution are. There is a rather curious defence in section 92(5) of
reasonable belief of non-infringement. In *R v Johnstone*,[186] it was held that the
prosecution had to show that the sign had been used as an indication of trade origin; the crime was not committed in circumstances where the accused could show
he had reasonable grounds to believe that use of band names to identify artists did
not constitute trade mark infringement. Given the consumer protection aspects of
the trade marks legislation, it not contrary to human rights legislation to place an
evidential burden on the accused to establish non-infringement.

The Trade Descriptions Act 1968 creates a number of further offences in   **28.121**
connection with the application to goods or other uses of false trade descriptions. Again, conviction can lead to the usual range of criminal penalties.
Trading Standards Officers, local government officials, have a duty to enforce the
Trade Descriptions Act and the criminal provisions of the Trade Marks Act
1994.[187]

---

[183] For example in *Priestly* [2004] EWCA Crim 2237 CA (Crim Div), the Court of Appeal
upheld a confiscation order in excess of £2 million where there had been counterfeiting on a 'factory
scale'.
[184] The Trade Marks and other registers are kept in electronic form. For evidential consequences
of this, cf *Houghton v Liverpool City Council* [2000] Crim LR 574 (QBD).
[185] This appears to be a fairly low threshold, in *R v Zaman* [2003] FSR 13, the Court of Appeal
upheld the trial judge's direction that 'the phrase "with a view to" simply means that the defendant
had something in his contemplation, not necessarily something that he wanted or intended to happen but something which might realistically occur'.
[186] [2003] 2 Cr App R 33; [2003] UKHL 28 HL—use of 'BON JOVI' trade mark on 'bootleg'
CDs.   [187] Cf eg *S v London Borough of Havering* [2002] EWCA Crim 2558 CA (Crim Div).

28.122   Forfeiture is available under the criminal provisions of the Trade Marks Act 1994 but has been held to be a civil remedy rather than a penalty.[188]

B. Pirated goods

28.123   As above,[189] the only customs remedy is forfeiture, but again the Copyright, Designs and Patents Act creates criminal offences in relation to the creation, importation, or dealing with goods known to infringe copyright or articles specifically designed for making such copies (s 107), illicit recordings (s 188), certain equipment for overcoming copy-protection or electronic rights management (ss 296, 296ZB, 296ZD, and 296ZG) or unauthorized decoders (ss 297A–298); again civil delivery up and forfeiture may be available (ss 108, 114, 114A, 195–7, 204A, and 297C,D).

C. Goods infringing a patent or a supplementary protection certificate

28.124   There are no criminal penalties relating to infringement of patents or supplementary protection certificates in the UK.

D. Goods infringing a plant variety right

28.125   There are no criminal penalties relating to infringement of plant breeders' or plant variety rights in the UK.

E. Goods infringing a designation of origin or a geographical indication

28.126   There are no criminal penalties relating to infringement of these rights, but misuse of a geographical indication is likely to constitute a false trade description, contrary to the Trade Descriptions Act 1968.[190]

---

[188] *Unic Centre Sarl v Harrow Crown Court and the London Borough of Brent and Harrow Trading Standards Service* [2000] FSR 667 QBD.   [189] Cf paras 28.119 and 28.120.
[190] Cf para 28.120 above.

VI. LIABILITY OF CUSTOMS AUTHORITIES AND RIGHT-HOLDERS

A. Liability of right-holders and sanctions

As it has been pointed out above, right-holders may be held liable for non-permitted use of the information provided by customs, under the action for breach of confidence.[191]   **28.127**

In order to impose liability for other breaches by right-holders of the Regulation (Article 19(3)), recourse could be made to the general law of tort (in Scotland, delict). It might be possible to argue that the right-holder owed a duty of care to a declarant or consignee of goods. Negligent behaviour causing damage might then be actionable under the tort of negligence.[192] There are torts of inducing breach of contract, and unlawful interference with trade which might perhaps be available where a right-holder engaged in fraudulent behaviour which interfered with supply contracts.[193] For registered intellectual property rights, there is a special form of action known as the 'threats' action, whereby someone aggrieved by groundless threats to sue for infringement may apply for an injunction to restrain threats and for damages.[194] In the case of registered rights other than trade marks, since the customs procedures require issue of proceedings,[195] it is possible that an improper application for customs measures could be characterized as a threat to sue.   **28.128**

B. Liability of customs authorities and sanctions

UK national law does not appear to entitle right-holders to compensation in the event that goods are not detected by a customs office and are released, or in the event that no action is taken to detain them once an application has been lodged by the right-holder.[196]   **28.129**

Customs Notice 34[197] states clearly 'we do not accept liability for any infringing goods covered by applications or Notices under either EC or UK legislation which   **28.130**

---

[191] At para 28.90.

[192] See, for example, Davies, *Tort*, ch 14 in Birks, ed, *English Private Law* (2002 and Supplement).

[193] See, for example, Carty, *An Analysis of the Economic Torts* (2001) Ch 3, Inducing Breach of Contract and Ch 5, Unlawful Interference with Trade.

[194] Registered Designs Act 1949, s 26; Patents Act 1977, s 70; Trade Marks Act 1994, s 21; Olympic Symbols etc (Protection) Act 1995, s 16. The burden of proof is reversed. Cf Lim 'The "Threats" Section In The UK Trade Marks Act 1994: Can A Person Still Wound Without Striking?' [1995] EIPR 138.   [195] SI 2004 No 1473, Reg 8.

[196] Cf Reg 1383/2003, Art 19(1).   [197] Para 5.4.

we do not detect'. Theoretically it might be possible to bring proceedings for judicial review,[198] but an especially good case would have to be brought in order to obtain leave to apply. In these circumstances it is unlikely that a complaint under Customs Notice 1000[199] would receive a sympathetic response.

28.131 As for the potential liability of a customs office or another authority to the persons involved or affected *by an ex-officio procedure* for damages suffered by them as a result of the authorities' intervention,[200] Customs Notice 1000[201] states at paragraph 6.1:

> If as a direct result of our mistake or unreasonable delay you are out of pocket, we will consider reimbursing your reasonable costs. These might include the costs of postage, phone calls, travelling expenses, professional fees or financial charges. We will not compensate you for the time you have spent unless you can show you lost earnings as a direct result.

Conclusion

28.132 In our view Regulation 1383/2003 has been successfully grafted on to the national customs system. Similar procedures apply in the case of counterfeit or pirate goods whether they emanate from inside or outside the EU. These may be dealt with swiftly under a simplified procedure. Although the use of Magistrates' Courts may involve non-specialist judiciary, the few reported decisions suggest that these courts are dealing competently with intellectual property rights. Extension of the customs procedure to rights such as patents, plant variety rights, and geographical indications sensibly involves the scrutiny of the expert courts, as envisaged by the Regulation. It remains to be seen, however, whether procedures under the Regulation are used more than their predecessors.

---

[198] See para 28.74 above.
[199] March 2002, available for consultation as a 'public notice' in the UK Customs website http://www.hmrc.gov.uk.   [200] Cf Reg 1383/2003, Art 19(2).
[201] March 2002, available for consultation as a 'public notice' in the UK Customs website http://www.hmrc.gov.uk.

Part V

CONCLUSION

29

INTELLECTUAL PROPERTY: BORDERS AND CROSSROADS

An overview of the issues

Jeremy Phillips

Introduction

The authors of the substantive chapters of this book have prepared a thorough and **29.01**
detailed analysis of the legal provisions governing the interception of infringing
products at the borders of the European Union. This chapter will not duplicate
any of that material. Instead it will attempt, by saying a little about the subject, to
explain why those chapters are so very important.

I. A SORT OF CHESS GAME

A review of the legislation governing the interception and suspension of goods from **29.02**
free circulation gives a very clear snapshot of the legal rules by which the actions of
intellectual property owners, their agents, the customs authorities, and other organs of
state must operate. But if you read the law you can easily forget that there is more to the
problem than just understanding and applying the rules. The real situation is something like a complex chess game, where each side's move is matched by the response of
others. The law reflects the dynamics of the conflict immediately before it is drafted;
but once it comes into force it creates a fresh dynamic, to which intellectual property
owners, customs officials, and infringers must all respond. It is out of the question for
intellectual property owners to cease playing and surrender their rights; but, while the
profits are great and outweigh the risk of obtaining them, the laws of economics and
the principles of game theory[1] ensure the continued participation of their adversaries.

---

[1] See eg James D Miller, *Game Theory at Work: How to Use Game Theory to Outthink and
Outmaneuver Your Competition* (New York, McGraw-Hill, 2003); Arun Agrawal, 'Rules, Rule

II. A CONFLUENCE OF INTERESTS

29.03 Although the provisions of the law do not explicitly state it, the arrival at the European Union's external borders of the goods that infringe intellectual property rights brings together, at that very moment, a confluence of interests. Some of these interests are in confluence with each other, while others are in conflict. Let us list the parties who meet at the crossroads when their separate interests are awakened by the arrival of infringing goods.

A. Intellectual property right-holders and users

29.04 It may appear obvious that, since counterfeiters and infringers damage intellectual property rights by importing and then selling unlawful goods, the owners of those rights would act with alacrity and enthusiasm to prevent such importation or, where it occurs, to minimize its consequences. Although this is generally the case, it often happens that the intellectual property owner acts slowly or without enthusiasm in seeking to protect incursions upon his intellectual domain. This may be for one or more of the reasons mentioned in the following non-exclusive list:

- The effort and expense of intercepting a small consignment of infringing goods might be disproportionate to the benefits derived from the interception. This can happen particularly where the intellectual property owner is faced with dealing with a large volume of infringing goods at the EEA's port of entry and his own resources are stretched.

One strategy employed by counterfeiters is to send large shipments that include both lawful and counterfeit goods but which contain only a few infringing items per right-holder—a strategy that aims to discourage right-holders from enforcing their rights. To counter this, right-holders must consider the following cost-reducing options: (i) create right-holders' associations that act on behalf of all of them; (ii) choose a lawyer who represents several companies in one field of activity (since many mixed shipments concern items of the same kind, such as telephone accessories); (iii) agree a fixed and minimal fee for small shipments; (iv) seek to recover their costs from the infringers. Sometimes it is clearly in the right-holder's interest to take action against even small quantities, for example for public health or consumer protection, where failure to act might impair the right-holder's goodwill and his brand's reputation.

Making and Rule Breaking: Examining the Fit between Rule Systems and Resource Use' in E Ostrom, R Gardner, and J M Walker, eds *Rules, Games, and Common-Pool Resources* (Ann Arbor, University of Michigan Press, 1994); M Boldrin and D K Levine, 'Intellectual Property and the Scale of the Market' (2004).

Right-holders may be forced to allow the importation of infringing goods because it is not economically viable to stop them, unless simplified legal frameworks are put in place and the mere fact of presenting infringing goods at the border becomes a customs offence that can be prosecuted by the authorities.[2]

- It may be difficult for the intellectual property proprietor to ascertain whether the goods are legitimate or not, for example where it has extensively licensed the manufacture outside the EEA of goods under its intellectual property rights but has not exercised tight control over its licensees and cannot easily distinguish between its licensees' products and those of distant infringers.[3]

- The infringing products may trespass upon the intellectual property rights of numerous rights owners, in circumstances where two or more of them each consider that a party other than themselves should take the necessary action (for example, where the works of two or more performers or composers are recorded on a sound recording in which the rights are owned by a third party).

- The intellectual property rights infringed may be of relatively small commercial or strategic value (for example, counterfeit pre-recorded tapes or reproductions of fashion goods that have themselves ceased to be fashionable[4]).

- On the basis of previous adverse experience of seeking to enforce rights against goods in the process of importation, the right-holder may prefer to allow the goods into the region and to take legal action further down the chain of distribution and sale. Although imported infringing goods may be more difficult to trace after importation, a large and profitable enterprise that subsequently resells those goods may be a more suitable target for litigation than the hapless carrier.

- It may be felt imprudent to court adverse publicity in the eyes of consumers through the pursuit of lawful rights. Consumers in the United Kingdom will remember how the powerful retail chain Tesco portrayed itself as the champion of the consumers' interests against the insensitive, greedy, and market-dividing pricing policy of trade mark owner Levi Strauss, which sold its products in the United Kingdom at a substantial premium over the shop-floor price of the same products across the Atlantic.[5]

---

[2] Several countries, including France and the United Kingdom, already have provisions of this nature with respect to trade mark infringements (the species of infringement that occurs most frequently).

[3] *Countering Counterfeiting: a guide to protecting and enforcing intellectual property rights* (ICC Counterfeiting Intelligence Bureau, 1997) gives some useful guidance as how right-holders can best keep control of licence and know-how agreements.

[4] For an example of the lengths that trade mark owners are prepared to go to in order to keep previous years' fashions out of the lucrative EU market, see the litigation before and after the reference to the European Court of Justice in Case C-355/96 *Silhouette International Schmied GmbH & Co KG v Hartlauer Handelsgesellschaft GmbH* [1998] ECR I-4799, [1998] ETMR 539.

[5] Levi Strauss won its trade mark infringement case against Tesco (see Joined Cases C-414/99 to C-416/99 *Zino Davidoff and Levi Strauss* [2001] ECR I-8691, [2001] ETMR 67 and *Levi Strauss & Co and Levi Strauss (UK) Ltd v Tesco Stores Ltd and others* [2002] ETMR), but at the cost of a loss of goodwill in a highly competitive sector. See eg http://news.bbc.co.uk/1/hi/business/1261060.stm and http://news.bbc.co.uk/1/hi/business/2163561.stm (websites verified on 28 April 2005).

29.05 These points should alert the reader to the fact that even the intellectual property owner, as one of the prime victims of infringement by importation, may be somewhat reticent about fighting to protect its own interests. Yet, given the fact that neither the Enforcement Directive nor the TRIPs Agreement require the State to take action against infringing acts, it is up to the intellectual property owner, as victim, to make his own arrangements to safeguard both his interests and those of his consumers.

B. Makers and sellers of infringing goods

29.06 The interests of those who make and sell infringing goods are served by their being able to get away with their unlawful activities.[6]

29.07 Yet even in this case there is an air of ambivalence in their position. The profitability of their operations depends upon their ability to trade in goods which incorporate protected technologies, which appropriate copyright work, or which exploit the goodwill or lifestyle aspirations created by a respected legitimate trader.

29.08 However, paradoxically, the interests of the counterfeiters may also be served by the good enforcement of intellectual property rights. Consumers often buy infringing goods either because (i) they believe them to be the desired or needed genuine products which they seek or because (ii) they know that they are buying fake products but that they are substantially cheaper than the genuine item. If consumer confidence in the genuine product is damaged, it loses its attraction for consumers. It is therefore in the best interests of any infringer that intellectual property rights are rigorously enforced against all infringers other than himself. That way, the quality, the desirability and the price of the genuine product may be kept high, along with the differential between their prices and the profits resulting from illicit trade.

C. Importers

29.09 When a merchant imports goods, it is generally for the purpose of selling them further down the chain of distribution, to wholesalers or retailers of those goods.

---

[6] Anecdotal evidence suggests that illicit cigarette trafficking remains profitable if even only 1 consignment out of 10 eludes the customs net. The profit margin of counterfeit goods (for example 900% for software) may be far higher than for narcotics (100% for cannabis). See 'Busting Software Pirates', *Times/Europe*, 18 November 2002, cited in Centre d'études internationales de la propriété industrielle (CEIPI), *Impacts de la contrefaçon et de la piraterie en Europe*, Juillet 2004, 28). The risk taken by traffickers in counterfeits is low since, in practice, they will often only lose the counterfeit goods and not be subject to criminal prosecution.

The prime concern of most importers is determined by the profit motive: they do not normally add value to goods but seek to source them as cheaply as possible and then sell them at the best price they can get. While some importers may be acutely sensitive to the need to deal only with legitimate product, many are less so and do not perform exercises in due diligence in order to ascertain the provenance of the goods they deal in. Paying, getting paid, organizing delivery, and making sure that the imported goods are insured at their risk for the shortest period possible are normally far greater priorities for them.

Goods that are detained and inspected are goods that cause inconvenience and annoyance to their importers. Accordingly, it is easy to understand if some importers, even if they themselves support the principle that only lawful goods be traded, are sometimes reluctant to see a consignment halted and opened up for careful inspection and possibly lengthy detention before being allowed to continue its journey or before being taken out of circulation completely. **29.10**

D. Trans-shippers

The transportation of goods into and through the countries of the European Union is a highly competitive market. Since the sector is a heavily regulated one, overheads and fixed costs incurred by competitors are high: vehicles must be procured, taxed, licensed, adequately serviced, and insured. Drivers must be trained, tested, licensed, and paid. Paperwork and documentation is substantial, and so on. It is therefore in the interests of trans-shippers to make sure that the movement of goods from one jurisdiction to another is effected as swiftly and efficiently as possible. The carriage of goods that might be detained even for inspection may substantially erode profit margins; how much more so where a driver is detained and interviewed at length and goods, having been inspected, are then separated from his cargo and held in suspense. **29.11**

It is not normally feasible for transporters to police intellectual property rights under any circumstances. Further, even where it is known by trans-shippers that the goods in transit are protected by intellectual property rights, that does not of itself raise the implication that goods so shipped are infringing any of those rights. **29.12**

In some countries the mere transportation of infringing goods is considered an act of infringement; in others the right-holder can sue the transporters and obtain the delivery up or the surrender of infringing goods. In response to this, transporters stipulate in their transportation contracts that they will surrender infringing goods if the right-holder has sent the holder of the goods a cease and desist letter which has remained unanswered. **29.13**

29.14 The suggestion has been made that transporters are actually liable under the Community Customs Code for any hidden defects found in the goods they transport, even where those goods infringe intellectual property rights.[7] This conclusion however requires further investigation.

29.15 The transportation industry is in general little inconvenienced by customers who pay for infringing products to be brought into the European Union: they designate the goods to be delivered, stipulate the places of pick-up and delivery, and pay the hauliers or shippers the agreed price. It is the customs officials, in the execution of their duties, who inconvenience drivers and trans-shippers by stopping them, examining their documentation, searching their cargo, detaining their containers, and interfering with the job they have been paid to perform. It follows accordingly that intellectual property right-holders cannot count on the support of the transport sector when seeking to protect their businesses.

E. Consumers

29.16 The position of individual consumers is impossible to summarize within a single generalized statement. This is because consumers, collectively and individually, adopt different, and frequently contradictory, attitudes towards infringing products. Consider the following propositions:

- No rational consumer would consider taking a counterfeit medicine or fitting his car with fake brake-pads. This is because the personal result for him could be fatal and the intellectual property rights (particularly the trade mark right) are viewed as a badge of quality and consequently of safety.

- A substantial proportion of consumers have no serious objection to purchasing underwear marked with designer labels, watches bearing prestigious trade marks, or recorded films and music, where in each case the manufacture is without the authorization of the relevant intellectual property rights owners, since the personal consequence of the use or purchase is generally regarded as being trivial or insignificant. In such cases the intellectual property rights (and again, particularly the trade mark right) are viewed as reflecting or aspiring towards a desirable image or lifestyle into which consumers wish to buy. Whether the goods are real or fake, the message of the brand or design is unchanged.

- Another substantial, though probably smaller, proportion of consumers does not welcome the wide-scale availability of unauthorized goods bearing prestige branding and design, since it devalues the exclusivity and respectability of those goods in their eyes.

---

[7] Per Christophe Zimmermann (Head of Intellectual Property in the European Commission's EC, Taxation and Customs Union DG).

- A very large proportion have no inhibition whatsoever with regard to the purchase of products which are genuine, having been manufactured by or with the licence of the intellectual property rights owner, but which have been imported into the European Economic Area from a market in which they were available at a much lower price. In such a case many consumers bitterly resent the enforcement of local intellectual property rights, which they perceive as means of forcing them to pay higher prices than those paid by consumers in other jurisdictions.[8]

It follows from this that the consumer may see himself as both the beneficiary and the victim of border controls on the importation of infringing goods. This has repercussions for intellectual property rights owners, who cannot rely consistently on the cooperation of consumers in the enforcement of their rights. **29.17**

F. Customs and local enforcement authorities

For the sake of their self-respect and *esprit de corps*, national enforcement agencies like to feel that they are performing a task that is important and that they are performing it well. They are acutely aware that their performance is monitored and that, if they do not identify or intercept infringing goods at the border, questions will be asked as to whether it is necessary to retain them at all, rather than leave 'policing' to civil actions or private prosecutions brought by the intellectual property owners themselves. It may be thought harsh to judge the enforcement agencies entirely by their results since the only results that are measurable are those which result from pathological behaviour such as infringement. Where the effect of good monitoring and swift, firm executive action is to deter the importation of counterfeit goods, statistics recording product seizures will show a decline and it is impossible to prove that any drop in seizures is caused by the successful implementation of an interventionist policy or by the unthinkable scenario of customs officers slumbering at their posts. **29.18**

In this context we must remember that, while statistics are an important source of information, they are difficult to interpret since counterfeiting is a shadow economy: those who practise its illicit arts do not file official returns or publish annual reports that boast their achievements. Likewise, figures for customs interventions are likely to record only the tip of the iceberg. We may also expect that, once figures in one country go up (reflecting efficient customs operations), the traffickers will vary their routes. In any event, the figures quoted by **29.19**

---

[8] Much the same reasoning applies to overruns, where infringers capitalize on the authentic source of an unlawful product by telling customers that the goods are made in the same factory or under similar circumstances.

right-holders tend to be overestimates since (i) they may be intended to persuade public opinion and (ii) they are frequently premised upon the assumption that every sale of an illicit product represents the loss of a corresponding sale of the genuine item—an assumption which is difficult to justify, particularly in sectors such as luxury goods and expensive watches.

G. National governments

29.20 The due enactment and the adequate and efficient enforcement of laws that guard against intellectual property infringement is a matter of pressing importance to national governments. Failure to do so has the following undesirable consequences:

- embarrassing public criticism for failure to protect against crime legitimate commercial interests, including not merely those of intellectual property owners but the distribution, wholesale, and retail channels through which legitimate goods are placed before the consumer;
- the risk of the government of another country initiating a complaint procedure with the World Trade Organization;
- an application by the European Commission for a declaration of non-compliance with European Union law;
- the tolerance of a criminal culture in which organized crime and money-laundering thrive;
- The loss of valuable tax revenue which arises from the sale of legitimate products, since 'black economy' transactions do not normally feature on the radar of the institutions responsible for the monitoring and taxation of commercial activity.

H. Countries of origin of infringing goods

29.21 Many developing countries do not see an immediate need for protecting intellectual property rights. In fact, counterfeiting creates industrial activity, employment (although often in 'sweatshops') and revenue to the State or the dominant class (often in the form of bribery). Where there is no effective sanction against counterfeiters, the local industry prefers to copy intellectual property rights than to be creative. A small-minded conclusion may be that 'fighting counterfeiting destroys the local economy'. This is not true, as the economic tissue that develops around counterfeiting is an unhealthy economic environment (women and children working at wages below the minimum in deplorable conditions, organized criminality, bribery, etc).

I. Balancing the interests

All the players listed above are involved in a game in which (i) the rules cannot easily **29.22** be changed but can be manipulated through interpretation; (ii) the players do not 'take turns' but play their parts simultaneously; (iii) the rewards of success are generously high and the price of failure can be catastrophic; and (iv) while participation is optional for counterfeiters and consumers, it is compulsory for intellectual property owners and for those who depend on those owners for their sustenance.

It is also a game in which the odds tend to favour the infringers. They do not have to **29.23** declare their hand (or even their existence) in advance, they have relative freedom with regard to manufacturing and outsourcing policies, they offer no guarantee of quality and they can switch their products, suppliers, and market targets almost at will.

In such circumstances it is important to get the balance right. Too little protection **29.24** for intellectual property owners and the incentive to make and sell new products, to develop brands, and to promote the commercialization of music, literature, and the arts will be gone. Too much protection and prices will be forced up and competition from even legitimate traders will become onerous and unprofitable and will ultimately fade away.

III. POLICING AND THE SCOPE OF INTELLECTUAL PROPERTY PROTECTION

While all intellectual property rights are equally capable of being infringed, not all **29.25** intellectual property rights are equally capable of being monitored. Some intellectual property rights are notoriously difficult to police. These rights include, for example,

- patents granted for manufacturing processes (where the same product may be made by either a patented process or by a process which is unpatented or which has fallen into the public domain); and
- items of clothing and footwear that are protected by design right or copyright (where the sheer volume of clothing shapes that exist in the public domain and the problem of proving copying militate against the establishment of clear proof of infringement).

To these rights we may add others where the scope of infringement has yet to be **29.26** established, such as

- trade marks for colours and combinations of colours
- trade marks for the shapes of goods and containers for goods
- trade marks for sounds and smells

where, in each case, it may be unclear as to what is a similar but non-identical mark and as to what level of similarity is likely to induce confusion on the part of the relevant consumer.

29.27   Precisely how customs authorities will respond to the challenge of 'non-traditional' marks is uncertain. It may well be that the unauthorized use of unusual marks that are not normally recognized by consumers as being trade marks will confer little or no advantage upon the counterfeit traders, in which case intellectual property owners may wish to consider the utility of maintaining such marks in their portfolios.

IV. COSTS FOR THE OWNERS, PROFITS FOR THE INFRINGERS

29.28   A further point to appreciate is that, for the intellectual property proprietor, every euro spent on the protection or enforcement of rights is an element of unwanted cost, unwillingly expended. This is so, not only in respect of the policing of the borders of the European Union but of all policing of intellectual property rights: these include the monitoring of the internet for signs of abuse, examining the goods and services of lawful competitors for evidence of impropriety, and imposing and asserting quality control and manufacturing restrictions upon lawful licensees. All of these activities cost money.

29.29   Policing and enforcement is only as good as the degree to which the intellectual property owner can commit his resources towards the gathering of accessible data relating to his own rights, the monitoring of the activities of his own licensees as well as unlicensed third parties, the marshalling of evidence, the payment of court and other official fees, the instruction of lawyers, and so on. In each case a decision must be made: policing must be cost-effective, which means that it is unlikely to be 100 per cent successful.

29.30   The law of diminishing returns means that policing will be geared towards catching or stopping those infringers who are cheapest and easiest to stop or who, in relation to the scale of damage they do, are the most expensive if they are allowed to continue. Smaller and more elusive infringers will generally have a much higher chance of survival. The only situation in which the law of diminishing returns does not apply is where the outlay in dealing with even a small number of infringers is seen as an investment in making an example of them and thus deterring potential future infringers from emulating their practices.[9]

---

[9] The efficacy of this practice in a non-border related context may be seen from the depressing effect upon unlicensed peer-to-peer file-sharing of the copyright infringement actions brought by

Some multinational corporations have indicated that, as a matter of financial pru- **29.31**
dence, their anti-counterfeiting campaigns should be self-funding, in other words
that every cost incurred in the detection, pursuit, and eradication of trade in illicit
produce should be balanced by income in terms of damages and costs awards.
While this is clearly a desirable end, such policies are rarely capable of being
achieved. Even assuming that costs awards are commensurate with costs incurred
(which, in practice, they never are), any awards of costs of damages occur a long
time after the event and take little or no account of internal labour and administration costs borne by the intellectual property rights owner. Such a strategy also
forgets that the protection of the value of a consumer brand, in terms of the goodwill invested in it and the reputation it enjoys in the eyes of consumers, is not easily quantifiable on a balance sheet that shows only the outflow of enforcement
expenditure and the inflow of damages and costs awards.

For infringers, however, each euro spent is aimed not at staunching their losses but **29.32**
at maximizing their profits. The greater the sum invested by illicit traders in the
procurement of unauthorized product, the greater the expectation that it will be
turned into pure gain. Without the costs associated with developing and testing
new products, popularizing new brands, instilling confidence into retailers and
the like, without the cashflow implications of value-added tax and the bottom-
line responsibility for the payment of corporation tax, counterfeiters and
infringers have little opportunity to commit their funds to anything other than
the pursuit of profit.

If funds will be committed sparingly and with reluctance by intellectual property **29.33**
owners in the protection of their intellectual estate, but more generously by
infringers in seeking to trespass upon that estate, it is clear that the latter will enter
combat with very much more enthusiasm and willingness to fight than will the
former.

Conclusions

It is apparent from the foregoing that, even in a favourable political and legal envir- **29.34**
onment and with the support of the customs authorities, intellectual property
rights owners will have a difficult enough task on their hands if they wish to keep
counterfeiters and infringers off their patch. Apart from ensuring that national
implementation of Regulation 1383/2003 is consistently effective throughout
the European Union it is unclear what more can or should be done for them since,

---

the RIAA in the United States against a very small number of individual large-scale home down-
loaders: see http://www.extremetech.com/article2/0,3973,1139108,00.asp. British Phonographic
Industry Ltd has adopted the same tactic in the United Kingdom: see http://ipkitten.blogspot.com/
2004/10/individual-downloaders-targeted-in-uk.html (both websites verified on 28 April 2005).

paradoxically, the greater the degree of protection they enjoy, the greater is their profitability and therefore the greater is the attraction of the unauthorized use of their rights for infringers.

29.35 No doubt the European Commission, the various intellectual property rights owners' groups, and the enforcement authorities will keep the situation under constant review. It may however be the case that the present regime represents the best means of keeping an acceptable balance between the interest groups described earlier in this chapter and that, accordingly, in the absence of any technological panaceas, future law reforms will be limited to mere fine-tuning of the legal regime now in place.

APPENDIX A

Council Regulation (EC) No 1383/2003
of 22 July 2003

concerning customs action against goods suspected of infringing certain
intellectual property rights and the measures to be taken against goods found to
have infringed such rights

The Council of the European Union,

Having regard to the Treaty establishing the European Community, and in particular Article 133 thereof,

Having regard to the proposal from the Commission,

Whereas:

(1) To improve the working of the system concerning the entry into the Community and the export and re-export from the Community of goods infringing certain intellectual property rights introduced by Council Regulation (EC) No 3295/94 of 22 December 1994 laying down measures to prohibit the release for free circulation, export, re-export or entry for a suspensive procedure of counterfeit and pirated goods,[1] conclusions should be drawn from experience of its application. In the interests of clarity, Regulation (EC) No 3295/94 should be repealed and replaced.

(2) The marketing of counterfeit and pirated goods, and indeed all goods infringing intellectual property rights, does considerable damage to law-abiding manufacturers and traders and to right-holders, as well as deceiving and in some cases endangering the health and safety of consumers. Such goods should, in so far as is possible, be kept off the market and measures adopted to deal effectively with this unlawful activity without impeding the freedom of legitimate trade. This objective is consistent with efforts under way at international level.

(3) In cases where counterfeit goods, pirated goods and, more generally, goods infringing an intellectual property right originate in or come from third countries, their introduction into the Community customs territory, including their transhipment, release for free circulation in the Community, placing under a suspensive procedure and placing in a free zone or warehouse, should be prohibited and a procedure set up to enable the customs authorities to enforce this prohibition as effectively as possible.

(4) Customs authorities should also be able to take action against counterfeit goods, pirated goods and goods infringing certain intellectual property rights which are in the process of being exported, re-exported or leaving the Community customs territory.

(5) Action by the customs authorities should involve, for the period necessary to determine whether suspect goods are indeed counterfeit goods, pirated goods or goods infringing certain intellectual property rights, suspending release for free circulation, export and re-export or, in the case of goods placed under a suspensive procedure, placed in a free zone or a free warehouse, in the process of being re-exported with notification, introduced into the customs territory or leaving that territory, detaining those goods.

1111

(6)   The particulars of the application for action, such as its period of validity and form, need to be defined and harmonised in all Member States. The same applies to the conditions governing the acceptance of applications by the customs authorities and the service designated to receive, process and register them.

(7)   Even where no application has yet been lodged or approved, the Member States should be authorised to detain the goods for a certain period to allow right-holders to lodge an application for action with the customs authorities.

(8)   Proceedings initiated to determine whether an intellectual property right has been infringed under national law will be conducted with reference to the criteria used to establish whether goods produced in that Member State infringe intellectual property rights. This Regulation does not affect the Member States' provisions on the competence of the courts or judicial procedures.

(9)   To make the Regulation easier to apply for customs administrations and right-holders alike, provision should also be made for a more flexible procedure allowing goods infringing certain intellectual property rights to be destroyed without there being any obligation to initiate proceedings to establish whether an intellectual property right has been infringed under national law.

(10)   It is necessary to lay down the measures applicable to goods which have been found to be counterfeit, pirated or generally to infringe certain intellectual property rights. Those measures should not only deprive those responsible for trading in such goods of the economic benefits of the transaction and penalise them but should also constitute an effective deterrent to further transactions of the same kind.

(11)   To avoid disrupting the clearance of goods carried in travellers' personal baggage, it is appropriate, except where certain material indications suggest commercial traffic is involved, to exclude from the scope of this Regulation goods that may be counterfeit, pirated or infringe certain intellectual property rights when imported from third countries within the limits of the duty-free allowance accorded by Community rules.

(12)   In the interests of this Regulation's effectiveness, it is important to ensure the uniform application of the common rules it lays down and to reinforce mutual assistance between the Member States and between the Member States and the Commission, in particular by recourse to Council Regulation (EC) No 515/97 of 13 March 1997 on mutual assistance between the administrative authorities of the Member States and cooperation between the latter and the Commission to ensure the correct application of the law on customs and agricultural matters.[2]

(13)   In the light of the experience gained in the implementation of this Regulation, inter alia, consideration should be given to the possibility of increasing the number of intellectual property rights covered.

(14)   The measures necessary for the implementation of this Regulation should be adopted in accordance with Council Decision 1999/468/EC of 28 June 1999 laying down the procedures for the exercise of implementing powers conferred on the Commission.[3]

(15)   Regulation (EC) No 3295/94 should be repealed,

Has adopted this Regulation:

CHAPTER I SUBJECT MATTER AND SCOPE

Article 1

1. This Regulation sets out the conditions for action by the customs authorities when goods are suspected of infringing an intellectual property right in the following situations:

(a) when they are entered for release for free circulation, export or re-export in accordance with Article 61 of Council Regulation (EC) No 2913/92 of 12 October 1992 establishing the Community Customs Code;[4]

(b) when they are found during checks on goods entering or leaving the Community customs territory in accordance with Articles 37 and 183 of Regulation (EEC) No 2913/92, placed under a suspensive procedure within the meaning of Article 84(1)(a) of that Regulation, in the process of being re-exported subject to notification under Article 182(2) of that Regulation or placed in a free zone or free warehouse within the meaning of Article 166 of that Regulation.

2. This Regulation also fixes the measures to be taken by the competent authorities when the goods referred to in paragraph 1 are found to infringe intellectual property rights.

Article 2

1. For the purposes of this Regulation, 'goods infringing an intellectual property right' means:

    (a) 'counterfeit goods', namely:

        (i) goods, including packaging, bearing without authorisation a trade mark identical to the trade mark validly registered in respect of the same type of goods, or which cannot be distinguished in its essential aspects from such a trade mark, and which thereby infringes the trade mark-holder's rights under Community law, as provided for by Council Regulation (EC) No 40/94 of 20 December 1993 on the Community trade mark[5] or the law of the Member State in which the application for action by the customs authorities is made;

        (ii) any trade mark symbol (including a logo, label, sticker, brochure, instructions for use or guarantee document bearing such a symbol), even if presented separately, on the same conditions as the goods referred to in point (i);

        (iii) packaging materials bearing the trade marks of counterfeit goods, presented separately, on the same conditions as the goods referred to in point (i);

    (b) 'pirated goods', namely goods which are or contain copies made without the consent of the holder of a copyright or related right or design right, regardless of whether it is registered in national law, or of a person authorised by the right-holder in the country of production in cases where the making of those copies would constitute an infringement of that right under Council Regulation (EC) No 6/2002 of 12 December 2001 on Community designs[6] or the law of the Member State in which the application for customs action is made;

    (c) goods which, in the Member State in which the application for customs action is made, infringe:

        (i) a patent under that Member State's law;

        (ii) a supplementary protection certificate of the kind provided for in Council Regulation (EEC) No 1768/92[7] or Regulation (EC) No 1610/96 of the European Parliament and of the Council;[8]

        (iii) a national plant variety right under the law of that Member State or a Community plant variety right of the kind provided for in Council Regulation (EC) No 2100/94;[9]

        (iv) designations of origin or geographical indications under the law of that Member State or Council Regulations (EEC) No 2081/92[10] and (EC) No 1493/1999;[11]

        (v) geographical designations of the kind provided for in Council Regulation (EEC) No 1576/89.[12]

2. For the purposes of this Regulation, 'right-holder' means:

    (a) the holder of a trade mark, copyright or related right, design right, patent, supplementary protection certificate, plant variety right, protected designation of origin, protected geographical indication and, more generally, any right referred to in paragraph 1; or

    (b) any other person authorised to use any of the intellectual property rights mentioned in point (a), or a representative of the right-holder or authorised user.

3. Any mould or matrix which is specifically designed or adapted for the manufacture of goods infringing an intellectual property right shall be treated as goods of that kind if the use of such moulds or matrices infringes the right-holder's rights under Community law or the law of the Member State in which the application for action by the customs authorities is made.

Article 3

1. This Regulation shall not apply to goods bearing a trade mark with the consent of the holder of that trade mark or to goods bearing a protected designation of origin or a protected geographical

indication or which are protected by a patent or a supplementary protection certificate, by a copyright or related right or by a design right or a plant variety right and which have been manufactured with the consent of the right-holder but are placed in one of the situations referred to in Article 1(1) without the latter's consent.

It shall similarly not apply to goods referred to in the first subparagraph and which have been manufactured or are protected by another intellectual property right referred to in Article 2(1) under conditions other than those agreed with the right-holder.

2. Where a traveller's personal baggage contains goods of a non-commercial nature within the limits of the duty-free allowance and there are no material indications to suggest the goods are part of commercial traffic, Member States shall consider such goods to be outside the scope of this Regulation.

Chapter II Applications for Action by the Customs Authorities

Section 1 Measures prior to an application for action by the customs authorities

Article 4

1. Where the customs authorities, in the course of action in one of the situations referred to in Article 1(1) and before an application has been lodged by a right-holder or granted, have sufficient grounds for suspecting that goods infringe an intellectual property right, they may suspend the release of the goods or detain them for a period of three working days from the moment of receipt of the notification by the right-holder and by the declarant or holder of the goods, if the latter are known, in order to enable the right-holder to submit an application for action in accordance with Article 5.

2. In accordance with the rules in force in the Member State concerned, the customs authorities may, without divulging any information other than the actual or supposed number of items and their nature and before informing the right-holder of the possible infringement, ask the right-holder to provide them with any information they may need to confirm their suspicions.

Section 2 The lodging and processing of applications for customs action

Article 5

1. In each Member State a right-holder may apply in writing to the competent customs department for action by the customs authorities when goods are found in one of the situations referred to in Article 1(1) (application for action).

2. Each Member State shall designate the customs department competent to receive and process applications for action.

3. Where electronic data interchange systems exist, the Member States shall encourage right-holders to lodge applications electronically.

4. Where the applicant is the right-holder of a Community trade mark or a Community design right, a Community plant variety right or a designation of origin or geographical indication or a geographical designation protected by the Community, an application may, in addition to requesting action by the customs authorities of the Member State in which it is lodged, request action by the customs authorities of one or more other Member States.

5. The application for action shall be made out on a form established in accordance with the procedure referred to in Article 21(2); it must contain all the information needed to enable the goods in question to be readily recognised by the customs authorities, and in particular:

   (i) an accurate and detailed technical description of the goods;
   (ii) any specific information the right-holder may have concerning the type or pattern of fraud;
   (iii) the name and address of the contact person appointed by the right-holder.

The application for action must also contain the declaration required of the applicant by Article 6 and proof that the applicant holds the right for the goods in question.

In the situation described in paragraph 4 the application for action shall indicate the Member State or States in which customs action is requested as well as the names and addresses of the right-holder in each of the Member States concerned.

By way of indication and where known, right-holders should also forward any other information they may have, such as:

(a) the pre-tax value of the original goods on the legitimate market in the country in which the application for action is lodged;
(b) the location of the goods or their intended destination;
(c) particulars identifying the consignment or packages;
(d) the scheduled arrival or departure date of the goods;
(e) the means of transport used;
(f) the identity of the importer, exporter or holder of the goods;
(g) the country or countries of production and the routes used by traffickers;
(h) the technical differences, if known, between the authentic and suspect goods.

6. Details may also be required which are specific to the type of intellectual property right referred to in the application for action.

7. On receiving an application for action, the competent customs department shall process that application and notify the applicant in writing of its decision within 30 working days of its receipt.

The right-holder shall not be charged a fee to cover the administrative costs occasioned by the processing of the application.

8. Where the application does not contain the mandatory information listed in paragraph 5, the competent customs department may decide not to process the application for action; in that event it shall provide reasons for its decision and include information on the appeal procedure. The application can only be re-submitted when duly completed.

Article 6

1. Applications for action shall be accompanied by a declaration from the right-holder, which may be submitted either in writing or electronically, in accordance with national legislation, accepting liability towards the persons involved in a situation referred to in Article 1(1) in the event that a procedure initiated pursuant to Article 9(1) is discontinued owing to an act or omission by the right-holder or in the event that the goods in question are subsequently found not to infringe an intellectual property right.

In that declaration the right-holder shall also agree to bear all costs incurred under this Regulation in keeping goods under customs control pursuant to Article 9 and, where applicable, Article 11.

2. Where an application is submitted under Article 5(4), the right-holder shall agree in the declaration to provide and pay for any translation necessary; this declaration shall be valid in every Member State in which the decision granting the application applies.

Article 7

Articles 5 and 6 shall apply mutatis mutandis to requests for an extension.

Section 3 Acceptance of the application for action

Article 8

1. When granting an application for action, the competent customs department shall specify the period during which the customs authorities are to take action. That period shall not exceed one year. On expiry of the period in question, and subject to the prior discharge of any debt owed by

the right-holder under this Regulation, the department which took the initial decision may, at the right-holder's request, extend that period.

The right-holder shall notify the competent customs department referred to in Article 5(2), if his right ceases to be validly registered or expires.

2. The decision granting the right-holder's application for action shall immediately be forwarded to those customs offices of the Member State or States likely to be concerned by the goods alleged in the application to infringe an intellectual property right.

When an application for action submitted in accordance with Article 5(4) is granted, the period during which the customs authorities are to take action shall be set at one year; on expiry of the period in question, the department which processed the initial application shall, on the right-holder's written application, extend that period. The first indent of Article 250 of Regulation (EEC) No 2913/92 shall apply mutatis mutandis to the decision granting that application and to decisions extending or repealing it.

Where an application for action is granted, it is for the applicant to forward that decision, with any other information and any translations that may be necessary, to the competent customs department of the Member State or States in which the applicant has requested customs action. However, with the applicant's consent, the decision may be forwarded directly by the customs department which has taken the decision.

At the request of the customs authorities of the Member States concerned, the applicant shall provide any additional information necessary for the implementation of the decision.

3. The period referred to in the second subparagraph of paragraph 2 shall run from the date of adoption of the decision granting the application. The decision will not enter into force in the recipient Member State or States until it has been forwarded in accordance with the third subparagraph of paragraph 2 and the right-holder has fulfilled the formalities referred to in Article 6.

The decision shall then be sent immediately to the national customs offices likely to have to deal with the goods suspected of infringing intellectual property rights.

This paragraph shall apply mutatis mutandis to a decision extending the initial decision.

CHAPTER III CONDITIONS GOVERNING ACTION BY THE CUSTOMS AUTHORITIES AND BY THE AUTHORITY COMPETENT TO DECIDE ON THE CASE

Article 9

1. Where a customs office to which the decision granting an application by the right-holder has been forwarded pursuant to Article 8 is satisfied, after consulting the applicant where necessary, that goods in one of the situations referred to in Article 1(1) are suspected of infringing an intellectual property right covered by that decision, it shall suspend release of the goods or detain them.

The customs office shall immediately inform the competent customs department which processed the application.

2. The competent customs department or customs office referred to in paragraph 1 shall inform the right-holder and the declarant or holder of the goods within the meaning of Article 38 of Regulation (EEC) No 2913/92 of its action and is authorised to inform them of the actual or estimated quantity and the actual or supposed nature of the goods whose release has been suspended or which have been detained, without being bound by the communication of that information to notify the authority competent to take a substantive decision.

3. With a view to establishing whether an intellectual property right has been infringed under national law, and in accordance with national provisions on the protection of personal data, commercial and industrial secrecy and professional and administrative confidentiality, the customs office

or department which processed the application shall inform the right-holder, at his request and if known, of the names and addresses of the consignee, the consignor, the declarant or the holder of the goods and the origin and provenance of goods suspected of infringing an intellectual property right.

The customs office shall give the applicant and the persons involved in any of the situations referred to in Article 1(1) the opportunity to inspect goods whose release has been suspended or which have been detained.

When examining goods, the customs office may take samples and, according to the rules in force in the Member State concerned, hand them over or send them to the right-holder, at his express request, strictly for the purposes of analysis and to facilitate the subsequent procedure. Where circumstances allow, subject to the requirements of Article 11(1) second indent where applicable, samples must be returned on completion of the technical analysis and, where applicable, before goods are released or their detention is ended. Any analysis of these samples shall be carried out under the sole responsibility of the right-holder.

Article 10

The law in force in the Member State within the territory of which the goods are placed in one of the situations referred to in Article 1(1) shall apply when deciding whether an intellectual property right has been infringed under national law.

That law shall also apply to the immediate notification of the customs department or office referred to in Article 9(1) that the procedure provided for in Article 13 has been initiated, unless the procedure was initiated by that department or office.

Article 11

1. Where customs authorities have detained or suspended the release of goods which are suspected of infringing an intellectual property right in one of the situations covered by Article 1(1), the Member States may provide, in accordance with their national legislation, for a simplified procedure, to be used with the right-holder's agreement, which enables customs authorities to have such goods abandoned for destruction under customs control, without there being any need to determine whether an intellectual property right has been infringed under national law. To this end, Member States shall, in accordance with their national legislation, apply the following conditions:

— that the right-holder inform the customs authorities in writing within 10 working days, or three working days in the case of perishable goods, of receipt of the notification provided for in Article 9, that the goods concerned by the procedure infringe an intellectual property right referred to in Article 2(1) and provide those authorities with the written agreement of the declarant, the holder or the owner of the goods to abandon the goods for destruction. With the agreement of the customs authorities, this information may be provided directly to customs by the declarant, the holder or the owner of the goods. This agreement shall be presumed to be accepted when the declarant, the holder or the owner of the goods has not specifically opposed destruction within the prescribed period. This period may be extended by a further ten working days where circumstances warrant it;

— that destruction be carried out, unless otherwise specified in national legislation, at the expense and under the responsibility of the right-holder, and be systematically preceded by the taking of samples for keeping by the customs authorities in such conditions that they constitute evidence admissible in legal proceedings in the Member State in which they might be needed.

2. In all other cases, for example where the declarant, holder or owner objects to or contests the destruction of the goods, the procedure laid down in Article 13 shall apply.

Article 12

A right-holder receiving the particulars cited in the first subparagraph of Article 9(3) shall use that information only for the purposes specified in Articles 10, 11 and 13(1).

Any other use, not permitted by the national legislation of the Member State where the situation arose, may, on the basis of the law of the Member State in which the goods in question are located, cause the right-holder to incur civil liability and lead to the suspension of the application for action, for the period of validity remaining before renewal, in the Member State in which the events have taken place.

In the event of a further breach of this rule, the competent customs department may refuse to renew the application. In the case of an application of the kind provided for in Article 5(4), it must also notify the other Member States indicated on the form.

Article 13

1. If, within 10 working days of receipt of the notification of suspension of release or of detention, the customs office referred to in Article 9(1) has not been notified that proceedings have been initiated to determine whether an intellectual property right has been infringed under national law in accordance with Article 10 or has not received the right-holder's agreement provided for in Article 11(1) where applicable, release of the goods shall be granted, or their detention shall be ended, as appropriate, subject to completion of all customs formalities.

This period may be extended by a maximum of 10 working days in appropriate cases.

2. In the case of perishable goods suspected of infringing an intellectual property right, the period referred to in paragraph 1 shall be three working days. That period may not be extended.

Article 14

1. In the case of goods suspected of infringing design rights, patents, supplementary protection certificates or plant variety rights, the declarant, owner, importer, holder or consignee of the goods shall be able to obtain the release of the goods or an end to their detention on provision of a security, provided that:

    (a) the customs office or department referred to in Article 9(1) has been notified, in accordance with Article 13(1), that a procedure has been initiated within the period provided for in Article 13(1) to establish whether an intellectual property right has been infringed under national law;

    (b) the authority empowered for this purpose has not authorised precautionary measures before the expiry of the time limit laid down in Article 13(1);

    (c) all customs formalities have been completed.

2. The security provided for in paragraph 1 must be sufficient to protect the interests of the right-holder.

Payment of the security shall not affect the other legal remedies available to the right-holder.

Where the procedure to determine whether an intellectual property right has been infringed under national law has been initiated other than on the initiative of the holder of a design right, patent, supplementary protection certificate or plant variety right, the security shall be released if the person initiating the said procedure does not exercise his right to institute legal proceedings within 20 working days of the date on which he receives notification of the suspension of release or detention.

Where the second subparagraph of Article 13(1) applies, this period may be extended to a maximum of 30 working days.

Article 15

The conditions of storage of the goods during the period of suspension of release or detention shall be determined by each Member State but shall not give rise to costs for the customs administrations.

CHAPTER IV PROVISIONS APPLICABLE TO GOODS FOUND TO INFRINGE AN INTELLECTUAL PROPERTY RIGHT

Article 16

Goods found to infringe an intellectual property right at the end of the procedure provided for in Article 9 shall not be:

— allowed to enter into the Community customs territory,
— released for free circulation,
— removed from the Community customs territory,
— exported,
— re-exported,
— placed under a suspensive procedure or
— placed in a free zone or free warehouse.

Article 17

1. Without prejudice to the other legal remedies open to the right-holder, Member States shall adopt the measures necessary to allow the competent authorities:

(a) in accordance with the relevant provisions of national law, to destroy goods found to infringe an intellectual property right or dispose of them outside commercial channels in such a way as to preclude injury to the right-holder, without compensation of any sort and, unless otherwise specified in national legislation, at no cost to the exchequer;

(b) to take, in respect of such goods, any other measures effectively depriving the persons concerned of any economic gains from the transaction.

Save in exceptional cases, simply removing the trademarks which have been affixed to counterfeit goods without authorisation shall not be regarded as effectively depriving the persons concerned of any economic gains from the transaction.

2. Goods found to infringe an intellectual property right may be forfeited to the exchequer. In that event, paragraph 1(a) shall apply.

CHAPTER V PENALTIES

Article 18

Each Member State shall introduce penalties to apply in cases of violation of this Regulation. Such penalties must be effective, proportionate and dissuasive.

CHAPTER VI LIABILITY OF THE CUSTOMS AUTHORITIES AND THE RIGHT-HOLDER

Article 19

1. Save as provided by the law of the Member State in which an application is lodged or, in the case of an application under Article 5(4), by the law of the Member State in which goods infringing an intellectual property right are not detected by a customs office, the acceptance of an application shall not entitle the right-holder to compensation in the event that such goods are not detected by a customs office and are released or no action is taken to detain them in accordance with Article 9(1).

2. The exercise by a customs office or by another duly empowered authority of the powers conferred on them in order to fight against goods infringing an intellectual property right shall not render them liable towards the persons involved in the situations referred to in Article 1(1) or the persons affected by the measures provided for in Article 4 for damages suffered by them as a result of the

authority's intervention, except where provided for by the law of the Member State in which the application is made or, in the case of an application under Article 5(4), by the law of the Member State in which loss or damage is incurred.

3. A right-holder's civil liability shall be governed by the law of the Member State in which the goods in question were placed in one of the situations referred to in Article 1(1).

Chapter VII Final Provisions

Article 20

The measures necessary for the application of this Regulation shall be adopted in accordance with the procedure referred to in Article 21(2).

Article 21

1. The Commission shall be assisted by the Customs Code Committee.

2. Where reference is made to this paragraph, Articles 4 and 7 of Decision 1999/468/EC shall apply.

The period laid down in Article 4(3) of Decision 1999/468/EC shall be set at three months.

Article 22

Member States shall communicate all relevant information on the application of this Regulation to the Commission.

The Commission shall forward this information to the other Member States.

The provisions of Regulation (EC) No 515/97 shall apply mutatis mutandis.

The details of the information procedure shall be drawn up under the implementing provisions in accordance with the procedure referred to in Article 21(2).

Article 23

On the basis of the information referred to in Article 22, the Commission shall report annually to the Council on the application of this Regulation. This report may, where appropriate, be accompanied by a proposal to amend the Regulation.

Article 24

Regulation (EC) No 3295/94 is repealed with effect from 1 July 2004.

References to the repealed Regulation shall be construed as references to this Regulation.

Article 25

This Regulation shall enter into force on the seventh day following that of its publication in the Official Journal of the European Union.

It shall apply with effect from 1 July 2004.

This Regulation shall be binding in its entirety and directly applicable in all Member States.

Done at Brussels, 22 July 2003.

For the Council

The President

G. Alemanno

[1] OJ L 341, 30.12.1994, p. 8. Regulation as last amended by Regulation (EC) No 806/2003 (OJ L 122, 16.5.2003, p. 1).

[2] OJ L 82, 22.3.1997, p. 1. Regulation as last amended by Regulation (EC) No 807/2003 (OJ L 122, 16.5.2003, p. 36).

3 OJ L 184, 17.7.1999, p. 23.
4 OJ L 302, 19.10.1992, p. 1. Regulation as last amended by Regulation (EC) No 2700/2000, of the European Parliament and of the Council (OJ L 311, 12.12.2000, p. 17).
5 OJ L 11, 14.1.1994, p. 1. Regulation as last amended by Regulation (EC) No 807/2003.
6 OJ L 3, 5.1.2002, p. 1.
7 OJ L 182, 2.7.1992, p. 1.
8 OJ L 198, 8.8.1996, p. 30.
9 OJ L 227, 1.9.1994, p. 1. Regulation as last amended by Regulation (EC) No 807/2003.
10 OJ L 208, 24.7.1992, p. 1. Regulation as last amended by Regulation (EC) No 806/2003.
11 OJ L 179, 14.7.1999, p. 1. Regulation as last amended by Regulation (EC) No 806/2003.
12 OJ L 160, 12.6.1989, p. 1. Regulation as last amended by Regulation (EC) No 3378/94 of the European Parliament and of the Council (OJ L 366, 31.12.1994, p. 1).

Commission Regulation (EC) No 1891/2004

of 21 October 2004

*laying down provisions for the implementation of Council Regulation (EC)
No 1383/2003 concerning customs action against goods suspected of infringing
certain intellectual property rights and the measures to be taken against goods
found to have infringed such rights*

The Commission of the European Communities,

Having regard to the Treaty establishing the European Community,

Having regard to Council Regulation (EC) No 1383/2003 of 22 July 2003 concerning customs action against goods suspected of infringing certain intellectual property rights and the measures to be taken against goods found to have infringed such rights,[1] and in particular Article 20 thereof,

Whereas:

(1) Regulation (EC) No 1383/2003 introduced common rules with a view to prohibiting the entry, release for free circulation, exit, export, re-export or entry for a suspensive procedure of counterfeit and pirated goods, and to dealing effectively with the illegal marketing of such goods without impeding the freedom of legitimate trade.

(2) Since Regulation (EC) No 1383/2003 replaced Council Regulation (EC) No 3295/94 of 22 December 1994 laying down measures concerning the entry into the Community and the export and re-export from the Community of goods infringing certain intellectual property rights,[2] it is also necessary to replace Commission Regulation (EC) No 1367/95,[3] which laid down provisions for the implementation of Regulation (EC) No 3295/94.

(3) For the different types of intellectual property rights, it is necessary to define the natural and legal persons who may represent the holder of a right or any other person authorised to use the right.

(4) It is necessary to specify the nature of the proof of ownership of intellectual property required under the second subparagraph of Article 5(5) of Regulation (EC) No 1383/2003.

(5) In order to harmonise and standardise the content and format of applications for action under Article 5(1) and (4) of Regulation (EC) No 1383/2003 and the information to be entered on the application form, a standardised version of the form should be established. The language requirements for applications for action under Article 5(4) of the Regulation should also be laid down.

(6) The type of information to be included in applications for action should be specified in order to enable the customs authorities to recognise more readily goods that may infringe an intellectual property right.

(7) It is necessary to define the type of right-holder liability declaration which must accompany the application for action.

(8) In the interests of legal certainty, it is necessary to specify when the time periods laid down in Article 13 of Regulation (EC) No 1383/2003 commence.

(9) Procedures should be laid down for the exchange of information between Member States and the Commission, so that it is possible, on the one hand, for the Commission to monitor the

effective application of the procedure laid down by Regulation (EC) No 1383/2003, to draw up in due course the report referred to in Article 23 thereof and to try to quantify and describe patterns of fraud, and, on the other hand, for the Member States to introduce appropriate risk analysis.

(10) This Regulation should apply from the same date as Regulation (EC) No 1383/2003.

(11) The measures provided for in this Regulation are in accordance with the opinion of the Customs Code Committee,

Has adopted this Regulation:

Article 1

For the purposes of Article 2(2)(b) of Regulation (EC) No 1383/2003, hereinafter 'the basic Regulation', the right-holder or any other person authorised to use the right may be represented by natural or legal persons.

The persons referred to in the first paragraph shall include collecting societies which have as their sole or principal purpose the management or administration of copyrights or related rights; groups or representatives who have lodged a registration application for a protected designation of origin or a protected geographical indication; and plant breeders.

Article 2

1. If an application for action within the meaning of Article 5(1) of the basic Regulation is lodged by the right-holder himself, the proof required under the second subparagraph of Article 5(5) shall be as follows:

(a) in the case of a right that is registered or for which an application has been lodged, proof of registration with the relevant office or proof that the application has been lodged;

(b) in the case of a copyright, related right or design right which is not registered or for which an application has not been lodged, any evidence of authorship or of the applicant's status as original holder.

A copy of registration from the database of a national or international office may be considered to be proof for the purposes of point (a) of the first subparagraph.

For protected designations of origin and protected geographical indications, the proof referred to in point (a) of the first subparagraph shall, in addition, consist in proof that the right-holder is the producer or group and proof that the designation or indication has been registered. This subparagraph shall apply mutatis mutandis to wines and spirits.

2. Where the application for action is lodged by any other person authorised to use one of the rights referred to in Article 2(1) of the basic Regulation, proof shall, in addition to the proof required under paragraph 1 of this Article, consist in the document by virtue of which the person is authorised to use the right in question.

3. Where the application for action is lodged by a representative of the right-holder or of any other person authorised to use one of the rights referred to in Article 2(2) of the basic Regulation, proof shall, in addition to the proof referred to in paragraph 1 of this Article, consist in his authorisation to act.

A representative, as referred to in the first subparagraph, must produce the declaration required pursuant to Article 6 of the basic Regulation, signed by the persons referred to in paragraphs 1 and 2 of this Article, or a document authorising him to bear any costs arising from customs action on their behalf in accordance with Article 6 of the basic Regulation.

Article 3

1. The documents on which applications for action are made pursuant to Article 5(1) and (4) of the basic Regulation, the decisions referred to in Article 5(7) and (8) and the declaration required

pursuant to Article 6 of the basic Regulation must conform with the forms set out in the Annexes to this Regulation.

The forms shall be completed by electronic or mechanical means, or legibly by hand. Handwritten forms shall be completed in ink and in block capitals. Whatever method is used, forms shall contain no erasures, overwritten words or other alterations. Where the form is filled in electronically, it shall be made available to the applicant in digital form on one or more public sites that are directly accessible by computer. It may subsequently be reproduced on private printing equipment.

Where additional sheets are attached, as referred to in boxes 8, 9, 10 and 11 of the form on which the application for action provided for in Article 5(1) is to be made out, or in boxes 7, 8, 9 and 10 of the form on which the request for action provided for in Article 5(4) is to be made out, they shall be deemed to be an integral part of the form.

2. Forms for applications for action under Article 5(4) of the basic Regulation shall be printed and completed in one of the official languages of the Community designated by the competent authorities of the Member State in which the application for action has to be submitted, together with any translations that may be required.

3. The form shall be made up of two copies:

(a) the copy for the Member State in which the application is lodged, marked '1';
(b) the copy for the right-holder, marked '2'.

The application forms, duly completed and signed, accompanied by one extract of the form for each Member State indicated in box 6 of the form, as well as the documentary proof referred to in boxes 8, 9 and 10, shall be presented to the competent customs department, which, after accepting the form, shall retain it for at least one year longer than its legal period of validity.

If the extract of a decision granting an application for action is addressed to one or more Member States pursuant to Article 5(4) of the basic Regulation, the Member State which receives the extract shall complete without delay the 'acknowledgement of receipt' section of the form by indicating the date of receipt and shall return a copy of the extract to the competent authority indicated in box 2 of the form.

So long as his application for Community action remains valid, the right-holder may, in the Member State where the application was originally lodged, enter a request for action to be taken in another Member State not previously mentioned. In such cases, the period of validity of the new application shall be the period remaining under the original application, and it may be renewed in accordance with the conditions applying to the original application.

Article 4

For the purposes of Article 5(6) of the basic Regulation, the place of manufacture or production, the distribution network or names of licensees and other information may be requested by the department responsible for receiving and processing applications for action in order to facilitate the technical analysis of the products concerned.

Article 5

If an application for action is lodged in accordance with Article 4(1) of the basic Regulation before expiry of the time limit of three working days and accepted by the customs service designated for that purpose, the time limits referred to in Articles 11 and 13 of that Regulation shall be counted only from the day after the application is received.

If the customs service informs the declarant or holder of goods that the goods are suspected of infringing an intellectual property right and that, pursuant to Article 4(1) of the basic Regulation, they have been detained, or their release suspended, the time limit of three working days shall be counted only from the time the right-holder is notified.

Article 6

In the case of perishable goods, the procedure for suspension of release or for detention of the goods shall be initiated primarily in respect of products for which an application for action has already been lodged.

Article 7

1. Where Article 11(2) of the basic Regulation applies, the right-holder shall notify the customs authority that proceedings have been initiated to determine whether, under national law, an intellectual property right has been infringed. Except in the case of perishable goods, if insufficient time remains to apply for such proceedings before the expiry of the time-limit laid down in the first subparagraph of Article 13(1) of the basic Regulation, the situation may be deemed an appropriate case within the meaning of the second subparagraph of that provision.

2. If an extension of ten working days has already been granted under Article 11 of the basic Regulation, no further extension may be granted under Article 13 thereof.

Article 8

1. Each Member State shall inform the Commission as soon as possible of the competent customs department, referred to in Article 5(2) of the basic Regulation, responsible for receiving and processing applications for action from right-holders.

2. At the end of each calendar year, each Member State shall send the Commission a list of all the written applications for action under Article 5(1) and (4) of the basic Regulation, giving the name and details of each right-holder, the type of right for which each application was submitted, and a summary description of each product concerned. The applications that have not been granted shall be included in that list.

3. In the month following the end of each quarter, each Member State shall send the Commission a list, by product type, giving detailed information on the cases in which the release of goods has been suspended or goods have been detained. The information shall include the following details:

(a) the name of the right-holder; a description of the goods; if known, the origin, provenance and destination of the goods; the name of the intellectual property right infringed;

(b) for each item, the quantity of goods whose release was suspended or which were detained; their customs status; the type of intellectual property right infringed; the means of transport used;

(c) whether commercial or passenger traffic was involved and whether the procedure was initiated ex officio or as the result of an application for action.

4. The Member States may send the Commission information concerning the real or estimated value of the goods for which release has been suspended or which have been detained.

5. At the end of every year, the Commission shall, in an appropriate manner, communicate to all Member States such information as it receives pursuant to paragraphs 1 to 4.

6. The Commission shall publish the list of departments within the customs authority, as referred to in Article 5(2) of the basic Regulation, in the C series of the Official Journal of the European Union.

Article 9

Applications for action lodged before 1 July 2004 shall remain valid until their legal expiry date and shall not be renewed. However, they must be accompanied by the declaration required under Article 6 of the basic Regulation, the model for which is set out in the Annexes to this Regulation. The declaration shall release any deposit and fee payable in the Member States.

Where proceedings brought before the competent authority on a matter of substance before 1 July 2004 are still under way on that date, the deposit shall not be released before the close of those proceedings.

Article 10

Regulation (EC) No 1367/95 is repealed. References to the repealed Regulation shall be construed as references to this Regulation.

Article 11

This Regulation shall enter into force on the day of its publication in the Official Journal of the European Union.

It shall apply from 1 July 2004.

This Regulation shall be binding in its entirety and directly applicable in all Member States.

Done at Brussels, 21 October 2004.

For the Commission

Frederik Bolkestein

Member of the Commission

[1] OJ L 196, 2.8.2003, p. 7.

[2] OJ L 341, 30.12.1994, p. 8. Regulation as last amended by Regulation (EC) No 806/2003 (OJ L 122, 16.5.2003, p. 1).

[3] OJ L 133, 17.6.1995, p. 2. Regulation as last amended by the 2003 Act of Accession.

ANNEX I

NATIONAL APPLICATION FOR ACTION	
1. Date of receipt of the application for action by the designated customs department (within the meaning of Article 5(2) of the Regulation (EC) 1383/2003) DD/MM/YY:	**INTELLECTUAL PROPERTY RIGHTS** **APPLICATION FOR ACTION BY CUSTOMS AUTHORITIES** Under Article 5(1) of Regulation **(EC) No 1383/2003**
3. Details of applicant (i.e. right-holder within the meaning of Article 2(2) of the Regulation (EC) 1383/2003 NAME:... FUNCTION:... ADDRESS:... TOWN:.................................... POSTCODE:.............................. COUNTRY:................................ VAT No:..................................... TEL.:.. MOBILE:................................... FAX:... E-MAIL:... INTERNET ADDRESS:..	**2. Name & address of competent authority to which application is made (see Annex I-C for details):**

4. Status of applicant (within the meaning of Article 2(2) of the Regulation (EC) 1383/2003)[1]
☐ Right-holder ☐ Right-holder's representative *
☐ Authorised user of the right* ☐ Representative of authorised user *

5. Type of right to which application refers[1]:
☐ Trademark ☐ Design right ☐ Copyright or related right ☐ Patent
☐ Supplementary protection certificate ☐ Protected designation of origin ☐ Protected geographical indication ☐ Plant variety right ☐ Geographical designations for spirit drinks[2]

6. Name and address of contact person (administrative matters):	7. Name and address of contact person (technical matters):
TEL.:	TEL.:
Fax:	Fax:
e-mail:	e-mail:
Mobile:	Mobile:
Internet address:	Internet address:

---

* **See box 10 (for further information see "Notes on completion", Annex I-A).**
[1] Tick the appropriate box(es).
[2] Reg. EEC No 1576/89.

8. I attach essential data on the authentic goods:
Number of documents attached[3]:   **Number of photos attached[3]:**
9. I attach specific information concerning the type or pattern of fraud:
Number of documents attached[3]:   **Number of photos attached[3]:**
10. I attach document(s) attesting to the fact that applicant holds the right for the goods in question within the meaning of Article 2(2) of Regulation (EC) No 1383/2003*:
Number of documents attached[3]:
11. I attach the undertaking laid down in Article 6 of Regulation (EC) No 1383/2003, assuming liability in the situations outlined in that Article *:
Undertaking attached:

---

[3] Insert the relevant number; if none are attached, insert 0 .

For further information see "Notes on completion", Annex I-A.

12. Any other information in the right holder's possession, e.g.:

- Country or countries of production   Number of documents attached:[4]

- Routes used by traffickers   Number of documents attached:[5]

- Technical differences between the authentic and the suspect goods:
  Number of documents attached:[5]

- CN tariff heading:

- Other useful information   Number of documents attached:

---

13. Date of filing application:

Date on which drawn up   Place   Applicant's signature and stamp ⇒

DD/MM/YY _____

---

[4] Insert the relevant number, if none are attached, insert 0.
⇒ If the applicant is a representative of the right-holder, he must provide proof that he is empowered to represent the right-holder.

14. DECISION BY CUSTOMS AUTHORITIES (within the meaning of Article 5(7) and (8) of Regulation (EC) No 1383/2003)

☐ **The application is approved**   **Registration number of application for action** _____

Date   **Place**   **Signature and stamp**

DD/MM/YY   __/__/__   _____

_____

☐ **The application is valid until: __/__/__. Any request for extension of the validity period should be sent to the competent authority of box 2, at the latest 30 working days before the validity of the application expires.**

☐ **The application has been refused**

A reasoned decision stating the grounds for refusal and information concerning the appeal procedure are attached.

Date   **Place**   **Signature and stamp**

DD/MM/YY   _____

ANNEX I-A

NOTES ON COMPLETION

I. OBLIGATORY INFORMATION ON RIGHTS AND ABILITY TO ACT

a) Where the holder of the right makes the application himself:
  — in the case of a right that is registered or for which an application has been lodged, proof of registration with the relevant office or lodging of the application,
  — in the case of a copyright, related right or design right which is not registered or for which an application has not been lodged, any evidence of authorship or of his status as original holder;

b) Where the application is made by any other person referred to in Article 2 (2)(b) authorised to use one of the rights referred to in Article 2 (1) (a), (b) and (c) of the basic Regulation, in addition to the proof required under point (a) of this Article, the document by virtue of which the person is authorised to use the right in question;

c) Where a representative of the holder or of any other person referred to in Article 2 (2) (a,b) authorised to use one of the rights referred to in Article 2 (1) (a), (b) and (c) of the basic Regulation applies, in addition to the proof required under points (a) and (b) of this Article, proof of authorisation to act.

The natural or legal person who fills in box 3 of the Application for action must, in all cases, be the one who will provide the documents foreseen in box 11 of the Application for action.

d) Box 5 contains all geographical indications. Protected designation of origin (PDO) and protected geographical indication (PGI) mean the official indications according to Council Regulations (EEC) No 2081/92 (OJ L 208, 24.7.1992, p. 1) Commision Regulations (EC) No 1107/96 (OJ L 148, 21.6.1996, p. 1) and (EC) No 2400/96 (OJ L 327, 18.12.1996, p. 11). 'Geographical designations for spiritous beverages' means the official designations according to Regulation (EEC) No 1576/89.

e) Individual producers as well as groups or their representatives are entitled to make an application.

Registration and specifications are required when an application is made: for protected designation of origin and protected geographical indication.

II. WHAT DOES THE APPLICATION FOR ACTION HAVE TO CONTAIN?

An application for action can be used by the right-holder, free of charge, either as a preventive measure or where he has reason to think that his intellectual property right or rights have been or are likely to be infringed. The application must contain all the information needed to make the goods in question readily recognisable by the customs authorities, and in particular:

— an accurate and detailed technical description of the goods,
— any specific information the right holder may have concerning the type or pattern of fraud,
— the name and address of the contact person appointed by the right holder,
— the undertaking required of the applicant by Article 6 of the basic Regulation and proof that the applicant holds the right for the goods in question.

• The right holders must imperatively return the proof of receipt of the notification which was addressed to them by the Customs Service, according to Articles 4 (ex-officio) and 9. It must be done *immediately after* having received this notification. The legal deadlines (3 working days— 10 working days) start from the moment of receipt of the notification. It is imperative that the right-holder, as soon as he is contacted by the customs authorities, *immediately* confirms the receipt of the notification.

• Within the meaning of the basic Regulation 'working day' (Council Regulation (EEC, Ecuatom) No 1182/71 (OJ L 124, 8.6.1971, p. 1)) is considered every day other than public holidays, Saturdays and Sundays. Moreover, the calculation of working days as included in Articles 4 and 13, has to be carried out taking into account the fact that the day of receipt of the notification is not included. The deadlines to be taken into account within the meaning of the basic Regulation commence therefore as from the day after the receipt of the notification.

The application for action can be submitted electronically if an electronic data exchange system is available. In all other cases, the form is to be completed by mechanical means or in legible handwriting and must not contain erasures or overwriting.

III. How to file an application for action

The right-holder must submit his application for action to the relevant office referred to in box 2 of the form. On receipt of the application, the competent customs office will process it and inform the applicant of its decision by writing within 30 working days. If the office refuses the application by reasoned decision, the applicant has the right of appeal. The period during which the customs authorities will take action is set at one year, renewable annually.

IV. Explanations of the main boxes to be filled in by the applicant

Box 3: Name, address and capacity of the applicant. Within the meaning of Article 2(2), the applicant may be the right-holder himself, a person authorised to use the intellectual property right or a designated representative.

Box 4: Status of the applicant. Tick the appropriate box.

Box 5: Type of right concerned by the application for action. Tick the appropriate box.

Boxes 6 and 7: Contact details for the applicant's contact person dealing with administrative matters should be entered in Box 6. Box 7 is for the contact details of the person who would be responsible for meeting the customs authorities to discuss technical details of the goods detained. The person concerned must be easily contactable at short notice.

Box 8, 9 and 12: Box 8 is for specific and accurate information which would enable the customs authorities to identify the authentic goods correctly and for any information the right-holder may possess concerning the type or pattern of fraud (documents, photos etc.).

The information should be as detailed as possible to allow the customs authorities to identify suspect consignments simply and effectively using risk analysis principles.

Various types of information should be entered in these boxes to help improve customs intelligence on products and patterns of fraud. Additional supporting details can be provided such as: the pretax value of the legal goods, the location of the goods or their intended destination, particulars identifying the consignment or packages, the scheduled arrival or departure date of the goods, the means of transport used, the identity of the importer, exporter or holder.

Box 11: The natural or legal person who fills in box 3 of the Application for action must, in all cases, be the one who will provide the documents foreseen in box 11 of the Application for action.

Box 13: By signing this box, the right-holder certifies that he accepts the terms of the Regulation and his obligations.

ANNEX I-B

DECLARATION IN ACCORDANCE WITH ARTICLE 6 OF COUNCIL REGULATION (EC) No 1383/2003

I, the undersigned . . . .

right-holder, within the meaning of Article 2(2) of Council Regulation (EC) No 1383/2003 (hereinafter 'the basic Regulation'), of the intellectual property rights certified by the attached documents, hereby undertake in accordance with Article 6 of the Regulation to assume liability towards the persons involved in a situation referred to in Article 1(1) in the event that a procedure initiated pursuant to present Regulation is discontinued owing to an act or omission on my part or in the event that the goods in question are subsequently found not to infringe an intellectual property right.

- I hereby undertake to pay all costs incurred under the basic Regulation by keeping goods under customs control pursuant to Article 9, and where applicable Article 11, including costs occasioned by the destruction of goods infringing an intellectual property right pursuant to Article 17.
- I confirm that I have taken note of Article 12 of the basic Regulation and undertake to notify the department indicated in Article 5(2) of any alteration to or loss of my intellectual property rights.

Done at . . . .

on . . ./. . ./20. .

. . . .

(Signature)

ANNEX I-C

NAMES AND ADDRESSES FOR THE SUBMISSION OF ABILITY TO ACT

[Note of the editors: the details listed in this Annex may no longer be up to date. It is therefore recommended to refer to the respective chapters of this book]

BELGIUM

Monsieur le Directeur général des douanes et accises
Service Gestion des Groupes cibles—Régimes divers—Direction 1 (Contrefaçon-Piraterie)
Boîte 37 Boulevard du Jardin Botanique 50-1010 Bruxelles
Tel.: (32-2)210.31.38 / Fax: (32-2) 210 32 13
e-mail: org.contr.reg.div@minfin.fed.be

* * *

De heer Directeur-generaal van de Administratie der Douane en
Accijnzen Dienst Diverse regelingen
Directie 1 'Namaak en Piraterij'
bus 37 Kruidtuinlaan 50-1010 Brussel
Tel.: (32-2) 210 31 38 Fax: (32-2) 210 32 13
e-mail: org.contr.reg.div@minfin.fed.be

[Note of the editors: no longer up to date: please refer to the Belgian chapter of this book]

DENMARK

Central Customs and Tax Administration
Customs Control
Østbanegade 123
DK-2100 Copenhagen
Tel.: +45 72379000
Fax: + 45 72372917
e-mail: toldskat@toldskat.dk
Internet: www.erhverv.toldskat.dk

GERMANY

Oberfinanzdirektion Nürnberg Zentralstelle Gewerblicher Rechtsschutz
Sophienstraße 6 D—80333 München
Tel.: (49-89) 59 95 (23 49)
Fax: (49-89) 59 95 23 17
e-mail: zgr@ofdm.bfinv.de
Internet: www.zoll.de/e0_downloads/b0_vordrucke/e0_vub/index.html

SPAIN

Departamento de Aduanas e Impuestos Especiales
Subdirección General de Gestión Aduanera
Avenida del Llano Castellano 17
E—28071 Madrid
Tel.: (34) 917 28 98 54
Fax: (34) 917 29 12 00

1135

FRANCE

Direction générale des douanes
Bureau E4—Section de la propriété intellectuelle
8 rue de la Tour des dames
F—75436 Paris Cedex 09
Tel.: (33) 1 55074860
Fax: (33) 1 55074866

IRELAND

Office of the Revenue Commissioners
Customs Branch
Unit 2
Government Offices
Nenagh
Co Tipperary
Tel.: 353 67 63238
Fax: 353 67 32381
e-mail: tariff@revenue.ie
Internet: www.revenue.ie

ITALY

Agenzia Delle Dogane
Ufficio Antifrode
Via Mario Carucci, 71
I—00144 Roma
Tel.: (39-6) 50 24 20 81—50 24 65 96
Fax: (39-6) 50 95 73 00—50 24 20 21
e-mail: dogane.antifrode@agenziadogane.it

LUXEMBOURG

Direction des douanes et accises
Division 'Attributions Securitaires'
Boîte postale 1605
L—1016 Luxembourg
Tel.: (352) 29 01 91
Fax: (352) 49 87 90

NETHERLANDS

Douane-Noord / kantoor Groningen, afdeling IER
P.O. Box 380
9700 AJ Groningen
Nederland
Tel.: (31) 50 5232175
Fax: (31) 50 5232176
e-mail: Douane.hier@tiscalimail.nl
Internet: www.douane.nl

AUSTRIA

Zollamt Villach
Competence Center Gewerblicher Rechtsschutz
Ackerweg 19
A-9500 Villach
Austria
Tel.: (43) 4242 3028-(39, 41 or 52)
Fax: (43) 4242 3028-71 or 73
e-mail: post.425-pdp.zaktn@bmf.gv.at

PORTUGAL

Ministério das Finanças
Direcção-Geral das Alfândegas e dos Impostos
Especiais sobre o Consumo
Direcção de Servicos de Regulação Aduaneira
Rua da Alfândega, n°5 R/C
P—1149-006 Lisboa
Tel.: (351) 21 881 3890
Fax: (351) 21 881 3984
e-mail: dsra@dgaiec.min-financas.pt
Internet: www.dgaiec.min-financas.pt

FINLAND

Tullihallitus
Valvontaosasto
PL 512
FI—00101 Helsinki
Tel.: (358) 20-492 2748
Fax: (358) 20 492 2669
Enforcement Department
National Board of Customs
Box 512
FI—00101 Helsinki

SWEDEN

Tullverket
Kc Ombud
Specialistenheten
Box 850
S—201 80 Malmö

Tel.: (46) 771 520520
Fax: (46 40) 6613013
Internet: www.tullverket.se

UNITED KINGDOM

HM Customs & Excise
CITOPS1st Floor West
Alexander House
21 Victoria Avenue
Southend-on-Sea
Essex SS99 IAA
Tel.: (44 1702) 367221
Fax: (44 1702) 366825
Internet: www.hmce.gov.uk

GREECE

ATTIKA CUSTOMS DISTRICT
Pl. Ag. Nikolaou
GR—18510 Pireas
Tel.: (30 210) 4282461, 4515587
Fax: (30 210) 451 10 09
Internet: www.e-oikonomia.gr

SLOVAK REPUBLIC

Customs Directorate of the Slovak Republic
Mierova 23
SK—815 11 Bratislava
Slovakia
Tel.: (421) 2 48273101
Fax: (421) 2 43336448
Internet: www.colnasprava.sk

ESTONIA

Maksu- ja Tolliamet
Narva mnt 9j
EE—15176 Tallinn
Tel.: (372) 683 5700
Fax: (372) 683 5709
E-mail: toll@customs.ee

LITHUANIA

Customs Department under the Ministry of Finance of the Republic of Lithuania
A. Jaksto 1/25
LT—2600 Vilnius
Tel.: (370) 5 2666111
Fax: (370) 5 2666005

CZECH REPUBLIC

Customs Directorate Hradec Kralove
ul. Bohuslava Martinu 1672/8a
P.O.BOX 88
CZ—501 01 HRADEC KRALOVE
Tel.: 00420 49 5756 111, 00420 495756214, 00420 495756267
Fax: 00420 49 5756 200
e-mail: posta0601@cs.mfcr.cz
Internet: www.cs.mfcr.cz

MALTA

Director general of Customs
Customs House
Lascaris Wharf Valletta
Tel.: (356) 25685101
Fax: (356) 25685243
e-mail: carmel.v.portelli@gov.mt
Internet: www.customs.business-line.com

SLOVENIA

Customs Administration of Republic of Slovenia
General Customs directorate
Šmartinska 55
SLO—1523 Ljubljana
Slovenia
Tel.: (386) 1 478 38 00
Fax: (386) 1 478 39 04
e-mail: ipr.curs@gov.si

CYPRUS

Customs Headquarters
M. Karaoli, 1096 Nicosia, Cyprus
Postal address: Customs Headquarters, 1440 Nicosia, Cyprus
Tel.: 00357-22-601652, 00357-22-601858
Fax: 00357-22-602769
e-mail: headquarters@customs.mof.gov.cy

REPUBLIC OF LATVIA

Intellectual Property Rights Subdivision
Enforcement Division
National Customs Board
State Revenue Service
Republic of Latvia
Kr. Valdemara Street 1a, LV-1841 Riga
Tel.: (371) 7047442, (371) 7047400
Fax: (371) 7047440
e-mail: customs@dep.vid.gov.lv
Internet: www.vid.gov.lv

HUNGARY

17. sz. Vámhivatal (Customs Office no.17)
Dirección: H-1143 Budapest, Hungária krt. 112-114.
Dirección postal: H-1591 Budapest, Pf. 310.
Tel.: +361 470-42-60
    +361 470-42-61
Fax:+361 470-42-78
    +361 470-42-79
E-mail: vh17000@mail.vpop.hu

POLAND

The Customs Chamber in Warsaw
Str. Modlińska 4
PL—03 216 Warsaw
Poland
Tel.: +48 22 5104611
Fax: +48 22 8115745

ANNEX II

COMMUNITY APPLICATION FOR ACTION	
1.Date of receipt of the application for action by the designated customs department (within the meaning of Article 5(2) of Regulation (EC) No 1383/2003) DD/MM/YY: .../.../...	**INTELLECTUAL PROPERTY RIGHTS** **APPLICATION FOR ACTION BY CUSTOMS AUTHORITIES** Under Article 5(4) of Regulation (EC) No 1383/2003
3. Details of applicant (i.e. right-holder within the meaning of Article 2(2) of Regulation (EC) No 1383/2003 NAME:... .... FUNCTION: .... ADDRESS: .... TOWN:............... POSTCODE: .... COUNTRY:.................. VAT NO: .... TEL.: .... MOBILE: .... FAX: .... E-MAIL: .... INTERNET ADDRESS:	**2. Name & address of competent authority to which application is made (see Annex II-C for details):**
4. Status of applicant (within the meaning of Article 2(2) of Regulation (EC) No 1383/2003[1] ☐ Right-holder * ☐ Right-holder's representative * ☐ Authorised user of the right * ☐ Representative of authorised user *	

See box 9 (for further information see "Notes on completion", Annex II - A).
[1] Tick the appropriate box(es).

5. Type of right to which application refers:

☐ Community trademark[2]   ☐ Community design[3] right

☐ Supplementary protection certificate[4]   ☐ Designation of origin protected by the
                                                Community[5]
☐ Geographical indication protected by the Community[5]

☐ Community protected plant variety right[6]   ☐ Geographical designations for spirit drinks[7]

6. Member State(s) in which action by customs authorities is requested

☐ AT	☐ DK	☐ FR	☐ FI	☐ LU
☐ BE	☐ EL	☐ IE	☐ SE	☐ NL
☐ DE	☐ ES	☐ IT	☐ UK	☐ PT
☐ CY	☐ HU	☐ MT	☐ CZ	☐ EE
☐ LV	☐ LT	☐ PL	☐ SI	☐ SK

7. I attach essential technical data on the authentic goods.:

☐ Number of documents attached[8]   ☐ Number of photos attached:[8]

8. I attach specific information concerning the type or pattern of fraud:

☐ Number of documents attached[8]   ☐ Number of photos attached:[8]

9. I attach document(s) attesting to the fact that applicant holds the right for the goods in question within the meaning of Article 2(2) of the Regulation (EC) No 1383/2003

☐ Number of documents attached[8]

10. I attach the undertaking laid down in Article 6 of Regulation (EC) No 1383/2003, assuming liability in the situations outlined in that Article:

Undertaking attached:

---

[2] Council Regulation (EC) No 40/94 (OJ L 11, 19.11.1994, p.1).
[3] Council Regulation (EC) No 6/2002 (OJ L 3, 5.1.2002, p.1).
[4] Council Regulation (EEC) No 1768/92 or Regulation (EC) No 1610/96 of the European Parliament and of the Council (OJ L 198,, 8.8.1996, p.30).
[5] Council Regulation (EEC) No 2081/92 and (EC) No 1493/99 (OJ L 179, 14.7.1999, p.1).
[6] Council Regulation (EC) No 2100/94 (OJ L 287, 1.9.1994, p.1).
[7] Council Regulation (EEC) No 1576/89 (OJ L 60, 19.6.1989, p.1).
[8] Insert the relevant number, if none are attached, insert 0.
Important: for further information see "Notes on completion", Annex II - A.

11. Right-holder's contact person in the other Member States where action is requested[9]

ADMINISTRATIVE QUESTIONS (lawyer, for example)

☐ BE	☐ DK	☐ DE	☐ EL
Name:	Name:	Name:	Name:
Address:	Address:	Address:	Address:
Tel.: Mobile: Fax: e-mail: ☐ see attached list	Tel.: Mobile: Fax: e-mail: ☐ see attached list	Tel.: Mobile: Fax: e-mail: ☐ see attached list	Tel.: Mobile: Fax: e-mail: ☐ see attached list
☐ ES	☐ FI	☐ FR	☐ IE
Name:	Name:	Name:	Name:
Address:	Address:	Address:	Address:
Tel.: Mobile: Fax: e-mail: ☐ see attached list	Tel.: Mobile: Fax: e-mail: ☐ see attached list	Tel.: Mobile: Fax: e-mail: ☐ see attached list	Tel.: Mobile: Fax: e-mail: ☐ see attached list
☐ IT	☐ LU	☐ AT	☐ NL
Name:	Name:	Name:	Name:
Address:	Address:	Address:	Address:
Tel.: Mobile: Fax: e-mail: ☐ see attached list	Tel.: Mobile: Fax: e-mail: ☐ see attached list	Tel.: Mobile: Fax: e-mail: ☐ see attached list	Tel.: Mobile: Fax: e-mail: ☐ see attached list
☐ PT	☐ SE	☐ UK	☐ CY
Name:	Name:	Name:	Name:
Address:	Address:	Address:	Address:
Tel.: Mobile: Fax: e-mail: ☐ see attached list	Tel.: Mobile: Fax: e-mail: ☐ see attached list	Tel.: Mobile: Fax: e-mail: ☐ see attached list	Tel.: Mobile: Fax: e-mail: ☐ see attached list
☐ HU	☐ MT	☐ SK	☐ CZ
Name:	Name:	Name:	Name:
Address:	Address:	Address:	Address:
Tel.: Mobile: Fax: e-mail: ☐ see attached list	Tel.: Mobile: Fax: e-mail: ☐ see attached list	Tel.: Mobile: Fax: e-mail: ☐ see attached list	Tel.: Mobile: Fax: e-mail: ☐ see attached list

[9] Tick the appropriate box(es).

☐ EE	☐ LV	☐ LT	☐ PL
Name:	Name:	Name:	Name:
Address:	Address:	Address:	Address:
Tel.: Mobile: Fax: e-mail: ☐ see attached list	Tel.: Mobile: Fax: e-mail: ☐ see attached list	Tel.: Mobile: Fax: e-mail: ☐ see attached list	Tel.: Mobile: Fax: e-mail: ☐ see attached list
☐ SI			
Name:			
Address:			
Tel.: Mobile: Fax: e-mail: ☐ see attached list			

12. Right-holder's contact person in the other Member States where action is requested[10]

TECHNICAL QUESTIONS (for example, expert)

☐ BE	☐ DK	☐ DE	☐ EL
Name:	Name:	Name:	Name:
Address:	Address:	Address:	Address:
Tel.: Mobile: Fax: e-mail: ☐ see attached list	Tel.: Mobile: Fax: e-mail: ☐ see attached list	Tel.: Mobile: Fax: e-mail: ☐ see attached list	Tel.: Mobile: Fax: e-mail: ☐ see attached list
☐ ES	☐ FI	☐ FR	☐ IE
Name:	Name:	Name:	Name:
Address:	Address:	Address:	Address:
Tel.: Mobile: Fax: e-mail: ☐ see attached list	Tel.: Mobile: Fax: e-mail: ☐ see attached list	Tel.: Mobile: Fax: e-mail: ☐ see attached list	Tel.: Mobile: Fax: e-mail: ☐ see attached list
☐ IT	☐ LU	☐ AT	☐ NL
Name:	Name:	Name:	Name:
Address:	Address:	Address:	Address:
Tel.: Mobile: Fax: e-mail: ☐ see attached list	Tel.: Mobile: Fax: e-mail: ☐ see attached list	Tel.: Mobile: Fax: e-mail: ☐ see attached list	Tel.: Mobile: Fax: e-mail: ☐ see attached list

---

[10] Tick the appropriate box(es).

☐ PT	☐ SE	☐ UK	☐ CY
Name:	Name:	Name:	Name:
Address:	Address:	Address:	Address:
Tel.: Mobile: Fax: e-mail: ☐ see attached list	Tel.: Mobile: Fax: e-mail: ☐ see attached list	Tel.: Mobile: Fax: e-mail: ☐ see attached list	Tel.: Mobile: Fax: e-mail: ☐ see attached list
☐ HU	☐ MT	☐ SK	☐ CZ
Name:	Name:	Name:	Name:
Address:	Address:	Address:	Address:
Tel.: Mobile: Fax: e-mail: ☐ see attached list	Tel.: Mobile: Fax: e-mail: ☐ see attached list	Tel.: Mobile: Fax: e-mail: ☐ see attached list	Tel.: Mobile: Fax: e-mail: ☐ see attached list
☐ EE	☐ LV	☐ LT	☐ PL
Name:	Name:	Name:	Name:
Address:	Address:	Address:	Address:
Tel.: Mobile: Fax: e-mail: ☐ see attached list	Tel.: Mobile: Fax: e-mail: ☐ see attached list	Tel.: Mobile: Fax: e-mail: ☐ see attached list	Tel.: Mobile: Fax: e-mail: ☐ see attached list
☐ SI			
Name:			
Address:			
Tel.: Mobile: Fax: e-mail: ☐ see attached list			

13. Any other information in the right-holder's possession, e.g.:

- Country or countries of production   Number of documents attached[11]

- Routes used by traffickers   Number of documents attached[11]

- Technical differences between the authentic and the suspect goods:

- Number of documents attached[11]

- CN tariff heading:

- Other useful information   Number of documents attached[11]

---

[11] Insert the relevant number, if none are attached, insert 0.

14. Date of filing application:

Date on which drawn up   Place   Applicant's signature

DD/MM/YY: .../.../...   ....

15. DECISION BY CUSTOMS AUTHORITIES (within the meaning of Article 5(7) and (8) of Regulation (EC) No 1383/2003)

☐ **The application is approved**   **Registration number of application for action:** ....

Date   **Place**   **Signature and stamp**

DD/MM/YY   ....

☐ **The application is valid until: ../../....., Any request for extension of the validity period should be sent to the competent authority of box 2, at the latest 30 working days before the validity of the application expires.**

☐ **The application has been refused**

A reasoned decision stating the grounds for refusal and information concerning the appeal procedure are attached.

Date   **Place**   **Signature and stamp**

DD/MM/YY   ....

16.   **ACKNOWLEDGEMENT OF RECEIPT**
Concerning application made by .... **(name of the applicant)**

☐ AT	☐ DK	☐ FR	☐ FI	☐ LU	**NAME:**
☐ BE	☐ EL	☐ IE	☐ SE	☐ NL	
☐ DE	☐ ES	☐ IT	☐ UK	☐ PT	**PLACE AND DATE OF RECEPTION:**
☐ CY	☐ HU	☐ MT	☐ SK	☐ CZ	
☐ EE	☐ LV	☐ LT	☐ PL		
☐ SI					**SIGNATURE AND STAMP:**

If the applicant is a representative of the right holder, he must provide proof that he is empowered to represent the right-holder.

ANNEX II-A

NOTES ON COMPLETION

I. Obligatory information on rights and ability to act

a) Where the holder of the right makes the application himself:
   — in the case of a right that is registered or for which an application has been lodged, proof of registration with the relevant office or lodging of the application,
   — in the case of a copyright, related right or design right which is not registered or for which an application has not been lodged, any evidence of authorship or of his status as original holder;

b) Where the application is made by any other person referred to in Article 2(2)(a) authorised to use one of the rights referred to in Article 2(1)(a), (b), and (c) of the basic Regulation, in addition to the proof required under point (a) of this Article, the document by virtue of which the person is authorised to use the right in question;

c) Where a representative of the holder or of any other person referred to in Article 2(2)(a) and (b) authorised to use one of the rights referred to in Article 2(1)(a), (b), and (c) of the basic Regulation applies, in addition to the proof required under points (a) and (b) of this Article, proof of authorisation to act.

The natural or legal person who fills in box 3 of the Application for action must, in all cases, be the one who will provide the documents foreseen in box 10 of the Application for action.

d) Box 5 contains all geographical indications. Protected designation of origin (PDO) and protected geographical indication (PGI) mean the official indications designated in accordance with Regulations (EEC) No 2081/92, (EC) No 1107/96 and (EEC) No 2400/96. 'Geographical indication for wines' means indications within the meaning of Regulation (EC) No 1493/99. 'Geographical designation for spiritous beverages' means the official designations according to Regulation (EEC) No 1576/89. Individual producers as well as groups and their representatives are entitled to make an application.

e) Registration and specifications are required when an application is made: for protected designation of origin and protected geographical indication.

II. What does the application for action have to contain

(Art. 5(4): 'Where the applicant is the holder of a Community trademark, a Community design, a Community plant variety right or a designation of origin or geographical indication protected by the Community, an application may, in addition to requesting action by the customs authorities of the Member State in which it is lodged, request action by the customs authorities of one or more other Member States.').

An application for action can be used by the right holder, free of charge, either as a preventive measure or where he has reason to think that his intellectual property right or rights have been or are likely to be infringed. The application must contain all the information needed to make the goods in question readily recognisable by the customs authorities, and in particular:

— an accurate and detailed technical description of the goods,
— any specific information the right holder may have concerning the type or pattern of fraud,
— the name and address of the contact person appointed by the right-holder,
— the undertaking required of the applicant by Article 6 of the basic Regulation and proof that the applicant holds the right for the goods in question.

The application for action can be submitted electronically if an electronic data exchange system is available. In all other cases, the form is to be completed by mechanical means or in legible handwriting and must not contain erasures or overwriting.

• The right-holders must imperatively return the proof of receipt of the notification which was addressed to them by the Customs Service, according to Articles 4 (ex-officio) and 9. It must be done *immediately after* having received this notification. The legal deadlines (3 working days—10 working days) start from the moment of receipt of the notification. It is imperative that the right-holder, as soon as he is contacted by the customs authorities, confirms immediately the receipt of the notification.

- Within the meaning of the basic Regulation 'working day' (reference to Regulation (EEC) No 1182/71) is considered every day other than public holidays, Saturdays and Sundays. Moreover, the calculation of working days as included in Articles 4 and 13, has to be carried out taking into account the fact that the day of receipt of the notification is not included. The deadlines to be taken into account within the meaning of the basic regulation commence therefore as from the day after the receipt of the notification.

III. How to file an application for action

The right-holder must submit his application for action to the relevant office referred to in box 2 of the form. On receipt of the application, the competent customs office will process it and notify the applicant in writing of its decision within 30 working days. If the office refuses the application by reasoned decision, the applicant has the right of appeal. The period during which the customs authorities will take action is set at one year, renewable annually.

IV. Explanations of the main boxes to be filled in by the applicant

Box 3: Name, address and capacity of the applicant. Within the meaning of Article 2(2), the applicant may be the right-holder himself, a person authorised to use the intellectual property right or a designated representative.

The natural or legal person who fills in box 3 of the Application for action must, in all cases, be the one who will provide the documents foreseen in box 10 of the Application for action.

Box 4: Status of the applicant. Tick the appropriate box.

Box 5: Type of right concerned by the application for action. Tick the appropriate box.

Box 6: Tick the box for the Member States in which action by the customs authorities is requested. You are strongly advised to file an application for action in every Member State.

Boxes 7, 8, and 9: These boxes are very important. Accurate, practical details must be provided to enable the customs authorities to quickly identify the goods detained (photos, documents, etc.).

Specific information relating to the type or pattern of fraud will facilitate risk analysis.

The information should be as detailed as possible to allow the customs authorities to identify suspect consignments simply and effectively using risk analysis. These boxes should be used to provide customs with more accurate intelligence in relation to products and so improve its understanding of trafficking. Additional supporting details can be provided such as: the pre-tax value of the legal goods, the location of the goods or their intended destination, particulars identifying the consignment or packages, the scheduled arrival or departure date of the goods, the means of transport used, the identity of the importer, exporter or holder.

Boxes 11 and 12: Contact details for the applicant's contact persons dealing with administrative matters and questions of technical expertise should be entered in Boxes 11 and 12. Box 12 is for the contact details of the person who would be responsible for meeting the customs authorities to discuss technical details of the goods detained. The person concerned must be easily reachable at short notice.

Box 14: By signing this box, the right-holder certifies that he accepts the terms of the Regulation and his obligations.

Box 15: The duly completed and signed form, together with as many extracts as the number of Member States indicated in Box 6, must be submitted to the customs office specified in Article 5(2) of the basic Regulation. The application for action may have to be translated into the language of the Member States where it is to be filed.

The customs offices listed in Annex II-C are at your disposal for any further information.

ANNEX II-B

DECLARATION ARTICLE 6 OF COUNCIL REGULATION (EC) ACCORDING TO NO 1383/2003

I, the undersigned . . . .

right-holder, within the meaning of Article 2(2) of Council Regulation (EC) No 1383/2003 (hereinafter 'the basic Regulation'), of the intellectual property rights certified by the attached documents, hereby undertake in accordance with Article 6 of the Regulation to assume liability towards the persons involved in a situation referred to in Article 1(1) in the event that a procedure initiated pursuant to the present Regulation is discontinued owing to an act or omission on my part or in the event that the goods in question are subsequently found not to infringe an intellectual property right.

- I hereby undertake to pay all costs incurred under the basic Regulation by keeping goods under customs control pursuant to Article 9, and where applicable Article 11, including costs occasioned by the destruction of goods infringing an intellectual property right pursuant to Article 17.
- I hereby certify that the undertaking is given in every Member State in which the decision granting the application applies. I further agree to bear any translation costs required.
- I confirm that I have taken note of Article 12 of the basic Regulation and undertake to notify the department indicated in Article 5(2) of any alteration to or loss of my intellectual property rights.

Done at . . . .

on. . ./. . ./20. .

. . . .

(Signature)

ANNEX II-C

NAMES AND ADDRESSES FOR THE SUBMISSION OF AN APPLICATION FOR ACTION

[Note of the editors: the details listed in this Annex may no longer be up to date. It is therefore recommended to refer to the respective chapters of this book]

BELGIUM

Monsieur le Directeur général des douanes et accises
Service 'Gestion des Groupes cibles'—Régimes divers—Direction 1 (Contrefaçon-Piraterie)
Boîte 37 Boulevard du Jardin Botanique 50 B-1010 Bruxelles
Tel.: (32–2)210 31 38 Fax: (32–2) 210 32 13

[Note of the editors: no longer up to date: please refer to the Belgian chapter of this book]

* * *

De heer Directeur-generaal van de Administratie der Douane en
Accijnzen Dienst Diverse regelingen
Directie 1 'Namaak en Piraterij'
Rijksadministratief Centrum
Financietoren
bus 37 Kruidtuinlaan 50 B-1010 Brussel
Tel.: (32–2) 210 31 38 Fax: (32–2) 210 32 13
e-mail: org.contr.reg.div@minfin.fed.be

[Note of the editors: no longer up to date: please refer to the Belgian chapter of this book]

DENMARK

Central Customs and Tax Administration
Customs Control
Østbanegade 123
DK-2100 Copenhagen
Tel. (45) 72379000
Fax: (45) 72372917
e-mail: toldskat@toldskat.dk
Internet: www.erhverv.toldskat.dk

GERMANY

Oberfinanzdirektion Nürnberg Zentralstelle Gewerblicher Rechtsschutz
Sophienstraße 6
D-80333 München
Tel.: (49–89) 59 95 23 49
Fax: (49–89) 59 95 23 17
e-mail: zgr@ofdm.bfinv.de
Internet: www.zoll.de/e0_downloads/b0_vordrucke/e0_vub/index.html

SPAIN

Departamento de Aduanas e impuestos Especiales
Subdirección General de Gestión Aduanera
Avenida del Llano Castellano 17
E-28071 Madrid
Tel.: (34) 917 28 98 54
Fax: (34) 917 29 12 00

FRANCE

Direction générale des douanes
Bureau E4—Section de la propriété intellectuelle
8 rue de la Tour des dames
F—75436 Paris Cedex 09
Tel.: (33) 1 55074860
Fax: (33) 1 55074866

IRELAND

Office of the Revenue Commissioners
Customs Branch
Unit 2
Government Offices
Nenagh
Co Tipperary
Tel.: (353 67 63238)
Fax: (353 67 32381)
e-mail: tariff@revenue.ie
Internet: www.revenue.ie

ITALY

Agenzia Delle Dogane
Ufficio Antifrode
Via Mario Carucci, 71
I—00144 Roma
Tel.: (39–6) 50 24 20 81—50246596
Fax: (39–6) 50 95 73 00—50242021
e-mail: dogane.antifrode@agenziadogane.it

LUXEMBOURG

Direction des douanes et accises
Division 'Attributions Securitaires'
Boîte postale 1605
L—1016 Luxembourg
Tel.: (352) 29 01 91
Fax: (352) 49 87 90

NETHERLANDS

Douane-Noord / kantoor Groningen, afdeling IER
P.O. Box 380
9700 AJ Groningen
Tel.: (31) 50 5232175
Fax: (31) 50 5232176
e-mail: douane.hier@tiscalimail.nl
Internet: www.douane.nl

AUSTRIA

Zollamt Villach
Competence Center Gewerblicher Rechtsschutz
Ackerweg 19
A-9500 Villach
Austria
Tel.: (43) 4242 3028-(39, 41 or 52)
Fax: (43) 4242 3028-71 or 73
e-mail: post.425-pdp.zaktn@bmf.gv.at

PORTUGAL

Ministério das Finanças
Direcção-Geral das Alfândegas e dos Impostos
Especiais sobre o Consumo
Direcção de Servicos de Regulação Aduaneira
Rua da Alfândega, n ° 5 R/C
1149–006 Lisboa
Tel.: (351) 21 881 3890
Fax: (351) 21 881 3984
e-mail: dsra@dgaiec.min-financas.pt
Internet: www.dgaiec.min-financas.pt

FINLAND

Tullihallitus
Valvontaosasto
PL 512
FI—00101 Helsinki
Tel.: (358) 20 492 2748
Fax: (358) 20 492 2669
Enforcement Department
National Board of Customs
Box 512
FI—00101 Helsinki

SWEDEN

Tullverket
Kc Ombud
Specialistenheten
Box 850
S—201 80 Malmö

Tel.: (46) 771 520520
Fax: (46-40) 6613013
Internet: www.tullverket.se

UNITED KINGDOM

HM Customs & Excise
CITOPS1st Floor West
Alexander House
21 Victoria Avenue
Southend-on-Sea
Essex SS99 IAA
United Kingdom
Tel.: (44) 1702 367221
Fax: (44) 1702 366825
Internet: www.hmce.gov.uk

GREECE

ATTIKA CUSTOMS DISTRICT
Pl. Ag. Nikolaou
GR—18510 Pireas
Tel.: (30 210) 4282461, 4515587
Fax: (30 210) 451 10 09
Internet: www.e-oikonomia.gr

SLOVAK REPUBLIC

Customs Directorate of the Slovak Republic
Mierova 23
SK—815 11 Bratislava
Slovakia
Tel.: (421) 2 48273101
Fax: (421) 2 43336448
Internet: www.colnasprava.sk

ESTONIA

Maksu- ja Tolliamet
Narva mnt 9j
EE—15176 Tallinn
Tel.: (372) 683 5700
Fax: (372) 683 5709
e-mail: toll@customs.ee

LITHUANIA

Customs Department under the Ministry of Finance of the Republic of Lithuania
A. Jaksto 1/25
LT—2600 Vilnius
Tel.: (370) 5 2666111
Fax: (370) 5 2666005

CZECH REPUBLIC

Customs Directorate Hradec Kralove
ul. Bohuslava Martinu 1672/8a
P.O.BOX 88
CZ—501 01 HRADEC KRALOVE
Tel.: 00420 49 5756 111, 00420 495756214, 00420 495756267
Fax: 00420 49 5756 200
e-mail: posta0601@cs.mfcr.cz
Internet: www.cs.mfcr.cz

MALTA

Director general of Customs
Customs House
Lascaris Wharf Valletta,
Tel.: (356) 25685101
Fax: (356) 25685243
e-mail: carmel.v.portelli@gov.mt
Internet: www.customs.business-line.com

SLOVENIA

Customs Administration of the Republic of Slovenia
General Customs directorate
Šmartinska 55
SLO—1523 Ljubljana
Slovenia
Tel.: (386) 1 478 38 00
Fax: (386) 1 478 39 04
e-mail: ipr.curs@gov.si

CYPRUS

Customs Headquarters
M. Karaoli, 1096 Nicosia, Cyprus
Postal address: Customs Headquarters, 1440 Nicosia, Cyprus
Tel.: 00357–22–601652, 00357–22–601858
Fax: 00357–22–602769
e-mail: headquarters@customs.mof.gov.cy

REPUBLIC OF LATVIA

Intellectual Property Rights Subdivision
Enforcement Division
National Customs Board
State Revenue Service
Republic of Latvia
Kr. Valdemara Street 1a,
LV 1841–Riga
Latvia
Tel.: (371) 7047442, (371) 7047400
Fax : (371) 7047423
e-mail: customs@dep.vid.gov.lv
Internet: www.vid.gov.lv

HUNGARY

17. sz. Vámhivatal (Customs Office no.17)
Address: H—1143, Budapest, Hungária krt. 112-114.
Postal address: H—1591 Budapest, Pf. 310.
Tel.: (361) 470-42-60, (361) 470-42-61
Fax: (361) 470-42-78, (361) 470-42-79
e-mail: vh17000@mail.vpop.hu

POLAND

The Customs Chamber in Warsaw
Str. Modlinska 4
PL—03 216 Warsaw
Poland
Tel.: (48) 22 5104611
Fax: (48) 22 8115745

Agreement on Trade-Related Aspects of Intellectual Property Rights

[. . .]

Section 4: Special requirements related to border measures[12]

Article 51
Suspension of Release by Customs Authorities

Members shall, in conformity with the provisions set out below, adopt procedures[13] to enable a right-holder, who has valid grounds for suspecting that the importation of counterfeit trade mark or pirated copyright goods[14] may take place, to lodge an application in writing with competent authorities, administrative or judicial, for the suspension by the customs authorities of the release into free circulation of such goods. Members may enable such an application to be made in respect of goods which involve other infringements of intellectual property rights, provided that the requirements of this Section are met. Members may also provide for corresponding procedures concerning the suspension by the customs authorities of the release of infringing goods destined for exportation from their territories.

Article 52
Application

Any right-holder initiating the procedures under Article 51 shall be required to provide adequate evidence to satisfy the competent authorities that, under the laws of the country of importation, there is *prima facie* an infringement of the right-holder's intellectual property right and to supply a sufficiently detailed description of the goods to make them readily recognizable by the customs authorities. The competent authorities shall inform the applicant within a reasonable period whether they have accepted the application and, where determined by the competent authorities, the period for which the customs authorities will take action.

---

[12] Where a Member has dismantled substantially all controls over movement of goods across its border with another Member with which it forms part of a customs union, it shall not be required to apply the provisions of this Section at that border.

[13] It is understood that there shall be no obligation to apply such procedures to imports of goods put on the market in another country by or with the consent of the right-holder, or to goods in transit.

[14] For the purposes of this Agreement:

(a) 'counterfeit trade mark goods' shall mean any goods, including packaging, bearing without authorization a trade mark which is identical to the trade mark validly registered in respect of such goods, or which cannot be distinguished in its essential aspects from such a trade mark, and which thereby infringes the rights of the owner of the trade mark in question under the law of the country of importation;

(b) 'pirated copyright goods' shall mean any goods which are copies made without the consent of the right-holder or person duly authorized by the right-holder in the country of production and which are made directly or indirectly from an article where the making of that copy would have constituted an infringement of a copyright or a related right under the law of the country of importation.

Article 53
Security or Equivalent Assurance

1. The competent authorities shall have the authority to require an applicant to provide a security or equivalent assurance sufficient to protect the defendant and the competent authorities and to prevent abuse. Such security or equivalent assurance shall not unreasonably deter recourse to these procedures.

2. Where pursuant to an application under this Section the release of goods involving industrial designs, patents, layout-designs or undisclosed information into free circulation has been suspended by customs authorities on the basis of a decision other than by a judicial or other independent authority, and the period provided for in Article 55 has expired without the granting of provisional relief by the duly empowered authority, and provided that all other conditions for importation have been complied with, the owner, importer, or consignee of such goods shall be entitled to their release on the posting of a security in an amount sufficient to protect the right-holder for any infringement. Payment of such security shall not prejudice any other remedy available to the right-holder, it being understood that the security shall be released if the right-holder fails to pursue the right of action within a reasonable period of time.

Article 54
Notice of Suspension

The importer and the applicant shall be promptly notified of the suspension of the release of goods according to Article 51.

Article 55
Duration of Suspension

If, within a period not exceeding 10 working days after the applicant has been served notice of the suspension, the customs authorities have not been informed that proceedings leading to a decision on the merits of the case have been initiated by a party other than the defendant, or that the duly empowered authority has taken provisional measures prolonging the suspension of the release of the goods, the goods shall be released, provided that all other conditions for importation or exportation have been complied with; in appropriate cases, this time-limit may be extended by another 10 working days. If proceedings leading to a decision on the merits of the case have been initiated, a review, including a right to be heard, shall take place upon request of the defendant with a view to deciding, within a reasonable period, whether these measures shall be modified, revoked or confirmed. Notwithstanding the above, where the suspension of the release of goods is carried out or continued in accordance with a provisional judicial measure, the provisions of paragraph 6 of Article 50 shall apply.

Article 56
Indemnification of the Importer and of the Owner of the Goods

Relevant authorities shall have the authority to order the applicant to pay the importer, the consignee and the owner of the goods appropriate compensation for any injury caused to them through the wrongful detention of goods or through the detention of goods released pursuant to Article 55.

Article 57
Right of Inspection and Information

Without prejudice to the protection of confidential information, Members shall provide the competent authorities the authority to give the right-holder sufficient opportunity to have any goods detained by the customs authorities inspected in order to substantiate the right holder's claims. The competent authorities shall also have authority to give the importer an equivalent opportunity to have any such goods inspected. Where a positive determination has been made on the merits of a case, Members may provide the competent authorities the authority to inform the right-holder of the names and addresses of the consignor, the importer and the consignee and of the quantity of the goods in question.

Article 58
Ex Officio Action

Where Members require competent authorities to act upon their own initiative and to suspend the release of goods in respect of which they have acquired *prima facie* evidence that an intellectual property right is being infringed:

(a) the competent authorities may at any time seek from the right-holder any information that may assist them to exercise these powers;

(b) the importer and the right-holder shall be promptly notified of the suspension. Where the importer has lodged an appeal against the suspension with the competent authorities, the suspension shall be subject to the conditions, *mutatis mutandis*, set out at Article 55;

(c) Members shall only exempt both public authorities and officials from liability to appropriate remedial measures where actions are taken or intended in good faith.

Article 59
Remedies

Without prejudice to other rights of action open to the right-holder and subject to the right of the defendant to seek review by a judicial authority, competent authorities shall have the authority to order the destruction or disposal of infringing goods in accordance with the principles set out in Article 46. In regard to counterfeit trade mark goods, the authorities shall not allow the re-exportation of the infringing goods in an unaltered state or subject them to a different customs procedure, other than in exceptional circumstances.

Article 60
De Minimis Imports

Members may exclude from the application of the above provisions small quantities of goods of a non-commercial nature contained in travellers' personal luggage or sent in small consignments.

Section 5: Criminal procedures
Article 61

Members shall provide for criminal procedures and penalties to be applied at least in cases of wilful trade mark counterfeiting or copyright piracy on a commercial scale. Remedies available shall include imprisonment and/or monetary fines sufficient to provide a deterrent, consistently with the level of penalties applied for crimes of a corresponding gravity. In appropriate cases, remedies available shall also include the seizure, forfeiture and destruction of the infringing goods and of any materials and implements the predominant use of which has been in the commission of the offence. Members may provide for criminal procedures and penalties to be applied in other cases of infringement of intellectual property rights, in particular where they are committed wilfully and on a commercial scale.

INDEX

1189